The Cumulated Indexes
to the
Public Papers of the Presidents
of the
United States

HARRY S. TRUMAN
1945–1953

kto press

A U.S. Division of Kraus-Thomson Organization Ltd.
Millwood, New York
1979

ISBN 0-527-20754-3

Composition by Vance Weaver Composition, Inc., New York

First Printing
Printed in the United States of America

PREFACE

Although the words spoken by a president during the course of his administration are directed to the citizens of his own time, they become invaluable to future generations of Americans who look to the past for help in understanding their present world. *The Cumulated Indexes to the Public Papers of the Presidents of the United States* provide, for the first time in one volume, full access to the papers of each presidential administration published in the government series, the *Public Papers of the Presidents*. The *Public Papers* offer a remarkable view of the American presidents and of American history. The character of a president, the individuals with whom a president interacts, the historical events that are shaped by a president and that, in turn, shape his presidency, are all to be found within the pages of the *Public Papers*.

A resolution passed by the United States Congress on July 17, 1894, provided that a compilation of "all the annual, special, and veto messages, proclamations, and inaugural addresses" of all the presidents from 1789 to 1894 be printed. The publication was to be prepared by James D. Richardson, a representative from Tennessee, under the direction of the Joint Committee on Printing, of which Richardson was a member. The official set was issued in two series of ten volumes each. A joint resolution of May 2, 1896, provided for the distribution of the set to members of Congress, with the remainder to be delivered to the compiler, James Richardson. An act passed about a year later provided that the plates for *A Compilation of the Messages and Papers of the Presidents* be delivered to Richardson "without cost to him." Representative Richardson then made arrangements for the commercial publication of the set. Several other compilations of presidential papers were commercially published in the first half of the nineteenth century; these usually contained only selected documents.

The Richardson edition of the *Messages and Papers*, however, was the only set authorized by Congress and published by the government until 1957, when the official publication of the public messages and statements of the presidents, the *Public Papers of the Presidents of the United*

States, was initiated based on a recommendation made by the National Historical Publications Commission (now the National Historical Publications and Records Commission). The Commission suggested that public presidential papers be compiled on a yearly basis and issued in a uniform, systematic publication similar to the *United States Supreme Court Reports* and the *Congressional Record*. An official series thus began in which presidential writings and statements of a public nature could be made promptly available. These presidential volumes are compiled by the Office of the Federal Register of the General Services Administration's National Archives and Record Service.

As might be expected, the ''public papers'' vary greatly in importance and content; some contain important policy statements while others are routine messages. They include, in chronological order, texts of such documents as the president's messages to Congress, public addresses, transcripts of news conferences and speeches, public letters, messages to heads of state, remarks to informal groups, etc. Executive orders, proclamations, and similar documents that are required by law to be published in the *Federal Register* and *Code of Federal Regulations* are not reprinted, but are listed by number and subject in an appendix in each volume.

The *Public Papers of the Presidents* are kept in print, and are available from the Superintendent of Documents, United States Government Printing Office. The *Papers* of each year are published in single volumes, with each volume containing an index for that calendar year. *The Cumulated Indexes to the Public Papers of the Presidents* combines and integrates the separate indexes for a president's administration into one alphabetical listing.

References to all of the volumes of a president's public papers can thus be found by consulting this one-volume cumulated index. *See* and *see also* references have been added and minor editorial changes have been made in the process of cumulating the separate indexes.

References in *The Cumulated Indexes to the Public Papers of the Presidents* are to item numbers. Individual volumes are identified in the *Index* by year, as are the actual volumes of the *Papers*. The year identifying the volume in which a paper is located appears in boldface type. When page references are used, they are clearly noted in the entry.

Other volumes in the set of *The Cumulated Indexes to the Public Papers of the Presidents* include Richard M. Nixon, 1969–1974; Lyndon B. Johnson, 1963–1969; John F. Kennedy, 1961–1963; and Dwight D. Eisenhower, 1953–1961. Forthcoming volumes will index the papers of Herbert C. Hoover and Gerald R. Ford, as well as those of future presidents when their administrations are completed.

KTO Press

HARRY S. TRUMAN
1945–1953

A-bomb.
  See Atomic bomb.
A. and H. Kroeger Organization, Businessmen's
    Dinner Forum, **1949:** 240ftn. (p. 533)
Abaca, import controls, **1947:** 18
  Production of, **1950:** 114
Abbot, Charles G., **1946:** 201
Abbott, Arthur J., **1948:** 228 [7]
Abbott, Douglas C., **1951:** 219n.
Abbott, Robert S., memorial award, acceptance,
    1949: 109
Abdul Ilah, Legion of Merit, citation, **1945:** 47
Aber, Dr., **1948:** 122 [4]
Aberdeen Proving Ground, Md., **1951:** 37 [1], 38,
    50
Abraham Lincoln, Carl Sandburg, **1952–53:** 136 [17]
Abramson, Dr. Arthur, **1950:** 156
Accident prevention, **1947:** 82; **1949:** 197
  Aviation, **1952–53:** 40, 351
  Coal mines, **1952–53:** 18 (p. 94), 19, 150, 206
  Federal aid, **1949:** 55
  Federal programs, **1950:** 9 (p. 99), 74
  Fires, **1949:** 55
  Forest fires, **1950:** 121 [9]
  Government employees, **1952–53:** 150
  Highway, **1949:** 114; **1950:** 229; **1951:** 9, 13 (p.
    81), 42, 121; **1952–53:** 93, 243, 249
  Industrial, **1948:** 5 (p. 54); **1949:** 8 (p. 90), 55;
    1950: 9 (p. 99), 74, 155; **1951:** 9, 13 (p.
    80); **1952–53:** 18 (p. 92), 150, 243, 367 (p.
    1151)
  Traffic, **1948:** 227 [2], 279; **1949:** 26, 55
Accidents
  Compensation, **1947:** 7 (p. 73)
    Federal employees, **1949:** 8 (p. 70)
  Fire, **1948:** 113
  Traffic, **1945:** 62, 208 [10], 224; **1946:** 96, 106;
    1947: 118; **1948:** 24, 89
Accounting practices, Federal, **1950:** 9 (pp. 51, 52)
Accounting Program, Joint, **1950:** 244
Acheson, Dean, **1945:** 150; **1946:** 95 [3], 119 [21],
    136 [6], 141 [3], 257 [18]; **1947:** 39, 47, 132,

Acheson, Dean — *continued*
    145 [1], 146n.; **1948:** 43, 278 [10]; **1949:** 11
    [18], 94n.
  See also State, Secretary of.
  News conference remarks on, **1945:** 106 [11], 208
    [12]
Acosta, Maj. Manuel, **1951:** 151
Acreage allotments, **1950:** 9 (p. 87); **1952–53:** 277
    [6]
  Cotton, **1949:** 269 [21]; **1950:** 83
  Peanuts, **1950:** 83
  Suspension, **1951:** 11
Act of Chapultepec, **1946:** 102; **1947:** 101, 105, 188;
    1951: 125
Act for International Development, **1950:** 240, 282,
    294; **1952–53:** 18 (p. 76), 20
Action Program, Highway Safety Conference,
    1947: 118
A.D.A.
  See Americans for Democratic Action.
Adams, Abigail, **1946:** 21 [2]
Adams, Alva, **1948:** 198 [5]
Adams, J. Alston, **1947:** 173, 174 [1]
Adams, John, **1948:** 261 [1]; **1949:** 122 [16]; **1951:**
    127n.
Adams, John Quincy, **1948:** 11 [11]; **1951:** 56 [25],
    127n.; **1952–53:** 26 [18]
Adams, Sherman, **1952–53:** 292 [13], 295n., 312,
    370
Adams, M. Sgt. Stanley T., Congressional Medal of
    Honor, **1951:** 146
Adams, Wis., campaign remarks, **1948:** 235 [1]
Adamson Act, **1948:** 240 [3]
Addonizio, Hugh J., **1948:** 227 [7]; **1952–53:** 303 [3]
Addresses or remarks, election campaign.
  See Election campaign.
Addresses or remarks on commemorative or ded-
    icatory occasions
  Aberdeen Proving Ground, weapons demon-
    stration, **1951:** 38
  Aero Club of Washington, Wright Memorial
    Dinner, **1952–53:** 351

Addresses or remarks — *continued*
  American Association for the Advancement of
    Science, centennial, **1948:** 186
  American Legion, dedication of headquarters,
    1951: 191
  Americans for Democratic Action, national con-
    vention banquet, **1952–53:** 129
  AMVETS Headquarters, Washington, dedica-
    tion, **1952–53:** 101
  Arbor Day, diamond anniversary, **1947:** 69
  Arlington National Cemetery memorial carillon,
    dedication, **1949:** 268
  Armed Forces Day Dinner, **1950:** 138; **1951:**
    109; **1952–53:** 128
  Arnold Engineering Development Center, ded-
    ication, **1951:** 138
  Atomic Energy Act, second anniversary, **1948:**
    164
  Augustana Lutheran Church, national conven-
    tion, **1950:** 158
  Bastille Day, **1945:** 81; **1946:** 167
  Battery D, 129th Field Artillery
    Executive committee meeting, **1950:** 161 [2]
    Reunion breakfast, **1949:** 18; **1950:** 161 [1]
  Better Business Bureaus, dinner, **1950:** 157
  Bolívar, Simón, statue, dedication, **1948:** 158
  Boyle, William, dinners honoring, **1949:** 190, 220
  Carter Barron Amphitheater, dedication, **1951:**
    116
  Central Intelligence Agency orientation course,
    1952–53: 335
  Chapel of the Four Chaplains, dedication, **1951:**
    30
  Chinese Republic, 34th anniversary, **1945:** 166
  Civil Air Patrol dinner, **1952–53:** 125
  Civil Defense Conference, dinner, **1951:** 96
  Civil Service, 69th anniversary, **1952–53:** 14
  Clark, Tom C., swearing in as Associate Justice
    of the Supreme Court, **1949:** 189
  Coffelt, Pvt. Leslie, dedication of memorial
    plaque, **1952–53:** 134
  Columbia Scholastic Press Association, conven-
    tion, **1952–53:** 63
  Commission on Internal Security and Individual
    Rights, swearing-in, **1951:** 35
  Congress
    Buffet supper for Democratic Members, **1951:**
      8
    Supper for new members, **1949:** 70
  Constitution Day, address at Library of Cong-
    ress, **1951:** 225
  Credit Union National Association, dedication
    of headquarters, **1950:** 131 [4], 132
  Cuban independence, 50th anniversary, **1948:** 81
  Czechoslovak Republic, anniversary of inde-
    pendence, **1945:** 173; **1946:** 245
  Declaration of Independence, 175th anniversary,
    1951: 144

Addresses or remarks — *continued*
  Democratic luncheon, San Francisco, **1951:** 215
  Democratic National Committee
    100th anniversary, **1948:** 32
    Reception, **1952–53:** 71
  Democratic National Congressional Committee,
    dinner, **1951:** 27
  Democratic Women's Day, **1948:** 211; **1949:**
    219; **1950:** 255; **1951:** 238
  Democratic Women's National Council, **1950:**
    139
  Detroit, Mich., 250th anniversary, **1951:** 174
  Dill, Sir John, unveiling of statue, **1950:** 275
  DiSalle, Michael V., dinner honoring, **1952–53:**
    34
  82d Airborne Division, remarks to members of,
    1951: 46
  Elks lodge, Pasco, Wash., dedication, **1950:** 121
    [13]
  Equestrian statues from Italy, dedication, **1951:**
    235
  Evans, Joshua, dinner honoring, **1951:** 21
  Everglades National Park, dedication, **1947:** 231
  Federal Bar Association, 30th anniversary, **1950:**
    94
  Forrestal, James, dinner for, **1949:** 56
  Franklin D. Roosevelt, aircraft carrier, commis-
    sioning, **1945:** 177
  Friendship International Airport, dedication,
    1950: 171
  General Accounting Office, cornerstone laying
    for new building, **1951:** 221
  Girard College centennial, **1948:** 104
  Gompers, Samuel, centennial dinner, **1950:** 4
  Gompers Square, Washington, dedication, **1951:**
    279
  Grand Coulee Dam, dedication, **1950:** 125
  Grandview, Mo., Baptist Church, dedication,
    1950: 315
  Greek independence, 128th anniversary, **1949:**
    61
  Greek-Turkish aid program, third anniversary,
    1950: 142
  Harriman, W. Averell, departure for Iran, **1951:**
    155
  High school essay contest winners, **1951:** 203
  Howard University, commencement, **1952–53:**
    169
  Hungry Horse Dam, Mont., dedication, **1952–
    53:** 271
  Idlewild International Airport, dedication, **1948:**
    168
  Independence Day address, **1947:** 138
  Industrial Safety, President's Conference on,
    1950: 155
  Industry Advisory Councils, Interior Depart-
    ment, **1951:** 98
  Interior Department, centennial, **1949:** 43

Addresses or remarks — *continued*
Jackson Day, **1946:** 67
Japanese peace conference, **1951:** 216, 127
Jefferson Day Dinner, **1947:** 68
Jefferson-Jackson Day Dinner, **1948:** 32; **1949:** 38, 39; **1950:** 39; **1951:** 80; **1952–53:** 69
Jefferson-Jackson Executive Committee, buffet supper, **1949:** 74
Jefferson Jubilee, **1950:** 134
Jefferson National Expansion Memorial, dedication, **1950:** 162
Jefferson Papers, publication of first volume, **1950:** 136
Jewish National Fund dinner, **1952–53:** 144
Johnson, Louis A., dinner for, **1949:** 64
Kentucky Dam, dedication, **1945:** 165
Kiel Auditorium, St. Louis, Mo., **1950:** 279
Knights of the Red Cross of Constantine, dinner, **1950:** 312
Korea, Republic of, second anniversary, **1950:** 211
Kosciusko, Thaddeus, 200th anniversary of birth, **1946:** 34
Labor Day, **1952–53:** 241
Law Enforcement Problems, Attorney General's Conference on, **1950:** 37
Lehman for Senator, Independent Citizens Committee for, dinner, **1949:** 251
Liberty Bell, dedication of replica, **1950:** 280, 281
Marshall, Gen. George C., dinner for, **1949:** 116
McIntire, Vice Adm. Ross T., luncheon for, **1951:** 281
Methodist Ministers, Washington Institute, **1951:** 31
Monument to Presidents Polk, Jackson, and Johnson, dedication, **1948:** 245
Motion picture industry, 50th anniversary, **1951:** 249
National Archives, dedication of shrine at, **1952–53:** 347
National Capital sesquicentennial, **1948:** 47
National Civil Service League, 70th anniversary meeting, **1952–53:** 117
National Community Christmas Tree, lighting, **1950:** 317; **1951:** 306
National Democratic Conference and Jefferson Jubilee, **1950:** 134
National Foundation for Infantile Paralysis, 10th anniversary, **1948:** 18
National Guard Association, **1950:** 272; **1951:** 270
National Housing Conference, 21st annual banquet, **1952–53:** 120
National Institutes of Health clinical center, dedication, **1951:** 135
National Music Week, **1951:** 99
New York Avenue Presbyterian Church, cornerstone laying, **1951:** 68

Addresses or remarks — *continued*
North Atlantic Treaty Organization
Remarks to Secretaries Acheson and Snyder on return from meeting, **1952–53:** 48
3d anniversary, **1952–53:** 77
Organized Reserve Corps Armory, Kansas City, dedication, **1951:** 218
Pakistan wheat loan document, signing, **1952–53:** 252
President's Committee on National Employ the Physically Handicapped Week, **1950:** 208
Princeton University bicentennial, **1947:** 117
Red Cross, District of Columbia building, cornerstone laying, **1951:** 271
Roosevelt, Franklin D.
4th anniversary of death, **1949:** 76
Home at Hyde Park, dedication, **1946:** 81
Memorial program, **1947:** 71
Rural Electrification Administration, 15th Anniversary, **1950:** 124 [4]
St. Patrick's Day, **1948:** 53
San Martín, Gen. José de, 100th anniversary of death, **1950:** 212
Savings bond drive, **1951:** 133, 213
Volunteers' dinner, **1949:** 82
Secretary of the Interior, luncheon for the President, **1951:** 32
Shrine of North America, 75th anniversary, **1949:** 160
Smithsonian Institution, centennial, **1946:** 201
Steel industry, meeting with management and labor leaders, **1952–53:** 118
Student Citizenship Seminar, **1951:** 139
Swedish pioneer centennial, **1948:** 115
Thirty-fifth Division, reunion, **1947:** 110; **1948:** 117; **1949:** 119; **1952–53:** 157, 158
Truman-Barkley Dinner, **1949:** 15
"Truman Day" reception, **1949:** 250
Turkey, national holiday, **1948:** 263
25th Infantry Division Association, **1951:** 148
Union Station, Washington, dedication of Presidential Lounge as servicemen's center, **1951:** 186
United Nations
General Assembly, **1950:** 271
Headquarters, laying of cornerstone, **1949:** 237
Second anniversary, **1947:** 129
United Nations Day, **1949:** 238
University of California, commencement, **1948:** 129
University of Missouri, commencement, **1950:** 159
U.S. Courts Building, District of Columbia, dedication, **1950:** 174
U.S. Military Academy, sesquicentennial convocation, **1952–53:** 130, 131
U.S.S. *Nautilus*, keel-laying ceremony, **1952–53:** 170

[References are to items except as otherwise indicated]

Addresses or remarks — *continued*
  V-E Day, first anniversary, **1946:** 107
  Veterans of Foreign Wars
    Dinner, **1952–53:** 29
    50th anniversary, **1949:** 184
  Voice of America radio transmitting ship, dedication, **1952–53:** 54
  Voice of Democracy contest winners, **1951:** 40
  Wagner, Sen. Robert F., dinner honoring, **1948:** 261 [15]
  War memorials
    Omaha, Neb., dedication, **1948:** 116 [1]
    West Frankfort, Ill., wreath-laying, **1948:** 218
  War Memorial Opera House, San Francisco, Cal., **1950:** 269
  War Memorial Park, Little Rock, Ark., dedication, **1949:** 120
  Washington, George
    Dedication of statue, **1950:** 42
    Masonic breakfast, **1950:** 41
  Washington Hebrew Congregation temple, cornerstone laying, **1952–53:** 330
  Washington Pilgrimage of American Churchmen, **1951:** 241
  Washington Student Citizenship Seminar, **1950:** 178
  Westminster Presbyterian Church, Alexandria, Va., cornerstone laying, **1952–53:** 337
  White House Conference on Children and Youth, **1950:** 299
  Winston-Salem, N.C., **1951:** 255
    Wake Forest College, groundbreaking, **1951:** 256
  "Women in the Armed Services" commemorative stamp, issuance, **1952–53:** 248
  World Day of Prayer, broadcast, **1950:** 316
Addresses or remarks to foreign or international groups
  Agricultural and Cooperative Credit, International Conference on, **1952–53:** 261
  Ancient and Accepted Scottish Rite, Supreme Council, **1951:** 259
  Boy Scout Jamboree, Valley Forge, Pa., **1950:** 185
  Brazilian Press Association, **1949:** 105
  British publishers and editors, **1951:** 88
  Business and Professional Women, International Federation of, **1952–53:** 188
  Christian Endeavor, International Society of, **1952–53:** 168
  Church of England bishops, **1949:** 207
  Colombia, industrialists from, **1951:** 267
  Council of the Organization of American States, ambassadors, **1949:** 230
  Displaced persons from Europe, **1952–53:** 94
  Exchange teachers, **1951:** 194; **1952–53:** 234
  Exchange teachers from United Kingdom, **1949:** 187

Addresses to foreign groups — *continued*
  Food and Agriculture Organization, U.N., **1948:** 276
  Foreign journalists, **1951:** 94, 160
  Foreign ministers meeting, American republics, **1951:** 59, 67, 76
  German editors and publishers, **1949:** 165
  India, motion picture industry representatives, **1952–53:** 256
  Inter-American Bar Association, **1949:** 115
  Inter-American Conference, Rio de Janeiro, **1947:** 188
  Inter-American Conference on Conservation of Renewable Resources, **1948:** 198 [1]
  International Boys Camp, Inc., Danish representatives, **1951:** 166
  International Council, Independent Order of Odd Fellows, **1951:** 220
  International Monetary Fund and International Bank for Reconstruction and Development, joint annual meeting, **1949:** 210; **1951:** 219
  Korean army officers, **1951:** 236
  Marshall plan countries, representatives, **1949:** 27
  NATO
    Foreign ministers, **1949:** 68, 69
    Trainees, **1951:** 36
  Organization of American States, Council of, **1952–53:** 92
  Pan American Sanitary Organization, Directing Council, **1951:** 243
  Pan American Union, Governing Board, **1946:** 83
  Point 4 agricultural trainees, **1951:** 262
  United Nations, **1946:** 236; **1947:** 61, 129; **1949:** 237; **1950:** 271
  Veterans of U.N. forces in Korea, **1951:** 272
  World Land Tenure Conference, delegates and trainees, **1951:** 296
  World's Christian Endeavor Union, **1950:** 197
Addresses or remarks to national groups
  Agricultural Editors Association, **1949:** 91
  American Association for the Advancement of Science, **1948:** 186
  American Dental Association, Board of Trustees, **1951:** 258
  American Hospital Association convention, **1952–53:** 249
  American Hungarian Federation, representatives, **1951:** 253
  American Legion
    Boys Forum of National Government, **1949:** 170
    Convention, **1948:** 244; **1949:** 194, 195
    Dedication of headquarters, **1951:** 191
    Representatives, **1949:** 49
  American Newspaper Guild, **1950:** 177

[References are to items except as otherwise indicated]

Addresses to national groups — *continued*
  American Society of Civil Engineers, **1949**: 249
  American Society of Newspaper Editors, **1947**: 74; **1948**: 80; **1950**: 92
  American Veterans of World War II, **1949**: 203
  Archives, Eighth Annual Institute on the Preservation and Administration of, **1952–53**: 174
  Associated Church Press, **1949**: 83; **1951**: 61; **1952–53**: 100
  Associated Press, annual luncheon, **1947**: 76
  Association of Immigration and Nationality Lawyers, **1952–53**: 350
  Association of Military Surgeons, **1952–53**: 333
  Attorneys Association, United States, **1952–53**: 165
  Boy Governors, National Conference of, **1949**: 125
  Boys Nation, American Legion, **1946**: 198; **1951**: 168
  Christians and Jews, National Conference of, **1949**: 254
  Citizens Food Committee, **1947**: 198
  Conference on Emergency Problems in Higher Education, **1946**: 162
  Conference of U.S. Attorneys, **1951**: 115
  Defense Advisory Committee on Women in the Services, **1951**: 289
  Democratic National Committee
    Finance Committee, **1949**: 16
    100th anniversary, **1948**: 32
    Reception, **1952–53**: 71
    Women's Division, **1949**: 20
  Democratic Party, **1946**: 67
  Federal Council of Churches of Christ, **1946**: 52
  Fire Prevention, Conference on, **1947**: 86
  Girls Nation, American Legion, **1949**: 191; **1951**: 178; **1952–53**: 220
  Marine Corps League, **1950**: 237
  Masons, **1951**: 41; **1952–53**: 45
  Mayors, U.S., conference of, **1949**: 54
  National Advisory Committee on the Selection of Physicians, Dentists, and Allied Specialists, **1951**: 9
  National Association for the Advancement of Colored People, **1947**: 130
  National Association of Postal Supervisors, **1950**: 247
  National Association of Postmasters, **1951**: 226
  National Association of Radio Farm Directors, **1949**: 90; **1950**: 163
  National Cartoonists Association, **1951**: 290
  National Citizens Committee for United Nations Day, **1949**: 212; **1950**: 239; **1951**: 223; **1952–53**: 259
  National Conference of Business Paper Editors, **1946**: 218; **1948**: 86; **1952–53**: 339
  National Conference on Citizenship, **1950**: 144; **1951**: 107; **1952–53**: 251

Addresses to national groups — *continued*
  National Conference on Family Life, **1948**: 92
  National Conference on Israel, **1951**: 229
  National Council of Churches, **1952–53**: 260
  National Council of Negro Women, **1949**: 256
  National Emergency Civil Rights Mobilization, **1950**: 15
  National 4-H Club, **1949**: 123; **1951**: 122; **1952–53**: 176
  National Guard Association, 73d General Conference, **1951**: 270
  National Health Assembly, **1948**: 89
  National Jewish Welfare Board, **1952–53**: 297
  National Newspaper Publishers Association, Directors, **1952–53**: 329
  National Planning Association, **1949**: 25
  National Plowing Match, **1948**: 195
  National Rural Electric Cooperative Association, **1952–53**: 62
  Polish Legion of American Veterans, **1951**: 291
  Political Action Committee, CIO, rally, **1952–53**: 230
  Presidential Electors Association, **1949**: 17
  President's Committee on Employment of the Physically Handicapped, **1950**: 208; **1951**: 195; **1952–53**: 243
  President's Highway Safety Conference, **1946**: 106; **1947**: 82, 118; **1951**: 42, 121
  Publishers' associations, **1947**: 82
  Reserve Officers Association, **1949**: 36; **1950**: 176
  Science Talent Search, contest winners, **1949**: 44; **1950**: 48; **1951**: 50; **1952–53**: 52
  Shrine of North America, **1949**: 159, 160
  Society of Business Magazine Editors, **1951**: 18
  Syrian and Lebanese American Federation, **1951**: 245
  Task Force Smith, **1952–53**: 172
  Theater Owners Convention, **1952–53**: 250
  Thirty-fifth Division, reunion, **1947**: 110
  U.S. National Commission for UNESCO, **1946**: 222; **1950**: 87
  United Defense Fund, **1951**: 180
  United Jewish Appeal, **1946**: 42
  Veterans of Foreign Wars, **1949**: 33
  Women's Bureau Conference, **1948**: 30
  Women's National Democratic Club, **1949**: 252; **1951**: 297
  Womens Patriotic Conference on National Defense, **1950**: 21
  Young Democrats, **1948**: 101
  Young Men's Christian Association and Government Assembly, **1952–53**: 184
  Youth Conference on Famine Relief, **1946**: 168
Addresses or remarks at presentation ceremonies. *See also* Awards and citations.
  Agriculture Department honor awards, **1952–53**: 126

[References are to items except as otherwise indicated]

Addresses at presentation ceremonies — *continued*
American Legion's Distinguished Service Medal, acceptance, **1949:** 195
Association of Immigration and Nationality Lawyers, acceptance of citation, **1952–53:** 350
Capital Press Club plaque, acceptance, **1952–53:** 153
Carillon from the Netherlands, acceptance, **1952–53:** 78
Chair used while Cabinet officer, gift to Gen. George C. Marshall, **1951:** 263
Collier Trophy, joint award, **1951:** 301
Collier's Congressional Awards
Committee, **1946:** 60
Monroney, Repr. Mike, **1946:** 80
Vandenberg, Sen. Arthur H., **1946:** 80
Congressional Medal of Honor presentations. *See under* Medals, presentation.
Corregidor, rock fragment from, acceptance, **1951:** 151
Danish arm band, acceptance, **1946:** 6 [18]
Defense bond, floral replica of, acceptance, **1951:** 210
Distinguished Service Medal. *See under* Medals, presentation.
Fleet Sonar School graduates, presentation of diplomas, **1949:** 53
4-H Club pin, acceptance, **1949:** 123
Franklin D. Roosevelt Memorial Brotherhood Medal, acceptance, **1952–53:** 290
Gift from French Ambassador, acceptance, **1952–53:** 99
Gold medal, Enrico Gaspar Dutra, **1949:** 103
Gonzaga University, Certificate of Merit, acceptance, **1950:** 126
Grand champion prize ribbon, acceptance, **1950:** 124 [6]
Harmon International Trophy, Col. David C. Schilling, **1951:** 268
Histadrut Humanitarian Award, acceptance, **1951:** 274
Honorary degrees, **1945:** 68; **1946:** 112; **1947:** 52, 117; **1948:** 129, 228 [9]; **1949:** 51; **1950:** 160 [1]
Legion of merit. *See under* Medals, presentation.
National Conference on Israel, acceptance of plaque from, **1951:** 229
National Forensic League medal, acceptance, **1952–53:** 173
National Newspaper Publishers Association plaque, acceptance, **1952–53:** 329
Overmantel for White House, acceptance, **1951:** 288
Papers of Thomas Jefferson, first volume, acceptance, **1950:** 136
Piano, acceptance, **1951:** 99

Addresses at presentation ceremonies — *continued*
Replica of statue, The God of Peace, acceptance, **1948:** 256 [6]
Robert S. Abbott memorial award, acceptance, **1949:** 109
Roosevelt, Franklin D., posthumous award for, acceptance, **1948:** 265
7th Regimental Citation, Nisei regiment, **1946:** 170
Silver Quill award, Paul Wooton, **1951:** 18
Speaker Rayburn, presentation of gavel to, **1951:** 24
Teacher of the Year award, Mrs. Geraldine Jones, **1952–53:** 133
Testimonial scroll, Brig. Gen. Benjamin O. Davis, **1948:** 162
Unit citations, aircraft carriers, **1946:** 171
Variety Clubs International, award to Secretary Marshall, **1948:** 196
Vice President Barkley, presentation of gavel to, **1951:** 51
Wendell Willkie journalism awards, **1947:** 48
White House correspondents gift of money to Warm Springs Foundation, acceptance, **1945:** 208 [1]
White House Photographers' Association, awards, **1951:** 43
Woodrow Wilson Foundation award, acceptance, **1951:** 6
Young American Medal for Bravery and Young American Medal for Service, **1952–53:** 181
Adenauer, Konrad, **1951:** 247 [8]
Adkins, Judge Jesse C., **1946:** 229 [1]
Administration for Research, report, **1947:** 201
Administrative Management, President's Committee on, **1952–53:** 84, 85
Administrative Procedures Act (1946), **1947:** 120; **1950:** 54, 75, 123; **1952–53:** 148
Admiralty Islands, **1945:** 45
Advertising matter, postal rates, **1951:** 45; **1952–53:** 367 (p. 1144)
Advisory Board on International Development, **1950:** 282, 289, 294
Chairman (Nelson Rockefeller), **1951:** 53
Advisory Board on Mobilization Policy, National, **1951:** 56 [2, 4], 74n., 137
Advisory Board for the Post Office Department, establishment, **1949:** 130
Advisory Commission to the Council of National Defense, **1945:** 55
Advisory Commission on Education, **1950:** 92
Advisory Commission on Educational Exchange, **1950:** 227
Advisory Commission on Information, U.S., **1950:** 190ftn. (p. 521)
Advisory Commission on International Information, **1950:** 227

Advisory Commission on Universal Training, President's, **1947:** 106; **1948:** 5 (p. 26), 86; **1950:** 138

Advisory Committee, National, savings bond drive, **1949:** 82

Advisory Committee on Civil Rights, **1947:** 130

Advisory Committee on Education, **1946:** 117

Advisory Committee on Management, **1952–53:** 18 (p. 115)

Advisory Committee on Management Improvement, **1949:** 167, 242

Advisory Committee on Merchant Marine, President's, **1948:** 4 [13]; **1949:** 133

Advisory Committee on Voluntary Foreign Aid, **1950:** 285

AEC.
  See Atomic Energy Commission.

Aero Club of Washington, Wright Memorial Dinner, **1952–53:** 351

Aeronautics, National Advisory Committee for, **1947:** 241; **1948:** 5 (p. 50); **1949:** 8 (p. 86); **1950:** 9 (pp. 64, 66); **1951:** 13 (p. 70); **1952–53:** 18 (p. 73), 367 (p. 1135)

Aeronautics, Radio Technical Commission for, **1948:** 175

Aeronautics research, **1948:** 5 (pp. 27, 50), 7, 60, 175

Afforestation, **1945:** 165

AFL.
  See American Federation of Labor.

Africa, **1946:** 29, 78 [14], 86 [4]; **1947:** 208
  See also specific countries.
  Assistance, **1952–53:** 15, 55
    Economic, **1951:** 4
    Technical, **1951:** 13 (p. 75), 83, 262
  Barbary pirates, Jefferson's expedition against, **1951:** 80
  Cobalt imports from, **1950:** 124 [7]
  Communism in, **1952–53:** 81
  Economic development, **1950:** 159
  Emergence of new nations, **1952–53:** 366
  Invasion of North Africa, **1945:** 45, 178
  Land reform, **1951:** 179 [13]
  Point 4 program in, **1951:** 83

Afton, Okla., campaign remarks, **1948:** 216 [12]

Agave fiber and cordage, import controls, **1947:** 18

Aggression, **1946:** 68, 83
  Dictators in 1930's, **1951:** 78

Agramonte, Arístides, **1948:** 81

Agricultural Act of 1948, approval, **1948:** 155

Agricultural Act of 1949, **1950:** 249; **1952–53:** 210

Agricultural Adjustment Act, **1948:** 138 [5], 222 [4, 6]; **1950:** 83, 110 [7]; **1952–53:** 267, 277 [6], 285, 312, 315 [4]

Agricultural Adjustment Administration, **1946:** 118; **1947:** 7 (pp. 80, 81)

Agricultural colleges, State, **1950:** 110 [3]

Agricultural commodities, **1947:** 7 (p. 94); **1948:** 1, 99, 175; **1950:** 6
  See also Agriculture; *specific commodities.*
  Campaign remarks, **1948:** 194 [11], 204 [2], 218 [8, 11], 222 [1, 8], 226, 228 [8], 233 [1], 261 [8]
  Conservation program, **1948:** 214 [5]
  Consumption, **1949:** 5; **1950:** 111
  Demand for, **1951:** 11, 13 (p. 87)
  Exchanges, **1947:** 209 [11, 12, 16], 226 [13, 15]
  Fruits and vegetables, exemption from price control, **1952–53:** 190
  Imports and exports, **1947:** 4 (p. 32), 7 (pp. 80, 81), 52; **1948:** 5 (p. 44), 8 (pp. 77, 93), 195, 213, 233 [1], 246, 276; **1949:** 2, 8 (p. 79); **1950:** 9 (p. 84), 83, 111
  Loans, **1952–53:** 267
  Marketing, **1948:** 2, 8 (pp. 77, 92, 93), 117
    Programs, **1947:** 80; **1948:** 101; **1949:** 2; **1950:** 9 (p. 87), 83, 110 [7], 111, 121 [2], 279
    Research, **1952–53:** 367 (p. 1150)
  Perishable, **1952–53:** 267
  Production payments, **1951:** 12 [15]
  Price supports.
    See main heading, Price supports.
  Prices, **1947:** 76, 107 [2]; **1948:** 5 (pp. 42–44), 8 (pp. 88, 94), 80, 99, 117, 181 [9], 183 [6], 195, 213, 218 [8, 11, 14], 222 [3, 8], 226, 228 [8], 261 [8], 276; **1949:** 5, 45 [3], 250 [3]; **1950:** 83, 111, 121 [7], 279; **1951:** 7 [10], 199; **1952–53:** 18 (p. 91), 315 [4], 321 [3–5]
  Production **1949:** 2, 5, 77, 151, 154, 203, 250 [3], 263; **1952–53:** 18 (p. 78), 367 (pp. 1148–1150)
    Distribution, **1951:** 11, 122, 167
    Payments, **1950:** 110 [7], 121 [2, 7], 127 [5]
  Purchase for overseas relief, **1947:** 226 [14]
  Sales, **1952–53:** 215
  Speculation in, **1948:** 165, 233 [1]; **1949:** 5
    Measures to curb, **1950:** 194
  Storage, **1948:** 195, 204 [2]; **1949:** 2; **1950:** 111
  Subsidies, **1951:** 12 [15, 22], 13 (pp. 88, 89), 70 [2]
  Surpluses.
    See main heading, Agricultural surpluses.
  U.S. territories and possessions, **1947:** 35

Agricultural and Cooperative Credit, International Conference on, **1952–53:** 261

Agricultural Credit Corporation, Regional, **1949:** 8 (p. 81)

Agricultural Editors Association, **1949:** 91

Agricultural Extension Service, **1948:** 5 (pp. 42, 44), 276

Agricultural implements, shipment to Europe, **1947:** 210 [6]

Agricultural Marketing Agreements Act **1947:** (1937), 80; **1952–53:** 367 (p. 1150)

Agricultural research.
  See under Agriculture.
Agricultural Research Administration, **1946:** 116;
    1947: 80
Agricultural Research Center, **1946:** 116; **1947:** 80
Agricultural surpluses, **1947:** 7 (pp. 80, 81), 35, 70
    [18]; **1948:** 5 (p. 44), 8 (p. 92), 99, 222 [6],
    237 [5]; **1950:** 9 (p. 87), 29 [7], 86 [18, 24],
    1·10 [2], 111; **1951:** 13 (p. 88); **1952–53:** 18
    (p. 91), 367 (p. 1148)
  See also specific commodities.
  Distribution to relief agencies, **1950:** 249
  Relief shipments to Yugoslavia, **1950:** 293
  Use in European recovery program, **1949:** 45 [9]
  Use for school lunch program, **1948:** 240 [5]
Agricultural workers
  Draft deferment, **1952–53:** 185–87
    Veto, **1945:** 23
  Unemployment insurance coverage, **1950:** 84
  Wages and hours, statistics, **1949:** 13
Agriculture, **1945:** 38, 128; **1946:** 18 (pp. 58–60, 80,
    81), 193; **1947:** 2 (pp. 3, 7, 12), 4 (pp. 31,
    32), 7 (pp. 58, 78), 51, 99, 110, 152, 181
    (pp. 402, 405), 183, 204, 212, 219, 224,
    225; **1948:** 2, 5 (pp. 25, 42), 8 (pp. 64, 75,
    77, 78, 85, 90), 12, 117, 134, 175; **1950:** 2,
    9 (pp. 84–88), 84, 86ftn. (p. 255), 92, 111,
    306; **1951:** 13 (p. 87), 163, 296; **1952–53:**
    18 (pp. 90–92)
  See also Agricultural commodities; Farm econ-
    omy.
  Acreage allotments, **1949:** 269 [21]; **1950:** 9 (p.
    87),83; **1952–53:** 277 [6]
    Suspension, **1951:** 11
  Allocations and priority agreements, **1948:** 1
  Budget, decrease, **1951:** 12 [50]
  Capacity, **1952–53:** 215
  Census of (1954), **1952–53:** 367 (p. 1156)
  Chinese, **1946:** 265
  Conservation, **1947:** 231; **1948:** 2, 5 (pp. 25, 44),
    8 (p. 67), 175, 199; **1949:** 8 (pp. 47, 78);
    1950: 9 (pp. 49, 84–88), 111; **1951:** 13 (pp.
    87, 90), 206; **1952–53:** 267, 277 [6]
  Cooperatives, **1950:** 132; **1952–53:** 15, 267
    See also main heading, Cooperatives.
  Credit, **1948:** 276; **1950:** 114; **1951:** 202, 296
    See also main heading, Credit.
  Crop conservation program, **1948:** 214 [5]
  Crop failures, **1947:** 191 [3]
  Crop insurance, **1948:** 2, 99, 194 [11], 246;
    1952–53: 367 (p. 1148)
  Crop loans, **1948:** 267 [3]
  Dairy products, restrictions on imports of,
    1952–53: 360
  Defense effort, contribution to, **1952–53:** 126
  Development projects, India, **1951:** 63 [2]
  Economy, **1952–53:** 367 (pp. 1148–1150)
  Education, **1950:** 110 [3]

Agriculture — *continued*
  Electric power, increased use on farms, **1951:** 11;
    1952–53: 126
  Employment
    European refugees on U.S. farms, proposed,
      1952–53: 65
    Manpower needs, **1951:** 15; **1952–53:** 15, 18 (p.
      94), 186, 187
  European, **1947:** 197, 238; **1951:** 25
  Expenditures for, **1952–53:** 231, 367 (p. 1131)
  Family vs. corporate farms, **1950:** 111, 121 [3]
  Farm income.
    See Income.
  Farm programs.
    See main heading, Farm programs.
  Farmers, defense program demands on, **1951:** 11
  Farmland prices, **1947:** 97
  Federal aid, **1948:** 5 (p. 44)
  Fertilizers, increased demand for, **1951:** 11;
    1952–53: 388
  Grain conservation, **1948:** 14, 19
  Grain crop failure, India, **1951:** 34
  Hybrid seed development, **1950:** 177
  Irrigation projects, **1952–53:** 388
  Legislation, proposed, **1951:** 4
  Marketing quotas, suspension, **1951:** 11
  Mechanization, growth of, **1951:** 11
  Message to Congress, **1948:** 99
  Migratory labor, **1951:** 16 [5], 75, 154
    Mexican, **1952–53:** 367 (pp. 1150–1151)
  Philippines, agrarian reform, **1945:** 176
  Production, **1947:** 4 (p. 33), 76, 127 [16], 152, 191
    [3], 236 [10]; **1948:** 2, 5 (p. 44), 8 (pp. 62,
    68, 70, 77, 92–94), 99, 120 [5], 134, 137 [3],
    138 [5], 167, 174 [14], 182, 194 [5, 6, 11],
    195, 213, 216 [1, 5], 217, 223, 234, 246,
    276; **1950:** 92, 106, 157, 163, 232, 303;
    1951: 11, 167; **1952–53:** 5, 15, 18 (p. 90),
    62, 126, 185, 187, 190, 210, 215, 315 [4]
  Republican stand, campaign remarks on, **1952–
    53:** 316
  Research, **1945:** 128; **1946:** 207; **1947:** 7, 80, 183,
    194; **1948:** 5 (p. 44), 8 (pp. 86, 92), 117,
    186, 234, 239, 246; **1950:** 6, 110 [3], 111;
    1951: 13 (p. 90), 297; **1952–53:** 5, 18 (p.
    92), 126, 267, 367 (p. 1150)
  Resources, conservation and development,
    1952–53: 289 [1], 367 (p. 1149), 376
  Southern, growth and diversification, **1952–53:**
    194
  Southern Hemisphere, **1947:** 210 [3]
  Subsidies, **1946:** 86 [19, 32]; **1947:** 6 [24]; **1951:**
    12 [15, 22]
  Surpluses.
    See Agricultural surpluses.
  Technical assistance abroad, **1950:** 177
  Technology, **1948:** 8 (pp. 85, 92), 276
  Yugoslavia, crop failures in, **1950:** 290, 293

Agriculture, Dept. of, **1945:** 128, 135; **1946:** 18 (pp. 80, 82, 86), 29, 99, 116, 118, 119 [3], 207; **1947:** 7 (pp. 58, 78, 85), 18, 39, 47, 80, 181 (p. 398), 186, 224, 241, 242; **1948:** 4 [7], 5 (pp. 42, 44, 46), 8 (p. 70), 14, 42, 105, 216 [7], 246; **1949:** 13, 185, 196, 206; **1950:** 54, 163n., 164; **1951:** 154, 158, 269, 296n.; **1952–53:** 81, 185, 221 [1], 263
  Appropriations, **1946:** 238
  Commodity exchanges, regulation, **1951:** 11; **1952–53:** 15
  Conservation functions, **1950:** 9 (p. 87); **1951:** 13 (p. 90); **1952–53:** 3
  Cowart, Jack, dismissal of, **1951:** 209 [12]
  Cranberries, marketing promotion, **1948:** 237 [5]
  Disaster relief loans, **1952–53:** 18 (p. 100)
  Farm housing contributions, **1949:** 126
  Flood control projects, **1947:** 144
  Food purchasing policies, **1951:** 205
  Foreign assistance functions, **1949:** 22 [3]
  Hill, Grover B., **1945:** 52 [7]
  Honor awards presentation, address, **1952–53:** 126
  Industrial development program, **1946:** 18 (p. 49)
  Key agricultural commodities, financing of production expansion, **1952–53:** 18 (p. 78)
  Marshall plan functions, **1947:** 238
  Missouri River Basin program, **1951:** 183n.; **1952–53:** 98 [9]
  National garden program, **1946:** 40
  Natural resources, role in development of, **1952–53:** 388
  News conference remarks on, **1947:** 107 [3], 177 [10], 210 [3, 4], 218 [6]; **1949:** 22 [3], 161 [1], 226 [4]
  Price control functions, **1946:** 232
  Programs review, **1950:** 196
  Reorganization, **1950:** 53, 54, 58
  Report on prices, **1951:** 49 [21]
  Rural housing functions, **1950:** 9 (p. 80)
  Soil conservation program, **1948:** 231 [7]
  Stevenson, Gov. Adlai, former service in, **1952–53:** 317 [4]
  Water resources development functions, **1950:** 140
Agriculture, Secretary of (Clinton P. Anderson), **1945:** 193 [9]; **1946:** 40n., 49, 87n., 99, 195n., 232; **1947:** 35, 47, 64, 139n., 202, 229; **1948:** 1, 14
  Directive, **1946:** 23
  Grain control order, **1948:** 19
  Letter, **1946:** 71; **1947:** 97
  News conference remarks on, **1946:** 30 [2], 41 [15], 43 [9], 78 [10], 84 [10, 17, 19, 23], 95 [24], 119 [3], 143 [2], 223 [1], 237 [21]; **1947:** 155 [7], 177 [10], 205 [2], 221 [1], 236 [4]
  Reports, **1946:** 144, 165, 255

Agriculture, Secretary of (Anderson) — *continued*
  Resignation, **1948:** 94
  Senate candidacy, question of, **1948:** 49 [10]
  Successor, question of, **1948:** 84 [13], 88 [11], 93 [15], 97 [1]
Agriculture, Secretary of (Charles F. Brannan), **1948:** 136 [2], 170 [1], 198 [1], 204 [4], 206 [3], 214 [7]; **1949:** 8 (pp. 80, 81), 90, 157; **1950:** 83, 111, 124 [1, 6], 145, 163; **1951:** 113 [3], 122, 202, 205, 209 [12]; **1952–53:** 15, 126, 186, 268 [2], 282 [7], 285n., 292n., 360
  Campaign remarks, **1952–53:** 292 [11]
  Cotton price control, consideration by, **1951:** 33 [4]
  Dairy product imports, imposition of additional restrictions, **1952–53:** 359 [2, 14]
  Farm plan, **1951:** 12 [15, 45], 22 [13], 227 [22]; **1952–53:** 17 [30], 285
  Farm prices survey, **1951:** 7 [16]
  Grain storage program, Republican charges concerning, **1952–53:** 267
  Letters and memorandums, **1949:** 149n.; **1950:** 192, 196, 259, 265; **1951:** 55
  News conference remarks on, **1949:** 30 [5], 72 [13], 122 [4], 182 [3], 269 [21]; **1950:** 86 [18–20, 28], 191 [11]; **1952–53:** 31 [17, 18]
  Price support plan, **1949:** 72 [13], 90n., 122 [4], 182 [3]; **1950:** 86 [18–20, 28]
  Resignation, **1952–53:** 385
Agriculture, Secretary of (Claude R. Wickard)
  Letter, **1945:** 38
  Resignation, **1945:** 40 [1], 44 [6]
Ahern, James T., **1945:** 163
Aiken, Sen. George D., **1948:** 276n.; **1949:** 7 [34], 94n.
Aiken, Paul, **1950:** 206 [3]
Air Coordinating Committee, **1947:** 40, 148, 149; **1952–53:** 155, 328
  Chairman (Donald W. Nyrop), letter, **1952–53:** 155
Air Force, **1945:** 45, 178; **1946:** 7, 18 (p. 48), 137, 138, 223 [6]; **1947:** 35, 50; **1948:** 5 (pp. 26–29), 175; **1949:** 8 (pp. 57, 60), 223, 244; **1951:** 138; **1952–53:** 131
  Aircraft for President-elect, provision of, **1948:** 285 [15]
  Aircraft procurement, **1948:** 175
  Appropriations, question of impounding by the President, **1951:** 224 [2]
  Authorized strength, **1949:** 7 [16, 21], 8 (p. 58), 11 [13, 20], 231 [19]; **1950:** 9 (p. 63), 80 [4], 169 [14], 194, 303
  B-36 bomber controversy, **1949:** 118ftn. (p. 280)
  Bases, **1952–53:** 217, 367 (p. 1137)
    Northwest, **1950:** 121 [13]
  Chief of Staff (Gen. Carl Spaatz), **1947:** 191 [22]
  Department for, proposed, **1945:** 218

Air Force — *continued*
European command, **1950:** 310
Expenditures for, **1950:** 8 [24], 9 (p. 61)
Food conservation in, **1947:** 202
Football team, question of, **1947:** 226 [2]
Formosa, use in neutralization of, **1950:** 209 [11]
Functions, **1947:** 159
Increase in strength, **1951:** 4, 13 (pp. 64, 69), 92, 167, 224 [2]; **1952–53:** 17 [2, 10, 17], 18 (pp. 64, 69), 158, 275, 367 (pp. 1134, 1137)
Intelligence report, **1948:** 285 [6]
Land transactions, veto of bill to restrict, **1951:** 105, 108 [1]
Matador (B-61) missile, **1951:** 224 [6], 247 [1, 12]
News conference remarks, **1949:** 7 [16, 21], 11 [13, 20], 89 [7], 200 [7], 231 [19]; **1950:** 8 [24], 80 [4], 169 [14], 209 [11], 295 [1]
North Korean targets, strikes against, **1950:** 184, 193
Petroleum products, use of, **1952–53:** 379
Preparedness, **1947:** 110
Racial discrimination, elimination, **1952–53:** 290, 315 [6]
Reserves, **1949:** 7 [16], 8 (p. 58), 174; **1950:** 9 (pp. 63, 64), 193
Retirement benefits, **1948:** 145
Status of, **1948:** 243 [1]
Review at dedication of Idlewild International Airport, **1948:** 168
Size, **1948:** 55 [5], 71 [9], 77 [5], 84 [9]
Subsidization of technical schools, **1951:** 85 [9]
Air Force, Department of the, **1945:** 218n.; **1947:** 10n., 202, 241; **1948:** 3, 43; **1949:** 50, 158, 174, 177
Judge Advocate, question of appointment, **1948:** 181 [7]
Air Force, Secrétary of the (Thomas K. Finletter), **1950:** 259; **1951:** 93n.; **1952–53:** 125, 128, 131
Air Force, Secretary of the (Stuart Symington), **1947:** 182 [1]; **1948:** 77 [5, 7, 10]; **1949:** 35 [24], 205 [9], 236ftn. (p. 525); **1950:** 80 [7, 8]
Air Force Association, **1950:** 138n.; **1951:** 109n.
Air forces, allied, in Korean war, **1950:** 232
Air Judge Advocate, question of appointment, **1948:** 181 [7]
Air National Guard, **1949:** 7 [16], 8 (p. 58); **1950:** 9 (p. 63)
Air navigation, **1946:** 133; **1947:** 7 (p. 58), 148; **1948:** 5 (pp. 47, 50), 7, 175
Air Policy Commission, President's, **1947:** 148, 149, 161; **1948:** 7, 9 [12]
Air Pollution
U.S. Technical Conference on, **1950:** 101
Victims, evacuation of, **1948:** 274 [10]
Air power, U.S., **1945:** 45, 178, 218
Defense emphasis on, **1949:** 8 (p. 56)

Air routes, North Pacific, **1946:** 95 [14]
Air safety, **1947:** 19 [18], 82, 180 [12], 115
Air traffic control, **1948:** 7, 175; **1952–53:** 40
Air Transport Agreement, U.S.-U.K., **1946:** 43 [2], 44
Air Transport Command, **1945:** 45
Air transportation, safety measures, **1948:** 5 (p. 49)
Air travel priorities, termination, **1945:** 129 [1]
Sacred Cow, Presidential plane, **1947:** 95 [18]
Aircraft, military, **1946:** 137, 138; **1947:** 148, 161; **1948:** 5 (p. 50), 7; **1949:** 7 [16, 21]; **1950:** 9 (p. 63)
See also Aviation; Aviation, civil.
Bombers, **1945:** 45; **1946:** 7; **1949:** 200 [7]
B-29, **1946:** 229 [15]; **1949:** 22 [8], 45 [15]
Interception by Soviet Union, **1950:** 86ftn. (p. 254)
B-36, **1949:** 118 [4], 205 [9]; **1951:** 153 [2]; **1952–53:** 158
B-50, **1949:** 45 [7, 12]
Budget allocations for, **1952–53:** 17 [31, 34]
C-54, gift to General de Gaulle, **1945:** 147 [3]
C-124 transport, **1951:** 252
Carriers
Strategic need for, **1949:** 45 [12]
Unit citations, **1946:** 171
Construction, **1949:** 200 [7]
Expenditures for, **1950:** 258 [15]
F-84E Thunderjet, first nonstop transatlantic crossing, **1951:** 268n.
Jet engines, development, **1952–53:** 275
Materiel and ordnance for, **1947:** 11
Navy Privateer, disappearance over Baltic, **1950:** 86 [23], 97 [9]
News conference remarks, **1950:** 105 [13], 258 [15]
Nuclear propulsion, development, **1951:** 13 (p. 86)
Procurement, **1947:** 181 (p. 398); **1948:** 5 (pp. 20, 26–29), 60, 98, 106, 175; **1949:** 8 (p. 60), 200 [7], 244; **1950:** 9 (p. 64), 105 [13]; **1951:** 13 (p. 69), 92; **1952–53:** 18 (pp. 70–71)
Production, **1947:** 94; **1950:** 256, 303; **1951:** 4, 11, 80, 91, 252; **1952–53:** 5, 17 [17], 158, 238 [12]
Research and development, **1951:** 13 (p. 70)
Senate investigation of, **1952–53:** 175 [10]
Surplus disposal, **1946:** 18 (p. 75)
Transport planes, **1945:** 45; **1951:** 252
U.N., assistance in Korean defense, **1950:** 193, 194
U.S. plane, destruction by Soviets, **1951:** 298 [5]
Aircraft industry, **1952–53:** 158
Labor dispute, **1951:** 252
Airlines
Federal aid, **1948:** 8 (pp. 67, 81, 82)
Labor dispute, **1951:** 132 [1], 140 [10]

Airlines — *continued*
  Mail transportation rates, **1951:** 13 (p. 83), 45
  Mexico, service to, **1952–53:** 246
  Strike, **1946:** 110 [11]
  Subsidies, **1952–53:** 367 (p. 1144)
Airmail, payments to carriers, **1950:** 9 (p. 94);
    1952–53: 18 (p. 83), 367 (p. 1144)
Airport Act, Federal, **1950:** 68
Airport Commission, President's, **1952–53:** 40, 41,
  155
Airport construction, **1945:** 128
Airports, **1946:** 18 (pp. 53, 81, 82); **1947:** 19 [15],
  35; **1948:** 5 (p. 25), 7, 175
  See also Aviation, civil.
  Alaska, **1948:** 5 (p. 50), 105
  Federal aid, **1947:** 7 (p. 86), 35, 180 [12], 181;
    1948: 5 (pp. 48, 50), 8 (p. 82), 105; **1950:** 9
    (p. 50), 171; **1951:** 13 (p. 83); **1952–53:** 18
    (p. 83), 155, 351, 367 (p. 1144)
  Friendship International Airport, Baltimore,
    dedication, **1950:** 97 [16], 171
  Idlewild International Airport, dedication, **1948:**
    168
  Location and use, study of, **1952–53:** 40
  Safety equipment, **1947:** 19 [18]; **1948:** 175
Airpower, issue in election campaign, **1952–53:** 156
  [8]
Akers, Robert W., **1952–53:** 98 [18]
Akron, Colo., remarks at, **1952–53:** 282 [8]
Akron, Ohio, campaign address, **1948:** 232
Alabama, **1947:** 104; **1949:** 205 [16]
  Folsom, Gov. James E., **1948:** 15 [4]
  Manasco, Repr. Carter, **1945:** 175 [18], 208 [14],
    221 [2], 222
  Peanut acreage allotments, **1950:** 83
  Primary elections, **1948:** 93 [13]
Alamo, the President's visit to, **1948:** 210 [1]
Alaska, **1946:** 27 [18], 223 [6]; **1947:** 7 (pp. 83, 91),
  35, 78 [2]; **1948:** 8 (p. 78)
  Airports.
    See under main heading, Airports.
  Assistance, **1951:** 262
  Defense, **1950:** 29 [23], 80 [4], 105 [14]
  Elective governorship, proposed, **1952–53:** 35
    [15]
  Gruening, Gov. Ernest, **1945:** 64 [3]; **1948:** 11 [7],
    49 [9]; **1949:** 112 [16]; **1950:** 11 [7], 29 [23]
  Highways, **1945:** 64 [3], 175 [12]; **1946:** 18 (p. 81)
    Construction, **1948:** 5 (p. 50), 105
  Housing, **1948:** 105; **1949:** 8 (p. 75); **1950:** 112;
    1951: 118 [5]
  Korean war casualties, **1950:** 291
  Lead and zinc production, **1950:** 124 [7]
  Message to Congress, **1948:** 105
  Military preparedness, **1950:** 291
  Natural resources, **1949:** 8 (p. 84)
    Development of, **1948:** 5 (p. 47); **1950:** 9 (p.
    91)

Alaska — *continued*
  News conference remarks, **1950:** 29 [23], 52 [9],
    80 [4], 105 [14], 179 [6], 206 [12], 230 [3],
    273 [5]
  Public works, **1949:** 8 (p. 75), 192 [8]; **1950:** 53,
    69, 70
  Purchase of, **1952–53:** 107 [10]
  Road Commission, **1945:** 64 [3]
  Statehood, Proposed, **1945:** 147 [23]; **1946:** 18 (p.
    66); **1948:** 2 (p. 3), 20, 105; **1949:** 4 [7], 112
    [9]; **1950:** 2, 52 [9], 107, 121 [13], 179 [6],
    206 [12], 230 [3], 267, 273 [5], 267, 291;
    1951: 168; **1952–53:** 5, 35 [15], 49 [8], 149
    [15], 274 [5]
  Taxes, **1950:** 291
  Transportation, **1948:** 105
  Visit to, question of, **1948:** 285 [11]
  Water resources development, **1950:** 140
  Williams, Llewellyn, dismissal from office in,
    1951: 224 [5]
Alaska Housing Act of 1949, **1952–53:** 18 (p. 99)
Alaska Housing Authority, **1949:** 8 (p. 75)
Alaska Railroad, **1948:** 5 (p. 50), 105; **1950:** 69
Albania, **1946:** 186 [12]
  Aid to Greek Communists, **1948:** 129
  Relief for, **1945:** 186
  Soviet domination, **1948:** 53
  Violation of Greek border, **1947:** 56
Albany, N.Y., **1948:** 170 [2]
  Campaign remarks, **1948:** 228 [1]; **1952–53:** 289
    [9]
  Corning, Mayor Erastus, **1948:** 228 [1]
Albany, Oreg., campaign remarks, **1948:** 126 [3]
Albert, Repr. Carl, **1948:** 214 [4, 5], 216 [5]
Albuquerque, N. Mex., **1949:** 248
  Campaign remarks, **1948:** 136 [3]
  Everly, Mayor Ernest W., **1948:** 136 [3]
Alcoa Aluminum Corp., **1952–53:** 274 [2]
Alcohol
  Proposed conversion of surplus potatoes into,
    1951: 2 [22]
Alcohol, ethyl, allocation and control of grain for
    production of, **1948:** 19
  Message to Congress, **1948:** 14
Alcohol, industrial, **1947:** 35
Alcohol laws, local, Federal enforcement aid, **1951:**
  63 [1]
Alcoholic beverages, production, **1946:** 29
Aldrich, Winthrop W., **1946:** 142; **1950:** 11 [8];
    1952–53: 317 [5]
Alemán, Miguel (President of Mexico), **1947:** 14 [8,
    17], 51, 79, 83, 84, 91n., 95 [17]; **1949:** 200
    [1]
Aleutian Islands, **1946:** 223 [6]
  Battle at, **1945:** 45
Alexander, Archibald S., **1948:** 225 [3], 227 [6, 7];
    1952–53: 303 [2–7]
Alexander, Field Marshal, message, **1945:** 21

Alexander, Viscount, **1947:** 19 [11], 111
Alexander the Great, **1950:** 138
Alexandria, Va., **1950:** 42, 44 [2, 10]; **1951:** 255
Alexandrian Library, destruction of, **1951:** 225
Alfange, Dean, **1948:** 253n.
Alfson, George, **1952–53:** 313 [1, 2]
Algonquin, **1946:** 188
Ali, Mohammed, **1952–53:** 252
Ali Khan, Liaquat, **1949:** 253 [10, 15]; **1950:** 102
   Death of, **1951:** 257
Alice of Old Vincennes, Maurice Thompson, **1948:**
   233 [3]
Alien property, Philippines, **1945:** 176
Alien Property Administration, Philippine, **1947:**
   80
Alien Property Custodian, Office of, **1946:** 84 [9],
   229 [27], 231; **1947:** 31 [12], 80; **1949:** 144
   [5]
   Vacancy, **1950:** 16 [8]
Alien Property Custodian (James E. Markham),
   1946: 231
   Letter, **1945:** 176
Alien and Sedition Acts, **1949:** 122 [13, 16]; **1950:**
   37, 203 [8], 207, 254; **1952–53:** 182
Aliens, **1952–53:** 182, 367 (p. 1163)
   Migrating to U.S. from Europe, **1945:** 225
   Resident, status of, **1948:** 142
   Security control, **1950:** 94, 203 [8], 207, 254
   Subversive, deportation of, **1948:** 215
Alkaloids, cinchona, import controls, **1947:** 18, 99
All-American Canal Project, **1948:** 206 [4]
Allegheny County Free Fair, Pittsburgh, Pa., **1949:**
   202
Allen, Repr. A. Leonard, **1952–53:** 312
Allen, George E., **1945:** 116n.; **1946:** 229 [14], 262
   [11]; **1947:** 6 [31]; **1948:** 77 [18]; **1951:** 27,
   251ftn. (p. 568)
   Appointment as Personal Representative on liq-
      uidation of war agencies, letter, **1945:** 117
Allen, George V., **1946:** 84 [1, 3, 16]; **1949:** 240 [4],
   269 [13]
Allen, Repr. Leo E., **1948:** 233 [4]; **1951:** 239 [2]
Allen, Richard F., **1947:** 107 [1]
Allen, Richard, Housing Project, Philadelphia, Pa.,
   1948: 225 [2]
Allentown, Pa.
   Campaign remarks, **1948:** 227 [3]
   Hock, Mayor Donald V., **1948:** 227n.
Allied Commission for Italy, abolition, **1947:** 25
Allied forces, withdrawal from Italy **1947:** 239
Allied leaders
   Joint report on Potsdam conference, **1945:** 91
   Joint statement against mistreatment of prison-
      ers held in Germany, **1945:** 9
Allied Middle East Command, proposed, **1952–53:**
   6
Allis, Barney, **1950:** 273 [16], 313n.

Allis-Chalmers Manufacturing Co., labor dispute,
   1946: 129 [12], 136 [5], 141 [16], 143 [5]
Allison, Emery W., **1950:** 3 [8], 16 [9], 23 [5], 160 [2],
   169 [5], 203 [2], 206ftn. (p. 568)
Alpine, Tex, campaign remarks, **1948:** 208 [7]
Altmeyer, Arthur J. (Commissioner for Social Se-
   curity), **1948:** 4 [8]
Altoona, Pa.
   Campaign remarks, **1948:** 139 [1]; **1952–53:** 306
      [6]
   Postmasters convention, **1948:** 139 [1]
Altoona, Wis., **1950:** 131 [1]
   Campaign remarks, **1948:** 235 [2]
Aluminum Company of America, **1949:** 4 [6];
   1952–53: 22
Aluminum industry
   Labor dispute, **1952–53:** 22
   National security, effect of strike on, **1952–53:** 22
   Production, **1952–53:** 15, 22, 33, 271
   United Kingdom, agreement on imports from,
      1952–53: 6n.
   Western, **1948:** 201
Aluminum plants, Government-owned, **1945:** 172
   [7]
Aluminum production, **1948:** 122 [6], 125; **1949:** 4
   [6]; **1950:** 125, 202; **1951:** 13 (p. 86), 167
Aluminum Workers of America, International
   Council of, **1952–53:** 22
AMA.
   See American Medical Association.
Amalgamated Association of Street, Electric, Rail-
   way and Motor Coach Employees, Div.
   689, strike, **1945:** 195
Amalgamated Clothing Workers, **1948:** 261 [11]
Amalgamated Clothing Workers of America, **1951:**
   239ftn. (p. 544)
Ambassador-at-large, question of appointment,
   1950: 80 [1, 12]
Ambassadors, U.S., **1947:** 23, 100
   See also specific countries.
   Appointment of, **1946:** 6 [5]; **1947:** 31 [5, 13, 15,
      17, 19], 36 [6, 16, 27], 62 [4, 8], 67 [3], 88
      [9], 95 [4, 7, 20]
   News conference remarks on, **1947:** 95 [15], 107
      [7, 9, 12, 14], 127 [9, 12], 145 [16]
   Resignation, **1947:** 62 [3]
American Action Committee Against Mass De-
   portations in Rumania, remarks, **1952–53:**
   145
American Association for the Advancement of
   Science, **1948:** 186, 191
American Association for the United Nations,
   1950: 318ftn. (p. 762)
American Bankers Association, **1947:** 97; **1952–53:**
   266 [2]
American Bar Association, **1951:** 140 [12]
American Battle Monuments Commission, **1946:**
   229 [2]; **1947:** 236 [2]

American Chemical Society, **1950:** 238 [7]; **1952–53:** 117

American Church Eucharistic Congress, **1949:** 207n.

American Churchmen, Washington Pilgrimage of, **1951:** 241

American colonies, **1947:** 90 [1], 138; **1950:** 132

American Conference of Mayors, **1948:** 238

American Council of Voluntary Agencies for Foreign Service, **1947:** 43

American Dental Association, Board of Trustees, **1951:** 258

American Economic Review, **1952–53:** 305

American Export Lines, **1948:** 177; **1952–53:** 177

American Falls power project, **1952–53:** 367 (p. 1146)

American Farm Bureau Federation, **1949:** 234 [10] Convention, **1948:** 285 [5]

American Federation of Government Employees, **1952–53:** 390

American Federation of Labor, **1946:** 53 [2], 215 [10], 220n.; **1947:** 19 [1], 20, 62 [2], 122, 236 [3]; **1948:** 140, 183 [6], 184; **1950:** 4; **1951:** 153 [16], 204, 214; **1952–53:** 22, 37,58, 266 [3], 286 [8], 336

American Fork, Utah, campaign remarks, **1948:** 200 [6]

American Hospital Association, **1952–53:** 268 [8]

American Hungarian Federation, **1951:** 253

American Institute of Architects, **1946:** 15 [8], 43 [10]

American Legion, **1945:** 163, 202 [2]; **1946:** 182, 229 [22]; **1948:** 228 [6]; **1949:** 64, 191; **1950:** 203 [16]; **1951:** 168, 178, 191, 261 [1]; **1952–53:** 220, 238 [1]

  Convention, **1948:** 244; **1949:** 194, 195

  Invitation, **1947:** 182 [3]

  Eberts Post No. 1, Little Rock, Ark., **1949:** 119 [3]

  Remarks to representatives, **1949:** 49

  Wewoka, Okla., post, honorary membership, **1948:** 216 [3]

American Legion, Boys Forum of National Government, **1949:** 170

American Legion Rehabilitation Commission, **1949:** 49n.

American Lithofold Corp., **1951:** 171 [2], 179 [1], 188 [3], 227 [10]

American Medical Association, **1949:** 118 [14]; **1952–53:** 2 [3], 135, 143, 167, 194, 213, 249, 258 [9, 15], 268 [8], 278, 284 [5]

American Mission for Aid to Greece, **1948:** 28, 188; **1950:** 142

American Municipal Association, **1949:** 226ftn. (p. 503)

American Newspaper Guild, **1950:** 177

American Newspaper Publishers Association, **1950:** 105ftn. (p. 286)

American Political Science Association, **1951:** 261 [5]; **1952–53:** 68

American President Lines, **1948:** 177

American Production Mission in China, termination, statement, **1945:** 151

American Railroads, Association of, **1946:** 56

American Red Cross, report on foreign relief activities, **1945:** 85

American Republics, **1945:** 120; **1946:** 18 (p. 42), 76, 77, 83, 116; **1947:** 51, 79, 83, 84, 105; **1948:** 282; **1949:** 9, 10

  See also Latin America; Organization of American States; *specific countries.*

  Assistance, **1950:** 9 (p. 59)

  Council of Foreign Ministers, **1951:** 16 [12], 59, 67

  Economic and social development, **1949:** 35

  European exports to, **1947:** 238

  Military cooperation, **1946:** 102; **1947:** 101

  Mutual security, **1947:** 188

  News conference remarks on, **1947:** 14 [19]

  Organization of American States Charter, ratification, **1951:** 125

  Reciprocal assistance, treaty of, **1947:** 230

  Solidarity, resolution by OAS, **1950:** 179 [22]

  U.S. relations with, **1949:** 80

American Revolution, **1947:** 110, 138; **1948:** 261 [9]; **1950:** 37, 42, 174, 185, 269; **1951:** 114, 144; **1952–53:** 81

American River, Calif., **1948:** 6; **1949:** 41

American Samoa, **1947:** 119

  Civil rights in, **1947:** 130; **1948:** 20

  Civilian administration, **1950:** 9 (p. 102); **1951:** 141

    Transfer to, **1949:** 101

  Trusteeship agreement, **1947:** 151

American Smelting and Refining Co., **1951:** 169, 204, 214, 277; **1952–53:** 37

American Society of Civil Engineers, **1949:** 249

American Society of Newspaper Editors, **1946:** 86; **1947:** 74, 218 [2]; **1948:** 80; **1949:** 86; **1950:** 92, 190n.; **1951:** 85 [1]; **1952–53:** 88 [1], 98

American States, International Conference of, **1947:** 221 [4]; **1948:** 55 [13], 77ftn. (p. 215); **1949:** 9, 10

American States, Organization of.

  See Organization of American States.

American Telephone and Telegraph Co., **1950:** 43n.

American Theatres Association, **1946:** 160

American Typographical Union, **1948:** 187n.

American Veterans, Polish Legion of, **1951:** 291

American Veterans Committee, **1946:** 214

American Veterans of World War II, **1949:** 268n.

American Volunteer Group, **1946:** 113

Americans for Democratic Action, **1952–53:** 129, 136 [7], 197 [19]

America's Democratic Club, Reading, Pa., membership in, **1948:** 227 [2]

Ames, Iowa, **1950:** 110 [3]

Amir Saud, Crown Prince, **1947:** 34

Ammunition, trade in, **1947:** 72

Amnesty Board, President's, **1946:** 270

Amphibious operations, **1945:** 45, 178

Amsterdam, N.Y.
   Campaign remarks, **1948:** 228 [3]; **1952–53:** 289 [7]
   Carter, Mayor Arthur, **1948:** 228 [3]

AMVETS Headquarters, Washington, dedication, **1952–53:** 101

Anaconda Copper and Mining Co., **1951:** 204, 214; **1952–53:** 37

Anchorage, Alaska, airport construction, **1948:** 105

Anderson, Maj. Gen. Alexander E., **1948:** 264 [5]

Anderson, Gov. C. Elmer, **1952–53:** 97

Anderson, Chester W., **1951:** 158

Anderson, Clinton P., **1948:** 136 [2, 3, 4], 208 [1, 2]; **1949:** 231 [24]; **1950:** 270 [11]; **1951:** 16 [5], 27, 251 [27, 29]; **1952–53:** 146
   See also Agriculture, Secretary of.
   Appointment as Secretary of Agriculture, **1945:** 40 [1]

Anderson, Dewey, **1949:** 240 [3]

Anderson, Eugenie, **1952–53:** 217, 313 [2]

Anderson, Gov. Sigurd, **1952–53:** 97

Anderson, Ind., campaign remarks, **1952–53:** 286 [2]

Andrews, Bert, **1946:** 126 [9], 250 [4]; **1947:** 31 [3], 67 [8], 243 [13, 17]; **1950:** 258 [2]; **1951:** 56 [14]; **1952–53:** 98 [42]

Andrews, M. Neal, **1950:** 209ftn. (p. 582), 258 [11]

Andrews, Repr. Walter G., **1948:** 33

Angaur island, U.S. capture of, **1945:** 161

Anglo-American-Canadian declaration on atomic energy, **1945:** 193 [7, 8, 10]

Anglo-American Committee of Inquiry (Palestine commission), **1945:** 187; **1946:** 5, 18 (p. 44), 132, 155; **1947:** 41; **1948:** 97ftn. (p. 253); **1952–53:** 297
   Members, question of, **1945:** 193 [6], 202 [4, 8], 208 [4]
   News conference remarks, **1946:** 15 [17], 66 [2], 95 [7, 9]
   Report, **1946:** 89, 92, 95 [7, 9], 163 [5], 227
   Statement, **1945:** 210

Anglo-American financial and trade conference, **1945:** 202 [10]

Anglo-American petroleum agreement, **1945:** 214
   News conference remarks, **1945:** 76 [9], 107 [3]

Anglo-Iranian Oil Co., **1951:** 132ftn. (p. 347)

Animal diseases, control of, **1949:** 263

Animal Industry, Bureau of, **1948:** 5 (p. 45)

Annapolis, Md., U.S. Naval Academy, **1951:** 200 [9]; **1952–53:** 130, 142
   Admission of Canadians, **1948:** 112
   Centennial, **1945:** 132 [9]

Annecy, France, **1950:** 273 [16], 280, 281
   Liberty Bell replica, presentation to Independence, Mo., **1950:** 280, 281
   Trade negotiations, **1949:** 217
   Volland, Mayor Georges, **1950:** 280, 281

Annual Inventory of Traffic Activities, **1951:** 42

Antarctica, question of Navy expedition, **1949:** 171 [6]

Anthracite Health and Welfare Fund, **1948:** 248

Antibiotics, **1947:** 6 [25]

Anti-lynching bill, question of, **1946:** 186 [10]

Antimony
   Import controls, **1947:** 18, 99
   Stockpiling, **1948:** 8 (p. 78)

Anti-Racketeering Act, **1946:** 131

Antisubmarine warfare, **1945:** 45

Antitrust laws, **1945:** 11; **1946:** 131; **1947:** 2 (p. 6), 4 (pp. 29, 35), 7 (p. 87), 70 [2, 11, 15], 152, 177 [7], 232 [6, 10], 242; **1948:** 2, 5 (p. 52), 8 (pp. 68, 89), 37, 127, 165, 220, 251, 252, 257 [2]; **1949:** 2, 149; **1950:** 2, 3 [16], 9 (p. 97), 118, 166, 319; **1951:** 254; **1952–53:** 204, 215

Antoine, Frank, **1948:** 237 [5]

Apache Indians, **1948:** 208 [2]

Apartment Owners Association, National, **1948:** 259 [3], 261 [2], 264 [1]

Appeals Board, Employees' Compensation, **1950:** 74; **1952–53:** 208

Appleby, Paul H., **1946:** 17, 145, 192

Apple-growing industry, Washington State, **1948:** 122 [4]

Appley, Lawrence A., **1949:** 167n.

Appointments, letters
   Allen, George E., Personal Representative on liquidation of war agencies, **1945:** 117
   Jackson, Robert H., U.S. Chief of Counsel, war crimes trials, **1945:** 22 [5]
   Kramer, Gen. Hans, U.S. Representative in Colorado-Kansas negotiations for division of waters of Arkansas River, **1945:** 194
   Lubin, Isador, Reparations Commission, **1945:** 14
   Pauley, Edwin W., Personal Representative on Reparations Commission, **1945:** 13
   Price, Byron, Personal Representative to study relations between U.S. occupation forces and German people, **1945:** 119
   Stettinius, Edward R., Jr., U.S. Representative on the Preparatory Commission of the United Nations, **1945:** 96
   Wyatt, Wilson, Housing Expediter, **1945:** 212

Apprentice Training Service, **1948:** 10

Apprenticeship, Bureau of, **1952–53:** 367 (p. 1151)

Apprenticeship programs, **1949:** 8 (p. 90)
   Building trades, **1946:** 263

Appropriations, **1946:** 18, 94; **1947:** 7 (pp. 68, 80), 11, 181 (pp. 396, 397, 400, 401, 403); **1948:**

Appropriations — *continued*
    4 [1, 5], 5 (pp. 24, 28, 29, 31, 34, 37, 40–42,
      44, 47, 53, 54, 56, 57, 59), 6, 15 [6, 11],
      175; **1949:** 7 [13, 47], 96, 247; **1951:** 228
Administrative expenses, Federal, **1952–53:** 231
Agriculture, Department of, **1946:** 238
Air Force, question of impounding by the President, **1951:** 224 [2]
Antitrust laws enforcement, **1951:** 254
Armed Forces, delay in voting, **1951:** 2 [19]
Atomic Energy Commission, **1949:** 155 [19];
    1950: 187; **1952–53:** 17 [1], 147, 170
Campaign of Truth, **1951:** 197
Certain, for fiscal year 1946, **1945:** 226
Civil defense, **1952–53:** 106
Civilian war agencies, **1945:** 124
Compensation and pensions, veterans, **1952–53:**
    18 (p. 109)
Congressional actions, **1949:** 112 [13], 144 [11],
    179 [27]
Defense, **1950:** 193n.; **1951:** 12 [2, 7], 92, 228, 300
    [12]; **1952–53:** 88 [10], 98 [38], 101, 123 [7],
    125, 128, 131, 144, 149 [5], 158, 170, 178,
    268 [5, 7], 273, 275, 283, 295 [8], 298 [8,
    10], 304, 313 [4], 315 [4], 322
Defense aid program, **1945:** 50
Deficiency, **1951:** 12 [4, 7]
Deficiency bill, approval, **1947:** 60
District of Columbia sesquicentennial, **1949:** 161
    [4]
Executive reduction after enactment, congressional requirement, **1950:** 234
Federal Civil Defense Administration, **1951:**
    131n.
Flood control, **1951:** 183, 185, 196; **1952–53:** 109,
    267 [6, 9]
Foreign assistance, **1950:** 179 [23], 204, 220, 230
    [14], 238 [17], 240; **1951:** 209 [10, 13];
    1952–53: 65, 149 [20], 156 [12], 268 [5],
    281, 295 [1], 307
General Appropriations Act, approval, **1950:** 234
General Services Administration, **1950:** 190
Housing, defense, **1952–53:** 18 (p. 97)
Immigration and Naturalization Service, **1951:**
    154
Independent offices, **1952–53:** 201
Information programs abroad, **1950:** 44 [14], 227
Interior Department, **1951:** 120
Internal Revenue Bureau, reduction, **1947:** 135
Labor Department, **1951:** 192
Loyalty program, Government employees, **1947:**
    89
Marshall plan, **1947:** 238; **1948:** 15 [6, 8, 11]
Migratory farm labor, recruiting and reception
    centers, **1952–53:** 18 (p. 94)
Military, **1950:** 193, 194, 204, 205 [1, 7], 296
National Housing Agency, **1947:** 131
Navy, **1945:** 134; **1946:** 66 [10], 238

Appropriations — *continued*
  News conference remarks on, **1947:** 6 [6], 62 [19],
    174 [2], 177 [18], 180 [12]
  Omnibus bill, question of, **1950:** 8 [8]
  Overseas relief, **1948:** 11ftn. (p. 104)
  Pan American Union, **1951:** 184
  Power projects, **1950:** 193; **1951:** 120
  Power and water resources development, **1952–
    53:** 18 (p. 89)
  Presidential discretion in spending, **1950:** 258
    [15]
  Public housing, **1951:** 111
  Reductions, **1948:** 175
    Proposed, **1946:** 10, 130; **1951:** 132 [13, 15]
  Relief grain shipments to India, **1951:** 34, 63 [2]
  Rent control, **1949:** 182 [4]
  Rescissions, **1947:** 11, 134
  River and harbor development, **1951:** 185;
    1952–53: 109
  Rural Electrification Administration, **1952–53:**
    282 [3]
  Single item veto, question of, **1950:** 8 [9]
  Soil conservation, **1952–53:** 242 [4]
  State Department, **1950:** 190
  Supplemental, **1951:** 12 [34], 117, 254n., 285;
    1952–53: 200, 205, 231
  Supplemental appropriations bill, **1950:** 252
  Tennessee Valley Authority, **1952–53:** 147
  Treasury Department, **1950:** 8 [46]
  Unexpended, **1952–53:** 17 [11]
  United Nations, U.S. participation, **1951:** 184,
    187
  Veterans Administration, **1952–53:** 135
  War agencies, **1946:** 130
  War department, **1945:** 146; **1946:** 238
Approval of acts of Congress, statements.
  See Legislation, statements upon approval.
Aquitania, **1945:** 45
Arab-Israeli dispute, **1948:** 253, 274 [7]; **1949:** 40
    [2], 193, 274; **1950:** 2, 25, 143, 147, 148;
    1951: 172; **1952–53:** 297
  Peace conference, **1949:** 122 [23]
Arab States, **1945:** 106 [18]
  Economic assistance, **1951:** 114
  Technical assistance, **1952–53:** 18 (p. 76)
Arabia.
  See Saudi Arabia.
Arabs, **1945:** 187, 210; **1946:** 129 [11], 215 [7], 227,
    241
  Palestine, **1946:** 92
Arbela, battle of, **1950:** 138
Arbor Day, diamond anniversary, **1947:** 69
Architects, American Institute of, **1946:** 15 [8], 43
    [10]
Archival and records functions, reorganization
    plans, **1950:** 53, 75
Archives, Eighth Annual Institute on the Preservation and Administration of, remarks to,
    1952–53: 174

Archives, National, **1951:** 127
Archivist of the United States, **1946:** 118
   Grover, Wayne C., **1952–53:** 347
Arco, Idaho, **1952–53:** 170
   Atomic plant, **1950:** 121 [1, 13]
   Campaign remarks, **1948:** 120 [1]
   Marvel, Mayor W. S., **1948:** 120 [1]
Ardahan, Turkey, **1946:** 53 [10]
Ardmore, Okla., campaign remarks, **1948:** 214 [5]
Area redevelopment, **1947:** 152; **1948:** 175
Arends, Henry, **1948:** 122 [6]
Argentina, **1945:** 157 [8]; **1948:** 283 [14]; **1950:** 212
   Beef exports, **1946:** 229 [9]
   Bruce, James, U.S. Ambassador, **1949:** 28 [8], 32
      [9], 40 [4], 205 [12, 14], 236 [17]
   Cereijo, Ramón A. (Finance Minister), **1950:** 86
      [5], 97 [6], 105 [12]
   FAO membership, question of, **1948:** 276
   Ibarra Garcia, Oscar (Ambassador to U.S.),
      1945: 22 [13]
   Ivanissevich, Oscar (Ambassador to U.S.), **1947:**
      105
   Loan to, **1950:** 105 [12], 137 [5, 16], 287 [20]
      Question of, **1947:** 221 [12]; **1949:** 45 [8]
   Medal, award to Maj. Gen. Harry H. Vaughan,
      1949: 32 [3]
   News conference remarks, **1946:** 37 [8], 72 [10,
      12], 86 [8, 27], 126 [26], 229 [9], 257 [18],
      266 [15]; **1950:** 105 [12], 137 [5, 16], 179
      [18], 287 [20]
   Perón, Juan, **1946:** 86 [8], 199 [10]; **1948:** 9 [6];
      1949: 40 [18]
   Rio Pact, approval by Chamber of Deputies,
      1950: 179 [18]
   Trade agreement with U.K., **1949:** 122 [7], 144
      [24]
   Trade with U.S., **1949:** 144 [22]
   Messersmith, George S., U.S. Ambbassador,
      1946: 78 [12]; **1947:** 14 [15], 95 [5, 15], 107
      [7, 9, 12, 14]
   Wheat shipments abroad, **1946:** 23, 86 [27]
   White paper on, **1946:** 37 [8]
Argentina-U.S. Joint Commission on Commercial
   Studies, **1949:** 113 [5]
Argentine grain, relief shipments to India, **1951:** 34
Arizona, **1947:** 35, 229; **1949:** 32 [6]
   All-American Canal Project, **1948:** 206 [4]
   Campaign remarks, **1948:** 136 [1], 206 [4], 207
   Candidates for public office, **1948:** 207
   Colorado River water rights, dispute with Cali-
      fornia, **1950:** 34 [17]
   Davis Dam, **1948:** 207
   Garvey, Gov. Dan E., **1948:** 136 n., 206 [4], 207n.
   Navajo Indians, **1950:** 9 (p. 91)
   Reclamation projects, **1948:** 206 [4]
Arkansas, **1945:** 147 [9], 163; **1947:** 104
   Campaign remarks, **1952–53:** 193, 194, 195 [1–3]
   Candidates for public office, **1952–53:** 197 [5]

Arkansas — *continued*
   Flood control, **1952–53:** 194, 195 [1, 2]
   Fulbright, Sen. J. William, **1945:** 69, 202 [14]
   Grand Prairie area irrigation project, **1949:** 183
   Laney, Gov. Ben, **1945:** 147 [9]
   McMath, Gov. Sydney S., **1949:** 119 [2–4], 120;
      1951: 261 [3]; **1952–53:** 193, 194, 195 [3],
      197 [5], 228 [2]
   Power projects, **1950:** 3 [9], 125; **1952–53:** 194,
      195 [1, 2]
   Primary election, **1952–53:** 228 [2]
   River basins, development, **1950:** 33, 129 [1], 140,
      164
   Rural electrification, **1952–53:** 194
Arkansas Gazette, **1952–53:** 228 [2]
Arkansas Power and Light Co., **1952–53:** 194
Arkansas River
   Colorado-Kansas negotiations for division of
      waters, **1945:** 194
   Development, **1945:** 128
   Flood control, **1947:** 144
   Kansas-Missouri dispute re, **1948:** 86
Arkansas River Basin, **1951:** 13 (pp. 86, 87), 185
Arkansas Valley development, **1946:** 18 (p. 61)
Arlington County, Va., **1947:** 35
Arlington National Cemetery, **1949:** 254
   Memorial carillon, dedication, **1949:** 268
   Unveiling of Sir John Dill statue, **1950:** 275
Arm band from Danish newsmen, acceptance,
   1946: 6 [18]
Armaments, **1947:** 72, 181 (p. 402); **1948:** 46
   See also Atomic bomb; Disarmament.
   Atomic, development, **1951:** 13 (p. 85); **1952–53:**
      17 [4, 6, 8], 170, 275, 367 (pp. 1145, 1146)
      Korean war, question of use in, **1952–53:** 166
      [12]
   Demonstration, Aberdeen Proving Ground,
      1951: 38, 50
   Delivery to allies, **1952–53:** 18 (pp. 64, 74), 231
   Expenditures for, **1950:** 105 [6]
   Exports under mutual security program, **1951:**
      114
   Howitzer carriages, World War II contract for,
      1951: 284
   Limitation and control, **1950:** 34 [16, 18], 42, 143,
      271
      See also Disarmament.
   Procurement, **1951:** 4, 13 (pp. 68, 69), 167; 18
      (pp. 70–71), 275, 367 (p. 1130)
   Production, **1950:** 204; **1951:** 4, 11, 80, 298 [6];
      1952–53: 15, 17 [2], 18 (pp. 64, 70–71, 74),
      55, 215
   Provision to European forces, **1951:** 13 (pp. 72,
      73)
   Research and development, **1951:** 13 (p. 70), 215;
      1952–53: 275, 367 (p. 1137)
   Rifles and ammunition, proposed NATO stan-
      dardization, **1952–53:** 6

Armaments — *continued*
  Shipments to allies, **1952–53:** 367 (p. 1139)
  Soviet, increase, **1951:** 54
  Trade in, **1950:** 38 [17], 147, 148, 252; **1951:** 63 [10], 114, 117
Armco Steel Corp., **1951:** 305
Armed Forces, Associated Services for, **1950:** 95
Armed Forces, Industrial College of the, **1949:** 144 ftn. (p. 339); **1952–53:** 127 [13], 349
Armed Forces, President's Committee on Equality of Treatment and Opportunity in, **1948:** 265
Armed Forces, President's Committee on Religion and Welfare in, **1950:** 32, 95; **1951:** 17, 180; **1952–53:** 297
Armed forces, U.S., **1945:** 34, 44 ftn. (p. 77), 45, 58, 93, 98, 101, 114, 122, 125, 154, 158, 192, 217; **1946:** 18 (pp. 38, 47, 48, 75), 124, 125, 268; **1947:** 35, 63, 68, 94, 101, 117; **1948:** 3, 5 (pp. 20, 26), 183 [1]; **1949:** 127, 154; **1950:** 78, 165; 13 (pp. 63–68), 107
  See also Military personnel; *Specific services.*
  Addresses, **1945:** 5, 123
  Administrative economy and efficiency, **1952–53:** 287
  Appropriation bill, delay in voting, **1951:** 2 [19]
  Bases, question of visits by the President, **1951:** 37 [1]
  Caribbean maneuvers, **1949:** 40 [14]
  Chaplaincy, **1950:** 297
  Civilian control of, **1950:** 138; **1952–53:** 286 [3]
  Civilian personnel, **1948:** 5 (p. 28)
    Temporary, **1947:** 50
  Collier Trophy, joint award to, **1951:** 301
  Comments on, **1951:** 186
  Community services to members, **1949:** 73; **1950:** 32, 95
  Congressional Medal of Honor presentations. *See under* Medals, presentation.
  Deaths from sickness, **1945:** 45
  Demobilization, **1945:** 107 [17], 128, 178, 201n., 202 [3], 218; **1946:** 6 [9], 8, 15 [15], 17 [13], 18 (pp. 47, 48, 71, 75), 43 [3], 61 [2], 84 [26], 86 [32], 193; **1947:** 2 (p. 8), 7 (p. 69), 18, 88 [1], 233; **1948:** 86, 236, 243 [1]
    Postwar, **1950:** 162; **1951:** 54
    Statement, **1945:** 138
  Dinner, remarks, **1950:** 138
  Disaster relief assistance, **1949:** 22 ftn. (p. 118)
  Dispatch abroad, **1952–53:** 44 [1, 13]
    Power of President to order, **1951:** 2 [18], 7 [5, 9], 16 [15], 70 [1]
  Dispatch to Palestine, question of, **1948:** 9 [17], 41 [1], 84 [20], 178 [9]
  Draft.
    See main heading, Draft.
  Enlistments, **1945:** 128

Armed forces, U.S., — *continued*
  Equal opportunity in, **1948:** 110 [8], 166 [4]; **1949:** 226 [3]; **1950:** 141; **1952–53:** 169
  Expansion, **1948:** 84 [9], 221, 236
  Expenditures for, **1950:** 133; **1952–53:** 231, 367 (p. 1136)
    Pressure on price level, **1951:** 107
  Experimental Training Unit, Fort Knox, Ky., **1948:** 190
  Facilities, operation and maintenance, **1950:** 9 (p. 63), 121 [13], 213; **1952–53:** 18 (p. 71), 367 (p. 1137)
  Firemen in, need for, **1947:** 86
  Functions, **1947:** 159
  Increase in strength, **1950:** 193, 232, 262, 269, 292, 296, 302, 303; **1951:** 11, 13 (pp. 63–68), 80, 91, 92, 98, 114, 144, 167, 294; **1952–53:** 5, 12, 15, 17 [2], 18 (pp. 64, 65, 69–73), 128, 231, 317 [7], 319 [3], 349, 366, 367 (pp. 1130, 1134)
    Telegram to General Marshall, **1951:** 57
  Integration, **1948:** 166 [1, 4], 185 [7]
  Land transactions, veto of bill to restrict, **1951:** 105, 108 [1]
  Leave bonds, interest payments, **1948:** 5 (p. 56)
  Manpower needs, **1951:** 15
  Military Justice, Uniform Code of, **1950:** 108
  Mobilization, **1950:** 295 [2, 15]
  Naturalization of foreigners serving in, **1947:** 18
  News conference remarks, **1945:** 44 [2], 52 [3], 107 [17], 137 [9, 12], 193 [11], 202 [3, 9, 16], 208 [16], 221 [5]; **1946:** 6 [9], 15 [15], 17 [13], 43 [3], 61 [2, 15], 70 [16], 75 [18], 78 [16, 18], 84 [4, 12, 14, 26], 86 [2, 32], 95 [16, 19], 119 [2], 126 [16], 129 [20], 141 [5], 223 [6]; **1947:** 6 [9, 11]; **1948:** 11 [12], 77 [7], 84 [9, 20], 110 [8], 166 [1, 4], 174 [3], 178 [9], 185 [7], 243 [1], 285 [6]; **1950:** 8 [33], 29 [3], 97 [12], 179 [5], 209 [11], 230 [15], 295 [1, 2, 15], 309 [10, 12]
  Occupation duties, **1946:** 76; **1947:** 2 (p. 11), 7 (p. 62), 209 [13], 234, 239; **1948:** 2; **1949:** 8 (pp. 54, 56, 59), 32 [12], 117, 154; **1950:** 274
  Officer corps, World War II, **1948:** 243 [1]
  Overseas, **1948:** 11 [12]
  Personnel.
    See Military personnel.
  Personnel policies, **1945:** 218
  Powers of President as Commander in Chief, **1949:** 148 [4]; **1951:** 27
  Procurement, **1948:** 60, 175; **1949:** 50
  Public works construction, **1949:** 8 (p. 60), 192 [8]
  Public works programs, **1950:** 8 [33], 9 (p. 65); **1951:** 13 (p. 68), 92
  Racial discrimination, elimination, **1952–53:** 290, 315 [6]

Armed forces, U.S., — *continued*
  Real property, acquisition, **1952–53:** 18 (p. 71)
  Recruitment, **1946:** 18 (pp. 47, 48); **1947:** 50, 54;
      1948: 5 (p. 27), 53; **1949:** 8 (p. 59); **1950:**
      194
  Red Cross services to, **1951:** 47
  Redeployment to Pacific theater, **1945:** 45, 52 [3],
      53, 54
  Reduction, **1947:** 7 (p. 62), 50; **1948:** 5 (p. 26);
      1949: 8 (p. 55)
    Proposed, **1951:** 247 [13]
  Refugees, European, proposed enlistment,
      1952–53: 65
  Religion and welfare in, **1951:** 17, 100
  Repatriation, **1947:** 18
  Research and development program, **1952–53:**
      18 (p. 72)
  Reserves.
    See Reserve forces.
  Rivalry, interservice, **1949:** 233 [1]
  Selective Service inductions, question of re-
      sumption, **1948:** 174 [3]
  Service academies, **1951:** 188 [14, 16], 193 [6], 200
      [9]
  Shoes for, wartime production in Brockton,
      Mass., **1948:** 261 [2]
  Statement commending, **1952–53:** 377 [2]
  Steel procurement, **1948:** 151
  Students, deferment of induction, **1952–53:** 18
      (p. 103)
  Supplies for, **1945:** 45, 49
  Surplus property, disposition, **1951:** 14
  Training, **1949:** 50
  Unification, **1945:** 202 [16], 208 [16], 221 [5];
      1946: 18 (p. 52), 70 [16], 76, 78 [16, 18], 84
      [4, 12, 14], 86 [2], 95 [16, 19], 126 [16], 129
      [20], 137, 138, 141 [5]; **1947:** 6 [9], 10, 12,
      36 [17], 42, 110, 145 [21], 159, 177 [5];
      1948: 77 [7], 243 [1], 285 [6]; **1949:** 8 (p.
      56), 50, 95 [3], 155 [18], 171 [13], 192 [13],
      234 [1], 241n., 267ftn. (p. 580); **1950:** 9 (p.
      51), 29 [3], 108, 138, 176, 245; **1951:** 38,
      218
    Message to Congress, **1945:** 218
  Voting rights, **1952–53:** 38, 68, 96, 124
  War mobilization planning, **1948:** 284
  Women, role in, **1951:** 294; **1952–53:** 248
  World War II dead, cemeteries overseas, **1947:**
      92
Armed Forces, U.S., in foreign countries
  Austria, **1950:** 218
  China, **1945:** 216; **1946:** 265
  Europe, **1950:** 242, 309 [10, 12]; **1952–53:** 57
    Question of reinforcement, **1951:** 2 [18], 7 [5, 9,
        17], 16 [15], 37 [17], 56 [15], 71, 114
  Formosa, question of, **1950:** 209 [11]
  Germany, **1945:** 193 [11], 201, 202 [9]
    Junction with Soviet forces, **1945:** 12
    Question of increase, **1950:** 230

Armed Forces in foreign countries — *continued*
  Italy, withdrawal, **1947:** 234, 239
  Japan, **1945:** 137 [9, 12], 138; **1949:** 32 [5, 18]
    Negotiations concerning, **1951:** 84, 216
  Korea, **1950:** 179 [5], 184, 193, 194, 211, 232, 260,
      263, 267, 269, 279, 296, 299, 303, 317;
      1951: 13 (p. 63), 80, 92, 109, 138, 148, 170,
      208, 213, 295 [3], 298 [1], 306; **1952–53:** 18
      (p. 69), 56, 57, 107 [2], 128, 131, 135, 139,
      172, 268 [5], 290, 356, 378
    Change in command, **1951:** 77, 95 [2, 4, 6], 101
        [4], 108 [2, 4, 13], 113 [3, 12], 118ftn. (p.
        324)
    Memorial Day prayers for, **1951:** 113 [1]
    Question of withdrawal, **1949:** 118 [19]; **1952–**
        53: 295 [8], 299, 300, 310, 316, 319 [1], 320,
        321 [4], 322, 323
  Latin America, World War II, **1951:** 114
  Philippines, strengthening, **1950:** 173
  Ryukyu Islands, **1951:** 84
Armed Forces Day dinner, remarks, **1951:** 109;
    1952–53: 128
Armed Forces Leave Act of 1946, **1947:** 158
Armed Forces Medical Policy Council, **1951:** 307
Armed Forces and Veterans, Committee on Service
    to, **1950:** 95
Armed Services, President's Committee on Equal-
    ity of Treatment and Opportunity in the,
    1952–53: 315 [6]
Armistice control commissions, termination, **1947:**
    114
Armistice Day, **1951:** 294
Arms embargo to Israel, **1948:** 110 [7, 22], 253
Arms limitation and control, **1946:** 86 [5], 102;
    1947: 101, 238; **1948:** 2, 243 [4]; **1949:** 19,
    148 [1]
  See also Disarmament.
  Soviet proposals, **1949:** 226 [22]
Arms race, **1947:** 101; **1949:** 226 [22]
Arms trade, **1947:** 72; **1948:** 253
Armstrong, Repr. O. K., **1951:** 85 [10]
Army, **1945:** 34, 41, 45, 57, 128, 139, 142, 178, 192,
    215, 218; **1946:** 7, 76, 102, 124, 135, 137,
    138, 193, 242 [2], 268; **1947:** 7 (pp. 57, 64),
    35, 80, 101; **1948:** 5 (pp. 26, 27, 29, 31),
    175, 283 [6]; **1949:** 8 (p. 57), 223, 234 [1];
    1952–53: 131
  Air forces, **1945:** 45
  Atomic bomb program, **1945:** 93
  Authorized strength, **1949:** 8 (p. 58); **1950:** 9 (p.
      63)
  Bases, funds to reactivate, **1948:** 274 [17]
  Chief of Staff, **1947:** 221 [7], 226 [3]
  Chief of Staff (Gen. J. Lawton Collins), **1950:**
      194, 226, 230 [7], 303; **1951:** 93n., 148
  Civilian personnel, temporary, **1947:** 50
  Contract surgeons, appointment, **1947:** 35
  Deaths from sickness, **1945:** 45
  Demobilization, **1945:** 45, 101, 137 [9], 138,

Army — *continued*
  Demobilization — *continued*
        146n.; **1946:** 8, 18 (p. 47), 43 [3], 84 [26], 86 [32]; **1947:** 2 (p. 11)
  Divisions in Germany, rotation of, **1952–53:** 345 [1]
  8th Army, Korean operations, **1950:** 320; **1951:** 77, 113 [13]
  82d Airborne Division, remarks to members of, **1951:** 46
  Engineers.
    See Engineers, Corps of.
  Enlisted Reserve Corps, **1947:** 35
  European command, **1946:** 18 (p. 46); **1950:** 310
  Expenditures for, **1950:** 8 [24], 9 (p. 61)
  Flood relief activities, **1950:** 129 [7]
  Food distribution overseas, **1947:** 32, 46 [4], 180 [15], 202
  Food stockpiles, **1946:** 86 [32]
  Functions, **1947:** 159
  Hospitals, surplus, **1952–53:** 212
  Increase in strength, **1950:** 194, 303; **1951:** 4, 13 (p. 64), 92, 167; **1952–53:** 17 [2], 18 (pp. 64, 69), 158, 275, 367 (p. 1134)
  Information program in Japan, transfer to State Department, **1952–53:** 18 (p. 77)
  Integration, **1948:** 166 [1]
  Land transactions, veto of bill to restrict, **1951:** 105, 108 [1]
  Manpower requirements, letter, **1945:** 114
  Materiel reclamation program, **1952–53:** 287
  Military cemeteries, grave markers, **1951:** 247 [4], 251 [8, 11]
  News conference remarks, **1945:** 22 [17], 44 [3], 106 [19], 116, 118 [5, 12, 14, 17], 129 [10], 137 [9]; **1946:** 15 [20], 43 [3], 78 [15, 18], 84 [12, 26], 86 [2, 32], 95 [4], 119 [11], 126 [15], 129 [20, 22], 192 [4, 8, 10, 25], 226 [19]; **1947:** 6 [3, 9, 14, 27, 29], 14 [6], 95 [18]; **1950:** 8 [24], 29 [9], 295 [1]
  Occupation duties, **1947:** 2 (p. 11), 38, 46 [2], 180 [15]; **1948:** 5 (pp. 29, 31), 175; **1949:** 8 (54, 59), 92, 117; **1950:** 9 (p. 58), 274
  Officers, appointment and retirement, **1947:** 35
  Operation and control of railroads, termination, **1948:** 159n.
  Operation of Montgomery Ward, **1945:** 22 [17]
  Optometry Corps, veto, **1946:** 109
  Pay, **1946:** 192 [8]
  Personnel policies, **1945:** 218
  Petroleum products, use of, **1952–53:** 379
  Postwar organization, **1945:** 174
  Preparedness, **1947:** 110
  Procurement program, **1945:** 126; **1947:** 35, 181, 208
  Public works, **1948:** 5 (pp. 26, 28)
  Public works construction, **1949:** 8 (p. 60)
  Public works program, **1947:** 181 (p. 339)

Army — *continued*
  Racial discrimination, elimination, **1952–53:** 290 315 [6]
  Railroads, emergency operation, **1951:** 33 [1, 15]; **1952–53:** 136ftn. (p. 359)
    Termination, **1952–53:** 141
  Recruitment, **1946:** 15 [20], 18 (pp. 47, 48); **1947:** 35, 50, 54
  Reduction in forces, **1945:** 45, 101; **1947:** 50
  Regulations (1835), book on, **1950:** 29 [9]
  Reorganization, **1946:** 78 [15], 95 [4]
  Report on Pearl Harbor attack, **1948:** 116, 118 [5, 12, 14, 17], 129 [10]
  Reserve forces, **1949:** 8 (p. 59), 174; **1950:** 9 (pp. 63, 64), 193
    Retirement benefits, **1948:** 145
    Status of, **1948:** 243 [1]
  Retired enlistees, credit for foreign service, veto, **1945:** 205
  Service forces, **1945:** 45
  35th Division, reunion, **1951:** 108 [7], 113 [16]
  36th Division, World War II casualties in Italy, **1951:** 275 [18]
  Training schools, attendance by Korean soldiers, **1951:** 236
  25th Infantry Division, **1951:** 148
Army, Department of the, **1945:** 218n.; **1947:** 10n., 202, 241; **1948:** 6, 43, 46; **1949:** 118 [18]; **1950:** 164
  Austrian occupation zone, transfer of functions, **1950:** 274
  Panama Canal, functions, **1950:** 28
  Programs review, **1950:** 196
  Real estate transactions, **1951:** 105, 108 [1]
  Reorganization, **1949:** 50, 158, 177
  Water resources development functions, **1950:** 140
Army, Secretary of the (Gordon Gray), **1949:** 118 [3], 122ftn. (p. 295), 179 [11], 185; **1950:** 34 [9, 14], 81
Army, Secretary of the (Frank Pace, Jr.), **1950:** 267, 268; **1951:** 46n., 93n., 188ftn. (p. 457), 254; **1952–53:** 128, 131, 163, 169, 193, 320
  Letters and memorandums, **1950:** 196, 259, 265; **1952–53:** 141
  Railroad strike, intervention in, **1951:** 33 [1]
  Railroads, emergency operation, **1950:** 188, 221
Army, Secretary of the (Kenneth C. Royall), **1947:** 182 [1], 208; **1948:** 6, 20, 95, 111, 162n., 166[1], 285 [13]; **1949:** 101
  News conference remarks on, **1949:** 32 [5, 18], 45 [1, 22], 72 [1], 78 [11, 15], 84 [1, 2]
  Resignation, **1949:** 84 [1, 2]
Army and Air Force Vitalization and Retirement Equalization Act of 1948, **1949:** 174
Army Day address, **1946:** 76
Army-Navy football game, **1945:** 202 [16]
  President's plans to attend, **1947:** 226 [2]

Army and Navy Munitions Board, **1947:** 182 [1]
Army Nurse Corps, **1947:** 35
Army Personnel Centers, **1945:** 45
Army Separation Centers, **1945:** 45
Army Transportation Corps, **1945:** 45
Arnall, Gov. Ellis G., **1945:** 129 [13]; **1946:** 72 [21]; **1952–53:** 26 [6, 15, 29], 31 [1], 34, 221 [3]
Arnold, Benedict, **1952–53:** 296
Arnold, Gen. Henry H., **1945:** 2, 45, 193 [3]; **1946:** 7, 21 [11], 70 [1]; **1951:** 138
Arnold, Mrs. Henry H., **1951:** 138
Arnold, Laurence, letter, **1945:** 228
Arnold, Brig. Gen. Milton W., **1947:** 115n.
Arnold, Thurman, **1945:** 132 [1]
Arnold Engineering Development Center, Tullahoma, Tenn., **1951:** 138
Art, Austrian, exhibition in U.S., **1949:** 253 [11]
Art, modern, comments on, **1951:** 99
Art, National Gallery of, **1947:** 31 [1]
Artukovic, Andrija, **1951:** 227 [12]
Arvey, Jacob M., **1951:** 171 [8], 275 [5]
Asapansa-Johnson, C., **1952–53:** 290n.
Ashburton, Lord, **1948:** 198 [6]; **1949:** 80; **1952–53:** 268 [4]
Ashland, Ky., campaign remarks, **1948:** 222 [8]
Ashraf, Princess, **1947:** 203n.
Asia, South Asia, and Southeast Asia, **1947:** 7 (p. 57), 188, 240; **1948:** 49 [17], 114 [2]; **1950:** 17n., 42; **1951:** 70 [3, 4]
    See also Far East; *specific countries.*
    Assistance, **1947:** 238; **1948:** 4 [2], 110 [6, 15], 160; **1949:** 117n., 160; **1950:** 11 [16], 78, 119, 154, 201, 204; **1952–53:** 57, 242 [2], 313 [2]
        Economic, **1951:** 4, 66, 114; **1952–53:** 5, 18 (pp. 76–77), 55, 144, 205, 367 (p. 1140)
        Military, **1951:** 4, 13 (pp. 73, 74), 25, 59, 66, 84, 114, 167, 216; **1952–53:** 15, 18 (pp. 76–77), 55, 196, 354, 367 (p. 1140)
        Technical, **1951:** 83, 114; **1952–53:** 18 (pp. 76–77), 55, 144, 205
    Bradley-Bohlen mission to, **1951:** 239 [1]
    Communism in, **1950:** 78, 92, 151, 162; **1951:** 13 (pp. 61, 62), 34, 59, 78, 90 [1], 92, 96, 216; **1952–53:** 5, 6, 12, 55, 81, 131, 295 [8], 307, 366, 367 (p. 1140)
    Defense, **1950:** 151; **1951:** 59, 153 [3], 216, 224 [1]; **1952–53:** 354
    Economic and political development, **1949:** 178, 256; **1950:** 159
    Emergence of new nations, **1952–53:** 366
    European refugees in, immigration to U.S., **1950:** 167
    Hoover report on, **1947:** 46 [2]
    Immigration to U.S., **1952–53:** 182
    Independence movement, **1950:** 151, 232; **1951:** 216
    Intelligence report concerning, **1951:** 78

Asia, South Asia, Southeast Asia — *continued*
    Land reform, **1951:** 179 [13]
    Limitation of conflict in, **1951:** 96
    News conference remarks, **1946:** 86 [4], 95 [3]; **1950:** 11 [16], 80 [1], 206 [1, 7, 14], 209 [2], 270 [2], 287 [1], 295 [17]
    Occupied areas, **1948:** 144
    Pacific union, question of, **1949:** 179 [14, 20]
    Policy on, **1949:** 171 [1], 179 [4], 260 [17]; **1950:** 11ftn. (p. 109), 80 [1], 206 [1, 7, 14], 239, 291, 301; **1951:** 56 [26], 78, 85 [2]; **1952–53:** 288
        Address by Justice Douglas, **1951:** 37 [5]
        Harriman mission to, **1950:** 209 [2]
        Meeting with Gen. MacArthur on, **1950:** 269, 270 [2]
    Regional conference of U.S. mission chiefs, **1949:** 260ftn. (p. 571)
    Rubber production, **1952–53:** 12
    Soviet military capabilities in, estimate by Gen. MacArthur, **1951:** 95 [11]
    UNICEF activities in, **1951:** 187
    U.S. relations with, **1950:** 252
    U.S. relief for, **1946:** 29, 45, 87, 124, 125; **1947:** 6 [26], 15
    Visits by U.S. political figures, **1951:** 113 [18], 224 [1], 230
Aspinall, Repr. Wayne N., **1948:** 200 [1]; **1952–53:** 32, 280 [4–6], 282 [1, 2]
Assassination attempt on the President, **1950:** 278 [4, 13]; **1952–53:** 134
Assignment of Claims Act of 1940, **1951:** 106
Associated Church Press, **1949:** 83; **1951:** 61
    Remarks, **1952–53:** 100
Associated General Contractors of America, **1947:** 20
Associated Press, **1947:** 76, 78 [22], 88 [3], 90 [3, 4]; **1951:** 247 [1], 298 [1]
Associated Press Managing Editors Association, **1951:** 302
Associated Services for the Armed Forces, **1950:** 95
Associated States.
    See Indochina.
Association of American Railroads, **1945:** 221 [9]; **1946:** 56
Association of Immigration and Nationality Lawyers, remarks, **1952–53:** 350
Association of Military Surgeons, remarks, **1952–53:** 333
Association of Radio News Analysts, **1949:** 234
    News conference with, **1947:** 90
Atherton, Ray, **1947:** 111
Athletics, at service academies, **1951:** 193 [6]
Atkins, T. A., Congressional Medal of Honor presentation, **1945:** 167n.
Atkinson, Eli, **1952–53:** 157n.
Atlantic Charter, **1945:** 177; **1946:** 248; **1951:** 290
Atlantic City, N.J., **1948:** 29

Atlantic City, N.J. — *continued*
American Farm Bureau Federation convention, **1948:** 285 [5]
Atlantic Command, allied, **1952–53:** 6, 16, 25
Atlantic Community, **1949:** 68, 188; **1951:** 4
Atlantic Monthly, **1948:** 278 [1]
Atlantic naval campaign, **1945:** 45
Atlantic Ocean, **1947:** 196
Atlantic-Pacific canal through Nicaragua, proposed, **1950:** 146 [11]
Atlantic-Pacific Oceans, connecting sea-level canal proposed, **1948:** 5 (p. 48)
Atlantic Pact.
See North Atlantic Treaty.
Atlantic Union, proposed, **1950:** 38 [19]
Atlas, H. Leslie, **1947:** 48n.
Atomic age, **1946:** 76, 83, 112; **1948:** 126 [6]; **1950:** 78
Atomic bomb, **1945:** 122, 155, 191; **1946:** 112; **1947:** 36 [3], 177 [9]; **1949:** 169; **1952–53:** 170
See also Hydrogen bomb; Nuclear weapons.
Civil defense against, **1951:** 96, 131
Control, **1945:** 97, 156, 178, 164 [4], 175 [14]
Decision for use, **1948:** 170 [11], 257 [3]
Against Japan, **1949:** 70
Development, **1945:** 93, 97, 164 [9], 179, 193 [8, 10]
History of, **1948:** 239
First explosion, **1950:** 121 [1]
Information, secrecy, **1945:** 164 [1, 4, 9], 175 [14], 193 [10], 208 [8]
Manhattan project, **1945:** 106 [2]; **1947:** 6 [1, 14], 7 (pp. 64, 81)
News conference remarks, **1945:** 106 [2], 147 [7, 21], 157 [4, 17, 18], 164 [1, 4, 9], 172 [12], 175 [14], 193 [8, 10], 208 [8]; **1946:** 6 [3, 6], 17 [23], 41 [1, 3, 21], 53 [14], 70 [6], 86 [15, 17], 163 [1], 226 [19], 229 [11], 237 [15]; **1949:** 30 [10], 45 [25], 66 [4], 72 [10], 166 [1, 10], 231 [19]; **1950:** 3 [2], 179 [5, 26], 203 [10], 209 [18], 250 [16], 273 [8, 13], 295 [12, 14]; **1951:** 16 [21], 165 [1], 247 [1, 9, 12], 251 [12], 295 [3]
Presidential responsibility for use of, **1952–53:** 283
Reports, **1946:** 163 [1]
Soviet explosions of, **1949:** 166 [10], 226 [8, 13], 234 [4], 236 [1], 253 [13]; **1950:** 3 [2], 34ftn. (p. 151), 97ftn. (p. 275), 273 [13]; **1951:** 96, 165 [1], 189, 246, 247 [1, 9, 12]; **1952–53:** 5, 158, 366
Soviet possession, question of, **1946:** 6 [3], 41 [21]
Tests, **1946:** 41 [1], 53 [14], 70 [6], 82, 86 [15, 17], 226 [19]
Bikini, **1949:** 45 [25], 66 [4], 166 [1]
Question of release of information re, **1948:** 278ftn. (p. 951), 283 [3]

Atomic bomb — *continued*
Tests — *continued*
Eniwetok, **1948:** 88 [4], 103, 164
U.S. arsenal, **1950:** 250 [16]
U.S. monopoly (1945–1949), **1952–53:** 366
Use in war
Korean war, question of, **1950:** 179 [5, 26], 203 [10], 295 [12, 14]; **1951:** 251 [12], 295 [3]
World War II, **1950:** 121 [1], 138, 209 [18], 273 [8]
Against Japan, **1945:** 93, 97, 156, 163, 174, 178; **1952–53:** 366, 378
Atomic energy, **1945:** 128; **1946:** 52, 76, 82, 83, 112, 218, 262, [1]; **1947:** 110; **1948:** 5 (pp. 21, 25, 45), 8 (p. 80), 175, 186; **1949:** 8 (p. 81)
Administration of program, **1948:** 191
"Big Three" conference, question of, **1945:** 181 [3], 208 [2]
Budget allocations for, **1952–53:** 17 [1, 4, 6, 8, 12, 16, 25, 29]
Civilian control of, **1952–53:** 298 [10]
Commission for control of, proposed, **1945:** 93, 156, 157 [4], 193 [8]
Control and development, **1945:** 156, 163, 181 [3]; **1946:** 6, [6, 10], 18 (pp. 42, 52), 28, 61 [15, 18], 70 [12], 119 [21], 136 [6], 141 [3, 6], 236, 242 [2]; **1947:** 2 (p. 10), 21, 132; **1948:** 34, 129, 164, 175, 259 [3]; **1949:** 70, 112 [2], 148 [1], 161 [2, 7], 216, 226 [13, 21], 234 [4], 237; **1950:** 8 [44], 9 (pp. 49, 64, 84, 89), 23 [17], 26, 34 [16, 18], 38 [20] and ftn., 42 (p. 162), 44 [2], 52 [6], 121 [1, 13], 162, 187, 271; **1951:** 54, 56 [16], 138, 246, 256, 293; **1952–53:** 18 (pp. 64, 87), 170, 366, 367 (pp. 1145, 1146), 376
Citizens commission on, proposed, **1950:** 34 [12]
Civilian vs. military, in U.S., **1948:** 164, 239
International, **1948:** 239; **1950:** 35ftn. (p. 152), 143
May-Johnson bill, **1945:** 172 [15]
Public vs. private, **1948:** 239
Cooperation, talks with U.K. and Canada, **1949:** 179 [18]
Expenditures for development, **1952–53:** 231
Facilities, collective bargaining at, **1948:** 140
First nuclear reaction, **1952–53:** 367 (p. 1145)
Fissionable materials, production facilities, **1952–53:** 367 (p. 1145)
Industrial application, **1948:** 2
Information on developments, availability, **1948:** 9 [12]
International cooperation, **1945:** 156, 178, 191, 193 [7, 8]
Investigation of program, **1949:** 118 [6]
Joint declaration with Prime Ministers of U.K. and Canada, **1945:** 191
Labor disputes at facilities, **1951:** 239 [18]

[References are to items except as otherwise indicated]

Atomic energy — *continued*
  Labor-management relations at installations,
      1949: 81, 87
  Manhattan project, **1945:** 106 [2]; **1947:** 6 [11,
      14], 7 (pp. 64, 81)
  Materials, procurement, **1952–53:** 18 (p. 87)
  Message to Congress, **1945:** 156
  News conference remarks, **1945:** 106 [2], 157 [4],
      172 [15], 181 [3], 193 [7, 8, 10], 208 [2];
      1946: 6 [6, 10], 17 [23], 41 [24, 26], 61 [15,
      18], 70 [12], 86 [15], 119 [21], 136 [6], 141
      [3, 6], 242 [4]; **1947:** 6 [11, 14], 180 [8, 9];
      1950: 8 [44], 23 [17], 34 [12, 16, 18], 38
      [20], 44 [2], 46 [20], 52 [6], 209 [18], 214 [8]
  Peaceful uses, **1945:** 106 [2], 157 [4], 165, 181 [3],
      191, 193 [10]; **1946:** 17 [23], 28, 86 [15],
      236; **1947:** 2 (p. 11), 7 (p. 81); **1948:** 5 (p.
      46), 88 [1], 104, 122 [3], 164, 239; **1949:**
      154, 169; **1950:** 2, 9 (p. 89), 42, 121 [1, 13],
      122, 138; **1951:** 135, 297; **1952–53:** 170,
      218, 219, 280 [4], 333, 366, 367 (p. 1146)
  Policy on, **1949:** 112 [1], 161 [2], 166 [1], 169
  Power projects, **1951:** 13 (p. 85); **1952–53:** 170,
      275
  Production facilities, **1948:** 110 [20], 239
  Quebec agreements, **1945:** 181 [3]
  Radioactive materials, research uses, **1948:** 239
  Reports, **1946:** 136 [6], 141 [3, 6]
  Research, **1945:** 93, 156, 193 [10]; **1948:** 156, 164,
      239; **1949:** 169; **1950:** 9 (p. 84), 121 [1];
      1951: 13 (pp. 84–85), 50, 135, 227 [5] and
      ftn. (p. 527), 246, 256, 293; **1952–53:** 147,
      170, 275, 280 [4], 366, 367 (p. 1146)
  Scientists, hampering by charges of Communist
      leanings, **1948:** 215
  Secret papers, disappearance, **1947:** 141 [11]
  Secrets, transmission to Soviet Union, **1950:** 34
      [18], 46 [20]; **1951:** 261 [9]
  Soviet attitude on, **1948:** 230, 239
  Soviet development, **1952–53:** 156 [10]
  Statement, **1946:** 242 [2]
Atomic Energy, Committee on, report, **1946:** 136
      [6], 141 [3]
Atomic Energy Act of 1946, **1946:** 242 [2], 262 [1];
      1947: 2 (p. 11); **1948:** 88 [1], 102, 164, 239;
      1949: 112ftn. (p. 267), 169
  Amendment, approval, **1948:** 156
Atomic energy bill, May-Johnson.
  See under Atomic energy.
Atomic Energy Commission, **1946:** 242 [3], 243;
      1947: 2 (p. 11), 7 (pp. 58, 64, 81, 83), 11,
      21, 181 (pp. 401, 403), 241; **1948:** 5 (pp.
      42, 47), 88 [1], 103, 140, 186, 239, 278 [1];
      1949: 8 (p. 81), 81, 87, 169; **1950:** 15ftn.
      (p. 118); **1951:** 50; **1952–53:** 18 (p. 87),
      117, 170, 249, 333, 340
  Air maps of installations, publication, **1952–53:**
      35 [3]

Atomic Energy Commission — *continued*
  Appropriations, **1949:** 155 [19]; **1950:** 187, 296;
      1952–53: 147, 170, 200
  Character investigations of nominees, veto, **1948:**
      102
  Communist activities in, question of, **1948:** 110
      [20]
  Facilities, **1950:** 121 [1, 13]
    Expansion, **1949:** 236 [1]
  Fissionable materials production program,
      1952–53: 17 [1]
  General Advisory Committee, **1946:** 262 [1]
  Hydrogen bomb, directive to continue devel-
      opment, **1950:** 26
  News conference remarks, **1946:** 6 [6], 41 [2], 61
      [15, 18], 141 [2], 186 [15], 199 [13], 216
      [20], 223 [4], 226 [17], 229 [29], 237 [20],
      242 [4, 7]; **1948:** 88 [1], 110 [20], 150 [4],
      278 [1], 283 [3]; **1949:** 11 [12], 58 [7], 84
      [18], 112 [1], 122 [6], 155 [19], 236 [1], 260
      [4], 267 [6]; **1950:** 34 [13], 52 [6], 146 [18],
      179 [10], 186 [3, 5, 7], 295 [1]
  Position on release of Bikini tests information,
      1948: 283 [3]
  Proposed, **1946:** 6 [6], 28, 41 [2], 61 [15, 18], 141
      [2]
  Rental housing near installations, **1951:** 13 (p.
      92)
  Report, **1948:** 164
  Research and development program, **1950:** 9
      (pp. 64, 89); **1951:** 13 (p. 85)
  Statement, **1946:** 242 [2]
  Terms of members, bill on extension, **1948:** 150
      [4], 156
  Vacancies, **1950:** 52 [6], 186 [3, 5, 7]
    Chairmanship, **1950:** 34 [13], 146 [18], 179 [10]
Atomic Energy Commission, Chairman (Gordon
      Dean), **1952–53:** 45, 170
Atomic Energy Commission, Chairman (David E.
      Lilienthal), **1947:** 31 [8, 11], 36 [21], 70
      [21], 132; **1948:** 88 [1]; **1950:** 16 [5, 15], 23
      [15], 29 [17]
  Appointment, **1946:** 242 [2], 243
  Memorandum, **1949:** 156
  News conference remarks on, **1947:** 31 [8, 11], 46
      [18]; **1949:** 30 [10], 112 [2, 18], 118 [9], 269
      [1]
Atomic Energy Commission, U.N., **1950:** 34ftn. (p.
      152); **1951:** 54
Atomic Energy Installations, President's Commis-
      sion on Labor Relations in, **1949:** 81
Atomic Energy Labor Relations Panel, **1949:** 81, 87
Atomic Trades and Labor Council (AFL), **1948:**
      140
Attlee, Clement R. (Prime Minister of Great Brit-
      ain), **1945:** 97, 107ftn. (p. 234), 187; **1946:**
      18 (pp. 41, 42), 92n., 212; **1947:** 19 [9, 17],
      29n., 41; **1948:** 239; **1949:** 71, 93 [12], 237;
      1950: 301; **1951:** 239 [15]

Attlee, Clement R. — *continued*
  Joint declaration on atomic energy, **1945:** 191
  Joint report on Potsdam conference, **1945:** 91
  Joint statement on Combined Food Board, **1946:** 108
  Joint statement on International Emergency Food Council, **1946:** 149
  Joint statement on removal of wartime trade controls, **1945:** 209
  Letter, **1945:** 188
  News conference remarks on, **1945:** 106 [8], 107 [18], 172 [10], 181 [3, 8]; **1946:** 27 [17], 41 [24], 126 [20], 186 [3], 199 [22], 215 [5], 229 [25]
Attorney General (Francis Biddle), resignation, **1945:** 40 [1]
  Letter, **1945:** 36
Attorney General (Tom C. Clark), **1945:** 172 [9]; **1946:** 186ftn. (p. 368), 189, 239, 246, 252; **1947:** 9, 77, 123, 124, 156, 202, 222, 242; **1948:** 1, 51n., 140, 171, 208 [4, 5], 209, 212 [2, 9], 215
  Appointment to Supreme Court, **1949:** 166 [4]
  Commodity exchanges investigation, **1947:** 209 [12]
  Letters, **1945:** 176; **1948:** 66, 179
  Lobbying investigation, **1948:** 208 [8], 278 [32]
  Memorandum, **1945:** 225; **1949:** 149n.
  News conference remarks on, **1946:** 43 [12], 223 [1], 237 [3, 8, 17, 18], 272; **1947:** 70 [4, 10, 11, 15], 78 [14, 24], 107 [6], 177 [7]; **1948:** 21 [3], 110 [12], 166 [8], 174 [4], 278 [32], 283 [1], 285 [14, 19]; **1949:** 28 [5], 84 [10], 122 [22], 166 [4]
  Report on enemy collaborators in the Philippines, **1946:** 63
  Report on patent practices and policies, **1947:** 109
  Report on war powers and war agencies, statutes governing, **1945:** 128 and ftn. (p. 275)
Attorney General (James P. McGranery), **1952–53:** 136 [9], 143, 161, 165, 182, 268 [3]
  Appointment and confirmation, **1952–53:** 75 [2, 4], 88 [19]
  Campaign remarks on, **1952–53:** 292 [11]
  Letters, **1952–53:** 177, 372
  Resignation, **1952–53:** 382
Attorney General (J. Howard McGrath), **1949:** 190, 220, 269 [14]; **1950:** 9 (p. 97), 49, 79, 94, 144; **1951:** 107, 115; **1952–53:** 7 [4, 6, 9], 26 [24], 37, 38, 45, 79
  Cooperation with Commission on Internal Security and Individual Rights, **1951:** 35
  Crime control functions, **1951:** 63 [1]
  Dismissal of Special Assistant Newbold Morris, **1952–53:** 75 [2, 4], 98 [36]
  Income tax returns, congressional request to examine, **1952–53:** 64 [6]

Attorney General (McGrath) — *continued*
  Law enforcement, conference on, **1950:** 37
  Letters and memorandums, **1950:** 35, 196, 259
  News conference remarks on, **1950:** 11 [3], 38 [9], 86 [2–4, 6, 7], 152 [9], 230 [9]
  Organized crime investigation, **1950:** 86 [2, 4, 6]
  Resignation, question of, **1951:** 300 [1, 2, 5, 8–10, 21]; **1952–53:** 2 [4], 75 [2, 4]
  Segregation, views on, **1950:** 86 [3]
  Special Assistant to, subpoena power for, **1952–53:** 35 [1], 36, 44 [10], 64 [15]
  Subpoena by congressional subcommittee, **1950:**82
  Telegram concerning injunction in copper strike, **1951:** 214
Attorney General, Office of the, Congressional investigation of, **1952–53:** 91
Attorney General's Conference on Law Enforcement Problems, **1950:** 37
Attorneys, U.S., Conference of, **1951:** 115
Attorneys Association, United States, remarks to, **1952–53:** 165
Attorneys General of the U.S., National Association of, **1950:** 37n.
Auburn, N.Y., campaign remarks, **1948:** 228 [9]
Auchincloss, Repr. James C., **1947:** 218 [3]; **1951:** 54n.
Augusta, U.S.S., **1945:** 79n., 82n., 91n., 93n.; **1951:** 282, 290
Augustana Lutheran Church, national convention, **1950:** 158
Auriol, Paul, **1951:** 58
Auriol, Vincent (President of France), message, **1947:** 13; **1950:** 152 [10]; **1951:** 58, 62, 63 [9], 65, 67, 157, 295 [1]; **1952–53:** 99
Auriol, Mme. Vincent, **1951:** 58, 65
Austin, Sen. Warren R., **1946:** 173 [1], 257 [7]; **1951:** 22 [1], 184, 266
  See also United Nations, U.S. Representative.
Austin, Tex.
  Campaign remarks, **1948:** 212 [2]
  McCloskey Army Hospital, **1948:** 212 [4]
  Miller, Mayor Tom, **1948:** 212 [2]
Australia, **1946:** 57, 247; **1947:** 7 (p. 65)
  Appointment of U.S. Ambassador, **1948:** 93 [14]
  Attitude toward Japan, **1951:** 132 [5]
  Curtin, John, death of, **1945:** 73
  Evatt, Herbert V., **1946:** 141 [14, 17]
  Grain, relief supplies for India, **1951:** 34
  Japanese peace mission in, **1951:** 49ftn. (p. 176)
  Korean war, participation, **1950:** 193, 194, 232, 296; **1951:** 170
  Military assistance, **1951:** 193 [2]; **1952–53:** 95
  Mission to, small business study, **1945:** 228
  Mutual defense treaty, **1951:** 84, 85 [8], 153ftn. (p. 387), 216; **1952–53:** 5, 26 [21], 95
  News conference remarks, **1945:** 132 [5], 157 [13]; **1946:** 30 [2], 86 [4]; **1950:** 179 [3], 250 [12]

Australia — *continued*
  Refugees, immigration to, **1952–53:** 65
  Wheat shipments to Europe, **1946:** 23
Austria, **1945:** 91; **1946:** 18 (p. 46), 172; **1947:** 7 (p. 67)
  Allied Commission for, **1950:** 218
  Art exhibit in U.S., **1949:** 253 [11]
  Assistance, **1947:** 47, 195, 224, 238; **1948:** 5 (p. 29), 147; **1952–53:** 55
  Attack by Germany (1938), **1951:** 4
  Communist aggression in, **1952–53:** 69
  Displaced persons in, **1947:** 38, 140
  Economic assistance, **1951:** 13 (p. 72), 114
  Figl, Leopold, **1952–53:** 127 [14]
  Mass deportations in, **1952–53:** 145
  News conference remarks, **1950:** 203 [19], 250 [1, 20]
  Occupied areas, **1949:** 8 (p. 59), 136
  Peace settlements, **1948:** 2
  Peace treaty, proposed, **1947:** 2 (p. 10); **1949:** 136
  Peace treaty, question of, **1950:** 218, 250 [1, 20]
  Relief for, **1945:** 186
  Soviet occupation zone, **1947:** 114
  Soviet policy in, **1951:** 197
  Trade with Soviet bloc, **1951:** 117n.
  U.S. Ambassador Walter J. Donnelly, **1952–53:** 98 [40]
  U.S. Minister and High Commissioner, **1950:** 217 [2], 218, 274
  U.S. relief for, **1947:** 47
Automation, **1948:** 104
Automobile, Aircraft and Agricultural Implement Workers of America, United, **1951:** 252
Automobile accidents, **1945:** 62, 208 [10], 224; **1947:** 8, 27
Automobile industry
  Labor contract, **1948:** 110 [17]
  Production, **1951:** 11, 42
Automobile Workers of America, United, **1946:** 2; **1948:** 110 [17]; **1949:** 269 [14]; **1950:** 202
  Labor dispute, **1945:** 204, 206
Automobiles
  Credit controls on purchase of, **1949:** 45ftn. (p. 156)
  Price control, **1950:** 318 [3]; **1952–53:** 33
  Prices, **1946:** 152, 153
  Production, **1946:** 72 [2]
  Sales, suspension by General Motors Corp., **1950:** 309 [7, 9]
  Shortage, **1947:** 4 (p. 28), 18
Aviation, **1946:** 137, 138; **1947:** 51, 148, 149, 159; **1948:** 7, 8 (p. 82), 175
  See also Aircraft; Aircraft, military; Aviation, civil.
  Aeronautical developments, secrecy respecting, **1948:** 9 [12, 14]
  Civil.
    See Aviation, civil.

Aviation — *continued*
  Coast Guard activities, **1947:** 7 (p. 85)
  Commercial, **1945:** 52 [16]
  Defense, **1948:** 5 (p. 29)
  Federal airways system, **1948:** 175
  Military airpower, defense emphasis on, **1949:** 8 (p. 56)
  Naval, question of expansion, **1951:** 224 [2]
  Navy and Marine units, question of transfer to Air Force, **1949:** 89 [7]
  News conference remarks, **1949:** 78 [17], 89 [7]
  Problems of, study by Congress, **1947:** 161
  Research and development, **1948:** 5 (27, 50), 7, 60, 175
  Round-the-world flight, Milton Reynolds and William Odom, **1947:** 74
  Safety, **1947:** 82, 115, 180 [12]
Aviation, civil, **1946:** 17 [30], 18 (pp. 81, 82, 86); **1947:** 7 (pp. 58, 84, 85), 148, 149; **1948:** 5 (p. 50), 7, 9 [12], 175; **1949:** 8 (p. 85); **1950:** 9 (pp. 49, 94), 171; **1952–53:** 125, 328, 351
  See also Aircraft, military; Airports.
  Air Coordinating Committee, report, **1947:** 40
  Air safety board, appointment, **1947:** 115
  Air traffic defense control, **1952–53:** 18 (p. 83)
  Air Transport Agreement, **1946:** 43 [2], 44
  Airline strike, **1946:** 110 [11]
  Airlines, assistance to, **1952–53:** 18 (p. 83)
  Airmail, payments to carriers, **1952–53:** 18 (p. 84)
  Airports, **1946:** 18 (pp. 53, 81, 82)
  Airways, **1951:** 13 (p. 83)
  Awards for contributions to, **1952–53:** 351n.
  Congressional study, **1947:** 161
  Federal aid, **1952–53:** 367 (p. 1144)
  Growth, **1952–53:** 351
  Helicopter industry, joint award of Collier Trophy to, **1951:** 301
  International conferences
    Bermuda, **1946:** 43 [2], 44
    Chicago (1944), **1946:** 133
  Mexico, air service to, **1952–53:** 246
  Navigation and safety aids, **1952–53:** 18 (p. 83)
  North Pacific air routes, **1946:** 95 [14]
  Safety, **1947:** 82, 180 [12]; **1952–53:** 40, 351
Aviation Policy Board, **1947:** 161
Awards and citations.
  See also Addresses or remarks at presentation ceremonies.
  Agriculture Department honor awards, **1952–53:** 126
  Allied officers, **1951:** 115
  American Legion, acceptance, **1949:** 195n.
  Association of Immigration and Nationality Lawyers, acceptance, **1952–53:** 350
  Boy Scout silver buffalo award, acceptance, **1950:** 185n.

Awards and citations — *continued*
  Civil aviation, awards for contributions to, **1952–53:** 351n.
  Collier's Congressional Awards
    Monroney, Repr. Mike, **1946:** 80
    Vandenberg, Sen. Arthur H., **1946:** 80
  Congressional Medal of Honor.
    See under Medals, presentation.
  Danish arm band, acceptance, **1946:** 6 [18]
  Distinguished Service Medal.
    See under Medals, presentation.
  Franklin D. Roosevelt Award, acceptance, **1948:** 265
  Gold Medal, Veterans of Foreign Wars, acceptance, **1949:** 184n.
  Honorary degrees, acceptance, **1945:** 68; **1946:** 112; **1947:** 52, 117; **1948:** 124 [1], 128 [4], 194 [5]
  Humanitarian Award, George C. Marshall, **1948:** 196
  Legion of Merit.
    See under Medals, presentation.
  Medal for Merit.
    See under Medals, presentation.
  National Health Assembly scroll
    Capp, Al, **1948:** 89n.
    Edwards, Ralph, **1948:** 89n.
    Robinson, Bill, **1948:** 89n.
    Winchell, Walter, **1948:** 89n.
  National Newspaper Publishers Association, acceptance of plaque, **1952–53:** 329
  Robert S. Abbott memorial award, acceptance, **1949:** 109
  7th Regimental Citation, Nisei regiment, **1946:** 170
  Statement, **1947:** 103
  Teacher of the Year award, Mrs. Geraldine Jones, **1952–53:** 133
  Testimonial scroll, Brig. Gen. Benjamin O. Davis, **1948:** 162
  Unit citations, aircraft carriers, **1946:** 171
  Wendell Willkie journalism awards, **1947:** 48
Axis aggression, **1945:** 2, 3, 10, 75, 186
Axis powers, **1945:** 66, 91, 177, 196n.; **1946:** 7, 68, 83, 172, 236; **1947:** 33, 34, 38, 238
  Surrender.
    See Unconditional surrender of Axis powers.
Axtell, Enos, **1946:** 173 [8, 18], 177 [8], 199 [2, 15]
Aydelotte, Frank, **1945:** 210
Ayers, Eben A., **1946:** 30 [2]; **1950:** 250 [14]

B-29 bomber
  Interception by Soviet Union, **1950:** 86ftn. (p. 254)
  Question of sale to U.K., **1949:** 22 [8], 45 [15]

B-36 bomber, **1949:** 118 [4], 205 [9]; **1951:** 153 [2]; **1952–53:** 158
B-50 bomber, round-the-world flight, **1949:** 45 [7, 12]
Baade, Maj. Gen. Paul W., **1947:** 110
Babcock, Charles E., **1951:** 255n.
Babelsberg, Germany, **1945:** 83n.
Bach, Johann Sebastian, **1951:** 99
Bacher, Robert F., **1946:** 242 [2]; **1948:** 88 [1]; **1949:** 84 [19]
Bailey, Cleveland M., **1952–53:** 242 [3]
Bailey, Joseph W., Jr., **1948:** 214 [3]
Bailey, Steve, "Congress Makes a Law," **1952–53:** 292 [3]
Baird, Spencer F., **1946:** 201
Baker, Bryant, **1950:** 42n.
Baker, George P., **1947:** 148n.; **1948:** 7n.
Baker, Roy G., **1948:** 101, 214 [1]
Baker, Oreg., **1950:** 121 [8]
Bakeries, grain conservation by, **1947:** 191 [5], 209 [2]; **1948:** 14
Bakersfield, Calif., campaign remarks, **1948:** 204 [4]
Balance of payments, **1947:** 4 (p. 26), 152; **1948:** 167, 175; **1950:** 6, 80 [8, 9], 81n., 159, 202; **1951:** 11, 167; **1952–53:** 15
  Foreign nations, **1952–53:** 203, 215
  France, **1952–53:** 15
  India, **1951:** 34
  United Kingdom, **1952–53:** 15
Balch, Richard, **1952–53:** 359 [11]
Baldhill Dam, **1950:** 130
Baldwin, Joseph C., **1946:** 229 [2]
Baldwin, Raymond, **1952–53:** 298 [9]
Balkan Commission, United Nations, **1948:** 28
Balkans, **1945:** 225
  Reported Soviet troop movements in, **1949:** 200 [10]
Ball, Sen. Joseph H., **1948:** 137ftn. (p. 363), 236, 237 [1]
  Federal labor relations bill, **1945:** 172 [1]
Ball-Burton-Hatch-Hill resolution (1943). **1948:** 137ftn. (p. 363)
Ballot boxes, theft of, **1950:** 86 [7]
Ball's Bluff, Civil War battle, **1950:** 121 [8]
Baltic countries, political refugees from, **1947:** 140; **1948:** 174 [4], 178 [12], 283 [5]
Baltimore, Lord, **1951:** 241
Baltimore, Md.
  Campaign remarks, **1948:** 139[4]
  Democratic National Convention (1912), **1951:** 6
  Election in, **1947:** 88 [5]
  Friendship International Airport, dedication, **1950:** 97 [16], 171
  Mayor Thomas D'Alesandro, Jr., **1948:** 139n., 228 [1]; **1950:** 97 [16], 171n.
Baltimore Sun, **1947:** 210 [2]; **1949:** 45 [6], 205 [3]; **1950:** 44 [11]

Bangkok, Thailand, regional conference of U.S.
mission chiefs in Asia, **1949:** 260ftn. (p.
571)
Bank of America National Trust and Savings
Association, **1951:** 284
Bank credits, restrictions, **1946:** 72 [3]
Bank for Reconstruction and Development.
See Bretton Woods agreements.
Bank of the U.S., Andrew Jackson's controversy
with, **1948:** 264 [5]
Bankers
Comment on, **1951:** 21
Contributions to Republican campaign fund,
1948: 251
Bankers Association, American, **1947:** 97
Bankhead, Sen. John H., **1946:** 84 [22]; **1948:** 247
Bankhead, Tallulah, **1948:** 247
Bankhead, William B., **1948:** 247
Bankhead-Jones Farm Tenant Act, **1950:** 121 [3]
Banking Act, Emergency, of 1933, **1951:** 44
Banknote, gift to President, **1948:** 271 [2]
Bankruptcy Act, **1946:** 205
Bankruptcy referees, in claims against U.S., **1947:**
168
Banks, Frank A., **1948:** 122 [3], 125; **1949:** 106n.
Distinguished Service Medal.
See under Medals, presentation.
Banks, **1947:** 7 (p. 88), 116, 152; **1948:** 175; **1949:** 5
Commercial, monopoly on deposits, **1948:** 220
Credit, **1948:** 4 [18], 8 (pp. 72, 73, 95, 96), 13
Deposit insurance, **1948:** 219, 231 [5], 255; **1949:**
5, 151, 154; **1950:** 110 [5], 157; **1952–53:**
276
Deposits, **1951:** 11
Farm credit operations, **1952–53:** 367 (p. 1149)
Federal Reserve, **1948:** 5 (p. 57); **1950:** 14
Government security holdings, **1947:** 75; **1948:** 5
(pp. 23, 57), 8 (p. 95), 175
Holding company, hearing on monopoly
charges, **1949:** 40 [6]
Interest rates, **1951:** 11, 91
Investments, **1952–53:** 215
Loans, **1949:** 151; **1952–53:** 15, 215
Policy, **1951:** 11, 37 [15], 91, 167
Defense contractors, **1951:** 106, 284
Small business, **1950:** 106, 118
News conference remarks, **1948:** 4 [18], 9 [4], 77
[9], 84 [16], 178 [5]
Policies, **1948:** 77 [9], 84 [16], 178 [5]; **1949:** 2, 5,
151
Reform, **1948:** 219
Reserves, **1947:** 232 [5]; **1948:** 8 (pp. 72, 95), 9 [4]
Requirements, **1950:** 6; **1951:** 11, 44, 91;
1952–53: 15
Role in European economy, **1947:** 238
Stability, **1948:** 121, 124 [5], 228 [5], 231 [5], 259
[5], 262; **1952–53:** 291
Baptist missionaries, remarks to, **1950:** 31

Bar Association, Inter-American, **1949:** 115
Barbary pirates, Jefferson's expedition against,
1951: 80
Barbosa, Ruy, **1947:** 189
Bard, Judge Guy K., **1952–53:** 286 [8], 303 [9, 10],
304, 305, 306 [1–3, 5, 6], 308 [2, 4–6]
Bard, Ralph A., **1946:** 37 [4]
Barden, Repr. Graham A., bill for aid to education,
1949: 144 [12]
Baring, Walter S., **1948:** 202 [1, 2]
Barker, James, **1949:** 253 [4]
Barkley, Sen. Alben W., **1945:** 165; **1946:** 15 [2], 43
[4]; **1947:** 78 [11], 125, 141 [1], 180 [10];
1948: 12n., 222 [5], 227 [4], 234, 269, 272;
1949: 15, 226 [7]
See also Vice President (Alben W. Barkley).
Candidacy for Vice President, **1948:** 160, 208 [2],
218 [12], 220, 222 [3, 8], 266, 269, 272, 274
[14]
Letter, **1945:** 89
News conference remarks on, **1945:** 8 [4], 129 [7];
1948: 163 [10], 174 [5], 274 [14], 285 [3]
Barkley, Mrs. Alben W., **1951:** 136n.
Barley, conservation, **1948:** 14
Barnard, Chester I., **1951:** 307n.
Barr, George, **1951:** 195; **1952–53:** 243
Barre, Isaac, **1948:** 249
Barrett, Repr. William A., **1952–53:** 304
Barro Colorado Island, Gatun Lake, **1946:** 118;
1947: 35
Barron, Carter T., **1948:** 196; **1950:** 77n., 137 [22],
287 [3]; **1951:** 116n.
Barrows, Arthur S., **1947:** 191 [1]
Barry, Commodore John, **1948:** 53
Barrymore, Ethel, **1948:** 247
Bartenders' Union, **1951:** 261 [7]
Bartlett, E. L., **1952–53:** 149 [15]
Bartley, Robert T., **1952–53:** 49 [1, 15]
Bartley, Mrs. Samuel E. (Meddie Rayburn), **1952–
53:** 49 [1]
Barton, Clara, **1951:** 47
Baruch, Bernard M., **1945:** 208 [13]; **1946:** 70 [14],
136 [6], 141 [3, 6], 226 [4]; **1947:** 1, 78 [6];
1948: 11 [1, 4], 71 [19]; **1949:** 144 [1, 10];
1951: 179 [7], 251 [23]; **1952–53:** 127 [13],
149 [12]
Atomic energy control plan, **1950:** 34 [18]
News conference remarks on, **1950:** 34 [18], 203
[1, 5, 9]
Baseball, comments on, **1948:** 194 [6]; **1949:** 192
[18]
Bases abroad, U.S., **1945:** 97; **1947:** 6 [39], 7 (p. 64);
1949: 8 (p. 59), 45 [12]; **1950:** 74
Air Force, **1952–53:** 367 (p. 1137)
Far East, **1945:** 129 [3]
Galapagos Islands, World War II offer by Ecua-
dor, **1951:** 136n.
Greenland, **1952–53:** 217

Bases abroad — *continued*
  News conference remarks, **1946:** 27 [7], 37 [1], 141 [14, 17], 216 [21], 226 [14]
  Pacific, **1946:** 141 [14, 17], 226 [14], 265
  Panama, **1946:** 216 [21]
  Philippines, **1948:** 283 [20]; **1951:** 84
  Tripoli, **1948:** 9 [15]
  United Kingdom, **1952–53:** 6
Bashore, Harry W., **1945:** 211 [10]
Bastille Day, **1946:** 167; **1951:** 157
  Statement, **1945:** 81
Bastille key, proposed return to France, **1951:** 165 [7]
Bataan, **1945:** 174; **1946:** 159
  Death march, **1945:** 45
Batavia, N.Y., campaign remarks, **1948:** 228 [13]; **1952–53:** 289 [1]
Batavia Daily News, **1952–53:** 289 [1]
Batcheller, Hiland, **1947:** 122
Bates, Joe B., **1948:** 222 [5, 8]
Batesville, Ark., campaign remarks, **1952–53:** 195 [2]
Batt, Dann, **1948:** 231 [6, 7]; **1952–53:** 311 [2], 319 [2]
Battery B, 129th Field Artillery, **1949:** 211 [7]
Battery D, 129th Field Artillery, **1949:** 18, 119 [4]; **1950:** 161 [1, 2]; **1951:** 138, 298 [1]
Battle, Repr. Laurie, **1951:** 54n.
Battle Act.
  See Mutual Defense Assistance Control Act of 1951.
Battle Monuments Commission, American **1946:** 229 [2]
Baughman, U. E., Jr., **1949:** 265
Baumann, Col. Julian, **1945:** 24
Bay, Charles U., **1950:** 52 [2]
Bay of Fundy tidal power project, **1950:** 121 [13]; **1951:** 16 [13], 239 [9]
  See also Passamaquoddy tidal power project.
Bayard, Alexis I., **1952–53:** 303 [1]
Baylor University, **1947:** 52
Bayonne, N.J., Mayor Charles Heiser, **1948:** 189n.
Bayou Meto irrigation project, Arkansas, **1949:** 183
Beans, **1947:** 18, 32
  Price supports, **1950:** 9 (p. 86)
Beard, growth by President, **1947:** 145 [14]
Beardsley, Gov. William S., **1952–53:** 97
Beau, Maj. Gen. Lucas V., **1952–53:** 351
Bebell, Clinton J., **1952–53:** 286 [8]
Bech, Joseph, **1949:** 68
Beck, Earl W., **1951:** 251 [6]; **1952–53:** 44 [7]
Beckworth, Repr. Lindley, **1952–53:** 123 [11], 238 [4]
Beene, Sim, **1948:** 212 [10]
Beer production, **1946:** 29
Beethoven, Ludwig van, **1951:** 99
Beggs, David W., **1952–53:** 321 [4]
Beggs, Lyall T., **1949:** 184n.

Begley, Owen, **1948:** 228 [2]
Belair, Felix, **1946:** 215 [5]
Belasco Theatre, Washington, D.C., **1948:** 21 [5]
Belgium, **1945:** 186; **1946:** 18 (p. 84); **1949:** 68, 78 [9], 113 [9], 118 [8], 192 [9]
  Assistance, **1947:** 195, 238
    Military, **1950:** 22
  Korean war, participation, **1950:** 296; **1951:** 170
  Lend-lease agreements, **1945:** 50; **1947:** 7 (p. 65)
  Liberation, **1945:** 45
  Prince Charles, **1948:** 71 [7], 85
  Spaak, Paul-Henri, **1948:** 71 [7, 16]; **1949:** 69n.
Bell, Daniel W., **1945:** 202 [11]; **1952–53:** 203n.
  Economic mission to Philippines, **1950:** 179 [11], 180
    Report, **1950:** 238 [5], 270 [9], 273 [2, 10], 278 [11]
  Report of Philippine economic survey, implementation, **1951:** 49 [5]
Bell, Repr. Jasper C., **1946:** 173 [9]
Belleau Wood, **1946:** 171n.
Bellefontaine, Ohio, campaign remarks, **1948:** 267 [1]; **1952–53:** 286 [4]
Bells, Tex., campaign remarks, **1948:** 212 [11]
Belt, Guillermo, **1948:** 81
Belton, Mont., campaign remarks, **1952–53:** 268 [9]
Belton Reservoir, Leon River, Tex., **1948:** 212ftn. (p. 584)
Ben-Gurion, David, **1951:** 95 [1]
Ben Hur, **1945:** 64 [1]
Bend, Oreg., **1946:** 6 [7]
Bendetsen, Karl R., **1951:** 93n.
Benediktsson, Bjarni, **1949:** 68
Benes, Eduard, **1945:** 173; **1946:** 245
Benevolent and Protective Order of Elks, **1948:** 130 [3]
Bennett, Edward A., Congressional Medal of Honor presentation, **1945:** 167n.
Bennett, Henry G., **1951:** 16 [1], 83, 262, 296n.; **1952–53:** 5, 144, 261
Bentley, Elizabeth, **1948:** 170ftns. (pp. 432, 433); **1949:** 32ftn. (p. 137); **1950:** 152ftn. (p. 450)
Benton, Sen. William, **1946:** 86 [1], 222; **1950:** 92; **1951:** 247 [1]; **1952–53:** 31 [12], 170, 292 [1–5, 7, 8], 293, 298 [7–11]
Berle, Adolf A., **1948:** 283 [1]
Berlin, **1945:** 133
  Airlift, **1950:** 80 [4], 232; **1951:** 138; **1952–53:** 107 [2], 366, 378
  Allied occupation, **1949:** 136
  Clay, Gen. Lucius D., release from duty in, **1949:** 92
  Communism in, **1950:** 92
    East German Communists, demonstration in Western sector, **1950:** 97 [13]
  Communist aggression, **1949:** 162; **1952–53:** 69, 107 [2]

Berlin — *continued*
  Control Council, **1945:** 91, 201n.
  Destruction of, **1945:** 97
  Flag raising over U.S. Group Council head-
    quarters, remarks, **1945:** 86
  Mayor Ernst Reuter, **1949:** 54
  News conference remarks, **1945:** 67 [2]; **1950:** 23
    [18], 80 [4], 97 [13], 179 [20]; **1952–53:** 149
    [8]
  Soviet blockade, **1948:** 150 [7], 163 [1, 11], 166 [2,
    11], 185 [6, 8], 230, 274 [3, 6], 278 [19];
    1949: 78 [3], 84 [24], 89 [6, 11], 92, 93 [4, 6,
    14], 95 [18]; **1950:** 23 [18], 80 [4], 232;
    1951: 78, 266; **1952–53:** 279, 366
    Electric power stoppage, **1950:** 179 [20]
  U.S. policy in, **1952–53:** 279
  U.S. Political Adviser, **1947:** 210 [4]
  U.S.-Soviet talks on, **1948:** 71 [18]
  Visit to, **1947:** 74
Berlin conference.
  See Potsdam conference.
Berlin, East, **1951:** 116
  Communists, demonstration against U.S., **1951:**
    197
Bermuda, Civil Aviation Conference, **1946:** 43 [2],
  44
Bermúdez, Antonio J., **1949:** 66 [11]
Bernadotte, Count Folke, **1945:** 22 [20], 40 [5];
  1948: 193 [2]
  Report on Palestine, **1948:** 274 [7]
Bernadotte, Countess, **1948:** 193 [2], 193n.
Bernhard, Prince, **1952–53:** 73, 74, 77n., 78
Berreta, Tomás, **1947:** 30, 31 [7]
Berryman, Jim, cartoon of President, **1948:** 55ftn.
  (p. 194)
Bersell, Dr. Petrus O., **1950:** 158n.
Berthold, N. Dak., campaign remarks, **1952–53:**
  266 [8]
Bertil, Prince, **1948:** 115
Bethlehem, Pa., campaign remarks, **1948:** 227 [4]
Bethlehem Steel Co., **1948:** 177; **1949:** 155 [12];
  1951: 305
Bethesda, Md., **1947:** 73n.; **1952–53:** 135
Bethune, Mary McLeod, **1949:** 256
Bethune-Cookman College, **1949:** 256
Better Business Bureaus, **1950:** 157
Bevin, Ernest (U.K. Foreign Minister), **1945:** 91,
  208 [2]; **1946:** 129 [11], 136 [14], 265;
  1947: 41, 46 [19], 191 [4]; **1948:** 166 [2];
  1949: 68, 72 [14]; **1951:** 88
Biak Island, **1945:** 45
Bibles
  Gift to the President, **1952–53:** 260
  Used at inaugural ceremony, **1949:** 19n.
Bidault, Georges, **1945:** 107 [5], 113
  Discussion with, statement, **1945:** 33
  Legion of Merit, citation, **1945:** 110
Biddle, Francis, **1946:** 251; **1952–53:** 129

Biddle, Francis — *continued*
  Appointment as U.S. representative on Interna-
    tional Military Tribunal, **1945:** 132 [1]
  News conterence remarks on, **1945:** 40 [1], 132
    [1]
  Resignation as Attorney General, **1945:** 36, 40 [1]
Biddle, M. E., Congressional Medal of Honor
  presentation, **1945:** 167n.
Biemiller, Andrew J., **1948:** 237 [6]
Bierut, Boleslaw, **1946:** 64
Biffle, Leslie L., **1945:** 8 [4], 22 [3], 107 [15], 129 [6];
  1946: 125, 250 [9]; **1952–53:** 174, 193, 253
  [5]
Big Bend National Park (Texas), **1948:** 208 [6–8]
"Big Three" (U.S., U.K., Soviet Union), meetings.
  See Heads of state and government, meetings.
Bigotry, racial and religious, **1947:** 9; **1948:** 21 [14],
  256
Bikini atomic bomb tests, **1948:** 278ftn. (p. 951),
  283 [3]; **1949:** 45 [25], 66 [4], 166 [1]
Bilbo, Sen. Theodore G., death of, **1947:** 182 [2]
Bill of rights, international, **1945:** 66
Bill of Rights, U.S., **1945:** 66; **1947:** 90 [1], 130, 210
  [1], 243 [2]; **1948:** 21 [3], 178 [15], 193 [1],
  214 [7], 265; **1951:** 18, 35, 116, 174, 178,
  191, 225, 241, 247 [1], 278; **1952–53:** 63,
  117, 165, 288, 313 [4, 5], 322, 347, 366, 373
Bill of Rights Conference, **1949:** 155 [2]
Billings, Josh, **1951:** 21, 27; **1952–53:** 127 [1]
Binaggio, Charles, **1950:** 86 [2, 4, 12]
Bingham, Barry, **1949:** 84 [4]; **1952–53:** 98 [4]
Bingham, Hiram, **1951:** 37 [12]; **1952–53:** 362n.
Binghamton, N.Y., **1949:** 144 [5]
Biography, American Dictionary of, **1952–53:** 7
  [10]
Birds, migratory, **1946:** 211
Birdzell, Donald T., **1950:** 278ftn. (p. 695)
Birmingham Veterans Hospital, Van Nuys, Calif.,
  1950: 137 [10], 146 [14]
Birthday, the President's, **1945:** 26 [1]; **1947:** 88
  [11]; **1950:** 110 [5], 111n., 124 [7]; **1952–
  53:** 123 [1, 9]
Bituminous Coal Operators' Association, **1952–53:**
  341
Bituminous Coal Operators Negotiating Commit-
  tee, **1946:** 252n.
Black, Justice Hugo L., **1945:** 52 [20]; **1946:** 126
  [21], 136 [8, 10]; **1952–53:** 161
Black, James B., **1947:** 55n., 236 [3], 237
Black market, **1945:** 44 [1]; **1946:** 95 [24], 99, 179;
  1947: 191 [24]
Black Sea Straits, free navigation of, **1948:** 86
Blackfoot, Idaho, campaign remarks, **1948:** 120 [2]
Blackfoot Indians, gifts to the President, **1950:** 217
  [7]
Blackmore, Dwight, **1948:** 231 [8, 9], 257 [4]
Blaine, James G., **1952–53:** 127 [18]
Blair, Lt. Gov. James T., Jr., **1948:** 138 [3];
  1952–53: 127 [1]

Blair-Buck, Mrs. J. L., **1947:** 191 [3]
Blair House, **1949:** 11 [1], 28 [23], 84 [15]; **1950:** 86
 [1]
  Meetings at, **1949:** 155 [13], 161 [2, 13]
  Occupancy of, **1952–53:** 378
Bland, Richard Parks, **1952–53:** 127 [18]
Blandford, John B., **1946:** 27 [1]
Blanding, Sarah G., **1952–53:** 203n.
Blatt, Solomon, **1945:** 147n.
Blatnik, Repr. John A., **1948:** 235 [5]; **1952–53:** 313
 [6], 314
Blind persons
  Assistance for, **1945:** 99
  Federal aid, **1948:** 107
  Occupational training, **1952–53:** 243
  Social security coverage, **1948:** 131, 152
  Vocational rehabilitation, **1946:** 117
Block, Rev. Karl Morgan, **1951:** 22 [2], 278n.
Block, william, **1949:** 202n.
Bloedorn, Dr. Walter A., **1947:** 21
Bloom, Repr. Sol, **1945:** 10; **1946:** 141 [7], 173 [1];
 1947: 19 [18]
  Nomination as Alternate U.S. Representative to
   U.N. General Assembly, **1945:** 219n.
Blooming mill, export to Yugoslavia, **1949:** 182 [11]
Bloomsburg, Pa., campaign remarks, **1952–53:** 306
 [3]
Blossom Time, **1947:** 14 [23]
Blough, Roy, **1951:** 44n.
Blue, Gov. Robert D., **1947:** 209 [2]; **1948:** 194 [6]
Blythe, Joseph L., **1947:** 205 [4]; **1948:** 110 [18];
 1949: 16
Board of Commissioners, Sedgwick County, Kan-
 sas, **1950:** 256
Board of Foreign Scholarships, **1951:** 103
Board of Trade, Chicago, **1947:** 196, 209 [11]
Boatner, Gen. Haydon L., **1952–53:** 127ftn. (p. 337)
Boeing Airplane Co., **1950:** 256
  Labor dispute, **1948:** 88 [5]
Boettiger, Mrs. John, **1947:** 204n.
Bogotá
  Pan American conference, **1948:** 198 [1]
  Political riots, **1948:** 77 [1, 8]
Bogotá, Act of, **1949:** 70; **1950:** 137 [26]
Bogotá, International Conference of American
   States, **1947:** 221 [4]; **1949:** 9, 10; **1950:**
   218; **1951:** 125
Bohlen, Charles E., **1949:** 112 [1]; **1951:** 239 [1]
Boise, Idaho, **1950:** 121 [4]
  Speech by Gen. Eisenhower, comments on,
   1952–53: 233 [15], 319 [4]
Boke, Richard L., **1949:** 58 [20], 96n.
Boland, Edward P., **1952–53:** 292 [9]
Bolívar, Simón, **1948:** 150 [9], 158
  Memorial Foundation, **1948:** 158
  Transfer of statue to New York, **1951:** 87
Bolivar, Mo.
  Mayor Doyle McCraw, **1948:** 158

Bolivar, Mo. — *continued*
  Memorial statue of Simón Bolívar, gift by Ven-
   ezuela, **1948:** 150 [9], 158
Bolivia, **1949:** 253 [19]
  Lend-lease settlement, **1951:** 244
  Offer by Chile of corridor to sea, **1950:** 191 [6]
  Tin, negotiations concerning, **1952–53:** 2 [8, 14],
   26 [14]
Bolling, Repr. Richard, **1951:** 196
Bolte, Charles G., **1946:** 214
Bolte, Maj. Gen. Charles L., **1952–53:** 310
Bolton, Repr. Frances P., **1951:** 54n.
Bombers, **1945:** 45; **1946:** 7
  See also under Aircraft, military.
Bombing, strategic and tactical, **1945:** 45
Bombs, atomic and hydrogen.
  See also Atomic bomb; Hydrogen bomb.
  Grand Slam, **1945:** 93
Bonds, **1947:** 6 [4], 116; **1948:** 8 (pp. 69, 72, 95, 96),
   175; **1949:** 11
  Armed forces leave, **1948:** 5 (p. 56)
  Interest on, **1947:** 90 [8]; **1948:** 175; **1949:** 154;
   1952–53: 15, 18 (pp. 68, 115)
  Investment, **1948:** 5 (p. 24)
  News conference remarks, **1952–53:** 17 [3, 9, 13]
  Railroad, **1946:** 205
  Road construction, **1950:** 213
  Savings, **1945:** 76 [3], 171, 213; **1946:** 17 [2], 18
   (p. 73); **1947:** 4 (p. 24), 7 (pp. 61, 91), 68,
   76, 90 [8], 180 [13, 14], 224; **1948:** 5 (pp.
   24, 25, 56), 8 (p. 74), 26 [3, 10], 76, 175;
   1949: 5, 7 [41], 37, 40 [16], 82, 98; **1950:** 8
   [25], 9 (p. 103), 127 [6], 133, 281n.; **1951:**
   11, 12 [13], 13 (p. 105), 60, 91, 133, 153 [1,
   13], 167, 210, 213, 290; **1952–53:** 367 (pp.
   1133, 1161)
  Terminal leave, **1947:** 145 [17], 158, 181 (pp. 404,
   406, 407)
Bonham, Tex., **1952–53:** 49 [1]
  Campaign address, **1948:** 213
Bonner, Gov. John W., **1950:** 80 [10], 124 [8], 127
   [4, 7], 128, 129 [1]; **1952–53:** 266 [13], 268
   [2–4, 7–9], 269, 270 [1, 4–8], 271, 274 [4],
   278
Bonners Ferry, Idaho, campaign remarks, **1952–53:**
   270 [9]
Bonnet, Henri, **1947:** 110; **1950:** 161 [2, 3]; **1951:**
   160; **1952–53:** 99
Bonnet, Mme. Henri, **1947:** 110
Bonnet, Indian, gift to the President, **1950:** 127 [7]
Bonneville Dam, **1946:** 18 (p. 60); **1948:** 201; **1950:**
   121 [4], 125
Bonneville Power Administration, **1946:** 18 (p. 82);
   1947: 7 (p. 81); **1948:** 5 (pp. 46, 47), 149;
   1949: 77; **1950:** 9 (p. 90); **1951:** 13 (p. 87);
   1952–53: 18 (p. 89), 388
Bonus, veterans, question of, **1949:** 40 [13]
Books, gift to the President, **1950:** 29 [9]

Boone, Vice Adm. Joel T., **1952–53:** 135
Borah, William E., **1947:** 191 [14]
Borax, extraction from Mojave Desert, **1948:** 204 [6]
Bosone, Mrs. Reva Beck, **1948:** 200 [5]; **1952–53:** 280 [1]
Boston, Mass., **1949:** 267 [2]
  Baltic emigrants, **1948:** 174 [4], 178 [12]
  Campaign address, **1948:** 260; **1952–53:** 296
  Internal Revenue collectorship, **1951:** 300 [5]
  Longshoremen's strike, **1951:** 276
  Mayor James M. Curley, **1947:** 127 [6]
  Speaking engagements, cancellation, **1949:** 58 [23]
  Visit to, **1949:** 231 [12], 236 [19]
Botanic Garden, U.S., **1949:** 8 (p. 76)
Bott, George J., **1950:** 258 [1]
Boulder Dam, **1950:** 3 [9]
Boundary and Water Commission, International, **1951:** 239 [7]
Boundary waters, U.S.-Canada, antipollution measures, **1947:** 171
Boundary Waters Treaty of 1909, U.S.-Canada, **1952–53:** 23, 102
Bourgholtzer, Frank, **1949:** 28 [21], 265; **1950:** 179 [24]; **1952–53:** 98 [40]
Bowers, Claude, **1950:** 137 [8]
Bowl, silver, gift to President, **1951:** 255
Bowles, Chester, **1945:** 17; **1946:** 36, 37 [12, 14], 173 [11], 250 [12]; **1947:** 78 [16, 21], 95 [12, 21, 23]; **1948:** 259 [2, 3], 261 [6, 7, 8, 9]; **1950:** 253 [9]; **1952–53:** 34, 298 [7]
  See also Economic Stabilization, Office of, Director.
Bowling shoes, the President's, **1947:** 62 [14]
Bowman, Dr. Isaiah, letter, **1945:** 223
Bowron, Fletcher, **1948:** 134n.; **1951:** 227 [3]; **1952–53:** 233 [13]
Boxcars, shortage, **1947:** 36 [8]
Boxer Rebellion, **1950:** 233; **1951:** 181
Boy Governors, National Conference of, **1949:** 125
Boy Scouts, **1948:** 120 [3]; **1950:** 121 [5], 185
Boycotts
  See Labor disputes.
Boyd, James (Director, Bureau of Mines), **1950:** 23 [16]
Boyd, Julian P., **1950:** 136n.
Boyd Orr, Lord, **1949:** 263
Boyington, Lt. Col. Gregory, Congressional Medal of Honor award, **1945:** 160n.
Boyle, William M., Jr. (Chairman, Democratic National Committee), **1949:** 166 [4], 190, 192 [20], 220, 226 [7]; **1950:** 12n.; **1951:** 27, 110, 113 [3], 118 [7], 171 [2], 179 [1, 10], 183 [3, 5, 15], 227 [10, 18], 239 [14]; **1952–53:** 149 [17]
  News conference remarks on, **1950:** 11 [12], 169 [6], 258 [9], 273 [15]

Boys Forum of National Government, American Legion, **1949:** 170
Boys Nation, **1946:** 198
Boys Nation, American Legion, **1951:** 168
Boys State, **1948:** 118 [6]
Boys Town, Nebr, campaign remarks, **1948:** 116 [2]
Braddock, Pa., campaign remarks, **1952–53:** 308 [2]
Braden, Spruille, **1946:** 257 [18]; **1947:** 14 [15]
Bradley, Gen. Omar N., **1947:** 184, 191 [19], 226 [1, 3]; **1948:** 162n.; **1949:** 36, 64, 72 [20], 179 [1, 10]; **1950:** 121 [1], 176, 184, 193, 238 [14], 242, 258 [3], 267, 268; **1951:** 93n., 108 [2, 4], 138, 239 [1], 251 [28], 261 [9], 275 [20]; **1952–53:** 128, 130, 131, 320, 353 [5, 8], 377 [18], 378
  See also Veterans Affairs, Administrator of.
  Appointment as Administrator of Veterans Affairs, **1945:** 52 [8]
Brady, Matthew, **1947:** 205 [12]
Brandt, Raymond P., **1946:** 17 [18], 61 [21], 78 [2], 257 [6, 21]; **1949:** 7 [32], 32 [12], 58 [17]; **1950:** 11 [14], 46 [13], 186 [7]; **1951:** 188 [3], 227 [18], 247 [1], 300 [1, 21]; **1952–53:** 17 [34], 35 [1], 75 [5], 98 [30, 34], 107 [6], 115 [16], 123 [14], 127 [6], 377 [7, 16]
Braniff Airways, **1952–53:** 246
Brannan, Charles F., **1947:** 123, 124; **1948:** 15 [2], 84 [13]
  See also Agriculture, Secretary of.
Brannan, Ray, **1952–53:** 342 [3]
Brannan plan, **1951:** 12 [15, 45], 22 [13], 227 [22]; **1952–53:** 17 [30], 285
Branscomb, Harvie, **1950:** 92, 227
Braverman, A. Marvin, **1951:** 186
Brazil, **1945:** 211 [7]; **1946:** 21 [8, 20], 53 [23], 61 [23], 247
  Barbosa, Ruy, **1947:** 189
  Congress, address to, **1947:** 189
  Cultural exchange program, **1949:** 108 [2]
  De Fernandes, Raul, **1949:** 103n.
  De Sousa Costa, Arthur, **1949:** 103n.
  Dom Pedro II, **1947:** 189
  Dutra, Enrico Gaspar, **1947:** 188, 189; **1949:** 93 [10], 95 [5], 102, 103, 105, 107, 108, 148 [20]
  Economic development, **1949:** 108 [1], 148 [20]
  Inter-American Conference, address, **1947:** 188
  Journalists, remarks to, **1949:** 105
  Lend-lease settlement, **1951:** 244
  News conference remarks, **1947:** 127 [10, 11], 141 [3], 145 [20, 22], 155 [1], 174 [4, 7], 177 [15]
  President-elect Getulio Vargas, **1950:** 273 [1], 287 [13]
  Proposed visit by Secretary Acheson, **1952–53:** 166 [14]
  Steel industry, **1951:** 59
  Technical assistance, **1951:** 259
  U.S. Ambassador William D. Pawley, **1947:** 62 [6, 9], 127 [9]

Brazil — *continued*
    Viana, Melo, **1947:** 189n.
    Visit to, **1947:** 188, 189; **1948:** 198 [1]; **1949:** 102, 105, 107
    World Wars I and II, participation in, **1949:** 102, 103n.
Brazilian Press Association, **1949:** 105
Bread
    Conservation, **1946:** 29, 144; **1947:** 191 [7], 196
    Prices, **1946:** 18 (p. 55)
    Rationing in France, **1947:** 195
Breckinridge, Minn., **1950:** 129 [7]
    Campaign remarks, **1952–53:** 266 [1]
Breen, Edward, **1948:** 231 [1, 2, 3]
Bremerhaven, Germany, **1946:** 267
Bremerton, Wash., **1950:** 121 [13]
    Campaign remarks, **1948:** 124 [1]
    Mayor L. Kean, **1948:** 124 [1]
    Navy Yard, **1948:** 124 [2]
Brennan, Earl, **1946:** 84 [3]
Bretton Woods Agreement Act, **1946:** 25, 47, 169n.
Bretton Woods agreements, **1945:** 128, 213; **1946:** 2, 17 [21], 18 (pp. 85, 86), 25, 47, 67
    International Bank for Reconstruction and Development, **1945:** 31 [3], 50, 76 [7], 128, 213
    International Monetary Fund, **1945:** 50, 128, 213
    News conference remarks, **1945:** 4 [4], 52 [1], 64 [2], 76 [3, 7], 118 [8]
Bretton Woods conference (1945), **1949:** 103
Brewer, Harrison, **1950:** 116n.
Brewer Trophy, **1952–53:** 351n.
Brewers, grain conservation by, **1948:** 14
Brewster, Sen. Owen, **1947:** 14 [4]; **1949:** 64; **1950:** 29 [7], 137 [18]; **1952–53:** 26 [10, 11], 149 [20]
Brian, Donald, **1951:** 99
Bricker, Sen. John W., **1952–53:** 304, 312, 315 [3]
Bridgeport, Conn., campaign remarks, **1952–53:** 298 [9]
Bridgeport, Pa., campaign remarks, **1948:** 227 [1], 261 [8]; **1952–53:** 303 [9]
Bridges, Sen. Styles, **1948:** 77 [4], 109, 171, 283 [9]; **1949:** 89 [5]; **1952–53:** 129, 266 [13], 268 [2]
    Bipartisanship in foreign policy, talks on, **1950:** 89
    Letter, **1947:** 197
    News conference remarks on, **1950:** 80 [5], 97 [17]
Brierley, Daniel S., **1945:** 24
Briggs, Ellis O., **1952–53:** 115 [15]
Briggs, Sen. Frank P., **1946:** 61 [21]
Briggs, Lyman J., retirement as Director, National Bureau of Standards, letter, **1945:** 179
Brigham, Utah, **1952–53:** 135
Brigham Young University, **1952–53:** 281
British-American loan conferences, **1947:** 177 [4]

British Columbia
    Alaska highway, **1945:** 64 [3]
    Lead and zinc production, **1950:** 124 [7]
British Commonwealth, **1946:** 76
British Museum, **1951:** 225
Broadcast to the Nation, announcement of, **1952–53:** 359 [1, 4, 5, 7]
Broadcasters, National Association of, **1952–53:** 43n.
Broadcasting industry
    Promotion of highway safety program, **1948:** 280
    Security responsibilities, **1950:** 207
Broadcasts.
    See Messages to the American people.
Broadcasts, Communist, proposed identification requirement, **1950:** 254
Brockton, Mass., campaign remarks, **1948:** 261 [2]; **1952–53:** 298 [1]
Broken Bow, Nebr., **1950:** 110 [9]
Bronk, Detlev W., **1951:** 89
Bronx, N.Y., campaign remarks, **1948:** 264 [3]
Brookings Institution, **1948:** 15 [6]
Brooklyn, N.Y., campaign address, **1948:** 266
Brooklyn-Battery Tunnel, **1947:** 174 [9]; **1949:** 8 (p. 75)
Brooks, Sen. C. Wayland, **1948:** 254, 274 [19]
Brotherhood of Locomotive Engineers, **1946:** 120, 121, 124, 125; **1948:** 95, 159n.; **1952–53:** 136ftn. (p. 359)
Brotherhood of Locomotive Firemen and Enginemen, **1948:** 95, 159n.; **1951:** 49 [6]; **1952–53:** 136ftn. (p. 359)
Brotherhood of Railway Trainmen, **1946:** 120, 121, 124, 125; **1948:** 11ftn. (p. 105); **1950:** 209ftn. (p. 580), 221; **1952–53:** 136ftn. (p. 359)
Brotherhood Week, 1950, **1949:** 224, 254
Broughton, Mel, **1948:** 246
Browdy, Benjamin, **1952–53:** 35 [2]
Brown, Cecil, **1947:** 90n.
Brown, Repr. Clarence J., **1946:** 199 [17]; **1949:** 94n.
Brown, Courtney C., **1946:** 255n.
Brown, Dudley M., **1948:** 125
Brown, Francis, **1946:** 166n.
Brown, Fred, **1952–53:** 295 [2]
Brown, George Rufus, **1951:** 19n.
Brown, Harrison S., **1948:** 191n.
Brown, Harvey W., **1947:** 236 [3], 237
Brown, John Nicholas, **1946:** 242 [1]; **1947:** 31 [19]
Brown, Matilda, **1945:** 8 [2]
Brown, Perry, **1949:** 195n.
Brown, Vice Adm. Wilson, **1945:** 175ftn. (p. 416); **1952–53:** 335
Browne, Sir Thomas, **1945:** 88
Brownell, Herbert, **1948:** 163 [4]
Browner, Vincent, **1948:** 194 [6]
Browning, Charles P., **1947:** 48n.

Browing, Gov. Gordon, **1951:** 138; **1952–53:** 221 [1]
Brownout, wartime, **1945:** 4 [21]
Bruce, David K. E., **1949:** 84 [1]
Bruce, Howard, **1945:** 125n.; **1946:** 84 [2]
  Distinguished Service Medal, citation, **1945:** 126
Bruce, James, **1949:** 28 [8], 32 [9], 40 [4], 205 [12, 14], 236 [17]
Brucker, Herbert, **1952–53:** 98 [12]
Brunner, George E., **1948:** 225n.
Brunsdale, Gov. C. Norman, **1952–53:** 97
Brussels, NATO foreign ministers meeting, **1950:** 305, 309 [1], 311
Brussels, Treaty of, **1949:** 162
Brussels agreement on economic cooperation, **1948:** 52, 53
Bryan, Charles W., **1950:** 111
Bryan, William Jennings, **1951:** 166n.; **1952–53:** 63, 127 [18], 274 [1], 315 [1], 317 [1]
Bryans, Henry B., **1949:** 194n.
Buchanan, Repr. Frank, **1949:** 202n.; **1952–53:** 308n.
Buchanan, James, **1948:** 139 [3]
Buchanan, Robert Earle, **1947:** 122
Buchanan, Repr. Vera, **1952–53:** 308 [2]
Buchenwald concentration camp, **1948:** 283 [3]
Buckley, Repr. Charles A., **1951:** 95 [7]; **1952–53:** 102
Buckley, Oliver E., **1951:** 89
Budenz, Louis, **1948:** 170ftn. (p. 432); **1951:** 227 [7]; **1952–53:** 362n.
Budget, **1945:** 129 [11]; **1946:** 67; **1948:** 4 [1], 101, 121, 243 [1, 4, 7]; **1949:** 2, 5, 119, 151, 154; **1950:** 2, 6, 39, 54, 110 [1], 121 [4, 6], 122, 127 [1], 129 [1, 7], 200, 234; **1952–53:** 33, 117
  Balancing, prospects of, **1951:** 12 [17, 24], 28; **1952–53:** 15, 366
  Cash budget, **1952–53:** 215
  Cash surplus, **1952–53:** 15
  Defense Department, military functions, **1951:** 92, 93
  News conference remarks, **1949:** 11 [13], 58 [12], 66 [12], 72 [2, 16], 78 [18], 95 [11], 179 [23], 200 [20], 236 [1], 260 [2, 22], 267 [3, 9], 269 [16]; **1950:** 8 [27, 39, 40], 44 [11], 46 [13], 80 [3], 105 [13], 137 [7]
  1938, **1947:** 6 [1]
  1939, **1947:** 4 (p. 17)
  1944, **1946:** 18 (p. 69); **1947:** 4 (p. 17)
  1945, **1947:** 68; **1948:** 86
  1946, **1945:** 22 [16, 19]; **1946:** 78 [1], 79; **1947:** 4 (pp. 17, 19), 180 [1]; **1949:** 86, 160
  1947, **1946:** 187, 194; **1947:** 6 [14, 15, 17], 7 (pp. 80, 95), 46 [2], 68, 96
    Annual message, **1946:** 18
    Tables, **1946:** 18 (pp. 67, 68, 70, 72)
    Government corporations, **1946:** 94

Budget — *continued*
  1947 — *continued*
    News conference remarks, **1946:** 15 [1, 11], 17, 41 [16], 72 [5, 7], 186 [1], 192, 199 [1, 11, 17], 226 [2], 229 [26], 237 [2]
    Statements, **1946:** 79, 193; **1947:** 75
    Surplus, **1947:** 75, 180 [1, 7], 181 (p. 395), 236 [9]
  1948, **1946:** 187, 192 [5], 257 [15], 266 [21]; **1947:** 2 (pp. 3, 7), 4 (p. 26), 11, 31 [4], 36 [14], 38, 46 [2], 67 [7], 68, 70 [3, 16], 96, 147, 174 [2], 177 [18]; **1948:** 4 [1, 9], 5 (pp. 19, 20, 22, 23), 75, 175
    Message to Congress, **1947:** 7
    News conferences on, **1947:** 6, 180
    Statement, **1947:** 181
    Surplus, **1947:** 70 [5], 180 [1, 4, 5, 11, 13]
  1949, **1947:** 177 [18], 180 [3, 19], 181 (p. 396), 243 [7, 10, 19]; **1948:** 6, 7, 8 (p. 98), 9 [4, 10], 15 [6], 21 [6, 11, 12], 60, 63, 79, 80, 106, 108, 228 [8], 243 [1], 278 [26], 283 [7, 13], 285 [3, 18], 288 [8]; **1949:** 7 [50], 58 [12], 78n., 175
    Message to Congress, **1948:** 5
    Midyear review, **1948:** 175
    News conference on, **1948:** 4
  1950, **1948:** 175, 243 [4]; **1949:** 11 [13], 66 [12], 72 [2, 16], 78 [18], 95 [11], 151, 244, 260 [22]
    Message to Congress, **1949:** 8
    News conference on, **1949:** 7
  1951, **1949:** 236 [1], 260 [22], 267 [9], 269 [16]; **1950:** 18, 3 [20]; **1952–53:** 367 (p. 1130), 368
    CED report on, **1950:** 11 [10]
    Message to Congress, **1950:** 9
    News conference on, **1950:** 8
  1952, **1950:** 105 [13], 318 [9]; **1951:** 11, 28, 45, 91–93, 111, 167, 185; **1952–53:** 97, 367 (p. 1130), 368
    Anticipated and cash budgets, **1951:** 12 [3]
    Message to Congress, **1951:** 13
    News conference on, **1951:** 12
    Nondefense spending, curtailment, **1951:** 12 [14, 16, 22]
    Obligational authority, advance, **1951:** 12 [3]
    Reduction by Congress, question of, **1951:** 33 [6]
  1953, **1951:** 12 [30]; **1952–53:** 21 [23], 85, 109, 128, 135
    Carryover figure, **1952–53:** 17 [18]
    Cash budget, consolidated, **1952–53:** 231
    Difficulty of drafting, **1952–53:** 17 [19]
    Increase, **1952–53:** 17 [2], 18 (p. 63)
    National security emphasis, **1952–53:** 17 [2]
    News conference remarks, **1952–53:** 17, 31 [9], 334 [7, 17]
    Obligational authority, **1952–53:** 18 (pp. 65, 66), 231

Budget — *continued*
1953 — *continued*
Receipts, miscellaneous, **1952–53:** 18 (pp. 67, 68)
Reduction by Congress, question of, **1952–53:** 17 [23]
Review statement, **1952–53:** 231
Water resources development, allocations, **1952–53:** 3
1954, **1952–53:** 275, 388
Long term planning, need for, **1952–53:** 367 (p. 1164)
Messages to Congress
Fiscal 1953, **1952–53:** 18
Fiscal 1954, **1952–53:** 367
Obligational authority, **1952–53:** 367 (pp. 1129, 1130)
Receipts, estimates, **1952–53:** 367 (p. 1133)
Public debt, fluctuations during President's term, **1952–53:** 368
Reduction, question of, **1952–53:** 17 [2], 218
Summary booklet, **1951:** 12 [1], 22 [5]
Surplus, **1951:** 118 [1], 221, 227 [19]; **1952–53:** 215, 272
Study by citizens, appeal for, **1951:** 221, 224 [12]
Budget, Bureau of the, **1945:** 70, 107 [1], 128, 194, 207, 226; **1946:** 18 (p. 77), 195, 238, 249, 262 [4]; **1947:** 4 (p. 34), 95 [9], 96, 180 [10], 201n.; **1948:** 4 [1, 9], 5 (p. 58), 21 [12]; **1949:** 7 [15], 72 [7, 19], 112 [7], 145, 167, 236 [1]; **1950:** 9 (p. 51), 203 [23]; **1951:** 108 [3], 119, 152, 161; **1952–53:** 18 (pp. 67–68, 114), 86, 98 [9], 147, 338, 370
Government corporations, study, **1946:** 94
Joint accounting program for executive agencies, **1951:** 221
Jones, J. Weldon, **1945:** 24
Manpower utilization control, **1951:** 93
News conference remarks, **1946:** 17 [28], 177 [7], 192 [9], 226 [18]
Panama Canal and Railroad Co., recommendations, **1950:** 28
Budget, Bureau of the, Acting Director (Paul H. Appleby), **1946:** 130, 145
Budget, Bureau of the, Director, vacancy in office, **1946:** 143 [14]
Budget, Bureau of the, Director (Frederick J. Lawton), **1950:** 9 (p. 51), 36, 192, 196, 288, 303; **1951:** 12, 55, 93, 119, 131, 177; **1952–53:** 17, 18 (p. 89), 38, 67, 79, 325, 388
Agency programs review, **1950:** 196
Letters, **1951:** 26, 119
Water resources development programs, establishment of standards, **1952–53:** 367 (p. 1147)
Budget, Bureau of the, Director (Frank Pace, Jr.), **1948:** 284; **1949:** 127, 145n., 167; **1950:** 8n.

Budget, Bureau of, Director (Pace) — *continued*
Appointment as Secretary of the Army, **1950:** 80 [8]
Memorandum, **1949:** 156
News conference remarks on, **1949:** 32 [6], 265
Budget, Bureau of the, Director (Harold D. Smith), **1945:** 50, 124, 134, 146, 185n., 223; **1946:** 10, 17
Letters, **1946:** 139, 140
News conference remarks on, **1946:** 21 [2], 66 [10]
Resignation, **1946:** 140
Budget, Bureau of the, Director (James E. Webb), **1946:** 192n., 238; **1947:** 6, 11n., 89, 174 [2], 177 [18], 180, 221 [3]; **1948:** 4, 60, 75, 98, 106; **1949:** 7n.
See also Webb, James E.
Budget and Accounting Act, **1946:** 17 [17]
Budget and Accounting Procedures Act of 1950, **1952–53:** 18 (p. 116)
Approval, **1950:** 244
Budget in Brief, pamphlet, **1951:** 221, 224 [12]; **1952–53:** 26 [2], 368
Buenos Aires Conference (1936), **1947:** 51
Buffalo, N.Y., campaign address, **1948:** 229; **1952–53:** 288
Buford-Trenton irrigation project, N. Dak., **1950:** 129 [3]
Building codes, **1947:** 86; **1948:** 5 (p. 38), 8 (p. 84), 37
Building and Construction Trades Department (AFL), **1947:** 19 [1]
Building materials, **1946:** 18 (p. 49), 75 [30], 178; **1947:** 2 (p. 7), 7 (pp. 74, 75); **1949:** 5, 45 [3], 179 [9]
Conservation for defense needs, **1950:** 192
Controls, **1945:** 208 [5], 211 [1]; **1947:** 58, 131
Development and use of improved materials, **1948:** 5 (p. 38)
Export controls, **1946:** 263
Exports, **1947:** 58
Premium payments, **1946:** 48, 94
Prices, **1946:** 67, 152, 153, 249; **1947:** 4 (pp. 25, 29), 44, 76, 214; **1948:** 8 (p. 64); **1950:** 202
Production, **1945:** 212; **1946:** 258, 263; **1947:** 18, 60; **1948:** 5 (p. 40), 37
Shortage, **1947:** 4 (p. 26); **1948:** 8 (pp. 82, 83)
Supply, **1948:** 8 (p. 82)
Building and space management, reorganization plans, **1950:** 53, 73
Building trades, apprenticeship program, **1946:** 263
Buildings, Federal, **1945:** 128
Bukowski, Peter I., **1952–53:** 2 [4], 31 [6]
Bulgaria, **1946:** 6 [2], 18 (pp. 41, 42)
Agreements on, **1945:** 91, 97
Aid to Greek Communists, **1948:** 129
Armed forces, **1951:** 174
Communism in, **1951:** 253
Peace treaty with, **1947:** 2 (p. 9), 114

Bulgaria — *continued*
  Soviet domination, **1948:** 53, 86
  Violation of Greek border, **1947:** 56
  Yalta agreement on, **1947:** 56
Bull Moose Party, **1952–53:** 280 [6]
Bull Shoals Dam, Ark., **1952–53:** 193, 194, 195 [1]
Bullis, Harry A., **1947:** 191 [3]
Bullitt, Stimpson, **1952–53:** 275
Bullitt, William C., **1947:** 88 [8]
Bulwinkle, Alfred L., **1948:** 251
Bulwinkle antitrust bill, **1948:** 110 [3], 251; **1949:** 149
Bulwinkle bill, **1946:** 72 [21], 84 [6], 86 [13]
Bulwinkle bill re railroads, **1945:** 221 [9]
Bunch, John Forrest, **1947:** 209 [8]
Bunche, Ralph J., **1949:** 32 [10], 40 [2], 58 [13, 30], 256; **1951:** 171 [13]; **1952–53:** 290n.
Bunker, Arthur H., **1951:** 19n.
Bunker Hill, **1946:** 171n.
Bunyan, Paul, legend, **1952–53:** 270 [10]
Burbank, Calif., campaign remarks, **1948:** 204 [7]
Burdick, Repr. Usher L., **1952–53:** 266 [11]
Bureau of Reclamation, **1948:** 175
Bureaucrat, definition of, **1950:** 178
Burgess, Paul S., **1950:** 1n., 306n.
Burgess, W. Randolph, **1947:** 122
Burke, Capt. Arleigh A., **1949:** 267 [8]
Burke, 1st Lt. Lloyd, Congressional Medal of Honor, **1952–53:** 90
Burke, Thomas A., **1949:** 240 [5]; **1952–53:** 287n.
Burke, Thomas H., **1948:** 258; **1952–53:** 319 [1]
Burke, Vincent, **1948:** 9 [1, 5, 7]; **1949:** 167n.
Burlington, Iowa, **1950:** 110 [2]
  Mayor Thomas J. Smith, **1950:** 110 [2]
Burma, **1946:** 30 [2]; **1952–53:** 55
  Communism in, **1951:** 96, 114
  Economic assistance, **1951:** 13 (p. 74)
  Grain, relief supplies for India, **1951:** 34
  Independence, **1950:** 119
Burma Road, **1946:** 113
Burnett, Robert A., **1951:** 40n.
Burnham, D. H., **1949:** 249
Burns, Frances, **1945:** 118n.
Burns, WAVE Seaman Shirley, **1951:** 186
Burns, William H., **1952–53:** 292 [9]
Burpo, Luther, **1948:** 218n.
Burrowes, Arthur V., **1952–53:** 98 [13]
Burt, Capt. J. M., Congressional Medal of Honor presentation, **1945:** 167n.
Burton, Frank W., **1945:** 210
Burton, Harold H., **1948:** 137ftn. (p. 363)
  Appointment to U.S. Supreme Court, **1945:** 137 [6]
  Federal labor relations bill, **1945:** 172 [1]
  News conference remarks on, **1945:** 137 [6], 172 [1]
Bush, Robert E., Congressional Medal of Honor award, **1945:** 160n.

Bush, Vannevar, **1947:** 109, 191 [1], 192; **1950:** 120
  See also Scientific Research and Development, Office of, Director.
Business, Census of, **1949:** 8 (p. 88)
Business, U.S., **1946:** 18 (pp. 38, 40, 48–51, 54, 56, 57, 72, 74, 86), 192 [7], 218; **1947:** 2 (p. 3), 4 (pp. 16, 32), 7 (pp. 56, 59, 86, 94), 116, 131, 147, 152, 212, 214, 219, 224, 225, 231; **1948:** 2, 4 [6], 5 (p. 23), 8 (pp. 78, 81, 90), 32, 37, 167, 175, 223; **1949:** 5; **1951:** 13 (p. 65); **1952–53:** 266 [3]
  See also Small business.
  Advertising circulars, postal rates, **1952–53:** 18 (p. 85)
  Advertising matter, postal rates, **1951:** 45, 226
  Allocations and priority agreements, **1947:** 236 [8]; **1948:** 1
  Amortization, tax treatment, **1951:** 11, 167
  Antitrust laws, **1950:** 2, 3 [16], 6, 9 (p. 97), 18, 118, 166, 319; **1951:** 254; **1952–53:** 215
  Assistance to, **1950:** 9 (pp. 96–97), 114; **1951:** 39, 82, 91, 106, 167; **1952–53:** 18 (pp. 77–79, 80–81), 367 (pp. 1131, 1142)
    Loans and guarantees, **1950:** 6, 9 (p. 96), 157, 202; **1951:** 11, 13 (pp. 76, 78), 39, 205, 284
  Bank borrowing, volume of, **1952–53:** 215
  Bank credit, **1951:** 91
  Campaign remarks, **1948:** 121, 183 [6, 7], 184, 195
  Census, **1948:** 5 (pp. 52, 53); **1952–53:** 367 (p. 1156)
    Report on, **1952–53:** 363n.
  Commercial premises, rent control, **1951:** 91
  Communication with businessmen abroad, **1950:** 92
  Competition, stimulus of, **1950:** 106
  Corporate structure, FTC study, **1948:** 220
  Depletion exemptions and depreciation allowances, **1950:** 18, 257
  Development of atomic energy, question of, **1948:** 239
  Economic outlook of, **1952–53:** 215
  Economic reports, **1950:** 6, 202
  Enterprise system, **1952–53:** 15, 215, 218, 376
  Ethical standards, **1950:** 157
  Executives in politics, **1948:** 86
  Fair trade legislation, approval, **1952–53:** 204
  Foreign assistance, study of effect on domestic economy, **1947:** 122
  Government policy toward, **1949:** 2
  Growth, **1952–53:** 366, 376
  Income and profits, **1950:** 122, 134, 157, 279; **1952–53:** 5, 33
  Inventories, **1949:** 5, 151; **1952–53:** 15, 215
  Investments, **1948:** 4, 8 (pp. 63, 79, 91), 18
    See also main heading Investments.
  Management, relations with labor and Government, **1951:** 11, 98, 212, 279; **1952–53:** 15, 215 367 (p. 1150)

Business, U.S. — *continued*
  Marshall plan, advisory participation, **1948:** 15 [6]
  Monopolies in, **1948:** 220
  News conference remarks on, **1947:** 70 [2, 11, 13, 15], 78 [22], 196; **1949:** 7 [40], 32 [7], 40 [6], 171 [11]; **1950:** 3 [16], 217 [20]
  Political influence, **1948:** 256
  Pricing practices, **1950:** 166, 243
  Price-wage policy, **1947:** 224
  Profits, **1948:** 228 [4], 262
    See also Profits, corporate.
  Recovery from 1949 recession, **1951:** 11
  Regional conference on, **1949:** 171 [11]
  Regulation, **1950:** 9 (p. 97)
  Relations with administration, **1948:** 278 [18]
  Relationship to Government, **1950:** 157
  Republican campaign contributions, **1948:** 251
  Republican sympathies, **1952–53:** 218
  Responsibilities to national economy and defense effort, **1950:** 84, 106, 202
  Safety programs, **1950:** 155
  Sales volume, wholesale and retail, **1952–53:** 215
  Security issues, **1952–53:** 15, 215
  Tax treatment, **1950:** 18, 257
  Trade and business press, news conference with editors, **1947:** 196
  Transportation facilities, allocation by, **1947:** 242; **1948:** 8 (p. 74)
  Unincorporated, income, **1952–53:** 15
  Unincorporated, profits, **1951:** 167
Business Magazine Editors, Society of, **1951:** 18; **1952–53:** 339n.
Business Paper Editors, National Conference of, **1946:** 218; **1949:** 80
Business and Professional Women, International Federation of, **1952–53:** 188
Business and trade paper editors, news conference with, **1947:** 196
Business Week magazine, **1952–53:** 308 [1], 317 [1]
Businessmen's Dinner Forum, A. and H. Kroeger Organization, **1949:** 240ftn. (p. 533)
Butler, Sen. Hugh, **1949:** 144 [7]; **1952–53:** 35 [15]
Butler, Repr. John C., Defense Production Act amendment, **1951:** 199; **1952–53:** 33
Butler, John Marshall, **1951:** 49ftn. (p. 176); **1952–53:** 69n.
Butte, Mont., **1950:** 128
  Campaign address, **1948:** 121
  Mayor Thomas R. Morgan, **1950:** 128
  Mayor Barry O'Leary, **1948:** 121
Butter
  Prices, **1946:** 18 (p. 55); **1947:** 221 [8], 242
  Substitutes, **1947:** 35
Butterworth, W. Walton, **1949:** 112 [1], 260ftn. (p. 571)
Butyl, synthetic rubber, **1950:** 13; **1952–53:** 12
Buy America Act, **1946:** 174

Buyers' strikes, comment on, **1947:** 70 [10]
Byrd, Sen. Harry Flood, **1949:** 95 [2]; **1950:** 46ftn. (p. 181); **1951:** 85 [9], 188 [4], 247 [2]
  News conference remarks on, **1950:** 23 [6], 29 [19], 44 [11], 46 [13], 169 [4], 295 [13], 318 [9]
Byrne, James A., **1952–53:** 304
Byrne, Repr. William T., **1948:** 228 [1]
Byrnes, James F., **1947:** 74; **1948:** 278 [20, 21]; **1949:** 144 [10]; **1950:** 16 [21], 46 [7], 121 [1], 206 [13]; **1951:** 16 [2], 247 [2], 251 [10]; **1952–53:** 64 [18], 221 [6], 303 [6], 304, 315 [6], 316, 378
  See also State, Secretary of.
  Article in Colliers magazine, **1952–53:** 98 [30]
  News conference remarks on, **1945:** 4 [13, 21], 8 [1], 60 [6], 67 [2]; **1947:** 46 [9], 95 [5], 209 [10]
  Recommendation re administration of surplus property disposal, **1945:** 84
  Resignation, letter, **1947:** 3
  Speaking Frankly, **1947:** 209 [10]
  Support of Gov. Stevenson, **1952–53:** 221 [6]

CAA.
  See Civil Aeronautics Administration.
CAB.
  See Civil Aeronautics Board.
Cabinet, the President's, **1945:** 100n., 128, 218; **1946:** 95 [21], 250 [6]; **1951:** 41
  Bipartisan membership, **1951:** 224 [10]
  Briefing of Presidential candidates, **1952–53:** 227
  Campaign remarks on, **1952–53:** 292 [11]
  Conferences with, **1949:** 52 [12], 269 [22]
  Designations by President-elect, **1952–53:** 342 [11]
  Farewell lunch with, the President's plans for, **1952–53:** 377 [15]
  Lunches with members, **1948:** 285 [4]
  Memorandum, **1949:** 156
  News conference remarks, **1945:** 4 [20], 64 [6]; **1949:** 11 [18], 45 [22, 24], 52 [12], 269 [22]
  Resignations or retirements, question of, **1948:** 274 [5, 6, 11], 278 [3, 11, 13, 15]; **1951:** 300 [13, 19]
  Salary increases for members, question of, **1948:** 285 [10]
  Succession to Presidency, **1945:** 63
Cabinet Committee on Palestine and Related Problems, **1946:** 132, 136 [14], 186 ftn. (p. 367), 227
Cabinet Committee on World Food Programs, **1947:** 46 [1], 47, 139, 191 [3, 5, 8]; **1948:** 1
Cabinet Gorge, Idaho, **1950:** 124 [7]
Cabinet officers, appearance before Congress, **1950:** 152 [2]

Cabot, **1946:** 171n.
Caccia, Harold, **1950:** 218
Cadet Nurse Corps, United States, **1945:** 130n.
Cadillac, Antoine de la Mothe, **1951:** 174
Caeiro da Matta, José, **1949:** 68n.
Caffery, Jefferson, **1947:** 88 [8], 95 [15]; **1949:** 66 [15], 84 [1]
Caffrey, James J., **1948:** 26 [1]
Cain, Sen. Harry P., **1949:** 45 [5, 10]; **1952–53:** 49 [11], 129, 228 [8]
Cairo, **1946:** 85, 87n.; **1947:** 36 [16]; **1950:** 186 [13]
Cairo Declaration (1943), **1945:** 143, 177, 216; **1949:** 117; **1950:** 3 [1], 301
Calder, Curtis E., **1949:** 89 [3, 10], 113 [8], 118 [12]
Caldwell, Horace K., **1946:** 14
Caldwell, Millard, **1947:** 231n.; **1950:** 303; **1951:** 10, 96; **1952–53:** 9, 21 [27], 44 [8]
Calf, gift to President, **1946:** 84 [19]
Calhoun, David R., **1945:** 137n.
Calhoun, Galloway, **1951:** 90 [2]
Calhoun, John C., **1948:** 245; **1951:** 8
California, **1947:** 30; **1950:** 4, 121 [8]; **1951:** 120
   Campaign remarks, **1948:** 128 [1–3], 130 [1–3], 133 [1–3], 134, 202 [3–6], 203, 204 [2–7], 205, 206 [1–3]; **1952–53:** 277 [2–6], 278, 279
   Candidates for public office, **1948:** 202 [4], 203, 204 [1, 2], 206 [1–3]; **1949:** 58 [6, 9], 260 [18, 20]; **1950:** 52 [3], 105 [5], 179 [8]; **1952–53:** 156 [15]
   Canneries, labor disputes, **1946:** 61 [4], 66 [3], 70 [7]
   Central Valley, **1950:** 3 [9, 22], 125, 129 [1]
   Central Valley Authority, proposed, **1947:** 31 [10]
   Central Valley project, **1948:** 6, 201, 203, 204 [4]
   Central Valley reclamation, **1949:** 8 (p. 83), 41
   Democratic National Convention, delegates to, **1952–53:** 136 [13]
   Democratic Party, **1947:** 205 [6]
   Dispute with Arizona over Colorado River water rights, **1950:** 34 [17]
   Downey, Sen. Sheridan, **1945:** 147 [15, 18]
   Economic progress, **1952–53:** 277 [4]
   Folsom Dam project, **1949:** 41
      Construction, **1948:** 6
   Irrigation projects, **1949:** 32 [6]
   Nazi war criminal, discovery in, **1951:** 227 [12]
   News conference remarks, **1950:** 3 [9, 22], 34 [17], 52 [3], 105 [5], 179 [8], 278 [12]
   Offshore lands, **1952–53:** 146, 377 [11]
   Power projects, **1952–53:** 277 [3, 4]
   Primary elections, **1951:** 298 [3]
   River development, **1945:** 128, 155
   San Francisco.
      See main heading, San Francisco, Calif.
   Visit to, proposed, **1948:** 84 [5], 88 [9]
   Warren, Gov. Earl, **1947:** 31 [10]; **1948:** 150 [6],

California — *continued*
   Warren, Gov. Earl — *continued*
      170 [13], 231 [1], 242 [2], 261 [7], 267 [2]; **1951:** 216, 295 [6]; **1952–53:** 242 [4], 277 [3, 6], 278, 279
   Water resources development, **1945:** 165; **1946:** 18 (p. 61), 97
California, University of, **1945:** 31 [7]; **1948:** 84 [5], 128 [4], 129; **1951:** 130; **1952–53:** 261, 262
Callaghan, Alfred, **1948:** 210 [1]
Callaghan, Adm. Dan, **1948:** 53
Calmer, Ned, **1947:** 90n.
Cambodia, **1952–53:** 18 (p. 76)
Camden, N.J.
   Brunner, Mayor George E.,**1948:** 225n.
   Campaign remarks, **1948:** 225 [3]; **1952–53:** 303 [7]
Cameras, excise tax on, **1950:** 23 [3]
Camp Donovan, **1949:** 36
Campaign of Truth, **1950:** 227
   Appropriation, **1951:** 197
   U.S. information programs abroad, **1952–53:** 18 (p. 77)
Campbell, Alex M., **1948:** 174 [13]; **1950:** 16 [11], 169 [4]
Campbell, James A., **1952–53:** 390
Campbell, Thomas D., **1947:** 218 [6]
Camptown Races, Stephen Foster, **1950:** 139
Canada, **1947:** 18, 51; **1948:** 198 [1]; **1949:** 159; **1952–53:** 44 [2]
   Aid to Europe, **1947:** 238
   Alaska highway, **1945:** 64 [3]
   Alexander, Viscount, **1947:** 111
   Ambassador H. H. Wrong, **1952–53:** 23n.
   Assistance, **1949:** 162
   Atomic bomb, **1945:** 97
      Cooperation in development, **1948:** 239
      Proposed discussion re, **1945:** 178
   Atomic energy, **1945:** 156, 164 [1], 181 [3]
      Cooperation with U.S., **1949:** 166 [1], 179 [18]
      Joint declaration with Prime Ministers of Canada and U.K., **1945:** 193 [7, 8, 10]
   Bay of Fundy tidal power project, joint development with U.S. **1951:** 16 [13], 239 [9]
   Boundary waters, joint development agreement, **1949:** 77, 80; **1951:** 11, 13 (p. 63)
   British Columbia, lead and zinc production, **1950:** 124 [7]
   Citizens, admission to U.S. service academies, **1948:** 112
   Combined Food Board, **1946:** 108, 119 [16], 149
   Community Chest campaign, **1950:** 262
   Defense, **1948:** 12; **1951:** 13 (p. 63)
   Economic talks with U.S. and U.K., **1949:** 195
   Economy, **1948:** 12
   Espionage activities in, **1946:** 41 [24, 26]
   Exchange teachers, **1951:** 194; **1952–53:** 234
   Floods, **1950:** 129 [7]

Canada — *continued*
  Food shipments abroad, **1946:** 23, 30 [2]
  Foreign trade, **1947:** 226 [5], 235
  Grain, relief supplies for India, **1951:** 34
  Great Lakes disarmament **1947:** (1817), 111
  Highway links with Alaska, **1948:** 105
  Inter-American military cooperation, **1946:** 102
  International Joint Commission, **1947:** 171;
      1948: 93 [10, 11]; **1950:** 34 [10]
  Iron ore deposits, **1950:** 9 (p. 94); **1951:** 11, 13 (p.
      83)
  Iron ore reserves, **1952–53:** 18 (p. 88)
  King, W. L. Mackenzie, **1945:** 107ftn. (p. 234),
      157 [17]; **1946:** 18 (p. 42), 41 [26], 108,
      149, 242 [6]; **1947:** 111, 112; **1948:** 11 [8],
      43, 239, 273; **1949:** 237
    Death of, **1950:** 198
    Joint declaration, **1945:** 191
    Joint statement, **1945:** 209
  Korean war, participation, **1950:** 193, 194, 232,
      296; **1951:** 170
  Military collaboration with, **1947:** 101, 111;
      1948: 9 [22], 239; **1949:** 162, 166 [1]
  Natural gas, exchange with U.S., **1952–53:** 377
      [25]
  Natural resources in northeast, joint develop-
      ment with U.S., **1950:** 265
  News conference remarks, **1945:** 64 [3], 157, [17],
      164 [1], 181 [3], 193 [7, 8, 10]; **1946:** 21 [8],
      30 [2], 41 [24, 26], 43 [12], 86 [4], 136 [9];
      1947: 19 [11], 46 [26], 67 [16]; **1949:** 166
      [1], 179 [18], 205 [8], 211 [8]; **1950:** 3[12],
      34 [10], 46 [2], 97 [2], 105 [3]
  Niagara power facilities, treaty concerning,
      1952–53: 18 (p. 88)
  Niagara River, joint development with U.S.,
      1950: 33, 46 [2], 99, 105 [3]
  Ottawa, **1945:** 209n.
  Parliament, address to, **1947:** 111
  Pearson, Lester B., **1948:** 9 [22]; **1949:** 68;
      1952–53: 98 [32], 102
  Permanent Joint Board on Defense, **1946:** 21 [8];
      1947: 111; **1948:** 43
  Power projects development, **1948:** 93 [10]; **1949:**
      80
  Quebec, **1945:** 177, 181 [3]
  Refugees, immigration to, **1952–53:** 65
  St. Laurent, Louis, **1948:** 273; **1949:** 22 [2]; **1951:**
      239 [17], 240; **1952–53:** 23, 175 [7]
  St. Lawrence Bridge, U.S. Commission, veto,
      1947: 172
  St. Lawrence River development, **1945:** 148, 155
  St. Lawrence Seaway, **1951:** 13 (p. 83), 240
    Question of joint development with U.S.,
        1952–53: 17 [27], 18 (p. 88), 23, 98 [32],
        102, 175 [7], 189, 367 (p. 1147)
  St. Lawrence Seaway project.
    See main heading, St. Lawrence Seaway
        project.

Canada — *continued*
  U.S. Ambassador Ray Atherton, **1947:** 111
  U.S. Ambassador Stanley Woodward, **1950:** 97
      [2], 138
  U.S. relations with, **1949:** 80; **1951:** 203n., 267;
      1952–53: 377 [25]
  U.S.-U.K.-Canada
    Combined boards, **1945:** 107ftn. (p. 234), 198,
        209
    Trade agreement, **1949:** 217
  Visit to, **1947:** 111, 112
  Visit by Sen. Taft, **1952–53:** 317 [3]
Canaday, Ward, **1949:** 148 [10]
Canal Zone, applicability of international conven-
    tion on wages and hours, **1951:** 97
Canal Zone Biological Area, **1946:** 118
Canberra, Australia, **1951:** 84
Cancer, **1952–53:** 249, 268 [8], 333
  Prevention, **1951:** 135
  Research on prevention, **1945:** 192; **1947:** 98
Candidacy for second term, **1945:** 181 [12]
Candidates for public office, **1946:** 84 [18, 20], 221;
      1949: 192 [2–4, 6], 205 [4, 18]; **1950:** 255;
      1951: 261 [2]
  Arizona, **1948:** 207
  California, **1948:** 202 [4], 203, 204 [1, 2], 206
      [1–3]; **1949:** 260 [18, 20]; **1950:** 52 [3], 105
      [5], 179 [8]; **1952–53:** 136 [13], 156 [15]
  Colorado, **1948:** 198 [4–7], 200 [1]; **1952–53:** 280
      [4–6], 282,[1–4, 7, 8]
  Connecticut, **1948:** 259 [2], 261 [6–9]; **1952–53:**
      31 [12], 292, 293, 298 [6–11]
  Delaware, **1948:** 225 [1]; **1952–53:** 303 [1]
  Democratic nominees, President's influence on
      choice of, **1952–53:** 197 [9]
  Idaho, **1952–53:** 270 [9, 10]
  Illinois, **1948:** 194 [1], 218 [1, 6–8], 219, 233 [4–6],
      234, 256, 267 [3]; **1950:** 16 [13]; **1951:** 171
      [8]; **1952–53:** 315 [6], 316, 321 [3–7]
  Indiana, **1948:** 218 [10], 233 [1–3], 210, 254, 255,
      257 [1, 2], 267 [2]; **1950:** 16 [11]; **1952–53:**
      107 [5], 286 [1–3], 311 [3], 312, 321 [2]
  Iowa, **1948:** 194 [1–4, 6, 9–11]; **1952–53:** 284 [1,
      2], 285, 315 [1–4]
  Kansas, **1948:** 197; **1950:** 206 [3]
  Kentucky, **1948:** 218 [11–14], 222 [1–8]
  Massachusetts, **1948:** 259 [1, 4, 5], 261 [1];
      1952–53: 292 [9–12], 295 [7–9], 296, 298
      [1–3]
  Michigan, **1948:** 181 [6]; **1952–53:** 317 [1–7]
  Minnesota, **1948:** 235 [5], 236, 237 [1–4]; **1952–
      53:** 266 [1], 313, 314
  Missouri, **1948:** 194 [12, 13], 216 [13–15]; **1949:**
      240 [9, 11]; **1950:** 3 [8, 13], 16 [9, 11], 23
      [5], 160 [2], 203 [2], 206 [2], 279; **1952–53:**
      21 [8], 26 [18], 35 [6], 75 [5], 98 [39], 149
      [3], 156 [1], 197 [12], 284 [4, 5], 322
  Montana, **1952–53:** 266 [13], 268 [1–5, 7–9], 269,
      270 [1, 5–8], 271

Candidates for public office — *continued*
 Nevada, **1948:** 202 [1, 2]
 New Hampshire, **1952–53:** 292 [13], 294, 295 [1, 3, 5, 6]
 New Jersey, **1948:** 225 [3], 227 [6–8]; **1949:** 144 [18]; **1952–53:** 303 [2–7]
 New Mexico, **1948:** 136 [2, 4], 208 [1, 2]
 New York, **1948:** 228 [2–5, 9], 264 [2]; **1949:** 144 [9], 148 [3], 155 [8], 192 [4], 200 [4], 231 [11, 17], 251; **1952–53:** 21 [30], 221 [7], 288, 289 [1–8, 11], 298 [12, 14], 300
 North Carolina, **1948:** 246
 North Dakota, **1952–53:** 266 [3–11]
 Ohio, **1948:** 114 [1], 193 [2], 231 [1–10], 253 [4, 5], 258; **1950:** 3 [13], 11 [12], 38 [5], 86 [9], 146 [9], 169 [1]; **1951:** 298 [2]; **1952–53:** 34, 253 [8], 277 [1], 286 [4–6], 287, 311 [1, 2], 319 [1–6], 320
 Oklahoma, **1948:** 213, 214 [4, 5, 7, 8], 216 [1–7, 10–12], 217
 Oregon, **1952–53:** 277 [1]
 Pennsylvania, **1948:** 227 [1, 5], 248, 249, 251; **1950:** 3 [13], 38 [5, 13], 270 [11]; **1951:** 179 [5]; **1952–53:** 240 [1], 286 [8], 303 [9, 10], 304, 305, 306 [1–3, 5, 6], 308 [2–6]
 Presidential, **1952–53:** 7 [2, 5, 7, 10, 12], 17 [20], 21 [4, 5, 8, 9, 11, 13, 15, 17, 20, 28, 31, 32], 26 [3, 7, 8, 15], 28, 31 [10, 13, 15], 35 [2], 44 [12], 49 [4, 6, 13, 14, 16], 64 [2, 9, 10], 69, 75 [11], 88 [18], 98 [2, 4, 7, 23, 24, 29, 31], 107 [4], 115 [3, 11, 20], 125, 127 [8, 15], 136 [8, 11, 16, 18], 149 [18, 20], 156 [3], 166 [16], 175 [5, 8, 13, 14], 197 [8, 12], 218, 221 [6, 9, 12, 14], 227, 228 [8, 7, 12], 233 [4, 7, 11, 12, 15, 17], 238 [3, 8], 240 [1, 2], 241 242, 247 [1], 253 [3, 6, 8, 9, 11, 12], 258 [1, 7, 11, 12], 266 [1–11, 13], 268 [2–5, 7–9], 270 [1, 5–10], 271–273, 274 [1–5, 7], 275– 301, 303–308, 310–324
 Rhode Island, **1948:** 261 [5]; **1952–53:** 298 [5], 299
 South Carolina, **1950:** 16ftn. (p. 119), 137 [23]
 Texas, **1948:** 208 [7], 212 [1, 4, 5, 11], 213, 214 [2]; **1952–53:** 98 [33], 238 [5]
 Utah, **1948:** [5, 6]; **1952–53:** 280 [1, 3]
 Virginia, **1949:** 166 [2]
 Washington, **1951:** 108 [10, 14]; **1952–53:** 272, 274 [1–3, 5, 7], 275, 276
 West Virginia, **1948:** 222 [9, 10], 223, 242 [2, 3]; **1952–53:** 242 [3–6], 308 [1, 8]
 Wisconsin, **1948:** 237 [5, 7], 238, 239; **1950:** 44 [4]; **1952–53:** 253 [10]
Cane, gift to the President, **1951:** 224 [3]
Canham, Erwin D., **1949:** 86; **1950:** 92
Cannae, battle of, **1950:** 138
Canneries, labor disputes, **1946:** 61 [4], 66 [3], 70 [7]
Cannon, Cavendish, **1952–53:** 31 [8]
Cannon, Repr. Clarence, **1948:** 216 [1]; **1949:** 20,

Cannon, Repr. Clarence — *continued*
 64, 78 [17]; **1950:** 160 [2], 252; **1952–53:** 358
 Letters, **1945:** 185; **1952–53:** 105, 180, 217
Cannon, Joseph G., **1948:** 233 [4]
Cannonball River, N. Dak., **1950:** 129 [5]
Canol oil project, **1946:** 215 [3]
Canon City, Colo., campaign remarks, **1948:** 198 [6]; **1952–53:** 282 [3]
Canton, Ohio, **1952–53:** 286 [5]
Canyon Ferry Dam, **1950:** 127 [4]
Cape, Ed M., **1948:** 212 [1]
Cape Girardeau, Mo., **1952–53:** 18 (p. 88), 367 (p. 1146)
Capehart, Sen. Homer E., **1948:** 110 [10]; **1952–53:** 31 [6], 287n., 312
 Defense Production Act amendment, **1951:** 176, 199, 261 [14], 279; **1952–53:** 33, 82, 287, 305, 319 [1]
Capeless, Robert, **1948:** 259n.
Capital, national, question of relocation, **1950:** 46 [5]
"Capital Comment," **1947:** 107 [13]
Capital gains tax, **1950:** 18; **1951:** 28, 228
Capital improvement program, **1950:** 9 (p. 49)
Capital improvement program for Khmer Indians, **1948:** 57
Capital Issues Committee, World War I, **1951:** 1, 44
Capital police force, **1947:** 35
Capital Press Club plaque, acceptance, **1952–53:** 153
Capital Transit Co. (D.C.), Government operation, **1945:** 195n., 208ftn. (p. 528)
Capp, Al, **1948:** 89
Capper, Sen. Arthur, **1948:** 234
Caraway, Hattie W., **1946:** 199 [7]; **1949:** 119 [2]
Carbide and Carbon Chemicals Corp., **1948:** 140
Carbondale,Ill.
 Campaign address, **1948:** 219
 Mayor John I. Wright, **1948:** 219
Cardinals, St. Louis, baseball team, **1949:** 192 [18]
Cardiovascular disease, **1948:** 22
CARE.
 See Cooperative for American Remittances to Europe.
CARE-for-Korea campaign, **1950:** 285
Career Compensation Act of **1949:** 1949, 218n.
Carey, James B., **1947:** 122; **1952–53:** 203n.
Caribbean area
 Public works in, **1950:** 69
 Visit to, question of, **1948:** 174 [8]
Caribbean maneuvers, U.S. forces, **1949:** 40 [14]
Carillon from the Netherlands, acceptance, **1952– 53:** 78
Carlock, Lyle S., **1951:** 93n.
Carlsen, Capt. Henrik Kurt, **1952–53:** 29n.
Carlson, Gov. Frank, **1950:** 312, 313; **1951:** 196

Carlson, Harry, **1948:** 9 [20]
Carlson, William E., **1952–53:** 266 [1], 313, 314
Carmi, Ill., campaign remarks, **1948:** 218 [8]
Carnahan, Repr. A. S. J., **1951:** 54n.
Caroline Islands, U.S. navy operations, World War II, **1945:** 161
Carpenter, Donald F., **1949:** 144 [21]
Carr, Albert Z., **1945:** 151n.
Carr, John C., **1952–53:** 295 [9]
Carrick, Jimmy, **1952–53:** 154
Carrier Congress, National, **1951:** 133n.
Carriers, unit citations, **1946:** 171
Carroll, Maj. Gen. Franklin O., **1951:** 138
Carroll, John Albert, **1952–53:** 282 [7]
Carry, Champ, **1946:** 142
Cartels, German, **1948:** 278 [23, 28]
Cartels, international oil, **1952–53:** 372
Carter, Amon G., **1948:** 212 [7]
Carter, Arthur, **1948:** 228 [3]
Carter, John Franklin, **1948:** 278ftn. (p. 954)
Carter, John Franklin, Jr., **1949:** 4ftn. (p. 11)
Carter, Oliver J., **1948:** 203
Carter Barron Amphitheater, dedication, **1951:** 116
Carthage, ancient, **1949:** 64
Carthaginian senate, cartoon concerning, **1951:** 18
Cartoon collection, the President's. **1951:** 43
Cartoonists Association, National, **1951:** 290
Cartoons, political, comments on, **1948:** 55 [12], 199, 228 [9], 267 [2]; **1949:** 119 [5], 122 [4, 8], 144 [11], 192 [24]
Caruthersville, Mo., **1945:** 147 [9], 163; **1946:** 216 [14]
Carvel, Gov. Elbert N., **1952–53:** 303 [1]
Carver Village housing project, bombing of, **1952–53:** 290
Carvey, John C., **1952–53:** 286n.
Casa Marina, Miami, Fla., **1951:** 56 [12]
Casablanca, **1945:** 177
Case, Everett C., **1949:** 260ftn. (p. 571)
Case, Francis, **1950:** 44 [16]; **1952–53:** 297
Case, Norman S., **1945:** 60 [2]
Case Against the New Deal, Thomas E. Dewey, **1948:** 247
Case (Repr. Francis) bill, **1946:** 157; **1947:** 2 (p.5)
News conference remarks, **1946:** 27 [9], 72 [8], 110 [4], 119 [7], 126 [2], 129 [5, 7], 136 [15]
Veto, **1946:** 131
Casey, James B., **1952–53:** 7 [1]
Cash, Albert D., **1948:** 231 [1]
Cashmore, John, **1952–53:** 288n., 289 [1–11], 298 [12–14], 300
Casper, Wyo., **1950:** 116
Cassini, Austine, **1951:** 70 [11]
Casualties, military, proportionate decline with development of weapons, **1950:** 138
Cates, Gen. Clifton B., **1947:** 226 [1]; **1950:** 165, 235, 237
Catholic University dramatic group departing for Korea, remarks to, **1952–53:** 56

Cato, senator of ancient Rome, **1949:** 64
Cats, **1947:** 19 [3–5]
Cattle, **1952–53:** 15, 33
  See also Livestock.
Caudle, T. Lamar, **1951:** 298 [4], 300 [8, 10, 21]; **1952–53:** 31 [20], 247 [5], 258 [3]
Caufield, Stanley W., **1948:** 208 [6]
Cawthorn, Joseph, **1951:** 99
CCC.
  See Commodity Credit Corporation.
CED.
  See Committee for Economic Development.
CEEC.
  See Committee of European Economic Cooperation.
Cedar Rapids, Iowa, campaign remarks, **1952–53:** 315 [2]
Celler, Repr. Emanuel, **1947:** 78 [4]; **1949:** 149; **1952–53:** 300, 373
Cemeteries, World War II, **1947:** 92
Censorship, **1948:** 11 [13]
Censorship, Office of, **1946:** 13
Censorship, wartime, **1946:** 13
Census, **1949:** 249; **1950:** 9 (p. 84)
  Municipal records, veto of bill to amend, **1950:** 210
  Seventeenth decennial, **1948:** 5 (p. 42); **1951:** 5
Census, Bureau of the, **1946:** 117; **1947:** 7 (p. 77), 65; **1948:** 5 (p. 42); **1949:** 8 (pp. 76, 93), 175; **1950:** 210; **1952–53:** 68, 367 (pp. 1155, 1156)
  Director (Roy V. Peel), letter, **1952–53:** 363
Census of Business, **1949:** 8 (p. 88)
Census of Manufactures, **1952–53:** 363n.
Census records, elimination of searching fee, veto, **1949:** 175
Centennial Exposition, Philadelphia **1949:** (1876), 102
Central Intelligence Agency, **1946:** 137, 138; **1947:** 10n.; **1950:** 152 [12]; **1951:** 95 [9], 171 [11], 247 [1]; **1952–53:** 69, 227, 228 [3, 7], 296, 299, 303 [2], 335
  Director (Gen. Walter Bedell Smith), **1951:** 95 [9], 128; **1952–53:** 335
  Internal security bill, advisory opinion against, **1950:** 254
Central Intelligence Group, **1946:** 19, 86 [3]
Central Valley, Calif., **1946:** 18 (p. 61), 97
Central Valley Authority (California), proposed, **1947:** 31 [10]
Central Valley project, Calif., **1948:** 6, 201, 203, 204 [4]
Centralia, Ill., mine disaster, **1952–53:** 19
Cereijo, Ramón A., **1950:** 86 [5], 97 [6], 105 [12]
Ceylon, independence, **1950:** 119
Chalk River, Canada, heavy water reactor at, **1949:** 166 [1]
Chamber of Commerce, St. Louis, Mo., **1949:** 205 [11]

Chamber of Commerce, U.S., **1947:** 88 [14]; **1948:** 114 [3]; **1951:** 101 [5]; **1952–53:** 43n.
Chambers, Lenoir, **1952–53:** 98 [21]
Chambers, Whittaker, **1948:** 170ftn. (p. 432), 283 [1]
Chang, John M., **1950:** 222n.
Changchun, Manchuria, **1946:** 265
Chapel of the Four Chaplains, dedication, **1951:** 30
Chaplains, World War II, **1948:** 131 [1]
Chapman, Oscar L., **1946:** 43 [4], 177 [2]; **1948:** 136 [2]; **1949:** 167n.
    See also Interior, Secretary of the.
Chapman, Repr. Virgil, **1948:** 218 [11–14], 222 [1–6, 8]
Chapultepec, Act of, **1946:** 102; **1947:** 101, 105, 188; **1951:** 125
Chapultepec, Mexico, **1948:** 210 [2]
Chariton, Iowa, campaign remarks, **1948:** 194 [11]
Charles, Prince, **1948:** 71 [7], 85
Charles I of England, **1951:** 18
Charles Evans Hughes, Merlo J. Pusey, **1951:** 285ftn. (p. 630)
Charles University, Czechoslovakia, **1952–53:** 47
Charleston, S.C., **1947:** 35; **1952–53:** 35 [7]
    Mayor Edwin Wehman, **1945:** 147n.
Charleston, W. Va., campaign address, **1948:** 223
Charlotte Amalie, Virgin Islands, **1948:** 36
Charlottesville, Va., **1947:** 138n.
Chartres, France, **1951:** 160
Chatham, Repr. Thurmond, **1949:** 118 [3]
Chavez, Sen. Dennis, **1948:** 136 [3], 208 [2]; **1949:** 115n., 144 [19, 22], 183n., 200 [1]; **1952–53:** 3
Cheese prices, **1946:** 18 (p. 55)
Chelf, Repr. Frank L., **1948:** 218 [13, 14], 222 [1]; **1952–53:** 64 [6], 75 [2], 91
Chelsea, Okla., campaign remarks, **1948:** 216 [10]
Chemical Society, American, **1950:** 238 [7]; **1952–53:** 117
Chemicals
    Export controls, **1947:** 58
    Price increase, **1951:** 11
Chenery, William L., **1946:** 80
Cherry, Judge Francis, **1952–53:** 228ftn. (p. 518)
Cherry, Gov. R. Gregg, **1948:** 245n., 246
Cherwell, Lord, **1952–53:** 6
Chesapeake and Ohio Canal, **1948:** 11 [11]
Chester Springs, Pa., **1945:** 76 [4]
Cheyenne, Wyo., **1950:** 118
    Campaign remarks, **1948:** 118 [5]
    Nelson, Mayor Ben, **1950:** 118n.
Chiang Kai-shek, **1945:** 4 [14], 118 [18], 147 [3], 151n., 172 [21]; **1948:** 49 [21], 274 [9], 278ftn. (p. 952), 288 [7]; **1949:** 118 [10], 155 [22], 171 [1]; **1950:** 3 [1], 46 [3], 318 [6]
    News conference remarks on, **1945:** 4 [14], 118 [18], 147 [3], 172 [2]

·Chiang Kai-shek, Madame, **1945:** 118, [6, 18]; **1948:** 278 [4, 24], 283 [15], 285 [16], 288 [13]
Chicago, Ill., **1945:** 163; **1946:** 75, 76, 86 [33], 133; **1949:** 148 [16], 166 [3], 226ftn. (p. 503), 249; **1951:** 113 [2], 247 [1], 275 [1, 3]
    Board of Trade, **1947:** 196
    Campaign address, **1948:** 256; **1952–53:** 315 [6], 316
    Election, **1947:** 88 [5]
    Hog prices, **1947:** 242
    Mayor Edward J. Kelly, **1945:** 44 [12]; **1946:** 15 [12], 76n.
    Mayor Martin H. Kennelly, **1947:** 67 [5]; **1948:** 115; **1950:** 134n.
    National Democratic Conference and Jefferson Jubilee, **1950:** 134
    News conference remarks, **1947:** 70 [8], 78 [8], 88 [5], 209 [11, 12]; **1950:** 46 [16], 52 [3], 86 [20, 26], 137 [18]
    Newspapers, reading by President, **1947:** 210 [2]
    Political corruption in, charges by newsman, **1952–53:** 342 [3]
    Radio Station WBBM, **1947:** 48n.
    Republican National Convention, **1952–53:** 267, 293, 317 [3]
    Visit to, question of, **1948:** 84 [5], 88 [9], 93 [3]
Chicago, Rock Island and Pacific Railroad, Government operation, **1950:** 188
Chicago, University of, **1952–53:** 367 (p. 1145)
Chicago Bar Association, **1951:** 165 [8], 275 [1]
Chicago Daily News, **1951:** 7 [3]
Chicago Defender, **1947:** 48n.; **1949:** 109n.
Chicago Sun-Times, **1947:** 210 [2]; **1951:** 165ftn. (p. 403); **1952–53:** 342 [3]
Chicago Tribune, **1949:** 36; **1950:** 137 [25, 26], 309 [3]; **1952–53:** 45
Chief of Engineers, **1948:** 126 [1]
    Pick, Maj. Gen. Lewis A., **1950:** 129 [1, 2]
Chief Joseph Dam, **1950:** 125
Chief Justice of the United States, vacancy in office, **1946:** 95 [3, 5, 6, 7, 25], 110 [1, 6], 119 [6], 126 [13, 19]
Chief Justice of the United States (Harlan F. Stone), **1945:** 1n.; **1946:** 27 [13]
    Death of, **1946:** 88
Chief Justice of the United States (Fred M. Vinson), **1948:** 230; **1949:** 19, 64, 173, 189, 254n.; **1950:** 94, 174; **1951:** 24, 27, 67, 145 [9], 225, 261 [2], 295 [8]; **1952–53:** 306 [5], 347
    Appointment, **1946:** 129 [1, 4], 136ftn. (p. 301)
    Mission to Soviet Union, question of, **1950:** 38 [1, 20]
Chief Magistrate, The, William Howard Taft, **1950:** 82
Chief of Staff, Army, **1947:** 221 [7], 226 [3]

Chief of Staff, Army — *continued*
 Collins, Gen. J. Lawton, **1950:** 194, 226, 230 [7], 303; **1951:** 93n., 148
Chiefs of Police, International Association of, **1945:** 62
Chiefs of Staff, Combined, U.S.-U.K., **1945:** 197, 198; **1946:** 7, 53 [5], 216 [16, 18], 272
Chiefs of Staff, Joint.
 See Joint Chiefs of Staff.
Children
 Child care centers, Federal aid, **1945:** 157[10]
  Letter, **1945:** 159
 Child care programs, **1946:** 117
 Dependent, public assistance payments to, **1948:** 131
 East German, Soviet indoctrination, **1950:** 162
 Greek, abduction to eastern Europe, **1950:** 7, 90, 261
 Guidance and supervision, **1946:** 52
 Health and welfare, **1945:** 99, 192; **1946:** 18 (p. 83), 128; **1947:** 98; **1948:** 18, 181 [2], 237 [3]; **1949:** 8 (p. 68), 85, 151, 159, 198, 219; **1950:** 9 (p. 75); **1951:** 11, 13 (pp. 97, 99), 191, 307; **1952–53:** 293
 Kidnapping in East Germany, **1951:** 116
 Labor
  Abolition, **1948:** 32, 70, 219, 228 [5], 240 [1], 255, 268; **1949:** 239
  Labor laws, enforcement, **1950:** 9 (p. 98), 18; **1952–53:** 18 (p. 94)
 Migrant workers', educational aid for, **1952–53:** 18 (p. 102)
 Moral and religious training, **1950:** 37, 299
 Public assistance, **1952–53:** 367 (p. 1156)
 School lunch program, **1950:** 135; **1952–53:** 18 (p. 105)
 Schoolchildren, Tehachapi, Calif., remarks to, **1948:** 204 [5]
 Schools.
  See main heading, Schools.
 U.N. emergency fund, **1949:** 257
 U.N. programs for, **1950:** 154; **1952–53:** 51
 War orphans, immigration to U.S., **1950:** 167
Children and Youth, White House Conference on, **1949:** 198, 204; **1950:** 5, 299
Children's Bureau, **1946:** 117; **1950:** 5n.; **1952–53:** 18 (p. 106)
Children's Fund, International, **1948:** 144
Chile, **1945:** 150n.; **1946:** 66 [4], 229 [3]
 Ambassador Felix Nieto del Rio, **1950:** 231; **1952–53:** 123 [13], 127 [2]
 Copper
  Discussions concerning, **1952–53:** 123 [5, 13], 127 [2]
  Exports, **1949:** 122 [9], 144 [28]
 Corridor to sea, offer to Bolivia, **1950:** 191 [6]
 Economic development, **1951:** 59
 Endorsement of Point 4 program, **1949:** 28 [11]

Chile — *continued*
 González Videla, President Gabriel, **1949:** 269 [17]; **1950:** 46 [8], 85, 86 [1, 8], 104, 152 [4], 191 [6]; **1952–53:** 123 [13]
 Liberation by San Martín, **1950:** 212
 News conference remarks, **1950:** 46 [15], 137 [8], 152 [4, 6], 191 [6], 270 [1]
 Power project, U.S.-financed, **1950:** 46 [15]
 Rios, Juan Antonio, **1945:** 56, 170; **1946:** 143 [9]
 Tax on copper imports from, question of suspension, **1950:** 152 [4, 6], 231
 U.S. Ambassador, appointment, **1947:** 95 [7]
 U.S. Ambassador Claude Bowers, **1950:** 137 [8]
 Visit to, question of, **1950:** 46 [15], 137 [8], 270 [1]
China, **1945:** 100, 136, 178; **1946:** 18 (pp. 42, 44, 45), 76, 85, 113, 172, 247; **1947:** 111; **1948:** 239
 See also China, Communist; China, Republic of.
 American Production Mission, termination, statement, **1945:** 151
 Assistance, **1946:** 4, 265, 266 [11]; **1947:** 7 (p. 65), 238; **1948:** 2, 4 [2], 5 (pp. 20, 29), 31, 81, 144, 160, 175, 202 [6], 274 [9], 278 [31], 283 [15], 288 [7, 13]; **1949:** 8 (p. 54), 86, 234 [8]
 Atomic energy declaration of U.S., U.K., and Canada, reaction to, **1945:** 193 [8]
 Boxer Rebellion, **1950:** 233; **1951:** 181
 Chiang Kai-shek, **1945:** 4 [14], 118 [18], 147 [3], 151n., 172 [2]; **1948:** 49 [21], 274 [9], 278ftn. (p. 952), 288 [7]; **1949:** 118 [10], 155 [22], 171 [1]; **1950:** 3 [1], 46 [3], 318 [6]
 Chiang Kai-shek, Madame, **1945:** 118 [6, 18]; **1948:** 278 [4, 24], 283 [15], 285 [16], 288 [13]
 Civil war, **1946:** 18 (p. 44), 265; **1948:** 31, 278ftn. (p. 952)
 Communism in, **1946:** 119 [10], 266 [17], 265
 Communists, inclusion in government, question of, **1948:** 49 [17, 19, 21]
 Council of Foreign Ministers, membership, **1945:** 91, 97
 Formosa.
  See main heading, Formosa.
 Hurley, Gen. Patrick J., mission to, **1949:** 171 [1]
 Japanese occupation, **1948:** 31
 Locke, Edwin A., mission of, **1946:** 15 [24], 41 [12]
 MacArthur, Gen. Douglas, mission by, question of, **1948:** 278 [34]
 Marshall, Gen. George C., mission to, **1945:** 202 [12, 15], 211 [8]; **1946:** 15 [24], 18 (p. 44), 37 [3], 41 [12], 53 [22], 78 [8], 86 [30], 119 [10], 172, 265, 266 [5, 7, 17]; **1949:** 171 [1]
 Mission (U.S.) on development of small business, **1945:** 228
 Nationalist forces, abandonment of Nanking by, **1949:** 84ftn. (p. 224)
 Naval patrol of, **1947:** 36 [25]

China — *continued*
  News conference remarks, **1945:** 107 [11, 16], 118
    [6], 157 [13], 193 [8], 202 [12, 15], 208 [17],
    211 [8]; **1946:** 6 [12], 15 [24], 27 [1], 37 [3],
    41 [12], 53 [22], 78 [8], 84 [27], 86 [4, 30],
    119 [8, 10], 266 [1, 3, 5, 9, 11, 17, 22];
    1947: 14 [5], 221 [16]; **1948:** 4 [2], 49 [17,
    19, 21], 274 [9], 278 [5, 31, 34], 283 [15],
    288 [7, 13]; **1949:** 58 [11], 84 [16], 89 [2, 5,
    13], 113 [6], 118 [10], 171 [1, 12], 179 [22],
    269 [15]
  Relief for, **1945:** 186
  Sino-Soviet treaty and agreements, **1945:** 118 [6],
    216
  Spoong, T.V., **1945:** 107 [11]
  34th anniversary of Republic, statement, **1945:**
    166
  U.S. Ambassador Patrick J. Hurley, **1945:** 202 [6,
    11], 208 [12]
  U.S. embassy in Nanking, reported violation of,
    1949: 89 [2, 13]
  U.S. policy toward, **1945:** 202 [12]; **1946:** 266 [1,
    3, 5, 9, 11, 17]; **1949:** 58 [11], 89 [5], 113
    [6], 171 [1, 12], 179 [22], 269 [15]
    Statement, **1945:** 216; **1946:** 265
  Wedemeyer, Lt. Gen. Albert C., mission of,
    1947: 209 [4]
    Report on, **1949:** 171 [1]
      Question of release, **1948:** 49 [21]
China, Communist, **1950:** 78, 232; **1952–53:** 232,
    354, 366
  Arrests and executions in, **1951:** 96
  Attack by Nationalists, question of, **1951:** 16 [9]
  Designation as aggressor by U.N., U.S. efforts
    for, **1951:** 16 [8]
  Diplomatic recognition, question of, **1949:** 234
    [5, 8], 240 [8], 260 [13]
  Food for famine relief in, **1950:** 119
  Formosa, prevention of invasion by, **1950:** 209
    [11]
  Fur imports from, question of restriction, **1951:**
    165 [3]
  Korean war, intervention in, **1950:** 230 [7], 287
    [1], 295 [1, 7], 296, 299, 301, 303; **1951:** 95
    [9], 96, 113 [7], 117, 199; **1952–53:** 5, 6, 12,
    345 [1]
  Mao Tse-tung, **1950:** 273 [7]
  News conference remarks, **1949:** 179 [22, 26], 240
    [8], 260 [3, 13]; **1950:** 38 [7], 146 [13], 209
    [11], 230 [7], 270 [2], 273 [7], 287 [1], 295
    [1, 7, 14]
  Soviet military assistance to, **1951:** 174
  Statement by Gen. MacArthur on, **1951:** 77n.
  Treaty with Soviet Union, **1950:** 38 [7]
  U.N.
    Authorization to bomb, question of **1951:** 2 [7,
      10]
    Membership, question of, **1951:** 261 [1]

China — *continued*
  U.S. consulates
    Closing of, **1949:** 234 [5]
    Imprisonment of U.S. consul, **1949:** 260 [3]
  War materials, imports through Hong Kong,
    1951: 63 [10]
China, Republic of.
  See also Formosa (Taiwan).
  Assistance, **1950:** 8 [4], 154; **1952–53:** 18 (p. 76),
    279, 366
    Military, **1951:** 114, 138, 247 [6], 251ftn. (p.
      568)
  Attack on Chinese mainland, question of, **1951:**
    16 [9]
  Chiang Kai-shek.
    See main heading, Chiang Kai-shek.
  "China lobby," proposed investigation of, **1950:**
    97 [5]
  Communist aggression, **1952–53:** 354, 366
  Invasion of Communist China, question of,
    1950: 318 [6]
  Korean war, question of participation, **1951:** 33
    [3], 85 [10]
  Li, Tsung-jen, **1950:** 46 [3]
  Military operations against mainland, cessation
    of, **1950:** 193
  Mission of Gen. George C. Marshall (1946),
    1950: 253 [1]
  News conference remarks, **1950:** 3 [1], 8 [4], 97
    [5], 186 [15], 253 [1], 295 [5], 318 [6]
  Troops, question of use in Korea, **1950:** 186 [15],
    295 [5]
  U.K. recognition of, **1950:** 301
  U.N. membership, question of, **1950:** 146 [13],
    270 [2], 273 [7], 301
  U.S. policy on, **1950:** 3 [1], 223, 232; **1951:** 251
    [25]; **1952–53:** 362n.
  U.S. relations with, **1952–53:** 54
Chinese-American Agricultural Collaboration
    Commission, **1946:** 265
Chinese Communists, **1945:** 216
Chinese-Japanese war, **1945:** 166, 216
Chinchy, Everett R., **1949:** 254n.
Ching, Cyrus S., Director, Federal Mediation and
    Conciliation Service, **1947:** 174 [1,3], 237;
    1948: 72, 93 [5], 252, 259 [1]; **1949:** 152,
    209, 213; **1950:** 43; **1951:** 204, 304; **1952–
    53:** 37
Chinook, Mont., campaign remarks, **1952–53:** 268
    [4]
Chiperfield, Repr. Robert B., **1952–53:** 312
Choate, Clyde L., **1948:** 218n.
Chopin, Frederic, **1951:** 99
Christian Citizenship, Crusade for, **1952–53:** 39
Christian Endeavor, International Society of, re-
    marks to, **1952–53:** 168
Christian Endeavor Union, World, **1950:** 197
Christian Leadership, National Committee for,
    1949: 28 [15]

Christian Rural Overseas Program, **1951:** 124
Christians and Jews, National Conference of, **1949:** 224
Christmas
    Eggnog for, **1947:** 221 [2]
    Exchange of greetings with newsmen, **1952–53:** 353 [10, 17]
Christmas plans, the President's, **1945:** 211 [13]
Christmas proclamation, preparation of, **1950:** 309 [6]
Christmas Seal campaign, **1950:** 286
Christmas Tree, National Community, **1945:** 227; **1946:** 271; **1947:** 240; **1948:** 287; **1949:** 271; **1950:** 317; **1951:** 306; **1952–53:** 356
Christopher, George H., **1948:** 216 [15]
Chromite, imports, **1948:** 8 (p. 78)
Chrysler Motor Co., **1952–53:** 175 [12]
    Labor dispute, **1950:** 202
Chudoff, Repr. Earl, **1952–53:** 304
Church, Stanley W., **1952–53:** 298 [12]
Church attendance, the President's, **1949:** 83
Church Press, Associated, **1949:** 83; **1951:** 61
Churches
    Aid in housing shortage, **1946:** 46
    Bombing of, **1952–53:** 290
    Ecumenical movement, **1951:** 241
    Role in national life, **1951:** 68
Churches of Christ, Federal Council of, **1946:** 52
Churchill, Winston, **1945:** 44ftn. (p. 80), 93; **1946:** 18 (p. 41), 27 [17], 37 [8], 41 [19], 43 [6], 53 [3, 20], 61 [5, 10], 237 [6]; **1947:** 19 [17]; **1948:** 15 [10]; **1949:** 52 [17], 260 [13], 273; **1950:** 38 [10], 121 [1], 203 [4], 230 [6]; **1951:** 70 [10], 295 [2]
    Attendance at Potsdam conference, **1945:** 91, 97
    Joint statement with, **1945:** 9
    Message, **1945:** 29
    News conference remarks on, **1945:** 4 [14], 26 [5], 31 [4], 44 [7], 60 [6], 67 [1], 76 [8], 106 [8], 147 [3], 181 [3]; **1950:** 38 [10], 203 [4], 230 [6]
    Visit to U.S., **1952–53:** 5, 378
        Joint statements, **1952–53:** 6, 16
        News conference remarks on, **1952–53:** 2 [7, 10, 17], 7 [8], 17 [22], 44 [1, 13], 149 [10], 359 [20]
        Welcoming remarks, **1952–53:** 4
Churchmen, American, Washington Pilgrimage of, **1951:** 241
CIA.
    See Central Intelligence Agency.
Cicero, Ill., riots at, **1952–53:** 290
Cielito Lindo, **1951:** 76
Cina, Fred, **1948:** 235 [5]
Cinchona bark and alkaloids, import controls, **1947:** 18, 99

Cincinnati, Ohio
    Campaign remarks, **1948:** 231 [1]; **1952–53:** 242 [1], 320
    Mayor Albert D. Cash, **1948:** 231 [1]
    Postelection remarks in, **1948:** 271 [3]
CIO.
    See Congress of Industrial Organizations.
Citations.
    See Awards and citations.
Cities Service Oil Corp., **1952–53:** 58, 238 [7]
Citizens' commission on atomic energy policy, proposed, **1950:** 34 [12]
Citizens Committee for the Hoover Report, **1951:** 56 [1]
Citizens' Committee for United Nations Day, National, **1950:** 239
Citizens Food Committee, **1947:** 198, 207, 225; **1948:** 14
    Chairman (Charles Luckman), **1947:** 202, 218 [6], 236 [1]
    News conference remarks, **1947:** 191 [3, 8], 209 [2], 210 [4, 5]
    Report, **1947:** 218 [6], 236 [1]
Citizens' Food Committee, St. Louis, **1950:** 3 [4]
Citizens' organizations, Communist attempts to infiltrate, **1950:** 207
Citizenship, **1947:** 204
    Responsibilities of, **1951:** 107, 168; **1952–53:** 98 [16], 100, 251, 270 [4]
Citizenship, Conference on, **1950:** 144; **1951:** 107; **1952–53:** 251
Citizenship Day, **1952–53:** 251
Citizenship Seminar, Washington Student, **1950:** 178; **1951:** 139; **1952–53:** 183
Citron, William M., **1952–53:** 292 [4], 298 [7]
City charter movement, origins, **1948:** 231 [1]
Civic affairs, participation in, **1946:** 75 [8]
Civil Aeronautics Act of 1938, **1952–53:** 351
Civil Aeronautics Administration, **1946:** 17 [30], 192 [8]; **1947:** 7 (p. 86), 181 (p. 402); **1948:** 175, 274 [10]; **1950:** 53, 76; **1951:** 13 (p. 83); **1952–53:** 18 (p. 83), 35 [3]
Civil Aeronautics Administrators
    Horne, Charles F., **1952–53:** 40, 351
    Wright, Theodore P., **1948:** 26 [6]
Civil Aeronautics Board, **1946:** 6 [16], 44, 237 [1]; **1947:** 243 [4]; **1948:** 3, 9 [3], 11 [3], 26 [5], 49 [11]; **1949:** 8 (p. 88); **1951:** 13 (pp. 83, 84), 45; **1952–53:** 18 (p. 84), 246, 351n., 367 (p. 1144)
    Reorganization, **1950:** 53, 54, 67
Civil Aeronautics Board, Chairman (James M. Landis), **1947:** 115n., 218 [8]
Civil Aeronautics Board, Chairman (Donald W. Nyrop), **1952–53:** 155, 246
Civil Aeronautics Board, Chairman (L. Welch Pogue), **1946:** 95 [14]

Civil Affairs Committee, Combined, **1945:** 198
Civil Air Patrol, dinner remarks, **1952–53:** 125, 351n.
Civil aviation.
    See Aviation, civil.
Civil Aviation, International Convention on, **1946:** 133
Civil Aviation Organization, International, **1946:** 133; **1947:** 21; **1950:** 9 (p. 102)
Civil defense, **1949:** 48, 231 [19], 260 [4]; **1950:** 203 [14], 251, 303; **1951:** 13 (pp. 90–92); **1952–53:** 5, 106, 125
    Accelerated program, proposed, **1951:** 131
    Administration program, news conference remarks on, **1952–53:** 353 [3]
    Air raid warning system, **1952–53:** 367 (p. 1154)
    Appropriations, **1951:** 285; **1952–53:** 106, 205
    Atomic attack on U.S., defense measures, **1951:** 96, 131
    CONELRAD plan, **1952–53:** 344n.
    Engineering supplies, stockpiling, **1952–53:** 367 (p. 1154)
    Expenditures for, **1952–53:** 231, 367 (p. 1154)
    Federal aid, **1951:** 10, 131; **1952–53:** 18 (pp. 96, 97, 99)
    First anniversary of Federal legislation, statement, **1952–53:** 9
    Girl Scouts, role in, **1951:** 48
    Ground Observer Corps, Operation Skywatch, **1952–53:** 202
    Land transactions by agencies, veto of bill to restrict, **1951:** 105, 108 [1]
    Manpower needs, **1951:** 15
    Master plan for, **1951:** 10
    Public works, **1951:** 13 (p. 92)
    Red Cross role in, **1951:** 47
Civil Defense, Office of, proposed, **1949:** 48
Civil Defense Administration, Federal, **1951:** 10, 13 (p. 92), 105, 131, 17 [1]; **1952–53:** 9, 18, 106
    Proposed, **1950:** 251
Civil Defense Administrator (Millard F. Caldwell), **1951:** 10, 96; **1952–53:** 21 [27], 44 [8]
Civil Defense Conference, **1951:** 96
Civil Defense Corps, U.S., **1951:** 96
Civil Defense Directors, National Association of State, **1952–53:** 353 [3]
Civil Engineers, American Society of, **1949:** 249
Civil Functions Appropriations Act, **1948:** 6n.
Civil laws, **1949:** 233
Civil rights, **1945:** 4 [8]; **1947:** 2 (p. 9), 130, 138, 215, 222; **1948:** 2; **1949:** 224, 237; **1950:** 2, 94, 174, 241, 280; **1951:** 7 [12], 18; **1952–53:** 129, 175 [15], 273, 313 [4], 329, 347
    Address, **1948:** 265
    American Samoa, **1947:** 130
    Anti-lynching laws, **1952–53:** 290
    Armed Forces, compliance, **1952–53:** 169

Civil rights — *continued*
    Commission on Internal Security and Individual Rights, **1951:** 20, 22 [2, 4, 6], 35, 37 [12]
    Communists, question of equal protection, **1948:** 71 [2]
    Constitutional guarantees, **1950:** 37, 176, 207, 254, 266; **1951:** 178, 194, 225, 241; **1952–53:** 288, 290, 297, 308 [7]
    Covenants, restrictive, prohibition of, **1948:** 265
    Democratic stand on, **1952–53:** 290
    Demonstration at Anacostia swimming pool, **1949:** 144 [14]
    Education, equal opportunity, **1952–53:** 290
    Educational facilities, **1946:** 214
    Employment.
        See under Employment.
    Fair employment practices, **1945:** 51, 128, 204; **1946:** 2, 18 (pp. 40, 52), 21 [17], 78 [5], 154, 199 [15]
    Government contracts, compliance, **1951:** 299; **1952–53:** 389
    Government employees, protection in loyalty and security programs, **1951:** 104, 156, 191
    Guam, **1947:** 130
    International protection of, **1950:** 174
    Issue in election campaign, **1952–53:** 303 [3]
    Legislation, proposed, **1948:** 20, 49 [8], 160, 165; **1949:** 2, 52 [4, 6], 214 [7]; **1950:** 8 [41], 9 (p. 102), 16 [16], 23 [13, 18], 52 [10]; **1952–53:** 5
    Message to Congress, **1948:** 20
    Michigan program, defeat by legislature, **1952–53:** 318
    Mob violence, protection against, **1952–53:** 290
    News conference remarks, **1948:** 21 [1, 3, 5], 26 [12], 49 [8], 71 [2], 163 [2], 285 [18]; **1949:** 52 [4, 6, 8], 89 [8], 144 [14], 155 [2], 211 [4], 214 [7]; **1950:** 8 [41], 16 [16], 23 [13, 18], 34 [1], 38 [9], 46 [12], 52 [10], 86 [3]
    Racial and religious discrimination, elimination, **1946:** 75 [22]; **1947:** 9, 48; **1948:** 2, 166 [1, 4], 185 [7], 219, 256, 257 [1], 258, 265; **1949:** 109n., 246, 250 [3], 254, 256; **1950:** 37, 86 [3], 126, 134; **1951:** 4, 116, 144, 171 [9], 241, 286, 299; **1952–53:** 169, 218, 288, 289 [7], 290, 297, 300, 303 [3, 4], 304, 315 [6], 317 [8], 318, 321 [2], 336, 366, 376, 378
    Republican stand on, **1952–53:** 218, 316
    Segregation
        Bill to abolish in Virginia, **1950:** 34 [1]
        Views of Attorney General on, **1950:** 86 [3]
    Voting.
        See Voting rights.
Civil Rights, Commission on, proposed, **1948:** 20; **1950:** 8 [41], 9 (p. 102)
Civil Rights, President's Committee on, **1947:** 2 (p. 9), 9, 130; **1948:** 2, 20, 265; **1952–53:** 169, 290, 315 [6], 317 [8], 329

Civil Rights, President's Committee — *continued*
    News conference remarks, **1947:** 218 [4]
    Report, **1947:** 215
Civil Rights Mobilization, National Emergency,
    1950: 15
Civil service, **1950:** 170, 283; **1952–53:** 76, 117, 137
    See also Government employees.
    Customs employees, transfer to, **1952–53:** 86
    Internal Revenue collectorships, proposed civil
        service status, **1951:** 239 [11, 13], 251 [21],
        300ftn. (p. 641); **1952–53:** 1, 2 [13], 11, 59,
        117
    Merit system, **1952–53:** 14, 84, 117, 390
    Personnel procedures for national defense,
        1952–53: 370
    Postmasterships, proposed civil service status,
        1952–53: 18 (p. 85), 85
    Reconversion, **1946:** 33
    Retirement system, **1952–53:** 18 (pp. 110, 113),
        207
    69th anniversary, statement, **1952–53:** 14
    Suppression in Communist bloc, **1951:** 253
    Trust funds, retirement and disability, **1952–53:**
        231
    U.S. Marshals, transfer to, **1952–53:** 87
Civil Service Commission, **1946:** 199 [7], 216 [1,
        10]; **1947:** 89, 222; **1948:** 5 (p. 56), 88 [6];
        1949: 127, 132, 201, 228, 242; **1950:** 9 (pp.
        51, 100), 53, 79, 182; **1951:** 119, 152, 156,
        161, 278, 299; **1952–53:** 18 (p. 112), 26 [5],
        137, 160, 169, 185, 222, 243, 290, 367 (p.
        1162), 370
    Recruitment of veterans, **1945:** 44 [1]
    Report, message transmitting, **1948:** 44
    Veterans preference, recommendations, **1945:**
        108
Civil Service Commission, Chairman (Harry B.
        Mitchell), **1950:** 82, 283, 288
Civil Service Commission, Chairman (Robert
        Ramspeck), **1952–53:** 59, 114, 117, 223,
        243
    Letters, **1952–53:** 222, 338
Civil Service Commission, President (Arthur S.
        Flemming), **1947:** 146n.
Civil Service Commission, President (Harry B.
        Mitchell), **1946:** 146
Civil Service League, National, **1952–53:** 117
Civil Service Retirement and Disability Fund,
        1952–53: 367 (p. 1163)
Civil War, **1945:** 45, 164 [3]; **1946:** 162; **1947:** 31 [1],
        51, 90 [1], 181 (p. 405), 243 [1]; **1948:** 139
        [3], 245; **1950:** 37, 87, 121 [8], 266; **1951:** 8,
        47, 90 [16], 181, 270
Civilian Defense, Office of, **1946:** 104
    Termination, **1945:** 19, 22ftn. (p. 37)
Civilian Defense, Office of, Director (William N.
        Haskell), **1945:** 19
Civilian defense material, disposal **1945:** 44 [12]

Civilian goods, production, **1945:** 180
Civilian Production Administration, **1946:** 43 [7],
        72 [2], 260, 262 [3]; **1947:** 4 (p. 25), 7 (p.
        86), 18, 60
Civilian Production Administrator (John D.
        Small), **1946:** 70 [19], 119 [5], 260
Civilian Public Service Camps, **1946:** 270
Civilian War Services, **1945:** 19
Civilians, Committee to Award Medals of Merit to,
        1945: 137 [4]
    See also Medal of Merit Board.
Claimants against Government, representation of,
        1947: 168
Claims, public land, **1948:** 105
Claims Commission, Motor Carrier, **1950:** 209ftn.
        (p. 582)
Clapp, Gordon R., **1946:** 242 [3], 243, 244; **1947:** 46
        [18], 141 [2]; **1949:** 122 [19], 156, 167, 193,
        274; **1950:** 25, 154, 196; **1952–53:** 144
Claremore, Okla., campaign remarks, **1948:** 216 [9]
Clark, Bennett Champ, **1945:** 31 [6], 129 [4], 132 [1,
        11]; **1950:** 160 [2]
Clark, D. Worth, **1950:** 209ftn. (p. 581)
Clark, Dean A., **1951:** 307n.
Clark, Dwight, Jr., **1952–53:** 43n.
Clark, Gilmore D., **1949:** 200 [12]
Clark, John D., **1946:** 177 [2], 183n.; **1950:** 118;
        1951: 44n.; **1952–53:** 377 [16]
Clark, Joseph S., Jr., **1952–53:** 249n., 304
Clark, Gen. Mark W., **1945:** 21; **1949:** 223; **1950:**
        16ftn. (p. 116); **1952–53:** 131, 288 [4], 295
        [8], 320
    Appointment to U.N. command, Korea, **1952–
        53:** 113
    Appointment as U.S. Ambassador to Vatican,
        1951: 275 [7, 18, 20], 300 [16]
Clark, Sheldon, **1946:** 45n., 255n.
Clark, Tom C., **1948:** 190
    See also Attorney General.
    Appointment as Attorney General, **1945:** 40 [1]
    Swearing in as Associate Justice, **1949:** 189
Clark, Vernon L., **1949:** 82n.
Clarksburg, W. Va., campaign remarks, **1948:** 242
        [1]; **1952–53:** 242 [3]
Classification Act, **1948:** 44, 153, 157; **1949:** 7 [35],
        8 (p. 48), 132, 218, 228, 242; **1950:** 9 (p.
        51); **1951:** 152, 161; **1952–53:** 11, 114, 137,
        160, 367 (p. 1162)
Clay, Henry, **1946:** 126 [21]; **1951:** 8, 24
Clay, Gen. Lucius D., **1945:** 119; **1947:** 210 [4];
        1948: 163 [1], 170 [9, 12]; **1949:** 28 [9], 93
        [6]; **1950:** 98n.; **1952–53:** 279, 308 [3]
    Berlin assignment, release from, **1949:** 92
    Distinguished Service Medal award, **1949:** 99
    News conference remarks on, **1945:** 118 [1], 181
        [2]
Clayton Act, **1950:** 2, 166, 319; **1951:** 254, 279
    Amendment, proposed, **1947:** 4 (p. 35)

Clayton, William L., **1946:** 186 [2]; **1947:** 31 [17], 39, 182 [7]; **1948:** 55 [14]
Clements, Earle C., **1948:** 218 [14], 220; **1952–53:** 3
Cleveland, Grover, **1947:** 6 [6], 117; **1948:** 101, 183 [5], 223, 228 [3], 231 [10], 233 [2, 4], 248; **1950:** 82, 94, 110 [1]; **1951:** 8, 56 [25], 108 [11]; **1952–53:** 45, 136 [19], 282 [1], 321 [3]
Cleveland, Miss., **1951:** 209 [13]
Cleveland, Ohio
    Campaign address, **1948:** 258; **1952–53:** 287
    Mayor Thomas A. Burke, **1948:** 258; **1949:** 240 [5]; **1952–53:** 287n.
Clifford, Clark M., **1946:** 84 [14], 129 [18], 143 [1]; **1949:** 267 [11], 269 [1]; **1950:** 23 [1], 24; **1951:** 56 [24]
Clinch River, **1945:** 165
Cline, John W., **1952–53:** 2 [3]
Clinical Center, National Institutes of Health, dedication, **1951:** 135
Clinton, Mass., campaign remarks, **1952–53:** 292 [11]
Clock for White House, acceptance, **1952–53:** 99
Clothing
    Consumer buying, **1947:** 4 (p. 23)
    Industry, **1947:** 152
    Overseas relief, **1946:** 4
    Prices, **1946:** 152, 153, 179; **1947:** 4 (p. 15), 76, 214, 224, 232 [6], 242; **1948:** 21 [12]
    Production, **1946:** 2, 72 [2]
    Relief supplies, **1947:** 56, 229
    Shortage in Europe, **1947:** 238
Clothing Collection, United National
    Letter to Henry J. Kaiser, **1945:** 144
    Statement, **1945:** 74
Clothing Workers, Amalgamated, **1948:** 261 [11]; **1951:** 239ftn. (p. 544)
Coal, **1947:** 217; **1948:** 1, 5 (p. 47), 8 (pp. 67, 70, 78–80), 200 [3], 218 [2]
    Conservation, **1947:** 231
    European production, **1947:** 238
    Exports, **1946:** 23, 264; **1947:** 29, 47, 228
    Imports by China, **1948:** 31
    Liquid fuel derivatives, **1949:** 8 (p. 84), 226 [6]
    Prices, **1946:** 252n.; **1947:** 142, 145 [13, 24], 152
    Shortage in Cleveland, Ohio, **1949:** 240 [5]
    Stockpile, **1947:** 127 [15]
    Supplies in Midwest, **1946:** 228
    U.S. shipments for Europe, **1945:** 135
Coal Association, National, **1947:** 145 [13]
Coal Association, Retail, St. Louis, Mo., **1950:** 3 [4]
Coal industry.
    See also Coal miners; Coal mines.
    Commission of inquiry, proposed, **1950:** 49, 50
    Emergency conservation measures, **1950:** 49
    Labor dispute, **1950:** 6, 11 [1], 16 [10, 17, 20], 23 [7, 16], 29 [19], 35, 38 [14], 44 [8, 16], 50, 202; **1952–53:** 341, 342 [7]

Coal industry — *continued*
    Labor dispute — *continued*
        Government seizure of mines, question of, **1950:** 34 [2], 46 [4, 9], 49, 50
        Injunction, **1950:** 35, 38 [14], 49
        Message to Congress, **1950:** 49
        Telegram to management and labor leaders, **1950:** 27
    Mine safety, **1952–53:** 18 (p. 94), 19, 206
    News conference remarks, **1950:** 11 [1], 16 [10, 17, 20], 23 [7, 16], 29 [19], 34 [2], 38 [14], 44 [8, 16], 46 [4, 9], 137 [1]
    Prices, **1952–53:** 341
    Research, **1952–53:** 305
    Supplies above ground, **1952–53:** 341
    Unemployment, **1952–53:** 305
    Wages in, **1952–53:** 342 [7]
    Workweek, **1950:** 29 [19]
Coal Mine Safety Act, **1952–53:** 367 (p. 1151)
Coal miners, **1948:** 200 [3]
    See also Coal industry.
    Labor disputes, **1948:** 55 [9], 66, 71 [5], 77 [4], 171, 198
    Labor movement, **1948:** 248
    Occupational diseases, prevention, **1948:** 248
    Retirement trust fund, **1948:** 171
    Wages, **1948:** 66, 171, 223
Coal mines.
    See also Coal industry.
    Chinese, **1946:** 265
    Federal operation, **1947:** 6 [16]
    Government operation, **1946:** 95 [20, 23], 110 [11, 14], 119 [24], 141 [16], 252
    Labor contracts, **1946:** 126 [25], 237 [5], 252, 262 [21]; **1947:** 121, 142, 152; **1949:** 118 [13, 20], 155 [15], 214 [8], 226 [5], 231 [1, 14, 20], 236 [2], 240 [5], 253 [12, 14], 260 [1, 6, 9, 11]
    Seizure by Government, question of, **1949:** 231 [1], 236 [2]
    Wages, **1947:** 142, 152
    Workweek, 3-day, question of, **1949:** 155 [14], 269 [10, 12]
Coal Mines Administration, **1946:** 252
Coal Operators' Association, Bituminous, **1952–53:** 341
Coal Organization, European, **1947:** 29
Coal and steel community, European, proposed, **1950:** 137 [1], 281; **1952–53:** 5, 55, 151
Coal strikes, **1945:** 31 [8], 172 [6]; **1946:** 124, 228, 252; **1947:** 36 [11], 127 [5, 10, 15]
    News conference remarks, **1946:** 70 [18, 19], 72 [4, 6], 78 [13], 86 [12], 95 [15, 20, 23], 110 [3, 5, 7, 11, 14, 20], 119 [17, 24, 27], 163 [2], 237 [5, 16], 242 [5, 8], 257 [3, 4]
    Statement, **1946:** 114
Coal Wage Agreement of 1947, National Bituminous, **1948:** 171

Coast and Geodetic Survey, **1947:** 7 (p. 77), 35; **1950:** 76; **1952–53:** 266 [9, 10]

Coast Guard, **1945:** 34, 45, 215; **1946:** 66ftn. (p. 164), 118, 126 [15], 129 [13], 135, 194; **1947:** 7 (p. 85), 181 (p. 402); **1948:** 5 (p. 49), 62, 105; **1949:** 8 (p. 87); **1950:** 8 [46], 9 (p. 93), 76; **1952–53:** 18 (pp. 81, 83), 255

Appropriations, **1947:** 11

Collier Trophy, joint award to, **1951:** 301

Construction and repair contracts, **1947:** 35

Demobilization, **1946:** 8, 18 (p. 47)

Ports, antisabotage mission, **1951:** 13 (p. 83)

Private boats, purchase for, **1947:** 35

Reservists, retirement benefits, **1948:** 145

Transfer to Treasury, proposed, **1945:** 157 [14], 208 [15]

Transfer of vessels, etc., to War or Navy Departments, **1947:** 35

Coast Guard Academy, United States, **1948:** 261 [6]; **1952–53:** 255

Cobalt, shortage, **1950:** 124 [7]

Cobb, John B., **1950:** 161 [2]

Cobo, Albert E., **1951:** 174

Cochran, H. Merle, **1949:** 272

Cochran, John, **1948:** 90; **1950:** 203 [3]

Cochran, Robert LeRoy, **1950:** 111

Cochrane, Vice Adm. Edward L., **1947:** 55

Cochrane, Mrs. Elizabeth, letter, **1952–53:** 167

Cocke, Erle, Jr., **1951:** 191n.

Coconut oil, **1946:** 29
Shortage, **1947:** 18

Coconuts, duty on, **1947:** 35

Code of Military Justice, Uniform, **1950:** 108

Coffelt, Pvt. Leslie, **1950:** 278ftn. (p. 695)
Dedication of memorial plaque, **1952–53:** 134

Coffey, Robert L., Jr., **1948:** 251

Cohans, vaudeville performers, **1949:** 205 [6]

Cohen, Benjamin V., **1950:** 219; **1951:** 266n.

Cohen, I. T., **1951:** 300 [23]

Coinage of commemorative 50-cent pieces, approval, **1946:** 196

Coins, commemorative, **1947:** 162; **1948:** 90

Coke, priorities, allocations, and inventory control, **1948:** 1

Colby (Pfc. Robert A.) case, **1945:** 118 [7]

Cold war, **1949:** 200 [8, 16], 234 [2], 249; **1950:** 38ftn. (p. 162), 80 [4], 105 [9], 138; **1951:** 227 [2]

Cole, Repr. Albert M., **1950:** 217 [17]

Cole, David L., **1950:** 27n.

Coleman, John A., **1948:** 53n.

Collazo, Oscar, **1950:** 278ftn. (p. 695)

Collective bargaining, **1945:** 104, 128, 180, 184, 204, 206; **1946:** 2, 9, 12, 15 [6], 16, 18 (pp. 40, 51, 52), 24, 35, 53 [2], 95 [10], 131, 213, 232, 249, 252; **1947:** 2 (pp. 4, 5), 7 (p. 88), 19 [1], 120, 121, 152; **1948:** 2, 8 (p. 90), 110 [17], 140, 159, 171, 179, 182, 183 [5, 7],

Collective bargaining — *continued*
184, 218 [7], 219, 222 [7], 223, 227 [9], 228 [4], 232, 235 [4], 236, 240 [3], 247, 248, 252, 255, 261 [15], 264 [2], 267 [3], 268; **1949:** 2, 8 (p. 90), 39, 151, 152, 209, 213, 234 [3], 240 [15]; **1950:** 2, 27, 43, 49, 128, 281
See also Labor.
News conference remarks, **1945:** 157 [5], 181 [11]

Collective security, **1947:** 2 (pp. 11, 12), 21, 51, 188, 197, 198, 207, 214, 220, 224, 230, 234

Collectivism, **1949:** 179 [5]

College textbooks, investigation by Un-American Activities Committee, **1949:** 122 [8]

Colleges and universities, **1946:** 75 [26]; **1947:** 169; **1948:** 8 (p. 86)
Agricultural, **1950:** 110 [3]
Community, **1950:** 9 (p. 84)
Federal aid, **1948:** 186; **1950:** 8 [34], 9 (pp. 83, 84); **1952–53:** 18 (pp. 102–103), 231
Football, intercollegiate, proposed de-emphasis, **1951:** 188 [14]
Housing, **1947:** 7 (p. 69), 44
Loans, **1952–53:** 367 (p. 1154)
Land-grant, **1946:** 18 (p. 84)
Federal aid, **1952–53:** 367 (p. 1155)
Negroes, admission to, **1952–53:** 290
Norwich University, **1945:** 92
Role in public affairs, **1947:** 117
Scholarships, **1950:** 8 [34]
Proposed, **1952–53:** 231
Students, Federal aid, **1951:** 13 (p. 96)
University of California, **1945:** 31 [7]; **1948:** 84 [5], 128 [4], 129; **1951:** 130; **1952–53:** 261, 262
University of Iowa, **1948:** 194 [3]
University of Kansas City, **1945:** 68
University of Missouri, **1950:** 159, 160 [1]
University of North Carolina, **1950:** 80 [8], 81
University of Southern Illinois, address, **1948:** 219
University of Utah, **1948:** 200 [5]
University of Virginia, **1948:** 77 [13]
University of Wisconsin, **1948:** 238
University of Wyoming, **1950:** 119

Collet, John C., **1946:** 37 [15] and ftn. (p. 123); **1947:** 141 [4], 174 [1, 3]

Collier Trophy, **1952–53:** 351n.
Presentation, **1951:** 301

Collier's Congressional Awards, presentation, **1946:** 80

Collier's Congressional Awards Committee, **1946:** 60

Colliers' magazine, **1951:** 70ftn. (p. 216)

Collingwood, Charles, **1951:** 2 [17]

Collins, Gen. J. Lawton, **1949:** 234 [1]; **1950:** 194, 226, 230 [7], 303; **1951:** 93n., 148; **1952–53:** 128, 320

Collyer, John L., **1947:** 122

Colombia, South America, **1946:** 129 [2]; **1948:** 55 [13]; **1951:** 130n.
  Industrialists from, remarks to, **1951:** 267
  Korean war, participation, **1950:** 296
  Lend-lease settlement, **1951:** 244
  Ospina Perez, Mariano, **1950:** 181 [4]
  President's visit, question of, **1947:** 221 [4]
Colombo plan, aid to less developed Asian countries, **1951:** 114
Colonies, American, **1947:** 90 [1], 138
Colonies, former Italian, U.S. policy on, **1948:** 185 [6, 11], 278 [14, 41]
Colorado, **1947:** 104
  Campaign remarks, **1948:** 198 [1–7], 199, 200 [1]; **1952–53:** 280 [4, 6], 282, 283
  Candidates for public office, **1948:** 198 [4–7], 200 [1]; **1952–53:** 280 [4–6], 282 [1–4, 7, 8]
  Economic progress, **1952–53:** 280 [4], 282 [4, 6, 8]
  Knous, Gov. William Lee, **1948:** 118 [7], 198 [4, 5], 199; **1949:** 260 [14]
  Mineral deposits, **1952–53:** 282 [1]
  Oil production, **1952–53:** 280 [5]
  Power projects, **1950:** 116; **1952–53:** 280 [4, 6]
  Reclamation projects, **1948:** 201
  San Luis irrigation project, **1949:** 245
  Water rights, dispute between California and Arizona, **1950:** 34 [17]
Colorado-Big Thompson irrigation project, **1948:** 199
Colorado-Big Thompson reclamation project, **1949:** 232
Colorado-Kansas negotiations for division of Arkansas River waters, **1945:** 194
Colorado River Basin, **1950:** 121 [13], 125
  Development, **1948:** 207, 212 [2]
Colorado River
  Development, **1945:** 165
  Storage project, **1952–53:** 280 [4, 6]
Colorado Springs, Colo., campaign remarks, **1952–53:** 283
Colson, Brig. Gen. Charles F., **1952–53:** 127ftn. (p. 337)
Colton, Calif., campaign remarks, **1948:** 206 [3]
Columbia, Mo., **1950:** 160 [1], 169 [5]
Columbia Broadcasting System, **1947:** 48n.
Columbia Falls, Mont., campaign remarks, **1952–53:** 270 [1]
Columbia River, **1946:** 18 (p. 60), 86 [16]; **1947:** 243 [18]
Columbia River Basin, **1948:** 119, 201, 214 [7]; **1949:** 8 (p. 83), 22 [1]; **1950:** 121 [11, 13], 129 [1], 140, 217 [1]
  Power projects, **1951:** 13 (p. 85, 86)
  Water resources and power development, **1952–53:** 97, 271, 274 [1], 294, 388
Columbia River development, **1945:** 128, 155, 164 [8], 165

Columbia Scholastic Press Association, **1952–53:** 63
Columbia University, **1947:** 226 [3]; **1950:** 80ftn. (p. 233); **1952–53:** 283, 284 [2], 289 [6]
Columbia Valley Administration, proposed, **1949:** 40 [9], 77, 78 [14], 106, 144 [19]; **1950:** 2, 6, 9 (p. 90), 121 [4, 8, 13], 124 [1], 125; **1951:** 183
  Power project, **1950:** 3 [9]
Columbia Valley Authority, **1945:** 64 [5]; **1946:** 6 [7]
Columbus, Christopher, **1952–53:** 291
Columbus, Ohio, **1946:** 52; **1948:** 71 [2]
  Campaign remarks, **1948:** 138 [8]
  Mayor James Rhodes, **1948:** 138 [8]
Columbus Day, **1949:** 230
Columnists, comments on, **1948:** 278 [20, 27, 38, 42]; **1951:** 113 [17]
Colvin, Howard T., **1947:** 182 [4]
Colyer, Air Marshal Douglas, Legion of Merit, citation, **1945:** 199
Combined Chiefs of Staff, U.S.-U.K., **1945:** 197, 198; **1946:** 7, 53 [5], 216 [16, 18], 272
Combined Civil Affairs Committee, **1945:** 198
Combined Displaced Persons Executive, **1945:** 152
Combined Food Board, **1945:** 107ftn. (p. 234), 209; **1946:** 108, 119 [16], 149
Combined Production and Resources Board, **1945:** 107ftn. (p. 234), 198, 209
Combined Raw Materials Board, **1945:** 107ftn. (p. 234), 209
Comintern, **1947:** 205 [7]
Commager, Henry Steele, **1951:** 193ftn. (p. 467)
Commemorative occasions.
  See Addresses or remarks on commemorative or dedicatory occasions.
Commerce, Department of, **1945:** 87, 228n.; **1946:** 17 [30], 18 (pp. 49, 56, 57, 86), 118, 192 [8], 197, 266 [4]; **1947:** 4 (p. 35), 7 (pp. 59, 77, 85, 86, 87), 18, 39, 53, 180 [12], 181 (p. 399), 186, 210 [4], 241; **1948:** 5 (pp. 42, 50, 52), 37, 42, 55 [2], 83, 84 [17]; **1949:** 8 (p. 88); **1950:** 106, 112, 114, 164; **1952–53:** 225, 226
  Foreign assistance functions, **1949:** 22 [3]
  Maritime functions, **1950:** 76
    War-risk insurance, **1950:** 236
  Materials controls, administration of, **1952–53:** 18 (p. 79)
  News conference remarks, **1950:** 152 [3], 217 [15, 18, 20]
  Panama Canal, functions, **1950:** 28
  Personal income estimates, **1951:** 12 [8]
  Program review, **1950:** 196
  Remington (William W.) case, **1950:** 152 [3]
    Clearance of disloyalty charges, **1949:** 32 [14]
  Reorganization, **1949:** 127, 134; **1950:** 53, 54, 59; **1951:** 226

Commerce, Department of — *continued*
RFC, question of transfer to, **1951:** 33 [2]
Small business
Assistance to, **1952–53:** 15, 18
Services for, **1950:** 118
Transportation, aid and regulatory functions,
1952–53: 18 (pp. 82–84)
Commerce, Secretary of (W. Averell Harriman),
1947: 122, 123, 124, 139n., 143, 148, 202,
212, 217, 219; **1948:** 1, 23, 37
See also Harriman, W. Averell.
Letter, **1947:** 53
News Conference remarks on, **1947:** 191 [4], 218
[7], 221 [1]
Report on natural resources, **1947:** 210 [5]
Resignation, **1948:** 83
Commerce, Secretary of (Charles W. Sawyer),
1948: 151, 170 [1]; **1949:** 266; **1950:** 9 (pp.
92, 97), 210; **1952–53:** 82, 98 [25], 115 [16],
118, 122, 135 [19], 155n., 177, 225
See also Sawyer, Charles W.
Campaign remarks on, **1952–53:** 292 [11]
Depressed areas, investigation of, **1949:** 155 [1]
Economic aid to Europe, proposal to end, **1952–
53:** 353 [13]
Letter on report of Water Resources Policy
Commission, **1951:** 55
Letters, **1950:** 196, 265; **1952–53:** 93, 226, 257
Maritime tax benefits study, **1952–53:** 211
Memorandum, **1949:** 149n.; **1950:** 259
News conference remarks on, **1949:** 155 [1], 161
[12], 171 [11], 267 [3]; **1950:** 152 [3], 217
[18]
RFC Loan Policy Board, ex-officio membership,
1951: 39
Resignation, **1952–53:** 374
Steel industry, question of control procedures,
1952–53: 88 [13]
Commerce, Secretary of (Henry A. Wallace), **1946:**
27 [3], 49, 66 [7], 216 [5, 13], 219
See also Wallace, Henry A.
Letter, **1945:** 11
Commercial Company, U.S., **1947:** 7 (p. 67), 181
(p. 400)
Commercial Policy, U.S.-U.K., Joint Statement on,
1946: 25
Commercial Standards, Division of, **1946:** 118
Commercial Studies, U.S.-Argentine Joint Com-
mission, **1949:** 113 [5]
Commercy, France, **1949:** 223
Commission on Civil Rights, proposed, **1948:** 20;
1950: 8 [41], 9 (p. 102)
Commission to the Council of National Defense,
Advisory, **1945:** 55
Commission of Fine Arts, **1946:** 21 [2]
Commission on the Health Needs of the Nation,
1951: 307; **1952–53:** 2 [3], 5, 15, 249, 278,
284 [5], 333, 352, 353 [1], 367 (p. 1158)

Commission on Higher Education, National, **1946:**
166, 214, 262 [2]
Commission on Immigration and Naturalization,
1952–53: 367 (p. 1163)
Commission on Internal Security and Individual
Rights, **1951:** 20, 35, 104, 156, 278
Criticism by Sen. Ferguson, **1951:** 22 [6]
Letter, **1951:** 278
News conference remarks on, **1951:** 22 [2, 4, 14],
37 [12], 108 [6]
Commission on labor-management relations, pro-
posed, **1947:** 2 (p. 5)
Commission on Labor Relations in Atomic Energy
Installations, President's, **1949:** 81
Commission on Migratory Labor, **1951:** 75; **1952–
53:** 18 (94, 102), 367 (p. 1151)
Commission on the Organization of the Executive
Branch, **1947:** 145 [1], 191 [2], 195; **1948:**
62, 135, 274 [1], 278 [10], 285 [6]; **1949:** 12,
25, 47, 49n., 50, 127–134, 137, 140, 158,
167, 177, 181, 242; **1950:** 1, 9 (pp. 52, 101),
28, 53, 54, 68, 69, 74, 76, 97 [3], 112–115,
149, 150; **1951:** 104n., 175, 226, 251 [4];
1952–53: 2 [13], 11, 18 (p. 116), 59, 84, 98
[6, 34], 107ftn. (p. 293), 292 [11], 366, 377
[30]
News conference remarks, **1949:** 93 [3], 122 [21]
Reports, **1949:** 94, 111
Commission on Renovation of the Executive Man-
sion, **1949:** 249
Commission to Superintend Construction of White
House, **1949:** 89 [1]
Commission on Universal Training, President's
Advisory, **1946:** 268; **1947:** 2 (p. 12), 7 (p.
63); **1948:** 86
Commissioner of Education, appointment and stat-
utory authority, **1950:** 150
Commissioner of Education (Earl James
McGrath), **1950:** 47
Commissioner of Social Security, appointment and
statutory authority, **1950:** 150
Commissions, regulatory, **1950:** 9 (pp. 95, 96)
Committee on Atomic Energy, report, **1946:** 136
[6], 141 [3]
Committee to Award Medals of Merit to Civilians,
1945: 137 [4]
See also Medal of Merit Board.
Committee on Civil Rights, President's, **1947:** 2 (p.
9); **1948:** 2, 20, 265
Committee for Constitutional Government, **1952–
53:** 294
Committee on Deferment of Government Em-
ployees, Review, report, letter, **1945:** 183
Committee for Economic Development, **1946:** 72
[3]; **1949:** 269 [20]; **1950:** 11 [10]
Committee on Equality of Treatment and Opportunity in the Armed Forces, President's,
1948: 265

Committee of European Economic Cooperation, news conference remarks, **1947:** 191 [4, 5]
Paris meeting, **1947:** 217, 219, 238
Committee on Export Transportation, Interagency, **1946:** 264
Committee on Fair Employment Practice, **1945:** 128; **1946:** 2, 154; **1950:** 8 [41]
Houston, Charles H., resignation, **1945:** 208 [18]
Letter to Repr. Sabath re, **1945:** 51
News conference remarks, **1945:** 60 [11], 137 [7]
Committee for Financing Foreign Trade, **1946:** 142
Committee on Foreign Economic Policy, Executive, **1946:** 71
Committee on Government Contract Compliance, **1951:** 299; **1952–53:** 7 [1, 6], 18 (p. 94), 26 [1], 169
Committee of Inquiry, Anglo-American (Palestine commission), **1945:** 187
See also Anglo-American Committee of Inquiry.
Members, question re, **1945:** 193 [6], 202 [4, 8], 208 [4]
Statement, **1945:** 210
Committee on the Integration of the Medical Services of the Government, President's, **1946:** 139
Committee on National Employ the Physically Handicapped Week, President's **1949:** 197; **1950:** 208
Committee on Palestine and Related Problems, Cabinet, **1946:** 132, 136 [14], 186ftn. (p. 367), 227
Committee on Racial Democracy, **1947:** 14 [23]
Committee on Refugees, Intergovernmental, **1945:** 152, 188
Committee on Religion and Welfare in the Armed Forces, President's, **1949:** 73; **1950:** 32; **1951:** 17, 100
Committee on Retirement Policy for Federal Personnel, **1952–53:** 367 (p. 1163)
Committee on Service to the Armed Forces and Veterans, **1950:** 95
Committee for United Nations Day, National Citizens, **1949:** 212; **1950:** 239
Committee on World Food Programs, Cabinet, **1947:** 191 [3, 5, 8]; **1948:** 1
Commodities
Conservation, **1947:** 242
Speculation in, **1947:** 232 [3], 236 [4], 243 [11]
Commodity Credit Corporation, **1945:** 128; **1946:** 18 (pp. 67, 80), 57, 79, 94, 118; **1947:** 7 (pp. 78, 80, 81, 95), 64, 128, 181, 195, 209 [15]; **1948:** 5 (pp. 25, 43, 57), 155, 195, 204 [2], 206 [3], 217, 218 [7, 8], 228 [12], 233 [1, 4], 234, 237 [4, 7], 240 [5, 6], 246, 259 [5], 267 [1, 3], 268; **1949:** 2, 7 [34], 8 (p. 79); **1950:** 9 (pp. 55, 86, 87), 114, 191 [11], 279; **1951:** 13 (pp. 87, 90); **1952–53:** 18 (p. 91), 31 [18], 231, 266 [5, 7], 267, 268 [2], 285, 312, 367 (p. 1148)

Commodity Exchange Authority, **1950:** 9 (p. 88); **1951:** 13 (p. 90)
Commodity exchanges, **1948:** 1, 5 (p. 52), 8 (pp. 65, 74), 167; **1949:** 2, 5
Control of trading margins, **1952–53:** 15
Investigation and regulation, **1947:** 209, [11, 12, 16], 226 [13, 15]; **1951:** 11, 91, 167
Commodity Groups, International, **1951:** 25
Communicable diseases, conquest of, **1945:** 192
Communications, **1946:** 18 (pp. 46, 81); **1947:** 7 (pp. 58, 84, 86); **1948:** 5 (p. 50), 175, 280; **1949:** 8 (pp. 47, 84–88); **1950:** 40, 207; **1951:** 13 (pp. 64, 80–84)
Broadcasting facilities, construction, **1951:** 13 (p. 75)
Communist media, proposed identification requirement, **1950:** 254
Excise taxes on, **1950:** 18
Expenditures for, **1952–53:** 231, 367 (pp. 1142, 1144)
Government control, question of, **1952–53:** 107 [1, 8, 9]
Industry, assistance to, **1952–53:** 18 (pp. 81–84)
Information programs abroad, **1950:** 127 [5]
Facilities for, **1952–53:** 18 (p. 77)
International, **1950:** 92
Interstate facilities, prohibition of use to transmit gambling information, **1951:** 63 [1]
Less developed areas, **1950:** 177
Radio and television frequency allocation, **1950:** 34 [8], 40
Radio waveband allocation, agreement with Mexico, **1949:** 84 [8]
Role in democratic society, **1950:** 92
Telecommunications convention, international, **1948:** 29
Telephone industry, labor dispute, **1950:** 43
Television coverage of Congressional hearings, question of, **1952–53:** 49 [7]
Communications Act (1934), **1947:** 35
Communications Commission, Federal.
See Federal Communications Commission.
Communications Policy Board, President's, **1950:** 40n.
Communications Workers of America, **1950:** 43
Communism, **1947:** 196, 222; **1948:** 165, 205, 215, 241, 252, 266; **1950:** 78, 134, 177, 197
Administration measures against, **1952–53:** 297
Africa, **1952–53:** 81
Asia, **1951:** 90 [1]; **1952–53:** 12, 81
Atheistic character of, **1951:** 68
Bulgaria, **1951:** 253
Burma, **1951:** 96, 114
Campaign remarks, **1948:** 195, 231 [2], 254, 256, 257 [3], 261 [1, 6]; **1952–53:** 283
China, **1946:** 119 [10], 265, 266 [17]; **1949:** 84ftn. (p. 224), 171 [1, 12], 179 [22, 26], 234 [5]; **1950:** 232; **1952–53:** 232
Comments on, **1952–53:** 246 [1], 251, 261

Communism — *continued*
  Czechoslovakia, **1948:** 256
  Electoral defeat in Italy (1948), **1952–53:** 291
  Europe, **1950:** 303
    Reverses due to Marshall plan, **1951:** 4
  Expectation of capitalist collapse, **1952–53:** 291
  Free world defense against, **1952–53:** 317 [3]
  Front organizations, **1950:** 241
  Greece, **1950:** 90
  Hawaii, charges of influence in, **1949:** 144 [7]
  Hungary, **1949:** 30ftn. (p. 131)
  Infiltration of world trade union movement, **1950:** 177
  Labor organizations, **1948:** 252
  Labor unions, **1947:** 120
  News conference remarks, **1947:** 14 [6], 31 [11], 67 [10], 90 [1], 205 [7]; **1948:** 71 [2], 170 [4, 6], 181 [12, 14, 16], 283 [1], 285 [2, 19]; **1949:** 89 [18], 112 [2], 118 [22], 144 [7], 171 [1, 12], 179 [22, 26], 231 [9]; **1950:** 38 [2, 18], 97 [5], 105 [10, 15]
  North Korea, **1952–53:** 232
  Propaganda, **1950:** 92, 127 [5], 190, 207, 227, 231, 254, 340; **1952–53:** 145, 215, 217
  Refugees from, **1947:** 140; **1948:** 142
    Immigration to U.S., **1952–53:** 317 [7]
  Rumania, **1951:** 174
  Soviet Union, **1951:** 225
  Spain, **1946:** 86 [9]
  Suppression of civil rights by, **1950:** 94
  Sympathizers with, question of barring from teaching profession, **1949:** 118 [22]
  United States, **1952–53:** 251, 295 [8]
    Arrest of Party members, **1951:** 132 [14]
    Attempts to infiltrate Government, **1952–53:** 296, 362n.; **1951:** 227 [7]
    Defense against, **1950:** 94, 146ftn. (p. 439); **1951:** 191; **1952–53:** 296, 303 [2]
    Influence in Democratic Party, charges of, **1952–53:** 69
    Influence in Government, charges of, **1948:** 110 [20], 170 [4, 6], 181 [12, 14, 16], 260, 283 [1], 285 [2, 19]; **1950:** 38 [18], 97 [5], 105 [10], 279; **1952–1953:** 89 [2]
    Congressional investigation of, **1949:** 112 [2]
    Opposition to free trade union movement, **1951:** 279; **1952–53:** 251
    Predictions of U.S. depression, **1950:** 157
    President's attitude toward, **1950:** 38 [2]; **1952–53:** 39
    "Softness" toward, Republican charges of, **1952–53:** 300, 303 [2], 313 [4]
  Versus democracy, **1948:** 115, 184, 215, 257 [3], 261 [1]; **1949:** 19, 50, 51, 159, 184; **1950:** 92, 94, 116, 119, 121 [5], 127 [1, 5], 132, 157, 171, 177, 207, 220, 228, 232, 240, 269, 299, 317; **1951:** 18, 20; **1952–53:** 295 [8], 366, 378

Communist aggression and expansion, **1947:** 238; **1948:** 53, 61, 86, 260; **1949:** 19, 120, 195; **1950:** 2, 42, 92, 110 [1], 111, 119, 126, 127 [5], 159, 162, 185, 207, 220, 228, 232, 243, 255, 281; **1951:** 11, 13 (pp. 61, 62), 18, 20, 59, 78, 80, 96, 98, 107, 118 [1], 123, 138, 144, 167, 197, 199, 216, 256, 271, 278, 293; **1952–53:** 54, 57, 74, 101, 144, 170, 196, 215, 232, 242 [2], 266 [8], 268 [5], 274 [7], 275, 279, 280 [1], 282 [7], 288, 289 [2], 292 [4], 297, 313 [1–3], 314, 316, 317 [2], 321, 327, 347, 354, 366, 369
  Administration measures to halt, Republican opposition, **1952–53:** 218
  Asia, **1950:** 78, 92, 151, 162; **1951:** 4, 13 (pp. 61, 62, 73, 74), 34, 92, 96, 114, 216; **1952–53:** 5, 6, 12, 55, 81, 131, 295 [8], 307, 366, 367 (p. 1140)
  Burma, **1952–53:** 55
  China, **1948:** 31; **1952–53:** 354, 366
  Japan, **1952–53:** 354
  Korea, **1950:** 151, 172, 175, 177, 181, 184, 189, 193, 194, 201, 202, 204, 211, 223, 232, 243, 269, 271, 279, 282. 284, 291, 294, 296, 301, 303, 304; **1951:** 4, 6, 13 (p. 68), 22 [1], 25, 57, 91, 109, 114, 137, 138, 144, 170, 174, 199, 213, 293, 297; **1952–53:** 6, 12, 15, 17 [2], 18 (p. 64), 69, 81, 107 [2], 121, 131, 132, 135, 158, 196, 217, 251, 259, 266 [2, 11], 268 [5], 276, 279, 295 [8], 299, 305, 308, 313 [1, 3, 5], 315 [2, 4], 318, 319 [1], 321 [1, 4], 322, 345 [4], 349, 354, 366, 378
  India, **1952–53:** 144, 303 [2]
  Indochina, **1951:** 78; **1952–53:** 18 (p. 76), 49 [9], 55, 345 [4], 367 (p. 1140)
  Intelligence reports on, **1951:** 78
  Malaya, **1952–53:** 55
  Philippines, **1949:** 89 [18]; **1952–53:** 18 (p. 76), 55, 367 (p. 1140)
  Campaign remarks, **1952–53:** 282 [2], 317 [1, 6], 319 [6]
  Defense against, **1951:** 13 (pp. 68, 70–75), 96, 219; **1952–53:** 319 [1, 3], 366
  Europe, **1948:** 49 [4], 52, 129, 166 [2]; **1949:** 86, 162; **1950:** 151, 301; **1951:** 96, 114, 209 [13]
  Austria, **1952–53:** 69
  Balkans, **1950:** 92
  Czechoslovakia, **1950:** 92; **1952–53:** 47, 309
  Germany, **1952–53:** 354
    Berlin, **1949:** 162; **1950:** 92; **1952–53:** 69, 107 [2]
  Greece, **1947:** 56, 243 [14]; **1948:** 28, 52, 53, 61, 129, 188; **1949:** 162, 184, 261; **1950:** 90, 142; **1951:** 138; **1952–53:** 69, 107 [2], 303 [2], 303 [2], 354, 366, 378
  Hungary, **1947:** 107 [8]
  Italy, **1951:** 138; **1952–53:** 69, 288
    Trieste, **1952–53:** 107 [2]

Communist aggression — *continued*
  Europe — *continued*
    Yugoslavia, **1951:** 292; **1952–53:** 107 [2]
  Issue in election campaign, **1952–53:** 322
  Latin America, **1951:** 76
  Middle East, **1948:** 129
  Near East, **1951:** 4, 13 (pp. 73, 74), 96, 114
    Iran, **1948:** 202 [6]; **1949:** 162, 184; **1950:** 151,
      232; **1952–53:** 69, 107 [2, 11, 14, 16]
    Turkey, **1949:** 162, 184; **1951:** 138; **1952–53:**
      69, 107 [2], 303 [2], 354, 378
  News conference remarks, **1950:** 191 [5], 309 [1];
    1952–53: 345 [4]
  Point 4 program, role in combating, **1951:** 83
  Soviet, **1952–53:** 319 [6], 320, 332
  Western Hemisphere, **1948:** 77 [8]
Communist bloc, **1947:** 196; **1948:** 52, 53, 86, 266;
  1949: 200 [8, 16]; **1950:** 119, 138, 269;
  1951: 116, 174; **1952–53:** 366
  See also specific countries.
  Agreements with, comment on, **1950:** 143
  Campaign of truth in nations of, **1950:** 267;
    1951: 72
  Civil rights, suppression in, **1951:** 253
  Defectors from, asylum in U.S., **1950:** 254
  Foreign trade of, **1952–53:** 105, 180, 217, 358
  Greek children, detention in, **1950:** 7, 90, 261
  Internal tension and unrest in, **1951:** 96; **1952–
    53:** 5
  Military strength, **1950:** 269, 299; **1951:** 54
  Peaceful liberation, question of, **1952–53:** 238 [6,
    16]
  Refugees and escapees from, **1951:** 96; **1952–53:**
    65, 164, 207, 288
  Restrictions on trade with, **1951:** 117, 118 [14]
  Ships from, refusal of longshoremen to unload,
    1950: 230 [4]
  Strategic materials, exports to, **1950:** 230ftn. (p.
    607), 252
  Uprisings in, U.S. position on, **1952–53:** 88
  U.S. information program in, **1952–53:** 18 (p. 77)
  U.S. relief program, **1952–53:** 288
  Western representatives, exclusion from, **1950:**
    162
  Yugoslavia, split from, **1950:** 293
Communist International, **1947:** 205 [7]
Communist Party, United States, **1948:** 266
  Indicted members, plans to prosecute, **1949:** 45
    [20]
  Front organizations, identification criteria, **1950:**
    254
  Leaders, conviction of, **1950:** 46 [11], 94, 207,
    254, 279
  Members in Government, alleged, **1949:** 32 [14]
    Testimony on, **1948:** 170ftns. (pp. 432, 433)
  Membership in, charges against William W.
    Remington, **1950:** 152ftn. (p. 450)

Communist Party, U.S. — *continued*
  News conference remarks, **1948:** 110 [12], 163
    [19], 170 [6], 283 [1]
  Outlawing, proposed, **1947:** 62 [20]; **1948:** 115
  Polling strength in U.S. elections, **1948:** 215, 260;
    1950: 207
  Stand in event of Soviet attack, **1949:** 45 [14, 16,
    20]
  U.S. leaders, trial of, **1948:** 163 [19], 170 [6], 215,
    283 [1]
Community Chest campaigns, **1945:** 154; **1946:**
  225; **1947:** 193; **1948:** 221; **1949:** 34, 221;
  1950: 262; **1951:** 3, 242; **1952–53:** 264, 280
  [4]
Community development, **1947:** (p. 74), 35, 102;
  1948: 5 (pp. 25, 38, 40), 175; **1950:** 6, 9
  (pp. 49, 81), 53, 69, 72; **1951:** 11, 13 (pp.
  64, 79, 90–94), 285; **1952–53:** 18 (pp.
  95–100)
  Defense, **1952–53:** 18 (pp. 97, 106), 367 (p. 1152)
  Expenditures for, **1952–53:** 231, 367 (pp. 1152–
    1154)
  Federal aid, **1952–53:** 18 (p. 96)
Community health services and facilities, **1948:** 146
Community property taxes, **1948:** 9 [2]
Community War Fund campaign
  Address, **1945:** 154
  National Capital area, memorandum, **1945:** 171
Compact, interstate, oil and gas conservation,
  1947: 104
Compensation Act, Federal Employees', **1950:** 74
Competition, business, **1946:** 18 (pp. 56, 57)
Compton, Colonel, **1949:** 223
Compton, Dr. Karl T., **1946:** 268n.; **1948:** 191n.;
  1952–53: 131
Compton, Wilson, **1952–53:** 54n.
Comptroller of the Currency, reorganization of
  functions, **1950:** 149
Comptroller General of the United States (Lindsay
  C. Warren), **1949:** 174; **1950:** 9 (p. 51);
  1951: 221; **1952–53:** 177
Conant, James B., **1946:** 43 [3], 262 [1]; **1951:** 89
Concannon, David, **1948:** 261 [1]
Conciliation and Mediation Service, Federal, **1947:**
  20, 120, 174 [1], 181 (p. 403), 182 [4], 221
  [6], 236 [3]; **1948:** 72, 88 [3], 252, 259 [1, 2]
Conciliation Service, United States, **1945:** 104, 202
  [3], 204; **1946:** 18 (p. 50), 131; **1948:** 134,
  135, 232
Condon, Edward U. (Director, Bureau of Stan-
  dards), **1948:** 84 [18], 97 [9]; **1949:** 122 [22]
CONELRAD (Control of Electromagnetic Radi-
  ation), **1952–53:** 344n.
Conference on Children and Youth, White House,
  1949: 198, 204; **1950:** 5, 299
Conference on Community Responsibility to
  Peacetime Servicemen and Women, President's, **1949:** 110

Conference on Emergency Problems in Higher Education, **1946:** 162
Conference on Industrial Safety, President's, **1949:** 55; **1950:** 155; **1952–53:** 150
Conference on Law Enforcement Problems, Attorney General's, **1950:** 11 [3], 37
Conference on Problems of War and Peace (1945), **1947:** 51
Conference of State School Lunch Officals, National, **1946:** 235n.
Conference of U.S. Attorneys, **1951:** 115
Conflict-of-interest legislation
  Proposed, **1952–53:** 258 [13]
  Proposed exemptions, **1951:** 104, 237
Conflicts of interests in Federal Government, **1947:** 168
Conger, Dr. John, **1950:** 110 [1]
Congress, **1947:** (pp. 68, 80), 212, 219; **1948:** 15 [6, 11], 19, 119, 150 [4], 189, 245, 270, 278 [5], 288 [2, 12]; **1949:** 15; **1950:** 272
  See also Legislative branch.
  Address before joint session, **1945:** 2
  Address by Gen. MacArthur, **1951:** 79, 85 [2]
  Address before Senate, **1945:** 69
  Adjournment, **1947:** 127 [11, 13], 141 [14]; **1949:** 112 [8, 10, 12], 179 [16], 192 [23], 214 [7], 231 [3], 234, 235; **1952–53:** 149 [11, 15]
  Appropriation bills, **1949:** 112 [13], 179 [27], 182 [4]
  Aviation problems, study of, **1947:** 161
  Budget, anticipated action on, **1951:** 28, 33 [6]
  Budget reduction by, question of, **1952–53:** 17 [23]
  Cloture rule, **1949:** 45 [18, 21]
    Views of Gov. Stevenson, **1952–53:** 221 [14]
  Committee sessions, question of television coverage, **1952–53:** 49 [7]
  Conflict-of-interest legislation.
    See main heading, Conflict-of-interest legislaton.
  Congressional districts, reapportionment, **1951:** 5
  Copper import tax, action on, **1950:** 152 [4]
  Dispatch of troops abroad, consultations on, **1951:** 2 [4, 6, 7, 18], 7 [5, 7, 9], 16 [15], 49 [17], 56 [15], 70 [1], 71
  Economic policy, coordination, **1952–53:** 376
  Economies effected by, **1947:** 174 [2]
  Elections.
    See main heading, Elections; Election campaigns.
  Executive information, question of disclosure to, **1950:** 79, 82, 94
  Executive reorganization plans, action on, **1950:** 97 [3], 137 [2, 17], 146 [7], 149, 150
  50th anniversary of Cuban independence, address, **1948:** 81
  Filibustering in, **1947:** 232 [12]

Congress — *continued*
  Government real estate transactions, action on veto of bill respecting, **1951:** 108 [1]
  House of Representatives
    Churchill, Winston S., request for information on Presidential talks with, **1952–53:** 44 [1, 13]
    Defeat of Korean aid bill, **1950:** 17
    Impeachment of President, rumors of, **1952–53:** 107 [3]
    Pay of members, **1952–53:** 207
    Proposed change in rules, **1950:** 16 [7]
    Reorganization bill, adverse vote, **1951:** 56 [1, 3, 8]
    Rules Committee, proposed changes in, **1951:** 2 [1]
  Information, privileged, availability to, **1948:** 97 [9, 10, 13]
  Information on food crisis, availability to, **1947:** 191 [14]
  Investigations by, **1947:** 14 [3, 21], 77; **1948:** 170 [4], 178 [15], 257 [5]
    Antitrust laws, **1949:** 149
    Atomic energy program, **1949:** 118 [6]
    Communist influence in Government, **1948:** 283 [1], 285 [2]; **1949:** 112 [2]; **1951:** 227 [7]
    Condon, Edward U., **1948:** 84 [18], 97 [9]
    Crime, **1950:** 152 [9], 168; **1951:** 49 [8], 63 [1, 4], 95 [3, 5], 115
    Defense program, World War II.
    See Truman Committee.
    Ethical standards, **1951:** 227 [10]
    "Five percenters," activities of, **1949:** 161 [5], 231 [21]; **1950:** 16ftn. (p. 119)
    Government employees, loyalty, **1950:** 44 [6, 9], 46 [11], 97 [5]; **1951:** 22 [14], 295 [12], 300 [21]; **1952–53:** 5, 26 [5, 24], 377 [24]
    Holding companies, public utility, **1950:** 124 [4]
    John Carter Vincent loyalty case, **1952–53:** 362n.
    Katyn Forest massacre, **1952–53:** 317 [7]
    Korean war, conduct of, **1951:** 90 [5, 7, 16], 95 [2, 4, 6], 101 [4], 113 [12]; **1952–53:** 345 [1]
    Lobbying, proposed, **1948:** 277, 278 [22], 285 [14, 19]
    Rearmament program, **1950:** 206 [5]
    Reconstruction Finance Corporation, **1950:** 97 [4]; **1951:** 33 [2, 12], 49 [4, 11], 56 [11, 17, 24], 63 [11, 13]
    Textbooks, school and college, **1949:** 122 [8]
    Un-American activities, **1951:** 22 [11]
    Watch imports, **1949:** 32 [1]
    Wiretapping, **1950:** 217 [12]
    World War II defense program (Truman Committee).
    See Truman Committee.

Congress — *continued*
  Leaders, conference with, **1947:** 46 [11], 191 [4], 195
  Legislative record, **1949:** 200 [5, 13], 202, 203, 219, 220, 231 [16], 234 [3, 9], 235, 236 [13], 252, 267 [3]; **1950:** 39, 110 [2, 7], 116, 121 [11], 134, 137 [4, 6], 253 [11], 279; **1951:** 113 [14], 118 [12]; **1952–53:** 218, 241, 242 [3, 5, 6], 266 [4, 7, 13], 267, 268 [2], 280 [1, 3], 288, 289 [1], 297, 298 [13], 303 [9], 306 [5], 308 [3], 319 [3, 5]
  Campaign remarks, **1948:** 114 [3], 117, 120 [2, 3], 121, 122 [2, 4], 124 [1, 4, 5], 125, 126 [1, 3, 4], 128 [1, 2], 134, 136 [3, 5], 137 [3], 138 [2–8], 139 [1–3], 160, 183 [1, 2, 5, 6], 184, 194 [1–4, 6, 10–13], 195, 198 [3–7], 199, 200 [1, 3, 5, 9], 201, 202 [1, 2, 4, 6], 203, 204 [2, 3, 6, 7], 205, 206 [1–3], 207, 208 [2, 5–8], 211, 212 [2, 3, 5–7, 9, 10], 213, 214 [1, 3–7, 9], 215, 216 [1–7, 11, 12, 15], 217, 218 [3, 7, 8, 10, 11, 14], 220, 222 [2, 5, 9, 10], 225 [1, 3], 226, 227 [1, 4–7, 9], 228 [2–4, 6–8, 11–13], 229, 231 [1–5, 7–10], 232, 233 [2, 4–6], 234, 235 [3, 4], 237 [1–5, 7], 238, 240 [1, 3–6], 241, 242 [1–3], 246, 248–252, 254–256, 257 [1–3], 258, 259 [1, 3–5], 260, 261 [2, 3, 6–9, 11, 14, 15], 262, 264 [1–3, 5], 266, 267 [2], 268
  Comments on, **1946:** 2; **1948:** 142, 146, 148, 149, 155, 156, 176, 219
  Library of.
    See Library of Congress.
  Maine delegation, proposal on disposition of surplus potatoes, **1951:** 2 [22]
  Members of
    Absenteeism, **1951:** 113 [15]
    Democratic, buffet supper for, **1951:** 8
    Ethical standards, **1951:** 300 [18]
    Expense allowances, **1945:** 52 [19], 128
    Lawyers among, **1950:** 94
    Letters on behalf of constituents, **1951:** 56 [24]
    Meetings with, **1949:** 16, 52 [12], 58 [2, 24, 28, 31], 70, 78 [6], 93 [3, 10], 148 [12], 155 [13], 166 [1], 171 [4], 186, 214 [7]; **1950:** 12, 29 [2], 89, 96, 103, 184, 295 [1, 8], 302; **1951:** 32
    Retirement, **1945:** 128
    Salaries, **1945:** 52 [19], 59, 128; **1946:** 17 [7], 191; **1947:** 6 [4], 62 [19]; **1948:** 11 [3]; **1949:** 137, 218; **1951:** 22 [10]; **1952–53:** 258 [14]
    Service as delegates to U.N. General Assembly, **1950:** 219; **1951:** 266n.
    Tax-free expense accounts, question of termination, **1951:** 22 [10]
    Texas delegation, President's dinner with, **1951:** 27
    Wives of, **1951:** 70 [7]

Congress — *continued*
  Mexican migrant labor agreement, question of action on, **1952–53:** 2 [5]
  News conference remarks, **1945:** 129 [7, 10], 181 [6], 211 [9]; **1947:** 14 [3], 31 [3], 70 [22], 90 [2], 145 [12], 155 [5], 180 [7]; **1949:** 11 [7, 13], 32 [1], 45 [18, 21], 52 [5, 6, 8, 12, 15], 58 [2, 24, 28, 31], 72 [3], 78 [6], 93 [3, 10], 95 [7, 15], 112 [2, 5, 8, 10, 12–14], 113 [12], 118 [6, 17], 122 [8, 21], 144 [11], 148 [12, 15], 155 [13], 161 [5, 9], 166 [1], 171 [4], 179 [16, 27], 182 [4], 192 [10, 15, 22, 23], 200 [5, 13, 20], 214 [7], 226 [7], 231 [2, 3, 5, 16, 21], 269 [16]; **1950:** 11 [13], 16 [7, 16], 29 [2], 38 [12], 44 [6, 9], 46 [11], 97 [3–5, 10], 137 [2, 4, 6, 17], 146 [7], 152 [2, 4, 9], 169 [12], 206 [5], 209 [17], 217 [12], 253 [11], 258 [15], 273 [4, 18], 278 [10], 287 [5, 12, 16, 21], 295 [1, 8]; **1952–53:** 64 [3]
  Pacific security arrangements, discussions with, **1951:** 84
  Parties, voting record in, **1952–53:** 319 [3, 4]
  Pearl Harbor investigation, **1945:** 129 [7, 10], 202 [15]
  President's relations with, Republican statement, **1948:** 258
  President's service in, **1947:** 46 [18], 127 [12], 232 [12]; **1948:** 122 [2], 200 [3], 228 [4], 231 [1], 262, 267 [2]; **1949:** 148 [15], 160, 192 [10]
  Procedural rules, **1952–53:** 290
  Recess, question of, **1945:** 181 [6], 211 [9]
  Relations with, **1946:** 172, 250 [1]; **1947:** 2 (p. 2); **1949:** 11 [7], 54, 58 [31], 94; **1951:** 70 [7]
  Relationship to Presidency, **1950:** 258 [15]
  Remarks at presentation of Congressional Medal of Honor to Jake W. Lindsey, **1945:** 34
  Reorganization, **1946:** 61 [22], 191; **1947:** 7 (p. 93)
  Resolution on repatriation of Greek children detained in eastern Europe, **1950:** 90n., 261
  St. Lawrence Seaway project, postponement of action on, **1951:** 251 [7]
  Senate
    Clerical help, **1947:** 35
    Committee assignments for freshman members, reform of, **1952–53:** 377 [12]
    Confirmation of Presidential appointments, **1948:** 84 [10]
    Equal representation of States in, **1950:** 107
    Filibuster, question of repeal of Rule **1952–53:** 22, 359 [18, 19]
    Former Presidents, proposed membership, **1952–53:** 26 [10, 11], 75 [8], 377 [30]
    Majority leadership, **1950:** 287 [12]
    Missouri seat, question of the President's candidacy, **1951:** 56 [14]; **1952–53:** 75 [5], 197 [12], 377 [29]

Congress — *continued*
  Senate — *continued*
    Presidential nominations and appointments, action on, **1949:** 161 [9], 231 [2, 5]; **1950:** 97 [10], 169 [12], 209 [17]; **1951:** 227 [11, 13, 17], 251 [2, 22, 23], 261 [22]
    Resolution of friendship for Soviet people, **1951:** 147, 188 [6], 197
    Secretary (Leslie Biffle), **1952–53:** 193
    Sergeant at Arms (Joseph C. Duke), **1951:** 239 [7]
    Service in, the President's, **1950:** 12, 15, 21, 38 [12], 97 [10], 124 [4], 139; **1951:** 18, 27, 32, 33 [2], 46, 51, 56 [24], 98; **1952–53:** 318, 377 [12]
    Southern bloc, **1950:** 287 [5]
    Southern Democratic leaders, civil rights strategy meeting, **1950:** 23ftn. (p. 134)
    Special session, **1947:** 141 [7], 177 [14], 182 [6], 195, 196 [6, 8, 10], 209 [3], 210 [4], 213, 214, 218 [5, 7, 9, 10, 14, 15], 221 [10], 226 [6]; **1948:** 110 [16], 150 [2], 160, 163 [3, 10, 15, 22], 166 [7], 170 [1, 2], 174 [1], 183 [1, 6], 199, 205, 206 [1], 208 [6], 211, 212 [4, 5, 9], 225 [3], 227 [1], 229, 231 [1–3], 240 [1], 251, 252, 257 [5], 258, 259 [3], 261 [6–8], 264 [3], 267 [2], 268, 274 [9]; **1950:** 273 [4, 18], 278 [10], 287 [16, 21]
    Message to, **1948:** 165
    Proposed, **1949:** 52 [8], 122 [21]
    Question of, **1946:** 163 [9], 192 [5], 215 [6, 13], 223 [2], 237 [19], 250 [10]; **1952–53:** 221 [4], 228 [9], 233 [16]
    White House summary of action, **1948:** 165n.
  Unity in, appeal for, **1951:** 4
  Water resources development, authorization of projects, **1950:** 140
  Women Representatives, **1946:** 75 [21]
Congress, letters to Members of.
  See also Congress, messages to.
  Andrews, Repr. Walter G., disability retirement of military personnel, **1948:** 33
  Barkley, Sen. Alben W.
    Eighth anniversary as Senate majority leader, **1945:** 89
    St. Lawrence Seaway, **1948:** 12n.
    Taft-Hartley bill, **1947:** 125
  Bridges, Sen. Styles
    European relief, **1947:** 197
    TVA steam plant, **1948:** 109
  Buckley, Repr. Charles A., St. Lawrence Seaway project, **1952–53:** 102
  Cannon, Repr. Clarence
    Foreign assistance, **1952–53:** 105, 180, 217, 358
    Funds for advance planning of public works, **1945:** 185
    Supplemental appropriations bill, **1950:** 252
    U.N. Palestine refugee program, **1951:** 172

Congress, letters to Members of — *continued*
  Celler, Repr. Emanuel, investigation of antitrust laws, **1949:** 149
  Chavez, Sen. Dennis, Federal aid highway bill, **1950:** 213
  Chelf, Repr. Frank L., request for information from executive agencies, **1952–53:** 60
  Connally, Sen. Tom
    Foreign assistance, **1952–53:** 27, 105, 180, 217, 358
    Genocide convention, **1950:** 222
    Mutual Security Director, powers of, **1952–53:** 67
    Refugees in Europe, assistance, **1952–53:** 66
    St. Lawrence Seaway project, **1952–53:** 102
    Yugoslavia, aid to, **1950:** 290; **1951:** 81, 292
  Cooper, Repr. Jere, expense allowances for President, Vice President, and Speaker of House, **1952–53:** 361
  Doughton, Repr. Robert L.
    Excess profits taxes, **1950:** 284
    Extension of Trade Agreements Act, **1949:** 6
  Eaton, Repr. Charles A.
    European relief, **1947:** 197
    International Development Advisory Board, **1951:** 53
  Flanders, Sen. Ralph E.
    Campaign of Truth, **1950:** 227
    Disarmament, **1951:** 54
  George, Sen. Walter F.
    Drug control bill, **1951:** 201
    Expense allowances for President, Vice President, and Speaker of House, **1952–53:** 361
    Extension of Trade Agreements Act, **1949:** 6
    Tax bills, **1950:** 200, 284
  Gurney, Sen. Chan, disability retirement of military personnel, **1948:** 33
  Halleck, Repr. Charles A., St. Lawrence Seaway, **1948:** 12n.
  Hayden, Sen. Carl
    Military personnel, voting rights, **1952–53:** 124
    Power projects legislation, **1951:** 120
  Johnson, Sen. Edwin C., confirmation of Presidential appointee, **1949:** 222
  Johnston, Sen. Olin D., Federal pay increase, **1951:** 152
  Kee, Repr. John
    Economic assistance to Yugoslavia, **1951:** 81
    Foreign assistance, **1950:** 78, 290
    International Development Advisory Board, **1951:** 53
  Lesinski, Repr. John, Federal aid to education, **1950:** 47
  Manasco, Repr. Carter, full employment bill, **1945:** 222
  May, Repr. Andrew J.
    Army manpower requirements, **1945:** 114
    Unification of armed forces, **1946:** 137

Congress, letters to Members of — *continued*
  Maybank, Sen. Burnet R.
    Annual leave for Government employees,
      1952–53: 108
    Atomic energy program, **1952–53:** 147
    Defense production bill, **1950:** 205
    Public housing appropriation, **1951:** 111
    Rent control extension, **1950:** 292
    Steel strike, **1952–53:** 159
  McCarran, Sen. Pat, Commission on Internal
      Security and Individual Rights, **1951:** 104
  McClellan, Sen. John L.
    Bureau of Internal Revenue, reorganization,
      1952–53: 53
    Reorganization legislation, **1951:** 175
  McCormack, Repr. John W., housing bill, **1946:**
      178
  McKellar, Sen. Kenneth
    Flood control, appropriations, **1951:** 185;
      1952–53: 109
    Foreign assistance, **1952–53:** 105, 180, 217, 358
    United Nations, U.S. contributions, **1951:** 172,
      184
  McMahon, Sen. Brien, control of atomic energy,
      1946: 28
  Millikin, Sen. Eugene D., expense allowances for
      President, Vice President, and Speaker of
      House, **1952–53:** 297
  Murray, Sen. James E., national health program,
      1946: 91
  Murray, Repr. Tom, Federal pay increase, **1951:**
      152
  O'Mahoney, Sen. Joseph C.
    Folsom Dam, **1949:** 41
    Publication of "Economic Indicators," **1949:**
      137
    Statehood for Alaska and Hawaii, **1950:** 107
    Wool price support program, **1946:** 57
  Pittenger, Repr. William, coal supplies in Mid-
      west, **1946:** 228
  Powell, Repr. Adam C., Jr., DAR refusal of
      permission for wife's use of Constitution
      Hall, **1945:** 168
  President pro tempore of the Senate and Speaker
      of the House of Representatives
    Barry, Commodore John, statue, **1947:** 154
    Civilian member, Permanent Joint Board on
      Defense, U.S.-Canada, **1948:** 43
    European recovery program, **1948:** 75
    European relief, **1947:** 197
    Federal aid to education, **1948:** 108
    Gifts to United Nations, tax exemption, **1947:**
      26
    Kuter, Maj. Gen. Laurence S., nomination as
      member of the Civil Aeronautics Board,
      1948: 3
    Loyalty program, Government employees,
      1947: 89

Congress, letters to Members of — *continued*
  President pro tempore — *continued*
    Military training, universal, **1947:** 106
    National Defense, Department of, **1947:** 12
    National Military Establishment, appropria-
      tions, **1948:** 98
    National Security Act, **1947:** 42
    National security program, appropriations,
      1948: 60
    Pacific Islands Trust Territory, administration,
      1947: 119
    Philippine Army veterans, benefits, **1947:** 134
    Presidency, succession to, **1947:** 22
    Reorganization Act of 1945, extension, **1948:**
      62
    St. Lawrence Seaway, **1948:** 12, 12n.
  President of the Senate, benefits for Philippine
      veterans, **1946:** 122
  President of Senate and Speaker of House of
      Representatives
    Antitrust laws enforcement, appropriation,
      1951: 254
    Appropriation bill, supplemental, **1952–53:**
      200
    Appropriations
      Civilian war agencies, **1945:** 124
      Navy, **1945:** 134
      Proposed reductions, **1946:** 10, 130
      War Department, **1945:** 146
    Child care centers, Federal aid for, **1945:** 159
    Civil defense, **1951:** 131
    Coal industry, proposed commission of in-
      quiry, **1950:** 50
    Defense aid program, **1945:** 50
    Defense Department, budget for military
      functions, **1951:** 92
    Defense Production Act amendments, **1952–
      53:** 148
    Defense production bill, **1950:** 215
    Disabled veterans, vocational rehabilitation,
      1950: 298
    Displaced Greek children, repatriation, **1950:**
      90, 261
    District of Columbia, home rule, **1949:** 164
    Emergency legislation, **1950:** 307
    Emergency Powers Continuation Act, **1952–
      53:** 38, 79
    Federal executives, salary increase, **1949:** 3,
      218
    Foreign war relief activities, report, **1945:** 85
    Germany, termination of state of war, **1951:**
      149
    Housing bill, **1946:** 178; **1949:** 125
    Internal Revenue Bureau, reorganization,
      1952–53: 59
    Legislative accomplishments, commendation,
      1949: 235
    Materials Policy Commission, report, **1952–
      53:** 192

Congress, letters to Members of — *continued*
  President of Senate — *continued*
    Military assistance, supplemental appropriations estimate, **1950:** 204
    Mine safety legislation, **1952–53:** 19
    National Advisory Board on Mobilization Policy, report, **1951:** 137
    Natural resources development, New England and New York, **1950:** 33
    Palestine refugees, assistance, **1950:** 25
    Panama Canal and Panama Railroad Co., **1950:** 28
    Philippine veterans, benefits, **1946:** 122
    Point 4 program, appropriations, **1950:** 220
    Price, wage, and production controls, **1951:** 143
    Public assistance payments, increase, **1951:** 159
    Reorganization plans, **1949:** 181; **1950:** 12, 123
    River and harbor development, **1949:** 183
    St. Lawrence Seaway and power project, **1952–53:** 189
    Salaries of Members of Congress, **1945:** 59
    Statehood, Hawaii and Alaska, **1950:** 291
    Steel strike, **1952–53:** 103, 159
    Tax increase, **1951:** 228
    Truth campaign to combat Communist propaganda, **1950:** 190
    UNICEF, U.S. contribution, **1951:** 187; **1952–53:** 51
    Veterans housing, **1946:** 48
    Veterans of Korean war, extension of benefits to, **1951:** 102
    Walker, Lt. Gen. Walton H., posthumous promotion to rank of General, **1950:** 320
    Wallace correspondence on 1944 Far Eastern trip, transmittal, **1951:** 230
    White House renovation, **1949:** 31, 59
  Ramspeck, Repr. Robert, reduction in hours of work, **1945:** 48
  Reed, Repr. Daniel A., expense allowances for President, Vice President, and Speaker of House, **1952–53:** 361
  Richards, Repr. James P.
    Economic assistance to Yugoslavia, **1951:** 292
    Foreign assistance, **1952–53:** 27n., 105, 180, 217, 358
    International Development Advisory Board, **1951:** 53
    Mutual Security Director, powers of, **1952–53:** 67
    Refugees in Europe, assistance, **1952–53:** 66
  Russell, Sen. Richard B.
    Economic assistance to Yugoslavia, **1951:** 81, 292
    Foreign assistance, **1952–53:** 27n., 105, 180, 217, 358

Congress, letters to Members of — *continued*
  Russell, Sen. Richard B. — *continued*
    Korean prisoner-of-war camps, uprising in, **1952–53:** 163
    Military construction, **1952–53:** 178
    Refugees in Europe, assistance, **1952–53:** 66
    St. Lawrence Seaway, **1952–53:** 175ftn. (p. 432)
  Sabath, Repr. Adolph J., Committee on Fair Employment Practice, **1945:** 51
  Somers, Repr. Andrew L., Folsom Dam, **1949:** 41
  Spence, Repr. Brent
    Defense production bill, **1950:** 205
    Housing bill, **1946:** 178
    Rent control extension, **1950:** 292
  Stanley, Repr. Thomas B., military personnel, voting rights, **1952–53:** 124
  Taber, Repr. John, European relief, **1947:** 197
  Thomas, Sen. Elbert D.
    Army manpower requirements, **1945:** 114
    Unification of armed forces, **1946:** 137
  Thomas, Sen. Elmer, surplus food distribution to welfare agencies, **1950:** 249
  Tydings, Sen. Millard E.
    Aid to Yugoslavia, **1950:** 290
    Appointment of General Marshall as Defense Secretary, **1950:** 246
    Confidential loyalty program files, refusal to release, **1950:** 79, 82
    Universal military training, **1950:** 225
  Vandenberg, Sen. Arthur H., International Development Advisory Board, **1951:** 53
  Vinson, Repr. Carl
    Aid to Yugoslavia, **1950:** 290; **1951:** 81, 292
    Appointment of General Marshall as Defense Secretary, **1950:** 246
    Foreign assistance, **1952–53:** 27n., 105, 180, 217, 358
    Refugees in Europe, assistance, **1952–53:** 66
    Unification of armed forces, **1946:** 137
    Universal military training, **1950:** 225
  Wagner, Sen. Robert F., full employment bill, **1945:** 222
  Walsh, Sen. David I., unification of armed forces, **1946:** 137
  Wherry, Sen. Kenneth S., reclamation projects, **1947:** 96
  Wiley, Sen. Alexander, International Development Advisory Board, **1951:** 53
Congress, Library of.
  See Library of Congress.
Congress, messages to.
  See also Congress, letters to Members of.
  Acreage allotments and marketing quotas, **1950:** 83
  Agriculture, **1948:** 99

Congress, messages to — *continued*
  Alaska, statehood, **1948:** 105
  Atomic energy, **1945:** 156
  Budget, **1946:** 18; **1947:** 7; **1948:** 5; **1949:** 8;
      1950: 9; **1951:** 13
    Fiscal 1953, **1952–53:** 18
    Fiscal 1954, **1952–53:** 367
    Government corporations, **1946:** 94
  China, assistance to, **1948:** 31
  Civil rights, **1948:** 20
  Civil Service Commission, report, **1948:** 44
  Coal industry
    Labor dispute settlement, **1948:** 171
    Strike, **1950:** 49
  Columbia Valley Administration, proposed,
      1949: 77
  Conflict-of-interest legislation, **1951:** 237
  Defense appropriations, **1950:** 296
  Defense Production Act
    Amendments, **1951:** 199
    Extension and broadening, **1951:** 91
    Proposed extension, **1952–53:** 33
  Department of National Defense, establishment,
      1945: 218
  Dependent territories, ILO recommendations,
      1946: 180
  Economic reports, **1947:** 4, 152; **1948:** 8, 167;
      1949: 5, 151; **1950:** 6, 202; **1951:** 11, 167;
      1952–53: 15, 215, 376
  Election districts, reapportionment, **1951:** 5
  European freedom, threat to, **1948:** 52
  Executive branch, reorganization, **1945:** 41;
      1949: 12, 94
  Export controls, **1947:** 58
  Financial Agreement, U.S.-U.K., **1946:** 25
  Flood control, **1947:** 144
  Flood damage insurance, **1952–53:** 119
  Flood rehabilitation, appropriation, **1951:** 196
  Folsom Dam, construction, **1948:** 6
  Foreign aid program, reports, **1948:** 91, 147
  Foreign loan policy, **1946:** 47
  Friendship resolution, Soviet reply, **1951:** 197
  Genocide, convention on prevention and pun-
      ishment, **1949:** 121
  Germany, conventions on relations with, **1952–
      53:** 151
  Government property management, **1948:** 46
  Grain controls, **1948:** 14
  Greece and Turkey
    Admission to NATO, protocol on, **1952–53:** 8
    Assistance to, **1947:** 56, 220; **1948:** 28
  Health needs, national, **1949:** 85
  Health program, **1945:** 192; **1947:** 98
  Highway construction, **1948:** 24
  Housing, **1948:** 37
  Housing and Rent Act, **1947:** 131
  India, food relief for, **1951:** 34

Congress, messages to — *continued*
  Institute of Inter-American Affairs, extension,
      1949: 35
  Inter-American Convention on the Granting of
      Political Rights to Women, **1949:** 10
  Inter-American military cooperation, **1946:** 102;
      1947: 101
  Inter-American Treaty of Reciprocol Assistance,
      1947: 230
  Internal security, **1950:** 207
  International Convention on Civil Aviation,
      1946: 133
  International Labor Conference, convention,
      1947: 126
  International Refugee Organization, U.S. partic-
      ipation, **1947:** 38
  International Telecommunication Convention,
      report, **1948:** 29
  International Trade Organization, **1949:** 88
  Interstate commerce, felony to obstruct, **1946:**
      157
  Italy, U.S. treaty with, **1948:** 73
  Japan, winning of war with, **1945:** 45
  Korea
    Assistance, **1949:** 117
    Defense of, **1950:** 193
  Labor, international conventions on, **1948:** 70
  Labor-management relations, **1945:** 204
  Land and water resources development, **1952–
      53:** 388
  Latin America, economic aid, **1948:** 69
  Liberated countries, relief for, **1947:** 37n.
  Maritime employment, ILO recommendations,
      1947: 123, 124
  Marshall plan, **1947:** 238
  Mexico, employment of agricultural workers
      from, **1951:** 154
  Military aid program, **1949:** 162
  Military assistance and defense support, **1950:**
      151
  Military personnel, voting rights, **1952–53:** 68
  Mutual security program, **1951:** 114; **1952–53:** 55
  National Military Establishment, reorganization,
      1949: 50
  Niagara River, U.S.-Canadian treaty on uses of,
      1950: 99
  North Atlantic Treaty, **1949:** 75
  Oak Ridge National Laboratory, labor dispute,
      1948: 140
  Oil and gas conservation, interstate compact,
      1947: 104
  Organization of American States, Charter, **1949:**
      9
  Pacific Islands Trust Territory, **1947:** 137
  Palestine refugees, relief, **1949:** 21
  Pay raise of Federal executives, **1949:** 137
  Philippines, general relations treaty, report,
      1946: 185

Congress, messages to — *continued*
  Plans respecting, the President's, **1952–53:** 345
      [3], 353 [7, 9], 359 [5, 16]
  Point-4 legislation, recommendation, **1949:** 139
  Post Office Department, reorganization, **1949:**
      140
  Postal rates, increase, **1951:** 45
  Portal-to-Portal Act, approval, **1947:** 93
  Price Control Act, extension, **1946:** 179
  Presidency, succession to, **1945:** 63
  Puerto Rico
      Constitution, **1952–53:** 104
      Form of government, **1945:** 169
  Railroad strike, **1946:** 125
  Reconversion program, **1945:** 128
  Refugees and displaced persons, **1952–53:** 65
      Admission to U.S., **1947:** 140
  Rent control, **1950:** 93
      Extension, **1947:** 65
  Reorganization Plans, **1946:** 116, 117, 118; **1947:**
      80, 81, 102; **1948:** 10; **1949:** 127–134, 158;
      1950: 53–76, 112–115, 149, 150; **1951:** 39;
      1952–53: 11, 84–87, 114
  Rivers and harbors bill, approval, **1950:** 140
  Rubber, controls on, **1947:** 24
  St. Lawrence Seaway, **1945:** 155; **1952–53:** 23
  Selective Service
      Discontinuance, **1947:** 50
      Records, **1947:** 54
  Ships, Government operation, **1947:** 228
  Small business, **1950:** 106
  Social security, **1948:** 107
  Special session, **1947:** 224
  State Department, reorganization, **1949:** 47
  State of the Union, **1946:** 18; **1947:** 2; **1948:** 2;
      1949: 2; **1950:** 2; **1951:** 4; **1952–53:** 5, 366
  Steel strike, **1952–53:** 83, 161
  Subpoena power for Special Assistant to Attor-
      ney General, **1952–53:** 36
  Surplus military property, disposition, **1951:** 14
  Surplus Property Act of 1944, amendment pro-
      viding for single administrator, **1945:** 84
  Synthetic rubber production, **1950:** 13
  Tax policy, **1950:** 18; **1951:** 28
  Trade Agreements Act, extension, **1948:** 42
  Unemployment compensation, **1945:** 42
  Unemployment insurance system, **1950:** 84
  United Nations
      Headquarters, control and administration,
          1947: 136
      Nominations of U.S. representatives, **1945:**
          219
      Ratification of Charter, address before Senate,
          1945: 69
      Relief and Rehabilitation Administration,
          U.S. participation, **1945:** 186
      Report, **1946:** 65

Congress, messages to — *continued*
  United Nations — *continued*
      U.S. loan for construction of headquarters,
          1948: 68
      U.S. participation, **1947:** 21; **1948:** 34
  Universal military training, **1945:** 174
  Venezuela, trade agreement with, **1952–53:** 239
  Veterans' benefits, **1952–53:** 138
  Veterans' housing, **1947:** 44
  Vetoes.
      See Veto Messages and Memorandums of
          Disapproval.
  Wage and hour statistics, international conven-
      tion on, **1949:** 13; **1951:** 97
  War materials, trade in, **1947:** 72
  War powers, **1947:** 18, 35, 99
  Wartime economic controls, extension, **1948:** 23
  World Health Organization, U.S. participation,
      1947: 59
  Yugoslavia, assistance to, **1950:** 293
Congress, reports to, lists, App. C, **1945:** p. 613;
      1946: p. 533; **1947:** p. 557; **1948:** p. 996;
      1949: p. 611; **1950:** p. 785; **1951:** p. 677;
      1952–53: p. 1240
Congress, reports to, messages transmitting.
  See also Congress, letters to Members of; Cong-
      ress, messages to.
  Air Coordinating Committee, **1947:** 40
  Civil defense, **1950:** 251
  Civil Defense Administration, Federal, **1952–53:**
      106
  Civil Service Commission, **1948:** 44; **1951:** 161;
      1952–53: 137
  Economic reports, **1947:** 4, 152; **1948:** 8, 167;
      1949: 5, 151; **1950:** 6, 202; **1951:** 11, 167;
      1952–53: 15, 215, 376
  Federal Works Agency, **1949:** 31
  Foreign aid program, **1948:** 91, 147
  Foreign war relief activities, **1945:** 85
  Greece and Turkey, assistance to, **1948:** 28
  Health Needs of the Nation, President's Com-
      mission on, **1952–53:** 369
  Highway needs for national defense, **1949:** 142
  Immigration and Naturalization, President's
      Commission on, **1952–53:** 373
  International Telecommunication Convention,
      1948: 29
  Lend-lease operations, **1951:** 244
  Metals industry, nonferrous, labor dispute,
      1952–53: 37
  Mutual security program, **1952–53:** 61, 332
  National Advisory Board on Mobilization Pol-
      icy, **1951:** 137
  National Science Foundation, **1952–53:** 13
  North Atlantic Treaty, **1949:** 75
  Philippines, general relations treaty, **1946:** 185
  Rubber production, **1952–53:** 12
      Synthetic, **1950:** 13

Congress, reports to — *continued*
  Trade agreements, escape clauses in, **1952–53:** 10
  United Nations, **1946:** 65
    U.S. participation, **1947:** 21; **1949:** 97; **1950:** 143; **1951:** 170; **1952–53:** 196
    Veterans, training under Servicemen's Readjustment Act, **1950:** 36
    War Claims Commission, **1950:** 100
Congress of Industrial Organizations, **1945:** 22 [8]; **1946:** 53 [2], 215 [10], 262 [12]; **1947:** 19 [1], 122, 177 [12], 236 [3]; **1948:** 26 [8], 93 [5], 183 [6], 184, 278 [36], 288 [12]; **1949:** 30 [3], 152, 211 [6], 240 [2]; **1950:** 38 [21], 43, 177n.; **1951:** 132 [16], 153 [16], 183, 252, 261 [8], 277, 298 [8], 304, 305; **1952–53:** 22, 58, 88 [9], 216, 230
"Congress Makes a Law," Steve Bailey, **1952–53:** 292 [3]
Congressional Awards Committee, Collier's, **1946:** 60
  Presentation, **1946:** 80
Congressional Committee, Democratic National, **1951:** 27
Congressional Medal of Honor.
  See under Medals, presentation.
Congressional Record, **1947:** 180 [10]; **1952–53:** 266 [1], 269, 270 [10], 274 [1], 280 [4], 282 [3], 289 [6, 7, 10], 295 [9], 306 [7], 319 [1]
Congressmen.
  See Congress, members of.
Conkling, Roscoe, **1952–53:** 127 [18]
Connally, Sen. Tom, **1945:** 10; **1946:** 70 [14], 173 [1]; **1948:** 212 [2], 213; **1949:** 16, 103n.; **1950:** 11ftn. (p. 109), 96; **1951:** 7 [5], 53, 81, 179 [11], 275ftn. (p. 603), 300 [16]; **1952–53:** 27n., 217, 262, 358
  Letters, **1950:** 222, 290; **1952–53:** 66, 67, 102, 105, 180
  News conference remarks on, **1950:** 97 [17], 318 [8]; **1952–53:** 44 [11], 98 [33], 334 [18]
  Nomination as U.S. representative to U.N. General Assembly, **1945:** 219n.
  Resolution on international cooperation, **1945:** 69
Connally-Smith Antistrike Act, **1945:** 172 [6]
Connecticut
  Campaign remarks, **1948:** 259 [2, 3], 261 [6–9]; **1952–53:** 292, 293, 298 [6–11]
  Candidates for public office, **1948:** 259 [2], 261 [6–9]; **1952–53:** 31 [12], 292, 293, 298 [7–11]
  Gov. Chester Bowles, **1950:** 253 [9]
  Gov. John D. Lodge, **1952–53:** 170
  War production record of, **1948:** 261 [7]
Connecticut River, power projects, **1950:** 121 [4], 129 [1], 140
Connecticut River Basin, **1952–53:** 292 [7]

Connellsville, Pa., campaign remarks, **1952–53:** 308 [4]
Connelly, Matthew J., **1945:** 4 [2]; **1948:** 200 [2], 214 [4]; **1949:** 16, 36; **1950:** 97 [2], 110 [9]; **1952–53:** 2 [19], 45, 292 [11], 377 [15]
Connors, John T., **1948:** 138 [4]
Connors, Tom, **1947:** 182 [8]
Conolly, Rear Adm. Richard L., **1950:** 86 [23]
Conscientious objectors, **1946:** 270
Conservation, **1947:** 7 (p. 58)
  Food, **1947:** 209 [1, 2, 3, 5, 14]; **1948:** 1, 23
  Fuel, **1948:** 55 [10]
  Grain, **1948:** 19
Conservation and Domestic Allotment Act, **1952–53:** 277 [6]
Conservation of natural resources, **1945:** 128, 150; **1947:** 4 (p. 34), 7 (pp. 81, 83), 144; **1948:** 2, 8 (pp. 65, 73), 25, 32, 117, 175, 219; **1949:** 2, 5, 19, 43, 77, 120, 154, 202, 219, 250; **1950:** 2, 9 (pp. 49, 88–91), 33, 39, 84, 116, 118, 121 [8], 122, 124 [7, 8], 126, 127, [4], 129 [1], 130, 140, 157, 281; **1951:** 11, 13, (pp. 64, 65, 84–87, 90), 55, 98, 215; **1952–53:** 5, 69, 98 [9], 126, 179, 242 [4], 268 [2], 277 [4, 6], 281, 285, 366, 388
  Campaign remarks, **1948:** 198 [1, 4, 6], 199, 200 [9], 201, 202 [1, 5], 203, 206 [4], 207, 214 [5, 7], 233 [1], 235 [4, 5], 257 [4]
  Federal aid, **1952–53:** 388
  Issue in election campaign, **1952–53:** 221 [15]
  Letter to heads of Federal agencies, **1950:** 265
Conservation of Renewable Resources, Inter-American Conference on, **1948:** 198 [1]
Constantine, Knights of Red Cross of, **1950:** 312
Constanza, Rumania, **1947:** 32
Constitution, British, slow evolution of, **1951:** 88
Constitution, Puerto Rican, message to Congress, **1952–53:** 104
Constitution, U.S., **1945:** 66, 68, 97; **1946:** 39, 198, 199 [22], 218, 250 [1]; **1947:** 2 (pp. 1, 9), 90 [1], 104, 137, 159, 185, 243 [1]; **1948:** 20, 21 [3], 32, 92, 101, 102; **1949:** 32 [12, 15, 17], 96, 219, 237, 238, 250 [3], 256; **1950:** 21, 126; **1951:** 18, 116, 191; **1952–53:** 63, 117, 123 [10], 136 [17, 19], 161, 165, 169, 249, 251, 268 [8], 270 [4], 274 [7], 277 [2], 313 [5], 322, 330, 331, 373
  Amendments
    Publication of, **1950:** 75
    Twentieth, **1952–53:** 367 (p. 1129)
  Amendments, proposed, **1950:** 8 [9], 29 [18, 24], 52 [8]
    Anti-poll tax **1949:** 118 [23]; **1951:** 16 [20]
    Presidency, prohibition of third term, **1951:** 49 [13]
    Treaties and executive agreements, **1952–53:** 140

Constitution, U.S. — *continued*
  Approval and disapproval of bills, Presidential responsibility, **1945:** 226
  Bill of Rights, **1945:** 66
  Campaign remarks, **1948:** 193 [1], 194 [2], 200 [7], 202 [1], 210 [2], 214 [7], 261 [1], 265, 269
  Civil rights guarantees, **1950:** 144, 174, 207, 266; **1951:** 20, 35, 178; **1952–53:** 129, 290
  Comments on, **1950:** 158; **1951:** 88, 225, 270
  Electoral college, purpose of, **1948:** 41 [3]
  Exhibition on Freedom Train, **1948:** 193 [1]
  Foreign relations, President's responsibility for conduct, **1948:** 244; **1951:** 33 [3]
  General welfare clause, **1950:** 18; **1951:** 225
  News conference remarks, **1949:** 28 [5], 32 [12, 15, 17], 45 [20, 21], 118 [17, 23], 148 [4]; **1950:** 8 [9], 29 [18, 24], 38 [9], 52 [8], 97 [10], 146 [4]
  Police powers, State and Federal, **1951:** 63 [1]
    Limitation, **1948:** 71 [2]
  Popular sovereignty principle, **1952–53:** 89 [3, 11], 292 [13]
  Presidential powers under, **1949:** 28 [5], 148 [4]; **1950:** 37, 82; **1952–53:** 110
  Prohibition of titled nobility, **1948:** 245
  Representation in Congress, provisions on, **1950:** 107; **1951:** 5
  Separation of powers, **1948:** 102; **1949:** 96; **1950:** 182; **1951:** 105, 168, 225
  Shrine at National Archives, dedication, **1952–53:** 347
  State of the Union, provisions respecting messages, **1952–53:** 353 [9]
  Treason, definition in, **1949:** 45 [20]
  War powers of Congress, **1949:** 118 [17]
  War powers of President and Congress under, **1951:** 2 [4, 6, 7], 7 [5], 49 [17], 56 [15]
  Washington's part in framing, **1950:** 42
  Women's suffrage amendment, 25th anniversary, statement, **1945:** 111
Constitution Day, **1951:** 225
Constitution Hall, controversy over use, **1945:** 168
Constitutional Convention, **1945:** 66; **1949:** 33; **1950:** 107
Constitutional Government, Committee for, **1952–53:** 294
Construction industry, **1947:** 4 (pp. 24, 25, 28, 30), 102, 152; **1948:** 8 (pp. 62, 82, 84), 37, 165, 167, 172, 175; **1949:** 8 (p. 72), 151, 156; **1950:** 6, 9 (pp. 77, 80, 81, 97), 121 [9], 128, 202; **1951:** 11, 167; **1952–53:** 15, 178, 366
  Contracts, channeling to depressed areas, **1949:** 155 [1]
  Controls, **1947:** 4 (p. 16), 131
  Cost reduction, **1949:** 2, 54
  Employment, **1947:** 131
  Labor contracts, **1947:** 19 [1]

Construction industry — *continued*
  Materials, conservation for defense needs, **1950:** 192
  National Joint Conference Committee, **1947:** 19 [1], 20
  Research, **1951:** 13 (p. 90)
  Residential, curtailment, **1951:** 13 (p. 90)
  Wages and hours, statistics, **1949:** 13
Consular offices, **1945:** 225
Consumer Price Index, **1947:** 4 (p. 22); **1948:** 63; **1949:** 5; **1951:** 91; **1952–53:** 18 (p. 95), 110
Consumers
  Credit, **1946:** 18 (pp. 49, 52), 193; **1947:** 4 (pp. 15, 19, 21, 24), 152, 155 [6], 176, 224; **1948:** 5 (p. 51), 8 (pp. 63, 71), 165, 166 [8], 167, 218 [1]; **1949:** 2, 5, 32 [8], 45 [3], 66 [7], 122 [5], 151; **1950:** 6, 193, 194, 202, 203ftn. (p. 560), 303; **1951:** 11, 44, 91, 118 [1]; **1952–53:** 15, 190, 215
  Demand, **1949:** 5; **1950:** 6, 84, 106; **1951:** 4, 11, 80, 91, 118 [1], 123, 167, 176, 215; **1952–53:** 15, 33, 55, 289 [2, 8], 292 [10]
    Subordination to military needs, **1950:** 193, 202, 243
  Distribution controls on goods, **1950:** 205
  Goods and services, **1948:** 84 [1], 167
  Income, **1946:** 18 (p. 57), 193; **1947:** 4 (pp. 15, 16, 17, 19, 20, 21, 22, 24), 7, 152, 181 (p. 406); **1948:** 2, 8 (pp. 63, 64, 68, 88, 91), 167, 176; **1949:** 5; **1950:** 6; **1952–53:** 15, 289 [2]
  Protection, **1948:** 184
  Purchasing power, **1949:** 5, 154
  Rationing, **1947:** 224, 225
  Sales tax, Federal, question of, **1951:** 12 [49], 16 [7]
  Savings, **1947:** 4 (pp. 21, 23, 24), 107 [2]; **1951:** 11, 91, 167, 213, 290; **1952–53:** 15, 148
  Spending, **1945:** 42; **1946:** 18 (pp. 51, 69, 71), 164, 193, 226 [1]; **1947:** 4 (pp. 15, 17, 19, 20, 22, 23, 25), 76, 107 [2], 210 [3], 214; **1948:** 8 (pp. 63, 64, 72, 80, 91), 30, 63, 80, 99, 101, 166 [8], 167, 176, 227 [7], 241; **1949:** 5; **1950:** 6, 84, 122, 157, 202; **1952–53:** 15, 215, 263, 266 [7]
Continental Congress, **1947:** 138; **1951:** 144
Continental shelf, **1946:** 189
  Oil reserves, **1949:** 7 [33]; **1952–53:** 379
  U.S. policy on subsoil and sea bed resources, proclamation, **1945:** 150
Contingent Services, Office of, **1945:** 129 [13]
Contract Compliance, Committee on Government, **1951:** 299; **1952–53:** 7 [1, 6], 18 (p. 94), 26 [1], 389
Contract Settlement, Director of (Robert H. Hinckley), memorandum, **1945:** 115
Contract Settlement, Office of, **1946:** 116, 119 [3], 262 [4]; **1947:** 80; **1949:** 150

Contract Settlement Act, **1950:** 183
  Veto of amendment, **1949:** 150
Contract surgeons, Army, **1947:** 35
Contracts, Government, **1946:** 226 [18]; **1947:** 11,
    35, 181 (pp. 396, 398, 401), 208; **1948:** 5
    (pp. 25, 28, 29), 8 (p. 71), 27, 175; **1949:** 8
    (pp. 51, 75); **1950:** 9 (p. 54)
  Atomic energy development, **1952–53:** 17 [1, 12,
    29]
  Civil rights provision, compliance, **1951:** 299;
    1952–53: 389
  Construction and repair, Coast Guard, **1947:** 35
  Cost-plus contracts, **1947:** 81
  Defense.
    See Defense contracts.
  Depressed areas, channeling to, **1949:** 155 [1],
    156, 161 [12], 179 [7]
  Employees of contractors, wages, hours, and
    working conditions, **1950:** 53, 74
  Ethical standards in relations with bidders, **1951:**
    300 [12]
  "Five percenters," offers of influence, **1949:** 144
    [6], 161 [5], 231 [21]; **1950:** 16ftn. (p. 119)
  Housing, **1949:** 8 (p. 75), 126
  Minerals, **1949:** 150
  Printing and binding, **1949:** 147
  Public health program, **1948:** 5 (p. 37)
  Public works, **1950:** 68
  Reimbursement of war contractors for wages
    paid on August 15 and 16, **1945:** 115
  Shipbuilding, **1947:** 223; **1948:** 79, 177; **1949:** 8
    (p. 87)
  Strategic and critical materials, **1948:** 60, 151
  War contracts, **1946:** 18 (pp. 71, 75, 77, 78), 116,
    130n., 177ftn. (p. 357); **1947:** 7 (pp. 59,
    65), 11, 18, 35, 80
    Termination, **1945:** 128, 202 [3]
  War plants, sale of, **1948:** 71 [14]
Contracts, labor.
  See Labor contracts.
Control Commissions, armistice, termination,
    1947: 114
Controlled Materials Plan, **1952–53:** 15, 18 (p. 79)
Controls, Government, **1945:** 128, 180, 184, 204;
    1947: 2 (p. 2), 4 (p. 31), 7 (p. 86), 18, 20,
    24, 58, 68, 76, 99, 143, 152, 181 (p. 401),
    224; **1948:** 8 (p. 74), 11ftn. (p. 104), 15 [6],
    114 [3], 176, 183 [1, 2]; **1949:** 2, 5, 8 (p.
    88); **1951:** 11, 13 (pp. 64–65), 98, 279
  See also Price controls; Rent control; Wage
    controls.
  Agricultural, **1950:** 111
  Allocation and limitation orders, **1952–53:** 15
  Building materials, **1945:** 208 [5], 211 [1]
  Campaign remarks, **1952–53:** 319 [1]
  Commodity exchanges, **1950:** 6; **1951:** 91
    Trading margins, **1952–53:** 15
  Credit, **1950:** 6, 193, 194, 196, 202, 215, 243, 303;

Controls, Government— *continued*
  Credit — *continued*
    1951: 11, 13 (pp. 90–92), 44, 91, 118 [1],
    137n., 140 [2], 143, 167; **1952–53:** 15, 18
    (p. 77), 33, 190, 291, 376
  Defense production, **1950:** 243; **1952–53:** 190
  Defense Production Act, proposed extension of
    controls, **1951:** 70 [6]
  Exports, **1951:** 11, 13 (p. 78)
  Extension
    Message to Congress, **1948:** 23
    Need for, **1951:** 107, 113 [14]
    Proposed, **1952–53:** 345 [5]
  Fiscal, **1951:** 93
  Investments, private, **1951:** 44
  Letters, **1950:** 205, 215
  Manpower resources, **1951:** 15, 93
  Natural gas, **1950:** 88
  News conference remarks, **1945:** 202 [3, 5], 208
    [5, 19], 211 [1]; **1947:** 36 [5, 23], 155 [6],
    191 [11], 209 [2, 11, 16, 17], 226 [13, 15],
    232 [8]; **1949:** 32 [8], 45 [3], 66 [17], 95
    [13]; **1950:** 203 [9], 209 [16], 217 [15, 18,
    20], 253 [6, 7], 295 [2], 318 [10]; **1951:** 132
    [5], 145 [2, 4], 153 [21], 179 [3]
  Opposition by special interests, **1951:** 107, 123
  Police-state methods, **1947:** 232 [8]
  Priorities and allocations, **1950:** 194, 202, 203 [9]
    and ftn. (p. 560), 217 [15, 18, 20]; **1951:**
    11, 15, 44
  Production and distribution, **1951:** 13 (pp. 76–
    77), 93, 98, 140 [2], 143, 176
  Profits, **1951:** 28
  Real estate prices, **1945:** 208 [19]
  Relaxation, prospect of, **1952–53:** 15
  Resources, allocation, **1952–53:** 18 (pp. 77, 79)
  Statement, **1948:** 1
  Strategic and critical materials, **1951:** 13 (pp. 27,
    75, 76, 77), 91, 92, 93, 199, 285; **1952–53:**
    15, 190, 367 (p. 1141)
  Synthetic rubber, **1950:** 13
  Trade with Communist bloc, **1952–53:** 358
  Transportation, **1951:** 13 (p. 81)
    Question of, **1950:** 209 [16]
    Railroads, emergency operation, **1950:** 221
  Termination, **1947:** 156
Conventional Armaments, Commission on, U.N.,
    1951: 54
Conventions, international, maritime employment,
    1947: 123, 124
Conway, Capt. Granville, **1946:** 23, 264; **1947:** 29,
    47, 122, 139
Conway cabal, **1951:** 90 [16]
Cook, Donald C., **1949:** 226ftn. (p. 503)
Cook, Lyle, **1952–53:** 278n.
Cookbook, U.N., gift to the President, **1951:** 223
Cooke, Morris L., **1950:** 1n., 306n.; **1952–53:** 388
Cooke, Thornton, **1951:** 21

Coolbaugh, Melville F., **1947:** 122

Cooledge, Belle, **1948:** 128 [2]

Cooley, Repr. Harold D., **1952–53:** 49 [4]

Coolidge, Calvin, **1948:** 201, 223; **1950:** 82; **1951:** 16 [17], 300ftn. (p. 641); **1952–53:** 195 [3]

Coombs, George, **1948:** 261 [13]

Coombs, George Hamilton, **1947:** 90n.

Cooper, Repr. Jere, **1952–53:** 361

Cooper, John Sherman, **1950:** 80 [12], 195, 219; **1951:** 266n.

Cooper, Prentice, **1947:** 127 [12]; **1948:** 77 [2]

Cooperative for American Remittances to Europe, **1946:** 105; **1951:** 124

Cooperatives, **1949:** 250 [3]

  Congressional investigation, question of, **1948:** 257 [5]

  Electric, **1952–53:** 194

  Farm, **1948:** 99, 117, 218 [1, 11], 234, 235 [4], 237 [1, 5], 246, 257 [5]; **1949:** 203; **1950:** 124 [7], 132; **1951:** 206; **1952–53:** 15, 62, 267

  Housing, **1949:** 8 (p. 72); **1950:** 9 (p. 79), 132

  Taxes on, **1950:** 191 [2]; **1951:** 206; **1952–53:** 62, 267

    Tax exemption, proposed, **1949:** 182 [10]

  Telephone, rural, **1950:** 9 (p. 86)

Coordinating Committee, State-War-Navy, **1945:** 218

Copeland Act, **1947:** 81

Coplon, Judith, **1949:** 122ftn. (p. 296)

Copper

  Import tax, **1949:** 122 [9], 144 [28]

    Proposed waiver, **1951:** 11

    Question of suspension, **1950:** 152 [4, 6], 209 [10], 231, 250 [18], 318 [13]

  Mining, **1950:** 128

  Prices, **1949:** 144 [28]; **1950:** 202

  Production, **1951:** 204

  Stockpiling, **1948:** 8 (p. 78)

  Subsidies, **1945:** 107 [10]; **1947:** 175

  Tax suspension bill, **1947:** 78 [10, 18]

Copper industry

  Chile, discussions with, **1952–53:** 123 [5, 13] 127 [2]

  Labor dispute, **1951:** 169, 209 [1], 214; **1952–53:** 37

    Letter to Chairman of Wage Stabilization Board, **1951:** 204

    Settlement, **1951:** 277

Copra, **1946:** 29

Coral Sea, battle, **1945:** 45, 178

Corcoran, Thomas J., **1952–53:** 289 [3]

Cordon, Sen. Guy, **1948:** 88 [8]

Corkery, Rev. Francis E., **1950:** 126

Corn, Herbert F., **1951:** 302

Corn

  Conservation, **1948:** 8 (p. 70), 14

  Crops, **1948:** 167, 214 [7]

  Exports, **1947:** 155 [6], 177 [6]

Corn — *continued*

  Marketing quota, **1947:** 35

  Overseas relief, **1946:** 86 [4]; **1947:** 177 [6]

  Prices, **1948:** 80, 218 [7, 8, 11, 14], 228 [12], 259 [5], 267 [1, 3], 268; **1949:** 5, 8 (p. 79); **1950:** 111; **1952–53:** 210, 367 (p. 1148)

  Production, **1951:** 11; **1952–53:** 315 [4], 367 (p. 1148)

  Shortage, **1947:** 191 [3], 210 [3]

  Surplus, **1950:** 191 [11]

  Whisky distilling abroad, use for, **1948:** 15 [5]

Corning, Erastus, **1948:** 228 [1]

Corporate profits.

  See under Profits.

Corporate taxes.

  See under Taxes.

Corporation Control Act, Government, approval, **1945:** 207

Corporations, Government.

  See Government corporations.

Corps of Engineers, **1945:** 148, 149, 155; **1946:** 18 (p. 82), 238; **1947:** 7 (pp. 70, 81, 85), 144; **1948:** 5 (pp. 46, 49), 6, 105, 111, 175; **1949:** 8 (pp. 80, 81, 83), 22ftn. (p. 118), 32 [16], 41, 77, 183; **1950:** 3ftn. (p. 15), 9 (pp. 90, 93, 94), 121 [4, 8], 129 [1, 5], 164, 191 [6]; **1951:** 13 (pp. 81, 83, 85, 86), 183n., 185; **1952–53:** 18 (pp. 83, 88), 231, 367 (pp. 1143, 1146, 1149), 388

Corps of Engineers, Chief (Maj. Gen. Lewis A. Pick), **1949:** 183; **1950:** 129 [1, 2]

Correa, Maj. M. F., **1945:** 116n.

Corregidor, battle of, **1945:** 131; **1946:** 159; **1951:** 151, 208

Correspondents' Association, White House, **1949:** 82

Corrupt Practices Act, Federal, **1952–53:** 143

Cost-of-living, **1946:** 18 (pp. 53, 55), 152; **1947:** 4 (pp. 15, 22, 30), 76, 131, 152, 191 [9], 202, 213, 214, 224, 232 [6], 242; **1948:** 2, 5 (p. 22), 8 (pp. 64, 65, 71, 73), 30, 37, 63, 80, 107, 157, 165, 167, 175, 176, 189; **1949:** 5; **1950:** 84, 253 [7], 258 [5], 303; **1951:** 11, 63 [24], 123, 167, 176, 188ftn. (p. 458), 199; **1952–53:** 82, 138, 263, 268 [5], 305

  Campaign remarks, **1948:** 114 [3], 136 [4], 138 [2, 4, 8], 184, 195, 199, 201, 205, 215, 226, 227 [3, 4, 6], 228 [3, 8] 231 [4, 6], 233 [6], 237 [4, 7], 238, 240 [1], 242 [1], 248, 257 [1], 258, 264 [5], 268

  News conference remarks, **1948:** 4 [5, 8, 14, 16], 9 [18], 21 [12], 170 [1]

Cost-of-living index, **1945:** 202 [3, 5]

Costa Rica

  Lend-lease settlement, **1950:** 244

  Otilio Ulate, **1950:** 181 [1]

Costello, Frank, **1951:** 95 [5]

Costigan, Edward, **1952–53:** 282 [7]

Costs, industrial, **1946:** 179
Cotlow, Augusta, **1951:** 99
Cotton, **1948:** 175
   Acreage allotments, **1949:** 269 [21]; **1950:** 83
   Exchanges, investigation, **1947:** 209 [12], 226 [15]
   Exports, **1946:** 18 (p. 85); **1947:** 7 (p. 78), 238;
      1948: 8 (p. 93), 213, 246; **1950:** 159, 270
      [7]
   Imports by China, **1948:** 31
   Loan to Hungary for purchase of, **1947:** 107 [8]
   Loan to Spain for purchase, question of, **1949:**
      113 [10]
   Marketing quota, **1947:** 35
   News conference remarks, **1950:** 191 [11], 270 [7]
   Prices, **1948:** 212 [10], 213, 246; **1950:** 111
      Control, question of, **1951:** 22 [9], 33 [4]
      Supports, **1947:** 70[18]; **1949:** 8 (p. 79); **1950:** 9
      (p. 86); **1952–53:** 210
   Production, **1951:** 11
   Storage, **1950:** 191 [11]
   Surplus, **1950:** 111, 191 [11]; **1951:** 12 [50]
   Textiles, **1946:** 237 [21]
   Shortage, **1945:** 209
Coudert, Repr. Frederic R., Jr., **1951:** 2 [4]
Coulee City, Wash., **1950:** 124 [1]
Council Bluffs, Iowa, relief of, veto, **1945:** 149
Council of Churches of Christ, Federal **1946:** 52
Council of Economic Advisers, **1946:** 183, 218;
      1947: 4 (pp. 13, 34, 39), 53, 122, 152n.,
      176, 212, 219, 238; **1948:** 8 (pp. 64, 79, 87,
      90), 241, 284; **1949:** 138; **1950:** 6, 9 (p. 97),
      118, 127 [4]; **1951:** 44, 113 [6], 118ftn. (p.
      321), 142, 167, 175n.; **1952–53:** 294, 376,
      377 [16]
   Committee of Experts on New England econ-
      omy, **1950:** 265
   Establishment, **1946:** 39
   News conference remarks, **1946:** 53 [13], 61 [13],
      95 [18], 126 [23], 129 [9], 143 [10], 173 [3],
      177 [2]; **1947:** 62 [17], 67 [4], 70 [12], 191
      [4], 218 [7]; **1949:** 7 [9], 22 [13], 32 [7], 45
      [3], 72 [3], 95 [8], 144 [23], 240 [3, 17], 260
      [21], 267 [13]
   Reports, **1946:** 266 [2, 4, 6, 8, 14, 16]; **1947:** 217;
      1948: 49 [12], 167; **1949:** 5; **1950:** 202
Council of Economic Advisers, Chairman (Leon H.
      Keyserling), **1950:** 137 [21]; **1951:** 44, 52,
      142
Council of Economic Advisers, Chairman (Edwin
      G. Nourse), **1946:** 266 [4]; **1948:** 284;
      1949: 234 [2]
   Letter, **1947:** 53
   Memorandum, **1949:** 156
   News conference remarks on, **1947:** 46 [10], 70
      [4]; **1949:** 66 [8], 72 [2, 17], 205 [1], 236 [7,
      12], 267 [13]
   Resignation, **1949:** 236 [7]

Council of Europe, **1949:** 195
Council of Foreign Ministers.
   See Foreign Ministers, Council of.
Council of Free Czechoslovakia, **1952–53:** 309
Council Grove, Kans., **1948:** 137 [4]
Council on International Monetary and Financial
      Problems, National Advisory, **1946:** 41
      [11], 47, 136 [7], 142
Council of National Defense, **1946:** 137, 138; **1947:**
      10n.
Counterfeiting, **1948:** 90
Courier, Voice of America vessel, **1952–53:** 54
Court of Justice, International.
   See International Court of Justice.
Court-martial death sentence imposed on U.S.
      soldier, **1946:** 27 [8]
Courts, attempts to influence by public demon-
      strations, **1950:** 254
Courts, Federal, **1946:** 203
   See also Judiciary, Federal; Supreme Court of
      the United States.
   Appeals from Subversive Activities Control
      Board, **1950:** 254
   Campaign remarks on, **1948:** 215
   Circuit Court of Appeals, Third, **1945:** 132 [1]
   Circuit courts, **1950:** 166; **1951:** 112n.
   Comment on, **1949:** 155 [21]
   Court of Appeals, **1947:** 174 [3]; **1950:** 166;
      1952–53: 116
   Court of Claims, **1945:** 39, 40 [1]; **1946:** 151;
      1947: 19 [7], 46 [16], 77
      Veto of bill to confer special jurisdiction on,
      1950: 256
   Customs Court, **1945:** 157 [15]
   District Courts, **1948:** 66, 179; **1950:** 16ftn. (p.
      117)
      District of Columbia, **1945:** 129 [4], 132 [1];
         1946: 229 [1]; **1948:** 171; **1950:** 46ftn. (p.
         182), 49, 174, 176
      Georgia, **1950:** 209ftn. (p. 582)
      Illinois, **1949:** 211 [2]
      Iowa, **1950:** 206ftn. (p. 570), 209ftn. (p. 582)
      Kansas, **1945:** 172 [9]
      Los Angeles, **1946:** 189
      Massachusetts, **1946:** 211
      Missouri, **1947:** 174 [1]
      New York, **1951:** 112n., 113 [10], 283
      North Carolina, **1948:** 181 [20]
      Tennessee, **1948:** 140
      Texas, **1947:** 78 [7]
      Vermont, **1949:** 211 [2]
   Injunctions in labor disputes.
      See Injunctions in labor disputes.
   News conference remarks, **1948:** 181 [20], 283
      [1]; **1950:** 44 [8, 15]
   Powers under Portal-to-Portal Act, **1947:** 93
   Prosecutions under internal security laws, **1950:**
      207

Courts, Federal — *continued*
  Ruling respecting employee loyalty program, **1952–53:** 362n.
  Rulings on President's power to send troops abroad, **1951:** 7 [5]
  Tax Court, **1946:** 78 [7]
Covenant on Human Rights, **1950:** 174
Covered wagons, **1949:** 82
Cowart, Jack, **1951:** 209 [12]
Cowen, Myron, **1949:** 28 [7]; **1950:** 180; **1951:** 113 [4]
Cox, Archibald, **1952–53:** 342 [4]
Cox, Charles M., **1952–53:** 127 [18]
Cox, Gov. Edward M., **1948:** 231 [3]
Cox, H. B., **1947:** 115n.
Cox, James M., **1945:** 4 [2], 8 [1]; **1948:** 41 [2, 9], 231 [2]; **1952–53:** 319n.
Cox, Mrs. James M., **1952–53:** 319n.
Cox, Lester E., **1952–53:** 157n.
Coy, Wayne (Chairman, Federal Communications Commission), **1949:** 149n.
  Resignation, **1952–53:** 49 [15]
CPA.
  See Civilian Production Administration.
Craft, C. B., Congressional Medal of Honor presentation, **1945:** 167n.
Craig, Lt. Gen. Howard A., **1952–53:** 354
Craig, May, **1947:** 14 [18], 31 [13], 46 [14], 62 [7]; **1948:** 4 [16], 11 [11], 77 [13, 16], 93 [11], 150 [10], 166 [12]; **1949:** 93 [16], 113 [12], 155 [16], 161 [5], 182 [1, 14], 253 [1]; **1950:** 3 [15], 86 [18], 203 [21], 250 [10], 258 [15]; **1951:** 2 [4, 6], 7 [5], 12 [13, 54], 16 [19], 22 [13], 33 [15], 49 [3], 63 [12], 70 [7], 85 [3], 90 [4], 101 [5], 167, 239 [9], 247 [1], 275 [20]; **1952–53:** 7 [10], 17 [22], 26 [4], 49 [7], 75 [4], 98 [26], 107 [12], 166 [18], 175 [12], 233 [8, 15], 258 [2]
Craig, William H., **1952–53:** 292 [13], 294, 295 [1, 3, 5, 6]
Cranberries, marketing promotion by Agriculture Department, **1948:** 237 [5]
Crane, Gov. Arthur Griswold, **1950:** 116, 117 [1, 4], 118
Crawford, Repr. Fred L., **1946:** 152, 153, 221
Crawfordsville, Ind., campaign remarks, **1948:** 233 [3]
Credit, **1947:** 2 (p. 6), 4 (pp. 15, 35, 39), 7 (p. 88), 76, 102, 152, 155 [6], 176, 224; **1948:** 5 (pp. 21, 24, 37, 38, 40, 44, 51, 52), 8 (pp. 63, 65, 69, 71, 73, 89, 91, 95), 13, 37, 80, 176; **1949:** 151
  See also Mortgages.
  Agricultural, **1948:** 276; **1949:** 203; **1950:** 6, 111, 114, 121 [7]; **1952–53:** 18 (p. 91), 126, 215, 231, 367 (p. 1149)
  Banks, policy on, **1948:** 77 [9], 178 [5]

Credit — *continued*
  Consumer, **1946:** 18 (pp. 49, 52), 193; **1952–53:** 5 (p. 51), 8 (pp. 63, 71), 165, 166 [8], 167, 218 [1]; **1949:** 32 [8], 78 [13, 16]; **1950:** 6, 194, 203ftn. (p. 560); **1951:** 118 [1]; **1952–53:** 15, 190, 215
    Regulation W, **1949:** 32 [8], 66 [7], 122 [5]
  Controls, **1948:** 9 [18], 165, 166 [8, 10]; **1949:** 2, 5, 32 [8], 45 [3], 66 [7]; **1950:** 193, 196, 202, 215, 243, 303; **1951:** 11, 44, 137n., 140 [2], 143, 167; **1952–53:** 18 (pp. 77, 80), 33, 190, 291, 376
  Corporate, **1949:** 8 (p. 89)
  Expansion, **1950:** 202
  Farm, **1951:** 13 (p. 89), 202, 296
  Federal Reserve Board, policy on, **1951:** 37 [4, 9]
  Housing, **1950:** 9 (p. 46), 128, 192, 194; **1951:** 13 (p. 90–92); **1952–53:** 18 (pp. 97, 98), 120, 123 [18], 190
  Indians, facilities for, **1951:** 13 (pp. 86, 87); **1952–53:** 18 (p. 90)
  Mortgage, **1951:** 118 [5], 167; **1952–53:** 231
  News conference remarks, **1948:** 4 [18], 77 [9], 84 [16]
  Restraint program, voluntary, **1952–53:** 15
  Small business, **1950:** 118; **1952–53:** 18 (p. 79)
Credit Administration, Farm, **1948:** 218 [1]
Credit Union National Association, dedication of headquarters, **1950:** 131 [4], 132
Credit unions, **1946:** 116; **1947:** 80
Creedon, Frank R., **1946:** 262 [5, 11]; **1947:** 196, 205 [8, 10, 17]
Crestline, Ohio, campaign remarks, **1948:** 114 [1], 193 [2]; **1952–53:** 240 [2]
Creston, Iowa, **1950:** 110 [4]
Crick, Wilfred P., **1945:** 210
Crime
  Antiracketeering law, proposed, **1950:** 11 [3]
  Conference on, **1950:** 37
  Congressional investigation of, **1950:** 152 [9], 168; **1951:** 49 [8], 63 [1, 4], 95 [3, 5], 115
  Control, **1947:** 7 (p. 58); **1949:** 8 (p. 70); **1951:** 63 [1]
  Criminal justice, elimination of administrative abuses, **1951:** 115
  District of Columbia, **1952–53:** 233 [4], 238 [3]
  Ingram case in Georgia, **1948:** 55 [4]
  Interstate, congressional investigation, **1951:** 63 [1, 4]
  Interstate syndicates, Justice Department investigation, **1949:** 226 [14]
  Organized, investigations of, **1950:** 86 [2, 4, 6, 7, 12], 152 [9]
  Persons accused of, legal rights, **1950:** 37
Crimea conference.
  See Yalta conference.
Critical and strategic materials.
  See Strategic and critical materials.

Criticism, public, comment on, **1947:** 74
Crockett, Gib, **1951:** 275 [18]
Crommelin, Capt. John G., **1949:** 211 [10], 226 [9]
Cromwell, Oliver, **1952–53:** 296, 303 [2]
Crook, Thurman C., **1948:** 257 [1, 2]
Crop insurance, **1945:** 128; **1946:** 18 (p. 53), 94;
        1948: 2, 8 (pp. 69, 92), 99, 194 [11], 246
Crops, farm.
    See Agricultural commodities.
Cross, Wilbur J., **1948:** 261 [7]
Crosser, Repr. Robert, **1948:** 258; **1949:** 260 [16];
        1952–53: 287
Crossman, Richard H. S., **1945:** 210
Crowley, David J., **1952–53:** 296, 298 [1]
Crowley, Leo T., **1945:** 175 [13], 181 [9], 202 [2]
    See also Federal Deposit Insurance Corporation,
        Chairman, Board of Directors; Foreign
        Economic Administrator.
Crowlie, Mrs. Philip L., **1947:** 204n.
Crum, Bartley C., **1946:** 66 [2]; **1950:** 250 [4]
Crusade for Christian Citizenship, **1952–53:** 39
Crusade in Europe, Dwight D. Eisenhower, **1951:**
        188 [11]; **1952–53:** 7 [10]
Crusade for Freedom, **1950:** 254
Cuba
    Ambassador Guillermo Belt, **1948:** 81
    50th anniversary of independence, address, **1948:**
        81
    Grau San Martín, Ramón, **1947:** 14 [6]
    Prío Socarrás, Carlos, **1948:** 170 [5], 282, 283 [16]
    Rice exports to, **1947:** 18
    Sugar, **1947:** 18, 64, 181 (p. 401); **1948:** 5 (p. 43)
Cullen, Helen, **1952–53:** 292 [12]
Cullman, Howard S., **1948:** 168
Cullum, Paul F., **1948:** 189n.
Culp, Fred, **1952–53:** 286 [3]
Cultural exchange program, U.S.-Brazil, **1949:** 108
        [2]
Cumberland, Md., **1950:** 135
    Campaign remarks, **1952–53:** 308 [7]
Cumberland River power project, **1950:** 3 [5]; **1951:**
        13 (pp. 85, 86), 185
Cummings, Walter J., **1946:** 142
Cunningham, Ben, **1948:** 118 [1]
Cunningham, Glenn, **1948:** 116 [1]
Curfew, wartime, **1945:** 4 [21]
Curley, Mayor James M., **1947:** 127 [6]
Currencies, **1949:** 151; **1952–53:** 15, 215, 319 [1],
        367 (pp. 1133, 1134, 1141)
    Bank holdings, **1951:** 11
    Control, **1950:** 97 [7]
    Money supply, **1951:** 167
Currencies, foreign, **1947:** 197; **1949:** 214 [5]
    China, **1946:** 265
    Counterpart funds, Marshall plan, **1947:** 238
    Dollar exchange, shortage abroad, **1950:** 81
    Exchange restrictions, reduction, **1951:** 219

Currencies, foreign — *continued*
    France, **1947:** 208, 209 [3]
    Greece, **1947:** 220
    India, **1951:** 34
    Mexico, **1947:** 83
    Payments union, European, proposed, **1950:** 169
        [9]
    Philippines, **1946:** 31
        Reduction of required gold coverage, **1945:**
            189
    Stabilization, **1947:** 51, 238
Curtin, John, death of, **1945:** 73
Cushing, Dr. E. H., **1952–53:** 31 [3]
Customs, Bureau of, **1946:** 118; **1947:** 7 (p. 91);
        1948: 5 (p. 56)
    Reorganization, **1952–53:** 84, 86, 117, 137
Customs duties, **1947:** 35; **1948:** 5 (p. 23); **1949:** 7
        [40]; **1950:** 9 (p. 53); **1951:** 13 (pp. 104,
        105)
CVA.
    See Columbia Valley Administration, proposed.
Cut Bank, Mont., campaign remarks, **1952–53:** 268
        [8]
Czechoslovakia, **1946:** 245
    Anniversary of independence, **1945:** 173; **1952–
        53:** 309
    Benes, Eduard, **1945:** 173
    Communism in, **1948:** 41 [4], 52, 53, 142, 256;
        1950: 92; **1951:** 253; **1952–53:** 47, 309
    Conspiracy and espionage trials, **1951:** 145 [7],
        153 [6], 209 [14]
    Council of Free Czechoslovakia, **1952–53:** 309
    Embargo on trade with, proposed, **1951:** 224 [4]
    Korean armistice commission membership,
        1952–53: 121
    Lidice, destruction by Nazis, **1945:** 52 [2]
    Mass deportations, **1952–53:** 145
    Oatis, William N., imprisonment, **1952–53:** 49
        [12], 115 [15]
    Refugees from, **1950:** 146 [20]
    Relief for, **1945:** 186
    Trade with, **1948:** 55 [6], 84 [21]
    Transfer of German population, **1945:** 91
    U.N. delegate, request for political asylum in
        U.S., **1950:** 137 [14]
    U.S. Ambassador Ellis O. Briggs, **1952–53:** 115
        [15]

Daily Treasury Statement, **1947:** 75
Dairy products, **1946:** 86 [22], 119 [20]; **1948:** 8 (pp.
        70, 92)
    Import restrictions, **1951:** 199; **1952–53:** 359 [2,
        14], 360
    Price supports, **1950:** 9 (p. 86)
    Shortage, **1947:** 18

Dalesandro, Peter, **1948:** 228 [1]
D'Alesandro, Thomas, Jr., **1948:** 139n., 228 [1];
    1950: 97 [16], 171n.
Dallas, Tex., campaign remarks, **1948:** 212 [9]
Dalles, The, power project, **1951:** 13 (pp. 85, 86)
Dalton, Neil, **1945:** 132 [1]
Dana, Charles A., **1951:** 8
Danaher, John A., **1951:** 22 [2], 278n.
Daniel, prophet, **1949:** 259
Daniel, Robert P., **1950:** 294n.
Daniels, Jonathan, **1945:** 26 [2, 5]; **1949:** 66 [13], 89
    [3], 93 [17], 95 [14], 118 [3], 166 [5]; **1951:**
    70 [7], 132 [7], 209 [9]; **1952–53:** 203n.
    News conference remarks on, **1945:** 4 [2], 8 [3]
    The Man of Independence, **1950:** 258 [2]
Daniels, Josephus, **1946:** 86 [2]; **1948:** 245
Danna, Howard, **1945:** 147n.
Danville, Ill.
    Campaign remarks, **1948:** 233 [4]; **1952–53:** 321
    [3]
    Mayor G.N. Hicks, **1948:** 234
Danville (Ill.) Commercial-News, **1952–53:** 321 [3]
Danzig, transfer to Poland, **1945:** 91
Dardanelles, **1945:** 132 [10]
Darmstadt, Germany, **1945:** 97
Darst, Joseph M., **1950:** 161 [2, 3], 162; **1952–53:**
    322
Daubin, Rear Adm. Freeland A., **1945:** 177
Daugherty, Richard E., **1949:** 249
Daughters of the American Revolution, **1945:**
    168n.; **1952–53:** 98 [28]
Davenport, Repr. Harry J., **1949:** 202n.
Davenport, Iowa, campaign remarks, **1948:** 194 [2];
    1952–53: 315 [4]
David Dam reclamation project, Colorado, **1948:**
    201
Davies, John C., **1948:** 228 [5]
Davies, Joseph E., **1945:** 97; **1946:** 268n.; **1948:** 178
    [1]
    Mission to United Kingdom, **1945:** 44 [8], 52
    [15], 60 [6]
    News conference remarks on, **1945:** 44 [8], 52
    [15], 60 [6], 67 [2]
Davies, Ralph K., **1946:** 95 [27], 101
    Medal for Merit, citation, **1945:** 214
Da Vinci, Leonardo, 500th anniversary of birth,
    statement, **1952–53:** 89
Davis, Brig. Gen. Benjamin O., **1948:** 162
Davis, Bette, **1952–53:** 273
Davis, Chester C., **1946:** 45n., 58, 255n.; **1947:** 122,
    191 [3]
Davis, Dowdal H., **1952–53:** 7 [1]
Davis, Elmer, **1947:** 90n.; **1949:** 40 [18], 52 [2];
    1951: 16 [18], 247 [1]; **1952–53:** 136 [18]
    See also War Information, Office of, Director
    (Elmer Davis).
Davis, John F., **1948:** 227 [1]
Davis, Monnett B., **1950:** 250 [4]

Davis, Thomas W. S., letter, **1952–53:** 328
Davis, Watson, **1950:** 48n.; **1951:** 50n.
Davis, William H., **1945:** 202 [5]; **1948:** 140n.;
    1949: 81, 87
    See also Economic Stabilization, Office of, Di-
    rector.
Davis, Calif., campaign remarks, **1948:** 128 [3];
    1952–53: 277 [6]
Davis, Okla., campaign remarks, **1948:** 214 [6]
Davis-Bacon Act, **1947:** 20, 81
    Public works contracts, **1950:** 68
Davis Dam, Ariz., **1948:** 207
Davis Mountains (Tex.), **1948:** 208 [7]
Dawes, Charles G., **1950:** 21
Dawson, Donald S., **1951:** 33 [2, 12, 14], 49 [11], 56
    [17, 24], 63 [11, 13, 18], 90 [9]
Dawson, Repr. William L., **1949:** 256; **1952–53:**
    315 [6], 317
Daylight saving time, **1946:** 61 [24]; **1948:** 55 [10];
    1949: 84 [8]
Dayton, Ohio, **1951:** 85 [9]
    Campaign remarks, **1948:** 231 [3]; **1952–53:** 319
    [5]
    Mayor Louis Lohrey, **1952–53:** 319n.
Dean, Gordon, **1949:** 58 [7]; **1950:** 15ftn. (p. 118),
    146ftn. (p. 441), 186ftn. (p. 516), 273 [11];
    1952–53: 45, 170
Dean, Maj. Gen. William F., **1952–53:** 29n.
    Congressional Medal of Honor award, **1950:** 263
Dean, Mrs. William F., **1950:** 263n.
Dean, William F., Jr., **1950:** 263n.
Dearden, Rt. Rev. John F., **1949:** 202n.
Death rate, reductions in, **1945:** 192
Deaths of noted persons, statements
    Curtin, John, **1945:** 73
    Pyle, Ernie, **1945:** 6
Debt, Bureau of the Public, **1952–53:** 367 (p. 1161)
Debt, national, **1946:** 18 (pp. 67, 68, 72–74), 73, 79,
    193; **1947:** 181 (p. 405); **1948:** 8 (pp. 72,
    94), 175, 176, 183 [6], 223; **1951:** 13 (p.
    68); **1952–53:** 272, 349
    Fluctuations during President's term, **1952–53:**
    368
    Increase, **1950:** 8 [42], 9 (pp. 48, 54, 103);
    1952–53: 17 [3], 18 (p. 68), 215, 367 (p.
    1133)
    Interest on, **1946:** 18 (pp. 73, 78, 79); **1947:** 2 (p.
    7), 6 [12], 7 (pp. 57, 61, 91), 76, 180 [1], 181
    (p. 401); **1948:** 4 [1], 5 (pp. 20, 21, 23, 25,
    56, 71, 175); **1949:** 7 [10, 41], 8 (pp. 47,
    94); **1950:** 217 [10]; **1951:** 12 [3], 13 (pp.
    64, 105, 106), 221; **1952–53:** 15, 18 (pp.
    114–115), 231, 367 (pp. 1163, 1164)
    Limit, **1950:** 8 [37]; **1951:** 12 [17]; **1952–53:** 17 [5]
    Management, **1947:** 4 (p. 39), 152; **1948:** 5 (pp.
    23, 24), 8 (pp. 69, 88, 95), 13, 167; **1949:** 7
    [10, 50], 11; **1950:** 8 [25], 39; **1951:** 44, 52;
    1952–53: 15, 215

Debt, national — *continued*
  News conference remarks, **1946:** 17 [2, 5, 11], 192
    [8, 21]; **1949:** 7 [1, 2, 4, 10, 11, 36, 41, 50],
    95 [19], 253 [2]; **1950:** 8 [25, 37, 42], 217
    [10]
  Reduction, **1946:** 17 [2, 5, 11], 18 (p. 72), 67, 187,
    192 [8, 21], 193, 195; **1947:** 2 (pp. 3, 7), 6
    [12, 19, 23, 37], 7 (pp. 56, 61), 36 [13], 68,
    75, 76, 116, 147, 152, 180 [1, 5, 13, 14, 16,
    18, 19], 181; **1948:** 5 (pp. 20, 22, 23, 25), 8
    (pp. 69, 94), 63, 124 [4], 138 [5–7], 167,
    175, 241; **1949:** 2, 7 [1, 2, 4, 10, 11, 36], 8
    (pp. 45, 48, 49), 95 [19], 151, 154, 253 [2];
    1950: 8 [37], 18; **1952–53:** 17 [3], 366
Debt, personal, **1949:** 151
Decatur, Ill.
  Campaign remarks, **1948:** 233 [6]; **1952–53:** 321
    [4]
  Mayor James A. Hedrick, **1948:** 234
Decker, Clarence R., **1945:** 68n.
Declaration of Independence, **1947:** 130, 138, 215;
    1948: 20, 36, 193 [1], 265, 269; **1950:** 280;
    1951: 116, 144, 145 [9], 174, 225, 241;
    1952–53: 169, 182, 347, 366
Decontrol Acts, **1947:** 58n., 99n., 143
  Second, **1948:** 23
Decorations.
  See Awards and citations.
Dedicatory occasions.
  See Addresses or remarks on commemorative or
    special occasions.
Deen, Edgar, **1948:** 212 [7]
Deep Rock Oil Corp., **1952–53:** 58
Deer Creek reclamation project, **1948:** 56; **1952–53:**
    367 (p. 1146)
Defense, Department of, **1949:** 8 (p. 56), 67, 177,
    244; **1950:** 9 (pp. 61, 63), 108; **1951:** 7 [3],
    13 (p. 66), 118 [17], 107, 153 [17], 165 [6],
    247 [1, 12], 251 [11], 272n., 301; **1952–53:**
    55, 79, 96, 117, 146, 228, 257, 333
  Administration of voting by military personnel,
    1952–53: 68
  Appropriations, **1950:** 193, 296
  Appropriations Act (1953), **1952–53:** 367 (p.
    1136)
  Budget, **1951:** 13 (pp. 68–70), 93
  Civilian employees, increase, **1952–53:** 18 (p. 71)
  Defense plants, construction by, **1951:** 12 [2], 13
    (pp. 76, 77)
  Establishment, proposed, **1945:** 218; **1946:** 18 (p.
    74), 137, 138; **1947:** 2 (p. 12), 7 (p. 63), 12,
    80, 155 [3]; **1949:** 158
  Fissionable materials production program,
    1952–53: 17 [1]
  Fund for purchase of industrial facilities, pro-
    posed, **1952–53:** 367 (p. 1138)
  Highway transportation, emergency plans, **1950:**
    229

Defense, Department of — *continued*
  Internal security bill, advisory opinion against,
    1950: 254
  Korean aid bill, testimony on, **1950:** 17n.
  Management improvement program, **1952–53:**
    18 (pp. 115–116)
  Manpower mobilization functions, **1951:** 15
  Military aid program, administration, **1951:** 114
  Military functions, budget for, **1951:** 92, 93;
    1952–53: 231, 367 (pp. 1134, 1135)
  Mobilization planning, **1950:** 9 (p. 65); **1951:**
    120, 123, 137, 143, 163, 177, 185, 189;
    1952–53: 33, 276
  News conference remarks, **1949:** 72 [7], 84 [9],
    226 [4], 236 [1]; **1950:** 46 [10], 186 [3, 11],
    206 [17], 250 [5], 253 [5], 270 [8]
  Personnel changes in, **1949:** 84 [9]
  Position on release of information on Bikini
    atomic bomb tests, **1948:** 283 [3]
  Public addresses by officials, policy on, **1950:**
    186 [11]
  Real estate transactions, **1951:** 105, 108 [1]
  Reduction in force, **1949:** 201
  Reorganization, **1951:** 56 [1, 3, 8], 226
    Proposed, **1949:** 50
  Research and development program, **1950:** 9 (p.
    64); **1952–53:** 18 (p. 72), 367 (p. 1137)
  Welfare programs for military personnel, **1950:**
    32
Defense, national.
  See National security.
Defense, Secretary of
  Functions, **1949:** 158, 177
  St. Lawrence Seaway project, support of, **1952–
    53:** 23
Defense, Secretary of (James Forrestal), **1947:** 192,
    221 [1], 229, 232 [2]; **1948:** 5 (p. 26), 20,
    60, 79, 98, 106, 151; **1949:** 50, 56
  Armed forces disability retirement, views on,
    1948: 33
  Distinguished Service Medal, **1949:** 63
  Letter on disaster relief, **1949:** 22ftn. (p. 118)
  Memorandum to, **1949:** 48
  News conference remarks on, **1948:** 9 [14], 71 [9],
    77 [5, 7, 10], 84 [9], 110 [13], 274 [5, 11],
    278 [1, 11, 13, 21, 40], 283 [3], 285 [4];
    1949: 11 [5], 45 [1]
  Resignation, **1949:** 46
    Question of, **1948:** 274 [5, 11], 278 [11, 13]
Defense, Secretary of (Louis A. Johnson), **1949:** 64,
    67, 73n., 142, 145n., 195n., 201, 231ftn. (p.
    511) 241n., 244; **1950:** 22, 138, 161 [1–3],
    176, 184, 193, 242
  Criticism of, **1950:** 230 [1], 250 [2, 3]
  Japan, visit to, **1950:** 137 [12]
  Korea, conference on, **1950:** 172
  Memorandums, **1949:** 149n.; **1950:** 259

Defense, Secretary of (Johnson) — *continued*
  News conference remarks on, **1949:** 84 [21], 89
      [7], 93 [17], 118 [18], 144 [6], 161 [5], 192
      [10], 200 [7], 226 [3, 4], 240 [18], 269 [6];
      1950: 29 [23], 97 [8], 105 [13], 137 [12], 186
      [11], 203 [11], 206 [10], 214 [15], 217 [16,
      22], 230 [1, 10, 13], 250 [2, 3]
  Resignation, **1950:** 245
Defense, Secretary of (Robert A. Lovett), **1951:** 93,
      272, 301n.; **1952–53:** 6, 27, 38, 48, 64 [9],
      68, 79, 88 [4], 101, 124, 128, 155n., 161,
      228 [7], 233 [14], 292 [11], 320, 331
  Denmark, endorsement of continued aid to,
      1952–53: 217
  Letter and memorandums, **1952–53:** 96, 162, 387
  Resignation, **1952–53:** 371
Defense, Secretary of (George C. Marshall), **1951:**
      41, 77n., 109, 123, 138, 155n.
  Armed Forces, telegram of congratulations on
      strength of, **1951:** 57
  Europe, consultations with Congress on dispatch
      of troops to, **1951:** 7 [9], 37 [17]
  Japan, security negotiations with, **1951:** 84
  Korean war, testimony and statements on, **1951:**
      63 [6, 7, 25], 101 [3–5], 108 [13]
    Advice on removal of Gen. MacArthur, **1951:**
      108 [2]
  Meeting with President and congressional lead-
      ers on national security, **1950:** 302
  News conference remarks on, **1950:** 309 [1, 2];
      1951: 132 [10], 165 [10], 209 [13]
  Psychological Strategy Board, directive on es-
      tablishment, **1951:** 128
  Resignation, **1951:** 222
  Water Resources Policy Commission, letter on
      report of, **1951:** 55
Defense, U.S.-Canadian Permanent Joint Board
      on, **1947:** 111; **1948:** 43
Defense Advisory Committee on Women in the
      Services, **1951:** 289
Defense aid program, letter to Speaker Rayburn,
      1945: 50
Defense contracts, **1948:** 79, 140; **1949:** 8 (p. 58);
      1950: 9 (pp. 54, 61), 284, 307; **1951:** 11, 13
      (pp. 69, 70, 76, 77), 15, 153, 189
  Aircraft, military, **1949:** 8 (p. 60); **1950:** 105 [13]
  Emergency powers, **1950:** 307
  Loans and guarantees, **1951:** 13 (pp. 76, 78), 106
  Military assistance abroad, **1950:** 151
  Policy, **1951:** 11
  Postwar cancellation, **1949:** 160
  Review by Renegotiation Board, **1952–53:** 18 (p.
      112)
  Small business, awards to, **1952–53:** 15, 18 (pp.
      79–80)
  War Contractors Relief Act, veto of amend-
      ments, **1950:** 183, 216
  World War II, veto of private bill respecting,
      1951: 284

Defense Fund, United, **1951:** 3, 180, 242
Defense Highway Act of 1941, **1947:** 35
Defense Homes Corporation, **1947:** 7 (pp. 75, 95);
      1948: 5 (p. 40)
Defense Housing and Community Facilities and
      Services Act, **1951:** 211, 286
Defense Materials Administration, **1951:** 205
Defense Materials Procurement Agency, **1951:** 177,
      205; **1952–53:** 18 (pp. 78, 89, 115)
Defense Minerals Administration, **1951:** 177
Defense mobilization, **1952–53:** 366
Defense Mobilization, Office of, **1951:** 13 (p. 65),
      44, 49 [10], 89, 93, 119, 163, 169, 204, 252,
      305, 307; **1952–53:** 18 (p. 78), 22, 58, 245,
      338
  Establishment, **1950:** 303
  Fissionable materials production program,
      1952–53: 17 [1]
  Steel dispute, mediation, **1952–53:** 82
Defense Mobilization, Office of, Director (Henry
      H. Fowler), **1952–53:** 245, 257, 341
Defense Mobilization, Office of, Director (John R.
      Steelman), **1952–53:** 118n., 161, 185–187
Defense Mobilization, Office of, Director (Charles
      E. Wilson), **1950:** 303, 307; **1951:** 11, 23,
      41, 52, 89, 93, 109, 123, 137n., 143, 158,
      169, 174, 177, 189, 196, 204, 205, 252, 276,
      298 [6], 299, 305; **1952–53:** 6, 34, 58
  Appointment as Chairman, National Advisory
      Board on Mobilization Policy, **1951:** 56
      [2]
  Debt management and credit controls, memo-
      randum, **1951:** 44
  Flood relief, letter, **1951:** 163
  Korean war, policy statement, **1951:** 63 [7]
  Labor criticism of, **1951:** 63 [8]
  Manpower mobilization functions, **1951:** 15
  National economy, report on, **1951:** 113 [6]
  News conference remarks on, **1951:** 37 [14], 49
      [2, 14], 118 [2, 9], 298 [6]
  Price control amendments, proposed, **1951:** 16
      [3], 22 [9]
  Resignation, **1952–53:** 70
  St. Lawrence Seaway project, support of, **1952–
      53:** 23
  Successor, question of appointment, **1952–53:** 75
      [9], 88 [8], 123 [8]
Defense Mobilization Board, **1951:** 188ftn. (p. 458)
Defense Plant Corporation, **1947:** 94; **1949:** 4 [4],
      150; **1950:** 256
Defense plants, construction by Government, ques-
      tion of, **1949:** 4 [4]
Defense procurement, **1949:** 8 (pp. 57, 60, 61), 50
Defense Production Act, **1950:** 243, 259, 288; **1951:**
      11, 13 (pp. 65, 76, 78–80), 23, 123, 143,
      161, 167, 199, 205, 285; **1952–53:** 18 (pp.
      77, 80, 94, 116), 82, 136 [19], 148, 231, 305,
      338, 359 [2], 360, 367 (pp. 1129, 1141)

Defense Production Act — *continued*
  Amendments of 1952, **1952–53:** 115 [10], 123 [18], 136ftn. (p. 361), 148, 190
  Approval, **1950:** 205n.
  Extension and strengthening, proposed, **1951:** 91, 92, 98; **1952–53:** 15, 33
  Import restriction provisions, criticism of, **1952–53:** 203
  Letters, **1950:** 205, 215
  Message to Congress, **1952–53:** 33
  News conference remarks, **1950:** 238 [3, 6]; **1951:** 2 [19], 22 [9], 37 [14], 63 [17], 70 [6], 85 [5], 113 [14], 118 [1], 140 [2], 145 [2, 4], 153 [21], 171 [6], 261 [14]
  1951 amendments, **1951:** 137, 176, 177, 199, 261 [14], 279
Defense Production Administration, **1951:** 13 (pp. 65, 76), 37 [14], 93, 177; **1952–53:** 18 (pp. 79, 115)
Defense Production Administrator (Manly Fleischmann), resignation, **1952–53:** 122
Defense Production Administrator (Henry H. Fowler), **1952–53:** 122
Defense Production Administrator (Edwin T. Gibson), **1951:** 41, 205
Defense Program, National, **1947:** 77
Defense spending, **1947:** 31 [4], 35; **1948:** 98, 167; **1949:** 8 (pp. 46–62), 50, 154, 177, 244; **1950:** 9 (pp. 46–48, 60–66), 110 [1], 121 [13], 151, 193, 202, 243; **1951:** 12 [1, 7, 19, 30, 39], 13 (pp. 62, 68–70), 28, 92, 93, 107, 118 [1], 123, 138, 167, 174, 176, 199, 221, 247 [13], 279; **1952–53:** 15, 17 [2, 34], 18 (p. 69), 55, 89 [4], 98 [11], 101, 196, 215, 231, 268 [7], 272, 274 [5], 282 [4], 289, 295 [1], 304, 317 [2, 3], 318, 319 [5], 322, 349, 353 [3], 366, 367 (pp. 1135–1138), 368, 376
  Alaska, **1950:** 9 (p. 91)
  News conference remarks, **1948:** 55 [5, 15], 77 [10], 86, 243 [1, 4, 7], 278 [2]; **1949:** 66 [12], 72 [2, 7, 16, 19], 192 [10, 13, 15], 200 [20], 234 [2], 269 [18]; **1950:** 8 [43], 105 [13], 146 [12, 17]
  Postwar reduction, **1949:** 86
Defense support.
  See Military assistance and defense support.
Defense Transportation, Office of, **1946:** 124, 228; **1947:** 18, 47, 60
  Operation of Capital Transit Co., **1945:** 195n.
  Operation of Great Lakes Towing Co. of Cleveland, Ohio, **1945:** 202 [1]
  Wartime controls, reduction, **1945:** 202 [3]
Defense Transportation, Office of, Director (J. Monroe Johnson), **1945:** 52 [3]; **1946:** 23, 54n., 55, 56n., 120; **1948:** 1; **1949:** 64
  Letter, **1945:** 53
De Fernandes, Raul, **1949:** 103n.

Deficit spending, **1945:** 128; **1946:** 72 [7], 79, 187, 193, 194, 229 [26]; **1947:** 4 (p. 24), 6 [10, 20], 68, 180 [19]; **1948:** 124 [4], 167, 175, 278 [2]; **1949:** 5, 151, 154; **1950:** 6, 9 (pp. 44, 45, 47, 54, 103), 18, 200, 202; **1951:** 13 (pp. 66, 68), 91, 228; **1952–53:** 15, 17 [2, 34], 18 (p. 63), 215, 231, 367 (p. 1132), 368
  News conference remarks, **1949:** 7 [50], 30 [11], 58 [12], 66 [3], 78 [18], 95 [19], 144 [17], 182 [7], 234 [2], 236 [12], 260 [5], 267 [3]; **1950:** 8 [31], 105 [9], 137 [7]; **1951:** 12 [24], 227 [20]
  Postal service, **1951:** 45
Deflation, **1945:** 42, 180, 202 [3]; **1946:** 2, 18 (pp. 49, 51); **1947:** 68, 116, 180 [21], 224; **1948:** 26 [10]; **1949:** 5, 7 [28, 30], 148 [19]; **1952–53:** 123 [3, 18]
De Gasperi, Alcide (Prime Minister of Italy), **1947:** 14 [20], 15, 239; **1948:** 192; **1951:** 231, 232, 235, 239 [19]
De Gaulle, Gen. Charles, **1945:** 33; **1948:** 84 [4]; **1950:** 203 [4]; **1951:** 160
  Gift of C-54 aircraft from the President, **1945:** 147 [3]
  Joint statement with, **1945:** 113
  Legion of Merit, citation, **1945:** 109
  Message, **1945:** 29
  News conference remarks on, **1945:** 4 [14], 26 [5], 31 [4], 44 [7], 76 [11], 107 [5], 118 [4], 147 [3]
Dejoie, C. C., **1947:** 48n.
De Kauffmann, Henrik, **1951:** 166n.
Delaney, Edward K., **1948:** 236; **1949:** 250n.
De Lattre de Tassigny, Gen. Jean, death of, **1952–53:** 7 [14]
Delaware
  Campaign remarks, **1948:** 225 [1]; **1952–53:** 303 [1]
  Candidates for public office, **1948:** 225 [1]; **1952–53:** 303 [1]
  Gov. Elbert N. Carvel, **1952–53:** 303 [1]
Delaware River Port Authority, **1952–53:** 209
Delgado, Francisco A., **1946:** 119 [1, 14]; **1951:** 64n.
Dellwo, Robert, **1952–53:** 272, 274 [2]
De los Monteros, Antonio, **1947:** 95 [17]
Demetriades, Anthony, **1949:** 27
Deming, N. Mex., campaign remarks, **1948:** 208 [2]
Democracy, **1947:** 30, 51, 76, 79, 90 [1]
  Comments on, **1946:** 83, 271
"Democracy, U.S.A.," radio program, **1947:** 48n.
Democracy, Voice of, remarks to contest winners, **1951:** 40
Democratic Action, Americans for, **1952–53:** 129, 136 [7]
Democratic Club, New York City, campaign remarks, **1948:** 261 [14]

Democratic Club, Women's National, **1951**: 297
Democratic Conference, Midwest, **1949**: 122 [4]
Democratic Farm Labor Party, **1949**: 250n.
Democratic Farm Leaders, **1949**: 113 [3]
Democratic National Committee, **1945**: 4 [2], 208
    [6]; **1946**: 199 [5], 223 [1]; **1947**: 67 [8], 107
    [10], 177 [1, 10, 17], 204n., 205 [4]; **1948**:
    211n.; **1949**: 190, 219n.; **1950**: 279; **1951**:
    63 [3], 227 [10, 16, 18], 275 [6, 9]; **1952–53**:
    26 [3, 28], 71, 88 [22], 115 [21], 127 [4, 16],
    166 [13], 228 [12], 247 [4], 253 [3], 266 [11],
    303 [9], 308 [6]
    Centennial, address, **1948**: 32
    Chairmanship, question of change in, **1952–53**:
        334 [4]
    Deficit, **1952–53**: 342 [12]
    Finance Committee, **1949**: 16
    News conference remarks, **1949**: 166 [4], 182 [9],
        192 [20], 226 [7]
    State chairmen, qualifications for, **1952–53**: 342
        [5]
    Treasurer (Joseph L. Blythe), **1948**: 110 [18]
    Women's Division, **1949**: 20
Democratic National Committee, Chairman
    (William Boyle), **1949**: 190, 192 [20], 220,
    226 [7]; **1950**: 12n.; **1951**: 27
    Letter, **1951**: 110
    News conference remarks on, **1950**: 11 [12], 169
        [6], 258 [9], 273 [15]; **1951**: 113 [3], 183 [3,
        5, 15], 227 [10, 18], 239 [14], 261 [3, 10, 12,
        15, 19]
    Successor, question of, **1951**: 261 [3, 12], 275 [6,
        9, 10, 16, 19]
Democratic National Committee, Chairman
    (Robert E. Hannegan), **1945**: 22 [3, 4, 7];
    1946: 37 [5], 53 [16], 67n., 84 [5, 8], 173
    [14], 223 [1]; **1947**: 14 [16, 18, 22], 31 [3],
    155 [2], 177 [10]
Democratic National Committee, Chairman (Sen.
    J. Howard McGrath), **1948**: 21 [8], 49 [6],
    84 [11], 101, 110 [18], 150 [5], 163 [6], 174
    [5], 261 [5] **1949**: 16, 20, 38, 39, 74
Democratic National Committee, Chairman
    (Frank E. McKinney), **1951**: 300 [1, 3, 4,
    8, 20, 23]; **1952–53**: 2 [6], 7 [3], 28, 64 [2, 5,
    10, 11, 16], 69, 71, 88 [15], 127 [4, 16], 136
    [7]
Democratic National Committee, Chairman
    (Stephen A. Mitchell), **1952–53**: 342 [8],
    377 [29]
Democratic National Congressional Committee,
    1951: 27
Democratic National Convention, **1947**: 78 [8], 177
    [1, 17]; **1949**: 190; **1950**: 12, 39; **1952–53**:
    98 [42], 123 [19], 149 [18], 175 [3], 197 [3]
    Attendance, the President's, **1952–53**: 88 [18, 20],
        98 [42], 127 [1, 6, 16], 156 [7]

Democratic National Convention — *continued*
    California delegates to, **1952–53**: 136 [13]
    Humphrey, Sen. Hubert H., suggested appoint-
        ment as keynoter, **1952–53**: 88 [15]
    News conference remarks on, **1948**: 11 [11], 150
        [6, 10]; **1952–53**: 64 [10, 11, 13]
    1912, **1951**: 6
    1952, **1951**: 63 [3], 113 [2]
    Nomination, acceptance address, **1948**: 160
    Stevenson, Gov. Adlai E., nomination, **1952–53**:
        218, 318
    Texas delegation, **1952–53**: 197 [15]
    Voting plans, the President's, **1952–53**: 197 [17]
Democratic Party, **1946**: 67, 70 [13], 173 [8, 12],
    221; **1947**: 31 [6], 46 [14], 62 [10], 67 [8],
    68, 70 [23], 107 [10, 13], 205 [7], 218 [1],
    243 [8, 12, 17]; **1949**: 15, 39, 74, 220; **1950**:
    39, 134, 279; **1952–53**: 71, 129, 240 [1], 241
    Administration records, custody and disposition,
        1952–53: 334 [11, 15]
    Campaign remarks on, **1952–53**: 266 [1], 280 [3,
        4], 281, 284 [5], 286 [3, 5, 6], 287, 288, 289
        [2, 11, 12], 292 [3, 7, 9, 13], 294, 295 [2],
        298 [5, 12], 303 [6], 306 [2, 7], 308 [4], 311
        [1], 312, 314, 315 [5], 316, 317 [4, 5, 7], 218,
        321 [7], 322
    Congressional leadership, resolution on dispatch
        of troops to Europe, **1951**: 16 [15]
    Communism in, charges of, **1952–53**: 69
    Communist view of, **1948**: 266
    Cooperatives, encouragement of, **1951**: 206
    Dissension within, **1948**: 77 [14], 150 [6], 163 [8],
        198 [3], 278 [5]
    "Dixiecrats".
        See main heading, "Dixiecrats".
    Election campaign, conduct of, **1952–53**: 253 [14]
    Election prospects, **1952–53**: 197 [19]
    Farm program, **1952–53**: 267
    "Favorite son" Presidential candidates, **1952–53**:
        26 [16]
    Jefferson-Jackson Day dinner, **1951**: 80
    Leadership role, the President's, **1951**: 27
    Legislative program, **1948**: 160, 194 [10], 201, 212
        [9], 216 [3, 13, 16], 218 [3], 228 [1, 5, 8, 10,
        11], 232, 233 [3], 235 [4, 5], 236, 237 [1],
        259 [6], 261 [5, 8], 262, 264 [2], 269, 270,
        274 [4, 12, 13]
    Special interest opposition to, **1951**: 215
    Luncheon, San Francisco, **1951**: 215
    Majorities in States, predictions by President,
        1948: 266
    Members of Congress, supper for, **1950**: 12;
        1951: 8
    Missouri, **1950**: 16 [12], 38 [12]
    New York, influence of Frank Costello in, **1951**:
        95 [5]
    New York State, **1950**: 270 [10]
        Chairman, **1952–53**: 359 [11]

Democratic Party — *continued*
  News conference remarks on, **1948:** 21 [1, 8], 55
    [11], 77 [14], 93 [2], 150 [6], 163 [6], 170 [1],
    174 [5], 278 [5]; **1949:** 52 [6], 89 [14, 19], 93
    [8], 122 [4], 144 [4], 226 [11], 253 [5], 267
    [15]; **1950:** 11 [12], 16 [12], 29 [15], 34 [13],
    38 [12], 44 [7, 13], 152 [1], 270 [10];
    1952–53: 123 [21], 377 [21]
  Nominees, President's influence on choice of,
    1952–53: 197 [9]
  Ohio, **1950:** 11 [12]
  Organization, **1948:** 240 [7]
  Pennsylvania, **1952–53:** 26 [3]
  Platform (1944), **1948:** 268; **1949:** 16, 38, 39, 89
    [14], 122 [4], 144 [4], 190, 219, 220, 250 [2],
    252, 253 [5]; **1950:** 12, 39, 110 [2], 134,
    135, 139; **1951:** 7 [2], 227 [22]; **1952–53:** 98
    [5, 18], 123 [7, 18], 127 [1, 16], 175 [15],
    218, 221 [14], 230, 241, 242 [3], 247 [10],
    266 [4, 5, 7, 9, 10], 267, 268 [4], 270 [5], 280
    [1, 3], 282 [6], 284 [6], 285, 288, 289, 290,
    295 [9], 298 [3, 9, 12, 14], 299, 303 [4, 9],
    304, 306 [1, 2, 6, 7], 308 [8], 311 [2], 313 [3],
    315 [4, 6], 317 [8], 319 [5], 321 [2]
  Pledge of future assistance to, the President's,
    1952–53: 377 [29]
  Political philosophy, **1948:** 247, 258; **1950:** 39,
    134; **1951:** 297; **1952–53:** 129, 284 [6]
  Position on Israel, **1948:** 253, 264 [3]
  Post-election plans, **1952–53:** 342 [9]
  Presidential candidate in 1952, question of, **1951:**
    113 [5]
  Record in office, **1948:** 160, 206 [2], 207, 208 [1,
    2, 8], 209, 212 [2, 3, 9], 214 [5, 6, 8, 9], 216
    [2, 3, 5–7, 11, 14], 217, 218 [1, 3, 11], 219,
    220, 227 [5], 228 [13], 229, 237 [4, 5], 240
    [2, 3, 5–7], 241, 242 [1, 2], 246, 252, 255,
    256, 257 [2–5], 258, 259 [1–3, 5, 6], 260,
    261 [2–4], 262, 264 [2, 5], 266, 267 [2, 3],
    268; **1949:** 38, 220; **1950:** 12, 39, 279;
    1951: 80, 215, 238; **1952–53:** 69, 129, 194,
    195 [2, 3], 197 [16], 218, 233 [7], 240 [2],
    241, 242 [1, 3], 266 [2–6, 11], 268 [3, 5, 7,
    8], 269, 270 [1, 5, 7, 10], 271–273, 274 [2],
    276–278, 280 [1, 3], 281, 282 [1, 6, 8], 285,
    286 [1, 2, 5, 8], 288, 289 [1–3, 8], 290, 291,
    292 [3, 5, 11, 12], 295 [6, 7, 9], 298 [1, 6, 8,
    12, 14], 303 [1, 2, 4, 9, 10], 305, 306 [4–6],
    308 [2, 6, 8], 311 [3], 312, 313 [1, 6], 315 [1,
    3], 317 [1, 6, 7], 318, 319 [1, 3, 5, 6], 321 [1,
    3, 5, 7], 324
  Regional conferences, **1951:** 110, 113 [2, 3]
  Relationship of Postmaster General Hannegan,
    1945: 181 [12]
  Reorganization, **1952–53:** 342 [5]
  Southern candidates, prospects of nomination
    and election, **1952–53:** 98 [18]

Democratic Party — *continued*
  Southern wing, civil rights strategy meeting,
    1950: 23ftn. (p. 134)
  Stevenson, Gov. Adlai E., leadership, **1952–53:**
    334 [4]
  Women, role of, **1948:** 211; **1949:** 219, 252; **1950:**
    139, 255; **1951:** 238
Democratic Women's Club, Bronx, N.Y., cam-
    paign remarks, **1948:** 264 [3]
Democratic Women's Day, **1947:** 204n.; **1948:** 211;
    1950: 255; **1951:** 238
Democratic Women's National Council, **1950:** 139
DeMolay, Order of, **1950:** 41n., 42; **1951:** 41n.
De Morgenstierne, Wilhelm Munthe, **1949:** 116n.
Denfeld, Adm. L. E., **1945:** 160n.; **1947:** 221 [1];
    1948: 110 [13]; **1949:** 179 [1], 231 [18], 240
    [1, 18], 241n.
Denham, Robert N., **1947:** 145 [2], 182 [5], 218 [14];
    1949: 240 [2]; **1950:** 16 [10, 14, 20, 23], 38
    [21], 146 [7]
De Nicola, Enrico, **1947:** 15
Denmark, **1945:** 186; **1949:** 30 [13], 68, 113 [11], 162
  Ambassador Henrik de Kauffmann, **1951:** 166n.
  Assistance, **1947:** 238; **1952–53:** 217
  International Labor Organization, meeting,
    1945: 181 [10]
  Korean war, participation, **1951:** 170
  Meeting with newsmen, **1946:** 6 [18]
  Military assistance, **1950:** 22
  NATO contribution, **1952–53:** 217
  Soviet bloc, trade with, **1952–53:** 217, 358
  U.S. Ambassador Eugenie Anderson, **1952–53:**
    217, 313 [2]
Dennison, Rear Adm. Robert L., **1949:** 36; **1950:**
    156
Denny, Charles R., Jr., **1946:** 36, 43 [1], 66 [1], 147
Dental Association, American, board of trustees,
    1951: 258
Dental education, **1950:** 9 (p. 75)
Dentists, **1946:** 1
  Shortage, **1947:** 98; **1952–53:** 367 (p. 1158)
Denton, Winfield K., **1948:** 218 [9, 10]
Denver, Colo.
  Campaign remarks, **1948:** 198 [3]; **1952–53:** 282
    [7]
  Democratic regional conventions in, **1951:** 110n.,
    113 [2, 3]
  Inter-American Conservation Conference, **1948:**
    198 [1]
  Mayor Quigg Newton, **1948:** 198n.
De Pachmann, Vladimir, **1951:** 99
Dependent territories, social policy, **1946:** 180
Depreciation allowances, **1951:** 91
Depressed areas, **1947:** 4 (p. 34); **1948:** 37
  Federal aid, **1949:** 151; **1950:** 6, 135
  Government contracts, channeling to, **1949:** 155
    [1], 161 [12], 179 [7]
  Procurement, concentration in, **1949:** 156

Depressions, **1947:** 4 (p. 13), 76, 95 [21, 23, 27], 107 [2], 152, 214, 224; **1948:** 80, 99, 101, 165, 183 [5], 184, 241, 261 [6]; **1949:** 25, 66 [3], 154; **1951:** 202, 279
See also Economy, national.
1919, **1948:** 2, 117, 183 [6], 223
1920, **1946:** 2, 18 (p. 53), 39, 153, 193; **1947:** 4 (p. 32), 51, 76, 152; **1949:** 5 ; **1950:** 111
1921, **1949:** 39
1929, **1947:** 152; **1948:** 32, 189, 195, 198 [4, 7], 199, 212 [10], 215, 223, 227 [7, 9], 231 [5], 233 [2], 234, 240 [4], 241, 246, 248, 255, 257 [5], 258, 260, 262; **1949:** 39, 195; **1950:** 39, 110 [5], 111, 118, 122, 127 [4, 7], 128, 157, 279
Home mortgages, foreclosures, **1950:** 51
Prevention, **1949:** 5, 54
Dermond, Philip, **1952–53:** 286 [2]
Desalinization, water, **1950:** 9 (p. 90)
DeSapio, Fred M., **1948:** 189n.
Deshler, Ohio, campaign remarks, **1948:** 231 [7]; **1952–53:** 311 [2]
Des Moines, Iowa, **1949:** 113 [3], 179 [12]
Campaign remarks, **1948:** 194 [6, 9]
Midwest Democratic Conference, **1949:** 122 [4]
Veterans convention, **1949:** 203
Des Moines River, **1947:** 141 [2]
De Sousa Costa, Arthur, **1949:** 103n.
Despotism, struggle against, **1951:** 225
Destroyers, wartime transfer to U.K., **1947:** 132
Detroit, Mich., **1946:** 53 [2]; **1951:** 174
Attempted bombing of UAW headquarters, **1949:** 269 [14]
Campaign address, **1948:** 184; **1952–53:** 317 [8], 318
Eisenhower, Gen. Dwight D., comments on campaign speech in, **1952–53:** 319 [1], 320
Mayor Albert E. Cobo, **1951:** 174
Mayor Eugene I. Van Antwerp, **1948:** 184
Visit by the President, recollections of, **1951:** 38
Detroit River, **1947:** 171
Deupree, R. R., **1947:** 122
De Valera, Eamon, **1948:** 49 [20]
Development Advisory Board, International.
See International Development Advisory Board.
Dever, Paul, **1948:** 259 [5]; **1949:** 32 [1]; **1952–53:** 292 [9, 11, 12], 295 [7–9], 296, 298
Devils Lake, N. Dak., campaign remarks, **1952–53:** 266 [6]
Deviny, John J. (Public Printer), **1949:** 147
Devlin, William F., **1948:** 124 [2], 125
De Weldon, Felix, **1949:** 20n.
Dewey, Bradley, **1948:** 278 [1]
Dewey, Gov. Thomas E., **1945:** 147 [2]; **1946:** 229 [13]; **1948:** 168; **1949:** 14, 30 [6–8], 237; **1950:** 157, 175, 270ftn. (p. 681); **1951:** 7 [11], 188 [10, 13], 224 [1]; **1952–53:** 26 [21],

Dewey, Gov. Thomas E. — *continued*
127 [17], 129, 143, 233 [15], 242 [1], 267, 268 [3], 283, 289 [8], 289 [10, 11], 295 [6], 298 [14], 303 [6], 304, 306 [1], 313 [4]
Atomic energy, position on development, **1948:** 239
Candidacy for President, **1948:** 150 [6], 225 [3], 231 [1, 3, 7, 8], 233 [1, 4, 6], 234, 236, 237 [5], 240 [1], 241, 247, 252–254, 257 [2–5], 258, 259 [2, 4–6], 260, 261 [4–8, 11, 12, 15], 262, 264 [1, 3, 5], 266, 267 [1, 2], 268
Case Against the New Deal, The, **1948:** 247
Communism in Government, charges of, **1948:** 181 [12]
Congress, endorsement of legislative record, **1948:** 246
Israel, position on, **1948:** 253n.
News conference remarks on, **1948:** 11 [11], 150 [6], 163 [20], 166 [7], 168, 174 [1], 178 [4, 14], 243 [5, 9], 278 [16, 42], 285 [6, 9, 15]
Telegram, **1945:** 148
Dexter, Iowa, **1950:** 110 [3]
Campaign remarks, **1948:** 194 [8], 195
Diabetes, prevention, **1951:** 135
Diamantopoulos, Cimon, death of, **1946:** 261
Dickerson, Col. Edwin, **1950:** 121 [8]
Dickinson, Mrs. La Fell (Emily G.), **1946:** 45n., 255n.
Dickman, Barnard F., **1950:** 23 [5]; **1951:** 226n.
Dickson, Cecil B., **1947:** 155 [6]
Dictatorship, **1947:** 138; **1948:** 256
Comment on, **1946:** 52; **1951:** 18, 116
Indoctrination of youth by, **1950:** 299
Dill, Sir John, unveiling of statue, **1950:** 275
Dill, Lady, **1950:** 275n.
Dillon, C. Douglas, **1950:** 23 [10]
Dillon, Montana, campaign remarks, **1948:** 120 [5]
Dilworth, Richardson, **1952–53:** 49 [10]
Dimock, Edward J., **1951:** 113 [10]
Dingell, Repr. John D., social security bill, **1945:** 44 [16]
Dinosaur National Monument, Colo., **1952–53:** 280 [4]
Diphtheria, prevention, **1951:** 135
Diplomas, Fleet Sonar School, presentation, **1949:** 53
Diplomats, U.S., salary, **1945:** 52 [19]
Directive on immigration to U.S. of displaced persons and refugees in Europe, **1945:** 225
Dirksen, Sen. Everett McK., **1952–53:** 21 [3], 283, 317 [2]
Disability compensation, **1947:** 98
Government employees, **1947:** 6 [2]
Veterans, **1947:** 2 (p. 8)
Disability insurance, **1948:** 5 (pp. 33, 34), 107, 175, 181 [2]; **1949:** 8 (pp. 49, 66), 135; **1950:** 74, 224

DiSalle, Michael V., **1948:** 257 [3]; **1950:** 287ftn. (p. 716); **1951:** 37 [7], 49 [21], 56 [5], 101 [8], 118 [2, 4], 123, 275 [10]; **1952–53:** 15, 26 [31], 34, 286 [4–6], 287, 311 [1, 2], 319, 320, 345 [5], 348

Disarmament, **1947:** 2 (p. 11); **1948:** 243 [4]; **1949:** 148 [1], 226 [22]; **1950:** 80ftn. (p. 233), 162, 271, 303; **1951:** 54, 56 [16], 140 [14], 170, 256, 275 [4, 21], 293; **1952–53:** 5, 170, 196

    Rush-Bagot agreement (1817), **1947:** 111

    U.S. and Soviet proposals, **1947:** 1, 21

Disarmament Commission, United Nations, **1952–53:** 196

Disaster Relief Act of 1950, **1951:** 163, 196

Disasters, natural

    Droughts, **1947:** 198, 202, 238; **1951:** 34, 63 [2], 81, 124; **1952–53:** 166 [10], 221 [1]

        Yugoslavia, **1950:** 290, 293

    Dust storms, **1950:** 110 [8]

    Earthquakes, **1951:** 34, 124

        Ecuador, **1949:** 182 [5]

    Emergency funds, **1948:** 126 [1]

    Floods, **1947:** 181 (p. 398), 198, 202, 231, 238; **1948:** 111, 119, 214 [7]; **1949:** 22 [1], 77, 236 [3]; **1950:** 129 [1, 3, 5, 7], 130, 306

      See also Flood control.

    Red Cross services, **1948:** 40; **1951:** 47, 124, 162, 196, 271

    Relief programs, **1949:** 8 (p. 75), 22 [1], 28 [2], 42, 182 [5]; **1952–53:** 18 (pp. 56–57), 50, 221 [1], 231

    Use of surplus property for, **1948:** 45

    Snowstorms, **1949:** 22 [1], 28 [2, 4]

Discrimination.

    See Civil rights.

Disease prevention, **1949:** 8 (p. 70), 54; **1950:** 9 (p. 75); **1951:** 13 (pp. 98, 99), 135, 184, 297; **1952–53:** 2 [3], 170, 249, 367 (p. 1157)

    See also Health programs.

    Animal diseases, **1949:** 263

    Cardiovascular, **1949:** 29

    Heart disease, **1950:** 30

    Livestock, **1948:** 208 [6]

    Malaria

        Northern India, **1950:** 177

        Sardinia, **1951:** 235

    Occupational, **1948:** 248

    Plant and animal, **1950:** 177; **1951:** 13 (p. 90)

    Poliomyelitis, **1949:** 205 [2]

    Puerto Rico, **1951:** 243

    Tuberculosis, **1950:** 9 (p. 75), 286

Disloyalty in Philippines, **1945:** 176

Displaced Persons Act, **1949:** 8 (p. 55); **1950:** 9 (p. 58), 167; **1952–53:** 65, 288, 289 [7], 297, 301

    See also Immigration laws.

Displaced Persons Act — *continued*

    Amendment, proposed, **1948:** 165, 249, 256, 257 [1], 258, 261 [7]

    Approval, **1948:** 142

Displaced Persons Commission, **1950:** 9 (p. 58), 167; **1952–53:** 65

Displaced persons in Europe, **1945:** 210; **1946:** 236; **1947:** 7 (pp. 57, 66), 38; **1952–53:** 78, 94, 145, 164, 182, 244

    See also Refugees and escapees.

    Assistance, **1952–53:** 65, 66

    Germany, **1946:** 136 [14], 267

        General Eisenhower, letter to, **1945:** 152

        Joint statement with Allied leaders, **1945:** 9

        Prime Minister Attlee, letter to, **1945:** 188

        Relief and rehabilitation, **1945:** 186

    Greek children, repatriation, **1950:** 261

    Harrison (Earl G.) report, **1945:** 152, 187, 188; **1946:** 227

    Immigration to U.S., **1946:** 18 (p. 44), 136 [14], 212, 227, 241, 267; **1947:** 2 (p. 10), 95 [22, 24], 140, 182 [10]; **1948:** 2, 115, 142, 160, 165, 174 [4], 178 [12], 236, 249, 256, 257 [1], 258, 261 [7]; **1949:** 2, 58 [5, 31], 144 [2]; **1950:** 2, 134, 167; **1952–53:** 65

    Statement and directive, **1945:** 225

    Jews.

      See main heading, Jews.

    NATO forces, proposed enlistment in, **1952–53:** 65

    News conference remarks on, **1947:** 141 [6], 155 [4]

    Occupational skills of, **1947:** 140

    President's visit to camp (1945), **1948:** 257 [1]

    Repatriation, **1946:** 18 (p. 46); **1947:** 38

    U.S. Armed Forces, service in, **1952–53:** 65

    U.S. relief for, **1947:** 43

Displaced Persons Executive, Combined, **1945:** 152

Distillers, grain conservation by, **1947:** 202, 205 [14, 18], 209 [2], 210 [3], 236 [1], 242; **1948:** 14, 19

Distillers Coordinating Committee, **1948:** 14

Distinguished Service Medal awards.

    See under Medals, presentation.

District of Columbia, **1946:** 118; **1948:** 247, 272; **1950:** 110 [2]

    Air photos of defense installations, press publication of, **1951:** 247 [1]

    American legion, dedication of headquarters, **1951:** 191

    Anacostia, civil rights demonstration at swimming pool, **1949:** 144 [14]

    Budget, **1949:** 58 [2]

    Butter prices, **1947:** 242

    Campaign remarks, **1952–53:** 308 [9], 330

    Capital, question of relocation, **1950:** 46 [5]

    Carter Barron Amphitheater, dedication, **1951:** 116

District of Columbia — *continued*
  Circumferential highway, proposed, **1952–53:** 18 (p. 113)
  Civil defense, **1950:** 203 [14]
  Commissioner, vacancy in office, **1951:** 22 [7]
  Commissioners, **1946:** 43 [10]
    Donohue, F. Joseph, **1952–53:** 308n., 353 [16]
    Mason, Guy, **1947:** 243 [3]
    Young, Brig. Gen. Gordon R., **1947:** 70 [7]
    Young, John R., **1946:** 66 [1]; **1949:** 26n., 40 [8], 93 [2, 11], 113 [1]
  Communist spy ring in, question of, **1948:** 170 [4, 6]
  Community War Fund campaign, **1945:** 171
  Courts, **1950:** 46ftn. (p. 182), 49, 174, 176
    District Court of the United States, **1945:** 132 [1]; **1948:** 171
  Crime in, remarks by Gov. Stevenson, **1952–53:** 233 [4], 238 [3]
  Decision to leave Washington, the President's, **1952–53:** 342 [17]
  Dispersal of Government from, AEC recommendation, **1949:** 260 [4, 22]
  Engineer Commissioner (Brig. Gen. Charles W. Kutz), **1945:** 129 [13]
  Equestrian statues from Italy, dedication, **1951:** 235
  Expenditures for U.S. Park Police, reimbursement, **1947:** 165
  Federal agencies, question of dispersal, **1950:** 214 [10], 230 [5], 273 [9]; **1952–53:** 18 (p. 113)
  Federal contribution to, **1946:** 136 [16]
  First Baptist Church, President's attendance, **1949:** 83
  Freedom Fair project, abandonment, **1950:** 77n.
  Gambling, enforcement of laws against, **1950:** 38 [9]
  Gompers Square, dedication, **1951:** 279
  Government, reorganization, **1952–53:** 114
  Government buildings, management, **1950:** 73
  Government offices, dispersal, **1951:** 13 (p. 104)
  Home rule, **1948:** 9 [11], 20; **1949:** 11 [7], 164; **1950:** 2, 214 [3]
    Proposed, **1951:** 209 [3]; **1952–53:** 5, 114, 160
  Hospital and research facilities, **1948:** 5 (pp. 35, 37)
  Industrial employees in, compensation and safety programs, **1950:** 74
  Jailbreaks, **1946:** 72 [15]
  Judicial vacancies, **1949:** 205 [13], 231 [2], 236 [6], 267 [15]
  Law enforcement bill, veto, **1945:** 80
  Library and museum services, Federal, **1952–53:** 367 (p. 1155)
  National Capital Sesquicentennial Commission, **1949:** 79
  National Theatre, **1947:** 14 [23]

District of Columbia — *continued*
  News conference remarks, **1949:** 11 [7], 58 [2], 66 [22], 72 [11, 21], 112 [7, 17], 144 [14, 31], 161 [4], 205 [13], 231 [2], 236 [6], 260 [4, 22], 267 [15, 17]; **1950:** 38 [9], 46 [5], 137 [12], 146 [5], 203 [14], 214 [3], 230 [5]
  Newspapers, President's reading of, **1947:** 210 [2]
  New York Avenue Presbyterian church, cornerstone laying, **1951:** 68
  Police brutality, charges of, **1947:** 209 [8]
  Primary elections, question of, **1952–53:** 44 [4], 175 [5, 13]
  Public Utilities Commission, vacancy on, **1949:** 267 [17]
  Racial discrimination, elimination, **1951:** 171 [9]; **1952–53:** 303 [3, 4], 353 [16]
  Recorder of Deeds
    Appointment authority, **1952–53:** 98 [27], 156 [13], 160
    Nomination, **1951:** 251ftn. (p. 565)
  Red Cross building, cornerstone laying, **1951:** 271
  Redevelopment land Agency, **1949:** 8 (p. 94)
  River and harbor construction, **1947:** 35
  Sales tax, **1949:** 58 [2], 112 [17]
  Sesquicentennial, **1948:** 47; **1949:** 72 [11], 79, 144 [31], 161 [4]; **1950:** 77, 137 [12], 146 [5]
  Technical schools, subsidization by Air Force, **1951:** 85 [9]
  Traffic laws, **1949:** 114
  Transit strike, **1945:** 195, 208ftn. (p. 528)
  Union Station, dedication of servicemen's center, **1951:** 186
  U.S. Court of Appeals, **1945:** 129 [4], 132 [1]
  U.S. District Court, **1946:** 229 [1]
  Urban development, **1950:** 9 (p. 102); **1951:** 116
  Voting rights, **1945:** 193 [4]; **1946:** 18 (p. 66), 237 [23, 25]
    Presidential elections, **1948:** 20
  West Executive Avenue, removal of pillars, **1947:** 95 [1]
Dividends
  Tax withholding, **1950:** 200, 202
  Veterans, insurance, **1950:** 202; **1951:** 12 [52]
"Dixiecrats," **1949:** 144ftn. (p. 343); **1950:** 44 [7], 105 [19]; **1952–53:** 129, 290, 306 [2], 318
  Coalition with Republicans, **1949:** 269 [8]
  News conference remarks on, **1948:** 278 [5]; **1949:** 52 [7], 89 [19], 182 [9], 269 [8]; **1951:** 179 [2]
Dixon, Sherwood, **1952–53:** 315 [6], 321
Dixon, Mrs. Sherwood, **1952–53:** 315n.
Docherty, Rev. George M., **1951:** 68n.
Doctors, shortage of, **1948:** 181 [2], 233 [6], 241, 257 [1]; **1949:** 2, 219; **1950:** 2, 129 [4]; **1951:** 135, 307; **1952–53:** 284 [5], 333, 367 (p. 1158), 369

Documents, historical, library custody of, **1951:** 225

Documents, public, preservation and publication, **1950:** 53

Dodd, Brig. Gen. Francis T., **1952–53:** 127ftn. (p. 337)

Dodd, Norris E., **1949:** 263n.; **1951:** 259, 262

Dodd, Thomas J., **1952–53:** 292 [5, 7, 8], 293

Dodds, Harold W., **1946:** 139n., 268n.; **1947:** 117; **1950:** 136n.

Dodero, Alberto, **1948:** 9 [6]

Dodge, Joseph, **1949:** 118 [2]; **1952–53:** 331, 334 [7]

Dodge City, Kans., campaign remarks, **1948:** 137 [1]

Doenitz, Adm. Karl, **1945:** 22 [14]

Dollar, U.S., **1950:** 80 [8, 9], 122
　See also Currencies.
　Exchange, shortage abroad, **1947:** 191 [13], 197; **1949:** 5, 139, 151
　Stability, **1948:** 114 [3], 163 [17]; **1951:** 176, 199, 290

Dollar-a-year men, **1947:** 35, 46 [22]

Dom Pedro II, **1947:** 189; **1949:** 102

Domestic Commerce, Office of, **1946:** 118

Dominican Republic, Rafael L. Trujillo Molina, **1950:** 181 [2]

Donahue, Repr. Harold D., **1952–53:** 292 [10]

Donaldson, Jesse M., **1945:** 76 [1]
　See also Postmaster General.

Donaldson, Sgt. Mike, **1948:** 53

Dondero, Repr. George A., **1948:** 217, 232
　"Wanted: A New Federal Power Policy," **1948:** 209

Donnelly, Eugene P., **1949:** 119 [4]

Donnelly, Phil M., **1948:** 138 [3], 158, 268n.; **1952–53:** 156 [1], 284 [4, 5], 322

Donnelly, Walter J., **1950:** 217 [2, 4], 218; **1952–53:** 98 [40]

Donohue, F. Joseph, **1952–53:** 88 [8], 308 [9], 353 [16]

Donohue, Repr. Harold D., **1948:** 259 [5, 6]

Donora, Pa., **1950:** 101

Donovan, Gen. William J., **1946:** 11
　Letter, **1945:** 140

Doolan, Edward F., **1952–53:** 298 [2, 3]

Doolittle, Lt. Gen. James H., **1952–53:** 40, 155, 351

Dorchester, World War II troopship, **1951:** 30n.

Dorfman, Ben D., **1945:** 24

Dorr, Goldthwaite, **1946:** 136ftn. (p. 303)

Dorrance Brooks Park, New York City, campaign remarks, **1952–53:** 290

Doss, Desmond T., Congressional Medal of Honor presentation, **1945:** 167n.

Dougherty, Carroll R., **1949:** 240 [12]

Dougherty, Cardinal Dennis J., **1949:** 253 [17]

Dougherty, Richard Erwin, **1949:** 89 [1]

Doughton, Repr. Robert L., **1945:** 132 [8]; **1947:**

Doughton, Repr. Robert L. — *continued*
　218 [5]; **1949:** 6n., 95 [19]; **1950:** 284; **1952–53:** 2 [11], 213

Douglas, Repr. Helen Gahagan, **1946:** 173 [1]; **1948:** 4ftn. (p. 17), 88 [12]; **1950:** 278 [12]; **1952–53:** 310

Douglas, James M., **1946:** 20

Douglas, Lewis W., **1946:** 78 [3], 110 [10]; **1947:** 210 [4]; **1948:** 110 [9]; **1949:** 118 [7]

Douglas, Paul H., **1948:** 194 [1], 218 [1, 5–8], 219, 233 [4–6], 234, 256, 267 [3]; **1949:** 260 [22]; **1950:** 134; **1951:** 56 [14], 118 [8], 165 [8], 171 [8], 179 [8], 188 [7], 193 [1, 15], 251 [17], 275 [1]; **1952–53:** 3, 7 [10], 98 [24, 41]

Douglas, Stephen A., **1948:** 236

Douglas, Justice William O., **1946:** 41 [7, 13, 15]; **1948:** 278 [36]; **1950:** 121 [9]; **1951:** 37 [5]

Douglas Aircraft Co., **1951:** 252

Douglas County, Nebr., war memorial, **1948:** 116 [1]

Dover, N.H., campaign remarks, **1952–53:** 295 [3]

Downey, D. K., **1948:** 200 [3]

Downey, Sen. Sheridan, wage increase bill, **1945:** 147 [15, 18]

Downs, Joseph, **1950:** 278ftn. (p. 695)

Doyle, Michael F., **1949:** 17n.

Draft, **1945:** 114, 128; **1947:** 46 [12, 13, 20]; **1951:** 13 (p. 71); **1952–53:** 283, 295 [8], 307, 312
　Campaign remarks, **1948:** 200 [2]
　Deferment policy, **1951:** 15, 63 [15]; **1952–53:** 185–187
　Doctors, **1952–53:** 333
　Executive clemency for violators, **1946:** 270
　Extension, **1947:** 31 [18], 36 [24]; **1949:** 8 (p. 55); **1950:** 97 [12]
　International conscription, **1946:** 41 [20]
　Legislation, proposed, **1951:** 63 [22]
　News conference remarks, **1945:** 64 [7], 106 [14], 137 [12]; **1946:** 15 [20], 41 [20], 53 [4, 9], 75 [6, 17], 84 [24], 86 [11], 110 [16], 119 [4, 11]; **1947:** 36 [4]; **1948:** 71 [19], 93 [16], 110 [8], 174 [3]
　Quota increase, **1950:** 303
　Railroad strikers, proposed, **1946:** 125
　Reduction
　　Question of, **1952–53:** 313 [5]
　　Statement, **1945:** 101
　Rejectees, World War II, **1951:** 258
　Scientists, question of deferment, **1950:** 238 [7]
　Statement, **1946:** 119 [2]

Draft Act.
　See Selective Training and Service Act.

Drake, Henry, **1952–53:** 286 [5, 6]

Draper, Claude L., **1946:** 70 [1]

Draper, William H., Jr., **1952–53:** 55n., 217

Drawings by GI artists, **1946:** 41 [14]

Drees, Willem, **1952–53:** 21 [21]

Dress, William H., **1948:** 218 [10]
Drew, Dr. Charles, **1952–53:** 169
Driscoll, Gov. Alfred E., **1952–53:** 303 [6]
Driver training, **1947:** 118
Driving safety, statement, **1945:** 62
Drought control, **1948:** 217
Droughts
    India, **1951:** 34, 63, 124
    Yugoslavia, **1951:** 81
Drucker, Joseph J., **1952–53:** 35ftn. (p. 155)
Drug addicts, deportation, **1952–53:** 182
Drugs
    Chinese imports, **1948:** 31
    Letter on control of, **1951:** 201
Drum, Robert A., **1948:** 117
Drury, Newton B., **1946:** 81n.; **1947:** 165
Dryden, Hugh, **1951:** 89
Drydock, New Orleans, La., **1947:** 35
DuBois, Arthur E., **1945:** 175ftn. (p. 417)
DuBridge, Lee A., **1946:** 262 [1]; **1950:** 40n.; **1951:**
    89
Dudkin, Harry, **1948:** 227 [7]
Dudley, Dr. Benjamin Winslow, **1948:** 222 [3]
Duff, Gov. James H., **1949:** 194; **1950:** 29 [15], 137
    [20, 24], 185
Duffy, F. Ryan, **1948:** 228 [4]
Duggan, I. W., **1951:** 202
Duke, Joseph C., **1951:** 239 [7]
Duke of Edinburgh, **1951:** 282, 288
Duke University, **1951:** 256
Dulles, John Foster, **1946:** 173 [1]; **1947:** 14 [10];
    1949: 144 [29], 205 [4], 253 [9]; **1950:** 80
    [12], 219, 287 [6], 318 [12]; **1951:** 49ftn. (p.
    176), 84, 193 [3], 216, 247 [15]; **1952–53:**
    310, 353 [2]
    Nomination as Alternate U.S. Representative to
        U.N. General Assembly, **1945:** 219n.
Duluth, Minn.
    Campaign remarks, **1948:** 235 [5]; **1952–53:** 313
        [6]
    Mayor George W. Johnson, **1952–53:** 313n.
Duluth-Superior, harbor improvement, **1952–53:**
    367 (p. 1143)
Dumbarton Oaks Conference, **1945:** 67 [1], 69, 97,
    177
Dungess, John, **1948:** 225 [3]
Dunlap, John B., **1951:** 239 [13]; **1952–53:** 35 [9]
Dunlop, John T., **1950:** 27n., 36n.
Dunn, Eddie, **1948:** 116 [2]
Dunn, James C., **1946:** 84 [3]
Dunsmuir, Calif., campaign remarks, **1952–53:** 277
    [2]
Durand, Mich., campaign remarks, **1952–53:** 317
    [4]
Durbin, Andrew, **1948:** 231 [8]
Durham, Repr. Carl T., **1950:** 44 [2]
Durkin, Martin P., **1952–53:** 342ftn. (p. 1070)
Durr, C. J., **1948:** 84 [7]

Durr, Clifford, **1949:** 155 [2]
Durr, Robert, **1947:** 48n.
Dutchess County, N.Y., **1945:** 76 [2]
Dutra, Enrico Gaspar (President of Brazil), **1947:**
    188, 189; **1949:** 102, 103, 105, 107, 108
    News conference remarks on, **1949:** 93 [10], 95
        [5], 148 [20]
Dyke, Nathaniel, Jr., **1947:** 173, 174 [1]

Earle, George H., **1947:** 67 [10]
Earlham College, **1948:** 233 [1]
Early, Jubal, **1945:** 31 [7]
Early, Stephen T., **1945:** 8 [1]; **1949:** 76, 167;
    1952–53: 378
    Death of, **1951:** 190
    News conference remarks on, **1945:** 4 [2], 31 [7],
        157 [3]
    Resignation, letter, **1945:** 43
Earthquakes
    Ecuador, **1949:** 182 [5]
    India, **1951:** 34, 124
Easley, John F., **1948:** 214 [5]
East Indies, **1945:** 45
East Newark, N.J., Mayor Harry F. Lawson, **1948:**
    189n.
East St. Louis, Ill.
    Campaign remarks, **1948:** 138 [4]
    Mayor John T. Connors, **1948:** 138 [4]
Eastern Air Lines, Inc., **1952–53:** 246
Eastern Star, Order of the, **1950:** 266, 314
Eastland, Sen. James O., **1946:** 6 [8]; **1949:** 211 [4]
Easton, Pa., campaign remarks, **1948:** 227 [5]
Eaton, Repr. Charles A., **1945:** 10; **1946:** 173 [1];
    1947: 197; **1951:** 53
    Nomination as Alternate U.S. representative to
        U.N. General Assembly, **1945:** 219n.
Eaton, E. T., **1948:** 121
Eban, Abba S., **1952–53:** 144
Eberharter, Repr. Herman P., **1949:** 202n.
ECA.
    See Economic Cooperation Administration.
Eccles, Marriner S., **1947:** 232 [5]; **1948:** 13, 15 [1,
    9], 77 [9], 97 [14]; **1951:** 33 [11]
    Letter, **1948:** 13
    News conference remarks on, **1948:** 15 [1, 9], 77
        [9], 88 [2], 93 [17], 97 [14]
Eckdall, Frank F., **1952–53:** 236n.
Economic Advisers, Council of.
    See Council of Economic Advisers.
Economic assistance, **1946:** 47, 236; **1947:** 15, 21,
    29, 46 [5], 47, 56, 57, 62 [10], 76, 83, 90 [1],
    95 [11, 13, 16, 26], 99, 100, 107 [2, 8], 116,
    122, 131, 138, 143, 145 [12], 152, 180 [10],
    181 (pp. 395, 398, 405), 188, 195, 197, 198,
    202, 207, 212, 214, 217, 219, 220, 224, 228,
    232 [9, 11], 238, 243 [19]; **1948:** 5 (p. 21),

Economic assistance — *continued*
   260, 263; **1949:** 8 (pp. 46, 53, 54), 19, 71,
      117, 120, 139, 159, 160, 178, 184; **1950:** 6,
      9 (pp. 56, 58, 59), 81, 132, 159, 180, 193,
      204, 232, 269, 289, 294; **1951:** 11, 13 (pp.
      63, 73–75), 80, 96, 205, 290; **1952–53:** 15,
      18 (p. 19), 55, 81, 101, 144, 307, 315 [5],
      322, 376
   See also Foreign assistance; Military assistance
      and defense support; Mutual security
      program; Point 4 program; Technical
      assistance to less developed countries;
      Truman Doctrine.
   Africa, **1951:** 4
   Appropriation, **1951:** 117
   Arab states, **1951:** 114
   Asia, **1950:** 162; **1951:** 4, 13 (p. 74), 66, 114;
      1952–53: 18 (p. 76), 55, 57
      Burma, **1951:** 13 (p. 74)
      Colombo plan, **1951:** 114
      Formosa, **1951:** 13 (p. 74)
      India, **1952–53:** 18 (p. 76), 367 (p. 1140)
      Indochina, **1951:** 13 (p. 75)
      Indonesia, **1951:** 13 (p. 74)
      Japan, **1951:** 13 (p. 74)
      Korea, **1952–53:** 296, 310, 320, 321 [2]
      Philippines, **1951:** 13 (p. 74), 64
      Thailand, **1951:** 13 (p. 74)
   Denial to nations trading with Communist bloc,
      1951: 117, 118 [14]; **1952–53:** 358
   Europe, **1951:** 4, 13 (p. 73), 59, 114, 167, 209 [13],
      256, 297; **1952–53:** 5, 15, 18 (p. 74), 27, 55,
      295 [8], 298 [8], 315 [5], 317 [2], 354
      See also European recovery program; Mar-
         shall plan.
      Austria, **1951:** 13 (p. 72), 114; **1952–53:** 55
      France, **1951:** 25; **1952–53:** 358, 367 (p. 1140)
      Germany, **1951:** 114
      Italy, **1951:** 232, 235n.; **1952–53:** 358
      Termination of, proposal by Secretary Sawyer,
         1952–53: 353 [13]
      Trieste, **1951:** 114
      Yugoslavia, **1951:** 81, 114, 292
   Expenditures for, **1952–53:** 231, 367 (p. 1139)
   IBRD loans for, **1951:** 219
   Indians, American, **1950:** 91
   Latin America, **1951:** 4, 13 (p. 75), 114; **1952–53:**
      55, 367 (p. 1140)
      Ecuador, **1951:** 134
   Less developed countries and new nations, **1951:**
      11, 41, 50, 53, 114, 250; **1952–53:** 15, 57,
      367 (p. 1139), 376, 378
      See also Point 4 program.
   U.N. program, **1950:** 143
   Middle East, **1950:** 25; **1952–53:** 18 (p. 76)
      Israel, **1951:** 114, 229
   Near East, **1951:** 4, 13 (p. 73), 114

Economic assistance — *continued*
   News conference remarks, **1950:** 3 [1], 8 [6], 11
      [16], 34 [15], 179 [1]; **1951:** 12 [37], 209 [10]
   United Kingdom, **1952–53:** 358
   U.N. program, **1951:** 170, 219
Economic Bill of Rights, **1945:** 192
Economic Commission for Europe, proposed,
   1947: 21
Economic Committee, Temporary National, **1947:**
   2 (p. 6), 4 (p. 35); **1948:** 8 (pp. 89, 90)
Economic Cooperation Act of 1948, **1948:** 75, 175;
   1949: 8 (p. 53); **1951:** 81; **1952–53:** 67
Economic Cooperation Administration, **1947:** 238;
   1949: 8 (pp. 53, 61), 84ftn. (p. 223); **1951:**
   34, 66, 114, 160, 177, 179 [11], 205, 296n.;
   1952–53: 18 (p. 115)
   Advisory board, proposed, **1948:** 110 [1]
   Aid cargoes, shipment on U.S.-flag vessels, **1948:**
      283 [9]
   Appropriations, **1950:** 86 [14], 206 [9], 230 [14],
      238 [17]; **1951:** 209 [10]
      Proposed reduction, **1949:** 112 [13]
   German aid functions, **1950:** 9 (p. 58)
   Korean activities, **1950:** 269
      Testimony on aid bill, **1950:** 17n.
   Mission to India, proposed, **1951:** 34
   News conference remarks, **1948:** 71 [10], 88 [10],
      110 [1], 274 [3], 283 [9]; **1949:** 22 [3], 40 [1],
      84 [4], 112 [13], 155 [23], 205 [15], 253 [8];
      1950: 3 [1], 86 [14], 206 [9], 230 [14], 238
      [17]
   Staff appointments, question of, **1948:** 71 [10], 88
      [10]
   Termination, question of, **1951:** 12 [25, 28]
   Textile purchase funds, **1949:** 253 [8]
   U.S. Special Representative in Europe (W.
      Averell Harriman), **1948:** 274 [3]; **1949:**
      84ftn. (p. 223), 86, 205 [15]; **1950:** 169 [9],
      203 [11]
   Yugoslavia, relief food shipments to, **1950:** 293
Economic Cooperation Administrator (William C.
   Foster), **1951:** 177
Economic Cooperation Administrator (Paul G.
   Hoffman), **1948:** 88 [15], 174 [9], 175, 283
   [9]; **1949:** 84ftn. (p. 223); **1950:** 169 [9],
   230 [14]
   See also Hoffman, Paul G.
   Memorandum, **1949:** 156
   News conference remarks on, **1949:** 144 [16], 171
      [3]
Economic Cooperation Agreement, U.S.-Italy,
   1948: 192
Economic Council, **1947:** 62 [17]
Economic Development, Committee for, **1946:** 72
   [3]; **1949:** 269 [20]
Economic Foreign Policy, Executive Committee
   on, **1946:** 71

Economic growth, U.S., **1947:** 76; **1948:** 2, 8 (pp. 63, 66, 75, 84, 86, 88, 94), 32, 182, 183 [5, 6], 184, 202 [2], 259 [5], 260; **1949:** 5, 120, 151, 154, 250; **1950:** 6, 9 (pp. 49, 96, 97), 18, 39, 84, 106, 110 [5], 118, 122, 127 [4], 157, 159, 171, 193, 202, 243, 303; **1951:** 11, 13 (p. 62), 28, 44, 91, 167, 177; **1952–53:** 15, 17 [2], 18 (pp. 64, 79), 62, 289 [2, 3], 349, 355, 366, 376

Economic Indicators, publication of, **1949:** 138

Economic reports to Congress, **1947:** 4, 152, 145 [17], 243 [7]; **1948:** 8, 167; **1950:** 6, 202

Economic and Social Council, Inter-American, **1950:** 52 [4]

Economic and Social Council (United Nations), **1949:** 237; **1950:** 10

Economic Stabilization, Office of, **1945:** 128; **1946:** 37 [10], 41 [22], 148, 177 [3]; **1947:** 80, 200

   Liquidation, **1945:** 137 [2]

   News conference remarks, **1945:** 137 [2], 157 [5], 202 [5]

   Reestablishment, **1946:** 36

   Termination, **1946:** 262 [3]

Economic Stabilization, Office of, Director (Chester Bowles), **1946:** 84 [23], 99, 119 [28], 129 [3], 148

Economic Stabilization, Office of, Director (William H. Davis), **1945:** 76 [10], 137 [8, 11]

Economic Stabilization Agency, **1950:** 243, 303; **1951:** 13 (p. 65), 23, 37 [14], 74, 188ftn. (p. 458), 209 [15]; **1952–53:** 18 (pp. 80, 115), 20, 205, 342 [15], 346, 348

Economic Stabilization Agency, Administrator (Michael V. DiSalle), letter of appointment, **1952–53:** 348

Economic Stabilization Agency, Administrator (Eric Johnston)

   Letter on transportation labor disputes, **1951:** 74

   News conference remarks on, **1951:** 49 [20], 56 [5], 118 [2], 188 [17]

Economic Stabilization Agency, Administrator (Roger L. Putnam), **1952–53:** 118n., 292 [9], 341

   Letter, **1952–53:** 346

Economic Stabilization Agency, Administrator (Alan Valentine), **1951:** 7 [13]

Economic stabilization bill, **1949:** 66 [10]

Economic Stabilization Board, **1946:** 262 [4]

Economic Stabilization Board, Chairman (John W. Snyder), **1945:** 172 [3], 175 [7, 19]

Economic Survey Mission to Middle East, U.N., **1949:** 274

Economic warfare, **1947:** 51

Economy, national, **1945:** 18, 35, 98, 184; **1946:** 18 (pp. 37, 39, 40, 48–57, 71, 73, 81, 82), 35, 39, 79, 93, 124, 125, 131, 152, 179,183, 187, 193, 194, 234, 249, 256, 258, 272; **1947:** 2

Economy, national — *continued*

   (pp. 2, 6, 12), 7 (p. 56), 35, 58, 68, 76, 85, 99, 110, 116, 120, 131, 142, 143, 144, 147, 148, 183, 186, 187, 200, 212, 214, 224; **1948:** 2, 5 (pp. 23, 50), 7, 12, 13, 23, 24, 63, 76, 80, 94, 98, 101, 107, 114 [3], 117, 136 [5], 138 [5], 175–177, 182, 183 [5], 195, 199, 204 [1], 205, 214 [5], 215, 216 [16], 218 [1–10], 226, 227 [6, 9], 228 [1, 12], 231 [2, 6], 233 [3], 237 [5], 240 [2, 4], 241, 261 [6]; **1949:** 2, 25, 39, 120, 138, 149, 159, 195, 199, 266; **1950:** 2, 9 (pp. 45, 96, 97), 39, 83, 106, 110 [1–3, 8, 10], 118, 121 [7, 9], 122 124 [8], 129 [3, 7], 134, 155, 157, 228; **1951:** 13 (pp. 75–78), 163, 174, 176, 199, 202, 215, 221; **1952–53:** 5, 13, 33, 55, 82, 98 [10, 12], 118, 123 [3, 18], 128, 147, 230, 237, 245, 266 [7, 11], 268 [4, 7], 272, 273, 274 [2, 5], 276, 277 [5], 280 [4], 303 [7], 304, 306 [4], 313 [5], 315 [2, 4], 351

See also Production.

Alaskan statehood, effect on, **1948:** 105

Budget, effect on, **1950:** 18

Campaign remarks, **1952–53:** 284 [1, 4], 285, 295 [6, 7], 305, 307, 313 [6], 314, 321 [1, 3, 6, 7], 324

Census report, **1952–53:** 363

Civilian sector, strength of, **1952–53:** 292 [10], 294

Coal strike, adverse effect on, **1950:** 49

   Coal industry study, proposed, **1950:** 50

Communist predictions of collapse, **1952–53:** 215

Concentration of control, danger to, **1948:** 256

Controls.

   See Controls, Government.

Council of Economic Advisers, divergent viewpoints on, **1952–53:** 377 [16]

Defense needs, adjustment to, **1950:** 194, 205, 301; **1952–53:** 5, 15, 17 [13], 33, 101, 215, 268 [7], 272, 282 [4], 283, 289 [8], 292 [10], 293, 294, 300, 307, 313 [6], 349, 366

Defense program, demands on, **1951:** 4, 11, 12 [20], 28, 59, 91–93, 107, 118 [1], 143, 145 [2], 199

Depressions and recessions, **1952–53:** 126, 268 [7], 272, 274 [5], 289 [8], 292 [3, 9, 10], 293, 294, 298 [2], 306 [2, 7], 308 [3], 313 [6], 314

   1920, **1952–53:** 286 [2], 321 [3]

   1921, **1952–53:** 282 [4]

   1928, **1952–53:** 296, 306 [5]

   1929, **1952–53:** 69, 286 [5], 318, 321 [6], 376

   1932, **1952–53:** 266 [10], 276, 278, 281, 282 [4], 287, 321 [2, 3, 4, 6]

   1949, **1952–53:** 286 [2], 366

   Preventive measures, **1952–53:** 316, 318, 376

Domestic prosperity and foreign policy, interdependence, **1950:** 121 [3]

Electric power, effect on, **1952–53:** 388

Economy, national — *continued*
  Farm and industrial prosperity, interdependence, **1948:** 233 [1], 237 [1], 242 [3]; **1949:** 202, 203, 219; **1950:** 111
  Foreign assistance, effect on, **1947:** 122, 212, 217, 219
  Foreign trade, dependence on, **1948:** 213; **1950:** 130
  Free enterprise system, **1952–53:** 69
  Free world defense, role in, **1952–53:** 319 [3]
  Goods and services, fair distribution, **1952–53:** 376
  Inflation.
    See main heading, Inflation.
  Issue in election campaign, **1952–53:** 268 [7], 300
  Korean war effort, effect on, **1950:** 243, 269
  Labor disputes, effect on, **1949:** 231 [14], 234 [3]; **1952–53:** 341
  Materials supply problem, appointment of commission to study, **1951:** 19
  Message to American people, **1949:** 154
  Messages to Congress, **1947:** 4, 152; **1948:** 8, 167; **1949:** 5, 151; **1950:** 6, 202; **1951:** 11, 167; **1952–53:** 15, 215, 376
  Minimum-wage law, effect on, **1950:** 18
  Mobilization planning, **1952–53:** 349
  National product, **1952–53:** 292 [10]
  News conference remarks, **1946:** 41 [18], 163 [2], 216 [19], 266 [4, 8, 10, 14, 16]; **1947:** 70 [1, 6, 9], 95 [27], 107 [2], 127 [1], 145 [9, 17], 180 [19], 191 [4]; **1948:** 11 [1, 2], 26 [3, 10, 16]; **1949:** 32 [21], 66 [10, 17, 20], 89 [12], 93 [5], 95 [10], 122 [10, 14, 17], 148 [17], 179 [5], 205 [1], 231 [14]; **1950:** 86 [17], 238 [3, 13], 250 [8], 253 [5, 6]; **1951:** 7 [1], 90 [15], 118 [1], 227 [19]
  Oil strike, effect on, **1952–53:** 58
  Policy coordination, **1952–53:** 376
  Postwar reconversion.
    See Reconversion, postwar.
  Post-World War I, **1948:** 260
  Prosperity, **1952–53:** 289 [1, 8], 292 [10], 293, 317 [1], 318, 319 [1]
    Need for combating Communism, **1948:** 215
  Public health, relationship to, **1949:** 181 [2]
  Report by Defense Mobilization Director, **1951:** 113 [6]
  Role of foreign trade in, **1947:** 52
  St. Lawrence Seaway project, importance to, **1952–53:** 23
  Stabilization, **1945:** 128; **1946:** 18 (pp. 49, 73, 79), 73, 152, 156, 216 [19], 232, 249; **1947:** 176; **1949:** 2, 8 (p. 79), 66 [10], 89 [12]; **1950:** 39, 121 [5, 8], 127 [6], 128, 145, 157, 163, 238 [13], 250 [8], 253 [6], 303; **1951:** 11, 23, 44, 91, 93, 107, 137, 143, 167, 279, 285, 290; **1952–53:** 15, 17 [3], 190, 215, 231, 292 [9], 341, 345 [5], 348, 367 (p. 1141), 376

Economy, national — *continued*
  Agency appropriations, reduction, **1952–53:** 205
  Steel strike, effect on, **1951:** 304, 305
  Strategic and critical materials, effective use and conservation, **1952–53:** 191, 192
  Strength of, **1952–53:** 215, 291
  Wage increases, effect on, **1948:** 110 [17]
  Weakness of, charges by Communist propaganda, **1950:** 92
  World War II, effect on, **1952–53:** 293
Ecuador
  Earthquake, in **1949:** 182 [5]
  Economic assistance, **1951:** 134
  History of, **1951:** 130
  Lend-lease settlement, **1951:** 244
  Plaza, Galo, **1951:** 118 [3], 129, 130, 132 [4, 6, 8], 134, 136
  Straw hat from, gift to the President, **1951:** 132 [17]
Eden, Anthony, **1945:** 22ftn. (p. 36), 31 [4], 91; **1952–53:** 6
Edinburgh, Duke of, **1951:** 145 [3], 153 [11], 193 [7], 282, 288
Edinburgh, Scotland, **1950:** 38ftn. (p. 162)
Edison, Irving, **1952–53:** 297
Editors, Business Paper, National Conference of, **1949:** 80
Editors Association, Agricultural, **1949:** 91
Editors and editorial writers, news conferences with, **1947:** 196, 210
Education, **1945:** 128; **1946:** 18 (pp. 40, 64, 65, 84), 75 [3, 20, 24, 26], 112, 117, 209; **1947:** 4 (p. 36), 7 (pp. 58, 76), 110, 204, 219; **1948:** 2, 5 (pp. 20, 21, 25, 41, 42), 8 (pp. 67, 76, 78, 84–86, 98), 32, 104, 115, 126 [4], 183 [1], 194 [3], 200 [5], 203, 215, 220, 241, 242 [3], 248, 257 [2]; **1949:** 5, 154; **1950:** 9 (pp. 82–84), 39, 127 [4, 7], 279; **1951:** 13 (pp. 64, 94), 256; **1952–53:** 69, 215
  See also Colleges and universities; Schools; Students; Teachers.
  Agricultural, **1950:** 110 [3]
  Alaska, **1948:** 105
  Budget, **1948:** 4 [19]
  Commission on Higher Education, report, **1947:** 235
  Conference on Emergency Problems in Higher Education, **1946:** 162
  Conservation, role in, **1947:** 186
  Driver training, **1951:** 121
  Equal opportunity, **1947:** 130; **1948:** 2, 20, 228 [8], 236; **1949:** 50 [3]; **1951:** 13 (p. 96); **1952–53:** 169, 378
  Exchange programs, **1949:** 139, 187; **1950:** 92, 190, 227; **1951:** 13 (pp. 75, 76), 124, 194; **1952–53:** 234
    See also main heading, Exchange programs.

Education — *continued*
  Expenditures for, **1952–53:** 376
  Federal aid, **1946:** 18 (pp. 64, 65, 83, 84); **1947:** 7
    (p. 76), 8 [13], 206, 235n.; **1948:** 2, 5 (pp.
    25, 41), 8 (pp. 67, 86), 99, 105, 108, 134,
    138 [1], 160, 165, 174 [1], 175, 176, 183 [5,
    6], 186, 203, 205, 211, 212 [9], 214 [9], 219,
    228 [2, 8, 12], 231 [1], 232, 233 [5], 247,
    249, 251, 257 [4], 258, 259, 262, 268; **1949:**
    2, 5, 7 [49], 8 (pp. 45, 47, 76–78), 51, 144
    [12], 179 [16] 202, 204, 208, 219; **1950:** 2,
    6, 8 [34], 9 (p. 82), 47, 52 [11, 13], 53, 69,
    71, 110 [2], 127 [7], 134, 160 [2]; **1951:** 4,
    11, 12 [32], 13 (pp. 93–96), 135; **1952–53:**
    5, 17 [15], 18 (pp. 100–103), 218, 231, 281,
    284 [5, 6], 313 [4], 333, 367 (pp. 1155,
    1156)
    Subordination to defense needs, **1952–53:** 15
  Federally affected areas, **1950:** 9 (p. 83)
  Fellowships, scientific, **1952–53:** 18 (p. 103)
  Handicapped, **1949:** 8 (p. 76)
  Indians, **1947:** 7 (p. 77), 229; **1949:** 8 (p. 76);
    1950: 91
  Institutions
    Housing for, **1952–53:** 18 (p. 99)
    Loans to, **1951:** 12 [6], 13 (p. 68)
    Tax exemption, **1950:** 18
  Jefferson's plan for, **1947:** 138
  Medical, **1945:** 192; **1946:** 18 (p. 83); **1947:** 98;
    1948: 89, 181 [2], 237 [3]; **1949:** 85; **1950:**
    9 (p. 75); **1951:** 4, 13 (p. 98), 135; **1952–
    53:** 15, 18 (p. 106), 249, 284 [5], 333, 367
    (p. 1158), 369
  Military, **1946:** 137, 138; **1947:** 106, 117; **1948:**
    89; **1950:** 32
  National Commission on Higher Education,
    1946: 166, 214, 262 [2]
  News conference remarks, **1949:** 7 [49], 122 [8],
    144 [12], 179 [16]; **1950:** 8 [34], 52 [11, 13]
  Point 4 program, contribution to, **1951:** 83
  Racial discrimination, **1946:** 214
  Role in combating crime, **1950:** 37
  Rural facilities, **1948:** 234, 237 [5]; **1950:** 6, 110
    [9], 127 [7]
  Scholarship program, **1952–53:** 17 [35]
  Schools.
    See main heading, Schools.
  School-age population, increase, **1952–53:** 18 (p.
    100)
  U.S. programs abroad, **1952–53:** 367 (p. 1144)
  Scientific, **1947:** 169, 183, 211; **1948:** 186; **1950:**
    48, 120
  Technical, **1947:** 169
  Textbooks, investigation by Un-American Ac-
    tivities Committee, **1949:** 122 [8]
  Veterans, **1946:** 18 (pp. 79, 84), 112, 166, 193, 226
    [1]; **1947:** 7 (pp. 56, 57, 69, 76), 134, 181
    (pp. 401, 405); **1948:** 2, 21, 32, 42, 228

Education — *continued*
  Veterans — *continued*
      [10], 259 [4]; **1949:** 8 (p. 63); **1950:** 9 (pp.
      68, 69), 36, 2̇8; **1951:** 13 (pp. 100, 101);
      1952–53: 18 (p. 108), 231, 366
  Vocational.
    See Occupational training.
  Women, **1948:** 30
  World progress of, **1950:** 87, 92
Education, Advisory Committee on, **1946:** 117;
    1950: 92
Education, Assistant Commissioner of, termination
    of office, **1946:** 117
Education, Commissioner of (Earl J. McGrath),
    1950: 8 [34]
Education, Office of, **1946:** 18 (p. 84), 117; **1950:**
    47, 69; **1952–53:** 18 (p. 102)
Education, President's Commission on Higher,
    1947: 206
Education Association, National, **1948:** 113n.;
    1950: 144n.; **1951:** 107n.
Educational Exchange, Advisory Commission on,
    1950: 227
Educational Exchange Act of 1948, United States
    Information and, **1951:** 194n.
Edwards, B. M., **1945:** 147n.
Edwards, Mrs. India, **1948:** 211n.; **1949:** 20, 219n.;
    1951: 275 [10], 297
Edwards, Ralph, **1948:** 89
Eggers, Frank H., **1948:** 189, 227n.
Eggs
  Conservation, **1947:** 205 [3, 19], 209 [2], 221 [2]
  Eggnog, Christmas, **1947:** 221 [2]
  Price supports, **1948:** 5 (p. 43); **1949:** 8 (p. 79)
  Prices, **1948:** 246
Eglin Air Force Base, **1950:** 165
Egypt, **1946:** 247; **1950:** 186 [13]
  Ambassador, appointment to, **1947:** 36 [16]
  Armistice with Israel, **1949:** 40 [2]
  British withdrawal, **1947:** 174 [10]
  King Farouk, **1946:** 110 [17], 141 [9]
  Policy on, **1952–53:** 6
  Stamp issue, **1946:** 110 [17]
  Suez Canal, dispute with U.K. concerning, **1951:**
    188 [12], 275 [14]
  Visit by W. Averell Harriman, question of, **1951:**
    188 [12], 200 [14]
Eidam, John, **1950:** 131n.
Eielson, Harry, **1948:** 234
Eiffel Tower, **1945:** 76 [11]
Eighth Army, Korea, change in command, **1951:**
    77
Eighty-second Airborne Division, remarks to mem-
    bers of, **1951:** 46
Eire.
  See Ireland.
Eisenhower, Gen. Dwight D., **1945:** 2, 12, 27, 45,
    86, 114, 119; **1946:** 6ftn. (p. 11), 15 [15,

Eisenhower, Gen. Dwight D. — *continued*
      20], 53 [4], 61 [8], 70 [1], 138, 216 [16], 225,
      250 [7]; **1947:** 31 [15], 110, 127 [17], 226
      [3]; **1949:** 36, 145n., 252; **1950:** 121 [1],
      254; **1951:** 91, 117, 138, 293; **1952–53:** 55,
      57, 79, 107 [2, 14], 129, 144, 250, 319n.,
      335, 373, 378
  See also President-elect.
  Administration, transition to, **1952–53:** 367 (p.
      1129)
  Appointment as Chief of Staff, U.S. Army, **1945:**
      193 [1]
  Boise, Idaho, campaign remarks, **1952–53:** 233
      [15], 319 [4]
  Budget, Federal, criticism of, **1952–53:** 166 [6]
  Cabinet meeting, invitation to attend, **1952–53:**
      227, 228 [3, 7, 12]
  Candidacy for President, question of, **1948:** 15
      [3], 150 [6]; **1949:** 269 [9]; **1951:** 153 [12],
      165 [5], 179 [7, 14], 188 [11], 193 [1], 275
      [5, 17], 295 [4]; **1952–53:** 7 [2, 10, 13], 21
      [28], 64 [9], 98 [7], 115 [20], 136 [8, 18], 175
      [14], 221 [13], 227, 228 [3, 7, 12], 233 [7, 12,
      15, 17], 241, 242 [1, 2, 4, 5], 247 [3, 9, 12],
      253 [6, 8], 258 [1, 7], 266, 267, 268 [2, 4, 5,
      8, 9], 269–272, 274–301, 303–308, 310–323
  Communism in Government, views on charges
      of, **1948:** 174 [2]
  Crusade in Europe, **1951:** 188 [11]; **1952–53:** 7
      [10]
  Directive on Germany, **1945:** 147 [20]
  Distinguished Service Medal, **1952–53:** 152, 157
  Educational aid (1949), support of Republican
      stand on, **1952–53:** 284 [6]
  Election victory, statement, **1952–53:** 325
  Endorsement of Senator Jenner, **1952–53:** 247 [7]
  European defense efforts, report on, **1951:** 30
  Health of, **1952–53:** 115 [20]
  Korea
      Armed Forces, role in withdrawal of (1947–
          1949), **1952–53:** 310, 323
      Peace efforts, **1952–53:** 247 [9, 12]
      Visit to, **1952–53:** 320, 321 [4], 345 [1, 4], 353
          [4]
  Letter on displaced persons in Germany, **1945:**
      152
  Letter on Joint Chiefs of Staff, **1949:** 180
  Meeting with the President, **1951:** 290
  Message on surrender of Germany, **1945:** 26 [5],
      29
  Mission to Soviet Union, question of, **1948:** 77
      [18]
  NATO command, **1951:** 7 [9, 17], 12 [22], 22 [3],
      56 [15], 69, 71, 80, 91, 117, 138, 165 [5],
      179 [7, 14], 293; **1952–53:** 18 (p. 74)
      Appointment, **1950:** 308, 309 [1, 10, 12], 311
      Letter, **1950:** 310
      Resignation, **1952–53:** 44 [9], 64 [9], 88 [4], 112

Eisenhower, Gen. Dwight D. — *continued*
  NATO command — *continued*
      Successor, question of appointment, **1952–53:**
          88 [12, 14, 17]
      News conference remarks on, **1945:** 26 [1, 5], 31
          [1], 60 [5, 7], 64 [8], 106 [10, 17], 118 [1],
          137 [12], 147 [20], 181 [2], 193 [12]; **1948:**
          15 [3], 26 [20], 77 [18], 110 [15], 150 [6],
          174 [2]; **1949:** 72 [18], 179 [1], 269 [9];
          1950: 80 [3], 258 [7], 309 [1, 10, 12]; **1951:**
          2 [5], 7 [9, 17], 12 [42], 22 [3], 56 [15], 118
          [8], 153 [6, 12, 14], 165 [5], 171 [8], 179 [7,
          14], 188 [11], 193 [1], 261 [9], 275 [4, 5, 17],
          295 [4]; **1952–53:** 64 [9], 115 [20], 149 [13],
          156 [2, 8], 166 [8], 175 [14], 221 [13]
      Parade in honor of, **1945:** 60 [5]
      Railroad labor dispute (1946), role in, **1952–53:**
          253 [2, 4]
      Recommendation on participation by civil au-
          thorities in government of Germany,
          1945: 181 [2]
      Republican National Convention, views on,
          1952–53: 197 [16]
      Republican presidential nomination, contest
          with Sen. Taft for, **1952–53:** 35 [8]
      Retirement, views on, **1948:** 26 [20]
      Spain, opposition to NATO membership for,
          1952–53: 31 [7]
      Taft-Hartley Act, support of, **1952–53:** 175 [16]
      Truman administration, criticism of, **1952–53:**
          156 [2]
      Visit with the President, **1952–53:** 149 [2, 6]
      Visit to White House, invitation, **1948:** 110 [15]
Eisenhower, Milton S., **1945:** 211 [2]; **1946:** 9n.
Eisler, Gerhart, **1949:** 113 [4]
El Alamein, **1945:** 177
  Campaign remarks, **1948:** 218 [7]
  Mayor John D. Upchurch, **1948:** 218 [7]
  Election campaign (1944), **1948:** 126 [4], 214 [5],
      231 [1], 236, 240 [1], 256, 258, 259 [1], 261
      [11], 262, 264 [3, 5], 268; **1950:** 39, 157;
      1952–53: 68, 69, 286 [6]
  Candidacy of Governor Dewey, **1948:** 260
  Candidacy for Vice President, **1945:** 163
  Republican platform, **1948:** 261 [15]
  Voter participation, **1948:** 261 [7]
  Election campaign (1946), **1946:** 216 [9, 12], 221,
      226 [10], 229 [6, 7, 10], 237 [9, 12, 24], 250
      [1]; **1949:** 250 [3]; **1950:** 39, 255, 279, 281
  Low voter participation, **1948:** 121, 122, 124,
      137–139, 194, 200, 202–204, 206–209, 212,
      214, 216, 218, 219, 227–229, 231, 233–235,
      237, 240, 242, 248, 250, 254, 257, 259,
      260–262, 264, 268
  Republican campaign, **1948:** 240 [7]
  Election campaign (1948), **1946:** 37 [5], 66 [11], 86
      [28], 266 [24]; **1947:** 70 [23], 205 [11], 218
      [1, 12], 226 [2]; **1949:** 4 [2, 3], 7 [39], 16, 17,

Election campaign (1948) — *continued*
    39, 52 [5], 155 [2], 190, 202, 252, 253 [5],
    269 [9]; **1950:** 12, 38 [1], 39, 87, 105 [5],
    110 [2, 3, 7–10], 121 [1, 3, 6, 11, 13], 124
    [8], 134, 157, 219 [7], 255, 267, 279; **1951:**
    56 [6], 113 [5], 200 [10], 215, 275 [5];
    1952–53: 7 [10], 69, 98 [31], 117, 126, 129,
    143, 218, 221 [2], 230, 233 [2], 242 [6], 253
    [5], 266 [2], 268 [3, 5], 269, 270 [8, 9], 272,
    273, 274 [7], 277 [1, 2], 280 [1, 3], 281, 284
    [2], 287, 289 [10], 290, 295 [2], 299, 303 [2],
    317 [8], 318, 321 [7], 322
  See also Candidates for public office.
Campaign train, news conference on, **1948:** 243
Candidacy, the President's, **1948:** 41 [7], 49 [6],
    55 [11], 77 [14, 16]
Communist Party, voting strength in, **1948:** 215
Conduct of, **1948:** 267 [2]
Foreign and domestic affairs, effect on, **1948:** 41
    [7, 9, 12, 17]
Foreign policy, effect of election on, **1948:** 278
    [21]
Funds, Republican solicitations for, **1948:** 242 [1,
    3]
"Housewives for Truman," **1948:** 264 [3]
Itinerary, the President's, **1948:** 21 [2], 150 [6, 10],
    163 [15, 18, 20], 166 [9], 170 [2], 174 [1, 12],
    178 [2], 181 [4, 6, 8, 13], 185 [1, 3, 9], 243
    [11], 250
Nebraska primary, **1948:** 117
News conference remarks, **1948:** 11 [11], 15 [4],
    21 [2], 41 [7, 9, 12, 17], 49 [6], 55 [11], 77
    [14, 16], 86, 93 [12], 150 [6, 10], 163 [6, 15,
    18, 20], 166 [9], 170 [2, 13], 174 [1, 12], 178
    [2], 181 [4, 6, 8, 9, 11, 13], 185 [1, 3, 9], 243
    [6, 11], 278 [5, 21, 42], 288 [5]
Pre-election polls, **1948:** 243 [6], 258, 261 [3, 5,
    14]
Press and radio opinion on, **1948:** 261 [12, 14],
    266
Television, role in, **1948:** 288 [5]
Tour, comments on, **1948:** 216 [15, 16], 261 [7],
    268
Victory, remarks following, **1948:** 270–272, 275
Election campaign (1948), major addresses
  June 8, Butte, Mont., **1948:** 121
  June 10, Seattle, Wash., **1948:** 125
  June 14, Los Angeles, Calif., **1948:** 134
  July 15, Philadelphia, Pa., acceptance of nomi-
    nation, **1948:** 160
  September 6, Detroit, Mich., **1948:** 184
  September 18, Dexter, Iowa, **1948:** 195
  September 20, Denver, Colo., **1948:** 199
  September 21, Salt Lake City, Utah, **1948:** 201
  September 22, Oakland, Calif., **1948:** 203
  September 23, Los Angeles, Calif., **1948:** 205
  September 24, Phoenix, Ariz., **1948:** 207
  September 25, El Paso, Tex., **1948:** 209

Election campaign (1948), addresses — *continued*
  September 27
    Bonham, Tex., **1948:** 213
    Democratic Women's Day, **1948:** 211
  September 28, Oklahoma City, Okla., **1948:** 215
  September 29, Tulsa, Okla., **1948:** 217
  September 30
    Carbondale, Ill., **1948:** 219
    Louisville, Ky., **1948:** 220
  October 1, Charleston, W. Va., **1948:** 223
  October 6, Philadelphia, Pa., **1948:** 226
  October 8, Buffalo, N.Y., **1948:** 229
  October 11, Akron, Ohio, **1948:** 232
  October 12, Springfield, Ill., **1948:** 234
  October 13, St. Paul, Minn., **1948:** 236
  October 14
    Madison, Wis., **1948:** 238
    Milwaukee, Wis., **1948:** 239
  October 15, Indianapolis, Ind., **1948:** 241
  October 19, Raleigh, N.C., **1948:** 246
  October 21, broadcast from White House, **1948:**
    247
  October 23
    Johnstown, Pa., **1948:** 251
    Pittsburgh, Pa., **1948:** 252
    Scranton, Pa., **1948:** 248
    Wilkes-Barre, Pa., **1948:** 249
  October 25
    Chicago, Ill., **1948:** 256
    Gary, Ind., **1948:** 255
  October 26, Cleveland, Ohio, **1948:** 258
  October 27, Boston, Mass., **1948:** 260
  October 28 and 29, New York City, **1948:** 262,
    265, 266
  October 30, St. Louis, Mo., **1948:** 268
  November 1, Independence, Mo., **1948:** 269
Election campaign (1948), rear platform and other
    informal remarks
  June 4, Ohio and Indiana, **1948:** 114
  June 5, Nebraska, **1948:** 116
  June 6, Nebraska and Wyoming, **1948:** 118
  June 7, Idaho, **1948:** 119
  June 8, Idaho and Montana, **1948:** 120
  June 9 and 10, Washington, **1948:** 122, 124
  June 11, Oregon, **1948:** 126
  June 12–14, California, **1948:** 128, 130, 133
  June 15, Arizona and New Mexico, **1948:** 136
  June 16, Kansas, **1948:** 137
  June 17, Missouri, Illinois, Indiana, and Ohio,
    1948: 138
  June 18, Pennsylvania and Maryland, **1948:** 139
  September 6, Michigan and Ohio, **1948:** 183
  September 17, Pennsylvania and Ohio, **1948:** 193
  September 18, Illinois, Iowa, and Missouri, **1948:**
    194
  September 19, Kansas, **1948:** 197
  September 20, Colorado, **1948:** 198
  September 21, Colorado and Utah, **1948:** 200

Election campaign (1948), remarks — *continued*
   September 22, Nevada and California, **1948:** 202
   September 23, California, **1948:** 204
   September 24, California and Arizona, **1948:** 206
   September 25, New Mexico and Texas, **1948:** 208
   September 26 and 27, Texas, **1948:** 210, 212
   September 28, Texas and Oklahoma, **1948:** 214
   September 29, Oklahoma and Missouri, **1948:** 216
   September 30, Illinois, Indiana, and Kentucky, **1948:** 218
   October 1, Kentucky and West Virginia, **1948:** 222
   October 6, Delaware, Pennsylvania, and New Jersey, **1948:** 225
   October 7, Pennsylvania and New Jersey, **1948:** 227
   October 8, New York, **1948:** 228
   October 11, Ohio, **1948:** 231
   October 12, Indiana and Illinois, **1948:** 233
   October 13 and 14, Wisconsin and Minnesota, **1948:** 235, 237
   October 15, Indiana, **1948:** 240
   October 16, West Virginia, **1948:** 242
   October 23, Pennsylvania, **1948:** 250
   October 25, Indiana, **1948:** 254
   October 26, Indiana and Ohio, **1948:** 257
   October 27, Massachusetts and Connecticut, **1948:** 259
   October 28, Massachusetts, Rhode Island, Connecticut, and New York, **1948:** 261
   October 29, New York, N.Y., **1948:** 264
   October 30, Ohio, Indiana, Illinois, and Missouri, **1948:** 267
Election campaign (1950), **1949:** 45 [26], 148 [7], 192 [2, 6], 205 [3, 18], 236 [13]; **1950:** 11 [12], 12, 16 [13], 38 [5], 39, 44 [4], 80 [4], 86 [9], 87, 97 [15], 152 [8], 160 [2], 203 [17], 214 [13], 230 [16], 237, 250 [10], 253 [12], 255, 258 [4], 270 [10, 11, 12], 273 [15, 16], 278 [12], 279, 287 [7, 9, 14, 15, 17] 309 [1]; **1952–53:** 251, 308 [7]
   Maryland campaign of Sen. Tydings, **1951:** 49 [19]
Election campaign (1952), **1949:** 122 [11], 192 [3], 269 [9]; **1950:** 38 [11], 86 [9], 105 [19], 157, 287 [8]; **1951:** 215, 297; **1952–53:** 29, 68, 69, 107 [15], 236
   Comments on, **1952–53:** 166 [8], 258 [16]
   Conduct of, **1952–53:** 5, 233 [11], 240 [1], 253 [5, 14], 268 [5], 303 [5], 304, 306 [3], 312, 313 [4, 6], 322, 324, 325
   Democratic nominees, President's influence on choice of, **1952–53:** 197 [9]
   Democratic prospects, **1951:** 227 [19]; **1952–53:** 197 [19]
   Democratic women, role in, **1951:** 238
   Farm vote, **1952–53:** 267

Election campaign (1952) — *continued*
   "Favorite son" Presidential candidates, **1952–53:** 26 [16]
   Issues, **1951:** 261 [2], 295 [14]; **1952–53:** 221 [15], 240 [1], 241, 242 [1, 2, 4], 258 [12], 266 [2, 3, 7, 8, 11], 268 [5, 7, 8], 270 [5], 273, 275, 276, 277 [3], 278, 279, 280 [6], 282 [7, 8], 283, 285, 286 [1], 287, 289 [2, 12], 292 [3], 295 [1, 3], 296, 298 [5, 9, 10, 13, 14], 299, 300, 303 [1, 3, 6, 7, 9, 10], 304, 306 [1, 2, 5, 6], 307, 308 [2, 3, 5, 6, 8, 9], 312, 313 [3–6], 315 [5], 317 [1], 321 [1, 5, 7], 322, 324
   Airpower, **1952–53:** 156 [8]
   Defense spending, **1952–53:** 98 [11]
   Korean war, **1952–53:** 64 [2], 299, 300
   Republican evasion of, **1952–53:** 289 [10], 291, 316, 317 [6, 7], 319 [4]
   Military men in politics, comments on, **1952–53:** 377 [18]
   News conference remarks, **1951:** 70 [13], 90 [13], 179 [2, 6], 200 [4], 275 [5, 17], 295 [4, 6], 300 [20]
   Participation, the President's, **1952–53:** 31 [11, 12], 88 [18, 20, 22], 98 [42], 126, 127 [4, 16], 149 [20], 156 [7], 166 [13], 221 [12], 228 [6, 11], 233 [10], 238 [10, 13], 247 [4], 253 [3, 11, 15]
   Presidential candidates.
     See Candidates for public office.
   President's candidacy, question of, **1951:** 16 [17], 56 [14, 18], 63 [3], 113 [3, 5, 9], 132 [7], 153 [7], 171 [12], 188 [11], 193 [1], 209 [9], 224 [9, 11], 227 [8, 14], 247 [2], 261 [2, 7, 16, 18], 295 [11]
   Republican tactics, **1951:** 227 [19, 21]
   Republican victory, **1952–53:** 334 [13], 342 [18]
   Southern Democrats, prospects of, **1952–53:** 98 [18]
   Speech and travel plans, the President's, **1951:** 16 [18], 37 [1, 11], 49 [2], 63 [20], 70 [11], 113 [3, 5], 132 [18], 140 [15, 17], 153 [23], 179 [9], 193 [10, 19, 21], 200 [12], 209 [5], 227 [23], 261 [16, 18], 298 [10]
   Taft, Sen. Robert A.
     See main heading, Taft, Sen. Robert A.
   Television coverage, adjustment of President's itinerary to, **1952–53:** 166 [13]
   United Press poll on, **1951:** 56 [14]
Election campaign (1952), major addresses
   July 2, Bull Shoals, Ark., **1952–53:** 194
   July 26, Chicago, Ill., **1952–53:** 218
   September 1, Milwaukee, Wis., **1952–53:** 241
   September 29, Grand Forks, N. Dak., interview at, **1952–53:** 267
   September 30, Tiber Dam, Mont., **1952–53:** 269
   October 1
     Broadcast on trade union radio program, **1952–53:** 273

Election campaign (1952), addresses — *continued*
  October 1 — *continued*
    Spokane, Wash., **1952–53:** 272
  October 2
    Seattle, Wash., **1952–53:** 275
    Tacoma, Wash., **1952–53:** 276
  October 4
    Oakland, Calif., **1952–53:** 279
    San Francisco, Calif., **1952–53:** 278
  October 6, Provo, Utah, **1952–53:** 281
  October 7, Colorado Springs, Colo., **1952–53:** 283
  October 8, Shenandoah, Iowa, **1952–53:** 285
  October 9
    Buffalo, N.Y., **1952–53:** 288
    Cleveland, Ohio, **1952–53:** 287
  October 10, Albany, N.Y., **1952–53:** 289
  October 11, New York City, **1952–53:** 290, 291
  October 16
    Hartford, Conn., **1952–53:** 293
    Manchester, N.H., **1952–53:** 294
  October 17, Boston, Mass., **1952–53:** 296
  October 18
    New York, N.Y., **1952–53:** 300
    Providence, R.I., **1952–53:** 299
  October 21
    Philadelphia, Pa., **1952–53:** 304
    Pottsville, Pa., **1952–53:** 305
  October 22, Pittsburgh, Pa., **1952–53:** 307
  October 27, Gary, Ind., **1952–53:** 312
  October 28, Hibbing, Minn., **1952–53:** 314
  October 29, Chicago, Ill., **1952–53:** 316
  October 30, Detroit, Mich., **1952–53:** 318
  October 31, Cincinnati, Ohio, **1952–53:** 323
  November 1, St. Louis, Mo., **1952–53:** 322
  November 3, Kansas City, Mo., **1952–53:** 324
Election campaign (1952), rear platform and other informal remarks
  July 1 and 2, Arkansas, **1952–53:** 193, 195
  September 1, Pennsylvania and Ohio, **1952–53:** 240
  September 2, Ohio and West Virginia, **1952–53:** 242
  September 29, Minnesota, North Dakota, and Montana, **1952–53:** 266
  September 30, Montana, **1952–53:** 268
  October 1, Montana and Idaho, **1952–53:** 270
  October 2, Washington and North Dakota, **1952–53:** 274
  October 3, Oregon and California, **1952–53:** 277
  October 6, Utah and Colorado, **1952–53:** 280
  October 7, Colorado, **1952–53:** 282
  October 8, Iowa and Missouri, **1952–53:** 284
  October 9, Indiana, Ohio, and Pennsylvania, **1952–53:** 286
  October 10, New York, **1952–53:** 289
  October 16, Connecticut, Massachusetts, and New Hampshire, **1952–53:** 292

Election campaign (1952), remarks — *continued*
  October 17, New Hampshire and Massachusetts, **1952–53:** 295
  October 18, Massachusetts, Rhode Island, Connecticut, and New York, **1952–53:** 298
  October 21, Delaware, New Jersey, and Pennsylvania, **1952–53:** 303
  October 22, Pennsylvania, **1952–53:** 306
  October 23, West Virginia, Pennsylvania, Maryland, and the District of Columbia, **1952–53:** 308
  October 27, Ohio and Indiana, **1952–53:** 311
  October 28, Minnesota, **1952–53:** 313
  October 29, Iowa and Illinois, **1952–53:** 315
  October 30, Michigan, **1952–53:** 317
  October 31, Ohio, **1952–53:** 319
  November 1, Indiana and Illinois, **1952–53:** 321
Election campaign (1956), **1951:** 70 [13]
Elections
  Costs, **1949:** 16, 74, 112 [5], 148 [21]
  Future campaigns, question of participation by the President, **1952–53:** 377 [29]
  Labor union, **1947:** 120
  Municipal, **1947:** 88 [5]
  Presidential, proposed amendment, **1950:** 52 [8]
  Primary.
    See Primary elections.
  Television, role of, **1952–53:** 26 [28]
Elections, foreign
  French, **1950:** 281
  Greek, **1950:** 142n.
  Italian (1948), **1952–53:** 288, 291
  Korean, question of, **1950:** 193, 194, 258 [13]
  United Kingdom, **1950:** 44 [13], 46 [17]
Elections, past
  1840, **1952–53:** 289 [9]
  1848, **1952–53:** 289 [9]
  1852, **1952–53:** 289 [9], 238 [14], 287
  1864, **1952–53:** 289 [9]
  1876, **1948:** 227 [2]
  1892, **1950:** 110 [1]
  1916, **1950:** 4
  1920, **1948:** 231 [2, 3], 236, 266
  1928, **1948:** 260, 261 [4], 262; **1952–53:** 296
  1932, **1948:** 198 [4], 215, 260; **1950:** 139; **1952–53:** 69, 251, 296, 314
  1934, **1950:** 39, 139; **1952–53:** 31 [11]
  1936, **1948:** 198 [4], 258, 264 [5]; **1950:** 39; **1952–53:** 69, 78, 286 [6], 292 [12]
  1940, **1948:** 236, 258; **1950:** 39; **1952–53:** 69, 286 [6]
Electoral college, constitutional purpose, **1948:** 41 [3]
Electric Boat Division, General Dynamics Corp., Groton, Conn., **1952–53:** 170
Electric Bond and Share Co., **1952–53:** 143
Electric Consumers Conference, address, **1952–53:** 143

Electric Cooperative Association, National Rural, message, **1952–53:** 62
Electric power.
   See Power projects.
Electric power industry
   Expansion, **1949:** 4 [6]
   Rates for, **1950:** 33
Electric power production, **1945:** 202 [3]; **1950:** 134, 193, 202; **1952–53:** 33, 271
Electrical workers, welfare fund, **1946:** 110 [8]
Electricity, national consumption of, **1945:** 155
Electrification, rural.
   See Rural areas.
Electronics equipment, production, **1950:** 303
Elephant Butte Dam, N. Mex., **1948:** 208 [2]
Eliot, Charles W., **1946:** 43 [3]
Eliot, George Fielding, **1947:** 90n.
Elizabeth, Princess, **1951:** 145 [3], 153 [11], 193 [7], 282, 288
Elizabeth II, Queen, **1952–53:** 30, 74, 342 [13]
Elizabeth, N.J.
   Campaign remarks, **1948:** 227 [6]
   Mayor James T. Kirk, **1948:** 227 [6]; **1952–53:** 303 [4]
   Remarks at, **1952–53:** 303 [4]
Elizalde, Joaquin M., **1951:** 49 [5], 151
Elk Refuge, National, **1950:** 248
Elkhart, Ind., campaign remarks, **1948:** 257 [2]
Elks lodge, Pasco, Wash., dedication, **1950:** 121 [13]
Ellender, Sen. Allen J., **1946:** 116, 119 [3], 215 [6], 258, 263
   Housing bill.
      See Taft-Ellender-Wagner housing bill.
   Invitation to President to visit South, **1948:** 110 [5]
El Paso, Tex., **1947:** 78 [7]
   Campaign address, **1948:** 209
   Mayor Dan R. Ponder, **1948:** 209
El Paso Times, **1952–53:** 197 [9]
Elroy, Wis., campaign remarks, **1948:** 237 [6]
El Salvador, lend-lease settlement, **1951:** 244
Elroy, Wis., **1950:** 131 [2]
Elston, Repr. Charles H., **1948:** 33
Ely, Lt. Gen. Paul, **1952–53:** 88ftn. (p. 258)
Elyria, Ohio, campaign remarks, **1948:** 257 [5]
Emancipation Proclamation, **1947:** 130; **1948:** 36
Emergency, national.
   See National emergency.
Emergency Banking Act of 1933, **1951:** 44
Emergency Export Programs, **1946:** 264; **1947:** 29, 139, 195
Emergency Export Programs, Coordinator (Capt. Granville Conway), **1947:** 139
Emergency Housing Act, Veterans, **1947:** 131
Emergency powers, the President's, **1949:** 234 [3]
Emergency powers, termination, **1947:** 14 [13], 156

Emergency Powers Continuation Act, proposed, **1952–53:** 38, 68, 79
Emergency Relief Assistance Act, Yugoslav, **1951:** 81
Emmerich, Herbert, **1949:** 167n.
Emory, Alan S., **1952–53:** 98 [32]
Employee Loyalty, President's Temporary Commission on, **1947:** 89n.
Employee loyalty program, **1952–53:** 76
Employees' Compensation, Bureau of, **1950:** 53, 74
Employees' Compensation Appeals Board, **1950:** 74; **1952–53:** 208
Employees Compensation Commission, **1946:** 117; **1950:** 74
Employees compensation functions, reorganization plans, **1950:** 53, 74
Employers records, availability to fact-finding boards in labor disputes, **1945:** 204, 221 [1, 3, 14, 21, 23]
Employment, **1945:** 122, 184; **1946:** 2, 18 (pp. 37, 40, 48, 49, 51, 54–57, 69), 39, 73, 164, 213, 218, 226 [1], 232, 260; **1947:** 2 (p. 2), 4 (pp. 14, 15, 17, 20, 25, 26, 28, 30, 39), 7 (p. 57), 20, 21, 58, 68, 76, 81, 87, 93, 110, 116, 126, 142, 147, 152, 177 [16], 204; **1948:** 2, 4 [6], 8 (pp. 62, 63, 66–70, 75, 77, 79, 81, 83, 84, 87–89, 91, 93), 10, 63, 97 [16], 99, 114 [3], 117, 124 [5], 126 [1], 128 [2], 176, 182, 183 [5], 184, 212 [5], 222 [3, 9], 227 [4], 234; **1949:** 5, 151, 154, 205 [1]; **1950:** 2, 6, 84, 106, 202; **1951:** 174, 279; **1952–53:** 5, 33, 98 [10], 266 [10], 272, 273, 276, 277 [5], 280 [3], 281, 298 [11], 312
See also Unemployment.
Agricultural, **1952–53:** 15
Coal mines, conditions, **1946:** 252
Communists, prohibitions against, **1950:** 254
Conditions on public works or Federally assisted projects, **1950:** 68, 74
Construction industry, **1947:** 131
Defense industries, **1950:** 303; **1951:** 11, 13 (pp. 78, 79), 15; **1952–53:** 15, 150
Disabled persons, **1951:** 13 (p. 98), 195; **1952–53:** 137, 243
Eight-hour laws, **1950:** 68
Equal opportunity, **1947:** 4 (p. 31); **1948:** 2, 5 (p. 54); **1949:** 8 (p. 90); **1951:** 13 (p. 80); **1952–53:** 5, 18 (p. 94), 169, 336, 378
   Armed forces, **1948:** 265; **1949:** 226 [3]
   Government employees, **1948:** 97 [16]
   Message to Congress, **1948:** 20
   National commission on, proposed, **1948:** 175
   Women, **1948:** 30
Fair employment practices, **1945:** 51, 128, 204; **1946:** 2, 18 (pp. 40, 52), 21 [17], 78 [5], 154, 199 [15]; **1947:** 4 (pp. 31, 32); **1948:** 8 (pp. 53, 88), 265; **1949:** 239, 256; **1950:** 9 (p. 99), 23 [8] and ftn. (p. 134), 29 [2, 12], 37,

Employment — *continued*
  Fair employment practices — *continued*
      44 [1], 86 [14], 126, 134, 137 [3], 141, 146
      [6]; **1951:** 12 [29], 13 (p. 80), 16 [11];
      1952–53: 169, 290, 300, 303 [3], 316
  Federal.
      See Government employees.
  Federal-State cooperation, **1945:** 226
  Full employment.
      See main heading, Full employment.
  Government.
      See Government employees.
  Handicapped persons, **1946:** 217; **1947:** 184;
      1948: 134, 152, 169; **1949:** 197; **1950:** 208
  "High level" versus "full" employment legisla-
      tion, **1945:** 208 [14]
  Increase, **1945:** 202 [3]; **1947:** 214, 224; **1948:** 8
      (pp. 85, 91), 131 [1], 167, 198 [7], 206 [4],
      216 [5], 219, 227 [5, 9], 228 [1, 2, 4–6, 12],
      231 [4], 252, 259 [5], 260, 261 [4], 267 [3],
      268; **1950:** 6, 125, 127 [4], 193, 232, 243;
      1951: 11, 91, 167; **1952–53:** 15, 215, 289
      [2], 293, 366, 368, 376, 378
  Indians, **1947:** 229
  International Conference on Trade and Em-
      ployment, **1946:** 18 (pp. 45, 46), 248
  Labor standards enforcement functions, reor-
      ganization, **1950:** 53, 68
  Maritime, ILO recommendations, **1947:** 123, 124
  Migratory workers, **1950:** 153
      Agricultural, **1951:** 16 [5], 75, 154, 192
      Mexican, **1952–53:** 21 [26], 31 [14], 367 (p.
      1151)
  Minimum-wage law, effect on, **1950:** 18
  National commission against discrimination,
      proposed, **1948:** 175
  News conference remarks, **1945:** 22 [18], 106 [4],
      107 [4], 175 [18], 202 [3], 208 [14], 221 [2,
      16, 23]; **1946:** 17 [11, 17, 18, 19], 61 [2],
      119 [2], 163 [2]; **1950:** 8 [20], 23 [8], 29 [2,
      12], 44 [1], 86 [14], 137 [3], 146 [6]
  Older persons, **1948:** 107; **1950:** 243; **1952–53:** 18
      (p. 104)
  Payroll taxes, **1949:** 8 (pp. 49, 67)
  Placement services, **1949:** 8 (p. 91), 127, 129, 181,
      201; **1950:** 9 (p. 97), 84, 208; **1951:** 13 (pp.
      79, 80), 154; **1952–53:** 18 (pp. 93, 94), 231,
      367 (p. 1150)
  Public employment offices, **1948:** 5 (pp. 25, 53,
      54)
  Public services, **1947:** 4 (p. 31), 81, 181 (pp. 402,
      406), 236 [1]
  Public works, Hawaii, **1947:** 35
  Railroad workers, conditions under Government
      control, **1950:** 221
  Stabilization, **1947:** 53
  Statistics, **1949:** 13, 138; **1952–53:** 18 (p. 92)

Employment — *continued*
  Taxes.
      See Social security; Taxes.
  Veterans, **1945:** 107 [4], 108, 128, 226; **1946:** 18
      (p. 65), 61 [2], 62, 119 [2], 164, 217, 226 [1],
      232; **1948:** 2; **1949:** 129, 181; **1952–53:**
      137
  Wage and hour statistics, international conven-
      tion on, **1951:** 97
  War Workers, **1945:** 226; **1946:** 62
  Women, **1950:** 243
  Working conditions, **1952–53:** 5
  Youth, **1948:** 70
Employment Act (full employment bill), **1946:** 218;
      1947: 4 (13, 15, 19, 22, 28, 31), 152; **1948:**
      8 (pp. 62, 65, 69, 75, 81, 89, 90, 98), 121,
      167, 219, 241; **1949:** 2, 5, 25, 45 [3], 138,
      151; **1950:** 6; **1952–53:** 376
  Approval, **1946:** 39
  News conference remarks, **1946:** 41 [10], 95 [18],
      126 [23], 143 [10], 177 [2]
Employment Commissioner, proposed, **1948:** 10
Employment offices, transfer to States, disapprov-
      al, **1945:** 226
Employment Security, Bureau of, **1948:** 10, 135;
      1949: 129, 181; **1950:** 53, 74
Employment Service, United States, **1945:** 128,
      180; **1946:** 18 (p. 52), 61 [2], 62, 118, 217;
      1947: 4 (p. 31), 81, 236 [1]; **1948:** 10, 101,
      134, 135, 138 [4], 175, 259 [1, 2]; **1949:**
      129, 201; **1951:** 11; **1952–53:** 117
  Bill providing for return to States, **1945:** 211 [11],
      221 [6]
  News conference remarks, **1945:** 137 [1], 211 [11],
      221 [6]
Employment services, State, **1947:** 181 (pp. 402,
      406); **1948:** 175
Emporia, Kans., campaign remarks, **1948:** 137 [4]
Enderis, Dorothy, **1949:** 73n., 110n.; **1950:** 32n.
Engel, Irving, **1952–53:** 7 [1]
Engineers, Chief of, **1950:** 34 [17]
  Report on Savannah Harbor and Two Harbors
      projects, **1945:** 90
Engineers, Chief of (Lt. Gen. Raymond A.
      Wheeler), **1948:** 126 [1]
Engineers, Corps of, **1945:** 148, 149, 155; **1946:** 18
      (p. 82), 238; **1948:** 5 (pp. 46, 49), 6, 105,
      111, 175; **1949:** 8 (pp. 80, 81, 83), 22ftn.
      (p. 118), 32 [16], 41, 77, 183; **1950:** 3ftn.
      (p. 15), 9 (pp. 90, 93), 121 [4, 8], 129 [1, 5],
      164, 191 [6]; **1951:** 13 (pp. 81–83, 85, 86),
      183, 185; **1952–53:** 18 (pp. 83, 88), 98 [34],
      107 [6], 231, 367 (pp. 1143, 1146, 1149),
      388
Engineers, shortage of, **1948:** 8 (p. 85)
England.
  See United Kingdom.

Engle, Repr. Clair, **1952–53:** 199, 277 [4]
English Channel, **1945:** 178
Engraving and Printing, Bureau of, **1948:** 59
Eniwetok atomic bomb tests, **1948:** 88 [4], 103, 164
Enterprise system, **1945:** 37, 128, 184; **1946:** 18 (pp.
        39, 40, 50, 56, 63), 39, 67, 125, 152; **1947:**
        2 (pp. 2, 3, 6, 12), 4 (pp. 32, 35, 39), 7 (pp.
        59, 86), 52, 68, 70 [10, 15, 20], 76, 102, 116,
        121, 152, 209 [2], 214; **1948:** 2, 8 (pp. 66,
        80, 83, 89, 90), 32, 37, 76, 182, 184, 220,
        229, 241, 262; **1949:** 2, 5, 8 (p. 88), 149,
        156, 195; **1950:** 2, 6, 9 (pp. 77, 79), 13, 18,
        39, 77, 106, 121 [3], 122, 125, 134, 154,
        157, 216, 259, 279, 289; **1951:** 215, 284
Entezam, Nasrollah, **1950:** 271n.
Ephrata, Wash., campaign remarks, **1948:** 122 [3];
        1952–53: 274 [1]
Epstein, Eliahu, **1948:** 141, 253
Equal opportunity, **1952–53:** 194
    Economic, **1952–53:** 288
    Employment.
        See under main heading, Employment.
    Negroes, **1952–53:** 169, 290, 353 [16]
Equality of Treatment and Opportunity, Presi-
        dent's Committee on, **1951:** 299
Equality of Treatment and Opportunity in the
        Armed Forces, President's Committee on,
        1948: 265; **1950:** 141
Equestrian statues, Italian, dedication, **1951:** 235
Erhardt, John G., **1950:** 218
Erickson, Judge Leif, **1946:** 53 [1]
Erie, Pa., campaign remarks, **1952–53:** 286 [8]
Erie County, Ohio, savings bond campaign, **1948:**
        76
Erlander, Tage, **1952–53:** 98 [37]
Ernie Pyle, **1946:** 267
ERP.
    See European recovery program.
Erskine, Maj. Gen. G. B., **1946:** 182
Erwin, John D., **1947:** 62 [4]
ESA.
    See Economic Stabilization Agency.
Espionage in U.S., **1946:** 41 [24, 26]
    Comments on, **1950:** 199, 203 [8], 207, 254
    Communist in U.S., charges of, **1948:** 170 [4, 6],
        181 [14, 16], 215, 285 [21]
    Rosenberg case, **1952–53:** 377 [10]
Essex, **1946:** 171n.
Estate taxes, **1947:** 116; **1949:** 2, 5, 151; **1950:** 18;
        1951: 28
Estonia, Soviet domination of, **1948:** 53, 86
Estonian refugees in U.S., **1946:** 237 [17], 239, 246
Ethical standards
    Business, **1950:** 157
    Cabinet members, **1949:** 231 [9]
    Government employees, **1949:** 179 [9, 11, 13, 15,
        19, 21]; **1951:** 56 [24], 239 [3], 251 [9, 15],
        295 [12], 298 [4], 300 [1, 12, 21], 303;

Ethical standards — *continued*
    Government employees — *continued*
        1952–53: 1, 5, 7 [6, 9, 11], 11, 14, 21 [19],
        26 [5], 36, 59, 69, 117, 143, 266 [2], 295 [8],
        357
    Consultants, proposed exemption from con-
        flict-of-interest statutes, **1951:** 104, 237
    Morris investigation, **1952–53:** 75ftn. (p. 231)
    International relations, **1950:** 313
    National committeemen, political parties, **1951:**
        188 [3, 15], 227 [10, 16, 18]
Ethiopia
    Attack by Italy (1935), **1951:** 4
    Korean war, participation, **1951:** 170; **1952–53:**
        196
    Technical assistance, **1951:** 245, 259, 262
Ethridge, Mark, **1950:** 92, 227
Eucharistic Congress, American Church, **1949:**
        207n.
Eufaula, Okla., campaign remarks, **1948:** 216 [6]
Eugene, Oreg., campaign remarks, **1948:** 126 [4]
Euphrates River, **1949:** 252
Euphrates Valley, **1951:** 245
Eureka, Mont., remarks at, **1952–53:** 270 [6]
Europe, **1945:** 225; **1946:** 18 (pp. 38, 41, 46), 30 [1];
        1947: 7 (p. 57), 31 [20], 88 [12], 90 [1], 188,
        240; **1949:** 19, 148 [6]
    See also specific countries.
    Agricultural tools, U.S. shipment to, **1947:** 210
        [6]
    Allied occupation, **1947:** 224
    Assistance, **1947:** 177 [22], 202, 214, 217, 219, 221
        [16], 238
    Banking services, **1947:** 238
    CEEC, Paris meeting, **1947:** 217, 219
    Clothing for, **1945:** 74
    Coal shortage, **1945:** 135, 209
    Communism in, **1950:** 303
    Crop failures in, **1947:** 197
    Currency stabilization, **1947:** 238
    Displaced persons in.
        See Displaced persons in Europe; Jews.
    Drought in, **1947:** 191 [3]
    Economy, **1947:** 21, 188, 191 [4, 5], 197, 213, 238
    Economy of Northwest Europe, letter to heads
        of war agencies, **1945:** 35
    Foreign trade, **1947:** 238
    Imports from U.S., **1950:** 159
    Inland waterways, unrestricted navigation, **1945:**
        97
    Jewish refugees in.
        See Jews.
    Liberated areas, **1947:** 140
    Marshall plan, message to Congress, **1947:** 238
    Reconstruction, **1947:** 218 [7]; **1950:** 42, 87
    Redeployment of U.S. armed forces to Pacific
        theater, **1945:** 53, 54
    Shipping services, **1947:** 238

Europe — *continued*
  U.S. policy in, **1950:** 239
  U.S. relief for liberated countries, **1945:** 33, 35, 74, 97, 118 [8], 128, 135, 186; **1946:** 4, 23, 29, 30 [2], 45, 76, 85, 86 [4, 22, 24, 27, 32], 87, 105, 124, 125; **1947:** 6 [26], 15, 29, 46 [2], 47, 107 [1], 127 [3], 139, 145 [12], 152, 191 [3], 195, 196, 197, 198, 202, 205 [15], 209 [3], 210 [1, 3, 6, 7], 213, 214, 217, 219, 224, 225, 238
  War casualties, **1947:** 210 [6]
  War destruction, **1945:** 97
Europe, Council of, **1949:** 195
Europe, Eastern, **1947:** 140; **1949:** 86, 200 [10]
  See also specific countries.
  Communism in, **1948:** 41 [10], 53, 86, 129; **1950:** 92; **1952–53:** 182, 242 [2]
  Displaced persons in.
    See Displaced persons in Europe; Jews.
  Greek children, detention by Communists in, **1950:** 7, 90, 261
  Immigration to U.S., **1952–53:** 182, 289 [7], 292 [5], 317 [7]
  Marshall plan rejection, **1947:** 141 [17]
  Military strength, **1951:** 174
  News conference remarks on, **1947:** 90 [1]
  U.S. crusade for freedom, **1950:** 98
Europe, Western, **1952–53:** 297
  See also European recovery program; Marshall plan; *specific countries.*
  Assistance, **1948:** 4 [2], 5 (pp. 20, 21, 29), 8 (p. 69), 53, 75, 85, 144, 147, 160, 175, 202 [6], 231 [3], 244, 260, 276, 283 [9]; **1949:** 7 [6, 9, 11], 8 (pp. 46, 53, 54), 71, 72 [2, 7, 16, 19], 89 [9], 159, 171 [9], 179 [17], 184, 236 [17], 260ftn. (p. 569); **1952–53:** 242 [2], 313 [2], 366
    Appropriations cuts, danger of, **1952–53:** 205
    Economic, **1952–53:** 5, 15, 18 (pp. 74, 75), 27, 55, 295 [5], 298 [8], 315 [5], 353 [13], 354, 367 (p. 1140)
    Military, **1952–53:** 5, 15, 18 (pp. 74, 75), 144, 158, 288, 295 [8], 298 [8], 367 (p. 1140)
  Coal and steel community, proposed, **1950:** 137 [1, 19], 162, 281; **1952–53:** 5, 55
  Communism in, **1948:** 41 [10], 49 [4], 115; **1950:** 301; **1951:** 96, 114, 209 [13]; **1952–53:** 288, 295 [8], 354
  Defense, **1949:** 72 [20], 120, 155 [3], 162, 184; **1950:** 151, 154, 162, 201, 203 [4, 11], 295 [1], 303, 309 [8]; **1951:** 13 (pp. 64, 72), 25, 59, 65, 69, 96, 167; **1952–53:** 217, 291
    Economic and political stability, relationship to, **1952–53:** 15
    European army, proposed, **1951:** 25; **1952–53:** 158
    German participation, negotiations for, **1952–53:** 18 (p. 75)

Europe, Western — *continued*
  Defense — *continued*
    Military assistance and defense support, **1948:** 52, 71 [16, 22], 88 [13], 278 [40]; **1951:** 4, 12 [42], 13 (pp. 72, 73), 59, 66, 114, 167
    Military procurement by U.S., **1952–53:** 367 (p. 1140)
    Military strength, **1952–53:** 18 (p. 75), 55
    Mutual defense assistance, **1950:** 22, 232, 242, 303; **1952–53:** 55
    NATO.
      See North Atlantic Treaty Organization.
    Report of Gen. Eisenhower on, **1951:** 30
    U.S. forces in **1950:** 242, 309 [10, 12]; **1951:** 2 [18], 7 [5, 9], 16 [15], 37 [17], 56 [15], 70 [1], 114; **1952–53:** 57
  Discussions with President-elect on, **1952–53:** 334 [14]
  Displaced persons in.
    See Displaced persons in Europe; Jews.
  Economy, **1948:** 2, 52, 84 [6], 92, 144, 202 [6], 244; **1949:** 8 (p. 53), 71, 116, 120, 139, 159, 162, 184, 195; **1950:** 52 [7], 154, 159, 162, 169 [9]; **1952–53:** 15, 18 (p. 75), 55
    Assistance, **1950:** 9 (pp. 56–59), 78, 110 [1], 119, 193; **1951:** 4, 13 (pp. 72, 73), 59, 114, 167, 209 [13], 256, 297
    See also European recovery program, Marshall plan.
    Balance of payments, **1952–53:** 55
    Campaign remarks, **1952–53:** 281
    Inflation, **1952–53:** 5
  Ewing, Oscar R., visit of, **1952–53:** 334 [10]
  Immigration to U.S., **1952–53:** 288
  Industrial progress, mission to study, **1952–53:** 257
  Integration, military and economic, **1952–53:** 358
  Lend-lease, **1948:** 97 [7]
  Message to Congress on, **1948:** 52
  News conference remarks, **1948:** 4 [2], 41 [10], 49 [4], 71 [16, 22], 84 [6], 88 [13], 97 [7], 278 [40], 283 [9], 288 [4]; **1949:** 7 [6, 9, 11], 72 [2, 7, 16, 19, 20], 89 [9], 155 [3], 171 [9], 179 [17], 211 [3], 236 [17]; **1950:** 52 [7], 137 [1, 19], 169 [9], 203 [4, 11], 273 [14], 295 [1], 309 [8, 10, 12]
  Occupied areas, **1948:** 144
  Payments union, proposed, **1950:** 169 [9]
  Political and economic integration, **1951:** 25, 235; **1952–53:** 55, 131, 366
  Public health, **1951:** 135
  Rearmament program, **1952–53:** 55, 125
  Relief shipments, **1948:** 5 (p. 48)
  Strategic importance, **1951:** 114
  U.S. labor unions, information programs in, **1950:** 92
  U.S. policy in, **1950:** 301; **1952–53:** 55

Europe, Western — *continued*
  U.S. Special Representative (William H. Draper,
      Jr.), **1952–53:** 217
  Vice President-elect, visit to, **1948:** 288 [4]
  War, possibilities of, **1950:** 273 [14]; **1952–53:**
      156 [14]
  World wars, casualties and devastation, **1951:** 36
      [26], 65
European Advisory Commission, **1945:** 91
European Coal Organization, **1947:** 29
European Defense Community, **1952–53:** 6, 55, 78,
      151, 366
  German progress toward acceptance of, state-
      ment, **1952–53:** 343
European Economic Cooperation, Committee of,
      1947: 191 [4, 5], 217, 219, 238
European Economic Cooperation, Organization
      for, **1949:** 71, 155 [23]; **1952–53:** 55
European Payments Union, **1952–53:** 55
European Recovery Act of 1948, **1952–53:** 203n.
European Recovery and American Aid, report,
      1947: 219
European recovery program, **1947:** 217, 219; **1948:**
      2, 5 (pp. 20, 21, 29, 31), 8 (pp. 69, 96), 28,
      31, 52, 63, 80, 83, 85, 91, 96, 101, 114 [2],
      175, 192, 202 [6], 244, 260, 266, 276; **1949:**
      5, 8 (p. 53), 19, 71, 75, 116, 120, 154, 159,
      160, 162, 184, 195, 202, 263; **1950:** 2, 8 [6,
      22, 23], 9 (pp. 57, 58), 42, 81, 119, 134,
      151, 154, 159, 162, 204; **1951:** 13 (p. 73),
      209 [13]; **1952–53:** 55
  Agricultural surpluses, use in, **1949:** 45 [9]
  Appropriations for, **1948:** 75, 144; **1949:** 66 [2]
  Counterpart funds, use in African territories,
      1951: 13 (p. 75)
  Message to Congress, **1947:** 238
  News conference remarks on, **1947:** 232 [9, 11];
      1948: 15 [6, 8, 11], 49 [3, 5], 71 [7], 86, 88
      [6], 174 [11]; **1949:** 45 [9], 66 [2], 86, 118
      [19]
  Third anniversary, statement, **1951:** 66
  U.S. representative, proposed, **1947:** 238
Evacuation claims, Japanese-Americans, **1948:** 20
Evaluation Board, Joint Chiefs of Staff, **1948:** 278
      [1]
Evaluation Commission, President's, **1946:** 163 [1]
Evans, Joshua, **1951:** 21
Evans, Luther H., **1951:** 225; **1952–53:** 347
Evans, Silliman, **1949:** 112 [4]
Evansville, Ind.
  Campaign remarks, **1948:** 218 [10]
  Mayor William H. Dress, **1948:** 218 [10]
  Wallace supporters, attacks on, **1948:** 71 [2]
Evatt, Herbert V., **1946:** 141 [14, 17]; **1948:** 274 [3,
      6]
Evening Star (Washington, D.C.), **1945:** 147 [12]
Everett, Edward, **1951:** 8

Everett, Glenn, **1952–53:** 233 [2]
Everett, Wash.
  Campaign remarks, **1948:** 122 [6]; **1952–53:** 274
      [5]
  Mayor Henry Arends, **1948:** 122 [6]
Everglades City, Fla., **1947:** 231n.
Everglades National Park, **1947:** 221 [10], 231
Everitt, William L., **1950:** 40n.
Everly, Ernest W., **1948:** 136 [3]
Evins, Repr. Joseph L., **1951:** 138
Ewing, Capt. Charles G., letter on repatriation of
      Korean prisoners-of-war, **1952–53:** 232
Ewing, Oscar R., **1947:** 184; **1948:** 16, 89, 181 [2],
      237 [3]; **1950:** 47, 196, 265, 299n.; **1951:**
      55, 135, 194; **1952–53:** 169, 234, 334 [10]
Excelsior Springs, Mo., **1949:** 17
Excess profits tax, **1945:** 42; **1946:** 18 (p. 80), 192
      [27]; **1947:** 4 (p. 16), 6 [36], 7 (p. 56), 221
      [15]; **1948:** 4 [15, 16, 18], 5 (p. 23), 8 (p.
      71), 165, 167, 170 [1], 176, 264 [5], 274 [8];
      1949: 4 [5]; **1950:** 203 [9], 209 [8], 273 [5],
      284, 303; **1951:** 1, 12 [10, 12], 13 (pp. 66,
      67), 28, 228
  See also Taxes.
Excess Profits Tax Act of 1950, **1951:** 1, 13 (pp. 66,
      67); **1952–53:** 231
Exchange programs
  Canada, **1951:** 194
  Ecuador, **1951:** 134
  Educational, **1949:** 139, 187; **1950:** 92, 190, 227
  France, **1951:** 194
  Fulbright program, **1951:** 103
  NATO, remarks to trainees, **1951:** 36
  Point 4 program, **1951:** 262
  Public health teams, **1951:** 135
  Teachers, **1951:** 103, 124, 194; **1952–53:** 234
  U.S.-Brazil, **1949:** 108 [2]
  U.S.-U.K., **1949:** 187; **1951:** 194
Excise taxes, **1947:** 2 (p. 7), 6 [12, 37], 7 (pp. 55, 60,
      92), 116; **1948:** 5 (p. 23), 63; **1951:** 11, 13
      (p. 66), 28; **1952–53:** 33
  See also Taxes.
Executive agreements, **1952–53:** 140
Executive Avenue, removal of pillars, **1947:** 95 [1]
Executive branch, **1946:** 250 [1], 268; **1947:** 7 (pp.
      59, 90), 35, 56, 115, 132, 156, 161, 169,
      172, 190, 197, 219, 223, 224; 238, 242;
      1948: 5 (p. 54), 20, 26 [10], 102, 187; **1949:**
      131; **1951:** 26
  Appointments
    Delays in Senate confirmation, **1950:** 97 [10],
        169 [12], 209 [7]
    Plans of President-elect, **1952–53:** 334 [19], 342
        [10, 11]
  Appropriations, **1950:** 234
  Cabinet officers, appearance before Congress,
      1950: 152 [2]

Executive branch — *continued*
  Campaign remarks on, **1952–53:** 292 [11]
  Civil rights, measures to implement, **1952–53:** 290
  Civilian employment, **1948:** 4 [1]
  Cooperation with congressional crime investigating committee, **1951:** 115
  Decentralization of agencies, proposed, **1951:** 90 [10]
  District of Columbia activities, dispersal in emergency, **1952–53:** 18 (p. 113)
  Documents, publication and codification of, **1950:** 75
  Economic policy, coordination, **1952–53:** 376
  Economy by, **1947:** 11, 134, 180 [2, 7]
  Financial management, **1952–53:** 367 (p. 1161)
  Food relief for India, study of, **1951:** 34
  Foreign aid programs, administration, **1951:** 114
  Foreign policy consultations with Congress, **1950:** 89, 103
  GAO joint accounting program, **1951:** 221
  Information
    Availability to Special Assistant to Attorney General, **1952–53:** 35 [1], 36, 44 [10], 64 [15]
    Privileged, **1951:** 35, 108 [4, 11]; **1952–53:** 60, 64 [6], 76, 91, 182, 238 [2]
    Security, classification and protection, **1951:** 233, 234, 247 [1, 5, 10, 12], 248, 302
    Services, **1952–53:** 335
    Release to Congress, **1948:** 97 [14]
  Italy, consultations on aid to, **1952–53:** 180
  Joint accounting program, **1952–53:** 18 (p. 116)
  Management improvement program, **1949:** 8 (p. 48), 167; **1950:** 8 [48], 9 (pp. 51, 52); **1952–53:** 1, 18 (pp. 115, 116), 367 (p. 1132)
  News conference remarks on, **1947:** 6 [7, 28], 62 [19], 155 [5], 177 [23], 182 [5], 191 [4]; **1948:** 4 [1], 97 [14], 274 [1], 278 [10], 285 [6]; **1949:** 28 [12, 18], 45 [23], 93 [3], 122 [21, 22], 155 [18], 166 [1], 182 [8], 226 [4]; **1950:** 97 [3], 105 [15], 137 [2, 17], 209 [12], 318 [2, 4]
  Officials, proposed salary increases, **1949:** 3
  Privileged papers, protection of, **1949:** 122 [22]
  Property and records management, **1952–53:** 367 (pp. 1161–1162)
  Real estate transactions, **1951:** 105, 108 [1]; **1952–53:** 18 (p. 114)
  Regulatory agencies, expenditures for, **1952–53:** 367 (p. 1131)
  Relations with Congress, **1947:** 31 [3]
  Remarks to officials on budget for military functions of Defense Department, **1951:** 93
  Reorganization, **1945:** 128; **1946:** 110 [2], 116, 118, 119 [3]; **1947:** 36 [10], 70 [9], 80, 102,

Executive branch — *continued*
  Reorganization — *continued*
    145 [1], 146, 232 [1, 4]; **1948:** 46, 62, 135, 160, 274 [1], 278 [10], 285 [6]; **1949:** 2, 25, 28 [12, 18], 45 [23], 47, 93 [3], 122 [21], 127–134, 145, 155 [18], 158, 167, 177, 181, 182 [8]; **1950:** 1, 9 (pp. 51, 100, 101), 28, 53–72, 74, 76, 112–115, 123, 149, 150, 307; **1951:** 33 [2], 39, 56 [1, 3, 8, 11], 82, 175, 209 [15], 226; **1952–53:** 1, 2 [4, 11], 5, 11, 18 (pp. 112, 115, 116), 53, 59, 84–87, 107 [6], 114, 115 [14], 117, 137, 287, 292 [11], 366, 367 (p. 1132)
    Messages to Congress, **1945:** 41; **1949:** 12, 94
    Resignations among Presidential appointees, **1952–53:** 334 [12]
    Strategic and critical materials, conservation efforts, **1952–53:** 191, 192
    Supergrade positions, limitation, **1950:** 288
    Transfer of functions, discussions concerning, **1952–53:** 233 [14], 326, 331, 334 [1, 7], 341, 342 [15], 366, 378
  Water resources development projects, coordination with Congress, **1950:** 140
Executive Branch, Commission on Organization. *See* Commission on the Organization of the Executive Branch of the Government.
Executive Committee on Economic Foreign Policy, **1946:** 71
Executive Mansion, Commission on Renovation of, **1949:** 31n., 249
Executive Office of the President, **1947:** 7 (p. 59); **1949:** 151, 156; **1950:** 115
  Reorganization, **1949:** 127, 131; **1950:** 53; **1951:** 175
The Presidency and the Executive Office of the President, George A. Graham, **1951:** 270
Executive orders, **1945:** 19n., 41, 102n., 104, 115, 120, 140, 141, 150n., 158n., 180, 195n., 228n., 230
  Armed forces, functions, **1947:** 159
  List, Appendix B, **1945:** p. 604; **1946:** p. 526; **1947:** p. 551; **1948:** p. 990; **1949:** p. 606; **1950:** p. 779; **1951:** p. 670; **1952–53:** p. 1233
  News conference remarks, **1945:** 22 [5], 137 [10], 157 [3, 5], 172 [3], 175 [5], 202 [1]
Executive privilege, **1950:** 44 [6, 9, 15], 46 [11], 79, 82, 94, 152 [9], 182, 217 [12], 254; **1951:** 108 [4, 11]; **1952–53:** 60, 64 [6], 76, 91, 182, 238 [2]
Exeter, N.H., campaign remarks, **1952–53:** 295 [5]
Exodus, Book of, **1947:** 86; **1950:** 37; **1951:** 241
Experiment Stations, Office of, **1946:** 116; **1947:** 80
Experimental Training Unit, Fort Knox, Ky., **1948:** 190
Export Control Act, **1947:** 18, 58, 99; **1948:** 8 (p. 74)

Export controls, **1945:** 202 [3]
Export-Import Bank of Washington, **1945:** 50, 128;
        1946: 17 [5, 22], 18 (pp. 45, 85, 86), 25, 47,
        76, 79, 94, 136 [7], 173 [10], 192 [19, 23],
        193, 265; **1947:** 2 (p. 10), 6 [27], 7 (pp. 57,
        67, 68, 94, 95), 46 [21], 83, 95 [25], 138, 181
        (p. 400), 195, 209 [3]; **1948:** 5 (pp. 29, 57),
        69, 110 [21], 178 [11]; **1949:** 8 (p. 54), 113
        [10], 139, 151; **1950:** 6, 9 (p. 59); **1951:** 12
        [3], 13 (pp. 72, 75), 81, 114, 205; **1952–53:**
        18 (pp. 77, 79), 55, 367 (p. 1140)
    Appointment of Wm. McC. Martin, Jr., as
        Chairman, Board of Directors, **1945:** 202
        [2]
    Appointments to Board, question of, **1945:** 175
        [13], 181 [9]
    Loans
        Argentina, **1950:** 137 [5, 15], 287 [20]
        Spain, **1950:** 287 [2]
        Yugoslavia, **1950:** 293
    News conference remarks, **1950:** 137 [5, 15], 179
        [14], 206 [9], 238 [2, 17], 287 [2, 20]
    President (Wayne C. Taylor), letter, **1945:** 176
Export Transportation, Interagency Committee on,
        1946: 264
Exports, **1946:** 18 (pp. 48, 69), 193; **1947:** 4 (pp. 26,
        37), 238; **1948:** 8 (pp. 63, 91, 96, 97), 42,
        99, 234; **1949:** 2, 5, 8 (pp. 79, 88), 151;
        1950: 6, 81, 111, 159; **1952–53:** 215
    See also Balance of payments; Imports; Tariffs;
        Trade, international; *specific commodities.*
    Agricultural, **1945:** 128; **1946:** 18 (pp. 58, 59);
        1948: 8 (pp. 77, 93), 31, 233 [1], 246; **1950:**
        9 (p. 84)
        Corn, **1946:** 86 [4]
        Cotton, **1946:** 18 (p. 85)
        Food.
            See main heading, Food.
        Grain, **1946:** 143 [2], 144, 168, 223 [1], 255, 264
        Wheat, **1946:** 23, 30 [2], 86 [4, 27], 87, 95 [1],
            119 [16]
    Assistance program, **1951:** 167
    Building materials, **1946:** 263
    Capital goods, **1952–53:** 15
    Coal, **1946:** 23, 264
    Controls, **1947:** 18, 36 [5, 23], 46 [10], 58, 76, 99,
        143, 155 [6], 224, 226 [9, 11], 242; **1948:** 1,
        5 (pp. 51–53), 23; **1950:** 9 (pp. 96, 97), 230
        [6], 270 [7]; **1951:** 11, 13 (p. 78); **1952–53:**
        18 (p. 79)
    Decrease, **1950:** 202; **1951:** 11
    Emergency programs, **1946:** 264; **1947:** 29, 47
    European, **1947:** 238
    Increase, **1952–53:** 15
    Natural gas to Canada, **1952–53:** 377 [25]
    News conference remarks, **1950:** 230 [6], 270 [7]
    Profiteering, **1947:** 224
    Prohibition by Canada, **1947:** 226 [5]

Exports — *continued*
    Raw materials, **1952–53:** 55
    Strategic materials, restrictions on shipment to
        Communist bloc, **1952–53:** 105, 180, 217,
        358
    To Soviet Union, **1947:** 226 [10]; **1948:** 55 [2]
    Transportation for, **1947:** 47
    War materials, **1947:** 72
        Embargo to Communist bloc, **1950:** 252; **1951:**
            117
Extension Service, **1947:** 7 (p. 80)
    Agricultural, **1948:** 5 (pp. 42, 44), 276
Ezra, Book of, **1951:** 68

Fabian, S. H., **1946:** 160
Factfinding boards in labor disputes, **1945:** 204,
        206; **1946:** 2, 18 (p. 52); **1949:** 155 [12, 15],
        179 [6], 240 [7, 12, 15]; **1950:** 49, 188, 221
    See also Labor-management relations.
    Airline strike, **1946:** 110 [11]
    Coal industry, **1950:** 27n., 35n.
    General Motors strike, **1946:** 9, 15 [6, 14], 16, 27
        [9], 53 [2]
    News conference remarks, **1945:** 211 [2, 4, 5], 221
        [3, 12, 14, 18, 21, 23]; **1950:** 34 [4], 46 [9],
        186 [1]
    Railroad strike, **1946:** 53 [1]
    Statement, **1945:** 221 [1]
    Steel strike, **1946:** 16, 20
Facts and Figures, Office of, **1946:** 21 [13]
Fahey, John H., **1947:** 173, 174 [1]
Fair, international trade, proposed, **1949:** 171 [3]
Fair Deal, **1949:** 52 [13]; **1950:** 163; **1951:** 7 [2, 4],
        295 [10, 14]; **1952–53:** 63, 129, 175 [5, 13],
        194, 230, 270 [7], 272, 274 [2], 276, 278,
        284 [1], 295 [3, 9], 296, 298 [1, 2, 6, 9, 13,
        14], 300, 303 [5], 304, 305, 306 [1, 7], 307,
        308 [1, 3], 311 [1], 313 [4, 6], 315 [1, 3], 321
        [3, 6, 7], 322
Fair Employment Board, **1952–53:** 169, 290
Fair Employment Practice, Committee on, **1945:**
        128; **1946:** 2, 154
    Houston, Charles H., **1945:** 208 [18]
    Letter to Representative Sabath re, **1945:** 51
    News conference remarks, **1945:** 60 [11], 137 [7]
Fair Employment Practice Act, proposed, **1946:** 18
        (p. 52)
Fair Employment Practice Commission, proposed,
        1948: 20; **1950:** 9 (pp. 99, 102), 23ftn. (p.
        134), 141; **1951:** 12 [29], 13 (p. 80), 16 [11],
        132 [16]; **1952–53:** 18 (p. 95), 98 [5], 123
        [17], 290, 317 [8]
    News conference remarks, 8 [41], 11 [13], 23 [8],
        29 [2, 12], 44 [1], 86 [14], 137 [3], 146 [6]
Fair employment practices, **1945:** 51, 128, 204;
        1946: 2, 18 (pp. 40, 52), 21 [17], 78 [5], 154

Fair employment practices — *continued*
    199 [15]; **1947:** 4 (p. 31); **1948:** 8 (p. 88);
    1949: 239, 256
  Bill, **1950:** 141
Fair Labor Standards Act, **1946:** 18 (p. 58), 117;
    1947: 4 (p. 29); **1948:** 183 [5], 227 [3], 228
    [5, 6, 12], 232, 233 [6], 240 [1], 255, 261 [4,
    10], 268; **1949:** 151; **1950:** 9 (p. 98), 18,
    19n.; **1952–53:** 376
  Amendment, proposed, **1945:** 128
Fair Labor Standards Amendments of 1949, **1949:**
    239
Fair Trade Practices Act, **1952–53:** 197 [4]
Fairbanks, Alaska, **1948:** 105
Fairchild, Thomas, **1952–53:** 253 [10]
Fairfield Base hospital, San Francisco, Korean
    casualties at, **1950:** 267
Fairless, Benjamin F., **1945:** 206n.; **1946:** 12, 15 [7],
    16, 21 [3, 5, 9]; **1947:** 236 [3], 237; **1948:** 84
    [1]; **1949:** 152n., 153; **1952–53:** 116, 216
Fairs, the President's attendance at, **1949:** 202
Faith of Our Fathers, **1951:** 116
Fall River, Mass.
  Campaign remarks, **1948:** 261 [4]; **1952–53:** 298
    [3]
  Mayor William P. Grant, **1948:** 261n.
Family Life, National Conference on, address,
    1948: 92
Famine, **1947:** 2 (p. 7), 32
Famine Emergency Committee, **1946:** 58, 85, 87,
    144, 255; **1952–53:** 98ftn. (p. 270), 377ftn.
    (p. 1196)
Famine Emergency Council, National, **1946:** 58
Famine Relief, Youth Conference on, **1946:** 168
FAO.
  See Food and Agriculture Organization.
Far East, **1945:** 118 [6], 186; **1946:** 18 (p. 44), 30 [2],
    76, 172
  See also Asia, South Asia, and Southeast Asia;
    specific countries.
  Assistance, **1948:** 4 [2]
  Clothing for, **1945:** 74
  Communism in, **1952–53:** 5
Far Eastern Advisory Commission, **1945:** 172 [5],
    175 [5], 181 [4]; **1946:** 95 [22]; **1950:** 250
    [1, 6]
Far Eastern Economic Assistance Act of 1950,
    1949: 117n.; **1950:** 17n.
Fargo, **1946:** 143 [15]
Fargo, N. Dak., **1950:** 130
  Campaign remarks, **1952–53:** 266 [2]
Farley, James A., **1946:** 15 [3]; **1948:** 41 [15], 261n.,
    264 [5]; **1949:** 226 [7]; **1952–53:** 7 [6], 359
    [11]
Farm Board, Federal, **1950:** 111
Farm Bureau Federation, American, **1949:** 234
    [10]; **1950:** 145
  Convention, **1948:** 285 [5]

Farm cooperatives, **1948:** 99, 117, 218 [1, 11], 234,
    235 [4], 237 [1, 5], 246, 257 [5]; **1949:** 203
Farm Credit Administration, **1945:** 76 [3]; **1946:** 18
    (p. 81); **1947:** 7 (p. 78), 80; **1948:** 218 [1];
    1950: 114; **1951:** 13 (p. 89), 202; **1952–53:**
    18 (p. 92)
Farm Credit Administration, Governor (I. W.
    Duggan), **1951:** 202
Farm economy, **1945:** 42, 128; **1946:** 18 (pp. 58,
    59), 61 [12], 152, 153, 226 [1]; **1947:** 2 (pp.
    3, 7), 4 (pp. 32, 33), 7 (pp. 58, 78), 97, 110,
    152, 202, 214, 224, 231; **1948:** 2, 5 (pp. 42,
    44), 8 (pp. 62, 65, 88, 92–94), 25, 32, 80,
    94, 99, 219, 285 [5]; **1949:** 2, 8 (p. 79), 90,
    91, 93 [5], 120, 123, 151, 203, 219; **1950:** 2,
    6, 9 (pp. 84, 85), 86 [17], 110 [7, 10], 111,
    121 [3, 5, 7], 122, 127 [4–6], 134, 145, 157,
    163, 202, 279, 281; **1951:** 7 [16], 13 (pp.
    87–89), 91, 167, 199, 202, 296; **1952–53:** 5,
    33, 69, 110, 126, 194, 215, 263, 266 [3, 4, 7,
    9], 268 [2, 5], 271, 272, 274 [2, 4], 276, 277
    [5, 6], 281, 282 [4, 6, 8], 284 [1, 2, 4], 285,
    289 [1, 2], 293, 300, 307, 312, 313 [1–4],
    314, 315 [1, 4], 321, 322, 360, 366, 367 (p.
    1148), 388
  See also Agriculture; Agricultural commodities.
  Campaign remarks, **1948:** 117, 136 [5], 137 [3],
    138 [3, 5], 160, 183 [5], 184, 194 [4, 6], 195,
    198 [3], 204 [1, 2], 206 [4], 208 [2], 212 [5,
    7, 10], 214 [8], 216 [3, 5, 7, 10, 13], 218 [1,
    7, 8, 14], 222 [1–5, 9, 10], 223, 227 [2, 5, 9],
    228 [1, 4–6, 8, 13], 231 [5–7], 232, 233 [5,
    6], 234, 236, 237 [1, 4, 5, 7], 240 [3–6], 242
    [3], 246, 257 [5], 259 [5], 267 [3], 268, 281
    [1]
  Census report, **1952–53:** 363n.
  Credit, **1952–53:** 18 (p. 92)
  Floods, danger to, **1947:** 144
  News conference remarks, **1947:** 107 [2], 210 [3]
  Stabilization, **1952–53:** 18 (pp. 91, 92)
Farm equipment, improvement, **1949:** 263
Farm exports, **1946:** 18 (pp. 58, 59)
Farm housing, **1948:** 5 (p. 38)
Farm income.
  See Farm economy.
Farm Journal, The, **1952–53:** 274 [4], 282 [4], 284
    [1]
Farm Loan Association, National, **1948:** 218 [1]
Farm machinery, **1948:** 8 (pp. 72, 77, 92), 167
  Exports to Soviet Union, **1947:** 226 [10]
Farm Mortgage Corporation, Federal, **1951:** 202
Farm mortgages, **1948:** 99, 117, 138 [3], 195, 212 [3],
    214 [7, 8], 216 [13], 218 [1, 14], 219, 227 [5],
    228 [4, 5, 10, 13], 240 [3], 268
Farm Placement Service, **1948:** 135; **1951:** 154
Farm prices and income.
  See Farm economy.

Farm program, **1948:** 5 (p. 54), 8 (pp. 72, 81), 285 [5]; **1949:** 2, 8 (p. 47), 90, 91, 151, 154, 203, 234 [10]; **1950:** 2, 6, 83, 110 [2, 5, 7], 111, 121 [2, 3, 7], 124 [6, 8], 127 [2, 4, 5], 134, 145, 157; **1951:** 13 (pp. 87–89)
    Bipartisanship, **1952–53:** 277 [6]
    Brannan plan, **1951:** 12 [15, 45], 22 [13]; **1952–53:** 17 [30], 285
    Budget, decrease, **1951:** 12 [50]
    Campaign remarks on, **1948:** 138 [3], 194 [11], 195, 204 [4], 216 [5, 6, 13], 217, 218 [1, 3], 228 [3, 5, 6, 10, 12], 231 [6], 233 [2], 234, 240 [2, 5], 246, 259 [5], 267 [1]; **1952–53:** 221 [15], 247 [10], 267, 285, 286 [5], 279 [6], 304, 311, 313 [2], 314, 315 [4, 5], 318, 321 [3, 7], 376
    Family farms, assistance, **1952–53:** 388
    Legislation, proposed, **1948:** 165
    News conference remarks, **1949:** 118 [24], 200 [21], 226 [11], 231 [24], 236 [15]
Farm real estate prices, **1947:** 97
Farm Security Administration, **1946:** 17 [12], 18 (pp. 80, 81); **1947:** 7 (p. 79)
Farm Security Administrator, **1945:** 193 [9]
Farm Support Act, **1948:** 228 [12]
Farm Tenant Purchase Program, **1948:** 216 [5]
Farmers Home Administration, **1947:** 7 (p. 79), 181 (p. 402); **1948:** 5 (pp. 43, 44); **1950:** 9 (pp. 54, 86), 121 [3]; **1951:** 13 (p. 89); **1952–53:** 18 (p. 92), 231
Farmers Home Administration Act, **1947:** 7 (p. 79)
Farmers' Home Corporation Act, approval, **1946:** 206
Farmers' Union Central Exchange, Billings, Mont., **1952–53:** 58n.
Farouk, King, **1946:** 110 [17], 141 [9]
Farrington, Joseph R., **1952–53:** 149 [15]
Fascism, **1945:** 66, 91, 178, 187, 210, 218; **1946:** 18 (pp. 38, 43), 83; **1947:** 90 [1], 113, 132, 222; **1948:** 256; **1949:** 195; **1951:** 225
Fast, Howard, conviction of, **1948:** 150 [6]
Fats and oils, controls, **1947:** 18, 99
Fawcett, Val, **1948:** 124 [4]
FBI.
    See Federal Bureau of Investigation.
FCC.
    See Federal Communications Commission.
FEA.
    See Foreign Economic Administration.
Featherbedding, **1947:** 120
Fechteler, Adm. William M., **1952–53:** 128, 320
Federal-Aid Highway Act, **1947:** 7 (p. 85), 118; **1948:** 24n., 175
Federal aid to States, **1945:** 99, 128; **1946:** 117, 203; **1947:** 4 (p. 34), 6 [4], 7 (pp. 76, 77); **1948:** 5 (pp. 34, 35, 37, 38, 40, 44, 45, 48, 50, 54), 82

Federal aid to States — *continued*
    Accident prevention, **1950:** 9 (p. 99), 74
    Agricultural experiment stations, **1952–53:** 367 (p. 1150)
    Airports, **1950:** 9 (p. 50), 171; **1951:** 13 (p. 83)
    Atomic energy development, **1949:** 154
    Aviation, **1952–53:** 367 (p. 1144)
    Civil defense, **1950:** 303; **1951:** 10, 131; **1952–53:** 18 (pp. 96, 97, 99)
    Conservation of natural resources, **1952–53:** 388
    Crime control, **1951:** 63 [1]
    Depressed areas, **1949:** 151, 161 [12]; **1950:** 6, 135
    Disaster relief, **1949:** 22 [1], 28 [2]
    Drought relief, **1952–53:** 221 [1]
    Education, **1946:** 18 (pp. 64, 65, 83, 84); **1947:** 7 (p. 76), 8 [13], 206, 235n.; **1948:** 2, 5 (pp. 25, 41), 8 (pp. 67, 86), 99, 105, 108, 134, 138 [1], 160, 165, 174 [1], 175, 176, 183 [5, 6], 186, 203, 205, 211, 212 [9], 214 [9], 219, 228 [2, 8, 12], 231 [1], 232, 233 [5], 247, 249, 251, 257 [4], 258, 259, 262, 268; **1949:** 2, 5, 7 [49], 8 (pp. 45, 47, 76–78), 51, 144 [12], 179 [16], 202, 204, 208, 219; **1950:** 2, 6, 8 [34], 9 (p. 82), 47, 52 [11, 13], 53, 69, 71, 110 [2], 127 [7], 134, 160 [2]; **1951:** 4, 11, 12 [32], 13 (pp. 93–96), 135; **1952–53:** 5, 17 [15], 18 (pp. 100–103), 218, 231, 281, 284 [5, 6], 313 [4], 333, 367 (pp. 1155, 1156)
    Employment services, **1947:** 7 (p. 89); **1949:** 8 (p. 91); **1950:** 9 (p. 97); **1951:** 13 (p. 79); **1952–53:** 18 (p. 93), 231
    Flood control, **1949:** 154; **1950:** 129 [5], 130; **1951:** 162, 163, 165 [4], 196, 224 [7], 261 [6], 269; **1952–53:** 97, 366, 388
    Health and welfare, **1948:** 5 (pp. 34, 35), 8 (pp. 87, 88), 105; 107, 152, 175; **1949:** 8 (pp. 47, 68, 69), 85, 151, 154; **1950:** 8 [32, 47], 9 (pp. 50, 75); **1951:** 13 (pp. 98, 99), 135, 221, 307; **1952–53:** 249, 268 [8], 273, 284 [5], 306 [1], 333, 366, 367 (pp. 1157–1158), 369
        Public health programs, **1952–53:** 18 (p. 106)
    Highways, **1946:** 18 (pp. 61, 81); **1947:** 7 (pp. 58, 85), 35, 118, 181 (p. 402); **1948:** 5 (pp. 47, 48, 50), 8 (p. 81), 24, 105, 175; **1949:** 8 (p. 87), 142 151, 154; **1950:** 9 (pp. 49, 50, 92, 94, 95), 121 [6], 213; **1951:** 13 (p. 84), 221; **1952–53:** 231, 277 [4], 367 (pp. 1143, 1144)
    Housing, **1948:** 5 (p. 38), 163 [13]; **1949:** 54, 126, 157, 269 [11]
    Industrial safety programs, **1947:** 7 (p. 89); **1950:** 9 (p. 99)
    Irrigation projects, **1949:** 168; **1952–53:** 388
    Labor programs, **1949:** 8 (p. 90); **1952–53:** 367 (p. 1150)
    Maritime schools, **1947:** 7 (p. 86)

Federal aid to States — *continued*
  Occupational training, **1951:** 13 (p. 98); **1952–53:** 367 (p. 1155)
  Public assistance programs, **1947:** 181 (p. 399); **1950:** 6, 9 (pp. 50, 73, 74); **1951:** 159; **1952–53:** 5, 18 (pp. 105–106), 213, 231, 367 (p. 1156)
  Public works, **1946:** 18 (pp. 61, 62, 69); **1947:** 7 (p. 92); **1950:** 9 (pp. 50, 81), 69, 171; **1951:** 13 (p. 94)
  Safety programs, **1949:** 55
  Soil conservation, **1949:** 154
  Unemployment insurance, **1949:** 151; **1950:** 84; **1952–53:** 231
  Urban redevelopment, **1949:** 8 (p. 72)
  Vocational training, **1947:** 7 (p. 58); **1950:** 9 (p. 74)
  Water pollution control, **1950:** 69
  Water resources development, **1949:** 154
Federal Airports Act of 1946, **1948:** 8 (p. 82); **1950:** 68
Federal Bar Association, **1950:** 94
Federal Board of Hospitalization, **1945:** 128
Federal Board of Vocational Education, termination, **1946:** 117
Federal Budget in Brief, pamphlet, **1951:** 22 [5], 221
Federal Bureau of Investigation, **1945:** 176; **1946:** 17 [10], 54, 86 [3], 192 [8]; **1947:** 89, 222; **1948:** 20, 50, 102, 178 [13], 215, 283 [1]; **1949:** 8 (p. 70), 269ftn. (p. 585); **1950:** 94, 254; **1952–53:** 69, 75 [4], 117, 169, 251, 290, 296, 300, 303 [2]
  Authority in cases of felony committed in D.C. park areas, **1945:** 80
  Espionage, sabotage, and subversion, reporting of information to, **1950:** 199
  Investigation of, proposed, **1949:** 122 [1], 155 [2]
  Loyalty files, question of disclosure to Congress, **1950:** 79, 82, 94, 254
  News conference remarks, **1949:** 122 [1], 155 [2], 211 [12]; **1950:** 16 [6], 86 [2]
  Wiretapping by, **1949:** 211 [12]
Federal Bureau of Investigation, Director (J. Edgar Hoover), **1946:** 54, 55n., 56n., 229 [22]; **1948:** 102, 215; **1949:** 122 [22], 269 [14]; **1950:** 79, 82, 94, 309 [4]; **1951:** 35, 300 [1]; **1952–53:** 26 [20], 75 [4], 296
Federal Bureau of Investigation, The, Max Lowenthal, **1950:** 309 [4]
Federal Civil Defense Act of 1950, approval, **1951:** 10; **1952–53:** 9n.
Federal Civil Defense Administration, **1951:** 10, 105, 131; **1952–53:** 9, 18 (p. 99), 106
Federal Civil Defense Administrator (Millard Caldwell), **1952–53:** 9
Federal Committee on Highway Safety, **1947:** 118
Federal Communications Commission, **1946:** 36, 41 [25], 43 [1], 66 [1], 84 [13], 147, 250 [11],

Federal Communications Comm. — *continued*
  257 [19]; **1947:** 14 [4], 31 [9, 14], 46 [17], 218 [10]; **1948:** 84ftn. (p. 228); **1949:** 8 (p. 88), 84 [8]; **1951:** 175, 283; **1952–53:** 281, 367 (p. 1144)
  Appointments to, **1952–53:** 49 [1, 15]
  William H. Wills, **1945:** 60 [2]
  Reorganization, **1950:** 53, 54, 65
  Television stations, proposed halt to construction of, **1952–53:** 26 [13]
Federal Communications Commission, Acting Chairman (Charles R. Denny, Jr.), **1946:** 66 [1], 147
Federal Communications Commission, Chairman (Wayne Coy), **1948:** 149n.
Federal Communications Commission, Chairman (Paul A. Porter), **1946:** 41 [22, 25]
Federal Conciliation and Mediation Service, **1948:** 252
Federal Corporation Control Bill, **1945:** 52 [11]
Federal Corrupt Practices Act, **1952–53:** 143
Federal Council of Churches of Christ, **1946:** 52
Federal Crop Insurance Corporation, **1946:** 18 (p. 81), 118
Federal Deposit Insurance Corporation, **1946:** 116, 119 [3]; **1947:** 6 [38], 7 (p. 95), 80; **1949:** 5; **1950:** 6, 110 [5]
Federal Deposit Insurance Corporation, Chairman (Leo T. Crowley), resignation, **1945:** 175 [13], 181 [7]
Federal Deposit Insurance Corporation, Chairman (Maple T. Harl), **1950:** 192
Federal Deposit Insurance Corporation, chairmanship of Board, question re, **1945:** 172 [11], 175 [17]
Federal Deposit Insurance Corporation Act, **1948:** 183 [5], 219, 231 [5], 255; **1952–53:** 266 [3]
Federal Employees, National Federation of, **1947:** 190
Federal Employees' Compensation Act, **1949:** 8 (p. 70); **1950:** 74; **1952–53:** 208
Federal Employees Salary Act of 1948, **1949:** 8 (pp. 54, 94)
Federal Farm Board, **1950:** 111
Federal Farm Mortgage Corporation, **1946:** 18 (p. 81), 94; **1947:** 7 (pp. 78, 94); **1951:** 202
Federal history program, **1951:** 26
Federal Home Loan Bank Administration, **1946:** 116; **1947:** 7 (p. 75)
Federal Home Loan Bank Board, **1946:** 116; **1947:** 102, 173, 174 [1]; **1948:** 5 (pp. 39, 40); **1949:** 8 (p. 72); **1950:** 9 (pp. 54, 80), 192
Federal Home Loan Bank Board, Chairman (John H. Fahey), **1947:** 174 [1]
Federal home loan banks, **1949:** 8 (pp. 74, 76)
Federal Housing Administration, **1946:** 18 (p. 63), 116, 257 [6], 262 [6], 263; **1947:** 7 (p. 75), 102, 173; **1948:** 5 (pp. 39, 58), 37, 150 [1],

Federal Housing Administration — *continued*
175, 225 [1]; **1949:** 8 (pp. 72, 74); **1950:** 9
(p. 77), 113 ; **1951:** 13 (p. 93), 158;
1952–53: 18 (p. 98), 367 (p. 1152)
Federal Housing Administration, Commissioner
(Franklin D. Richards), **1947:** 173, 174 [1]
Federal Inter-Agency Basin Committee, **1950:** 164
Federal Loan Administrator (John W. Snyder),
1945: 60 [3]; **1951:** 33 [2]
Federal Loan Agency, **1946:** 18 (p. 56); **1947:** 102;
1950: 112
Federal Maritime Board, **1950:** 53, 76, 236; **1952–
53:** 18 (p. 82), 177
Federal Mediation Board, proposed, **1946:** 131
Federal Mediation and Conciliation Service, **1947:**
141 [16], 145 [3], 181 (p. 403), 209 [7], 236
[3]; **1948:** 5 (p. 54), 66n., 72, 88 [3], 140,
171n., 252, 259 [1, 2]; **1951:** 13 (p. 80),
169, 204, 252, 305; **1952–53:** 18 (p. 93), 22,
37, 58
Federal Mediation and Conciliation Service, Director (Cyrus S. Ching), **1947:** 174 [1, 3],
237; **1948:** 72, 93 [5], 252, 259 [1]; **1949:**
152, 209, 213; **1950:** 43; **1951:** 204, 276,
304; **1952–53:** 37, 341
Federal Narcotics Hospital, **1951:** 201
Federal National Mortgage Association, **1948:** 175;
1949: 8 (p. 74); **1950:** 9 (p. 79), 192; **1951:**
12 [47], 13 (p. 93); **1952–53:** 18 (p. 98), 367
(p. 1153)
Reorganization, **1950:** 112
Federal Open Market Committee, **1951:** 29
Federal Personnel Recruitment Act, **1952–53:** 137
Federal Power Commission, **1946:** 70 [1]; **1947:** 7
(p. 87); **1949:** 222, 226 [7, 15], 231 [2];
1950: 3 [6], 99, 164; **1951:** 165 [2], 183n.;
1952–53: 175 [7], 314
Appointment of members, **1945:** 132 [1]
Natural gas, regulatory functions, **1950:** 88
Nomination to, **1952–53:** 26 [25]
Reorganization, **1950:** 53, 54, 63
St. Lawrence Seaway, proceedings concerning,
1952–53: 23, 189
Water resources development functions, **1950:**
140
Federal Power Commission, Chairman (Nelson
Lee Smith), **1949:** 149n.
Federal Power Commission, Chairman (Mon C.
Wallgren), **1950:** 265, 266
Letter, **1951:** 55
News conference remarks on, **1951:** 108 [10, 14],
165 [2], 251 [18]
Federal Property and Administrative Services Act,
1949: 134, 145; **1950:** 9 (p. 100), 69, 73;
1951: 14, 105; **1952–53:** 18 (p. 112), 367
(p. 1161)
Federal Public Housing Authority, **1946:** 116

Federal Public Housing Authority, Commissioner
(Dillon S. Myer), **1947:** 173, 174 [1], 226
[4], 232 [7]
Federal Records Act of 1950, **1952–53:** 149 [16]
Federal Register, **1949:** 265; **1950:** 75, 254
Federal Register Act, **1950:** 75
"Federal Research Program, The," report, **1947:**
194
Federal Reserve Act, **1950:** 117 [1]
Federal Reserve Bank, New York, **1947:** 221 [12]
Federal Reserve System, **1946:** 18 (p. 73); **1947:** 6
[38], 7 (p. 95), 18, 35, 97, 224, 226 [13];
1949: 5, 151; **1950:** 6, 9 (p. 103), 106, 217
[10]; **1951:** 44, 113 [6]
Bank chairmen and directors, remarks, **1950:** 14
Federal Reserve System, Board of Governors,
1947: 7 (p. 95), 176; **1948:** 5 (pp. 24, 57), 8
(pp. 71, 72, 95), 9 [4], 11 [5], 13, 77 [9], 84
[16], 93 [17], 165, 166 [8], 167, 178 [5];
1949: 5, 28 [12], 32ftn. (p. 136), 40 [6], 45
[3], 66 [7]; **1951:** 11, 37 [4, 6, 9], 56 [21], 91,
167; **1952–53:** 15, 123 [18]
Federal Reserve System, Board of Governors,
Chairman (Marriner S. Eccles), **1947:** 232
[5]
Letter, **1948:** 13
News conference remarks on, **1948:** 15 [1, 9], 77
[9]
Federal Reserve System, Board of Governors,
Chairman (Thomas B. McCabe), **1948:**
166 [8]; **1949:** 149n.; **1950:** 14, 192, 259;
1951: 37 [6, 9]
Fiscal policy, joint announcement with Secretary
Snyder, **1951:** 52
Letter and memorandum to, **1951:** 29, 44
Resignation, **1951:** 56 [21]
Federal Savings and Loan Insurance Corporation,
1946: 116, 208; **1947:** 102, 173; **1948:** 5
(pp. 39, 40); **1949:** 8 (pp. 74, 76); **1950:** 9
(pp. 55, 80)
Federal Security Agency, **1945:** 157 [1]; **1946:** 117,
118; **1947:** 7 (pp. 71, 77), 81, 241; **1948:** 5
(p. 35), 10, 62, 135, 154; **1949:** 7 [29], 94,
127–129, 181; **1950:** 8 [32, 47], 47, 164;
1951: 13 (p. 96), 135; **1952–53:** 185
Programs review, **1950:** 196
Reorganization, **1950:** 9 (p. 73), 69, 71, 74, 150
Federal Security Agency, Administrator (Oscar R.
Ewing), **1947:** 184; **1948:** 16, 89, 181 [2],
237 [3]; **1949:** 73n., 156, 198; **1950:** 47,
196, 265, 299n.; **1951:** 55, 135, 194, 195,
243, 251 [1]; **1952–53:** 169, 234, 334 [10]
Federal Security Agency, Administrator (Watson
B. Miller), **1947:** 123, 124
Federal-State-local governmental responsibilities,
1945: 128, 192; **1946:** 117
Aviation safety, **1952–53:** 40

Federal-State-local government — *continued*
    Civil defense, **1950:** 251, 303; **1951:** 10, 96;
        1952–53: 18 (p. 96), 106
    Civil rights, **1947:** 130; **1948:** 2, 20, 265; **1952–53:**
        290
    Community development, **1950:** 9 (p. 81); **1952–
        53:** 18 (p. 96)
    Conservation and development of natural re-
        sources, **1952–53:** 388
    Crime prevention, **1950:** 37; **1951:** 63 [1]
    Depressed areas, **1950:** 6
    Disaster relief, **1952–53:** 18 (p. 99)
    Education, **1946:** 18 (p. 84); **1950:** 9 (p. 82)
    Electric power development, **1950:** 110 [4]
    Espionage, sabotage, and subversion, reporting
        of information on, **1950:** 199
    Fair employment legislation, **1946:** 78 [5]
    Fire prevention, **1947:** 86
    Flood control and relief, **1950:** 129 [5, 7]; **1951:**
        162, 163, 165 [4], 196, 261 [6], 269
    Food, relief distribution, **1950:** 249
    Food conservation, **1947:** 225
    Forest conservation, **1947:** 69
    Handicapped, employment of, **1950:** 208; **1951:**
        195
    Health, **1948:** 16, 152, 181 [2], 237 [3]; **1949:** 8 (p.
        69); **1950:** 9 (p. 75); **1951:** 135, 307
    Highways, **1946:** 96, 106; **1948:** 24, 279; **1950:**
        121 [6], 229; **1951:** 42; **1952–53:** 367 (pp.
        1143–1144)
    Housing, **1946:** 18 (pp. 62, 63), 263; **1947:** 44,
        131; **1948:** 5 (p. 38), 37, 261 [2]; **1949:** 126,
        157
    Labor standards, **1952–53:** 18 (p. 94)
    Manpower mobilization, **1951:** 15
    Migratory workers, **1950:** 153
    Narcotics laws enforcement, **1951:** 287
    National defense program, **1950:** 304
    Natural resources development, **1950:** 121 [4],
        265
    Navajo rehabilitation, **1947:** 229
    Public assistance, **1951:** 159
    Public services, **1950:** 9 (p. 52)
    Public works, **1946:** 18 (p. 61); **1948:** 8 (p. 98),
        175; **1949:** 151; **1950:** 9 (p. 81), 69, 171
    Regional development, **1948:** 8 (pp. 67, 77, 83),
        125, 261 [2]
    Rent control, **1947:** 131; **1950:** 93
    Schools, **1952–53:** 18 (p. 102)
    Taxation, **1949:** 54
    Traffic safety, **1949:** 114
    Transportation, **1950:** 9 (p. 92)
    Unemployment, **1949:** 54, 260 [12]
    Water resources development, **1950:** 9 (p. 90),
        116; **1951:** 55
Federal Supply, Bureau of, **1948:** 5 (p. 56), 46, 60;
    1949: 145n.

Federal Surplus Commodities Corporation, **1947:** 7
    (p. 95)
Federal Trade Commission, **1946:** 218; **1947:** 4 (p.
    35), 7 (p. 87), 182 [9]; **1948:** 5 (p. 52), 220;
    1949: 8 (p. 89), 28 [6], 171 [3, 16], 192 [16],
    200 [17], 240 [14]; **1950:** 9 (p. 97), 166,
    169ftn. (p. 485), 186ftn. (p. 516), 209ftn.
    (p. 582); **1951:** 254; **1952–53:** 88 [8], 197
    [6, 13], 221 [11], 263, 282 [8]
    Antitrust laws, enforcement, **1950:** 319
    Lowell B. Mason, appointment to, **1945:** 157 [1]
    News conference remarks, **1950:** 52 [1], 186 [7],
        206 [15], 253 [14]
    Pricing practices, regulation, **1950:** 166
    Reorganization, **1950:** 54, 62
Federal Trade Commission, Chairman (Lowell B.
    Mason, Acting), **1949:** 149n.
Federal Trade Commission, Chairman (James M.
    Mead), **1950:** 259
    Letter, **1952–53:** 263
Federal Trade Commission Act, approval of fair-
    trade amendments, **1952–53:** 204
Federal Water Power Act of 1920, **1952–53:** 388
Federal Works Agency, **1945:** 128, 159, 185; **1946:**
    195n.; **1947:** 7 (pp. 76, 85, 86, 91), 35, 102;
    1948: 5 (pp. 35, 38, 40, 42), 46, 175; **1949:**
    8 (pp. 62, 75), 31, 134; **1950:** 69
    Termination, **1950:** 53
Federal Works Agency, Administrator (Maj. Gen.
    Philip B. Fleming), letter, **1945:** 224;
    1946: 96, 103, 106, 195n., 262 [3, 11];
    1947: 19 [2], 27, 35, 82, 86, 118n., 243 [16];
    1948: 24, 45, 46, 105, 111, 113, 126 [1],
    279n.; **1949:** 28 [2], 31, 89 [1], 114, 142,
    249
Federalist Papers, **1949:** 164
Federalist Party, **1950:** 207
Federally-owned property, tax exemption, **1949:**
    146
Federation of Western nations, proposed, **1947:**
    205 [16]
Feed grains, **1948:** 1, 8 (p. 70), 14, 167
    Conservation, **1947:** 205 [3, 14, 18], 209 [2], 218
        [6]
    Export controls, **1947:** 58
Feeney, Al, **1948:** 138 [6], 240 [7], 241
Feeney, Joseph, **1949:** 265
Fees for Government services
    Budget Bureau study, **1952–53:** 18 (p. 67)
    Policy on, **1949:** 175
Feighan, Repr. Michael A., **1948:** 258; **1952–53:**
    287
Feinsinger, Nathan P., **1946:** 20; **1947:** 87n.; **1951:**
    252, 277, 305; **1952–53:** 22, 58
Feldman, Maj. Gen. H., **1949:** 179 [11], 200 [6];
    1951: 200 [5]
Feller, White House dog, **1948:** 71 [6]

Fellers, Col. Bonner F., **1947:** 177 [9]
Fellowships, **1947:** 169, 206n.; **1948:** 5 (p. 42);
    1949: 5; **1950:** 120, 143
Felt, Truman, **1948:** 97 [10]
Fenton, Francis P., **1948:** 130 [1]
FEPC.
    See Fair Employment Practice Commission.
Ferguson, Garland, **1949:** 28 [6], 200 [17]
Ferguson, Sen. Homer, **1948:** 178 [13], 181 [6];
    1950: 11 [15]; **1951:** 22 [6]; **1952–53:** 129,
    297
Ferguson, Joseph T., **1950:** 146 [9], 169 [1]
Fermi, Enrico, **1946:** 262 [1]
Fertilizer, **1947:** 58, 99, 217
    Exports to China, **1948:** 31
FHA.
    See Federal Housing Administration.
Fibers, production, **1951:** 13 (p. 87)
Field, Eugene, **1950:** 110 [1]
Figg, Robert, **1945:** 147n.
Figl, Leopold, **1952–53:** 127 [14]
Filene, Edward A., **1950:** 131n.
Filene House, Credit Union National Association,
    dedication, **1950:** 131 [4], 132
Filibusters, **1946:** 21 [17]; **1947:** 232 [11]; **1949:** 45
    [18, 21]
Fillmore, Abigail, **1948:** 9 [21]
Fillmore, Millard, **1952–53:** 268 [4], 282 [7], 289
Fillmore, Mrs. Millard, **1952–53:** 249
Films, Government informational, **1946:** 160
Financial Agreement, U.S.-U.K., **1946:** 18 (pp. 45,
    85, 86), 25, 47, 51, 76; **1947:** 6 [27], 7 (pp.
    57, 67, 68), 52, 181 (p. 400)
    News conference remarks, **1946:** 15 [22], 17 [4,
        14, 22], 21 [18], 84 [21], 86 [29], 110 [4],
        192 [9, 19]
    Statement, **1946:** 169
Financial and trade conference, U.S.-U.K., **1945:**
    202 [10]
Findling, David P., **1948:** 187
Fine Arts, Commission of, **1946:** 21 [2]; **1947:** 154;
    1948: 26 [18, 20], 77 [15]
    Chairmanship, **1949:** 200 [12, 18]
Finland, **1946:** 18 (pp. 41, 42); **1948:** 41 [4], 52, 53,
    59
    Agreements on, **1945:** 91, 97
    Assistance, **1947:** 47
Finletter, Thomas K., **1947:** 148n.; **1948:** 7n.; **1950:**
    80ftn. (p. 237), 259
    Secretary of the Air Force, **1951:** 93n.
Finnegan, James P., **1951:** 251 [9, 13, 15], 300 [5, 6]
Finucane, Thomas G., **1952–53:** 244, 373
Fire prevention, **1947:** 82, 86, 231; **1948:** 113
Fire Prevention Conference, President's, **1949:** 55
Firearms, souvenir, **1946:** 15 [12]
Firefly, The, **1951:** 99
Firemen, National Association of, **1948:** 227 [2]

Firestone, Harvey S., Jr., **1949:** 104; **1950:** 294n.;
    1951: 22 [2], 278n.
First War Powers Act, **1951:** 284
Fiscal controls, **1946:** 72 [3, 9]
Fiscal policy, **1947:** 2 (p. 7), 53, 70 [22], 83, 110,
    147, 152, 180 [1]; **1948:** 8 (p. 88), 13, 63,
    90, 98, 175; **1949:** 2, 5, 8 (p. 45), 54, 151,
    229; **1950:** 2, 6, 9 (pp. 45, 96, 97), 14, 18,
    39, 202; **1951:** 13 (pp. 104–106), 44, 93,
    113 [6], 221; **1952–53:** 15, 17 [9, 13], 18 (p.
    67), 215, 367 (p. 1161), 376
    Defense, **1951:** 12 [17, 31, 41], 28, 29
    Statement, **1951:** 52
Fish, shortage, **1947:** 18
Fish and wildlife resources, **1946:** 18 (p. 82); **1947:**
    7 (p. 83), 78 [11]; **1948:** 5 (p. 47), 8 (p. 78),
    201; **1949:** 43, 77, 185, 229, 232
Fish and Wildlife Service, **1949:** 185
Fishbein, Dr. Morris, **1949:** 118 [14]
Fisher, Adrian S., **1949:** 112 [1]; **1952–53:** 244, 373
Fisher, Ham, **1951:** 290
Fisheries, Columbia River, **1949:** 77
Fisheries, conservation, **1950:** 125
Fissionable materials, **1946:** 28, 206
Fitch, Col. Tom, **1948:** 261 [9]
Fitzpatrick, Paul E., **1946:** 53 [16], 70 [3], 81n., 163
    [5, 7], 216 [6, 9, 15]; **1948:** 77 [12], 261n.;
    1949: 78 [10]; **1950:** 287 [8]; **1951:** 140 [9],
    275 [10, 19]; **1952–53:** 21 [30], 44 [6]
"Five percenters," **1949:** 144 [5], 161 [5], 231 [21];
    1950: 16ftn. (p. 119)
Flag, Presidential, **1945:** 175 [5]
Flag, U.N., gift to the President, **1950:** 239n.
Flag Day ceremonies, San Francisco, **1948:** 130 [3]
Flag raising, U.S. Group Control Council head-
    quarters, Berlin, remarks, **1945:** 86
Flanagan, Rev. E. J., **1948:** 116 [2]
Flanders, Sen. Ralph E., **1946:** 266 [22]; **1947:** 127
    [16], 191 [16]; **1950:** 227; **1951:** 54; **1952–
    53:** 3
Flat Head River power project, **1949:** 32 [16]
Flaxseed, price supports, **1949:** 8 (p. 79)
Fleeson, Doris, **1951:** 7 [5]
Fleet Sonar School, **1949:** 53
Fleischmann, Manly, **1951:** 93n.; **1952–53:** 122
Fleming, Sir Alexander, **1945:** 88
Fleming, Charles F., **1948:** 255
Fleming, Maj. Gen. Philip B., **1946:** 96, 103, 106,
    195n., 262 [3, 11]; **1947:** 19 [2], 27, 35, 82,
    86, 118n., 243 [16]; **1948:** 24, 45, 46, 105,
    111, 113, 126 [1], 279n.; **1949:** 28 [2], 31,
    89 [1], 142, 156, 249; **1950:** 229; **1951:** 42,
    121
    Letter, **1945:** 224
Fleming, Mrs. Philip B., **1951:** 121
Flemming, Arthur S., **1947:** 145 [1], 146n.; **1949:**
    94n.
Fletcher, Adm. Frank J., **1952–53:** 142

Flight officers, Army Air Forces, **1947:** 35
Flint, Mich., campaign remarks, **1948:** 183 [6];
　　1952–53: 317 [5]
Flood, Repr. Daniel J., **1948:** 249; **1952–53:** 306 [2]
Flood control, **1945:** 128, 164 [8], 165; **1946:** 18 (pp.
　　60, 82), 86 [16], 97, 195, 226 [18]; **1947:** 4
　　(p. 34), 7 (p. 93), 181 (pp. 398, 402, 406),
　　231; **1948:** 2, 5 (pp. 21, 25, 46), 6, 8 (pp.
　　67, 78), 32, 175; **1949:** 2, 7 [24], 8 (p. 83),
　　41, 43, 77, 154, 183, 185, 196; **1950:** 3 [21],
　　9 (p. 87), 121 [4, 13], 125, 127 [1], 129 [1,
　　3–5, 7], 130, 135, 306; **1951:** 13 (pp. 84,
　　85), 47, 158, 162, 163; **1952–53:** 3, 5, 17
　　[14, 19], 18 (pp. 88, 99, 100), 26 [23], 32,
　　50, 97, 98 [3, 9, 34], 101, 109, 119, 127 [5],
　　194, 195 [1, 2], 231, 266 [6, 9], 268 [2], 270
　　[9, 10], 271, 277 [3], 292 [7], 313 [1], 366,
　　367 (pp. 1146, 1149), 376, 388
　　See also Rivers and harbors development; Water
　　　　resources development.
　　Appropriations, **1951:** 183, 185, 196
　　Approval of bill, **1946:** 176
　　Campaign remarks, **1948:** 119, 122 [2, 4, 6], 124
　　　　[1], 125, 126 [1–3], 128 [1], 136 [3, 4], 199,
　　　　201, 212 [2, 4], 214 [5, 7], 216 [11], 217, 219
　　CIO assistance, **1951:** 183
　　India, **1951:** 34, 124
　　Legislation, **1951:** 196, 269
　　　　Proposed, **1950:** 33
　　Message to Congress, **1947:** 144
　　Midwest, **1951:** 185, 261 [6]
　　News conference remarks, **1947:** 141 [2], 145 [8];
　　　　1948: 4 [7], 274 [17]; **1951:** 165 [4], 209 [5],
　　　　224 [7], 261 [6]
Flood Control Acts, **1947:** 144; **1948:** 6; **1949:** 41,
　　196; **1950:** 164
Florida, **1945:** 172 [13]; **1946:** 30 [5], 237 [17], 239;
　　1947: 104, 231; **1948:** 178 [2], 274 [17];
　　1952–53: 290
　　Everglades National Park, dedication, **1947:** 221
　　　　[10]
　　Gov. Millard Caldwell, **1947:** 231n.
　　Gov. Fuller Warren, **1949:** 51
　　Primary elections, **1950:** 105 [2, 11]
Florists Telegraph Delivery Association, **1951:**
　　210n.
Flour, **1946:** 30 [2]
　　Conservation, **1946:** 29, 84 [17]
　　Overseas relief, **1947:** 47
　　Shipment to Yugoslavia, **1950:** 293
Fly, James Lawrence, **1949:** 211 [12]
Flying, by the President, **1947:** 19 [16, 18]
Flying Enterprise, **1952–53:** 29n.
Flying saucers, **1947:** 141 [8]
Flying Tigers, **1946:** 113
Flynn, Edward J., **1946:** 30 [3], 70 [3]; **1948:** 77 [12],
　　264 [3]; **1951:** 95 [7], 227 [8]
Flynn, Michael J., **1951:** 118 [2]

Fogarty, Repr. John E., **1948:** 261 [5]; **1951:** 239
　　[2]; **1952–53:** 298 [5], 299
Foley, Edward H., Jr., **1947:** 123, 124
Foley, Raymond M., **1946:** 262 [6, 11]; **1947:** 173,
　　174 [1]; **1948:** 5 (pp. 38, 40), 111; **1949:** 8
　　(p. 72), 148 [22], 157, 267 [18], 269 [11];
　　1950: 9 (p. 81), 192, 259; **1951:** 11, 111,
　　163, 303; **1952–53:** 120n.
Folger, John C., **1951:** 271
Folliard, Edward T., **1948:** 41 [5]; **1950:** 152 [5, 7];
　　1951: 16 [17, 21], 90 [4], 140 [14], 179 [12,
　　14], 251 [27], 300 [1]; **1952–53:** 75 [4], 98
　　[23, 29], 136 [19], 197 [6], 233 [15], 377 [6]
Folsom, Gov. James E., **1948:** 15 [4]
Folsom, Marion B., **1947:** 55
Folsom Dam, **1948:** 6, 203; **1949:** 41
Food, **1947:** 51
　　See also specific commodities.
　　Army and Navy stockpiles, **1946:** 86 [32]
　　Black market, **1947:** 191 [24]
　　Cabinet Committee on World Food Programs,
　　　　1947: 177 [6], 191 [3, 5, 8], 196; **1948:** 1
　　Commodity exchanges, **1947:** 209 [11, 12, 16]
　　Conservation, **1946:** 30 [2], 45, 49, 58, 60, 70 [7],
　　　　84 [7, 17], 86 [24, 32]; **1947:** 191 [3, 5, 7,
　　　　12], 198, 202, 204, 207, 209 [1, 5, 11, 14],
　　　　210 [3], 214, 225, 231, 236 [1]; **1948:** 1, 14,
　　　　23
　　Consumption, **1947:** 4 (pp. 23, 32)
　　Controls, **1945:** 64 [10, 13, 16]; **1948:** 8 (p. 73),
　　　　11ftn. (p. 104)
　　Export controls, **1947:** 58
　　Food conference, remarks, **1946:** 49
　　Foreign production, **1947:** 242
　　Germany, daily food ration, **1945:** 201n.
　　Hoarding, condemnation of, **1950:** 191 [11], 194
　　Imports, **1947:** 220
　　India, **1952–53:** 55, 57, 144
　　Low-income families, **1947:** 4 (p. 33); **1950:** 135,
　　　　249
　　National garden program, **1946:** 40
　　Navajo Indians, **1947:** 229
　　Need for U.S. production, statement, **1945:** 49
　　News conference remarks, **1950:** 86 [18], 191 [11,
　　　　16], 318 [3]
　　Overseas relief, **1945:** 33, 35, 49, 118 [8], 135;
　　　　1946: 18 (pp. 46, 58, 59), 23, 29, 30 [2], 43
　　　　[9], 45, 49, 58, 60, 70 [20], 75 [28], 76, 78
　　　　[14], 84 [7, 10, 19], 85, 86 [4, 22, 24, 27, 32],
　　　　87, 95 [1], 105, 108, 119 [9, 16], 124, 125,
　　　　141 [8, 10], 143 [2, 3], 144, 149, 163 [2],
　　　　164, 165, 168, 223 [1], 255; **1947:** 2 (p. 10),
　　　　7 (p. 67), 18, 29, 32, 37, 46 [1, 4], 47, 56,
　　　　107 [2, 3], 110, 139, 155 [7], 177, 191 [3, 7,
　　　　8, 11, 12, 20], 195, 196, 197, 198, 202, 209
　　　　[2, 3, 11], 210 [3], 213, 214, 220, 224, 225,
　　　　226 [14], 238; **1948:** 19, 194 [5], 195; **1949:**
　　　　263; **1950:** 9 (p. 85), 111, 119, 130, 249,

Food — *continued*
  Overseas relief — *continued*
    290, 293; **1951:** 34, 63 [2], 124; **1952–53:** 5
  Prices, **1945:** 202 [3]; **1946:** 18 (pp. 54, 55, 60), 86 [4], 152, 153, 193, 249; **1947:** 4 (pp. 15, 29), 67 [15], 70 [10], 76, 90 [5], 131, 152, 202, 214, 224, 242; **1948:** 2, 8 (pp. 64, 73), 21 [12], 26 [10, 11, 13, 14], 88 [12], 121, 170 [1], 174 [14], 181 [9], 189, 195, 261 [8]; **1949:** 5, 22 [13]; **1950:** 6, 83, 86 [18], 202, 318 [3]; **1951:** 2 [14, 27], 7 [16], 12 [18], 33 [5], 37 [14], 56 [5], 91, 167, 199
  Production and distribution, **1946:** 2, 18 (pp. 59, 60), 118, 128; **1947:** 2 (pp. 2, 7), 4 (pp. 32, 33), 58, 99, 110; **1948:** 8 (pp. 68, 74, 92, 93), 23, 176; **1950:** 193, 202; **1951:** 11, 12 [15, 22], 13 (p. 87), 83, 114; **1952–53:** 126
  Program for reconversion period, **1945:** 128
  Rationing, **1946:** 30 [2], 66 [9], 70 [9], 86 [24], 95 [11]; **1947:** 191 [5, 8, 24], 209 [11, 14]; **1950:** 191 [16]
  School lunch program, **1950:** 135; **1952–53:** 18 (p. 105)
  Shortages, **1948:** 5 (p. 42), 167
  Subsidies, **1946:** 18 (pp. 54, 55), 86 [19, 32], 94, 193
  Surplus, **1947:** 196; **1950:** 86ftn. (p. 255)
Food and Agriculture Organization, United Nations, **1948:** 8 (p. 97), 276; **1949:** 8 (p. 55), 263; **1950:** 177, 287 [24]; **1952–53:** 51, 55
Food Board, Combined, **1945:** 107ftn. (p. 234), 209; **1946:** 108, 119 [16], 149
Food Committee, Citizens.
  See Citizens Food Committee.
Food Committee, St. Louis Citizens, **1950:** 3 [4]
Food Council, International Emergency, **1946:** 149; **1947:** 18, 99; **1948:** 23
Food and Drug Organization, United Nations, **1951:** 296n.
Foot-and-mouth disease, **1947:** 181, 399
  Eradication in Mexico, **1951:** 13 (p. 90)
Football, Army-Navy game, **1945:** 202 [16]
Forand, Repr. Aime J., **1948:** 261 [5]; **1952–53:** 299
Forbes, Russell, **1952–53:** 7ftn. (p. 19), 26 [1]
"Forced Labor in the Soviet Union," **1952–53:** 253 [1]
Ford, Henry, 2d., **1945:** 175 [10]; **1946:** 27 [16]; **1947:** 14 [9], 148n.; **1948:** 89; **1950:** 46 [9]; **1951:** 38
Ford Motor Co., **1947:** 62 [15]; **1952–53:** 175 [12]
Fordham University, **1946:** 112
Foreign affairs, **1946:** 61 [11, 17], 66 [11], 223 [7]; **1947:** 2 (p. 9), 6 [27], 7 (pp. 57, 66); **1948:** 4 [1], 5 (pp. 20, 21, 25), 41 [7, 9, 12, 17], 175
Foreign Agents Registration Act, **1950:** 207
Foreign Aid, President's Committee on, report, **1947:** 219

Foreign Aid Act of 1947, **1948:** 14, 91, 147
Foreign Aid Appropriation Act, 1949, approval, **1948:** 144
Foreign Aid Program, report, **1948:** 91
Foreign assistance, **1946:** 18 (p. 76), 47, 52, 236; **1947:** 7 (p. 66), 51, 58, 76, 99, 116, 143, 181 (pp. 395, 405), 207, 214, 224, 228; **1948:** 4 [1, 2], 5 (pp. 20, 29–31), 8 (pp. 62, 70, 71, 73), 11ftn. (p. 104), 31, 40, 60, 63, 64, 94, 129, 167, 168, 175, 182, 194 [5], 195, 215, 252, 266, 281; **1949:** 8 (pp. 52–55), 120, 151, 154, 244; **1950:** 6, 8 [23], 9 (pp. 46–48, 58, 59), 39, 78, 86 [14], 94, 132, 133, 154, 162; **1952–53:** 275, 303 [2], 315 [5], 349, 366

  See also Economic assistance; Military assistance and defense support; Relief programs abroad; Technical assistance.
  Africa, **1951:** 4, 13 (p. 75), 262
  Appropriations, **1952–53:** 149 [20], 156 [12], 268 [5], 281, 295 [1], 307
  Arab states, **1951:** 114
  Asia, **1947:** 6 [26], 238; **1948:** 4 [2], 110 [6, 15], 160; **1949:** 160; **1950:** 11 [16], 78, 119, 154, 162; **1951:** 4, 13 (pp. 73, 74), 25, 59, 66, 84, 114, 153 [3], 167; **1952–53:** 242 [2], 313 [2]
  Australia, **1951:** 193 [2]
  Austria, **1947:** 47, 195, 224; **1948:** 5 (p. 29), 147; **1951:** 13 (p. 72), 114
  Belgium, **1947:** 195
  Brazil, **1949:** 108 [1]; **1951:** 259
  Burma, **1951:** 13 (p. 74)
  Canada, **1949:** 162
  China, **1946:** 4, 265, 266 [11]; **1947:** 7 (p. 65), 238; **1948:** 2, 4 [2], 5 (pp. 20, 29), 31, 81, 144, 160, 175, 202 [6], 274 [9], 278 [31], 283 [15], 288 [7, 13]; **1949:** 8 (p. 54), 234 [8]; **1950:** 8 [4], 154; **1951:** 13 (p. 74), 114, 138, 247 [6], 251ftn. (p. 268); **1952–53:** 279
  Denial to exporters of war material to Communist bloc, **1950:** 252
  Denmark, **1952–53:** 217
  Ecuador, **1951:** 134
  Effect on domestic economy, **1947:** 122, 212, 217, 219
  Europe, **1946:** 4, 23, 29, 30 [2], 45, 76, 85, 86 [4, 22, 24, 27, 32], 87, 105, 124, 125; **1947:** 6 [26], 47, 145 [12], 152, 177 [22], 191 [4], 198, 202, 217, 219, 232 [9, 11], 238; **1948:** 4 [2], 5 (pp. 20, 21, 29), 8 (p. 69), 53, 75, 85, 144, 147, 160, 175, 202 [6], 231 [3], 244, 260, 276, 283 [9]; **1949:** 8 (pp. 46, 53–54), 19, 71, 159, 160, 184; **1950:** 9 (pp. 57, 58), 78, 110 [1], 119; **1951:** 4, 7 [5], 12 [42], 13 (pp. 72, 73), 16 [15], 59, 66, 114, 167, 191, 209 [13], 256, 297; **1952–53:** 242 [2], 295 [8], 313 [2], 366
  Expenditures, **1947:** 180 [13, 15, 22]

Foreign assistance — *continued*
  Formosa, **1950:** 3 [1], 11 [4]; **1952–53:** 366
  Finland, **1947:** 47
  France, **1946:** 95 [1, 21]; **1947:** 195, 196, 197, 205 [13], 210 [6], 213, 214, 224; **1948:** 5 (p. 29), 147, 160, 260; **1950:** 281; **1951:** 25, 138; **1952–53:** 27
  Germany, **1947:** 195, 238; **1948:** 260; **1949:** 8 (p. 54); **1950:** 9 (p. 58); **1951:** 114; **1952–53:** 354
  Greece, **1945:** 75, 186; **1947:** 46 [5], 56, 57, 62 [10], 67 [2, 11, 12], 90 [1], 95 [11, 26], 100n., 107 [2], 138, 180 [8, 10], 181 (pp. 398, 405), 188, 195, 210 [6], 220, 243 [19]; **1948:** 2, 28, 144, 160, 175, 188, 202 [6], 228 [1], 231 [2], 244, 260, 263, 278 [31]; **1949:** 8 (p. 54), 22 [3]; **1950:** 81, 86 [27], 142, 232; **1951:** 78, 138; **1952–53:** 27, 81, 242 [2], 354, 366
  History of, **1950:** 232
  Hungary, **1947:** 107 [8]
  India, **1951:** 124; **1952–53:** 242 [2]
  Indochina, **1951:** 13 (p. 75), 25, 114
  Indonesia, **1950:** 119; **1951:** 13 (p. 74)
  Iran, **1949:** 273; **1952–53:** 242 [2]
  Ireland, **1947:** 47
  Israel, **1948:** 110 [14, 21], 253; **1951:** 114, 229
  Italy, **1946:** 253; **1947:** 15, 25, 47, 195, 196, 197, 210 [6], 213, 214, 224; **1948:** 5 (p. 29), 147, 260; **1951:** 138, 232, 235n.; **1952–53:** 180, 298 [8]
  Japan, **1947:** 238; **1949:** 8 (p. 54); **1950:** 9 (p. 58); **1951:** 13 (p. 74), 193 [2]; **1952–53:** 354
  Korea, **1947:** 67 [11], 95 [13], 238; **1949:** 8 (p. 54), 117, 118 [19]; **1950:** 9 (p. 58), 17, 78, 81, 154, 268, 285; **1951:** 78, 80, 114, 138; **1952–53:** 242 [2], 296, 310
  Latin America, **1947:** 95 [10]; **1948:** 69; **1951:** 4, 13 (p. 75), 114, 167
  Less-developed and new nations, **1948:** 69, 276; **1949:** 19, 40 [10], 139, 193, 237, 263; **1950:** 18, 25, 87, 126, 132, 154, 289; **1951:** 170, 250
  Letter to Congressional leaders, **1947:** 197
  Liberated countries, **1947:** 37
  Marshall plan.
    See main heading, Marshall plan.
  Mexico, **1947:** 83
  Near East, **1949:** 193, 274; **1951:** 4, 13 (pp. 73, 74), 114
  Need for, **1950:** 122
  Netherlands, **1952–53:** 105
  New Zealand, **1951:** 193 [2]
  News conference remarks, **1947:** 6 [4], 107 [2, 8], 191 [4], 209 [9], 218 [9]
  Palestine, **1946:** 227
  Partisan opposition, **1952–53:** 288
  Philippines, **1946:** 18 (p. 66), 90, 173 [10], 192 [5];

Foreign assistance — *continued*
  Philippines — *continued*
    1947: 6 [27], 7 (p. 68); **1949:** 8 (p. 54), 178; **1950:** 9 (p. 60), 180; **1951:** 13 (p. 74), 64, 114, 193 [2]
  Point 4 program.
    See main heading, Point 4 program.
  Refugees, **1952–53:** 65, 66
  Report to Congress, **1948:** 91
  Rumania, **1947:** 32
  Ryukyu Islands, **1950:** 9 (p. 58)
  Soviet Union, question of, **1945:** 208 [13]
  Spain, **1949:** 155 [23]; **1950:** 234; **1951:** 165 [6]
  Stopgap relief, **1947:** 191 [8, 21], 195, 205 [9, 13], 209 [3], 213, 218 [13, 15, 18]
  Switzerland, **1947:** 47
  Thailand, **1951:** 13 (p. 74), 114
  Trieste, **1951:** 114
  Turkey, **1947:** 56, 67 [2, 11, 12], 90 [1], 95 [11, 16, 26], 100n., 107 [2], 138, 180 [10], 181 (pp. 398, 405), 188, 195, 220; **1948:** 2, 28, 144, 160, 175, 202 [6], 228 [1], 231 [2], 244, 260, 263; **1949:** 8 (p. 54), 22 [3]; **1950:** 81, 86 [27], 94, 142, 232; **1951:** 114, 138; **1952–53:** 27, 81, 242 [2], 354, 366
  United Kingdom, **1945:** 67 [4], 107 [22], 132 [4], 208 [11], 221 [4]; **1946:** 15 [22], 17 [4, 14, 22], 18 (pp. 45, 85, 86), 21 [18], 25, 47, 51, 76, 84 [21], 86 [29], 110 [4], 169, 192 [9, 19]; **1947:** 6 [27], 29; **1949:** 148 [5], 234 [11]; **1952–53:** 27
  Yugoslavia, **1950:** 290, 293, 295 [13]; **1951:** 81, 114, 292; **1952–53:** 27
Foreign Assistance Act of 1948, **1949:** 71
  Approval, **1948:** 64
Foreign Assistance Act of 1950, **1949:** 139n.; **1950:** 25n., 78, 119, 154
Foreign currencies
  China, **1946:** 265
  Philippines, **1946:** 31
Foreign Economic Administration, **1945:** 118 [16], 176; **1946:** 18 (p. 86)
Foreign Economic Administrator (Leo T. Crowley), **1945:** 107ftn. (p. 232), 116n., 128
  Chairman, Foreign Shipments Committee, **1945:** 35n.
  News conference remarks on, **1945:** 107 [22], 147 [14], 175 [13], 181 [7]
  Resignation, **1945:** 147 [14], 175 [13], 181 [7]
Foreign Funds Control, **1947:** 7 (p. 86)
Foreign information operations, **1945:** 120
Foreign intelligence program, **1945:** 140; **1946:** 17 [15], 18 (p. 86), 21 [10, 13], 86 [3]
  Directive, **1946:** 19
  Letter to Secretary Byrnes, **1945:** 141
Foreign Liquidation, Office of, **1947:** 7 (p. 68)
Foreign loan policy, **1946:** 47

Foreign Ministers, Council of, **1946:** 18 (p. 41), 126
[9], 181; **1949:** 93 [12], 118ftn. (p. 280),
122 [24], 136
  Establishment, **1945:** 91, 97
  News conference remarks, **1945:** 132 [10], 147 [6],
157 [6], 164 [2], 172 [5], 181 [4], 211 [12],
221 [13]
Foreign ministers meetings, **1950:** 238 [9]
  American Republics, **1951:** 16 [12], 59, 65, 67, 76,
85 [12], 125; **1952–53:** 94
  "Big Four," question of, **1951:** 2 [13, 17, 20]
  Brussels, **1950:** 309 [1], 311
  London, **1945:** 91, 132 [10], 147 [6], 157 [6], 164
[2], 172 [5], 181 [4]; **1946:** 6 [14], 18 (p.
41); **1947:** 236 [11]; **1950:** 146 [12, 16],
162, 218
    Arms shipments to Near East, policy state-
ment, **1950:** 147, 148
  Moscow, **1945:** 211 [12], 221 [13]; **1946:** 6 [2, 14],
18 (pp. 41, 42, 44), 265; **1947:** 2 (p. 10), 67
[17, 19], 74, 78 [23]; **1948:** 170 [12], 174
[11], 178 [3, 14]
  New York City, **1946:** 250 [14]; **1950:** 250ftn. (p.
640), 253 [10]
  News conference remarks, **1945:** 132 [10], 147 [6],
157 [6], 164 [2], 172 [5], 181 [4], 208 [2],
211 [12], 221 [13]
  Paris, **1946:** 95 [21], 110 [121, 141 [19], 143 [17],
163 [11], 173 [7], 181; **1947:** 74; **1948:** 185
[6]; **1949:** 93 [12], 112 [13], 118 [1], 122
[24], 136, 253 [18, 20], 260ftn. (p. 570);
1950: 162
    Peace conference, **1946:** 53 [19], 119 [25], 126
[22], 173 [2, 16], 199 [19], 202, 219; **1947:** 2
(p. 9)
  Potsdam, **1947:** 236 [6]
  Rio de Janeiro, **1947:** 188, 189, 230
  Washington, **1949:** 84ftn. (p. 223)
  Western Hemisphere, **1950:** 309 [13]
  World War II peace treaties, proposed meeting
on, **1950:** 250 [20]
Foreign policy, U.S., **1945:** 120, 141, 178, 218;
1946: 2, 18 (pp. 41–45), 21 [10], 76, 81, 110
[19], 202, 216 [5], 226 [11], 236, 250 [1];
1947: 39, 56, 68, 76, 83, 99, 117, 128, 137,
143, 188, 214, 238; **1948:** 5 (pp. 19, 31), 8
(p. 98), 34, 52, 80, 96, 101, 129, 165, 195,
215, 236, 244, 245; **1949:** 2, 8 (pp. 52–55),
120, 159, 184, 199, 225, 230, 251; **1950:** 2,
31, 39, 41, 81, 87, 110 [8–10], 116, 126, 127
[5, 7], 130, 134, 151, 159, 160 [1], 161 [3],
162, 228, 239, 305; **1951:** 13 (p. 61), 18, 34,
36, 138, 174; **1952–53:** 5, 18 (pp. 73–77),
26 [17], 63, 156 [15], 261, 291, 292 [4], 320
  Address to American Society of Newspaper
Editors, **1950:** 92
  Address to Civil Defense Conference, **1951:** 96
  Address by John Foster Dulles, **1950:** 318 [12]

Foreign policy, U.S. — *continued*
  Address by Herbert Hoover, **1950:** 318 [5, 12]
  Africa, **1951:** 179 [13]
  Allies, need for solidarity with, **1951:** 107, 114
  Appeasement, repudiation of, **1950:** 232, 301,
303; **1951:** 80
  Asia, **1950:** 80 [1], 232, 252, 301; **1951:** 4, 56 [26],
78, 90 [1], 96, 179 [13]
    Address by Justice Douglas, **1951:** 37 [5]
  Assistance programs.
    See Foreign assistance.
  Bipartisanship, **1946:** 266 [15]; **1947:** 74; **1948:**
64, 121, 137 [3, 4], 139 [3], 160, 185 [6, 11],
202 [6], 213, 227 [5], 235 [2], 236, 245, 266;
1949: 32 [13], 144 [29], 253 [9]; **1950:** 44 [2,
10], 80 [1, 4, 5, 7], 89, 96, 97 [17], 193, 201,
202, 214 [11], 219, 253 [3], 258 [10], 279;
1951: 7 [5], 56 [15], 80, 109, 138, 215, 297;
1952–53: 5, 34, 129, 228 [3], 283, 291, 292
[4], 319 [1], 320, 334 [1]
  Briefing of Presidential candidates and President-elect, **1952–53:** 227, 334 [8]
  China, **1945:** 202 [12], 216; **1946:** 265; **1948:** 49
[17, 19, 21]; **1949:** 58 [11], 113 [6], 144 [29],
171 [1, 12], 179 [22]; **1950:** 223, 232; **1951:**
95 [11], 251 [25]; **1952–53:** 362n.
  Collective security, principle of, **1952–53:** 366
  Communist aggression, measures to counter,
1951: 114; **1952–53:** 319 [6]
  Conduct of, **1949:** 7 [1], 47, 94
  Consultations with Congress on, **1951:** 49 [17], 70
[1]
  Democratic record on, **1948:** 160, 256
  Domestic criticism of, **1951:** 80, 108 [4]
  Economic, **1946:** 18 (pp. 45, 46, 84–86), 47, 71;
1947: 4 (p. 37), 52, 58; **1948:** 5 (p. 31), 23,
42; **1949:** 88, 139, 151, 192 [7, 24], 195, 211
[8], 214 [5]; **1950:** 6, 25, 46 [6], 78, 122,
130, 159, 231, 282, 289; **1952–53:** 15, 20,
215
    Advisory Board on International Develop-
ment, statement on, **1950:** 294
    Gray (Gordon) report, **1950:** 273 [3], 282
  Eisenhower, Gen. Dwight D., views on, **1952–53:**
289 [4], 293
  Europe, **1950:** 301; **1951:** 4, 96, 116; **1952–53:** 55,
291, 317 [2]
    NATO, U.S. participation and support, **1951:**
71
  Far East, **1949:** 170 [4], 260 [17]
  Formosa, **1950:** 232
  France, joint statement with Prime Minister
Pleven, **1951:** 25
  Germany, **1950:** 119; **1951:** 149; **1952–53:** 288
  Information, Executive privilege, **1951:** 77n.
  Iran, **1945:** 208 [12]
  Isolationism, repudiation of, **1948:** 160, 210 [2],
213, 260; **1950:** 39, 78, 80 [4, 5], 110 [1],

Foreign policy, U.S. — *continued*
  Isolationism, repudiation of — *continued*
    119, 122, 132, 139, 151, 159, 162, 279, 280,
    281 [5], 309 [3, 5]; **1951:** 110
  Israel and Palestine, **1948:** 253, 262, 264 [3]
  Issues in election campaign, **1952–53:** 69, 129,
    218, 242 [2], 266 [8], 268 [5], 279, 283, 286
    [8], 307, 320
  Japan, **1950:** 119
  Korea, **1949:** 117; **1950:** 17n., 179 [2, 5], 186 [8],
    232, 264, 303; **1951:** 33 [3], 78, 116, 144,
    170, 298 [1]; **1952–53:** 5, 279
  Latin America, **1951:** 76, 179 [13]; **1952–53:** 94
  Moral standards in international relations, **1951:**
    31, 41
  Near East, **1950:** 252; **1951:** 4
  News conference remarks, **1947:** 36 [12], 74, 210
    [1]; **1948:** 49 [15–19, 21], 88 [6], 170 [2],
    185 [6, 11], 278 [22, 36], 285 [8], 288 [8];
    1949: 4 [2, 3], 32 [13], 58 [11], 86, 113 [6],
    144 [29], 170 [4], 171 [1, 12], 179 [22], 192
    [7, 24], 211 [8], 214 [5], 253 [9], 260 [17],
    267 [16], 269 [16]; **1950:** 44 [2, 10], 46 [6],
    80 [1, 4, 5, 7], 86 [19, 27], 97 [17], 179 [2, 5],
    186 [8], 203 [13], 214 [5, 11], 230 [4], 253
    [3], 258 [10], 273 [3], 281 [5], 309 [1, 3, 5],
    318 [5, 12]
  Soviet Union, **1951:** 227 [2, 4]; **1952–53:** 318, 320
  Spain, **1951:** 165 [6]
  Statement, **1946:** 219; **1950:** 103
  Truman Doctrine.
    See main heading, Truman Doctrine.
  U.S. role of world leadership, **1948:** 116 [2], 122
    [6], 126 [1, 6], 128 [4], 130 [2], 136 [5], 137
    [3], 139 [3], 231 [3], 269; **1949:** 70, 159,
    160, 220; **1950:** 14, 121 [3], 133, 139, 162,
    255, 267, 279, 303; **1951:** 18, 20, 30, 31, 80,
    91, 109, 290; **1952–53:** 55, 57, 81, 130, 236,
    255, 268 [9], 275, 277 [4], 295 [5, 8, 9], 298
    [8, 10], 303 [1, 4, 6], 304, 306 [7], 312, 313
    [1, 4, 5], 315 [2], 316, 317 [2], 321 [2, 6, 7],
    322, 335
  Western Hemisphere, **1951:** 4
  World peace, administration efforts for, **1951:** 2
    [8], 30, 56 [26], 68; **1952–53:** 5, 34, 42, 69,
    88 [16], 98 [10], 101, 107 [2], 118, 123 [2],
    125, 128, 129, 131, 144, 158, 170, 175 [9],
    188, 196, 215, 218, 242 [2, 3], 247 [9, 12],
    266 [8, 11], 280 [4], 281, 282 [2, 7, 8], 283,
    288, 289 [4], 291, 292 [1, 4], 307, 314, 315
    [1], 317 [6], 318, 321 [3, 5], 324, 354, 358,
    359 [6, 10, 12], 366, 378
Foreign relations, **1951:** 13 (pp. 70–76); **1952–53:**
  351, 360
  Allies, **1952–53:** 315 [1, 2, 4, 7]
  Canada, **1952–53:** 377 [25]
  Conduct of, **1951:** 13 (p. 75); **1952–53:** 182

Foreign relations — *continued*
  Expenditures for, **1952–53:** 231, 367 (pp. 1138–
    1141)
  France, **1951:** 58, 62, 63 [9], 65
  Germany, **1952–53:** 151, 258 [5]
  Latin America, **1951:** 132 [8], 259, 267; **1952–53:**
    377 [23]
  Philippines, **1951:** 64
  Soviet Union, **1951:** 2 [17], 4, 227 [2, 4], 261 [13],
    293
  United Kingdom, **1951:** 288
Foreign Relief and Rehabilitation Operations, Of-
  fice of, **1946:** 68
Foreign Scholarships, Board of, **1951:** 103
Foreign Service, **1947:** 7 (p. 68), 35; **1949:** 8 (p. 54),
  234 [5, 6]; **1952–53:** 362n.
Foreign Service, Voluntary, American Council of
  Agencies for, **1947:** 43
Foreign Service Act of 1946, **1947:** 7 (p. 68); **1949:**
  47
  Approval, **1946:** 202
Foreign service retirement credit for 1898–1912,
  military enlistees, veto, **1945:** 205
Foreign Shipments Committee, **1945:** 35n.
Foreign Trade, Committee for Financing, **1946:**
  142
Foreign war relief, reports on, letters re, **1945:** 85
Foreign Wars, Veterans of, **1951:** 108 [4], 203n.
Foreman, Herbert E., **1947:** 20n.
Forensic League, National, medal acceptance,
  1952–53: 173
Forest Congress, **1947:** 69
Forest conservation, **1950:** 9 (p. 90), 33, 116, 121 [4,
  9], 125, 248
Forest fires, prevention, **1947:** 18, 35, 86
Forest Products Laboratory, **1948:** 37
Forest Service, **1946:** 18 (pp. 81, 86); **1947:** 7 (pp.
  68, 83)
Forests, national, **1945:** 128; **1946:** 18 (pp. 81, 82);
    1947: 68, 69; **1948:** 8 (pp. 66, 78), 105, 199
  Conservation, **1947:** 231; **1948:** 2, 5 (pp. 45, 46),
    99, 201, 237 [4]; **1949:** 2, 8 (p. 84);
    1952–53: 376
  Highways, **1947:** 7 (p. 85); **1948:** 24; **1952–53:** 18
    (p. 84)
  Management and development, **1952–53:** 18 (p.
    89)
Formosa, Taiwan, **1946:** 265; **1949:** 269 [15]
  See also China, Republic of.
  Assistance, **1952–53:** 18 (p. 76), 366, 367 (p.
    1140)
    Economic, **1950:** 3 [1], 11 [4]; **1951:** 13 (p. 74)
    Military, **1950:** 175n.; **1951:** 114, 153 [3]
  Cairo Declaration (1943), applicability to, **1950:**
    301
  News conference remarks, **1950:** 3 [1], 11 [4, 15],
    209 [11], 230 [7, 11], 270 [2], 295 [6]

Formosa, Taiwan — *continued*
    Relief for, **1945:** 186
    Sugar exports, **1947:** 64
    U.S. policy on, **1950:** 3 [1], 173, 209ftn. (p. 580),
        230 [7, 11], 232, 270 [2]
        Neutralization, **1950:** 173, 193, 223; **1951:** 78
        Views of Gen. MacArthur on, **1951:** 95 [11], 108
            [4], 261 [1]
Forrest, Wilbur, **1947:** 74
Forrestal, James, **1949:** 64, 94n., 205 [9]; **1952–53:**
    310, 323n.
    See also Defense, Secretary of; Navy, Secretary
        of.
    Death of, **1949:** 56n.
Forrestal Diaries, The, James Forrestal, **1951:** 251
    [3, 28], 261 [9]
Forster, Rudolph, Medal for Merit, posthumous
        citation, **1945:** 61
Fort, Jardine C., **1945:** 221 [9]
Fort Bliss, Tex., **1949:** 223
Fort Bragg, N.C., **1949:** 223; **1951:** 46
Fort Knox, Ky.
    Experimental Training Unit, **1948:** 190
    Gold reserves at, **1952–53:** 98 [28]
Fort Lewis, Wash., **1945:** 64 [11]; **1950:** 121 [13]
Fort Logan, Colo., disapproval of Veterans Ad-
        ministration facility at, **1952–53:** 212
Fort McHenry Military Reservation, **1947:** 35
Fort Peck Dam, Mont, **1950:** 121 [1], 129 [2, 3];
    1952–53: 268 [2]
Fort Riley, Kans., **1948:** 197
Fort Sill, Okla., **1949:** 36; **1951:** 38
Fort Sumner, N. Mex., irrigation project, **1949:**
    168, 185
Fort Wayne, Ind., campaign remarks, **1948:** 114 [2]
Fort Worth, Tex., **1947:** 209 [12]
    Campaign remarks, **1948:** 212 [7]
    Mayor Edgar Deen, **1948:** 212 [7]
Fortas, Abe, **1945:** 157 [2]
Fortifications, acquisition of land for, **1947:** 35
Fortune magazine, **1951:** 247 [1]
Fosdick, Raymond B., **1949:** 260ftn. (p. 571)
Foskett, Capt. James H., **1946:** 143 [1]
Foster, Stephen, **1950:** 139
Foster, Wally C., **1952–53:** 123 [12]
Foster, William C., **1947:** 47; **1949:** 40 [1]; **1950:**
    169 [9]; **1951:** 177
Fostoria, Ohio, campaign remarks, **1948:** 231 [8]
Foundations, tax-exempt, **1948:** 158, 280
Founding fathers, religious faith of, **1951:** 241
Four Chaplains chapel, dedication, **1951:** 30
Four Freedoms, **1945:** 66; **1946:** 236; **1947:** 204;
    1948: 205; **1949:** 184
4-H Club, **1949:** 123
    Girls, presentation of flag to the President, **1950:**
        239
    National Camp, **1951:** 122; **1952–53:** 176
Four-leaf clovers, the President's, **1948:** 163 [16]

Fourth of July, statement, **1945:** 72
Fowler, Harry W., **1949:** 202n.
Fowler, Henry H., **1952–53:** 122, 123ftn. (p. 324)
    See also Defense Mobilization Director (Henry
        H. Fowler).
Fox, Lt. George L., **1951:** 30n.
Fox, Joseph A., **1945:** 100, 106 [22]; **1947:** 95 [1],
    180 [11]; **1949:** 40 [17], 66 [21, 22], 72 [21],
    192 [24], 267; **1948:** 15 [11], 41 [5]; **1950:**
    238 [6]; **1951:** 12 [11, 17]; **1952–53:** 7 [7],
    136 [19]
Fox, Martin S., **1952–53:** 303 [3]
Framingham, Mass., campaign remarks, **1948:** 259
    [6]
France, **1945:** 33, 91, 178, 186; **1946:** 18 (pp. 42,
    84), 181, 247; **1947:** 111; **1948:** 239; **1949:**
    78 [9], 84ftn. (p. 223), 217, 223, 250 [3]
    Amphibious landings, **1945:** 45
    Armed forces, withdrawal from Syria and
        Lebanon, **1948:** 202 [6]
    Assistance, **1947:** 195, 197, 210 [6], 214, 224, 238;
        1948: 5 (p. 29), 147, 160, 260; **1950:** 22,
        193, 281; **1952–53:** 18 (p. 76), 27, 358, 367
        (pp. 1140, 1141)
        Economic, **1951:** 25
        Military, **1951:** 25, 138
    Atomic energy declaration of U.S., U.K., and
        Canada, reaction to, **1945:** 193 [8]
    Auriol, Paul, **1951:** 58
    Auriol, Vincent, **1947:** 13; **1950:** 152 [10]; **1951:**
        58, 62, 63 [9], 65, 67, 157, 295 [1]; **1952–
        53:** 99
    Auriol, Mme. Vincent, **1951:** 58, 65
    Balance of payments, **1952–53:** 15
    Bastille Day, **1946:** 167
        Message to President Auriol, **1951:** 157
        Statement, **1945:** 81
    Berlin Control Council, action in, **1945:** 201n.
    Bidault, Georges, **1945:** 33, 107 [5], 110, 113
    Bonnet, Henri, **1947:** 110; **1950:** 161 [2, 3]; **1951:**
        160; **1952–53:** 99
    Bread ration in, **1947:** 195
    Coal and steel industries, proposal to pool with
        German, **1950:** 137 [1]
    Communist-inspired strikes, failure of, **1951:** 4
    Council of Foreign Ministers, membership, **1945:**
        91, 97
    Defense effort in NATO, **1952–53:** 358
    De Gaulle, Gen. Charles.
        See main heading, De Gaulle, Gen. Charles.
    De Lattre de Tassigny, Gen. Jean, **1952–53:** 7
        [14]
    Diplomatic recognition of Communist China,
        question of, **1949:** 234 [5]
    Disarmament discussions with, **1951:** 293
    Displaced persons of Europe, assistance to, **1945:**
        225
    Dollar exchange shortage, **1952–53:** 18 (p. 75)

France — *continued*
    Early investments in U.S., **1952–53:** 218
    Economy, **1947:** 214
    Elections, **1950:** 281
    Ely, Lt. Gen. Paul, **1952–53:** 88ftn. (p. 258)
    Exchange teachers, **1951:** 194
        Remarks, **1952–53:** 234
    Forces in Indochina, **1951:** 96, 114
    Gifts for White House, acceptance, **1952–53:** 99
    Imports, **1947:** 208
    Japanese peace treaty, discussions with, **1951:** 84n.
    Jefferson papers, search for, **1950:** 12
    Joint declaration on Israeli arms policy, **1950:** 147
    Key to Bastille, proposed return to, **1951:** 165 [7]
    Korean war, participation, **1950:** 194, 232, 296; **1951:** 170
    Lend-lease agreements, **1945:** 50; **1947:** 7 (p. 65)
    Letourneau, Jean, **1952–53:** 175 [4]
    Liberation, **1945:** 29, 45
    Liberty Bell replica, gift to Independence, Mo., **1950:** 270 [12], 273 [16], 280, 281
    Loan to, **1946:** 95 [1, 21]
    Louis XIV, **1951:** 18
    News conference remarks, **1945:** 44 [7], 52 [9], 76 [6], 107 [5], 147 [3], 193 [8]; **1946:** 6 [8], 78 [14], 86 [22], 95 [1, 21]; **1950:** 137 [1], 270 [12], 273 [16]
    Occupation zone in Germany, **1948:** 244
    Paris.
        See main heading, Paris.
    Persche, Maurice (Minister of Finance and Economic Affairs), **1949:** 210n.
    Pleven, René, **1951:** 22 [12]
        Joint statement with, **1951:** 25
    Procurement in, **1947:** 208
    Provincial press representatives, visit to U.S., **1951:** 160
    Relations with Germany, conventions, **1952–53:** 151
    Resistance movement, **1945:** 109, 110
    Schuman, Maurice, **1949:** 72 [14]
    Schuman, Robert, **1949:** 68; **1950:** 137 [1], 162, 169 [9], 250ftn. (p. 640), 281, 311; **1951:** 58
    Strategic materials, export to Communist bloc, **1952–53:** 358
    Syrian-French controversy, **1945:** 44 [7], 52 [15]
    U.S. Ambassador David K. E. Bruce, **1949:** 84 [1]
    U.S. Ambassador Jefferson Caffery, **1947:** 88 [8], 95 [15]; **1949:** 66 [15], 84 [1]
    U.S. food for, **1945:** 33
    U.S. relations with, **1945:** 33, 113; **1951:** 58, 62, 63 [9], 65
    U.S. relief for, **1947:** 107 [1], 196, 205 [13], 209 [3], 213
    Veterans' reunions, **1950:** 161 [2]

France — *continued*
    Visit of Margaret Truman, **1951:** 160
    Visit by the President, question of, **1951:** 65 [20]
    World wars
        Casualties, **1947:** 210 [6]; **1951:** 65
        Financial drain on, **1952–53:** 218
    Zone of occupation in Germany, **1945:** 33
Franchise, civic duty to exercise, **1947:** 204
Francis, Clarence, **1946:** 45n., 255n.
Franco, Francisco, **1945:** 107 [18], 221 [19]; **1946:** 86 [9]; **1947:** 90 [1]; **1949:** 155 [23], 211 [3]; **1951:** 165ftn. (p. 403); **1952–53:** 31 [21]
Frankfort, Ill., mine explosion, **1952–53:** 150
Frankfort, Ky., campaign remarks, **1948:** 222 [2]
Frankfurt, Germany, **1945:** 97, 181 [2]
Frankfurter, Justice Felix, **1952–53:** 161, 342 [6]
Franklin, Benjamin, **1946:** 198; **1951:** 127, 241
Franklin, Jay, **1949:** 4 [2, 3]
    Column by, **1948:** 278 [21]
Franklin D. Roosevelt, aircraft carrier, commissioning, address, **1945:** 177
Franks, Oliver, **1949:** 11 [2, 8]; **1950:** 275n.
Fraser, James E., **1951:** 235
Fraser, Willard, **1952–53:** 266 [13], 268 [2–4, 8], 269
Frear, Allen J., Jr., **1948:** 225 [1]
Frech, Col. Frederic F., **1950:** 265n.
Free enterprise.
    See Enterprise system.
Free Europe, National Committee for, **1950:** 98
Free Trade Unions, International Confederation of, **1952–53:** 253 [1]
Freedom, Crusade for, **1950:** 254
Freedom Council of Denmark. **1946:** 6 [18]
Freedom Fair, National Capital Sesquicentennial, **1949:** 79
Freedom Fair, proposed, **1950:** 77, 137 [22]
Freedom of information, Geneva conference on, **1948:** 49 [2]
Freedom of the press, **1947:** 76
Freedom of religion, Jefferson's statute for, **1947:** 138
Freedom of the seas, **1945:** 178
Freedom Train, 1st anniversary, **1948:** 193 [1]
Freehof, Rabbi Solomon B., **1949:** 202n.
Freeman, David, **1952–53:** 173n.
Freeman, Douglas S., **1947:** 48n.
Friedlander, Leo, **1951:** 235n.
Freeman, Orville L., **1949:** 250; **1952–53:** 266 [1], 313, 314
Freight cars, shortage, **1947:** 18; **1948:** 8 (pp. 70, 79, 80)
Freight rates, class rate, ICC ruling, **1945:** 208 [3]
Freight rates, railroad, requested increase, **1946:** 84 [25]
French, Jack, interview with the President, **1952–53:** 267
French Revolution, **1950:** 281
Fresno, Calif., campaign remarks, **1948:** 204 [2]

Friant, Mrs. Julien, **1949:** 252n.
Friendship International Airport, Baltimore, dedication, **1950:** 97 [16], 171
Frilot, George A., III, **1952–53:** 43n.
Frontier, spirit of, **1950:** 122
Frontier Days, pageants, Cheyenne, Wyo., **1950:** 118
Fruit exports, **1948:** 8 (p. 93)
  Dried, **1950:** 159
Fruits, exemption from price control, **1952–53:** 190
Fry, Celia, **1952–53:** 173n.
Frydrysiak, Bernard, **1951:** 291n.
FTC.
  See Federal Trade Commission.
Fuchs, Klaus, **1950:** 34 [18], 46 [20]
Fuel, **1948:** 8 (p. 80)
  Conservation, **1948:** 55 [10]
  Oil rationing, end of, **1945:** 128
  Overseas relief, **1947:** 29, 56, 191 [13], 195, 196, 197, 213, 214, 224
  Prices, **1947:** 224; **1948:** 8 (p. 64), 170 [1, 8]
  Shortage, **1947:** 191 [13], 238, 243 [16]
  Synthetic liquids, **1948:** 5 (p. 47); **1949:** 8 (p. 84), 226 [6]; **1952–53:** 18 (p. 89), 199
Fulbright, Sen. J. William, **1945:** 202 [14]; **1946:** 250 [3]; **1949:** 119n.; **1950:** 97ftn. (p. 276); **1952–53:** 31 [6]
  Educational exchange program, **1951:** 103
  Report on RFC, **1951:** 16 [10], 33 [2, 12], 49 [4, 11]
  Resolution on international cooperation, **1945:** 69
Full employment, **1945:** 128, 203; **1946:** 17 [11, 18, 19], 18 (pp. 37, 40, 48, 49, 51, 52, 57, 59, 64, 72, 73), 193; **1947:** 107 [2], 131, 147, 183; **1948:** 5 (pp. 23, 37), 8 (pp. 70, 89), 80, 175, 176, 232; **1949:** 5, 8 (p. 49), 154; **1950:** 6, 128; **1951:** 118 [1]; **1952–53:** 241, 289 [1], 292 [3], 294, 305, 307, 314, 317 [5], 319 [1], 321 [6], 376
Full Employment Act, **1948:** 232; **1952–53:** 268 [7], 289 [1], 294, 318
Full employment bill, **1945:** 22 [18], 106 [4], 175 [18], 180, 208 [14], 221 [2, 16, 23], 222; **1946:** 2, 17 [17, 18], 18 (p. 37)
  See also Employment Act.
  Approval, **1946:** 39
  News conference remarks, **1945:** 22 [18], 106 [4], 175 [18], 208 [14], 221 [2, 16, 23]
Full employment board.
  See Council of Economic Advisers.
Fuller, Enoch D., **1952–53:** 28
Fulton, Repr, James G., **1949:** 202n.
Fulton, Robert, **1952–53:** 170
Fulton, Mo., **1946:** 53 [3, 18]
Fundraising campaigns
  CARE-for-Korea, **1950:** 285
  Christmas Seal, **1950:** 286

Fundraising campaigns — *continued*
  Community Chest, **1946:** 225; **1947:** 193; **1948:** 221; **1949:** 221; **1950:** 262; **1951:** 242; **1952–53:** 264
  Community War Fund, **1945:** 154, 171
  March of Dimes, **1946:** 26; **1947:** 17; **1948:** 18
  Poliomyelitis, emergency drive, **1949:** 205 [2]
  Red Cross, **1946:** 50; **1947:** 5, 49; **1948:** 40; **1949:** 42; **1950:** 45; **1951:** 47, 73; **1952–53:** 50
  Savings bond drive, **1949:** 37, 40 [16], 82, 98; **1951:** 11, 13 (pp. 105, 106), 60, 133, 167, 210, 213, 290
  United Service Organizations, **1946:** 225
Funkhouser, Frank, **1950:** 124 [6]
Furcolo, Foster, **1948:** 259 [4]: **1952–53:** 292 [9]
Furniture, prices, **1947:** 76, 214
Furs, Soviet and Chinese, question of import restriction, **1951:** 165 [3]

Gabrielson, Guy G. (Chairman, Republican National Committee), **1950:** 105 [19], 250 [3], 273 [7]
Gadsden Purchase, commemorative coin, **1947:** 162
Gainesville, Tex., campaign remarks, **1948:** 214 [3]
Galapagos Islands, **1951:** 136n.
Galassi, Margaret, **1952–53:** 181n.
Galesburg, Ill., **1950:** 110 [1]
Galion, Ohio, campaign remarks, **1952–53:** 286 [6]
Gallager, Phil, **1952–53:** 274 [2]
Gallagher, Buell, **1948:** 203
Gallagher, Charles E., **1952–53:** 98 [16]
Gallagher, Manuel C., **1951:** 67n.
Gallegos, Rómulo (President of Venezuela), **1948:** 150 [9], 158
Gallegos, Señora, **1948:** 158
Gallup, George H., **1946:** 45n., 58n., 255n.; **1949:** 17; **1950:** 86 [25]; **1952–53:** 143
Gallup, N. Mex., campaign remarks, **1948:** 136 [2]
Gallup public opinion poll, **1945:** 193 [4]; **1949:** 22 [7]; **1950:** 86 [25], 152 [5, 7]; **1952–53:** 35 [8], 143
  President's popularity, **1951:** 56 [6]
Galveston, Tex., harbor improvement, **1952–53:** 367 (p. 1143)
Galvin, Michael, **1951:** 63 [3]; **1952–53:** 7ftn. (p. 19), 26 [1]
Gambling, control of, **1950:** 38 [9]
Gambling information, prohibition of interstate transmission, **1951:** 63 [1]
Gandhi, Mohandas K., **1950:** 20
  Assassination, **1948:** 17
Gannon, Rev. Robert I., **1946:** 112
GAO.
  See General Accounting Office.
Garbage, disposal in territorial waters, **1947:** 171

Garber, John N., **1950:** 157n.
Garcia, Gen. Calixto, **1948:** 81
Garden program, national, **1946:** 40
Gardens, victory, **1945:** 49
Gardner, Edward J., **1948:** 131 [1]
Gardner, O. Max, **1945:** 210; **1946:** 51n., 136 [2], 177 [2], 216 [20], 257 [1, 8, 13], 262 [16], 266 [18]; **1948:** 246; **1951:** 56 [4]
   Statement on death of, **1947:** 23
Garfield, James A., **1952–53:** 127 [18], 136 [16], 282 [7], 289
Garfield, Utah, **1951:** 169, 277
Gargotta, Charles, **1950:** 86 [2, 4, 12]
Garman, Phillips L., **1947:** 87n.
Garment industry, unemployment in, **1951:** 239 [8]
Garner, John Nance, **1948:** 214 [2], 216 [9, 11, 13]; **1949:** 186
Garrett, Ind., campaign remarks, **1948:** 254; **1952–53:** 311 [3]
Garrison, Lloyd K., **1946:** 9n.; **1947:** 87n.
   See also National War Labor Board, Chairman.
Garrison, Mont, **1950:** 127 [2]
Garrison Dam, **1950:** 129 [3]
Garsson, Henry M., **1946:** 177 [11]
Garsson, Murray W., **1946:** 177 [11]
Garvey, Gov. Dan E., **1948:** 136n., 206 [4], 207n.
Gary, Ind.
   Campaign remarks, **1948:** 114 [3], 255; **1952–53:** 312
   Mayor Peter Mandich, **1952–53:** 312
   School strikes, **1946:** 75 [16]
Gas, **1946:** 101
   Manufactured, **1948:** 1
   Natural, **1948:** 1, 5 (p. 47), 8 (p. 78); **1952–53:** 289 [11]
     Conservation, interstate compact, **1947:** 104
     Consumption, **1947:** 145 [9]
     Leases on public lands, **1947:** 35
     Regulation of interstate sale, **1950:** 88
   Poison, **1947:** 36 [3]
Gasoline
   Prices, **1947:** 242
   Rationing, **1945:** 62
     End of, **1945:** 128, 224
   Tax, **1950:** 86 [10]
Gaston, Captain, **1948:** 26 [19]
Gaston, Herbert, **1946:** 136ftn. (p. 303)
Gaston, William, **1948:** 261 [8, 9]
Gatch, Adm. T. L., **1945:** 116
Gates, Gen, Horatio, **1951:** 85 [10]
Gatun Lake, Barro Colorado Island, **1946:** 118
GATT.
   See General Agreement on Tariffs and Trade.
Gaulle, Gen. Charles de.
   See DeGaulle, Gen. Charles.
Gauss, Christian, **1952–53:** 362n.
Gavels, presentation to Vice President Barkley and Speaker Rayburn, **1951:** 24, 27, 51

Gavin, Repr. Leon H., **1948:** 214 [7]
Gavin, Tom, **1952–53:** 197 [17]
Gavins Point power project, **1951:** 13 (p. 87)
Gazette des Beaux-Arts, **1952–53:** 229
Geelan, James P., **1952–53:** 298 [8]
General Accounting Office, **1945:** 207; **1947:** 6 [4], 7 (p. 59), 205 [12]; **1949:** 7 [15], 127, 145; **1951:** 12 [36], 221, 224 [12]; **1952–53:** 86
General Agreement on Tariffs and Trade, **1948:** 8 (p. 97), 42, 84 [23], 88 [6, 18, 21], 143; **1949:** 6, 120, 217; **1951:** 126
   Statement, **1947:** 216
General Aniline & Film Corp., **1949:** 144 [5]
General Appropriations Act, **1950:** 234, 240
General Assembly, U.N.
   See United Nations General Assembly.
General Ceiling Price Regulation, **1951:** 167
General Defense Appropriation, **1951:** 12 [2]
General Electric Co., **1947:** 243 [2]; **1948:** 11 [2]; **1950:** 303; **1952–53:** 270 [8], 277 [2], 303 [10], 308 [3]
General Federation of Jewish Workers in Israel, **1951:** 274n.
General Foods Corp., **1952–53:** 270 [8], 277 [2], 303 [10], 308 [3]
General Land Office, termination, **1946:** 118
General Motors Corp., **1948:** 11 [2], 110 [17]; **1950:** 146 [19], 202, 309 [7]; **1952–53:** 270 [8], 277 [2], 303 [10]
General Motors strike, **1946:** 2
   Factfinding board, **1945:** 204, 206, 208 [7], 211 [4], 221 [14, 21]; **1946:** 9, 15 [6, 14], 16, 27 [9], 53 [2]
     Members, **1945:** 211 [2]
   News conference remarks, **1945:** 193 [5], 202 [5], 208 [7], 211 [2, 4], 221 [14, 21]; **1946:** 15 [6, 14, 23], 21 [14], 27 [9], 41 [23], 53 [2]
General Services Administration, **1949:** 94, 111, 127, 134, 145; **1950:** 9 (pp. 51, 81, 100), 80 [10], 129 [5]; **1951:** 13 (p. 105), 14, 105, 127n., 177, 205, 226; **1952–53:** 18 (p. 112), 367 (p. 1161)
   Appropriations, **1950:** 190
   Government records, transfer of custody from State Department, **1950:** 75
   Programs review, **1950:** 196
   Reorganization, **1950:** 53, 69–73, 75
General Services Administrator (Jess Larson), **1949:** 145, 147, 156; **1951:** 177, 205; **1952–53:** 347, 387
   Letters, **1950:** 196; **1951:** 127
   Memorandum, **1950:** 259
   Successor, question of appointment, **1951:** 188 [18]
Genêt, Edmond C. E., **1952–53:** 45
Geneva, International Red Cross, **1950:** 191 [12]
Geneva, N.Y., campaign remarks, **1948:** 228 [11]

Geneva conferences
    Freedom of information, **1948:** 49 [2]
    International Labor Conference, **1949:** 13
    Tariffs and trade, **1947:** 39, 51, 52, 128, 138, 182
        [7], 216; **1948:** 42
Geneva Convention, **1947:** 35
Genghis Khan, **1950:** 313
Genocide, **1947:** 21
Genocide, Convention on Prevention and Pun-
        ishment, **1949:** 121, 237, 254; **1950:** 2, 174,
        222, 270 [3]
Geological Survey, **1945:** 194; **1947:** 7 (p. 83); **1948:**
        5 (p. 47); **1949:** 8 (p. 83), 150; **1951:** 13 (p.
        87), 177; **1952–53:** 18 (p. 89)
George II, King, **1946:** 261
    Death of, **1947:** 66
George VI, King, **1945:** 91n.
    Death of, **1952–53:** 30
    Funeral, U.S. delegation to, **1952–53:** 31 [19]
George, Sen. Walter F., **1945:** 31 [5], 52 [18]; **1949:**
        6n., 66 [3], 144 [127], 182 [7]; **1950:** 200,
        284; **1951:** 12 [20], 54n., 201; **1952–53:** 115
        [21], 361
George C. Marshall Research Foundation, Inc.,
        1952–53: 387
George Washington University, **1946:** 126ftn. (p.
        283); **1948:** 126 [4]; **1951:** 21
George Washington University Hospital, **1951:**
        298ftn. (p. 639)
Georgetown, S.C., Mayor H. L. Smith, **1945:** 147n.
Georgetown, Tex., campaign remarks, **1948:** 212 [3]
Georgetown University, **1951:** 130; **1952–53:** 29
Georgia, **1950:** 209ftn. (p. 582), 258 [11]
    Gov. Ellis Arnall, **1946:** 72 [21]
    Ingram case, **1948:** 455 [4]
    Lynchings in, **1946:** 186 [10], 199 [16]
    Power projects, **1950:** 121 [4, 13]
    Ramspeck, Repr. Robert, **1945:** 48
    Savannah Harbor, improvement, veto, **1945:** 90
    Visits to, comments on, **1945:** 132 [8], 172 [13]
    Warm Springs, **1945:** 172 [13]
Gerard, James W., **1950:** 294n.
Gerber, Calif., campaign remarks, **1952–53:** 277 [5]
Germany, **1945:** 2, 3, 34, 45, 50, 66, 123, 125, 177,
        186, 196; **1946:** 7, 18 (pp. 41, 42, 44, 46),
        64n., 167, 172; **1947:** 14 [5], 138, 236 [11];
        1948: 8 (p. 96); **1949:** 122ftn. (p. 295), 195
    Adenauer, Konrad, **1951:** 247 [8]
    Air Force, proposed, **1950:** 309 [8]
    Allied Control Council, **1945:** 91, 135
    Allied Occupation, **1947:** 7 (p. 67), 209 [13], 214;
        1948: 5 (pp. 29, 30), 15 [7], 244; **1951:** 114,
        197; **1952–53:** 151
    Allied political and economic policy toward,
        1945: 91, 97
    Allied prisoners of war, internees, or deported
        citizens, warning against mistreatment,
        1945: 9

Germany — *continued*
    Army, question of creation, **1949:** 260 [15]; **1950:**
        203 [20]; **1952–53:** 197 [7]
    Art, tour of U.S., **1948:** 71 [1]
    Assets in Switzerland, **1946:** 134
    Assistance, **1947:** 195, 238; **1948:** 260; **1950:** 8
        [6]; **1952–53:** 354
    Atomic bomb, research on, **1945:** 93, 97; **1948:**
        239
    Attack on Austria (1938), **1951:** 4
    Babelsberg, **1945:** 83n.
    Berlin.
        See main heading, Berlin.
    Cartels, industrial, **1948:** 278 [23, 28]
    Clay, Gen. Lucius D., services in, **1949:** 99
    Coal and steel industry, proposal to pool with
        French, **1950:** 137 [1]
    Communism in, **1952–53:** 354
    Confiscated property, disposition, **1952–53:** 258
        [5]
    Crop failure, **1948:** 5 (p. 29)
    Darmstadt, **1945:** 97
    Defense, **1951:** 13 (p. 73), 25, 247 [7]; **1952–53:**
        151
    Democracy, progress toward, **1950:** 119
    Disarmament, **1946:** 18 (pp. 46, 47), 236
    Displaced persons in, **1945:** 9, 152, 186, 188, 225;
        1946: 18 (p. 46), 136 [14], 267; **1947:** 38,
        140
    Economic assistance, **1951:** 114
    Economy, **1947:** 140, 238
    Editors and publishers, remarks to, **1949:** 165
    Elections, question of, **1951:** 247 [8]
    European defense, negotiations for participation,
        1952–53: 18 (p. 75)
    European Defense Community, **1952–53:** 342
        [16], 343
    Foreign ministers meeting on, **1949:** 93ftn. (p.
        243), 118ftn. (p. 280), 122 [24]
    Four-power talks on, question of, **1949:** 78ftn. (p.
        214)
    Frankfurt, **1945:** 97, 181 [2]
    German-Russian state papers, publication, **1948:**
        11 [15]
    Grain exports to, **1947:** 18
    Hitler, Adolf.
        See main heading, Hilter, Adolf.
    Integration with free Europe, **1950:** 119
    Investments in U.S., **1952–53:** 218
    Joint report with Allied leaders, **1945:** 91
    Junction of Soviet and Anglo-American forces,
        statement, **1945:** 12
    Kassel, **1945:** 97
    Magdeburg, **1945:** 97
    Mass deportations, **1952–53:** 145
    Militarism in, **1947:** 238
    NATO membership, proposed, **1952–53:** 5, 6,
        158

Germany — *continued*
   Nazis, **1945:** 3, 26 [5], 31 [1], 45, 52 [2], 91, 152,
      173, 187, 188, 201n., 210, 218
     Rise to power (1933), **1948:** 256
     Trade policy, **1947:** 51
     War criminals, **1951:** 33 [8], 227 [12]
   Nazism, **1945:** 26 [5], 29, 91, 97, 178
   News conference remarks, **1945:** 16, 22 [6, 11, 20,
      22], 26 [1, 4, 5], 31 [1, 2], 40 [2, 4], 60 [9],
      64 [8], 67 [2], 106 [10], 118 [1, 9, 13], 147
      [11, 19, 20], 181 [2], 193 [11], 202 [9], 221
      [11]; **1946:** 6 [8], 27 [13], 30 [2], 37 [2], 78
      [11], 84 [15], 86 [32], 110 [18, 21], 126 [3],
      136 [14], 141 [11], 163 [11], 186 [11], 215
      [1], 226 [13], 229 [13, 14], 257 [14]; **1947:**
      90 [7]; **1948:** 11 [15], 15 [7], 71 [1, 4], 181
      [14], 278 [23, 28], 283 [6]; **1949:** 28 [9], 32
      [12, 15, 17], 58 [15], 122 [24], 214 [2], 236
      [4], 253 [8, 18], 260 [15]; **1950:** 8 [6], 34 [5],
      137 [1], 146 [20], 203 [20], 230 [15], 250 [1,
      20], 309 [8]
   Occupation, **1945:** 106 [10]; **1946:** 18 (pp. 41, 44,
      46), 78 [11], 110 [18], 257 [14]; **1949:** 8 (pp.
      54, 59), 28 [9], 58 [15], 84 [3], 92, 136, 214
      [2]
     U.S. forces, relations with German people,
      Byron Price study, **1945:** 118 [1, 9, 13],
      119, 193 [11], 201, 202 [9]
     Zones, **1945:** 33, 91, 97, 181 [2], 221 [11]
   Occupation of Greece, **1947:** 56
   Peace settlements, **1948:** 2
   Peace treaty with, question of, **1947:** 2 (p. 10);
     1950: 250 [20]; **1951:** 149, 273
   Political structure, five-point program, **1948:** 71
     [4]
   Population growth, **1952–53:** 65
   Potsdam conference.
     See main heading, Potsdam conference.
   Refugees, immigration to U.S., **1950:** 167; **1952–
     53:** 65
   Refugees in, **1950:** 146 [20]
   Reparations, **1945:** 13, 91, 97, 106 [10], 182
     Statement, **1945:** 32
   Reunification, question of, **1949:** 136; **1952–53:**
     151
   Ruhr coal production, **1947:** 238
   Soviet policy in, **1950:** 119; **1951:** 149, 273;
     1952–53: 151
   State Department, political functions in, **1950:** 9
     (p. 56)
   State of war with, termination, **1951:** 149, 273;
     1952–53: 151
   Surrender, **1945:** 26 [1, 4, 5], 28, 45, 91, 97; **1947:**
     74, 88 [1], 110, 200, 210 [1]; **1948:** 268;
     1949: 86, 160; **1952–53:** 378
     Broadcast, **1945:** 27
     Messages, **1945:** 29
     Proclamation, **1945:** 26 [4], 27

Germany — *continued*
  Surrender — *continued*
    Rumor of, **1945:** 16
    Timing of announcement, statement, **1945:** 25
  Surrender of forces in Italy
    Messages to allied commanders, **1945:** 21
    Statement, **1945:** 20
  Textile tariff negotiations with U.S., **1950:** 34 [5]
  U.S. forces in, **1952–53:** 345 [1]
    Question of increase, **1950:** 230 [15]
  U.S. High Commissioner (John J. McCloy),
    1949: 122 [3], 234 [6], 260 [15]; **1950:** 23
    [18], 238 [9]; **1951:** 33 [8]
  U.S. policy in, **1951:** 273; **1952–53:** 151, 288
  U.S. relations with, **1952–53:** 151, 258 [5]
  U.S. relief for, **1947:** 46 [2]
  War assets and claims, disposition and settle-
    ment, **1948:** 154
  War casualties, **1947:** 210 [6]
  War crimes, **1948:** 283 [6]; **1952–53:** 292 [8]
    Trials, **1946:** 18 (pp. 46, 47), 42, 215 [1], 226
      [13], 229 [13], 230, 233, 251
  Wartime spies in U.S., **1948:** 181 [14]
    Trial of, **1949:** 32 [15]
  World wars, financial drain on, **1952–53:** 218
Germany, East, **1949:** 234 [6]
  Communists, demonstration in West Berlin,
    1950: 97 [13]
  Kidnapping by Communist regime in, **1951:** 116
  News conference remarks, **1950:** 97 [13], 146 [20]
  Refugees from, **1950:** 146 [20]; **1952–53:** 65
  School children, Soviet indoctrination, **1950:** 162
  Soviet policy in, **1951:** 149
Gerspach, Lorenz, **1948:** 126 [5]
Gerstenfeld, Rabbi Norman, **1952–53:** 330
Gestapo, **1945:** 9
Gettysburg, battle of, **1947:** 177 [9], 231; **1951:** 90
  [16]
Gettysburg Address, **1948:** 193 [1]; **1952–53:** 45
  Contemporary press criticism of, **1951:** 8
GI bill of rights, **1945:** 42, 107 [4], 114; **1946:** 38,
    122, 226 [1]; **1947:** 44, 134, 206n.; **1948:**
    259 [4]; **1949:** 8 (pp. 62, 64), 151; **1950:** 9
    (pp. 69, 70, 79), 36; **1951:** 12 [51], 13 (p.
    102)
Giannini, L. M., **1946:** 142
Gibson, Edwin T. (Defense Production Adminis-
    trator), **1951:** 41, 93n.
Gibson, Gov. Ernest W., **1948:** 170 [7]; **1949:** 211
  [2]
Gibson, John W. (Acting Secretary of Labor),
    1948: 130 [1]
Gibson, Judge Philip S., **1946:** 119 [6]
Gibson, Truman, **1949:** 73n., 110n.; **1950:** 32n.
Gibson, Truman K., Jr., **1946:** 268n.
Gideonse, Harry D., **1951:** 6n.
Gift taxes, **1948:** 63; **1949:** 2, 5, 151; **1950:** 18
  Exemption on gifts to U.N., **1947:** 26

Gifts to the President, **1951:** 8, 68, 99, 224 [3], 253n., 255, 299n.; **1952–53:** 99, 171n., 260
Gila reclamation project, **1948:** 206 [4]
Gilbert and Sullivan operettas, **1951:** 99
Gilbertsville, Ky., **1945:** 165; **1946:** 6 [7]
Gildersleeve, Dean, **1945:** 10
Gillem, Maj. Gen. Alvan C., Jr., **1949:** 223
Gillette, Guy M., **1948:** 194 [1–4, 6, 9–11]; **1949:** 226 [10]; **1952–53:** 3
    Resignation as Chairman, Surplus Property Board, **1945:** 44 [13], 52 [5]
Gilmer, Dixie, **1948:** 216 [10, 11], 217
Girard, Stephen, **1948:** 104
Girard College, centennial celebration, **1948:** 104
Girl From Utah, musical show, **1951:** 99
Girl Scouts, 39th anniversary, statement, **1951:** 48
Girls Nation, **1949:** 191; **1951:** 178; **1952–53:** 220
Girls State, **1948:** 118 [6]
Glacier National Park, **1949:** 32 [16]; **1950:** 124 [8]; **1952–53:** 268 [9]
    Acquisition of property, veto, **1946:** 150
Glacier View Dam, **1949:** 32 [16]
Glade, Earl J., **1952–53:** 280 [1, 3]
Glasgow, Mont., **1950:** 129 [2]
    Campaign remarks, **1952–53:** 268 [2]
Glasses, the President's, **1952–53:** 123 [1]
Glen Elder Dam, Kans., **1952–53:** 18 (p. 88)
Glenns Ferry, Idaho, **1950:** 121 [3]
Glenwood Springs, Colo., campaign remarks, **1952–53:** 280 [6]
Globe, in President's office, **1949:** 252
GNP (gross national product).
    See National product.
Godwin, Earl, **1946:** 223 [1]; **1947:** 145 [14]; **1949:** 30 [9], 192 [24]
Goering, Hermann, **1945:** 76n.
Gold
    Prices, **1949:** 253 [2]
    Reserves, **1947:** 7 (p. 95), 232 [5]; **1948:** 163 [17]
    Shortage abroad, **1947:** 197
Gold key, acceptance, **1949:** 16
Goldberg, Rube, **1951:** 290
Golden, Clinton S., **1947:** 236 [3], 237
Golden Rule, **1946:** 52; **1947:** 51, 185
    Application to world leadership, **1945:** 163, 164 [2], 178
Golder, Boyd E., **1948:** 228 [5]
Goldman, Mrs. Olive Remington, **1948:** 233 [5, 6]
Goldmann, Nahum, **1946:** 155
Goldsborough, T. Alan, **1948:** 66n., 171
Golob, Richard, **1951:** 122n.
Gómez, Gen. Máximo, **1948:** 81
Gompers, Samuel, **1951:** 279
    Centennial dinner, **1950:** 4
Gompers, Mrs. Samuel, **1951:** 279
Gonzaga University, **1950:** 126
González Videla, Gabriel, **1949:** 269 [17]; **1950:** 46 [8], 85, 86 [1, 8], 104, 152 [4], 191 [6]

Good Neighbor Policy, **1946:** 77, 83, 102; **1947:** 51, 73, 79, 83, 84, 101, 188; **1948:** 69, 198 [1]; **1949:** 35, 105, 230; **1950:** 137 [26]; **1951:** 76; **1952–53:** 55, 92, 377 [23]
Good Samaritan, **1952–53:** 264
Goode, Lt. Alexander D., **1951:** 30n.
Goodloe, John D., **1946:** 262 [11]
Gordy, Irving, **1952–53:** 117
Gore, Repr. Albert, **1945:** 208 [13]; **1949:** 231 [24]
Gorgas, Gen. William C., **1948:** 81
Gorrie, Jack, **1951:** 101 [7]; **1952–53:** 38n., 355, 375
Gorski, Chester C., **1952–53:** 288n.
Gospel, St. Matthew's, **1951:** 241
Goss, Albert S., **1947:** 191 [3]
Gossett, Repr. Ed, proposed amendment of Presidential election procedure, **1950:** 52 [8]
Government agencies, dispersal from Washington, question of, **1950:** 214 [10], 230 [5], 273 [9]
Government contracts.
    See Contracts, Government.
Government controls.
    See Controls, Government.
Government Corporation Control Act, approval, **1945:** 207; **1946:** 18 (pp. 68, 81), 94; **1947:** 7 (pp. 95, 97); **1948:** 5 (pp. 57, 58); **1949:** 77, 140
Government corporations, **1945:** 207; **1946:** 17 [8], 18 (pp. 67, 68, 76, 78), 94, 186 [7], 193; **1947:** 6 [5, 13, 38], 7 (pp. 62, 93, 94, 97), 31 [12], 80, 94, 180 [1], 181 (p. 403); **1948:** 5 (pp. 24, 25, 57, 58), 175; **1949:** 7 [15], 8 (p. 51); **1950:** 112
Government Corporations Appropriation Act, **1948:** 146
Government employees, **1945:** 122; **1946:** 18 (pp. 65, 66), 146; **1947:** 135
    See also Civil service.
    Accident compensation, **1949:** 8 (p. 70)
    Accident prevention, **1950:** 74
    Annual leave, **1947:** 35; **1952–53:** 108, 201
    Appeals board, establishment, **1946:** 117
    Cafeteria and recreational services for, **1950:** 9 (p. 102)
    Career, appointment to executive positions, **1950:** 247
    Civil Service Commission report, **1948:** 44
    Civil Service System, anniversary statements, **1952–53:** 14, 390
    Claims against U.S., **1948:** 43
    Commendation of, **1945:** 102; **1950:** 139
    Comments on, **1951:** 271; **1952–53:** 14, 69, 126, 266 [2], 281
    Communists among
        Defense against, **1952–53:** 296
        Prohibitions against, **1950:** 254
    Conflicts of interest, **1947:** 168
    Congressional committees, appearance before, **1952–53:** 49 [5, 7]

Government employees — *continued*
  Corruption among, Republican charges of, **1952–53:** 69
  Defense Department, increase, **1952–53:** 18 (p. 71)
  Defense mobilization personnel, roster of, **1952–53:** 338
  Defense utilization, administrative procedures, **1951:** 15, 156, 161
  Dollar-a-year men, **1947:** 35
  Efficiency, **1951:** 226
  Employee organizations, **1947:** 190
  Equal employment opportunities, **1948:** 20, 97 [16], 265
  Ethical standards, **1949:** 179 [9, 11, 13, 15, 19, 21]; **1951:** 104, 237, 239 [3], 251 [9, 15], 295 [12], 298 [4], 300 [1, 10, 17, 21], 303; **1952–53:** 1, 5, 11, 14, 21 [19], 26 [5], 36, 59, 69, 117, 143, 266 [2], 295 [8], 357
    Morris investigation, **1952–53:** 75ftns. (p. 231)
  Fair employment practices, **1952–53:** 169, 290
  Handicapped persons, **1952–53:** 137, 243
  Holidays, **1945:** 102, 107 [2]
  Inaugural holiday, question of, **1948:** 278 [17]
  Increase, **1948:** 174 [9]; **1949:** 5
  Insurance, **1948:** 182
  Internal Revenue Bureau, proposed increase, **1952–53:** 231
  Leaves of absence, **1945:** 107 [2]
  Legislation, proposed, **1950:** 9 (p. 51)
  Loyalty, **1947:** 67 [10], 89, 222; **1948:** 5 (p. 56), 50, 110 [12], 170 [4], 178 [13, 15], 181 [12], 191, 215; **1949:** 32 [14], 118 [5, 6], 122 [13, 16, 18, 19, 22]; **1950:** 79, 82, 94, 207, 279; **1951:** 20, 22 [6, 14], 35, 37 [12], 104, 156, 188 [19], 226, 278, 295 [12], 300 [5, 7, 21]; **1952–53:** 26 [5, 24], 36, 69, 76, 117, 222, 223, 289 [2], 296, 303 [2, 5], 323, 353 [12, 14], 359 [3], 362n., 377 [24]
    Republican attacks on, **1952–53:** 320
  Merit system, **1946:** 33; **1952–53:** 14, 390
  Military service, retirement credit for, **1950:** 170
  News conference remarks, **1946:** 17 [7, 29, 31], 143 [10], 177 [15], 192 [8, 16]; **1947:** 6 [28, 30], 180 [1]; **1950:** 38 [8, 12], 44 [6, 8], 46 [11, 12], 80 [4]
  Oath of office, **1952–53:** 347
  Occupational training, **1952–53:** 18 (p. 112)
  Overseas, judicial safeguards for, **1949:** 32 [17]
  Panama Canal, bill concerning compensation claims, **1952–53:** 208
  Patronage appointments, Republican, **1952–53:** 317 [3]
  Pay, **1945:** 128; **1946:** 17 [7], 18 (pp. 52, 65, 66, 86), 143 [10], 187, 192 [18]; **1947:** 7 (p. 57), 62 [19], 117; **1948:** 5 (p. 22), 63, 150 [3], 153, 157, 165, 174 [9], 175, 261 [12]; **1949:** 3, 7 [35], 8 (p. 48), 58 [20], 94, 95 [1], 96,

Government employees — *continued*
  Pay — *continued*
    127, 137, 218, 228, 236 [16], 242; **1951:** 152, 226; **1952–53:** 1, 11, 18 (pp. 71, 113), 86
    Terminal leave, **1947:** 7 (p. 89)
  Personnel management, **1952–53:** 18 (p. 112), 366, 367 (p. 1162)
  Personnel procedures in interest of national defense, **1950:** 283
  Political activity, **1947:** 18
    Restrictions on, **1950:** 38 [12], 182
  Postal.
    See under Postal service.
  Public criticism of, **1952–53:** 117
    Comment on, **1950:** 237, 247
  Reclamation projects, work on, **1946:** 209
  Recreation and cafeteria services, **1949:** 8 (p. 94)
  Reduction, **1945:** 22 [19]; **1946:** 17 [29, 31], 18 (p. 65), 192 [8, 16], 193; **1947:** 6 [28, 30], 7 (pp. 56, 93); **1948:** 2, 4 [1]; **1949:** 201; **1951:** 132 [15]
  Retirement, **1947:** 6 [2], 7 (pp. 73, 91); **1948:** 5 (pp. 22, 54, 56), 175; **1949:** 8 (pp. 71, 91–93), 132; **1950:** 9 (pp. 50, 76, 100, 101), 170; **1951:** 13 (pp. 104, 105); **1952–53:** 18 (pp. 110, 113), 213, 367 (p. 1163)
  Review Committee on Deferment of Government Employees, report, **1945:** 183
  Safety, **1952–53:** 150
  Scientists, recruitment and retention, **1948:** 191
  Security, **1952–53:** 222, 223
  Southern States, appointments from, **1949:** 269 [4]
  Supergrade positions, limitation, **1950:** 288
  Tickets to Jefferson-Jackson Day dinner, sale to, **1950:** 38 [8]
  Training, **1947:** 117
  Unemployment compensation, **1948:** 107; **1952–53:** 18 (p. 113), 108, 137
  Unemployment insurance, **1950:** 9 (pp. 99, 100, 102), 84
    Proposed, **1945:** 42, 128; **1949:** 8 (p. 91)
  Veterans, **1952–53:** 137
    Preference, **1950:** 108
  Workmen's compensation, **1950:** 74; **1951:** 118 [17]
  Workweek, **1951:** 118 [9]
    Reduction, **1945:** 48, 70, 107 [1]
Government Employees, American Federation of, **1952–53:** 390
Government facilities, dispersal, **1951:** 13 (pp. 103, 104)
Government funds, handling of, memorandum, **1945:** 79
Government Information Service, **1946:** 262 [4]
Government Manual, United States, **1945:** 120

Government offices, dispersal from Washington, **1949:** 260 [4, 22]

Government Printing Office, **1949:** 147; **1951:** 224 [12]

Government programs review, letter to agency heads, **1950:** 196

Government reorganization, **1945:** 228

Government Reports, Office of, **1946:** 262 [4]

Government services, Budget Bureau study of fees charged for, **1952–53:** 18 (p. 67)

Government Services Corporation, proposed, **1949:** 8 (p. 93); **1950:** 9 (p. 102)

Government spending.
    See Spending by Government.

Governments, State and local, financial operations, **1952–53:** 215

Governors, **1947:** 19 [13], 207
    Highway Safety Conference, **1949:** 26
    Inaugural parade, **1949:** 22 [14]
    National Conference of Boy Governors, **1949:** 125
    Northern, suit re ICC freight rate ruling, **1945:** 208 [3]

Governors Conference, National, **1948:** 259 [4]; **1950:** 169ftn. (p. 485), 229; **1951:** 247 [2]; **1952–53:** 150

Governors' Conference (1945), Mackinac Island, Mich., **1945:** 64 [9]

GRS synthetic rubber, **1950:** 13; **1952–53:** 12

Grady, Henry F., **1946:** 136 [14], 186ftn. (p. 367), 199 [8, 22], 215 [5, 7], 227; **1947:** 67 [3]; **1950:** 142; **1952–53:** 279n.

Grafton, W. Va., campaign remarks, **1948:** 242 [2]; **1952–53:** 242 [4]

Graham, Evarts A., **1951:** 307n.

Graham, Frank P., **1947:** 87n.; **1949:** 11 [12], 58 [26]; **1950:** 179 [13], 250 [19], 270 [15]

Graham, George A., *The Presidency and the Executive Office of the President*, **1951:** 270

Graham, J. W., **1950:** 266

Graham, Newt, **1948:** 216 [7]

Graham, Brig. Gen. Wallace H., **1947:** 243 [11]; **1948:** 71 [6]; **1949:** 36, 95 [6], 223, 265, 267 [1]; **1950:** 52ftn. (p. 195), 266; **1952–53:** 333

Grain, **1946:** 29, 108; **1949:** 5, 203
    Chinese imports, **1948:** 31
    Conservation, **1947:** 202, 205 [3, 14, 18], 209 [2–5, 14], 210 [3], 218 [6], 224, 225, 242; **1948:** 14, 19
    Controls, **1948:** 19
    Crop failures, **1946:** 86 [4, 27]
        In Europe, **1947:** 198, 238
    Exchanges, **1947:** 209 [11, 12], 218 [16], 226 [13]
    Exports, **1947:** 47, 139, 155 [6], 191 [3], 198, 209 [11], 210 [3], 228; **1948:** 19
    Feed grains, **1947:** 58, 205 [3, 14, 18]; **1948:** 1, 8 (p. 70), 14, 167

Grain — *continued*
    Loans to farmers on, **1948:** 267 [3]
    Overseas relief, **1946:** 143 [2], 144, 168, 223 [1], 255, 264; **1947:** 15, 18, 29, 32, 47n., 107 [3], 110, 139, 155 [7], 191 [3], 195, 196, 198, 205 [3, 14, 18], 209 [2, 3, 11], 214, 220, 225, 238; **1948:** 14, 19
        UNRRA shipments to Poland, **1946:** 64
    Prices, **1947:** 202; **1948:** 217, 240 [5, 6]
        Supports, **1950:** 9 (p. 86)
    Relief supplies for India, **1951:** 34, 63 [2], 124
    Shortage, **1948:** 8 (p. 73)
    Speculation in, **1947:** 191 [16], 196, 243 [11]; **1948:** 228 [12], 233 [4], 237 [4]
    Storage, **1948:** 155, 217, 218 [7, 8], 228 [12], 233 [4], 234, 237 [4, 7], 240 [5, 6], 259 [5], 267 [3]; **1950:** 9 (p. 86), 279; **1952–53:** 233 [2], 266 [5, 7], 267, 268 [2], 314
    Surplus, **1950:** 111

Granahan, Repr. William T., **1952–53:** 304

Grand Central Station, New York City, campaign remarks, **1952–53:** 289 [12]

Grand Coulee Dam, **1946:** 18 (p. 60); **1948:** 122 [3], 124 [1], 201; **1949:** 77, 106; **1950:** 121 [4, 6], 122, 124 [1, 4, 7], 127 [2, 4], 128, 129 [1], 134; **1952–53:** 129
    Dedication, **1950:** 125
    Distinguished Service Medal, presentation to District Manager, **1950:** 124 [3]
    News conference remarks, **1950:** 44 [10], 52 [3], 86 [26]

Grand Cross of the Military Willems Order award, **1948:** 87

Grand Forks, N. Dak.
    Campaign remarks, **1952–53:** 266 [3]
    Interview at, **1952–53:** 267

Grand Island, Nebr., **1950:** 110 [7]
    Campaign remarks, **1948:** 118 [1]
    Mayor Ben Cunningham, **1948:** 118 [1]

Grand Junction, Colo., campaign remarks, **1948:** 200 [1]; **1952–53:** 280 [4]

Grand juries, investigations of organized crime, **1950:** 86 [2, 4, 6, 7, 12]; **1951:** 63 [1]

Grand Mufti (Haj Amin el Husseini), **1946:** 141 [9]

Grand Prairie, Tex., campaign remarks, **1948:** 212 [8]

Grand Prairie irrigation project, Arkansas, **1949:** 183

Grand Rapids, Mich.
    Campaign remarks, **1948:** 183 [1]; **1952–53:** 317 [2]
    Mayor George Welsh, **1948:** 183 [1]; **1949:** 26, 54n.

Grand River, Okla., flood control and power project, **1948:** 216 [11], 217

"Grand Slam" bomb, **1945:** 93

Grand Teton National Park, reestablishment, **1950:** 248

Grand Theater, Kansas City, Mo., **1949:** 205 [6]
Grandview, Mo., **1951:** 158; **1952–53:** 149 [19], 344ftn. (p. 1059)
    Baptist Church, dedication, **1950:** 315
    Order of the Eastern Star, remarks, **1950:** 314
Granger, Lester B., **1947:** 191 [3]
Granger, Repr. Walter K., **1948:** 200 [2, 3]; **1952–53:** 21 [10], 280 [1, 3]
Granite City, Ill., campaign remarks, **1952–53:** 321 [7]
Grant, Gen. Ulysses S., 3d, **1946:** 104; **1947:** 31 [1]; **1951:** 90 [16]; **1952–53:** 127 [18], 282 [7], 289, 295 [3]
Grant, William P., **1948:** 261n.
Grapes, **1947:** 30
Grasslands, conservation, **1950:** 125
Grau San Martín, Ramón, **1947:** 14 [6]
Gray, Carl R., Jr., **1947:** 226 [1, 13]; **1949:** 8 (p. 65); **1950:** 192, 196, 203 [3]; **1951:** 251 [26], 260; **1952–53:** 31 [3, 16], 135
Gray, Floyd L., **1950:** 124 [7]
Gray, Gordon, **1949:** 95ftn. (p. 248); **1950:** 289, 294; **1951:** 53, 171 [11], 256; **1952–53:** 203, 253 [7]
    See also Army, Secretary of the.
    Appointment as Special Assistant to the President, **1950:** 80 [8, 11]
    Balance of payments study, **1950:** 159
    Foreign economic policy, report, **1950:** 273 [3], 282
Gray, J. Copeland, **1947:** 141 [4], 145 [2], 218 [14]; **1949:** 260 [10], 267 [7], 269 [2]; **1950:** 29 [1]
Gray, James A., **1949:** 118 [3]
Gray, Richard, **1947:** 20n.
Grazing lands, **1948:** 8 (p. 77), 25, 199
Grazing Service, **1946:** 118; **1947:** 7 (p. 83)
Great Britain.
    See United Kingdom.
Great Falls, Mont., **1950:** 127 [5]
Great Falls, N.H., medical fees in 19th century, **1952–53:** 249
Great Lakes, **1945:** 148, 155; **1948:** 12; **1947:** 111, 171; **1950:** 125
    Coal supplies, **1946:** 228
Great Lakes Steel Corp., **1951:** 305
Great Lakes Towing Co. of Cleveland, Ohio, seizure order, **1945:** 202 [1]
Great Plains, **1950:** 110 [8]
Greece, **1946:** 86 [4], 268
    American Mission for Aid to, **1948:** 28, 188
    Ancient, legacy to U.S. political system, **1950:** 87
    Ancient, Persian aggression against, **1951:** 8
    Archbishop Michael, exchange of messages, **1950:** 7
    Assistance, **1945:** 75, 186; **1947:** 46 [5], 56, 57, 62 [10], 67 [2, 11, 12], 90 [1], 95 [11, 16, 26], 100n., 107 [2], 138, 180 [8, 10], 181 (pp.

Greece — *continued*
  Assistance — *continued*
    398, 405), 188, 195, 210 [6], 220, 238, 243 [19]; **1948:** 2, 28, 144, 160, 175, 188, 202 [6], 228 [1], 231 [2], 244, 260, 263, 278 [31]; **1949:** 8 (p. 54), 86, 162, 184; **1950:** 86 [27], 81, 94, 232; **1952–53:** 81, 242 [2], 354, 366
    Economic, **1951:** 114; **1952–53:** 18 (p. 75), 27, 317 [2]
    Military, **1950:** 9 (p. 59), 151, 201, 204; **1951:** 78, 114, 138; **1952–53:** 18 (p. 75), 27, 55, 288, 317 [2]
    Third anniversary, letters, **1950:** 142
  Children abducted from, **1950:** 7, 90, 261
  Communist aggression in, **1947:** 56, 243 [14]; **1948:** 28, 52, 53, 61, 129, 188; **1949:** 162, 261; **1950:** 90; **1951:** 138; **1952–53:** 69, 107 [2], 303 [2], 354, 366, 378
  Economy, **1947:** 220
  Elections (1945–46), **1950:** 142n.
  German occupation, **1947:** 56
  Griswold, Dwight, mission to, **1949:** 122 [3]
  Immigration to U.S., **1950:** 167; **1952–53:** 182
  Imports, **1947:** 220
  Independence, 128th anniversary, **1949:** 61
  King George II, **1946:** 261
    Death of, **1947:** 66
  King Paul I, message, **1948:** 61
  Korean war, participation, **1950:** 296; **1951:** 170
  Mass deportations in, **1952–53:** 145
  Maximos, Demetrios, **1947:** 57
  Mission of Paul A. Porter **1947:** 95 [6], 107 [1], 221 [10]
  NATO membership, **1951:** 227ftn. (p. 527); **1952–53:** 18 (p. 75), 77
    Question of admittance to, **1952–53:** 5, 8
  News conference remarks, **1947:** 6 [27], 46 [3, 5], 62 [12]
  Political arrests in, **1947:** 141 [12]
  Population growth, **1952–53:** 65
  Sofianopoulos, John, discussions with, **1945:** 75
  Sophoulis, Themistocles, **1947:** 57
  Truman Doctrine, reaction to, **1947:** 57
  Tsaldaris, Constantin, **1949:** 261
  U. N. operations in, **1948:** 34, 202 [6]
  U.N. resolution on, **1949:** 162
  U.S. Ambassador Lincoln MacVeagh, **1947:** 56, 100; **1948:** 48; **1950:** 142
  Venizelos, Sophocles, **1949:** 261
Greek National Army, **1948:** 28
Greeley, Horace, **1951:** 8
Green, Mrs. David, **1951:** 123
Green, Gov. Dwight H., **1948:** 115
Green, Sen. Theodore F., **1945:** 60n.; **1948:** 261 [5]; **1949:** 253 [8]; **1951:** 225; **1952–53:** 3, 298 [5], 299
Green, William, **1945:** 175 [3]; **1946:** 37 [14], 220n.; **1947:** 191 [3], 236 [3], 237; **1948:** 252;

Green, William — *continued*
     1949: 144 [26]; **1950:** 4, 38 [17], 287 [24];
          1951: 279
     Death of, **1952–53:** 336
Green, Repr. William J., Jr., **1952–53:** 304
Greenfield, Albert, **1949:** 194n.
Greenfield, Ind., campaign remarks, **1948:** 233 [2]
Greenfields irrigation district, Montana, **1952–53:**
          80
Greenland, **1945:** 107 [21]
     Campaign remarks, **1948:** 212 [10]
     Mayor Sim Beene, **1948:** 212 [10]
     U.S. bases in, **1952–53:** 217
Greer, Lt. Col. Dewitt, **1946:** 14
Gregory, Lt. Gen. Edmund B., **1945:** 221 [20];
          1946: 141 [13], 192 [22]
Gregory, Repr. Noble J., **1945:** 165
Grew, Joseph C., **1945:** 60 [15], 67 [2]; **1950:** 98
Gridiron Club, **1946:** 86 [33], 110 [18]
Griffin, Cardinal Bernard, **1946:** 112n.
Griffis, Stanton, **1949:** 205 [12]; **1950:** 318 [8]
Griffith, Paul H., **1950:** 272
Grinnell, Iowa, campaign remarks, **1948:** 194 [5]
Grinnell College, **1948:** 194 [5]
Griswold, Dwight P., **1947:** 107 [1, 11]; **1948:** 188;
          1949: 122 [3]; **1950:** 111, 142
Gromyko, Andrei (Ambassador from Russia),
          1945: 172 [5]; **1946:** 66 [5], 177 [13]; **1951:**
          140 [5] and ftn. (p. 364), 193 [9]
Gross, Ernest A., **1949:** 112 [1]; **1950:** 219; **1951:**
          266n.
Gross, Repr. H. R., **1952–53:** 334 [10]
Gross national product (GNP).
     See National product.
Grosz, Archbishop Josef, conspiracy charges by
          Hungary, **1951:** 153ftn. (p. 385)
Groton, Conn., **1952–53:** 170
Ground Observer Corps, "Operation Sky watch,"
          1952–53: 202, 344
Grover, Wayne C., **1952–53:** 347
Groves, Maj. Gen. Leslie R., **1946:** 242 [2]
Groves, Brig. Gen. R. Dinwiddie, **1951:** 218
Gruening, Gov. Ernest, **1945:** 64 [3]; **1948:** 11 [7],
          49 [9]; **1949:** 112 [16]; **1950:** 11 [7], 29 [23]
Gruenther, Gen. Alfred M., **1952–53:** 112
Grundy, Joseph R., **1948:** 178 [1], 213, 227 [3], 266;
          1950: 137 [20, 24]
Guadalcanal, battle, **1945:** 45, 174, 178
Guam, **1945:** 45; **1948:** 20, 26 [7]
     Administration, **1947:** 119
          Civil, **1949:** 101; **1950:** 9 (p. 102), 203 [7];
               1951: 141
     Civil rights in, **1947:** 130
     Trusteeship agreement, **1947:** 151
     U.S. capture of, **1945:** 161, 178
Guaranteed wages, report, **1947:** 53
Guatemala
     Flood relief, **1949:** 236 [3]

Guatemala — *continued*
     U.S. Ambassador Richard C. Patterson, **1950:**
          146 [10]
Guay, John, **1952–53:** 292 [13], 294
Guerrilla warfare, **1947:** 243 [14]
     In Greece, **1948:** 28
Gulf Oil Corp., **1952–53:** 58
Gullixson, Rev. Thaddeus F., **1952–53:** 244, 373
Gundersen, Dr. Gunnar, **1951:** 307n.; **1952–53:** 2
          [3]
Gunnison-Arkansas power project, **1948:** 198 [5]
Gunther, John, **1950:** 273 [8]
Gurney, Sen. Chan, **1948:** 33
Gustaf Adolf, Prince, death of, **1947:** 16
Gustaf V, King, **1947:** 16
Guttenberg, N.J., Mayor Andrew Johnstone, **1948:**
          189n.
Guyer, Mrs. C. Irving, letter on inflation control,
          1951: 164

Habeas corpus, writ of, **1950:** 254
Hadley, Paul, **1950:** 278 [7]
Hagan, Douglas, **1952–53:** 173n.
Hague, Frank, **1948:** 227 [8, 9]; **1949:** 155 [8]
Hague, Rear Adm. W. McL., **1952–53:** 349n.
Hague conference on Indonesian independence,
          1949: 272
Hailer, Frederick C., **1952–53:** 296
Haines Cutoff Road, Alaska-Canada, **1948:** 105
Haiti, **1951:** 193 [13]
Haj Amin el Husseini (Grand Mufti), **1946:** 141 [9]
Hale, Repr. Robert, **1951:** 54n.
Hall, Gov. John H., **1948:** 88 [8]
Halleck, Repr. Charles A., **1948:** 12n., 214 [1], 227
          [6], 240 [2], 259 [2]; **1952–53:** 315
Hals, Frans, **1948:** 71 [1]
Halsey, Edwin A., **1950:** 29 [9]
Halsey, Adm. William F., **1946:** 70 [1]
Halstead, Charles L., **1948:** 236
Hamburg, Iowa, campaign remarks, **1952–53:** 284
          [2]
Hamilton, Alexander, **1946:** 268; **1948:** 32, 236;
          1949: 98; **1951:** 127n.; **1952–53:** 255
Hamilton, Brig. Gen. P.M., **1952–53:** 310
Hamilton, Ohio, campaign remarks, **1948:** 231 [2];
          1952–53: 319 [6]
Hamilton College, **1952–53:** 289 [6]
Hammond, Ind., campaign remarks, **1948:** 240 [1]
Hammurabi, code of, **1950:** 313
Hamtramck, Mich.
     Campaign remarks, **1948:** 183 [4]; **1952–53:** 317
          [7]
     Mayor Stephen S. Skrzycki, **1948:** 183 [4]
Hand, Judge Learned B., **1952–53:** 362n.
     Retirement, **1951:** 112
Handicapped persons, **1946:** 217

Handicapped persons — *continued*
  Community Chest services, **1950:** 262
  Disabled veterans
    Automobiles for, **1952–53:** 18 (p. 110)
    Vocational rehabilitation, **1950:** 9 (p. 67), 298
  Education, **1949:** 8 (p. 76); **1952–53:** 367 (p. 1155)
  Employment, **1945:** 226; **1949:** 197; **1950:** 208; **1951:** 15, 195; **1952–53:** 137, 243
  Health and Welfare, **1947:** 98; **1948:** 89; **1949:** 8 (p. 68), 85; **1951:** 13 (pp. 97, 98); **1952–53:** 18 (p. 106), 293, 367 (p. 1158)
  Old age and survivors insurance rights, **1952–53:** 213
  Public assistance, **1952–53:** 367 (p. 1156)
  Rehabilitation, **1951:** 281
  Social security provisions, **1948:** 131, 152, 215
Handicapped Week, President's Committee on National Employ the, **1948:** 169
Handshaking, comments on, **1949:** 119; **1950:** 87
Hanes, John W., **1947:** 70 [5]; **1950:** 137 [18]
Hanford, Wash., atomic plant, **1948:** 110 [20], 239; **1950:** 121 [13]
Hanlon, James T., **1948:** 248; **1952–53:** 306n.
Hanna, John A., **1950:** 294n.; **1952–53:** 81
Hanna Co., M. A., **1947:** 236 [3]
Hannegan, Robert E., **1946:** 15 [12]; **1949:** 220
  See also Democratic National Committee, Chairman; Postmaster General.
  News conference remarks on, **1945:** 22 [3, 4, 7]; **1947:** 31 [3], 70 [24]
  Nomination as Postmaster General, **1945:** 22 [3]
Hannibal, **1950:** 138; **1951:** 8, 18
Hanrahan, Edmond M. (Chairman, Securities and Exchange Commission), **1949:** 149n.
Hapsburg art collection, exhibition in U.S., **1949:** 253 [11]
Harbach, Otto, **1951:** 99
Harbor and river construction, **1946:** 18 (p. 81), 176, 195
Harbor and river development.
  See Rivers and harbors, development.
Harbor workers, **1946:** 117
Harding, Warren G., **1948:** 201, 223; **1949:** 128; **1951:** 297; **1952–53:** 129, 267, 286 [6]
Hardy, Repr. Porter, Jr., **1952–53:** 177
Harkness, Richard, **1947:** 90n.; **1949:** 17
Harl, Maple T. (Chairman, Federal Deposit Insurance Corporation), **1950:** 192n.
Harlem, N.Y.
  Address, **1948:** 265
  Campaign remarks, **1952–53:** 290
Harmon, Marcia Anne, **1951:** 40n.
Harmon International Trophy, presentation, **1951:** 268
Harper, Roy, **1946:** 216 [14]; **1947:** 174 [1, 5], 236 [5]
Harper, R. S., *Lincoln and the Press*, **1951:** 56 [25]

Harpers Ferry, W. Va., campaign remarks, **1952–53:** 308 [8]
Harrell, William G., Congressional Medal of Honor award, **1945:** 160n.
Harriman, E. Roland, **1950:** 278 [1]; **1951:** 47n., 73, 162
Harriman, W. Averell, **1945:** 97, 181 [4]; **1946:** 6 [5], 27 [14], 61 [7]; **1948:** 274 [3]; **1949:** 86, 205 [15]; **1950:** 189 [9], 203 [11], 206 [1, 7, 14], 209 [2, 7], 253 [3], 268, 278 [1]; **1951:** 66; **1952–53:** 6, 21 [22], 27, 55, 65, 66, 67, 180, 203, 217, 279, 292 [11], 342 [5], 358
  See also Commerce, Secretary of.
  Dinner honoring, question of President's attendance, **1952–53:** 44 [6], 88 [21]
  District of Columbia primary election victory, **1952–53:** 175 [5, 13]
  Mission to Iran, **1951:** 150, 153 [9, 19], 155
  News conference remarks on, **1951:** 108 [2], 118 [10], 165 [11], 200 [2, 7, 11, 14], 239 [10, 12]; **1952–53:** 98 [23, 31], 175 [8], 221 [7, 9]
  Presidential candidacy, **1952–53:** 98 [23, 31], 107 [4], 127 [8], 136 [16], 175 [5, 8, 13]
  Visit to Egypt, question of, **1951:** 188 [12], 200 [14]
Harrington, Cornelius J., **1952–53:** 35ftn. (p. 155)
Harris, Edward A., **1952–53:** 26 [8]
Harris, Franklin, **1952–53:** 281
Harrisburg, Pa., campaign remarks, **1948:** 139 [2]
Harrison, Earl G., **1952–53:** 244, 373
  Reports, **1945:** 152, 187, 188; **1946:** 227
Harrison, Pat, **1949:** 226 [7]
Harrison, William Henry, **1950:** 217 [15]; **1951:** 93n.; **1952–53:** 282 [7], 289
Harrison, N.J., Mayor Frank E. Rodgers, **1948:** 189n.
Harsch, Joseph C., **1947:** 90n.
Hart, Repr. Edward J., **1948:** 227 [8]; **1952–53:** 303 [2]
Hartford, Conn., **1949:** 66 [5]
  Campaign remarks, **1948:** 259 [3]; **1952–53:** 293
Hartke, Rev. Gilbert V., **1952–53:** 56n.
Hartley, Repr. Fred A., Jr., **1947:** 121, 127 [1], 182 [4]; **1952–53:** 298 [1], 314
  Labor act.
    See Taft-Hartley Act.
  Our National Labor Policy, the Taft-Hartley Act and the Next Steps, **1948:** 232, 247, 261 [11]
Hartwell Reservoir, S.C., **1952–53:** 18 (p. 88)
Harvard University, **1946:** 43 [3]; **1949:** 116n.; **1951:** 209 [13]
Harvey, Capt. Raymond, Congressional Medal of Honor, **1951:** 146
Harvey, William, **1945:** 88
Harwell, Coleman, **1952–53:** 98 [10]
Haseltine, Herbert, **1950:** 275n.

Haskell, William N. (Director, Office of Civilian Defense), **1945:** 19; **1946:** 105n.
Haslett, Dame Caroline, **1952–53:** 188
Hassett, William D., **1945:** 4 [2]; **1946:** 199 [11]; **1949:** 265; **1951:** 22 [2]; **1952–53:** 45n.
Hastie, Gov. William H., **1948:** 36, 38; **1949:** 40 [15]
Hastings, Rev. J. Warren, **1951:** 241
Hastings, Minn., campaign remarks, **1952–53:** 313 [3]
Hat, gift to President, **1948:** 118 [5]
Hatch, Sen. Carl A., **1946:** 163 [1]; **1947:** 90 [2]; **1948:** 136 [2, 3], 137ftn. (p. 363); **1949:** 112 [5]
   Labor relations bill, **1945:** 172 [1]
Hatch, William H., **1950:** 110 [3]
Hatch Act, **1947:** 18; **1948:** 110 [12]; **1949:** 112 [5], 148 [21]
   Agricultural experiment stations, **1950:** 121 [3]
   Restricting political activity of Federal employees, **1950:** 38 [12], 182
Havana, **1947:** 236 [7]; **1949:** 88
Havana, International Trade Organization, Charter signing, **1948:** 54
Haverhill, Mass., campaign remarks, **1952–53:** 295 [7]
Havre, Mont., **1950:** 127 [7]
   Campaign remarks, **1952–53:** 266 [6], 268 [5]
Hawaii
   Congressional Medal of Honor winners, World War II, **1950:** 267
   Elective governorship, proposed, **1952–53:** 35 [15]
   Gov. Ingram M. Stainback, **1950:** 11 [7], 267, 278 [9]; **1951:** 37 [3]
   Korean war casualties, **1950:** 291
   Maritime strike, **1949:** 118 [16], 144 [20], 148 [9, 11], 155 [17]
   Military cemeteries, grave markers, **1951:** 247 [4], 251 [8, 11]
   Military preparedness, **1950:** 291
   News conference remarks, **1949:** 4 [7], 112 [9], 118 [16], 144 [7, 20], 148 [9, 11], 155 [17]; **1950:** 52 [9], 179 [6], 206 [12], 230 [3], 273 [5]
   Public works, employment on, **1947:** 35
   Statehood proposed, **1946:** 18 (p. 66), 30 [6]; **1948:** 2, 20, 88 [8, 14]; **1949:** 4 [7], 112 [9], 144 [7, 20]; **1950:** 2, 52 [9], 107, 121 [13], 179 [6], 206 [12], 230 [3], 267, 273 [5], 291; **1951:** 168; **1952–53:** 5, 35 [15], 49 [8], 149 [15]
   Taxes, **1950:** 291
   Tidal wave, **1946:** 72 [18]
   Transfer of lands to, **1947:** 35
Hawesville, Ky., campaign remarks, **1948:** 218 [13]
Hawkes, Sen. Albert W., **1947:** 46 [28]
Hawley, Joseph Roswell, **1947:** 51
Hawley, Maj. Gen. Paul R., **1952–53:** 135n.

Hawley-Smoot tariff, **1947:** 51; **1949:** 195
Hayden, Sen. Carl, **1948:** 136 [1], 207; **1949:** 32 [6], 179 [23]; **1951:** 32
Hayden, Martin S., **1952–53:** 136 [19]
Hayes, A. J., **1951:** 307n.
Hayes, Rutherford B., **1945:** 175ftn. (p. 417); **1952–53:** 127 [18], 136 [17]
Hays, Repr. Brooks, **1951:** 16 [20], 54n.
Hays, Repr. Wayne L., **1952–53:** 2 [6]
Haywood, Allan S., **1947:** 236 [3], 237
Hayworth, Donald, **1952–53:** 317 [3]
Hayworth, Harold, **1952–53:** 317 [5]
Heads of state and government, joint statements with.
   See Joint statements with heads of state and government.
Heads of state and government, meetings, **1946:** 41 [4], 53 [21], 61 [6], 66 [13], 70 [4], 126 [8, 11, 20], 226 [8], 250 [14]; **1947:** 112
   Atomic energy control, **1948:** 239
   "Big Three" conference, question of, **1948:** 15 [10]; **1949:** 93 [12]
   Cairo conference (1943), **1950:** 3 [1]
   Crimea conference.
     See Yalta conference.
   East-West meeting, prospects of, **1950:** 209 [13, 15, 19]
   News conference remarks, **1945:** 31 [4], 44 [5, 14, 17], 52 [15], 60 [6], 64 [8], 67 [1, 2], 147 [5], 193 [13], 202 [13], 208 [2]
   Potsdam conference, **1946:** 18 (p. 41), 27 [7, 17], 30 [2], 53 [10], 126 [3, 8]; **1947:** 46 [7], 74, 90 [7], 196, 210 [1], 236 [6]; **1948:** 86, 126 [4], 239; **1949:** 28 [20], 86; **1950:** 80 [4], 121 [1]; **1951:** 88, 232, 253
     See also main heading, Potsdam conference.
   Proposed, **1945:** 31 [4], 44 [5, 14, 17], 52 [15], 164 [10], 172 [5], 181 [3], 193 [13], 202 [13], 208 [2]; **1947:** 19 [9]; **1951:** 251 [24], 295 [1]
   Teheran conference, **1945:** 97; **1949:** 273; **1950:** 80 [4]
   Three-nation (U.S.-U.K.-Canada) Declaration (1945), **1949:** 216
   Truman-Stalin meeting, question of, **1949:** 214 [3], 234 [13]
   Yalta conference.
     See main heading, Yalta conference.
Heads of state and government, messages to.
   See Messages to heads of state and government.
Health, national, **1946:** 26; **1947:** 28, 86, 98, 110, 171; **1948:** 2, 4 [19], 5 (pp. 25, 37), 8 (pp. 67, 68, 78, 84, 93, 98), 20, 175
   Legislative programs.
     See Health programs.
Health, the President's, **1946:** 78 [6]; **1947:** 14 [18]; **1948:** 243 [3]; **1949:** 36; **1950:** 238 [1]; **1951:** 56 [10], 153 [20], 295 [13]

Health, Education and Security, Department of, proposed, **1950:** 150
Health, Education, and Welfare, Department of, proposed, **1947:** 7 (p. 71); **1949:** 7 [29]
Health Assembly, National, **1948:** 89, 181 [2]
Health Council, Inter-Agency, **1951:** 307
Health insurance, **1947:** 7 (pp. 58, 72) 187, 211; **1948:** 2, 4 [8], 5 (pp. 20, 21, 23, 25, 34, 37), 8 (pp. 68, 88), 181 [2], 182, 237 [3], 251; **1949:** 8, 85, 250 [3]; **1950:** 2, 9 (pp. 46, 54, 76, 77), 279; **1951:** 4, 135; **1952–53:** 5, 237, 249
    Campaign remarks, **1948:** 205, 257 [3], 262, 268
    News conference remarks, **1949:** 7 [4, 48], 22 [12], 40 [3], 66 [6], 95 [6]; **1951:** 12 [26]; **1952–53:** 17 [28]
    Payroll tax for, proposed, **1949:** 7 [4]; **1951:** 13 (p. 99)
    President's physician, views on, **1949:** 95 [6]
    Program, proposed, **1945:** 192
    Trust fund, **1946:** 18 (p. 69); **1949:** 7 [48]
    Under social security, proposed, **1946:** 18 (p. 64); **1947:** 98; **1950:** 9 (p. 73); **1951:** 13 (p. 99), 135; **1952–53:** 258 [9, 15], 268 [8], 278, 284 [5], 369
    See also Social security.
Health Needs of the Nation, Commission on the, **1951:** 307; **1952–53:** 2 [3], 5, 15, 249, 268 [8], 278, 284 [5], 333, 352, 353 [1], 367 (p. 1158), 369
Health Organization, World, **1947:** 7 (p. 67), 21
    U.S. membership, **1948:** 132
Health programs, **1945:** 128; **1946:** 18 (pp. 52, 64, 83), 91, 117; **1947:** 2 (p. 8), 4 (pp. 35, 36), 7 (pp. 58, 71, 73), 86n., 110, 152, 181 (p. 405), 187, 193, 194, 204, 211; **1948:** 8 (p. 87), 248, 257 [2, 3], 259 [6], 268; **1949:** 2, 5, 8 (pp. 45, 47, 67, 69), 154, 181, 202; **1950:** 2, 6, 9 (pp. 72, 73, 75), 39, 129 [4], 134; **1951:** 13 (pp. 64, 65, 96–99); **1952–53:** 2 [3], 5, 18 (pp. 103, 106), 69, 215, 218, 278, 293, 352, 369
    See also Disease prevention; Hospitals and medical care facilities; Medical care.
    Alaska, **1948:** 105
    Campaign remarks on, **1948:** 117, 134, 160, 205, 228 [10], 231 [1], 232, 237 [3, 7], 241, 242 [3]
    Children, **1946:** 18 (p. 83), 128; **1947:** 17, 98; **1948:** 18, 181 [2], 237 [3]; **1949:** 85, 204, 219; **1950:** 9 (p. 75); **1951:** 13 (p. 98), 307; **1952–53:** 367 (p. 1157)
    Defense needs, adjustments to, **1951:** 11; **1952–53:** 15
    Disease prevention.
        See main heading, Disease prevention.
    Drug addiction, cure of, **1951:** 201, 287
    Expansion, **1948:** 247; **1951:** 11
Health programs — *continued*
    Expenditures for, **1952–53:** 231, 367 (pp. 1156–1159)
    Federal aid, **1949:** 85, 154; **1950:** 8 [32, 47], 9 (pp. 50, 75); **1951:** 135, 307; **1952–53:** 273, 306 [1], 333
    Federal-State cooperation, **1948:** 16
    Handicapped persons, **1948:** 89; **1951:** 281
    Indians, **1947:** 229; **1950:** 91
    Insurance.
        See Health insurance.
    International cooperation, **1948:** 132; **1951:** 184
    Issue in election campaign, **1952–53:** 268 [8], 280
    Legislation, proposed, **1948:** 160, 165
    Maternal, **1948:** 181 [2], 237 [3]; **1949:** 85; **1950:** 9 (p. 75); **1951:** 13 (p. 99), 307; **1952–53:** 367 (p. 1157)
    Medical and dental education, **1951:** 4, 9, 13 (p. 98)
    Medical supplies, stockpiling for civil defense, **1952–53:** 367 (p. 1154)
    Mental health, **1948:** 89; **1949:** 204; **1950:** 9 (p. 75); **1951:** 9
    Message to Congress, **1945:** 192; **1947:** 98; **1949:** 85
    Military personnel, **1952–53:** 333
    News conference remarks, **1949:** 58 [33], 84 [17], 118 [14]
    Physical fitness, **1951:** 9
    Public health, **1951:** 13 (p. 98); **1952–53:** 15, 18 (pp. 105, 106), 249, 333, 367 (p. 1157)
    Reorganization plans, **1950:** 53, 69, 71
    Research, **1950:** 9 (p. 84); **1951:** 13 (pp. 98, 99), 135, 297, 307; **1952–53:** 333, 367 (p. 1157), 376
    Rural, **1948:** 117
    Special interest opposition to, **1952–53:** 194
    Statement, **1948:** 181 [2]
    United Defense Fund for, **1951:** 3
    Veterans, **1948:** 228 [10]; **1949:** 8 (pp. 62, 64, 65); **1951:** 260; **1952–53:** 135, 333
Health Resources Advisory Committee, **1952–53:** 249
Healy, George P. A., **1947:** 31 [1]
Hearst, William Randolph, **1949:** 253 [9]
Hearst newspapers, treatment of the President, 1944 campaign, **1948:** 268
Heart disease, **1948:** 22, 205; **1949:** 29; **1952–53:** 249, 268 [8], 333
    Prevention, **1951:** 135
    Statement, **1947:** 28
Heart River, N. Dak., **1950:** 129 [5]
Hébert, Repr. F. Edward, **1950:** 309ftn. (p. 753)
Hebrews, legacy to U.S. political system, **1950:** 87
Hedrick, James A., **1948:** 234
Heinkel, Fred V., **1952–53:** 32
Heiser, Charles, **1948:** 189n.
Helena, Mont., **1950:** 127 [4]

Heller, Mrs. Eleanor, **1951:** 215n.
Heller, Repr. Louis B., **1952–53:** 298 [14], 300
Hell's Canyon Dam, **1950:** 121 [4, 8]
   Power project, **1951:** 13 (pp. 85, 86); **1952–53:** 270 [9], 367 (p. 1146)
Helmstedt, Germany, checkpoint for Allied vehicles, **1950:** 23ftn. (p. 135)
Helper, Utah
   Campaign remarks, **1948:** 200 [3]; **1952–53:** 280 [3]
   Mayor D. K. Downey, **1948:** 200 [3]
Henderson, Charles B., letter, **1945:** 176
Henderson, David, **1948:** 181 [20]
Henderson, Ky., campaign remarks, **1948:** 218 [11]
Hendren, John H., **1950:** 38 [6, 12]
Hendrickson, Sen. Robert C., **1951:** 54n.
Hennings, Thomas C., Jr., **1950:** 169ftn. (p. 485), 206 [2], 279, 287 [7]; **1951:** 196; **1952–53:** 3, 21 [17], 32, 98 [39]
Hennock, Frieda B., **1951:** 140 [12], 251 [14], 261 [22], 283
Henry, Bill, **1947:** 90n.
Henry, Joseph, **1946:** 201
Henry, Patrick, **1950:** 144
Henry Modell and Co., **1946:** 78ftn. (p. 192)
Henson, Harry F., **1952–53:** 274 [4, 5]
Herlong, Repr. A. S., Jr., Defense Production Act, amendment, **1951:** 199; **1952–53:** 33
Hernandez, Cpl. Rodolfo, Congressional Medal of Honor, **1952–53:** 90
Herr, Harrington, **1952–53:** 304
Herrin, Ill.
   Campaign remarks, **1948:** 218 [3]
   Mayor John Murray, **1948:** 218 [3]
Herron, W. W., **1952–53:** 88 [11]
Hersey, John, **1951:** 16 [21], 70 [8]
Hershey, Maj. Gen. Lewis B., **1945:** 107 [4, 13]; **1946:** 119 [2]; **1952–53:** 185, 187
Herter, Repr. Christian A., **1951:** 54n.
Herzog, Paul, **1947:** 145 [2]
   Appointment as Chairman, National Labor Relations Board, **1945:** 52 [4]
Heselton, Repr. John W., **1950:** 86 [24]; **1951:** 54n.
Hess, Myra, **1951:** 99
Hester, E. D., **1945:** 24
Heyerdahl, Thor, *Kon-Tiki*, **1951:** 130
Hibbing, Minn., campaign remarks, **1952–53:** 314
Hickenlooper, Sen. Bourke B., **1947:** 141 [12]; **1948:** 88 [1]; **1949:** 112 [2]; **1950:** 214ftn. (p. 588); **1952–53:** 129, 297
Hickerson, John T., **1949:** 112 [1]
Hickey, Margaret A., **1950:** 294n.
Hicks, G. N., **1948:** 234
Higgins, Brig. Gen. Gerald J., **1946:** 224
High Commissioner to the Philippines.
   See United States High Commissioner to the Philippines.
High schools, **1946:** 75 [11, 26]

Higher Education, President's Commission on, report, **1947:** 235
"High-level" versus "full" employment legislation, **1945:** 208 [14]
Highway program, **1945:** 128
Highway Safety, Federal Committee on, **1947:** 118
Highway Safety Conference, President's, **1946:** 96, 106; **1947:** 8, 82; **1948:** 279; **1949:** 26, 55, 114; **1950:** 229; **1951:** 42, 121; **1952–53:** 93
Highways, **1946:** 18 (pp. 61, 81), 238; **1947:** 4 (p. 34), 7 (pp. 84, 85, 86), 35; **1948:** 5 (pp. 25, 48), 8 (pp. 67, 81), 234
   Access roads program, **1947:** 35
   Accident prevention, **1951:** 9, 13 (p. 81), 42, 121; **1952–53:** 93, 243, 249
   Alaska, **1945:** 64 [3], 175 [12]; **1948:** 5 (p. 50), 105
   Circumferential, District of Columbia, proposed, **1952–53:** 18 (p. 113)
   Defense facilities, access roads, **1951:** 13 (pp. 83, 84)
   Federal aid, **1947:** 7 (pp. 58, 85), 35, 181 (pp. 401, 402); **1948:** 5 (pp. 48, 50), 8 (p. 81), 24, 105; **1949:** 8 (p. 87), 142, 151, 154, 192 [5], 269 [3]; **1950:** 9 (pp. 49, 50, 92, 94, 95), 121 [6], 213; **1951:** 13 (p. 84), 221; **1952–53:** 5, 18 (p. 84), 231, 277 [4], 367 (pp. 1143–1144)
   Forest roads, **1949:** 8 (p. 84); **1950:** 116, 121 [9]
   Indian lands, **1952–53:** 18 (p. 90)
   Inter-American Highway, **1945:** 128
   Interstate system, **1950:** 9 (p. 95), 160 [2]; **1951:** 13 (p. 83); **1952–53:** 18 (p. 84)
   Jackson County, Mo., **1950:** 121 [6]
   Japanese, **1948:** 288 [6]
   Korean, reopening of, **1950:** 268
   Military facilities and defense plants, access roads, **1952–53:** 18 (p. 84)
   National forest, **1952–53:** 18 (p. 84)
   News conference remarks, **1947:** 6 [24]
   Oregon, **1950:** 121 [6]
   Rural, **1948:** 117, 237 [5]
   Safety, **1947:** 8, 27, 82, 86, 118; **1948:** 279; **1949:** 26, 55, 114; **1950:** 229
      Conference, **1945:** 224
   Tolls, use to finance other transportation facilities, **1952–53:** 209
   Traffic accidents, **1945:** 62, 208 [10], 224; **1946:** 96, 106
Hill, Arthur M. (Chairman, National Security Resources Board), **1948:** 109, 148; **1949:** 28 [1]
Hill, Grover B., **1945:** 52 [7]
Hill, Vice Adm. Harry W., **1952–53:** 142
Hill, Sen. Lister, **1948:** 137ftn. (p. 363); **1951:** 54n.; **1952–53:** 3, 127 [3]
Hill, Oliver, **1952–53:** 7 [1]

Hill-Burton Act.
   See Hospital Survey and Construction Act.
Hillenkoetter, Rear Adm. Roscoe H., **1949:** 182 [2];
   1950: 152 [12]
Hillman, Ernest, **1949:** 202n.
Hillman, Sidney, **1948:** 261 [11]
   Death of, **1946:** 161
Hillman, William, **1947:** 90n.; **1949:** 234, 265
   "Mr. President," **1952–53:** 31 [5], 64 [4, 18]
Hillsboro, Tex., campaign remarks, **1948:** 212 [6]
Hilton, Frank C., **1952–53:** 29
Himmler, Heinrich, **1945:** 22 [20], 40 [5]
Hinckley, Robert H., **1952–53:** 203n.
   Memorandum, **1945:** 115
Hines, Brig. Gen. Frank T., resignation as Admin-
   istrator of Veterans Affairs, **1945:** 52 [8],
   112
Hines, Lewis G., **1950:** 294n.
Hinsey, Joseph C., **1951:** 307n.
Hirohito, Emperor, **1945:** 143, 145
   News conference remarks on, **1945:** 100, 172 [2]
   Soviet demand for trial, **1950:** 29 [14]
Hiroshima, Japan, **1946:** 112
   Atomic bomb target, **1945:** 97, 174, 178; **1950:**
   209 [18]
   Statement, **1945:** 93
Hise, Harley A. (Chairman, Reconstruction Fi-
   nance Corporation), **1950:** 192, 196, 259
Hiss, Alger, **1950:** 23 [2, 4]
   Trial of, **1949:** 155 [21]
Histadrut Humanitarian Award, **1951:** 274
Historical documents, publication program, **1950:**
   136
History, Marxist interpretation of, **1952–53:** 366
History program, Federal, **1951:** 26, 127
Hitler, Adolf, **1945:** 2, 12, 27, 45, 66, 91, 186; **1946:**
   42, 86 [31]; **1947:** 110; **1948:** 236, 256;
   1950: 80 [4], 185, 232; **1951:** 18, 138, 256;
   1952–53: 261, 276, 279, 295 [8], 296
   News conference remarks on, **1945:** 22 [21], 26
   [1], 31 [1], 40 [5]
Hitler Youth organization, **1945:** 201n.
H.M.S. *Renown*, **1945:** 91n.
Hoan, Daniel W., **1948:** 235n.
Hoarding, **1945:** 211 [1], 229
Hobbs (Repr. Sam) labor bill, **1946:** 15 [5], 143 [16]
   Approval, **1946:** 157
Hoboken, N.J., Mayor Fred M. DeSapio, **1948:**
   189n.
Hobson, Rear Adm. Richmond P., **1948:** 81
Hoch, Daniel K., **1948:** 227n.
Hock, Donald V., **1948:** 227n.
Hod Carriers, Building, and Common Laborers
   Union, **1949:** 240ftn. (p. 532)
Hodge, Lt. Gen. John C., **1949:** 223
Hodges, Charles, **1947:** 90n.
Hodges, George, **1952–53:** 7 [10]
Hodgins, Eric, **1951:** 19n.

Hoey, Sen. Clyde R., **1949:** 161 [5], 179 [19], 182 [1]
Hoffman, Paul G., **1946:** 142; **1947:** 122, 236 [3],
   237; **1948:** 88 [15], 174 [9], 175, 283 [9];
   1949: 171 [3]; **1951:** 90 [12]; **1952–53:** 278
   See also Economic Cooperation Administrator.
Hogness, T. R., **1948:** 191n.
Hogs
   Marketing of, **1946:** 223 [1]
   Prices, **1947:** 76, 242
Holbein, Hans, *The Merchant*, **1948:** 71 [1]
Holdenville, Okla., campaign remarks, **1948:** 216
   [4]
Holding Company Act, Public Utility, **1952–53:**
   143
   Bank, hearing on monopoly charges, **1949:** 40 [6]
   Public utility, bill to prohibit, **1948:** 233 [3]
Holiday, 2-day, in celebration of end of war, **1945:**
   100, 102, 115
Holidays for Government employees, **1946:** 18 (p.
   65)
Holland, Sen. Spessard, **1947:** 231n.; **1951:** 16 [20],
   90 [10]
Holland.
   See Netherlands.
Holling, Thomas L., **1946:** 163 [4]
Hollis, Everett L., **1952–53:** 7ftn. (p. 19), 26 [1]
Holmes, Horace, **1952–53:** 57
Holmes, John, **1947:** 191 [3]
Holt, Hamilton, **1949:** 51
Holtzoff, Alexander, **1945:** 132 [1]
Holum, Kenneth, **1952–53:** 32
Home Builders, National Association of, **1946:** 48
Home Loan Bank Board, Federal, **1947:** 102, 173,
   174 [1]; **1948:** 5 (pp. 39, 40); **1950:** 9 (pp.
   54, 80)
Home Loan Bank Board, Federal, Chairman (John
   H. Fahey), **1947:** 173, 174 [1]
Home mortgages, **1948:** 218 [1], 219
Home Owners' Loan Act, **1948:** 183 [5]; **1950:** 51
Home Owners' Loan Association, **1952–53:** 278
Home Owners Loan Corporation, **1946:** 94, 116;
   1947: 7 (p. 75), 102, 173; **1948:** 5 (p. 40),
   227 [9]; **1950:** 9 (p. 80), 51; **1951:** 13 (p.
   93)
Home relief funds, under social security, question
   of, **1949:** 32 [2]
Homer, Arthur B., **1949:** 152n., 153; **1952–53:** 116
Homestead Act (1862), **1948:** 115
Homestead steel strike (1892), **1948:** 198 [5]
Honduras, U.S. Ambassador John D. Erwin, **1947:**
   62 [4]
Hong Kong, **1945:** 106 [10]
   Arms trade with Communist China, **1951:** 63 [10]
Honorary degrees, acceptance, **1946:** 112; **1947:** 52,
   117; **1948:** 124 [1], 128 [4], 194 [5], 216 [3],
   227 [2], 228 [9]; **1949:** 51; **1950:** 159n., 166
   [1]
Hook, Frank, **1948:** 184; **1950:** 209ftn. (p. 582)

Hooper rating on broacast re wages and prices in reconversion period, **1945:** 181 [1]

Hoover, Calvin B., **1947:** 122

Hoover, Herbert, President, **1945:** 64 [10, 13]; **1946:** 45, 49, 85, 86 [4, 24], 87, 141 [8, 10], 255n.; **1947:** 47; **1948:** 201, 223, 236, 247, 262, 278 [10]; **1949:** 25, 94n., 181, 234 [1]; **1950:** 105 [15], 137 [27], 318 [5, 12]; **1951:** 7 [5], 33 [9], 135, 179 [6]; **1952–53:** 26 [17], 96 [6], 107 [6], 284 [2], 285, 298 [2], 306 [7], 322, 366

Campaign (1928), **1948:** 260

Commemorative coins, policy on, **1947:** 162; **1948:** 90

Letter, **1948:** 274 [1]

News conference remarks on, **1947:** 46 [2, 4, 8], 232 [4]; **1948:** 11 [1, 9], 274 [1], 278 [10]

Services to Nation following Presidential term, **1952–53:** 377 [30]

Hoover, J. Edgar, **1946:** 54, 55n., 56n., 229 [22], **1948:** 102, 215; **1949:** 122 [22], 269 [14]; **1950:** 79, 82, 94, 309 [4]; **1951:** 35, 300 [1]

See also Federal Bureau of Investigation, Director.

"Hoover carts," **1948:** 246

Hoover Commission.

See Commission on the Organization of the Executive Branch of the Government.

Hoover Dam, **1950:** 127 [1]; **1952–53:** 277 [3]

Hoover Report, Citizens Committee on, **1951:** 56 [1]

Hope, Repr. Clifford R., **1952–53:** 32, 33

Defense Production Act amendment, **1951:** 176, 199

Hopi Indians, **1947:** 229n.; **1948:** 40; **1949:** 226 [19], 231 [23], 233; **1950:** 9 (p. 91); **1952–53:** 46

Hopkins, Harry L., **1945:** 126n.

Distinguished Service Medal, citation, **1945:** 125

Letters, **1945:** 71, 153

Mission to Soviet Union, **1945:** 44 [8, 18], 52 [15], 60 [6, 10, 12, 15]; **1947:** 74

News conference remarks on, **1945:** 44 [8, 18], 52 [15], 60 [6, 10, 12, 15], 67 [2], 127

Resignation as Special Assistant to the President, **1945:** 71

Hopkins, John Jay, **1952–53:** 171

Hopkins, Robert, **1948:** 249

Hopkinson, Edward, Jr., **1946:** 142

Hopson, Howard C., **1952–53:** 143

Horne, Charles F., **1952–53:** 40, 351

Horner, F. V., Congressional Medal of Honor presentation, **1945:** 167n.

Horner, Henry, **1948:** 256

Hornet, **1946:** 171n.

Horseracing, ban on, **1945:** 4 [18, 21]

Horseshoes, game of, **1946:** 72 [13], 78 [10]

Horton, Maj. John E., **1950:** 21n.

Horton, Mrs. John E., **1952–53:** 156 [14]

Horvitz, Aaron, **1948:** 140n.; **1949:** 81

Hospital Survey and Construction Act, **1949:** 35; **1950:** 68; **1952–53:** 268 [8]

Approval, **1946:** 203

Hospital survey and construction program, **1952–53:** 249, 268 [8]

Hospitalization, Federal Board of, **1945:** 128

Hospitals and medical care facilities, **1945:** 107 [9], 128, 192; **1946:** 18 (p. 83), 199 [20]; **1947:** 6 [4], 7 (p. 73), 98, 110; **1948:** 2, 8 (p. 68); **1950:** 2, 9 (pp. 73, 75)

See also Health insurance; Health programs; Medical care.

Approval of bill, **1946:** 203

Campaign remarks, **1948:** 205, 212 [4], 228 [12], 236, 237 [3], 268

Construction, **1948:** 89; **1949:** 8 (p. 70), 85; **1950:** 134; **1951:** 13 (p. 99), 135; **1952–53:** 15, 268 [8], 273, 284, 366, 367 (pp. 1156, 1157), 376

Expansion, **1948:** 257 [3]

Federal aid, **1945:** 192; **1948:** 5 (pp. 35, 37); **1950:** 9 (pp. 50, 73, 75); **1951:** 135, 307; **1952–53:** 249, 268 [8], 273, 284 [5], 366, 369

Federal Narcotics Hospital, **1951:** 201

Indians, New Mexico, **1949:** 248

Infantile paralysis, **1947:** 17

Military, **1949:** 34

Personnel shortage, **1952–53:** 367 (p. 1158)

Rural, **1948:** 242 [3]

Shortage, **1948:** 181 [2], 233 [6], 241, 257 [1]; **1949:** 2, 85, 219; **1950:** 129 [4]

Veterans, **1945:** 112, 128; **1946:** 18 (p. 79), 195; **1947:** 5, 7 (pp. 70, 72), 131, 134, 181 (pp. 398, 404); **1948:** 5 (pp. 21, 33, 34), 218 [5]; **1949:** 8 (pp. 47, 62, 64–65), 11 [11], 49n., 104, 192 [17]; **1950:** 9 (p. 70), 137 [10], 146 [14], 156, 203 [3], 233; **1951:** 101 [1], 260; **1952–53:** 18 (p. 110), 135, 212, 367 (p. 1160)

Virgin Islands, **1948:** 146

Houghton, Amory, **1950:** 185

Houmann, Borge, **1946:** 6 [18]

Hours of work, reduction, **1945:** 175 [11], 180

Government employees, **1945:** 48, 70, 107 [1]

House of Commons, **1945:** 181 [3]

Household furnishings, prices, **1947:** 76, 214

"Housewives for Truman," 1948 campaign, **1948:** 264 [3]

Housing, **1945:** 128; **1946:** 2, 18 (pp. 48, 49, 62, 63), 52, 67, 73, 116, 124, 164, 262 [6]; **1947:** 4 (pp. 15, 22, 24, 25, 26, 28, 30), 7 (pp. 73, 92), 18, 35, 76, 80, 110, 152, 173, 174 [1]; **1948:** 2, 5 (pp. 20, 21, 25, 37), 8 (pp. 63, 67, 74, 83, 84), 32, 101, 172, 175, 200 [5], 231 [1, 8], 234, 236, 257 [2, 4], 258, 261 [1];

Housing — *continued*
1949: 2, 5, 8 (pp. 45, 47, 72–76), 54, 126, 151, 154, 157, 250 [3], 256; **1950:** 9 (pp. 49, 50, 77–82), 69, 93, 114, 134; **1951:** 13 (pp. 90–94), 106); **1952–53:** 5, 18 (pp. 95–99), 69, 120, 215, 218, 296
Administration programs, Republican opposition, **1952–53:** 218
Alaska, **1948:** 105; **1950:** 112; **1951:** 118 [5]; **1952–53:** 18 (p. 99)
Appropriations, **1947:** 131
Building materials, controls, **1945:** 208 [5], 211 [1]
Carver Village project, bombing of, **1952–53:** 290
Census statistics on, **1952–53:** 363n.
Construction, **1947:** 2 (pp. 3, 6), 131; **1948:** 5 (p. 37), 8 (pp. 83, 84), 150 [1], 165, 167, 172, 248, 259 [6]; **1950:** 2, 9 (pp. 77, 80, 97), 93, 110 [2], 121 [9], 128, 192; **1951:** 13 (pp. 48, 90, 92, 93), 111 167; **1952–53:** 15, 18 (p. 95), 215, 276, 366, 367 (pp. 1152–1155)
Cooperative, **1950:** 9 (p. 79), 132
Credit, **1950:** 9 (p. 46), 112, 118, 194, 243; **1951:** 11, 12 [67], 13 (pp. 45, 47, 92–94), 118 [5]; **1952–53:** 18 (pp. 97, 98), 120, 123 [18], 190
Controls, **1950:** 192, 202, 215
Defense, **1951:** 4, 11, 12 [6], 13 (pp. 19, 80, 90–92), 15, 107, 111, 211, 285; **1952–53:** 5, 15, 18 (pp. 97, 102), 231, 367 (pp. 1152–1154)
Demand for, **1951:** 167; **1952–53:** 237
Educational institutions, **1952–53:** 18 (p. 99)
Colleges, **1947:** 7 (p. 69), 44; **1948:** 183 [2]
Construction loans, **1951:** 12 [6], 13 (pp. 93, 94); **1952–53:** 367 (p. 1154)
Election, effect on program, **1948:** 41 [17]
Equal opportunity, **1947:** 130; **1948:** 20; **1952–53:** 169, 290
Expenditures for, **1952–53:** 231, 369 (pp. 1152–1154)
Farm, **1951:** 13 (pp. 90, 93); **1952–53:** 126
Federal aid, **1948:** 5 (p. 38), 163 [13]; **1949:** 8 (pp. 72–76), 54, 126, 157
Fire prevention, **1947:** 86
Government programs, special interest opposition to, **1952–53:** 194
Home ownership, increase, **1952–53:** 376
Housing bills, **1946:** 78 [20], 119 [13], 178, 186 [8], 215 [6], 258, 263; **1947:** 2 (p. 7), 65, 95 [19], 131; **1948:** 92, 110 [2], 134, 138 [6, 8], 139 [1, 2], 150 [1], 183 [1, 2, 5], 199, 202 [2], 203, 205, 225 [1–3], 227 [6], 228 [3], 229, 238, 242 [3], 261 [7], 268; **1949:** 148 [22], 236 [9]
Taft-Ellender-Wagner bill.
See Taft-Ellender-Wagner housing bill.
Indiana, **1951:** 171 [6]
Integration, **1949:** 267 [18], 269 [11]
Investment in, **1948:** 8 (p. 84)

Housing — *continued*
Issue in election campaign, **1952–53:** 278
Legislation, proposed, **1950:** 9 (p. 77), 86 [21], 93, 110 [5]
Low-income, **1949:** 5, 8 (pp. 75, 76), 219; **1950:** 2, 6, 9 (pp. 77, 79), 93, 127 [4, 5], 128, 134; **1951:** 13 (p. 90), 111; **1952–53:** 169, 241, 273, 278, 313 [4], 321 [2], 366, 367 (p. 1153)
Lustron Corp., question of RFC loan to, **1950:** 29 [16], 217 [17]
Messages to Congress, **1947:** 44; **1948:** 37, 165
Military personnel, **1948:** 5 (p. 28); **1949:** 8 (p. 60); **1950:** 32; **1952–53:** 5
Mortgage insurance, **1947:** 221 [11]; **1948:** 5 (pp. 38, 39), 37, 150 [1], 175, 227 [9]
News conference remarks, **1945:** 208 [5, 19], 211 [1]; **1946:** 75 [27, 30], 78 [20], 86 [18], 119 [3, 13], 163 [2], 250 [8], 257 [6, 11], 262 [11], 266 [12]; **1949:** 148 [22], 179 [9], 236 [9], 267 [4, 18], 269 [11]; **1950:** 29 [16], 86 [21], 117 [17]
Patman bill, **1945:** 208 [19]
Prefabricated, **1946:** 258, 263; **1947:** 14 [12]; **1950:** 29 [16], 113; **1951:** 13 (p. 90)
Price controls, **1945:** 208 [19], 211 [1]; **1946:** 18 (p. 62), 35, 67, 250 [8]; **1948:** 5 (pp. 38, 40), 8 (p. 84), 37, 189, 205, 220, 262; **1951:** 13 (p. 93); **1952–53:** 18 (p. 97), 366, 367 (p. 1154)
Public, **1948:** 5 (p. 40), 183 [6]; **1949:** 5, 8 (pp. 74–75), 126, 267 [18]; **1950:** 9 (pp. 54, 80), 135; **1951:** 13 (pp. 93, 94), 171 [6], 111, 171 [6], 174; **1952–53:** 18 (p. 98), 120, 169, 241, 276, 289 [3], 298 [14], 304, 366, 367 (pp. 1153–1154)
Rent control.
See main heading, Rent control.
Rental units, **1946:** 18 (p. 63), 257 [6], 258, 263; **1947:** 2 (p. 7), 4 (p. 30), 7 (pp. 74, 76), 44, 65, 131; **1949:** 2, 5, 8 (pp. 74, 75), 39, 54, 126, 157; **1950:** 93, 121 [11], 157; **1951:** 11, 13 (p. 92)
See also Rental housing.
Reorganization Plan, **1947:** 102
Reports, **1946:** 32, 250 [8]
Research, **1948:** (p. 38), 8 (p. 84); **1950:** 9 (p. 81)
Richard Allen Project, Philadelphia, Pa., **1948:** 225 (2)
Rural, **1945:** 128; **1947:** 131; **1948:** 5 (p. 38), 8 (pp. 83, 84), 99, 117, 165, 172, 205, 216 [3], 220, 227 [2], 231 [2, 3, 5, 6], 235 [4], 237 [4, 5], 238, 249, 257 [4], 264 [1]; **1949:** 2, 8 (pp. 74, 76), 126, 157; **1950:** 6, 9 (p. 80), 110 [9]
See also Rural areas.
Shortage, **1945:** 212; **1947:** 2 (p. 2), 131; **1948:** 5 (p. 52), 8 (p. 83), 121, 134, 165, 183 [1], 194

Housing — *continued*
  Shortage — *continued*
    [3], 199, 203, 205, 206 [1], 227 [2, 3, 7], 235
      [4], 237 [4], 252, 257 [1, 3], 259 [3], 261 [2,
      7–9], 264 [1], 267 [2]
  Slum.
    See Slum clearance.
  Statements, **1946:** 32, 46, 258, 263
  Urban.
    See under Urban areas.
  Veterans, **1945:** 211 [1], 212; **1946:** 18 (p. 62), 32,
      46, 48, 67, 75 [30], 94, 116, 152, 153, 178,
      182, 193, 195, 226 [1], 249, 257 [6], 258,
      263; **1947:** 2 (p. 6), 4 (pp. 25, 30), 7 (pp.
      58, 69, 74, 75, 94), 18, 44, 60, 131, 181 (pp.
      398, 405); **1948:** 2, 5 (pp. 25, 37, 40, 41),
      37, 150 [1], 165, 175, 183 [1, 2], 203, 205,
      220, 227 [7], 228 [10], 231 [3], 259 [3, 4];
      1949: 179 [9]; **1950:** 9 (pp. 69, 70, 78, 79,
      81); **1951:** 13 (pp. 93, 94), 111, 171 [6],
      174; **1952–53:** 18 (p. 98), 231, 366, 367 (p.
      1152, 1153)
  War-built, **1948:** 5 (pp. 40, 41)
Housing Act, National, **1947:** 221 [11]; **1948:** 37
Housing Act of 1937, **1949:** 54, 126
Housing Act of 1948, **1949:** 8 (p. 72)
  Approval, **1948:** 172
Housing Act of 1949, **1949:** 65, 126; **1951:** 111;
      1952–53: 120, 367 (p. 1154)
Housing Act of 1950, **1951:** 13 (p. 93)
Housing acts, **1950:** 2, 68, 69, 86ftn. (p. 254), 93n.,
      113, 118, 292
Housing Administration, Public.
  See Public Housing Administration.
Housing Agency, National, **1947:** 131
Housing Authority, Alaska, **1949:** 8 (p. 75)
Housing Authority, U.S., **1946:** 116; **1947:** 102
Housing Conference, National, address, **1952–53:**
      120
Housing Corporation, U.S., termination, **1946:** 116
Housing Council, National, **1947:** 102, 173; **1948:** 5
      (p. 38); **1950:** 112
Housing Expediters, **1945:** 211 [1]
  Creedon, Frank R., **1947:** 205 (8, 10, 17); **1948:** 5
      (pp. 40, 52), 58
  Woods, Tighe E., **1948:** 71 [13, 15]; **1951:** 12 [55];
      1950: 93, 278 [5]; **1949:** 22 [5], 65, 179 [9],
      182 [4]
  Wyatt, Wilson W., **1946:** 48; **1947:** 60
    News conference remarks on, **1946:** 70 [19], 75
      [27], 86 [18], 250 [8], 257 [6]
    Reports, **1946:** 32, 250 [8]
    Resignation, **1946:** 258, 259
Housing and Home Finance Agency, **1947:** 102,
      131n., 173; **1948:** 37, 62, 111; **1950:** 53,
      112, 114; **1951:** 211, 303; **1952–53:** 18 (p.
      100), 221 [1]
  Reorganization, **1950:** 69, 113

Housing and Home Finance Agency, Administra-
      tor (Raymond M. Foley), **1947:** 173, 174
      [1]; **1948:** 5 (pp. 38, 40), 111; **1949:** 8 (p.
      72), 148 [22], 156, 157, 267 [18], 269 [11];
      1950: 9 (p. 81), 192, 259; **1951:** 11, 111,
      163, 196, 303; **1952–53:** 120n.
Housing and Rent Act, **1949:** 54n.
  Approval, **1947:** 131; **1948:** 58; **1948:** 58
Houston, Charles H., resignation from Committee
      on Fair Employment Practice, **1945:** 208
      [18]
Houston, Frank, **1948:** 138
Houston, John, **1947:** 145 [2]
Houston, Tex., **1952–53:** 197 [12]
Howard, Nathaniel R., **1948:** 80n.
Howard, Roy, **1951:** 298 [1]
Howard University, **1947:** 7 (p. 77); **1948:** 5 (p. 42);
      1949: 8 (p. 76); **1952–53:** 169, 367 (p.
      1155)
Howell, Repr. Charles R., **1952–53:** 303 [6]
Howington, James T., letter, **1945:** 228
Howitzer carriages, World War II contract for,
      1951: 284
Howse, Alfred E., **1951:** 196
Hoyer, Eric G., **1949:** 250
Hoyt, Palmer, **1947:** 148n.; **1948:** 7n.
Huber, Repr. Walter B., **1948:** 257 [5], 258
Hudson, Henry, **1952–53:** 74
Hudson, N.Y., campaign remarks, **1952–53:** 289
      [10]
Hudson County, N.J., **1948:** 189
Hudson River, **1952–53:** 74
Huffman, James W., **1947:** 182 [11]
Hughes, Charles Evans, **1949:** 103n.; **1951:** 295 [8]
  Death of, **1948:** 180
Hughes, Howard, **1950:** 217ftn. (p. 593)
Hughes, R. O., **1950:** 209ftn. (p. 580)
Hughes, Sarah, **1950:** 253 [14]
Hulihan, Mrs. Albert C., **1949:** 219n.
Hull, Cordell, **1945:** 10, 100n.; **1946:** 83; **1947:** 39,
      52, 73, 74; **1948:** 213, 245, 266; **1950:** 80
      [1], 97 [17]; **1951:** 200 [13]
  News conference remarks on, **1945:** 60 [1], 67 [1],
      118 [2, 12]
Human rights, **1947:** 21, 138, 153, 185, 188, 215,
      224; **1948:** 2, 20, 130 [3]
  See also Civil rights.
  Violations by Hungary, **1951:** 173
Human Rights, Covenant on, **1950:** 174
Human Rights, Declaration of, **1949:** 237, 254, 256;
      1950: 2, 126, 138, 174
Human Rights, United Nations Commission on,
      1947: 130, 138; **1948:** 30; **1949:** 237, 256
Humanitarian Award dinner, Variety Clubs of
      America, **1945:** 88; **1948:** 196
Humphrey, George D., **1950:** 119n.
Humphrey, George M., **1947:** 236 [3], 237

Humphrey, Hubert H., **1948:** 235 [5], 236, 237 [1–4]; **1949:** 148 [2], 250; **1950:** 46 [1], 129 [7], 146 [7], 152 [1]; **1951:** 153 [8], 193 [19]; **1952–53:** 3, 7 [3], 115 [8], 204, 297, 313 [1, 4, 5, 6], 314

   Democratic National Convention, suggested appointment as keynoter, **1952–53:** 88 [15]

   Former Presidents, proposed Senate membership for, **1952–53:** 75 [8]

Humphrey, Tom, **1952–53:** 233ftn. (p. 530)

Humphrey's Executor v. U.S., cited, **1948:** 102

Hungarian Federation, American, **1951:** 253

Hungary, **1946:** 18 (pp. 41, 42); **1947:** 107 [8]

   Agreements on, **1945:** 91, 97

   Armed forces, **1951:** 174

   Communism in, **1947:** 107 [8]; **1949:** 30ftn. (p. 131); **1951:** 173, 253

   Conspiracy and espionage trials, **1951:** 153 [4]

   Mass deportations in, **1951:** 153 [16], 173, 253n.; **1952–53:** 145

   Mindszenty, Cardinal Josef, arrest of, **1948:** 288 [1]; **1949:** 28 [19], 30 [9]

   Nagy, Ferenc, **1947:** 107 [8]

   Peace treaty with, **1947:** 2 (p. 9), 114

   Soviet domination, **1948:** 53, 86

Hungry Horse, Mont., campaign remarks, **1952–53:** 270 [2]

Hungry Horse Dam, **1949:** 32 [16], 77; **1950:** 124 [7], 125, 127 [1, 2]; **1952–53:** 268 [5], 271, 388

Hunsaker, Jerome C., **1947:** 115n.; **1952–53:** 40

Hunt, Col. James V., **1949:** 171 [7, 15]

Hunt, Lester C., **1948:** 118 [5, 7]; **1949:** 112 [7]; **1951:** 54n.

Huntington, Oreg., **1950:** 121 [7]

Huntington, W. Va., campaign remarks, **1948:** 229 [9]

Hurley, Patrick J., **1945:** 202 [6, 11], 208 [12]; **1949:** 171 [1]

Hursh, Vern, **1948:** 202 [1]

Hutcheson, Joseph C., **1945:** 210; **1946:** 89

Hutcheson, William L., **1946:** 53 [6]; **1947:** 236 [3], 237

Hutchinson, Martin A., **1950:** 52 [1], 169 [4], 186 [2, 7], 206 [15], 209 [6, 17]

Hutchinson, Kans., **1951:** 185

   Campaign remarks, **1948:** 137 [2]

Hutchison, Claude B., **1946:** 265

Hutchison, Knox T., **1952–53:** 126n.

Hutson, John B., **1945:** 52 [7]

Hyde, Rosel H., **1946:** 66 [1]

Hyde Park, N.Y., **1946:** 81n., 118; **1947:** 71; **1951:** 251 [27]

Hyde Park Agreement (1941), **1947:** 111

Hydroelectric dams, Soviet, war destruction of, **1947:** 226 [10]

Hydroelectric power projects, **1947:** 7 (p. 81), 144,

Hydroelectric power projects — *continued* 177 [3]; **1948:** 2, 5 (p. 46), 6, 8 (p. 80); **1949:** 43; **1950:** 2, 9 (p. 90), 121 [8], 124 [7], 127 [1, 2, 4], 128, 129 [1, 3, 5], 134, 157, 171

   See also Power projects.

   Bay of Fundy, **1950:** 121 [4, 13]

   Boulder Dam, **1950:** 3 [9]

   Campaign remarks, **1948:** 119, 125, 175, 176, 198 [6], 199, 200 [1], 201, 202 [1, 4], 203, 233 [6]

   Central Valley, Calif., **1950:** 3 [9]

   Colorado-Big Thompson, **1948:** 199

   Colorado River, **1950:** 121 [13]

   Columbia River, **1950:** 3 [9], 121 [11, 13], 125

   Connecticut River, **1950:** 121 [4]

   Creston, Iowa, **1950:** 110 [4]

   Cumberland River, **1950:** 3 [5]

   Folsom Dam, **1948:** 6

   Grand Coulee Dam, **1948:** 122 [4]; **1949:** 106; **1950:** 124 [1, 4], 125

   Grand River, **1948:** 216 [11]

   Gunnison-Arkansas project, **1948:** 198 [5]

   Mississippi Valley, **1950:** 3 [9, 11], 121 [13]

   Missouri Valley, **1950:** 3 [9, 11], 121 [13]

   New England, **1950:** 3 [5, 9, 15], 33, 34 [10], 140

   News conference remarks, **1950:** 3 [5, 6, 9, 11, 12, 15, 21], 34 [10], 46 [2]

   Niagara River, **1950:** 3 [9, 12], 46 [2], 99, 265

   Ohio Valley, **1950:** 3 [9, 11], 121 [13]

   Oklahoma, **1950:** 3 [9]

   Passamaquoddy tidal power project, **1948:** 55 [8], 93 [11]; **1950:** 121 [4, 13]

   Role in Latin American economy, **1948:** 69

   St. Lawrence Seaway and power project, **1948:** 12, 93 [7, 10], 181 [10], 235 [5], 278 [39], 285 [9]; **1949:** 5, 7 [24], 30 [6]; **1950:** 2, 3 [6, 9, 12, 15], 6, 9 (p. 94), 33, 121 [4, 13], 140, 265

   Savannah River, **1950:** 3 [9], 121 [13]

   Snake River, **1950:** 3 [9]

   South Carolina, **1950:** 3 [9], 121 [13]

   Tennessee Valley Authority, **1948:** 109, 236, 258; **1950:** 121 [4, 13]

   Texas, **1950:** 3 [9]

   Weber Basin, Utah, **1949:** 196

   Western, **1950:** 116

   Wyoming, **1950:** 117 [4]

Hydrogen bomb.

   See also Atomic bomb.

   Control, **1950:** 23 [17], 29 [10, 12]

     U.S.-Soviet negotiations, question of, **1950:** 16 [5]

   News conference remarks, **1950:** 3 [10], 16 [5, 18], 23 [14, 17], 29 [10, 12, 20], 34 [14]

   U.S. development, **1950:** 3 [10], 16 [18], 23 [14], 26, 29 [20], 34 [14], 187

Hydrographic Office, **1946:** 118

Ibarra Garcia, Oscar (Ambassador from Argentina), **1945:** 22 [13]
Ibn-Saud, Abdul-Aziz, **1945:** 147 [3, 13]; **1946:** 110 [13], 241; **1947:** 33
IBRD.
    See International Bank for Reconstruction and Development.
Icarus, **1952–53:** 125
ICC.
    See Interstate Commerce Commission.
Ice Harbor power project, **1951:** 13 (p. 85); **1952–53:** 18 (p. 88), 367 (p. 1146)
Iceland, **1945:** 107 [21]
    Assistance, **1947:** 238
    Bjarni Benediktsson, **1949:** 68
Ickes, Harold L., **1946:** 53 [7], 78 [4]; **1952–53:** 146, 266 [10], 292n.
    See also Interior, Secretary of the (Harold L. Ickes).
    Column by, **1948:** 278 [38]
Idaho
    Addresses or remarks in, **1950:** 121 [1–5], 124 [7]
    Campaign remarks, **1948:** 119, 120 [1–4]; **1952–53:** 270 [9, 10]
    Candidates for public office, **1952–53:** 270 [9, 10]
    Floods, control and relief, **1952–53:** 270 [9]
    Gov. C.A. Robins, **1948:** 120n.
    News conference remarks, **1950:** 105 [16], 209 [9]
    Power projects, **1952–53:** 270 [9], 367 (p. 1146)
Idlewild International Airport, dedication, **1948:** 168
Ijams, George E., **1945:** 24
Illinois, **1947:** 104, 221 [5]; **1949:** 122ftn. (p. 292), 211 [2]; **1950:** 110 [1, 9], 121 [8]
    Campaign remarks, **1948:** 138 [4], 194 [1], 218 [1–3, 5–8], 219, 233 [4–7], 234, 256, 267 [3]; **1952–53:** 315 [5, 6], 316, 321 [3–7]
    Candidates for public office, **1948:** 194 [1], 218 [1, 6–8], 219, 233 [4–6], 234, 256, 267 [3]; **1950:** 16 [13]; **1951:** 171 [8]; **1952–53:** 315 [6], 321 [3–7]
    Chicago.
        See main heading, Chicago.
    Eisenhower, Gen. Dwight D., campaign remarks in, comment on, **1952–53:** 317 [2]
    Federal judgeships, nominations for, **1951:** 179 [8], 227 [11, 13, 17]
    Floods, **1951:** 162, 185
    Gov. Dwight H. Green, **1948:** 115
    Gov. Adlai E. Stevenson.
        See Stevenson, Adlai E.
    Judiciary, Federal, vacancies, **1952–53:** 35 [4, 7], 88 [8]
    Methodist ministers from, remarks, **1951:** 31
    National Guard, **1952–53:** 290
    News conference remarks, **1950:** 16 [13], 169 [6, 10]
    Primary elections, **1952–53:** 21 [12]

Illinois — *continued*
    Sabath, Repr. Adolph, **1945:** 51
    State fair, **1951:** 140 [17]
Illinois Bar Association, **1951:** 165ftn. (p. 403)
Illiteracy in U.S., reduction, **1948:** 215
ILO.
    See International Labor Organization.
Immigration laws, **1946:** 136 [14], 227; **1948:** 142, 160, 165, 236, 249, 257 [1]
Immigration and Nationality Act, **1952–53:** 136 [5], 166 [15], 291, 292 [5], 289 [7], 297, 298 [14], 300, 301, 303 [4], 367 (pp. 1141, 1163), 373
    Veto of proposed revision, **1952–53:** 182
Immigration and Nationality Lawyers, Association of, remarks, **1952–53:** 350
Immigration and Naturalization, President's Commission on, **1952–53:** 244, 251, 364, 367 (p. 1163), 373
Immigration and Naturalization Service, **1946:** 237 [17]; **1948:** 174 [4]; **1950:** 153; **1951:** 154; **1952–53:** 18 (p. 94), 367 (p. 1163)
    Study on admission of immigrants from Europe, **1945:** 225
Immigration to U.S., **1952–53:** 136 [5], 350
    Anti-foreign hysteria, history of, **1952–53:** 288
    Asian, **1952–53:** 182
    Baltic escapees, **1948:** 174 [4], 178 [12], 283 [5]
    Communist defectors, **1950:** 254
    Defense workers, **1951:** 15
    Displaced persons, **1946:** 18 (p. 44), 136 [14], 212, 227, 241, 267; **1947:** 2 (p. 10), 95 [22, 24], 140, 182 [10]; **1948:** 2, 115, 142, 160, 165, 249, 256, 257 [1], 258, 261 [7]; **1949:** 2, 58 [5, 31], 144 [2]; **1950:** 2, 134, 167; **1952–53:** 65, 94
        Statement and directive, **1945:** 225
    Drug addicts, deportation, **1952–53:** 182
    European, **1952–53:** 182, 291, 317 [7]
    Greek, **1952–53:** 182
    Indians and Chinese, **1946:** 6 [12]
    Investigations and clearances, **1952–53:** 367 (p. 1141)
    Issue in election campaign, **1952–53:** 298 [9, 14], 300
    Italian, **1951:** 235; **1952–53:** 182
    Laws, **1949:** 58 [5], 144 [2]; **1950:** 2, 134, 167, 207, 254; **1952–53:** 65, 166 [15], 182, 244, 251, 288, 291, 292 [5], 297, 298 [9, 14], 299, 300, 307, 317 [7], 373
    Migratory workers, **1950:** 153; **1951:** 75, 154, 192; **1952–53:** 21 [26]
    Orphans, **1948:** 142
    Quotas, **1945:** 225; **1948:** 142; **1952–53:** 182, 244, 288, 289, 299
    Refugees and escapees, **1946:** 237 [17]; **1947:** 140; **1948:** 142, 174 [4], 178 [12]; **1952–53:** 288

Immigration to U.S. — *continued*
  Republican stand on, **1952–53:** 288, 291, 292 [5], 301
  Scandinavian, **1948:** 59
  Subversives, exclusion, **1950:** 254
  Transportation facilities, **1952–53:** 182
  Turkish, **1952–53:** 182
Impellitteri, Vincent R., **1952–53:** 63n., 290n., 291n.
Imports **1946:** 18 (p. 69); **1947:** 4 (p. 37), 35, 152; **1948:** 8 (pp. 63, 96, 97), 42; **1949:** 5, 122 [9], 151, 195; **1950:** 130, 159; **1952–53:** 215
  See also Balance of payments; *Specific commodities.*
  Canadian, **1947:** 111
    Natural gas, **1952–53:** 377 [25]
  Cobalt, **1950:** 124 [7]
  Controls, **1945:** 202 [3]; **1947:** 18, 64, 99, 143; **1948:** 5 (pp. 52, 53), 23, 42
  Copper, proposed suspension of tax, **1950:** 209 [10], 231, 250 [18], 318 [13]; **1951:** 11
  Critical materials, **1952–53:** 15
  Dairy products, **1951:** 199; **1952–53:** 359 [2, 14], 360
  Defense materials, **1952–53:** 33
  European, **1947:** 238
  Filberts, shelled, **1952–53:** 302
  Food, **1947:** 220
  Increase, **1951:** 11; **1952–53:** 15
  Iron ore, **1951:** 11; **1952–53:** 175ftn. (p. 432)
  Mexican livestock, **1946:** 232
  Mineral, **1948:** 8 (p. 67); **1952–53:** 15, 55, 57
  NATO countries, **1952–53:** 15
  News conference remarks, **1950:** 23 [9], 29 [25], 209 [10], 230 [6], 250 [18], 318 [13]
  Oil, **1950:** 23 [9], 29 [25]; **1951:** 199
  Petroleum products, **1952–53:** 239
  Raw materials, growth of, **1952–53:** 192
  Sugar, **1947:** 64
  War materials, **1947:** 72
  Wheat from Argentina, **1946:** 86 [27]
  Wool, **1947:** 128; **1952–53:** 359 [15]
Inaugural, **1949:** 52 [5]; **1952–53:** 353 [15], 377 [6, 8, 15, 20]
  Address, **1949:** 19
  Government holiday for, question of, **1948:** 278 [17]
  Greetings from Governor Dewey, message, **1949:** 14
  Parade, **1949:** 22 [14]
  Platform, nickname for, **1948:** 274 [19]
  Preparations for, **1948:** 285 [12]
Inchon, Korea, **1950:** 268
Income
  Business, unincorporated, **1952–53:** 15
  Consumers, **1948:** 167
  Corporate, **1948:** 268; **1951:** 122, 127 [4]; **1952–53:** 17 [24], 33

Income — *continued*
  Farm, **1949:** 2, 90; **1950:** 6, 111, 121 [7], 122, 127 [4, 5], 134, 202; **1951:** 199, 202; **1952–53:** 15, 289 [1, 2], 293, 367 (p. 1148)
    See also Farm economy.
  Government officials, **1952–53:** 258 [13]
    Disclosure by, proposed legislation, **1951:** 237, 239 [3]
  National.
    See main heading, National income.
  Personal, **1948:** 2, 5 (p. 23), 21 [12], 37, 63, 99, 107, 175, 176, 182, 183 [6], 184, 195, 228 [1, 5]; **1949:** 5, 7 [45], 77, 151; **1950:** 2, 6, 8 [18, 21], 84, 111, 121 [5], 122, 127 [4], 134, 202; **1951:** 11, 12 [8], 91, 123, 159, 167, 176, 215, 221, 279; **1952–53:** 15, 17 [24], 33, 63, 69, 98 [10], 194, 215, 270 [7], 272, 273, 277 [5], 292 [9], 293, 305, 313 [5], 314, 315 [5], 319, [1], 321 [1, 5], 349, 366, 376, 378
  Professional, **1952–53:** 15
  Western Hemisphere, **1951:** 59
Income taxes, **1947:** 9 (p. 92), 152, 181 (p. 402), 210 [3]; **1948:** 2, 4 [5, 8, 18], 5 (pp. 23, 57), 8 (p. 94), 11 [14]; **1949:** 2, 8 (p. 49); **1950:** 9 (pp. 52, 53), 18, 202, 243; **1951:** 13 (p. 65), 28, 228, 264; **1952–53:** 110, 231
  Increase, proposed, **1949:** 5, 11 [6]; **1950:** 200; **1952–53:** 367 (p. 1132)
  News conference remarks, **1949:** 7 [8, 18, 36, 37], 11 [6]; **1950:** 8 [36, 38], 152 [9], 203 [9], 217 [12]
  Reduction, **1948:** 5 (p. 23), 8 (p. 71), 63, 167
    Disapproval, **1947:** 116, 145 [10], 147
  Refund to Indians, disapproval, **1947:** 163
  Returns, inspection by Senate committees, **1950:** 152 [9], 217 [12]
Indemnity Act of 1951, Servicemen's, **1952–53:** 367 (p. 1160)
Independence, Mo., **1945:** 67; **1946:** 61 [21]; **1948:** 246; **1949:** 40 [16], 271; **1950:** 21n.; **1952–53:** 63, 149 [19], 170
  Campaign remarks, **1948:** 269
  Christmas message from, **1948:** 287
  Liberty Bell replica, gift from France, **1950:** 270 [12], 273 [16], 280, 281
  Mayor Roger T. Sermon, **1948:** 270n.
  Mayor Robert P. Weatherford, **1950:** 280, 281
  News conference remarks, **1945:** 8 [2], 64 [9], 76 [9]; **1950:** 270 [12], 273 [16], 309 [11]
  Note on First National Bank, gift to President, **1948:** 271 [2]
  Postelection remarks in, **1948:** 270
  President's homecoming after assuming office, **1948:** 138 [1]
  Return to, the President's, **1952–53:** 75 [7], 342 [17], 377 [19]

Independence, Mo. — *continued*
  Truman family dentist in, **1951:** 258
  Truman Library, **1950:** 43n., 79n.; **1951:** 251
      [27]; **1952–53:** 334ftn. (p. 1059)
  Visit to, question of, **1948:** 285 [17]
  William Chrisman High School, **1952–53:** 173
Independence Day, **1952–53:** 197 [14]
Independence Hall, Philadelphia, **1950:** 281
Independence of nations, **1951:** 4, 59, 114, 116,
    216; **1952–53:** 88, 366
Independent Offices Appropriation Act, **1951:** 111,
    254; **1952–53:** 201
Independent Order of Odd Fellows, International
    Council, **1951:** 220
India, **1946:** 78 [14], 85; **1948:** 20
  Ambassador, appointment, **1947:** 36 [6], 67 [3]
  Assistance, **1952–53:** 205, 242 [2]
    Economic, **1952–53:** 18 (p. 76), 367 (p. 1140)
    Technical, **1952–53:** 57
  Communism in, **1952–53:** 144, 303 [2]
  Conference on Japanese peace treaty, refusal to
      attend, **1951:** 209 [16]
  Dispute with Pakistan, **1948:** 202 [6]; **1950:** 143
  Economic development, **1951:** 34, 63 [2]
  Ewing, Oscar R., visit of, **1952–53:** 334 [10]
  Exchange programs with, **1951:** 124
  Food relief for, **1951:** 33 [9], 34, 63 [2], 124
  Food supply, **1952–53:** 5, 55, 57, 144
  Gandhi, Mohandas K., statement on assassina-
      tion, **1948:** 17
  Immigration of persons to U.S., **1946:** 6 [12]
  Independence, **1950:** 20, 119; **1951:** 34
  Industry, **1951:** 34
  Korean prisoner-of-war camps, investigation of
      uprising in, **1952–53:** 162
  Korean war, participation, **1951:** 170
  Lend-lease settlement, **1947:** 7 (p. 65)
  Malaria prevention, **1950:** 177
  Mineral resources, **1951:** 34
  Motion picture industry representatives, re-
      marks, **1952–53:** 256
  Mountbatten, Earl (Governor General), **1948:** 17
  Natural disasters, **1951:** 34, 63 [2], 124
  Nehru, Jawaharlal, **1949:** 45 [19], 227, 231 [10,
      22], 236 [5], 252, 264
  Pandit, Madam Vijaya Lakshmir, **1949:** 256
  Point 4 program in, **1952–53:** 55, 57
  Prasad, Rajendra, **1950:** 20
  Rice crop failure, **1946:** 30 [2], 86 [4]
  U.N. police action in Korea, support of, **1950:**
      179 [16]
      Hospital units, participation, **1950:** 296
India Emergency Food Aid Act of 1951, **1951:** 124
Indian Affairs, Bureau of, **1946:** 18 (p. 82); **1947:**
    229; **1952–53:** 18 (p. 106)
Indian Claims Commission, **1946:** 204
Indian Wars, **1947:** 181 (p. 405); **1951:** 181

Indiana, **1947:** 104; **1949:** 122 [16]
  Campaign remarks, **1948:** 114 [2, 3], 138 [5–7],
      218 [9, 10], 233 [1–3], 240, 241, 254, 255,
      257 [1, 2], 267 [2]; **1952–53:** 286 [1–3], 311
      [3], 312, 321, [1, 2]
  Candidates for public office, **1948:** 218 [10], 233
      [1–3], 240, 254, 255, 257 [1, 2], 267 [2];
      1950: 16 [11]; **1952–53:** 107 [5], 286 [1–3],
      311, 312, 321 [2]
  Gov. Henry F. Schricker, **1950:** 203 [16]; **1952–
      53:** 286 [1–3], 311 [3], 312, 321 [2]
  Housing in, **1951:** 171 [6]
  News conference remarks, **1950:** 16 [11], 169 [4]
  Postelection remarks in, **1948:** 271 [2]
  "Wallaceites" (Henry Wallace), attacks on, **1948:**
      71 [2]
Indianapolis, Ind., **1950:** 203 [16]
  Campaign remarks, **1948:** 138 [6], 240 [7], 241;
      1952–53: 286 [1]
  Mayor Al Feeney, **1948:** 138 [6], 240 [7], 241
Indianapolis Times, **1952–53:** 319 [5]
Indians
  Apache, **1948:** 208 [2]
  Attacks on forebears, recollections of the Pres-
      ident, **1951:** 289
  Blackfoot tribe, gifts to the President, **1950:** 127
      [7]
  Cherokee, letter from Jefferson, **1950:** 12
  Credit facilities for, **1951:** 13 (p. 87); **1952–53:** 18
      (p. 90)
  Economic rehabilitation, **1950:** 91
  Education, **1947:** 7 (p. 77); **1949:** 8 (p. 76); **1950:**
      91
  Hopi, **1947:** 229n.; **1948:** 40; **1949:** 226 [19], 231
      [23], 233; **1950:** 9 (p. 91), 91; **1952–53:** 46
  Income tax refund, veto, **1947:** 163
  Klamath, capital reserve funds, **1948:** 57
  Land resources development, **1950:** 9 (p. 91);
      1952–53: 18 (p. 90), 231
  Medical care, **1949:** 248
  Navajo, **1947:** 229; **1948:** 40; **1949:** 226 [19], 231
      [23], 233; **1950:** 9 (p. 91), 91; **1952–53:** 46
  Property rights, **1946:** 204
  Red Cross services for, **1948:** 40
  Reservations
    Highway construction on, **1948:** 24
    Land disposal, veto, **1948:** 25
  Salish and Kootenai tribes, claims against U.S.,
      1946: 151
  Self-government, **1950:** 91
  Sioux, **1948:** 118 [1]
  Utes, use of tribal funds, approval, **1951:** 198
  Welfare programs, **1952–53:** 18 (p. 106), 367 (p.
      1158)
Individual Rights, Commission on Internal Secu-
    rity and, **1951:** 278
Indochina, **1945:** 107 [21]; **1946:** 30 [2], 86 [4], 265;
    1952–53: 18 (p. 76), 175 [4]

Indochina — *continued*
  Assistance, **1952–53:** 5, 18 (p. 76), 27, 57, 367 (p. 1140)
    Economic, **1951:** 13 (p. 74)
    Military, **1950:** 173, 175n., 193; **1951:** 25, 114
    Public health, **1951:** 135
  Communist aggression in, **1951:** 78, 96, 114; **1952–53:** 18 (p. 76), 49 [9], 55, 345 [4], 367 (p. 1140)
  Discussion with Gen. MacArthur on, **1950:** 270 [2]
  French forces in, **1951:** 114
  French High Commissioner, death of, **1952–53:** 7 [14]
  Point 4 program in, **1952–53:** 57
Indonesia
  Assistance, **1950:** 119
    Technical, **1952–53:** 18 (p. 76)
  Dispute with Netherlands, **1948:** 202 [6]; **1950:** 2, 143
    Truce, **1948:** 124 [1]
  Independence, **1949:** 272; **1950:** 119
  Korean prisoner-of-war camps, investigation of uprising in, **1952–53:** 162
  Sukarno, Achmed, **1949:** 272
  U.S. Ambassador H. Merle Cochran, **1949:** 272
Industrial College of the Armed Forces, **1949:** 144ftn. (p. 339); **1952–53:** 127 [13], 349
Industrial Conference Board, National, **1950:** 23ftn. (p. 133)
Industrial development, **1946:** 18 (pp. 48, 49)
Industrial disputes.
  See Labor disputes.
Industrial materials, export priorities, **1947:** 99
Industrial peace in reconversion period, statement, **1945:** 104
Industrial reconversion, postwar, **1945:** 80, 202 [3, 7]
Industrial Safety, President's Conference on, **1949:** 55; **1950:** 155; **1952–53:** 150
Industry, U.S., **1947:** 68, 142, 204, 211, 231; **1948:** 4 [10], 5 (pp. 20, 25, 38, 40, 48, 52), 8 (pp. 64, 75–77, 85), 12, 32, 76, 80, 175, 177, 184; **1949:** 5, 203, 219; **1950:** 9 (pp. 96, 97), 13; **1951:** 13 (p. 65), 279; **1952–53:** 98 [10], 123 [2], 257, 271
See also specific industries.
  Accident prevention, **1948:** 5 (p. 54); **1949:** 55; **1952–53:** 18 (p. 92), 150, 243, 367 (pp. 1150, 1151)
  Air pollution from, prevention, **1950:** 101
  Allocations and priority agreements, **1948:** 1
  Aluminum, plants affected by labor dispute, **1952–53:** 22
  Apprentices, draft deferment, **1952–53:** 185
  Atomic energy development, **1948:** 9 [12], 164, 239; **1950:** 187; **1952–53:** 18 (p. 85)

Industry, U.S. — *continued*
  Capacity, **1947:** 4 (pp. 20, 27, 31, 32), 58, 102; **1948:** 2, 8 (pp. 67, 79, 80, 90), 98; **1950:** 6, 122, 155, 194, 202, 232, 243; **1951:** 4, 11, 13 (pp. 62, 64, 65, 76), 91, 167; **1952–53:** 15, 18 (p. 79), 33, 215, 275
  Conservation, role in, **1947:** 186
  Controls, production and distribution, **1951:** 13 (pp. 76, 77), 98
  Corporate structure, FTC study, **1948:** 220
  Decentralization, **1947:** 2 (p. 6)
  Defense
    Federal aid to, **1952–53:** 18 (p. 77)
    Mediation of labor disputes, **1952–53:** 18 (p. 92)
    Production **1950:** 193, 194, 215, 243, 303; **1951:** 4, 11, 13 (pp. 76, 77), 39, 59, 63 [7], 80, 91, 93, 98, 167, 174, 189, 205, 284; **1952–53:** 18 (pp. 64, 68–70, 74, 77–79), 158, 275, 367 (pp. 1137, 1138, 1141)
  Dependence on farm economy, **1948:** 233 [1], 237 [1]
  Depreciation allowances, **1951:** 91
  Development in West, **1948:** 200 [3, 5], 201
  Dispersal, **1951:** 189, 193 [4], 200 [3]
  Earnings in, average hourly, **1952–53:** 215
  Economic report to Congress, **1948:** 167
  Expansion, **1948:** 8 (pp. 67, 78–80, 89), 125; **1952–53:** 339
  Exports to Europe, **1947:** 238
  Five-year censuses of, **1952–53:** 367 (p. 1156)
  Flood damage, reconstruction, **1951:** 196
  Government-possessed facilities, **1947:** 87
  Grain conservation, **1948:** 14
  Growth of, **1947:** 187
  Inventories, manufacturers and distributors, **1952–53:** 15
  Investments.
    See main heading, Investments.
  Labor disputes, effect on economy, **1948:** 93 [6]
  Leaders, meetings with, **1949:** 45 [2]
  Manpower needs, **1951:** 13 (p. 68), 15
  Market development, **1952–53:** 215
  Materials supply problem, appointment of commission to study, **1951:** 19
  Mobilization planning, **1949:** 8 (pp. 56, 58, 61), 144 [1]; **1950:** 9 (p. 65), 186 [14], 191 [3, 8]; **1951:** 92, 137n., 189; **1952–53:** 349
  Modernization of plant and equipment, **1948:** 8 (pp. 67, 70, 72, 79, 80), 63, 167
  Monopolies in, **1948:** 202 [5], 203, 220
  New England, problems of, **1952–53:** 294
  News conference remarks, **1949:** 4 [4], 45 [2], 144 [1], 155 [15], 205 [1], 240 [15]
  Oil, refusal of companies to release books, **1952–53:** 377 [26]
  Pension and insurance plans, **1950:** 9 (p. 72); **1951:** 12 [44, 48]

Industry, U.S. — *continued*
  Plant and equipment
    Government construction or operation, **1951:**
      11, 12 [2], 91
    Modernization, **1947:** 4 (pp. 17, 20, 24); **1949:**
      5, 51; **1950:** 6, 84, 134, 202; **1951:** 91, 167;
      1952–53: 15, 289 [2], 376
  Plant fires, prevention, **1947:** 86
  Prices, **1948:** 8 (p. 88)
    Proposed conference on, **1947:** 177 [12]
  Production, **1947:** 76; **1948:** 2, 5 (p. 45), 8 (pp. 62,
    65–67, 70, 79, 81, 88, 94), 9 [12], 148, 167,
    182, 218 [2], 223, 240 [1], 252; **1949:** 2, 5,
    39, 77, 151, 154, 155 [15], 205 [1], 250 [3];
    1950: 2, 6, 9 (p. 46), 84, 92, 106, 118, 134,
    157, 163, 194, 202, 232; **1952–53:** 15, 57,
    215, 289 [2], 376
    Curtailment due to coal strike, **1950:** 49
    Incentives, proposed, **1950:** 203ftn. (p. 560)
  Profits, **1948:** 262
  Refugees, employment of, **1952–53:** 65
  Research, **1947:** 183, 194; **1948:** 8 (p. 86), 37, 186,
    239; **1951:** 297
  Reserve, question of, **1948:** 71 [20]
  Safety, **1950:** 9 (p. 99), 74, 155; **1951:** 9, 13 (p. 80)
  Salaries, **1949:** 13, 137, 218
  Seizure, Presidential power of, **1952–53:** 136 [9,
    14, 17, 19], 156 [4], 161, 175 [16]
  Shortage of materials, **1948:** 170 [1], 178 [6];
    1951: 11
  South, growth in, **1952–53:** 194
  Steel strike, effect on, **1952–53:** 175 [12]
  Stimulus from conservation of natural resources,
    1948: 199
  Technology, **1948:** 8 (p. 85)
  Wage guarantees, **1947:** 53
  Wage security plans, **1948:** 8 (p. 87)
  Wage Stabilization Board, industry members,
    1952–53: 345 [5]
  Wages.
    See main heading, Wages.
  War mobilization **1947:** 94, 199; **1948:** 183 [6],
    284
  Water resources, use of, **1950:** 306
  Work stoppages, **1952–53:** 15
Industry Advisory Councils, **1951:** 98
Industry and Military Liaison Committee, **1948:**
  177
Infant mortality, **1951:** 135; **1952–53:** 249
Infantile paralysis, **1946:** 26
Infantile Paralysis, National Foundation for, **1946:**
  26; **1947:** 17
  Gift from White House correspondents, accep-
    tance, **1945:** 208 [1]
  10th anniversary, **1948:** 18
Inflation, **1945:** 17, 128, 180, 202 [3], 229; **1946:** 2,
  18 (pp. 40, 48, 53–55, 62, 72, 74), 35, 67,
  73, 79, 94, 124, 125, 131, 148, 152, 153,

Inflation — *continued*
    156, 164, 179, 187, 193, 194, 195, 213, 220,
    232, 249, 256; **1947:** 4 (p. 15), 62 [17], 68,
    75, 76, 88 [14], 97, 107 [2, 15], 116, 142,
    143, 147, 152, 158, 176, 180 [2, 21, 23] 213,
    214, 218 [9, 13, 15], 224, 238, 242, 243 [2,
    20]; **1948:** 2, 5 (pp. 19, 21, 23, 38, 51), 8
    (pp. 62–66, 69–75, 81, 82, 91, 92, 97, 98),
    24, 31, 37, 58, 63, 80, 107, 167, 175, 182;
    1949: 2, 5, 151, 154; **1950:** 6, 202, 287 [19];
    1951: 8, 25, 98, 144, 167, 199; **1952–53:**
    83, 110, 118, 215
  Anti-inflation bill, **1948:** 174 [14]
  Bank credit, **1948:** 77 [9], 84 [16], 166 [8], 178 [5]
  Campaign remarks on, **1948:** 114 [3], 115, 117,
    124 [4], 183 [6], 194 [1], 195, 199, 202 [2],
    205, 214 [5], 215, 220, 222 [3, 9], 223, 231
    [2, 3], 236, 237 [4], 240 [6], 241, 246, 249,
    251, 255, 256, 257 [3], 259 [3], 260, 268;
    1952–53: 287, 293
  China, **1946:** 265
  Control measures, **1950:** 194, 200, 215, 232, 243,
    303; **1951:** 44, 91, 93, 107, 133, 137, 143,
    176, 221, 290, 304; **1952–53:** 5, 15, 17 [9],
    18 (p. 79), 33, 190, 205, 215, 341, 376
    Opposition by special interests, **1951:** 164
    Report to Nation, **1951:** 123
    Savings, **1951:** 11, 60
    Tax program to curb, **1950:** 284; **1951:** 37 [13]
  Correspondence with citizens, **1951:** 123, 164
  Effect of tax bill on, **1948:** 170 [1]
  Effect of wage increase on, **1948:** 110 [17]
  Europe, **1952–53:** 5
  Message to Congress, **1948:** 165
  Military spending, danger from, **1950:** 193; **1951:**
    11, 13 (p. 66), 28, 93, 199, 279; **1952–53:**
    15, 55
  News conference remarks, **1945:** 22 [8], 211 [1];
    1946: 6 [15], 27 [16], 37 [16], 72 [2, 3], 163
    [2], 192 [18], 216 [4], 226 [6]; **1948:** 4 [1, 10,
    18], 21 [11–13], 26 [3, 10], 41 [6], 77 [9], 84
    [1, 16], 110 [17], 163 [17], 166 [8], 170 [1,
    4], 174 [14], 178 [5], 185 [2]; **1949:** 7 [30],
    22 [13], 30 [2, 11], 32 [21], 45 [3], 66 [17],
    148 [19]; **1951:** 2 [25], 118 [1, 5], 132 [5],
    140 [2], 153 [13], 188 [17], 298 [8]; **1952–
    53:** 123 [3, 18]
  Philippines, **1945:** 176
  Post-World War II, **1952–53:** 319 [1]
  Return to gold standard as means to combat,
    1948: 163 [17]
  Savings bonds as means to combat, **1948:** 76
  Statement, **1948:** 176
Information.
  See also Voice of America.
  Aeronautical developments, **1948:** 9 [12, 14]
  Atomic energy technology, **1948:**164

Information — *continued*
  Atomic weapons, **1948:** 9 [12, 14], 278ftn. (p.
    951), 283 [3]; **1949:** 30 [10], 161 [7], 166 [1]
  Bikini tests, **1948:** 278ftn. (p. 951), 283 [3];
    1949: 45 [25], 66 [4]
  Availability, **1947:** 21, 138, 218 [2]; **1948:** 11 [13],
    71 [18], 278 [1]; **1949:** 86, 161 [7]
    To Soviet people, **1948:** 266
    To Special Assistant to Attorney General,
      1952-53: 35 [1], 44 [10], 64 [15]
  Briefing of Presidential candidates, **1952-53:** 227
  Campaign of truth in Communist bloc nations,
    1950: 190, 267
  Churchill meeting, House Resolution on, **1952-
    53:** 44 [1, 13]
  Classified, respecting 1949 U.S. troop withdraw-
    al from Korea, **1952-53:** 320
  Census records, **1949:** 175
  Defense plants, opposition to publication of list,
    1950: 258 [12]
  Executive privilege, **1950:** 44 [6, 9, 15], 46 [11],
    79, 82, 94, 152 [9], 182, 217 [12], 254;
    1951: 108 [4, 11]; **1952-53:** 60, 64 [6], 76,
    91, 182, 238 [2]
  Farm radio broadcasts, **1950:** 163
  Foreign informational and cultural programs,
    1948: 5 (p. 31)
  Free exchange of, **1950:** 254, 269
  FTC report on oil cartel, security classification,
    1952-53: 197 [13], 221 [11]
  Government programs, statement, **1945:** 120
  Labor statistics, **1952-53:** 18 (p. 95)
  Private media
    Cooperation with Government programs
      abroad, **1950:** 127 [5]
    Role in democratic society, **1950:** 92
  Privileged, **1947:** 236 [4]; **1949:** 122 [22]
  Relief food shipments to Yugoslavia, publicity
    for, **1950:** 293
  Scientific, collection and dissemination by De-
    partment of Commerce, **1950:** 106
  Scientific and technological issues, public un-
    derstanding of, **1948:** 191
  Security, safeguarding of, **1951:** 233, 234, 247 [1,
    5, 10, 12], 248, 302; **1952-53:** 303 [2]
  Security classification, **1950:** 29 [3, 5, 9]
  Soviet restrictions on freedom of, **1951:** 188 [6]
  Subversives, communication of information to
    FBI, **1950:** 94, 199
  U.S. programs abroad, **1949:** 8 (p. 54); **1950:** 92,
    127 [5], 227; **1951:** 13 (pp. 63, 75, 76), 70
    [1], 197
    Broadcasting facilities, **1951:** 72
  Wake Island meeting with General MacArthur
    1951: 90 [11]
  War information, utilization, **1947:** 18
  World food crisis, **1947:** 191 [14]

Information, U.S. Advisory Commission on, **1950:**
  92, 190n.
Information Agency, U.S., **1950:** 92
Information and Educational Exchange Act of
  1948, U.S., **1951:** 194n.
Informational films, Government, **1946:** 160
Ingman, Corp. Einar H., Congressional Medal of
  Honor, **1951:** 146
Ingram, Charlotte, **1950:** 239n.
Ingram case, Georgia, **1948:** 55 [4]
Injunctions in labor disputes, **1948:** 179, 184; **1949:**
  28 [5]
  Coal industry, **1947:** 127 [15]; **1948:** 66, 171;
    1950: 35, 38 [14], 49
  Copper industry, **1951:** 214
  Maritime, **1948:** 179
  Oak Ridge National Laboratory, **1948:** 140
  Taft-Hartley Act provisions, **1947:** 120
Inland Steel Corp., **1951:** 305
Inland waterways, **1948:** 2
Inland Waterways Corporation, **1946:** 94; **1947:** 7
  (p. 95); **1949:** 8 (p. 87); **1950:** 8 [15], 76;
  1952-53: 18 (p. 83)
Innes, Guy, **1945:** 106n.
Inonu, Ismet, **1948:** 263
Inside Strategy of the Campaign, Jay Franklin,
  1949: 4ftn. (p. 11)
Installment buying, **1948:** 166 [8]
Institute of Inter-American Affairs, **1947:** 7 (p. 16);
  1952-53: 18 (p. 115), 72
Institute of Inter-American Transportation, **1947:**
  (p. 95)
Institute of Pacific Relations, **1952-53:** 362n.
Insurance, **1947:** 68; **1948:** 175
  Bank deposits, **1948:** 219, 231 [5], 255; **1949:** 5,
    151, 154; **1950:** 110 [5], 157; **1952-53:** 276
  Bank loans to small business, proposed, **1950:**
    106, 118
  Crop, **1945:** 128; **1946:** 18 (p. 53), 94; **1948:** 2, 99,
    194 [11], 246; **1952-53:** 267, 367 (p. 1148)
  Disability, **1947:** 98; **1948:** 5 (pp. 33, 34), 107,
    175, 181 [2]; **1949:** 5, 8 (pp. 49, 66), 250
    [3]; **1950:** 74, 224; **1952-53:** 5, 231
  Firms, opposition to social security, **1952-53:**
    289 [3]
  Flood, **1952-53:** 17 [14], 119
    Proposed, **1951:** 196, 269
  Government programs, stimulus to private in-
    surance business, **1950:** 157
  Health.
    See Health insurance.
  Life.
    See Life insurance.
  Loan guarantees
    Defense contractors, **1951:** 13 (pp. 76, 78)
    Housing construction, **1951:** 13 (p. 92)
  Marine, **1950:** 76, 236; **1952-53:** 17 [32]

Insurance — *continued*
  Military personnel, **1951:** 12 [36]
  Mortgage, **1946:** 18 (p. 63), 94, 263; **1947:** 7 (p.
    75), 97, 102, 131, 221 [11]; **1948:** 5 (pp. 38,
    39), 37, 150 [1], 175, 227 [9]; **1949:** 8 (p.
    72); **1950:** 51, 68, 76, 112, 192; **1951:** 13
    (pp. 90, 93), 202; **1952–53:** 18 (pp. 95, 96),
    367 (pp. 1152, 1153)
  National Service Life.
    See Life Insurance, National Service.
  Old-age and survivors, **1945:** 99; **1946:** 18 (pp.
    64, 83); **1947:** 4 (p. 30), 7 (p. 58), 181 (p.
    406); **1948:** 4 [8], 5 (pp. 34, 36, 37, 59), 8
    (pp. 68, 87, 88), 107, 131, 165, 175, 241,
    252, 255; **1949:** 5, 8 (pp. 49, 66, 71), 151,
    250 [3]; **1950:** 2, 9 (pp. 46, 53, 54, 68, 71,
    72, 76, 77), 84, 127 [5], 128, 157, 281;
    1951: 4, 12 [54], 159, 280; **1952–53:** 15, 18
    (pp. 70, 104, 105), 213, 215, 218, 237, 241,
    266 [3], 276, 278, 293, 300, 306 [1], 312,
    366, 367 (p. 1157), 376
  Private plans, **1950:** 6, 9 (p. 72)
  Railroad retirement, **1951:** 280; **1952–53:** 270 [5]
  Savings and loan premiums, **1946:** 208
  Special groups, Government and private plans
    for, **1951:** 12 [44, 48]
  Trust funds, **1951:** 13 (p. 99)
  Unemployment.
    See Unemployment insurance.
  U.S. programs abroad, **1952–53:** 18 (p. 77), 54,
    367 (p. 1141)
  Veterans, **1947:** 2 (p. 8), 6 [2], 7 (p. 70), 134;
    1948: 5 (p. 33), 175; **1949:** 7 [30], 8 (pp. 48,
    64–65); **1950:** 9 (pp. 70, 71), 202, 236;
    1951: 12 [52], 13 (pp. 102, 103); **1952–53:**
    18 (pp. 109, 110), 367 (p. 1160)
    Trust funds, **1952–53:** 18 (p. 100)
  War damage, **1952–53:** 18 (p. 100)
    Profits, **1948:** 4 [10]
  War risk, **1952–53:** 17 [14, 32]
Insurance Act of 1951, **1952–53:** 18 (pp. 109, 110)
Insurance companies, **1947:** 116; **1948:** 5 (p. 53)
Integration
  Armed Forces, **1948:** 166 [1, 4], 185 [7]; **1949:**
    226 [3]
  Housing, **1949:** 267 [18], 269 [11]
  Schools, **1950:** 38 [16]
    On Federal property, **1951:** 286
    Virginia, bill to abolish segregation in, **1950:** 34
    [1]
Intelligence Advisory Board, **1946:** 19
Intelligence program, foreign, **1945:** 140; **1946:** 17
    [15], 18 (p. 86), 21 [10, 13], 86 [3]; **1948:**
    285 [6]; **1950:** 254; **1951:** 13 (p. 76), 95 [9]
  Directive, **1946:** 19
  Letter to Secretary Byrnes, **1945:** 141
Inter-Agency Committee, New York-New Eng-
    land, **1952–53:** 294

Inter-Agency Committee on Export Transporta-
    tion, **1946:** 264
Interagency committee for resources survey, pro-
    posed, **1950:** 265
Inter-Agency Health Council, **1951:** 307
Inter-American Affairs, Institute of, **1948:** 5 (p.
    57); **1949:** 35; **1952–53:** 18 (p. 115)
Inter-American Affairs, Office of, **1945:** 120; **1946:**
    77, 94, 116, 119 [3]
Inter-American Association, **1947:** 79
Inter-American Bar Association, **1949:** 115
Inter-American Conference for Maintenance of
    Continental Peace and Security, **1947:**
    188
Inter-American Conference on Problems of War
    and Peace, **1946:** 18 (p. 42), 83; **1947:** 105
Inter-American Congress (1825), **1948:** 158
Inter-American Conservation Conference, **1948:**
    198 [1]
Inter-American Convention on the Granting of
    Political Rights to Women, **1949:** 10
Inter-American Defense Board, **1946:** 102
Inter-American Economic and Social Council,
    1950: 52 [4]
Inter-American Educational Foundation, **1947:** 7
    (p. 95)
Inter-American Highway, **1945:** 128
Inter-American military cooperation, **1946:** 102;
    1947: 101; **1948:** 5 (p. 29)
Inter-American military standardization bill, **1949:**
    11 [19]
Inter-American Navigation Corporation, **1947:** 7
    (p. 95)
Inter-American Press Conference, **1950:** 273 [6]
Inter-American System, **1947:** 51, 188
Inter-American Treaty of Reciprocal Assistance,
    Rio Pact, **1946:** 27 [5]; **1947:** 230; **1949:**
    19, 70, 162, 184; **1950:** 119, 179 [18]; **1951:**
    59, 65, 114, 125; **1952–53:** 55, 196, 366,
    378
Interdenominational Ministers Meeting, **1952–53:**
    290
Interdenominational religious program, address,
    1949: 62
Interdepartmental committee on domestic and for-
    eign economic policy, proposed, **1950:** 46
    [6]
Interdepartmental Committee on Internal Security,
    1951: 233, 234
Interdepartmental Committee on Narcotics, **1951:**
    287
Interdepartmental Committee on Scientific Re-
    search and Development, **1947:** 201n.;
    1948: 27, 186
Interdepartmental Safety Council, Policy Board,
    1950: 74
Interdepartmental water resources development
    commission, proposed, **1950:** 140

Interest on Government bonds, **1947:** 90 [8]
Interest on national debt, **1946:** 18 (pp. 73, 78, 79);
    1947: 2 (p. 7), 6 [2], 7 (pp. 57, 61, 91), 76,
    180 [1], 181 (p. 401); **1948:** 4 [1], 5 (pp. 20,
    21, 23, 25, 56), 175; **1949:** 7 [10, 41], 8 (p.
    94); **1950:** 9 (pp. 48, 103); **1951:** 12 [3, 13],
    13 (pp. 64, 105); **1952–53:** 15, 18 (pp. 114,
    115), 231, 367 (pp. 1163–1164)
Interest rates, **1948:** 37, 175, 228 [10]; **1949:** 151,
    154; **1950:** 128; **1951:** 33 [11, 13], 44, 91
  On railroad bonds, **1946:** 205
Inter-Governmental Committee on Refugees, **1945:**
    152, 188
Inter-Governmental Joint Wool Organization,
    1946: 57
Interim aid program, **1947:** 218 [13, 15, 18]
Interior, Department of the, **1945:** 194; **1946:** 18
    (pp. 86, 87), 118, 150, 211, 252; **1947:** 7
    (pp. 77, 83, 85), 11, 35, 95 [9], 119n., 144,
    165, 186, 229, 241; **1948:** 4 [7], 5 (pp. 42,
    46, 51), 6, 26 [7], 105; **1949:** 43, 96n., 101,
    248; **1950:** 54, 203 [7]; **1951:** 141, 177,
    205; **1952–53:** 98 [34]
  Appropriation act, 1949, approval, **1948:** 149
  Appropriations, **1951:** 120
  Columbia Valley Administration, study of, **1949:**
    40 [9]
  Fortas, Abe, **1945:** 157 [2]
  Hester, E. D., **1945:** 24
  Industry Advisory Councils, remarks, **1951:** 98
  Mine safety, **1952–53:** 19, 150, 206
  Mineral resources development assistance,
    1952–53: 18 (p. 77)
  Natural resources development functions, **1952–
    53:** 388
  News conference remarks, **1946:** 37 [11, 13], 43
    [4], 61 [19]; **1949:** 40 [9], 118 [21]
  Pacific territories, administration, **1950:** 9 (p.
    102)
  Petroleum policies coordination, **1946:** 101
  Programs review, **1950:** 196
  Public land exchanges, veto, **1946:** 190
  Reclamation program, **1946:** 238
  Reorganization, **1950:** 53, 54, 57, 69, 70; **1951:**
    226; **1952–53:** 107 [6]
  Research programs, **1952–53:** 199
  Strauss, Michael W., **1945:** 211 [10]
  Water resources development functions, **1950:**
    140
Interior, Secretary of the
  Authority over U.S. park police, **1945:** 80
  Vacancy in office, **1946:** 37 [11, 13], 41 [7, 13]
Interior, Secretary of the (Oscar L. Chapman),
    1950: 23ftn. (p. 135), 121 [9], 124 [1],
    265n.; **1951:** 98, 141, 177, 235, 279; **1952–
    53:** 62, 78n., 80, 199, 271, 280 [4, 6], 282
    [7], 292 [11]
  Disloyalty charges against, **1950:** 238 [10]

Interior, Secretary of the (Chapman) — *continued*
  Letters, **1950:** 196, 265; **1951:** 55
  Luncheon for the President, **1951:** 32
  Memorandum, **1950:** 259
  Mine disaster, report on, **1952–53:** 19
  News conference remarks on, **1950:** 52 [3], 238
    [10]; **1951:** 108 [3]
  Resignation, **1952–53:** 384
Interior, Secretary of the (Harold L. Ickes), **1946:**
    27 [18], 30 [3], 31, 37 [1, 2, 4, 6, 17], 43 [8]
  Mission to London re oil agreement renegotia-
    tion, **1945:** 76 [9], 107 [3]
  News conference remarks on, **1945:** 64 [4], 67 [3],
    76 [9], 107 [3], 129 [2], 175 [2], 211 [10]
  Solid Fuels Administrator for War, **1945:** 35n.
  U.S. assistance for Philippines, discussions on,
    1945: 175 [2]
Interior, Secretary of the (Julius A. Krug), **1946:** 43
    [4], 53 [7], 61 [19], 81n., 195n., 237 [5, 16];
    1947: 5, 119, 122, 212, 217, 219, 229,
    231n., 238; **1948:** 1, 25, 26 [7], 105, 111,
    124 [1, 4], 136 [4], 170 [1], 207, 238; **1949:**
    185, 196, 229, 232, 233
  Coal mines labor dispute, **1946:** 252
  Letters, **1946:** 101; **1947:** 186; **1948:** 56, 57; **1949:**
    101
  Medal for Merit, citation, **1946:** 93
  Memorandum, **1949:** 149n.
  News conference remarks on, **1947:** 67 [14], 191
    [4], 218 [7], 221 [1]; **1949:** 32 [6], 144 [20],
    253 [6]
  Report, **1947:** 209 [8], 210 [5]
  Resignation, **1949:** 255
    Question of, **1948:** 278 [13]
Interior Department Appropriation Act, 1952,
    1951: 120
Internal Revenue, Bureau of, **1946:** 17 [30], 116;
    1947: 7 (p. 90), 80, 135, 181 (p. 402); **1948:**
    4 [1], 5 (p. 55), 175; **1949:** 8 (p. 93); **1950:**
    8 [36], 9 (p. 100); **1951:** 13 (p. 105), 115;
    1952–53: 35 [9], 127 [9], 238 [2], 266 [2]
  Collectorships, **1951:** 251 [9], 300 [5, 6, 21]
    Proposed civil service status, **1951:** 239 [11,
      13], 251 [15, 21], 300ftn. (p. 641); **1952–53:**
      11, 59, 117
  Investigation of, **1951:** 295ftn. (p. 630), 298 [4];
    1952–53: 31 [17]
  Reorganization, **1952–53:** 1, 2 [4, 11, 13], 5, 11, 18
    (pp. 112, 116), 53, 59, 84, 117, 367 (p.
    1161)
  Staff increase, proposed, **1952–53:** 231
  Tax enforcement program, **1945:** 44 [1]
Internal Revenue, Commissioner of (John B. Dun-
    lap), **1952–53:** 35 [9]
Internal Revenue, Commissioner of (George J.
    Schoeneman), **1947:** 135
Internal Revenue Code, **1947:** 26; **1949:** 229

Internal security
  Message to Congress, **1950:** 207
  Veto of bill, **1950:** 254
Internal Security, Interdepartmental Committee
    on, **1951:** 233, 234
Internal Security Act, **1950:** 270 [6]; **1951:** 20;
    1952–53: 182
Internal Security and Individual Rights, Commis-
    sion on.
  See Commission on Internal Security and Indi-
    vidual Rights.
International agreements
  Charter of United Nations.
    See United Nations Charter.
  Publication of, **1950:** 75
International agreements (1945)
  Bretton Woods agreements (International Bank
    for Reconstruction and Development and
    International Monetary Fund).
    See Bretton Woods agreements.
  Potsdam agreement, **1945:** 91, 97, 186, 202 [9],
    221 [19]
  U.S.-Mexico, Water Utilization Treaty, **1945:** 7
International agreements (1946)
  International Convention on Civil Aviation,
    1946: 133
  U.S.-Philippines, general relations treaty, **1946:**
    185
  U.S.-Philippines, trade agreement, **1946:** 90n.
  U.S.-U.K., Air Transport Agreement, **1946:** 43
    [2], 44
  U.S.-U.K., Financial Agreement.
    See Financial Agreement, U.S.-U.K.
International agreements (1947)
  Inter-American Treaty of Reciprocal Assistance,
    1947: 230
  Pacific Islands Trust Territory, **1947:** 137, 151
  Tariffs and Trade, General Agreement on, **1947:**
    216
  U.N. headquarters, control and administration,
    1947: 136
  U.S.-Bulgaria, peace treaty, **1947:** 114
  U.S.-Canada, trade agreement, **1947:** 111
  U.S.-Hungary, peace treaty, **1947:** 114
  U.S.-Italy, peace treaty, **1947:** 113
  U.S.-Mexico, currency stabilization, **1947:** 83
  U.S.-Rumania, peace treaty, **1947:** 114
International agreements (1948)
  Brussels, European economic cooperation, **1948:**
    52, 53
  International Trade Organization, **1948:** 54
  Telecommunications convention, **1948:** 29
  U.S.-Italy, economic cooperation, **1948:** 192
  U.S.-Italy, friendship, commerce and navigation,
    1948: 73
International agreements (1949)
  International Trade Organization, **1949:** 88
  International Wheat Agreement, **1949:** 202

International agreements (1949) — *continued*
  North Atlantic Treaty, **1949:** 68, 69, 75, 162, 188,
    202
  U.S.-Canada
    Boundary waters development, **1949:** 77
    Trade agreement, **1949:** 217
International agreements (1950)
  U.S.-Canada, Niagara River water and power
    development, **1950:** 46 [2], 99, 105 [3]
International agreements (1951)
  Brazil, supplemental lend-lease accord, **1951:** 244
  Japan, peace treaty, **1951:** 49 [18], 216, 217,
    227ftn. (p. 527)
  Mutual defense treaties
    Australia and New Zealand, **1951:** 84, 85 [8],
      153ftn. (p. 387), 216
    Philippines, **1951:** 208
International agreements (1952)
  Mutual defense treaties, Australia and New
    Zealand, Japan, Philippines, **1952–53:** 95
  Japan, peace treaty, **1952–53:** 95, 111
  Pakistan wheat loan document, **1952–53:** 252
International Association of Chiefs of Police,
    1945: 62
International Association of Machinists, **1948:** 277
International Bank for Reconstruction and De-
    velopment, **1946:** 18 (pp. 45, 85, 86), 25,
    47, 67, 76, 78 [3], 110 [10], 126 [13], 140,
    192 [19], 202, 236, 248, 266 [19]; **1947:** 2
    (p. 10), 4 (p. 38), 7 (p. 67), 21, 46 [24], 138;
    1948: 8 (p. 97), 276; **1949:** 84ftn. (p. 223),
    139, 151, 195, 210, 273; **1950:** 6, 9 (p. 59);
    1951: 13 (p. 75), 114, 219; **1952–53:** 6, 18
    (p. 77), 55
  See also Bretton Woods agreements.
International bill of rights, **1945:** 66; **1947:** 130
International Boundary and Water Commission,
    U.S.-Mexico, **1946:** 18 (p. 82); **1947:** 7 (p.
    82); **1948:** 5 (p. 46); **1951:** 239 [7]
International Boys Camp, Inc., **1951:** 166
International Broadcasting Division, **1946:** 167n.
International Children's Fund, **1948:** 144
International Civil Aviation Organization, **1946:**
    133; **1947:** 21; **1950:** 9 (p. 102)
International Claims Commission, U.S., **1950:**
    146ftn. (p. 439)
International Commodity Groups, **1951:** 25
International Confederation of Free Trade Unions,
    1951: 153 [16]; **1952–53:** 253 [1]
International Conference on Agricultural and Co-
    operative Credit, **1952–53:** 261
International Conference of American States,
    1947: 221 [4]; **1948:** 55 [13], 77ftn. (p.
    215); **1949:** 9, 10
International Conference on Trade and Employ-
    ment, **1946:** 18 (pp. 45, 46), 248
International Convention on Civil Aviation, **1946:**
    133

International cooperation, **1945:** 66; **1946:** 25, 68, 81, 83, 236, 248; **1947:** 7 (pp. 56, 68), 21, 37, 38, 51, 72, 101, 138, 181 (p. 407), 185; **1948:** 5 (p. 19), 129, 183 [1], 236, 266; **1950:** 87, 132–134, 159; **1951:** 144, 271; **1952–53:** 55, 72, 281, 283, 285, 303 [1], 307, 321 [2], 366

    Atomic energy, **1945:** 156, 178, 191, 193 [7, 8]

    Connally resolution, **1945:** 69

    Fulbright resolution, **1945:** 69

    News conference remarks, **1945:** 193 [7, 8], 202 [6]

International Council, Independent Order of Odd Fellows, **1951:** 220

International Council of Aluminum Workers of America, **1952–53:** 22

International Court of Justice, **1947:** 21; **1949:** 103n.; **1950:** 143; **1951:** 140 [19], 150

International Court of Justice, Statute of Ratification, **1945:** 69

    Signing at San Francisco conference, **1945:** 68

International Development, Act for, **1950:** 240, 282, 294; **1952–53:** 18 (p. 76), 20

International Development Advisory Board, **1950:** 289, 294; **1952–53:** 20

International Development Advisory Board, Chairman (Nelson Rockefeller), **1951:** 53

International disputes, peaceful settlement of, **1950:** 271, 281, 296, 301, 303

International Economic and Social Development, National Conference on, address, **1952–53:** 81

International educational exchange, **1949:** 139

International Emergency Food Council, **1946:** 149; **1947:** 18, 99; **1948:** 23

International Federation of Business and Professional Women, **1952–53:** 188

International groups.

    See Addresses or remarks to foreign or international groups.

International Harvester Co., **1946:** 173 [17]; **1947:** 62 [15]

International Information, Advisory Commission on, **1950:** 227

International Information and Cultural Affairs, Office of, **1946:** 159n.

International Joint Commission, U.S. and Canada, **1947:** 171; **1948:** 93 [10, 11]; **1950:** 34 [10]; **1952–53:** 189, 367 (p. 1147)

International Labor Conference, **1947:** 123, 124, 126; **1949:** 13

    Message to Congress, **1948:** 70

International Labor Office, **1947:** 126

International Labor Organization, **1945:** 132 [11], 181 [10]; **1946:** 18 (p. 87), 180, 215 [10], 236; **1947:** 21, 123, 124, 126; **1948:** 70, 130 [1]

International Ladies Garment Workers Union, **1952–53:** 273

International law, **1946:** 133, 233, 236, 251; **1947:** 21; **1950:** 174, 222

International Longshoremen's Association, **1948:** 179; **1951:** 276n.

International Materials Conference, **1952–53:** 190

International Military Tribunal, **1945:** 129 [8], 132 [1, 2]; **1946:** 230, 233, 236, 251; **1947:** 21; **1950:** 174

International Monetary and Financial Problems, National Advisory Council on, **1946:** 41 [11], 47, 136 [7], 142

International Monetary Fund, **1946:** 18 (pp. 45, 85, 86), 25, 47, 67, 79, 192 [9, 17, 19], 193, 202, 236, 248; **1947:** 2 (p. 10), 4 (p. 38), 7 (p. 67), 21, 52; **1948:** 8 (p. 97); **1949:** 195, 210; **1951:** 219

    See also Bretton Woods agreements.

International monetary stabilization, **1945:** 76 [3]

International organizations, **1950:** 42, 81

    U.S. membership, **1948:** 5 (p. 31); **1950:** 9 (p. 56)

International and Public Affairs, Woodrow Wilson School of, **1947:** 117

International Radio Conference, **1948:** 29

International Red Cross, **1950:** 191 [12]

International Refugee Organization, **1946:** 236; **1947:** 7 (pp. 66, 68), 21, 38, 133, 140; **1948:** 115, 144, 202 [6]; **1949:** 8 (p. 55); **1950:** 9 (p. 58); **1952–53:** 65

International Scientific Conference on Conservation and Utilization of Natural Resources, **1947:** 186

International security, **1948:** 52, 239; **1951:** 13 (pp. 70–75); **1952–53:** 18 (pp. 73–77)

International Security Affairs Committee, **1951:** 114

International Smelting and Refining Co., **1951:** 204, 214

International Society of Christian Endeavor, remarks to, **1952–53:** 168

International Telecommunication Convention, **1948:** 29

International trade.

    See Trade, international.

International trade fair, proposed, **1949:** 171 [3, 16]

International Trade Organization, **1948:** 2, 8 (p. 97), 42, 54, 202 [6], 213; **1949:** 5, 8 (p. 55), 88, 217, 263; **1950:** 2, 6, 9 (p. 56), 42, 130, 159

    Proposed, **1946:** 236, 248; **1947:** 4 (p. 38), 7 (p. 67), 21, 51, 52, 111, 128, 138, 155, 182 [7]

International Union of Mine, Mill and Smelter Workers, **1951:** 204, 214; **1952–53:** 37

International wage and hour statistics, convention on, **1951:** 97

International Wheat Agreement, **1948:** 99, 165,

International Wheat Agreement — *continued*
    195, 213, 233 [1], 240 [5], 246, 276; **1949:**
    5, 8 (p. 80), 202, 203, 263; **1950:** 9 (p. 87),
    130, 134; **1951:** 13 (pp. 41, 42, 88, 89);
    1952–53: 18 (p. 91), 367 (pp. 1148–1149)
Interstate commerce, **1946:** 157; **1947:** 118
Interstate Commerce Act, veto of amendment,
    1947: 160; **1948:** 127
Interstate Commerce Commission, **1946:** 84 [25];
    1947: 7 (p. 85), 18, 160; **1948:** 127; **1949:**
    28 [12]; **1950:** 86 [13], 209 [16]; **1951:** 13
    (pp. 83, 84), 45; **1952–53:** 123 [11], 367 (p.
    1144)
  Freight rate ruling, **1945:** 208 [3]
  Lee, William E., **1945:** 202 [2]
  News conference remarks, **1951:** 56 [24], 188 [17]
  Patterson, William J., **1945:** 202 [2]
  Reorganization, **1950:** 53, 54, 61; **1951:** 175
Interstate Commerce Commission, Chairman (J.
    Monroe Johnson), **1950:** 259
Interstate Commerce Commission, Chairman
    (Charles D. Mahaffie), **1949:** 149n.
Interstate Compact to Conserve Oil and Gas, **1947:**
    104
Interstate Highway System, **1950:** 9 (p. 95), 160 [2]
Interstate transportation, **1948:** 20
Inventory controls, **1945:** 128
Investigations, congressional.
  See Congress.
"Investigation of Government Patent Practices and
    Policies, 1947," report, **1947:** 109n.
Investment opportunities, **1948:** 8 (pp. 82–84)
Investments, **1946:** 18 (pp. 56, 69); **1947:** 152
  Bonds, savings, **1952–53:** 15
  Capital goods, **1947:** 4 (pp. 24, 25, 28), 116, 152;
    1948: 2, 4 [18], 8 (pp. 63, 67, 68, 71, 79, 80,
    91), 37, 63, 69, 167, 175ftn. (p. 441); **1949:**
    5, 139, 151; **1950:** 2, 6, 84, 118, 122, 125,
    134, 154, 157, 243; **1951:** 11, 167; **1952–**
    53: 15, 215, 289 [2]
  Dividends, **1950:** 200, 202
  Foreign in U.S., **1949:** 252
  Government bonds, **1947:** 116; **1951:** 28, 29, 37
    [6], 44, 60
  Housing, **1950:** 6
  Increase, **1952–53:** 349
  International, **1950:** 122
  Nationally chartered investment companies, pro-
    posed, **1950:** 106
  Private, **1950:** 202; **1951:** 44, 176
    Deferment of nonessential types, **1952–53:** 15
  Shipbuilding, **1948:** 177
  Small business, **1950:** 106, 118
  Tax incentives, **1949:** 151; **1950:** 6, 18
    Defense, **1951:** 13 (pp. 76, 77)
  U.S. abroad, **1945:** 31 [3]; **1947:** 4 (pp. 37, 38);
    1948: 8 (pp. 63, 97), 69, 167; **1949:** 5, 19,
    108 [1], 139, 151, 195, 237, 273; **1950:** 6,

Investments — *continued*
  U.S. abroad — *continued*
    18, 42, 81, 119, 154, 159; **1951:** 13 (p. 75),
    114, 229; **1952–53:** 18 (p. 77), 215, 367 (p.
    1140)
    European, **1947:** 238
    Less developed countries and new nations,
      1949: 151; **1950:** 2, 9 (pp. 48, 59)
    Virgin Islands, **1949:** 141
Iowa, **1949:** 226 [10]; **1950:** 110 [2–5], 209ftn. (p.
    582), 258 [11]
  Campaign remarks, **1948:** 194 [2–11], 195; **1952–**
    53: 284 [1, 2], 285, 315 [1–4]
  Candidates for public office, **1948:** 194 [1–4, 6,
    9–11]; **1952–53:** 284 [1, 2], 285, 315 [1–4]
  Council Bluffs, **1945:** 149
  Floods, control and relief, **1952–53:** 97
  Gov. William S. Beardsley, **1952–53:** 97
  Gov. Robert D. Blue, **1947:** 209 [2]; **1948:** 194 [6]
Iowa City, campaign remarks, **1948:** 194 [3]
  Statehood, commemorative coin, **1947:** 162
Iowa State Agricultural College, **1950:** 110 [3]
Iran
  Assistance, **1949:** 162, 273; **1952–53:** 242 [2]
    Economic, **1951:** 114
    Military, **1950:** 151, 201, 204; **1951:** 114;
      1952–53: 144
    Technical, **1950:** 177; **1951:** 259, 262; **1952–53:**
      18 (p. 76), 55, 281
  Communist aggression, **1949:** 162, 184; **1952–53:**
    69, 107 [2, 11, 14, 16]
  Discussions at meeting with President-elect,
    1952–53: 334 [16]
  Doctors, shortage of, **1951:** 135
  Economic and social development, **1949:** 273
  Jones, W. Alton, visit of, **1952–53:** 238 [7]
  Mosadeq, Mohammed, **1951:** 140 [4], 150, 200 [2]
    Nationalization of industry, **1951:** 153 [19],
      165 [11]
  News conference remarks, **1946:** 53 [11], 61 [7],
    70 [2], 72 [17], 86 [14]
  Oil dispute with U.K., **1951:** 113 [8], 118 [11], 132
    [11], 140 [4, 6, 19], 153 [19], 165 [11], 200
    [2], 239 [6, 15], 251 [19], 275 [11]; **1952–53:**
    5, 6
  Harriman, W. Averell, mission to, **1951:** 150,
    153 [9, 19], 155, 239 [10]
  Point 4 program in, **1952–53:** 5
  Princess Ashraf, **1947:** 203n.
  Shah Mohammad Reza Pahlavi, **1947:** 203;
    1949: 258, 259, 262, 273
  Soviet forces in, **1946:** 53 [11], 61 [7]
    Invasion and withdrawal from, **1948:** 202 [6];
      1952–53: 378
    Ultimatum on (1946), **1952–53:** 107 [2, 11, 14,
      16]
  Soviet pressure on, **1950:** 151
  Teheran, **1945:** 177

Iran — *continued*
U.N. operations (1946), **1950:** 232
U.N. policy in, **1952–53:** 366
U.S. Ambassador George V. Allen, **1946:** 84 [1, 3, 16]
U.S. foreign policy, **1945:** 208 [12]
Iraq
Assistance, **1952–53:** 55
Technical, **1951:** 262
Prince Abdul Ilah, **1945:** 47
Ireland, **1947:** 47, 154, 238; **1950:** 11 [6]
Eamon de Valera, **1948:** 49 [20]
McBride, Sean, **1951:** 63 [5]
Matthews, Francis P., appointment as U.S. Ambassador to, **1951:** 113 [11], 140 [1], 180n.
Unity, resolution of U.S. Congress, **1951:** 239 [2]
U.S. relations with, **1951:** 63ftn. (p. 203)
Iron, European production, **1947:** 238
Iron Curtain.
See Communist bloc.
Iron ore
Imports, **1952–53:** 175ftn. (p. 432)
Stockpiling, **1948:** 8 (p. 78)
U.S. reserves, **1950:** 9 (p. 94); **1952–53:** 18 (p. 88)
Iron ore deposits
Labrador, **1951:** 11, 13 (pp. 81–83)
Lake Superior, **1951:** 11
Quebec, **1951:** 13 (pp. 81–83)
Venezuela, **1951:** 11
Iron and Steel Institute, **1952–53:** 110
Irrigation projects, **1945:** 164 [8]; **1946:** 18 (pp. 60, 61, 82), 97, 176, 209; **1947:** 144; **1948:** 5 (p. 46), 6, 8 (p. 77), 32; **1949:** 2, 32 [6], 41, 43, 77, 168, 183, 185, 196, 245; **1950:** 2, 116, 121 [3, 4], 125, 127 [1, 2, 6], 129 [1, 5]; **1951:** 183; **1952–53:** 3, 21 [23], 80, 268 [2, 3, 7], 269, 271, 274, [1], 277 [3], 280 [6], 291, 307, 366, 388
Campaign remarks on, **1948:** 128 [1], 136 [3, 4], 198 [5], 199, 200 [1, 9], 201, 203, 206 [3, 4], 207, 208 [2, 7], 209, 218 [14], 219
Irving, Maj. Gen. Frederick A., **1952–53:** 130, 131
Irving, Repr. Leonard, **1949:** 240 [9]
Irvington, Ky., campaign remarks, **1948:** 218 [14]
Irwin, Maj. Gen. Leroy, **1950:** 218
Isaiah, **1945:** 227; **1946:** 52, 271; **1948:** 101; **1950:** 37
Ismay, Lord, **1952–53:** 6
Isolationism, **1945:** 147 [12]; **1946:** 236; **1947:** 2 (p. 10), 138, 196
Repudiation of, **1948:** 2, 160, 210 [2], 213, 231 [3], 236, 266; **1949:** 120, 184, 195
Israel, **1951:** 188 [12]; **1952–53:** 144
Ambassador Abba S. Eban, **1952–53:** 144
Ancient, **1951:** 241
Religious legacy to West, **1950:** 158
Arab-Israeli dispute, **1948:** 124 [1], 253, 274 [7]; **1949:** 193; **1950:** 2, 25, 143, 147, 148

Israel — *continued*
Arab refugees, **1949:** 122 [23]
Armistice with Egypt, **1949:** 40 [2]
Arms embargo, question of modification, **1948:** 110 [7, 22], 253
Arms shipments to, tripartite declaration on, **1950:** 147, 148
Assistance, **1948:** 110 [14, 21], 253
Economic, **1951:** 114, 229; **1952–53:** 144
Technical, **1952–53:** 18 (p. 76), 55
Ben-Gurion, David, **1951:** 95 [1]
Boundaries, definition of, **1948:** 253
Diplomatic recognition of, **1948:** 100, 110 [23], 141, 185 [10], 253
Election in, **1948:** 185 [10]
Epstein, Eliahu, **1948:** 141, 253
Kfar Truman, village of, **1952–53:** 144
Loan to, question of, **1948:** 110 [14, 21], 178 [9], 278 [25]
National Conference on, **1951:** 229
News conference remarks, **1949:** 11 [9], 22 [4], 40 [2], 52 [16], 122 [23]
Statement on, **1948:** 253
United Nations operations, **1948:** 110 [7, 21], 178 [9], 253
U.S. Ambassador James G. McDonald, **1949:** 192 [21]; **1950:** 250 [4]
U.S. diplomatic recognition of government, **1949:** 24
U.S. troops to, question of, **1948:** 178 [9]
U.S.-U.K. policy on, **1948:** 110 [9, 21], 262
Weizmann, Chaim, **1948:** 110 [7, 21], 224; **1949:** 58 [1], 84 [1, 15]; **1952–53:** 144, 297
Italy, **1945:** 91, 97; **1946:** 18 (pp. 41, 42, 46), 100, 253; **1947:** 90 [7], 138; **1949:** 192 [1], 195; **1950:** 293; **1951:** 153 [16]
Allied Commission for, abolition, **1947:** 25
Allied troop withdrawal, **1947:** 234, 239
Ambassador Alberto Tarchiani, **1948:** 51n., 74, 278 [41]
Armistice, **1945:** 40 [3], 175 [16]
Assistance, **1947:** 15, 47, 195, 197, 210 [6], 214, 224, 238; **1948:** 5 (p. 29), 147, 260; **1952–53:** 180, 298 [8], 358
Economic, **1951:** 232, 235
Military, **1950:** 22; **1951:** 138, 232
Attack on Ethiopia (1935), **1951:** 4
Communist expansion, **1948:** 52, 53; **1952–53:** 69, 288
Communist-inspired strikes, failure of, **1951:** 4
De Gasperi, Alcide, **1947:** 14 [20], 15, 239; **1948:** 192; **1951:** 231, 232, 235, 239 [19]
De Nicola, Enrico, **1947:** 15
Displaced persons in, **1947:** 38, 140
Immigration to U.S., **1950:** 167; **1952–53:** 182
Economic Cooperation Agreement, **1948:** 192
Economy, **1947:** 214; **1949:** 162

Italy — *continued*
Elections in, **1948:** 77 [19], 84 [3, 19]; **1952–53:** 288, 291
Equestrian statues from, dedication, **1951:** 235
Fascism.
See main heading, Fascism.
Former colonies
Disposition of, **1948:** 178 [14], 278 [14, 41]
Independence, **1950:** 143
U.S. policy on, **1948:** 185 [6, 11]
Industrial capacity, **1951:** 235
Invasion, World War II, **1945:** 45, 178
King Umberto, **1946:** 126 [7]
Labor movement, **1951:** 235
Liberation, **1947:** 239
Mussolini, Benito, **1945:** 22 [21], 66; **1948:** 256
NATO effort of, **1951:** 232; **1952–53:** 358
News conference remarks, **1945:** 40 [3], 107 [21], 147 [11], 175 [16]; **1946:** 37 [2], 84 [3], 136 [13]
Partition of Trieste with Yugoslavia, proposed, **1951:** 239 [4]
Peace treaty with, **1947:** 2 (p. 9), 113
Revision, proposed, **1951:** 232, 235
Population growth, **1952–53:** 65
Refugees from, **1945:** 225
Relief for, **1945:** 186; **1947:** 47, 196, 213
Sforza, Count Carlo, **1949:** 68
Ships seized by U.S., return to, **1948:** 51
Stevenson rehabilitation mission (1943), **1952–53:** 289 [5], 291, 292 [1, 2], 317 [4]
Strategic materials, export to Communist bloc, **1952–53:** 358
Surplus population, problem of resettlement, **1951:** 232, 235
Surrender of German forces, **1945:** 20, 21
Trade treaty with U.S., **1948:** 73
Trade union movement, **1951:** 235
Trieste, return to, **1948:** 74; **1951:** 232
U.N. membership, proposed, **1951:** 235
U.S. Ambassador Alexander C. Kirk, **1946:** 129 [10, 15]
War casualties, **1947:** 210 [6]
Ithaca, N.Y., letter from mayor of, **1951:** 298 [11]
Iturbi, José, **1951:** 99
Ivanissevich, Oscar, **1947:** 105
Ives, Sen. Irving M., **1948:** 229; **1950:** 258 [5]; **1952–53:** 221 [7]
Iwo Jima, **1945:** 45
U.S. invasion. **1945:** 161, 178

Jabara, Capt. James, **1952–53:** 279, 319 [5]
Jackman, Art, **1948:** 216 [14]
Jackson, Andrew, **1945:** 227; **1946:** 67, 126 [21]; **1947:** 68; **1948:** 9 [21], 26 [20], 32, 53, 84ftn. (p. 230), 101, 227 [7], 231 [10], 236,

Jackson, Andrew — *continued*
242 [1], 245, 261 [4], 264 [5]; **1949:** 28 [5], 38, 39, 123; **1950:** 12, 39, 44 [15], 94, 312; **1951:** 80; **1952–53:** 136 [17], 282 [7], 289
Anecdote respecting, **1951:** 8
News conference remarks on, **1951:** 56 [25], 108 [11], 251 [22]
Press attacks on, **1951:** 8
Jackson, Lt. Arthur J., Congressional Medal of Honor award, **1945:** 160n.
Jackson, Repr. Henry M., **1949:** 40 [9]; **1952–53:** 156 [10], 272, 274 [1–5, 7], 274 [7], 275, 276
Jackson, Justice Robert H., **1946:** 136 [8, 10], 141 [4], 186 [11], 233, 237 [3, 8]; **1948:** 50n.; **1950:** 79; **1951:** 295 [8]; **1952–53:** 161
Appointment as U.S. Chief of Counsel, war crimes trials, statement, **1945:** 22 [5]
News conference remarks on, **1945:** 22 [5, 14], 31 [2], 44 [9], 52 [2, 9], 60 [9], 67 [2], 157 [1]
War crimes report, **1945:** 52 [2, 9], 60 [9]
Jackson, Mich., **1950:** 313
Jackson County, Mo., **1945:** 163; **1949:** 249
President's service as Judge for Eastern District, **1945:** 68
Visit, **1945:** 68
Jackson Day dinner, **1946:** 67; **1947:** 31 [6]
Jackson-Jefferson Day dinner.
See Jefferson-Jackson Day Dinners.
Jackson Hole National Monument, **1950:** 248
Jacobs, Repr. Andrew, **1950:** 169 [4]
Jacobson, Douglas T., Congressional Medal of Honor award, **1945:** 160n.
Jacobson, Edward, **1949:** 52ftn. (p. 171)
Jailbreaks, Washington, D.C., **1946:** 72 [15]
James, Wynn, Jr., **1948:** 227 [3]
James I, King, **1952–53:** 260
James River, N. Dak., **1950:** 129 [5]
Jamestown Island, **1947:** 231
Jane's Fighting Ships, **1949:** 269 [18]
Japan, **1945:** 2, 3, 20, 27, 30, 33, 34, 37, 50, 54, 66, 91, 125, 136, 146n., 161, 186, 190, 216, 218; **1946:** 2, 7, 18 (pp. 38, 42, 44–47), 76, 83, 85, 265; **1947:** 7 (p. 67), 35, 56, 90 [7], 138; **1948:** 8 (p. 96)
Aggression in Manchuria, **1945:** 139, 216
Attack (1931), **1951:** 4
Allied Control Commission, question of, **1945:** 147 [1]
Allied policy toward, **1945:** 132 [5], 147 [4]
Statement, **1945:** 143
Army, Soviet charges on, **1948:** 288 [6]
Assistance, **1947:** 238; **1950:** 9 (p. 58); **1952–53:** 95, 111, 354
Economic, **1951:** 13 (p. 74)
Military, **1951:** 193 [2]
Atomic bomb, use against, **1950:** 121 [1], 209 [18], 273 [8]; **1952–53:** 366, 378

Japan — *continued*
  Atomic bomb targets
    Hiroshima, **1945:** 93, 97, 156, 178
    Nagasaki, **1945:** 178
  China, occupation of, **1948:** 31
  CIA operations in, opposition by General Mac-
    Arthur, **1951:** 95 [9]
  Communism in, **1952–53:** 354
  Crop damage, **1948:** 5 (p. 29)
  Defense, negotiations concerning, **1951:** 84, 216,
    247 [15]
  Demobilization of U.S. forces, **1945:** 138
  Democracy, progress towards, **1950:** 119
  Disarmament, **1946:** 18 (pp. 46, 47), 236
  Economy, **1950:** 119; **1952–53:** 55, 366
  Emperor Hirohito, **1945:** 100, 143, 145, 172 [2]
    Soviet demand for trial, **1950:** 29 [14]
  Grain exports to, **1947:** 18
  Greece in state of war with, **1945:** 75
  Information program in, transfer to State De-
    partment, **1952–53:** 18 (p. 77)
  Mandated islands, **1946:** 15 [4, 9], 247; **1947:** 119
  May Day riots in Tokyo, **1952–53:** 115 [18]
  Message to Congress on winning war, **1945:** 45
  Militarism in, **1948:** 256; **1949:** 195
  Military code, decipherment, **1945:** 221 [10]
  Mutual defense treaty, **1952–53:** 95, 111
  News conference remarks, **1945:** 26 [2, 3], 40 [2],
    44 [2, 4], 64 [15], 94, 100, 106 [3, 5, 9, 10,
    13, 22], 132 [5, 6], 137 [9, 12], 147 [1, 4, 11,
    19], 157 [7], 181 [2, 4], 221 [7, 10]; **1946:** 6
    [14], 15 [4, 9, 21], 30 [2], 37 [2], 84 [27], 86
    [32], 95 [3, 22], 186 [7]; **1949:** 32 [5, 18],
    148 [9]; **1950:** 3 [1], 29 [14], 137 [12], 179
    [19], 203 [20], 206 [1, 7], 250 [1, 6, 9, 17,
    20], 270 [14, 16], 273 [8], 287 [6], 295 [10]
  Occupation, Allied, **1945:** 106 [10, 13, 22], 123,
    137 [9, 12], 143, 147 [4], 157 [7], 181 [2, 4],
    221 [7]; **1947:** 214; **1949:** 8 (pp. 54, 59);
    1951: 216
  Peace settlements, **1948:** 2
  Peace treaty with, **1951:** 49 [18], 84, 153 [22], 193
    [3, 8, 10, 11], 200 [6], 209 [16], 216, 217,
    224 [8], 227ftn. (p. 527), 247ftn. (p. 562),
    261 [17]; **1952–53:** 5, 38, 79, 111
    Question of, **1947:** 2 (p. 10); **1950:** 137 [12],
      179 [19], 250 [1, 6, 9, 17, 20], 269, 270 [14,
      16], 287 [6]
    Statement upon signing, **1952–53:** 95
  Pearl Harbor attack, **1947:** 110
  Philippines, occupation of, **1946:** 31
  Rearmament, question of, **1950:** 203 [20], 250
    [17]
  Reparations, **1945:** 32, 143, 147 [11]; **1946:** 37 [2],
    95 [3, 22]; **1947:** 36 [20]
    Mission of Ambassador Pauley on, statement,
      1945: 182
  Soviet declaration of war, **1945:** 94, 97

Japan — *continued*
  Soviet policy in, **1951:** 197
  Supreme Commander for the Allied Powers,
    authority of, **1945:** 143, 145
  Surrender, **1945:** 100, 106 [3, 5, 9], 128, 143, 145,
    196n.; **1947:** 88 [1], 110, 177 [8], 200, 210
    [1]; **1948:** 31, 88 [1], 89, 92, 181 [1], 268;
    1949: 86, 117, 160; **1950:** 110 [1], 194, 216,
    223
    Address to U.S. armed forces, **1945:** 123
    Broadcast on occasion of signing, **1945:** 122
    Demand for unconditional surrender, **1945:** 26
      [2, 3], 28, 45, 93, 97
    Potsdam Declaration, **1945:** 100, 145, 216
    Proclamation, **1945:** 105
  Tojo, Hideki, **1948:** 256; **1951:** 138
  Tokyo, **1945:** 45, 161; **1946:** 18, 141 [11]; **1947:**
    36 [20]
  Tongass National Forest, Alaska, logging op-
    erations in, **1952–53:** 247 [11]
  U.N. membership, proposed, **1951:** 216
  U.S. Ambassador, question of appointment,
    1952–53: 26 [30]
  U.S. policy in, **1950:** 267, 268; **1952–53:** 288
  U.S. prisoners of war, **1945:** 44 [2, 4], 97
  Visit of Secretary Johnson, **1950:** 137 [12]
  Visit by Senator Magnuson, **1951:** 85 [11]
  War assets and claims, disposition and settle-
    ment, **1948:** 154
  War crimes trials, **1946:** 18 (pp. 46, 47)
  Wartime espionage in U.S., **1948:** 181 [14]
Japanese-American evacuation claims, **1948:** 20
Japanese-Chinese war, **1945:** 166, 216
Java, sugar exports, **1947:** 64
Javits, Repr. Jacob K., **1949:** 231 [19]
Jay Treaty, **1952–53:** 45
Jefferson, Thomas, **1945:** 227; **1946:** 126 [21], 268;
    1947: 68, 138; **1948:** 32, 77 [13, 15], 86,
    213, 227 [7], 231 [10], 236, 242 [1], 245, 257
    [2], 259 [3], 261 [1, 4, 5]; **1949:** 38, 39, 122
    [16], 249, 250 [3]; **1950:** 39, 110 [3], 121 [6],
    134, 280; **1951:** 8, 56 [25], 80; **1952–53:** 45,
    131, 136 [17], 146, 174, 229n.
  Education, views on, **1952–53:** 284 [6]
  Louisiana Purchase, **1950:** 162; **1952–53:** 107 [10]
  Writings, publication of, **1950:** 12, 136
Jefferson, Thomas, Memorial Foundation, **1947:**
    138n.
Jefferson Barracks, Mo., **1949:** 118 [21]
Jefferson City, Mo.
  Campaign remarks, **1948:** 138 [3]; **1952–53:** 284
    [6]
  Mayor James T. Blair, Jr., **1948:** 138 [3]
  Visit to, question of, **1952–53:** 88 [20]
Jefferson-Jackson Day Committee, National, **1950:**
    34ftn. (p. 151)
Jefferson Day Dinners, **1947:** 31 [6], 68; **1948:** 32,
    41 [15]; **1949:** 38, 39; **1950:** 39; **1951:** 80;
    1952–53: 69, 88 [2]

[References are to items except as otherwise indicated]

Jefferson Day Dinners — *continued*
  Tickets, sale to Government employees, **1950:** 38
    [8]
Jefferson-Jackson Executive Committee, **1949:** 74
Jefferson Jubilee, **1950:** 134
Jefferson Memorial, **1946:** 21 [2]
Jefferson Memorial, St. Louis, Mo., **1949:** 253 [7]
  Proposed, **1948:** 283 [11, 13]
Jefferson National Expansion Memorial, dedication, **1950:** 162
Jenner, Sen. William E., **1952–53:** 280 [3], 283, 286
    [8], 289 [3], 291, 292 [8], 296, 297, 298 [9,
    10, 14], 300, 301, 303 [5], 304, 312, 313 [4],
    322
  Endorsement by General Eisenhower, **1952–53:**
    247 [7]
  Revenue Act of 1951, amendment, **1951:** 264
Jersey City, N.J.
  Campaign remarks, **1948:** 227 [8, 9]; **1952–53:**
    303 [2]
  Mayor Frank H. Eggers, **1948:** 189, 227n.
  Mayor John V. Kenny, **1952–53:** 303 [2]
Jerusalem, rebuilding of Temple, **1951:** 68
Jessel, George, **1949:** 82; **1952–53:** 273
Jessup, Philip C., **1949:** 11 [8], 30 [1], 260ftn. (p.
    571); **1950:** 80 [1, 6, 12], 268; **1951:** 227
    [15], 266; **1952–53:** 289 [6], 290, 303 [5]
Jester, Gov. Beauford H., **1948:** 208 [4–8], 209, 210
    [1, 2], 212 [2–7, 9], 213, 214 [1–5]
Jester, Mrs. Beauford H., **1948:** 212 [4], 214, [1, 3]
Jewish Agency for Palestine, **1946:** 155
Jewish Appeal, United, **1946:** 42
Jewish National Fund, dinner remarks, **1952–53:**
    144
Jewish New Year, **1946:** 210
  Statement, **1945:** 103; **1947:** 153; **1952–53:** 235
Jewish Welfare Board, National, **1952–53:** 297
Jewish Workers, National Federation of, Israel,
    1951: 274n.
Jews, **1945:** 210; **1947:** 108
  See also Israel; Palestine.
  Disloyalty, denial of press allegations, **1948:** 49
    [1]
  Immigration into Palestine, **1945:** 106 [18], 147
    [13], 152, 172, [10], 181 [8], 187, 188, 210;
    1946: 92, 129 [11, 16], 136 [14], 141 [18],
    155, 175, 177 [14], 215 [5], 226 [5], 227, 237
    [6], 241; **1947:** 41
  Immigration to U.S., **1946:** 212; **1948:** 2, 115,
    142, 160, 165, 249, 256, 257 [1], 258, 261
    [7]
  National Conference of Christians and, **1949:**
    224
  Nazi and Fascist persecution, **1945:** 152, 187,
    188; **1946:** 42, 241
  News conference remarks, **1945:** 106 [8, 18], 147
    [13], 172 [10], 181 [8] 202 [4]; **1946:** 95 [7],
    129 [11, 16], 136 [14], 141 [18], 177 [14],
    226 [5], 237 [6]

Jews — *continued*
  Refugees in Europe, **1946:** 5, 95 [7], 132, 136 [14],
    186ftn. (p. 367), 212, 227, 241
    Letter to Prime Minister Attlee, **1945:** 188
    Statement, **1945:** 187
J. I. Case Co., labor dispute, **1946:** 129 [12], 136 [5],
    141 [16], 173 [17], 199 [3]
John Sevier steamplant, TVA, **1952–53:** 367 (p.
    1146)
Johns Hopkins University, **1950:** 80 [6]
Johnson, Andrew, **1945:** 63; **1948:** 245; **1951:** 108
    [11]; **1952–53:** 107 [10]
Johnson, Charles S., **1951:** 307n.
Johnson, Rev. Cliff R., **1952–53:** 337
Johnson, Sen. Edwin C., **1946:** 186 [9]; **1948:** 198
    [3–5, 7], 199, 200 [1]; **1950:** 186 [7];
    1952–53: 282 [6], 377 [12]
    Letter, **1949:** 222
Johnson, George, W., **1952–53:** 313n.
Johnson, Harold T., **1948:** 128 [1], 202 [4]
Johnson, Rev. Hewlett, **1946:** 30 [1]
Johnson, J. Monroe, **1948:** 1; **1949:** 64, 119 [4];
    1950: 259
  See also Defense Transportation, Office of, Director.
Johnson, James W., **1951:** 33ftn. (p. 147)
Johnson, James William, Jr., **1952–53:** 377 [22]
Johnson, Keen, **1946:** 186 [2]
Johnson, Louis, **1947:** 199; **1949:** 16, 45 [1, 13];
    1952–53: 26 [19], 242 [3], 378
  See also Defense, Secretary.
Johnson, Luther A., **1946:** 78 [7]
Johnson, Repr. Lyndon B., **1948:** 71 [14], 212 [1, 4,
    5], 213, 214 [2]; **1949:** 118 [11]; **1950:** 206
    [5]; **1951:** 2 [24]; **1952–53:** 175 [10], 238
    [5], 310, 377 [12]
Johnson, Mordecai, **1952–53:** 169
Johnson, Ole C., **1952–53:** 266 [3, 4, 7]
Johnson, Thomas, **1948:** 258
Johnson, Vilas, **1948:** 115
Johnson, Walter (Chairman, Board of Foreign
    Scholarships), letter, **1951:** 103
Johnson Debt Default Act
  News conference remarks, **1945:** 4 [6], 31 [3]
  Repeal, proposed, **1945:** 128; **1946:** 18 (p. 53)
Johnson-May atomic energy bill, **1945:** 172 [15]
Johnston, Alvanley, **1946:** 121, 124, 125
Johnston, Eric A., **1945:** 175 [3]; **1946:** 45n., 255n.;
    1948: 92; **1952–53:** 20, 21 [22], 203, 256
    Letter, **1951:** 74
    News conference remarks on, **1951:** 16 [4], 49
      [20], 56 [5], 123, 188 [17]
Johnston, Sen. Olin D., **1950:** 137 [23]; **1951:** 152
Johnston, Victor A., **1950:** 137 [18]
Johnston, W. Carl, **1952–53:** 321 [6]
Johnstone, Andrew, **1948:** 189n.
Johnstone, Mrs. Anne Hartwell, **1949:** 212
Johnstown, Pa., campaign address, **1948:** 251;
    1952–53: 306 [7]

Joint Accounting Program, **1950:** 244; **1952–53:** 86

Joint Brazil-U.S. Technical Mission, **1949:** 108 [1]

Joint Chiefs of Staff, **1945:** 145n., 218; **1946:** 7, 11, 63, 82, 137, 138, 215 [3]; **1947:** 10n., 42; **1948:** 110 [13], 278 [1]; **1949:** 50, 84ftn. (p. 223), 177, 179 [1], 180, 231 [7]; **1950:** 184, 193, 242; **1951:** 77n., 90 [7], 93, 95 [2, 9], 101ftn. (p. 276), 128, 132 [9], 138; **1952–53:** 128, 279, 310, 323n., 345 [1]

    Chairman (Gen. Omar N. Bradley), **1950:** 121 [1], 176, 184, 193, 238 [14], 242, 258 [3], 267, 268; **1952–53:** 128, 130, 131, 320, 353 [5, 8], 377 [18], 378

    Evaluation of Bikini atomic bomb tests, **1948:** 283 [3]

    Evaluation Board, **1948:** 278 [1], 283 [3]; **1949:** 66ftn. (p. 192)

        Report, **1946:** 163 [1]

    Korea, conference with President on, **1950:** 172

    Korean military policy, views on, **1952–53:** 320

    Marine Corps representation, proposed, **1950:** 235

    News conference remarks on, **1945:** 26 [2], 147 [4]; **1948:** 84 [9], 110 [13], 278 [1], 283 [3]; **1952–53:** 35 [8, 14]

    St. Lawrence Seaway project, support of, **1952–53:** 23

    Vandenberg, Gen. Hoyt S., question of reappointment, **1952–53:** 44 [3]

Joint Commission on Commercial Studies, U.S.-Argentina, **1949:** 113 [5]

Joint Philippine-American Finance Commission, **1949:** 178

Joint Statement on Commercial Policy, U.S.-U.K., **1946:** 25

Joint statements, with heads of state and government

    Allied leaders, **1945:** 9, 91

    Brazil, President Dutra, **1949:** 108

    Canada

        Prime Minister King, **1945:** 191, 209; **1946:** 108, 149

        Prime Minister St. Laurent, **1951:** 240

    Ecuador, President Plaza, **1951:** 134

    France

        President de Gaulle, **1945:** 113

        Prime Minister Pleven, **1951:** 25

    Iran, Shah Mohammad Reza, **1949:** 273

    Italy, Prime Minister De Gasperi, **1951:** 232

    Mexico, President Alemán, **1947:** 83

    Philippines, President Quirino, **1949:** 178

    Soviet Union, Marshal Stalin, **1945:** 9, 91

    United Kingdom

        Prime Minister Attlee, **1945:** 91, 191, 209; **1946:** 108, 149; **1950:** 301

        Prime Minister Churchill, **1945:** 9; **1952–53:** 6, 16

Joint U.S. Military Advisory and Planning Group, Greece, **1950:** 142n.

Jones, Alexander F., **1952–53:** 98 [1, 2], 107 [2]

Jones, Charles S. (Casey), **1952–53:** 110

Jones, Mrs. Geraldine, **1952–53:** 133

Jones, Harold, **1948:** 26 [5]

Jones, Cpl. Harvey D., **1952–53:** 321 [4], 322

Jones, J. Weldon, **1945:** 24; **1946:** 17 [9, 18, 26], 192 [1, 13, 20]; **1947:** 6; **1948:** 4 [7]

Jones, Jenkin L., **1952–53:** 98 [17]

Jones, Jesse, **1946:** 84 [21]; **1950:** 97 [11]; **1951:** 33 [2]

Jones, John G., **1952–53:** 277 [1]

Jones, Lewis, **1947:** 48n.; **1950:** 1n., 306n.; **1952–53:** 194

Jones, Marvin (War Food Administrator), **1945:** 35n.

    Resignation, **1945:** 39, 40 [1]

Jones, Repr. Robert E., Jr., **1952–53:** 127 [3]

Jones, W. Alton, **1952–53:** 238 [7]

Jones, Walter, **1952–53:** 98 [7]

Jones & Laughlin Steel Corp., **1951:** 305

Josefson, Nils S., **1952–53:** 243

Joy, Vice Adm. Charles T., **1950:** 260; **1952–53:** 131

Judd, Repr. Walter H., **1948:** 137 [4]; **1951:** 54n.

Judge Advocate, Air, question of appointment, **1948:** 181 [7]

Judiciary, Federal, **1946:** 192 [8], 268; **1947:** 7 (p. 59); **1948:** 5 [54], 20, 102; **1949:** 218; **1950:** 169 [12]

    See also Courts, Federal.

    Appointments to, **1949:** 161 [9, 10], 200 [4, 9], 211 [2], 226 [10]

    Hand, Learned, retirement, **1951:** 112

    Hennock, Frieda B., refusal of recess appointment, **1951:** 283

    Nominations, **1951:** 90 [2], 113 [10], 118 [6], 132 [12], 145 [6], 153 [5], 179 [8], 188 [7], 227 [3, 11, 13, 17], 251 [2, 17, 22], 261 [22], 275 [1, 3]

    Pay, **1945:** 128; **1946:** 17 [7]

    Presidential nominees, rejection by Senate, **1950:** 206ftn. (p. 570), 209ftn. (p. 582)

    Question of appointment, **1948:** 181 [20]

    Tenure in, **1949:** 205 [16]

    Vacancies, **1949:** 205 [13, 21], 231 [2], 260 [14]; **1952–53:** 35 [4, 7], 44 [5], 88 [8, 11], 166 [4]

Judson, Richard, **1952–53:** 289 [1]

Juliana, Queen, **1952–53:** 31 [4]

    Visit of, **1952–53:** 73, 74, 77, 78

Junction City, Kans., campaign remarks, **1948:** 197

Jungle Book, Rudyard Kipling, **1952–53:** 218

Junior Livestock Show, Spokane, Wash., **1950:** 124 [6]

Junior Police, Decatur, Ill., **1948:** 233 [6]

Jurisdictional strikes, **1945:** 184; **1947:** 2 (p. 4), 19 [1]

Justice, Department of, **1945:** 52 [13], 225; **1946:** 35, 52, 116, 118, 186ftn. (p. 368); **1947:** 2 (p. 9), 4 (p. 35), 7 (p. 87), 35, 70 [2, 4, 10], 77, 78 [14], 80, 89, 109; **1948:** 5 (p. 52), 20, 26 [8], 37, 78 [15], 102, 265, 283 [1]; **1949:** 8 (p. 89), 226 [14]; **1950:** 94, 144n.; **1952–53:** 60, 136 [9], 169, 181n., 296

See also Attorney General.

Alien control functions, **1952–53:** 367 (p. 1163)

Alien property functions, **1946:** 231

Chicago newsman, prosecution, **1952–53:** 342 [3]

Civil rights functions, **1952–53:** 290
    Proposed expansion, **1950:** 9 (p. 102)

Crime control functions, **1951:** 63 [1]

Deportable aliens, supervision over, **1950:** 207

Internal security bill, advisory opinion against, **1950:** 254

Investigations of, **1952–53:** 26 [24], 91, 247 [5]

McCarthy, Sen. Joseph R., investigation, **1952–53:** 377 [24]

News conference remarks, **1946:** 27 [13], 37 [4], 41 [5], 119 [3], 199 [16], 229 [27]

Officers, changes in title, **1950:** 54

Programs review, **1950:** 196

Questionnaire, distribution to employees, **1952–53:** 75ftn. (p. 231)

Reorganization, **1950:** 53, 54, 56; **1951:** 226; **1952–53:** 87, 137

Shea, Francis M., **1945:** 157 [1]

Sonnett, John F., **1945:** 157 [1]

Justice, International Court of, **1950:** 143; **1951:** 150

Justice, Military, Uniform Code of, **1950:** 108

Juvenile delinquency, **1946:** 229 [21]
    National conference for prevention (1946), **1951:** 63 [1]

Kaesong, Korea, cease-fire negotiations, **1951:** 153 [15], 165 [9], 171 [5], 200 [8]

Kaiser, Henry J., United National Clothing Collection, **1945:** 74n., 144

Kaiser, Philip M., **1949:** 161 [1]

Kaiser Wilhelm II, **1951:** 138

Kaiser Aluminum & Chemical Corp., **1952–53:** 22

Kaiser-Frazer Corp., **1946:** 15 [6]

Kaiser Steel Co., RFC loan to, **1951:** 13 (p. 78)

Kalbfus, Adm. Edward C., **1947:** 236 [2]

Kalispell, Mont., campaign remarks, **1952–53:** 270 [4]

Kaltenborn, H. V., **1947:** 90 [1]; **1949:** 17, 234 [14]

Kane, John J., **1948:** 189n., 252; **1952–53:** 240n., 307

Kane, Mrs. John J., **1949:** 202n.

Kangaroo, gift for the President, **1952–53:** 149 [7]

Kansas, **1947:** 104; **1950:** 110 [3], 206 [3]
    Campaign remarks, **1948:** 137, 197

Kansas — *continued*
    Candidates for public office, **1948:** 197
    Colorado-Kansas negotiations for division of Arkansas River waters, **1945:** 194
    Dispute with Missouri over Arkansas River, **1948:** 86
    Federal district court, judgeship appointment, **1945:** 172 [9]
    Flood relief, **1951:** 158, 162, 185, 196, 224 [7]; **1952–53:** 18 (p. 88), 32, 50, 109, 119
        Kansas River Basin, **1951:** 183, 185, 196
    Gov. Frank Carlson, **1950:** 312, 313; **1951:** 196
    High school essay contest winners, remarks to, **1951:** 203
    High school students, remarks, **1952–53:** 236
    Power projects, **1951:** 185
    Sedgwick County Board of Commissioners, **1950:** 256

Kansas City, Mo., **1945:** 68; **1946:** 37 [15], 61 [21]; **1947:** 71n., 107 [6], 110, 209 [12]; **1948:** 89, 183 [7]; **1949:** 98n., 206 [6], 211 [7], 220; **1951:** 21, 196, 209 [5]; **1952–53:** 29, 63, 170, 197 [17]
    Bank, President's boyhood employment in, **1948:** 194 [12]
    Campaign remarks, **1952–53:** 324
    Crime, grand jury investigation, **1950:** 86 [2, 6]; **1951:** 63 [1]
    Flood control levees, **1950:** 129 [3]
    Knights of the Red Cross of Constantine, dinner, **1950:** 312
    News conference remarks, **1950:** 86 [2, 6], 273 [16]
    Organized Reserve Corps Armory, dedication, **1951:** 218
    Press luncheon, **1950:** 313

Kansas City, University of, **1945:** 68

Kansas City Power and Light Co., **1952–53:** 143

Kansas City Star, **1947:** 210 [2]; **1952–53:** 284 [4], 292 [12]

Kansas-Nebraska Act, **1951:** 8

Karaberis, C. H., Congressional Medal of Honor presentation, **1945:** 167n.

Kars, Turkey, **1946:** 53 [10]

Kashmir dispute, **1948:** 202 [6]; **1950:** 143

Kassel, Germany, **1945:** 97

Katyn Forest massacre, **1952–53:** 312, 317 [7]

Kaufman, Judge Irving, **1949:** 155 [21]; **1952–53:** 377ftn. (p. 1192)

Kaufmann, Aloys P., **1948:** 283 [11]

Kean, L., **1948:** 124 [1]

Kearney, Nebr., campaign remarks in, **1948:** 118 [2]

Keating, Repr. Kenneth B., **1951:** 120

Keats, Harold A., **1949:** 203n.

Keck, Charles, **1948:** 245

Kee, Repr. John, **1950:** 11 [11, 14], 78; **1951:** 53, 81

Keech, Richmond B., **1946:** 229 [1]; **1950:** 46 [4]

Keegan, Frank A., **1952–53:** 303 [9]
Keen Teen Club, **1946:** 75, 86 [33]
Kefauver, Estes, **1950:** 168; **1951:** 49 [8], 54n., 95 [5], 138, 298 [3]; **1952–53:** 2 [9, 18], 3, 49 [11], 175ftn. (p. 432)
    Antitrust bill, **1948:** 252
    Government, charges of corruption in, **1952–53:** 21 [19]
    News conference remarks on, **1952–53:** 21 [3, 12, 15, 17, 32], 98 [42]
    Presidential candidacy, **1952–53:** 21 [4, 15, 17, 32], 26 [7], 88 [18], 98 [24, 41], 136 [11], 156 [3]
Keleher, Thomas J., **1952–53:** 284 [1, 2], 285
Keller, A. D., **1948:** 200 [2]
Keller, Harry, **1948:** 227 [1]
Keller, K. T., **1947:** 55n., 223
Keller, Kent, **1948:** 218 [6], 219
Kelley, Capt. Colin, **1948:** 53
Kelley, Nicholas, **1952–53:** 117n.
Kellogg, William Sparks, **1949:** 119n.
Kelly, Edna F., **1952–53:** 298n., 300
Kelly, Edward J., **1945:** 44 [12]; **1946:** 15 [12], 76n.; **1948:** 268
Kelly, Monsignor, **1948:** 227 [7]
Kelly, T. J., Congressional Medal of Honor presentation, **1945:** 167n.
Kelly, Walter A., **1952–53:** 320
Kelsey, Frank W., **1946:** 262 [11]
Kem, Sen. James P., **1949:** 192 [24]; **1951:** 118 [14]; **1952–53:** 21 [17], 26 [9], 266 [13], 280 [3], 312
Kennan, George F., **1949:** 112 [1]
Kennecott Copper Corp., **1951:** 204, 214; **1952–53:** 37
Kennedy, Repr. John F., **1948:** 174 [4]; **1949:** 231 [19]; **1952–53:** 292 [9–12], 295 [7–9], 296, 298 [1–3]
Kennedy, Joseph P., **1949:** 94n.
Kennedy, William J., **1946:** 72 [1]
Kennelly, Martin H., **1947:** 67 [5]; **1948:** 115; **1950:** 134n.
Kenney, John W., **1949:** 93 [1]
Kennon, Gov. Robert F., **1952–53:** 315 [6], 316
Kenny, Mayor John V., **1952–53:** 303 [2]
Kent, Wash., campaign remarks, **1952–53:** 274 [7]
Kentucky, **1945:** 163; **1946:** 266 [10]; **1947:** 145 [7], 218 [1]
    Barkley, Sen. Alben W., **1945:** 8 [4], 89, 129 [7], 165
    Campaign remarks, **1948:** 218 [11–14], 220, 222 [1–8]
    Candidates for public office, **1948:** 218 [11–14], 222 [1–8]
    Droughts, **1952–53:** 221 [1]
    Floods, control and relief, **1952–53:** 50
    Gilbertsville, **1945:** 165
    Gov. Earle C. Clements, **1948:** 218 [14], 220

Kentucky — *continued*
    Gov. Lawrence W. Wetherby, **1952–53:** 221 [1]
    Gregory, Repr. Noble J., **1945:** 165
    May, Repr. Andrew J., **1945:** 114, 118 [5]
    President's forebears in, **1948:** 222 [1]
Kentucky Dam, dedication, address, **1945:** 165
Kentucky Derby, **1951:** 70 [5]
Kenyon, Dorothy, **1948:** 30; **1950:** 10
Keogh, Repr. Eugene J., **1952–53:** 300
Keough, Archbishop Francis P., **1950:** 171n.
Keppel, Mrs. Francis, **1950:** 32
Kerr, Repr. John H., **1951:** 165 [2]
Kerr, Robert S., **1948:** 213, 214 [4, 5, 7, 8], 216 [1–7, 10–12], 217; **1952–53:** 3
Kerr bill, **1950:** 86 [22]
Kerstetter, D. J., Congressional Medal of Honor presentation, **1945:** 167n.
Kessler, Dr. Henry H., **1952–53:** 135, 243
Key, 4-H Club, gift to the President, **1951:** 122
Key West, Fla., **1948:** 274n.; **1949:** 45 [11], 52, 53, 265, 267
    News conferences at, **1950:** 80; **1951:** 56, 295, 297; **1952–53:** 64 [7]
    News conference remarks on, **1950:** 3 [18], 273 [18]
    Releases from, **1950:** 82–84
    Visits to, **1951:** 16 [18], 56 [23], 70 [11]
        Question of, **1952–53:** 49 [14]
Keyes, Lt. Gen. Geoffrey, **1950:** 218, 274
Keyser, W. Va., campaign remarks, **1948:** 242 [3]; **1952–53:** 242 [5]
Keyserling, Leon H., **1946:** 177 [2], 183n.; **1950:** 137 [21]
    Memorandum and letter to, **1951:** 44, 142
"Kid of the Year" award, remarks to winner, **1952–53:** 154
Kidney disease, **1948:** 22
Kilburn, Repr. Clarence E., **1952–53:** 115 [10]
Kilgore, Sen. Harley M., **1946:** 21 [3]; **1948:** 222 [9], 242 [2, 3]; **1949:** 64; **1950:** 238 [4]; **1952–53:** 242 [3–6], 308 [1, 8]
Killian, James R., Jr., **1950:** 40n.; **1951:** 89
Kimball, Dan A., **1951:** 93n., 140 [1, 7]; **1952–53:** 170, 171
Kimball, Lindsley F., **1948:** 190; **1949:** 73n., 110n.; **1950:** 32n.
Kimmel, Adm. Husband E., **1945:** 118 [5]
King, Repr. Cecil R., **1951:** 295 [9]; **1952–53:** 2 [13]
King, Adm. Ernest J., **1945:** 2, 45; **1946:** 70 [1], 215 [3]; **1948:** 257 [3]; **1950:** 121 [1]
    Distinguished Service Medal, citation, **1945:** 215
    News conference remarks on, **1945:** 107 [17], 116, 193 [1]
King, W. L. Mackenzie (Prime Minister of Canada), **1945:** 107ftn. (p. 234), 157 [17]; **1946:** 18 (p. 42), 41 [26], 108, 149, 242 [6]; **1947:** 111, 112; **1948:** 11 [8], 43, 239, 273; **1949:** 237

King, W. L. Mackenzie — *continued*
  Death of, **1950:** 198
  Joint declaration on atomic energy, **1945:** 191
  Joint statement, **1945:** 209
Kings River project, Calif., **1946:** 97
Kingston steamplant, TVA, **1952–53:** 367 (p. 1146)
Kinneman, John A., **1952–53:** 321 [3]
Kinney, J. L., **1948:** 194n.
Kinney, Michael, **1950:** 23 [5]
Kipling, Rudyard, *Jungle Book*, **1952–53:** 218
Kirk, Adm. Alan G., **1949:** 72 [4], 182 [13]; **1951:**
  140 [5]
Kirk, Alexander C., **1946:** 129 [10, 15]
Kirk, James T., **1948:** 227 [6]; **1952–53:** 303 [4]
Kirwan, Repr. Michael J., **1948:** 258; **1949:** 45 [26];
  1952–53: 269n.
Kitchin, Thurman, **1951:** 256
Kitty Hawk, N.C., **1952–53:** 125, 328
Klamath Falls, Oreg.
  Campaign remarks at, **1948:** 126 [6]; **1952–53:**
    277 [1]
  Mayor Ed Ostendorn, **1948:** 126 [6]
Klamath Indians, capital reserve funds, **1948:** 57
Klein, Repr. Arthur G., **1949:** 171 [4]; **1952–53:** 298
  [13, 14]
Kline, Allan B., **1952–53:** 203n.
Kniffen, Luther M., **1948:** 249n.; **1952–53:** 306 [2]
Knight, Frank A., **1952–53:** 98 [20]
Knight, Goodwin J., **1948:** 128 [2], 134
Knight, John S., **1946:** 86 [1]
Knights of the Red Cross of Constantine, **1950:** 312
Knous, Gov. William Lee, **1948:** 198 [4, 5], 199;
  1949: 260 [14]
Knowland, Sen. William F., **1949:** 148 [11]; **1951:**
  56 [24]; **1952–53:** 156 [15]
  Amendment to Social Security Act, **1950:** 224
Knowlson, James S., **1947:** 191 [3]
Know-Nothing Party, **1952–53:** 288
Kon-Tiki, Thor Heyerdahl, **1951:** 130
Knox, Frank, **1952–53:** 289 [5]
Knox, Harley E., **1948:** 206 [1]
Knox College, **1950:** 110 [1]
Knoxville, Tenn., **1948:** 110 [5]
Knudsen, Lt. Gen. Williams, **1945:** 157 [3]
  Retirement, letter, **1945:** 55
Knutson, Repr. Harold, **1946:** 192 [26], 215 [2];
  1947: 6 [28], 70 [5], 127 [2]; **1948:** 214 [4]
Koch, Ilse, **1948:** 283 [6]
Koenig, Robert, **1947:** 122
Koenigsberg, transfer to Soviet Union, **1945:** 91
Kohler, Gov. Walter J., Jr., **1952–53:** 97
Koje, Korea, uprising in prisoner-of-war camps,
  1952–53: 127 [12], 162, 163, 166 [3]
Kokomo, Ind., campaign remarks, **1948:** 240 [4]
Kolodny, Joseph, **1947:** 85n.
Kootenai Indians, **1946:** 151
Korea, **1945:** 138; **1946:** 18 (p. 44), 76, 95 [3]; **1947:**
  7 (p. 67), 90 [4]; **1950:** 119

Korea — *continued*
  See also Korea, North; Korean War.
  Airlift to, **1951:** 13 (p. 83); **1952–53:** 18 (p. 83)
  Ambassador John M. Chang, **1950:** 222n.
  Armed forces, **1950:** 232; **1951:** 170; **1952–53:**
    12, 107 [2], 131, 283, 295 [8], 299, 320, 321
    [4], 322
    Training in U.S., **1951:** 236
  Army officers in U.S., remarks to, **1951:** 236
  Assistance, **1947:** 67 [11], 95 [13], 238; **1949:** 8 (p.
    54), 117, 118 [19], 162; **1952–53:** 242 [2],
    310
    Economic, **1950:** 9 (p. 58), 17, 78, 81, 154, 264,
      268, 269, 285; **1952–53:** 296, 310, 320, 321
      [2]
    Military, **1950:** 175, 179 [4], 181, 184; **1951:**
      114, 138; **1952–53:** 295 [8], 307, 310, 315
      [5], 320, 354
  Communist aggression in, **1950:** 151, 172, 173,
    175, 177, 181, 184, 193, 194, 201, 202, 204,
    211, 223, 282, 284, 291, 294, 296, 301, 304;
    1951: 13 (p. 68), 57, 114, 137, 138, 144,
    170, 174, 199, 256, 293, 297
    See also Communist aggression and expan-
      sion; Korean War.
  Defense, **1949:** 162, 184
  Eisenhower, Gen. Dwight D., visit to, **1952–53:**
    354 [4], 316, 320, 321 [4], 345 [4]
  Elections (1947), **1952–53:** 310, 323
  Elections under U.N. supervision, question of,
    1950: 258 [13]
  Four-power conference on, question of, **1951:** 2
    [13, 17]
  Japanese forces in, World War II surrender
    arrangements, **1950:** 194
  Koje, uprising in prisoner-of-war camps, **1952–
    53:** 127 [12], 162, 163, 166 [3]
  Liberation, statement, **1945:** 136
  Messages and statements on, **1950:** 184, 193, 194,
    211, 232, 303
  Mission to, small business study, **1945:** 228
  News conference remarks, **1945:** 106 [8], 132 [6];
    1950: 179 [2, 4, 5, 9, 11, 15, 16, 19, 21, 24,
    26], 186 [6, 8, 10, 11–13, 15], 191 [5, 9, 12,
    13], 203 [5, 9, 10, 14, 18], 209 [5, 12–14,
    16], 217 [7, 16, 22], 230 [7], 238 [12, 14, 16,
    18], 253 [13], 258 [3, 6, 8, 13], 270 [2], 273
    [12, 14, 18], 287 [1, 18], 295 [1, 2, 4–7,
    9–12, 14–18]; **1951:** 140 [16], 153 [3], 171
    [1], 209 [11], 300 [15]
  Peace settlements, **1948:** 2
  Police action in.
    See Korean war.
  Red Cross services in, **1951:** 271; **1952–53:** 50
  Relief for, **1945:** 186
  Rhee, Syngman, **1950:** 211, 260n.; **1952–53:** 156
    [11], 166 [11]
  Soviet attitude on, **1948:** 129

Korea — *continued*
  Unification, **1949:** 117; **1951:** 78, 216
  United Nations operations, **1948:** 34; **1950:** 186
    [13], 193, 209ftn. (p. 579), 223, 264, 296,
    303
  United Nations Temporary Commission on,
    1948: 129; **1949:** 1, 117
  U.S. Ambassador John J. Muccio, **1950:** 193,
    222, 268, 269; **1952–53:** 299
  U.S. forces in, **1949:** 117, 118 [19]; **1950:** 179 [5],
    186 [10], 269, 279, 287 [18], 317, 320
  U.S. occupation, **1947:** 214
  U.S. policy on, **1950:** 179 [2, 5, 11], 186 [8, 11],
    232, 239, 303
    Meeting with General MacArthur, **1950:** 264,
      267–269
  Visit to, question of, **1952–53:** 49 [18], 345 [2, 4]
Korea, North, **1950:** 173, 206ftn. (p. 571), 232
  Attack on South Korea, **1950:** 193, 194, 211, 258
    [8, 13]; **1951:** 170; **1952–53:** 5, 12
  Broadcast of General MacArthur to, **1950:** 258
    [8, 13]
  Communism in, **1952–53:** 232
  Intelligence report concerning, **1951:** 78
  Military strength, **1951:** 174
  News conference remarks, **1950:** 179 [11, 15, 17],
    191 [12], 258 [3, 8, 13]
  Soviet military assistance to, **1950:** 296; **1951:**
    174
  U.S. prisoners of war, executions, **1951:** 295 [3]
  Yalu River, question of U.N. military operations
    to, **1951:** 63 [14, 16, 23], 95 [9]
Korean war, **1950:** 197, 214ftn. (p. 588), 223, 226,
    232, 237, 254, 263, 267, 271, 272, 279, 281,
    292, 296, 299; **1951:** 4, 6, 25, 30, 38, 59, 92,
    96, 109, 110, 170, 293; **1952–53:** 29, 35
    [10], 69, 81, 288, 315 [1], 318
  Air strikes on targets in north, authorization,
    1950: 184
  Air supremacy, U.S., **1952–53:** 158
  Atomic bomb, question of use in, **1950:** 179 [5,
    26], 203 [10], 295 [12, 14]; **1951:** 251 [12],
    295 [3]; **1952–53:** 166 [12]
  Bombing of Communist China, question of,
    1951: 2 [7, 10], 70 [15], 90 [5]
  Campaign remarks, **1952–53:** 283, 316, 317 [1, 2],
    319 [1, 3, 5], 320, 321 [4, 5, 7], 322
  Casualties, **1950:** 238 [18]; **1951:** 96, 109, 121,
    252; **1952–53:** 249
    Alaskan and Hawaiian, **1950:** 291
  Chinese Communist intervention, **1950:** 230 [7],
    287 [1], 295 [1, 7], 296, 301, 303; **1951:**
    90ftn. (p. 242), 95 [9], 117, 199; **1952–53:**
    6, 12
  Chinese Nationalist troops, question of use in,
    1950: 295 [5]; **1951:** 33 [3], 85 [10]
  Clark, Gen. Mark W., appointment to U.N.
    command, **1952–53:** 113

Korean war — *continued*
  Congressional hearings on, **1951:** 90 [5, 7, 16], 95
    [2, 4, 6]; **1952–53:** 345 [1]
  Disabled veterans, vocational rehabilitation,
    1950: 298
  Economic effects of, **1952–53:** 292[9], 294, 319
    [1], 376
  8th U.S. Army, combat record in, **1950:** 320
  Eisenhower, Gen. Dwight D., views on, **1952–53:**
    247 [9, 12], 289, 293, 318
  Enemy offensive, preparations for renewal, **1951:**
    78, 90 [1, 8]
  Ethiopian troops in, **1952–53:** 196
  Expansion, administration opposition to, **1952–
    53:** 316, 345 [1]
  Expenditures for, **1952–53:** 231, 367 (p. 1130),
    368
  Hoarding by consumers at outbreak, **1952–53:**
    287
  Home front effort, **1950:** 243; **1951:** 80, 91, 116
    Nondefense spending, curtailment, **1950:** 213
    Railroad strike, question of effect on, **1950:**
      186 [6]
  India, participation, **1950:** 179 [16]
  Issue in election campaign, **1952–53:** 64 [2], 299,
    300
  Legal status, **1952–53:** 127 [10]
  Limitation of, **1951:** 78, 96, 98
  Lowe, Maj. Gen. Frank E., interception of cables
    from, **1952–53:** 26 [4]
  MacArthur, Gen. Douglas.
    See main heading, MacArthur, Gen. Douglas.
  Marine units in, **1950:** 235
  Military situation, estimate by Gen. MacArthur,
    1950: 194n.
  Moral issues at stake in, **1951:** 68
  NATO forces in, **1951:** 114
  Naval blockade, **1950:** 184, 193
  News conference remarks, **1951:** 2 [3, 6], 37 [8],
    140 [3, 11, 16], 261 [2], 295 [7]; **1952–53:** 2
    [15], 149 [10], 345 [1], 353 [8]
  Payments for enemy desertions and surrenders,
    proposal by newsman, **1951:** 7 [18]
  Philippines, participation, **1950:** 217 [16]; **1951:**
    208
  "Police action" designation, comment on, **1952–
    53:** 334 [9]
  Policy statements on
    Defense Mobilization Director, Charles E.
      Wilson, **1951:** 63 [7]
    Secretary of Defense, Gen. George C. Mar-
      shall, **1951:** 63 [6, 7, 25]
    Secretary of State, Dean Acheson, **1951:** 2 [13],
      16 [6], 113 [7]
  Prisoners.
    See Prisoners of war, Korean.
  Radio report on, **1951:** 78

Korean war — *continued*
  Republican stand on, campaign remarks, **1952–53:** 316
  Ridgway, Lt. Gen. Matthew B., armistice proposal, **1952–53:** 121, 123 [20]
  Seoul, liberation of, **1950:** 260
  Soviet intervention, question of, **1951:** 95 [9], 275 [15]
  Soviet plane, destruction of, **1950:** 238 [12]
  Steel strike, effect on, **1952–53:** 103
  Swedish forces in, **1951:** 170
  Termination, negotiations for
    Armistice or cease-fire, **1951:** 16 [6, 8], 22 [1], 140 [3, 11, 13, 14, 18], 144, 153 [3, 15], 165 [9], 171 [5], 174, 193 [16], 200 [1, 8], 213, 227 [6], 298 [1], 300 [15]; **1952–53:** 5, 35 [13], 64 [5], 75 [1], 98 [17], 113, 121, 123 [20], 127 [11], 131, 132, 136 [6], 149 [8], 232n., 238 [9, 11, 15], 345 [1, 2, 4], 354, 359 [17]
    Peace settlement, **1951:** 2 [11, 13, 15], 56 [22], 77n., 78, 108 [8], 113 [7], 132 [3]
  Thirty-eighth parallel demarcation line
    Allied operations beyond, question of, **1950:** 191 [9], 230 [7], 253 [13], 258 [3, 6]; **1951:** 37 [8, 10], 56 [13], 63 [6, 12, 14, 16, 21, 23, 25], 95 [9]
    Violation by North Korea, **1950:** 193, 194
  Typhus among Communist forces, **1951:** 135
  U.N. operations in, **1950:** 226, 232, 264, 268, 269, 296, 301; **1951:** 7 [6], 50, 101 [5], 170, 171ftn. (p. 426), 184, 298 [1], 306; **1952–53:** 5, 6, 12, 121, 131, 132, 166 [9], 196, 232, 259, 299, 321 [4], 366
    Change in command, **1951:** 77, 78
    Designation of Gen. MacArthur to command, **1950:** 189
    Yalu River, operations to, **1951:** 63 [14, 16, 23], 95 [9]
  U.S. forces in, **1951:** 13 (pp. 63, 64), 109, 113 [1, 13], 138, 148, 170, 184, 208, 213, 256, 298 [1], 306; **1952–53:** 18 (p. 69), 56, 57, 107 [2], 128, 131, 135, 139, 172, 268 [5], 356, 378
    Medical facilities for, **1952–53:** 135, 333
    Withdrawal, **1952–53:** 295 [8], 299, 300, 310, 316, 319 [1], 320, 321 [4], 322, 323
  U.S. policy and objectives in, **1951:** 33 [3], 78, 80, 116, 144, 170, 298 [1]; **1952–53:** 5, 145, 266 [2], 272, 279, 310, 349, 366
  Veterans
    Benefits, **1951:** 13 (p. 99), 101 [1], 102; **1952–53:** 18 (p. 109), 135, 367 (p. 1160)
    Remarks to, **1951:** 38, 236, 272
  Wedemeyer, Lt. Gen. Albert C., report of, **1952–53:** 316
  White House conference with President-elect and Gen. MacArthur, proposed, **1952–53:** 345 [1]

Korean war — *continued*
  Women, role in war effort, **1950:** 255
Kortes, Andrew, **1950:** 116
Kortes Dam, Wyoming, **1950:** 116, 117 [4]
Kosciusko, Thaddeus, **1946:** 34
Kosenkina, Mrs. Oksana, **1948:** 178ftn. (p. 453)
Kozel, E. F., **1950:** 110 [8]
Kramer, Brig. Gen. Hans, U.S. representative in Colorado-Kansas negotiations for division of Arkansas River waters, letter, **1945:** 194
Krehel, Peter, **1952–53:** 305
Krock, Arthur, **1950:** 38 [20] and ftn. (p. 159); **1951:** 90 [6], 295 [4]
Kroeger, A. and H. Organization, Businessmen's Dinner Forum, **1949:** 240ftn. (p. 533)
Kroll, Jack, **1952–53:** 230n.
Kronheim, Milton S., Sr., **1952–53:** 144
Krug, Julius A.
  See Interior, Secretary of the; War Production Board, Chairman.
Kruppenbacher, Victor, **1952–53:** 289 [2]
Kruse, Edward H., Jr., **1948:** 254
Ku Klux Klan, in 1928 election campaign, **1948:** 260; **1949:** 122 [16]; **1952–53:** 169, 290
Kunkel, Repr. John C., **1950:** 137ftn. (p. 421)
Kurfees, Marshall C., **1951:** 255
Kurile Islands, **1946:** 27 [7]
Kuter, Maj. Gen. Laurence S., **1948:** 3, 11 [3]
Kutz, Brig. Gen. Charles W., **1945:** 129 [13]
Kuznets, Simon, **1952–53:** 305
Kwajalein Island, **1945:** 45

Labor, **1946:** 18 (pp. 40, 49–51), 125, 213, 226 [1], 257 [5], 266 [12]; **1947:** 4 (pp. 27, 29, 31), 7 (p. 88), 44, 70 [14], 76, 81, 93, 121, 142, 152, 174 [1, 3], 177 [23], 212, 214, 219, 225; **1948:** 2, 5 (pp. 20, 25, 38, 53), 8 (pp. 62, 70, 74, 77, 78, 81, 82, 84–87, 90), 10, 14, 32, 175, 182, 183 [1, 4, 5, 7], 184; **1949:** 5, 8 (p. 90), 199, 239, 250 [3]; **1950:** 9 (pp. 97–100), 202; **1951:** 13 (pp. 64, 78–80); **1952–53:** 18 (pp. 92–95), 98 [10], 237, 268 [5], 306 [2]
  Administration program, **1952–53:** 218, 367 (pp. 1150–1152)
    Contribution to World War II victory, **1948:** 218 [3]
  Agricultural
    Draft deferment, **1952–53:** 185–187
    Manpower needs, **1952–53:** 15, 18 (p. 94), 186, 187
  Apprenticeship standards, **1951:** 13 (p. 80)
  Building trades, **1946:** 263
  Child, **1949:** 239
    Abolition, **1948:** 219
  Closed shop, **1952–53:** 110

Labor — *continued*
Coal miners, **1952–53:** 341
Collective bargaining, **1951:** 11, 49 [6, 9], 74, 265, 277, 279; **1952–53:** 88 [3, 5], 148, 161, 215, 237, 289 [1], 292 [5], 304, 308 [1], 317 [5], 341, 376
Defense effort, cooperation with, **1951:** 11, 15, 63 [8], 212
Disputes.
See Labor disputes.
Fair standards laws, Republican opposition, **1952–53:** 218
Industrial, draft deferment, **1952–53:** 185
Labor force, expansion, **1951:** 11, 13 (pp. 78–80); **1952–53:** 215
Legislation, **1946:** 6 [13], 15 [23], 27 [9], 110 [14], 119 [5], 126 [5, 12, 18], 129 [14], 136 [15]; **1947:** 78 [4, 9], 90 [2], 95 [3], 107 [4], 120, 127 [1, 4, 10], 187; **1948:** 183 [6], 218 [8], 261 [4, 8, 9, 11, 15], 267 [2, 3], 268; **1949:** 2, 4 [8], 22 [11], 28 [5], 84 [23], 112 [15], 118 [16, 20], 144 [4], 202, 214 [6]; **1950:** 2, 49, 123, 127 [5], 128, 279; **1951:** 4, 7 [4], 279; **1952–53:** 237, 242 [5], 266 [3], 315 [1], 318
Taft-Hartley Act.
See main heading, Taft-Hartley Act.
Mediation and conciliation services, **1952–53:** 88 [3]
Migrant workers
Commission to study problems of, **1950:** 153; **1951:** 75, 154
Mexican, **1951:** 75, 154, 192; **1952–53:** 2 [5], 18 (p. 94–95), 31 [14], 367 (pp. 1150–1151)
Educational aid for children of, **1952–53:** 18 (p. 102)
Mobility of, **1950:** 84
News conference remarks, **1950:** 38 [17], 217 [20], 230 [4]
Productivity, **1951:** 11; **1952–53:** 215
Recruitment and training, **1952–53:** 18 (p. 92)
Relations with management and Government, **1951:** 11, 13 (pp. 79, 80), 98, 212, 279; **1952–53:** 15, 215, 237, 313 [5], 367 (p. 1150)
Legislation, proposed, **1952–53:** 215
Representation in mobilization agencies, **1951:** 49 [2, 10, 15, 20, 22, 23], 56 [4], 63 [8]
Republican stand on, **1952–53:** 286 [8]
Responsibility in reconversion period, **1945:** 180
Rights of, **1948:** 217, 236, 249; **1951:** 11, 212, 279; **1952–53:** 281, 306 [6]
Role in foreign policy, **1948:** 278 [36]
Soviet Union, forced, **1952–53:** 253 [1]
Standards, **1951:** 154; **1952–53:** 18 (p. 94), 237, 376
Enforcement functions, reorganization, **1950:** 53, 68

Labor — *continued*
Statistics, **1949:** 8 (pp. 90, 91), 13
Collection, **1952–53:** 18
Wage and hour, international convention on, **1951:** 97
Trade union movement, **1948:** 228 [13], 248, 261 [15]; **1950:** 4, 157, 177, 228, 279; **1951:** 212, 279; **1952–53:** 251, 291, 292 [13], 308 [1], 317, 336
International, **1950:** 177
Italian, **1951:** 235
Union shop, **1952–53:** 88 [7], 110, 166 [5], 270 [5]
Wage guarantee, **1947:** 53
Wages.
See Wage-price policy *under* Wages.
War effort, **1948:** 186 [6]
Work stoppages, **1952–53:** 215
Working conditions, improvement, **1948:** 219
Labor, Acting Secretary of, **1948:** 130 [1]
Labor, American Federation of, **1948:** 140, 183 [6], 184; **1952–53:** 336
Labor, Department of, **1945:** 104, 128, 206; **1946:** 117, 262 [4]; **1947:** 2 (p. 5), 7 (pp. 59, 74, 89), 20, 53, 67 [1], 78 [13], 81, 93, 120, 145 [23], 177 [16], 187, 232 [1, 4]; **1948:** 5 (pp. 25, 53), 10, 30, 42, 175, 182; **1949:** 8 (p. 90), 13; **1950:** 318 [3]; **1952–53:** 150, 185
Appropriation, **1951:** 192
Child labor law enforcement, **1952–53:** 18 (p. 95)
Cost-of-living index, **1945:** 202 [3, 5]
Creation (1913), **1948:** 259 [1, 2]
Defense production activities, **1952–53:** 18 (pp. 92–94)
Industrial development program, **1946:** 18 (p. 49)
Industrial safety training program, **1952–53:** 367 (p. 1151)
Labor extension service, proposed, **1950:** 9 (p. 99)
Labor market surveys, **1951:** 154
Labor mediation functions, **1946:** 131
Lubin, Isador, **1945:** 14, 15
Manpower mobilization activities, **1952–53:** 18 (pp. 92–94)
Mexican migrant workers, negotiations concerning, **1952–53:** 2 [5]
News conference remarks, **1945:** 106 [15], 132 [11], 137 [1, 7], 202 [3, 5]; **1946:** 70 [7], 72 [6], 129 [13], 136 [4], 192 [8], 199 [3], 215 [12]; **1949:** 155 [15], 161 [1, 12]
Placement services, **1952–53:** 18 (p. 92)
Programs review, **1950:** 196
Reorganization, **1945:** 137 [1, 7]; **1948:** 101, 121, 134, 135, 138 [4, 8], 139 [2], 160, 227 [9], 232, 252, 259 [1, 2]; **1949:** 2, 127, 129, 181; **1950:** 53, 54, 60, 68, 74
Safety programs for Federal employees, **1950:** 74
State labor programs, cooperation with, **1952–53:** 367 (p. 1150)

Labor, Migratory, President's Commission on, **1950:** 153; **1951:** 75, 154
Labor, Secretary of, **1945:** 204, 226
First (William B. Wilson), **1948:** 259 [1, 2]
Labor, Secretary of (Frances Perkins)
Letter, **1945:** 37
Resignation, **1945:** 40 [1]
Labor, Secretary of (Lewis B. Schwellenbach), **1945:** 137n.; **1946:** 12, 23, 41 [15], 61 [4], 66 [3], 78 [13], 136 [1, 14], 173 [17], 215 [10, 12]; **1947:** 20, 87, 93, 123, 124, 126; **1948:** 10, 30n., 70, 110 [19]
Death of, **1948:** 123, 124 [1], 125
Letters, **1947:** 53, 184
News conference remarks on, **1945:** 76 [1], 147 [16, 22], 175 [10]; **1947:** 62 [20], 221 [1]
Successor, question of, **1948:** 150 [5], 163 [7], 170 [10]
Labor, Secretary of (Maurice J. Tobin), **1948:** 178 [8], 259 [1, 2, 4, 5]; **1949:** 13, 55, 84 [23], 161 [12], 267 [2]; **1950:** 18, 155, 208; **1951:** 154, 195, 279; **1952–53:** 148, 150
Campaign remarks on, **1952–53:** 292 [11]
Conference with the President, **1951:** 49 [2, 3, 16]
International wage and hour statistics, letter, **1951:** 97
Memorandum, **1950:** 259
Programs review, letter, **1950:** 196
Resignation, **1952–53:** 386
Labor Conference, International, message to Congress, **1948:** 70
Labor contracts, **1945:** 181 [5], 184; **1946:** 73, 131; **1947:** 120; **1951:** 265
Automobile workers, **1948:** 110 [17]; **1950:** 146 [19], 202
Coal miners, **1946:** 126 [25], 237 [5], 252, 262 [21]; **1947:** 121, 141 [9], 142, 152; **1948:** 66, 171, 248; **1950:** 29 [19], 49, 50; **1952–53:** 342 [7]
Communications industry, **1950:** 43n.
Construction workers, **1947:** 19 [1]
General Motors Corp., **1946:** 9
Kaiser-Frazer Corp., **1946:** 15 [6]
Migratory workers, Mexican, **1951:** 154
Rubber workers, **1947:** 19 [1], 62 [18], 62 [19]
Steel workers, **1947:** 19 [1], 142; **1952–53:** 82
Transportation industry, **1951:** 74
Labor Day, **1949:** 199
Address, **1952–53:** 241
Statements, **1945:** 121; **1946:** 213; **1947:** 187; **1948:** 182; **1950:** 228; **1951:** 212; **1952–53:** 237
Labor disputes, **1945:** 104, 128, 180, 184, 202, [3], 204; **1946:** 2, 18 (pp. 50–52), 35, 164, 216 [4], 266 [12]; **1947:** 2 (pp. 3, 5), 4 (pp. 20, 25, 28), 7 (p. 89), 68; **1948:** 8 (p. 85), 183 [7], 184; **1949:** 2, 5, 8 (p. 90); **1951:** 13 (p. 80); **1952–53:** 263

Labor disputes — *continued*
Aircraft industry, **1951:** 252
Airlines, **1946:** 110 [11]; **1951:** 132 [1], 140 [10]
Allis-Chalmers Manufacturing Co., **1946:** 129 [12], 136 [5], 141 [16], 143 [5]
Aluminum industry, **1952–53:** 22
Atomic energy facilities, **1951:** 239 [18]
Automobile industry, **1948:** 110 [17]
Boeing Co., **1948:** 88 [5]
Boycotts, **1947:** 120, 2 (p. 4), 19 [1]
Canneries, **1946:** 61 [4], 66 [3], 70 [7]
Coal industry, **1948:** 66, 71 [5], 171, 198 [5]; **1949:** 118 [13, 20], 155 [15], 214 [8], 226 [5], 231 [1, 14, 20], 236 [2], 240 [5], 253 [12, 14], 260 [1, 6, 9, 11]; **1950:** 6, 16 [10, 17, 20], 23 [7, 16], 27, 29 [19], 34 [2, 4], 35, 44 [8, 16], 46 [4, 9], 49, 50, 202; **1952–53:** 341, 342 [7]
Injunction, **1950:** 35, 38 [14], 49
Message to Congress, **1950:** 49
Strikes.
See main heading, Coal strikes.
Communications industry, telegram to management and labor leaders, **1950:** 42
Committee for study of, proposed, **1946:** 125, 131
Communist-inspired strikes, failure in Europe, **1951:** 4
Copper industry, **1951:** 169, 204, 209 [1], 214; **1952–53:** 37
Settlement, **1951:** 277
D.C. transit strike, **1945:** 195, 208ftn. (p. 528)
Defense industries, **1951:** 167
Mediation, **1952–53:** 18 (p. 92)
Factfinding boards.
See Factfinding boards in labor disputes.
Federal mediation, record of, **1948:** 259 [1]
General Motors strike, **1945:** 193 [5], 202 [5], 204, 206, 208 [7], 211 [2, 4], 221 [14, 21]; **1946:** 2, 9, 15 [6, 14, 23], 16, 21 [14], 27 [9], 41 [23], 53 [2]
Great Lakes Towing Co., Cleveland, Ohio, **1945:** 202 [1]
Homestead steel strike (1892), **1948:** 198 [5]
Injunctions.
See Injunctions in labor disputes.
International Harvester Co., **1946:** 173 [17]
J. I. Case Co., **1946:** 129 [12], 136 [5], 141 [16], 173 [17], 199 [3]
Jurisdictional strikes, **1945:** 184; **1947:** 2 (p. 4), 19 [1], 120
Labor courts, question of, **1946:** 262 [14]
Lockouts, **1947:** 120
Longshoremen, **1948:** 178 [8]; **1951:** 276
Maritime industry, **1946:** 126 [15, 18], 129 [13], 136 [4], 215 [12], 216 [7, 11, 23], 220n.; **1948:** 110 [4], 179, 181 [19], 274 [18]; **1949:** 118 [16], 144 [20], 148 [9, 11], 155 [17]

Labor disputes — *continued*
  Meatpacking industry, **1946:** 15 [18], 21 [6]; **1948:** 71 [17], 72, 93 [5]
  Mediation and conciliation services, **1950:** 9 (p. 98); **1951:** 13 (p. 80), 169, 204, 252, 305; **1952–53:** 136 [20], 148
    Additional, veto of, **1946:** 131
    Legislation, question of need for, **1952–53:** 156 [5]
  Metals industry, nonferrous, **1952–53:** 37
  News conference remarks, **1945:** 31 [8], 147 [16], 157 [5], 164 [3], 172 [6], 193 [5], 202 [1, 5], 208 [7], 211 [2, 4], 221 [14, 21]; **1947:** 70 [10, 15]
  Oak Ridge National Laboratory, **1948:** 140
  Oil industry, **1952–53:** 58, 123 [6]
  Petroleum industry, **1945:** 158
  Presidential intervention, question of, **1949:** 148 [9, 11], 155 [7, 15], 234 [3], 236 [2], 240 [16], 260 [6]
  Pullman strike (1894), **1948:** 198 [5]
  Railroad, **1947:** 145 [15]; **1948:** 88 [3], 93 [1, 3, 6, 8], 95, 198 [5]; **1949:** 155 [15], 205 [11]; **1950:** 186 [1, 4, 6, 9], 188, 209 [4, 21], 214 [1, 6, 16], 217 [3, 6, 8, 21], 303; **1951:** 16 [14], 33 [1, 15], 37 [16], 49 [1, 6, 9], 74, 209 [2]; **1952–53:** 136 [2, 14]
    Federal control, statement, **1950:** 221
    1946, **1952–53:** 253 [2, 4]
    Settlement, **1948:** 159
  Railroad strike.
  See main heading, Railroad strike.
  Rubber industry, **1946:** 53 [2]
  Steel industry, **1945:** 204, 206; **1946:** 6 [15], 12, 15 [7, 10], 16, 20, 21 [3, 5, 7, 9, 14, 19], 27 [9], 30 [4, 5], 37 [9, 16, 19], 53 [2], 61 [9], 72 [4]; **1948:** 198 [5]; **1949:** 152, 153, 155 [5, 7, 12, 15], 179 [6], 200 [15], 205 [10, 20], 209, 211 [6], 213, 214 [9, 11], 226 [5], 231 [14], 236 [2], 240 [5, 7], 253 [14], 260 [6, 11]; **1950:** 6; **1951:** 304, 305; **1952–53:** 64 [14], 70, 75 [10], 82, 83, 88 [3, 5], 98 [14, 25], 107 [2, 12], 110, 115 [1, 5, 8, 10, 12, 13, 16, 17, 19], 116, 123 [2, 4], 129, 136 [3], 156 [4], 159, 161, 166 [1, 5, 7], 175 [12, 16], 197 [2], 215, 231, 233 [5], 242 [5]
    Address to American people, question of, **1952–53:** 115 [10]
    Government seizure, **1952–53:** 156 [4], 175 [16]
    Injunction, question of use, **1952–53:** 37, 115 [12]
    Settlement, **1952–53:** 216
  Strike ballots, termination, **1946:** 118
  Strikes against Government, **1946:** 95 [10, 15], 110 [7, 11], 125, 131
  Telephone industry, **1946:** 53 [2]; **1947:** 67 [1], 78 [13]
  Textile workers, **1951:** 85 [7]

Labor disputes — *continued*
  Threat to national economy, **1948:** 93 [6]
  Transit strike, Philadelphia, **1949:** 32 [19]
  Transportation industry, **1951:** 74
  Trucking industry, **1948:** 181 [19]
  Wage Stabilization Board functions, **1951:** 167; **1952–53:** 190
  "Wildcat" strikes, **1947:** 120
  Work stoppages, danger to defense production, **1951:** 13 (pp. 78, 79), 167
Labor Disputes Act, **1945:** 172 [6]
Labor extension service, proposed, **1950:** 9 (p. 99)
Labor Israel, National Committee for, **1951:** 274n.
Labor-Management Conference, National, **1945:** 104, 128, 180, 204; **1946:** 2; **1947:** 120
  Address, **1945:** 184
  News conference remarks, **1945:** 106 [21], 107 [19], 147 [22], 175 [3, 18], 193 [2]
Labor-Management Panel, National, **1947:** 236 [3], 237
Labor-management relations, **1945:** 180, 184, 203, 206; **1946:** 2, 9, 18 (pp. 40, 48–50), 73, 124, 125, 131, 161, 232, 250 [5]; **1947:** 2 (pp. 3, 5), 4 (pp. 14, 20, 28, 30), 7 (pp. 88, 89), 19 [1], 20, 68, 76, 110, 121, 125, 127 [1, 4, 10], 142, 152, 174 [1, 3], 177 [12], 179, 187, 221 [6], 237; **1948:** 2, 8 (p. 70), 37, 286; **1950:** 84, 127 [5]
  Atomic energy facilities, **1948:** 140; **1949:** 81, 87
  History in U.S., **1948:** 184
  Labor disputes.
  See main heading, Labor disputes.
  Legislation, **1948:** 182, 231 [1], 283 [8]
  Message to Congress, **1945:** 204
  News conference remarks, **1945:** 164 [5], 172 [1], 193 [2], 211 [2, 9]; **1948:** 93 [5], 178 [8], 283 [8]
  Record of, **1948:** 235 [4], 236
  Toledo plan, **1946:** 257 [17]
Labor Management Relations Act.
  See Taft-Hartley Act.
Labor Organization, International, **1945:** 132 [11], 181 [10]; **1946:** 18 (p. 87), 180, 215 [10], 236; **1947:** 21, 123, 124, 126; **1948:** 70, 131 [1]
Labor organizations, **1945:** 37, 104; **1946:** 15 [5], 110 [7], 131, 157; **1947:** 36 [11], 121, 205 [10]; **1948:** 8 (p. 85), 32, 182, 183 [1, 2], 222 [9], 223, 226, 242 [3]; **1949:** 39, 151; **1950:** 279; **1952–53:** 37, 69, 237, 308 [1], 312, 322
Amalgamated Association of Street, Electric, Railway and Motor Coach Employees, **1945:** 195
Amalgamated Clothing Workers, **1948:** 261 [11]; **1951:** 239ftn. (p. 544)
American Federation of Government Employees, **1952–53:** 390

Labor organizations — *continued*
American Federation of Labor, **1946:** 53 [2], 215 [10], 220n.; **1947:** 19 [1], 20, 62 [2], 122, 236 [3]; **1948:** 140, 183 [6], 184; **1950:** 4; **1951:** 153 [16], 204, 214; **1952–53:** 22, 37, 58, 286 [8], 336
American Newspaper Guild, **1950:** 177
Brotherhood of Locomotive Engineers, **1946:** 120, 121, 124, 125; **1948:** 95, 159n.; **1952–53:** 136ftn. (p. 359)
Brotherhood of Locomotive Firemen and Enginemen, **1948:** 95, 159n.; **1950:** 221n.; **1951:** 49 [6]; **1952–53:** 136ftn. (p. 359)
Brotherhood of Railway Trainmen, **1946:** 120, 121, 124, 125; **1948:** 11ftn. (p. 105); **1950:** 209ftn. (p. 580), 221; **1952–53:** 136ftn. (p. 359)
Carpenters Union, AFL, **1947:** 236 [3]
Coal industry, welfare funds, **1948:** 248
Communications Workers of America, **1950:** 42
Communists in, **1947:** 120; **1948:** 252; **1950:** 94, 207
Congress of Industrial Organizations, **1945:** 22 [8]; **1946:** 53 [2], 215 [10], 262 [12]; **1947:** 19 [1], 122, 177 [12], 236 [3]; **1948:** 26, 93 [5], 183 [6], 184, 278 [36], 288 [12]; **1949:** 30 [3], 152, 211 [6], 240 [2]; **1950:** 38 [21], 42, 177n.; **1951:** 132 [16], 153 [16], 183, 252, 261 [8], 277, 298 [8], 304, 305; **1952–53:** 22, 58, 216, 230
Agreement with, the President's alleged, **1952–53:** 88 [9]
German, suppression by Nazis, **1948:** 256
Gompers, Samuel, role in developing, **1951:** 279
Growth of, **1948:** 227 [7, 9], 228 [2, 5, 6, 12, 13], 261 [15], 268
Hod Carriers, Building, and Common Laborers Union, **1949:** 240ftn. (p. 532)
Information programs abroad, **1950:** 92
International Association of Machinists, **1947:** 236 [3]; **1948:** 277
International Confederation of Free Trade Unions, **1952–53:** 253 [1]
International Council of Aluminum Workers of America, **1952–53:** 22
International Labor Organization.
See main heading, International Labor Organization.
International Ladies Garment Workers Union, **1952–53:** 273
International Longshoremen's Association, **1948:** 179
International Union of Mine, Mill and Smelter Workers, **1951:** 204, 214; **1952–53:** 37
Lobbying, **1948:** 277
National Federation of Federal Employees, **1947:** 190

Labor organizations — *continued*
News conference remarks, **1945:** 175 [18], 211 [4], 221 [3, 12, 14, 18]
Oil Workers International Union, **1952–53:** 58
Order of Railway Conductors, **1950:** 209ftn. (p. 580), 221; **1952–53:** 136ftn. (p. 359)
Political activities, **1947:** 121
Railroads, **1948:** 240 [3], 257 [4]; **1951:** 33 [1, 15], 74, 214
Records, availability to factfinding boards in labor disputes, **1945:** 204, 211 [4], 221 [3, 12, 14, 18]
Safety programs, **1950:** 155
Switchmen's Union of North America, **1948:** 95; **1950:** 188
Taft-Hartley Act
Criticism of, **1950:** 123
Provisions respecting, **1947:** 120
Union shop elections, **1951:** 265
United Automobile, Aircraft and Agricultural Implement Workers of America, **1951:** 252
United Automobile Workers of America, **1945:** 204, 206; **1946:** 2; **1948:** 110 [17]; **1949:** 122 [10], 269 [14]; **1950:** 146 [19], 202
Labor dispute, **1945:** 204, 206
United Mine Workers, **1946:** 252; **1947:** 127 [15], 141 [9]; **1948:** 55 [9], 66n., 171, 248; **1950:** 16ftn. (p. 117), 27, 34 [2], 35, 49; **1951:** 153 [16]; **1952–53:** 341
United Rubber Workers Union, **1945:** 175 [18]
United Steel Workers of America, **1945:** 204, 206; **1946:** 12, 16; **1949:** 152, 209, 213; **1951:** 169, 277, 304, 305; **1952–53:** 22, 116n., 118n., 216
Welfare funds, **1947:** 120
Labor practices, unfair, **1947:** 120
Labor Policy Committee, United, **1951:** 49 [2], 70 [9]
Labor Problems, President's Panel on, **1947:** 87
Labor program, **1945:** 208 [9], 211 [6]
Labor Relations Act, National, **1947:** 120, 121
Labor Relations in Atomic Energy Installations, President's Commission on, **1949:** 81
Labor Relations Board, National, **1946:** 118, 131; **1947:** 127 [1], 141 [4], 145 [2], 174 [2], 177 [23], 181 (p. 403), 218 [14]; **1948:** 5 (p. 54), 140; **1952–53:** 18 (p. 93), 35 [11]
Reorganization, **1950:** 66
Labor Relations Panel, Atomic Energy, proposed, **1949:** 81
Labor Standards, Bureau of, **1950:** 74
Labor standards, public works and Federally assisted projects, **1950:** 68, 74
Labor Statistics, Bureau of, **1946:** 179; **1947:** 20, 65; **1948:** 10, 37, 101, 121, 134, 138 [4], 139 [2], 252, 259 [1, 2]; **1950:** 74, 93; **1952–53:** 18 (p. 95)

Laborers and mechanics on public works projects, **1947:** 81

Labrador, iron ore reserves, **1950:** 9 (p. 94); **1951:** 11, 13 (pp. 81–83); **1952–53:** 175ftn. (p. 433)

Lackey, E. Dent, **1952–53:** 228n.

Lafayette, Marquis de, **1950:** 185

LaFollette, Robert M., **1948:** 235 [1], 236, 238; **1949:** 53 [9]; **1951:** 174; **1952–53:** 241, 277 [1], 308 [1], 312

La Follette, Sen. Robert M., Jr., **1946:** 6 [8], 61 [22], 223 [4], 226 [17]; **1947:** 122, 127 [4]; **1951:** 174; **1952–53:** 241

La Grande, Oreg., **1950:** 121 [9]

La Guardia, Fiorello H., **1945:** 178; **1946:** 21 [8], 87n., 119 [16], 141 [1]; **1948:** 43

  News conference remarks on, **1945:** 44 [12], 76 [6]

Lake Erie, **1950:** 99

Lake Ontario, **1950:** 99

Lake Pontchartrain, Louisiana, **1952–53:** 367 (p. 1146)

Lake St. Clair, **1947:** 171

Lake Success, N.Y., **1950:** 296

Lake Superior, iron ore deposits, **1951:** 11

Lake Texoma (Oklahoma), **1948:** 214 [5]

Lakota, N. Dak., campaign remarks, **1952–53:** 266 [5]

"Lame duck" appointments, **1947:** 19 [12], 36 [26]

Land, Vice Adm. Emory S.
  See War Shipping Administrator (Vice Adm. Emory S. Land).

Land, Frank S., **1950:** 41n., 312; **1951:** 41n.; **1952–53:** 45

Land, veto of bill to restrict Government transactions in, **1951:** 105, 108 [1]

Land-grant colleges, **1946:** 18 (p. 84)

Land Management, Bureau of, **1946:** 118; **1949:** 8; **1952–53:** 18 (p. 89)

Land prices, farm, **1947:** 97

Land reclamation, **1945:** 128

Land reform, Africa, Asia, and Latin America, **1951:** 179 [13]

Land resources, **1947:** 4 (p. 34); **1952–53:** 231, 367 (pp. 1146, 1147), 388

  Agricultural, **1952–53:** 367 (pp. 1148–1150)

Land Tenure Conference, World, **1951:** 296

Land-use program, **1948:** 8 (pp. 67, 77, 78); **1950:** 9 (p. 85), 33, 111, 265

Landlords, pressure for termination of rent control, **1950:** 46 [18]

  Telegram, **1949:** 66 [19, 21]

Landis, Repr. Gerald W., **1947:** 36 [11]

Landis, James M., **1947:** 115n., 218 [8], 243 [4]

Landon, Alfred M., **1952–53:** 289 [8], 292 [12], 295 [6]

Landry, Brig. Gen. Robert B., **1949:** 36, 265

Lands
  Offshore, renunciation of U.S. claims, veto, **1946:** 189
  Private, water supply, **1949:** 245
  Virgin Islands, **1949:** 141

Lands, public, **1946:** 18 (p. 82), 190, 206; **1947:** 7 (p. 83), 35, 231; **1948:** 2, 5 (p. 46); **1950:** 9 (p. 90), 116, 121 [9]
  Alaska, claims to, **1948:** 105
  Indian, disposal of lands, veto, **1948:** 25
  Management and development, **1952–53:** 18 (p. 89)
  Offshore, **1952–53:** 115 [7], 136 [4], 146, 149 [4], 377 [11]
  Oil and gas leases, **1947:** 35
  Public mining claims, **1949:** 124
  Reclamation, **1947:** 110; **1948:** 32

Lane, Arthur Bliss, **1945:** 77, 78; **1947:** 62 [3, 8]

Lane, Repr. Thomas J., **1949:** 78 [4]; **1952–53:** 295 [8]

Lane, Gov. William P., **1948:** 259 [4]; **1949:** 26n.; **1950:** 97 [16], 135, 171

Laney, Gov. Ben, **1945:** 147 [9]

Lange, Halvard (Norwegian Foreign Minister), **1949:** 28ftn. (p. 128), 30 [13], 68

Langer, Sen. William, **1949:** 32 [13]; **1952–53:** 3, 266 [2, 3], 266 [6], 266 [9–11], 277 [1]

Langley, Samuel P., **1946:** 201

Langlie, Gov. Arthur B., **1950:** 124 [1], 125, 126

Language, universal, **1946:** 75 [9]

Lanham Act, **1947:** 44; **1950:** 69, 72

Lansing, Mich., campaign remarks, **1948:** 183 [2]; **1952–53:** 317 [3]

Laos, **1952–53:** 18 (p. 76)

Lapham, Lewis, **1947:** 236 [3], 237

Laramie, Wyo., **1950:** 119, 152 [7]
  Campaign remarks, **1948:** 118 [6]

Larrimore, N. Dak., campaign remarks, **1952–53:** 266 [4]

Larsen, Lt. Gen. Henry, **1952–53:** 353 [3]

Larson, Jess, **1947:** 226 [3], 229; **1948:** 88 [17]; **1949:** 89 [1], 145, 147; **1950:** 196, 259; **1951:** 177, 205; **1952–53:** 347
  Letter, **1951:** 127
  Successor, question of appointment, **1951:** 188 [18]

Las Vegas, N. Mex., campaign remarks, **1948:** 136 [4]

Latimer, Murray W., **1946:** 72 [1]

Latin America, **1945:** 120; **1947:** 14 [5]; **1948:** 15 [6]
  See also American Republics; Organization of American States; *specific countries.*
  Aid to Europe, **1947:** 191 [15, 18, 20]
  Ambassadorial appointments to, **1950:** 217 [5]
  Arms shipment to, question of, **1947:** 95 [10]
  Assistance, **1948:** 69; **1949:** 162; **1952–53:** 18 (pp. 76, 77), 55, 72, 367 (p. 1140)

Latin America — *continued*
  Assistance — *continued*
    Economic, **1951:** 4, 13 (p. 75), 114
    Military, **1951:** 114, 167
    Technical, **1951:** 13 (p. 75), 114, 262
  Capital investments in, **1948:** 69
  Communist propaganda in, **1950:** 231; **1951:** 76
  Defense, **1951:** 13 (pp. 64, 75)
  Donnelly, Walter J., diplomatic service in, **1950:** 218
  Economic and social development, **1948:** 69; **1950:** 52 [4], 159
  Foreign Ministers, Council of, **1952–53:** 94
  Foreign ministers meeting, **1951:** 16 [12], 59, 65, 67, 76, 85 [12], 125
  Foreign trade, **1947:** 238
  Good Neighbor Policy, **1946:** 77, 83, 102; **1947:** 73, 79, 83, 84, 101; **1948:** 69; **1949:** 35, 105, 230; **1950:** 137 [26]; **1951:** 76; **1952–53:** 94
  Independence
    Contribution of San Martín, **1950:** 212
    U.S. recognition (1821), **1951:** 8
  Land reform, **1951:** 179 [13]
  Mission of President Hoover, **1946:** 141 [8, 10]
  News conference remarks, **1946:** 21 [11, 20], 70 [20], 141 [8, 10]; **1950:** 52 [4], 137 [26], 217 [5], 250 [12], 278 [6]
  Pacific pact, proposed, **1950:** 250 [12]
  Point 4 program, **1950:** 278 [6]; **1952–53:** 55
  Refugees, immigration to, **1952–53:** 65
  U.S. forces in, World War II, **1951:** 114
  U.S. investments in, **1952–53:** 18 (pp. 76, 77)
  U.S. labor unions, information programs in, **1950:** 92
  U.S. policy in, **1950:** 239
  U.S. relations with, **1951:** 132 [8], 259, 267; **1952–53:** 94, 377 [23]
  Visit to, question of, **1947:** 95 [14]
  Visitors to news conference, **1951:** 70 [1]
Latta, Maurice C., **1947:** 78 [18], 182 [4]
  Death of, **1948:** 65
Lattimore, Owen, **1950:** 80 [6]; **1952–53:** 197 [10]
Latvia, Soviet domination, **1948:** 53, 86
Laughtenhauser, Dr. J., **1952–53:** 135
Laurel, José, **1949:** 240 [6]
Lauritsen, Charles G., **1948:** 191n.
Lausche, Frank J., **1948:** 84 [2], 114 [1], 231, 257 [4], 258; **1950:** 169 [1, 15]; **1952–53:** 253 [8], 286 [4, 6], 287, 311 [1, 2], 319 [1–6], 320
Lautier, Louis R., **1947:** 48n.
Lavalley, Georges Pierre, **1947:** 110
Law, Arthur, **1952–53:** 317 [6]
Law, comment on, **1950:** 37
Law, international, **1946:** 133, 233, 236, 251
Law, rule of, development, **1951:** 225
Law enforcement bill, District of Columbia, veto, **1945:** 80

Law Enforcement Problems, Attorney General's Conference on, **1950:** 11 [3], 37
Law School, University of Kansas City, President's attendance, **1945:** 68
Lawrence, David, **1945:** 147 [12]; **1948:** 252; **1949:** 202n.; **1950:** 38 [13]; **1952–53:** 7 [11], 307
Lawrence, James E., **1952–53:** 32, 269
Lawrence, William H., **1951:** 132 [10], 188 [11]; **1952–53:** 7 [10]
Lawrence, Mass., **1949:** 78 [4]
  Campaign remarks, **1952–53:** 295 [8]
Laws, Judge Bolitha J., **1950:** 174; **1951:** 35n.
Laws
  Colonial, **1947:** 138
  Emergency, termination, **1947:** 14 [13]
  Fire prevention, **1947:** 86
  International, **1947:** 21
  State, collection by Library of Congress, **1950:** 75
  Traffic, **1947:** 118
Lawson, Harry F., **1948:** 189n.
Lawton, Frederick J., **1949:** 4 [1], 7n.; **1950:** 8n.
  See also Budget, Bureau of the, Director.
Lawyers, U.S. Conference of, **1950:** 37n.
Lawyers Association, New York, **1951:** 113 [10]
Lawyers Guild, National, **1949:** 155 [2]; **1950:** 16 [6]
Lay, James S., Jr., letter, **1951:** 156
Leach, Paul R., **1948:** 41 [7]; **1951:** 295 [11], 300 [19]; **1952–53:** 98 [41, 42]
Lead
  Prices, **1949:** 58 [25]
  Stockpiling, **1948:** 8 (p. 78)
  Subsidies, **1947:** 175
Leadership, comments on, **1950:** 272
League of Nations, **1945:** 202 [9]; **1946:** 236; **1947:** 52, 126; **1948:** 101, 236, 245; **1949:** 120; **1950:** 10, 279; **1951:** 297; **1952–53:** 196, 378
  U.S. refusal to join, **1948:** 101, 117, 236, 245, 256, 266
League of Women Voters, **1947:** 121
Leahy, Adm. William D., **1945:** 2, 45, 94n., 97, 118n.; **1946:** 70 [1], 229 [3, 5]; **1947:** 88 [8], 107 [1], 110; **1948:** 30, 257 [3]; **1949:** 60; **1951:** 22 [2], 278n.; **1952–53:** 142, 335
  News conference remarks on, **1945:** 16, 60 [6], 67 [2], 127
Leather industry, **1947:** 152
Leather shortage, **1945:** 209
Lebanese American Federation, Syrian and, **1951:** 245
Lebanon
  Technical assistance, **1952–53:** 55
  Withdrawal of British and French troops, **1948:** 202 [6]
Lee, Gen. Charles, **1951:** 90 [16]

Lee, M. Sgt. Hubert L., Congressional Medal of
    Honor, **1952–53:** 24
Lee, Gen. Robert E., **1947:** 48n., 177 [9]; **1948:** 242
    [1]
Lee, Russel V., **1951:** 307n.
Lee, William E., reappointment to Interstate Com-
    merce Commission, **1945:** 202 [2]
Leesburg, Va., **1950:** 121 [8]
Lefever, Gregory, **1952–53:** 173n.
Leffingwell, Russell C., **1951:** 22 [2], 278n.
Leggett, Sir Frederick, **1945:** 210
Legion of Merit.
    See under Medals, presentation.
Legislation, statements upon approval.
    See also Congress.
    Acreage allotments and marketing quotas, **1950:**
        83
    Agricultural Act of 1948, **1948:** 155
    Agricultural price supports, **1952–53:** 210
    Agricultural research, expansion, **1946:** 207
    Aid to schools in Federal areas, **1949:** 208
    Aircraft, military, appropriation, **1948:** 106
    Appropriations bill, temporary, **1949:** 96
    Armed forces reservists, retirement benefits,
        1946: 145
    Atomic Energy Commission, extension of terms
        of members, **1948:** 156
    Aviation problems, study by Congress, **1947:** 161
    Budget and Accounting Procedures Act, **1950:**
        244
    Classification Act of 1949, **1949:** 242
    Clayton Act, amendment, **1950:** 319
    Coal mine safety, **1952–53:** 206
    Coinage of commemorative 50-cent pieces, **1946:**
        196
    Consumer credit regulation, **1947:** 176
    Decontrol Act, Second, **1947:** 143
    Defense contracts, financing, **1951:** 106
    Displaced Persons Act of 1948, **1948:** 142
        Amendment, **1950:** 167
    Defense Production Act Amendments of 1951,
        1951: 176
    Defense Production Act Amendments of 1952,
        1952–53: 190
    Delaware River Port Authority, **1952–53:** 209
    Documents, publication and codification of,
        1950: 75
    "Economic Indicators," publication of, **1949:**
        138
    Emergency powers, termination, **1947:** 156
    Employment Act, **1946:** 39
    Excess Profits Tax Act of 1950, **1951:** 1
    Fair Labor Standards Amendments of 1949,
        1949: 239
    Fair-trade amendments to Federal Trade Com-
        mission Act, **1952–53:** 204
    Farmers' Home Corporation Act, **1946:** 206
    Federal Civil Defense Act of 1950, **1951:** 10

Legislation — *continued*
    Flood control, **1946:** 176
    Flood Rehabilitation Act, **1951:** 269
    Foreign Aid Appropriation Act, 1949, **1948:** 144
    Foreign Assistance Act of 1948, **1948:** 64
    Foreign Economic Assistance Act, **1950:** 154 129
        [3]
    Foreign Service Act, **1946:** 202
    Fort Sumner irrigation project, New Mexico,
        1949: 168
    General Appropriations Act, **1950:** 234
    Government Corporations Appropriation Act,
        1949, **1948:** 148
    Government Corporation Control Act, **1945:** 207
    Government printing and binding, authorization
        of private procurement, **1949:** 147
    Grand Teton National Park, reestablishment,
        1950: 248
    Greece and Turkey, assistance, **1947:** 100
    Hospital care, New Mexico Indians, **1949:** 248
    Hospital Survey and Construction Act, **1946:** 203
    House of Representatives
        Communications and clerk hire allowance for
            members, **1949:** 137
        Pay of Members, **1952–53:** 207
    Housing Act of 1948, **1948:** 172
    Housing Act of 1949, **1949:** 157
    Housing and Rent Act, **1947:** 131
    Housing and Rent Act of 1949, **1949:** 65
    Housing and Rent Control Act of 1948, **1948:** 58
    Independent Offices Appropriation Act, **1952–
        53:** 201
    India Emergency Food Aid Act of 1951, **1951:**
        124
    Indian Claims Commission, establishment, **1946:**
        204
    Indians, economic rehabilitation, **1950:** 91
    Interdepartmental Committee for Scientific Re-
        search and Development, establishment,
        1947: 241
    Interior Department Appropriation Act, 1949,
        1948: 149
    International Refugee Organization, U.S. mem-
        bership, **1947:** 133
    Interstate commerce, felony to obstruct, **1946:**
        157
    Japan, peace treaty with, **1952–53:** 95
    Klamath Indians, capital reserve funds, **1948:** 57
    Legislative Reorganization Act, **1946:** 191
    Lend-Lease Act, extension, **1945:** 3
    Maritime war-risk insurance, **1950:** 236
    Medicine and Surgery, Department of, **1946:** 1
    Merchant Marine Act of 1936, amendment,
        1952–53: 211
    Mexico, employment of migratory workers from,
        1951: 192
    Military aid program, continuation, **1950:** 201
    Minimum wage, increase, **1950:** 18

Legislation — *continued*
  Mining claims, continuation of annual assess-
    ment work, **1949:** 124
  Mutual Defense Assistance Act of 1949, **1949:**
    225
  Mutual Security Act of 1951, **1951:** 250
  Narcotics laws, amendment, **1951:** 287
  National Military Establishment Appropriation
    Act of 1950, **1949:** 244
  National School Lunch Act, **1946:** 128
  National Science Foundation, **1950:** 120
  National Security Act, **1949:** 67
  National Security Act Amendments of 1949,
    1949: 177
  Pacific Islands Trust Territory, administration,
    1947: 151
  Palestine refugee relief, **1949:** 57
  Philippines
    Rehabilitation and trade, **1946:** 90
    Veterans pay bill, **1946:** 38
  Portal-to-Portal Act, **1947:** 93
  Postal Rate Revision and Federal Employees
    Salary Act, **1948:** 157
  Price control, **1947:** 242; **1948:** 176
  Price Control Act, extension, **1946:** 179
  Provo River reclamation project, Utah, **1948:** 56
  Puerto Rico
    Elective governorship, **1947:** 166
    Resolution approving constitution of, **1952–
      53:** 198
  Railroad retirement benefits, increase, **1951:** 280
  Recorder of Deeds, District of Columbia, **1952–
    53:** 160
  Reorganization Act of 1945, **1945:** 220
  Reorganization Act of 1949, **1949:** 127
  Reserve forces, disability compensation for
    members, **1949:** 135
  Revenue Act of 1951, **1951:** 264
  River and harbor construction, **1946:** 176
  Rivers and harbors bill, **1950:** 140
  Rural telephone facilities, improvement, **1949:**
    243
  Savings bonds, extension of interest-bearing life,
    1951: 60
  Second War Powers Act of 1942, extension,
    1945: 229
  Selective Training and Service Act of 1940,
    extension, **1945:** 30
  Social Security Act, amendments, **1950:** 224
    Amendments of 1952, **1952–53:** 213
  Strategic and Critical Materials Stockpiling Act,
    1946: 174
  Subsidy payments, **1945:** 65
  Sugar Control Extension Act, **1947:** 64
  Supplemental appropriation acts, **1951:** 117, 285;
    1952–53: 205
  Taft-Hartley Act, amendment, **1951:** 265
  Terminal leave bonds, redemption, **1947:** 158

Legislation — *continued*
  Trade Agreements Extension Act of 1948, **1948:**
    143; **1949:** 217
  Trade Agreements Extension Act of 1951, **1951:**
    126
  Trading With the Enemy Act, amendment, **1948:**
    154
  Uniform Code of Military Justice, **1950:** 108
  Urgent Deficiency Appropriation Bill, **1947:** 60
  Ute Indians, use of tribal funds, **1951:** 198
  Veterans Administration, pay raise for certain
    employees, **1949:** 228
  Veterans benefits, **1952–53:** 138
  Veterans priority for purchase of surplus prop-
    erty, **1946:** 98
  Virgin Islands Company, continuation, **1948:**
    146
  Virgin Islands Corporation, incorporation, **1949:**
    141
  Water desalination research, **1952–53:** 199
  Weber Basin reclamation project, Utah, **1949:**
    196 [*For citation to private bill (not in-
    cluded in this volume) see Appendix A under
    July 19, p. 600*]
  World Health Organization, U.S. membership,
    1948: 132
Legislation, Vetoes and Memorandums of Dis-
  approval.
  See Veto Messages and Memorandums of Dis-
    approval.
Legislative branch, **1946:** 250 [1], 268; **1947:** 7 (pp.
  59, 90), 56, 132, 146, 172, 182 [5], 190,
  242; **1948:** 5 (p. 54), 20, 102, 187; **1950:**
  79, 82, 89, 103, 140, 234
  See also Congress.
  Autonomy of, **1949:** 112 [14]
  Reorganization, **1946:** 61 [22], 191
Legislative program, **1947:** 2 (p. 5), 7 (p. 55); **1949:**
  2, 5, 8 (p. 47), 202; **1950:** 2, 6, 9 (pp.
  103–106), 121 [3, 5, 7], 122, 124 [8], 127
  [5], 134, 157, 193, 202, 207; **1951:** 4, 13
  (pp. 65, 77), 92, 225, 238; **1952–53:** 218
  Civil rights, **1952–53:** 290
  Comments on, **1946:** 95 [26], 192 [5]
  Congressional action on, **1949:** 231 [16], 235
  Economic, **1951:** 11, 167; **1952–53:** 15
  Emergency legislation, **1950:** 307
  Labor-management relations, **1952–53:** 15
  News conference remarks, **1949:** 32 [1, 11], 40 [3],
    45 [18, 21], 52 [10, 13], 95 [15], 112 [8, 10,
    12, 15], 113 [1, 12], 118 [11, 24], 144 [10],
    192 [23], 200 [5], 214 [10], 231 [16], 267
    [10]; **1950:** 8 [10], 137 [4], 287 [11, 16, 17,
    21]; **1951:** 7 [2, 4], 12 [33]
  Obstruction through appropriations reduction,
    1951: 285
  Republican opposition.
    See Republican Party.

Legislative program — *continued*
  Special interests, opposition to, **1952–53:** 62, 97, 277 [1], 278, 280 [6], 282 [4], 284 [4], 287, 295 [2, 9], 298 [5], 305, 306 [2, 5–7], 314, 322
  Taft, Sen. Robert A., comment on, **1952–53:** 359 [9]
Legislative program, the President's, **1948:** 2, 5 (pp. 20, 59), 175, 182
  Campaign remarks, **1948:** 117, 183 [1, 5, 6], 184, 215, 247–249, 251, 257 [2, 3], 258, 259 [3], 267 [2], 268
  Congressional inaction on.
  See Congress.
  Message to Congress, **1948:** 165
  News conference remarks, **1948:** 26 [11, 15], 181 [2], 274 [4, 16]
Legislative Reorganization Act, **1947:** 7 (p. 93)
  Approval, **1946:** 191
Lehman, Herbert H., **1946:** 61 [21], 66 [9], 68, 70 [9], 84 [10], 215 [9]; **1947:** 191 [3]; **1948:** 228 [1], 262; **1949:** 155 [9], 192 [4], 200 [4], 231 [11], 251; **1950:** 39, 105 [3], 214 [12], 287 [14]; **1951:** 227 [7]; **1952–53:** 3, 88, 89 [1, 2, 4, 5, 7, 11], 290, 291, 297, 298 [13, 14], 300
  Memorandum, **1945:** 225
Lehman, Orin, **1952–53:** 203n.
Leiserson, William M., **1947:** 87n.; **1950:** 153
LeMoyne College, **1948:** 228 [8]
Lend-lease, **1945:** 50, 71; **1946:** 18 (pp. 45, 76, 84), 192 [25], 265; **1947:** 7 (p. 65), 11, 132; **1948:** 97 [7]
  Discontinuance, **1945:** 107 [12, 22], 128
  News conference remarks, **1945:** 40 [2], 107 [12, 22]
  Report on operations, transmittal to Congress, **1951:** 244
  Soviet Union, **1945:** 40 [2]
  United Kingdom, **1945:** 107 [22]
  Use of funds for price supports, **1945:** 128
Lend-Lease Act, **1946:** 102; **1947:** 11, 35, 101
  Extension, approval, **1945:** 3
Lenin, Nikolai, **1952–53:** 366
Lenroot, Katherine F., **1950:** 5n.
Leon River, Tex., **1948:** 212 [4]
Leonard, Colvin T., **1952–53:** 98 [13]
LeSauvage, George R., **1947:** 191 [3]
Lesinski, Repr. John, **1949:** 11 [7]; **1950:** 29 [2, 12], 47
  Labor bills, **1949:** 89 [17], 93ftns. (pp. 242, 244), 214 [6]
Less-developed and new nations, assistance, **1948:** 69, 276; **1949:** 19, 35, 40 [10], 139, 193, 195, 237, 263; **1952–53:** 15, 20, 57, 101, 367 (p. 1139), 376, 378
See also Point 4 program; *specific countries.*

Less-developed and new nations — *continued*
  Economic, **1949:** 28 [11], 35, 40 [10], 88, 151; **1950:** 2, 6, 9 (pp. 48, 56, 59), 18, 25, 87, 94, 126, 132, 154, 159, 177, 193, 289; **1951:** 11, 41, 50, 53, 114, 250
    Private investment in, **1950:** 2, 9 (p. 48)
    U.N. program, **1950:** 143; **1951:** 170, 187
  Military, **1950:** 177; **1951:** 250
  Raw materials production, **1951:** 114, 167
  Technical, **1951:** 114
  Trade, **1949:** 88
Lesueur, Larry, **1947:** 90n.
Letourneau, Jean (French Minister of State), **1952–53:** 175 [4]
Letters, etc., to Federal agencies or officials.
  See Memorandums to Federal agencies or officials.
Leviero, Anthony H., **1949:** 32 [2], 231 [2], 265; **1950:** 137 [18], 179 [14]; **1951:** 90 [6]; **1952–53:** 98 [22, 37], 156 [2], 345 [1], 377 [8]
Leviticus, Book of, **1952–53:** 347
Levy, Mrs. David M., **1947:** 204n.; **1950:** 5n.
Lewis, Clyde A., **1950:** 226n.
Lewis, David N., **1950:** 16ftn. (p. 116)
Lewis, James Hamilton, **1949:** 70
Lewis, John L., **1945:** 172 [6], 175 [18]; **1946:** 53 [6], 72 [6], 78 [4], 86 [12], 95 [20], 110 [5, 20], 114, 119 [27], 237 [5], 242 [8], 252, 262 [21]; **1947:** 67 [14]; **1948:** 66n., 71 [5], 84 [8], 86, 171, 212 [9]; **1949:** 118 [13], 155 [16], 240 [15], 253 [12], 260 [1]; **1950:** 16ftn. (p. 117), 27n., 29 [19]
Lewis, Robert, **1946:** 216 [2]
Lewis, Sir Willmott, death of, **1950:** 3 [3]
Lewis and Clark expedition, **1950:** 136
Lexington, **1946:** 171n.
Lexington, Ky., **1951:** 201
  Campaign remarks, **1948:** 222 [3]
Leyte Gulf, battle, **1945:** 45, 161, 178
Leyte island, Japanese currency during military invasion, **1945:** 176
Lhevinne, Josef, **1951:** 99
Li, Tsung-jen, **1950:** 46 [3]
Liaison Committee, Military and Industry, **1948:** 177
Libby, Mont, campaign remarks, **1952–53:** 270 [7]
Libby Dam, Idaho, **1952–53:** 270 [9]
Liberalism, comments on, **1948:** 236
Liberated countries, U.S. relief for, **1947:** 37, 46 [4]
Liberia, **1948:** 162n.
  Assistance, **1952–53:** 55
    Technical, **1951:** 114
  Iron ore deposits, **1952–53:** 175ftn. (p. 433)
  Point 4 program in, **1952–53:** 5
  U.S. economic mission in, **1950:** 177
Liberty, Statue of, **1947:** 231

Liberty Bell, **1951:** 144; **1952–53:** 347
  Tolling to open Savings Bond drive, **1950:** 133
Liberty Bell replica, gift from Annecy, France,
  1950: 270 [12], 273 [16], 280, 281
Liberty League, **1950:** 157
Librarian of Congress (Luther H. Evans), **1952–53:**
  347
Libraries, Presidential, **1951:** 251 [27, 29]; **1952–53:**
  334ftn. (p. 1059)
Libraries, USIA, **1950:** 92
Library, Harry S. Truman, Independence, Mo.,
  1950: 43n., 79n.; **1951:** 251 [27]; **1952–53:**
  334ftn. (p. 1059)
Library of Congress, **1947:** 7 (p. 77); **1949:** 8 (p.
  76); **1950:** 12; **1951:** 90 [16], 127, 225;
  1952–53: 174, 347
  Expansion of services, **1948:** 5 (p. 42)
  State statutes, collection, **1950:** 75
Libya
  Independence, **1950:** 143
  Technical assistance, **1951:** 114
Lichfield, England, trial of U.S. soldiers, **1946:** 84
  [15]
Lidice, destruction by Nazis, **1945:** 52 [2]
Lie, Trygve, **1946:** 66 [14], 123; **1947:** 61, 133,
  136n.; **1948:** 274 [3, 6]; **1949:** 139, 193,
  237; **1950:** 105 [8], 146 [2], 152 [11], 209
  [13], 223, 226, 271; **1951:** 173
Life expectancy, **1948:** 89; **1952–53:** 249, 333
  Lengthening, **1951:** 135
Life insurance, **1947:** 90 [8], 97; **1950:** 18, 200, 202
Life Insurance, National Service, **1946:** 18 (p. 79);
  1947: 2 (p. 8), 75, 134; **1949:** 8 (pp. 48,
  66); **1951:** 12 [36]
  Trust fund, **1948:** 5 (p. 33), 175
Life insurance companies, taxation, **1951:** 28
Life of Lincoln, Carl Sandburg, **1951:** 90 [16]
Life magazine, **1948:** 77 [18]; **1949:** 4 [2, 3];
  1952–53: 143
Light metals plants in Pacific Northwest, opera-
  tion, **1945:** 208 [21]
Lilienthal, David E.
  See Atomic Energy Commission, Chairman;
    Tennessee Valley Authority, Chairman.
Lima, Ohio, campaign remarks, **1948:** 231 [5]
Limestone Air Force Base, Maine, **1951:** 268n.
Limon, Colo., campaign remarks, **1952–53:** 282 [6]
Lincoln, Abraham, **1945:** 5, 227; **1946:** 126 [21];
  1947: 30, 68, 130, 205 [1, 12], 31 [1]; **1948:**
  86, 194 [12], 233 [4, 5], 234, 236, 261 [11];
  1949: 28 [5]; **1950:** 309 [1]; **1952–53:** 45,
  107 [10], 136 [17], 143, 149 [16], 272, 282
  [7], 303 [4], 316, 318, 321 [3, 6]
  Gettysburg Address, press criticism of, **1951:** 8
  Lincoln-Douglas debates, **1950:** 110 [1]
  News conference remarks on, **1951:** 56 [25], 90
    [16], 108 [11]
  Writings, publication of, **1950:** 12

Lincoln, Mrs. Abraham, **1947:** 205 [1, 12]
Lincoln, Murray D., **1952–53:** 143
Lincoln, Robert Todd, **1947:** 31 [1]
Lincoln, Nebr., **1950:** 110 [2, 3, 5, 8], 111
Lincoln Finds a General, Kenneth P. Williams,
  1951: 90 [16]
Lincoln and the Press, R. S. Harper, **1951:** 56 [25]
Lindley, Ernest, **1947:** 90n.
Lindley, William C., **1949:** 211 [2]
Lindsey, Jake W., Congressional Medal of Honor
  award, **1945:** 34
Linkins, Carroll, **1949:** 265
Linseed oil, price supports, **1950:** 9 (p. 86)
Lippmann, Walter, **1946:** 110 [18, 21]; **1947:** 36 [3];
  1952–53: 64 [9], 295 [5], 304
Lipsky, Louis, **1946:** 155
Liquidation, Director of, termination of office,
  1946: 145, 146
Liquidation, Director of (Robert L. McKeever),
  1946: 143 [11], 145
Lisbon, NATO meeting, **1952–53:** 48, 49 [17], 55,
  57
List, Eugene, **1951:** 99, 116n.
Lister, Lord Joseph, **1945:** 88
Litchfield, Ill., campaign remarks, **1952–53:** 321 [6]
Litchfield (Ill.) News-Herald, **1952–53:** 321 [6]
Literary Digest poll, (1936), **1948:** 264 [5]
Literary Digest poll (1948), **1952–53:** 129
Lithuania, Soviet domination, **1948:** 53, 86
Litigation, labor-management, **1947:** 120
"Little Assembly" (United Nations), **1948:** 53, 129
Little Falls, N.Y., campaign remarks, **1948:** 228 [4]
Little Missouri River, **1952–53:** 367 (p. 1146)
Little Rock, Ark., **1947:** 35; **1949:** 112 [19]
  Mayor Sam M. Wassell, **1949:** 119 [3, 4], 120n.
  Thirty-fifth Division reunion, **1949:** 119
  War Memorial Park, dedication, **1949:** 120
Little Steel Formula, **1945:** 59
  News conference remarks, **1945:** 22 [8], 52 [17]
Littlejohn, Maj. Gen. Robert M., **1946:** 262 [11];
  1947: 226 [1, 3]
Litvinov, Maxim M., **1948:** 288 [4]
Livestock, **1946:** 30 [2], 99, 223 [1], 232; **1947:** 202,
  224, 231; **1952–53:** 15, 33
  Danger from snowstorms in West, **1949:** 28 [4]
  Disease control, **1947:** 45
  Disease, prevention of, **1948:** 208 [6]
  Feed, conservation, **1947:** 209 [2], 210 [3], 218 [6];
    1948: 14
  Food products, economy in buying, **1947:** 191 [3]
  Foot-and-mouth disease, **1947:** 181 (p. 399)
  Junior Livestock Show, Spokane, Wash., **1950:**
    124 [6]
  Markets, **1948:** 212 [7]
  Pasturing on White House grounds in past, **1948:**
    26 [19]
  Prices, **1947:** 209 [12], 242; **1948:** 218 [14]
  Supports, **1949:** 151

Livestock — *continued*
   Production, **1948:** 8 (pp. 68, 70, 92), 99, 167;
     1951: 11, 199
     Expansion, **1950:** 111, 117 [4]
     Shipments, curtailment by railroad strike, **1950:**
      186 [4], 188
     Shortage, **1948:** 136 [3]
Lloyd, David, **1949:** 265; **1952–53:** 26 [20]
Loan Agency, Federal, **1950:** 112
Loan Association, National Farm, **1948:** 218 [1]
Loan Policy Board, RFC, **1951:** 39
Loans
   Crop, **1948:** 267 [3]
   Price support, **1948:** 268
   Veterans, **1947:** 2 (p. 8); **1948:** 5 (pp. 32, 37)
Lobbying, **1948:** 278 [35]
   Congressional investigation, proposed, **1948:**
     277, 278 [22, 27], 285 [14, 19]
   Regulations, tightening of, **1948:** 278 [32]
Lobbyists, registration of, **1946:** 61 [22]
Lock Haven, Pa., campaign remarks, **1948:** 250
Locke, Edwin A., Jr., **1945:** 151n.; **1946:** 15 [24], 41
   [12], 269
Lockett, Edward B., **1945:** 164ftn. (p. 385); **1946:**
   78 [9]
Lockouts.
   See Labor disputes.
Locksley Hall, Alfred Tennyson, **1950:** 159; **1952–
   53:** 125
Locomotive Engineers, Brotherhood of, **1946:** 120,
   121, 124, 125; **1948:** 95, 159n.; **1952–53:**
   136ftn. (p. 359)
Locomotive Firemen and Enginemen, Brotherhood
   of, **1948:** 95, 159n.; **1950:** 221n.; **1951:** 49
   [6]
Locust plagues, in India, **1951:** 34, 124
Lodge, Sen. Henry Cabot, Jr., **1949:** 148 [21]; **1950:**
   29ftn. (p. 144), 52 [8], 214ftn. (p. 588),
   219; **1951:** 251 [12]; **1952–53:** 331
Lodge, Gov. John D., **1952–53:** 170, 310
Lodge Act of 1950, **1952–53:** 65
Loeb, Robert F., **1951:** 89
Loeb, William, **1952–53:** 35 [5]
Logan, John A., **1947:** 191 [3]
Logansport, Ind., campaign remarks, **1948:** 240 [3]
Lohrey, Louis, **1952–53:** 319n.
London, Mrs. George, **1949:** 219n.
London, **1945:** 12n., 209n., 210; **1946:** 53 [21];
   1947: 31 [15]
   Council of Foreign Ministers meetings, **1945:** 91,
     132 [10], 147 [6], 157 [6], 164 [2], 172 [5],
     181 [4]
   Foreign ministers meetings, **1946:** 6 [14], 18 (p.
     41); **1947:** 236 [11]; **1950:** 146 [12, 16],
     162, 218
     Arms shipments to Near East, tripartite dec-
      laration and statement, **1950:** 147, 148
   International trade meeting, **1946:** 248; **1947:** 51

London — *continued*
   Meetings on British financial crisis, **1949:** 148 [5]
   News conference remarks, **1945:** 60 [6, 8, 14, 16],
     132 [10], 147 [6], 157 [6], 164 [2], 172 [5],
     181 [4], 208 [2], 221 [10, 22]
   North Atlantic Council meeting, **1950:** 193, 195
   Palestine conference, **1946:** 143 [13], 177 [14], 227
   Polish government in exile, **1945:** 60 [6, 8, 14, 16]
   Trade negotiations by Marshall plan nations,
     1949: 144 [16]
   U.N. General Assembly meeting, **1945:** 219, 221
     [22]; **1946:** 15 [16], 65; **1947:** 21, 38
   U.N. Security Council meeting, **1945:** 219
   UNRRA Council meeting, **1945:** 128, 186
   World's Christian Endeavor Union, convention,
     1950: 197
London Symphony Orchestra, **1952–53:** 262
London tailors, comments on President's apparel,
   1951: 2 [26]
London Times, **1950:** 3ftn. (p. 12)
Lonejack, Mo., **1945:** 68
Long, Mary Anne, **1950:** 239n.
Long Island, landing of German spies, **1949:** 32
   [15, 17]
Long-range shipping bill, amendment to Merchant
   Marine Act of 1936, **1952–53:** 211, 225
Longshoremen, **1946:** 117
   Accident prevention and workmen's compensa-
     tion, **1950:** 74
   Refusal to unload ships from Communist bloc
     countries, **1950:** 230 [14]
Longshoremen's Association, International, **1948:**
   179; **1951:** 276n.
Longshoremen's labor dispute, **1948:** 178 [8]
Look magazine, **1949:** 211 [12]; **1951:** 16 [17], 193
   [14, 18]
Loran system of radio navigation, **1947:** 7 (p. 85)
Lord, Mrs. Oswald B., **1949:** 257
Lordsburg, N. Mex., campaign remarks, **1948:** 208
   [1]
Los Alamos, N. Mex., **1947:** 141 [11]; **1948:** 140n.
   Atomic bomb production, **1949:** 166 [1]
Los Alamos Scientific Laboratory, **1948:** 103
Los Angeles, Calif., **1946:** 189; **1947:** 242; **1949:** 8
   (p. 83); **1952–53:** 233 [13]
   Campaign remarks, **1948:** 134, 205
   Eisenhower, Gen. Dwight D., comments on
     campaign remarks in, **1952–53:** 291, 292
     [12]
   Mayor Fletcher Bowron, **1948:** 134n.; **1951:** 227
     [3]; **1952–53:** 233 [13]
   Rent control, **1950:** 278 [5, 12]
   Special grand jury for crime investigation, **1951:**
     63 [1]
Los Angeles Press Club, **1948:** 93 [2]
Los Angeles Times, **1952–53:** 233 [13]
Lost Battalion Hall, New York, campaign remarks
   in, **1948:** 264 [5]

Loughlin, Edward V., **1946:** 72 [20]
Louis, Joe, **1948:** 226
Louis XIV, **1951:** 18
Louisiana, **1947:** 104
　Gov. Robert M. Kennon, **1952–53:** 315 [6], 316
　Indictment of newsmen in, **1951:** 209 [6]
　New Orleans.
　　See main heading, New Orleans.
　Offshore lands, public ownership of, **1952–53:** 146
　River basin development, **1950:** 164
Louisiana Purchase, **1948:** 32, 245; **1949:** 249, 250; **1950:** 162; **1952–53:** 107 [10]
Louisville, Ky.
　Campaign address, **1948:** 220
　Interfaith service committee for military personnel, **1948:** 190n.
　Rent control in, **1947:** 205 [8, 10, 17]
Louisville Courier-Journal, **1950:** 227
Louvre museum, **1951:** 225
Love, George H., **1950:** 27n.
Love, Mrs. Paula, **1948:** 216 [9]
Lovell, Vivian, **1945:** 106 [10]
Lovett, Robert A., **1945:** 137 [5]; **1947:** 205 [7], 230; **1948:** 68, 70, 73, 95 [5], 288 [1, 7]; **1949:** 9, 10, 13, 21; **1950:** 309 [2]; **1951:** 93, 272, 301n.
　See also Defense, Secretary of (Robert A. Lovett).
　Resignation as Under Secretary of State, **1949:** 4 [1]
Loveless, Herschel C., **1952–53:** 284 [1, 2], 285, 315 [1–4]
Lowe, Gen. Frank E., **1945:** 24; **1950:** 206 [1]; **1952–53:** 26ftn. (p. 131)
　Appointment to Reparations Commission, **1945:** 15
　　Statement, **1945:** 14
　Cables from, report of interception, **1952–53:** 26 [4]
　News conference remarks on, **1945:** 31 [7], 32
Lowell, Mass., campaign remarks, **1952–53:** 292 [12]
Lowenthal, Max, *The Federal Bureau of Investigation,* **1950:** 309 [4]
Loyalty, comment on, **1946:** 75 [5]
Loyalty, Government employees, **1947:** 67 [10], 89; **1948:** 5 (p. 56), 50, 181 [12], 191, 215; **1949:** 32 [14], 118 [5, 6], 122 [13, 16, 18, 19, 22]; **1950:** 79, 82, 94, 207, 279; **1951:** 20, 22 [6, 14], 35, 37 [12], 104, 156, 188 [19], 226, 278, 295 [12], 300 [5, 7, 21]; **1952–53:** 26 [5, 24], 36, 69, 76, 117, 222, 223, 289 [2], 296, 303 [2, 5], 323, 353 [12, 14], 359 [3], 362n.
Loyalty Review Board, **1947:** 222; **1948:** 178 [13]; **1950:** 79, 82, 94, 152ftn. (p. 450); **1952–53:** 26 [5, 20], 76, 362n.; **1951:** 300 [5]

Loyalty Review Board, Chairman (Hiram Bingham), **1952–53:** 362n.
Loyalty Review Board, Chairman (Seth W. Richardson), **1950:** 79, 94
Lucas, Jacklyn H., Congressional Medal of Honor award, **1945:** 160n.
Lucas, Sen. Scott W., **1946:** 110 [5, 14]; **1947:** 78 [12], 221 [5]; **1948:** 26 [14], 84 [5], 234, 267 [3], 288 [12]; **1949:** 70, 74n., 76, 144ftn. (p. 343); **1950:** 12, 29ftn. (p. 141), 134; **1952–53:** 166 [16]
　News conference remarks on, **1949:** 95 [4], 112 [8, 12, 15], 192 [23], 214 [10], 226 [11]; **1950:** 16 [13], 46 [1], 86 [4], 206 [12], 230 [3]
Lucas Act, termination of war contracts, **1949:** 150
Luce, Mrs. Clare Boothe, **1948:** 150 [6]; **1952–53:** 143
Luce, Henry R., **1946:** 45n., 255n.; **1952–53:** 143n.
Lucedale, Miss., **1945:** 34
Lucey, Archbishop Robert E., **1950:** 153
Luckey, George, **1948:** 205; **1949:** 84 [11]; **1950:** 38 [11, 15]
Luckman, Charles, **1947:** 191 [3], 196, 198, 202, 218 [6], 225, 236 [1]; **1950:** 16 [4], 34 [13], 39n.
　Conservation, **1947:** 231
　Export controls, **1947:** 58
Lumber industry, **1950:** 121 [9]
　Prices, **1950:** 202
Lundy, Roy, **1948:** 217
Lustron Corp., **1947:** 14 [12]; **1950:** 29 [16], 217 [17]; **1951:** 227 [18]
Luther, Martin, **1948:** 101
Lutheran Church, Augustana, national convention, **1950:** 158
Luxembourg, **1949:** 148ftn. (p. 350)
　Assistance, **1947:** 238
　　Military, **1950:** 22
　Bech, Joseph, **1949:** 68
　Korean war, participation, **1950:** 296; **1951:** 170
　Liberation, **1945:** 45
　U.S. Minister Perle Mesta, **1951:** 101 [9]
　Visit of Margaret Truman, **1951:** 145 [5]
Lyford, Joseph P., **1952–53:** 298 [9–11]
Lynchings
　Georgia, **1946:** 186 [10], 199 [16]
　Prohibitory provision in civil rights bill, **1950:** 23ftn. (p. 134)
　Proposed Federal statute against, **1948:** 20
Lyon, A. E., **1952–53:** 203n.

M. A. Hanna Company, **1947:** 236 [3]
Mabry, Gov. Thomas I., **1948:** 136 [2, 3, 4], 208 [1, 2]
MacArthur, Gen. Douglas, **1945:** 2, 45, 114, 122, 138, 143n., 182; **1946:** 63, 70 [1], 186 [7],

MacArthur, Gen. Douglas — *continued*
265; **1947:** 177 [9]; **1948:** 110 [6, 15]; **1949:** 36, 179 [4]; **1950:** 272, 296; **1952–53:** 157, 270 [8], 277 [2], 289, 303 [10], 305, 310
Activities in Japan, Soviet announcement on, **1948:** 288 [6]
American Legion, address to, **1951:** 261 [1]
Authority in Japan, message, **1945:** 145
Conference with the President, **1950:** 264, 266, 267, 268, 270 [2, 14]
Congress, address to, **1951:** 79, 85 [2]
Dulles, John Foster, meeting with, **1952–53:** 353 [2]
Eisenhower, Gen. Dwight D., meeting with, **1952–53:** 353 [2]
Far East, discussions with officials on, **1950:** 206 [1, 7]
Formosa, views on, **1950:** 230 [11]
In Japan
    CIA operations, opposition to, **1951:** 95 [9]
    Occupation, achievements of, **1951:** 216
Korean war
    Comment on, **1952–53:** 359 [8]
    Enemy commander, ultimatum to, **1951:** 108 [2, 4, 8, 13]
    Ground forces, authorization for use in, **1950:** 184
    Manchurian targets, question of bombing, **1951:** 70 [15]
    North Korea, broadcast to, **1950:** 258 [8, 13]
    Policy in conducting, **1951:** 56 [22], 90 [4, 6, 14]
    Removal from commands, **1951:** 77, 95 [2, 4, 6], 101 [4], 108 [2, 4, 13], 113 [3, 12], 118ftn. (p. 324)
    Role in withdrawal of U.S. forces, **1952–53:** 320
    Seoul, exchange of messages on liberation of, **1950:** 260n.
    U.N. forces, designation to command, **1950:** 189, 194
    U.S. forces, report on, **1950:** 194n.
Letter to Repr. Martin, **1951:** 108 [2, 4]
Message to Veterans of Foreign Wars, letter on withdrawal of, **1950:** 226
Mission to China, question of, **1948:** 278 [34]
News conference, remarks on, **1945:** 100, 106 [5, 17, 22], 132 [6], 137 [9], 147 [4], 221 [7]; **1950:** 186 [10], 191 [9], 206 [1, 7], 209 [7], 230 [11], 258 [3, 6, 8, 13], 270 [2, 14], 273 [8], 287 [18], 295 [4, 11], 309 [12]; **1951:** 7 [3, 6], 33 [3], 63 [6, 23], 85 [10], 90 [4, 14], 132 [2], 140 [3], 171 [1, 4], 193 [3]; **1952–53:** 49 [6], 334 [15], 345 [1], 353 [5]
Relief from command, hearings on, **1952–53:** 362n.
Republican National Convention, appointment as keynoter, **1952–53:** 166 [2, 17], 175 [11]

MacArthur, Gen. Douglas — *continued*
Veterans of Foreign Wars, 1950 message to, **1951:** 108 [4]
Wake Island meeting with the President, **1951:** 90 [6, 11, 15], 95 [6, 9, 11], 108 [2, 4]
White House, question of invitation to, **1951:** 85 [14]; **1952–53:** 345 [1]
MacDonald, Comdr. Donald, **1949:** 265
MacDonald, Harry A., **1951:** 44n.
MacDonald, Thomas H., **1946:** 43 [10], 195n.; **1949:** 142
Maceo, Antonio, **1948:** 81
Machine tools, **1950:** 151, 159
Machinists, International Association of, **1948:** 277
Machinery, agricultural, **1947:** 217; **1948:** 8 (pp. 72, 77, 92)
Machrowitz, Repr. Thaddeus M., **1952–53:** 317 [7]
Mack, Repr. Peter F., **1952–53:** 321 [5]
Mack, Repr. Russell V., **1949:** 122 [21]; **1952–53:** 342 [1]
Mackinac Island, Mich., Governors Conference, **1945:** 64 [9]
Macmillan, Harold, **1946:** 41 [4]
Macready, Lt. Gen. Gordon N., Legion of Merit, citation, **1945:** 198
MacVeagh, Lincoln, **1947:** 56, 100; **1948:** 48
Macy, Repr. W. Kingsland, **1950:** 270ftn. (p. 681)
Madden, Repr. Ray J., **1948:** 114 [3], 240 [1], 255; **1952–53:** 312
Madison, Dolley, **1946:** 21 [2]
Madison, James, **1946:** 268; **1949:** 164; **1951:** 127; **1952–53:** 276
Madison, Wis., **1951:** 174
    Campaign address, **1948:** 238
    Dedication of Credit Union National Association, **1950:** 131 [4], 132
Madison Square Garden, N.Y., campaign address, **1948:** 262
Madrid, Spain, **1951:** 165 [6]
Magazines, postal rates, **1952–53:** 367 (p. 1144)
Magdeburg, Germany, **1945:** 97
Magee, Repr. Clare, **1952–53:** 3
Magee, Elizabeth S., **1951:** 307n.
Magee, Rev. J. Ralph, **1951:** 31n.
Magellan, Ferdinand, **1946:** 159
Magellan, Ferdinand, Presidential railroad car, **1952–53:** 377 [19]
Maginot Line, **1951:** 92
Magnuson, Don, **1952–53:** 272, 274 [1–5, 7], 275, 276
Magnuson, Dr. Paul B., **1949:** 11 [11]; **1951:** 307n.; **1952–53:** 2 [3], 135n.
Magnuson, Mrs. Paul B., **1952–53:** 262
Magnuson, Sen. Warren G., **1945:** 64 [3], 174 [12]; **1946:** 119 [23]; **1948:** 122 [2, 3, 5], 124 [1, 4]; **1950:** 124 [1, 4, 6], 125, 126; **1951:** 85 [11], 113 [18]; **1952–53:** 272, 274 [1, 4], 276

Maguire, Philip, **1949:** 265
Mahaffie, Charles D. (Chairman, Interstate Commerce Commission), **1949:** 149n.
Mahoney, George F., **1952–53:** 308 [7]
Mail
    Franked, reports by agencies of volume sent, **1947:** 35
    Second class, Federal subsidy, **1947:** 6 [10]
    Transportation, **1947:** 181 (p. 399)
Maine, **1948:** 278 [35]
    Admission to Union, **1951:** 8
    Election, **1946:** 216 [8]
    News conference remarks, **1950:** 29 [7], 250 [10]
    Passamaquoddy tidal power project, **1948:** 55 [8], 93 [11]
    Potatoes, **1950:** 29 [7], 121 [2]
        Surplus, disposition, **1951:** 2 [22]
Maine, U.S.S., **1948:** 81
Malaria
    Eradication in India, **1950:** 177
    Prevention, **1951:** 135
Malaya, **1946:** 86 [4]
    British forces in, **1951:** 114
    Communist aggression in, **1951:** 96; **1952–53:** 55
    Military assistance, **1952–53:** 5
Malden, Mass., campaign remarks, **1952–53:** 295 [9]
Malik, Jacob A., **1949:** 89ftn. (p. 237); **1950:** 209 [1], 287 [1]; **1951:** 140 [3, 5, 13, 18]
Mallery, Otto J., **1951:** 99n.
Mallory, E., **1948:** 124 [5]
Malone, Richard T., **1952–53:** 313 [3]
Maloney, Francis T., **1952–53:** 292 [3]
Maloney, Mrs. Francis T., **1952–53:** 292n.
Maloney, James J., **1948:** 278 [16]
Malta, Colo., campaign remarks, **1952–53:** 282 [1]
Malta, Mont., campaign remarks, **1952–53:** 268 [3]
Man of Independence, The, Jonathan Daniels, **1950:** 258 [2]
Management, **1947:** 120, 121
    See also Labor-management relations.
    Contribution to full employment, **1945:** 203
Management, Advisory Committee on, **1952–53:** 18 (p. 115)
Management, Society for the Advancement of, **1945:** 203
Management Improvement, Advisory Committee on, **1949:** 167, 242
Management improvement fund, Presidential, **1949:** 8 (p. 48)
Management improvement program, **1950:** 8 [48], 9 (p. 51); **1951:** 13 (p. 65)
    Federal, **1952–53:** 1, 18 (pp. 65, 115, 116)
Management-labor disputes.
    See Labor disputes.
Manasco, Carter, **1949:** 94n.
    Letter, **1945:** 222

Manasco, Carter — *continued*
    News conference remarks on, **1945:** 175 [18], 208 [14], 221 [2]
Manchester, N.H., campaign remarks, **1952–53:** 294
Manchuria, **1945:** 44 [2], 131n., 139, 151n., 216; **1946:** 95 [3], 265
    Attack from, on U.N. forces in North Korea, **1950:** 295 [1]
    Attack by Japan (1931), **1951:** 4
    Communist bases in, question of bombing, **1951:** 2 [7, 10], 70 [15], 90 [5]
    Troop movements in, **1951:** 70 [4, 12]
    U.N. military operations in, question of, **1950:** 295 [9, 11, 16]
    Mandated Islands, Japanese, trusteeship, **1946:** 15 [4, 9], 247
Mandich, Peter, **1952–53:** 312
Manhattan atomic project, **1945:** 106 [2]; **1946:** 242 [2]; **1947:** 6 [11, 14], 7 (pp. 64, 81)
Manhattan Engineer District, **1946:** 27 [3], 242 [2]
Manila, **1945:** 45, 106 [9]
    Demonstrations by U.S. soldiers, **1946:** 6 [9]
Manila rope, import controls, **1947:** 99
Mankato, Minn., campaign remarks, **1948:** 237 [1]
Mankin, Jack H., **1952–53:** 321 [2]
Manly, Basil, **1945:** 132 [1]; **1946:** 250 [5]
Manningham-Buller, Maj. Reginald E., **1945:** 210
Manpower controls, termination, **1947:** 18
"Manpower for Research," report, **1947:** 206
Manpower resources, **1948:** 22, 99
    Conservation and development, **1949:** 19; **1950:** 203 [9], 209 [14], 213, 229; **1951:** 4, 11, 12, 13 (pp. 78, 79), 44, 92, 119; **1952–53:** 15, 18 (pp. 92, 94, 102), 367 (p. 1150)
    Controls, **1951:** 11, 93
    Defense mobilization personnel, roster of, **1952–53:** 338
    Memorandum, **1951:** 15
    Waste due to educational deficiencies, **1952–53:** 18 (p. 101)
Manpower shortage of western railroads, statement, **1945:** 83
Mansfield, Repr. Mike, **1948:** 121; **1950:** 127 [1, 2, 4, 5, 7]; **1951:** 266n.; **1952–53:** 266 [13], 268, 269, 270 [1, 5, 7, 8], 271
Manston, England, **1951:** 268n.
Manufacturers, census of, **1952–53:** 363n.
Manufacturers, National Association of, **1946:** 110 [8]; **1948:** 114 [3], 194 [1, 11], 212 [9], 216 [7], 220, 226, 251, 261 [2, 8, 11]; **1951:** 164; **1952–53:** 294, 306 [2], 314, 319 [1], 321 [2]
Manuscripts, historical, library custody of, **1951:** 225
Manwell, Milton, **1948:** 237 [1]
Mao Tse-tung, **1950:** 273 [7]
Maps, topographical, **1947:** 7 (p. 83)

Maragon, John, **1949:** 192 [1], 200 [14]; **1950:** 16ftn. (p. 119)

Marbury v. Madison, cited, **1948:** 102

March, Charles H., **1945:** 157 [1]

March of Dimes, **1946:** 26; **1947:** 17; **1948:** 18

Marciano, Rocky, **1952–53:** 298 [1]

Marfa, Tex., campaign remarks, **1948:** 208 [6]

Margarine, tax on, **1947:** 221 [8]

Mariana Islands, **1945:** 161, 174

Marias River, **1950:** 127 [6]

Marietta, Okla., campaign remarks, **1948:** 214 [4]

Marine Band, **1948:** 89; **1951:** 99

Marine Corps, **1945:** 34, 45, 174, 215, 218; **1946:** 86 [2], 118, 135, 137, 138; **1947:** 2 (p. 11), 7 (p. 64), 35, 159, 221 [13]; **1948:** 11 [12], 145, 243 [1]; **1952–53:** 18 (p. 69), 131, 158, 367 (p. 1134)

  Air arm, transfer to Air Force, **1949:** 89 [7]

  Authorized strength, **1949:** 8 (p. 59); **1950:** 9 (p. 63)

  China, **1945:** 211 [8], 216; **1946:** 265

  Commandant (Gen. Clifton B. Cates), **1947:** 226 [1]; **1950:** 165, 235, 237

  Congressional Medal of Honor presentations, **1945:** 160

  Demobilization, **1946:** 8, 18 (p. 47)

  Increase in strength, **1951:** 13 (pp. 68, 69), 92

  Merger with Army, question of, **1949:** 234 [1]

  News conference remarks, **1950:** 8 [35], 238 [19]

  Officers, retirement, **1947:** 35

  Quantico base, remarks, **1950:** 165

  Recruitment, **1947:** 50

  Reserve, **1950:** 9 (p. 63)

  Retired enlistees, credit for foreign service 1898–1912, veto, **1945:** 205

  Tripoli expedition, **1951:** 80

Marine Corps League

  Letter to Commandant (Clay Nixon), **1950:** 235

  Remarks to members of, **1950:** 237

Marine Falcon, **1946:** 267

Marine Flasher, **1946:** 267

Marine Inspection and Navigation, Bureau of, **1946:** 118

Marine insurance, **1950:** 76, 236

Marine Marlin, **1946:** 267

Marion, Ill., campaign remarks, **1948:** 218 [5, 6]

Marion, Ohio, campaign remarks, **1952–53:** 286 [5]

Maritime Administration, **1950:** 53, 76; **1951:** 13 (pp. 81, 82); **1952–53:** 18 (p. 82), 367 (p. 1142)

Maritime Board, Federal, **1950:** 53, 76, 236; **1952–53:** 18 (p. 82), 177

Maritime Commission, U.S., **1945:** 128; **1946:** 18 (pp. 53, 74, 77, 78, 82), 21 [16], 84 [11], 95 [6], 119 [9], 187, 192 [10], 193, 257 [12], 267; **1947:** 7 (pp. 85, 86), 11, 18, 29, 31 [16], 35, 47, 55, 181 (pp. 404, 406, 407), 228; **1948:** 4 [1, 13], 5 (pp. 25, 48, 50), 77

Maritime Commission, U.S. — *continued* [11], 79n., 88 [19], 97 [5], 105, 175, 177; **1949:** 8 (p. 86); **1950:** 9 (pp. 92, 93)

  Brierley, Daniel S., **1945:** 24

  News conference remarks, **1949:** 84 [20], 89 [1]; **1950:** 8 [12], 146 [8]

  Reorganization, **1949:** 127, 133; **1950:** 53, 76

Maritime Commission, U.S., Chairman (Maj. Gen. Philip B. Fleming), **1949:** 156

Maritime Commission, U.S., Chairman (Vice Adm. Emory S. Land), **1946:** 3

Maritime Commission, U.S., Chairman (Vice Adm. William W. Smith), **1946:** 194n.; **1947:** 123, 124; **1948:** 51n., 79; **1949:** 78 [2]

Maritime employment, **1947:** 124

Maritime industry, tax benefits, **1952–53:** 211, 225, 226

Maritime labor disputes, **1946:** 126 [15, 18], 129 [13], 136 [4], 215 [12], 216 [7, 11, 23], 220n.; **1948:** 110 [4], 179, 181 [19], 274 [18]; **1951:** 276

  Hawaii, **1949:** 144 [20]

  News conference remarks, **1949:** 118 [16], 144 [20], 148 [9, 11], 155 [17]

Maritime schools, **1947:** 7 (p. 86)

Maritime workers, unemployment insurance, proposed, **1945:** 42, 128

Mark, George L., **1951:** 291n.

Markel, Lester, **1952–53:** 98 [6]

Marketing programs, **1947:** 111

Marketing research, **1948:** 5 (p. 45)

Markham, James E., **1946:** 231

  Letter, **1945:** 176

Marland, William C., **1952–53:** 308 [8]

Marsalis, John H., **1952–53:** 282 [3, 4], 283n.

Marshall, Gen. George C., **1945:** 2, 45, 174; **1946:** 53 [18, 22], 70 [1], 76, 224, 229 [2]; **1947:** 90 [4]; **1948:** 110 [15], 126 [3], 200 [2], 214 [4], 257 [3]; **1949:** 36, 78ftn. (p. 214); **1950:** 45, 110 [9], 121 [1, 8], 245, 275; **1951:** 271; **1952–53:** 107 [2], 135, 279, 283, 286n., 289 [6], 290n., 291, 293, 296, 303 [4, 5], 308 [4], 310, 313 [4], 316, 320, 322

See also Defense, Secretary of (George C. Marshall).

  Appointment as president of American Red Cross, **1950:** 278 [1]

  Bill to permit appointment as Defense Secretary, **1950:** 246

  Chair used while Cabinet officer, presentation to, **1951:** 263

  Criticism by Sen. McCarthy, **1950:** 105 [18]

  Dinner honoring, address, **1949:** 116

  Mission to China, **1945:** 202 [12, 15], 211 [8]; **1946:** 15 [24], 18 (p. 44), 37 [3], 41 [12], 53 [22], 78 [8], 86 [30], 119 [10], 172, 265, 266 [5, 7, 17]; **1950:** 253 [1]

Marshall, Gen. George C. — *continued*
  News conference remarks on, **1945:** 107 [17],
      116, 118 [14], 175 [8], 193 [1], 202 [12, 15],
      208 [17], 211 [8]; **1949:** 171 [1], 214 [1];
      1950: 80 [3], 105 [18], 191 [12], 250 [5, 15,
      19], 253 [1], 278 [1]; **1951:** 251 [28], 275
      [20]
  Proposal for European recovery program (1947),
      1951: 66
  Resignation as Secretary of Defense, **1951:** 222
Marshall, George C., Research Foundation, Inc.,
      1952–53: 387
Marshall, James D., **1947:** 20n.
Marshall, John, **1948:** 84 [18], 102; **1949:** 103n.
Marshall, Peter John, **1951:** 68
Marshall, Gen. Richard J., **1950:** 179 [1], 180
Marshall plan, **1947:** 177 [22], 180 [4, 13, 18], 191 [3,
      21], 195, 210 [1], 218 [7, 15, 18], 219, 221
      [16], 226 [8], 232 [9, 11]; **1948:** 52; **1949:**
      69n., 249, 252; **1950:** 78, 92, 94, 132, 159,
      162, 232, 269; **1951:** 4, 65, 66, 114, 209
      [13]; **1952–53:** 55, 69, 81, 203, 218, 281,
      283, 289 [5], 291, 298 [8], 303 [2], 304, 317
      [2], 366, 378
  Administration of, **1947:** 238
  Appropriations, **1948:** 15 [6, 8, 11]
  Arms for countries in, **1948:** 93 [9], 97 [6], 188,
      244, 263
  Campaign remarks, **1948:** 215, 228 [1], 260
  CEEC, Paris meeting, **1947:** 238
  Effect of trade modification on repayments,
      1948: 88 [18, 21]
  Effect on U.S. economy, **1947:** 238
  Financial arrangements, **1947:** 238
  Grain, etc., procurement for, **1947:** 155 [7]
  Latin American participation, question of, **1947:**
      191 [21]
  Message to Congress, **1947:** 238; **1948:** 75
  News conference remarks, **1947:** 141 [6], 145 [9,
      11]; **1949:** 22 [3], 40 [5, 11], 86, 144 [16],
      236 [4]; **1950:** 105 [9], 179 [23]
  Opposition by Sen. Taft, **1950:** 253ftn. (p. 643)
  Origins, **1947:** 238
  Paris conference on, **1947:** 141 [15, 17]
  Participating nations
      Agreement among, **1948:** 114 [2]
      Remarks to representatives, **1949:** 27
  Personnel, **1948:** 4 [3, 5]
  Second anniversary, dinner, **1949:** 116
  Soviet opposition, **1948:** 53
  Taxes to finance, **1947:** 221 [14]
Marshfield, Mo., campaign remarks, **1948:** 216 [16]
Martel, Charles, **1951:** 8
Martel, Frank, **1948:** 184
Martí, José, **1948:** 81
Martin, Crawford, **1948:** 212 [6]
Martin, Edward, **1947:** 191 [14]; **1948:** 81n.; **1949:**
      202n., 249n.; **1950:** 270 [13]

Martin, Harry, **1950:** 177n.
Martin, Repr. Joseph W., Jr., **1950:** 39; **1951:** 24,
      77n., 108 [2, 4]; **1952–53:** 312, 377 [15]
  See also Speaker of the House of Representa-
      tives.
Martin, L. C., **1947:** 6
Martin, Marian E., **1947:** 14 [4]
Martin, William McC., Jr., **1948:** 278 [25]; **1951:**
      44n., 56ftn. (p. 190)
  Appointment as Chairman, Board of Directors,
      Export-Import Bank, **1945:** 202 [2]
Martinsburg, W. Va., campaign remarks, **1952–53:**
      242 [6]
Marvel, W. S., **1948:** 120 [1]
Marx, Karl, interpretation of history, **1952–53:** 366
Maryland, **1947:** 35; **1950:** 135
  Campaign remarks in, **1948:** 139 [4]; **1952–53:**
      308 [7]
  Federal offices, dispersal to, question of, **1950:**
      214 [10]
  Gov. William P. Lane, Jr., **1948:** 259 [4]; **1949:**
      26n.; **1950:** 97 [16], 135, 171
  National capital region, coordinated develop-
      ment, **1950:** 9 (p. 102)
  Records, Hall of, **1952–53:** 174n.
  Senatorial election (1950), **1951:** 49 [19]; **1952–
      53:** 69, 308 [7]
  Sen. Millard E. Tydings, **1945:** 24
Masaryk, Jan, death of, **1948:** 49 [7]
Masaryk, Thomas G., **1952–53:** 309
Mason, Edward S., **1947:** 122; **1949:** 167n.; **1951:**
      19n.
Mason, Guy, **1947:** 243 [3]; **1951:** 22 [7]
Mason, Lowell B., **1945:** 157 [1]; **1947:** 182 [9];
      1949: 149n., 192 [16]
Mason, Repr. Noah M., **1952–53:** 285
Masonic order, Washington's birthday breakfasts,
      1950: 41; **1951:** 41; **1952–53:** 45
Masonic order, Philadelphia Grand Lodge, **1949:**
      194
Massachusetts, **1945:** 208 [10]; **1946:** 211
  Attorney General, campaign proposal for Pres-
      idential visit to Korea, **1952–53:** 345 [2]
  Campaign addresses or remarks, **1948:** 259 [1,
      4–6], 260, 261 [1–4]; **1952–53:** 292 [9–12],
      295 [7–9], 296, 298
  Candidates for public office, **1948:** 259 [1, 4, 5],
      261 [1]; **1952–53:** 292 [9–12], 295 [7–9],
      296, 298 [1–3]
  Congressmen, meeting with, **1949:** 78 [6]
  Gov. Paul A. Dever, **1949:** 32 [1]; **1952–53:** 295
      [7, 9], 296, 298 [1–3]
  State Democratic Chairman, **1948:** 21 [9]
  Unemployment in Lawrence, **1949:** 78 [4]
Masselink, Mara Gay, **1952–53:** 43n.
Matador (B-61) missile, **1951:** 224 [6], 247 [1, 12]
Matchbooks, mementos, **1949:** 171 [7, 15]
Materials Conference, International, **1952–53:** 190

Materials Policy Commission, President's, **1951:**
19; **1952–53:** 15, 179, 191, 192, 203, 355
Materiel, military, **1947:** 159
Maternity health services, **1945:** 192; **1946:** 18 (p.
83); **1947:** 98; **1948:** 181 [2], 237 [3]; **1949:**
85; **1950:** 9 (p. 76); **1951:** 135, 307
Mather, Rear Adm. Paul L., **1949:** 89 [1]
Mathias, Bob, **1948:** 204 [3]
Matthews, Francis P.
See Navy, Secretary of the (Francis P.
Matthews).
Matthews, Ralph, **1947:** 48n.
Matthiessen, C. H., **1945:** 24
Mattoon, Ill., campaign remarks, **1948:** 267 [3]
Maverick, Maury, **1950:** 29 [9]; **1952–53:** 175 [17],
197 [15]
Letter, **1945:** 228
Mission to Far East and Pacific countries, small
business study, **1945:** 228
Maw, Gov. Herbert B., **1948:** 200 [2–5, 7], 201, 259
[4]
Maximos, Demetrios, **1947:** 57
May, Repr. Andrew J., **1945:** 114, 118 [5]; **1946:** 41
[20], 137; **1947:** 14 [11]
May-Johnson atomic energy bill, **1945:** 172 [15]
Maybank, Sen. Burnet R., **1945:** 118 [10], 211 [7];
1946: 229 [2]; **1947:** 243 [16]; **1950:** 292;
1951: 22 [8], 33 [2], 108 [12]; **1952–53:** 31
[6], 108, 120, 159, 190
Mayors, American Conference of, **1948:** 238; **1949:**
54
Mayors Emergency Housing Committees, **1946:**
263
McAlester, Okla., campaign remarks, **1948:** 216 [5]
McBride, Sean, **1951:** 63 [5]
McCabe, Thomas B., Chairman, Federal Reserve
Board, **1948:** 15 [1]; **1949:** 149n.; **1950:**
14; **1951:** 37 [6, 9], 44
Fiscal policy, joint announcement with Secretary
Snyder, **1951:** 52
Letters, **1950:** 192; **1951:** 29
Memorandum, **1950:** 259
Resignation, **1951:** 56 [21]
McCandless, Comdr. Byron, **1945:** 175ftn. (p. 416)
McCardell, Lee, **1950:** 146 [16]
McCardle, Carl W., **1951:** 132 [7]; **1952–53:** 98 [24,
38]
McCarran, Sen. Pat, **1946:** 6 [8]; **1948:** 202 [1, 2];
1949: 211 [3, 4]; **1950:** 169 [12], 238 [4],
250 [7, 13], 258 [12], 270 [6]; **1951:** 22 [11];
1952–53: 88 [19], 136 [5], 291n., 298 [14],
301
McCarran-Walter Act.
See Immigration and Nationality Act.
McCarthy, Repr. Eugene J., **1952–53:** 313 [4], 314
McCarthy, Capt. Joseph J., Congressional Medal
of Honor award, **1945:** 160n.

McCarthy, Sen. Joseph R., **1950:** 38 [18], 44 [6, 9],
52 [12], 79, 80 [4], 86 [9], 97 [5], 105 [18],
137 [11, 15], 152ftn. (p. 451); **1951:** 132
[10], 188 [19], 193 [12, 15, 17], 227 [15], 275
[12]; **1952–53:** 129, 170, 266 [13], 280 [3],
283, 286 [8], 289 [3, 6], 291, 292 [8], 293,
296, 297, 298 [9, 10, 14], 300, 301, 303 [5],
304, 308 [7], 312, 313 [4], 318, 319 [1], 322
Disloyalty charges against Government employees, investigation of, **1952–53:** 377 [24]
Marshall, Gen. George C., criticism of, **1952–53:**
293
News conference remarks on, **1952–53:** 26 [20,
22], 35 [5], 247 [2], 253 [10]
McCarthy, Martin, **1952–53:** 315n.
McChord Air Force Base, **1950:** 121 [13]
McClellan, Gen. George B., **1951:** 90 [16]; **1952–53:**
282 [7], 289 [9]
McClellan, Sen. John L., **1949:** 94n., 119n., 200
[20]; **1950:** 137 [2]; **1952–53:** 53
Letter, **1951:** 175
McClendon, Sarah, **1952–53:** 98 [33]
McCloskey, Mark A., **1949:** 73n., 110n.; **1950:** 32n.
McCloskey Army Hospital, visit to, **1948:** 212 [4]
McCloy, John J., **1945:** 137 [5]; **1946:** 27 [14]; **1947:**
46 [24]; **1949:** 84 [3], 122 [3], 234 [6], 260
[15]; **1950:** 23 [18], 238 [9]; **1951:** 33 [8];
1952–53: 362n.
McCone, John A., **1948:** 7n.
McConnell, Raymond A., Jr., **1952–53:** 98 [9]
McConnell, Repr. Samuel K., FEPC amendment,
1952–53: 290
McCord, Gov. Jim Nance, **1948:** 245n.
McCormack, Chauncey, **1950:** 5n.
McCormack, Repr. John W., **1946:** 178, 223 [2];
1948: 259 [4], 288 [12]; **1949:** 93ftn. (p.
241), 148 [13], 253 [8]; **1950:** 29ftn. (p.
141); **1951:** 24, 27; **1952–53:** 143n., 292
[12], 296
McCormick, Edward T., **1949:** 226ftn. (p. 503)
McCormick, Fowler, **1946:** 142
McCormick, Adm. Lynde D., **1952–53:** 25
McCormick, Col. Robert R., **1949:** 253 [9]; **1952–
53:** 129, 238 [14], 317 [2]
McCraw, Doyle, **1948:** 158
McDonald, Harry A., **1952–53:** 31 [6]
McDonald, James G., **1945:** 210; **1948:** 141; **1949:**
192 [21]; **1950:** 250 [4]; **1951:** 229n.
McDonough, Repr. Gordon L., **1950:** 235
McDonough, Patrick W., letter, **1945:** 228
McDonough, Roger I., **1946:** 20
McEnery, John, **1948:** 130 [2]
McFarland, Archie J., **1949:** 152n., 153
McFarland, Sen. Ernest W., **1946:** 61 [21]; **1948:**
136 [1], 207; **1951:** 2 [24]; **1952–53:** 123
[17], 143n., 159n.
McGaha, Charles L., Congressional Medal of
Honor award, **1946:** 69

McGhee, George C., **1949:** 112 [1]

McGowan, Patrick A., **1952–53:** 306 [3, 5]

McGowan, Wilbur J., **1948:** 189n.

McGrady, Edward F., **1947:** 87n.

McGranery, James P., **1951:** 179 [12]; **1952–53:** 136 [9], 143, 161, 165, 268 [3]

   See also Attorney General (James P. McGranery).

McGrath, Earl J. (Commissioner of Education), **1950:** 8 [34], 47

McGrath, J. Howard, **1946:** 237 [4]; **1952–53:** 75ftn. (p. 230)

   See also Attorney General (J. Howard McGrath); Democratic National Committee, Chairman (Sen. J. Howard McGrath).

   News conference remarks on, **1952–53:** 156 [6], 258 [6, 8]

McGraw, Curtis W., **1946:** 172n.

McGraw, James H., Jr., **1947:** 191 [3]

McGraw-Hill Publishing Co., **1946:** 172; **1949:** 32 [10]

McGregor, Repr. J. Harry, **1949:** 249n.

McGuire, Arthur, **1952–53:** 289 [3]

McGuire, John A., **1948:** 261 [7]; **1952–53:** 292 [1–3], 298 [8]

McGuire, Peter J., **1952–53:** 237

McHale, Frank, **1948:** 240 [1, 3]; **1952–53:** 107 [5]

McIntire, Adm. Ross T., **1948:** 169; **1949:** 197n.; **1950:** 208n.; **1951:** 195, 281; **1952–53:** 135, 243

McKay, Ernest R., **1952–53:** 280 [1, 3]

McKeesport, Pa., campaign remarks, **1952–53:** 308 [3]

McKeever, Robert L., **1946:** 143 [11], 145

McKellar, Sen. Kenneth, **1947:** 31 [11]; **1949:** 249n.; **1950:** 252; **1951:** 172, 184, 185; **1952–53:** 105, 109, 180, 217, 358

   See also President Pro Tempore of the Senate.

McKelway, B.M., **1950:** 92n.

McKeough, Raymond S., **1946:** 119 [19]; **1950:** 146 [8]; **1952–53:** 88 [8]

McKim, Edward D., **1945:** 60 [3]; **1948:** 116 [1], 117n.

McKim, Mead and White, **1952–53:** 229n.

McKinley, William, **1946:** 158; **1948:** 65; **1950:** 39; **1952–53:** 129, 286 [5], 306 [2, 4], 311 [3]

McKinney, Frank, **1951:** 275 [16, 19]; **1952–53:** 2 [6], 7 [3], 28, 64 [2, 5, 10, 11, 16], 69, 71, 88 [15], 127 [4, 16], 136 [7]

McKinnon, Clinton D., **1948:** 206 [1, 2]; **1952–53:** 26 [14]

McLean, Robert, **1947:** 76n.

McMahon, Sen. Brien, **1946:** 28, 61 [18], 119 [21]; **1948:** 239, 259 [3], 261 [9]; **1949:** 30 [10], 214 [3], 234 [13]; **1950:** 29 [20], 34 [14], 46 [14]; **1951:** 227 [2, 5], 247 [13]; **1952–53:** 21 [3], 115 [3], 170, 219, 292 [2, 5], 293n., 298 [9, 10, 11]

McMahon, John A., **1950:** 247n.

McMath, Gov. Sydney S., **1949:** 119 [2–4], 120; **1951:** 261 [3]; **1952–53:** 193, 194, 195 [3], 197 [5], 228 [2]

McMeekin, Dr. Thomas L., **1952–53:** 117

McMillin, Lucille F., **1946:** 199 [7], 216 [1]

McMorland, Maj. Gen. Edward E., **1951:** 38n.

McNamara, Fred A., **1952–53:** 249

McNarney, Gen. Joseph T., **1945:** 193 [1]

McNary Dam, **1949:** 77; **1950:** 121 [11], 125

McNary-Haugen farm bills, 1920's, **1952–53:** 267

McNutt, Paul V., **1946:** 254, 257 [20]; **1948:** 231 [4], 278 [29]

   See also United States High Commissioner to the Philippines (Paul V. McNutt).

   Appointment as U.S. High Commissioner to the Philippines, **1945:** 129 [2, 5]

McQuillan, Claude, **1948:** 237 [3]

McSpaden, Richard, **1948:** 264 [2]

McVane, John, **1947:** 90n.

McVeagh, Lincoln, **1950:** 142

Mead, Dewey, **1948:** 202 [6]

Mead, George H., **1947:** 145 [1], 146n.; **1949:** 94n.; **1952–53:** 203n.

Mead, Sen. James M., **1946:** 61 [21], 70 [3, 5, 10], 72 [20], 84 [20], 141 [1], 163 [6, 10], 177 [11, 16], 186 [13], 199 [12], 215 [3, 9], 257 [16]; **1947:** 14 [15], 155 [2], 177 [2], 243 [4]; **1948:** 9 [3]; **1949:** 45 [27]; **1950:** 247, 259; **1952–53:** 263

Meade, Gen. George G., **1947:** 177 [9]; **1951:** 90 [16]

Meadows, Lester, **1948:** 138n.

Means, Coatsworth, **1945:** 147n.

Meany, George, **1947:** 122; **1950:** 4n.; **1952–53:** 7 [1], 203n.

Meat, **1946:** 18 (p. 55)

   Conservation, **1947:** 191 [12], 205 [3, 19], 224; **1948:** 21 [11, 12], 26 [15]

   Consumption, **1948:** 8 (p. 92)

   News conference remarks, **1946:** 30 [2], 86 [22], 95 [24], 163 [3], 226 [12, 15], 229 [4, 6, 9, 12, 16, 18]

   Packers, investigation of, **1947:** 209 [12]

     Labor disputes, **1946:** 15 [18], 21 [6]; **1948:** 71 [17], 72, 93 [5]

   Price and distribution controls, **1945:** 64 [10]; **1946:** 99, 163 [3], 223 [1], 229 [12, 16], 232, 249; **1947:** 127 [16]; **1948:** 8 (p. 73); **1951:** 95 [8], 101 [8], 118 [2, 4], 123, 145 [8], 176, 247 [11]; **1952–53:** 33, 282 [8]

   Production and sale, **1952–53:** 33

   Rationing, question of, **1947:** 127 [16]; **1948:** 15 [2]

   Shortage, **1946:** 223 [1], 226 [12, 15], 229 [4, 6, 9, 18], 232; **1947:** 18; **1948:** 8 (pp. 70, 73), 167

   Slaughter controls, **1946:** 95 [24], 99

Meat — *continued*
  Statement, **1946:** 223 [1]
  United Kingdom, availability of, **1952–53:** 57
Mechanics and laborers on public works projects,
  1947: 81
Medals, commemorative, **1947:** 162; **1948:** 90
Medals, military, **1950:** 272
Medals, presentation.
  See also Addresses or remarks at presentation
    ceremonies; Awards and citations.
  Congressional Medal of Honor, **1948:** 183 [1],
    228 [1]; **1950:** 165, 267; **1951:** 115; **1952–
    53:** 35 [12], 125, 157, 250
    Adams, M. Sgt. Stanley T., **1951:** 146
    Atkins, T. A., **1945:** 167n.
    Bennett, Edward A., **1945:** 167n.
    Biddle, M. E., **1945:** 167n.
    Boyington, Lt. Col. Gregory, **1945:** 160n.
    Burke, 1st Lt. Lloyd, **1952–53:** 90
    Burt, Capt. J. M., **1945:** 167n.
    Bush, Richard E., **1945:** 160n.
    Bush, Robert E., **1945:** 160n.
    Craft, C. B., **1945:** 167n.
    Dean, Maj. Gen. William F., **1950:** 263
    Doss, Desmond T., **1945:** 167n.
    Harrell, William G., **1945:** 160n.
    Harvey, Capt. Raymond, **1951:** 146
    Hernandez, Cpl. Rodolfo, **1952–53:** 90
    Horner, F. V., **1945:** 167n.
    Ingman, Corp. Einar H., **1951:** 146
    Jackson, Lt. Arthur J., **1945:** 160n.
    Jacobson, Douglas T., **1945:** 160n.
    Karaberis, C. H., **1945:** 167n.
    Kelley, T. J., **1945:** 167n.
    Kerstetter, D. J., **1945:** 167n.
    Lee, M. Sgt. Hubert L., **1952–53:** 24
    Lindsey, Jake W., **1945:** 34
    Lucas, Jacklyn H., **1945:** 160n.
    McCarthy, Capt. Joseph J., **1945:** 160n.
    McGaha, Charles L., **1946:** 69
    Millett, Capt. Lewis L., **1951:** 146
    O'Kane, Comdr. Richard H., **1946:** 69
    Oresko, N., **1945:** 167n.
    Rodriguez, C., **1945:** 167n.
    Rodriguez, Sgt. Joseph C., **1952–53:** 24
    Sigler, Franklin E., **1945:** 160n.
    Silk, Lt. E. A., **1945:** 167n.
    Sjogren, Lt. J. C., **1945:** 167n.
    Soderman, W. A., **1945:** 167n.
    Street, Lt. Comdr. George L., **1945:** 160n.
    Wahlen, George E., **1945:** 160n.
    Wainwright, Gen. Jonathan M., **1945:** 131
    Watson, Wilson D., **1945:** 160n.
    Williams, Hershel W., **1945:** 160n.
    Wilson, T. Sgt. Harold E., **1952–53:** 90
    Wilson, Maj. Louis H., **1945:** 160n.
  Distinguished Service Medal
    American Legion, acceptance, **1949:** 195

Medals, presentation — *continued*
  Distinguished Service Medal — *continued*
    Arnold, Gen. Henry H., **1946:** 7
    Banks, Frank A., **1950:** 124 [3]
    Bruce, Howard, **1945:** 126
    Byrnes, James F., **1945:** 98
    Clay, Gen. Lucius D., **1949:** 99
    Donovan, Maj. Gen. William J., **1946:** 11
    Eisenhower, Gen. Dwight D., **1952–53:** 152
    Fleming, Maj. Gen. Philip B., **1946:** 103
    Forrestal, James, **1949:** 63
    Hopkins, Harry L., **1945:** 125
    King, Adm. Ernest J., **1945:** 215
    Leahy, Fleet Adm. William D., **1949:** 60
    Nimitz, Adm. Chester W., **1945:** 161; **1947:**
      233
    Ridgway, Lt. Gen. Matthew B., **1952–53:** 132
    Souers, Rear Adm. Sidney W., **1952–53:** 340
    Stimson, Henry L., **1945:** 142
    Watson, Maj. Gen. Edwin M., posthumous
      citation, **1945:** 57
    Wilson, Field Marshal Henry M., **1945:** 197
  Legion of Merit
    Abdul Ilah, **1945:** 47
    Alemán, Miguel, **1947:** 84
    Amir Saud, Crown Prince, **1947:** 34
    Auriol, President Vincent, **1951:** 62
    Bidault, Georges, **1945:** 110
    Caldwell, Horace K., **1946:** 14
    Colyer, Air Marshal Douglas, **1945:** 199
    De Gaulle, Gen. Charles, **1945:** 109
    Grant, Maj. Gen. Ulysses S., 3d, **1946:** 104
    Greer, Lt. Col. Dewitt, **1946:** 14
    Ibn Saud, King Abdul Aziz, **1947:** 33
    Macready, Lt. Gen. Gordon N., **1945:** 198
    Olav, Crown Prince, **1945:** 196
    Shah of Iran, **1947:** 203
    Somerville, Fleet Adm. James F., **1945:** 200
    Stoner, Frank G., **1946:** 14
  Medal of Merit, **1951:** 136n.
    Acheson, Dean, **1947:** 132
    Davies, Ralph K., **1945:** 214
    Forster, Rudolph, posthumous citation, **1945:**
      61
    Hoover, J. Edgar, **1946:** 54
    Hull, Cordell, **1947:** 73
    Johnson, J. Monroe, **1946:** 55
    Johnson, Louis, **1947:** 199
    Krug, Julius A., **1946:** 93
    McNutt, Paul V., **1946:** 254
    Morgenthau, Henry, Jr., **1945:** 213
    Niles, David K., **1947:** 179
    Pawley, William D., **1946:** 113
    Pelley, John J., **1946:** 56
    Plaza, Galo, President of Ecuador, **1951:** 136n.
    Price, Byron, **1946:** 13
    Rosenman, Samuel I., **1946:** 22
    Snyder, John W., **1947:** 94

Medals, presentation — *continued*
  Medal of Merit — *continued*
    Taylor, Myron C., **1948:** 286
    Vinson, Fred M., **1947:** 200
  Medal of Merit Board, **1945:** 157 [3]
    See also Committee to Award Medals of Merit to
      Civilians.
Mediation Board, National, **1950:** 186 [1]
Mediation and Conciliation Service, Federal, **1947:**
  145 [3], 174 [1], 181 (p. 403), 209 [7], 236
  [3]; **1948:** 5 (p. 54), 66n., 72, 88 [3], 140,
  171n., 252, 259 [1, 2]; **1950:** 43; **1951:** 13
  (p. 80), 169, 204, 252, 305; **1952–53:** 18 (p.
  93), 22, 37, 58
Medical care, **1945:** 128, 192; **1946:** 18 (pp. 40, 52,
  64, 83), 91; **1947:** 2 (p. 8); **1948:** 2, 5 (pp.
  21, 34), 8 (pp. 68, 76, 86); **1949:** 85, 202,
  250; **1950:** 39, 129 [4]; **1951:** 135, 258;
  1952–53: 2 [3], 18 (pp. 108, 110), 135, 249,
  268 [8], 273, 278, 284 [5], 333
  See also Health insurance; Hospitals and med-
    ical care facilities.
  Approval of bill, **1946:** 203
  Campaign remarks, **1948:** 115, 134, 205, 215, 220,
    257 [4], 262
  Equal opportunity, **1947:** 130
  Inadequate facilities, loss of life due to, **1948:** 241
  Indians, **1949:** 248
  Insurance, **1948:** 237 [3]
  Legislation, proposed, **1948:** 160
  Mental patients, **1946:** 118
  Message to Congress, **1947:** 98; **1949:** 85
  Military personnel, **1946:** 109; **1948:** 60
  Older persons, **1950:** 233; **1951:** 307
  Rural areas, **1950:** 6
  Seamen, **1947:** 123
  Under social security, proposed, **1946:** 18 (p. 64)
  Veterans, **1946:** 18 (p. 79), 27 [11], 91, 122, 139;
    1947: 2 (p. 8); **1948:** 2, 5 (p. 33), 228 [10];
    1950: 156; **1951:** 13 (pp. 100, 101), 260
Medical Corps, **1945:** 45
Medical education, **1946:** 18 (p. 83); **1947:** 98;
  1948: 89, 181 [2], 237 [3]; **1950:** 9 (p. 75);
  1952–53: 5
Medical Education, National Fund for, **1951:** 135
Medical personnel
  Government, proposed pay raise, **1949:** 228
  Shortage, **1948:** 8 (p. 85); **1949:** 85; **1950:** 9 (p.
    75), 129 [4]
Medical research, **1946:** 18 (p. 83); **1947:** 2 (p. 11),
  98, 211; **1948:** 18, 22, 89, 181 [2], 186, 205,
  237 [3], 239; **1949:** 8 (p. 70); **1950:** 9 (pp.
  75, 84)
Medical Services of the Government, President's
  Committee on the Integration of the,
  1946: 139
Medical supplies for liberated countries, **1947:** 37
Medicine and Surgery, Department of, **1946:** 1

Medill, Joseph, **1951:** 8
Mediterranean, dispatch of Marines to, **1948:** 11
  [12]
Medora, N. Dak., **1946:** 200
"Meet the Press," **1948:** 21 [8]; **1951:** 98
Megis, Mrs. Edward, **1949:** 252n.
Meister, John G. **1948:** 189n.
Melcher, Iowa, campaign remarks, **1948:** 194 [10]
Mellon, Andrew, **1952–53:** 69
Memoirs, the President's plans for writing, **1952–
  53:** 377 [17]
Memorandums to Federal agencies or officials.
  See also Congress, letters to Members of.
  Airport Commission, recommendations, **1952–
    53:** 155n.
  Antitrust laws, Congressional investigation,
    1949: 149n.
  Civil defense planning, **1949:** 48
  Coal industry wage dispute, **1952–53:** 341
  Community War Fund campaign, **1945:** 171
  Copper strike, injunction, **1951:** 214
  Crime, Senate investigation, **1950:** 168
  Critical materials, **1952–53:** 355
  Debt management and credit controls, request
    for study, **1951:** 44
  Defense mobilization, **1952–53:** 245
  Depressed areas, Federal procurement in, **1949:**
    156
  Economic study by FTC, request for, **1952–53:**
    263
  Employee loyalty records, **1948:** 50
  Enterprise system, protection during defense
    emergency, **1950:** 259
  European industrial progress survey, **1952–53:**
    257
  Flood relief, **1951:** 163
  General Services Administration, establishment,
    1949: 145
  George C. Marshall Research Foundation,
    1952–53: 387
  Government employees
    Holidays and leaves of absence, **1945:** 107 [2]
    Personnel procedures, **1950:** 283
    Reduction in workweek, **1945:** 70, 107 [1]
    Security, **1952–53:** 223
    Supergrade positions, limitation in defense
      agencies, **1950:** 288
    Veteran preference, **1945:** 108
  Government funds, handling of, **1945:** 79
  Government programs, review, **1950:** 196
  Highway safety, **1952–53:** 93
  Housing credit restriction, **1950:** 192
  Industrial dispersal policy, **1951:** 189
  John Carter Vincent loyalty case, **1952–53:** 362n.
  Legislative requests for Executive information,
    1952–53: 60, 76, 91
  Manpower mobilization, **1951:** 15
  Natural resources development, **1950:** 265

Memorandums to Federal agencies — *continued*
 Petroleum industry, labor dispute, **1952–53:** 58
 President's Airport Commission, **1952–53:** 41
 Price and wage stabilization, **1951:** 23
 Psychological Strategy Board, creation, **1951:** 128
 Red Cross campaign, **1947:** 5
 Reduction of expenditures, **1946:** 187
 Security information, classification and protection, **1951:** 234
 Shipping industry, tax benefits, **1952–53:** 225, 226
 Transportation industry, labor disputes, **1951:** 74
 Treaties and executive agreements, **1952–53:** 140
 Uprising in Korean prisoner-of-war camps, **1952–53:** 162
Memorandums of Disapproval.
 See Veto Messages and Memorandums of Disapproval.
Memorial Day, **1951:** 113 [1]
 Statement, **1952–53:** 139
Mencken, Henry L., **1947:** 210 [1]
Mendelssohn, Felix, **1951:** 99
Mental fitness of youth, **1946:** 268
Mental health, **1947:** 98; **1948:** 89
Mental illness and mental retardation, **1951:** 135; **1952–53:** 268 [8]
Mental patients, **1946:** 118
Merced, Calif., campaign remarks, **1948:** 204 [1]
Mercer, Clarence, **1952–53:** 117
Mercer, Leroy S., **1948:** 194n.
Merchant, The, Hans Holbein, **1948:** 71 [1]
Merchant marine, U.S., **1945:** 45, 122, 128, 154, 178; **1946:** 3, 18 (pp. 76, 82); **1947:** 7 (pp. 58, 84), 35, 123, 223, 228, 238; **1948:** 4 [13], 8 (p. 81), 177; **1950:** 9 (pp. 92, 93), 76; **1951:** 13 (pp. 81, 82, 83); **1952–53:** 18 (p. 82), 177, 226, 231, 367 (pp. 1142–1143)
Merchant Marine, Advisory Committee on, **1948:** 4 [13]; **1949:** 133; **1950:** 76
 Letter, **1947:** 55
 Report, **1947:** 223
Merchant Marine Act of 1936, **1947:** 35; **1948:** 5 (p. 48), 79, 177; **1949:** 133; **1950:** 9 (p. 92), 76, 236; **1952–53:** 17 [32], 177, 211, 225, 226
Merchant Ship Sales Act of 1946, **1949:** 133
 Veto of amendment, **1950:** 257
Merchant Tailors and Designers Association, **1946:** 86 [25]
Meredith, Margaret, **1952–53:** 173n.
Meriden, Conn., campaign remarks, **1952–53:** 292 [3]
Merit system, Civil Service, 70th anniversary, **1952–53:** 390
Merrill, Adm. Aaron Stanton, **1948:** 11 [3]
Merrill, Eugene H., **1952–53:** 281
Merrill, Joseph F., **1952–53:** 281

Merrimack River, **1952–53:** 294
 Power projects survey, proposed, **1950:** 140
Merrow, Repr. Chester E., **1947:** 182 [6]
Merry Widow, The, Franz Lehár, **1951:** 99
Messages to the American people
 Armistice Day, **1951:** 294
 Arms reduction, international, **1951:** 293
 Congress, special session, **1947:** 214
 Election eve, **1948:** 269
 Farewell address, **1952–53:** 378
 Food conservation, **1947:** 202
 Food for overseas relief, **1946:** 87; **1947:** 213
 Fundraising campaigns
  Community Chest, **1946:** 225; **1947:** 193; **1948:** 221; **1949:** 221; **1950:** 262; **1951:** 242; **1952–53:** 264
  March of Dimes, **1946:** 26
  National War Fund, **1945:** 154
  Red Cross, **1946:** 50; **1947:** 49; **1948:** 40; **1949:** 42; **1950:** 45; **1951:** 47; **1952–53:** 50
  Savings bonds, **1948:** 76; **1949:** 98; **1950:** 133
 Inflation controls, **1951:** 123
 Interdenominational religious program, **1949:** 62
 Korean situation, **1950:** 194, 232, 243, 303; **1951:** 78
 Meat shortage, **1946:** 232
 Mutual Security Program, **1952–53:** 57
 National Community Christmas Tree, lighting, **1946:** 271; **1947:** 240; **1948:** 287; **1949:** 271; **1950:** 317; **1951:** 306; **1952–53:** 356
 National economy, **1949:** 154
 Potsdam conference, **1945:** 97
 Price controls, **1946:** 153, 232
 Railroad strike, **1946:** 124
 Reconversion program, **1946:** 2
 Religion in American life, **1949:** 246
 Steel industry, need for Government operation of, **1952–53:** 82
 Surrender of Germany, **1945:** 27
 Surrender of Japan, **1945:** 122
 United Nations, second anniversary, **1947:** 129
 Veto of the Taft-Hartley bill, **1947:** 121
 Wages and prices in reconversion period, **1945:** 180
 Women of the United States, **1947:** 204
Messages of congratulation on election victory, response by the President, **1948:** 275
Messages to the Congress.
 See Congress, Messages to.
Messages to heads of state and government.
 See also Visitors, foreign leaders.
 Belgium, Prince Charles, **1948:** 85
 Canada, incoming and outgoing Prime Ministers, **1948:** 273
 Chile, President González Videla, **1950:** 104
 Colombia, President Mariano Ospina Perez, **1950:** 181 [4]

Messages to heads of state — *continued*
  Costa Rica, President Otilio Ulate, **1950:** 181 [1]
  Dominican Republic, President Rafael L. Trujillo Molina, **1950:** 181 [2]
  France
    President Auriol, **1947:** 13; **1951:** 157
    President de Gaulle, **1945:** 29
  Greece
    King George II, **1946:** 261
    King Paul I, **1948:** 61
  India
    President Rajendra Prasad, **1950:** 20
    Prime Minister Nehru, **1949:** 264
  Iran, Prime Minister Mohammed Mosadeq, **1951:** 150
  Israel, President Weizmann, **1948:** 224
  Italy
    President de Nicola, **1947:** 15
    Prime Minister de Gasperi, **1947:** 239
  Korea, President Syngman Rhee, **1950:** 211
  Mexico, President Alemán, **1947:** 91
  Netherlands, Queen Wilhelmina, **1948:** 87
  Nicaragua, President Anastasio Somoza, **1950:** 181 [3]
  Pakistan, Governor General Khwaja Nazimuddin, **1951:** 257
  Philippines, President Quirino, **1948:** 82; **1951:** 207
  Poland, President Bierut, **1946:** 64
  Polish Provisional Government of National Unity, Prime Minister Osobka-Morawski, **1945:** 78
  Saudi Arabia, King Ibn-Saud, **1946:** 241
  Soviet Union
    Marshal Stalin, **1945:** 29
    President Nikolai Shvernik, **1951:** 147
  Sweden, King Gustav V, **1947:** 16
  United Kingdom
    Prime Minister Attlee, **1949:** 71
    Prime Minister Churchill, **1945:** 29
  Vatican, Pope Pius XII, **1947:** 185; **1949:** 270
Messersmith, George S., **1946:** 78 [12]; **1947:** 14 [15], 95 [5, 15], 107 [7, 9, 12, 14]
Mesta, Perle, **1949:** 38, 148ftn. (p. 350); **1951:** 101 [9]
Mestrovic, Jan, **1951:** 6n.
Metallurgical Laboratory, Chicago, Ill., **1949:** 166
Metals
  Prices, **1947:** 175, 214, 224; **1950:** 202
  Shortages, **1948:** 8 (p. 70), 167
Metals industry
  Labor dispute, **1952–53:** 37
  Production, **1945:** 202 [3]
Metals Reserve Company, **1949:** 150
Metcalf, Lee, **1952–53:** 268 [9], 269n., 270 [1, 5, 6–8]
Methodist ministers, Illinois, **1952–53:** 42, 44 [2]
Methodist Ministers, Washington Institute of, **1951:** 31

Metzger, John William, **1952–53:** 280 [4, 5, 6], 282 [1–4, 6–8], 283n.
Mexican War, **1945:** 164 [3]; **1948:** 245
Mexico, **1946:** 247; **1949:** 159
  Air service to, **1952–53:** 246
  Alemán, Miguel, **1947:** 14 [8, 17], 51, 79, 83, 84, 91n., 95 [17]; **1949:** 200 [1]
  Ambassador Antonio de los Monteros, **1947:** 95 [17]
  Assistance, **1947:** 83
    Technical, **1951:** 259
  Border with U.S., immigration law enforcement, **1952–53:** 367 (p. 1163)
  Cattle imports from, **1946:** 232
  Chapultepec, Act of, **1947:** 101, 105, 188
  Economic Development, **1947:** 83
  Foot-and-mouth disease, eradication, **1951:** 13 (p. 90)
  International Boundary and Water Commission, **1946:** 18 (p. 82); **1947:** 7 (p. 82); **1948:** 5 (p. 46)
  Lend-lease operations, report on, **1951:** 244
  Livestock disease control, cooperation with U.S., **1947:** 45, 181 (p. 399)
  Loan to, **1950:** 146 [15], 179 [14], 191 [10], 217 [9], 238 [2]
  Migratory workers in U.S., **1950:** 153; **1951:** 16 [5], 75, 154, 192; **1952–53:** 2 [5], 18 (p. 94), 21 [26], 31 [14], 367 (pp. 1150–1151)
  News conference remarks, **1949:** 58 [6], 66 [11], 78 [8], 84 [6, 8], 122 [12, 25], 144 [13], 155 [6], 161 [6], 171 [10], 182 [6], 192 [11], 200 [1, 3, 11], 205 [17], 211 [9], 253 [16], 260 [16]; **1950:** 146 [15], 179 [14], 191 [10], 214 [5], 217 [9], 238 [2]
  Oil development loan, proposed, **1949:** 66 [11], 78 [8], 84 [6], 122 [12, 25], 144 [13], 155 [6], 161 [6], 171 [10], 182 [6], 192 [11], 200 [1, 3, 11], 205 [17], 211 [9], 253 [16], 260 [16]
  Radio waveband allocation, agreement with U.S., **1949:** 84 [8]
  Rio Grande dams, **1948:** 5 (p. 46)
  Tello, Manuel, **1951:** 75n.; **1952–53:** 2 [5]
  U.S. Ambassador William O'Dwyer, **1950:** 217 [9]; **1951:** 63 [4], 95 [3, 10], 101 [3], 227 [9]
    Question of resignation, **1952–53:** 115 [2]
  U.S. Ambassador Walter Thurston, **1947:** 145 [16]; **1950:** 214 [5, 7]
  U.S. relations with, **1950:** 214 [5]
  Visit to, **1947:** 19 [16], 46 [25], 51, 79, 112; **1948:** 198 [1], 210 [2]
Mexico, Mo., **1950:** 160 [2], 169 [5]
  Ledger, **1952–53:** 26 [9, 10]
  Mayor Herbert Morris, **1950:** 160 [2]
Mexico City, **1946:** 18 (p. 42), 83; **1947:** 19 [16]; **1952–53:** 262, 263
  Conference on Problems of War and Peace (1945), **1947:** 51

Mexico-United States, Water Utilization Treaty, **1945:** 7

Meyer, Eugene, **1946:** 45n., 58n.; **1947:** 191 [3]

Miami, Fla., **1949:** 267 [15]
  American Legion convention, address, **1948:** 244
  Grand jury for crime investigation, **1951:** 63 [1]
  Miami Herald, **1951:** 56 [6]
  News conference remarks, **1951:** 56 [6, 12], 63 [1], 261 [1]
  Visit to, question of, **1948:** 178 [2]

Miami, Okla., **1951:** 158

Mica, stockpiling, **1948:** 8 (p. 78)

Michael, Archbishop, exchange of messages, **1950:** 7

Michigan, **1946:** 197
  Campaign addresses or remarks, **1948:** 183 [1, 2, 4–6], 184; **1952–53:** 317, 318
  Candidates for public office, **1948:** 181 [6]; **1952–53:** 317 [1, 3–7]
  Dingell, Repr. John D., **1945:** 44 [16]
  Gov. Kim Sigler, **1948:** 183 [2]
  Gov. G. Mennen Williams, **1951:** 174; **1952–53:** 317 [1–7], 318
  Mackinac Island, **1945:** 64 [9]
  Vandenberg, Sen. Arthur H., **1945:** 10, 219n.
  Visit to, question of, **1948:** 170 [2], 174 [8, 12], 178 [2, 16]

Michigan Bell Telephone Co., **1950:** 43n.

Midcentury White House Conference on Children and Youth, **1950:** 5, 299

Middle East and Near East, **1945:** 47; **1946:** 76, 241; **1947:** 56; **1948:** 2, 129, 193 [2]; **1949:** 40 [2]; **1950:** 42; **1952–53:** 5
  See also specific countries.
  Allied command, proposed, **1952–53:** 6, 55
  Arms shipments to
    Opposition of British labor to, **1950:** 38 [17]
    Tripartite declaration on, **1950:** 147, 148
  Assistance, **1949:** 274; **1950:** 78; **1952–53:** 6, 15, 18 (p. 76), 55, 57, 73
    Economic, **1951:** 4, 13 (p. 73), 114
    Military, **1951:** 4, 13 (pp. 73, 74), 114, 167
    Technical, **1951:** 13 (p. 74), 83, 245
  Communism in, **1951:** 13 (p. 73), 96, 114
  Economic development, **1949:** 40 [10], 193, 274
  News conference remarks, **1945:** 76 [9], 208 [12]; **1950:** 38 [17], 80 [1]
  Oil reserves, **1951:** 114
  Proposed Anglo-American oil agreement, **1945:** 76 [9]
  Public works program, U.N., **1950:** 143
  Refugees, **1952–53:** 367 (p. 1140)
  Strategic importance, **1951:** 114
  U.N. Economic Survey Mission, **1949:** 274; **1950:** 25, 154
  U.S. relations with, **1950:** 252

Middlebush, Frederick A., **1950:** 159n., 160 [1]

Middletown, Conn.
  Campaign remarks, **1952–53:** 292 [4]
  Mayor Steve Bailey, **1952–53:** 292 [3]

Midway Islands, battle, **1945:** 45, 177, 178
  10th anniversary, **1952–53:** 142

Midwest
  Coal supplies, **1946:** 228
  Drought, **1952–53:** 166 [10]
  Floods, **1951:** 261 [6]; **1952–53:** 97, 98 [8], 101, 109, 119

Midwest Democratic Conference, **1949:** 122 [4]; **1951:** 110, 113 [2, 3]

Migrants from Europe, Provisional Inter-Governmental Committee for the Movement of, **1952–53:** 65, 164

Migratory Bird Conservation Commission, **1946:** 211

Migratory birds, **1946:** 211

Migratory Labor, Commission on, **1950:** 153; **1951:** 75, 154; **1952–53:** 18 (p. 94), 367 (p. 1151)

Mikhailovitch, Gen. Draja, **1946:** 95 [12]

Mikolajczyk, Stanislaw, **1947:** 218 [11]

Milan, Italy, **1951:** 153 [16]

Miles City, Mont., **1949:** 206

Militarism, German, **1947:** 238

Military Academy, U.S., **1946:** 224; **1947:** 226 [2]; **1950:** 29 [9]; **1951:** 188 [14, 16], 200 [9]; **1952–53:** 130, 131, 142
  Admission of Canadians to, **1948:** 112

Military aggressions of 1930's, lessons of, **1950:** 193, 194

Military aides, the President's, **1949:** 36

Military alliance, Western nations, question of, **1948:** 49 [16]

Military assistance and defense support, **1947:** 56, 57, 90 [1], 95 [10, 12, 16, 26], 100, 107 [2], 117, 220, 239; **1948:** 28, 52, 53, 60; **1949:** 8 (pp. 53, 54), 19; **1950:** 2, 6, 9 (pp. 48, 56, 65), 81, 94, 119, 126, 132, 134, 159, 161 [3], 162, 177, 194, 202, 232, 269, 279, 299, 301, 303; **1951:** 11, 13 (pp. 8, 62–64, 70–74), 53, 80, 91–93, 107, 167, 215, 239 [12]; **1952–53:** 15, 17 [2], 18 (pp. 64, 73–77), 55, 69, 101, 128, 144, 190, 259, 275, 279, 281, 283, 295 [1], 303 [2], 313 [2], 319 [6], 378
  See also Mutual Defense Assistance Program; North Atlantic Treaty; *individual countries.*
  Address to American people, **1952–53:** 57
  Africa, **1952–53:** 15
  Appropriations, supplemental estimate, **1950:** 204
  Asia, **1950:** 162, 201; **1951:** 4, 13 (pp. 73, 74), 25, 59, 66, 84, 114, 153 [3], 167; **1952–53:** 15, 18 (pp. 76, 77), 55, 196, 354
    China, **1951:** 114, 138; **1952–53:** 18 (p. 76)
    Formosa, **1950:** 175n.; **1952–53:** 18 (p. 76), 367 (p. 1140)

Military assistance — *continued*
  Asia — *continued*
    Indochina, **1950:** 173, 175n., 193; **1951:** 25,
      114; **1952–53:** 5, 27, 367 (p. 1140)
    Japan, **1951:** 193 [2]; **1952–53:** 95, 111
    Korea, **1949:** 162, 184; **1950:** 172, 175, 181,
      184, 186 [12], 189, 193, 201, 211; **1951:** 78,
      80, 114, 138; **1952–53:** 307, 310, 315 [5],
      320, 354
    Philippines, **1949:** 162, 184; **1950:** 173, 175n.,
      193, 204; **1951:** 114, 193 [2], 207, 208, 216;
      1952–53: 5, 18 (p. 76), 26 [21], 95, 367 (p.
      1140)
    Thailand, **1951:** 114
  Australia, **1951:** 84, 85 [8], 153ftn. (p. 387), 193
    [2], 216; **1952–53:** 5, 26 [21], 95
  Canada, **1949:** 162
  Europe, **1949:** 7 [6, 9, 11, 43], 72 [2, 7, 16, 19], 89
    [9], 120, 155 [3], 171 [9], 179 [17], 184, 236
    [17]; **1950:** 9 (p. 59), 22, 203 [11], 242, 303;
    1951: 4, 7 [5], 12 [42], 13 (pp. 72, 73), 16
    [15], 59, 66, 114, 167; **1952–53:** 5, 15, 18
    (pp. 74, 75), 144, 158, 288, 295 [8], 298 [8],
    317 [2]
    American Legion support of, **1951:** 191
    France, **1950:** 173; **1951:** 25, 138; **1952–53:** 27,
      367 (p. 1140)
    Greece, **1949:** 86, 162, 184; **1950:** 9 (p. 59),
      142, 201, 204, 232; **1951:** 78, 138; **1952–**
      53: 18 (p. 75), 27, 55, 288, 317 [2]
    Italy, **1951:** 138, 232
    North Atlantic area, **1950:** 195, 204, 230 [12]
    Yugoslavia, **1951:** 292; **1952–53:** 18 (p. 75), 55
  Europe, Western, **1948:** 71 [16, 22]
  Expenditures for, **1951:** 12 [37]; **1952–53:** 205,
    231, 367 (pp. 1139–1140)
  Latin America, **1949:** 162; **1951:** 114, 167; **1952–**
    53: 15, 18 (p. 77), 55
  Malaya, **1952–53:** 5
  Marshall plan nations, **1948:** 93 [9], 97 [6], 188,
    244, 263
  Message to Congress, **1949:** 162; **1950:** 151;
    1951: 114
  Military aid bill, approval, **1950:** 201
  Near East, **1951:** 4, 13 (p. 73); **1952–53:** 15, 18
    (pp. 75–77)
    Iran, **1949:** 162, 184, 273; **1950:** 201, 204, 232;
      1952–53: 144
    Turkey, **1949:** 86, 162, 184; **1950:** 9 (p. 59),
      142, 201, 204, 232; **1951:** 114, 138; **1952–**
      53: 18 (pp. 75, 76), 27, 55, 288, 317 [2]
  New Zealand, **1951:** 84, 85 [8], 153ftn. (p. 387),
    193 [2], 216; **1952–53:** 5, 26 [21], 95
  News conference remarks, **1948:** 71 [16, 22], 93,
    [9], 278 [5, 31, 40]; **1949:** 7 [6, 9, 11, 43], 58
    [10], 72 [2, 7, 16, 19], 78 [12], 84 [5, 7], 89
    [9], 155 [3, 18], 161 [8], 171 [9], 179 [17],
    214 [3], 236 [17]; **1952–53:** 17 [2], 123 [2]

Military assistance — *continued*
  Reduction, Republican proposals, **1952–53:** 319
    [5]
  Steel production, effect on, **1952–53:** 116
Military cemeteries, **1947:** 92
Military cooperation, Inter-American, **1947:** 101,
  127 [17]; **1948:** 5 (p. 29)
Military establishment, **1946:** 18 (p. 45), 130n., 137,
  138, 192 [10], 193, 194
  Single civilian control, proposed, **1945:** 218
Military Establishment, National.
  See National Military Establishment.
Military Housing Act, **1950:** 113
Military and Industry Liaison Committee, **1948:**
  177
Military information, security of, **1948:** 11 [13]
Military Justice, Uniform Code of, **1950:** 108
Military March, Franz Schubert, **1950:** 139
Military Order of the World Wars, **1950:** 138n.;
  1951: 109n.
Military personnel, **1946:** 135; **1947:** 7 (p. 64);
  1948: 175
  See also Armed forces, U.S.
  Appointment, **1947:** 35
  Community services for, **1949:** 73, 110; **1951:**
    186, 242
  Dependents, health services, **1946:** 18 (p. 83)
  Dependents, housing, **1951:** 111
  Equal opportunity, **1948:** 110 [8], 166 [4]; **1950:**
    141
  Expenditures for, **1952–53:** 367 (pp. 1135–1136)
  Foreign decorations, acceptance by, **1949:** 32 [3]
  Housing, **1948:** 5 (p. 28); **1949:** 8 (p. 60); **1950:**
    32; **1952–53:** 5
  Increase, **1952–53:** 18 (p. 69)
  Information and education programs, **1950:** 32
  Insurance, **1951:** 12 [36]
    Life Insurance, National Service, **1947:** 75
    Old age and survivors, extension to, **1952–53:**
      18 (p. 70)
  Integration, **1948:** 166 [1, 4], 185 [7]
  Medical care, **1946:** 109; **1948:** 60; **1952–53:** 333
  Medical personnel, **1945:** 192
  Mental patients, **1946:** 118
  Moral safeguards, **1948:** 190
  Morale, **1951:** 180
  Pay, **1946:** 192 [3, 5, 6, 14, 17, 21], 193, 194, 199
    [17]; **1948:** 5 (pp. 22, 26, 27), 60, 175;
    1949: 8 (pp. 57, 59), 40 [12], 112 [3], 218;
    1950: 9 (pp. 61, 63, 66); **1952–53:** 18 (pp.
    69, 70), 64 [17], 231, 275, 322
  Mustering-out, **1946:** 18 (p. 75); **1947:** 2 (p. 8),
    4 (pp. 15, 19), 7 (p. 68)
  Retired Generals of the Army and Admirals of
    the Fleet, **1951:** 108 [4]; **1952–53:** 377 [30]
  Terminal leave, **1947:** 2 (p. 8), 6 [3, 18, 21];
    1947: 5 (p. 26), 228 [10]
Physical rehabilitation, **1947:** 86

Military personnel — *continued*
Physically disabled, retirements, **1948:** 33
Postage rates for, **1947:** 18
Prisoners, question of Christmas clemency for, **1948:** 285 [13]
Promotions, **1949:** 267 [8]
Rank of Chiefs and Assistant Chiefs of naval bureaus, **1945:** 217
Religious and welfare programs, **1950:** 32, 95n., 262; **1951:** 3, 100
Reservists, **1949:** 135, 174; **1950:** 270 [5, 8]
Retirement benefits, **1948:** 145
Retired enlistees, credit for foreign service 1898–1912, veto, **1945:** 205
Retirement, **1947:** 35; **1949:** 174; **1950:** 9 (pp. 61, 66); **1952–53:** 18 (p. 70), 213, 367 (pp. 1135–1136)
Terminal leave bonds, **1947:** 145 [17]
Testimony before congressional committees, **1949:** 11 [13]
Uniform, pride in wearing, **1951:** 38
USO services for, **1949:** 34, 104, 221
Utilization, control by Defense Department, **1951:** 93
Voluntary enlistees, **1948:** 175
Voting rights, **1952–53:** 68, 96, 124
Welfare, **1948:** 5 (p. 27); **1952–53:** 297
Military policy, postwar, **1945:** 174
Military preparedness, **1945:** 174
Military procurement, **1946:** 137, 138; **1947:** 7 (p. 64); **1948:** 5 (pp. 28, 29), 60, 98; **1949:** 8 (pp. 57, 60, 61), 50; **1950:** 9 (pp. 54, 61, 64, 65), 193, 204; **1951:** 13 (pp. 69, 70), 177
Military research, **1945:** 218; **1946:** 18 (p. 75), 137, 138; **1947:** 7 (p. 64); **1948:** 5 (p. 26), 175, 186
National agency, proposed, **1945:** 174
Military spending, **1946:** 17 [13], 18 (pp. 67, 76), 192 [25], 193, 194, 238; **1947:** 2 (p. 7), 6 [14, 21], 7 (p. 64), 10n.; **1948:** 5 (pp. 28, 29), 98, 175, 243 [1, 4, 7], 278 [2]; **1949:** 66 [12], 72 [2, 7, 16, 19], 86, 179 [25], 192 [10, 13, 15], 200 [20], 269 [18]; **1950:** 110 [1], 133, 193, 194, 204, 243
News conference remarks, **1950:** 8 [24], 80 [3], 97 [8], 105 [6, 13], 146 [12, 16], 186 [10], 191 [4], 203 [23], 217 [7]
Military standardization bill, inter-American, **1949:** 11 [19]
Military strength, free world, **1951:** 83
Military strength, U.S., **1945:** 45, 178, 218; **1946:** 18 (p. 75), 76; **1947:** 2 (p. 11), 7 (p. 64), 50, 54, 68, 110, 117, 188, 233; **1948:** 5 (pp. 19, 21, 26, 27), 52, 53, 60, 63, 80, 98, 175, 186, 243 [1], 262; **1949:** 2, 7 [16], 8 (pp. 47, 55–62), 50; **1950:** 2, 9 (pp. 48, 61–63), 110 [1], 121 [5], 126, 133, 151, 155, 193, 194, 202, 225, 228, 232, 243, 292, 296, 299, 301,

Military strength, U.S. — *continued*
302; **1951:** 4, 11, 13 (pp. 61, 62 68–70), 54, 71, 80, 92, 98, 144, 167, 215, 294; **1952–53:** 5, 55, 57, 128, 131, 158, 275, 279, 293, 315 [4], 317 [7], 318, 319 [6], 366
News conference remarks, **1950:** 258 [3], 295 [7, 10]
Military Surgeons, Association of, remarks, **1952–53:** 333
Military training and education, **1945:** 174, 218; **1946:** 137, 138; **1947:** 31 [18], 50, 54; **1948:** 175, 190, 243 [4]; **1949:** 50; **1951:** 218
Korean soldiers, attendance at U.S. Army schools, **1951:** 236
Marine Corps, **1950:** 165
NATO forces, **1950:** 311; **1951:** 4, 69
Reserves, **1950:** 9 (pp. 63, 64); **1951:** 13 (p. 64)
Universal, **1945:** 44 [3], 106 [14, 16], 174, 218; **1946:** 18 (p. 52), 27 [6], 41 [20], 53 [4], 75 [3, 13], 76; **1947:** 2 (p. 12), 7 (p. 63), 36 [4, 7, 9], 46 [12], 88 [6], 106, 117, 127 [14]; **1948:** 2, 5 (pp. 20, 26–29), 52, 71 [19], 80, 86, 88 [16], 89, 93 [16], 114 [2], 165, 175, 243 [1]; **1949:** 2, 7 [17], 8 (pp. 55, 56); **1950:** 8 [45], 138n., 214 [2, 4, 15], 225n., 272, 318 [11]; **1951:** 63 [22], 107, 191; **1952–53:** 18 (p. 72)
Institution by NATO member states, **1951:** 4
World War II officers, continuation, **1948:** 243 [1]
Military Training and Service Act, Universal, **1945:** 174n.
Military Tribunal, International, **1947:** 21
Militia, Organized, retirement credit for service in, **1949:** 174
Milk, **1946:** 18 (pp. 55, 84), 84 [23]
Prices, **1948:** 99, 246
Supports, **1950:** 9 (p. 86)
Miller, Edward G., **1949:** 112 [1], 161 [6]
Miller, Frieda S., **1948:** 30
Miller, Joe Zach, **1951:** 21
Miller, Justin, **1945:** 132 [1]; **1946:** 45n., 255n.; **1947:** 191 [3]; **1952–53:** 7 [11]
Miller, Ray T., **1948:** 84 [2], 258n.
Miller, Tom, **1948:** 212 [2]
Miller, Watson B., **1947:** 123, 124, 184
Appointment as Federal Security Administrator, **1945:** 157 [1]
Miller, Wilbur K., **1945:** 132 [1]
Miller-Tydings Fair Trade Act of 1937, **1952–53:** 204
Millett, Capt. Lewis L., Congressional Medal of Honor, **1951:** 146
Milligan, Maurice Morton, **1948:** 71ftn. (p. 211)
Millikin, Sen. Eugene D., **1947:** 39; **1951:** 7 [5], 12 [20], 239 [3]; **1952–53:** 297
Milling industry, **1946:** 30 [2]

Millis, H. A., resignation as Chairman, National Labor Relations Board, **1945:** 52 [4]

Millis, Walter, **1951:** 251ftn. (p. 565), 261ftn. (p. 586)

Mills, Vice Adm. Earle W., **1946:** 119 [19]

Mills, Repr. Wilbur D., **1949:** 112 [6]; **1952–53:** 193n., 195 [3]

Miltonberger, Maj. Gen. Butler B., **1948:** 118 [3]

Milwaukee, Wis.
   Campaign address, **1948:** 239; **1952–53:** 241
   Eisenhower campaign speech, comment on, **1952–53:** 293
   Visit to, **1952–53:** 123 [15]

Mindszenty, Cardinal Joseph, **1946:** 41 [17]; **1948:** 288 [1]; **1949:** 28 [19], 30 [9]

Mine, Mill and Smelter Workers, International Union of, **1951:** 204, 214; **1952–53:** 37

Mine Workers, United, **1946:** 252; **1948:** 55 [9], 66n., 171, 248; **1950:** 16ftn. (p. 117), 27, 35, 49; **1951:** 153 [16]; **1952–53:** 341

Mineral resources, **1946:** 118, 206; **1947:** 7 (p. 83), 175, 231; **1948:** 2, 5 (pp. 45–47), 8 (pp. 62, 67, 78), 201; **1949:** 8 (pp. 83–84); **1950:** 9 (pp. 91, 94), 121 [4], 124 [7]
   See also Mining industry; *specific minerals.*
   Atomic energy source materials, **1945:** 156
      U.S. purchase of lands, **1945:** 157 [18]
   Conservation, **1950:** 116; **1952–53:** 5, 15, 18 (p. 89)
   Continental shelf deposits, **1945:** 150
   Depletion exemptions, **1950:** 18
   Exploration and development, **1951:** 13 (pp. 76, 81–83, 87)
      Subsidies, **1947:** 175; **1951:** 70 [2]
   Five-year censuses, **1952–53:** 367 (p. 1156)
   Imports, **1952–53:** 15, 55, 57
   India, **1951:** 34
   Labrador, **1951:** 11, 13 (pp. 81–83)

Minerva clock, White House, **1952–53:** 228 [1], 229

Mines, Bureau of, **1947:** 7 (p. 83); **1948:** 5 (p. 47), 105; **1949:** 8 (p. 84), 150; **1951:** 13 (p. 87), 177; **1952–53:** 18 (pp. 89, 94), 231, 280 [5]

Mines, Bureau of, Director (James Boyd), **1950:** 23 [16]

Mines, Government-possessed, **1947:** 87

Minidoka power project, **1952–53:** 367 (p. 1146)

Minimum wage, **1946:** 2, 18 (pp. 52, 57, 58), 177 [21]; **1947:** 53, 93, 110, 152, 187; **1948:** 2, 8 (pp. 93, 98), 182, 189; **1949:** 2, 8 (p. 90), 39, 151, 154, 219, 239; **1950:** 2, 157; **1952–53:** 215, 241, 242 [3], 273, 281, 289 [1], 291, 292 [5], 294, 296, 298 [1], 312, 366
   Campaign remarks, **1948:** 101, 138 [4], 139 [2], 183 [5], 184, 227 [2, 3, 9], 228 [5], 232, 233 [1], 236, 240 [1], 261 [10]
   Establishment by law, **1948:** 219
   Increase, **1948:** 160, 165, 176, 215, 247, 249, 251, 252, 255, 257 [2], 258, 259 [3], 261 [8], 262,

Minimum wage — *continued*
   Increase — *continued*
      267 [2], 268; **1950:** 9 (p. 98), 18, 128, 134, 279
   Proposed, **1945:** 128
   Legislative history, **1950:** 18

Mining industry, **1948:** 5 (p. 53), 80
   See also Mineral resources.
   Claims on public lands, **1949:** 124
   Copper, **1950:** 128
   Depletion exemptions, **1950:** 18
   Frankfort, Ill., explosion, **1952–53:** 150
   Lead, **1950:** 124 [7]
   Phosphate, **1950:** 124 [7], 127 [1]
   Production, **1949:** 150
   Safety legislation, proposed, **1952–53:** 19, 21 [2, 3], 150
   Taxation of, **1951:** 28
   Wages and hours, statistics, **1949:** 13

Ministers, Methodist, Washington Institute of, **1951:** 31

Ministers Meeting, Interdenominational, **1952–53:** 290

Minneapolis, Minn., **1947:** 226 [13]; **1949:** 50
   Campaign remarks, **1952–53:** 313 [5]
   Mayor Eric G. Hoyer, **1949:** 250 [2]
   Mayor Hubert H. Humphrey, **1948:** 235 [5], 236, 237 [1–4]

Minneapolis Tribune, **1952–53:** 35 [3]

Minnesota, **1947:** 35; **1950:** 129 [1, 3, 7], 130
   Ball, Sen. Joseph H., **1945:** 172 [1]
   Campaign remarks, **1948:** 235 [5, 6], 236, 237 [1–4]; **1952–53:** 266 [1], 313, 314
   Candidates for public office, **1952–53:** 266 [1], 313, 314
   Centennial, **1949:** 250 [2]
   Commemorative coin for, veto, **1948:** 90
   Flood relief in, **1952–53:** 97
   Gov. C. Elmer Anderson, **1952–53:** 97
   Gov. Luther W. Youngdahl, **1949:** 250 [2, 3]; **1951:** 153 [8]
   Mineral industry, contribution to World War II victory, **1948:** 235 [5], 236
   Primary elections, **1952–53:** 7 [3], 64 [8]
   Two Harbors, improvement, veto, **1945:** 90

Minnesota State Fair, **1950:** 127 [5]

Minot, N. Dak., **1950:** 129 [4]
   Campaign remarks, **1952–53:** 266 [7]

Mint, Bureau of the, Director (Mrs. Nellie Tayloe Ross), **1948:** 118 [6]; **1950:** 117 [1], 118

Minton, Sherman, **1949:** 211 [2]

Minuet in G, Ignace Paderewski, **1951:** 99

Missiles, **1947:** 194
   See also specific missiles.
   Procurement, **1950:** 9 (p. 65)

Missing Persons Act, **1947:** 134

Missionaries, Baptist, remarks to, **1950:** 31

Missionaries, U.S., in Korea, **1949:** 117

Mississippi
  Gov. Fielding L. Wright, **1950:** 169 [2]
  Lucedale, **1945:** 34
  Patronage for congressional delegation, **1949:** 95
    [7]
Mississippi River, **1945:** 165; **1947:** 141 [2], 144
Mississippi River Basin, **1949:** 8 (p. 83); **1950:** 3 [9,
    11, 25], 86 [15], 121 [4, 13], 125, 127 [2],
    129 [1]; **1951:** 183, 185
  Barge transportation in, **1952–53:** 18 (p. 83)
  Floods, control and relief, **1952–53:** 97, 109, 194
Mississippi River survey bill, **1949:** 182 [15]
Missoula, Mont., **1950:** 127 [1]
Missouri, **1946:** 41 [19], 53 [3, 18], 61 [21], 70 [5, 10],
    141 [1], 186 [13], 237 [24]; **1947:** 31 [6], 88
    [4], 174 [1], 236 [5]; **1948:** 89; **1950:** 37,
    110 [3, 5, 9]; **1951:** 8
  Addresses or remarks in, **1950:** 160 [1, 2], 161
    [1–3], 162
  Campaign remarks, **1948:** 138 [1–3], 194 [12, 13],
    216 [13–16], 267 [4], 268, 269; **1952–53:**
    284 [4–6], 322, 324
  Campaign for Senate seat, recollections by the
    President, **1952–53:** 193
  Candidates for public office, **1948:** 194 [12, 13],
    216 [13–15], 235 [5], 236, 237 [1–4]; **1950:**
    3 [8, 13], 16 [9], 23 [5], 160 [2], 203 [2], 206
    [2], 279; **1952–53:** 21 [8], 26 [18], 35 [6], 75
    [5], 98 [39], 149 [3], 156 [1], 197 [12], 284
    [4, 5], 322, 377 [29]
  Cannon, Repr. Clarence, **1945:** 185
  Caruthersville, **1945:** 147 [9], 163
  Delegation at Democratic National Convention,
    1952–53: 197 [17]
  Dispute with Kansas over Arkansas River, **1948:**
    86
  District Attorney, Eastern District, **1947:** 19 [10]
  Flood relief in, **1951:** 158, 162, 165 [4], 185, 196,
    209 [5], 224 [7], 269; **1952–53:** 3, 18 (p.
    88), 32, 50, 97, 109, 119
  Friends of President, presence at news confer-
    ence, **1948:** 178 [10]
  Gasoline tax, defeat, **1950:** 86 [10]
  Gov. Phil M. Donnelly, **1948:** 138 [3], 158, 268
  Gov. Forrest Smith, **1949:** 220; **1950:** 23 [5], 29
    [4], 38 [6], 86 [10], 160 [2], 161 [2, 3], 162,
    312; **1951:** 165 [4], 196; **1952–53:** 98 [13],
    157, 158
  Independence, **1945:** 8 [2], 64 [9], 67, 76 [9]
  Jackson County, **1945:** 68, 163
    President's service as official, **1948:** 214 [8],
    231 [1]; **1949:** 54, 249; **1950:** 121 [6]
  Jefferson Barracks, proposed national monu-
    ment, **1949:** 118 [21]
  Kansas City, **1945:** 68
  Lead and zinc production, **1950:** 124 [7]
  Lonejack, **1945:** 68

Missouri — *continued*
  National Guard, President's service in, **1948:** 237
    [5]; **1950:** 272
  Natural resources, conservation and develop-
    ment, **1952–53:** 3
  News conference remarks, **1945:** 64 [3, 9, 14];
    1949: 118 [21], 148 [7], 155 [11], 240 [9];
    1950: 3 [8, 13], 16 [9, 11, 19], 23 [5, 11], 38
    [5, 6], 86 [10], 169 [4, 5, 7], 203 [2, 15], 206
    [2]
  Postelection remarks in, **1948:** 270, 271 [1]
  Power projects, **1952–53:** 3, 62, 194
  President's forebears in, **1948:** 222 [1]
  Primary election, **1946:** 173 [6, 8, 9, 18], 177 [8],
    199 [2, 15]; **1947:** 107 [6]; **1950:** 16 [9, 19],
    23 [5, 11], 38 [5, 6], 86ftn. (p. 251), 169 [4,
    5, 7], 203 [15], 206 [2]; **1952–53:** 21 [12], 26
    [18], 75 [6], 221 [5]
  Public works projects in, **1951:** 32, 120
  Redistricting, proposed, **1952–53:** 26 [18]
  Visit to, comment on, **1945:** 172 [13]
Missouri, University of, **1951:** 122; **1952–53:** 98 [13]
Missouri, U.S.S., **1945:** 122; **1947:** 119 [14]; **1948:**
    181 [1]; **1949:** 36, 160; **1950:** 29 [6, 8, 10];
    1952–53: 255, 266 [4]
Missouri Compromise, **1951:** 8
Missouri Basin Survey Commission, **1952–53:** 3, 18
    (p. 88), 32, 269, 367 (p. 1147)
Missouri-Kansas-Texas Railroad, **1951:** 49 [6]
Missouri Pacific Railroad, labor dispute, **1949:** 205
    [11]
Missouri River, **1946:** 86 [16]
Missouri River Basin, **1949:** 7 [24], 8 (p. 83); **1950:**
    116, 121 [4, 13], 125, 127 [2], 129 [1]; **1951:**
    13 (p. 87), 120, 183, 185, 196; **1952–53:** 3,
    32, 101, 109, 266 [6], 269
  News conference remarks, **1950:** 3 [9, 11, 14, 25],
    86 [15]; **1952–53:** 26 [23], 98 [8, 9]
  Power projects, **1952–53:** 109
Missouri River Basin Commission, **1952–53:** 109,
    388
Missouri River development, **1945:** 128, 164 [8],
    165
Missouri Valley, flood control, **1947:** 144
Missouri Valley, President's Emergency Commis-
    sion on the, proposed, **1951:** 183n.
Missouri Valley Authority, **1945:** 4 [7, 9]; **1946:** 17
    [20, 25], 86 [16]; **1947:** 141 [2], 243 [18]
  Proposed, **1949:** 7 [24], 78 [14]; **1950:** 3 [11, 14];
    1951: 171 [7], 183
Missouri Valley development, **1946:** 18 (p. 61)
Missouri Waltz, **1946:** 86 [26]; **1948:** 71ftn. (p. 211);
    1949: 250 [2]
Mistral, Gabriela, **1946:** 66 [4]
Mitchell, Harry B., **1946:** 146; **1951:** 119
  Letter, **1950:** 288
  Memorandum, **1950:** 283
  Subpoena by Congress, **1950:** 82

[References are to items except as otherwise indicated]

Mitchell, Sen. Hugh B., **1945:** 64 [5], 208 [21]; **1946:** 257 [12]; **1952–53:** 272, 274–276
Mitchell, John, **1948:** 248; **1952–53:** 306 [1]
Mitchell, Julian, **1945:** 147n.
Mitchell, Stephen A., **1952–53:** 342 [8], 377 [27]
Mitscher, Adm. Marc A., **1946:** 171
Mobilization Policy, National Advisory Board on, **1951:** 74n., 137; **1952–53:** 110
Modell, Henry, **1946:** 78ftn. (p. 192)
Mojave, Calif., campaign remarks, **1948:** 204 [6]
Mojave Desert, borax extraction from, **1948:** 204 [6]
Molasses, controls, **1947:** 18
Moldavia, **1947:** 32
Moline, Ill., campaign remarks, **1952–53:** 315 [5]
Mollison, Irvin C., **1945:** 157 [15]
Mollohan, Robert H., **1952–53:** 242 [4], 308 [1]
Molotov, Vyacheslav M., **1945:** 91; **1946:** 126 [3, 9], 265; **1947:** 74; **1948:** 96, 97 [19]
   News conference remarks on, **1945:** 4 [11], 22 [10]
Monetary Commission, National, proposed, **1949:** 122 [2]
Monetary policy.
   See Fiscal policy.
Monetary stabilization, international, **1945:** 76 [3]
Monett, Mo., campaign remarks, **1948:** 216 [14]
Montana, Sen. James E. Murray, **1945:** 22 [18]
Money, Hernando, **1949:** 70
Monongahela River, **1950:** 3 [21]
Mongols, defeat at gates of Vienna, **1951:** 8
Monopolies
   Corporate, **1948:** 202 [5], 203, 220
   Laws against, **1951:** 254
   Program to curb, **1949:** 8 (p. 88), 149
   Restriction of, **1947:** 2 (pp. 3, 6, 12)
Monroe, James, **1947:** 68; **1950:** 82, 94; **1951:** 24; **1952–53:** 229
Monroe Doctrine, **1947:** 68, 189
Monroney, Repr. A.S. Mike, **1946:** 61 [22], 80; **1948:** 84 [14], 214 [7, 8]; **1951:** 54
Monrovia, Liberia, **1948:** 162n.
Montana, **1946:** 173 [5]; **1947:** 104; **1950:** 80 [10]
   Addresses or remarks in, **1950:** 124 [8], 127 [1, 2, 4–7], 128, 129 [1, 2]
   Campaign remarks, **1948:** 120 [5], 121; **1952–53:** 266 [13], 268–270
   Candidates for political office, **1952–53:** 266 [13], 268, 269, 270 [1, 5–8], 271
   Floods, **1952–53:** 268 [2]
   Gov. John W. Bonner, **1950:** 80 [10], 124 [8], 127 [4, 7], 128, 129 [1]; **1952–53:** 266 [13], 268 [2–4, 7–9], 269, 270 [1, 4–8], 271, 274 [4], 278n.
   Hungry Horse Dam, dedication, **1952–53:** 271
   Indian lands, veto of bill for disposal, **1948:** 25
   Mineral resources, **1950:** 124 [7], 127 [1]

Montana — *continued*
   Power projects, **1952–53:** 271
   Sun River irrigation project, **1952–53:** 80
Montana Power Co., **1952–53:** 270 [8], 271
Monte-Bello, Canada, **1947:** 112n.
Monteros, Antonio de los, **1947:** 95 [17]
Montevideo Conference (1933), **1947:** 51
Montgomery, Field Marshal, **1946:** 216 [16]; **1949:** 115
Montgomery, Gen. Bernard L., **1952–53:** 250
Montgomery, Ruth S., **1951:** 300 [15]; **1952–53:** 98 [34, 35]
Montgomery, W. Va., campaign remarks, **1948:** 222 [10]
Montgomery Ward, Army operation of, **1945:** 22 [17]
Montgomery Ward, Federal operation, **1947:** 6 [16]
Monticello, Va., **1947:** 138n.
Montoya, Joseph M., **1948:** 208 [1]
Montreal, Canada, **1946:** 133; **1948:** 70
Monuments, national, **1948:** 245; **1950:** 248
Moody, Sen. Blair, **1951:** 174; **1952–53:** 49 [7], 317, 318
Moody, Joseph E., **1950:** 27n.
Moore, A. Harry, **1948:** 227 [8]; **1952–53:** 303n.
Moore, Sen. E. H., **1948:** 214 [4]
Moore, Harry T., **1952–53:** 290
Moore, Mrs. Harry T., **1952–53:** 290n.
Moore, Leslie, **1947:** 210 [6]
Moral law, role in national and international life, **1951:** 61, 68, 256
Moran, Edward C., Jr., **1945:** 76 [1]
Moran, Joseph A., **1952–53:** 306 [6]
Moreell, Vice Adm. Ben, **1946:** 224; **1949:** 152n.; **1952–53:** 116
Morehead, Ky., campaign remarks, **1948:** 222 [6]
Morgan, Harcourt A., **1946:** 244
Morgan, Thomas, **1949:** 167n.; **1950:** 128; **1952–53:** 308 [4]
Morgenthau, Henry, Jr., **1945:** 127; **1946:** 78 [3]; **1947:** 71n., 243 [9, 11]; **1951:** 229, 251 [19]
   See also Treasury, Secretary of the (Henry Morgenthau, Jr.).
   Medal for Merit, citation, **1945:** 213
Mormons, **1948:** 201
Morning Register, **1947:** 210 [2]
Morotai Island, **1945:** 45
Morris, Herbert, **1950:** 160 [2]
Morris, Newbold, **1952–53:** 35 [1], 36, 44 [10], 64 [15], 75 [2, 4], 98 [3, 36]
Morris, Samuel B., **1950:** 1n., 306n.
Morrison, DeLesseps S., **1949:** 226 [14]
Morrison, Mrs. Fred W., **1951:** 297n.
Morrison, Herbert S., **1946:** 108n., 199 [8], 215 [5, 7], 227
Morrison, Harold A., **1952–53:** 266 [3, 4, 7]
Morrison, Howard L., **1952–53:** 311 [3]

Morrison, Lord Robert, **1945:** 210
Morrow, Dwight, **1948:** 212 [6]; **1949:** 93 [13], 118 [8]
Morrow, Mrs. Dwight, **1948:** 212 [6]
Morse, David A., **1948:** 130 [1]
Morse, Philip M., **1948:** 191n.
Morse, Sen. Wayne L., **1946:** 21 [3], 110 [5]; **1947:** 130, 236 [8]; **1948:** 88 [8], 226; **1949:** 52 [6]; **1950:** 121 [8]; **1952–53:** 107 [13], 129, 166 [5] and ftn. (p. 416), 175 [12], 277 [1, 3], 280, 284, [6], 293, 307, 312, 317 [3]
Mortgage Association, Federal National, **1949:** 8 (p. 74); **1951:** 12 [47], 13 (p. 93); **1952–53:** 18
   Reorganization, **1950:** 112
Mortgages, **1946:** 257 [6]; **1947:** 7 (p. 94); **1948:** 5 (pp. 25, 40, 44), 8 (p. 72), 175
   Credit control, **1950:** 202; **1951:** 118 [5], 167
   Farm, **1948:** 99, 117, 138 [3], 195, 212 [3], 214 [7, 8], 216 [13], 218 [1, 14], 219, 227 [5], 228 [4, 5, 10, 13], 240 [3], 268; **1951:** 202
     Foreclosures in depression, **1950:** 110 [5]; **1952–53:** 284 [1, 2], 285
   Home, **1948:** 218 [1], 219; **1950:** 9 (pp. 46, 69, 77, 78, 79), 51, 192; **1951:** 11
   Insurance, **1946:** 18 (p. 63), 94, 263; **1947:** 7 (p. 75), 97, 102, 131, 221 [11]; **1948:** 5 (pp. 38, 39), 37, 150 [1], 175, 227 [9]; **1949:** 8 (p. 72); **1950:** 51, 68, 112, 192; **1951:** 13 (pp. 90, 93); **1952–53:** 18 (pp. 95, 97), 231, 367 (pp. 1152–1153)
     Ships, **1950:** 76
   Interest on, **1948:** 228 [10]
Morton, Julius Sterling, **1947:** 69
Mosadeq, Mohammed, **1951:** 140 [4], 150, 200 [2]
Mosaic law, **1950:** 37, 313; **1952–53:** 45
Moscow, **1946:** 141 [11]; **1947:** 14 [5], 74
   Foreign ministers meetings, **1945:** 211 [12], 221 [13]; **1946:** 6 [2, 14], 18 (pp. 41, 42, 44), 265; **1947:** 2 (p. 10), 67 [17, 19], 74, 78 [23]; **1948:** 170 [12], 174 [11], 178 [3, 14]
   Special emissary to, question of, **1948:** 244, 274 [2]
   U.N. General Assembly meeting in, proposed, **1950:** 46ftn. (p. 184)
   Visit by the President, question of, **1950:** 46 [14, 19]
Moscow conference, (1943), **1945:** 67 [1]; **1949:** 136
Moscow Declaration, **1945:** 22 [5], 91, 186
Moses, Harry M., **1950:** 27n.
Moses, Herbert, **1949:** 105n.
Moses, Robert, **1947:** 67 [6]; **1951:** 87n.
Moses, Sidney, **1948:** 261 [13]
Moses, Divine command to, **1951:** 256
Moses, Rembrandt, **1948:** 71 [1]
Moses Lake Air Force Base, **1950:** 121 [13]
Mosher, Ira, **1945:** 175 [3]
Moss, John E., Jr., **1952–53:** 277 [6]

Motion Picture Association, **1952–53:** 20
Motion picture industry, **1946:** 160
   50th anniversary, **1951:** 249
Motor Carrier Claims Commission, **1950:** 209ftn. (p. 582)
Mott, Marshall A., **1950:** 157n.
Motz, Clarence E., **1948:** 232
Moulder, Repr. Morgan M., **1952–53:** 284 [5]
Moulton, Harold G., **1947:** 122
Mountbatten, Earl, **1948:** 17
Mount Vernon, Ill., campaign remarks, **1948:** 218 [1]
Mount Vernon, Ind., campaign remarks, **1948:** 218 [9]
Mount Vernon, Va., **1951:** 165 [7]
Mt. Sterling, Ky., campaign remarks, **1948:** 222 [5]
Movement Coordinating Committee, establishment, **1946:** 23
Movies, viewing by President, **1947:** 218 [17]
Mowrey, Corma, **1951:** 107n.
Mozart, Wolfgang Amadeus, **1951:** 99
Mr. President, William Hillman, **1952–53:** 31 [5], 64 [4]
Muccio, John J., **1950:** 193, 222, 268, 269; **1952–53:** 299
Mudaliar, Sir Ramaswami, **1952–53:** 253 [1]
Mukden, Manchuria, Soviet detention of U.S. consul in, **1949:** 234 [5]
Mules, shipment to Greece, **1947:** 210 [6]
Mullaney, T. W., **1952–53:** 315 [2]
Multer, Repr. Abraham J., **1952–53:** 300
Muncie, Ind., campaign remarks, **1952–53:** 286 [3]
Mundt, Karl E., **1948:** 97 [18], 170 [6], 174 [2], 283 [1]; **1951:** 179 [2]; **1952–53:** 129
Mundt-Nixon Communist-control bill, **1948:** 97 [18], 110 [12]
Munich, military trials in, **1949:** 32 [12]
Munich pact (1938), **1950:** 303
Municipal Association, American, **1949:** 226ftn. (p. 503)
Municipal Law Officers, National Institute of, **1950:** 37n.
Municipalities, veto of bill to amend census records, **1950:** 210
Munitions
   Procurement, **1946:** 18 (p. 75); **1947:** 35
   Production, **1945:** 42, 45; **1947:** 199
   Question of shipment to China, **1948:** 274 [9]
   Reduced spending for, **1947:** 7 (p. 62)
   Trade in, **1947:** 72
Munitions Assignments Board, U.S.-U.K., **1945:** 125, 198, 199
Munitions Board, **1948:** 21 [4]; **1949:** 50, 148 [10], 226 [17], 253 [4]; **1951:** 93
Munitions Board, Army and Navy, **1947:** 182 [1]
Munitions Board, Chairman (John D. Small), **1951:** 93n., 189; **1952–53:** 26 [1]
Munitions Control Board, National, **1947:** 72

Muñoz Marín, Gov. Luis, **1948:** 278 [12], 283 [10]; **1950:** 11 [5], 52 [5], 277; **1951:** 275 [2]

Murdock, Abe, **1947:** 145 [2], 218 [14]

Murdock, Repr. John R., **1948:** 207

Murmansk Coast, **1945:** 178

Murphy, Charles S., **1949:** 265, 269 [1, 5]; **1950:** 23 [1]; **1951:** 44n.; **1952–53:** 45

Murphy, Justice Frank, **1949:** 161 [10]; **1952–53:** 318

Murphy, James J., **1948:** 228 [2, 3]; **1952–53:** 300

Murphy, Joseph M., **1952–53:** 63

Murphy, Robert, **1945:** 106 [17]; **1947:** 210 [4]; **1949:** 192 [9]; **1952–53:** 26 [30]

Murphy, Thomas F., **1951:** 37 [7]; **1952–53:** 2 [20], 7 [11]

Murphy, Vincent J., **1948:** 227 [7]

Murray, Sen. James E., **1946:** 91, 266 [22]; **1947:** 141 [2]; **1948:** 121; **1949:** 148 [2]; **1950:** 124 [8], 127 [7], 128; **1951:** 56 [24]; **1952–53:** 3, 32, 266 [13], 268, 269, 270 [1, 6, 7], 271

    Full employment bill, **1945:** 22 [18]

Murray, Mrs. James E., **1950:** 124 [8], 127 [7]

Murray, John, **1948:** 218 [3]

Murray, Philip, **1946:** 12, 15 [7], 16, 21 [3, 9], 37 [14, 19]; **1947:** 191 [3], 236 [3], 237; **1948:** 26 [8], 163 [6], 252; **1949:** 152n., 202n., 211 [6], 240 [2]; **1950:** 38 [17], 287 [24]; **1951:** 132 [16], 171 [7], 183; **1952–53:** 116, 216, 230n.

    Message, **1945:** 206

    News conference remarks, **1945:** 175 [3], 208 [9]

Murray, Repr. Tom, **1951:** 152

Murray, Thomas E., **1948:** 171

Murray, Wallace, **1946:** 84 [3]

Muscle Shoals dam and power project, **1952–53:** 69, 267

Museum services, **1948:** 5 (p. 42)

Music appreciation, the President's, **1946:** 75 [23, 25]; **1949:** 194

Music Week, National, **1951:** 99

Muskegon, Mich, campaign remarks, **1952–53:** 317 [1]

Muskogee, Okla., campaign remarks, **1948:** 216 [7]

Mussolini, Benito, **1945:** 22 [21], 66; **1948:** 256; **1950:** 185; **1951:** 18

Mustering-out pay, veterans, **1947:** 2 (p. 8), 4 (pp. 15, 19), 7 (p. 68)

Mutual Defense Assistance Act of 1949, **1949:** 225; **1950:** 9 (p. 59), 22, 151n., 290; **1951:** 81, 292; **1952–53:** 310

Mutual Defense Assistance Control Act of 1951, **1952–53:** 105, 180, 217

Mutual Defense Assistance Program, **1950:** 42, 119, 172, 193, 204; **1952–53:** 47, 67

    See also Military assistance and defense support.

    Funds, use for relief food shipments to Yugoslavia, **1950:** 293

Mutual defense treaties

    Australia, **1952–53:** 95

    Japan, **1952–53:** 95, 111

    New Zealand, **1952–53:** 95

    Philippines, **1952–53:** 95

Mutual Security Acts

    1951, **1951:** 172n., 250, 292; **1952–53:** 27, 55, 61, 65–67, 367 (p. 1138, 1141)

    1952, **1952–53:** 123 [7], 149 [5, 11, 20], 156ftn. (p. 403)

Mutual Security Agency, **1952–53:** 18 (p. 115), 55, 67, 81, 257

Mutual Security Director (W. Averell Harriman), **1952–53:** 27, 48n., 55, 65–67, 105, 107 [4], 127 [8], 136 [16], 180, 331, 358

Mutual Security Director (W. Stuart Symington), **1952–53:** 75 [6]

Mutual security program, **1952–53:** 18 (pp. 73–76), 61, 69, 217, 218, 367 (pp. 1138–1141)

    See also Military assistance and defense support.

    Africa, **1952–53:** 55

    Appropriations of, **1952–53:** 205

    Asia, **1952–53:** 55, 57

    Europe, **1952–53:** 55, 57

    Latin America, **1952–53:** 55

    Message to Congress, **1952–53:** 55

    Middle East, **1952–53:** 55, 57

    Public Advisory Board, **1952–53:** 203

    Report to Congress, message transmitting, **1952–53:** 332

    Republican stand on, **1952–53:** 291

MVA.

    See Missouri Valley Authority.

Myer, Dillon S., **1946:** 186 [8]; **1947:** 173, 174 [1], 226 [4], 232 [7]

Myer, John, **1948:** 213

Myers, Sen. Francis J., **1948:** 226, 250 [1], 252; **1949:** 148ftn. (p. 351), 202n.; **1950:** 3 [13], 38 [13], 270 [11]; **1952–53:** 305

Myers, Col. Henry T., **1947:** 19 [16]

Myers, Victor A., **1952–53:** 274n.

Myers, William I. **1946:** 45n., 255n.; **1947:** 122, 191 [3]

Myersdale, Pa., campaign remarks, **1952–53:** 308 [6]

NAACP.

    See National Association for the Advancement of Colored People.

Nabuco, Joaquin, **1947:** 189

Nacy, Richard, **1949:** 155 [11]

Nagasaki, Japan, atomic bomb target, **1945:** 178

Nager, Charles, **1948:** 264 [2]

Nagy, Ferenc, **1947:** 107 [8]

NAM.

    See National Association of Manufacturers.

Nampa, Idaho, **1950:** 121 [5]
Nangle, John J., **1951:** 179 [12]; **1952–53:** 21 [20]
Nanking, China, **1948:** 278ftn. (p. 952)
    Abandonment by Nationalist forces, **1949:** 84ftn. (p. 224)
    U.S. Embassy, reported violation of, **1949:** 89 [2, 13]
Napoleon, **1949:** 50 [3]
Napoleonic wars, starvation following, **1947:** 210 [3]
Narcotics, Bureau of, **1951:** 201
Narcotics, Interdepartmental Committee on, **1951:** 287
Narcotics Hospital, Federal, **1951:** 201
Narcotics laws
    Amendment, approval, **1951:** 287
    Local, Federal enforcement aid, **1951:** 63 [1]
Nash, Philleo, **1952–53:** 26 [20]
Nashua, N.H., campaign remarks, **1952–53:** 292 [13]
Nashville, Tenn., **1949:** 107
Nashville Tennessean, **1952–53:** 284 [5]
Nathan, Robert R., **1946:** 61 [13], 262 [12], 266 [13]
National Advisory Board on Mobilization Policy, **1951:** 56 [2, 4], 74n., 137; **1952–53:** 110
National Advisory Committee, savings bond drive, **1949:** 82
National Advisory Committee for Aeronautics, **1947:** 241; **1948:** 5 (p. 50); **1949:** 8 (p. 86); **1950:** 9 (pp. 64, 66); **1951:** 13 (p. 70); **1952–53:** 18 (p. 18), 367 (p. 1135)
National Advisory Committee on Selective Service, **1951:** 9
National Advisory Council on International Monetary and Financial Problems, **1946:** 41 [11], 47, 136 [7], 142
National Apartment Owners Association, **1948:** 259 [3], 261 [2], 264 [1]
National Archives and Records Service, **1950:** 75; **1951:** 127, 251 [27]; **1952–53:** 149 [16], 174, 347, 387
National Association for the Advancement of Colored People, **1947:** 130; **1950:** 15n.
National Association of Attorneys General of the U.S., **1950:** 37n.
National Association of Broadcasters, **1952–53:** 43n.
National Association of Firemen, **1948:** 227 [2]
National Association of Home Builders, **1946:** 48
National Association of Manufacturers, **1946:** 110 [8]; **1948:** 114 [3], 194 [1, 11], 212 [9], 216 [7], 220, 226, 251, 261 [2, 8, 11]; **1951:** 123, 164; **1952–53:** 294, 306 [2], 314, 319 [1], 321 [2]
National Association of Postal Supervisors, **1950:** 247
National Association of Postmasters, **1951:** 226

National Association of Radio Farm Directors, **1949:** 90, 93 [5]
National Association of Real Estate Boards, **1948:** 212 [9]; **1949:** 66ftn. (p. 195)
National Association of State Civil Defense Directors, **1952–53:** 353 [3]
National Association of Wholesalers, **1947:** 85
National Bank of Commerce, Kansas City, Mo., **1948:** 194 [12]
National Bituminous Coal Wage Agreement of 1947, **1948:** 66, 171
National Blood Program, **1952–53:** 249
National Broadcasting Co., **1948:** 110ftn. (p. 280)
National Bureau of Standards, **1946:** 118; **1949:** 8 (p. 76)
National Bureau of Standards, Director (Lyman J. Briggs), retirement, letter, **1945:** 179
National Cancer Institute, **1945:** 192
National Capital Park and Planning Commission, **1946:** 15 [8], 21 [2], 43 [10]; **1949:** 8 (p. 94); **1950:** 9 (p. 102)
National Capital Park System, **1945:** 80
National Capital Sesquicentennial Commission, **1948:** 47; **1949:** 79, 144 [31]; **1950:** 146 [5]
    Statement, **1950:** 77
National Carrier Congress, **1951:** 133n.
National Catholic Community Service, **1950:** 95n.
National cemeteries, **1947:** 92
National Citizens Committee for United Nations Day, **1949:** 212; **1950:** 239; **1951:** 223; **1952–53:** 259
National Civil Service League, address, **1952–53:** 117
National Coal Association, **1947:** 145 [13]
National Commission on Higher Education, **1946:** 166, 214, 262 [2]
National Committee for Christian Leadership, **1949:** 28 [15]
National Committee for a Free Europe, **1950:** 98
National Committee for Labor Israel, **1951:** 274n.
National Community Christmas Tree, **1946:** 271; **1947:** 240; **1948:** 287; **1949:** 271; **1950:** 317; **1951:** 306; **1952–53:** 356
National Conference of Boy Governors, **1949:** 125
National Conference of Business Paper Editors, **1946:** 218; **1949:** 80
National Conference of Christians and Jews, **1949:** 224
National Conference on Citizenship, **1951:** 107; **1952–53:** 251
National Conference of Editorial Writers, **1947:** 210
National Conference on Family Life, address, **1948:** 92
National Conference on International Economic and Social Development, address, **1952–53:** 81

National Conference on Israel, **1951:** 229
National Conference of State School Lunch Officials, **1946:** 235n.
National conventions.
  See Political parties.
National Council, Democratic Women's, **1950:** 139
National Council of Churches, **1952–53:** 260
National Council of Negro Women, **1949:** 256
National day of prayer, proposed, **1949:** 28 [15]; **1950:** 309 [5]
National debt.
  See Debt, national.
National defense.
  See National security.
National Defense, Advisory Commission to the Council of, **1945:** 55
National Defense, Council of, **1946:** 137, 138; **1947:** 10n.
National Defense, Department of, proposed, **1946:** 18 (p. 74), 137, 138; **1947:** 2 (p. 12), 7 (p. 63), 10n., 12, 80, 155 [3]
  Message to Congress, **1945:** 218
National Defense, Women's Patriotic Conference on, **1950:** 21
National Defense Act, **1946:** 192 [25]
National Defense Program, Special Senate Committee to Investigate Contracts under.
  See Truman Committee.
National Democratic Club, Women's, **1949:** 252; **1951:** 297
National Democratic Conference and Jefferson Jubilee, **1950:** 134
National Economic Committee, Temporary, **1947:** 2 (p. 6), 4 (p. 35)
National economy.
  See Economy, national.
National Education Association, **1948:** 113n.; **1950:** 144n.; **1951:** 107n.
National Elk Refuge, **1950:** 248
National emergency.
  See also National security.
  Citizens' responsibilities in, **1951:** 107, 110
  Comments on, **1951:** 41
  Consumer demand, subordination to defense needs, **1951:** 4, 11, 80
  Declaration in coal strike, question of, **1950:** 16 [20], 23 [16], 44 [16], 46 [9]
  Defense Production Act.
    See main heading, Defense Production Act.
  Government consultants, proposed exemption from conflict-of-interest statutes, **1951:** 104
  Highway transportation plans, **1950:** 229
  Industry Advisory Councils, remarks to conference, **1951:** 98
  Labor, cooperation of, **1951:** 49 [16]
  Message to American people on, **1950:** 303
  Mobilization plans, **1951:** 92; **1952–53:** 122

National emergency — *continued*
  News conference remarks, **1951:** 49 [16], 63 [7], 70 [3]; **1952–53:** 175 [9]
  Nonpartisan response to, need for, **1951:** 80
  Presidential powers during, **1952–53:** 107 [1, 7, 10, 12, 13]
  Procurement problems, **1951:** 82
  Question of declaration in labor disputes, **1949:** 155 [15], 260 [1, 9, 11], 269 [12]
  White House announcement of discussions with congressional leaders, **1950:** 302
National Emergency Civil Rights Mobilization, **1950:** 15
National Employ the Physically Handicapped Week, **1952–53:** 243
  President's Committee on, **1949:** 197
National Evening Hymn Memorial Carillon, **1949:** 268n.
National Famine Emergency Committee, **1952–53:** 98ftn. (p. 270), 377ftn. (p. 1196)
National Famine Emergency Council, **1946:** 58
National Farm Loan Association, **1948:** 218 [1]
National Federation of Federal Employees, **1947:** 190
National Forensic League medal, acceptance, **1952–53:** 173
National forests, **1945:** 128
National Foundation for Infantile Paralysis, **1946:** 26; **1947:** 17; **1948:** 18
  Gift from White House correspondents, acceptance, **1945:** 208 [1]
National 4-H Club Camp, **1949:** 123; **1951:** 122; **1952–53:** 176
National Fund for Medical Education, **1951:** 135
National Gallery of Art, **1947:** 31 [1]; **1949:** 8 (p. 76)
  German collection, **1948:** 71 [1]
National Government, American Legion Boys Forum of, **1949:** 170
National Governors Conference, **1948:** 259 [4]
National groups.
  See Addresses or remarks to national groups.
National Guard, **1945:** 174; **1947:** 35, 86; **1948:** 243 [1, 4]; **1950:** 9 (p. 63), 194, 303; **1951:** 13 (p. 69), 92, 218, 270
  Air, **1949:** 7 [16], 8 (p. 58); **1950:** 9 (p. 63)
  Authorized strength, **1949:** 8 (p. 58); **1950:** 9 (63)
  Call to active duty, **1950:** 44 [16], 186 [10], 191 [15], 193, 303
  Disability compensation, **1949:** 135
  Flood relief activities, **1950:** 129 [7]
  President's service in, **1947:** 36 [9]; **1948:** 89; **1949:** 211 [7]; **1950:** 272
  Puerto Rican, message respecting members killed or wounded, **1950:** 277
  Recruiting campaign, **1949:** 211 [7]
  Retirement, **1949:** 174
  Thirty-fifth Division, World War I, **1948:** 117

National Guard, Illinois, **1952–53:** 290
National Guard Association, **1950:** 272
  73d General Conference, **1951:** 270
National Health Assembly, **1948:** 89, 181 [2]
National Heart Act of 1948, **1949:** 8 (p. 70)
National heroes, commemoration of, **1948:** 210 [2]
National Historical Publications Commission,
  1950: 136; **1951:** 127
National Housing Act, **1947:** 221 [11]; **1948:** 37;
  1949: 236 [9]; **1950:** 68, 112, 113, 118
National Housing Agency, **1946:** 18 (p. 63), 94, 116,
  119 [3], 182, 262 [6], 263; **1947:** 35, 102,
  131
National Housing Agency, Administrator (John B.
  Blandford), **1946:** 27 [1]
National Housing Conference, address, **1952–53:**
  120
National Housing Council, **1947:** 102, 173; **1948:** 5
  (p. 38); **1950:** 112
National income, **1946:** 17 [5], 192 [7, 19], 226 [1];
  1947: 2 (p. 2), 76, 116, 147, 180 [6, 11, 13,
  16, 20], 181 (p. 406), 183, 187, 214, 224,
  238; **1948:** 2, 4 [5, 17, 20], 5 (p. 23), 8 (pp.
  66, 76, 84, 91, 92), 63, 124, [5], 126 [1], 128
  [2], 138 [5–7], 160, 175, 182, 183 [5, 6], 194
  [6], 195, 198 [3, 6], 200 [6], 206 [3], 208 [6],
  209, 212 [5, 7], 214 [5, 8], 216 [2, 7, 15], 218
  [8, 14], 222 [2, 3, 8], 227 [2], 228 [1, 4, 6, 8,
  12], 231 [1, 3–5], 233 [1–3, 6], 237 [4], 238,
  240 [3, 6], 241, 246, 252, 255, 257 [2], 259
  [5], 261 [3, 4], 267 [2], 268; **1949:** 7 [8, 45],
  8 (p. 79), 91, 95 [19], 151, 154, 220; **1950:**
  6, 8 [18, 21], 110 [8], 163; **1951:** 215;
  1952–53: 17 [3, 24], 101, 266 [7], 268 [7],
  274 [5], 368
  See also Income.
National independence movement, **1951:** 4, 59,
  114, 116, 216
National Industrial Conference Board, **1950:** 23ftn.
  (p. 133)
National Industrial Recovery Act, **1950:** 18
National Institute of Municipal Law Officers,
  1950: 37n.
National Institutes of Health, dedication of clinical
  center, **1951:** 135
National Intelligence Authority, **1946:** 19, 21 [10,
  13]
National Jefferson-Jackson Day Committee, **1950:**
  34ftn. (p. 151)
National Jewish Welfare Board, **1950:** 95n.; **1952–
  53:** 297
National Joint Conference Committee, **1947:** 19
  [1], 20
National Labor-Management Conference, **1945:**
  104, 128, 180, 204; **1946:** 2; **1947:** 120
  Address, **1945:** 184
  News conference remarks, **1945:** 106 [21], 107
  [19], 147 [22], 175 [3, 18], 193 [2]

National Labor-Management Panel, **1947:** 237
National Labor Relations Act, **1946:** 110 [7, 14],
  131, 262 [15]; **1947:** 2 (p. 4), 120, 121;
  1948: 200 [3], 218 [1, 3, 7, 10], 222 [7, 8],
  227 [7], 228 [2–6], 232, 233 [1, 6], 247, 248,
  252, 255, 261 [3, 4, 8, 9, 11], 267 [1, 3], 268,
  274 [4]; **1949:** 2, 11ftn. (p. 99), 202; **1950:**
  123; **1951:** 279; **1952–53:** 315 [1]
National Labor Relations Board, **1946:** 118, 131;
  1947: 7 (p. 89), 120, 127 [1], 141 [4], 145
  [2], 174 [2], 177 [23], 181 (p. 403), 218 [14];
  1948: 5 (p. 54), 140, 178 [8], 187, 255;
  1949: 240 [2], 260 [10], 267 [7], 269 [2];
  1951: 175, 265; **1952–53:** 18 (p. 93), 35
  [11], 37
  News conference remarks, **1950:** 3 [7], 11 [9], 16
  [10], 23 [20], 29 [1], 38 [21], 146 [7], 253 [4],
  258 [1]
  Reorganization, **1950:** 53, 54, 66, 123, 146 [7]
  Vacancies on, **1950:** 11 [9], 23 [20], 253 [4]
National Labor Relations Board, Chairman (H. A.
  Millis), resignation, **1945:** 52 [4]
National Lawyers Guild, **1949:** 155 [2]; **1950:** 16 [6]
National Manpower Mobilization Policy, **1951:** 15
National Mediation Board, **1946:** 24; **1948:** 26 [2];
  1950: 186 [1]
National Military Establishment, **1947:** 10n., 12n.,
  159n., 241; **1948:** 3, 5 (pp. 26–28, 42), 42,
  46, 60, 98, 103, 175, 177; **1949:** 22ftn. (p.
  118), 50, 142, 145n.
  News conference remarks, **1949:** 7 [16], 155 [18]
  Reorganization plan for, **1949:** 155 [18], 158, 177
National Military Establishment Appropriation
  Act of 1950, approval, **1949:** 244
National Monetary Commission, proposed, **1949:**
  122 [2]
National Munitions Control Board, **1947:** 72
National Music Week, **1951:** 99
National Newspaper Publishers Association, re-
  marks, **1952–53:** 329
National Old Trails Association, **1948:** 137 [1, 4],
  233 [1]
National Park Service, **1946:** 18 (p. 81), 118; **1948:**
  5 (p. 47), 208 [7]; **1949:** 32 [16]
National Parks.
  See Parks, national.
National Petroleum Council, **1951:** 108 [5]
National Planning Association, **1949:** 25
National Plowing Match, **1948:** 194 [8], 195
  Question of President's attendance, **1952–53:** 228
  [6]
National Press Club, **1947:** 48n.; **1950:** 11ftn. (p.
  109); **1951:** 18; **1952–53:** 136 [16]
National product, **1946:** 17 [6], 18 (p. 69); **1947:** 4
  (p. 26); **1948:** 8 (pp. 63, 66, 75), 167; **1950:**
  6, 122, 127 [4], 157, 202, 243; **1951:** 11, 92,
  98, 167, 221; **1952–53:** 15, 17 [3, 24], 55,
  274 [5], 282 [4], 292 [10], 313 [6], 321 [5],
  349, 376

National Production Authority, **1952–53:** 18 (p. 79)
National Production Authority, Administrator
    (Manly Fleischmann), **1951:** 93n.
National Professional Committee for Eisenhower
    and Nixon, **1952–53:** 284 [5]
National Prohibition Act, **1946:** 116; **1947:** 80
National Railway Labor Panel, **1951:** 74
National Recreation Association, **1951:** 99n.
National resources, **1947:** 122
National resources and foreign aid, report, **1947:**
    209 [9], 212, 217, 219
National Rifle Association, **1947:** 157
National Rural Electric Cooperative Association,
    message, **1952–53:** 62
National Safety Council, **1952–53:** 93
National School Lunch Act, **1946:** 128, 235
National Science Board, **1950:** 120, 278 [2]
National Science Foundation, **1945:** 223n.; **1946:**
    28; **1947:** 7 (p. 76), 183, 201n., 206n; **1949:**
    8 (p. 78), 94; **1950:** 2, 9 (p. 84), 134; **1951:**
    13 (pp. 94, 95); **1952–53:** 13, 18 (p. 103),
    367 (p. 1156)
  Approval of bill, **1950:** 120
  News conference remarks, **1950:** 105 [20], 238 [7],
      278 [2]
  Proposed, **1948:** 5 (pp. 25, 41, 42), 175, 186
  Veto, **1949:** 169
National Science Foundation Act of 1950, **1950:**
    121 [1]
  Approval, **1950:** 120
National security, **1945:** 128, 156, 158, 174, 218;
    1946: 18 (p. 37), 19, 61 [15], 82, 86 [3], 192
    [25], 193, 194, 234; **1947:** 2 (p. 12), 4 (p.
    35), 6 [3, 9, 21], 7 (pp. 56, 57, 62, 64, 81)
    42, 50, 54, 55, 56, 77, 78 [14, 19, 24], 98,
    106, 110, 117, 130, 147, 148, 149, 159, 161,
    167, 169, 180 [1], 181 (pp. 398, 400, 401,
    404, 405, 407), 183, 193, 194, 196, 198,
    199, 204, 211, 212, 217, 223, 224, 233, 235,
    237, 238, 241; **1948:** 2, 4 [1], 5 (pp. 20, 21,
    25, 26, 28, 46, 47, 50), 7, 8 (pp. 71, 78, 81,
    86, 97, 98), 9 [12, 14], 11 [10, 13], 12, 14,
    18, 24, 27, 42, 43, 46, 50, 52, 53, 79, 80, 86,
    92, 102, 103, 106, 108, 109, 140, 145, 148,
    164, 167, 177, 186, 191, 215, 239, 244, 257
    [3], 263, 266; **1949:** 2, 5, 8 (pp. 46, 55–62),
    19, 47, 50, 94, 100, 120, 127, 142, 151, 154,
    158, 266, 268; **1950:** 6, 9 (pp. 48, 60–66,
    92, 94), 26, 39, 42, 78, 107, 110 [8, 10], 121
    [5, 9, 13], 124 [7, 8], 126, 129 [7], 133, 151,
    155, 162, 176, 194, 204, 228, 232, 282;
    1951: 7 [2], 13 (pp. 67–76), 54, 92, 110,
    137, 167, 199, 246; **1952–53:** 13, 18 (pp.
    64, 65), 35 [3], 38, 40, 55, 57, 66, 222, 223,
    268 [5], 289 [2], 101, 131, 144, 147, 170,
    180, 182, 215, 237, 273, 366, 379
  See also Civil defense; National emergency.

National security — *continued*
  Administration measures, Republican opposi-
      tion, **1952–53:** 218
  Agencies
    Management and organization, **1951:** 13 (p.
        65), 56 [1, 3, 8], 109
    Representation of labor groups in, **1951:** 49 [2,
        10, 15, 20, 22, 23], 56 [4], 63 [8]
  Allies, dependence on, **1952–53:** 55, 57, 101
  Aluminum industry strike, threat to, **1952–53:** 22
  American Legion, efforts for, **1951:** 191
  Antisubversion bills, **1950:** 238 [4], 250 [7, 13],
      253 [2], 258 [12]
  Appropriations, **1948:** 60; **1951:** 285; **1952–53:**
      125, 170, 273, 275
    Danger from cuts, **1952–53:** 205
  Atomic Energy Commission construction pro-
      gram, **1952–53:** 200
  Atomic energy development for, **1952–53:** 18 (p.
      87)
  Bipartisan commission on, proposed, **1950:**
      146ftn. (p. 439)
  Budget emphasis on, **1952–53:** 17 [2]
  Campaign remarks on, **1952–53:** 287, 319 [5]
  Coal industry, proposed study of security as-
      pects, **1950:** 50
  Communist subversion, measures against, **1952–
      53:** 288
  Congressional leaders, meeting with, **1950:** 302
  Defense, postwar, **1945:** 193 [12]
  Defense installations, security of, **1950:** 207
    Barring of Communists from employment in,
        1950: 254
    Proposed publication of list, opposition to,
        1950: 254
  Defense program, **1952–53:** 123 [2], 128, 147, 149
      [11, 12], 158, 275, 276, 295 [8], 307, 313 [5,
      6], 367 (pp. 1129, 1130)
    Aid to schools in areas affected by, **1952–53:**
        18 (p. 102), 367 (pp. 1155, 1156)
    Congressional action on, **1952–53:** 125
    Economy, adjustment to, **1952–53:** 5, 15, 17
        [3], 33, 101, 215, 268 [7], 272, 282 [4], 283,
        289 [8], 292 [10], 293, 294, 300, 307, 313
        [6], 349, 366
    Financing, **1952–53:** 18 (pp. 66, 67, 68)
    Issue in election campaign, **1952–53:** 275
    Joint statement with Prime Minister Attlee,
        1950: 301
    Progress of, **1951:** 80
    Soviet reaction to, **1951:** 56 [9]
  Dispersal program
    Government, **1951:** 13 (pp. 103, 104)
    Industry, **1951:** 189, 200 [3]
  Economic requisites for, **1951:** 11
  Economic stabilization, importance to, **1952–53:**
      341

National security — *continued*
  Eisenhower, Gen. Dwight D., views of, **1952–53:** 293
  Electric power, effect on, **1952–53:** 388
  Emergency powers
    Proposed continuation, **1952–53:** 79
    Request for, **1950:** 307
  European defense, relationship to, **1952–53:** 217, 358
  Expenditures for.
    See Spending by Government.
  Federal personnel procedures in interest of, **1950:** 283; **1952–53:** 370
  Federal programs
    Management improvement, **1952–53:** 18 (pp. 115, 116)
    Review, **1950:** 234
  Fiscal program, **1951:** 1, 12 [1, 35], 13 (pp. 62, 64), 28, 29, 44, 221
  Hemispheric defense, integration with, **1951:** 59
  Highway transportation plans, emergency, **1950:** 229
  Highways, defense, **1952–53:** 18 (p. 84)
  Homefront, efforts required of, **1951:** 11, 107, 212
  Individual rights, protection in security and defense effort, **1951:** 20, 35, 37 [12], 104
  Information affecting, classification and protection, **1951:** 233, 234, 247 [1, 5, 10, 12], 248
  Internal security, message to Congress, **1950:** 207
  Internal security bill, veto, **1950:** 254
  Labor disputes, danger to defense effort, **1951:** 33 [1], 167, 204, 252, 276, 277, 304, 305; **1952–53:** 148
  Manpower mobilization, **1951:** 15, 156
  Marine Corps, role in, **1950:** 235
  Materials supply problem, appointment of commission to study, **1951:** 19
  Military aid abroad, relationship to domestic defense, **1951:** 11
  National emergency, proclamation, **1950:** 304
  News conference remarks, **1949:** 45 [23], 144 [1], 148 [4], 166 [1], 192 [10, 13, 15], 231 [4, 6, 7, 13], 234 [1], 269 [20]; **1950:** 8 [43, 46], 46 [10], 105 [6, 13, 14, 21], 146 [16], 186 [3], 206 [5, 12], 230 [3], 238 [4, 9], 250 [7, 13], 253 [2], 258 [8, 12, 14]
  Oil reserves, **1952–53:** 377 [11]
  Oil strike, effect on, **1952–53:** 58
  Pacific territories, importance to, **1950:** 267
  Ports, protection against sabotage, **1951:** 13 (p. 83)
  Railroad strike, threat to, **1950:** 188
  St. Lawrence Seaway project, importance to, **1952–53:** 23, 189
  Scientific research for, **1951:** 13 (pp. 69, 70), 89, 92

National security — *continued*
  Steel strike, effect on, **1952–53:** 82, 83, 103, 118, 161
  Tax program to finance, **1950:** 284; **1952–53:** 367 (p. 1132)
  Women's role in support of, **1951:** 193 [5], 289, 294
  Work stoppages, danger to defense program, **1952–53:** 215
National Security, Research Board for, **1945:** 128
National Security Act, **1945:** 218n.; **1947:** 10n., 12n., 42n., 192; **1948:** 2, 5 (pp. 26, 29), 284; **1949:** 8 (p. 56), 50, 67, 111, 127, 148 [4], 158; **1950:** 29 [3], 115, 235, 245; **1952–53:** 375
National Security Act Amendments of 1949, approval, **1949:** 177
National Security Council, **1948:** 5 (p. 26); **1949:** 50, 177, 244; **1950:** 46 [5], 207; **1951:** 117, 128, 156, 165 [6], 233, 234, 278, 298 [6]; **1952–53:** 147, 158, 222, 310, 323, 340, 366
  News conference remarks, **1949:** 182 [12], 236 [1], 269 [20]
  Transfer to Executive Office, **1949:** 127, 131
National Security Resources Board, **1946:** 137, 138; **1947:** 10n., 221 [1]; **1948:** 5 (p. 26), 284; **1949:** 48, 50, 142, 244; **1950:** 113; **1951:** 10n.; **1952–53:** 191, 192, 338, 355, 375
  News conference remarks, **1949:** 28 [1, 2], 58 [8, 17], 66 [16], 78 [5], 112 [4], 144 [21], 200 [7], 236 [16], 269 [20]; **1950:** 34 [13], 52 [2], 80 [8], 179 [25], 214 [10]; **1951:** 101 [6], 118 [10], 193 [4], 200 [3]
  Nomination of Mon C. Wallgren as Chairman, **1949:** 28 [1], 45ftn. (p. 157), 58 [8, 17], 66 [16], 78 [5], 100
  Reorganization, **1950:** 115
  St. Lawrence Seaway project, support of, **1952–53:** 23
  Transfer to Executive Office, **1949:** 127, 131
  Vice Chairman (Robert J. Smith), resignation, **1951:** 49 [12]
National Security Resources Board, Chairman (Jack Gorrie), **1952–53:** 38
  Letter, **1952–53:** 355, 375
National Security Resources Board, Chairman (Arthur M. Hill), **1948:** 109, 148
National Security Resources Board, Chairman (John R. Steelman), **1949:** 48, 260 [4]
National Security Resources Board, Chairman (W. Stuart Symington), **1950:** 162n., 243, 251; **1951:** 49 [12]; **1952–53:** 79
  Memorandum, **1950:** 259
  News conference remarks on, **1950:** 179 [25], 186 [14], 203 [6], 238 [8], 309 [2]
National Security Training Commission, **1952–53:** 18 (p. 73)

National Service Life Insurance, **1946:** 18 (p. 79); **1947:** 2 (p. 8), 7 (pp. 68, 70); **1948:** 175; **1949:** 8 (pp. 48, 66); **1951:** 12 [36]
　　Discontinuance, **1952–53:** 18 (p. 109, 110)
National Service Life Insurance Act, **1945:** 128; **1947:** 134
National Service Life Insurance Fund, **1947:** 75; **1948:** 5 (p. 33)
National Shipping Authority, **1951:** 13 (pp. 81, 82, 83); **1952–53:** 231, 367 (p. 1143)
National Social Welfare Assembly, **1950:** 95
National socialism.
　　See Nazism.
National Sojourners, **1952–53:** 134n.
National Symphony Orchestra, luncheon remarks, **1952–53:** 262
National Theatre, Washington, D.C., **1947:** 14 [23]
National Travelers Aid Association, **1951:** 186
National Tuberculosis Association, **1950:** 286
National Wage Policy Committee, **1952–53:** 216
National Wage Stabilization Board, **1946:** 35, 110 [8], 152, 153, 156, 179, 220, 229 [8, 23], 237 [14], 262 [4, 21]
　　Establishment, **1945:** 230
National War College, **1947:** 226 [1]
　　Address, **1952–53:** 354
National War Fund Campaign, address, **1945:** 154
National War Labor Board, **1945:** 104, 128; **1946:** 143 [10]; **1951:** 74
　　News conference remarks, **1945:** 106 [12], 137 [1], 157 [5]
　　Termination, **1945:** 230
National War Labor Board, Chairman (Lloyd K. Garrison)
　　Letter, **1945:** 230
　　News conference remarks on, **1945:** 172 [3], 211 [2]
National Youth Administration, **1949:** 256
Nationality Act of 1940, veto of amendment, **1950:** 241
NATO.
　　See North Atlantic Treaty Organization.
Natural gas, **1950:** 88; **1952–53:** 289 [11]
　　Conservation, **1949:** 8 (p. 84)
　　Exchange with Canada, **1952–53:** 377 [25]
Natural Gas Act of 1938, veto of amendment, **1950:** 88; **1951:** 165ftn. (p. 402)
Natural History Museum, **1952–53:** 88 [1]
Natural resources, **1946:** 18 (pp. 60, 61, 80–83), 189; **1947:** 2 (p. 9), 7 (pp. 58, 64, 83, 92), 191 [4], 212; **1948:** 2, 5 (pp. 20, 25, 45, 47), 8 (pp. 62, 77, 81, 88, 97, 98)
　　See also Irrigation projects; Reclamation projects; *specific resources.*
　　Alaska, **1948:** 105; **1949:** 8 (p. 84)
　　Conservation and development, **1945:** 128, 150, 165; **1947:** 4 (p. 34), 7 (pp. 81, 83), 68, 69,

Natural resources — *continued*
　　Conservation and development — *continued*
　　　　104, 110, 144, 181 (pp. 401, 402, 405), 204, 231; **1948:** 2, 4 [7], 5 (pp. 45, 46), 8 (pp. 66, 98), 12, 32, 117, 122 [6], 125, 175, 198 [1, 4, 6], 199, 200 [2, 9], 201, 202 [1, 5], 203, 206 [4], 207, 214 [5, 7], 219, 233 [1], 235 [4, 5], 257 [4]; **1949:** 2, 5, 8 (pp. 47, 81–84), 19, 43, 77, 120, 154, 202, 219, 250 [3]; **1950:** 2, 9 (pp. 49, 88–91), 33, 39, 84, 116, 118, 121 [8], 122, 124 [7, 8], 126, 127 [2, 4, 5], 129 [1], 130, 134, 135, 140, 157, 265, 281; **1951:** 11, 13 (pp. 64, 65, 84–87), 55, 98, 215; **1952–53:** 3, 15, 17 [19], 18 (p. 87), 98 [9], 129, 146, 179, 194, 215, 218, 231, 267, 367 (pp. 1145–1147, 1149–1150), 376, 388
　　　　U.N. conference on, **1947:** 186
　　Destruction by fire, **1947:** 86
　　Report by Secretary Harriman, **1947:** 210 [4]
Natural rights, **1951:** 225
Natural rubber, **1947:** 31 [2]
　　Stockpiling, **1950:** 13; **1952–53:** 12
Naturalization, equality in, **1948:** 20
Naturalization laws, **1950:** 207, 241, 254; **1952–53:** 182
Nautilus, U.S.S., **1952–53:** 156 [6]
　　Gift of model to President, **1952–53:** 171n.
　　Keel-laying ceremony, **1952–53:** 170
Navajo Indians, **1949:** 226 [19], 231 [23], 233; **1950:** 9 (p. 91)
　　Report, **1947:** 229
　　Tribal Council representatives, remarks to, **1952–53:** 46
Naval Academy, U.S., **1947:** 35, 226 [2]; **1951:** 200 [9]; **1952–53:** 130
　　Admission of Canadians, **1948:** 112
　　Luncheon remarks, **1952–53:** 142
Naval Medical Center, **1947:** 73n.
Naval Observatory, **1946:** 118; **1949:** 8 (p. 76)
Naval Operations, Chief of (Adm. Louis E. Denfeld), **1949:** 241n.
Naval Operations, Chiet of (Fleet Adm. Chester W. Nimitz), **1947:** 221 [1], 233
Naval Operations, Chief of (Adm. F. P. Sherman), **1950:** 29 [8], 226, 235; **1951:** 98n., 165 [6], 171 [14]
Naval Operations, Office of Chief, **1946:** 118
Naval Personnel, Bureau of, **1946:** 118
Naval War College, **1947:** 236 [2]
Navigation, **1945:** 165, 178; **1946:** 18 (pp. 43, 60, 82), 86 [16], 176; **1947:** 4 (p. 34), 18, 144
　　Aids to, **1947:** 7 (pp. 59, 93); **1948:** 219; **1950:** 9 (p. 92), 125, 129 [1]; **1951:** 13 (pp. 34, 81, 83), 183, 185; **1952–53:** 18 (p. 83), 40, 292 [7], 367 (p. 1143), 376
　　Air, **1946:** 133; **1947:** 7 (p. 58); **1948:** 5 (pp. 47, 50), 7, 175

Navigation — *continued*
  Loran system, **1947:** 7 (p. 85)
  Missouri River project, **1945:** 164 [8]
  Water, **1948:** 8 (p. 78)
Navy, **1945:** 34, 45, 128, 138, 177, 178, 192, 215,
      216, 217; **1946:** 18 (pp. 47, 48, 76), 76, 102,
      130n., 135, 137, 138, 193, 194, 268; **1947:** 2
      (p. 11), 6 [3, 9, 11, 14, 29], 7 (p. 57), 18, 35,
      80, 101; **1948:** 5 (pp. 26–28); **1949:** 8 (pp.
      57, 59, 60), 223; **1950:** 9 (p. 61), 24;
      1952–53: 131
  Air arm, transfer to Air Force, **1949:** 89 [7]
  Air review, Idlewild International Airport, **1948:**
      168
  Aircraft carrier, construction, **1952–53:** 17 [21]
  Aircraft procurement, **1947:** 181 (p. 404); **1948:** 5
      (p. 26)
  Alaskan ports, development, **1948:** 105
  Antarctica, expedition to, **1949:** 171 [6]
  Appropriations, **1945:** 134; **1946:** 66 [10], 238;
      1947: 11
  Atlantic and Pacific campaigns, **1945:** 45, 161
  Aviation, question of expansion, **1951:** 224 [2]
  B–36 bomber controversy, **1949:** 118ftn. (p. 280),
      205 [9]
  Barbary pirates, expedition against, **1951:** 80
  Bases in Northwest, **1950:** 121 [13]
  Bases in Spain, question of, **1951:** 165 [6]
  Civilian personnel, temporary, **1947:** 50
  Congressional Medal of Honor presentations,
      1945: 160
  Demobilization, **1945:** 134; **1946:** 8, 18 (p. 47), 43
      [3], 86 [32]; **1947:** 2 (p. 11), 233
  Dispatch of ships to Chinese waters, question of,
      1948: 274 [9]
  European command, **1950:** 310
  Evacuation of U.S. civilians from China, **1949:**
      89 [2]
  Expenditures for, **1951:** 107
  Fleet Reserve members, retirement pay, **1947:** 35
  Fleet Sonar School, **1949:** 53
  Functions, **1947:** 159
  Hospitals, surplus, **1952–53:** 212
  Increase in strength, **1947:** 35; **1950:** 9 (p. 63),
      121 [13], 303; **1951:** 4, 13 (pp. 63, 64, 69),
      92, 167; **1952–53:** 18 (p. 69), 158, 275, 367
      (p. 1134)
  Korean operations, **1950:** 184, 193
  News conference remarks, **1945:** 44 [3], 106 [19],
      116, 118 [5, 12, 14], 129 [3, 10], 221 [10];
      1946: 15 [15], 43 [3], 66 [10], 84 [14], 86 [2,
      32], 126 [15], 129 [13, 20, 22], 192 [4, 10,
      25], 229 [3]; **1949:** 78 [1], 82 [2], 84 [12, 22],
      89 [7], 171 [6], 200 [2], 205 [9], 231 [4, 18,
      19], 267 [8]; **1950:** 8 [24], 209 [11], 230 [7],
      295 [1]
  Officers
    Retirement, **1947:** 35

Navy — *continued*
  Officers — *continued*
    Testimony at defense policy hearings, **1949:**
      231 [4, 18, 19]
    Offshore oil lands, transfer to, **1952–53:** 377 [11,
      14]
    Pacific Fleet, **1947:** 221 [1]
    Personnel policies, **1945:** 218
    Petroleum products, use of, **1952–53:** 379
    Postwar organization, **1945:** 174
    Preparedness, **1947:** 110
    Privateer aircraft, disappearance over Baltic,
      1950: 86 [23], 97 [9]
    Promotion list, **1949:** 267 [8]
    Public works program, **1947:** 11, 181 (p. 399);
      1948: 5 (pp. 26, 28)
    Racial discrimination elimination, **1952–53:** 290,
      315 [6]
    Recruitment, **1947:** 50, 54
    Reduction in strength, **1947:** 50
    Report on Pearl Harbor attack, **1945:** 116, 118 [5,
      12, 14], 129 [10]
    Reserve ships, reactivation, **1951:** 13 (p. 69);
      1952–53: 17 [2], 18 (p. 64)
    Reserves, **1948:** 243 [1]; **1950:** 9 (pp. 63, 64), 193
    Retirement benefits, **1948:** 145; **1949:** 174
    Retired enlistees, credit for foreign service
      1898–1912, veto, **1945:** 205
    Ship construction, **1948:** 5 (pp. 26, 28); **1950:** 9
      (p. 64), 76
    6th Fleet, question of visit to Spanish port, **1949:**
      200 [2]
    7th Fleet, **1946:** 265; **1950:** 173, 193, 209 [11], 230
      [7], 232
    Supercarrier, construction, **1949:** 78 [1], 84 [12,
      22]
    Withdrawal from Chinese waters, report of,
      1947: 36 [25]
  Navy, Department of the, **1945:** 30, 70, 128, 143n.,
      145n., 218; **1946:** 18 (pp. 47, 74, 75, 77),
      29, 59, 118, 187, 193, 194, 242 [2]; **1947:** 7
      (pp. 56, 93), 10n., 35, 39, 50, 55, 75, 80, 92,
      151, 157, 181 (pp. 401, 404), 202, 241;
      1948: 4 [1], 5 (p. 42), 43, 46; **1949:** 173,
      174, 241, 267 [8]; **1950:** 235; **1952–53:** 170
    American Samoa, transfer to civilian adminis-
      tration, **1951:** 141
    Bureau Chiefs and Assistants, raise in rank, veto,
      1945: 217
    Civilian advisory committee, **1946:** 70 [16]
    Correa, Maj. M. F., **1945:** 116n.
    News conference remarks, **1945:** 64 [7], 157 [14],
      175 [5], 208 [15], 221 [5, 10]; **1946:** 70 [16],
      78 [18, 19], 119 [4], 126 [24], 129 [1], 192
      [8]; **1947:** 6 [32, 34, 39]
    Pacific Trust Territory, administrative functions,
      1947: 119n.
    Real estate transactions, **1951:** 105, 108 [1]

[References are to items except as otherwise indicated]

Navy, Department of the — *continued*
  Reorganization, **1949:** 50, 158, 177
  Stevenson, Gov. Adlai, wartime service in,
    1952–53: 289 [5], 292 [2], 317 [4]
Navy, Secretary of the (James Forrestal), **1945:**
    158n.; **1946:** 82, 193; **1947:** 12, 35, 42, 50,
    119, 146n., 148, 151
  Directives, **1946:** 19, 23
  Letters, **1945:** 201; **1946:** 138, 194; **1947:** 10
  News conference remarks on, **1945:** 26 [2], 107
    [6, 17], 116, 221 [8]; **1946:** 37 [2, 4], 70 [16],
    84 [4], 95 [16, 19], 119 [2], 126 [16], 129
    [19], 141 [5], 192 [4, 10], 229 [3], 237 [8],
    250 [4]; **1947:** 31 [15], 88 [10], 127 [17], 145
    [1, 21], 155 [3], 177 [5]
  Report, **1946:** 137, 138
Navy, Secretary of the (Dan A. Kimball), **1952–53:**
    128, 131, 170, 171
Navy, Secretary of the (Francis P. Matthews),
    1949: 95ftn. (p. 248), 241; **1950:** 29 [8],
    259; **1951:** 93n., 140 [1, 7], 141, 180
  News conference remarks on, **1949:** 211 [10], 226
    [9], 240 [1, 18]
Navy, Secretary of the (John L. Sullivan), **1947:**
    182 [1]; **1948:** 170ftn. (p. 433); **1949:** 101
  News conference remarks on, **1949:** 45 [22], 72
    [8], 78 [11, 15], 89 [7]
Navy-Army football game, **1945:** 202 [16]; **1947:**
    226 [2]
Navy Day, address, **1945:** 178
Navy League, **1950:** 138n.; **1951:** 109n.
Navy-War-State Coordinating Committee, **1945:**
    218
Nazimuddin, Khwaja, **1951:** 257
Nazis, **1945:** 3, 26 [5], 31 [1], 45, 52 [2], 152, 173,
    187, 188, 201n., 210, 218; **1946:** 215 [1],
    241, 251
  Persecution of Jews by, **1952–53:** 297
Nazism, **1945:** 26 [5], 29, 91, 97, 178; **1946:** 6 [18],
    18 (pp. 38, 41, 43), 42, 83, 236; **1947:** 51,
    90 [1], 113, 114, 210 [6]; **1948:** 256; **1949:**
    195; **1951:** 225
Near East.
  See Middle East and Near East; *specific coun-
    tries.*
Near East, U.N. Economic Survey Mission, **1950:**
    154
Near East Foundation, technical assistance in Iran,
    1950: 177
Nebraska, **1951:** 223
  Addresses or remarks in, **1950:** 110 [7–10], 111
  Campaign remarks, **1948:** 116 [1, 2], 117, 118
    [1–4]
  Floods, **1950:** 129 [1]
  Gov. Val Peterson, **1948:** 116n.; **1950:** 111;
    1952–53: 97
  Power projects, **1950:** 116
  Primary election, **1948:** 77 [3], 117

Nebraska — *continued*
  Sioux Indians, **1948:** 118 [1]
  Wherry, Sen. Kenneth S., **1945:** 60 [13]
Nebuchadnezzar, **1949:** 252
Neckties, the President's, **1946:** 70 [15]
  Comment by London tailors, **1951:** 2 [26]
Neely, Matthew M., **1948:** 222 [9], 242 [2, 3]; **1949:**
    113 [1]; **1952–53:** 242 [3, 4]
Neff, Pat Morris, **1947:** 52; **1948:** 212 [5]
Negligence, laws on, **1947:** 86
Negro Women, National Council of, **1949:** 256
Negroes
  Education, **1952–53:** 169
  Equal rights, **1947:** 48; **1949:** 226 [3]; **1950:** 15, 34
    [1]; **1951:** 286; **1952–53:** 169, 290, 353 [16]
  NAACP, address, **1947:** 130
  Press, awards to, **1947:** 48
Nehru, Jawaharlal, **1949:** 45 [19], 227, 231 [10, 22],
    236 [5], 252, 264
Nelson, Ben., **1950:** 118n.
Nelson, Donald M., **1946:** 141 [13]
Nelson, Herbert U., **1949:** 66 [21]
Nelson, Otto, **1949:** 167n.
Neosho, Mo., campaign remarks, **1948:** 216 [13]
Nephews, the President's, **1950:** 145, 163
Nesemeir, Edward, **1952–53:** 266 [3, 4, 7]
Netherlands, **1945:** 186; **1946:** 18 (p. 84), 247; **1950:**
    273 [14]
  Assistance, **1947:** 195, 238; **1952–53:** 105
  Carillon, gift to U.S., **1952–53:** 78
  Dairy products, restrictions on imports to U.S.,
    1952–53: 360
  Dispute with Indonesia, **1949:** 272; **1950:** 2, 143
    Truce in, **1948:** 124 [1], 202 [6]
  Drees, Willem, **1952–53:** 21 [21]
  Investments in U.S., **1952–53:** 218
  Korean war, participation, **1950:** 193, 194, 232,
    296; **1951:** 170
  Lend-lease agreements, **1945:** 50; **1947:** 7 (p. 65)
  Liberation, **1945:** 45
  Military assistance, **1950:** 22
  NATO participation, **1952–53:** 78, 105
  Oil drilling equipment, shipment to Poland,
    1952–53: 105
  Point 4 trainees from, **1951:** 262
  Population growth, **1952–53:** 65
  Posthumous award to Franklin D. Roosevelt,
    1948: 87
  Press, **1945:** 107 [21]
  Prince Bernhard, **1952–53:** 73n., 74n., 77n., 78
  Queen Juliana, **1952–53:** 31 [4], 73, 74, 77, 78
  Queen Wilhelmina, **1948:** 87
  Stikker, Dirk, **1949:** 68
  Strategic materials, export to Communist bloc,
    1952–53: 358
  U.S. relations with, **1952–53:** 78
  World War II resistance efforts, **1952–53:** 78
  World wars, financial drain on, **1952–53:** 218

Neutrality Act, **1947:** 72
Nevada
    Campaign remarks, **1948:** 202 [1, 2]
    Candidates for public office, **1948:** 202 [1, 2]
    Gov. Vail Pittman, **1948:** 202 [1, 2]
Nevada, U.S. Attorney, commission for, **1952–53:** 377 [22]
New Britain, Conn.
    Campaign remarks, **1952–53:** 292 [5]
    Mayor John L. Sullivan, **1952–53:** 292n.
New Brunswick, N.J., campaign remarks, **1952–53:** 303 [5]
New Deal, **1946:** 81; **1950:** 39, 110 [8]; **1952–53:** 69, 129, 175 [5, 13], 241, 270 [7], 272, 274 [2], 276, 278, 280 [4], 281, 284 [1], 295 [3, 9], 296, 298 [1, 2, 6, 9, 13, 14], 300, 303 [2, 5], 304, 305, 306 [1, 5, 7], 307, 308 [1, 3], 311 [1], 313 [4, 6], 315 [1, 3], 321 [3, 6, 7], 322, 366
    Campaign remarks, **1948:** 236, 247
New Deal, Case Against the, Thomas E. Dewey, **1948:** 247
New England
    Business conditions in, **1949:** 171 [11]
    Economy, **1951:** 142; **1952–53:** 294
    Natural resources, conservation and development, **1950:** 33, 140, 265
    News conference remarks, **1949:** 155 [1], 171 [11], 236 [4]; **1950:** 3 [5, 9, 15], 29 [21], 34 [10], 137 [21], 203 [21]
    Oil shortage, **1947:** 232 [10]
    Power projects, **1950:** 3 [5, 9, 15], 29 [21], 34 [10], 125, 203 [21]
    River and harbor development, **1951:** 13 (p. 87)
    Textiles, purchase by foreign countries, **1949:** 236 [4]
    Unemployment in, **1950:** 137 [21]
    Visit to, question of, **1948:** 150 [10], 163 [20]
New England-New York Commission, proposed, **1950:** 34 [10]
New England town meeting, anecdote on, **1948:** 259 [2]
New Freedom, **1952–53:** 366
New Guinea, **1945:** 45
New Hampshire
    Campaign remarks, **1952–53:** 292 [13], 294, 295 [1–6]
    Candidates for public office, **1952–53:** 292 [13], 294, 295 [1, 3, 5, 6]
    Gov. Sherman Adams, **1952–53:** 292n., 295 [1], 312
    Primary elections, **1952–53:** 26 [3, 8], 28, 31 [13, 15], 49 [13], 64 [8]
New Hampshire Democratic chairman, **1948:** 21 [9]
New Haven, Conn., campaign remarks, **1948:** 261 [7]; **1952–53:** 298 [8]

New Jersey, **1949:** 144 [18], 155 [8]
    Campaign remarks, **1948:** 225 [3], 227 [6–9]; **1952–53:** 303 [2–7]
    Candidates for public office, **1948:** 225 [3], 227 [6–8]; **1952–53:** 303 [2–7]
    Eaton, Repr. Charles A., **1945:** 10, 219n.
    Gov. Alfred E. Driscoll, **1952–53:** 303 [6]
    Hudson County municipalities, letters to mayors, **1948:** 189
New Johnsonville, Tenn., TVA steam generating plant, proposed, **1948:** 109, 148, 165, 218 [7, 9], 258
New London, Conn.
    Campaign remarks, **1948:** 261 [6]; **1952–53:** 298 [6]
    Luncheon remarks at U.S. Submarine Base, **1952–53:** 171
New Mexico, **1947:** 104, 229
    Anderson, Repr. Clinton P., **1945:** 40 [1]
    Campaign remarks in, **1948:** 136 [2–5], 208 [1, 2]
    Candidates for public office, **1948:** 136 [2, 4], 208 [1, 2]
    Fort Sumner irrigation project, **1949:** 168, 185
    Gov. Thomas I. Mabry, **1948:** 136 [2–4], 208 [1, 2]
    Hatch, Sen. Carl A., **1945:** 172 [1]
    Indians
        Bill to confer state citizenship on, **1949:** 226 [19]
        Hopi, **1950:** 9 (p. 91)
    Power projects, **1948:** 208 [2]
    River basin development, **1950:** 164; **1952–53:** 21 [23]
    Vermejo reclamation project, **1949:** 185
New Orleans, La., **1945:** 4 [7], 164 [6]; **1950:** 104
    Battle of, **1947:** 31 [6]
    Mayor DeLesseps S. Morrison, **1949:** 226 [14]
    Naval base, lease of, **1947:** 35
New Republic magazine, **1950:** 97 [5]
New Rochelle, N.Y.
    Campaign remarks, **1952–53:** 298 [12]
    Mayor Stanley W. Church, **1952–53:** 298n.
New Rockford, N. Dak., **1950:** 129 [5]
New Testament, gift to the President, **1951:** 68
New Year message, broadcast, **1950:** 316
New Years resolutions, the President's, **1947:** 243 [13]; **1952–53:** 359 [13]
New York, **1946:** 15 [3], 30 [3], 61 [21], 70 [3, 5, 10], 72 [20], 163 [5, 7], 173 [12], 186 [13], 199 [12], 215 [9], 216 [6, 9, 15], 229 [10], 237 [22]; **1947:** 104
    Bloom, Repr. Sol, **1945:** 10, 219n.
    Campaign remarks, **1948:** 228 [1–13], 229, 261 [10–15], 262, 264 [1–3, 5], 266; **1952–53:** 288, 289, 298 [12–14], 300
    Candidates for public office, **1948:** 228 [2–5, 9], 264 [2]; **1949:** 144 [8], 148 [3], 155 [9], 192

New York — *continued*
  Candidates for public office — *continued*
    [4], 200 [4], 205 [18], 231 [11, 17], 251;
    1952–53: 21 [30], 221 [7], 289, 298 [12, 14],
    300
  Collector of Internal Revenue, Third District,
    question of removal, **1951:** 33 [7]
  Communist Party leaders, prosecution of, **1949:**
    45 [20]
  Courts, **1951:** 112n., 113 [10], 283
  Democratic Party, influence of Frank Costello
    in, **1951:** 95 [5]
  Democratic State Chairman, **1952–53:** 359 [11]
  Dutchess County, **1945:** 76 [2]
  Elections, **1950:** 270 [10]
  Federal judgeships, vacancies, **1949:** 231 [2]
  Gov. Thomas E. Dewey, **1945:** 147 [2], 148;
    1946: 229 [13]; **1949:** 14, 30 [6, 7], 237;
    1950: 157, 175, 270ftn. (p. 681); **1951:** 7
    [11], 188 [10, 13], 224 [1]; **1952–53:** 26 [21],
    127 [17], 129, 143, 233 [15], 242 [1], 267,
    268 [3], 283, 289 [10, 11], 295 [6], 298 [14],
    303 [6], 304, 306 [1], 313 [4]
    See also Dewey, Gov. Thomas E.
  Land and water resources development, **1950:**
    33, 265
  News conference remarks, **1950:** 3 [6], 105 [3],
    214 [12], 270 [10], 287 [8, 14]
  Niagara River project.
    See Niagara River, power and water resources
    development.
  Oswego, **1945:** 225
  Powell, Repr. Adam C., Jr., **1945:** 168
  Power Authority, **1945:** 148, 155
  Power projects development, **1948:** 93 [10]
  River and harbor development, **1951:** 13 (p. 87)
  St. Lawrence Seaway and power projects, **1945:**
    147 [2], 148, 155; **1952–53:** 175 [7]
    See also main heading, St. Lawrence Seaway
    power project.
  Federal-State accord on, **1951:** 37 [2]
  Senatorial election, **1949:** 253 [5]
  Visit to, question of, **1948:** 150 [10], 163 [20], 170
    [2]
  Wagner, Sen. Robert F., **1945:** 44 [16], 202 [4],
    221 [2], 222
New York Avenue Presbyterian Church, Wash-
    ington, cornerstone laying, **1951:** 68
New York Central Railroad, **1951:** 209 [2]
New York City, **1945:** 177, 178, 203n.; **1946:** 85,
    123, 173 [1], 236, 237 [22], 267; **1949:** 107
  Air photos of defense installations, press pub-
    lication of, **1951:** 247 [1]
  Arrest and indictment of Communist Party
    members, **1948:** 163 [19], 170 [6]
  Associated Press, address, **1947:** 76
  Avenue of the Americas, transfer of Bolívar
    statue to, **1951:** 87

New York City — *continued*
  Brooklyn-Battery Tunnel, **1949:** 8 (p. 75)
    Proposed, **1947:** 174 [9]
  Campaign remarks, **1948:** 261 [10–15], 262, 264
    [3, 5], 266; **1952–53:** 289 [12], 290, 291,
    298 [13, 14], 300
  Career of Margaret Truman in, **1949:** 28 [21]
  Federal Reserve Bank, **1947:** 221 [12]
  Financial interests, influence in Eisenhower
    nomination, **1952–53:** 319 [5], 320
  Foreign ministers meeting, **1946:** 250 [14]; **1950:**
    250ftn. (p. 640), 253 [10]
  Harbor improvement, **1952–53:** 367 (p. 1143)
  Jews, press allegation of statement on disloyalty
    of, denial, **1948:** 49 [1]
  Longshoremen, refusal to unload Communist
    bloc ships, **1950:** 230 [4]
  Longshoremen's strike, **1951:** 276
  Mayor Vincent R. Impelliteri, **1952–53:** 290n.,
    291n.
  Mayor Fiorello H. La Guardia, **1945:** 44 [12], 76
    [6], 178
  Mayor William O'Dwyer, **1947:** 174 [9]; **1948:**
    168, 261n., 264n.; **1949:** 155 [9], 237, 238,
    251; **1950:** 214 [5]
  News conference remarks on, **1951:** 22 [2], 247
    [1]
  Newspapers, President's reading of, **1947:** 210 [2]
  Police Commissioner Thomas F. Murphy, pro-
    posed appointment in Office of Price
    Stabilization, **1951:** 37 [7]
  St. Patrick's Day speech, question of, **1948:** 49
    [18]
  Soviet refugees in, **1948:** 178 [7]
  Speaking engagements, cancellation, **1949:** 58 [1,
    23]
  Stock Exchange, **1947:** 226 [13]
  Trucking strike, **1948:** 181 [19]
  United Nations
    General Assembly meeting, **1947:** 21, 38;
      1950: 217 [1, 19]
    Headquarters, **1947:** 26, 136; **1948:** 68, 101,
      165, 168, 173; **1949:** 8 (p. 55), 58 [1, 3], 231
      [11], 234 [12], 237, 238
    Visit by the President, question of, **1949:** 226 [20]
New York City Bar Association, **1951:** 140 [12]
New York Daily Mirror, **1948:** 49 [1]
New York Daily News, **1949:** 252
New York Herald Tribune, **1948:** 15 [11], 227 [6];
    1949: 27n., 66 [14], 144 [6]; **1951:** 275 [5,
    17]; **1952–53:** 45
New York Lawyers Association, **1951:** 113 [10]
New York-New England Inter-Agency Committee,
    1952–53: 294
New York-New England Resources Survey Com-
    mission, proposed, **1950:** 140
New York Shipbuilding Corp., **1948:** 177
New York Stock Exchange, **1947:** 226 [13]

New York Times, **1947:** 14 [15], 70 [5]; **1949:** 66
    [14], 72 [10], 252, 265ftn. (p. 576); **1950:**
    80 [1], 136, 203 [18]; **1951:** 77n., 90 [6];
    1952–53: 321 [4]
New York Trades and Labor Assembly, **1952–53:**
    237
New Yorker magazine, **1951:** 16 [21], 70ftn. (p. 216)
New Zealand, **1946:** 57, 247
    Dairy products, restrictions on imports to U.S.,
      1952–53: 360
    Japanese peace mission to, **1951:** 49ftn. (p. 176)
    Korean war participation, **1950:** 193, 194, 232,
      296; **1951:** 170
    Lend-lease settlement, **1947:** 7 (p. 65)
    Military assistance, **1951:** 193 [2]; **1952–53:** 95
    Mission to, small business study, **1945:** 228
    Mutual defense treaty, **1951:** 84, 85 [8], 153ftn.
      (p. 387), 216; **1952–53:** 5, 26 [21], 95
Newark, N.J.
    Campaign remarks, **1948:** 227 [7]; **1952–53:** 303
      [3]
    Grand jury for crime investigation, **1951:** 63 [1]
    Mayor Vincent J. Murphy, **1948:** 227 [7]
Newbrough, Norita, **1951:** 40n.
Newburyport, Mass., **1947:** 78 [17]
Newport, Ark., campaign remarks, **1952–53:** 193,
    195 [3]
Newport, R.I., **1947:** 236 [2]
Newport News, Va., **1945:** 79n., 91n., 97n.
News conferences, the President's
    1945
       April 17, **1945:** 4
       April 20, **1945:** 8
       April 27, **1945:** 15
       April 28, **1945:** 16
       May 2, **1945:** 22
       May 8, **1945:** 26
       May 15, **1945:** 31
       May 23, **1945:** 40
       June 1, **1945:** 44
       June 7, **1945:** 52
       June 13, **1945:** 60
       June 21, Olympia, Wash., **1945:** 64
       June 27, Independence, Mo., **1945:** 67
       July 5, **1945:** 76
       August 8, **1945:** 94
       August 14, **1945:** 100
       August 16, **1945:** 106
       August 23, **1945:** 107
       August 29, **1945:** 116
       August 30, **1945:** 118
       September 5, **1945:** 127
       September 6, **1945:** 129
       September 12, **1945:** 132
       September 18, **1945:** 137
       September 26, **1945:** 147
       October 3, **1945:** 157
       October 8, Tiptonville, Tenn., **1945:** 164

News conferences, the President's — *continued*
    1945 — *continued*
      October 18, **1945:** 172
      October 25, **1945:** 175
      October 31, **1945:** 181
      November 15, **1945:** 191
      November 20, **1945:** 193
      November 29, **1945:** 202
      December 7, **1945:** 208
      December 12, **1945:** 211
      December 20, **1945:** 221
    1946
      January 8, **1946:** 6
      January 15, **1946:** 15
      January 19, **1946:** 17
      January 24, **1946:** 21
      January 31, **1946:** 27
      February 7, **1946:** 30
      February 15, **1946:** 37
      February 21, **1946:** 41
      February 26, **1946:** 43
      March 8, **1946:** 53
      March 21, **1946:** 66
      March 28, **1946:** 70
      April 3, **1946:** 72
      April 6, Chicago, Ill., **1946:** 75
      April 11, **1946:** 78
      April 17, **1946:** 84
      April 18, **1946:** 86
      May 2, **1946:** 95
      May 9, **1946:** 110
      May 16, **1946:** 114, 119
      May 18, **1946:** 121
      May 31, **1946:** 126
      June 6, **1946:** 129
      June 14, **1946:** 136
      June 20, **1946:** 141
      June 27, **1946:** 143
      July 11, **1946:** 163
      July 18, **1946:** 173
      July 25, **1946:** 177
      August 1, **1946:** 186
      August 2, **1946:** 192
      August 9, **1946:** 199
      September 5, **1946:** 215
      September 12, **1946:** 216
      September 20, **1946:** 219
      September 26, **1946:** 223
      October 3, **1946:** 226
      October 10, **1946:** 229
      October 24, **1946:** 237
      October 28, **1946:** 242
      November 11, **1946:** 250
      December 3, **1946:** 257
      December 12, **1946:** 262
      December 18, **1946:** 266
      December 31, **1946:** 272

News conferences, the President's — *continued*
    1947
        January 8, **1947:** 6
        January 23, **1947:** 14
        February 1, **1947:** 19
        February 13, **1947:** 31
        February 20, **1947:** 36
        February 28, **1947:** 46
        March 26, **1947:** 62
        April 3, **1947:** 67
        April 10, **1947:** 70
        April 17, **1947:** 74
        April 24, **1947:** 78
        May 8, **1947:** 88
        May 13, **1947:** 90
        May 15, **1947:** 95
        June 5, **1947:** 107
        June 12, Monte-Bello, Canada, **1947:** 112
        June 26, **1947:** 127
        July 10, **1947:** 141
        July 17, **1947:** 145
        July 24, **1947:** 155
        August 1, **1947:** 164
        August 7, **1947:** 174
        August 14, **1947:** 177
        August 20, **1947:** 180
        August 21, **1947:** 182
        September 25, **1947:** 191
        September 29, **1947:** 195
        September 30, **1947:** 196
        October 9, **1947:** 205
        October 16, **1947:** 209
        October 17, **1947:** 210
        October 23, **1947:** 213
        November 6, **1947:** 218
        November 13, **1947:** 221
        November 21, **1947:** 226
        December 11, **1947:** 232
        December 18, **1947:** 236
        December 31, **1947:** 243
    1948
        January 10, **1948:** 4
        January 15, **1948:** 9
        January 22, **1948:** 11
        January 29, **1948:** 15
        February 12, **1948:** 26
        March 1, Key West, Fla., **1948:** 41
        March 25, **1948:** 55
        April 8, **1948:** 71
        April 15, **1948:** 77
        April 22, **1948:** 84
        April 23, **1948:** 86
        April 29, **1948:** 88
        May 6, **1948:** 93
        May 13, **1948:** 97
        May 27, **1948:** 110
        July 1, **1948:** 150
        July 22, **1948:** 163

News conferences, the President's — *continued*
    1948 — *continued*
        July 29, **1948:** 166
        August 5, **1948:** 170
        August 12, **1948:** 174
        August 19, **1948:** 178
        September 2, **1948:** 181
        September 7, **1948:** 185
        October 16, on campaign train, **1948:** 243
        November 16, Key West, **1948:** 274
        December 2, **1948:** 278
        December 9, **1948:** 283
        December 16, **1948:** 285
        December 30, **1948:** 288
    1949
        January 7, **1949:** 4
        January 8, **1949:** 7
        January 13, **1949:** 11
        January 27, **1949:** 22
        February 3, **1949:** 28
        February 10, **1949:** 30
        February 17, **1949:** 32
        February 24, **1949:** 40
        March 3, **1949:** 45
        March 18, Key West, Fla., **1949:** 52
        March 24, **1949:** 58
        March 31, **1949:** 66
        April 7, **1949:** 72
        April 14, **1949:** 78
        April 15, **1949:** 80
        April 21, **1949:** 84
        April 22, **1949:** 86
        April 28, **1949:** 89
        May 5, **1949:** 93
        May 12, **1949:** 95
        May 26, **1949:** 112
        June 2, **1949:** 113
        June 9, **1949:** 118
        June 16, **1949:** 122
        June 30, **1949:** 144
        July 7, **1949:** 148
        July 14, **1949:** 155
        July 21, **1949:** 161
        July 28, **1949:** 166
        August 4, **1949:** 171
        August 11, **1949:** 179
        August 18, **1949:** 182
        August 25, **1949:** 192
        September 1, **1949:** 200
        September 8, **1949:** 205
        September 15, **1949:** 211
        September 22, **1949:** 214
        October 6, **1949:** 226
        October 13, **1949:** 231
        October 19, **1949:** 234
        October 20, **1949:** 236
        October 27, **1949:** 240
        November 10, **1949:** 253

News conferences, the President's — *continued*
  1949 — *continued*
    November 17, **1949:** 260
    December 8, Key West, Fla., **1949:** 265
    December 15, Key West, Fla., **1949:** 267
    December 22, **1949:** 269
  1950
    January 5, **1950:** 3
    January 7, **1950:** 8
    January 12, **1950:** 11
    January 19, **1950:** 16
    January 27, **1950:** 23
    February 2, **1950:** 29
    February 9, **1950:** 34
    February 16, **1950:** 38
    February 23, **1950:** 44
    March 2, **1950:** 46
    March 9, **1950:** 52
    March 30, Key West, Fla., **1950:** 80
    April 13, **1950:** 86
    April 27, **1950:** 97
    May 4, **1950:** 105
    May 18, **1950:** 137
    May 25, **1950:** 146
    June 1, **1950:** 152
    June 22, **1950:** 169
    June 29, **1950:** 179
    July 6, **1950:** 186
    July 13, **1950:** 191
    July 27, **1950:** 203
    August 3, **1950:** 206
    August 10, **1950:** 209
    August 17, **1950:** 214
    August 24, **1950:** 217
    August 31, **1950:** 230
    September 7, **1950:** 238
    September 14, **1950:** 250
    September 21, **1950:** 253
    September 28, **1950:** 258
    October 19, **1950:** 270
    October 26, **1950:** 273
    November 2, **1950:** 278
    November 16, **1950:** 287
    November 30, **1950:** 295
    December 19, **1950:** 309
    December 28, **1950:** 318
  1951
    January 4, **1951:** 2
    January 11, **1951:** 7
    January 13, **1951:** 12
    January 18, **1951:** 16
    January 25, **1951:** 22
    February 8, **1951:** 33
    February 15, **1951:** 37
    March 1, **1951:** 49
    March 15, Key West, Fla., **1951:** 56
    March 29, **1951:** 63
    April 5, **1951:** 70

News conferences, the President's — *continued*
  1951 — *continued*
    April 18, **1951:** 85
    April 26, **1951:** 90
    May 3, **1951:** 95
    May 10, **1951:** 101
    May 17, **1951:** 108
    May 24, **1951:** 113
    June 7, **1951:** 118
    June 21, **1951:** 132
    June 28, **1951:** 140
    July 5, **1951:** 145
    July 12, **1951:** 153
    July 19, **1951:** 165
    July 26, **1951:** 171
    August 2, **1951:** 179
    August 9, **1951:** 188
    August 16, **1951:** 193
    August 23, **1951:** 200
    August 30, **1951:** 209
    September 13, **1951:** 224
    September 20, **1951:** 227
    September 27, **1951:** 239
    October 4, **1951:** 247
    October 11, **1951:** 251
    October 18, **1951:** 261
    October 25, **1951:** 275
    November 15, Key West, Fla., **1951:** 295
    November 29, Key West, Fla., **1951:** 298
    December 13, **1951:** 300
  1952
    January 3, **1952–53:** 2
    January 10, **1952–53:** 7
    January 19, **1952–53:** 17
    January 24, **1952–53:** 21
    February 7, **1952–53:** 31
    February 14, **1952–53:** 35
    February 20, **1952–53:** 44
    February 28, **1952–53:** 49
    March 20, Key West, **1952–53:** 64
    April 3, **1952–53:** 75
    April 10, **1952–53:** 88
    April 17, **1952–53:** 98
    April 24, **1952–53:** 107
    May 1, **1952–53:** 115
    May 8, **1952–53:** 123
    May 15, **1952–53:** 127
    May 22, **1952–53:** 136
    May 29, **1952–53:** 149
    June 5, **1952–53:** 156
    June 12, **1952–53:** 166
    June 19, **1952–53:** 175
    July 3, **1952–53:** 197
    August 7, **1952–53:** 221
    August 14, **1952–53:** 228
    August 21, **1952–53:** 233
    August 28, **1952–53:** 238
    September 11, **1952–53:** 247

New conferences, the President's — *continued*
  1952 — *continued*
    September 18, **1952–53:** 253
    September 25, **1952–53:** 258
    November 20, **1952–53:** 334
    December 4, **1952–53:** 342
    December 11, **1952–53:** 345
    December 18, **1952–53:** 353
    December 31, **1952–53:** 359
  1953
    January 15, **1952–53:** 377
News conferences, rules governing, **1945:** 4 [1, 16], 64
News vendors, veto of bill to exclude from social security, **1947:** 170; **1948:** 67
Newsmen, Allied, information from Soviet spheres of influence, **1945:** 60 [15], 97
Newsmen, Danish, meeting with, **1946:** 6 [18]
Newsome, Herschel D., **1952–53:** 203n.
Newspaper Editors, American Society of, **1946:** 86; **1947:** 74, 218 [2]; **1948:** 80; **1949:** 86; **1950:** 92; **1951:** 85 [1]; **1952–53:** 88 [1], 98
Newspaper editors, news conference remarks on, **1952–53:** 98 [20]
Newspaper Publishers Association, American, **1950:** 105ftn. (p. 286)
Newspaper Publishers Association, National, remarks, **1952–53:** 329
Newspapers, editorial opinion on election, **1948:** 262 [12, 14]
Newsweek magazine, **1949:** 95 [3]
Newton, Kans., campaign remarks, **1948:** 137 [3]
Newton, Louie, **1947:** 88 [12]
Newton, Quigg, **1948:** 198n.
Niagara River, power and water resources development, **1950:** 33, 99, 125, 265; **1951:** 11, 13 (p. 87), 185, 239 [20]; **1952–53:** 18 (p. 69)
  News conference remarks, **1950:** 3 [9, 12], 46 [2], 105 [3]
  U.S.-Canadian treaty, **1950:** 99
Nicaragua
  Ambassador Guillermo Sevilla-Sacasa, **1952–53:** 115 [4]
  Atlantic-Pacific canal, proposed, **1950:** 146 [11]
  Román y Reyes, Victor, death of, **1950:** 109
  Somoza, Gen. Anastasio, **1950:** 146 [11], 181 [3]; **1952–53:** 115 [4]
  U.S. Ambassador Capus M. Waynick, **1950:** 146 [10], 278 [8]
Nicholson, Henry J., **1949:** 234 [14]
Nicholson, Meredith, **1948:** 233 [3]
Nickell, Col. Joe, **1949:** 119n.
Nieces, the President's, visit to Washington, **1950:** 247
Nieto del Rio, Felix, **1950:** 231; **1952–53:** 123 [13], 127 [2]

Niles, David K., **1945:** 100n.; **1946:** 186 [9]; **1947:** 179; **1951:** 153 [10]
  Death of, **1952–53:** 265
  Letter, **1945:** 87
Nimitz, Adm. Chester W., **1945:** 2, 45; **1946:** 70 [1], 84 [4], 138, 141 [5], 225; **1947:** 221 [1], 233; **1948:** 110 [15]; **1950:** 80 [3], 121 [1]; **1951:** 20, 22 [2], 35, 104n.; **1952–53:** 136 [1]
  Distinguished Service Medal, citation, **1945:** 161
  News conference remarks on, **1945:** 64 [15], 193 [1, 12]
Nimitz Commission.
  See Commission on Internal Security and Individual Rights.
Niños Héroes monument, Mexico, wreathlaying by the President (1947), **1948:** 210 [2]
Ninth Sonata, Mozart, **1951:** 99
Nisei regiment, citation, **1946:** 170
Nitrates, shortage, **1947:** 99
Nitrogen production, **1952–53:** 33
Nixon, Clay (Commandant, Marine Corps League), **1950:** 235, 237n.
Nixon, Richard M., **1948:** 97 [18], 283 [1]; **1951:** 298 [4]; **1952–53:** 247 [3], 258 [1, 3, 13], 266 [7], 278, 282 [4], 284 [5], 288, 289 [7, 11], 291, 292 [5], 295 [9], 298 [9], 301, 304, 308 [1, 7], 312, 313 [1], 314, 315 [1], 319 [5], 320, 321 [2, 4, 7], 322
Nixon, Robert G., **1946:** 129 [21]; **1947:** 19 [1], 88; **1949:** 112 [15], 265, 267; **1950:** 217 [21], 278 [13]; **1951:** 2 [6, 14], 56 [15], 101 [9], 261 [7, 18]; **1952–53:** 88 [14], 342 [20]
NLRB.
  See National Labor Relations Board.
Nobel peace prize, **1949:** 40 [18], 263; **1950:** 138
Noblesville, Ind., campaign remarks, **1948:** 240 [6]
Nolan, Thomas B., **1948:** 27n.
Nold, Marjorie, **1951:** 122n.
Nonintervention, **1947:** 51
Norfork Dam, Ark., dedication, **1952–53:** 194
Norman, Okla., **1952–53:** 194
  Campaign remarks, **1948:** 214 [9]
Normandy invasion, **1945:** 45, 178
Norrell, Repr. W. F., **1952–53:** 271
Norris, Frank, *The Octopus,* **1948:** 202 [5]
Norris, George W., **1946:** 243, 244; **1948:** 236; **1952–53:** 277 [1], 312
Norris Dam, **1945:** 165
Norris-La Guardia Act, **1946:** 131, 157; **1951:** 279
Norstad, Lt. Gen. Lauris, **1950:** 206 [1]
North Africa, **1946:** 29, 78 [14], 86 [4]; **1947:** 208
  Invasion, **1945:** 45, 178
North America, settlement of, **1948:** 92
North American Holding Co., **1952–53:** 143
North Atlantic Council, **1950:** 22, 151, 201, 308; **1951:** 227ftn. (p. 527); **1952–53:** 112
  Deputy U.S. Representative, appointment of Charles M. Spofford, **1950:** 169 [13], 195

North Atlantic Council — *continued*
London meeting, **1950:** 193
Temporary Committee, **1952–53:** 18
North Atlantic Treaty, **1949:** 66 [18], 69, 70, 120,
159, 162, 184, 202, 225; **1950:** 22, 42, 94,
119, 134, 151, 159, 162, 193, 204, 232, 242;
1951: 13 (pp. 63, 64, 71, 72), 65, 96, 114;
1952–53: 21 [21], 354, 366, 378
Defense efforts by member states, **1952–53:** 15
Denmark, question of accession, **1949:** 30 [13]
Entry into force, statement, **1949:** 188
Imports from member states, proposed removal
of restrictions, **1952–53:** 15
Message to Congress, **1949:** 75
News conference remarks, **1949:** 22 [2], 30 [13],
32 [4], 58 [4, 27], 66 [18], 73 [5], 78 [12], 80,
112 [15], 118 [17], 148 [1], 155 [3, 14], 161
[7], 171 [9], 269 [13]; **1951:** 85 [8]
Norway, question of accession, **1949:** 28 [14], 30
[13]
Opposition by Senator Taft, **1950:** 253ftn. (p.
643)
Ratification, statement, **1949:** 162
Republican stand on, **1952–53:** 291
Second anniversary, statement, **1951:** 69
Senate Resolution 99 supporting, **1951:** 71
Signing, address, **1949:** 68
Third anniversary, remarks, **1952–53:** 77
U.S. commitments under, **1949:** 78 [12], 86, 155
[3], 171 [9]; **1950:** 201
War powers of Congress, relationship to, **1949:**
118 [17]
North Atlantic Treaty Organization, **1949:** 72 [15,
16], 161 [7]; **1950:** 204, 282, 301, 303;
1951: 13 (pp. 72, 73), 25, 91, 138, 145 [1],
167; **1952–53:** 5, 26ftn. (p. 133), and [21],
27, 47, 69, 81, 107 [2], 151, 152, 158, 180n.,
182, 196, 303 [2], 307, 317 [2], 358
Additional U.S. funds for, question of, **1950:** 230
[12]
American Legion support of, **1951:** 191
Anglo-American cooperation in, **1951:** 88
Appropriations for U.S. contribution, danger in
reduction of, **1952–53:** 205
Atlantic Command, joint statement on, **1952–53:**
16
Brussels meeting, **1950:** 305, 311
Correspondents from NATO countries, atten-
dance at news conference, **1951:** 188 [2]
Danish contribution to, **1952–53:** 217
Defense Committee, **1950:** 22
Defense plan, **1950:** 9 (pp. 59, 60), 204, 290
Editors from NATO countries, attendance at
news conference, **1952–53:** 149 [1]
Italian contribution to, **1951:** 232
Joint military forces, planning of, **1950:** 301, 303
Lisbon meeting, **1952–53:** 48, 49 [17], 55, 57

North Atlantic Treaty Organization — *continued*
Membership, admissions
Germany, **1952–53:** 6, 158
Greece, **1951:** 227ftn. (p. 527); **1952–53:** 5, 8,
18 (p. 75), 77
Spain, **1951:** 2 [9]; **1952–53:** 31 [7]
Turkey, **1951:** 227ftn. (p. 527); **1952–53:** 5, 8,
18 (p. 76), 77
Military Committee, **1950:** 22
Military strength, **1952–53:** 18 (p. 74), 55, 57, 367
(pp. 1139–1140)
Increase, **1951:** 4, 7 [5, 9, 17], 114
Netherlands, participation, **1952–53:** 78, 105
News conference remarks, **1950:** 38 [19], 191 [17],
203 [11], 230 [12], 295 [19]
Refugees, European, proposed enlistment in
forces of, **1952–53:** 65
Rifles and ammunition, proposed standardiza-
tion, **1952–53:** 6
Second anniversary, statement, **1951:** 69
Shipping mobilization plans, cooperation with
U.S., **1950:** 9 (p. 92)
Supreme Allied Commander, Atlantic (Adm.
Lynde D. McCormick), **1952–53:** 25
Supreme Commander (Gen. Dwight D. Eisen-
hower), **1951:** 69, 71, 80, 91, 117, 138, 293;
1952–53: 18 (p. 75), 55, 57, 79
Assumption of command, **1951:** 4
Designation of, **1950:** 301, 308, 310, 311
Inspection tour, **1951:** 22 [3]
News conference remarks on, **1951:** 7 [9, 17],
12 [42], 56 [15], 179 [7, 14]
Presidential candidacy, relief to permit, **1952–
53:** 7 [10]
Resignation, **1951:** 165 [5]; **1952–53:** 64 [9], 88
[4], 112
Successor, question of appointment, **1952–53:**
83 [12, 14, 17]
Supreme Allied Commander, Europe (Gen.
Matthew B. Ridgway), **1952–53:** 112
Third anniversary, remarks, **1952–53:** 77
Trade with Soviet bloc, reduction, **1952–53:** 217
Trainees, remarks to, **1951:** 36
U.S. forces for, **1951:** 7 [5, 9, 17]
U.S. participation and support, **1952–53:** 218,
288, 366
Yugoslavia
Food relief for, consultations on, **1950:** 290
Strategic relationship to, **1950:** 293; **1951:** 81
North Atlantic Union, proposed, **1950:** 23 [12], 38
[19]
North Bergen, N.J., Mayor Paul F. Cullum, **1948:**
189n.
North Carolina, **1947:** 205 (p. 460); **1949:** 58 [26],
118 [3]
Bulwinkle, Repr. Alfred L., **1945:** 221 [9]
Campaign address, **1948:** 246
Candidates for public office, **1948:** 246

North Carolina — *continued*
  Doughton, Repr. Robert L., **1945:** 132 [8]
  Gov. R. Gregg Cherry, **1948:** 245n., 246
  Gov. W. Kerr Scott, **1951:** 90 [13], 256
  Hostile reception to Henry A. Wallace, **1948:** 181ftn. (p. 461)
  Primary elections, **1950:** 23 [11], 179 [13]
  Visit to, **1945:** 132 [8]
    Question of, **1948:** 163 [18], 174 [6]
North Carolina, University of, **1952–53:** 98 [13]
North Dakota, **1950:** 129 [1]
  Addresses or remarks in, **1950:** 129 [3–5], 130
  Campaign remarks, **1952–53:** 266 [2–12], 267
  Candidates for public office, **1952–53:** 266 [3–11]
  Floods, **1950:** 129 [1, 3, 4, 5, 7], 130
  Gov. C. Norman Brunsdale, **1952–53:** 97
  Indian lands, veto of bill for disposal, **1948:** 25
  Oil, **1952–53:** 266 [9, 10]
North Haven, Conn., campaign remarks, **1952–53:** 292 [1]
North Judson, Ind., campaign remarks, **1948:** 240[2]
North Pacific air routes, **1946:** 95 [14]
North Platte, Nebr., campaign remarks, **1948:** 118 [3]
Northumberland, Pa., campaign remarks, **1952–53:** 306 [4]
Northwest Ordinance, **1946:** 204
Northwestern University, **1951:** 251 [1]
Norton, Garrison, **1947:** 149n.
Norwalk, Conn., campaign remarks, **1952–53:** 298 [10]
Norway, **1945:** 186; **1946:** 6 [18], 86 [4]
  Assistance, **1947:** 238
  Crown Prince Olav, **1945:** 196
  De Morgenstierne, Wilhelm Munthe, **1949:** 116n.
  Economy, **1949:** 162
  Korean war, participation, **1951:** 170
  Lange, Halvard (Foreign Minister), **1949:** 28ftn. (p. 128), 30 [13], 68
  Lend-lease settlement, **1947:** 7 (p. 65)
  Military assistance, **1950:** 22
  North Atlantic Treaty, question of accession to, **1949:** 28 [14], 30 [13]
  Torp, Oscar, **1952–53:** 258 [10]
  Trade with Soviet bloc, **1951:** 117n.
  U.S. Ambassador Charles U. Bay, **1950:** 52 [2]
Nourse, Edwin G., **1946:** 183, 266 [4]; **1947:** 46 [10], 53, 70 [4]; **1950:** 105 [6]
  Chairman, Council of Economic Advisers, **1948:** 284
    News conference remarks on, **1949:** 66 [8], 72 [2, 17], 205 [1], 234 [2], 236 [7, 12], 240 [3], 267 [13]
  Resignation, **1949:** 236 [7]
Norwich University, conveyance of certain Weather Bureau property to, veto, **1945:** 92

NSRB.
  See National Security Resources Board.
Nuclear reactor.
  See Atomic energy.
Nuclear war, **1946:** 112, 242 [2]
Nuclear weapons **1946:** 82
  See also Atomic bomb; Hydrogen bomb.
  News conference remarks, **1946:** 41 [1], 53 [14], 70 [6], 86 [15, 17], 163 [1], 226 [19]
  Reports, **1946:** 163 [1]
Nullification crisis (1832), **1948:** 245
Nürnberg trials, **1945:** 201n.; **1946:** 18 (pp. 46, 47), 42, 215 [1], 226 [13], 229 [13], 230, 233, 251
Nürnberg Tribunal.
  See International Military Tribunal.
Nurses, **1946:** 1
  Shortage of, **1947:** 98; **1948:** 8 (p. 85), 181 [2], 241; **1949:** 2; **1950:** 2, 129 [4]; **1951:** 135, 307; **1952–53:** 333, 367 (p. 1158), 369
Nurses training program, termination, **1945:** 130
Nutrition, **1948:** 99
Nyrop. Donald W., **1952–53:** 155, 246, 351

Oak Ridge, Tenn., atomic installation, **1945:** 93, 156
  Communist activities, investigation, **1948:** 110 [20]
  Labor dispute, **1948:** 140
  Operation, **1948:** 239
  Separation of U-235, **1949:** 166 [1]
  Visit to, question of, **1948:** 110 [5]
Oakland, Calif., campaign address, **1948:** 203; **1952–53:** 279
Oakridge, Oreg.
  Campaign remarks, **1948:** 126 [5]
  Mayor Lorenz F. Gerspach, **1948:** 126 [5]
OAS.
  See Organization of American States.
Oath of office, statement, **1945:** 1
Oatis, William N., **1952–53:** 49 [12], 115 [15]
  Espionage charges by Czechoslovakia, **1951:** 145 [7], 153 [4], 209 [14]
Oats, conservation, **1948:** 14
Oberg, Stuart W., **1952–53:** 181n.
O'Brien, David H., **1950:** 40n.
O'Brien, John L., **1950:** 157n.
O'Brien, Repr. Leo W., **1952–53:** 289
O'Brien, Michael P., **1952–53:** 287n.
Occupational disease, prevention, **1948:** 248
Occupational training, **1946:** 18 (p. 84), 75 [26]; **1947:** 4 (p. 31), 7 (pp. 58, 69, 77), 70 [4], 81; **1948:** 5 (p. 42); **1949:** 8 (p. 90), 256; **1950:** 9 (p. 74), 74, 127 [7], 208
  Defense workers, **1951:** 11, 13 (pp. 78, 80, 96), 15
  Disabled persons, **1951:** 13 (p. 98); **1952–53:** 243, 367 (p. 1158)

Occupational training — *continued*
  Federal aid, **1952–53:** 367 (pp. 1150, 1155)
  Government employees, **1952–53:** 18 (p. 112)
  Merchant seamen, **1950:** 76
  Older persons, **1952–53:** 18 (p. 104)
  Subsidies for, **1951:** 85 [9]
  Veterans, **1948:** 228 [10]; **1950:** 9 (pp. 68, 69), 36, 298; **1951:** 13 (pp. 99–101), 260; **1952–53:** 18 (p. 108), 231, 243
Occupied areas, **1947:** 36 [12], 38, 46 [2], 180 [15], 188; **1948:** 175; **1949:** 8 (pp. 54, 56, 59), 154
  See also specific countries.
  Assistance, **1950:** 8 [6], 9 (p. 58)
  Europe, **1947:** 224; **1948:** 144
    Austria, **1948:** 2; **1949:** 8 (p. 59), 136
    Germany, **1947:** 209 [13], 214, 238; **1948:** 2; **1949:** 8 (pp. 54, 59), 28 [9], 58 [15], 84 [3], 92, 122 [3], 136, 214 [2]; **1951:** 114, 149; **1952–53:** 151, 345 [1]
    Italy, U.S. troop withdrawal, **1947:** 234, 239
  Far East, **1948:** 144
    Japan, **1947:** 214; **1948:** 2; **1949:** 8 (pp. 54, 59); **1951:** 216
    Korea, **1947:** 214; **1948:** 2; **1949:** 117
  Relief programs, **1949:** 117
  U.S. expenditures in, **1947:** 6 [4, 11, 14, 27], 7 (p. 62); **1948:** 5 (pp. 26, 29, 31)
Ocean weather stations, **1948:** 5 (pp. 49, 50)
Oceanside, Calif., campaign remarks, **1948:** 206 [2]
O'Connell, John J., **1945:** 132 [1]; **1952–53:** 274 [3, 7], 276
O'Connor, Basil, **1949:** 73n., 110n., 205 [2], 214 [1]; **1950:** 32n.
O'Connor, Sen. Herbert R., **1949:** 76n., 112ftn. (p. 269); **1950:** 135
Octopus, The, Frank Norris, **1948:** 202 [5]
Odd Fellows, Independent Order of, remarks to International Council, **1951:** 220
Odegard, Peter H., **1950:** 153
Odgers, Merle M., **1948:** 104
Odom, Capt. William, **1947:** 74n.
O'Donnell, Gerald, **1952–53:** 313n.
O'Donnell, John A., **1951:** 64n.
O'Donnell, R. J., **1948:** 196n.
  Letter, **1945:** 88
ODT.
  See Defense Transportation, Office of.
O'Dwyer, William, **1947:** 174 [9]; **1948:** 168, 261n., 264n.; **1949:** 155 [9], 237, 238, 251; **1950:** 214 [5], 217 [9]; **1951:** 63 [4], 95 [3, 10], 101 [3], 227 [9]; **1952–53:** 64 [15], 115 [2]
OEEC.
  See Organization for European Economic Co-operation.
Office space, Federal, acquisition and management, **1950:** 53, 73

Office space, the President's, **1946:** 21 [2]
Official papers, definition, question of, **1947:** 19 [14]
Offshore lands.
  See Public lands.
Ofstie, Rear Adm. Ralph A., **1949:** 231 [19]
Ogden, Utah, campaign remarks, **1948:** 200 [9]
Ogden River irrigation project, Utah, **1948:** 200 [9]
Ogdensburg, N.Y., **1947:** 172
Ogdensburg Agreement (1940), **1947:** 111
O'Grady, John, **1948:** 233 [3], 240 [6], 267 [2]
O'Grady, Msgr. John, **1952–53:** 244, 373
Ohio, **1947:** 104, 182 [11]; **1949:** 45 [26], 122ftn. (p. 292)
  Burton, Sen. Harold H., **1945:** 137 [6], 172 [1]
  Campaign addresses or remarks in, **1948:** 114 [1], 138 [8], 183 [7], 193 [2], 231 [1–10], 232, 257 [3–5], 258, 267 [1]; **1952–53:** 240 [2], 242 [1], 311 [1, 2], 286 [4–6], 287, 319 [1–6], 320
  Candidates for public office, **1948:** 114 [1], 193 [2], 231 [1–10], 257 [4, 5], 258; **1950:** 3 [13], 11 [12], 38 [5], 86 [9], 146 [9], 169 [1]; **1951:** 298 [2]; **1952–53:** 34, 253 [8], 286 [4–6], 287, 311 [1], 319 [2–6], 320
  Farm Bureau group, remarks, **1950:** 145
  Floods, control and relief, **1952–53:** 50
  Gov. James M. Cox, **1948:** 231 [2, 3]
  Gov. Frank J. Lausche, **1950:** 169 [1, 15]; **1952–53:** 253 [8], 286n., 287n., 311 [1, 2], 319 [1–6], 320
  Hamilton County, property assessment system, **1948:** 231 [1]
  News conference remarks, **1950:** 3 [13], 11 [12], 38 [5], 86 [9, 26], 146 [9], 169 [1]
  Postelection remarks in, **1948:** 271 [3]
  Primary elections, **1948:** 84 [2], 93 [12]
  State Grange, **1950:** 127 [5]
Ohio River, **1945:** 165; **1947:** 141 [2], 144; **1950:** 3 [9, 11, 25], 121 [4, 13], 125, 127 [2], 129 [1]; **1952–53:** 50
Oil, **1946:** 101; **1947:** 145 [11], 237, 238; **1948:** 1, 8 (pp. 67, 70, 78, 79)
  See also Petroleum.
  Canol project, **1946:** 215 [3]
  Cartel in industry, allegations of, **1952–53:** 197 [6, 13], 221 [11], 372
  Companies, refusal to release books, **1952–53:** 377 [26]
  Conservation, **1947:** 104, 231; **1949:** 7 [33], 8 (p. 84)
  Consumption, **1947:** 145 [9]; **1952–53:** 379
  Continental shelf deposits, **1945:** 150
  Depletion exemptions, **1950:** 18
  Edible fats and oils, **1950:** 83
    Import controls, **1947:** 99
  Exports, **1950:** 34 [3]

Oil — *continued*
 First well in Oklahoma, **1948:** 216 [10]
 Imports, **1950:** 23 [9], 29 [25], 34 [3, 11]; **1951:**
  199; **1952–53:** 239
 Imports by free China, **1948:** 31
 Industry, question of Government operation,
  1952–53: 115 [9]
 Iran, dispute with U.K., **1951:** 118 [11], 132 [11],
  150, 153 [19], 165 [11], 239 [6]; **1952–53:** 5,
  6
 Labor dispute in industry, **1952–53:** 58, 123 [6]
 Lands suit filed by Department of Justice, **1945:**
  52 [13]
 Leases on public lands, **1947:** 35
 Manufacture from coal, **1948:** 200 [3]
 Mexican, **1949:** 58 [6]
  Development loan, **1949:** 66 [11], 78 [8], 84 [6],
   122 [12, 25], 144 [13], 155 [6], 161 [6], 171
   [10], 182 [6], 192 [11], 200 [1, 3, 11], 205
   [17], 211 [9], 253 [16], 260 [16]; **1950:** 146
   [15], 179 [14], 191 [10], 217 [9]
 Navy, transfer of offshore oil lands to, **1952–53:**
  377 [11, 14]
 North Dakota, **1952–53:** 266 [9, 10]
 Offshore, public ownership of, **1952–53:** 129,
  146, 238 [8], 266 [9, 10], 289 [11], 314, 321
  [2], 379
 Pipelines, **1947:** 35
 Production, **1950:** 202; **1952–53:** 58, 280 [5], 379
 Refining capacity, **1951:** 11
  Expansion, **1952–53:** 15
 Refining industry, **1948:** 8 (p. 79)
 Reserves, **1948:** 5 (p. 46)
 Roosevelt, Franklin D., letters on, **1947:** 78 [20]
 Saudi Arabia, **1946:** 110 [13]
 Shale, **1948:** 118 [7], 200 [3]; **1949:** 226 [6]; **1950:**
  116
 Shortage, **1947:** 110, 228, 232 [10], 243 [6]
 Taxation of industry, **1951:** 28
 Teapot Dome scandal, 1920's, **1950:** 116; **1952–**
  53: 277 [1]
 Termination of fuel oil rationing, **1945:** 128
 Tidelands, **1948:** 228 [12], 278 [37], 285 [7]; **1949:**
  2, 7 [33, 38] 113 [2], 122 [15]; **1952–53:**
  293, 317 [3]
 Tidelands bill, **1946:** 177 [6], 186 [5], 189
Oil Workers International Union, **1952–53:** 58
O'Kane, Comdr. Richard H., **1946:** 69
Okinawa, **1945:** 45
 News conference remarks, **1945:** 64 [15], 129 [3]
 U.S. forces in, **1951:** 84
 U.S. invasion, **1945:** 161, 178
Oklahoma, **1947:** 104
 Campaign remarks, **1948:** 214 [4–9], 215, 216
  [1–12], 217
 Candidates for public office, **1948:** 213, 214 [4, 5,
  7, 8], 216 [1–7, 10–12], 217
 Cherokee Indians, **1950:** 12

Oklahoma — *continued*
 First oil well in, **1948:** 216 [10]
 Flood relief, **1951:** 158, 162, 185, 196, 224 [7];
  1952–53: 119, 194
 Gov. Roy J. Turner, **1948:** 213, 214 [3–8], 216
  [1–6, 10–12], 217; **1951:** 118 [2], 145 [8]
 Lead and zinc mines, exhaustion, **1950:** 124 [7]
 News conference remarks, **1950:** 3 [9], 38 [16]
 Power projects, **1950:** 3 [9], 125; **1951:** 185
 River basin development, **1950:** 164
 School integration, **1950:** 38 [16]
Oklahoma, University of, **1952–53:** 266 [11]
Oklahoma City, Okla., **1949:** 22 [5]
 Campaign address, **1948:** 215
Olav, Crown Prince, Legion of Merit, citation,
 1945: 196
Old-age and survivors insurance, **1945:** 99; **1946:**
 18 (pp. 64, 83); **1947:** 4 (p. 30), 7 (pp. 58,
 73), 181 (p. 406); **1948:** 2, 4 [8], 5 (pp. 34,
 36, 37, 59), 8 (pp. 68, 87, 88), 107, 131,
 165, 175, 241, 252, 255; **1949:** 5, 8 (pp. 49,
 66, 71), 151, 250 [3]; **1950:** 2, 9 (pp. 46, 53,
 54, 68, 71, 72, 76, 77), 84, 127 [5], 128, 157,
 281; **1951:** 12 [54], 13 (p. 99), 159, 280
 See also Insurance.
Old Hickory power project, **1951:** 13 (pp. 85, 86)
Old Saybrook, Conn., campaign remarks, **1952–53:**
 298 [7]
Old Trails Association, National, **1948:** 137 [1, 4],
 233 [1]
Older persons, **1947:** 7 (pp. 58, 71); **1948:** 5 (p. 35),
 115
 Assistance, **1945:** 99; **1948:** 131; **1949:** 8 (p. 67),
  151; **1952–53:** 367 (pp. 1156, 1157)
 Community Chest programs for, **1950:** 262
 Employment, **1950:** 243; **1952–53:** 18 (p. 104)
  In defense production, **1950:** 303; **1951:** 15
  Part-time, **1948:** 107
 Medical care, **1950:** 233; **1951:** 307
  Under social security, proposed, **1950:** 9 (p.
   73)
 Pensions, **1949:** 267 [2]
 Social security.
  See main heading, Social security.
 Welfare programs, **1948:** 107; **1950:** 9 (p. 73)
Olds, Irving S., **1946:** 27 [9], 142
Olds, Leland, **1949:** 222, 226 [7, 15], 231 [2], 236
 [18]; **1950:** 1n., 306n.
O'Leary, Barry, **1948:** 121
Oleomargarine, repeal of tax on, **1949:** 5
Oleomargarine legislation, question of, **1948:** 166
 [12]
Oliphant, Charles, **1951:** 298 [4, 9]
Olive Hill, Ky., campaign remarks, **1948:** 222 [7]
Oliver, Harold, **1951:** 145 [9]
Oliver, Robert C., **1948:** 233 [1, 2]
Olsen, Arnold H., **1952–53:** 268n.
Olsen, Floyd B., **1948:** 236

Olson, Curtiss, **1952–53:** 266 [1]
Olympia, Wash., **1945:** 64
   Campaign remarks, **1948:** 124 [5]
   Mayor E. Malory, **1948:** 124 [5]
Olympic Junior College, Wash., **1948:** 124 [1]
Olympic National Park, **1952–53:** 342 [1], 365
Omaha, Nebr., **1947:** 209 [12]
   Campaign remarks, **1948:** 116 [1], 117; **1952–53:** 97
   Mayor Glenn Cunningham, **1948:** 116 [1]
   Steers, prices, **1947:** 242
O'Mahoney, Sen. Joseph C., **1948:** 37 [11], 43 [4], 57, 136 [16], 257 [10]; **1949:** 32 [6], 41, 138, 148ftn. (p. 351); **1950:** 107, 116, 117 [1, 4], 118, 119; **1951:** 168, 300 [12]; **1952–53:** 49 [8], 146, 199
   Antitrust bill, **1948:** 252
O'Malley, Patrick, **1948:** 259 [1]
Omar N. Bradley Gold Medal, **1952–53:** 29n.
"One Great Hour" religious program, address, **1949:** 62
O'Neal, Edward A., **1947:** 191 [3]
O'Neal, Emmet, **1947:** 88 [9], 95 [20], 134
O'Neal, Samuel A., **1947:** 46 [27]
Oneida, N.Y., campaign remarks, **1948:** 228 [7]; **1952–53:** 289 [4]
O'Neil, James F., **1946:** 270; **1948:** 244n.
O'Neil, Vice Adm. Merlin, **1951:** 301n.
O'Neill, Charles, **1946:** 114
O'Neill, Emmet, **1949:** 28 [7]
O'Neill, Harry P., **1948:** 248; **1952–53:** 306 [1]
O'Neill, James F., **1952–53:** 298 [3]
O'Neill, Thomas P., **1952–53:** 296
O'Neill, Vincent, **1952–53:** 317 [2]
Onondaga, **1946:** 188
Ontario, Canada, role in St. Lawrence Seaway project, **1952–53:** 23
Ontario, Oreg., **1950:** 121 [6]
OPA.
   See Price Administration, Office of.
OPA bill.
   See Price Control Act.
Open Market Committee, Federal, **1951:** 29
Opera, comments on, **1951:** 99
Oppenheimer, J. Robert, **1946:** 262 [1]; **1951:** 89
"Operation Skywatch," statements on, **1952–53:** 202, 344
Opportunity Savings Bond Drive, **1949:** 82, 98
Optometry Corps, Army, veto, **1946:** 109
OPS.
   See Price Stabilization, Office of
Order of the Eastern Star, **1950:** 266, 314
Order of Railway Conductors, **1950:** 221; **1952–53:** 136ftn. (p. 359)
Order of San Martín (Argentina), **1949:** 32ftn. (p. 135)
Ordnance Department, World War II contract, **1951:** 284

Oregon, **1947:** 236 [8]
   Acquistion by U.S. (1846), **1948:** 198 [6]
   Campaign remarks, **1948:** 126 [1–6]; **1950:** 121 [6–9, 11], 122; **1952–53:** 277 [1]
   Candidates for public office, **1952–53:** 277 [1]
   Gov. John H. Hall, **1948:** 88 [8]
   Gov. Leslie Scott (Acting), **1948:** 126 [2]
   Population growth, **1950:** 121 [6], 125
   Portland, **1945:** 64 [1, 14]
   Visit to, question of, **1948:** 88 [8]
Oregon Journal, **1952–53:** 233ftn. (p. 530)
Oregon Trail, **1950:** 121 [6, 7], 125
Oresko, N., Congressional Medal of Honor presentation, **1945:** 167n.
Organization of American States, **1949:** 9, 230; **1950:** 179 [22]; **1952–53:** 55
   Bogotá, International Conference of American States, **1951:** 125
   Charter, **1951:** 125, 132 [8], 134; **1952–53:** 92
   62d anniversary, **1952–53:** 94
   Technical assistance program, **1951:** 114
Organization of American States, Council of, **1949:** 230
   Remarks to, **1952–53:** 94
Organization for European Economic Cooperation, **1949:** 71, 155 [23], 195
Organization of the Executive Branch, Commission on.
   See Commission on Organization of the Executive Branch of the Government.
Organized Militia, retirement credit for service in, **1949:** 174
Organized Reserve, **1950:** 9 (p. 63)
Organized Reserve Corps Armory, Kansas City, **1951:** 209 [5], 218
Orphans, immigration from Europe, **1945:** 225
Orr, Douglas W., **1949:** 89 [1], 249
Osgood, Warren L., **1952–53:** 157n.
Oslo, Mayor Halfdan E. Stokke, **1949:** 54
Osmena, Sergio, **1945:** 24, 157 [2], 176; **1946:** 31, 111
   Discussions with, statement, **1945:** 175 [2]
   Letter, **1945:** 189
Osobka-Morawski, Edward, message, **1945:** 78
Ospina Perez, Mariano, **1950:** 181 [4]
OSS.
   See Strategic Services, Office of.
Ostendorn, Ed, **1948:** 126 [6]
Ostrich eggs, **1949:** 267 [14]
Oswego, N.Y., **1945:** 225
O'Toole, Repr. Donald L., **1952–53:** 300
Ottawa, Canada, **1945:** 209n.; **1947:** 51, 111, 112
   North Atlantic Council meeting, **1951:** 227ftn. (p. 527)
Ottawa, Ohio, campaign remarks, **1948:** 231 [6]; **1952–53:** 319 [2]
Ottumwa, Iowa, **1950:** 110 [3]

Our National Labor Policy, the Taft-Hartley Act and the Next Steps, Repr. Fred A. Hartley, Jr., **1948:** 232, 247, 261 [11]
Ouray Indian Reservation, **1951:** 198
Overseas Airways, **1950:** 169 [11]
Overton, Sen. John H., **1946:** 136 [16]
Owensboro, Ky., campaign remarks, **1948:** 218 [12]
OWMR.
   See War Mobilization and Reconversion, Office of.
Oxford, Iowa
   Campaign remarks, **1948:** 194 [4]
   Mayor J. L. Kinney, **1948:** 194n.
Ozark Hillbilly Medallion of the Springfield (Mo.) Chamber of Commerce, **1952–53:** 157n.

Pace, Frank, Jr., **1949:** 4[1]
   See also Army, Secretary of the; Budget, Bureau of the, Director.
Pace (Repr. Stephen A.) bill, **1946:** 61 [12]
Pachmann, Vladimir de, **1951:** 99
Pacific-Atlantic Oceans, sea-level canal connecting, **1948:** 5 (p. 48)
Pacific bases, U.S., **1946:** 141 [14, 17], 226 [14], 265
Pacific campaign, World War II, **1945:** 45, 218
Pacific coast ports, security measures, **1950:** 214 [9]
Pacific Fleet, **1947:** 221 [1]
Pacific Islands Trust Territory, **1947:** 119, 137, 151; **1949:** 101
   Civilian administration, **1950:** 9 (p. 102); **1951:** 141
Pacific Junction, Iowa, **1950:** 110 [5]
   Campaign remarks, **1952–53:** 284 [1]
Pacific Northwest, **1947:** 110
   Defense, **1950:** 105 [14]
   Electric generating facilities, **1952–53:** 18 (p. 89)
   Floods, **1948:** 111
   Power projects, **1951:** 11, 210, 185; **1952–53:** 277 [1], 367 (p. 1146)
   Resources development, **1949:** 77
Pacific pact for Latin America, proposed, **1950:** 250 [12]
Pacific Relations, Institute of, **1952–53:** 362n.
Pacific union, question of, **1949:** 179 [14, 20]
Paderewski, Ignace Jan, **1951:** 99, 291
Pahlavi, Princess Ashraf, **1947:** 203n.
Pahlavi, Shah Mohammad Reza, **1949:** 258, 259, 262, 273
   Legion of Merit award, **1947:** 203
Paine, Thomas, **1951:** 30
Paintings, the President's preferences, **1948:** 71 [1]
Pakistan
   Ambassador Mohammed Ali, **1952–53:** 252
   Assistance, **1952–53:** 55
   Dispute with India, **1948:** 202 [6]; **1950:** 143

Pakistan — *continued*
   Independence, **1950:** 119
   Liaquat Ali Khan, **1949:** 253 [10, 15]; **1950:** 102; **1951:** 257
   Nazimuddin, Khwaja, **1951:** 257
   Uprising in Korean prisoner-of-war camps, question of investigation by, **1952–53:** 162
   Wheat loan document, signing, **1952–53:** 252
Palau Islands, **1945:** 45
Palestine, **1946:** 5, 89, 132, 212; **1947:** 14 [5], 90 [6]; **1952–53:** 297
   See also Israel.
   Acts of terrorism, statements, **1946:** 175; **1947:** 108
   Arab-Israeli dispute, **1948:** 124 [1], 253; **1949:** 11 [8], 40 [2], 122 [23], 193, 274; **1950:** 2, 25, 143
   Arab population, **1946:** 92
   Arms, embargo, question of modification, **1948:** 71 [23]
   Arms shipments to, tripartite declaration on, **1950:** 147, 148
   Evacuation of Americans, question of, **1947:** 19 [8]
   Grady-Morrison plan, **1946:** 199 [8, 22], 215 [5, 7], 227
   Jewish immigration, **1945:** 106 [18], 147 [13], 152, 172 [10], 181 [8], 187, 188, 210; **1946:** 92, 129 [11, 16], 136 [14], 141 [18], 155, 175, 177 [14], 215 [5], 226 [5], 227, 237 [6], 241; **1947:** 41n.; **1948:** 55 [1]
   Jewish national state, proposed, **1945:** 106 [8, 18], 202 [4]; **1946:** 227, 241
   Loan to, question of, **1948:** 278 [25]
   London conference on, **1946:** 143 [13], 177 [14], 227
   News conference remarks, **1945:** 106 [18], 147 [13], 157 [9, 11], 172 [10], 181 [8], 202 [4]; **1946:** 95 [9], 110 [13], 129 [11, 16], 136 [14], 141 [18], 143 [13], 163 [5], 177 [14], 186 [3], 199 [4, 6, 8, 22], 215 [5, 7, 11], 226 [5], 229 [25], 237 [6], 266 [15]; **1948:** 9 [17, 19], 26 [9], 41 [1], 55 [1], 71 [23], 84 [20], 93 [4], 97 [4], 278 [25]; **1949:** 11 [8], 40 [2], 122 [23], 192 [21]
   Partition, proposed, **1948:** 26 [9], 34
   Provisional Israeli government, diplomatic recognition, **1948:** 100
   Refugees, **1949:** 21, 57, 122 [23], 192 [21]
      U.S. relief for, **1948:** 281; **1950:** 9 (p. 58), 25, 78, 154; **1951:** 13 (p. 74), 114, 172
   Statements on, **1948:** 39, 253
   U.K. withdrawal, question of, **1947:** 19 [17]; **1948:** 55 [1], 71 [23], 93 [4]
   U.N. mediator, death of, **1948:** 193 [2]
   U.N. operations, **1948:** 9 [19], 55 [1], 71 [23], 84 [20], 93 [4]; **1950:** 2

Palestine — *continued*
  U.N. resolution on, **1948:** 253
  U.S. forces in, question of, **1948:** 9 [17], 41 [1], 84 [20], 178 [9]
  U.S. policy, **1948:** 93 [4], 264 [3]; **1949:** 11 [8]
  U.S. recognition, question of, **1948:** 97 [4]
Palestine, Jewish Agency for, **1946:** 155
Palestine commission.
  See Anglo-American Committee of Inquiry.
Palestine Conciliation Commission (United Nations), **1949:** 11 [8], 40 [2], 57, 193, 274
Palestine and Related Problems, Cabinet Committee on, **1946:** 132, 136 [14], 186ftn. (p. 367), 227
Paley, William S., **1951:** 19; **1952–53:** 179, 203
Palm oil, shortage, **1947:** 18
Palmer, Dwight, **1952–53:** 7 [1]
Palmer, James, **1949:** 167n.; **1950:** 94n.
Pan American Airways, **1950:** 169 [11]
Pan American conference, Bogotá, **1948:** 198 [1]
Pan American Day, **1952–53:** 94
Pan American Sanitary Bureau, **1951:** 184; **1952–53:** 207
Pan American Sanitary Organization, Directing Council, **1951:** 243
Pan American Union, **1946:** 18 (p. 87), 83
  Appropriations, U.S. participation, **1951:** 184
  Foreign ministers, dinner, **1951:** 67
Pan Americanism, **1947:** 84
Panama, **1946:** 216 [21]
Panama, Inter-American Congress (1825), **1948:** 158
Panama Canal, **1945:** 70, 128; **1946:** 18 (p. 81), 43 [5]; **1947:** 7 (pp. 85, 96); **1948:** 4 [1]
  Administration, **1950:** 28
  Employee compensation claims, **1952–53:** 208
Panama Canal Company, **1950:** 28; **1952–53:** 18 (p. 83), 208
Panama Canal Zone, **1947:** 171; **1948:** 20
Panama City, **1948:** 158
Panama Railroad, **1948:** 4 [1]
Panama Railroad Company, **1946:** 94; **1947:** 7 (p. 96); **1948:** 5 (p. 57)
  Administration, **1950:** 28
Pandit, Madame Vijaya Lakshmir, **1949:** 256
Panic, Father Stephen, **1948:** 261 [8]
Panmunjom, Korea, **1950:** 263n.
  Armistice negotiations, **1952–53:** 75 [1]
Paraguay, point 4 program in, **1952–53:** 5
Paraplegics Manufacturing Co., **1952–53:** 243
Paper conservation, statement, **1945:** 58
Papers of Thomas Jefferson, publication of first volume, **1950:** 136
Paradise, Mont., **1950:** 124 [8]
Pardue, Bishop Austin, **1949:** 202n.
Paris, **1945:** 12n.; **1947:** 88 [8]; **1952–53:** 262
  CEEC meeting, **1947:** 191 [4], 217, 219, 238

Paris — *continued*
  Foreign ministers meetings, **1946:** 95 [21], 110 [12], 141 [19], 143 [17], 163 [11], 173 [7], 181; **1947:** 74; **1948:** 185 [6]; **1949:** 93 [12], 112 [13], 118 [1], 122 [24], 136, 253 [18, 20], 260ftn. (p. 570); **1950:** 162
  Peace conference, **1946:** 53 [19], 119 [25], 126 [22], 173 [2, 16], 181, 199 [19], 202, 219; **1947:** 2 (p. 9)
  ILO meeting, **1946:** 180
  Marshall plan conference, **1947:** 141 [15, 17], 177 [22]; **1948:** 52
  Meetings on British financial crisis, **1949:** 148 [5]
  NATO Defense Committee, meeting, **1950:** 22
  United Nations General Assembly meetings (1948), **1948:** 178 [14], 202 [6], 230, 239, 243 [8, 10], 248, 274 [3]; **1949:** 11 [8]; **1951:** 266, 293
  Visit by the President, question of, **1951:** 56 [20], 70 [11]
Paris, Treaty of (1899), **1952–53:** 104
Park and Planning Commission, National Capital, **1946:** 15 [8], 21 [2], 43 [10]; **1950:** 9 (p. 102)
Park police, U.S., **1947:** 165
  Jurisdiction over park areas in District of Columbia, **1945:** 80
Park Service, National, **1947:** 165; **1948:** 5 (p. 47), 208 [7]
Park Service, National, Director (Newton B. Drury), **1947:** 165
Park System, National Capital, **1945:** 80
Parker, John J., **1945:** 132 [1]; **1946:** 230
Parker River National Wildlife Refuge, **1946:** 211
Parkersburg, W. Va.
  Campaign remarks, **1952–53:** 242 [2]
  Veto of bill to amend census records, **1950:** 210
Parkhurst, Richard, **1948:** 77 [11]
Parks, national, **1946:** 18 (p. 82); **1947:** 7 (p. 83), 231; **1948:** 5 (p. 47), 199, 208 [6–8]; **1949:** 8 (p. 84), 43; **1950:** 9 (p. 91), 124 [8]; **1952–53:** 342 [1]
  See also specific parks.
  Everglades National Park, **1947:** 221 [10]
  Glacier National Park, **1946:** 150
  Grand Teton National Park, reestablishment, **1950:** 248
  Highways, **1948:** 24
  Roads, trails, **1948:** 5 (p. 47)
  Theodore Roosevelt National Park, disapproval, **1946:** 200
Parler, J. D., **1945:** 147n.
Parliament, Canadian, address to, **1947:** 111
Parran, Thomas, **1950:** 294n.
  See also Surgeon General, Public Health Service.
Parten, John P., **1946:** 143 [10]
Parten, Jubal R., **1945:** 31 [7]

Pasco, Wash., **1950:** 121 [13]
Pasha, Mustapha Kemal, **1948:** 263
Passamaquoddy tidal power project, **1948:** 55 [8], 93 [11]; **1949:** 80; **1950:** 33, 121 [4, 13]; **1951:** 16 [13], 239 [9]; **1952–53:** 31 [11]
　News conference remarks, **1950:** 3 [5], 34 [10]
Pastore, Gov. John O., **1948:** 261 [5]; **1949:** 260 [12]; **1952–53:** 298 [5], 299
Patent laws, letter to Secretary Wallace, **1945:** 11
Patent Office, **1946:** 18 (p. 57), 199 [18]; **1947:** 7 (p. 88); **1948:** 104, 126 [6], 128 [2, 4], 204 [3]; **1950:** 9 (p. 54), 118
Patents, **1947:** 4 (p. 35)
　Alien, disposal, **1946:** 84 [9]
　Applications for, **1947:** 7 (p. 88)
　Practices and policies, report, **1947:** 109
Paterson, Chat, **1952–53:** 287n.
Patman, Repr. Wright, **1948:** 212 [2], 213; **1950:** 23 [9], 34 [11]
Patman (Repr. Wright) bill on housing, **1945:** 208 [19]
Patman Housing Act, **1946:** 35, 263; **1947:** 99
Patronage, political, **1948:** 84 [12]
　Conference with Democratic leaders on, **1949:** 89 [14, 19]
　Mississippi congressional delegation, alleged denial to, **1949:** 95 [7]
　News conference remarks, **1949:** 78 [10], 89 [14, 19], 95 [7], 148 [15]
Patten, Harold A., **1948:** 207
Patterson, Richard C., Jr., **1947:** 62 [5, 8]; **1950:** 146 [10]
Patterson, Robert P., **1945:** 116n.; **1949:** 155 [21]; **1950:** 121 [1]; **1952–53:** 7 [6], 26 [27], 310
　See also War, Secretary of (Robert P. Patterson).
　Appointment as Secretary of War, **1945:** 137 [5]
　News conference remarks on, **1945:** 129 [4], 137 [5]
　Statement on World War II defense contract, **1951:** 284
Patterson, William J., **1945:** 202 [2]
Patterson-McCormick newspapers, denunciation of the President, 1944 campaign, **1948:** 268
Patteson, Okey L., **1948:** 222 [10], 242 [2, 3]
Patton, Gen. George S., Jr., **1950:** 121 [1]
Patton, James G., **1946:** 173 [17]; **1947:** 191 [3]; **1952–53:** 203n.
　Letter, **1951:** 206
Paul, Randolph, **1946:** 134
Paul, Saint, **1945:** 227
Paul I, King, **1948:** 61
Pauley, Edwin W., **1945:** 32, 97; **1946:** 30 [3], 37 [1, 2, 4], 41 [8], 43 [13], 53 [8], 59, 61 [16], 66 [12], 78 [11], 95 [3, 22], 119 [8], 141 [11], 199 [6]; **1947:** 31 [5], 36 [20], 46 [15], 243 [11]; **1948:** 21 [4], 128 [4]; **1949:** 58 [6], 200 [1]; **1950:** 179 [9], 206 [17]

Pauley, Edwin W. — *continued*
　Letter, **1945:** 13
　News conference remarks on, **1945:** 31 [7], 60 [6], 118 [3], 157 [12]
　Personal Representative on Reparations Commission
　　Appointment, **1945:** 13, 15
　　Mission to Japan, statement, **1945:** 182
Pauls Valley, Okla., campaign remarks, **1948:** 214 [7]
Pawley, William D., **1946:** 113; **1947:** 62 [6, 9], 127 [9]
Pay, **1948:** 182
　See also Wages.
　Army, **1946:** 192 [8]
　Cabinet, members of, **1948:** 285 [10]
　Congress, members of, **1945:** 52 [19], 128; **1946:** 17 [7], 191; **1947:** 6 [4], 62 [19]; **1948:** 11 [3]; **1949:** 137; **1951:** 22 [10]; **1952–53:** 207, 258 [14]
　　Letter, **1945:** 59
　Diplomats, **1945:** 52 [19]
　Federal judiciary, **1945:** 128; **1946:** 17 [7]
　Flag and general officers, retired, **1951:** 108 [4]
　Government employees, **1945:** 128; **1946:** 17 [7], 18 (pp. 52, 65, 66, 86), 143 [10], 187, 192 [8]; **1947:** 7 (p. 57), 62 [19], 102; **1948:** 5 (p. 22), 63, 150 [3], 153, 157, 165, 174 [9], 175, 261 [12]; **1949:** 3, 7 [35], 8 (p. 48), 94, 95 [1], 96, 127, 137, 218, 228, 242; **1951:** 152, 226; **1952–53:** 1, 11, 18 (pp. 71, 113), 86
　Executives, **1949:** 58 [20], 218
　Foreign Service personnel, **1946:** 202; **1949:** 8 (p. 54)
　Terminal leave, **1947:** 7 (p. 89)
　Government officials, **1948:** 11 [3]
　Industrial, **1950:** 202
　Laborers on public works projects, **1947:** 81
　Military personnel, **1946:** 18 (p. 75), 192 [3, 5, 6, 14, 17, 21], 193, 194, 199 [17]; **1948:** 5 (pp. 22, 26, 27), 60, 175; **1949:** 8 (pp. 57, 59), 40 [12], 112 [3], 218; **1950:** 9 (pp. 61, 63); **1952–53:** 18 (pp. 69, 70), 64 [17], 231, 275, 322
　　Mustering-out, **1947:** 4 (p. 15), 7 (p. 68), 2 (p. 8)
　　Terminal leave, **1947:** 2 (p. 8), 6 [3, 18, 21]; **1948:** 5 (p. 26), 228 [10]
　Overtime, **1949:** 155 [20], 239
　Philippine Army veterans, **1946:** 38
　Postal employees, **1946:** 18 (p. 87); **1948:** 175
　President's, **1952–53:** 377 [3, 30]
　　Increase, **1948:** 285 [10]; **1949:** 137
　Railroad employees, **1952–53:** 306 [6]
　Retired generals, **1952–53:** 377 [30]
　Teachers, **1948:** 108, 134, 157, 165, 183 [5], 203, 241, 258, 259 [4], 262, 268; **1949:** 2, 8 (p. 76)

Pay — *continued*
  Vice President's, increase, **1948:** 285 [10]; **1949:** 137
  War workers, **1946:** 18 (p. 69)
  Women, **1948:** 30
Payard, Jean, **1950:** 218
Payroll Savings Plan, **1948:** 76
Payroll taxes, **1947:** 4 (p. 37), 6 [35]; **1948:** 4 [8], 5 (pp. 23, 34, 35, 37), 8 (p. 88), 131, 220; **1949:** 5, 7 [2–4, 36, 42, 46], 8 (pp. 49, 67, 71), 151; **1950:** 8 [11, 30], 9 (pp. 50, 53, 76, 77), 84; **1951:** 13 (pp. 80, 99)
  See also Taxes.
Peace conferences
  Paris, **1946:** 53 [19], 119 [25], 126 [22], 173 [2, 16], 181, 199 [19], 202, 219; **1947:** 2 (p. 9)
  21-nation, proposed, **1946:** 126 [9]
Peace pipe and plaque, gift to President, **1948:** 118 [1]; **1950:** 127 [7]
Peace treaties, **1947:** 2 (p. 9), 88 [12], 114, 234
"Peacemakers", painting, **1947:** 31 [1]
Peanuts
  Marketing quota, **1947:** 35
  Price supports, **1950:** 9 (p. 86), 83; **1952–53:** 210
Pearl Harbor, **1947:** 35, 110, 111; **1952–53:** 344
  Attack, **1945:** 45, 51, 93, 97, 122; **1946:** 21 [13], 186 [6]; **1948:** 262; **1949:** 148 [9]; **1951:** 306
    Army and Navy reports, **1945:** 116, 118 [5, 12, 14, 17], 129 [10]
    Congressional investigation, **1945:** 129 [7, 10], 202 [15]
    News conference remarks, **1945:** 107 [6], 116, 118 [5, 12, 14, 17], 129 [7, 10], 202 [15]
    Trial of U.S. officers in command, question of, **1945:** 107 [6], 116, 118 [5, 14]
  Remarks at, **1950:** 267
Pearlstine, Milton, **1945:** 147n.
Pearson, Drew, **1946:** 61 [21]; **1949:** 40 [18]
Pearson, Lester B., **1948:** 9 [22]; **1949:** 68; **1952–53:** 98 [32], 102
Peas, shortage, **1947:** 18
Pease, Herbert H., **1946:** 142
Peck, Col. Harry, **1951:** 151
Peekskill, N.Y., riot at, **1949:** 205 [7]
Peel, Roy V., letter, **1952–53:** 363
Pegrum, George, **1948:** 191n.
Peiping, **1946:** 265
Peleliu Island, U.S. capture of, **1945:** 161
Pelley, John J., **1945:** 221 [9]; **1946:** 54n., 55n., 56
Pels, J. A., **1951:** 123
Pemiscot County (Mo.) Fair, remarks, **1945:** 163
Pendergast, James M., **1946:** 173 [8]; **1949:** 192 [19]; **1952–53:** 21 [6]
Pendergast, T. J. **1952–53:** 31 [11]
Pendleton, Oreg., **1950:** 122
Pendleton Act (1883), **1952–53:** 84
Penn, William, **1951:** 241

Pennekamp, John., **1947:** 231n.
Pennsylvania, **1947:** 104; **1949:** 211 [11]; **1950:** 121 [8]
  Campaign remarks, **1948:** 139 [1–3], 193 [1], 225 [2], 226, 227 [1–5], 248–252; **1952–53:** 240 [1], 286 [8], 303 [9, 10], 304–307, 308 [2–6]
  Candidates for public office, **1948:** 227 [1, 5], 248, 249, 251; **1950:** 3 [13], 38 [5, 13], 270 [11]; **1951:** 179 [5]; **1952–53:** 240 [1], 286 [8], 303 [9, 10], 304–306, 308 [2–6]
  Chester Springs, **1945:** 76 [4]
  Colonial assembly, **1951:** 144
  Democratic Party, **1952–53:** 26 [3]
  Floods, control and relief, **1952–53:** 50
  Gov. James H. Duff, **1949:** 194; **1950:** 29 [15], 137 [20, 24], 185
  Gov. George H. Earle, **1947:** 67 [10]
  News conference remarks, **1950:** 3 [13], 38 [5, 13], 270 [11]
  Primary elections, **1950:** 137ftn. (p. 421)
Pennsylvania, University of, **1952–53:** 305
Pensions, **1949:** 267 [2]
  Defense workers, **1951:** 11
  Industrial plans, **1950:** 9 (p. 72)
  Plans, Government and private, **1951:** 12 [44, 48, 54]
  Social security.
    See main heading, Social security.
  Steelworkers, **1949:** 214 [11]
  Veterans, **1947:** 6 [2]; **1948:** 5 (p. 33), 175; **1949:** 8 (p. 64), 40 [13], 58 [14]; **1950:** 9 (p. 70); **1951:** 13 (pp. 102, 103), 181, 182; **1952–53:** 18 (p. 109), 138, 367 (p. 1160)
Pepper, Sen. Claude, **1946:** 66 [6]; **1947:** 70 [23], 231n.; **1948:** 41 [7]; **1950:** 105 [2], 217 [12]
Perez, Leander, **1951:** 200 [10]
Perez, Manuel A., **1946:** 240
Perez Damera, Maj. Gen. Genovevo, **1947:** 14 [6]
Pericles, **1949:** 204
Periodicals, application fees, **1947:** 35
Perkins, Frances, **1946:** 216 [1, 10]; **1948:** 259 [1]
  News conference remarks on, **1945:** 40 [1], 127
  Resignation as Secretary of Labor, **1945:** 37, 40 [1]
Perkins, Fred W., **1947:** 180 [13]; **1952–53:** 98 [25]
Perkins, George W., **1949:** 112 [1]
Perlman, Philip B. (Solicitor General), **1949:** 267 [18]; **1950:** 34 [1], 38 [16]; **1952–53:** 244, 297, 373
Perlmeter, Irving, **1952–53:** 253 [1]
Permanent Appropriation Repeal Act of 1934, **1949:** 229
Permanent Joint Board on Defense, U.S.-Canada, **1946:** 21 [8]; **1947:** 111; **1948:** 43
Peron, Juan, **1946:** 86 [8], 199 [10]; **1948:** 9 [6]; **1949:** 40 [18]
Perry, Joseph S., **1952–53:** 35ftn. (p. 154)
Persche, Maurice, **1949:** 210n.

Pershing, Gen. John J., **1949:** 103n., 223, 234 [1]
  Death of, **1948:** 161
  85th birthday, message, **1945:** 133
Persia, aggression against Greek city-states, **1951:** 8
Persian empire, **1949:** 259, 262
Person, C. T., **1952–53:** 32
Personal property tax, **1949:** 126
Personnel directors, remarks, **1946:** 33
Personnel management, Federal, **1947:** 135
Personnel Recruitment Act, Federal, **1952–53:** 137
Peru
  Foreign Minister Manuel C. Gallagher, **1951:**
    67n.
  Liberation by San Martín, **1950:** 212
  U.S. Ambassador Prentice Cooper, **1947:** 127
    [12]; **1948:** 77 [2]
Peterson, Eric, **1948:** 277
Peterson, Harry J., **1952–53:** 32
Peterson, Gov. Val, **1948:** 116 [1]; **1950:** 111;
    1952–53: 44 [8], 97
Petroleum, **1945:** 150; **1946:** 101
  See also Oil.
  U.S. operation of refineries, statement, **1945:** 158
  U.S.-U.K. agreement, renegotiation, **1945:** 76 [9],
    107 [3], 214
  Wartime administration, **1945:** 214; **1946:** 37 [4],
    95 [27], 101
Petroleum Council, National, **1951:** 108 [5]
Petroleum products
  Armed forces, use of, **1952–53:** 379
  Consumption in U.S., **1952–53:** 379
  Imports from Venezuela, **1952–53:** 239
  Production, **1952–53:** 379
Pettit, H. Frank, **1952–53:** 303 [4]
Petropolis, Brazil, **1947:** 188n.
Pfost, Mrs. Gracie, **1952–53:** 269n., 270 [9, 10]
Phelan, Edward J., **1948:** 130 [1]
Phelps Dodge Corp., **1951:** 204, 214; **1952–53:** 37
Phi Beta Kappa key, honorary, presentation to the
    President, **1951:** 122
Philadelphia, Pa., **1947:** 138, 189; **1948:** 11 [11],
    101, 104, 183 [7]; **1952–53:** 49 [10], 63
  American Legion Convention, **1949:** 194, 195
  Campaign remarks, **1948:** 225 [2], 226; **1952–53:**
    304
  Centennial Exposition (1876), **1949:** 102
  Chapel of the Four Chaplains, dedication, **1951:**
    30
  Declaration of Independence, 175th anniversary,
    1951: 145 [9]
  Democratic National Convention, **1949:** 190;
    1950: 12
    President's address accepting nomination,
      1948: 160
  Liberty Bell, tolling to open Savings Bond drive,
    1950: 133
  Mayor Joseph S. Clark, Jr., **1952–53:** 249n.

Philadelphia, Pa. — *continued*
  Mayoralty election, **1951:** 179 [5]
  Republican National Convention, **1948:** 138 [3],
    139 [2], 160, 183 [6, 7], 227 [1], 229, 231 [1],
    232, 252, 258, 266
  Richard Allen Housing Project, **1948:** 225 [2]
  Special grand jury for crime investigation, **1951:**
    63 [1]
  Transit strike in, **1949:** 32 [19]
Philadelphia Bulletin, **1947:** 210 [2]
Philbin, Repr. Philip J., **1952–53:** 292 [11]
Philbrick, Herbert, **1952–53:** 300
Philippine Alien Property Administration, **1947:** 80
Philippine-American Finance Commission, Joint,
    1949: 178
Philippine Property Act, **1947:** 80
Philippine War Damage Commission, **1946:** 119 [1,
    14]; **1947:** 6 [2]
  Termination, **1951:** 64
Philippines, **1945:** 45, 131; **1946:** 247; **1947:** 171;
    1948: 20, 278 [29]; **1949:** 28ftn. (p. 127)
  Ambassador Joaquin M. Elizalde, **1951:** 49 [5],
    151
  Army veterans, benefits, **1947:** 134
  Assistance, **1946:** 4, 18 (p. 66), 90, 173 [10], 192
    [5]; **1947:** 6 [27], 7 (p. 68); **1949:** 8 (p. 54),
    162, 178; **1952–53:** 18 (p. 76), 95, 367 (p.
    1140)
    Economic, **1950:** 9 (p. 60), 34 [15], 179 [1], 180,
      238 [5], 270 [9], 273 [2, 10], 278 [11]; **1951:**
      13 (p. 74), 49 [5], 64
    Letter, **1945:** 176
    Military, **1950:** 173, 175, 193, 204; **1951:** 114,
      193 [2]
    Statement, **1945:** 175 [2]
  Commission on health and rehabilitation, **1945:**
    129 [2]
  Commonwealth, 10th anniversary, statement,
    1945: 190
  Communism in, **1951:** 96, 114; **1952–53:** 55, 367
    (p. 1140)
  Copra trade, **1946:** 29
  Corregidor, rock fragment from, acceptance,
    1951: 151
  Currency, reduction of required gold coverage,
    1945: 189
  Defense, **1949:** 184
  Economic development, **1949:** 178
  Elections, **1949:** 240 [6], 260 [8]
  General relations treaty, **1946:** 185
  Independence, **1945:** 169, 190; **1946:** 18 (p. 66),
    31, 63, 76, 86 [9], 90, 116, 119 [3], 141 [15];
    1950: 119, 151, 232
    Address, **1946:** 159
    Statements, **1945:** 24, 157 [2]; **1946:** 158
  Japanese occupation, **1945:** 190
    Currency, **1946:** 31

Philippines — *continued*
Japanese peace mission to, **1951:** 49ftn. (p. 176)
Korean war, participation, **1950:** 217 [16], 232, 296; **1951:** 170, 208
Manila, **1945:** 45, 106 [9]; **1946:** 6 [9]
Mission to, small business study, **1945:** 228
Mutual defense treaty with U.S., **1951:** 207, 208, 216; **1952–53:** 5, 26 [21], 95
News conference remarks, **1945:** 44 [2, 4], 129 [2], 157 [2]; **1946:** 84 [27], 86 [4, 6], 119 [3], 126 [17], 136 [11], 141 [15], 173 [10], 192 [5]; **1950:** 34 [15], 179 [1, 4], 217 [16], 238 [5], 270 [9]
Osmena, Sergio, **1945:** 24, 157 [2], 176; **1946:** 31, 111
Discussions with, statement, **1945:** 175 [2]
Letter, **1945:** 189
Philippine Insurrection, **1951:** 181
Quirino, Elpidio, **1948:** 82; **1949:** 11 [16], 22 [9], 113 [6], 144 [9], 155 [22], 171 [1, 8, 14], 172, 173, 176, 178, 179 [14, 20], 260 [8]; **1950:** 34 [15], 180, 273ftn. (p. 689), 278 [11]; **1951:** 130n., 136, 193 [8], 207, 208, 224 [3]
Recapture by U.S., **1945:** 161, 178
Rehabilitation, **1948:** 5 (p. 30)
Rice exports to, **1947:** 18
Romulo, Gen. Carlos P., **1951:** 40n., 49 [5], 208n.
Roxas y Acuña, Manuel, **1946:** 111, 122n.; **1947:** 226 [3]
Death of, **1948:** 78
Sugar exports, **1947:** 64
Trade with U.S., **1946:** 90; **1947:** 236 [7]
Trial of enemy collaborators, **1946:** 63
U.S. Ambassador, appointment, **1947:** 88 [9], 95 [20]; **1948:** 185 [5], 278 [8], 288 [9]
U.S. Ambassador Myron Cowen, **1950:** 180; **1951:** 113 [4]
U.S. Ambassador Paul V. McNutt, **1946:** 257 [20]
U.S. Ambassador Emmet O'Neal, **1947:** 134
U.S. bases, question of withdrawal, **1948:** 283 [20]
U.S. forces in, **1950:** 173
U.S. military facilities in, **1951:** 84
U.S. relations with, **1949:** 172, 240 [6]; **1951:** 64, 208
U.S. teachers in, **1949:** 187
Veterans benefits, **1946:** 38, 74, 122; **1948:** 5 (p. 31)
War damage restoration, **1947:** 7 (p. 57); **1948:** 5 (p. 30)
Philippines, U.S. High Commissioner.
See United States High Commissioner to the Philippines (Paul V. McNutt).
Phillips, William, **1945:** 210
Phillips Petroleum Co., **1951:** 165 [2]
Phoenix, Ariz., campaign address, **1948:** 207

Phosphate
Mining, **1950:** 124 [7], 127 [1]
Production, proposed in West, **1948:** 201
Stockpiling, **1948:** 8 (p. 78)
Photographers
Commendation of, **1947:** 164
Press, White House, dinner for, **1947:** 209 [1]
Photographers' Association, White House, award presentations, **1951:** 43
Photography, the President's interest in, **1951:** 43, 227 [9]
Physical fitness, **1950:** 48, 272; **1951:** 9
Youth, **1946:** 268; **1948:** 89
Physically handicapped persons, **1946:** 217
Employment, **1947:** 184
Veterans, **1948:** 2
Physicians, **1946:** 1
Role in health program, **1945:** 192
Shortage, **1947:** 98; **1948:** 181 [2]; **1949:** 85
Physicians, Dentists and Allied Specialists, National Advisory Committee on the Selection of, **1951:** 9
Pianetto, Mario, deportation proceedings against, **1950:** 253 [15]
Piano, gift to the President, **1951:** 99
Piano Manufacturers Association, **1951:** 99n.
Piano playing, the President's, **1946:** 86 [26]
Pick, Brig. Gen. Lewis A., **1947:** 141 [2]; **1949:** 183, 196; **1950:** 129 [1, 2]; **1951:** 158; **1952–53:** 97, 98 [8, 34], 194, 195 [1]
Pick-Sloan plan, Missouri valley development, **1950:** 3 [14]; **1952–53:** 3, 98 [8]
Pickens, Jane, **1949:** 82
Pickett, Clarence E., **1952–53:** 244, 373
Pickett, Repr. Tom, **1949:** 148 [15]
Pidgeon, Walter, **1951:** 116n.
Pieces of eight, Spanish, **1951:** 290
Pierce, Alfred R., **1952–53:** 303 [7]
Pierce, Franklin, **1952–53:** 7 [10]
Pierce, Walter, **1952–53:** 277 [1]
Piercey, John H., **1952–53:** 317 [1]
Pig iron, shortage of, **1948:** 170 [7]
Pike, Sumner T., **1946:** 242 [2]; **1947:** 46 [23]; **1948:** 88 [1]; **1950:** 15ftn. (p. 118), 179 [10], 186 [3, 5, 7]
Pilgrimage of American Churchmen, Washington, **1951:** 241
Pinchot, Gifford, **1952–53:** 277 [3]
Pincus River (Texas), **1948:** 208 [7]
Pine, Judge David E., **1952–53:** 136 [19]
Pinehurst, N.C., visit to, **1949:** 11ftn. (p. 98)
Piñero, Gov. Jesús T., **1946:** 163 [8], 177 [2], 186 [14], 240; **1947:** 14 [14], 166; **1948:** 26 [17], 35, 185 [5]; **1949:** 45 [17], 84 [13]; **1952–53:** 104
Pipelines, gas, **1950:** 88
Pipelines, oil, **1947:** 35

Piper, A. M., **1952–53:** 98 [8]
Pirates, Barbary, Jefferson's expedition against,
    1951: 80
Pittenger, Repr. William, **1946:** 228
Pittman, Sen. Key, **1948:** 202 [2]
Pittman, Gov. Vail, **1948:** 202 [1, 2]
Pittsburgh, Pa., **1947:** 242
    Allegheny County Free Fair, **1949:** 202
    Campaign remarks, **1948:** 193 [1], 252; **1952–53:**
        240 [1], 306 [8], 307
    Mayor David L. Lawrence, **1948:** 252; **1949:**
        202n.; **1950:** 38 [13]; **1952–53:** 240n., 307
    Newspapers, reading by President, **1947:** 210 [2]
Pittsburgh Pirates, baseball team, **1946:** 129 [6]
Pittsfield, Mass.
    Campaign remarks, **1948:** 259 [1]
    Mayor Robert Capeless, **1948:** 259n.
Pius XII, Pope, **1946:** 100, 253; **1947:** 178, 185n.,
    189; **1949:** 270; **1951:** 80
Pizarro, Francisco, **1951:** 130
Placement Service, Farm, **1951:** 154
Plaistow, N. H., campaign remarks, **1952–53:** 295
    [6]
Plambeck, Herbert, **1948:** 194 [8], 195
Planning Association, National, **1949:** 25
Plant breeding, **1948:** 8 (p. 77)
Platte, Casper, **1949:** 211 [2]
Plaza, Galo, visit of, **1951:** 118 [3], 129, 130, 132 [4,
    6, 8], 134, 136
Plaza, Señora Galo, **1951:** 136
Pleven, René, **1951:** 22 [12], 25
Plowing Match, National, **1948:** 194 [8], 195
Plutarch's Lives, **1949:** 204
Plymouth, England, **1951:** 282
Pneumonia, **1952–53:** 249
    Prevention, **1951:** 135
Po Valley, Italy, **1947:** 196
Poage, Repr. W. R., **1948:** 212 [4, 5]; **1952–53:** 7 [6],
    149 [4]
Pocatello, Idaho, **1950:** 121 [1]
    Campaign remarks, **1948:** 119
Pocket veto, use by the President, **1950:** 250 [14]
Poe, Clarence, **1951:** 307n.
Poe, Thomas, **1950:** 294n.
Pogue, L. Welch, **1946:** 95 [14]
Point 4 program, **1949:** 249, 252, 273; **1950:** 6, 25,
    42, 78, 92, 119, 143, 154, 159, 177, 269,
    289; **1951:** 53, 114, 134, 170, 259; **1952–
    53:** 5, 20, 55, 57, 72, 81, 107 [2], 144, 169,
    196, 218, 228 [10], 257, 261, 262, 274 [1],
    303 [2], 307, 313 [2], 315 [5], 322, 337, 354,
    366
    Administration, statement, **1950:** 240
    Administration by ECA, **1951:** 114
    Advisory Board on International Development,
        1950: 294
    Agricultural trainees, remarks to, **1951:** 262

Point 4 program — *continued*
    Appropriations, **1952–53:** 205, 281
        Letter, **1950:** 220
    Asia, **1952–53:** 144
    Campaign remarks, **1952–53:** 281
    India, **1952–53:** 55, 57
    Indochina, **1952–53:** 57
    Latin America, **1952–53:** 55
    News conference remarks, **1949:** 22 [3, 6], 28 [11],
        214 [10], 267 [5]; **1950:** 8 [23], 11 [8], 230
        [2], 278 [6]; **1951:** 16 [1], 56 [26]
    Report on, statement, **1951:** 83
    Turkey, **1952–53:** 57
Poirier, Peter, **1952–53:** 294, 295 [1, 3, 5, 6]
Poland, **1946:** 34, 247; **1947:** 21; **1951:** 253
    Bierut, Boleslaw, **1946:** 64
    Free elections in, question of, **1947:** 62 [3]
    Government in exile in London, **1945:** 60 [6, 8,
        14, 16]
    Katyn Forest massacre, **1952–53:** 317 [7]
    Korean armistice commission membership,
        1952–53: 121
    Mikolajczyk, Stanislaw, **1947:** 218 [11]
    Moscow conference of Polish leaders, **1945:** 60
        [6, 8, 14, 16]
    News conference remarks, **1945:** 4 [22], 20 [10],
        60 [6, 8, 14, 16]; **1946:** 30 [2], 78 [17], 86 [4,
        31]
    Oil drilling equipment, shipment from Nether-
        lands, **1952–53:** 105
    Osobka-Morawski, Edward, message, **1945:** 78
    Political refugees from, **1947:** 140
    Potsdam conference, action re Poland, **1945:** 91,
        97
    Provisional Government of National Unity,
        1945: 60 [6, 8, 14, 16], 78, 91, 97
        Establishment of diplomatic relations with,
            1945: 77, 78n.
    Relief for, **1945:** 186
    Soviet domination, **1948:** 53, 86
    UNRRA grain shipments, **1946:** 64
    U.S. Ambassador Arthur Bliss Lane, **1945:** 77, 78
        Resignation, **1947:** 62 [3]
    Yalta agreement on, **1947:** 56
Police, International Association of Chiefs, **1945:**
    62
Police, wiretapping by, **1949:** 211 [12]
Police state methods, **1947:** 209 [2, 11, 14, 16]
Police states, security problems of, **1950:** 207
Policy Board, Interdepartmental Safety Council,
    1950: 74
Poling, Lt. Clark V., **1951:** 30n.
Poling, Daniel, **1946:** 268n.; **1949:** 73n., 110n.;
    1950: 32n., 197; **1951:** 30n., 179 [5];
    1952–53: 7 [9]
Poliomyelitis, **1946:** 26
    Drive for funds to combat, **1949:** 205 [2]

Polish army in exile, veterans, immigration to U.S., **1950:** 167

Polish Legion of American Veterans, **1951:** 291

Polish Provisional Government of National Unity. *See* Poland.

Political Action Committee, CIO, remarks, **1952–53:** 230

Political parties.

    See also specific parties.

    Continuation in office, question of limit on, **1952–53:** 98 [15]

    Ethical standards, **1951:** 188 [3, 15], 237

    Income taxes, deduction of bad debt loans to political parties, **1952–53:** 127 [7, 9]

    Midterm conventions, proposed, **1951:** 261 [5]

    National conventions, unit rule respecting delegations, **1952–53:** 98 [41]

    Outlawing of, **1948:** 97 [18]

Political philosophy, the President's, **1949:** 220, 231 [8]

Political Science Association, American, **1951:** 261 [5]; **1952–53:** 68, 96

Political system, U.S., **1948:** 32; **1952–53:** 7 [10], 123 [10], 184, 286 [3], 289

    Party system, **1949:** 52 [5, 7]

    Separation of powers, **1949:** 27, 52 [6]

Politics, comments on, **1946:** 75 [14, 21]; **1952–53:** 69

Politics, women's role in, **1949:** 219

Polk, James, **1946:** 201; **1948:** 245; **1951:** 90 [16]; **1952–53:** 107 [10] 229n.

Poll tax, **1946:** 75 [29], 78 [5]; **1948:** 20, 166 [3]; **1949:** 52 [6], 118 [23]; **1950:** 23ftn. (p. 134)

    Proposed abolition, **1951:** 16 [20]; **1952–53:** 169

Pollard, James E., *Presidents and the Press*, **1948:** 86

Pollock, James K., **1949:** 94n.

Polls, political, **1952–53:** 35 [8], 129, 136 [8], 143, 218, 267

    Preelection, **1948:** 243 [6]), 258, 261 [7, 14], 264 [5]

    President's views on, **1951:** 56 [6, 14], 209 [7]

Polls, public opinion, **1945:** 193 [5]; **1947:** 218 [7]; **1949:** 22 [7], 36; **1950:** 86 [25], 152 [5, 7], 267

Polo, Mo., campaign remarks, **1948:** 194 [13]

Pomerene, Attlee, **1951:** 300ftn. (p. 641)

Ponder, Dan R., **1948:** 209

Pontiac, Mich., campaign remarks, **1948:** 183 [5]; **1952–53:** 317 [6]

Pope, Doyle, **1952–53:** 194

Pope, Fortune, **1952–53:** 291n.

Pope, James P., **1946:** 244; **1951:** 108 [9], 171 [10]

Pope Pius XII, **1946:** 100, 253; **1947:** 178, 185n. 189; **1949:** 270; **1951:** 80

Popularity, the President's, Gallup poll on, **1951:** 56 [6]

Population growth, Europe, **1952–53:** 65

Population growth, U.S., **1948:** 8 (pp. 75, 83–85,

Population growth, U.S. — *continued* 92); **1949:** 154, 249, 250 [3]; **1950:** 2, 9 (p. 46), 110 [8], 157, 193; **1951:** 5, 226

"Porgy and Bess," musical, **1952–53:** 221 [10]

Portal-to-Portal Act

    Approval, **1947:** 93

    News conference remarks, **1947:** 62 [16], 95 [3]

Porter, Adm. David D., **1947:** 31 [1]

Porter, Paul A., **1946:** 36, 41 [22, 25]; **1947:** 221 [9]; **1952–53:** 34

    See also Price Administrator.

Portland, Maine, **1950:** 243

    Harbor improvements, **1952–53:** 367 (p. 1143)

Portland, Oreg., **1945:** 64 [1, 14]

    Campaign remarks, **1948:** 126 [1]

    Mayor Earl Riley, **1948:** 126 [1]

    Rose festival, **1948:** 88 [8]

Portrait, gift to the President, **1951:** 291n.

Portrait of Himself, Titian, **1948:** 71 [1]

Ports, protection against sabotage, **1951:** 13 (p. 83); **1952–53:** 303 [2]

Portsmouth, N.H., **1952–53:** 171

    Campaign remarks, **1952–53:** 295 [1]

Portugal, **1949:** 155 [23]

    Assistance, **1947:** 238

    Caeiro da Matta, José, **1949:** 68

    U.S. Ambassador, question of appointment, **1952–53:** 31 [8]

    U.S. Ambassador Lincoln MacVeagh, **1948:** 48

Post Office Department, **1945:** 22 [1]; **1946:** 192 [8]; **1947:** 6 [10], 7 (pp. 86, 93), 135, 174 [2], 181 (pp. 399, 402, 403); **1948:** 4 [1], 175; **1949:** 8 (p. 85); **1950:** 9 (p. 51), 73, 170

    Advisory Board, establishment, **1949:** 130

    Donaldson, Jesse M., **1945:** 76 [1]

    Programs review, **1950:** 196

    Purdum, Smith, **1945:** 132 [1]

    Reorganization, **1949:** 127, 130, 140; **1950:** 53; **1951:** 45, 226; **1952–53:** 18 (p. 85), 84, 85, 115 [14], 117, 135, 137

Post Office Department Financial Control Act of 1950, **1949:** 140n.

Postal Rate Revision and Federal Employees Salary Act of 1948, approval, **1948:** 157

Postal rates, **1947:** 7 (p. 86); **1948:** 5, 157, 175; **1949:** 7 [32, 51], 8 (pp. 47, 85), 140; **1950:** 8 [13], 9 (pp. 46, 95); **1951:** 12 [53], 13 (pp. 81, 83–85), 45, 226; **1952–53:** 18 (p. 85), 231, 367 (p. 1144)

    Increase, **1947:** 7 (p. 55); **1951:** 45

    Military personnel, **1947:** 18

    Special services, fees for, **1951:** 45

Postal Supervisors, National Assciation of, **1950:** 247

Postal service, **1946:** 18 (p. 87); **1947:** 7 (p. 84), 180 [1], 181 (p. 399); **1948:** 5 (p. 50); **1949:** 7 [32], 8 (p. 85); **1950:** 9 (p. 95), 214 [3], 247; **1951:** 13 (p. 83), 226; **1952–53:** 18 (p. 85)

Postal service — *continued*
  Airmail, payments to carriers, **1952–53:** 18 (p. 83), 367 (p. 1144)
  Costs, **1951:** 13 (pp. 84, 85), 45
  Deficit, **1947:** 6 [8, 12, 37], 7 (p. 86); **1948:** 5 (p. 50), 175; **1949:** 7 [32], 8 (pp. 47, 85), 140; **1950:** 8 [13], 9 (p. 95), 170; **1951:** 12 [53], 13 (pp. 81, 84), 45, 226; **1952–53:** 18 (p. 85), 231, 367 (p. 1144)
  Efficiency, improvement, **1952–53:** 18 (pp. 85, 116)
  Employees, **1946:** 192 [8]; **1947:** 7 (p. 93), 180 [1]
    Pay, **1946:** 18 (p. 87); **1948:** 175; **1950:** 170; **1951:** 45, 152, 226
  Equipment, modernization, **1951:** 226
  Expenditures, **1948:** 175
  Laws against misuse, **1951:** 63 [1]
  Promotion of World War II veterans in, veto of bill, **1950:** 170
  Quarters for, authority of Postmaster General to lease, **1952–53:** 214
  Postmaster General (Jesse M. Donaldson), **1948:** 9 [7], 59; **1949:** 7 [51], 8 (p. 85); **1950:** 8 [13], 9 (p. 95), 196, 247; **1951:** 12 [53], 45, 226; **1952–53:** 155n., 248
  Campaign remarks on, **1952–53:** 292 [11]
  Post office quarters, authority to lease, **1952–53:** 214
  Resignation, **1952–53:** 383
  Postmaster General (Robert E. Hannegan), **1946:** 15 [12]; **1947:** 7 (p. 86), 14 [16, 18, 22], 35, 70 [24]
    See also Hannegan, Robert E.
  News conference remarks on, **1945:** 76 [1], 181 [12]
  Resignation, **1947:** 227
  Postmaster General (Frank C. Walker)
    Letter, **1945:** 22 [2]
    Resignation, **1945:** 22 [1, 2]
  Postmasters
    Appointment, **1949:** 89 [1, 4, 15], 113 [7]
    Senate confirmation of, **1948:** 88 [6], 139 [1]
  Postmasters, National Association of, **1951:** 226
Potatoes, **1947:** 76; **1948:** 5 (p. 43), 175
  Marketing quotas, proposed, **1950:** 121 [2]
  Price supports, **1949:** 8 (p. 79); **1950:** 9 (p. 86), 83, 111, 121 [2]
  Surplus, **1950:** 29 [7], 121 [2]
    Disposition, **1951:** 2 [22]
Poteat, W. L., **1951:** 256
Potofsky, Jacob, **1948:** 261 [11]; **1950:** 294n.; **1951:** 239 [8]
Potomac River bridges, **1946:** 43 [8, 10]
Potsdam agreement, **1945:** 97, 186
  News conference remarks, **1945:** 202 [9], 221 [19]
  Text, **1945:** 91
Potsdam conference, **1945:** 79n., 82n., 93, 163, 182, 188; **1946:** 18 (p. 41); **1947:** 74; **1948:** 86,

Potsdam conference — *continued*
    126 [4], 239; **1949:** 28 [20] 86, 136; **1950:** 121 [1]; **1951:** 88, 232, 253; **1952–53:** 107 [14], 378
  See also Potsdam agreement.
  Agreements, **1946:** 30 [2], 126 [3]; **1947:** 46 [7], 196, 210 [1]; **1949:** 86; **1950:** 80 [4]
  Broadcast on return, **1945:** 97
  Joint report with Allied leaders, **1945:** 91
  News conference remarks, **1945:** 67 [1, 2], 76 [8], 106 [8, 18], 132 [10], 147 [19, 20], 164 [4]; **1946:** 27 [7, 17], 30 [2], 53 [10], 126 [3, 8]; **1947:** 90 [7], 236 [6]
Potsdam Declaration on Japanese surrender, **1945:** 100, 145, 216; **1949:** 117
Pottsville, Pa., campaign remarks, **1952–53:** 305
Poultry, **1947:** 202, 209 [2], 224
  Conservation, **1947:** 205 [3, 19]
  Consumption, **1948:** 8 (p. 92)
  Feed, conservation, **1947:** 210 [3]; **1948:** 14
  Shortage, **1948:** 8 (p. 70)
Pound, British, devaluation of, **1949:** 214 [5]
Poundcake, gift to the President, **1951:** 223n.
Powell, Repr. Adam C., Jr., letter, **1945:** 168
Powell, Mrs. Ferdinand, Sr., **1949:** 73n., 110n.; **1950:** 32n.
Powell, Paul, **1948:** 218 [7]
Power Commission, Federal, Chairman (Mon C. Wallgren), **1950:** 265, 266; **1951:** 101 [6], 108 [10, 14], 165 [2]
  Letter, **1951:** 55
Power projects, **1946:** 18 (pp. 60, 61, 82), 86 [16], 94, 97, 176; **1947:** 4 (p. 33), 95 [28], 110, 231, 243 [18]; **1948:** 5 (p. 46), 8 (pp. 67, 78); **1950:** 121 [4], 134; **1951:** 13 (pp. 81–85), 55, 185; **1952–53:** 5, 15, 18 (pp. 88, 89), 129, 241, 274 [2, 5], 276, 280 [1], 291, 304, 376
  Appropriations, **1950:** 193; **1951:** 120
  Arkansas, **1945:** 128; **1952–53:** 193, 194, 195 [1, 2]
  Atomic, **1945:** 93; **1951:** 13 (p. 85); **1952–53:** 18 (p. 87), 170
  Bay of Fundy, **1951:** 16 [13]
  Bonneville Power Administration, **1952–53:** 388
  California, **1951:** 120; **1952–53:** 277 [3, 4]
  Campaign remarks on, **1948:** 122 [4], 124 [4], 126 [1, 2], 128; **1952–53:** 280 [6], 281, 298 [2, 3]
  Chile, **1950:** 46 [15]; **1951:** 59
  Colorado, **1952–53:** 280 [4, 6]
  Columbia River, **1945:** 128, 155, 164 [8], 165; **1951:** 13 (p. 85); **1952–53:** 271, 274 [1], 297, 388
  Connecticut River, **1952–53:** 292 [7]
  Cumberland River, **1951:** 13 (p. 85), 185
  Expenditures for, **1952–53:** 367 (pp. 1146–1147)
  Federal policy, **1952–53:** 62

Power projects — *continued*
  Generating capacity, **1952–53:** 62, 388
    Expansion, **1951:** 11, 13 (p. 76), 167
  Generating facilities, shortage, **1948:** 165
  Hells Canyon, **1952–53:** 18 (p. 88), 270 [9]
  Hydroelectric.
    See Hydroelectric power projects.
  IBRD loans for, **1951:** 219
  Idaho, **1952–53:** 270 [9]
  Kansas, **1951:** 185
  Kentucky Dam, Tennessee River, **1945:** 165
  Legislation, proposed, **1951:** 120
  Missouri River, **1945:** 128, 164 [8], 165; **1952–53:**
    3, 62, 109, 194, 266 [6]; **1951:** 120, 183, 185
  Montana, **1952–53:** 268 [5], 269, 271
  New England, **1950:** 3 [5, 9, 15], 29 [21], 34 [10],
    203 [21]; **1952–53:** 294
  New Mexico, **1948:** 208 [2]
  News conference remarks, **1945:** 164 [6, 8]
  Niagara River.
    See Niagara River, power and water resources
    development.
  Nuclear, **1948:** 122 [3]
  Oklahoma, **1951:** 185
  Pacific Northwest, **1951:** 11, 120, 185; **1952–53:**
    18 (p. 89), 277 [1], 367 (p. 1146)
  Passamaquoddy tidal project, **1950:** 3 [5], 34 [10];
    1951: 16 [13], 239 [9]; **1952–53:** 31 [11]
  Power pools, **1952–53:** 175ftn. (p. 432)
  Private vs. public, **1948:** 120 [3], 148, 149, 160,
    202 [5], 207, 208 [7], 209, 212 [2], 213, 214
    [3], 216 [2], 217, 218 [7–9, 14], 233 [3], 236,
    237 [1], 242 [3]; **1949:** 2, 112 [2], 155 [11],
    202; **1950:** 2, 3 [22], 46 [2], 124 [4], 125,
    127 [1], 129 [1], 157; **1951:** 11, 215;
    1952–53: 62, 69, 143, 149 [9], 194, 267, 289
    [3], 388
  Public utility holding companies, bill to prohibit,
    1948: 233 [3]
  Republican opposition, **1952–53:** 218
  St. Lawrence-Great Lakes System, **1947:** 111
  St. Lawrence River, **1945:** 148, 155
  St. Lawrence Seaway.
    See main heading, St. Lawrence Seaway.
  Sale of, proposed, **1952–53:** 315 [3]
  Seoul, Korea, **1950:** 268
  Transmission lines, public, **1948:** 200 [9], 201,
    202 [4, 5], 203, 228 [12]
  TVA.
    See Tennessee Valley Authority.
  Washington, **1952–53:** 62
Prasad, Rajendra, **1950:** 20
Prayer
  Comments on, **1950:** 317
  National day of, proposed, **1949:** 28 [15]; **1950:**
    309 [6]
    Victory in the East, **1945:** 105, 106 [1]
    Victory in Europe, **1945:** 26 [4], 27

Prefabricated housing, **1946:** 258, 263; **1947:** 14
  [12]; **1948:** 37; **1950:** 29 [16], 113
Prejudice, racial and religious, **1948:** 256
Prencinradio, **1947:** 7 (p. 95)
Preparedness, **1945:** 218
Presentation ceremonies, addresses or remarks.
  See Addresses or remarks at presentation
  ceremonies.
Presidency, **1950:** 37, 134
  Administration, President's assessment of,
    1952–53: 317 [8], 333, 378
  Candidates.
    See Candidates for public office.
  Civil rights enforcement, **1952–53:** 288
  Civilian nature of office, **1952–53:** 286 [6]
  Comments on, **1947:** 88 [11]; **1948:** 55 [12], 86,
    124 [1], 126 [3, 6], 210 [2]; **1949:** 25, 72 [6],
    119 [3, 4], 234 [12]; **1950:** 21, 127 [2], 315;
    1951: 27, 32, 56 [25], 270, 290; **1952–53:**
    45, 98 [2], 130, 184, 195 [2], 240 [2], 250,
    266 [5], 268 [4, 9], 270 [10], 283, 288, 291,
    295 [3, 9], 298 [10, 12], 308 [5], 319 [2], 321
    [2], 335, 366, 378
  Conduct of, **1947:** 31 [3]; **1948:** 21 [14], 243 [1]
  Constitutional responsibilities, **1947:** 169
  Daily routine, the President's, **1948:** 139 [3]
  Dignity of office, **1952–53:** 377 [30]
  Emergency powers, **1950:** 307; **1952–53:** 38, 79
  Executive Office.
    See Executive Office of the President.
  Executive privilege, **1951:** 108 [4, 11]
  Expense allowances for, **1952–53:** 361
  First year in office, **1946:** 78 [6, 9]
  Foreign policy
    Constitutional responsibility for, **1951:** 33 [3]
    Role in shaping, **1952–53:** 289 [4]
  Former Presidents
    Press attacks on, **1951:** 8, 56 [24, 25]
    Proposed Senate membership, **1952–53:** 26 [10,
      11], 75 [8], 377 [30]
  Inauguration Day plans, **1952–53:** 353 [15], 377
    [6, 8, 15]
  Incumbent, role in selection of successor, **1952–
    53:** 21 [18], 64 [13], 98 [21], 123 [19], 127
    [18], 156 [3, 7], 175 [3]
  Method of election to, proposed amendment,
    1950: 29 [18, 24], 52 [8]
  Military men in office, comments on, **1952–53:** 7
    [10], 282 [7], 289 [3, 9], 292 [2], 295 [3],
    307, 308 [5], 313 [1, 3], 321 [4], 377 [18]
  News conference remarks, **1950:** 29 [18, 24], 34
    [2], 38 [21], 44 [9, 15], 46 [9], 52 [8], 86 [17],
    209 [14], 258 [15]; **1952–53:** 342 [20], 377
    [1, 5, 7, 9]
  Party leadership role, **1952–53:** 286 [6]
  Plans upon leaving office, the President's, **1952–
    53:** 75 [7], 98 [6, 13, 39], 334 [6], 342 [14,
    17, 20], 353 [6], 377 [15, 17, 19, 29, 30]

Presidency — *continued*
  Powers of, **1948:** 92; **1949:** 28 [5], 94, 148 [4, 9],
      155 [7], 234 [3], 240 [15]; **1950:** 34 [2], 37,
      38 [21], 46 [9], 209 [14]; **1951:** 13 (p. 65),
      49 [17], 56 [15], 270; **1952–53:** 98 [14], 107
      [1, 7, 10, 12, 13], 110, 115 [13], 131, 136 [9,
      14, 17, 19], 142, 156 [4], 161, 175 [16], 270
      [4], 283, 335, 366
  Records, custody and disposition, **1952–53:** 64
      [4], 149 [14, 19], 174, 334 [11, 15] and ftn.
      (p. 1059)
  Reelection, question of President's candidacy,
      1952–53: 2 [6], 7 [2, 7, 10, 12], 17 [20], 21
      [1, 8, 9, 11, 20, 31], 26 [3, 8, 15, 18], 28, 31
      [13, 15], 35 [2], 44 [12], 49 [4, 13, 14, 16], 64
      [2, 10, 13, 16], 69, 88 [2], 98 [2, 29], 115 [3,
      11], 125, 127 [15], 195 [3], 197 [8]
  Relationship to Congress, **1950:** 258 [15]
  Responsibilities of office, **1945:** 163; **1952–53:**
      318
  Salary, the President's, **1952–53:** 377 [3, 30]
      Increase, **1948:** 285 [10]; **1949:** 137
  Subpoenas by legislative branch, protection
      from, **1950:** 44 [9, 15]
  Succession to, **1946:** 6 [17], 18 (p. 52); **1947:** 22
      Message to Congress, **1945:** 63
  Tax-free expense account, question of termina-
      tion, **1951:** 22 [10]
  Term of office, **1952–53:** 26 [8], 98 [29]
  Third term prohibition, proposed amendment,
      1951: 49 [13]
  Transition to new administration, **1952–53:** 342
      [15], 367 (p. 1129)
  Walks, the President's, **1952–53:** 377 [4]
*Presidency and the Executive Office of the President,
    The,* George A. Graham, **1951:** 270
President-elect (Gen. Dwight D. Eisenhower)
  Cabinet designations, **1952–53:** 334 [19], 342 [10,
      11]
  Civil defense, meeting with president of State
      directors' association, **1952–53:** 353 [3]
  Dulles, John Foster, meeting with, **1952–53:** 353
      [2]
  Election victory, statement, **1952–53:** 325
  Executive functions, discussions on transfer of,
      1952–53: 331, 366, 378
  Joint statement with President, **1952–53:** 331
  Korean war
      Prisoners, agreement with administration pol-
          icy, **1952–53:** 334 [1, 3, 5]
      Visit to front, **1952–53:** 345 [1, 4], 353 [4]
      White House conference, proposed, **1952–53:**
          345 [1]
  Letters
      Government Contract Compliance, transmit-
          ting report of Committee on, **1952–53:**
          389
      Government personnel procedures, **1952–53:**
          370

President-elect (Eisenhower) — *continued*
  MacArthur, Gen. Douglas, meeting with, **1952–
      53:** 353 [2]
  News conference remarks on, **1952–53:** 345 [1],
      353 [5]
  President Truman, meeting with, **1952–53:** 334
      [2, 5, 8, 14, 16]
  Railroad car, offer to President for return to
      Independence, **1952–53:** 377 [19]
  Telegram from the President, **1952–53:** 326
President Pierce, **1949:** 89 [2]
President Pro Tempore of the Senate, succession to
      Presidency, proposed, **1945:** 63
President Pro Tempore of the Senate (Kenneth
      McKellar), **1945:** 2, 34; **1946:** 125
  Letters, **1946:** 122
      Child care centers, Federal aid for, **1945:** 159
      Foreign war relief activities, report, **1945:** 85
      Salaries of Members of Congress, **1945:** 59
  News conference remarks on, **1946:** 21 [2], 143
      [10], 186 [4], 226 [18]
President pro tempore of the Senate (Arthur H.
      Vandenberg), **1947:** 2, 6 [35], 26, 39, 56,
      146, 151; **1948:** 15 [6], 81, 165, 183 [1]
  Letters.
      See Congress, letters to Members of.
  News conference remarks on, **1947:** 6 [35], 145
      [20], 191 [14]
President of the Senate.
  See Vice President (Alben W. Barkley).
President Van Buren, **1949:** 89 [2]
President Wilson, **1949:** 89 [2]
Presidential appointments, Senate confirmation,
      1948: 88 [6], 139 [1]
Presidential documents published in Federal Reg-
      ister, App. B, **1945:** p. 603; **1946:** p. 525;
      1947: p. 550; **1948:** p. 988; **1949:** p. 605;
      1950: p. 778; **1951:** p. 669
Presidential electors, certification, **1950:** 75
Presidential Electors Association, **1949:** 17
Presidential flag and seal, **1945:** 175 [5]
Presidential reports to Congress App. C, **1945:** p.
      613; **1946:** p. 533; **1947:** p. 557; **1948:** p.
      996; **1949:** p. 611; **1950:** p. 785; **1951:** p.
      677; **1952–53:** p. 1240
  See also Congress, reports to, messages trans-
      mitting.
Presidential Research Board, **1947:** 4 (p. 35)
President's Advisory Commission on Universal
      Training, **1946:** 268; **1947:** 2 (p. 12), 7 (p.
      63); **1948:** 5, 26, 86, 190; **1950:** 138
President's Advisory Committee on Civil Rights,
      1947: 2 (p. 9), 9, 130, 215, 218 [4]
President's Advisory Committee on the Merchant
      Marine, **1949:** 133; **1950:** 76
President's Air Policy Commission, **1947:** 148, 149,
      161
  Report, **1948:** 7, 9 [12]

President's Airport Commission, **1952–53:** 40, 41

President's Airport Commission, Chairman (James H. Doolittle), **1952–53:** 155

President's Amnesty Board, **1946:** 270

President's Commission on the Health Needs of the Nation, **1952–53:** 268 [8], 353 [1], 367 (p. 1158), 369

President's Commission on Higher Education, **1947:** 206

Report, **1947:** 235

President's Commission on Immigration and Naturalization, **1952–53:** 244, 251, 364, 373

President's Commission on Internal Security and Individual Rights, **1951:** 20, 35, 37 [12], 104, 108 [6]

President's Commission on Migratory Labor, **1951:** 75, 154

President's Commission on Water Resources Policy, **1950:** 34 [17]

President's Committee on Administrative Management, **1952–53:** 84, 85

President's Committee on Civil Rights, **1948:** 2, 20, 265; **1952–53:** 169, 290, 315 [6], 317 [8], 329

President's Committee on Employment of the Physically Handicapped, **1952–53:** 243

President's Committee on Equality of Treatment and Opportunity in the Armed Forces, **1948:** 265; **1951:** 299; **1952–53:** 315 [6]

President's Committee on Foreign Aid, **1947:** 219n.

President's Committee on the Integration of the Medical Services of the Government, **1946:** 139

President's Committee on National Employ the Handicapped Week, **1948:** 169; **1949:** 197; **1950:** 208; **1951:** 195

President's Committee on Religion and Welfare in the Armed Forces, **1949:** 73; **1950:** 32, 95; **1951:** 17, 100; **1952–53:** 297

President's Communications Policy Board, establishment, **1950:** 40

President's Conference on Community Responsibility to Peacetime Servicemen and Women, **1949:** 110n.

President's Conference on Industrial Safety, **1949:** 55; **1950:** 155; **1952–53:** 150

President's Emergency Commission on the Missouri Valley, proposed, **1951:** 183n.

President's Evaluation Commission, **1946:** 163 [1]

President's Fire Prevention Conference, **1949:** 55

President's Food Committee, **1947:** 209 [2]

President's grandfather, trips from Kansas City to San Francisco in mid-1800's, **1945:** 68

President's Highway Safety Conference, **1946:** 96, 106; **1947:** 8, 27, 82, 118; **1948:** 279; **1949:** 55, 114; **1951:** 42, 121; **1952–53:** 93

President's Highway Safety Conference, Chairman (Maj. Gen. Philip B. Fleming), **1950:** 229

President's Materials Policy Commission, **1951:** 19; **1952–53:** 179, 191, 192, 203, 355

President's Materials Policy Commission, Chairman (William S. Paley), **1952–53:** 179

President's National Labor-Management Panel, **1947:** 236 [3]

President's Panel on Labor Problems, **1947:** 87

Presidents and the Press, James E. Pollard, **1948:** 86

President's Scientific Research Board, **1946:** 234, 262 [2]; **1947:** 109, 183, 206; **1948:** 22, 186

Chairman (John R. Steelman), **1948:** 150 [5]

President's Soviet Protocol Committee, **1945:** 125

President's Special Board of Inquiry on Air Safety, **1947:** 115

President's Temporary Commission on Employee Loyalty, **1947:** 89n.

President's Water Resources Policy Committee, **1952–53:** 32

Presque Isle, Maine, **1950:** 121 [2]

Press

Accessibility after return to private life, the President's, **1952–53:** 377 [13]

American Newspaper Guild, address, **1950:** 177

American Society of Newspaper Editors

Address, **1950:** 92

Attendance at news conference, **1952–53:** 98

Associated Church Press, remarks, **1952–53:** 100

Associated Press, address, **1947:** 76

Awards to, **1947:** 48

Business, news conference with editors, **1947:** 196

Remarks to, **1952–53:** 339

Campaign remarks on, **1948:** 212 [6], 214 [1], 219

Cartoonists, remarks to, **1951:** 290

Columbia Scholastic Press Association, address, **1952–53:** 63

Columnist, **1949:** 58 [30, 31]

Comments on, **1951:** 113 [17]

News conference remarks on, **1948:** 278 [20, 21, 27, 37]

Comments on, **1947:** 62 [7], 74, 95 [2], 164; **1949:** 52 [1], 72 [10, 17], 220, 226 [18]

Communist, denunciation of the President in, **1948:** 215

Communist publications, proposed identification requirement, **1950:** 254

Correspondents from NATO countries, attendance at news conference, **1951:** 188 [2]; **1952–53:** 149 [1]

Criticism of President, **1949:** 36, 54; **1951:** 8, 56 [24, 25]; **1952–53:** 288

Editorial opinion on election, **1948:** 261 [12, 14]

Editorial writers, news conference with, **1947:** 210

Editors and publishers groups, addresses or remarks to, **1951:** 18, 61, 88, 94, 160

Farewell to press corps, the President's, **1952–53:** 377 [1, 30]

Press — *continued*
  Farm, **1949:** 91
  Foreign journalists
    Attendance at news conference, **1950:** 253 [16]
    German editors and publishers, remarks to,
      1949: 165
    Remarks to, **1951:** 94, 160
    Visit to U.S., **1949:** 105, 211 [1], 165
  Freedom of, **1946:** 75 [15]; **1950:** 254
  Government control, question of, **1952–53:** 107
    [1, 8, 9]
  Interviews, President's policy on granting, **1950:**
    38 [4]
  Labor, support of Democrats, **1948:** 257 [4]
  Look magazine, article on the President, **1951:**
    193 [14, 18]
  Luncheon, Kansas City, Mo., **1950:** 313
  Meeting with Senator Taft on labor relations,
    1948: 187
  News conferences
    Article on, **1951:** 70 [8]
    Change in setting for, **1950:** 117 [1]
    Comments on, **1952–53:** 342 [20], 359 [13], 377
      [1, 5, 7, 9]
    Statement by the President, failure to report,
      1951: 16 [15, 19]
    Transcripts.
      See News conferences, the President's.
  Newsmen
    Indictment in Louisiana, **1951:** 209 [6]
    Picnic at Key West for, **1950:** 80n.
  Newspaper column by the President, question of,
    1952–53: 342 [20]
  Postal rates for, **1949:** 7 [32]; **1951:** 45, 226;
    1952–53: 18 (p. 85)
  Photographers, White House, dinner for, **1947:**
    209 [1]
  Point 4 program, dissemination of information
    on, **1950:** 177
  Political views of, **1952–53:** 308 [2], 322
  Predictions on outcome of election, **1948:** 266
  Presidents, press attacks on, **1952–53:** 319 [2]
  President's reading of, **1947:** 210 [2]
  Relations with, the President's, **1950:** 38 [1–4];
    1951: 90 [6]; **1952–53:** 98 [26]
  Remarks to, on death of President's mother,
    1947: 164
  Republican control, comments on, **1952–53:** 69,
    247 [1, 8], 289 [2], 316, 317 [5, 7, 8], 318,
    319 [2]
  Religious, remarks to members, **1949:** 83
  "Road Back to America," editorial, **1950:** 146 [4]
  Role in traffic safety, **1947:** 82
  Security responsibilities, **1950:** 207; **1951:** 247 [1,
    5, 12], 298 [1], 300 [15], 302
  Stevenson, Gov. Adlai E., attitude toward,
    1952–53: 321 [6]

Press — *continued*
  Swedish, comments on Margaret Truman's visit,
    1952–53: 233 [1, 6, 9]
  Treatment of the President, 1944 campaign,
    1948: 268
  Vincent case, editorial comment on, **1952–53:**
    353 [14]
  Wartime censorship, **1946:** 13
  White House corps, comment on, **1951:** 37 [11]
  White House Photographers' Association,
    awards presentation, **1951:** 43
Press Association, Brazilian, **1949:** 105
  News conference remarks, **1949:** 30 [2], 66 [20]
Press Club, **1945:** 127
Press Club, Capital, acceptance of plaque, **1952–
  53:** 153
Press Club, National, **1950:** 11ftn. (p. 109); **1952–
  53:** 136 [16]
Press Conference, Inter-American, **1950:** 273 [6]
Press conference.
  See News conferences.
Press releases, list, Appendix A, **1945:** p. 591; **1946:**
  p. 515; **1947:** p. 539; **1948:** p. 973; **1949:**
  p. 595; **1950:** p. 765; **1951:** p. 657; **1952–
  53:** 1217
Prettyman, E. Barrett, **1945:** 129 [4], 132 [1]
Pribyson, Stanley J., **1952–53:** 292 [2, 4, 5, 7, 8],
  293, 298 [7–11]
Price, Byron, **1946:** 13; **1948:** 9 [14]
  Letter, **1945:** 119
  News conference remarks on, **1945:** 118 [1, 9,
    13], 127, 193 [11], 202 [9]
  Study on relations between U.S. occupation
    forces and German people, **1945:** 118 [1,
    9, 13]
    Appointment as Personal Representative for,
      1945: 119
    Report on, **1945:** 193 [11], 201, 202 [9]
Price, Repr. Melvin, **1952–53:** 321 [7]
Price, Utah
  Campaign remarks, **1948:** 200 [2]
  Mayor A. D. Keller, **1948:** 200 [2]
Price adjustments, **1948:** 8 (p. 62)
Price Administration, Office of, **1945:** 128, 180, 202
  [3]; **1946:** 18 (p. 74), 35, 36, 99, 148, 152,
  153, 156, 172, 179, 232, 256; **1947:** 7 (p.
  86), 36 [15, 19], 46 [28], 60, 65, 152, 160,
  209 [14], 232 [8]; **1948:** 220, 226, 227 [2],
  259 [3]; **1952–53:** 241, 305, 319 [1]
  Commendation, statement, **1945:** 17
  Expediting Committee, proposed, **1946:** 95 [8,
    13]
  News conference remarks, **1945:** 157 [5], 211 [1];
    1946: 27 [2, 10], 37 [16], 43 [7], 72 [2, 16],
    84 [22], 86 [7], 95 [8, 13], 177 [12, 19], 199
    [5], 262 [10]
  Reestablishment, question of, **1950:** 209 [12]
  Termination, **1946:** 262 [3]

Price Administrator (Chester Bowles), **1945:** 17
Price Administrator (Michael V. DiSalle), **1952–53:** 31 [1]
Price Administrator (Paul A. Porter), **1946:** 86 [7], 215 [4], 232, 237 [21], 249, 250 [11], 256
Price Control Act, extension, **1946:** 18 (pp. 53, 54), 148, 232
  Approval, **1946:** 179
  News conference remarks, **1946:** 129 [17], 136 [3], 141 [8, 10], 143 [6, 8], 163 [3], 173 [13], 177 [1, 5]
  Veto of bill, **1946:** 152
    Broadcast, **1946:** 153
Price Control Act, repeal, **1947:** 70 [4]
Price Control Act, Wherry amendment, comment on, **1945:** 60 [13]
Price controls, **1945:** 17, 104, 128, 203 [3]; **1946:** 2, 18 (pp. 49, 53–55, 62), 35, 67, 73, 99, 125, 148, 156, 164, 172, 193, 213, 256, 262 [3]; **1947:** 7 (pp. 75, 86), 64, 68, 76, 143, 224, 242; **1948:** 5 (pp. 22, 51, 52), 8 (pp. 65, 74), 80, 101, 167, 176, 189; **1949:** 2, 5, 8 (p. 88); **1950:** 205, 303; **1951:** 4, 11, 13 (p. 78), 23, 28, 44, 91, 98, 107, 123, 137n., 143, 164, 167, 176, 199, 279; **1952–53:** 5, 15, 18 (pp. 77, 79, 80), 33, 70, 82, 218, 231, 241, 268 [5], 272, 273, 289 [11], 292 [9], 293, 300, 305, 306 [6], 313 [5], 315 [2], 319 [1], 320, 321 [2], 322, 376
  See also Rent control; Wage controls; *specific commodities.*
  Agencies, question of reorganization, **1951:** 209 [15]
  Amending legislation, proposed, **1951:** 22 [9]
  Approval of bill, **1946:** 179
  Broadcasts, **1946:** 153, 232
  Campaign remarks, **1948:** 114 [3], 121, 124 [1, 4], 134, 136 [4, 5], 138 [2, 4, 7, 8], 183 [1, 2, 5, 6], 184, 194 [1], 198 [6], 199, 202 [2], 203, 205, 211, 212 [9], 215, 216 [5], 220, 226, 227 [1, 2, 4, 6], 228 [1], 229, 231 [1–3], 233 [1, 3], 235 [4], 240 [4], 242 [3], 247, 248, 249, 251
  Defense Production Act amendments, **1952–53:** 190
  Delay in implementing, **1951:** 2 [19], 22 [8]
  Extension, **1948:** 160
    Need for, **1951:** 108 [12]
  General Ceiling Price Regulation, **1951:** 23n., 167
  Housing, **1945:** 208 [19], 211 [1]
  Legislation, proposed, **1948:** 165
  Letter, **1950:** 215
  Message to the American people, **1951:** 123
  Message to Congress, **1946:** 179
  News conference remarks, **1945:** 64 [10] [16], 202 [5], 208 [19], 211 [1]; **1946:** 27 [16], 37 [16],

Price controls — *continued*
  News conference remarks — *continued*
    84 [22], 173 [13], 192 [18], 199 [5], 215 [6], 223 [1], 237 [21]; **1947:** 19 [1], 62 [17], 70 [11, 20], 107 [2], 191 [5], 209 [11, 14], 210 [3], 218 [15], 226 [7], 232 [6, 8]; **1948:** 11ftn. (p. 104), 15 [2], 26 [11], 71 [19], 163 [12, 14, 22], 170 [1, 8], 174, [14], 285 [3]; **1950:** 109 [14], 203 [6, 9, 22, 24], 206 [4], 217 [11], 238 [13, 15], 253 [9], 258 [5], 270 [13], 287 [19, 25], 309 [7, 9], 318 [3, 10]; **1951:** 2 [14, 16, 21, 27], 7 [10, 13, 16], 12 [18], 16 [3], 49 [21], 101 [8], 118 [1], 132 [5], 140 [2], 247 [11]
  Renewal, need for, **1948:** 252, 255, 258, 259 [3–5], 261 [1, 6], 264 [5], 267 [2], 268
  Termination, **1946:** 232, 249, 252; **1947:** 4 (pp. 15, 16, 23, 29), 18, 65, 75, 76, 152, 175; **1948:** 256
  Veto of bill, **1946:** 152
Price Decontrol Board, **1946:** 152, 177 [1, 12, 18], 179, 223 [1], 232; **1947:** 146n.
Price Index, Consumers, **1952–53:** 18 (p. 95)
Price Stabilization, Director of, filling of position, **1950:** 287 [26]
Price Stabilization, Director of (Ellis G. Arnall), **1952–53:** 221 [3]
Price Stabilization, Director of (Michael V. DiSalle), **1951:** 37 [7], 49 [21], 56 [5], 101 [8], 118 [2, 4], 123, 275 [10]; **1952–53:** 15, 34
  See also DiSalle, Michael V., Price Administrator.
Price Stabilization, Office of, **1951:** 23, 91, 118 [4], 123, 199, 247 [1, 11], 304; **1952–53:** 15, 18 (p. 80), 33, 82, 342 [15]
Price supports, **1945:** 42, 128; **1946:** 18 (pp. 59, 80), 57, 61 [12], 79, 94, 152, 193; **1947:** 4 (p. 33), 7 (pp. 58, 78, 94), 70 [16, 18], 76, 78 [25], 128; **1948:** 2, 5 (pp. 25, 42, 43), 8 (pp. 69, 93), 99, 194 [11], 234; **1949:** 2, 5, 8 (p. 79), 39, 151, 154, 202, 203, 226ftn. (p. 503); **1950:** 2, 6, 9 (pp. 46, 85, 86), 83, 111, 127 [5], 134, 202, 279; **1951:** 11, 13 (pp. 87–89), 33 [5], 91, 118 [15]; **1952–53:** 5, 15, 18 (p. 91), 69, 126, 129, 210, 218, 231, 266 [3, 4, 7, 9], 267, 268 [5], 274 [2], 276, 277 [6], 281, 282 [6], 284 [4], 285, 291, 300, 307, 311 [2], 312, 313 [1–4], 314, 315 [1, 4, 5], 321 [3–6], 322, 360, 367 (p. 1148)
  See also specific commodities.
  Brannan plan, **1949:** 72 [13], 90n., 122 [4], 182 [3]; **1950:** 86 [18–20, 28]; **1951:** 12 [15, 45], 22 [13], 227 [22]
  Campaign remarks, **1948:** 117, 134, 138 [5], 175, 194 [11], 195, 204 [2, 4], 206 [3], 213, 214 [7], 216 [2, 7], 217, 218 [7], 222 [1, 6, 7], 223, 228 [3, 10, 12], 231 [5–7], 233 [1, 2, 5,

Price supports — *continued*
  Campaign remarks — *continued*
      6], 234, 237 [4], 240 [5, 6], 242 [3], 246, 259
      [5], 267 [1, 3], 280 [6]
  Extension, **1948:** 155
  Legislative history, **1948:** 216 [5]
  Loans, **1948:** 268
  News conference remarks, **1948:** 181 [9], 285 [5];
      1949: 7 [34], 30 [5], 45 [4], 72 [13], 122 [4],
      182 [3], 231 [15]; **1951:** 7 [10, 16], 12 [15,
      45], 22 [13], 33 [5], 63 [17], 70 [6]
  Parity, question of revision, **1951:** 63 [17]
  Perishable commodities, **1950:** 121 [7]
  Reduction, question of, **1948:** 216 [1]
Price-fixing, **1947:** 70 [10]; **1952–53:** 204
Prices, **1945:** 128, 202 [3]; **1946:** 2, 18 (pp. 49–51,
    56, 62), 67, 153, 179, 193, 249; **1947:** 2 (pp.
    7, 12), 4 (pp. 15, 17, 22, 28, 29), 58, 62 [17],
    67 [4], 68, 76, 88 [3, 14], 90 [3], 97, 110,
    131, 141 [9], 145 [13, 24], 152, 158, 177 [7,
    12], 180 [21, 23], 181 (p. 406), 191 [3], 209
    [11, 14], 217, 220, 221 [8], 238; **1948:** 2, 8
    (pp. 68, 70, 73, 75, 77, 89, 90), 63, 76, 101,
    175, 181 [17], 183 [6], 184, 211, 212 [4, 5,
    9], 214, [5], 218 [8], 219, 220, 223, 225 [1],
    226, 231 [2, 3], 235 [4], 237 [4], 242 [1], 257
    [2], 258, 259 [3–5], 260, 261 [2, 6, 8], 264 [3,
    5], 267 [2]; **1950:** 6; **1952–53:** 33, 215, 221
    [4, 8], 287, 313 [5]
  See also Inflation; Price controls; *specific com-*
    modities.
  Agricultural.
    See under Agricultural commodities.
  Building materials, **1948:** 8 (p. 64)
  Campaign remarks, **1948:** 115, 117, 124 [4, 5],
    183 [7], 198 [6, 7], 200 [5], 222 [5, 9], 228
    [3, 8, 12], 229, 231 [1, 5], 236, 251
  Commission on, proposed, **1947:** 78 [16, 22]
  Critical raw materials, **1952–53:** 15
  Decrease, **1949:** 30 [2, 4], 32 [7], 151; **1951:** 107
  Effect of farm productivity on, **1948:** 174 [11]
  Electricity, **1948:** 8 (p. 64)
  Farm.
    See Farm economy.
  Fluctuations, **1952–53:** 15
  Food, **1947:** 67 [15], 214; **1948:** 8 (pp. 64, 73), 21
    [12], 26 [10, 11, 13, 14], 88 [12], 121, 170
    [1], 174 [14], 181 [9], 189, 195, 261 [8];
    1950: 83, 86 [18], 318 [3]; **1951:** 12 [18], 33
    [5], 37 [14], 91, 167, 199
  Fuel, **1948:** 8 (p. 64), 170 [1, 8]
  General price freeze, **1952–53:** 319 [1]
  Government surplus ships, **1950:** 257
  Housing, **1948:** 5 (pp. 38, 40), 8 (p. 34), 37, 189,
    205, 220, 262
  Increase, **1947:** 4 (p. 16), 75, 197, 198, 202, 224,
    242; **1948:** 2, 5 (p. 29), 8 (pp. 63–65, 72,

Prices — *continued*
  Increase — *continued*
    74), 21 [12], 121, 134, 157, 165, 167; **1949:**
    5, 8 (p. 61), 151; **1950:** 191 [11], 202, 318
    [3]; **1951:** 7 [13], 11, 25, 118 [1], 123, 167,
    176, 179 [3]; **1952–53:** 18 (p. 64), 33, 83,
    282 [8], 292 [9], 319 [1], 366
  Industrial, **1947:** 107 [2]; **1948:** 8 (p. 88)
  Investigation, **1947:** 177 [7]
  Labor-management conference on, **1947:** 177
    [12]
  News conference remarks, **1945:** 52 [10], 137 [11],
    157 [5], 172 [3], 181 [1], 202 [5], 221 [1, 3];
    1946: 30 [4], 37 [14, 15, 16, 18, 19], 72 [2,
    16], 86 [4], 173 [13], 192 [7, 15, 18, 21], 226
    [6], 262 [12]; **1947:** 14 [9], 62 [15, 17], 70 [2,
    4, 10, 11, 15, 22], 78 [17, 22], 90 [5], 95 [12,
    27], 107 [2, 15], 213; **1948:** 4 [1, 2, 3, 6, 16],
    26 [11, 13], 49 [12], 88 [12], 170 [1, 8], 174
    [11, 14], 181 [9, 17]; **1950:** 86 [18], 191 [11],
    318 [3]
  Pricing practices, application of Federal Trade
    Commission Act and Clayton Act, **1950:**
    166
  Public power, **1948:** 217
  Reconversion period, broadcast, **1945:** 180
    Hooper rating re, **1945:** 181 [1]
  Reduction, **1947:** 14 [9], 76, 85, 107 [2], 131, 176,
    214, 242, 243 [2]; **1948:** 8 (p. 90), 170 [1]
    To pre-Korean war level, prospects for, **1951:**
    63 [24]
  Retail, **1952–53:** 15, 215
  Stabilization, **1945:** 172 [3]; **1946:** 18 (pp. 53, 80),
    35, 152, 232; **1947:** 2 (p. 3), 62 [17], 147,
    152, 180 [6, 19], 196, 214, 224, 242; **1948:**
    1, 5 (p. 23), 21 [12], 37, 183 [1], 199, 212
    [5], 215, 226, 227 [3, 4, 6, 9], 231 [4, 8], 261
    [9]; **1949:** 5, 8 (p. 88), 93 [5], 151, 154;
    1950: 127 [4], 243, 303; **1951:** 11, 91, 118
    [15]; **1952–53:** 5, 33, 82, 83, 110, 118, 129,
    161, 190, 241, 367 (p. 1141)
  Statistics collection, **1952–53:** 18 (p. 92)
  Supports.
    See Price supports.
  Wage-price policy, **1946:** 18 (p. 51), 30 [4], 35, 36,
    67, 72 [2], 73; **1947:** 2 (p. 3), 62 [17], 76,
    107 [2], 116, 224, 242; **1948:** 8 (pp. 88–90),
    101, 165, 167, 183 [6], 195, 212 [5], 216
    [15], 217, 218 [3, 10], 226, 231 [6], 233 [3],
    234, 240 [4, 6], 242 [3], 246, 251, 268;
    1949: 2, 5, 90, 151, 250 [3]; **1950:** 6, 243,
    303; **1951:** 23, 118 [1], 304; **1952–53:** 15,
    82, 118, 161, 376
  Wholesale, **1952–53:** 15, 215
  World level of, **1952–53:** 15
Priest, Repr. J. Percy, **1950:** 206 [10]
Priestly, Joseph, **1952–53:** 306 [4]

Primary elections, **1952–53:** 169
　Alabama, **1948:** 93 [13]
　Arkansas, **1952–53:** 228 [2]
　California, **1951:** 298 [3]
　Direct presidential primaries, proposed, **1951:**
　　179 [15]
　District of Columbia, **1952–53:** 44 [4], 175 [5, 13]
　Florida, **1950:** 105 [2, 11]
　Idaho, **1950:** 209 [9]
　Illinois, **1952–53:** 21 [12]
　Indiana, **1950:** 16 [11], 169 [4]
　Kansas, **1950:** 206 [3]
　Minnesota, **1952–53:** 7 [3], 64 [8]
　Missouri, **1949:** 192 [6]; **1950:** 3 [8, 13], 16 [9, 11,
　　19], 23 [5, 11], 38 [5, 6], 86ftn. (p. 251), 169
　　[4, 5, 7], 203 [15], 206 [2]; **1952–53:** 21 [12].
　　26 [18], 75 [6], 221 [5]
　National, proposed, **1952–53:** 21 [14], 28, 44 [4]
　Nebraska, **1948:** 77 [3], 117
　New Hampshire, **1952–53:** 26 [3, 8], 28, 31 [13,
　　15], 49 [13], 64 [8]
　New York, **1949:** 200 [4]
　North Carolina, **1950:** 23 [11], 179 [13]
　Ohio, **1948:** 84 [2], 93 [12]
　Pennsylvania, **1950:** 3 [13], 137ftn. (p. 421)
　Republican, **1951:** 275 [13]
　South Carolina, **1950:** 16 [19]
　Utah, **1952–53:** 21 [10]
　"White primaries," elimination of, **1952–53:** 290
　Wisconsin, **1948:** 71 [11]; **1952–53:** 247 [2]
Prince, David E., **1952–53:** 289 [7, 8]
Princess Elizabeth, **1951:** 282, 288
Princeton University, **1947:** 117; **1950:** 12; **1952–**
　53: 45, 174
Princeton University Press, publication of Jeffer-
　son papers, **1950:** 136
Printing and Binding Acts, **1949:** 147
Prío Socarrás, Carlos, **1948:** 170 [5], 282, 283 [16]
Priorities, business agreements on, **1947:** 236 [8]
Prisoners of war, **1947:** 35
　German, **1945:** 40 [4]
　　Repatriation, **1946:** 18 (p. 46)
　Korean, **1952–53:** 121, 127 [12], 131, 162, 163,
　　166 [3], 232, 334 [1, 3, 5]
　U.S. citizens, **1945:** 44 [2, 4], 97; **1946:** 135
　U.S. in Korea, executions, **1951:** 295 [3]
　Warning to Germans against mistreatment,
　　1945: 9
Prisons, Bureau of, **1946:** 72 [15], 118
Prisons, Federal, **1949:** 8 (p. 70)
Private enterprise.
　See Enterprise system.
Privateer aircraft, disappearance over Baltic, **1950:**
　86 [23], 97 [9]
Prize ribbon, gift to the President, **1950:** 124 [6]
Proclamations
　Continental shelf, U.S. policy on subsoil and sea
　　bed resources, **1945:** 150

Proclamations — *continued*
　Death of Charles Evans Hughes, **1948:** 180
　Death of Harlan Fiske Stone, **1946:** 88
　Germany, termination of state of war, **1951:** 273
　List, Appendix B, **1945:** p. 603; **1946:** p. 525;
　　1947: p. 550; **1948:** p. 988; **1949:** p. 605;
　　1950: p. 778; **1951:** p. 669; **1952–53:** p.
　　1232
　National emergency, **1950:** 304
　Victory in the East, **1945:** 105
　Victory in Europe, **1945:** 26 [4], 27
　World War II, cessation of hostilities, **1946:** 273
Procurement, Federal, **1947:** 208; **1948:** 5 (pp. 21,
　　27–29), 8 (pp. 64, 74), 151; **1949:** 147;
　　1951: 13 (p. 104)
　Atomic energy, raw materials, **1951:** 13 (pp. 85,
　　86); **1952–53:** 18 (p. 87)
　Depressed areas, channeling to, **1949:** 155 [1],
　　156
　Grain for overseas relief, **1947:** 155 [7]
　Military, **1946:** 137, 138; **1947:** 7 (p. 64), 35;
　　1948: 46, 60, 175; **1949:** 8 (pp. 57, 60, 61),
　　50, 244; **1950:** 9 (pp. 54, 61, 64, 65), 179
　　[19], 193, 204; **1951:** 11, 13 (pp. 68–70),
　　82, 91–93, 98, 114, 167, 177, 199; **1952–53:**
　　18 (pp. 70, 75), 231, 275, 367 (pp. 1130,
　　1135, 1136–1139)
　Real property, **1951:** 105, 108 [1]
　Nondefense, curtailment of, **1950:** 196
　Strategic and critical materials, **1951:** 82, 205
Production, **1946:** 2, 18 (pp. 40, 48–51, 53–57, 62,
　　67, 69, 72, 73), 30 [4], 35, 73, 131, 152, 153,
　　164, 172, 221, 226 [1], 232, 249, 260, 268;
　　1947: 7 (p. 60), 20, 58, 68, 90 [5], 107 [2],
　　127 [1], 131, 142, 204; **1948:** 2, 4 [18], 5
　　(pp. 23, 53), 8, 11n., 23, 32, 63, 80, 101;
　　1949: 2, 138, 154; **1950:** 202, 304; **1952–**
　　53: 289 [8], 319 [1, 3]
　See also National product.
　Agricultural, **1947:** 217; **1948:** 2, 5 (p. 44), 8 (pp.
　　62, 68, 70, 77, 92–94), 99, 117, 120 [5], 134,
　　137 [3], 138 [5], 167, 174 [14] 182, 194 [5, 6,
　　11], 213, 216 [1, 5], 217, 223, 234, 246, 276;
　　1949: 2, 5, 77, 151, 154, 203, 250 [3], 263;
　　1950: 6, 92, 106, 157, 202, 232, 303; **1951:**
　　11, 122, 167; **1952–53:** 5, 15, 18 (p. 90), 62,
　　185, 187, 190, 210, 215, 315 [4]
　　Production payments, **1950:** 121 [7]
　Aircraft, military, **1952–53:** 5
　Allocation authority, need for, **1948:** 167
　Aluminum, **1952–53:** 22, 33, 271
　Armaments, **1952–53:** 17 [2]
　Civilian, subordination to defense needs, **1950:**
　　303; **1952–53:** 33
　Controls, **1951:** 13 (pp. 76–77), 93, 98, 140 [2],
　　143, 176
　Copper, **1951:** 204
　Decline due to strikes, **1946:** 125

Production — *continued*
  Decrease, **1948:** 21 [12]
  Defense, **1950:** 193, 194, 202, 204, 215, 232, 243,
        269, 301, 303; **1951:** 59, 63 [7], 91, 107,
        123, 143, 174, 176, 189, 195, 199, 205, 212,
        213, 277, 279, 285, 298 [6], 299, 304;
        1952–53: 5, 15, 18 (pp. 64, 69, 70, 74, 78,
        79), 33, 55, 122, 128, 131, 148, 158, 161,
        190, 175 [12], 215, 231, 238 [12], 245, 275,
        276, 313 [6], 319 [3], 349, 367 (pp. 1136–
        1137, 1141, 1142)
     Controls, **1951:** 15
     Manpower needs, **1951:** 15
     NATO, **1951:** 69
     Work stoppages, **1951:** 13 (pp. 78, 79)
  Farm, **1947:** 224
  Fissionable materials, **1952–53:** 17 [1]
  Food, **1952–53:** 126
  Increase, **1946:** 179; **1947:** 2 (pp. 2, 3), 4 (pp. 14,
        17, 20, 26, 28, 29), 76, 99, 152, 183, 214;
        1948: 184; **1950:** 194, 301; **1952–53:** 5, 55,
        148, 319 [1]
  Industrial, **1947:** 217, 224; **1948:** 2, 5 (p. 45), 8
        (pp. 62, 65–67, 70, 79, 81, 88, 94), 9 [12],
        148, 167, 182, 218 [2], 223, 240 [1], 252;
        1949: 2, 5, 39, 77, 151, 154, 155 [15], 205
        [1], 250 [3]; **1950:** 2, 6, 9 (p. 46), 84, 92,
        106, 118, 134, 157, 163, 194, 202, 232;
        1951: 11, 44, 144, 167; **1952–53:** 15, 57,
        215, 376
     Incentives, proposed, **1950:** 203ftn. (p. 560)
  Loss through illness and disability, **1948:** 241;
        1952–53: 2 [3]
  Minerals, **1949:** 150
     European, **1951:** 167
  Munitions, **1947:** 199
  Need for, **1945:** 184
  News conference remarks, **1946:** 17 [5, 18], 30 [4],
        41 [27], 72 [2, 3, 4], 86 [19, 20], 163 [2]
  Nitrogen, **1952–53:** 33
  Oil, **1952–53:** 58, 280 [5], 379
  Output per man-hour, **1950:** 202
  Petroleum products, **1952–53:** 379
  Relation to prices, **1948:** 165
  Rubber, synthetic, **1951:** 13 (p. 76)
  Steel, **1951:** 11, 304; **1952–53:** 23, 82, 103, 107 [2],
        116, 118, 161, 166 [5], 175 [16], 282 [4]
  Strategic and critical materials, **1951:** 13 (p. 75),
        25, 59, 82, 98, 114, 117, 134, 167
  Synthetic rubber, **1952–53:** 12
  Uranium, increase, **1952–53:** 280 [4]
  Wartime, **1948:** 240 [1]
  Weapons, **1952–53:** 5
Production Authority, National, **1952–53:** 18 (p.
        79)
Production controls, **1945:** 128
Production Credit Association, **1948:** 218 [1]

Production Management, Office of, **1945:** 55, 87
Production and Marketing Administration, **1946:**
        118; **1950:** 9 (p. 87)
Production and Resources Board, Combined,
        1945: 107ftn. (p. 234), 198, 209
Profiteering, **1946:** 179
  Elimination, **1950:** 194, 200, 243
Profits, **1946:** 152, 153, 179, 226 [1]; **1947:** 70 [15],
        107 [2], 152, 196; **1948:** 8 (pp. 65, 68, 74,
        80, 88–90), 11ftn. (p. 104), 32, 63, 71 [19],
        80, 182, 183 [5], 222 [7]
  Corporate, **1947:** 4, (pp. 15, 16, 25), 76; **1948:** 4
        [14, 16], 5 (p. 23), 8 (pp. 63, 65), 63, 167,
        214 [5], 219, 220, 226, 227 [2], 228 [4], 229,
        231 [3, 4], 232, 236, 242 [3], 246, 248, 251,
        252, 262, 264 [5], 267 [2]; **1949:** 5, 22 [10],
        151; **1950:** 6, 8 [22], 18, 84, 106, 134, 157,
        202, 279, 284; **1951:** 11, 13 (pp. 66, 67), 91,
        167, 215, 221; **1952–53:** 15, 18 (p. 112), 33,
        82, 88 [6], 110, 129, 215, 231, 272, 277 [5],
        289 [2, 3], 294, 376
  Excess, taxation of, **1950:** 284
  Industrial, **1948:** 262
  Real estate, **1948:** 227 [7]
  U.S. operation of railroads, **1946:** 125
Progress, technological, **1948:** 104, 126 [6]
Progressive Citizens of America, **1948:** 11ftn. (p.
        105)
Progressive Party, **1948:** 11ftn. (p. 105), 181ftn. (p.
        461); **1949:** 52 [9]; **1950:** 44 [7], 209ftn. (p.
        581)
  1948 campaign, **1948:** 205
  Support by Communist Party, **1948:** 215
Project X, **1948:** 84 [24]
Propaganda
  Anti-administration, **1950:** 157
  Communist, **1950:** 92, 207, 227, 254; **1951:** 256;
        1952–53: 57, 63, 145, 196
  Special-interest, **1949:** 205 [3, 5]
Prohibition Act, **1947:** 80
Property, destruction by fire, **1947:** 86
Property and Administrative Services Act, Federal,
        1950: 9 (p. 100), 73; **1951:** 14, 105;
        1952–53: 18 (p. 112), 367 (p. 1161)
Property management, Federal, **1949:** 8 (p. 93);
        1950: 9 (pp. 51, 100); **1951:** 13 (pp. 104,
        105); **1952–53:** 367 (pp. 1161–1162)
Prophets, role as conscience of Israel, **1951:** 241
Protestant groups, opposition to appointment of
        ambassador to Vatican, **1950:** 16ftn. (p.
        116)
Protocol, comments on, **1950:** 138
Providence, R.I., campaign remarks, **1948:** 261 [5];
        1952–53: 299
Provisional Inter-Governmental Committee for the
        Movement of Migrants from Europe,
        1952–53: 65, 164

Provo, Utah
Campaign remarks, **1948:** 200 [5]; **1952–53:** 281
Steel plant, **1946:** 21 [19]
Provo River reclamation project, **1948:** 56; **1952–53:** 367 (p. 030)
Pruden, Rev. Edward Hughes, **1949:** 83; **1950:** 31n.; **1951:** 241
Psychological Strategy Board, **1951:** 128; **1952–53:** 253 [7], 303 [2]
Psychological Warfare Board, **1951:** 171 [11]
Public Advisory Board for Mutual Security, **1952–53:** 203
Public assistance, **1947:** 4 (p. 29); **1948:** 5 (pp. 25, 34, 35), 8 (pp. 87, 88), 131, 175; **1949:** 8 (pp. 67–69), 151; **1950:** 9 (pp. 50, 72), 84; **1951:** 13 (pp. 97, 98), 159
Federal aid, **1950:** 6, 9 (pp. 50, 73, 74); **1952–53:** 5, 18 (pp. 104, 105), 213, 231, 367 (p. 1146)
Public Assistance, Bureau of, **1946:** 117
Public buildings, **1947:** 35
Maintenance, **1949:** 8 (pp. 91, 93)
Public Buildings Act of 1949, **1950:** 9 (p. 102), 73
Public Buildings Administration, **1946:** 118; **1948:** 46; **1949:** 146, 151
Public debt.
See Debt, national.
Public Debt, Bureau of, **1948:** 4 [1]; **1952–53:** 367 (p. 1161)
Public employment offices, **1948:** 5 (pp. 25, 53, 54)
Public employment service, **1948:** 8 (p. 87)
Public health, **1945:** 99, 192; **1947:** 98, 171; **1948:** 5 (pp. 25, 34, 35, 37), 175, 181 [2]; **1949:** 85; **1950:** 9 (p. 75); **1951:** 13 (pp. 98, 99), 83; **1952–53:** 5, 333
Public health scrolls, presentation, **1948:** 89
Public Health Service, **1945:** 128, 192; **1946:** 18 (p. 83), 117, 118; **1947:** 181 (p. 404); **1948:** 5 (pp. 37, 42); **1949:** 8 (p. 70); **1950:** 9 (p. 75), 30, 69, 74; **1951:** 13 (p. 99), 135; **1952–53:** 18 (p. 106), 81, 117, 268 [8], 333, 367 (p. 1157)
Public Health Service, Surgeon General (Dr. Thomas Parran)
Letter, **1945:** 130
Memorandum, **1945:** 225
Public Health Service Act, **1949:** 8 (p. 69), 85n.
Public Health Service Clinical Center, Bethesda, Md., **1952–53:** 249
Public Housing Administration, **1947:** 102, 173; **1949:** 8 (pp. 75, 76); **1950:** 9 (pp. 80, 81); **1952–53:** 367 (p. 1154)
Public Housing Administration, Commissioner (Dillon S. Myer), **1947:** 173, 174 [1]
Public housing programs, **1948:** 5 (p. 40), 183 [6]; **1950:** 9 (pp. 54, 80), 135
Public and International Affairs, Woodrow Wilson School of, **1947:** 117
Public lands, **1946:** 18 (p. 82), 190, 206; **1947:** 7

Public lands — *continued*
(p. 83), 35, 231; **1948:** 2, 5 (p. 46); **1950:** 9 (p. 90), 116, 121 [9]
Alaska, claims to, **1948:** 105
Indian, disposal of, veto, **1948:** 25
Management and development, **1952–53:** 18 (p. 89)
Offshore, **1952–53:** 115 [7], 136 [4], 146, 149 [4], 377 [11]
Renunciation of U.S. claims, veto, **1946:** 189
Oil and gas leases on, **1947:** 35
Public mining claims, **1949:** 124
Reclamation, **1947:** 110; **1948:** 32
Public opinion polls, **1947:** 218 [7]; **1949:** 22 [7]; **1950:** 86 [25], 152 [5, 7], 267
Gallup poll, remarks re, **1945:** 193 [5]
Washington Post, D.C. voting rights, **1945:** 193 [5]
Public Printer (John J. Deviny), **1949:** 147
Public Roads, Bureau of, **1949:** 151; **1950:** 9 (p. 95), 53, 76; **1951:** 13 (p. 84); **1952–53:** 18 (p. 84), 93, 367 (p. 1144)
Public Roads, Commissioner of (Thomas H. MacDonald), **1949:** 142
Public Roads Administration, **1945:** 224; **1947:** 35; **1948:** 5 (p. 51), 8 (p. 81); **1949:** 127, 134
Public Roads Administration, Commissioner (Thomas H. MacDonald), **1946:** 43 [10], 195n.
Public utilities, **1948:** 8 (p. 62), 233 [3]
Antistrike bill, **1947:** 88 [4]
Coal stockpiling, restrictions, **1946:** 228
Holding companies, **1950:** 110 [9], 124 [4]
Labor disputes, **1946:** 131; **1950:** 43
Public Utilities Fortnightly, **1948:** 209
Public Utility Holding Company Act, **1952–53:** 143
Public welfare, **1949:** 32 [2]
Public works, **1945:** 128; **1946:** 17 [24, 26], 18 (pp. 61, 62, 65, 69, 80), 79, 164, 193, 195, 238; **1947:** 4 (pp. 28, 34), 6 [14], 7 (pp. 56, 58, 76, 92), 35, 75, 96, 110, 180 [23]; **1948:** 4 [7], 8 (pp. 64, 74, 82, 98); **1949:** 8 (pp. 45, 57, 75), 154; **1950:** 127 [1]; **1952–53:** 291
Alaska, **1948:** 105; **1949:** 8 (p. 75); **1950:** 53
Civil defense, **1951:** 13 (pp. 92, 93)
Contracts, **1950:** 9 (p. 54)
Curtailment in favor of defense needs, **1950:** 196
Depressed areas, **1949:** 148 [2], 155 [1], 156
Employees, wages and hours, **1950:** 68, 74
Federal aid, **1947:** 181 (p. 406); **1948:** 5 (pp. 38, 40); **1950:** 9 (pp. 50, 81), 69, 171; **1951:** 13 (p. 94)
Federal-State-local governmental responsibilities, **1949:** 151
Hawaii, **1947:** 35
Letter to Representative Cannon, **1945:** 185
Military, **1947:** 181 (p. 399); **1948:** 5 (pp. 26, 28); **1949:** 8 (p. 60), 192 [8]; **1950:** 8 [33], 9

Public works — *continued*
  Military — *continued*
    (p. 65); **1951:** 13 (pp. 68, 69), 92, 93;
      1952–53: 18 (p. 70)
    Near East, U.N. program, **1950:** 143
    News conference remarks, **1950:** 8 [33], 209 [3]
    Public buildings, construction, **1950:** 9 (pp. 101,
      102)
      Curtailment, **1952–53:** 18 (p. 112)
    Reorganization plans respecting, **1950:** 53, 69,
      70, 72
    Virgin Islands, **1950:** 53
    Wages and hours of workers employed on, **1947:**
      81
    Wartime, management and disposition, **1950:** 53
Pueblo, Colo., campaign remarks, **1948:** 198 [5];
  1952–53: 282 [4]
Puerto Rico, **1946:** 18 (p. 66); **1947:** 35, 78 [2], 119
  Assistance, **1947:** 14 [14]
  Constitution, **1952–53:** 104, 197 [11], 198
  Disease prevention, **1951:** 243
  Disapproval of bills, **1946:** 115, 240
  Economic and social development, **1948:** 35
  Elective governorship, **1947:** 166; **1952–53:** 35
    [15]
  Form of government, message to Congress,
    1945: 169
  Gov. Luis Muñoz Marín, **1948:** 278 [12], 283
    [10]; **1950:** 11 [5], 52 [5], 277; **1951:** 275 [2]
  Gov. Jesús T. Piñero, **1946:** 163 [8], 177 [2], 186
    [14], 240; **1947:** 14 [14], 166; **1948:** 26 [17],
    35, 185 [5]; **1949:** 84 [13]
  Gov. Rexford G. Tugwell, **1945:** 208 [6], 221 [15,
    17]; **1946:** 141 [12], 143 [4], 163 [8], 240
  Nationalists, attempt on life of the President,
    1950: 277n., 278 [4, 13]
  News conference remarks, **1946:** 41 [6], 136 [12],
    163 [4, 8], 173 [4], 177 [2, 17], 186 [14], 199
    [14], 216 [22], 226 [7]; **1950:** 52 [5], 278 [3,
    4, 13]
  Population increase, **1951:** 243
  Rice exports to, **1947:** 18
  Self-government, **1948:** 35; **1950:** 52 [5], 278 [3]
    Growth of, **1952–53:** 104
  Sugar producers, **1948:** 5 (p. 44)
  Unemployment insurance legislation, proposed
    extension to, **1950:** 84
  Uprisings in, message to Governor, **1950:** 277
  U.S. relations with, **1948:** 35
  Visit to, **1947:** 36 [2]; **1948:** 26 [17], 35, 278 [12],
    283 [10]
Puget Sound, **1950:** 121 [13]
Pulaski, Casimir, **1950:** 185
Pulitzer, Joseph, **1945:** 8 [2]
Pullman strike (1894), **1948:** 198 [5]
Punch, cartoon in, **1951:** 18
Purcell, Buck, **1948:** 214 [8]
Purcell, Okla., campaign remarks, **1948:** 214 [8]

Purdum, Smith, **1945:** 132 [1]
Purchasing power, **1948:** 107
Purnell, Frank, **1949:** 152n., 153; **1952–53:** 116
Puryear, Edgar F., letter, **1945:** 183
Pusan, Korea, **1950:** 268
Pusey, Merlo J., *Charles Evans Hughes*, 295ftn. (p.
  630)
Putnam, Roger L., **1952–53:** 118n., 292 [9], 341, 345
  [5], 346
Pyle, Ernie, death of, **1945:** 6
Putnam County Sentinel, Ottawa, Ohio, **1952–53:**
  319 [2]

Quantico, Va., Marine base, **1950:** 165
Quartermaster Corps, **1947:** 35
Quartermaster General (Maj. Gen. H. Feldman),
  1949: 200 [6]
  Promotion, question of, **1951:** 200 [5]
Quebec, **1945:** 177; **1947:** 111
  Atomic energy agreements, **1945:** 181 [3]
  Iron ore reserves in, **1950:** 9 (p. 94); **1951:** 13 (pp.
    81–83)
Queen Elizabeth, **1945:** 45
Queen Mary, **1945:** 45
Queens, N.Y., campaign remarks, **1948:** 264 [5]
Quezon, Mrs. Manuel, murder of, **1949:** 89 [18]
Quick magazine, **1949:** 122 [11]
Quincy, Mass.
  Campaign remarks, **1948:** 261 [1]
  Mayor Charles A. Ross, **1948:** 261n.
Quinine, import controls, **1947:** 99
Quirimo, Elpidio, **1948:** 82; **1949:** 172, 173, 176,
  178; **1950:** 34 [15], 180, 273ftn. (p. 689),
  278 [11]; **1951:** 130n., 136, 193 [8], 207,
  208, 224 [3]
  News conference remarks on, **1949:** 11 [16], 22
    [9], 113 [6], 144 [9], 155 [22], 171 [1, 8, 14],
    179 [14, 20], 260 [8]

Rabaut, Repr. Louis C., **1949:** 249n.; **1951:** 153 [21]
Rabi, I. I., **1946:** 262 [1]
Racetrack, diversion of scarce materials for, **1949:**
  179 [9]
Racial Democracy, Committee on, **1947:** 14 [23]
Racial Discrimination.
  See Civil rights.
Radar net, development, **1950:** 8 [46]
Radford, Adm. Arthur W., **1949:** 231 [19]; **1950:**
  267, 268
Radio, question of Government control, **1952–53:**
  107 [1, 8, 9]
Radio addresses.
  See Messages to the American people.

Radio broadcasting companies, security responsibilities, **1950**: 207

Radio broadcasting facilities, construction, **1951**: 13 (pp. 75, 76)

Radio commentators, opinions on election, **1948**: 261 [12]

Radio Conference, International, **1948**: 29

Radio Farm Directors, National Association of, **1949**: 90, 93 [5]; **1950**: 163

Radio Free Europe, **1950**: 98

Radio frequency allocations, **1950**: 34 [8], 40

Radio News Analysts, Association of, **1947**: 90; **1949**: 234

Radio station WBBM, Chicago, **1947**: 48n.

Radio stations, promotion of highway safety program, **1948**: 280

Radio Technical Commission for Aeronautics, **1948**: 175

Radio-Television Manufacturers Association, **1952–53**: 43n.

Radio waveband allocation, agreement with Mexico, **1949**: 84 [8]

Radioisotopes, **1952–53**: 249, 333

Railroad Retirement Act, **1947**: 7 (p. 73); **1951**: 280; **1952–53**: 18 (p. 105)

Railroad Retirement Board, **1946**: 72 [1]; **1948**: 5 (p. 37); **1951**: 13 (p. 98); **1952–53**: 18 (p. 105)

Railroad strike, **1946**: 120
  Broadcast, **1946**: 124
  Message to Congress, **1946**: 125
  News conference remarks, **1946**: 53 [1], 95 [15], 110 [9], 119 [5, 12, 18, 22, 26], 121, 163 [2]

Railroad Trainmen, Brotherhood of, **1946**: 120, 121, 124, 125; **1948**: 11ftn. (p. 105); **1950**: 209ftn. (p. 580), 221; **1952–53**: 136ftn. (p. 359)

Railroad Unemployment Insurance Act, **1951**: 280

Railroads, **1946**: 24; **1947**: 99; **1948**: 8 (pp. 67, 80, 82)
  Army operation, **1951**: 33 [1, 15]; **1952–53**: 136ftn. (p. 359)
    Termination, **1948**: 159; **1952–53**: 141
  Contributions to Republican campaign fund, **1948**: 251
  Controls, **1947**: 143; **1948**: 1, 23
  Debtor corporations, **1946**: 205
  Equipment and modernization, **1948**: 8 (p. 82)
  Exemption from antitrust laws, **1948**: 220, 251, 252, 257 [2]
  Freight cars, production, **1951**: 13 (pp. 75, 76)
  Freight cars, shortage, **1947**: 18, 36 [8]; **1948**: 8 (pp. 70, 79, 80)
  Freight rates, **1946**: 84 [25]; **1951**: 188 [17]; **1952–53**: 266 [2], 270 [5]
    Basing point bill, **1949**: 148 [23]
  Government operation, **1946**: 110 [15], 119 [22, 26], 124, 126 [5]

Railroads — *continued*
  Government operation — *continued*
    Statement, **1946**: 120
  Interest rates on bonds, **1946**: 205
  Korean, reopening of, **1950**: 268
  Labor disputes, **1948**: 88 [3], 93 [1, 3, 6, 8], 95; **1949**: 155 [15], 205 [11]; **1950**: 186 [1, 4, 6, 9], 188, 209 [4, 21], 214 [1, 6, 16], 217 [3, 6, 8, 21], 221, 303; **1951**: 16 [14], 33 [1, 15], 37 [16], 49 [1, 6, 9], 74, 209 [2]; **1952–53**: 136 [2, 14], 253 [2, 4]
    Federal operation, **1950**: 186 [4], 209 [4], 221
    Settlement, **1948**: 159
  Labor organizations, **1948**: 11ftn. (p. 105), 240 [3], 257 [4]; **1951**: 33 [1, 15], 74, 214
  Legislation, **1948**: 261 [11]
  Mail rates, **1951**: 13 (pp. 83, 84), 45
  News conference remarks, **1946**: 85 [25], 110 [15], 119 [22, 26], 126 [5], 199 [9]
  Reorganization bill, **1946**: 199 [9]
  Restrictions on civilian travel, **1945**: 54
  Retirement expenditures, **1948**: 5 (pp. 34, 36)
  Retirement system, **1952–53**: 213
    Trust fund, **1947**: 7 (pp. 58, 73), 181 (p. 400); **1948**: 5 (pp. 34, 3 5), 175; **1949**: 8 (pp. 49, 69, 71); **1950**: 8 (1), 9 (pp. 50, 73, 74, 76); **1951**: 13 (pp. 55, 98, 99), 280; **1952–53**: 18 (pp. 104, 105), 231, 270 [5], 306 [6], 367 (p. 1156)
  Safety, **1947**: 82
  St. Lawrence Seaway construction, opposition to, **1952–53**: 23
  Securities, open-market sale of, **1951**: 56 [2]
  Sleeping car companies, **1947**: 160
  Stock issues, **1947**: 160
  Strike.
    See Railroad strike.
  Unemployment insurance program, **1949**: 8 (p. 91)
  Unions, **1952–53**: 37
  Wages, **1948**: 5 (p. 37), 159n.; **1952–53**: 277 [5], 306 [6]
  Western States, **1950**: 171
    Manpower shortage, statement, **1945**: 83
    Transportation of war material, **1945**: 54
  Work rules revision, **1948**: 159n.

Railroads, Association of American, **1945**: 221 [9]; **1946**: 56

Railway Conductors, Order of, **1950**: 209ftn. (p. 580), 221; **1952–53**: 136ftn. (p. 359)

Railway Labor Act, **1945**: 204; **1946**: 6 [13], 24, 110 [9], 120, 124; **1947**: 145 [15]; **1948**: 93 [3], 95; **1949**: 205 [11]; **1950**: 186 [9], 188, 221; **1951**: 74; **1952–53**: 136 [2]

Railway Labor Panel, National, **1951**: 74

Rains, Repr. Albert, **1951**: 200 [3]

Raleigh, N.C.
  Campaign address, **1948**: 246

Raleigh, N.C. — *continued*
  Monument to Presidents Jackson, Polk, and
     Johnson, dedication, **1948:** 245
Ramsay, Robert L., **1948:** 242 [2]
Ramsey, George E., **1951:** 93n.
Ramspeck, Robert, **1948:** 169; **1951:** 85 [9]; **1952–
     53:** 59, 114, 117, 222, 223, 243, 338
  Letter, **1945:** 48
Ramspeck Act (1940), **1952–53:** 87
Randall, Clarence B., **1952–53:** 88 [9], 116
Randolph, Repr. Jennings, **1946:** 177 [15]
Range Livestock Experiment Station, Miles City,
     Mont., **1949:** 206
Rangoon, Burma, **1946:** 113
Rankin, Repr. John E., **1946:** 257 [5]; **1949:** 58 [14]
Ransom, Ronald, **1948:** 13
Rappahannock River, **1951:** 290
Rash, Bryson B., **1948:** 288ftn. (p. 969)
Rasmussen, Gustav, **1949:** 68
Rationing, **1945:** 17, 128, 135, 202 [3]; **1946:** 30 [2],
     66 [9], 70 [9], 86 [24], 95 [11], 262 [3]; **1947:**
     7 (p. 86), 60, 64, 191 [5, 8, 24], 209 [2, 11,
     14], 224, 225, 226 [7], 242; **1948:** 5 (pp. 22,
     51, 52), 8 (pp. 65, 73), 15 [2], 21 [12], 114
     [3], 163 [22], 165 [167]; **1950:** 191 [16], 203
     [6, 9, 24] and ftn. (p. 560), 205
  Gasoline, **1945:** 62, 128, 224
  Grain, in India, **1951:** 34
  In U.S., question of, **1951:** 2 [21]
Raton, N. Mex., campaign remarks, **1948:** 136 [5]
Ravenna, Nebr., **1950:** 110 [8]
  Mayor E. F. Kozel, **1950:** 110 [8]
Raw materials, **1948:** 8 (pp. 69, 78, 80, 97)
  Conservation, **1948:** 14
  Exports, **1952–53:** 55, 57, 179
  Imports, **1947:** 18
  Increase in supply, **1950:** 84
  Marketing, Bernard Baruch recommendations,
     1948: 11ftn. (p. 104)
  Production by less developed countries, **1951:**
     167
  Shortage, **1951:** 11; **1952–53:** 179
  Strategic and critical, stockpiling, **1947:** 238
Raw Materials Board, Combined, **1945:** 107ftn. (p.
     234), 209
Rawlins, Wyo., **1950:** 117 [4]
  Campaign remarks, **1948:** 118 [7]
Rayburn, Miss Lou, **1948:** 214 [1]
Rayburn, Repr. Sam, **1947:** 68n.; **1948:** 12n., 163
     [10], 208 [4–6], 209, 210 [2], 212 [2, 4, 10,
     11], 213, 214 [1–3, 7], 216 [5, 6, 13], 278
     [18], 288 [12]
  See also Speaker of the House of Representatives
     (Sam Rayburn).
REA.
  See Rural Electrification Administration.
Reactors, nuclear.
  See Atomic Energy.

Reading, Pa.
  Campaign remarks, **1948:** 227 [2]; **1952–53:** 303
     [10]
  Mayor John F. Davis, **1948:** 227 [1]
Real estate
  Credit controls, **1951:** 44
  Government transactions, **1951:** 13 (pp. 104,
     105), 105, 108 [1]
  Price rise, **1946:** 18 (p. 53)
Real Estate Boards, National Association of, **1948:**
     212 [9]; **1949:** 66ftn. (p. 195)
Real estate credit controls, proposed, **1950:** 193,
     202
Real estate prices, **1945:** 52 [10], 202 [5]; **1947:** 97
  Control on, **1945:** 208 [19]
Real estate taxes, **1949:** 126; **1950:** 256
Real property, acquisition by Armed Forces,
     1952–53: 18 (p. 71)
Rearmament program, **1950:** 282; **1952–53:** 98 [12],
     349, 366
  American Legion support of, **1951:** 191
  Europe, **1952–53:** 55, 125
Receipts, Federal, **1952–53:** 215
Recession, question of, **1946:** 266 [8]
Recessions, **1947:** 6 [20], 7 (p. 56), 70 [19], 76, 107
     [2], 147, 152, 214; **1948:** 80, 176; **1950:** 6,
     18
  1949, **1951:** 11; **1952–53:** 366, 376
  Economic, **1949:** 30 [11], 144 [23]
Reciprocal Assistance, Inter-American Treaty of,
     1947: 230; **1949:** 19, 184; **1951:** 59, 65,
     114, 125; **1952–53:** 378
Reciprocal Trade Agreements Act.
  See Trade Agreements Act.
Reclamation, Bureau of, **1945:** 211 [10]; **1946:** 18
     (p. 82), 209; **1947:** 7 (p. 81), 11, 96, 144,
     181 (pp. 398, 402); **1948:** 5 (p. 46), 6, 149;
     1949: 8 (pp. 81, 83), 41, 77, 96, 185, 196;
     1950: 3ftn. (p. 15), 9 (p. 90), 121 [4, 8], 129
     [1, 5]; **1951:** 13 (pp. 85–87), 183n.; **1952–
     53:** 18 (pp. 88, 89), 199, 231, 367 (p. 1146)
Reclamation, Bureau of, Commissioner (Harry W.
     Bashore), **1945:** 211 [10]
Reclamation, Bureau of, Commissioner (Michael
     W. Straus), **1949:** 58 [20], 96n.
Reclamation Act of 1902, **1952–53:** 388
Reclamation Acts, **1948:** 198 [4], 200 [1]
Reclamation program, **1948:** 2, 5 (pp. 25, 46), 37
Reclamation projects, **1945:** 128; **1946:** 18 (pp. 60,
     82), 86 [16], 97, 238; **1947:** 7 (p. 93), 95
     [28], 96, 110, 144; **1948:** 56, 119, 149, 175;
     1949: 95 [17], 245; **1950:** 3 [22], 116, 121
     [3, 4, 8], 125, 127 [1, 2, 6], 129 [1, 7]; **1951:**
     13 (pp. 84, 85), 32; **1952–53:** 221 [15], 268
     [2], 277 [3], 280 [1, 6], 367 (p. 1146), 376
  Campaign remarks on, **1948:** 122 [3], 125, 126 [1],
     128 [1], 136 [3, 4], 198 [5, 6], 200 [1, 2, 9],
     201 [1], 202 [5], 203, 206 [3, 4], 208 [6, 7],
     209, 212 [4], 214 [5], 217, 218 [9, 14]

Reconstruction, Southern, report on (1869), **1950:** 29 [9]

Reconstruction Finance Corporation, **1945:** 41, 228n.; **1946:** 18 (pp. 57, 74, 80), 94, 229 [14], 257 [6], 263; **1947:** 6 [28, 31], 7 (pp. 58, 65, 68, 74, 75, 76, 80, 81, 88, 94, 95), 14 [12], 62 [10] 80, 174 [9], 175, 181 (pp. 400, 401, 403, 405); **1948:** 5 (pp. 40, 52, 53, 56, 57), 173, 175, 223; **1949:** 8 (pp. 62, 74, 75, 88, 89), 150, 151; **1950:** 6, 9 (pp. 55, 77, 79, 81, 96), 106, 112, 118, 256; **1951:** 13 (pp. 78, 92), 177, 205, 269; **1952–53:** 119

Activities in support of military services, **1952–53:** 18 (p. 73)

Appointment of W. Stuart Symington as Administrator, **1951:** 82

Assistance to small business, **1951:** 82

Business loans, **1952–53:** 367 (pp. 1141–1142)

Defense production loans, **1952–53:** 18 (pp. 79, 80)

Disaster relief loans, **1952–53:** 18 (p. 100)

Loan Policy Board, **1951:** 39

Loans, congressional investigation of, **1950:** 97 [4]

Loans to States for toll roads, **1949:** 269 [3]

News conference remarks, **1949:** 144 [31], 192 [5], 269 [3]; **1950:** 8 [42], 29 [16], 97 [4, 11], 217 [17], 318 [2, 4]; **1951:** 2 [12], 16 [10], 33 [2, 12], 49 [4, 11], 56 [11, 17, 24], 63 [11, 13], 171 [1], 179 [1], 188 [3, 15]; **1952–53:** 31 [6]

Programs review, **1950:** 196

Reorganization, **1950:** 113, 114, 318 [2, 4]; **1951:** 39, 82; **1952–53:** 18 (p. 116)

Small business, assistance to, **1952–53:** 15, 18 (p. 79)

Tin, policy on, **1952–53:** 2 [12, 14]

Tin and synthetic rubber, procurement functions, **1951:** 82

Reconstruction Finance Corporation, Chairman (Charles B. Henderson), letter, **1945:** 176

Reconstruction Finance Corporation, Chairman (Harley Hise), **1949:** 156; **1950:** 192

Letter directing programs review, **1950:** 196

Memorandum, **1950:** 259

Reconstruction Finance Corporation, Chairman (W. Stuart Symington), **1952–53:** 2 [4, 12]

Reconstruction Finance Corporation Act, **1950:** 113

Reconversion, postwar, **1945:** 42, 163, 184, 185, 204, 226, 229; **1946:** 18 (pp. 37, 40, 48–52, 57, 64, 67–69, 71, 79, 86), 35, 67, 73, 152, 193, 195, 213, 220, 226 [1], 260, 262 [3], 269, 272; **1947:** 2 (p. 2), 4 (pp. 16, 17, 31), 7 (pp. 56, 93), 18, 23, 35, 80, 120, 152, 156, 200; **1948:** 8 (p. 66), 182; **1950:** 122

Broadcast, **1946:** 2

First 100 days, statement, **1945:** 202 [3]

Industrial peace, statement, **1945:** 104

Reconversion, postwar — *continued*
Letter to Chairman, War Production Board, **1945:** 95

Message to Congress, **1945:** 128

News conference remarks, **1945:** 164 [7], 202 [7]; **1946:** 17 [5, 11, 18], 41 [27], 72 [2], 129 [21], 163 [2], 262 [8]

Statement, **1946:** 164

Wages and prices, broadcast, **1945:** 180

Records Act of 1950, Federal, **1952–53:** 149 [16]

Records and archival functions, reorganization plans, **1950:** 53, 75

Records management, Federal, **1952–53:** 367 (pp. 1161–1162)

Records of outgoing administration, custody and disposition, **1952–53:** 334 [11, 15]

Recreation Association, National, **1951:** 99n.

Recreation facilities, **1945:** 165; **1949:** 43, 185, 232; **1950:** 9 (p. 91), 33, 129 [1], 248; **1952–53:** 194

Community Chest programs for military personnel, **1950:** 262

Red Bluff, Calif., campaign remarks, **1952–53:** 277 [4]

Red Cross, **1945:** 85, 208 [20]; **1946:** 60, 80, 182n.; **1948:** 40, 45n., 126 [1]; **1949:** 214 [1], 215; **1950:** 7, 95n.; **1952–53:** 50, 249

Campaign, **1946:** 50; **1947:** 5, 49

Disaster relief, **1952–53:** 18 (p. 99)

District of Columbia building, cornerstone laying, **1951:** 271

Establishment in U.S., role of Clara Barton, **1951:** 47

Flood relief, **1950:** 129 [5, 7]

Flood relief assistance for Guatemala, **1949:** 236 [3]

Fundraising campaign, **1949:** 42; **1950:** 45; **1951:** 47, 73; **1952–53:** 50

Italian, **1946:** 253

News conference remarks, **1950:** 191 [12], 250 [19], 278 [1]

President (E. Roland Harriman), **1950:** 278 [1]; **1951:** 47n., 73, 162

Relief services, **1951:** 47, 124, 162, 196, 271
In Europe, **1947:** 107 [1]

Rumanian, **1947:** 32

Red River, **1948:** 214 [3, 4]; **1950:** 33, 129 [1, 5, 7], 130, 140, 164

Development, **1951:** 13 (p. 87)

Flood control, **1947:** 144; **1952–53:** 109

Red River Valley, Indochina, **1952–53:** 57

Red Wing, Minn., campaign remarks, **1952–53:** 313 [2]

Redding, Calif., campaign remarks, **1952–53:** 277 [3]

Redevelopment Land Agency, District of Columbia, **1949:** 8 (p. 94)

Redmond, John R., **1949:** 265

Redwood City, Calif., harbor improvement, **1952–
        53:** 367 (p. 1143)
Reece, Repr. B. Carroll, **1946:** 72 [11], 221; **1947:**
        67 [5]
Reed, Repr. Chauncey W., **1946:** 199 [9]
Reed, Sen. Clyde M., **1949:** 112ftn. (p. 269)
Reed, Repr. Daniel A., **1952–53:** 361
Reed, David A., **1947:** 236 [2]
Reed, Lowell J., **1951:** 307n.
Reed, Macon, Jr., **1951:** 247 [1]
Reed, Maj. Walter, **1948:** 81
Reed-Bulwinkle antitrust bill, **1949:** 149
Reelfoot Lake, Tenn., **1945:** 164n.
Reese, Ben H., **1952–53:** 98 [39]
Refugee Board, War, **1945:** 85
Refugee Organization, International, **1946:** 236;
        1947: 7 (pp. 66, 68), 21, 133, 140; **1948:**
        115, 144, 206 [6]; **1949:** 8 (p. 55); **1950:** 9
        (p. 58); **1952–53:** 65
    U.S. participation, **1947:** 38n.
Refugees, **1946:** 18 (p. 44); **1947:** 7 (p. 66), 133
    See also Displaced persons in Europe; Jews;
        Refugees and escapees.
    Estonian in U.S., **1946:** 237 [17], 239, 246
    German, **1946:** 18 (p. 46)
    Immigration to U.S., statement and directive,
        1945: 225
    Jewish, in Europe
        Letter to Prime Minister Attlee, **1945:** 188
        Statement, **1945:** 187
    Political, **1945:** 140
        Policy on, **1946:** 237 [17]
    U.S. relief for, **1947:** 43, 51
Refugees, Intergovernmental Committee on, **1945:**
        152, 188
Refugees and escapees.
    See also Displaced persons in Europe; Refugees.
    Arab, U.S. aid for, **1952–53:** 18 (p. 76)
    Assistance, **1952–53:** 66
        Message to Congress, **1952–53:** 65
    Australia, immigration to, **1952–53:** 65
    Baltic, question of U.S. asylum, **1948:** 174 [4],
        178 [12], 283 [5]
    Canada, immigration to, **1952–53:** 65
    Communist bloc, **1951:** 96; **1952–53:** 164, 244,
        288, 297
    Communist defectors, political asylum for, **1950:**
        137 [14], 254
    East German and Czech, **1950:** 146 [20]
    Europe, **1952–53:** 78, 145, 182
    Latin America, immigration to, **1952–53:** 65
    Middle East, **1952–53:** 367 (p. 1140)
    Palestine, **1948:** 281; **1949:** 21, 57, 122 [23], 192
        [21], 274; **1950:** 9 (p. 58), 25, 78, 143, 154;
        1951: 13 (p. 74), 114, 172; **1952–53:** 297
    Remarks to, **1952–53:** 94
    Service in U.S. and NATO forces, proposed,
        1952–53: 65

Refugees and escapees — *continued*
    Soviet, **1948:** 178 [7]
    U.S., immigration to, **1950:** 167; **1952–53:** 65,
        288
Regan, Repr. Ken, **1948:** 208 [5–8]
Regan, Phil, **1949:** 220
Regional Agricultural Credit Corporation, **1949:** 8
        (p. 81)
Regional development, **1948:** 8 (p. 78)
Regulation W, credit, **1948:** 166 [8]; **1949:** 32 [8], 66
        [7], 78 [13, 16], 122 [5]; **1951:** 11; **1952–53:**
        123 [18]
Regulation X, housing credit, **1951:** 11; **1952–53:**
        123 [18]
Regulatory agencies
    Budget, **1950:** 9 (p. 96)
    Chairmen, Presidential designation, **1950:** 54
    Reorganization, **1950:** 123
Rehabilitation Commission, American Legion,
        1949: 49n.
Reid, Gordon S., **1952–53:** 262n.
Reinsch, Leonard, **1945:** 4 [2], 8 [1, 3]
Reiser, Carlton, **1952–53:** 319 [3, 4]
Relief agencies, surplus food for, **1950:** 249
Relief programs, overseas, **1947:** 107 [1]; **1948:** 5 (p.
        29); **1949:** 8 (p. 54), 21, 117, 251; **1950:** 9
        (pp. 56, 58, 85), 25, 78, 110 [1], 111, 119,
        130, 154, 249, 264, 269, 285, 290, 293;
        1951: 124; **1952–53:** 5, 50, 65, 88, 366
    See also specific countries.
    UNICEF, **1951:** 187
Religion
    Comments on, **1946:** 52, 75 [2]
    Role in national life, **1949:** 246, 254; **1950:** 37,
        126, 299; **1951:** 30, 68, 241; **1952–53:** 42,
        330, 337
Religion and Welfare in the Armed Forces, Pres-
        ident's Committee on, **1949:** 73; **1950:** 32,
        95; **1951:** 17, 100; **1952–53:** 297
Religious freedom, **1948:** 2
    Jefferson's statute for, **1947:** 138
Rembrandt, **1948:** 71 [1]
Remington, William W., **1948:** 170 [4]; **1949:** 32
        [14]; **1950:** 152 [3]
Renegotiation Board, **1952–53:** 18 (p. 112)
Renfrow, Col. Louis H., **1949:** 166 [3]
Renne, Roland R., **1950:** 1n., 306n.
Rennebohm, Gov. Oscar, **1950:** 132n.
Reno, Nev.
    Campaign remarks, **1948:** 202 [2]
    Mayor Francis R. Smith, **1948:** 202 [2]
    Veto of act for relief of, **1949:** 146
Renown, H.M.S., **1945:**91n.; **1951:** 282
Rent control, **1946:** 2, 18 (pp. 49, 54, 62), 67, 152,
        153, 179, 213, 232, 249, 250 [8], 262 [3, 10],
        263; **1947:** 4 (p. 29), 7 (p. 86), 18, 36 [15],
        46 [28], 60, 76, 131, 152, 209 [14], 224;
        1948: 2, 5 (pp. 40, 51–53), 8 (pp. 64, 65,

Rent control — *continued*
74), 37, 58, 101, 167, 175; **1949:** 2, 5, 8 (p. 88), 65; **1950:** 2, 6, 203ftn. (p. 560), 243; **1951:** 4, 13 (p. 78), 91, 107, 123, 143, 167, 176; **1952–53:** 18 (pp. 77, 79, 80), 33, 231, 273, 287, 300, 305, 321 [2], 322, 367 (p. 1154)
  See also Price controls; Wage controls.
  Campaign remarks, **1948:** 194 [1], 259 [3], 261 [2], 264 [1]
  Defense Production Act Amendments, **1952–53:** 190
  Extension, **1951:** 11
    Message to Congress, **1947:** 65
    Proposed, **1950:** 9 (pp. 96, 97), 93, 292
  Landlord opposition to, **1948:** 259 [3], 261 [2], 264 [1]; **1949:** 54, 66 [19, 21]
  Legislation, proposed, **1948:** 165
  Los Angeles, Calif., **1950:** 278 [5, 12]
  Louisville, Ky., **1947:** 205 [8, 10, 17]
  News conference remarks, **1947:** 14 [1, 7, 21]; **1948:** 9 [18], 21 [12], 71 [13], 170 [1]; **1949:** 22 [5], 52 [11], 58 [21, 29], 66 [19, 21], 182 [4]; **1950:** 46 [18], 273 [5], 278 [5, 12]; **1951:** 12 [55], 140 [2]
  Reimposition, **1952–53:** 15
  Republican opposition, **1952–53:** 218, 289 [11]
  Stabilization, **1952–53:** 367 (p. 1141)
Rental housing, **1946:** 18 (p. 63), 257 [6], 258, 263; **1947:** 2 (p. 7), 4 (p. 30), 7 (p. 74), 19 [2, 6]; **1948:** 5 (pp. 38, 40, 41), 37, 58, 139 [1], 150 [1], 160, 165, 172, 176, 183 [1], 203, 205, 212 [9], 219, 220, 227 [2, 7], 229, 231 [2], 232, 233 [6], 235 [4], 237 [4], 238, 247, 249, 251, 257 [4], 259 [3], 261 [2], 264 [1], 268
  See also Rental units *under* Housing.
  Veterans, **1947:** 44
Rentschler, Gordon S., **1946:** 142
Reorganization Act of 1945, approval, **1945:** 220
Reorganization Act of 1949, **1949:** 128, 129, 131–134, 158; **1950:** 53, 55–68, 70–74, 76, 112, 115, 149; **1951:** 13 (p. 65); **1952–53:** 11, 18 (pp. 112, 116), 84, 85, 86, 87, 114, 367 (p. 1132)
  Approval, **1949:** 127
Reorganization Acts, **1948:** 10, 62
Reorganization bill, adverse vote by House, **1951:** 56 [1, 8]
Reorganization plans, **1949:** 158, 181; **1950:** 9 (p. 51); **1951:** 13 (p. 65); **1952–53:** 287, 367 (p. 1132)
  Advance planning and war public works, **1950:** 69, 72
  Agriculture Department, **1950:** 54, 58
  Bureau of Customs, **1952–53:** 84, 86, 117, 137
  Bureau of Employees' Compensation and Employees' Compensation Appeals Board, **1950:** 74

Reorganization plans — *continued*
  Bureau of Employment Security, **1949:** 127, 129
  Bureau of Internal Revenue, **1952–53:** 1, 2 [4, 11], 5, 11, 53, 59, 84, 117
  Civil Aeronautics Board, **1950:** 54, 67
  Civil Service Commission, **1949:** 127, 132
  Commerce Department, **1950:** 54, 59
  Department of Welfare, proposed, **1949:** 127, 128
  Department of Health, Education and Security, proposed, **1950:** 150
  District of Columbia government, **1952–53:** 114
  Executive Office of the President, **1949:** 127, 131
  Federal Communications Commission, **1950:** 54, 65
  Federal National Mortgage Association, **1950:** 112
  Federal Power Commission, **1950:** 54, 63
  Federal Trade Commission, **1950:** 54, 62
  General Services Administration, **1950:** 73
  General Services Administration and State Department, **1950:** 75
  Housing and Home Finance Agency, **1950:** 113
  Interior Department, **1950:** 54, 57
  Interstate Commerce Commission, **1950:** 54, 61
  Justice Department, **1950:** 54, 56; **1952–53:** 84, 87, 137
  Labor Department, **1950:** 54, 60, 68
  Messages, **1946:** 116, 117, 118; **1947:** 80, 81, 102
  National Labor Relations Board, **1950:** 54, 66, 123
  National Security Resources Board, **1950:** 115
  News conference remarks, **1949:** 45 [23], 122 [21], 155 [18], 182 [8]; **1950:** 97 [3, 7], 105 [15], 137 [2, 17], 146 [7], 209 [12], 318 [2, 4]
  Post Office Department, **1949:** 127, 130, 140; **1952–53:** 84, 85, 115 [14], 117, 137
  Public Roads Administration, **1949:** 127, 134
  Public works, Alaska and Virgin Islands, **1950:** 69, 70
  Reconstruction Finance Corporation, **1950:** 114; **1951:** 33 [2], 39, 56 [11], 82
  School districts and water pollution control, assistance, **1950:** 69, 71
  Securities and Exchange Commission, **1950:** 54, 64
  Senate action on, **1952–53:** 175 [1]
  Summary, **1950:** 53; **1952–53:** 84
  Treasury Department, **1950:** 54, 55, 149; **1952–53:** 11
  U.S. Employment Service, **1948:** 10
  U.S. Maritime Commission, **1949:** 127, 133; **1950:** 76
Reparations
  Axis powers, negotiations with Soviet Union, **1948:** 128 [4]
  German, **1945:** 13, 91, 97, 106 [10], 182; **1946:** 37 [2]
    Statement, **1945:** 32

Reparations — *continued*
  Italian, **1946:** 37 [2]
  Japanese, **1945:** 143, 147 [11]; **1946:** 37 [2], 95 [3, 22]; **1947:** 36 [20]; **1951:** 216
    Mission to Japan, statement, **1945:** 182
    News conference remarks, **1945:** 60 [6], 106 [10], 118 [3], 147 [11]
  Rumanian, **1947:** 32
  Soviet Union, for, **1945:** 60 [6]
  Reparations Commission, **1945:** 31 [7], 32, 91, 97; **1946:** 37 [2], 66 [12], 78 [11], 95 [3], 199 [6]; **1947:** 36 [20]
    Appointments to, **1945:** 13, 14, 15
Reports to the Congress.
  See also Congress, reports to, messages transmitting.
  List, Appendix C, **1945:** p. 613; **1946:** p. 533; **1947:** p. 557; **1948:** p. 996; **1949:** p. 611; **1950:** p. 785; **1951:** p. 677; **1952–53:** p. 1240
Reports to the President
  Advisory Board on International Development, **1951:** 53n.
  Advisory Commission on Universal Military Training, **1948:** 190
  Air Coordinating Committee, **1947:** 149n.
  Air Policy Commission, **1947:** 148n.; **1948:** 7
  Aldrich, Winthrop W., economic survey of Europe, **1950:** 11ftn. (p. 108)
  Anglo-American Committee of Inquiry, **1946:** 89, 92, 95 [7, 9], 163 [5], 227
  Armed forces unification, **1946:** 126 [16], 137, 138
  Atomic bomb tests, **1946:** 163 [1]
  Atomic Energy Commission, **1948:** 103, 164
  Attorney General Clark
    Patent practices and policies, **1947:** 109
    Statutes governing war powers and war agencies, **1945:** 128 and ftn. (p. 275)
  Bell, Daniel W., economy of Philippines, **1950:** 238 [5], 273 [2, 10], 278 [11]
  Bennett, Dr. Henry G., point 4 program, **1951:** 83
  Biddle, Francis, war crimes trials, **1946:** 251
  Bruce, Howard, surplus property, **1946:** 84 [2]
  Budget Bureau Director
    Coordination of Defense Department and General Services Administration, **1949:** 145n.
    Training of veterans, **1950:** 36
  Bush, Vannevar, "Science, the Endless Frontier," **1945:** 223n.
  Cabinet Committee on World Food Programs, **1947:** 47, 139
  Census Bureau, economic report, **1952–53:** 363
  Citizens Food Committee, **1947:** 218 [6], 236 [1]
  Civil Rights Committee, **1947:** 215, 218 [4]; **1948:** 20

Reports to the President — *continued*
  Commission on the Health Needs of the Nation, **1952–53:** 352
  Commission on Immigration and Naturalization, **1952–53:** 366
  Commission on Labor Relations in Atomic Energy Installations, **1949:** 81
  Commission on Migratory Labor, **1951:** 75
  Commission on Organization of the Executive Branch of the Government, **1949:** 47, 50, 94, 111; **1950:** 54
  Commission on Renovation of the Executive Mansion, **1949:** 31n.
  Committee on Equality of Treatment and Opportunity in the Armed Forces, **1950:** 141
  Committee of European Economic Cooperation, **1947:** 191 [4]
  Committee on Religion and Welfare in the Armed Forces, **1950:** 32n.; **1951:** 100
  Communications Policy Board, **1950:** 40n.
  Council of Economic Advisers, **1946:** 266 [2, 4, 6, 8, 14, 16]; **1948:** 167
  Debt management and credit control, **1951:** 44n.
  Department of the Interior, river valleys reclamation projects, **1948:** 119
  Dulles, John Foster, discussions on Japanese peace treaty, **1951:** 84
  Factfinding boards in labor disputes, **1949:** 144 [20]
    General Motors strike, **1946:** 9, 15 [6, 14], 16
    Steel strike, **1946:** 16
  Federal Security Administrator, national health plan, **1948:** 181 [2], 237 [3]
  Federal Works Administrator, fire prevention, **1948:** 113
  Firestone, Harvey S., Jr., reactivation of USO, **1949:** 104
  Foreign Aid, Committee on, **1947:** 219
  Gray, Gordon, foreign economic policy, **1950:** 273 [3], 282
  Harrison, Earl G.
    Displaced persons in Europe, **1946:** 227
    Displaced persons in Germany, **1945:** 152, 187, 188
  Higher Education, Commission on, **1947:** 235
  Jackson, Robert H., war crimes, **1945:** 52 [2, 9], 60 [9]; **1946:** 233
  Kaiser, Henry J., United National Clothing Collection, **1945:** 74n.
  Keyserling, Leon H., New England economy, **1951:** 142
  Korea, U.S. forces in, **1950:** 194
  Locke, Edwin A., Chinese economy, **1946:** 15 [24], 41 [12]
  Lovett, Robert A.
    Convention on wage and hour statistics in mining and manufacturing industries, **1949:** 13

Reports to the President — *continued*
  Lovett, Robert A. — *continued*
    Inter-American Convention on the Granting
      of Political Rights to Women, **1949:** 10
    Inter-American Treaty of Reciprocal Assis-
      tance, **1947:** 230
    OAS Charter, **1949:** 9
  MacArthur, Gen. Douglas, estimate of situation
    in Korea, **1950:** 194n.
  McKeever, R. L., liquidation of war agencies,
    1946: 145
  Materials Policy Commission, **1952–53:** 179, 191,
    192, 355
  Merchant Marine, Advisory Committee on,
    1947: 223
  Military chaplaincy, **1950:** 297
  Mine disaster, Secretary Chapman's report,
    1952–53: 19
  Missouri Basin Survey Commission, **1952–53:**
    3n.
  National Capital Sesquicentennial Commission,
    1950: 77
  National Historical Publications Commission,
    1951: 127
  National Security Resources Board, Chairman,
    1952–53: 375
  National Security Resources Board, civil de-
    fense, **1950:** 251
  News conference remarks, **1947:** 218 [3]
  Office of Alien Property Custodian, **1946:** 231
  Office of War Mobilization and Reconversion,
    1946: 18 (pp. 37, 52, 71), 72 [2, 4, 7, 8], 73,
    143 [2], 163 [2], 164, 226 [1, 6, 15]
    Guaranteed wage, **1947:** 53
  Pauley, Edwin W., Japanese reparations, **1946:**
    95 [3, 22]
  Philippine War Damage Commission, **1951:** 64
  President's Committee on the Integration of the
    Medical Services of the Government,
    1946: 139
  President's Scientific Research Board, **1948:** 22
  Price, Byron, relations between U.S. occupation
    forces and German people, **1945:** 193 [11],
    201n., 202 [9]
  Religion and Welfare in the Armed Forces,
    President's Committee on, **1949:** 73
  Review Committee on Deferment of Govern-
    ment Employees, letter, **1945:** 183
  Rosenman, Samuel I., economy of Northwest
    Europe, **1945:** 35
  Scientific Research Board, **1947:** 183, 194n., 201,
    206, 211; **1948:** 186
  Secretary Acheson
    Brussels NATO meeting, **1950:** 311
    Paris foreign ministers meeting, **1949:** 135
  Secretary Anderson, food shipments abroad,
    1946: 144, 165, 255

Reports to the President — *continued*
  Secretary Byrnes, treaty with Philippines, **1946:**
    185
  Secretary Harriman, natural resources, **1947:** 210
    [5]
  Secretary Krug
    National resources and foreign aid, **1947:** 209
      [9], 210 [5], 212, 217
    Navajo Indians, **1947:** 229
  Secretary Marshall
    Administration of the Pacific islands, **1947:**
      119
    Foreign Assistance, **1947:** 210 [1]
    International Labor Conference, **1947:** 126
    International telecommunications and radio
      regulations, **1948:** 29
    Maritime employment, **1947:** 123, 124
    U.N. meetings in Paris, **1948:** 230
  Secretary Sawyer
    Business conditions, **1949:** 171 [11]
    Federal transportation program, **1949:** 266
  Snyder, John W.
    Grain Shipments abroad, **1946:** 144
    Housing, **1945:** 211 [1]
    Postwar reconversion, **1945:** 128 and ftn. (p.
      265)
  Steel Industry Board, **1949:** 209
  Tennessee Valley Authority, **1947:** 243 [18]
  Trial of enemy collaborators in Philippines,
    1946: 63
  United Nations International Children's Emer-
    gency Fund, United States Committee
    for, **1949:** 257
  Universal Training Advisory Commission on,
    1947: 106
  Veterans Affairs Administrator, **1950:** 36
  Water Resources Policy Commission, **1950:** 306;
    1951: 55
  Wyatt, Wilson W., housing, **1946:** 32, 250 [8]
Repplier, T.S., **1947:** 191 [3]
Republic Steel Corp., **1949:** 155 [12]; **1951:** 305
Republican Fact Book, **1948:** 183 [6]
Republican National Committee, **1946:** 192 [26],
  262 [20]; **1949:** 161 [15], 171 [5]; **1950:** 39;
  1951: 63 [3]
Republican National Committee, Chairman (Guy
  G. Gabrielson), **1950:** 105 [19], 250 [3],
  273 [7]
Republican National Committee, Chairman (B.
  Carroll Reece), **1946:** 72 [11]; **1947:** 67 [5]
Republican National Committee, Chairman (Hugh
  Scott, Jr.), **1948:** 266; **1949:** 155 [10]
Republican National Convention, **1948:** 138 [3],
  139 [2], 160, 183 [6, 7], 227 [1], 229, 231 [1],
  232, 252, 258, 266; **1952–53:** 120, 267, 276,
  278, 279, 283, 293, 303 [4, 6], 317 [3], 318,
  320

Republican National Convention — *continued*
  Contest over nomination, **1952–53:** 286 [4]
  Eisenhower, Gen. Dwight D., views on, **1952–53:** 197 [16]
  Liberal and conservative party wings, contest between, **1952–53:** 292 [8]
  MacArthur, Gen. Douglas A., appointment as keynoter, **1952–53:** 166 [2, 17], 175 [11]
  News conference remarks on, **1952–53:** 197 [16]
"Republican News," **1948:** 183 [6]
Republican Party, **1946:** 67, 86 [9, 31], 250 [1]; **1947:** 14 [3], 31 [4], 36 [12, 18], 46 [14], 62 [10], 68, 78 [5, 9], 145 [2], 177 [16], 180 [7], 191 [14], 232 [6], 243 [12]; **1948:** 101, 121, 160, 172, 176, 247; **1949:** 190; **1950:** 134, 135; **1951:** 247 [15], 297; **1952–53:** 129, 218
  Campaign remarks, **1948:** 138 [6], 183 [1, 2, 4–7], 184, 194 [2], 195, 198 [3, 5], 199, 200 [4], 201, 202 [1, 2, 4–6], 203, 204 [3], 205, 206 [2–4], 207, 208 [1, 6–8], 209, 211, 212 [3–5, 7, 9], 213, 214 [1, 5, 7], 215, 216 [1–4, 7, 15], 217, 218 [1, 9, 12], 219, 220, 222 [1, 4–8, 10], 223, 225 [3], 226, 227 [1, 3, 6, 7], 228 [1, 8, 9, 11], 229, 231 [1, 6, 7], 232, 234, 236 [5, 6], 237 [5], 238, 239, 240 [2], 241, 242 [1, 3], 246–252, 254–256, 257 [2, 3, 5], 258, 259 [1–3, 5], 260, 261 [2–5, 9, 11, 12, 15], 262, 264 [1–3, 5], 266, 267 [1–3], 268; **1952–53:** 69, 218, 238 [14], 241, 242 [2], 247 [10, 12], 253 [6], 266 [1, 2, 10], 267, 268 [5], 269, 270 [8, 10], 272, 276, 278, 280 [3, 4, 6], 281, 284 [2, 6], 285, 286 [1, 3, 5, 6], 287, 288, 289 [1–4, 7–12], 290, 291, 292 [2–13], 293, 294, 295 [2, 3, 5–9], 296, 297, 298 [5], 304, 306 [3, 5, 7], 307, 308 [7], 312, 313 [3], 314, 315 [5], 316, 317 [4–7], 318, 319 [1, 4, 6], 320, 321 [5], 322, 334 [17]
  Campaign slogan, 1952, suggested, **1951:** 179 [6]
  Coalition with "Dixiecrats," **1949:** 269 [8]; **1951:** 179 [2]; **1952–53:** 318
  Congressmen, meetings with, **1949:** 58 [31]
  Criticism of administration foreign policy, **1951:** 108 [4]
  "Declaration of Conscience," issued by Republican Senators, **1950:** 152ftn. (p. 451)
  Electoral victory, **1952–53:** 334 [13], 342 [18]
  Foreign policy, criticism of, **1952–53:** 69, 129, 242 [2]
  Foreign policy statement, **1950:** 214 [11]
  News conference remarks, **1948:** 55 [2], 84 [10], 150 [1, 6], 163 [17], 170 [1, 3]; **1949:** 7 [39], 30 [7], 52 [6, 7], 58 [14, 17, 31], 155 [10], 179 [23], 269 [8]; **1950:** 3 [13], 29 [15], 34 [6], 44 [7, 12], 80 [1, 4, 12], 86 [20], 105 [19], 152 [1, 8], 186 [5], 214 [11], 270 [10], 309 [1]; **1952–53:** 156 [8], 197 [16, 19], 377 [21]

Republican Party — *continued*
  Opposition to administration measures, **1952–53:** 69, 213, 218, 240 [2], 241, 242, 266 [1–6, 9, 11, 13], 267, 268 [2–5, 7, 8], 269, 270 [1, 6, 8, 9, 10], 271, 272, 273, 274 [1–5], 276, 277 [1–3, 6], 278, 280 [1, 3, 4, 6], 281, 282 [1, 3, 4, 6, 8], 284 [5, 6], 285, 286, 287, 289, 290, 292 [3, 5, 9–13], 293, 294, 295 [3, 6, 7, 9], 296, 297, 298, 300, 303 [1, 2, 5, 9, 10], 304, 305, 306 [1, 4–7], 307–319, 321 [3, 6, 7], 322
  Platforms, **1950:** 34 [6], 39; **1952–53:** 69, 123 [18], 218, 266 [4, 7, 9], 267, 268 [7, 8], 276, 277 [1, 3], 278, 280 [1, 3], 282 [6], 284 [6], 285, 286 [6], 288, 289 [1, 7], 292 [13], 295 [5], 298 [12, 14], 299, 300, 301, 303 [4, 9], 304, 305, 306 [2, 6, 7], 307, 308 [8], 313 [1, 3, 4], 315 [1, 4], 317 [8], 321 [2]
  1948 platform, **1952–53:** 120
  Presidential candidate in 1952, question of, **1951:** 113 [5]
  Primary elections, **1951:** 275 [13]
  Record in office, **1950:** 34 [6], 279
Research, **1947:** 4 (p. 35), 219; **1948:** 5 (pp. 20, 25, 42), 175; **1949:** 8 (pp. 76–78); **1950:** 9 (p. 84); **1951:** 13 (pp. 64, 94, 95); **1952–53:** 18 (pp. 100–103)
  Administration of, **1947:** 201
  Aeronautical, **1948:** 5 (pp. 27, 50), 7, 60, 175
  Agricultural, **1945:** 128; **1946:** 207; **1947:** 7 (pp. 58, 59), 80, 183, 194; **1948:** 5 (p. 44), 8 (pp. 77, 86, 92), 117, 186, 234, 239, 246; **1950:** 6, 110 [3], 111; **1951:** 13 (p. 90), 297; **1952–53:** 5, 18 (p. 92), 126, 267, 367 (p. 1150)
  Atomic energy, **1945:** 93, 156, 193 [10]; **1948:** 156, 164, 239; **1949:** 166 [1], 169; **1950:** 9 (p. 84), 121 [1]; **1951:** 13 (pp. 84–85), 50, 135, 227 [5] and ftn. (p. 527), 246, 256, 293; **1952–53:** 170, 275, 280 [4], 366, 367 (p. 1146)
  Biology, **1952–53:** 18 (p. 87)
  Coal industry, **1952–53:** 305
  Conservation, **1947:** 186
  Construction industry, **1951:** 13 (p. 90)
  Defense, **1949:** 8 (pp. 56, 60)
  Economic, **1947:** 110, 122
  Expenditures for, **1948:** 27; **1952–53:** 231
  Federal agency, proposed, **1945:** 128, 192, 218; **1946:** 18 (p. 83)
  Fuels, liquid synthetic, **1949:** 226 [6]
  General purpose, **1952–53:** 367 (pp. 1155–1156)
  Health programs, **1951:** 13 (pp. 98, 99), 135, 297, 307
  Housing, **1946:** 18 (p. 63), 263; **1948:** 5 (p. 38), 8 (p. 84); **1949:** 2, 126, 157; **1950:** 9 (p. 81)
  Industrial, **1947:** 183, 194; **1948:** 8 (p. 86), 37, 186, 239; **1950:** 13; **1951:** 297

Research — *continued*
  Medical, **1945:** 192; **1946:** 18 (p. 83); **1947:** 2 (p. 11), 98, 183, 211; **1948:** 18, 22, 89, 181 [2], 186, 205, 237 [3], 239; **1949:** 8 (p. 70); **1950:** 9 (pp. 75, 84); **1951:** 13 (p. 98, 99), 135, 297, 307; **1952–53:** 18 (pp. 87, 106), 243, 249, 268 [8], 333, 367 (p. 1157), 376
  Military, **1945:** 174; **1946:** 18 (p. 75), 137, 138; **1947:** 7 (pp. 64, 65), 194; **1948:** 5 (p. 26), 175, 186; **1950:** 9 (pp. 64, 84); **1951:** 13 (pp. 69, 70), 89, 92; **1952–53:** 18 (p. 72), 275, 367 (p. 1137)
  Mineral, **1947:** 175; **1948:** 8 (p. 67); **1950:** 124 [7]
  Natural resources, **1947:** 212
  Public health, **1948:** 5 (p. 35)
  Salt water utilization, **1950:** 8 [17]; **1952–53:** 199
  Scientific, **1945:** 128, 218; **1946:** 18 (p. 52), 201, 234, 262 [2]; **1947:** 2 (p. 11), 7 (pp. 76, 77), 35, 109, 110, 169, 183, 192, 194, 201, 206, 211, 241; **1948:** 5 (pp. 20, 41), 8 (pp. 67, 68, 86), 104, 186, 195, 239, 246; **1949:** 8 (p. 78), 166 [1]; **1950:** 2, 9 (p. 84), 120; **1951:** 13 (pp. 85, 86, 95, 96), 89, 135; **1952–53:** 5, 13, 18 (pp. 87, 103), 218, 367 (p. 1156)
    Federal assistance, **1945:** 223
  Small business, **1950:** 106
  Synthetic liquid fuels, **1952–53:** 18 (p. 89)
Research Board, Presidential, **1947:** 4 (p. 35)
Research Board for National Security, **1945:** 128
Research and Development, Interdepartmental Committee on, **1948:** 27
Research and Development Board, **1947:** 191 [1]; **1949:** 50; **1950:** 29 [22]
Research and Development Board, Chairman (Vannevar Bush), **1947:** 192
Research and Marketing Act, **1947:** 7 (p. 80); **1948:** 5 (p. 45)
Reserve Association, **1949:** 234 [1]
Reserve forces, **1945:** 174; **1947:** 2 (p. 12), 7 (pp. 64, 65); **1948:** 5 (pp. 20, 26, 27), 53, 243 [1, 4]; **1949:** 8 (pp. 56, 58–59)
  Appointments to Naval Academy, **1947:** 35
  Authorized strength, **1950:** 9 (p. 63)
  Call to active duty, **1947:** 35; **1950:** 186 [10], 191 [15], 193, 194, 270 [5, 8], 303; **1951:** 13 (pp. 68, 69), 15, 92; **1952–53:** 18 (p. 72)
  Coast Guard, **1952–53:** 18 (p. 83)
  Drill pay, **1948:** 5 (p. 27)
  Expenditures for, **1952–53:** 367 (p. 1137)
  Increase in strength, **1952–53:** 18 (p. 72), 367 (p. 1137)
  Legislation, proposed, **1952–53:** 18 (p. 71)
  News conference remarks, **1949:** 7 [16], 211 [7], 234 [1]
  Officers, appointment of, **1952–53:** 38
  Organized Reserve Corps Armory, Kansas City, dedication, **1951:** 209 [5], 218

Reserve forces — *continued*
  Retirement, **1949:** 174
    Benefits, **1948:** 145
  Training, **1950:** 9 (p. 63); **1951:** 13 (pp. 63, 64)
Reserve Officers Association, **1949:** 36; **1950:** 176; **1951:** 218
Reserve Officers Training Corps, **1946:** 75 [13]; **1950:** 9 (p. 64); **1952–53:** 18 (p. 72)
Resignations, letters
  Acheson, Dean, **1952–53:** 380
  Anderson, Clinton P., **1948:** 94
  Baruch, Bernard, **1947:** 1
  Biddle, Francis, **1945:** 36; **1946:** 251
  Bowles, Chester, **1946:** 148
  Brannan, Charles F., **1952–53:** 385
  Briggs, Lyman J., **1945:** 179
  Byrnes, James F., **1947:** 3, 3n.
  Chapman, Oscar, **1952–53:** 384
  Clifford, Clark M., **1950:** 24
  Committee on Fair Employment Practice, **1946:** 154
  Donaldson, Jesse M., **1952–53:** 383
  Early, Stephen T., **1945:** 43
  Forrestal, James, **1949:** 46
  Griswold, Dwight, **1948:** 188
  Hand, Judge Learned, **1951:** 112
  Hannegan, Robert E., **1947:** 227
  Harriman, W. Averell, **1948:** 83
  Hopkins, Harry L., **1945:** 71
  Jackson, Justice Robert H., **1946:** 233
  Johnson, Louis A., **1950:** 245
  Jones, Marvin, **1945:** 39
  Kenyon, Dorothy, **1950:** 10
  Keyes, Lt. Gen. Geoffrey, **1950:** 274
  Knudsen, Lt. Gen. William S., **1945:** 55
  Krug, Julius A., **1945:** 162; **1949:** 255
  Land, Vice Adm. Emory S., **1946:** 3
  Lehman, Herbert H., **1946:** 68
  Lilienthal, David E., **1946:** 243
  Locke, Edwin A., Jr., **1946:** 269
  Lovett, Robert A., **1949:** 4 [1]; **1952–53:** 371
  Markham, James E., **1946:** 231
  Marshall, Gen. George C., **1949:** 4 [1]; **1951:** 222
  McGranery, James P., **1952–53:** 382
  Morgenthau, Henry, Jr., **1945:** 76 [3]
  O'Connor, Dr. Basil, **1949:** 214 [1], 215
  Parker, Judge John J., **1946:** 230
  Patterson, Robert P., **1947:** 150
  Paul, Randolph, **1946:** 134
  Perkins, Frances, **1945:** 37
  Porter, Paul A., **1946:** 256
  Roberts, Justice Owen J., **1945:** 76 [5]
  Rosenman, Samuel I., refusal to accept, **1945:** 46
  Sawyer, Charles, **1952–53:** 374
  Small, John D., **1946:** 260
  Smith, Harold D., **1946:** 140
  Snyder, John W., **1952–53:** 381

Resignations, letters — *continued*
    Stettinius, Edward R., Jr., **1945:** 67 [1]; **1946:** 127
    Stimson, Henry L., **1945:** 139
    Tobin, Maurice J., **1952–53:** 386
    Walker, Frank C., **1945:** 22 [2]
    Wickard, Claude R., **1945:** 38
    Wilson, Charles E., **1952–53:** 70
    Wyatt, Wilson W., **1946:** 259
Resources, national, **1947:** 122
Resources for Freedom, report of Materials Policy
        Commission, **1952–53:** 191, 192
Resources Survey Commission, New York-New
        England, proposed, **1950:** 140, 265
Restaurants
    Food conservation by, **1948:** 14
    Grain conservation by, **1947:** 209 [2]
    Prices, **1948:** 56 [5]
Retail Coal Association, St. Louis, **1950:** 3 [4]
Retail sales, **1945:** 202 [3]; **1952–53:** 33
Retirement, **1952–53:** 69
    Age reduction, **1948:** 8 (p. 85)
    Civil service, **1952–53:** 231
    Coal miners, trust fund, **1948:** 171
    Congressmen, **1945:** 128
    Employees of international organizations, **1952–
        53:** 207
    Government employees, **1947:** 6 [2], 7 (pp. 73,
        91); **1948:** 5 (pp. 22, 54, 56); **1949:** 8 (p.
        71), 132; **1950:** 9 (pp. 50, 76, 101), 170;
        1951: 13 (pp. 104, 105); **1952–53:** 18 (p.
        110), 367 (p. 1163)
    Income, **1948:** 8 (p. 87)
    Judges, Federal, **1949:** 205 [16]
    Military personnel, **1947:** 35; **1949:** 174; **1950:** 9
        (p. 61); **1952–53:** 18 (p. 70), 367 (p. 1136)
        Credit for foreign service 1898–1912, veto,
            1945: 205
        Disabled, **1948:** 33
    Pensions, private plans, **1950:** 6
    Personal plans, the President's, **1952–53:** 123 [9,
        14, 22], 156 [9], 184, 228 [5, 10]
    Railroad, **1952–53:** 213, 367 (p. 1156)
        Trust fund, **1947:** 7 (p. 58), 145 [2], 181 (p.
            400); **1948:** 5 (pp. 34, 36), 175; **1949:** 8
            (pp. 49, 69, 71); **1950:** 8 [10], 9 (pp. 50,
            73), 74, 76; **1951:** 13 (pp. 55, 98, 99), 280;
            1952–53: 18 (pp. 104–106), 231, 270 [5],
            306 [6], 367 (pp. 1158–1159)
    Special groups, plans for, **1951:** 12 [44]
    Veterans, **1949:** 72 [9]
Retirement and Disability Fund, Civil Service,
        1952–53: 367 (p. 1163)
Retirement Policy for Federal Personnel, Commit-
        tee on, **1952–53:** 367 (p. 1163)
Retraining and Reemployment Administration,
        1945: 128
Reuter, Ernst, **1949:** 54

Reuther, Walter, **1948:** 71 [2], 184; **1949:** 122 [10,
        14]; **1951:** 307n.; **1952–53:** 175 [16]
    Message, **1945:** 206n.
Revenue Act, **1946:** 18 (pp. 72, 74)
Revenue Act of 1948, **1948:** 175; **1949:** 8 (p. 49);
        1950: 18
Revenue Act of 1950, **1950:** 18n., 200n., 284; **1951:**
        13 (pp. 65, 66), 91
Revenue Act of 1951, **1951:** 22ftn. (p. 125), 264;
        1952–53: 18 (p. 112), 231
Revenue cutter crews, veteran status, veto, **1946:**
        188
Revercomb, William Chapman, **1952–53:** 297, 300,
        301, 313 [4]
Revere, Paul, **1948:** 199; **1949:** 192 [24]
Review Committee on Deferment of Government
        Employees, report, letter, **1945:** 183
Revolutionary War, **1945:** 164 [3]; **1950:** 37, 42,
        185, 269; **1951:** 30; **1952–53:** 296, 366
Revolutions, character of, **1951:** 225
Reynolds, James, **1947:** 145 [2]
Reynolds, Milton J., **1947:** 74
Reynolds, Quentin, **1947:** 191 [3]
Reynolds, Thomas F., **1946:** 37 [5]
RFC.
    See Reconstruction Finance Corporation.
Rhee, Syngman, **1950:** 211, 260n.; **1952–53:** 156
        [11]
    Voice of America broadcasts, prohibition,
        1952–53: 166 [11]
Rhine River, free navigation of, **1948:** 86
Rhode Island
    Campaign remarks, **1948:** 261 [5]; **1952–53:** 298
        [5], 299
    Candidates for public office, **1948:** 261 [5];
        1952–53: 298 [5], 299
    Gov. John O. Pastore, **1948:** 261 [5]; **1949:** 260
        [12]
    Gov. Dennis J. Roberts, **1952–53:** 298 [5], 299
    Sen. Theodore F. Green, **1945:** 60n.
Rhodes, George M., **1948:** 227 [2]; **1952–53:** 303
        [10]
Rhodes, James, **1948:** 138 [8]
Ribicoff, Repr. Abraham A., **1952–53:** 292, 293,
        298 [7–10]
Rice, Carl, **1950:** 206 [3]
Rice
    Crop failures, **1946:** 30 [2], 86 [4]
    Exports, **1948:** 8 (p. 93)
    Marketing quota, **1947:** 35
    Price controls, **1946:** 249, 262 [7]; **1947:** 18, 65;
        1950: 9 (p. 86)
Richards, Franklin D., **1947:** 173, 174 [1]
Richards, Repr. James P., **1951:** 53; **1952–53:** 27n.,
        107 [4], 217, 310, 358
    Letters, **1952–53:** 66, 67, 105, 180
Richardson, Lt. Gen. Robert C., Jr., **1946:** 41 [14]

Richardson, Robert O., **1952–53:** 284 [4]
Richardson, Seth (Chairman, Loyalty Review Board), **1950:** 79, 94
Richland, Wash., atomic installation, **1945:** 93, 156
Richmond, Ind.
  Campaign remarks, **1948:** 138 [7], 233 [1]
  Mayor Lester Meadows, **1948:** 138n.
Richmond, Va., **1947:** 31 [1]
Richmond (Va.) Times-Dispatch, **1949:** 119n.
Ridgway, Lt. Gen. Matthew B., **1951:** 85 [10], 144, 171ftn. (p. 426), 200 [1], 209 [11], 216, 300 [15]; **1952–53:** 131, 136 [6], 144, 158, 169, 320
  Appointment to U.N. command, Korea, statement, **1951:** 77
  Authorization to bomb Manchurian targets, question of, **1951:** 90 [5]
  Denmark, endorsement of continued aid, **1952–53:** 217
  Distinguished Service Medal, **1952–53:** 132
  Korean armistice proposal, **1952–53:** 121, 123 [20]
  Supreme Allied Commander, Europe, appointment, **1952–53:** 112, 113
Rifle, Colo., campaign remarks, **1952–53:** 280 [5]
Riggs, Robert L., **1951:** 300 [14]
Right-wing political views, comment on, **1950:** 134
Rights of nations, violation of, **1947:** 68
Riley, Earl, **1948:** 126 [1]
Riley, James Whitcomb, **1948:** 233 [2, 3]
Rio Branco, Gastão Paranhos do, **1947:** 189
Rio de Janeiro, **1949:** 105; **1952–53:** 262
Rio de Janeiro conference, **1947:** 14 [19], 127 [11], 141 [3], 145 [20], 155 [1], 174 [4, 7], 177 [13, 15], 188, 189; **1950:** 218
Rio Grande Basin irrigation project, **1948:** 209; **1951:** 108 [3], 154
Rio Grande River, development, **1947:** 7 (p. 82); **1948:** 5 (p. 46)
Rio Grande Valley, **1952–53:** 97
Rio Pact (1947).
  See Inter-American Treaty of Reciprocal Assistance.
Rios, Juan Antonio, **1945:** 56; **1946:** 143 [9]
  Visit of, statement, **1945:** 170
Ritter, Archbishop Joseph E., **1950:** 162n.
River and Harbor Act of 1950, **1949:** 183n.
River and harbor development, **1946:** 18 (p. 81), 176, 195; **1947:** 7 (pp. 58, 85), 35; **1948:** 2, 4 [20], 5 (pp. 25, 49), 175; **1949:** 8 (p. 87), 183; **1950:** 2, 6, 9 (pp. 49, 90, 93), 33, 129 [1]; **1951:** 11, 13 (pp. 63, 81, 82, 83), 183; **1952–53:** 18 (p. 83), 62, 270 [10], 271, 277 [3], 307, 366, 367 (pp. 1143, 1146), 376, 388
  See also Flood control; Water resources development.
  Appropriations, **1951:** 185; **1952–53:** 109

River and harbor development — *continued*
  Approval of bill, **1950:** 140
  Arkansas River, **1951:** 13 (pp. 86, 87), 185
  Arkansas-White-Red River Basins Inter-Agency Committee, **1950:** 164
  Campaign remarks, **1948:** 125, 126 [1], 128 [1], 134, 149, 214 [4]
  Colorado, **1950:** 121 [13]
  Columbia River, **1952–53:** 271
  Columbia Valley Administration, proposed, **1949:** 40 [9], 78 [14], 144 [19]; **1950:** 121 [4, 8, 13], 124 [1], 125
  Connecticut River, **1952–53:** 292 [7]
  Delaware River Port Authority, approval of bill, **1952–53:** 209
  Mississippi, **1949:** 182 [15]; **1950:** 3 [9, 11, 21], 86 [15], 121 [4, 13]; **1951:** 183, 185
  Missouri, **1950:** 3 [14, 21], 86 [15], 116, 121 [4, 13]; **1952–53:** 3, 26 [23]
  Monongahela, **1950:** 3 [21]
  New England, **1951:** 13 (p. 87)
  New York, **1951:** 13 (p. 87)
  Niagara River.
    See main heading, Niagara River.
  Ohio, **1950:** 3 [9, 11, 21], 121 [4, 13]
  Red River, **1951:** 13 (p. 87)
  Rio Grande, **1951:** 108 [3], 154
  Sacramento, **1950:** 125
  St. Lawrence.
    See St. Lawrence Seaway power project.
  San Joaquin, **1950:** 125
  Savannah, **1950:** 3 [24]
  Snake River, **1950:** 121 [13]
  White River, **1951:** 13 (p. 87)
River Queen, **1947:** 31 [1]
River valley authorities, **1948:** 4 [20]
Rivers, Herbert, **1947:** 20n.
Rivers and Harbors Act, **1950:** 265
"Road Back to America," editorial, **1950:** 146 [4]
Roanoke, Va., **1952–53:** 242 [6]
Roanoke Island, N.C., **1948:** 110 [5]
Roanoke River, **1950:** 125
Roberts, Gov. Dennis J., **1952–53:** 298 [5], 299
Roberts, Owen J., **1946:** 270; **1949:** 11 [12]; **1950:** 23 [12]; **1951:** 295 [8], 300ftn. (p. 641)
  Appointment as Chairman, Committee to Award Medals of Merit to Civilians, **1945:** 137 [4], 157 [3]
  News conference remarks on, **1945:** 76 [4, 5], 107 [7], 118 [11, 14], 129 [8], 132 [2], 137 [4], 157 [3]
  Resignation as Supreme Court Justice, **1945:** 76 [4]
    Letter, **1945:** 76 [5]
Roberts, Roy, **1950:** 312
Robertson, A. W., **1946:** 142; **1947:** 55; **1951:** 54n.
Robertson, Sen. Edward V., **1946:** 84 [12]
Robertson, Walter S., **1946:** 265

Robeson, Paul, **1949:** 155 [2]
Robinson, Bill, **1948:** 89
Robinson, Elmer E., **1948:** 130 [3]; **1950:** 269; **1951:** 216
Robinson, O. P., **1952–53:** 171
Rochambeau, Comte de, **1951:** 275 [8]
Rochester, Minn.
  Campaign remarks, **1948:** 237 [3]
  Mayor Claude McQuillan, **1948:** 237 [3]
Rochester, N.Y., campaign remarks, **1948:** 228 [12]; **1952–53:** 289 [2]
Rock Island, Ill., campaign remarks, **1948:** 194 [1]
Rockefeller, Nelson A., **1950:** 278 [6, 8], 282, 289, 294n.; **1951:** 16 [1], 53
Rockets, **1947:** 194
Rockingham, N.H., campaign remarks, **1952–53:** 295 [4]
Rockwood, Pa., campaign remarks, **1952–53:** 308 [5]
Rodgers, Frank E., **1948:** 189n.
Rodino, Peter, Jr., **1948:** 227 [7]; **1952–53:** 303 [3]
Rodriguez, C., Congressional Medal of Honor presentation, **1945:** 167n.
Rodriguez, Sgt. Joseph C., Congressional Medal of Honor award, **1952–53:** 24
Rodriguez Larreta, Eduardo, **1950:** 137 [26]
Rogers, Repr. Byron G., **1952–53:** 282 [7]
Rogers, Repr. Edith Nourse, **1951:** 247 [4]
Rogers, George, **1948:** 228 [12]
Rogers, Hugo E., **1948:** 261 [13]
Rogers, James Grafton, **1952–53:** 362n.
Rogers, Will, **1946:** 37 [5]
  Memorial to, **1948:** 216 [9, 10]
Rohde, Borge, **1951:** 166n.
Rohde, Ruth Bryan, **1951:** 166n.
Rollins College, **1949:** 51
Rolvaag, Karl F., **1948:** 237 [2–4]; **1952–53:** 313 [5]
Romagna, Jack, **1946:** 53 [14], 61 [11], 66 [1]; **1947:** 177 [7]; **1950:** 29 [15]; **1951:** 33 [12], 37 [9], 56 [25], 179 [7], 300 [17]; **1952–53:** 253 [4], 345 [1]
Román y Reyes, Victor, death of, **1950:** 109
Romans, ancient, legacy to U.S. political system, **1950:** 87
Rome, **1946:** 253, 268; **1947:** 67 [13], 185
Rome, ancient, **1951:** 8, 18, 218
Rome, N.Y., campaign remarks, **1948:** 228 [6]; **1952–53:** 289 [5]
Romero, Alice, **1948:** 208n.
Romulo, Brig. Gen. Carlos P., **1949:** 237; **1951:** 40n., 49 [5], 208n.
Romulo, Ricardo, **1951:** 40n.
Rooney, Repr. John J., **1952–53:** 300
Roosevelt, Franklin D., **1945:** 1n., 3, 5, 10, 12, 24, 27, 43, 45, 46, 56, 61, 63, 66, 68, 71, 74, 87, 93, 97, 122, 123, 128, 148, 153, 155, 163, 165, 177, 178, 179, 196n., 223n., 225;

Roosevelt, Franklin D. — *continued*
  1946: 3n., 18 (pp. 38, 53), 22, 25, 26, 67, 68, 76, 81, 83, 90, 97, 100, 112, 117, 131, 133, 188, 213, 222, 232, 243, 244, 272; **1947:** 17, 24, 68, 109, 162, 167; **1948:** 32, 43, 50n., 86, 90, 101, 125, 160; **1949:** 38, 86, 128, 134, 154, 172, 215n., 220, 251, 273; **1950:** 3ftn. (p. 15), 12, 82, 110 [5], 125, 137 [12], 138, 158; **1951:** 49 [6], 56 [25, 26], 70 [1], 190, 216, 230n., 251 [27], 275ftn. (p. 601); **1952–53:** 26 [15], 63, 78, 107 [10], 130, 136 [17], 144, 174, 233 [7], 242 [2], 266 [10, 13], 277 [3], 278, 281, 283, 284 [5], 289 [1, 2, 5, 11], 290, 291, 292 [1], 296, 298 [1, 8, 12, 14], 300, 303 [2], 305, 306 [1, 7], 307, 308 [2, 3], 311 [1], 312, 314, 315 [4], 318, 321 [2, 6], 366, 378
  Anti-depression program, **1948:** 258
  Atomic bomb project, inception by, **1948:** 239
  Campaign remarks on, **1948:** 122 [2], 126 [6], 128 [1], 130 [1, 2], 184, 198 [4–6], 199, 200 [1, 5], 201, 205, 212 [10], 216 [4], 217, 218 [7, 8], 222 [3], 226, 227 [3, 5–7], 228 [1, 11], 231 [3, 5], 233 [1, 2, 6], 236, 239, 240 [5, 7], 245, 246, 248, 249, 255, 256, 257 [3], 258, 259 [1, 2], 260, 261 [3, 4, 13], 262, 264 [5], 265, 268
  Commemorative coins, policy on, **1947:** 162
  Conservation program, **1948:** 216 [4]
  Farm programs, **1948:** 217, 240 [5], 246
  Foreign policy, bipartisan conduct of, **1948:** 245
  Fourth anniversary of death, remarks, **1949:** 76
  Human rights, championship of, **1948:** 265
  Income taxes, views on, **1949:** 11 [6]
  Influence of mother on, **1948:** 261 [13]
  Labor program, **1948:** 248, 259 [1], 261 [3]
  Letters on oil, **1947:** 78 [20]
  Memorial program, **1947:** 71
  Netherlands decoration, posthumous award, **1948:** 87
  News conference remarks on, **1945:** 4 [1, 8], 22 [1], 31 [3], 67 [1], 76 [2], 118 [12, 14], 147 [13], 164 [8], 172 [2], 175 [5], 181 [3]; **1946:** 21 [1], 27 [17], 37 [2, 4], 95 [20], 136 [13], 237 [11]
  Nomination (1932), **1948:** 256
  Program, President's commitment to continue, **1948:** 268
  "Public Papers and Addresses of Franklin D. Roosevelt," **1950:** 199n.
  Record in office, **1948:** 240 [7], 260, 264 [5]
  Vice-Presidential candidacy (1920), **1948:** 231 [3]
Roosevelt, Franklin D., Library, **1946:** 118; **1951:** 251 [27]
Roosevelt, Franklin D., U.S.S., **1951:** 275 [4]
Roosevelt, Mrs. Franklin D., **1945:** 177, 219n.; **1946:** 81, 173 [1]; **1947:** 71n., 130; **1948:**

Roosevelt, Mrs. Franklin D. — *continued*
   30, 150 [6], 211; **1949:** 76, 251n.; **1950:**
   5n., 219, 239; **1951:** 266n.; **1952–53:** 129,
   197 [3], 289 [5], 290, 378
  Disagreement with Cardinal Spellman, **1949:** 166
   [8], 171 [2]
  News conference remarks on, **1945:** 4 [3, 17];
   1949: 171 [2, 17], 205 [7], 226 [19]
  Newspaper column, comment on riots at Peekskill, N.Y., **1949:** 205 [7]
  U.N. position, offer to resign, **1949:** 171 [2, 17]
  Views on pending Indian legislation, **1949:** 226
   [19]
Roosevelt, Repr. Franklin D., Jr., **1950:** 105 [3]
Roosevelt, James, **1949:** 58 [9], 260 [20]; **1950:** 105
   [5], 179 [8]
Roosevelt, Sara Delano, **1948:** 261 [13]
Roosevelt, Theodore, **1948:** 65, 81, 199, 236; **1950:**
   94; **1951:** 215; **1952–53:** 62, 78, 136 [17],
   277 [1, 3], 280 [6], 312, 317 [3], 388
Roosevelt, Theodore, National Park, disapproval,
   1946: 200
Roosevelt Memorial Association, **1945:** 127
Roosevelt National Memorial Committee, **1945:**
   153
Root, Elihu, **1949:** 102n., 103n.
Roper, Elmo, poll, **1948:** 243 [6]; **1952–53:** 129, 143
Roper, Elmo B., Jr., **1952–53:** 143
Rosebud Indian Reservation, **1950:** 129 [2]
Rosenberg, Anna M., **1946:** 268; **1951:** 22 [14]
Rosenberg, Ethel, **1952–53:** 377ftn. (p. 1192)
Rosenberg, Julius, **1952–53:** 377ftn. (p. 1192)
Rosenman, Samuel I., **1946:** 21 [1], 22, 143 [1],
   268n.; **1950:** 199n.
  News conference remarks on, **1945:** 4 [2], 44 [19]
  Report on economy of Northwest Europe, **1945:**
   35
  Resignation, refusal to accept, letter, **1945:** 46
Roseville, Calif.
  Campaign remarks, **1948:** 128 [1], 202 [4]
  Mayor Harold T. Johnson, **1948:** 128 [1], 202 [4]
Ross, Betsy, **1948:** 130 [3]
Ross, Charles A., **1948:** 261n.
Ross, Charles G., **1945:** 64, 67n., 164 [1, 2]; **1946:**
   15 [7], 21 [4], 53 [2], 66 [1], 84 [20], 163
   [11], 250 [13]; **1947:** 6, 19 [14], 164, 180 [1],
   181 [1], 210 [5], 218 [14], 236 [1]; **1948:** 86,
   89 163 [5], 243 [1], 274 [1]; **1949:** 7 [1], 52
   [18], 72 [21], 82, 112 [1], 144 [1], 171 [14],
   223, 240 [16], 260 [17], 265, 267; **1950:** 8
   [1], 46 [1], 80 [8], 152 [10], 209 [3], 214 [2,
   6] and ftn. (p. 587), 250 [5] and ftn. (p.
   640), 266, 287 [1]; **1952–53:** 45, 63, 311n.
  Death of, **1950:** 300
  News conference remarks on, **1945:** 8 [2, 3, 4], 60
   [6], 106, 116, 132 [1], 202 [4]
Ross, John C., **1950:** 219
Ross, Malcolm, **1946:** 154

Ross, Nellie Tayloe (Director, Bureau of the Mint),
   1948: 118 [6]; **1950:** 117 [1], 118
ROTC.
  See Reserve Officers Training Corps.
Rowe, C. Edward, letter, **1945:** 228
Rowe, Hartley, **1946:** 262 [1]
Rowe, James H., Jr., **1949:** 94n.
Rowen, Paul R., **1948:** 26 [1, 4]
Roxas y Acuña, Manuel, **1946:** 111, 122n.; **1947:**
   226 [3]; **1949:** 172
  Death of, **1948:** 78
Royal Air Force, **1945:** 199
Royal Navy, **1945:** 200
Royall, Anne, **1948:** 11 [11]
Royall, Kenneth C.
  See Army, Secretary of the.
Rubber
  Crude, shortage, **1945:** 128, 209
  Prices, **1950:** 202
  Synthetic, **1950:** 13, 114
    Disposal of Federal plants, **1945:** 4 [19]
    Facilities operation by RFC, **1951:** 82
    Production, **1951:** 13 (p. 76)
Rubber Act, **1947:** 99
Rubber Act of 1948, **1950:** 13; **1952–53:** 12
Rubber Development Corporation, **1947:** 7 (p. 95)
Rubber industry, **1947:** 18, 24, 31 [2], 62 [18]
  Strike settlement, **1946:** 53 [2]
Rubber Survey Committee, **1947:** 24
Rubber Workers Union, United, **1945:** 175 [18]
Rubinstein, Anton, **1951:** 99
Rubinstein, Artur, **1951:** 99
Rules governing this publication, Appendix D,
   1945: p. 614; **1946:** p. 534; **1947:** p. 559;
   1948: p. 998; **1949:** p. 612; **1950:** p. 786;
   1951: p. 678; **1952–53:** p. 1241
Rumania, **1946:** 6 [2], 18 (pp. 41, 42)
  Agreements on, **1945:** 91, 97
  Armed forces, **1951:** 174
  Communism in, **1951:** 253
  Peace treaty with, **1947:** 2 (p. 9), 114
  Soviet domination, **1948:** 53, 86
  U.S. relief for, **1947:** 32
  Yalta agreement on, **1947:** 56
Rumania, American Action Committee Against
   Mass Deportations in, remarks, **1952–53:**
   145
Rural areas, **1950:** 111
  Development program, **1948:** 99
  Education, **1950:** 6, 110 [9], 127 [7]
  Employment in, **1950:** 9 (p. 98)
  Hospitals, **1948:** 242 [3]
  Housing, **1946:** 18 (p. 63); **1949:** 2, 8 (p. 76), 126,
   157; **1950:** 6, 9 (p. 80), 110 [9]; **1951:** 13
   (pp. 90, 93); **1952–53:** 126
   See also under Housing.
  Irrigation, **1949:** 245
  Medical care, **1950:** 6, 129 [4]

Rural areas — *continued*
  Schools, **1948:** 234, 242 [3]
  Slum clearance, **1949:** 157
  Telephone service, **1949:** 243; **1950:** 6, 9 (p. 86), 110 [9], 127 [6]; **1951:** 13 (p. 89); **1952–53:** 266 [5, 7, 13], 267 [12], 274 [1], 285
Rural electrification, **1946:** 18 (p. 81), 238; **1947:** 7 (pp. 58, 79, 94); **1948:** 2, 5 (p. 44), 8 (p. 94), 99, 117, 194 [11], 213, 214 [5], 216 [1, 2], 217, 218 [1, 11], 228 [9], 233 [1–3, 5, 6], 234, 236, 237 [5], 242 [3], 246; **1949:** 2, 8 (p. 80), 243; **1950:** 6, 9 (p. 86), 110 [4, 9], 121 [7], 124 [4, 7], 125, 127 [6], 132, 279; **1951:** 11, 13 (p. 89); **1952–53:** 5, 18 (p. 92), 62, 126, 194, 218, 241, 242 [4], 266 [3–7, 9, 13], 267, 268 [2], 270 [10], 271, 274 [1], 277 [3, 6], 282 [3, 6, 8], 284 [4], 285, 295 [7], 307, 311 [2], 313 [2], 314, 315 [2], 319 [4], 366, 367 (p. 1149), 388
Rural Electrification Act, **1948:** 237 [1]; **1949:** 243
Rural Electrification Administration, **1945:** 38; **1946:** 18 (pp. 80–82), 94; **1947:** 7 (p. 79), 181 (p. 405); **1948:** 5 (p. 44), 175, 213, 214 [3], 216 [2, 11], 218 [1], 228 [11], 233 [3], 237 [1]; **1949:** 8 (p. 80), 243; **1950:** 9 (pp. 86, 87), 110 [4, 9], 114, 124 [4, 7], 125, 127 [6]; **1951:** 13 (p. 89); **1952–53:** 18 (p. 92), 194, 266 [1, 3, 5, 6, 7, 9, 13], 267, 268 [2], 270 [10], 274 [1], 282 [3, 6], 285, 314, 315 [3], 388
Rural Electrification Administrator (Claude R. Wickard), **1952–53:** 266 [7]
Rush-Bagot Agreement (1817), **1947:** 111
Rusk, Dean, **1950:** 268
Rusk, Dr. Howard A., **1950:** 156; **1951:** 9n.; **1952–53:** 249
Russell, Bertrand, **1952–53:** 123 [16]
Russell, Sen. Richard B., **1948:** 110 [8]; **1949:** 66 [2], 226ftn. (p. 503); **1950:** 23 [13]; **1951:** 81, 247 [2]; **1952–53:** 27n., 162, 163, 166 [3], 175 [7], 178, 217, 358
  Letters, **1952–53:** 66, 105, 180
  Presidential candidacy, **1952–53:** 31 [10], 127 [8]
Russia.
  See Soviet Union.
Ruy Barbosa, **1947:** 189
Ryan, James V., **1952–53:** 305
Rye, conservation, **1948:** 14
Ryukyu Islands, **1947:** 7 (p. 67)
  Assistance, **1950:** 9 (p. 58)

Sabath, Repr. Adolph J., **1946:** 223 [1]; **1950:** 16 [7], 52 [8, 13]
  Death of, **1952–53:** 327
  Letter, **1945:** 51

Sabotage, measures to combat, **1950:** 46 [11], 199, 203 [8], 207, 254
Sabotage, protection of ports against, **1951:** 13 (p. 83)
Saboteur trials, release of transcript, **1945:** 129 [9]
Sachse, Richard, **1945:** 132 [1]
Sacred Cow, Presidential plane, **1945:** 67 [2]; **1947:** 95 [18]
Sacramento, Calif.
  Campaign remarks, **1948:** 128 [2], 202 [5]
  Mayor Belle Cooledge, **1948:** 128 [2]
Sacramento River, **1950:** 125
Saerchinger, Cesar, **1947:** 90n.
Safe driving, statement, **1945:** 62
Safety
  See also Accident prevention.
  Airway, **1947:** 19 [18], 180 [12]
  Highway, **1947:** 8, 27, 82, 118
  Industry, **1948:** 175
  Waterways, **1948:** 62
Safety, Industrial, President's conference on, **1949:** 55; **1950:** 155
Safety Conference, Highway, **1949:** 26, 114
St. Clair River, **1947:** 171
St. Croix, Virgin Islands, **1948:** 38
St. Croix River bridges, construction, **1947:** 35
St. Elizabeths Hospital, **1946:** 117, 118; **1947:** 35
St. Joseph, Mo., campaign remarks, **1952–53:** 284 [4]
St. Joseph (Mo.) News Press, **1952–53:** 284 [4]
St. Laurent, Louis, **1948:** 273; **1949:** 22 [2]; **1951:** 239 [17], 240; **1952–53:** 23, 175 [7]
St. Lawrence Bridge Commission, **1947:** 172
St. Lawrence Seaway, **1946:** 15 [19], 17 [26], 18 (p. 53), 266 [20]; **1947:** 111, 177 [3], 243 [18]; **1948:** 5 (p. 48), 165, 181 [10]; **1949:** 2, 5; **1951:** 13 (pp. 81–83), 95 [7]; **1952–53:** 15, 18 (p. 88), 23, 44 [11], 62, 98 [32], 102, 175 [7], 189, 266 [2], 294, 295 [2], 298 [2, 3], 313 [6], 314, 367 (p. 1147)
  Accord with New York State on, **1951:** 37 [2]
  Campaign remarks, **1948:** 228 [12], 235 [4, 5], 257 [4]
  Federal vs. State development, **1949:** 30 [6]
  Letters, **1948:** 12
  Message to Congress, **1945:** 155
  News conference remarks, **1945:** 4 [9], 52 [14], 118 [15], 129 [12], 147 [2, 10]; **1950:** 9 [16], 11 [10], 93 [7], 181 [10], 278 [39], 283 [19], 285 [9]; **1949:** 7 [24, 31], 30 [6], 78 [14], 80
  Telegram to Governor Dewey, **1945:** 148
St. Lawrence Seaway power project, **1945:** 148, 155; **1950:** 2, 3 [6, 9, 12, 15], 6, 9 (p. 94), 33, 99, 121 [4, 13], 125, 127 [2], 191 [6], 265; **1951:** 11, 13 (pp. 81–83), 167, 171 [3], 174, 239 [9, 18, 20], 240, 251 [7]; **1952–53:** 15, 21 [16], 44 [11], 62, 102, 175 [7], 189,

St. Lawrence Seaway — *continued*
266 [2], 294, 295 [2], 298 [2, 3], 313 [6], 314, 317 [7]
Canada, joint development with, **1952–53:** 17 [27], 18 (p. 88), 23, 98 [32], 102, 175 [7], 189, 367 (p. 1147)
Letter to President of Senate and Speaker of House, **1952–53:** 189
Message to Congress, **1952–53:** 23
1941 Agreement, **1952–53:** 23, 102
St. Lô, France, Mayor Georges Pierre Lavalley, **1947:** 110
St. Louis, Mo., **1947:** 19 [15], 88 [12]; **1949:** 249; **1950:** 23ftn. (p. 133), 161 [1–3], 162, 279; **1952–53:** 158
Campaign remarks, **1948:** 267 [4], 268; **1952–53:** 322
Chamber of Commerce, **1949:** 205 [11]
Internal Revenue collectorship, **1951:** 251 [9], 300 [5, 6]
Jefferson Memorial project, **1949:** 253 [7]
Proposed, **1948:** 283 [11, 13]
Mayor Joseph M. Darst, **1950:** 161 [2, 3], 162; **1952–53:** 322
Mayor Aloys P. Kaufmann, **1948:** 283[11]
News conference remarks, **1949:** 58 [17], 171 [7], 192 [18], 205 [11], 253 [7]; **1950:** 3 [4], 169 [7], 203 [3]
Post-election remarks, **1946:** 271 [1]
Postmaster Bernard F. Dickmann, **1951:** 226
St. Louis Cardinals, baseball team, **1949:** 192 [18]
St. Louis Citizens Food Committee, **1950:** 3 [4]
St. Louis Post-Dispatch, **1947:** 210 [2]; **1949:** 226 [16]; **1951:** 171 [2], 247 [1], 300 [6, 21]; **1952–53:** 26 [8], 45, 75 [5], 322
St. Louis Retail Coal Association, **1950:** 3 [4]
St. Louis Star Times, editorial, **1948:** 71 [3]
St. Marys River, **1947:** 171
St. Matthew, **1950:** 37
St. Matthew's Gospel, **1949:** 231 [8]; **1951:** 241
St. Patrick's Day
Address, **1948:** 53
News conference remarks, **1948:** 49 [18]
St. Paul, **1946:** 52; **1950:** 37; **1951:** 306; **1952–53:** 182, 337
St. Paul, Minn., **1947:** 209 [12], 226 [13]; **1949:** 250
Campaign remarks, **1948:** 235 [6], 236; **1952–53:** 313 [4]
Mayor Edward K. Delaney, **1948:** 236; **1949:** 250 [2]
St. Paul Pioneer Press, **1949:** 250 [2]
Saipan, U.S. invasion, **1945:** 45, 161, 178
Salary.
See Pay; Wages.
Salary Stabilization Board, **1952–53:** 18 (p. 80)
Salem, Oreg., campaign remarks, **1948:** 126 [2]
Salem College, N.C., **1947:** 46 [25]
Sales tax, Federal, proposed, **1951:** 12 [49], 16 [7]

Sales tax bill, District of Columbia, **1949:** 112 [17]
Salida, Colo., campaign remarks, **1948:** 198 [7]; **1952–53:** 282 [2]
Salina, Kans., **1951:** 158
Salish Indians, **1946:** 151
Salt Lake City, Utah, **1945:** 68; **1949:** 249; **1951:** 270
Mayor Earl J. Glade, **1952–53:** 280n.
Campaign remarks, **1948:** 200 [7], 201; **1952–53:** 280 [1]
Salt water utilization, research, **1950:** 8 [17]
Saltonstall, Sen. Leverett, **1950:** 80 [5]
Saltzman, Charles E., **1949:** 112 [1]
Samarin, Mikhail I., **1948:** 178ftn. (p. 453)
Samoa, American, **1948:** 20, 26 [7]; **1950:** 9 (p. 102)
Administration, **1947:** 119
Civil rights in, **1947:** 130
Transfer to civilian administration, **1949:** 101
Sampson, Edith S., **1950:** 219
San Antonio, Tex.
Campaign remarks, **1948:** 210 [1, 2]
Mayor Alfred Callaghan, **1948:** 210 [1]
San Bernardino, Calif., campaign remarks, **1948:** 133 [3]
San Diego, Calif.
Campaign remarks, **1948:** 206 [1]
Mayor Harley E. Knox, **1948:** 206 [1]
San Francisco, Calif., **1945:** 10, 66, 96; **1946:** 143 [18], 236; **1947:** 74, 88 [1], 129, 189; **1950:** 121 [8], 269
Air photos of defense installations, press publication of, **1951:** 247 [1]
Campaign remarks, **1948:** 130 [1–3], 193 [2], 202 [6]; **1952–53:** 278
Democratic luncheon, remarks, **1951:** 215
Eisenhower rally in, **1952–53:** 320
Internal Revenue collectorship, **1951:** 300 [5]
Japanese peace conference (1951), **1951:** 209 [16], 216, 217, 227ftn. (p. 527)
Mayor Dewey Mead (Acting), **1948:** 202 [6]
Mayor Elmer E. Robinson, **1948:** 130 [3]; **1950:** 269; **1951:** 216
News conference remarks, **1945:** 4 [10, 11, 13], 26 [3], 31 [4], 52 [15], 60 [1, 10], 64 [1], 67 [1], 157 [13]
United Nations conference, **1945:** 1 n., 2, 4 [10, 11, 13], 22ftn. (p. 36), 26 [3], 33, 52 [15], 60 [1, 10], 64 [1], 67 [1], 68, 75, 97, 177; **1948:** 130 [3], 137 [4], 139 [3], 193 [2], 227 [5], 268; **1949:** 160, 210; **1950:** 80 [4], 127 [4], 174, 232, 269; **1951:** 56 [26], 150, 213, 215, 216; **1952–53:** 196, 378
Addresses, **1945:** 10, 66
Visit by the President, **1951:** 179 [9], 193 [10]
San Jacinto, **1946:** 171n.
San Joaquin River, **1950:** 125
San Jose, Calif., **1951:** 284
San Jose Manufacturers, Inc., **1951:** 284

San Juan, P.R., **1952–53:** 104
San Luis Valley project, Colorado, **1949:** 245
San Marcos, Tex., campaign remarks, **1948:** 212 [1]
San Martín, José de, **1948:** 158; **1950:** 212
San Martín, Order of (Argentina), **1949:** 32 [3]
Sandburg, Carl, **1950:** 110 [1]
Sandburg, Carl, *Abraham Lincoln,* **1952–53:** 136
    [17]
Sandburg, Carl, *Life of Lincoln,* **1951:** 90 [16]
Sanderson, Julia, **1951:** 99
Sanderson, Tex., campaign remarks, **1948:** 208 [8]
Sandpoint, Idaho, **1950:** 124 [7]
    Campaign remarks, **1952–53:** 270 [10]
    Mayor Floyd L. Gray, **1950:** 124 [7]
Sandstone Creek watershed, Texas-Oklahoma,
    1952–53: 194
Sandusky, Ohio, **1948:** 76
    Campaign remarks, **1948:** 257 [4]
Santa Barbara, Calif., campaign remarks, **1948:** 133
    [1]
Santelmann, Maj. William F., **1951:** 99
Sara Delano Roosevelt Park, New York, campaign
    remarks, **1948:** 261 [13]
Sardinia, malaria eradication, **1951:** 235
Sargeant, Howland, **1952–53:** 297
Sarratt, A. Reed, Jr., **1952–53:** 98 [3]
Satellite nations, Soviet
    See Communist bloc.
Satti, Dr. C. John, **1952–53:** 298 [6]
Saturday Evening Post, **1952–53:** 143, 233 [2, 8],
    282 [4]
Saudi Arabia
    Crown Prince Amir Saud, **1947:** 34
    King Abdul-Aziz Ibn-Saud, **1945:** 147 [3, 13];
        1946: 110 [13], 241; **1947:** 33
    U.S. oil concessions, **1946:** 110 [13]
Savage, Henry, **1947:** 107 [10]
Savage, John L., **1950:** 294n.
Savage River Dam, **1950:** 135
Savannah, Ga., **1946:** 67
Savannah Harbor, Ga., improvement, veto, **1945:**
    90
Savannah River, **1950:** 3 [9, 24], 125
Savings, personal, **1950:** 6, 202, 243; **1951:** 91,
    137n.; **1952–53:** 15, 148
Savings bonds, **1945:** 76 [3], 171, 213; **1946:** 17 [2],
    18 (p. 73); **1947:** 4 (p. 24), 7 (pp. 61, 91),
    68, 76, 90 [8], 180 [13, 14], 224; **1948:** 5
    (pp. 24, 25, 26), 8 (p. 74), 26 [3, 10], 76,
    175; **1949:** 5, 7 [41], 37, 40 [16], 82, 98;
    1950: 8 [25], 9 (p. 103), 127 [6], 133, 281n.;
    1951: 11, 12 [13], 13 (p. 105), 60, 91, 133,
    153 [1, 13], 167, 210, 213, 290; **1952–53:**
    367 (pp. 1133, 1161)
Savings and loan associations, **1946:** 18 (p. 63);
    1947: 102; **1948:** 5 (p. 40)
Savings and Loan Insurance Corporation, Federal,
    1950: 9 (pp. 55, 80)

Savings and loan insurance premiums, **1946:** 208
Sawyer, Charles W., **1948:** 84 [2, 15], 151, 170 [1]
    See also Commerce, Secretary of.
Sayre, Francis B., **1945:** 129 [2]
Scandinavia, **1946:** 86 [22]; **1948:** 52
    See also specific countries.
Scannell, Joseph S., **1952–53:** 303 [1]
Shaub, William F., **1951:** 93n.
Scheele, Leonard A. (Surgeon General), **1951:** 135
Schenectady, N.Y.
    Campaign remarks, **1948:** 228 [2]; **1952–53:** 289
        [8]
    Mayor Owen Begley, **1948:** 228 [2]
Schilling, Col. David C., **1951:** 268
Schoeneman, George J., **1945:** 100n., 107ftn. (p.
    229); **1947:** 135
Schoeppel, Sen. Andrew F., **1950:** 238 [10]; **1952–
    53:** 129
Scholarships, **1947:** 169, 206n.; **1948:** 5 (p. 42), 186;
    1949: 5, 51; **1950:** 8 [34], 120; **1951:** 13 (p.
    98)
Scholarships, Board of Foreign, **1951:** 103
School Lunch Act, National, **1946:** 128, 235
School lunch program, **1946:** 18 (pp. 60, 81, 84),
    128, 235; **1947:** 4 (p. 33), 7 (p. 80); **1948:**
    2, 99, 117, 216 [1], 231 [7], 233 [2, 5], 234,
    240 [5]; **1950:** 135, 249; **1952–53:** 18 (p.
    105)
School strikes, Gary, Ind., **1946:** 75 [16]
Schools, **1948:** 2, 5 (p. 42), 8 (p. 85), 37, 160; **1950:**
    47, 69, 71; **1952–53:** 5
    See also Education; Teachers.
    Construction, **1949:** 2, 8 (p. 77), 202, 204; **1950:**
        6; **1952–53:** 18 (p. 102), 284 [6]
    Demand for, **1952–53:** 237
    Federal aid.
        See Education.
    Federal property, veto of bill to require segre-
        gation, **1951:** 286
    Federally affected areas, **1951:** 12 [38], 13 (p. 96)
    Fire safety instruction in, **1948:** 113n.
    High school essay contest winners, remarks to,
        1951: 203
    Integration, **1950:** 34 [1], 38 [16]
    Maritime, **1947:** 7 (p. 86)
    Medical, **1949:** 85
    Private and parochial, **1947:** 88 [13]
    Rural, **1948:** 234, 242 [3]
    Shortage of facilities, **1948:** 8 (p. 67), 183 [1, 5],
        219, 228 [8], 237 [3], 241, 257 [1, 3], 259
        [4]; **1950:** 9 (p. 83), 127 [7]
    Technical, subsidies for, **1951:** 85 [9]
    Textbooks, investigation by Un-American Ac-
        tivities Committee, **1949:** 122 [8]
    Virgin Islands, **1948:** 146
    War-affected communities, **1947:** 7 (p. 77)
Schram, Emil, **1946:** 6 [1]

Schricker, Henry F., **1948:** 233 [1–3], 240 [1, 2, 4–7], 254, 255n., 257 [1, 2], 267 [2]; **1950:** 203 [16]; **1952–53:** 286 [1–3], 311 [3], 312, 321 [2]

Schubert, Franz, **1950:** 139

Schubert, Paul, **1947:** 90n.

Schuman, Maurice, **1949:** 72 [14]

Schuman, Robert, **1949:** 68; **1950:** 137 [1], 162, 169 [9], 250ftn. (p. 640), 281, 311; **1951:** 58

Schuman plan for European economic integration, **1951:** 25, 85 [13], 235; **1952–53:** 5, 55, 131, 151, 366

Schwartz, Harold E., **1952–53:** 57

Schwellenbach, Lewis B., **1948:** 235 [4]; **1950:** 126; **1952–53:** 284 [5], 292 [11]
  See also Labor, Secretary of.
  Appointment as Secretary of Labor, **1945:** 40 [1]
  Death of, **1948:** 123, 124 [1], 125

Schwellenbach, Mrs. Lewis, **1950:** 126

Science, **1946:** 18 (p. 39); **1952–53:** 179, 366
  Achievements, **1950:** 159; **1951:** 297; **1952–53:** 13, 81
  Education, **1947:** 169, 183, 206, 211; **1948:** 186; **1950:** 48, 120
  Students, question of draft deferment, **1950:** 238 [7]

"Science, the Endless Frontier" (Bush report), **1945:** 223n.

Science Advisory Committee, **1951:** 89

Science Foundation, National, **1947:** 169, 183, 201n., 206n.; **1948:** 5 (pp. 25, 41, 42); **1949:** 8 (p. 78), 94; **1950:** 9 (p. 84), 105 [20], 120, 134, 238 [7]; **1951:** 13 (pp. 94, 95); **1952–53:** 13, 18 (p. 103), 367 (p. 1155)

"Science and Public Policy," report, **1947:** 183, 194, 201, 206, 211

Science Service, **1950:** 48n.

Science Talent Search, **1949:** 44; **1950:** 48; **1951:** 50; **1952–53:** 52

Scientific research, **1945:** 128, 218; **1946:** 18 (p. 52), 201, 234, 262 [2]; **1947:** 2 (p. 11), 7 (p. 76), 35, 169, 183, 201, 206, 211, 241; **1948:** 5 (pp. 20, 41), 8 (pp. 67, 68, 86), 104, 186, 195, 246; **1949:** 8 (p. 78), 166 [1]; **1950:** 2, 9 (p. 84), 120; **1951:** 13 (pp. 85, 86, 95, 96), 89, 135; **1952–53:** 5, 13, 18, 218, 367 (p. 1156)
  Federal assistance, **1945:** 223
  Radioactive materials, use in, **1948:** 239

Scientific Research Board, **1946:** 234, 262 [2]; **1947:** 7 (p. 76), 109, 183, 206, 211; **1948:** 22, 186

Scientific Research Board, Chairman (John R. Steelman), **1947:** 183, 194n. 201, 211, 241; **1948:** 150 [5]

Scientific Research and Development, Interdepartmental Committee for, **1947:** 201n., 241; **1948:** 27, 186

Scientific Research and Development, Office of, **1945:** 128; **1947:** 7 (p. 77)

Scientific Research and Development, Office of, Director (Vannevar Bush), **1945:** 175 [14]
  Report, "Science, the Endless Frontier," **1945:** 223n.

Scientists
  German, in Spain, issue re, **1945:** 175 [14]
  Government service, **1948:** 191
  Question of draft deferment, **1950:** 238 [7]
  Shortage of, **1949:** 44

Scofield, Frank, resignation, **1952–53:** 35 [9]

Scott, Hazel, **1945:** 168

Scott, Repr. Hugh, **1948:** 266; **1949:** 155 [10]

Scott, Kerr, **1948:** 246; **1951:** 90 [13], 256

Scott, Gov. Leslie (Acting), **1948:** 126 [1, 2]

Scott, John Thad, Jr., **1948:** 26 [2]

Scott, John W., **1945:** 132 [1]

Scott, Gen. Winfield, **1951:** 85 [10], 90 [16]; **1952–53:** 7 [10], 21 [29], 282 [7], 287, 289

Scottish Rite, Ancient and Accepted, Supreme Council, **1951:** 259

Scranton, Pa., **1947:** 182 [8]
  Campaign address, **1948:** 248; **1952–53:** 306 [1]
  Mayor James T. Hanlon, **1948:** 248; **1952–53:** 306n.
  Special grand jury for crime investigation, **1951:** 63 [1]

Scrap metals, customs duties, **1947:** 35

Scrolls, presentation of, **1948:** 89, 162; **1951:** 253n.

Seaborg, Glenn T., **1946:** 262 [1]

Seal, Presidential, **1945:** 175 [5]

Seamen, employment, ILO recommendations, **1947:** 123, 124

Seapower, U.S., **1945:** 178

Seattle, Wash., **1945:** 64 [11, 12]; **1947:** 123
  Air photos of defense installations, press publication of, **1951:** 247 [1]
  Campaign remarks, **1948:** 124 [2], 125; **1952–53:** 275
  Mayor William F. Devlin, **1948:** 124 [2], 125

SEC.
  See Securities and Exchange Commission.

Secaucus, N.J., Mayor John J. Kane, **1948:** 189n.

Secondary boycotts, **1947:** 2 (p. 4)

Secret Service, **1947:** 19 [16, 18]; **1948:** 278 [16]; **1949:** 234 [14]; **1950:** 44 [15], 278 [13]; **1952–53:** 255, 378

Secret Service, Chief (U. E. Baughman, Jr.), **1949:** 265

Securities
  Government, **1948:** 5 (pp. 23, 57), 8 (p. 95)
    Bank holdings, **1947:** 75
  Prices, **1945:** 52 [10]
  Railroad, marketing regulations, **1947:** 160
  Regulation of marketing, **1949:** 154

Securities and Exchange Commission, **1947:** 7 (p. 88); **1948:** 5 (p. 53), 26 [1, 4]; **1949:** 144

Securities & Exchange Commission — *continued*
    [3], 179 [3], 226 [12]; **1950:** 53, 54, 64;
    1951: 56 [24]; **1952–53:** 31 [6], 314
Securities and Exchange Commission, Chairman
    (Edmond M. Hanrahan), **1949:** 149n.
Securities and Exchange Commission, Chairman
    (Harry A. MacDonald), **1951:** 44n.
Security, national.
    See National security.
Security Act, National, **1947:** 42n.; **1948:** 5 (pp. 26,
    29); **1950:** 245
    Amendment, **1949:** 67
Security Council.
    See United Nations Security Council.
Security Council, National.
    See National Security Council.
Security loans, **1948:** 26 [3], 76
Security markets, regulation, **1950:** 157
Security sales, regulation, **1948:** 219
Sedalia, Mo., campaign remarks, **1948:** 138 [2];
    1952–53: 284 [5]
Sedgwick County Kans., Board of Commissioners,
    1950: 256
Seed, for Greek relief, **1947:** 56
Seeds, export controls, **1947:** 58
Segregation.
    See Civil rights; Integration.
Segregation of schools on Federal property, veto of
    bill requiring, **1951:** 286
Selective service, **1945:** 45, 101, 114, 122, 128, 183
    Rejection of applicants on medical grounds,
    1945: 192
Selective Service Act of 1948, **1948:** 151
    Steel industry, provisions for operation of,
    1952–53: 115 [13, 17], 166 [7]
Selective Service Records, Office of, **1947:** 54, 63
Selective Service System, **1945:** 174; **1946:** 15 [20],
    86 [10], 118, 119 [2, 4]; **1947:** 2 (p. 12), 35,
    54, 63; **1948:** 52, 53, 80, 174 [3]; **1949:** 8
    (p. 62); **1950:** 2, 9 (p. 61), 193, 194, 303;
    1951: 13 (pp. 70, 96); **1952–53:** 18 (p. 73),
    187, 367 (p. 1135)
    Extension, question of, **1947:** 31 [18], 36 [4, 24],
    46 [12, 20]
    Inductees, moral safeguards, **1948:** 190
    Legislation, proposed extension and revision,
    1951: 4
    Rejectees, **1951:** 258
    Termination, **1947:** 50, 54, 63
Selective Service System, Director (Maj. Gen.
    Lewis B. Hershey), **1946:** 119 [2]; **1952–
    53:** 185, 187
Selective Training and Service Act, **1945:** 107 [4,
    13], 128; **1946:** 18 (p. 48), 76, 119 [2, 4],
    270; **1947:** 50, 63; **1949:** 8 (p. 59)
    Extension, approval, **1945:** 30
Self-determination for nations, **1946:** 18 (pp. 41, 43)
Seminars, budget, **1947:** 6, 180

Seminoe Dam, Wyo., **1950:** 117 [4]
Seminole, Okla., campaign remarks, **1948:** 216 [2]
Senate Committee to Investigate the National
    Defense Program (World War II).
    See Truman Committee.
Seneca, Nebr., **1950:** 110 [10]
Seneca Falls, N.Y., campaign remarks, **1948:** 228
    [10]
Seneca Falls Convention, women's rights (1848),
    1948: 30
Sengstacke, John H., **1949:** 109n.; **1952–53:** 315 [6]
Seoul, Korea, **1950:** 258ftn. (p. 658), 260n., 268
Separation of church and state, **1951:** 275 [7]
Separation of powers of Government, **1946:** 21 [5],
    268
Sermon, Roger T., **1948:** 270n.; **1950:** 21n.
Sermon on the Mount, **1945:** 227; **1946:** 75 [2], 112;
    1949: 220, 231 [8]; **1950:** 158, 313; **1951:**
    8, 41, 241; **1952–53:** 45, 63
Servicemen's Indemnity Act of 1951, **1952–53:** 367
    (p. 1160)
Servicemen's Readjustment Act, **1946:** 18 (p. 79),
    122; **1947:** 7 (p. 68), 134, 206n.; **1948:** 5
    (pp. 31, 32), 150 [1], 259 [4]; **1949:** 8 (pp.
    62, 64), 151; **1950:** 9 (pp. 69, 70, 79), 36;
    1951: 13 (p. 99); **1952–53:** 18 (p. 108)
Servicemen's Voting Act of 1946, **1952–53:** 68, 96
Sesquicentennial Commission, National Capital,
    1948: 47; **1949:** 144 [31]
Sevareid, Eric, **1947:** 90n.
Sevilla-Sacasa, Guillermo, **1952–53:** 115 [4]
Sewage disposal, **1945:** 192
Seward, William H., **1950:** 309 [1]; **1952–53:** 107
    [10]
SFAW.
    See Solid Fuels Administration for War.
Sforza, Count Carlo, **1949:** 68
SHAEF.
    See Supreme Headquarters, Allied Expedition-
    ary Forces.
Shafter, Maj. Gen. William R., **1948:** 81
Shah Mohammad Reza Pahlavi, **1947:** 203
Shale oil, **1948:** 200 [3]; **1949:** 226 [6]; **1950:** 116
    Experimental station, Wyoming, **1948:** 118 [7]
Shanghai, evacuation of U.S. civilians, **1949:** 89 [2]
SHAPE.
    See Supreme Headquarters Allied Powers
    Europe.
Sharecroppers, **1948:** 99
Sharon Steel Corp., **1951:** 305
Shasta Dam, Calif., **1948:** 203; **1952–53:** 277 [3, 4]
Shatto, Sfc. James, **1952–53:** 321 [4], 322
Shaw, G. Grafton, **1952–53:** 362n.
Shaw, George Bernard, death of, **1950:** 276
Shaw, Mrs. George H., **1950:** 32
Shawnee, Okla., campaign remarks, **1948:** 216 [1]
Shays, Capt. Daniel, **1948:** 259 [4]
Shays' Rebellion, **1948:** 259 [4]

Shea, Francis M., **1945:** 157 [1]
Sheahan, Marion W., **1951:** 307n.
Sheehe, Mrs. Norman, **1950:** 21n.
Sheep, reduction in numbers, **1946:** 57
Sheil, Bishop Bernard J., **1946:** 173 [15]
Shelby, Mont., campaign remarks, **1952–53:** 268 [7]
Shelbyville, Ky., campaign remarks, **1948:** 222 [1]
Shell Oil Co., **1952–53:** 58
Shenandoah, Iowa
   Campaign remarks, **1952–53:** 285
   Taft, Sen. Robert A., comment on remarks in, **1952–53:** 291
Shepherd, Gen. Lemuel C., Jr., **1950:** 165
Sheppard, Repr. Harry R., **1948:** 206 [3]
Sherman, Adm. Forrest P., **1949:** 226ftn. (p. 502), 240 [1], 241n.; **1950:** 29 [8], 226, 230 [7]; **1951:** 165 [6], 171 [14]
Sherman, John, **1952–53:** 127 [18], 136 [16]
Sherman, Gen. W. T., **1947:** 31 [1]; **1952–53:** 115 [11]
Sherman, Tex., campaign remarks, **1948:** 214 [1]
Sherman Anti-Trust Act, **1947:** 177 [7]; **1948:** 8 (p. 89); **1950:** 118
Sheyenne River, **1950:** 130
Shimon, Joseph W., **1950:** 217 [12]
Ship construction, cutback, **1945:** 22ftn. (p. 37) and [19], 134n.
Ship Sales Act, **1947:** 228
Ship Warrants Act, veto of bill to repeal, **1947:** 167
Shipbuilding industry, **1948:** 8 (p. 81)
Shipping, role in European economy, **1947:** 238
Shipping Authority, National, **1951:** 13 (pp. 81, 82, 83); **1952–53:** 18 (p. 81), 231, 367 (p. 1143)
Ships, **1945:** 45, 128; **1946:** 118, 267; **1947:** 159, 181 (p. 404)
   See also Navy.
   Aircraft carriers, **1949:** 7 [27], 45 [12], 78 [1], 84 [12, 22]; **1950:** 29 [8]
      Citation, **1946:** 171
   Aquitania, **1945:** 45
   Augusta, **1945:** 79n., 82n., 91n., 93n.; **1951:** 282, 290
   Availability for relief shipments, **1947:** 29
   Charters, termination, **1947:** 35
   Communist bloc, refusal of longshoremen to unload, **1950:** 230 [4]
   Construction, **1946:** 18 (p. 82), 193; **1947:** 7 (pp. 64, 85), 11, 55, 145 [3], 223; **1948:** 4 [13], 5 (pp. 26, 28, 48, 50), 8 (p. 81), 79, 88 [20], 175, 177, 261 [1, 6]; **1949:** 7 [21, 25, 27], 8 (pp. 57, 60, 87), 269 [18]; **1950:** 8 [12, 26], 9 (pp. 64, 92), 76; **1952–53:** 18 (p. 82), 211
      Loans, **1951:** 13 (p. 81)
   Courier, VOA broadcast vessel, **1952–53:** 54
   Crew accommodations, **1947:** 123
   Destroyers, U.S., wartime transfer to U.K., **1947:** 132

Ships — *continued*
   Disposition under Lend Lease Act, **1947:** 35
   Dorchester, World War II troopship, **1951:** 30n.
   Fargo, **1946:** 143 [15]
   Flagships, transportation of ECA cargoes, **1948:** 283 [9]
   Flying Enterprise, **1952–53:** 29n.
   Foreign in U.S. ports, emergency control over, **1947:** 35
   Franklin D. Roosevelt, **1945:** 177
   Free access to waterways, **1948:** 86
   Garbage, discharge from, **1947:** 171
   Great Lakes region, **1946:** 228
   Maine, **1948:** 81
   Merchant
      Arming, **1947:** 35
      Construction, **1952–53:** 367 (pp. 1142–1143)
      Reserve fleet, **1951:** 13 (pp. 33, 68, 82), 34
   Merchant Ship Sales Act of 1946, veto of amendment, **1950:** 257
   Missouri, **1945:** 122; **1947:** 191 [14]; **1948:** 181 [1]; **1949:** 36, 160; **1950:** 29 [6, 8]; **1952–53:** 255, 266 [4]
   Nuclear powered
      Development, **1951:** 13 (pp. 85, 86)
      Nautilus, **1952–53:** 170, 171n.
   Officers and crews, citizenship, **1947:** 35
   Operation, **1947:** 7 (p. 84), 18, 31 [16], 228
      By National Shipping Authority, **1952–53:** 367 (p. 1143)
   President Pierce, **1949:** 89 [2]
   President Van Buren, **1949:** 89 [2]
   President Wilson, **1949:** 89 [2]
   Purchase from Maritime Commission, **1947:** 35
   Queen Elizabeth, **1945:** 45
   Queen Mary, **1945:** 45
   Radio operators, **1947:** 35
   Renown, HMS, **1945:** 91n.; **1951:** 282
   Repair and alteration, **1947:** 35
   Requisition of, **1947:** 35
   Reserve fleets, **1947:** 233
   Revenue cutters, **1946:** 188
   River Queen, **1947:** 31 [1]
   Roosevelt, Franklin D., **1951:** 275 [4]
   Sale of, **1946:** 18 (p. 53); **1947:** 7 (p. 85)
   Submarines, construction by Soviet Union, **1949:** 269 [18]
   Submarines, Soviet, containment in event of war, **1952–53:** 217
   Subsidies, **1950:** 9 (pp. 91, 92), 53
   Supercarrier, question of, **1948:** 110 [13]
   Tanker, sale by Denmark to Soviet Union, **1952–53:** 217
   Transfer to Europe, **1947:** 238
   Transfer to Italy, statement, **1948:** 51
   United Kingdom, **1950:** 217 [23]
   United States, **1952–53:** 177, 197ftn. (p. 470)

Ships — *continued*
  War-risk insurance, **1950:** 236
  Warrants, **1947:** 167
  Williamsburg, **1951:** 295 [8]; **1952–53:** 255
Shirts, **1946:** 72 [2, 16], 78 [2]
Shissler, Simon, **1948:** 139 [3]
Shivers, Gov. Allan, **1952–53:** 175 [17], 247 [3], 315 [6], 316
Shoemaker, Philip R., **1952–53:** 308 [5, 6]
Shoes
  Prices, **1947:** 242
  Wartime production in Brockton, Mass., **1948:** 261 [2]
Shoop, Duke, **1946:** 143 [16]; **1951:** 95 [10], 165 [4], 200 [11]; **1952–53:** 149 [2]
Shopping centers, **1950:** 37
Short, Repr. Dewey, **1949:** 64; **1952–53:** 312
Short, Joseph H., **1946:** 237 [17]; **1948:** 41 [8], 134; **1949:** 45 [6], 205 [3]; **1951:** 7 [1], 18, 22 [2, 3], 33ftn. (p. 143), 37 [9], 49 [13], 56 [10, 25], 70 [7], 85 [14], 95 [9], 113 [17], 118 [17], 145 [5], 153 [16, 21], 246n., 247 [1, 10], 251 [27], 275ftn. (p. 601), 298 [1, 11], 300 [10, 14], 302n.; **1952–53:** 2 [12, 19], 7 [1], 17 [7], 45, 49 [7, 15], 64 [1, 9], 75 [4], 98 [1, 19], 107 [2, 5, 14, 16], 115 [4, 16], 136n., 149 [7, 10], 197 [2], 228 [7], 238 [1], 242 [3], 254
Short, Maj. Gen. Walter C., **1945:** 118 [5]
Shortages, postwar, **1945:** 229; **1947:** 191 [3, 7, 12], 228, 238, 242, 243 [16]
Shoshone, Idaho, **1950:** 121 [2]
Shrine of North America, **1949:** 159, 160
Shriners meeting, **1946:** 143 [18]
Shulman, Harry, **1947:** 87n.
Shvernik, Nikolai M., **1951:** 147, 188 [6, 8], 197, 209 [4, 8]
Siam, **1946:** 30 [2]
  U.S. Ambassador Edwin F. Stanton, **1946:** 84 [1, 3]
Siberia, atomic bomb explosion, **1949:** 166 [10]
Sicily, **1947:** 196
  Invasion of, **1945:** 45
Sick, Emil G., **1948:** 125
Sidney, Ohio, campaign remarks, **1948:** 231 [4]; **1952–53:** 319 [3]
Sieminski, Repr. Alfred D., **1952–53:** 303 [2]
Sierra Blanca, Tex., campaign remarks, **1948:** 208 [4]
Sigler, Franklin E., Congressional Medal of Honor presentation, **1945:** 160n.
Sigler, Gov. Kim, **1948:** 183 [2]
Sikorsky, Igor I., **1951:** 301
Silicosis, prevention, **1948:** 248
Silk, Lt. E. A., Congressional Medal of Honor presentation, **1945:** 167n.
Silk, Japanese, **1946:** 186 [7]

Silver, Rabbi Abba H., **1946:** 155
Silver, Charles H., **1951:** 22 [2], 278n.
Silver Creek project, Oreg., **1946:** 190
Silver currency bill, **1946:** 177 [10]
Silver purchase program, **1950:** 8 [29]
Silver Quill, award to Paul Wooton, **1951:** 18
Simmons, Arthur, **1945:** 147n.
Simón Bolívar Memorial Foundation, **1948:** 158
Simplified Trade Practices, Division of, **1946:** 118
Simpson (Lt. Gen. William H.) report on Army reorganization, **1946:** 78 [15], 95 [4]
Sims (Repr. Hugo S., Jr.) labor bill, **1949:** 93 [9]
Sinclair Oil Corp., **1952–53:** 58
Singleton, Sir John E., **1945:** 210
Sinnott, Edmund W., **1948:** 186n.
Sino-Soviet agreements, **1945:** 216
Sioux Indians, **1948:** 118 [1]
Sirups, price controls, **1947:** 7 (p. 86), 18, 65
Siskind, Max, **1951:** 188 [15]
Sixth Fleet, question of visit to Spanish port, **1949:** 200 [2]
Sjogren, Lt. J. C., Congressional Medal of Honor presentation, **1945:** 167n.
Skelton, Byron, **1949:** 192 [12]
Skouras, Spyros, **1947:** 191 [3]
Skrzycki, Stephen S., **1948:** 183 [4]
Skykomish, Wash., campaign remarks at, **1948:** 122 [5]; **1952–53:** 274 [3]
"Skywatch Operation," Ground Observer Corps, **1952–53:** 202, 344
Slattery, Edward E., Jr., **1952–53:** 351
Slaughter, Repr. Robert C., **1946:** 173 [6, 8, 9], 199 [2]
Slaughter, Roger C., **1947:** 141 [13]
Slavery, **1948:** 36, 245
  Jefferson's statute prohibiting, **1947:** 138
Sleeping-car companies, regulation, **1947:** 160
Slichter, Sumner H., **1947:** 87n.
Sloan, Alfred P., **1948:** 280
Sloan, Alfred P., Foundation, **1948:** 280
Sloan, William G., **1952–53:** 98 [8]
Sloan-Pick plan, Missouri Valley development, **1950:** 3 [14]; **1952–53:** 3, 98 [8]
Sloman, Ernest G., **1951:** 307n.
Slot machines, regulation of interstate shipment, **1951:** 63 [1]
Slum clearance, **1945:** 128; **1946:** 18 (p. 63); **1947:** 7 (p. 74), 102, 131; **1948:** 8 (p. 83), 37, 160, 165, 172, 183 [1], 205, 219, 220, 227 [2], 229, 231 [2, 3], 232, 233 [6], 235 [4], 237 [4, 7], 238, 247, 249, 251, 257 [4], 258, 261 [2], 264 [1], 268; **1950:** 9 (pp. 77, 81), 37, 69, 134, 157; **1951:** 13 (pp. 90, 94); **1952–53:** 120, 273, 276, 278, 321 [2]
  See also Urban areas.
  Federal aid, **1949:** 2, 5, 8 (pp. 45, 72, 76), 54, 126, 151, 202

Small, John D., **1946:** 70 [19], 119 [5], 260; **1947:** 31 [12]; **1951:** 93n., 189; **1952–53:** 7ftn. (p. 19), 26 [1]

Small business, **1945:** 128; **1946:** 18 (pp. 51, 56, 57); **1947:** 4 (p. 35), 7 (p. 88); **1948:** 4 [17], 8 (p. 89), 46, 107, 184, 202 [5]; **1949:** 2, 250 [3]; **1950:** 3 [16]; **1952–53:** 289 [2]

Antitrust legislation, **1950:** 319

Assistance to, **1947:** 2 (pp. 3, 6); **1948:** 267 [3]; **1951:** 106; **1952–53:** 15, 18 (p. 79), 367 (p. 1142)

Bids for Government contracts, **1948:** 151

Capital investments, **1950:** 157

Controls, exemptions from, **1952–53:** 18 (p. 79)

Credit, **1952–53:** 215

Defense program, effect on, **1952–53:** 15

Defense program, participation, **1951:** 106

Employees, unemployment insurance for, **1950:** 84

Federal aid for, **1950:** 6, 9 (pp. 96, 97), 106, 114, 118, 124 [8], 134, 135

Reconversion problems, **1945:** 180

Republican stand, campaign remarks on, **1952–53:** 316

RFC functions, **1951:** 82

Study on, mission to Far East and Pacific countries, **1945:** 228

Tax treatment, **1950:** 18

Threat from corporate monopolies, **1948:** 256

World War II contracts with, **1951:** 284

Small Defense Plants Administration, **1951:** 179 [4], 239 [5]; **1952–53:** 15, 18 (pp. 79, 115)

Smaller War Plants Corporation, **1946:** 18 (p. 56); **1947:** 7 (p. 88), 80, 181 (pp. 400, 406)

Termination, **1945:** 228

Smallpox, **1951:** 135; **1952–53:** 249

Smathers, Repr. George A., **1950:** 105 [2]

Smazel, Clarence V., **1952–53:** 317 [4]

Smith, Alfred E., **1948:** 228 [1], 260, 261 [4], 262; **1952–53:** 289 [2], 296, 300, 303 [2]

Smith, Lt. Col. Charles B., **1952–53:** 172n.

Smith, Cyril S., **1946:** 262 [1]

Smith, Donald E., **1951:** 158

Smith, Forrest, **1948:** 194 [12, 13]; **1949:** 220; **1950:** 23 [5], 29 [4], 38 [6], 86 [10], 160 [2], 161 [2, 3], 162, 312; **1951:** 165 [4], 196; **1952–53:** 98 [13], 157, 158

Smith, Francis R., **1948:** 202 [2]

Smith, George A., **1948:** 200 [7], 201

Smith, Sen. H. Alexander, **1950:** 214ftn. (p. 588); **1951:** 54n.; **1952–53:** 303 [5], 310

Smith, H. L., **1945:** 147n.

Smith, Harold D.

  See Budget, Bureau of the, Director (Harold D. Smith).

Smith, James, **1945:** 147n.

Smith, John L., **1952–53:** 101

Smith, Kingsbury, **1949:** 28ftn. (p. 127)

Smith, Repr. Margaret Chase, **1948:** 55 [8]; **1949:** 30 [8]; **1950:** 152 [8]; **1951:** 239 [9]; **1952–53:** 3

Smith, Merriman, **1945:** 164ftn. (p. 387); **1946:** 110 [1], 216 [23]; **1947:** 67 [16], 88 [1], 145 [22], 191, 209 [3], 243 [11]; **1949:** 192 [24], 231 [2], 265, 267; **1950:** 38 [1]; **1951:** 2 [27], 16 [21], 22 [2], 33 [15], 49 [20], 63 [25], 90 [11], 108 [14], 140 [14], 145 [9], 224 [11], 247 [1], 261 [21], 275 [20]; **1952–53:** 7 [7, 10], 21 [32], 31 [2], 35 [15], 49 [18], 64 [12], 88 [5, 22], 98 [22, 27, 28, 34], 127 [11], 136 [10]

Smith, Nelson Lee (Chairman, Federal Power Commission), **1949:** 149n.

Smith, Robert J. (Vice Chairman, National Security Resources Board), resignation, **1951:** 49 [12]

Smith, Theodore J., **1948:** 240 [2, 3]

Smith, Thomas J., **1950:** 110 [2]

Smith, Tom K., **1946:** 142

Smith, Gen. Walter Bedell, **1946:** 37 [3], 226 [9]; **1947:** 210 [4]; **1948:** 96, 97 [3, 19], 288 [3]; **1949:** 11 [15], 32 [10], 58 [13, 15, 18]; **1950:** 152 [12]; **1951:** 95 [9], 128; **1952–53:** 227, 296, 335

Smith, Vice Adm. William W., **1946:** 119 [19], 194n.; **1947:** 123, 124; **1948:** 51n., 79; **1949:** 78 [2], 84 [20]

Smith, Willis, **1946:** 270; **1948:** 245n.

Smith Act of 1940, **1950:** 254; **1951:** 132 [14]

Indictment of Communists under, **1948:** 170ftn. (p. 434)

Smith-Connally Act.

  See War Labor Disputes Act.

Smithson, James, **1946:** 201

Smithsonian Institution, **1946:** 27 [13], 118, 201; **1947:** 241; **1949:** 8 (p. 76); **1951:** 151

Expansion of services, **1948:** 5 (p. 42)

Smithsonian Institution, Secretary (Alexander Wetmore), **1946:** 201

Smog victims, evacuation of, **1948:** 274 [10]

Smoot, I. A., **1952–53:** 115 [7]

Smoot, Reed, **1947:** 51

Smoot-Hawley Tariff (1930), **1949:** 195

Smuts, Jan C., **1946:** 257 [9]

Snake River, **1950:** 3 [9], 121 [13], 124 [7]; **1952–53:** 18 (p. 88)

Snohomish, Wash., campaign remarks, **1952–53:** 274 [4]

Sny Basin, Illinois, **1952–53:** 367 (p. 1146)

Snyder, Edith Cook, **1950:** 21n.

Snyder, John W.

  See Economic Stabilization Board, Chairman; Federal Loan Administrator; Treasury, Secretary of the; War Mobilization and Reconversion, Office of, Director.

Social evils, moral character of problem, **1951:** 68

Social policy in dependent territories, **1946:** 180

Social security, **1945:** 42, 99, 128; **1946:** 18 (pp. 40, 53, 63, 64, 83), 117, 192 [2, 3], 193; **1947:** 4 (pp. 29, 35, 36, 37), 6 [18], 7 (p. 58), 53, 98, 110, 152, 181 (p. 406), 187, 204; **1948:** 2, 4 [8], 5 (pp. 20–23, 25, 34), 8 (pp. 67, 68, 71, 76, 84, 88, 98) 32, 62, 67, 89, 101, 115, 134, 138 [8], 175, 176, 182, 183 [5–7], 184, 219, 227 [9], 236, 258; **1949:** 5, 154, 202; **1950:** 8 [10], 9 (p. 46), 39, 117 [1], 157, 279; **1951:** 13 (pp. 64, 65, 96–97), 159, 279; **1952–53:** 5, 18 (pp. 103–106), 69, 129, 135, 138, 241, 242 [3, 5], 266 [3], 268 [5], 270 [5], 281, 284 [2], 289 [1], 291, 293, 298 [3], 300, 304, 306 [6], 317 [5], 321 [6]
   Benefits, extension of, **1951:** 4, 11, 12 [48]; **1952–53:** 5, 167, 218, 273, 276, 278, 292 [12], 311 [1], 321 [2], 322, 376
   Blind persons, **1948:** 152
   Defense contractors, contributions, **1951:** 106
   Earning limit for eligibility, proposed increase, **1952–53:** 17 [33]
   Employment relationships under, **1948:** 67
   Expansion programs, subordination to defense needs, **1952–53:** 15
   Expenditures for, **1952–53:** 231, 367 (pp. 1156–1159)
   Extension of benefits, **1947:** 7 (p. 71), 170; **1949:** 2, 5, 8 (p. 45), 154, 219; **1950:** 2, 6, 9 (pp. 53, 67, 71, 72), 110 [5], 127 [4, 5], 128, 129 [4], 134, 224, 279
   Health insurance under, proposed, **1947:** 98; **1948:** 67, 107, 241; **1950:** 9 (p. 73); **1951:** 13 (p. 99), 135; **1952–53:** 258 [9, 15], 268 [8], 278, 284 [5], 369
   Increase in, **1949:** 7 [26, 28, 48]
   Insurance interests, opposition, **1952–53:** 289 [3]
   Issue in election campaign, **1952–53:** 278, 298 [14], 306 [1], 312, 313 [4]
   Liberalization of benefits or coverage, proposed, **1948:** 160, 189, 205, 215, 220, 227 [6], 228 [12], 231 [1, 3], 232, 241, 247–249, 251, 252, 257 [1, 2], 258, 259 [3], 262, 267 [2]
   Medical care inclusion, proposed, **1945:** 192
   Message to Congress, **1948:** 107
   News conference remarks, **1949:** 7 [22, 26, 28, 48], 22 [12], 32 [1, 2, 11, 20], 40 [3]
   News vendors, veto of bill to exclude, **1947:** 170
   Payroll taxes.
     See Taxes.
   Republican opposition, **1952–53:** 218, 286 [5]
   Restrictive legislation, vetoes, **1948:** 67, 131, 152
   Seamen, **1947:** 123
   Supplementation by private pension plans, **1951:** 12 [44, 48, 54]
   Trust fund, **1949:** 7 [22]
   Wagner-Dingell bill, **1945:** 44 [16]
Social Security, Commissioner of, **1950:** 150

Social Security, Commissioner of (Arthur J. Altmeyer), **1948:** 4 [8]
Social Security Act, **1947:** 98; **1948:** 107, 131, 152, 233 [6], 252, 255, 261 [11]; **1949:** 8 (p. 66); **1950:** 6, 224; **1951:** 13 (pp. 98, 99); **1952–53:** 18 (p. 103), 312
   Amendment, proposed, **1945:** 42
   Amendments of 1950, **1951:** 12 [44], 159
   Amendments of 1952, approval, **1952–53:** 213
   Tenth anniversary, statement, **1945:** 99
Social Security Board, **1946:** 117; **1947:** 81; **1948:** 10
Socialism, **1950:** 23 [6], 34 [6], 80 [4], 157, 279
   Republican charges against administration, **1952–53:** 62, 69, 126, 253 [13], 289 [3], 291, 298 [2], 307, 312, 317 [3], 322
Socialist Party, **1950:** 44 [7]
Socialized medicine, **1945:** 192
Society for the Advancement of Management, **1945:** 203
Society of Business Magazine Editors, **1951:** 18
Socony Vacuum Oil Co., **1952–53:** 58
Soderman, W. A., Congressional Medal of Honor presentation, **1945:** 167n.
Sofianopoulos, John, discussions with, statement, **1945:** 75
Soil conservation, **1945:** 128, 165; **1946:** 18 (pp. 80, 81); **1947:** 4 (p. 32), 7 (p. 80), 68, 110, 144, 181 (pp. 402, 405), 194, 231; **1948:** 2, 5 (p. 45), 8 (pp. 67, 68, 77, 92), 25, 99, 117, 194 [11], 195, 199, 200 [9], 201, 203, 208 [7], 214 [7, 8], 216 [1, 2, 4], 228 [9], 231 [7], 233 [1, 2, 5, 6], 234, 236, 237 [4, 5], 240 [2], 242 [3], 246; **1949:** 2, 154, 203; **1950:** 9 (p. 87), 110 [8], 111, 116, 121 [4], 125, 279; **1951:** 13 (p. 90), 55; **1952–53:** 5, 18 (p. 92), 126, 194, 215, 218, 241, 242 [4], 268 [2], 285, 291, 311 [2], 313 [2], 315 [2], 366, 376, 388
   Appropriations, **1952–53:** 242 [4]
   Indian lands, **1952–53:** 18 (p. 90)
Soil Conservation Act of 1936, **1948:** 237 [5], 240 [2]
Soil Conservation and Domestic Allotment Act of 1936, **1952–53:** 242 [4], 267, 285, 312
Soil Conservation Service, **1946:** 18 (p. 86); **1947:** 7 (p. 80), 144; **1948:** 5 (p. 44); **1949:** 8 (p. 80); **1950:** 9 (p. 87); **1951:** 13 (p. 90); **1952–53:** 18 (p. 92), 117, 367 (p. 1149)
Sojourners, National, **1952–53:** 134n.
Solicitor General (Philip B. Perlman), **1949:** 267 [18]; **1950:** 34 [1], 38 [16]; **1952–53:** 290
Solid Fuels Administration for War, **1946:** 228; **1947:** 7 (p. 87)
Solid Fuels Administration for War, Administrator (Harold L. Ickes), **1945:** 35n.
Solomon, King, **1945:** 2; **1950:** 158
Solomon Islands, battle, **1945:** 45, 178
Somaliland, Italian, independence, **1950:** 143

Somers, Repr. Andrew L., **1949:** 41
Somersworth, N. H., campaign remarks, **1952–53:** 295 [2]
Somervell, Gen. Brehon H., **1945:** 193 [3]
Somerville, Adm. James F., Legion of Merit, citation, **1945:** 200
Somoza, Anastasio, **1950:** 146 [11], 181 [3]
    Visit of, **1952–53:** 115 [4]
Sonar School, Fleet, **1949:** 53
Sonnett, John F., **1945:** 157 [1]
Soong, T. V., **1945:** 107 [11]
Sophoulis, Themistocles, **1947:** 57
Soucek, Capt. Apollo, **1945:** 177
Souers, Rear Adm. Sidney W., **1952–53:** 340
Souhan, Francis J., **1948:** 228 [9]
South Africa, **1946:** 57
    Crop failure, **1946:** 30 [2], 86 [4]
    Lend-lease settlement, **1947:** 7 (p. 65)
    Smuts, Jan C., **1946:** 257 [9]
South Africa, Union of
    Korean war, participation, **1950:** 296; **1951:** 170
    U.S. Ambassador John G. Erhardt, **1950:** 218
South America.
    See Latin America.
South Bend, Ind., campaign remarks, **1948:** 257 [1]
South Carolina, **1949:** 148 [8], 186, 231 [12]
    Byrnes, Gov. James F., **1951:** 16 [2], 247 [2], 251 [10]; **1952–53:** 64 [18], 98 [30], 221 [6], 303 [6], 304, 315 [6], 316
    Candidates for public office, **1950:** 16ftn. (p. 119), 137 [23]
    Democratic convention, **1952–53:** 221 [6]
    Judiciary, Federal
       Nominations, **1952–53:** 166 [4]
       Vacancies, **1952–53:** 44 [5]
    Maybank, Sen. Burnet R., **1945:** 118 [10], 211 [7]
    News conference remarks, **1950:** 3 [9], 16 [19], 137 [23], 169 [2]
    Nullification crisis (1832), **1948:** 245
    Poll tax, abolition of, **1952–53:** 169
    Power projects, **1950:** 3 [9], 121 [4, 13]
    Republican Party support, question of, **1952–53:** 253 [6]
    Thurmond, Gov. Strom, **1948:** 278 [5]; **1950:** 169 [2]
    Williams, Gov. Ransome J., **1945:** 147n.
South Dakota, **1950:** 129 [1]
    Disposal of Indian lands, veto of bill, **1948:** 25
    Gov. Sigurd Anderson, **1952–53:** 97
South Norwalk, Conn., campaign remarks, **1948:** 261 [9]
South Parkersburg, W. Va., veto of bill to amend census records, **1950:** 210
Southeastern Power Administration, **1951:** 13 (p. 87); **1952–53:** 18 (p. 89)
Southern Baptist Convention, **1947:** 88 [12]
Southern Democrats, **1946:** 86 [31]

Southern Hemisphere, crop failures in, **1947:** 210 [3]
Southern Pacific Railway, **1947:** 145 [15]
Southern States
    Federal appointments from, **1949:** 269 [4]
    Question of visit to, **1948:** 110[5], 163 [20]
Southwestern Gas and Electric Co., **1952–53:** 194
Southwestern Power Administration, **1946:** 18 (p. 82); **1947:** 7 (p. 81); **1949:** 155 [11]; **1950:** 9 (p. 90); **1951:** 13 (p. 87), 120; **1952–53:** 18 (p. 89), 129
Souvenir hunting, American propensity for, **1952–53:** 342 [19]
Souvenirs, war, **1947:** 157
Soviet Protocol Committee, President's, **1945:** 125
Soviet Union, **1945:** 97, 125, 136, 178; **1946:** 18 (pp. 41, 42, 44, 84), 76, 181, 247, 251, 265; **1947:** 2 (p. 10), 111; **1949:** 72ftn. (p. 202); **1950:** 206ftn. (p. 571); **1951:** 225, 256, 271; **1952–53:** 63
    See also Communist aggression and expansion.
    Aggression against free world, **1951:** 114, 235; **1952–53:** 170, 217
    Aggression in Eastern Europe and Middle East, **1948:** 52, 129, 202 [6]
    Agreements, violation, **1949:** 86, 160
    Aircraft, destruction in Korea, **1950:** 238 [12]
    Ambassador Georgi N. Zarubin, **1952–53:** 166 [18]
    Announcement on Gen. MacArthur's activities in Japan, **1948:** 288 [6]
    Anti-Zionist campaign in, **1952–53:** 377 [28]
    Armaments, control and limitation, **1951:** 293
    Armed forces, **1946:** 43 [11]
       In Balkans, **1949:** 200 [10]
       In Iran, **1946:** 53 [11], 61 [7]
       Junction with Anglo-American forces in Germany, **1945:** 12
    Atomic attack on U.S., capability, **1951:** 131
    Atomic bomb explosions, **1949:** 166 [10], 216, 226 [8, 13], 234 [4], 236 [1], 253 [13]; **1950:** 3 [2], 34ftn. (p. 151), 97ftn. (p. 275), 273 [13]; **1951:** 96, 165 [1], 189, 246, 247 [1, 9, 12]; **1952–53:** 5, 158, 366
    Atomic bomb possession, question of, **1946:** 6 [3], 41 [21]
    Atomic energy
       Control and development, **1947:** 21; **1948:** 230, 239; **1950:** 34 [18], 44 [2]; **1951:** 256; **1952–53:** 156 [10], 366
       Possession of information, question of, **1945:** 164 [4, 9]
       U.S.-U.K.-Canada declaration, Soviet reaction to, **1945:** 193 [8]
    Atomic secrets
       Rosenberg conspiracy for transmission to, **1952–53:** 377 [10]

Soviet Union — *continued*
  Atomic secrets — *continued*
    Transmission to, **1950:** 34 [18], 46 [20]; **1951:**
      261 [9]
  Austria, claims against, **1949:** 136
  Axis reparations, negotiations on, **1948:** 128 [4]
  Berlin blockade.
    See under Berlin.
  Big Three conferences.
    See Heads of state and government, meetings.
  Chinese-Soviet treaty, **1945:** 118 [6]
  Comments on, **1952–53:** 233 [3], 366
  Constitution, **1951:** 225
  Council of Foreign Ministers, membership, **1945:**
      91, 97
  Declaration of war on Japan, **1945:** 94, 97
  Dictatorship in, **1951:** 116
  Disarmament proposals, **1947:** 21; **1949:** 226 [22]
  Economic potential, **1952–53:** 366
  Espionage in U.S., **1948:** 215
  Exports to, **1948:** 55 [2]
  FAO membership, question of, **1948:** 276
  Far Eastern Advisory Commission, attendance,
      question of, **1945:** 175 [15], 181 [4]
  Forced labor in, **1952–53:** 253 [1]
  Foreign ministers meetings.
    See main heading, Foreign ministers meetings.
  Foreign policy, **1949:** 162, 195; **1950:** 159, 162,
      269, 296, 303; **1951:** 13 (p. 71), 78, 92, 110,
      167, 197; **1952–53:** 57, 131, 144, 151, 196,
      261, 316, 317 [2], 318, 319 [6], 320, 354,
      366
    Asia, **1951:** 96
    Cold war reverses, **1951:** 227 [2]
    Europe, **1951:** 96
    Germany, **1950:** 119; **1951:** 149, 273
    Korea, **1949:** 117; **1950:** 193, 194
    Propaganda, **1950:** 92
    United Nations, **1950:** 34 [18], 143, 162, 193,
      269
  Foreign relations
    Communist China, **1950:** 38 [7]
    U.S., **1948:** 96, 97 [3, 15, 17], 243 [10, 13], 266,
      288 [4]; **1950:** 105 [7], 144
    Western powers, **1948:** 244
    Yugoslavia, **1948:** 150 [8]; **1950:** 293; **1951:** 96
  Friendship for people of, resolution by U.S.
      Congress, **1951:** 147, 188 [6], 197
  German-Russian state papers, publication, **1948:**
      11 [15]
  German unification, opposition to, **1949:** 136
  Gromyko, Andrei, **1945:** 172 [5]; **1946:** 66 [5],
      177 [13]; **1951:** 140 [5] and ftn. (p. 364),
      193 [9]
  Hopkins (Harry) mission, **1945:** 44 [8, 18], 52
      [15], 60 [6, 10, 12, 15]
  Hydrogen bomb, development, **1950:** 16 [5], 29
      [10]

Soviet Union — *continued*
  Immigrants to U.S., **1948:** 178 [7]
  Information, restrictions on freedom of, **1951:**
      188 [6]
  International police force, opposition to, **1949:**
      184
  Iran, removal of troops from, **1952–53:** 107 [2,
      11, 14, 16], 378
  Iron Curtain, isolating effect on people of, **1948:**
      266
  Italian U.N. membership, opposition to, **1951:**
      235
  Japanese emperor, demand for trial of, **1950:** 29
      [14]
  Japanese forces in North Korea, World War II
      surrender, **1950:** 194
  Joint report on Potsdam conference, **1945:** 91
  Korean war
    Aircraft pilots in, **1951:** 275 [15]
    Intervention, question of, **1951:** 95 [9], 275 [15]
    Military aid for North Koreans, **1951:** 174
  Lend-lease negotiations, **1951:** 244
  Living standards, **1948:** 244
  Loan to
    Proposed, **1947:** 78 [3]
    Question of, **1952–53:** 64 [3]
  Machinery shipments to, **1947:** 226 [10]
  Malik, Jacob A., **1949:** 89ftn. (p. 237); **1950:** 209
      [1], 287 [1]; **1951:** 140 [3, 5, 13, 18]
  Marshall Plan, denunciation of, **1947:** 221 [16]
  Meetings and negotiations with, **1951:** 49 [7], 227
      [2, 4]
  Military strength, **1950:** 162, 269; **1951:** 13 (p.
      71), 54, 92, 95 [11], 138, 144, 174, 292,
      293; **1952–53:** 5, 158, 275, 366
  Mission by Chief Justice Vinson, question of,
      1950: 38 [1, 20]
  Molotov, Vyacheslav M., **1945:** 4 [11], 22 [10],
      91; **1946:** 126 [3, 9], 265; **1947:** 74; **1948:**
      96, 97 [19]
  Moscow.
    See main heading, Moscow.
  Navy, expansion of, **1949:** 269 [18]
  News conference remarks, **1945:** 40 [2], 44 [18],
      52 [9], 60 [6, 8, 10, 12, 15], 94, 100, 107
      [11], 118 [6], 147 [4, 19], 157 [7], 164 [4,
      19], 175 [15], 181 [4], 193 [8], 202 [6], 208
      [13], 221 [7]; **1946:** 6 [3, 8], 27 [7, 12], 41 [3,
      9, 11, 19, 21], 53 [10, 11], 61 [7], 66 [14], 70
      [8, 11], 72 [17], 75 [20], 86 [23], 110 [4, 19],
      141 [3], 143 [3, 12], 173 [10], 216 [13], 266
      [22]; **1947:** 74, 90 [1]; **1948:** 11 [15], 55 [2],
      71 [3, 18], 84 [22], 86, 97 [3, 15, 17, 19], 150
      [7, 8], 163 [1, 11], 166 [2, 11], 178 [1], 243
      [10, 13], 288 [3, 4, 6]; **1949:** 28 [14], 32 [18],
      45 [14, 16, 20], 66 [15], 78 [9], 84 [14], 93
      [6], 166 [10], 200 [10], 226 [8, 13, 22], 236
      [1], 253 [13, 20], 269 [18]; **1950:** 3 [2], 16

Soviet Union — *continued*
  News conference remarks — *continued*
    [5], 29 [10, 14], 34 [18], 38 [1, 7, 20], 44 [2],
    46 [14, 19, 20], 80 [4], 97 [9], 105 [7], 179
    [7], 209 [1, 19, 20], 230 [6], 238 [12], 250 [1,
    6, 9], 273 [12–14], 295 [1]
  Occupation of Japan, role in, **1945:** 147 [4], 157
    [7], 221 [7]
  Occupation zone in Austria, **1947:** 114
  Peace treaty discussions
    Austria, **1950:** 218, 250 [1]
    Japan, **1950:** 250 [6, 9]
  Polish leaders
    Arrest of 16 by Soviets, **1945:** 60 [6]
    Moscow conference, **1945:** 60 [6, 8, 14, 16]
  Propaganda, **1951:** 54, 144
    In U.S. press, **1947:** 205 [7]
  Satellite nations.
    See Communist bloc.
  Shvernik, Nikolai M., **1951:** 147, 188 [6, 8], 197,
    209 [4, 8]
  Siberian frontier with Korea, **1950:** 273 [12]
  Sino-Soviet agreements, **1945:** 216
  Special emissary to, question of, **1948:** 230, 244
  Stalin, Joseph V.
    See main heading, Stalin, Joseph V.
  Stalingrad, **1945:** 177
  Strategic and critical materials, exports to, **1950:**
    230 [6]
  Submarines
    Construction, **1949:** 269 [18]
    Containment in event of war, **1952–53:** 217
  Tanker, purchase from Denmark, **1952–53:** 217
  Troops in U.N. police force, question of, **1948:**
    84 [22]
  Ukraine, **1945:** 186
  U.N. disarmament plan, opposition to, **1951:** 54
  U.N. policy in Korea, opposition to, **1948:** 129
  U.N. Security Council delegation, **1950:** 209 [1,
    20]
  U.N. policies, **1951:** 197; **1952–53:** 196
  U.S. aircraft
    B-29 bomber, interception of, **1950:** 86ftn. (p.
      254)
    Destruction, **1951:** 298 [5]
    Privateer aircraft incident, **1950:** 97 [9]
  U.S. Ambassador W. Averell Harriman, **1945:**
    97, 181 [4]; **1946:** 6 [5], 27 [14], 61 [7]
  U.S. Ambasador Alan G. Kirk, **1949:** 182 [13,
    16]; **1951:** 140 [5]
  U.S. Ambassador Walter Bedell Smith, **1948:** 96,
    97 [3, 19], 288 [3]; **1949:** 11 [15], 32 [10], 58
    [13, 15, 18]
  U.S. broadcasts, jamming of, **1950:** 92; **1952–53:**
    18 (p. 77)
  U.S. consul in Mukden, Manchuria, detention
    of, **1949:** 234 [5]
  U.S. defense program, reaction to, **1951:** 56 [9]

Soviet Union — *continued*
  U.S. diplomats, restrictions on, **1952–53:** 21 [25]
  U.S. forces in Korea, influence on decision to
    withdraw, **1952–53:** 320
  U.S. negotiations with, question of, **1949:** 28 [13]
  U.S. relations with, **1947:** 210 [1]; **1949:** 93 [6],
    253 [20]; **1951:** 2 [17], 4, 227 [2, 4], 261
    [13], 293; **1952–53:** 54, 279
  Veto power in United Nations, **1946:** 143 [12];
    1949: 234 [4]
  Vishinsky, Andrei Y., **1951:** 261 [13], 295 [5];
    1952–53: 5, 268 [5, 9], 269n., 270 [7], 318
  Visit by the President, question of, **1950:** 46 [14,
    19]
  Voice of America broadcasts, interference with,
    1951: 72, 188 [6]
  War casualties, **1948:** 86
  White Russia, **1945:** 186
  World government conference, question of par-
    ticipation, **1948:** 71 [3]
Soybeans, **1950:** 83
Spaak, Paul-Henri, **1946:** 236n.; **1948:** 71 [7, 16];
  1949: 68, 69n.
Spaatz, Gen. Carl, **1946:** 21 [12]; **1947:** 191 [1, 19,
  22], 205 [5]; **1948:** 110 [13], 227 [2]; **1949:**
  95 [3]; **1952–53:** 125
Spain, **1945:** 190; **1946:** 53 [12], 78 [17], 86 [9]
  Assistance, question of, **1949:** 113 [10], 155 [23]
  Diplomatic recognition, question of, **1949:** 66
    [14], 95 [12], 211 [3]
  Falangist Party members, exclusion from U.S.
    under Internal Security Act, **1950:** 270 [6]
  Franco, Gen. Francisco, **1945:** 107 [18], 221 [19];
    1946: 86 [9]; **1947:** 90 [1]; **1949:** 155
    [23],211 [3]; **1951:** 165ftn. (p. 403); **1952–
    53:** 31 [21]
  Loan to, **1950:** 206 [9, 11], 217 [14], 230 [14], 234,
    238 [17], 287 [2]
    Question of, **1948:** 41 [16]
  NATO membership, question of, **1951:** 2 [9];
    1952–53: 31 [7]
  News conference remarks, **1945:** 107 [18], 175
    [14], 221 [19]; **1949:** 66 [14], 95 [12], 113
    [10], 155 [23], 200 [2], 211 [3]; **1950:** 11 [11,
    14], 206 [9, 11], 217 [14], 230 [14], 238 [17],
    270 [6], 278 [14], 287 [2], 318 [2]
  United Nations membership
    Prohibition, **1945:** 91
    Question of, **1950:** 278 [14]
  United Nations resolution on, **1950:** 278 [14]
  U.S. Ambassador, appointment, question of,
    1950: 278 [14], 287 [2]
  U.S. Ambassador Stanton Griffis, appointment,
    1950: 318 [8]
  U.S. naval bases, question of, **1951:** 165 [6]
  U.S. policy on, **1950:** 11 [11, 14]; **1945:** 221 [19]
  Withdrawal from Cuba, **1948:** 81

Spanish-American War, **1945:** 52 [8], 164 [3]; **1946:** 188; **1947:** 181 (p. 405); **1948:** 89, 162n.; **1951:** 181, 182

Spanish-American War veterans, veto of bill to broaden health services, **1950:** 233

Sparkman, Sen. John J., **1949:** 148 [2]; **1950:** 219; **1951:** 227 [15]; **1952–53:** 221 [6, 11], 224, 233 [7, 11], 240 [2], 241, 242 [3–5], 258 [11], 266, 268 [2, 3, 7, 8], 270 [1, 5, 7, 8, 10], 272, 274 [1–5], 277 [2, 4–6], 280 [1, 3–6], 282 [1, 4, 6–8], 284 [1, 2, 4, 6], 285, 286 [1, 3, 5, 6], 289 [1, 2, 4–9], 292 [2, 3, 5, 7–10], 293, 294, 295 [1, 5, 7, 8], 298 [1, 2, 5, 7, 9, 14], 299, 300, 304, 305, 306 [2, 6], 308 [1–3, 5, 6], 311 [3], 312, 313 [1–4, 6, 10], 315 [1, 6], 317 [3, 6, 8], 318, 319 [1], 320, 321 [2, 5–7], 322, 324

Sparks, Nev.
  Campaign remarks, **1948:** 202 [1]
  Mayor Vern Hursh, **1948:** 202 [1]

Sparta, kings of, **1951:** 18

Sparta, Wis., campaign remarks, **1948:** 237 [5]

Speaker of the House of Representatives, succession to Presidency, proposed, **1945:** 63

Speaker of the House of Representatives (Joseph W. Martin, Jr.), **1947:** 2, 56, 146, 151; **1948:** 77 [4], 81, 84 [8], 138 [1], 165, 213, 214 [1], 227 [6]
  Letters.
  See Congress, letters to Members of.

Speaker of the House of Representatives (Sam Rayburn), **1945:** 2, 34; **1946:** 70 [6], 125; **1949:** 16, 70, 93ftn. (p. 241), 103, 173; **1950:** 12, 94; **1951:** 8, 27, 67, 79, 80, 131, 209 [12]; **1952–53:** 2 [1, 16], 32, 45, 49 [1, 5, 7], 51n., 68, 69, 125, 143n., 144, 161, 218n., 225n., 314, 361, 378
  Letters.
  See also Congress, letter to Members of.
  Appropriations, reductions, **1946:** 10, 130
  Child care centers, Federal aid for, **1945:** 159
  Civilian war agencies, appropriations, proposed reductions, **1945:** 124
  Defense aid program, **1945:** 50
  Foreign war relief activities, **1945:** 85
  Housing bill, **1946:** 178
  Navy appropriations, proposed reductions, **1945:** 134
  Philippine veterans, benefits, **1946:** 122
  Salaries of Members of Congress, **1945:** 59
  Veterans housing, **1946:** 48
  War Department appropriations, proposed reductions, **1945:** 146
  News conference remarks on, **1949:** 112 [8], 113 [2]; **1950:** 3 [20], 16 [7], 29 [2, 12]
  Presentation of gavel to, **1951:** 24
  Statement on Far Eastern situation, **1951:** 70 [4]

Speaking engagements, the President's, **1950:** 44, [10], 138
  Cancellation, **1949:** 58 [1, 3, 23, 32], 66 [5], 148 [16]

Speaking Frankly, James F. Byrnes, **1947:** 209 [10]

Speaking tour by the President, question of, **1949:** 93 [15], 113 [14]

Special Board of Inquiry on Air Safety, President's, **1947:** 115

Special Senate Committee to Investigate Contracts under the National Defense Program.
  See Truman Committee.

Speculation
  Commodity, **1947:** 191 [16], 209 [11, 12, 16], 232 [3]
  Curbs on, **1945:** 76 [10]

Speech, freedom of, **1950:** 254

Spellman, Cardinal Francis, **1946:** 112n.; **1949:** 166 [8], 171 [2]

Spence, Repr. Brent, **1946:** 178, 226 [12]; **1950:** 292; **1952–53:** 120, 190, 320

Spending by Government, **1945:** 128; **1946:** 18, 79, 94, 164, 179, 187, 193, 194, 195, 220, 234, 238; **1947:** 4 (pp. 17, 19, 27), 7 (pp. 55, 62, 68), 75, 96, 116, 147, 169, 175, 181 (p. 395), 194, 208, 211, 217, 220, 223; **1948:** 2, 4 [1, 4, 7, 10, 12], 5, 8 (pp. 63, 71, 91, 98), 21 [6], 24, 25, 60, 63, 98, 106, 108, 167, 175, 186, 243 [1, 4, 7], 278 [2, 26]; **1949:** 5, 8, 77, 127, 151, 154, 226 [4]; **1950:** 6, 9 (p. 44), 11ftn. (p. 108), 18, 39, 46 [1], 121 [4, 6, 9], 122, 125, 127 [1], 129 [1, 7], 130, 193, 200, 202, 203 [23], 213, 303; **1951:** 11, 28, 45, 91, 167, 185, 228; **1952–53:** 147, 367 (pp. 1129–1130)
  See also Budget.
  Defense.
    See Defense spending.
  News conference remarks, **1946:** 17, 72 [7], 186 [1], 192, 226 [2], 229 [26], 257 [15]; **1947:** 6, 70 [10], 107 [2], 174 [2], 180 [19]
  Nondefense, **1951:** 101, 221
  Policy on, **1952–53:** 367 (pp. 1131–1132)
  Reduction, **1947:** 68; **1952–53:** 15, 17 [19], 18 (pp. 64, 65), 215, 231, 275, 295 [1], 318, 319 [5]

Spies, German in U.S., trial of, **1949:** 32 [15, 17]

Spingarn, Stephen J., **1949:** 265
  Letter, **1952–53:** 357

Spofford, Charles M., **1950:** 169 [13], 195

Spokane, Wash., **1950:** 121 [13], 124 [6], 125, 126
  Campaign remarks, **1948:** 122 [1, 2]; **1952–53:** 272

Spooner, Wis., campaign remarks, **1948:** 235 [3]

Sporting equipment, taxes on, **1949:** 220

Spring Valley Canal, Mont., **1952–53:** 80

Springfield, Ill.
  Campaign remarks, **1948:** 233 [7], 234

Springfield, Ill. — *continued*
  Mayor Harry Eielson, **1948:** 234
Springfield, Mass., campaign remarks, **1948:** 259
  [4]; **1952–53:** 292 [9]
Springfield, Mo., campaign remarks, **1948:** 216 [15]
Springville, Utah, campaign remarks, **1948:** 200 [4]
Sproul, Allan, **1951:** 44n.
Sproul, Robert G., **1945:** 31 [7]; **1947:** 122; **1948:**
  128 [4], 129
Spruance, Adm. Raymond A., **1945:** 193 [1];
  1952–53: 142
Spruce Production Corporation, **1947:** 7 (p. 95)
Spurs, gift to President, **1948:** 118 [1]
Squantum, Mass., naval base, lease of, **1947:** 35
Staats, Elmer B., **1950:** 80 [8]; **1951:** 12, 93n.
Stabilization Administrator (John C. Collet), **1946:**
  37 [15] and ftn. (p. 123)
Stabilization Agency, Economic, **1951:** 13 (p. 65),
  23, 37 [14], 74, 188ftn. (p. 458), 209 [15];
  1952–53: 346
Stabilization program, **1945:** 128; **1946:** 18 (pp. 49,
  73, 79), 73, 152, 156, 216 [19], 232, 249
Stack, John, **1952–53:** 351n.
Stack, Joseph M., **1946:** 181
Stacy, Judge Walter Parker, **1945:** 211 [2]; **1946:**
  9n.; **1947:** 87n.
Staggers, Harley O., **1948:** 242 [3]; **1952–53:** 242 [5,
  6, 8]
Stainback, Gov. Ingram M., **1950:** 11 [7], 267, 278
  [9]; **1951:** 37 [3]
Staley, A. E., Jr., **1947:** 191 [3]
Stalin, Joseph V., **1945:** 44ftn. (p. 80), 97; **1946:** 18
  (p. 41), 27 [17], 61 [5, 7, 10], 70 [11], 119
  [9], 126 [3, 6, 8, 10, 20, 22], 223 [7]; **1949:**
  273; **1950:** 38 [3, 10], 105 [6], 121 [1];
  1952–53: 107 [14, 16], 123 [2], 366, 378
  Joint statement with, **1945:** 9
  Meeting with, question of, **1947:** 19 [9], 236 [6];
    1949: 11 [3], 28 [20, 22, 23], 214 [3]
  Message, **1945:** 29
  News conference remarks on, **1945:** 4 [14, 22], 22
    [10, 12], 26 [5], 31 [4], 60 [6], 67 [1], 106 [8],
    164 [4], 172 [4, 5], 175 [15], 181 [4]; **1948:**
    41 [14], 49 [14], 77 [18], 84 [17], 86, 97 [9],
    110 [11], 274 [2], 288 [4]; **1949:** 11 [3], 28
    [10, 17, 20, 22, 23], 93 [12, 14], 182 [13],
    214 [3]
  Potsdam conference with, **1948:** 110 [11], 126 [4]
    Joint report on, **1945:** 91
  Renewed meeting with, question of, **1948:** 41
    [14], 49 [14], 77 [18], 84 [17], 86, 97 [9], 274
    [2]
  Special emissary to, question of, **1948:** 77 [18],
    244, 288 [4]
Stalingrad, **1945:** 177
Stambaugh, Lynn U., **1945:** 202 [2]
Stamford, Conn., campaign remarks, **1952–53:** 298
  [11]

Stamps
  Commemorative
    Four Chaplains, World War II, **1948:** 131 [1]
    Swedish pioneer centennial, veto of issue,
      1948: 59
  Designs, **1947:** 177 [2]
  Egyptian, **1946:** 110 [17]
  Standard of living, U.S., 2 (p. 2), 4 (pp. 14, 28), 76,
    83, 110, 152, 187, 202, 212, 214, 217, 224;
    1948: 2, 8 (pp. 68, 74, 77, 78, 91–93), 30,
    32, 42, 76, 99, 165, 167, 170 [1], 182, 183
    [7], 184, 195, 199, 205, 215, 216 [5], 219,
    222 [9], 234, 236, 244, 255, 259 [5], 261 [1];
    1949: 5, 85, 141, 154, 203, 250; **1950:** 18,
    92, 94, 110 [2, 8], 118, 121 [5], 122, 127 [4],
    128, 134, 155, 243; **1951:** 123, 143, 154,
    176, 279; **1952–53:** 5, 15, 63, 69, 81, 101,
    126, 215, 266 [2], 272, 276, 283, 284 [4],
    295 [6, 7], 300, 303 [2, 4], 304, 324, 339,
    349, 363, 366, 376
Standard Oil Co. (Ind.), **1952–53:** 58
Standard time, return to, **1945:** 107 [23]
Standards, National Bureau of, **1946:** 118; **1947:** 7
  (pp. 59, 77); **1948:** 5 (pp. 38, 42), 37; **1949:**
  8 (p. 76); **1952–53:** 367 (p. 1155)
Standards, National Bureau of, Director (Edward
  U. Condon), **1948:** 84 [18], 97 [9]
Stanley, Frank L., **1947:** 48n.
Stanley, N. Dak., campaign remarks, **1952–53:** 266
  [9]
Stanton, Edwin F., **1946:** 84 [1, 3]
Star, Evening (Washington, D.C.), **1945:** 147 [12]
Starch, Elmer, **1952–53:** 57
Stark, Adm. Harold R., **1945:** 118 [14]
Stark, Paul C., **1946:** 40n., 235n.
Stassen, Harold E., **1945:** 10; **1946:** 266 [12]; **1947:**
  232 [3]; **1948:** 93 [12], 181 [9], 185 [2, 4],
  204 [4], 206 [3], 214 [7], 216 [1, 5, 7], 231
  [7]; **1949:** 166 [9]; **1950:** 105 [4], 273 [7];
  1951: 153 [8], 247 [6], 251ftn. (p. 568);
  1952–53: 7 [7]
State, Department of, **1945:** 96n., 143n., 145n., 225,
  228; **1946:** 11, 18 (p. 75), 71, 77, 102, 116,
  159n., 167n., 202, 219, 239; **1947:** 6 [27], 7
  (pp. 68, 96), 14 [15], 18, 39, 72, 95 [10, 22],
  101, 104, 107 [8, 12], 119n., 123, 149n., 181
  (p. 402), 186, 212, 220, 221 [9], 243 [14];
  1948: 5 (pp. 31, 42), 42, 43; **1949:** 8 (p. 53),
  13, 249; **1950:** 17n., 22, 75, 254, 265, 289;
  1951: 16 [2], 153 [22], 173; **1952–53:** 55,
  79, 81, 166 [11], 246, 257, 296, 310
  Acheson, Dean, **1945:** 106 [11], 150, 208 [12]
  Appropriations, **1950:** 9 (p. 56), 190
  Austrian occupation zone, functions, **1950:** 274
  Berlin blockade negotiations, statement on,
    1949: 89 [6]
  China policy, publication of record on, **1949:** 171
    [1]

State, Department of — *continued*
  Documents, theft from, **1948:** 283 [1, 12]
  Employees, loyalty, **1950:** 38 [18], 44 [6], 79, 80
    [4], 82
    Republican attacks on, **1952–53:** 320
  "Forced Labor in the Soviet Union," booklet,
    1952–53: 253 [1]
  Fulbright exchange program, administration,
    1951: 103
  Genocide, report on convention to prevent and
    punish, **1949:** 121
  Germany, political functions in, **1949:** 28 [9],
    84ftn. (p. 223)
  Grew, Joseph C., **1945:** 60 [15], 67 [2]
  Information programs overseas, **1945:** 120, 140,
    141; **1949:** 8 (p. 54)
    Japan, **1952–53:** 18 (p. 77)
  Loyalty investigations, **1951:** 188 [19]
  Marshall Plan functions, **1947:** 238
  Mexican migrant workers in U.S., negotiations
    concerning, **1952–53:** 2 [5]
  News conference remarks, **1945:** 22 [6, 20], 40 [1],
    44 [7, 15], 118 [16], 181 [2], 221 [4]; **1946:**
    17 [15], 27 [5, 12], 70 [12], 84 [9], 119 [3],
    126 [9, 10], 129 [15], 141 [17], 143 [3], 216
    [17, 21], 237 [8, 17], 257 [2]; **1948:** 4 [1, 2],
    15 [6, 7], 41 [11, 14], 170 [9], 283 [1, 12];
    1949: 28 [9], 58 [10], 84 [8], 89 [6], 112 [1,
    2], 122 [7], 171 [1], 253 [16]; **1950:** 11 [1, 14],
    16 [1], 34 [14], 38 [17–19], 44 [6], 46 [6], 80
    [4], 97 [9, 14], 137 [14], 169 [13], 250 [1, 6],
    287 [24], 295 [4]
  Programs review, **1950:** 196
  Reorganization, **1949:** 47, 112 [2], 127; **1950:** 53,
    75; **1951:** 226
  Schuman Plan signing, statement on, **1951:** 85
    [13]
  Soviet proposal for truce in Korean war, state-
    ment on, **1951:** 140 [3, 13]
  Spanish Falange Party, suspension of visas for
    members, **1950:** 270ftn. (p. 680)
  Stevenson, Adlai, service in, **1952–53:** 317 [4]
  Surplus property disposition functions, **1948:** 46
  Technical assistance functions, **1952–53:** 18 (p.
    115)
  U.S. forces in Korea, role in decision to with-
    draw, **1952–53:** 316, 320
State, Secretary of, **1945:** 219
State, Secretary of, Acting (Robert A. Lovett),
  1949: 9, 10, 13
State, Secretary of (Dean Acheson), **1949:** 68, 101,
  230, 260ftn. (p. 571); **1950:** 17n., 22, 38ftn.
  (p. 161), 143, 162, 184, 194, 195, 219, 227,
  242, 250ftn. (p. 640), 264, 265n., 269, 302,
  308; **1951:** 59, 67, 90 [12], 101 [2], 118 [13,
  16], 132 [11], 153 [9], 155n., 165 [6], 184,
  187, 207n., 208n., 209 [13], 216, 226, 235,
  244, 251 [25]; **1952–53:** 6, 23n., 27, 48, 49

State, Secretary of (Acheson) — *continued*
  [17], 81n., 98 [37], 107 [2], 115 [6, 15], 128,
  149 [8, 10], 158, 279, 292 [4, 11], 310, 331,
  366, 378
  Address to U.S. Chamber of Commerce, **1951:**
    101 [5]
  Advice respecting removal of General Mac-
    Arthur, **1951:** 108 [2, 4]
  Appearances before Congress, **1950:** 82, 152ftn.
    (p. 450)
  Brazil, proposed visit to, **1952–53:** 166 [14]
  Continuation in office, **1951:** 224 [9, 11]
  Criticism of, **1950:** 179 [12], 214 [14, 17], 250 [3],
    309 [1]
    Comments on, **1951:** 138
  Denmark, endorsement of continued aid to,
    1952–53: 217
  Directive to, **1951:** 128
  Foreign aid coordination functions, **1949:** 22 [3]
  Foreign policy discussions, **1950:** 89, 96, 97 [17],
    103, 172
  Foreign travel procedures, question of tighten-
    ing, **1952–53:** 197 [10]
  Germany, conventions on relations with, **1952–
    53:** 151
  Hiss (Alger) case, remark on, **1950:** 23ftn. (p.
    132)
  Information programs abroad, **1950:** 92
  International Trade Organization, memorandum
    on, **1949:** 88n.
  Japanese peace negotiations, **1951:** 84
  Korean policy statement (1950), **1952–53:** 316
  Letters
    Administration of the loyalty-security pro-
      gram, **1952–53:** 76
    International wage and hours statistics con-
      vention, **1951:** 97
  Memorandums to
    George C. Marshall Research Foundation,
      Inc., organization, **1952–53:** 387
    John Carter Vincent loyalty case, **1952–53:**
      362n.
  Military aid to Europe, testimony to Congress,
    1949: 89 [9]
  NATO meeting, **1950:** 303, 305, 311
  News conference remarks on, **1949:** 22 [3], 28
    [10, 13, 17], 30 [9], 32 [4], 58 [27], 78 [3], 84
    [5], 89 [5, 9], 95 [12], 118 [1], 122 [24], 155
    [6], 161 [6], 182 [5], 253 [15], 260 [3, 15,
    17]; **1950:** 3 [1], 29 [14, 25], 34 [12, 16, 18],
    80 [1, 6, 12], 97 [3, 17], 137 [12], 179 [12],
    191 [13], 203 [11], 206 [10, 16], 214 [14, 17],
    217 [19], 250 [3], 270 [4], 287 [6, 10, 24],
    295 [17], 309 [1], 318 [8]
  Paris foreign ministers meeting, report, **1949:** 136
  Point 4 program, functions, **1950:** 240
  Policy statements
    Asia, **1950:** 11ftn. (p. 109)

State, Secretary of (Acheson) — *continued*
  Policy statements — *continued*
    Berlin blockade, **1949:** 78 [3]
    Chinese Communist detention of U.S. consul, **1949:** 260 [3]
    Ecuador, relief for earthquake victims, **1949:** 182 [5]
    Formosa, **1950:** 3 [1]
    German army, question of creation, **1949:** 260 [15]
    Hydrogen bomb, **1950:** 34 [12, 16, 18]
    Iran, controversy with U.K., **1951:** 113 [8]
    Korea, **1951:** 2 [13], 16 [6], 113 [7]
    Mindszenty case, **1949:** 30 [9]
    NATO, U.S. obligations as member, **1951:** 7 [5]
    North Atlantic Treaty, **1949:** 32 [4]
    Spain, **1949:** 95 [12]; **1950:** 11ftn. (p. 109)
    United Nations, unity of members, **1950:** 270 [4]; **1951:** 170
  Programs review, letter, **1950:** 196
  Resignation, **1952–53:** 238 [1], 377 [15], 380
  Troop commitments to Europe, consultations with Congress on, **1951:** 7 [9]
  U.S. delegation to U.N., chairmanship of, **1951:** 266n.
  Vatican, Presidential emissary to, telegram to U.S. Embassy in Rome, **1950:** 16ftn. (p. 116)
  Vice Chairmanship of Hoover Commission, **1952–53:** 377 [30]
  Vincent loyalty case, **1952–53:** 353 [14], 362n.
State, Secretary of (James F. Byrnes), **1945:** 91, 94n., 97, 105, 113, 116n., 118n., 120; **1946:** 65, 181, 202, 219, 246, 248, 250 [1], 265; **1947:** 1
  Directives, **1946:** 19, 23
  Distinguished Service Medal, citation, **1945:** 98
  Letters, **1945:** 141, 201
  Memorandum **1945:** 225
  News conference remarks on, **1945:** 76 [9], 100, 106 [11], 107 [5, 7, 16], 147 [4], 157 [6, 7], 164 [1], 175, [12, 15, 16], 202 [8], 208 [17], 211 [12]; **1946:** 6 [6, 10], 27 [7, 12, 14], 37 [8, 14], 41 [19], 43 [12], 53 [4, 18], 61 [1, 3, 20], 66 [14], 70 [2, 8, 11], 78 [12], 95 [1, 3, 21], 110 [12], 119 [6, 25], 126 [1, 3, 9], 129 [11], 136 [6, 14], 141 [19], 143 [17], 163 [11], 173 [1, 2, 7], 177 [4], 186 [3], 199 [19], 216 [13], 226 [11]
  Report, **1946:** 185
  Resignation, letter, **1947:** 3
State, Secretary of (George C. Marshall), **1947:** 59, 105, 119, 134, 136, 137, 139n., 148, 151, 202n., 220, 224, 238; **1948:** 29, 53, 64n., 137 [4], 202 [6], 229, 248; **1949:** 47, 57, 68
  Columnist's comment on, **1948:** 278 [20, 21]

State, Secretary of (Marshall) — *continued*
  Consultations with the President, **1948:** 266, 274 [3]
  Food for overseas relief, statement, **1947:** 198n.
  Humanitarian Award, Variety Clubs International, **1948:** 196
  News conference remarks on, **1947:** 14 [2, 5, 15, 19], 67 [19], 78 [23], 88 [10], 90 [4], 127 [3, 9, 17], 177 [13], 191 [4], 209 [4], 210 [4], 218 [7], 221 [16], 236 [11]; **1948:** 15 [6, 10], 41 [11], 49 [7, 21], 77 [8], 93 [9], 97 [5, 15, 19], 110 [21], 150 [7], 163 [1, 9, 11], 170 [12], 185 [6, 8, 11], 274 [3, 6], 278 [3, 11, 13, 20, 21], 283 [17]; **1949:** 4 [1], 11 [14]
  Policy statements, comment on, **1948:** 150 [7], 185 [8, 11]
  Recovery from illness, **1948:** 283 [17]
  Reports, **1947:** 119, 123, 124, 126, 210 [1]; **1948:** 70, 230
  Resignation, **1949:** 4 [1]
  Retirement, question of, **1948:** 274 [6], 278 [3, 11, 13]
State, Secretary of (Edward R. Stettinius, Jr.), **1945:** 10, 22ftn. (p. 36), 66n.
  News conference remarks on, **1945:** 26 [2], 60 [6], 64 [6], 67 [2, 3]
  Resignation, **1945:** 67 [2, 3]
    Letter, **1945:** 67 [1]
State Civil Defense Directors, National Association of, **1952–53:** 353 [3]
State dinners
  Apparel for, **1946:** 229 [20]
  Cancellation of, **1947:** 209 [1]
State papers, definition, question of, **1947:** 19 [14]
State Tuberculosis Hospital, Galen, Mont., **1952–53:** 268 [8]
State of the Union message, **1946:** 18; **1947:** 2, 19 [1], 62 [22], 95 [3], 218 [4, 5], 243 [7, 10, 15]; **1948:** 2; **1949:** 2; **1950:** 2; **1951:** 4; **1952–53:** 2 [1, 16], 5, 366
  Comments on, **1946:** 15 [1, 11]; **1951:** 2 [2, 19], 7 [2], 295 [10], 300 [11, 17]
State-War-Navy Coordinating Committee, **1945:** 218; **1952–53:** 323n.
Statehood, proposed
  Alaska, **1945:** 147 [23]; **1946:** 18 (p. 66); **1948:** 2, 20; **1949:** 4 [7], 112 [9]; **1950:** 2, 52 [9], 121 [13], 179 [6], 206 [12], 230 [3], 267, 273 [5], 291; **1951:** 168; **1952–53:** 5, 35 [15], 49 [8], 149 [15], 274 [5]
    Message to Congress, **1948:** 105
  Hawaii, **1946:** 18 (p. 66), 30 [6]; **1948:** 2, 20 88 [8, 14]; **1949:** 4 [7], 112 [9], 144 [7]; **1950:** 2, 52 [9], 121 [13], 179 [6], 206 [12], 230 [3], 267, 273 [5], 291; **1951:** 168; **1952–53:** 5, 35 [15], 49 [8], 149 [15], 274 [5]
Statements by the President.
  See also Legislation, statements upon approval.

Statements by the President — *continued*

Armed Forces, Committee on Equality of Treatment and Opportunity, report, **1950:** 141
Armed Forces, Committee on Religion and Welfare in
  Appointments, **1950:** 32
  Report of, **1951:** 100
Armed forces, religion and welfare in, **1949:** 73
Atomic bomb, Soviet explosion of, **1951:** 246
Atomic energy, administration program, **1949:** 112 [2], 166 [1], 169
Atomic Energy Act, second anniversary, **1948:** 164
Atomic Energy Commission
  Expansion of facilities, **1949:** 236 [1]
  Supplemental appropriations, **1950:** 187
Atomic energy installations, labor-management relations, **1949:** 81
Atomic Energy Labor Relations Panel, appointment of chairman, **1949:** 87
Bolívar statue, transfer to Avenue of the Americas in New York, **1951:** 87
Budget review, **1952–53:** 231
Canadians, admission to U.S. service academies, **1948:** 112
China policy, **1949:** 171 [1]
Christian Citizenship, Crusade for, **1952–53:** 39
Christmas Seal campaign, **1950:** 286
Civil defense, anniversary of Federal legislation, **1952–53:** 9
Civil Service, 69th anniversary, **1952–53:** 14
Clapp, Gordon, appointment as chairman of economic survey mission to Near East, **1949:** 193
Clark, Gen. Mark W., appointment to U.N. Command, Korea, **1952–53:** 113
Clay, Gen. Lucius D., release from Berlin duty, **1949:** 92
Commission on the Health Needs of the Nation, creation, **1951:** 307
Commission on Internal Security and Individual Rights, establishment, **1951:** 20
Commission on Migratory Labor, report, **1951:** 75
Committee on Government Contract Compliance, creation, **1951:** 299
Continental shelf, naval petroleum reserve, **1952–53:** 379
Czechoslovakia, Communist control of, 4th anniversary, **1952–53:** 47
Da Vinci, Leonardo, 500th anniversary of birth, **1952–53:** 89
Debt management and monetary policy, **1951:** 52
Defense Department employees, reduction in force, **1949:** 201
Defense housing, World War II, **1951:** 211

Statements by the President — *continued*

Defense Materials Procurement Agency, **1951:** 177, 205
Donnelly, Walter J., nomination as Minister and High Commissioner to Austria, **1950:** 218
Draft deferment policy, **1952–53:** 185
Early, Stephen T., death of, **1951:** 190
Election victory, **1948:** 275
Espionage, sabotage and subversion, reporting of information on, **1950:** 199
European recovery program, third anniversary, **1951:** 66
Executive branch, management improvement program, **1949:** 167
Executive Branch of the Government, Commission on Organization of, **1949:** 111
Far East security, **1951:** 84
Federal Farm Mortgage Corporation, **1951:** 202
Foreign policy
  Bipartisanship, **1950:** 89, 96
  Economic, **1950:** 282
  Legislation, **1950:** 103
Formosa, U.S. policy on, **1950:** 3 [1]
French and German steel and coal industries, proposed pooling, **1950:** 137 [1]
General MacArthur
  Invitation to address the Congress, **1951:** 79
  Removal from commands, **1951:** 77
George VI, King, death of, **1952–53:** 30
Germany, European Defense Community, progress toward acceptance of, **1952–53:** 343
Girl Scouts, 39th anniversary, **1951:** 48
Grand Coulee Dam, activation, **1949:** 106
Greek independence, 128th anniversary, **1949:** 61
Green, William, death of, **1952–53:** 336
Ground Observer Corps, "Operation Skywatch," **1952–53:** 202, 344
Health Needs of the Nation, Commission on the, report, **1952–53:** 352
Heart disease
  Crusade against, **1950:** 30
  Prevention, **1949:** 29
Highway safety, **1948:** 279
Highway Safety Conference, reconvening, **1951:** 42
Home Owners' Loan Corporation, record of, **1950:** 51
Hungary, mass deportations in, **1951:** 173
Hydrogen bomb, development, **1950:** 26
Immigration and Naturalization, President's Commission on, report, **1952–53:** 373
Immigration to U.S., Republican position on, **1952–53:** 301
Imports
  Dairy products, **1952–53:** 360
  Filberts, shelled, **1952–53:** 302

Statements by the President — *continued*
  Indonesian independence, **1949:** 272
  Information, security classification and protec-
    tion, **1951:** 233
  Inter-American Affairs, Institute of, 10th anni-
    versary, **1952–53:** 72
  Interior Department, centennial, **1949:** 43
  Internal Revenue, Bureau of, reorganization,
    1952–53: 1
  International broadcasting facilities, request for
    funds, **1951:** 72
  International Development, Advisory Board on,
    1950: 294
  Israel, policy on, **1948:** 141, 253
  Japan, termination of state of war with, **1952–53:**
    111
  Japanese peace treaty, **1950:** 250 [1]
  Jessup, Philip C., appointment to U.N. delega-
    tion, **1951:** 266
  Jewish New Year, **1952–53:** 235
  King, W. L. Mackenzie, death of, **1950:** 198
  Korea
    Aid bill, defeat in House of Representatives,
      1950: 17
    Armed forces withdrawal, **1952–53:** 310, 323
    Armistice proposal by General Ridgway,
      1952–53: 121
    CARE-for-Korea campaign, **1950:** 285
    Chinese Communist intervention, **1950:** 287
      [1], 295 [1]
    Communist aggression, **1950:** 172, 173
    United Nations command, appointment of
      General Clark, **1952–53:** 113
  Labor Day, **1949:** 199; **1950:** 228; **1951:** 212;
    1952–53: 237
  Longshoremen's strike, **1951:** 276
  MacArthur, Gen. Douglas
    Designation as commander of U.N. forces in
      Korea, **1950:** 189
    Meetings with, **1950:** 264, 268
  Materials Policy Commission, report, **1952–53:**
    191
  McMahon, Sen. Brien, death of, **1952–53:** 219
  Memorial Day, **1952–53:** 139
  Middle East, U.N. Economic Survey Mission,
    1949: 274
  Military chaplaincy, **1950:** 297
  Missouri Basin Survey Commission, **1952–53:** 3,
    32
  Mutual Defense Assistance Act, administration,
    1950: 22
  National Capital Sesquicentennial Commission,
    1949: 79; **1950:** 77
  National Security Act, amendment, **1949:** 67
  Near East, tripartite declaration on arms ship-
    ments to, **1950:** 148
  Niles, David K., death of, **1952–53:** 265

Statements by the President — *continued*
  North Atlantic Council, Deputy U.S. Represen-
    tative, appointment, **1950:** 195
  North Atlantic Treaty
    Entry into force, **1949:** 188
    Ratification, **1949:** 162
    Second anniversary, **1951:** 69
    Senate Resolution 99 supporting, **1951:** 71
  North Atlantic Treaty Organization meeting
    Departure of Secretary Acheson, **1950:** 305
    Report of Secretary Acheson, **1950:** 311
  Olympic National Park, enlargement, **1952–53:**
    365
  "Operation Skywatch," **1952–53:** 202, 344
  Organization of American States Charter, rati-
    fication, **1951:** 125
  Pacific Islands and American Samoa, civilian
    administration, **1951:** 141
  Paris foreign ministers meeting, **1949:** 135
  Pershing, Gen. John J., death of, **1948:** 161
  Philippines, Economics Survey Mission, **1950:**
    180
  Point 4 program, **1951:** 83
    Administration, **1950:** 240
  President-elect Eisenhower
    Election victory, **1952–53:** 325
    Joint statement with, **1952–53:** 331
  President of France, visit of, **1951:** 58
  Public debt, fluctuations during term, **1952–53:**
    368
  Railroads
    Federal control, **1950:** 221
    Labor dispute, **1950:** 188
  Ridgway, Lt. Gen. Matthew B.
    Korean armistice proposal, **1952–53:** 121
    NATO command appointment, **1952–53:** 112
  Román y Reyes, Victor, death of, **1950:** 109
  Ross, Charles G., death of, **1950:** 300
  Sabath, Repr. Adolph J., death of, **1952–53:** 327
  San Martín, Gen. José de, 100th anniversary of
    death, **1950:** 212
  Schwellenbach, Lewis B., death of, **1948:** 123
  Selective Service inductees, moral safeguards,
    1948: 190
  Shaw, George Bernard, death of, **1950:** 276
  Short, Joseph H., death of, **1952–53:** 254
  Soviet explosion of atomic bomb, **1949:** 216
  Spofford, Charles M., appointment as Deputy
    U.S. Representative, North Atlantic
    Council, **1950:** 195
  Steel industry labor dispute, **1951:** 304
    Settlement, **1952–53:** 216
  Steelman, John R., designation as Acting Chair-
    man, National Security Resources Board,
    1948: 284
  Transportation policy **1949:** 266
  Turkey, national holiday, **1948:** 263

[References are to items except as otherwise indicated]

Statements by the President — *continued*
U.N. General Assembly
Delegation, **1950:** 219
United Defense Fund, creation, **1951:** 3
Meeting, **1948:** 230
U.S. forces in Europe, increase, **1950:** 242
USO reactivation, **1949:** 34
Vandenberg, Sen. Arthur H., death of **1951:** 86
Veterans' hospitals, appointment of committee
on, **1950:** 156
Water Resources Policy Commission, report,
1950: 306
White House Conference on Children and
Youth, **1950:** 5
States, **1947:** 51
See also Federal-State-local governmental re-
sponsibilities; *specific States.*
Absentee voting for military personnel, **1952–53:**
68, 96, 124
Admission to Union, commemorative coins,
1947: 162
Agricultural experiment stations, **1950:** 110 [3]
Agricultural research stations, **1952–53:** 267
Antilynching laws, **1952–53:** 290
Civil rights responsibilities, **1947:** 130; **1948:** 2,
20
Colleges and universities, admission of Negroes,
1952–53: 290
Colorado River Basin, sharing of water rights,
1948: 207
Community property, taxation, **1947:** 141 [5], 145
[19]; **1948:** 9 [2], 63
Congressional reapportionment, **1951:** 5
Crime control, **1951:** 63 [1]
Criminal justice, elimination of administrative
abuses, **1951:** 115
Deficit spending, **1952–53:** 15
Democratic majorities, predictions by President,
1948: 266
Employees, **1952–53:** 213, 290
Employment, **1947:** 181 (p. 402)
Fair employment legislation, **1946:** 78 [5]
Services, **1949:** 201; **1950:** 208
Expenditures, **1948:** 167; **1949:** 5
"Fair-trade" laws, **1952–53:** 204
Federal aid.
See Federal aid to States.
Federal real estate acquisitions in, **1952–53:** 18
(p. 71)
Payments for, **1951:** 13 (p. 104)
Food conservation, telegram, **1947:** 207, 209 [2]
Governors, **1947:** 19 [13]
Conference on Industrial Safety, invitation,
1949: 55
Highway Safety Conference, invitation, **1949:**
26
White House Conference on Children and
Youth, telegram, **1949:** 198

States — *continued*
Governors Conference, **1948:** 259 [4]
Highway safety programs, **1947:** 27; **1950:** 229
Hospitals and medical care facilities, **1948:** 89
Housing, laws against discrimination in, **1952–
53:** 290
Industrial safety programs, **1950:** 155; **1951:** 13
(p. 80); **1952–53:** 206, 367 (p. 1151)
Laws, traffic, **1947:** 118
Living standards, **1947:** 187
Oil and gas conservation compact, **1947:** 104
Police forces, wiretapping by, **1949:** 211 [12]
Public assistance programs, **1951:** 159
Public works programs, **1946:** 18 (p. 61)
Rent control laws, **1950:** 93
School facilities, **1952–53:** 18 (p. 101), 284 [6]
Selective Service records, centers for, **1947:** 54
Southern
"Dixiecrat" States, barring of delegates by
Democratic National Committee, **1949:**
182 [9]
Economic and social development, **1952–53:**
194
Meetings with Congressmen, **1949:** 58 [31]
Plans for campaign in, **1948:** 243 [12]
Statutes, collection by Library of Congress,
1950: 75
Taxes, **1949:** 146
Tidelands
Dispute, **1946:** 177 [6], 186 [5], 189
Resources, question of rights to, **1948:** 9 [13];
1949: 113 [2]
Toll roads, RFC loans for, **1949:** 269 [3]
Traffic laws, **1947:** 8
Transfer of public employment offices to, dis-
approval, **1945:** 226
Unemployment insurance programs, **1945:** 128;
1950: 8 [3], 84
Vocational rehabilitation services, **1950:** 208
Water resources development programs, **1950:**
140
Statesman, definition of, **1951:** 8
Statism, **1949:** 205 [5], 211 [5]
Republican charges of, **1950:** 80 [4]
Statistical Agencies, Task Force on, **1952–53:** 18 (p.
116)
Statistics, collection of, **1952–53:** 18 (pp. 92, 116)
Statue of Liberty, **1948:** 168
Replica, dedication, **1950:** 121 [5]
Statues
Equestrian, gift from Italy, **1951:** 235
Simón Bolívar statue, transfer to New York City,
1951: 87
Statute of limitations, extension in espionage cases,
1950: 207
Statutes, State, collection by Library of Congress,
1950: 75
Steamplant, TVA, **1948:** 163 [5]

Steed, Tom, **1948:** 216 [1–4]
Steel
  Exports to U.K., agreement on, **1952–53:** 6n.
Steel Formula, Little, **1945:** 59
  News conference remarks, **1945:** 22 [8], 52 [17]
Steel industry, **1947:** 217; **1948:** 8 (pp. 79, 80)
  Brazil, **1951:** 59
  Capacity, **1947:** 4 (p. 10); **1948:** 8 (p. 67); **1949:** 4
    [4, 6], 7 [12, 14]; **1950:** 202; **1951:** 11, 13
    (pp. 75, 76), 167; **1952–53:** 5, 15
  Conservation, **1947:** 224
  European, **1947:** 238
  Export controls, **1947:** 58
  Federal-owned steel plants, **1946:** 21 [19]
  French and German, proposal to pool, **1950:** 137
    [1]
  Ingot production, **1945:** 202 [3]
  Investigation of, **1948:** 41 [6]
  Labor contracts, **1947:** 19 [1], 142
  Labor disputes, **1948:** 198; **1949:** 155 [5, 7, 12,
    15], 200 [15], 205 [10], 209, 211 [6], 214 [9,
    11], 226 [5], 231 [14], 236 [2], 240 [5, 7, 15],
    260 [6, 11]; **1950:** 6; **1951:** 304, 305;
    1952–53: 64 [4], 70, 75 [10], 82, 88 [3, 5],
    110, 115 [1, 5, 8, 10, 12, 13, 16, 17, 19], 123
    [2, 4], 129, 136 [3], 156 [4], 159, 161, 166 [1,
    5, 7], 175 [12, 16], 197 [2], 215, 231, 233 [5],
    242 [5]
    Address to American people, question of,
      1952–53: 115 [10]
    Factfinding board, **1949:** 155 [12], 179 [6]
    Government operation, **1946:** 21 [5, 7], 27 [9];
      1952–53: 82, 83, 88 [13], 98 [14, 25], 103,
      107 [2, 12], 110, 118, 156 [4], 161, 175 [16]
    Government seizure, **1949:** 236 [2]; **1951:**
      305n.
    Injunction, question of use, **1952–53:** 115 [12]
    Meeting with management and labor leaders,
      1952–53: 118
    Message to Congress, **1952–53:** 83
    Messages to management and labor leaders,
      1949: 152, 153, 213
    Settlement, **1952–53:** 216
    Telegram to management and labor leaders,
      1952–53: 116
  Monopoly in, **1948:** 220
  Prices, **1946:** 6 [11, 15], 15 [7, 13], 27 [2, 9, 10, 15],
    37 [14, 16, 19], 152, 153, 179; **1947:** 142,
    152; **1948:** 49 [12], 80, 226; **1949:** 22 [10];
    1950: 202, 287 [22]; **1951:** 304; **1952–53:**
    70, 83, 110, 118, 129
  Production, **1947:** 228; **1950:** 193, 202; **1951:** 11,
    304; **1952–53:** 23, 82, 103, 107 [2], 116,
    118, 161, 166 [5], 175 [16], 282 [4]
    Allocation to Armed forces, **1948:** 151
    Shortage, **1948:** 5 (p. 48), 8 (pp. 70, 79, 80), 167
  Profits, **1952–53:** 82, 88 [6], 110, 129

Steel industry — *continued*
  Republican campaign fund, contributions by,
    1948: 251
  Strike.
    See Steel strike.
  Taxes, **1952–53:** 110
  Wages, **1946:** 21 [5], 27 [9], 53 [2], 61 [9]; **1947:** 19
    [1]; **1948:** 84 [1], 226; **1951:** 304; **1952–53:**
    70, 82, 88 [5, 13], 110, 129
Steel Industry Board, **1949:** 209, 213, 240 [12, 15]
Steel strike, **1946:** 12, 20
  News conference remarks, **1946:** 6 [15], 15 [7, 10],
    21 [3, 5, 7, 9, 14, 19], 27 [9], 30 [4, 5], 37 [9,
    16, 19], 53 [2], 61 [9], 72 [4]
  Statement, **1946:** 16
Steel Workers of America, United, **1946:** 12, 16;
    1949: 152, 209, 213; **1951:** 169, 277, 304,
    305; **1952–53:** 22, 116n., 118n., 216
  Labor dispute, **1945:** 204, 206
Steelman, John R., **1945:** 175 [1]; **1946:** 12, 15n.,
    121, 136 [1], 262 [2, 8, 11]; **1951:** 141 [16],
    145 [8], 183, 194, 201, 206, 211, 241; **1948:**
    71 [8], 89, 93 [1], 284; **1949:** 28 [1, 2], 48,
    155 [1], 156, 171 [4], 179 [6], 260 [4]; **1950:**
    13n., 179 [25], 188n., 209 [21], 230 [4];
    1951: 16 [14], 49 [2], 101 [7], 153 [16];
    1952–53: 12n., 45, 122, 136 [2], 187, 245,
    292 [11]
  See also Defense Mobilization, Office of, Direc-
    tor; Scientific Research Board, Chair-
    man; War Mobilization and Reconver-
    sion, Office of, Director.
Steinemann, George C., **1952–53:** 311 [1]
Stelle, John, **1946:** 182
Stennis, Sen. John C., **1951:** 54n.
Sternhagen, John M., **1946:** 78 [7]
Stettinius, Edward R., Jr., **1945:** 157 [13]; **1946:**
    123, 126 [1, 14], 127
  See also State, Secretary of (Edward R.
    Stettinius, Jr.).
  Appointment as U.S. Representative on the
    Preparatory Commission of the United
    Nations, **1945:** 67 [1, 2]
    Letter, **1945:** 96
  Nomination as U.S. Representative to the Unit-
    ed Nations, the U.N. Security Council,
    and the U.N. General Assembly, **1945:**
    219n.
Steuben, Baron von, **1950:** 185
Stevens, Judge Harold M., **1950:** 174n.
Stevens, Samuel N., **1948:** 194 [5]
Stevens, Thaddeus, **1948:** 212 [6]
Stevenson, Adlai E., **1946:** 173 [1]; **1948:** 218 [6, 7],
    233 [4–6], 234, 256, 267 [3]; **1950:** 110 [1],
    134n.; **1951:** 140 [17]; **1952–53:** 21 [2, 3,
    13], 49 [6], 97, 98 [4], 197 [12], 230, 268n.,
    289n., 290n., 291n., 325

Stevenson, Adlai E. — *continued*
  Byrnes, Gov. James F., support by, **1952–53:** 221 [6]
  Cabinet meeting, invitation to attend, **1952–53:** 221 [12], 228 [3, 7, 12]
  Democratic Party, leadership, **1952–53:** 334 [4]
  Government service in World War II, **1952–53:** 289 [5]
  Italian rehabilitation mission (1943), **1952–53:** 291, 292 [1]
  Meeting with the President, **1952–53:** 224, 253 [9], 342 [2, 8, 12, 18], 334 [4]
  Presidential candidacy, **1952–53:** 21 [5, 13], 49 [6], 75 [11], 88 [18], 98 [4], 115 [3], 136 [8, 11, 18], 166 [16], 218, 221 [6, 12, 14], 227, 228 [3, 7, 12], 233 [4, 7, 11, 17], 238 [3, 8], 240 [1, 2], 241, 242, 247 [1], 253 [3, 8, 9, 11, 12], 258 [11, 12], 266, 268–270 [1, 5–10], 271–300, 303–308, 311–322, 324
  Record in office, **1952–53:** 290, 304
  United Nations, contribution to, **1952–53:** 289 [5]
  Washington, remarks on crime in, **1952–53:** 233 [4], 238 [3]
Stevenson, Adlai E., Sr., **1948:** 233 [4]
Steward, Luther C., **1947:** 190
Stewart, Irvin L., **1950:** 40
Stewart, Sen. Tom, **1946:** 41 [8]; **1951:** 251 [20]
Stigler, Repr. William G., **1948:** 216 [7]
Stikker, Dirk, **1949:** 68
Stimson, Henry L., **1947:** 150; **1948:** 239, 257 [3]; **1950:** 80 [5]; **1952–53:** 289 [5]
  See also War, Secretary of (Henry L. Stimson).
Stock Exchange, New York, **1947:** 226 [13]
Stock market, **1946:** 6 [1], 215 [14]; **1947:** 7 (p. 88), 152; **1949:** 5, 148 [17], 154; **1950:** 3 [19], 157, 279
  Activity, **1945:** 211 [3]
  Crash, **1945:** 180
Stockings, nylon and rayon, **1946:** 72 [19]
Stokke, Halfdan E., **1949:** 54
Stoltz, Mildred K., **1952–53:** 268 [8]
Stone, Adm. Ellery W., **1947:** 25
Stone, Harlan F., **1945:** 1n.; **1946:** 27 [13]; **1951:** 295 [8]; **1952–53:** 378
  Death of, **1946:** 88
Stone, Kimbrough, **1947:** 78 [15]
Stoner, Frank G., **1946:** 14
Stopgap relief, **1947:** 191 [8, 21], 205 [9, 13]
Storage facilities, military use of, **1947:** 35
Stoves, end of rationing, **1945:** 128
Stowe, David H., **1950:** 29 [16]
Stowe, Leland, **1947:** 90n.
Straat, Parker E., **1952–53:** 181n.
Strasbourg, Council of Europe meeting, **1949:** 195
Strategic bombing, **1945:** 45
Strategic and critical materials, **1946:** 93

Strategic and critical materials — *continued*
  Allocation, **1951:** 167, 199; **1952–53:** 367 (p. 1141)
  Atomic, procurement and processing, **1951:** 13 (pp. 85, 86)
  Building materials, **1950:** 192
  Conservation, **1950:** 192, 213, 229
  Controls, **1947:** 58, 99; **1948:** 23; **1950:** 230 [6], 243; **1951:** 13 (pp. 27, 75, 76, 77), 91–93, 199, 285; **1952–53:** 15, 190
  Development loans by Export-Import Bank, **1951:** 114
  Embargo on shipment to Communist bloc, **1952–53:** 105, 180, 217, 358
  Exports, **1950:** 9 (p. 97), 230 [6]; **1951:** 11
  Geological surveys for, **1952–53:** 18 (p. 89)
  Imports, **1952–53:** 15
  Mutual assistance, U.S.-U.K., **1952–53:** 6
  News conference remarks, **1950:** 8 [44], 230 [6]
  Prices, **1952–53:** 15
  Priorities and allocation, **1949:** 2, 5; **1950:** 193, 194, 202; **1951:** 11, 189
  Procurement, **1951:** 82, 205
  Production, **1951:** 13 (p. 75), 25, 59, 82, 98, 114, 117, 134, 167; **1952–53:** 15, 18 (p. 77)
  Reduction in civilian use, **1951:** 4
  Report of Materials Policy Commission, **1952–53:** 191, 192
  Shortage, **1948:** 170 [1, 7], 178 [6]; **1949:** 4 [4], 8 (p. 61); **1950:** 193, 202, 301; **1951:** 204n.; **1952–53:** 17 [17, 31]
  Trade in, **1951:** 13 (pp. 75, 76); **1952–53:** 105, 180, 217, 358
  Yugoslavia, assistance for imports, **1951:** 81
  Stockpiling, **1945:** 128; **1946:** 18 (p. 53), 174; **1947:** 7 (pp. 65, 83), 18, 24, 181 (p. 398), 196, 199, 238; **1948:** 5 (pp. 28, 29, 47), 8 (pp. 67, 78, 97), 60, 175; **1949:** 7 [17], 8 (pp. 56, 58, 61); **1950:** 8 [44], 9 (pp. 61, 66), 13, 124 [7], 193, 202; **1951:** 11, 12 [5], 13 (pp. 62, 70, 71), 92, 177; **1952–53:** 12, 15, 18 (p. 72), 33, 231, 367 (pp. 1138, 1154)
Strategic and Critical Materials Stockpiling Act, **1947:** 24
  Approval, **1946:** 174
Strategic Services, Office of, **1946:** 11
  Liquidation, **1945:** 141
    Letter to General Donovan, **1945:** 140
Stratemeyer, Lt. Gen. George E., **1950:** 260
Straus, Michael W., **1949:** 96n.
  Appointment as Commissioner of Reclamation, **1945:** 211 [10]
Strauss, Anna Lord, **1946:** 45n., 58n., 255n.; **1947:** 191 [3]; **1951:** 22 [2, 4], 266n., 278n.
Strauss, Lewis L., **1946:** 242 [2]; **1948:** 88 [1]; **1949:** 122 [6]
Straw hat, the President's, **1951:** 132 [17]

Street, Lt. Comdr. George L., Congressional Medal of Honor award, **1945**: 160n.
Street, Thaddeus, **1945**: 147n.
Streptomycin, shortage, **1947**: 18
Strikes.
   See Labor disputes.
Stryker, Lloyd P., **1951**: 113 [10]
Stuart, J. Leighton, **1949**: 260ftn. (p. 571)
Students
   Citizenship seminar, **1950**: 178; **1951**: 139; **1952–53**: 183
   College
      Federal aid, **1951**: 13 (p. 96)
      Question of draft deferment, **1951**: 63 [15]; **1952–53**: 18 (p. 103)
   Exchange, **1946**: 75 [20]; **1950**: 92; **1951**: 103, 124
   High school essay contest winners, remarks to, **1951**: 203
   Scholarships and loans for, proposed, **1952–53**: 18 (p. 103), 231
   Schools, payments to, **1951**: 85 [9]
   Science, question of draft deferment, **1950**: 238 [7]
   Science Talent Search, remarks to winners, **1950**: 48
   U.N. fellowships for, **1950**: 143
Styles, Paul L., **1950**: 23 [20], 29 [1]
Submarine warfare, **1945**: 45
Submarines, construction by Soviet Union, **1949**: 269 [18]
Subsidies, Federal, **1946**: 94, 152; **1947**: 6 [4]; **1949**: 7 [32, 34], 150, 151; **1950**: 53; **1951**: 7 [14], 227 [22]
   Agricultural, **1947**: 6 [24], 7 (p. 80), 70 [18]; **1950**: 83, 110 [7], 121 [2], 127 [5]; **1951**: 12 [15, 22], 13 (pp. 88, 89), 70 [2]
   Airlines, mail payments, **1951**: 13 (p. 83)
   Aluminum plants, question of, **1945**: 172 [7]
   Aviation, **1950**: 9 (p. 94); **1952–53**: 18 (p. 84), 367 (p. 1144)
   Copper and zinc, **1945**: 107 [10]
   Food, **1945**: 128; **1946**: 18 (pp. 54, 55), 86 [19, 32], 94, 193
   Industry, high-cost producers, **1951**: 91
   Mail, **1947**: 6 [10]
   Merchant marine, **1951**: 13 (pp. 81, 82, 83); **1952–53**: 18 (p. 82), 367 (pp. 1142–1143)
   Milk, **1946**: 84 [23]
   Minerals, **1951**: 70 [2]
   Mining, **1947**: 175
   Shipping, **1950**: 8 [12], 9 (p. 92), 76; **1952–53**: 211
   Soil management, **1946**: 18 (p. 81)
   Technical schools, **1951**: 85 [9]
Subsidy payments, approval of bill, **1945**: 65
Subversion, comments on, **1950**: 94, 199, 203 [8], 207, 250 [7], 253 [2], 254
Subversive activities, measures to combat, **1951**: 20
Subversive Activities Control Board, **1950**: 254

Subversive organizations, **1947**: 222
Suchow, China, **1948**: 278ftn. (p. 952)
Sudduth, Willis W., **1948**: 208 [8]
Suez Canal, Anglo-Egyptian dispute, **1951**: 188 [12], 275 [14]
Sugar
   Controls, **1947**: 7 (p. 86), 18, 64, 65
   Cuban, **1947**: 181 (p. 401)
      Imports from, **1948**: 5 (p. 43)
   Exports, **1947**: 64
   Legislation, **1947**: 7 (p. 80), 64, 65, 99
   Prices, **1946**: 18 (p. 55), 249; **1947**: 18
   Producers, payments to, **1948**: 5 (p. 44); **1951**: 13 (p. 89)
   Rationing, **1946**: 262 [3]; **1947**: 7 (p. 86), 60
   Subsidies, **1947**: 7 (p. 80)
Sugar Act, **1946**: 18 (p. 59)
Sugar Act of 1948, **1948**: 5 (p. 44); **1950**: 9 (p. 87); **1951**: 13 (p. 89); **1952–53**: 367 (p. 1148)
Sullivan, Mrs. Antoinette, **1948**: 264 [3]
Sullivan, Charles F., **1948**: 259 [5]; **1952–53**: 292n.
Sullivan, Gael E., **1945**: 132 [1]; **1946**: 143 [14]; **1947**: 62 [11, 13], 67 [8]
Sullivan, John L., **1946**: 129 [1, 19]; **1948**: 170 [4]; **1949**: 224, 254; **1951**: 80n., 261 [12], 275 [10]; **1952–53**: 292 [5]
   See also Navy, Secretary of the (John L. Sullivan).
Sullivan, Mark, **1947**: 141 [9]
Sullivan, William, **1952–53**: 274 [3]
Sun River, Mont., irrigation project, **1952–53**: 80
Sun Yat-sen, **1945**: 166, 216
Sunday Sun, Lowell, Mass., **1952–53**: 292 [12]
Supercarrier, question of construction, **1949**: 78 [1]
Superior, Wis., campaign remarks, **1948**: 235 [4]
Supervisory employees, **1946**: 131
Supplemental appropriation acts, **1952–53**: 103
   1951, **1950**: 204n.
   1952, approval, **1951**: 117, 285
   1953, approval, **1952–53**: 205
Supreme Court of Puerto Rico, **1947**: 166
Supreme Court of the United States, **1946**: 27 [13], 88, 136 [8], 189; **1947**: 70 [10], 77; **1951**: 41, 171 [9], 265, 305n.; **1952–53**: 127 [10], 129, 161, 169, 238 [8], 266 [9, 10], 270 [5], 314, 321 [2]
   See also Courts, Federal.
   Appointments to, **1949**: 166 [4], 211 [2]
   Chief Justice.
      See Chief Justice of the United States.
   Chief Justice Fred M. Vinson, **1950**: 38 [1, 20], 94, 174
   Decisions
      Business price-fixing agreements, **1952–53**: 204
      Employment relationships under social security, **1948**: 67
      Executive appointments, **1948**: 102

Supreme Court of the U.S. — *continued*
  Decisions — *continued*
    Housing, prohibition of restrictive covenants,
      1952–53: 290
    Negroes, admission to State colleges and uni-
      versities, **1952–53:** 290
    Restrictive covenants, prohibition, **1948:** 265
    Steel industry seizure, **1952–53:** 123 [4], 136 [3,
      17, 18], 156 [4], 161, 175 [16]
    Tidelands oil, **1952–53:** 293, 317 [3]
  Expansion, question of, **1949:** 253 [3]
  Justices
    Black, Hugo L., **1945:** 52 [20]
    Clark, Tom C., **1949:** 189
    Douglas, William O., **1950:** 121 [9]
    Frankfurter, Felix, question of resignation,
      1952–53: 342 [6]
    Jackson, Robert H., **1945:** 22 [5, 14], 31 [2], 44
      [9], 52 [2, 9], 60 [9], 67 [2], 157 [1]
    Murphy, Frank, **1949:** 161 [10]
    Religious faith of, **1949:** 166 [6]
    Roberts, Owen J., resignation, **1945:** 76 [4, 5]
    Stone, Harlan F., **1945:** 1n.
  News conference remarks, **1945:** 22 [5], 106 [6],
    107 [8], 129 [4], 132 [11], 137 [6]; **1952–53:**
    123 [4], 127 [10], 136 [3, 17, 19], 238 [8]
  Vacancy, **1945:** 106 [6], 107 [8], 129 [4], 132 [11];
    1946: 95 [3, 5, 6, 7, 25], 110 [1, 6], 119 [6],
    126 [13, 19]
    Appointment of Senator Burton, **1945:** 137 [6]
    Appointment of Fred M. Vinson, **1946:** 129 [1,
      4], 136ftn. (p. 301)
  Virginia school integration, brief on, **1950:** 34 [1]
Supreme Headquarters, Allied Expeditionary
    Forces, **1945:** 31 [1], 152; **1952–53:** 217
Supreme Headquarters, Allied Powers, Europe,
    1952–53: 217
Surgeon General
  Appointment, method of, **1950:** 150
  Council to advise, **1946:** 203
Surgeon General, (Dr. Thomas Parran)
  Letter, **1945:** 130
  Memorandum, **1945:** 225
Surgeon General (Leonard A. Scheele), **1951:** 135
Surplus, Treasury, **1947:** 36 [14]
Surplus Marketing Administration, **1946:** 118;
    1947: 35
Surplus property, **1946:** 18 (pp. 40, 45, 67, 71,
    74–76), 94, 193, 263; **1947:** 7 (pp. 58, 91),
    80; **1948:** 175
  Bruce (Howard) report, **1946:** 84 [2]
  China, aid to, **1946:** 265
  Disaster relief, use in, **1948:** 45
  Disposition, **1945:** 92, 128, 129 [6]; **1947:** 181 (p.
    402); **1948:** 5 (pp. 23, 25, 54–56), 31, 46;
    1949: 7 [19], 8 (pp. 91, 93); **1950:** 9 (p. 54),
    16 [8], 53, 69, 72; **1951:** 82

Surplus property — *continued*
  Defense housing, World War II, **1951:** 211;
    1952–53: 367 (p. 1154)
    Land, **1951:** 105, 108 [1]
    Military, **1951:** 14
  Enemy war assets, **1948:** 154; **1949:** 144 [5]
  Housing, **1945:** 211 [1]
  News conference remarks, **1946:** 41 [16], 84 [2],
    192 [22, 25]
  Philippines, aid to, **1945:** 176
  Ships, **1950:** 257
  Synthetic rubber plants, **1950:** 13
  Veterans, aid to, **1946:** 98
  War Assets Administration, liquidation, **1947:**
    226 [3]
  War plants, recovery, **1948:** 71 [8, 14]
Surplus Property Act of 1944, **1948:** 46
  Amendment providing for single administrator,
    message to Congress, **1945:** 84
Surplus Property Administration, **1946:** 18 (p. 75);
    1947: 80
Surplus Property Administrator, proposed, **1945:**
    128
Surplus Property Administrator (W. Stuart Sy-
    mington)
  Letter, **1945:** 176
  See also Symington, W. Stuart.
Surplus Property Board, **1945:** 84; **1947:** 80
Surplus Property Board, Chairman (Guy M. Gil-
    lette), resignation, **1945:** 44 [13], 52 [5]
Surrender of Axis powers.
  See Unconditional surrender of Axis powers.
Surveys, U.S. Supervisor of, **1946:** 118
Suwon, Korea, **1950:** 268
Swacker, Frank M., **1946:** 53 [1]
Swartz, Eugene, **1948:** 114 [3]
Sweden, **1946:** 6 [18]; **1949:** 260 [7]; **1950:** 296
  Assistance, **1947:** 238
  Dairy products, restrictions on imports to U.S.,
    1952–53: 360
  Erlander, Tage, **1952–53:** 98 [37]
  German-Swedish negotiations, **1945:** 22 [6, 20],
    40 [5]
  Immigration to U.S., **1948:** 59, 115
    Displaced persons and refugees, **1945:** 225
  King Gustaf V, **1947:** 16
  Korean War
    Armistice commission membership, **1952–53:**
      121
    Participation, **1951:** 170
    Prisoner-of-war camps uprising, question of
      investigation by, **1952–53:** 162
  Prince Bertil, **1948:** 115
  Prince Gustaf Adolf, **1947:** 16
Swedish Pioneer Centennial Association, **1948:** 115
Swing, Raymond, **1947:** 90n.
Switchmen's Union of North America, **1948:** 95;
    1950: 188

Switzer, Carroll, **1948:** 194 [2–4, 6, 9–11]; **1949:** 161 [9], 205 [21]; **1950:** 206 [15], 209ftn. (p. 582), 258 [11]
Switzerland, **1945:** 100; **1946:** 134
    Assistance, **1947:** 47, 238
    Immigration of displaced persons and refugees, **1945:** 225
    Korean armistice commission membership, **1952–53:** 121
    Korean prisoner-of-war camps uprising, question of investigation by, **1952–53:** 162
    Peace conference, Arab-Israeli dispute, **1949:** 122 [23]
Sydney, Nebr., campaign remarks, **1948:** 118 [4]
Symington, W. Stuart, **1952–53:** 2 [4, 12], 7 [6], 31 [6], 35 [6], 75 [6], 79, 149 [3], 221 [5], 284 [4, 5], 322
    See also Air Force, Secretary of the; National Security Resources Board, Chairman; Surplus Property Administrator
    Appointment as RFC Administrator, **1951:** 82
    Appointment as Surplus Property Administrator, **1945:** 137 [3]
    News conference remarks on, **1945:** 52 [5], 129 [6]
Synagogues, bombing of, **1952–53:** 290
Synthetic rubber facilities, **1950:** 13
    Federal, **1945:** 4 [19]
    RFC operation, **1951:** 82
Synthetic rubber industry, **1947:** 31 [2]
Syracuse, N.Y.
    Campaign remarks, **1948:** 228 [8]; **1952–53:** 289 [3]
    Mayor Thomas Corcoran, **1952–53:** 289 [3]
    Mayor Frank Costello, **1948:** 228 [8]
Syracuse University, **1948:** 228 [8]
Syria, withdrawal of British and French troops, **1948:** 202 [6]
Syrian-French controversy, **1945:** 44 [7], 52 [15]
Syrian and Lebanese American Federation, **1951:** 245
Szymczak, M.S., **1948:** 11 [5]

Taber, H. A. W., **1952–53:** 282 [1]
Taber, Repr. John, **1947:** 145 [18], 180 [10], 197; **1948:** 4 [12], 213, 214 [1, 4], 216 [1], 227 [6], 228 [9]; **1952–53:** 298 [1], 312, 334 [11]
Table Basin, Okla., **1948:** 214
Table Rock Dam, Mo., **1952–53:** 194
Tacoma, Wash.
    Campaign remarks at, **1948:** 124 [4]; **1952–53:** 276
    Mayor Val Fawcett, **1948:** 124 [4]
Tactical bombing, **1945:** 45
Taft, Charles P., **1952–53:** 253 [8]

Taft, Sen. Robert A., **1946:** 221, 229 [13]; **1947:** 131; **1948:** 93 [12], 166 [10], 187, 213, 214 [4, 7], 222 [9], 226, 227 [3, 6], 231 [1], 233 [3], 261 [9]; **1950:** 123, 169ftn. (p. 485)
    Administration legislative program, comment on, **1952–53:** 359 [9]
    Amendment to price control bill, **1946:** 152, 153, 179, 232
    Budget, views on balancing, **1952–53:** 334 [17]
    Campaign issues, unity with Gen. Eisenhower on, **1952–53:** 286 [8], 292 [2–5], 317 [3]
    Campaign remarks on, **1952–53:** 242 [1], 258 [7], 266 [2, 3], 268 [7], 270 [5], 275, 276, 277 [1–5], 280 [3], 281, 283, 284 [2, 6], 285, 286 [4], 289 [8, 11], 291–293, 295 [5–9], 298 [6–12], 303 [6], 304, 306 [1, 2, 4], 304, 308 [2, 3], 312, 313 [4, 6], 315 [4], 317, 319 [5], 320, 321 [3], 322, 377 [18]
    Criticism of administration, **1950:** 137 [25], 238 [11]
    Defense spending reduction proposed, **1952–53:** 289
    Full employment bill, opposition to, **1952–53:** 317 [5]
    Housing bill.
        See Taft-Ellender-Wagner housing bill.
    Joint Chiefs of Staff, criticism of, **1952–53:** 35 [8, 14]
    Korean war, criticism of, **1952–53:** 35 [10]
    Labor act.
        See Taft-Hartley Act.
    Meeting with Gen. Eisenhower, **1952–53:** 291, 303 [4]
    News conference remarks on, **1947:** 36 [13], 70 [14], 78 [11], 107 [2, 5, 15], 127, [1], 180 [10], 221 [16], 226 [6, 9]; **1949:** 28 [5], 32 [21], 45 [26], 66 [2, 18] 144 [4], 155 [3, 15]; **1950:** 11 [4, 12], 16 [10], 86 [9], 137 [25, 27], 179 [12], 238 [11], 253 [3], 287 [7, 15, 19]; **1951:** 2 [2, 23], 7 [5, 8], 188 [11], 251 [3, 5], 261 [2, 4, 11], 295 [7], 298 [2]; **1952–53:** 7 [5, 7, 10], 149 [20], 156 [8], 166 [6], 253 [8, 13], 258 [7], 342 [10]
    Postwar economy, views on, **1952–53:** 292 [10]
    Presidential candidacy, **1952–53:** 7 [5, 7, 10], 35 [8], 149 [20], 242 [1]
    Price supports, position on, **1952–53:** 267
    Republican leadership role, **1952–53:** 289 [3], 292 [8, 10]
    Voting record, **1950:** 253 [3]
Taft, Mrs. Robert A., **1951:** 251 [3]
Taft, William Howard, **1950:** 82; **1952–53:** 295 [7]
Taft-Ellender-Wagner housing bill, **1946:** 116, 119 [3], 215 [6], 258, 263; **1947:** 95 [19], 131; **1948:** 92, 121, 138 [6, 8], 139 [1, 2], 150 [1], 160, 165, 172, 174 [1, 14], 183 [1, 2, 5], 199, 202 [2], 203, 205, 206 [2], 212 [9], 216 [3], 225 [1], 229, 238, 252, 257 [4], 258, 259 [3], 261 [1, 7], 262, 268; **1952–53:** 120

Taft-Hartley Act, **1947:** 121, 182 [4], 237; **1948:** 2, 5
    (pp. 13, 50), 66, 122 [1], 140, 160, 183 [5],
    184, 187n., 198 [5], 218 [3], 218 [7, 10, 14],
    222 [7–9], 223, 225 [3], 227 [1, 2, 7, 9], 228
    [3, 5, 6, 12], 231 [1, 3], 233 [1], 236, 240 [3,
    4], 241, 242 [3], 248, 252, 257 [2], 259 [3, 5],
    260, 261 [8], 267 [1, 3]; **1949:** 153, 202;
    1950: 279; **1952–53:** 5, 110, 129, 215, 218,
    241, 258 [7], 266 [3], 277 [5], 286 [8], 298
    [3], 299, 300, 303 [4, 9, 10], 306 [2, 6], 307,
    308 [1, 2], 313 [4], 314, 315 [1, 2], 321 [2],
    322
  Amendment, approval, **1951:** 265
  Amendment or repeal, **1948:** 165, 226, 227 [6],
    232, 235 [4, 5], 237 [7], 247, 255, 259 [6],
    261 [1, 3, 4], 262, 264 [2], 274 [4, 13], 278
    [9], 288 [11]; **1949:** 2, 11 [7], 30 [3], 39, 89
    [16], 93 [7, 9, 16, 18], 144 [4, 26], 148 [9, 12,
    14], 236 [11]; **1950:** 9 (p. 98), 123, 128, 134
    Lesinski bills, **1949:** 89 [17], 93ftns. (pp. 242,
      244), 214 [6]
    Thomas bill, **1949:** 93 [18]
  Effect on labor unions, **1952–53:** 292 [13]
  Effect on New England economy, **1952–53:** 294
  Indictment of Philip Murray under, **1948:** 26 [8]
  Invocation in labor disputes, **1950:** 11 [1], 16 [10],
    29 [19], 35, 49; **1951:** 214
  Question of, **1949:** 155 [15], 240 [5, 15], 260 [1,
    6, 11]; **1952–53:** 37, 82, 103, 107 [12], 110,
    123 [6], 148, 156 [4], 161, 166 [1], 175 [12,
    16], 312
  News conference remarks, **1947:** 127 [1, 4, 10],
    182 [4], 236 [3]; **1948:** 26 [8], 71 [5, 17], 178
    [8], 274 [4, 13], 278 [9], 288 [11]; **1949:** 4
    [8], 11 [7], 30 [3], 89 [16, 17], 93 [7, 9, 16,
    18], 118 [13], 144 [4, 26], 148 [9, 12, 14],
    155 [15], 214 [6], 236 [11], 240 [5, 15], 253
    [14], 260 [1, 6, 11]; **1950:** 11 [1], 16 [10], 29
    [19], 250 [11], 287 [23]; **1951:** 7 [4], 295 [14]
  Republican endorsement, **1952–53:** 218, 289 [11],
    317 [5]
  Veto, **1947:** 120
    Letter to Senator Barkley, **1947:** 125
    Passage over veto, **1948:** 183 [7], 256, 261 [9],
      268
*Taft-Hartley Act and the Next Steps, The National
    Labor Policy,* Repr. Fred A. Hartley, Jr.,
    1948: 232
Tailors, English, comments on President's apparel,
    1951: 2 [26]
Taiwan.
    See China, Republic of; Formosa.
Talbot, Tom, **1952–53:** 319 [5, 6]
Tamerlane, **1950:** 313
Tandy, Delores, **1952–53:** 173n.
Tanguay, Eva, **1949:** 205 [6]
Tarawa, battle, **1945:** 45, 178
Tarchiani, Alberto, **1948:** 51n., 74, 278 [41]

Tariff Act of 1930, **1949:** 195; **1952–53:** 239
Tariff Commission, U.S., **1947:** 7 (p. 87), 39; **1948:**
    42; **1950:** 34 [11]; **1952–53:** 239, 359 [15]
  Ben D. Dorfman, **1945:** 24
Tariffs, **1947:** 4 (p. 38), 51; **1948:** 32, 195; **1949:**
    195; **1950:** 130; **1951:** 11, 126; **1952–53:**
    115 [6], 203, 239, 266 [2], 302
    See also Trade Agreements Act.
  Concessions to Czechoslovakia, **1948:** 84 [21]
  Copper, Chilean, **1949:** 122 [9]
  Geneva conference, **1947:** 52; **1948:** 42
  High level following World War I, **1948:** 260, 266
  News conference remarks, **1950:** 34 [5], 137 [21],
    206 [6], 217 [13]
  Philippine imports, **1947:** 236 [7]
  Reduction, **1947:** 138; **1948:** 2, 8 (p. 97), 213;
    1949: 120, 217; **1950:** 159
  "Tariff of Abominations" (1828), **1948:** 245
  Textiles, negotiations, **1950:** 34 [5]
  Wool imports, **1947:** 128
Tariffs and Trade, General Agreement on.
    See General Agreement on Tariffs and Trade.
Tarquins, expulsion from Rome, **1951:** 18
Tarrant, Vice Adm. W. T., **1945:** 24
Tarver, Malcolm C., **1947:** 46 [16]
Task Force Smith, campaign remarks, **1952–53:**
    172
Task Force on Statistical Agencies, **1952–53:** 18 (p.
    116)
Taunton, Mass., campaign remarks, **1948:** 261 [3];
    1952–53: 298 [2]
Tauriello, Anthony F., **1950:** 230 [1]; **1952–53:**
    288n.
Tax Court of the United States, **1946:** 78 [7]
  Vacancy on, **1952–53:** 35 [4]
Taxes, **1946:** 18 (pp. 51, 67, 71, 72), 79, 179, 193;
    1947: 4 (pp. 30, 39), 7 (pp. 55, 72, 73), 36
    [14], 53, 95 [27], 107 [2], 110, 180 [12, 13,
    21], 181 (pp. 402, 403, 406), 217, 243 [12,
    15]; **1948:** 8 (pp. 66, 69, 88, 89, 94, 95),
    101, 124 [4], 175, 183 [5]; **1949:** 5, 8 (p.
    93), 151, 240 [10], 269 [16]; **1950:** 157, 243,
    248; **1951:** 44, 98, 123, 137n., 221; **1952–
    53:** 17 [7], 101, 117, 158, 272, 277 [5], 287,
    307, 314
  Adjustments, **1948:** 8 (p. 98)
  Alaska, **1950:** 291
    Reform of tax structure, **1948:** 105
  Budget recommendations, **1952–53:** 367 (pp.
    1132–1133)
  Capital gains, **1950:** 18; **1951:** 28, 228
  Capital investments, tax incentives for, **1949:**
    151; **1950:** 6, 18
  Collection, **1951:** 13 (pp. 104, 105), 28
    Internal Revenue collectorships, proposed civ-
    il service status, **1951:** 239 [11, 13], 251
    [15, 21], 300ftn. (p. 641); **1952–53:** 1, 2
    [13], 117

Taxes — *continued*
  Collection system, administration, **1952–53:** 18 (p. 112)
  Community property, **1948:** 9 [2]
  Congressional inspection of returns, **1946:** 163 [10], 177 [16]
  Convention with Brazil, proposed, **1949:** 108 [1]
  Cooperatives, **1949:** 182 [10]; **1950:** 191 [2]; **1951:** 206; **1952–53:** 62, 267
  Copper tax suspension bill, **1947:** 78 [10, 18]
  Corporate, **1945:** 180; **1946:** 18 (pp. 71, 79), 21 [9], 192 [24]; **1947:** 6 [36], 7 (pp. 61, 92), 116, 152; **1948:** 2, 4 [5, 14, 16, 18], 5 (pp. 23, 25, 57), 8 (pp. 71, 94), 11 [14], 63, 67, 175; **1949:** 2, 5, 7 [36, 37], 8 (p. 49), 112 [6], 151; **1950:** 9 (pp. 52, 53), 18, 191 [2], 200, 202, 203 [9], 243, 257; **1951:** 11, 13 (p. 66), 28, 228, 264; **1952–53:** 110, 231, 367 (p. 1132)
  Cost-of-living credits, proposed, **1948:** 2, 4 [14, 16], 8 (p. 71)
  Deductions, **1952–53:** 127 [7, 9]
  Defense industries, tax treatment of, **1951:** 11, 13 (pp. 76, 77), 106, 167
  Delinquent, expenditures for collection, **1952–53:** 367 (p. 1161)
  District of Columbia, **1949:** 58 [2], 112 [17]
  Estate, **1947:** 116; **1948:** 63; **1949:** 2, 5, 151; **1950:** 18; **1951:** 28
  Excess profits, **1945:** 42; **1946:** 18 (p. 80), 192 [27]; **1947:** 4 (p. 16), 6 [36], 7 (pp. 56, 90), 70 [17], 221 [15]; **1948:** 4 [15, 16, 18], 5 (p. 23), 8 (p. 71), 165, 167, 170 [1], 176, 264 [5], 278 [30]; **1949:** 4 [5]; **1950:** 203 [9], 209 [8], 273 [5], 284, 303; **1951:** 1, 12 [10, 12], 13 (pp. 66, 67), 28, 228; **1952–53:** 367 (p. 1132)
  Excise, **1947:** 2 (p. 7), 6 [12, 37], 7 (pp. 55, 60, 61, 92), 116, 181 (pp. 403, 406); **1948:** 5 (p. 23), 63; **1949:** 5, 7 [23, 36, 40], 8 (p. 49), 144 [15, 25], 171 [4], 182 [7, 10], 229, 267 [3], 269 [22]; **1950:** 9 (p. 53), 18, 23 [3], 191 [2], 200, 202, 231; **1951:** 11, 13 (p. 66), 28; **1952–53:** 33
    Copper imports, **1950:** 152 [4, 6], 209 [10], 231, 250 [18], 318 [13]; **1951:** 11
    Gasoline, **1950:** 86 [10]
  Exempt organizations, proposed review of status, **1951:** 28
  Exemptions, **1947:** 26, 172; **1949:** 126, 146
    Charitable organizations, **1950:** 18
    Communist organizations, denial of exemptions, **1950:** 254
  Expense allowances for President, Vice President, and Speaker of House, **1952–53:** 361
  Gift, **1948:** 63; **1949:** 2, 5, 151; **1950:** 18
  Hawaii, **1950:** 291

Taxes — *continued*
  Income.
    See main heading, Income taxes.
    Increase, **1950:** 3 [17], 8 [5], 105 [9], 191 [14], 193, 194, 200, 202, 243, 303; **1951:** 1, 4, 7 [15], 11, 12 [11, 17, 20], 13 (pp. 12, 62, 66, 67), 28, 44, 70 [14], 91, 92, 98, 107, 118 [1], 167, 227 [1, 20], 228; **1952–53:** 5, 11, 15, 17 [34], 18 (p. 80), 33, 215, 293, 349, 367 (p. 1132), 376
    Proposed, **1949:** 2, 5, 7 [2, 7, 36, 39, 46], 8 (p. 48), 30 [11], 32 [1, 11], 66 [3], 72 [12], 95 [11, 13, 19], 112 [8, 14], 144 [27], 236 [12, 14], 260 [2, 5], 267 [3, 4]
    Question of, **1948:** 278 [2], 285 [3], 288 [10]
  Knutson bill, **1947:** 127 [2]
  Legislation, **1947:** 107 [4]
  Legislation, proposed, **1950:** 3 [16], 8 [39, 48], 9 (pp. 44, 47, 73), 11 [2], 16 [2], 18, 106, 284; **1951:** 12 [9, 12, 21, 40], 16 [16], 28, 37 [13], 177, 227 [1, 20], 228, 261 [8, 21]; **1952–53:** 18 (p. 67), 367 (p. 1132)
    Tax bills, **1950:** 137 [7, 9], 169 [3], 203 [12], 318 [7]
  Life insurance companies, **1951:** 28
  Local, **1949:** 126
  Local improvements, use to finance, **1952–53:** 209
  Loopholes and special privileges, elimination, **1952–53:** 5, 15
  Margarine, **1947:** 221 [8]
  Marshall Plan, financing by, **1947:** 221 [14]
  Merchant marine, tax benefits, **1951:** 13 (pp. 81–83); **1952–53:** 18 (p. 82), 211, 226
  Message to Congress, **1950:** 18; **1951:** 28
  National economy, impact of tax program on, **1951:** 28, 45
  News conference remarks, **1945:** 22 [15], 31 [5], 44 [1], 52 [18], 106 [7]; **1946:** 17 [2, 19], 21 [9], 75 [29], 78 [5], 163 [10], 177 [16], 192 [7, 11, 13, 24, 26, 27], 215 [2], 262 [19]; **1947:** 6 [8, 12, 20, 35, 36], 141 [1, 5], 145 [10, 19], 218 [5]; **1948:** 4 [1, 5, 8, 11, 14, 16, 18], 9 [2], 11 [14], 21 [10], 26 [14], 55 [3], 170 [1], 274 [8], 278 [2, 30]; **1950:** 3 [16, 17], 8 [5, 11, 22, 30, 39, 48], 11 [2], 16 [2], 23 [3], 46 [7], 86 [10], 105 [9], 137 [7, 9], 152 [4, 6], 169 [3], 191 [2, 14], 203 [9, 12], 209 [8, 10], 250 [18], 273 [5], 287 [19], 318 [7, 13]
  Payroll, **1947:** 4 (p. 37), 6 [35]; **1948:** 4 [8], 5 (pp. 23, 34, 35, 37), 8 (p. 88), 131, 220; **1949:** 5, 7 [2–4, 36, 42, 46], 8 (pp. 49, 67, 71), 151; **1950:** 8 [11, 30], 9 (pp. 50, 53, 76, 77), 84; **1951:** 13 (pp. 80, 99); **1952–53:** 17 [26], 18 (pp. 95, 104, 113)
  Personal property, **1949:** 126

Taxes — *continued*
  Poll, **1946:** 75 [29], 78 [5]; **1948:** 20, 166 [3]; **1949:** 52 [6], 118 [23]
    Proposed abolition, **1951:** 16 [20]; **1952–53:** 290
  Railroad, transfer of receipts to retirement trust fund, **1952–53:** 231
  Real estate, **1949:** 126; **1950:** 256
  Receipts, **1947:** 36 [14], 135, 180 [13, 19]; **1948:** 4 [11, 18], 5 (pp. 20, 22, 23, 34–36), 8 (p. 71); **1949:** 5, 7 [5, 8, 10, 37, 39], 8 (pp. 48, 49); **1950:** 9 (pp. 46, 47, 52–54, 100); **1952–53:** 11, 17 [2, 24], 231
    Estimated, **1951:** 12 [10], 13 (p. 66)
  Reduction, **1945:** 22 [15], 31 [5]; **1946:** 17 [2, 19], 18 (pp. 72, 74), 192 [26], 193, 215 [2], 262 [19]; **1947:** 4 (p. 30), 7 (pp. 56, 60), 36 [13], 62 [22], 68, 75, 78 [26], 90 [8], 116, 147, 152, 180 [3, 19], 191 [15], 221 [8], 236 [9]; **1948:** 2, 11ftn. (p. 104), 11 [14], 21 [10], 26 [14], 55 [5], 63, 80, 138 [7], 175, 183 [4, 6], 184, 223, 242 [1, 3], 259 [5], 261 [3], 264 [5], 267 [2], 268; **1949:** 5, 6, 144 [15, 25], 154, 182 [7], 234 [2], 236 [12], 267 [3]; **1950:** 2, 11ftn. (p. 108), 18, 23 [3], 39; **1952–53:** 170, 175 [2, 6], 283, 295 [8], 313 [5], 319 [5], 334 [17], 368
  Refunds, **1946:** 18 (pp. 78, 79), 192 [11, 13], 193; **1947:** 6 [36], 7 (pp. 57, 92), 163, 180 [8], 181 (p. 399); **1948:** 4 [1], 5 (pp. 20, 21, 25, 57), 8 (p. 71), 121, 175; **1949:** 7 [8, 15, 22, 39], 8 (p. 49), 234 [2]
    Interest on, **1951:** 13 (p. 106)
  Republican stand on, **1952–53:** 289 [2, 11], 319 [5], 334 [17]
  Returns, inspection by congressional committees, **1952–53:** 64 [6], 91
  Revision, **1945:** 128; **1947:** 147; **1948:** 2, 5 (pp. 22, 23)
  Sales tax, Federal, question of, **1951:** 12 [49], 16 [7]
  Securities, proposed review of exemptions, **1951:** 28
  Tax bills, **1948:** 55 [3], 138 [4, 7], 160, 183 [2, 6, 7], 198 [5, 7], 200 [3], 212 [7], 218 [7], 219, 227 [6], 228 [12], 231 [3], 235 [4], 238, 240 [6], 242 [3], 255, 259 [5], 264 [5], 267 [2], 268, 285 [10]; **1949:** 7 [1], 144 [17], 148 [13], 182 [10]
  Tax-free expense account, the President's, question of termination, **1951:** 22 [10]
  Tax structure, elimination of inequities, **1950:** 6, 18, 193, 194, 200, 202; **1951:** 28, 264
  Tax substitute bill, **1947:** 78 [12]
  Transportation, **1949:** 151
  Treasury Committee Study, **1949:** 267 [12]
  Wartime program, **1945:** 213

Taxes — *continued*
  Withholding
    Abolition proposed, **1950:** 46 [7]
    Dividends, **1950:** 200, 202
Taylor, George, **1946:** 143 [10], 177 [2]; **1951:** 169, 204
Taylor, Sen. Glen H., **1950:** 105 [16], 209 [9]
Taylor, Harry E., **1948:** 38
Taylor, J. E., **1952–53:** 21 [6], 149 [3], 156 [1], 221ftn. (p. 511)
Taylor, Jack, **1952–53:** 274 [2]
Taylor, Maj. Gen. Maxwell D., **1946:** 224
Taylor, Myron C., **1946:** 100, 129 [8], 136 [13], 173 [16], 2531947: 67 [13], 88 [12], 178, 185; **1948:** 286; **1949:** 269 [7], 270n.; **1950:** 16 [1], 44 [3], 86 [11], 206 [8]; **1951:** 188 [9]
Taylor, Telford, **1951:** 239 [5]
Taylor, Wayne C., letter, **1945:** 176
Taylor, Zachary, **1952–53:** 282 [7], 289
Taylorville, Ill., campaign remarks, **1952–53:** 321 [5]
Teacher of the Year award, presentation, **1952–53:** 133
Teachers.
  See also Education; Schools.
  Communist, question of barring from college faculties, **1949:** 118 [22]
  Exchange, **1949:** 187; **1951:** 103, 124, 194; **1952–53:** 234
  Pay, **1948:** 108, 134, 157, 165, 183 [5], 203, 241, 258, 259 [4], 262, 268; **1949:** 2, 8 (p. 76), 93 [5]; **1952–53:** 284 [6]
  Shortage, **1947:** 235; **1948:** 2, 8 (pp. 67, 85), 160, 183 [1, 5], 194 [3], 200 [5], 203, 214 [9], 219, 228 [8], 241; **1949:** 2, 204; **1950:** 2, 9 (p. 83), 92, 127 [7]; **1952–53:** 284 [6]; **1948:** 138 [1]
Teapot Dome oil scandal, 1920's, **1950:** 116; **1951:** 300ftn. (p. 641); **1952–53:** 69, 129, 143, 277 [1]
Technical assistance to less developed countries and new nations, **1949:** 139, 151, 193, 195; **1950:** 2, 6, 9 (pp. 48, 56, 59), 18, 25, 42, 132, 154, 177, 185; **1951:** 13 (p. 74), 96, 114, 135, 250, 259, 262; **1952–53:** 18 (p. 74), 20, 55, 57, 72, 81, 101, 169, 281, 354, 367 (p. 1139)
  See also Economic assistance; Foreign assistance; Point 4 program.
  Africa, **1951:** 13 (p. 75), 262
  Arab states, **1952–53:** 18 (p. 76)
  Asia, **1952–53:** 18 (p. 76)
  Indonesia, **1952–53:** 18 (p. 76)
  Iran, **1952–53:** 18 (p. 76)
  Israel, **1952–53:** 18 (p. 76)
  Latin America, **1951:** 13 (p. 75), 114, 262; **1952–53:** 18 (p. 76), 367 (p. 1140)

Technical assistance — *continued*
  Latin America — *continued*
    Brazil, **1951:** 259
    OAS program, **1951:** 114
  Middle East, **1952–53:** 18 (p. 76)
  Near East, **1951:** 13 (p. 74)
  State Department functions, **1952–53:** 18 (p. 115)
  United Nations program, **1950:** 143, 177, 240;
    1951: 114, 170; **1952–53:** 18 (p. 77)
Technical Commission for Aeronautics, Radio,
    1948: 175
Technical Conference on Air Pollution, U.S., **1950:**
    101
Technical Cooperation Administration, **1952–53:**
    18 (p. 115), 55
Technical Cooperation Administrator (Henry G.
    Bennett), **1951:** 16 [1], 83, 262, 296n.
Technical Mission, Joint U.S.-Brazil, **1949:** 108 [1]
Technological development, **1945:** 218
Technological progress, **1952–53:** 33, 179
Techachapi, Calif., campaign remarks, **1948:** 204
    [5]
Teheran, **1945:** 177
Teheran agreements, **1950:** 80 [4]
Teheran conference, **1945:** 97
Teheran Declaration (1943), **1949:** 273
Telecommunication Convention, International,
    1948: 29
Telephone facilities for rural areas, **1949:** 243
Telephone industry
  Labor dispute, **1950:** 43
  Strike, **1946:** 53 [2]; **1947:** 67 [1], 78 [13]
Telephone service, rural, **1950:** 6, 9 (p. 86), 110 [9],
    127 [6]; **1951:** 13 (p. 89); **1952–53:** 266 [5,
    7, 13], 274 [1], 285, 367 (p. 1149)
Television, **1952–53:** 274 [5]
  Comment on, **1951:** 63 [4]
  Congressional hearings, question of use in,
    1952–53: 49 [7]
  Election campaigns, role in, **1948:** 288; **1952–53:**
    26 [28], 166 [13]
  Frequency allocations, **1950:** 34 [8]
  Stations, proposed halt to construction of,
    1952–53: 26 [13]
Tello, Manuel, **1951:** 76; **1952–53:** 2 [5]
Temple, Tex., campaign remarks, **1948:** 212 [4]
Templeton, Fay, **1951:** 99
Templeton, W. L., **1950:** 157n.
Temporary Controls, Office of, **1946:** 262 [3, 13];
    1947: 7 (pp. 56, 74, 86), 60, 65; **1948:** 5 (p.
    52)
Temporary Emergency Railroad Wage Panel,
    1951: 74n.
Temporary National Economic Committee, **1947:**
    2 (p. 6), 4 (p. 35); **1948:** 8 (pp. 89, 90)
Ten Commandments, **1945:** 178
Tenant farmers, **1948:** 99

Tennessee, **1945:** 163; **1946:** 186 [4]; **1947:** 104;
    1950: 3 [5], 105 [19]
  Browning, Gov. Gordon, **1951:** 138; **1952–53:**
    221 [1]
  Droughts, **1952–53:** 221 [1]
  Gore, Repr. Albert, **1945:** 208 [13]
  McCord, Gov. Jim Nance, **1948:** 245n.
  McKellar, Sen. Kenneth, **1945:** 2, 34, 59, 85, 159
  Oak Ridge, **1945:** 93, 156
  Poll tax, abolition of, **1952–53:** 169
  President's forbears in, **1948:** 222 [1]
  Reelfoot Lake, **1945:** 164n.
  Tiptonville, **1945:** 164
  Visit to, question of, **1948:** 178 [2]
Tennessee River, **1946:** 86 [16]; **1950:** 157
  Development, **1945:** 165
  Power projects, **1952–53:** 294
Tennessee Valley, **1947:** 110; **1949:** 8 (p. 83)
Tennessee Valley Associated Cooperatives, **1947:** 7
    (p. 95)
Tennessee Valley Authority, **1945:** 70, 128, 155, 164
    [8], 165; **1946:** 18 (pp. 61, 82), 94, 223 [5],
    238, 242 [3], 243, 244; **1947:** 7 (p. 82), 46
    [18], 243 [18]; **1948:** 2, 5 (p. 46), 101, 109,
    148, 163 [5], 165, 175, 218 [7, 8, 9, 14], 236,
    258; **1949:** 8 (p. 83), 77, 107, 236 [1]; **1950:**
    3 [5], 9 (p. 90), 121 [4, 13], 125, 196; **1951:**
    11, 13 (pp. 84–86), 108 [9], 171 [10], 183,
    251 [16], 261 [20]; **1952–53:** 8 (p. 88), 62,
    117, 129, 143, 194, 267, 271, 277 [3, 6],
    294, 298 [2], 388
  Appointment of chairman, question of, **1952–53:**
    26 [26]
  Appropriations, **1952–53:** 147
  Steam powerplants, **1952–53:** 367 (p. 1146)
Tennessee Valley Authority, Chairman (Gordon R.
    Clapp), **1949:** 156; **1950:** 25, 154, 196;
    1952–53: 144
Tennessee Valley Authority, Chairman (David E.
    Lilienthal), **1946:** 136 [6], 195n., 226 [17],
    242 [2, 3], 243, 244
  News conference remarks on, **1945:** 4 [7], 22 [4]
  Reappointment to TVA, **1945:** 22 [4]
Tennyson, Alfred, *Locksley Hall*, **1950:** 159; **1952–
    53:** 125
Terminal leave pay, **1946:** 192 [3, 5, 6, 14, 17, 21],
    194, 199 [17]; **1947:** 2 (p. 8), 6 [3, 18, 21], 7
    (pp. 65, 68, 89), 145 [17], 181 (pp. 404,
    406, 407)
Terre Haute, Ind.
  Campaign remarks at, **1948:** 138 [5], 267 [2];
    1952–53: 321 [2]
  Mayor Ralph Tucker, **1948:** 138 [5]
Territories, dependent, social policy, **1946:** 180
Territories and possessions, U.S., **1950:** 9 (p. 102)
  See also specific territory.
  Agricultural commodities for, **1947:** 35

Territories and possessions, U.S. — *continued*
  Civil rights, **1948:** 2, 20
  Isolation by maritime strikes, **1949:** 118 [16]
  Self-government, **1950:** 2
  Statehood, proposed, **1950:** 267
  Transfer to civilian administration, **1949:** 101
  Virgin Islands, assistance, **1949:** 40 [15]
  Welfare programs, **1948:** 146
Teton National Forest, **1950:** 248
Texas, **1946:** 6 [17]; **1947:** 78 [7], 104; **1949:** 148 [15]
  Admission into Union, **1952–53:** 107 [10]
  Big Bend National Park, **1948:** 208 [6–8]
  Campaign remarks, **1948:** 208 [4–9], 209, 210, 212, 213, 214 [1–3]
  Candidates for public office, **1948:** 208 [7], 212 [1, 4, 5, 11], 213, 214 [2]; **1952–53:** 98 [33], 238 [5]
  Congressional delegation, President's dinner with, **1951:** 27
  Connally, Sen. Tom, **1945:** 10, 69, 219n.
  Delegation at Democratic National Convention, **1952–53:** 197 [15]
  Flood control, **1952–53:** 194
  Gov. Beauford H. Jester, **1948:** 208 [4–8], 209, 210 [1, 2], 212 [2–7, 9], 213, 214 [1–5]
  Gov. Allan Shivers, **1952–53:** 175 [17], 315 [6], 316
    Endorsement of General Eisenhower, **1952–53:** 247 [3]
    Natural gas, export to Canada, **1952–53:** 377 [25]
  Irrigation projects, **1948:** 208 [7], 209
  Judicial vacancy in, **1951:** 90 [2]
  Martial tradition of, **1948:** 212 [2]
  News conference remarks, **1950:** 3 [9], 29 [9], 38 [16]
  Offshore lands, **1952–53:** 146, 377 [11]
  Patman, Repr. Wright, **1945:** 208 [19]
  Peanut acreage allotments in, **1950:** 83
  Power projects, **1950:** 3 [9], 125
  Rayburn, Repr. Sam, **1945:** 2, 34, 50, 59, 85, 124, 134, 146, 159
    See also, Rayburn, Repr. Sam; Speaker of the House of Representatives (Sam Rayburn).
  River basin development, **1950:** 164
  Waco, **1945:** 175 [6]
Texas, Republic of, **1952–53:** 149 [4]
Texas City, Tex., **1947:** 86
  Tin smelter at, **1950:** 114
Texas Oil Co., **1952–53:** 58
Textbooks, investigation by Un-American Affairs Committee, **1949:** 122 [8]
Textiles, **1949:** 236 [4], 253 [8]
  Cotton, **1946:** 237 [21]
  Decrease in consumer demand, **1952–53:** 15
  Exports, **1950:** 159
  Japanese silk, **1946:** 186 [7]

Textiles — *continued*
  Labor dispute in industry, **1951:** 85 [7]
  Prices, **1947:** 4 (p. 15), 76, 214, 224; **1948:** 8 (p. 64), 285 [3]
    Increase, **1951:** 11
  Production, **1946:** 72 [2]
  Tariff negotiations, **1951:** 34 [5]
Thailand **1945:** 107 [21]
  Assistance, **1952–53:** 55
    Economic, **1951:** 13 (p. 74)
    Military, **1951:** 114
  Korean War, participation, **1950:** 232, 296; **1951:** 170
Thanksgiving Day, **1949:** 260 [19], 263
  U.S. tradition of, **1948:** 276
Theatres Association, American, **1946:** 160
Theater Owners Convention, remarks, **1952–53:** 250
Theodore Roosevelt National Park, disapproval, **1946:** 200
There Is No Other Vehicle, Republican booklet, **1948:** 183 [6]
Third world war, danger of, **1951:** 70 [4]
Thirty-fifth Division, World War I, **1948:** 117, 118 [3], 217
  Reunion, **1947:** 110; **1949:** 119; **1950:** 161; **1951:** 108 [7], 113 [16]; **1952–53:** 157, 158
This is Our Story, Red Cross pamphlet, **1947:** 49
Thomas, Charles A., **1950:** 238 [7]; **1951:** 89
Thomas, Sen. Elbert D., **1946:** 137; **1948:** 130 [1]; **1949:** 155 [17]; **1951:** 297; **1952–53:** 281, 322
  Labor bill, **1949:** 93 [18]
  Letter, **1945:** 114
Thomas, Sen. Elmer, **1948:** 214 [8]; **1949:** 260 [7]; **1950:** 191 [4], 249
Thomas, Repr. J. Parnell, **1947:** 205 [16]; **1948:** 86ftn. (p. 235)
Thomas, Lowell, **1947:** 90n.
Thomas, R. J., message, **1945:** 206n.
Thomason, Repr. Robert Ewing, **1947:** 78 [7]
Thompson, C. Mildred, **1948:** 30
Thompson, Carl, **1948:** 237 [5, 8], 238n., 239n.
Thompson, Dr. L. E., **1948:** 198 [7]
Thompson, Mrs. Marguerite Peyton, **1948:** 198 [7]
Thompson, Maurice, *Alice of Old Vincennes*, **1948:** 233 [3]
Thompson, Roy L., **1947:** 177 [10]
Thompsonville, Conn., campaign remarks, **1948:** 259 [2]; **1952–53:** 292 [8]
Thought clinics, **1947:** 67 [8]
Thourot, Harry J., **1948:** 189n.
Thurman, Samuel, **1949:** 11 [9]
Thurmond, Gov. Strom, **1948:** 278 [5]; **1950:** 169 [2]; **1952–53:** 35 [7]
Thurston, Walter, **1947:** 145 [16]; **1950:** 214 [5, 7]
Thye, Sen. Edward J., **1951:** 54n.
Thyroid diseases, **1952–53:** 333

Tiber Creek, **1948:** 11ftn. (p. 106)
Tiber Dam, Mont., **1950:** 127 [6]
  Campaign remarks, **1952–53:** 269
Tidal wave in Hawaii, **1946:** 72 [18]
Tidelands oil, **1948:** 228 [12], 278 [37], 285 [7];
    1949: 2, 7 [33, 38], 113 [2], 122 [15]
Tidelands oil bill, **1946:** 177 [6], 186 [5]
  Veto, **1946:** 189
Tientsin, China, **1946:** 265
Tiernan, Msgr. L. Curtis, **1951:** 218n.
Tighe, B. C. B., **1950:** 130n.
Tigris River, **1949:** 252
Tilden, Samuel Jr., **1948:** 227 [2]
Tillett, Mrs. Charles, **1949:** 20
Timber resources, **1948:** 5 (p. 46), 8 (pp. 67, 78)
Timberman, Brig. Gen. T. S., **1952–53:** 310
Time magazine, **1947:** 19 [13]; **1950:** 163, 279
Tin
  Bolivian, **1952–53:** 2 [8, 14], 26 [14]
  Import controls, **1947:** 18, 99
  Imports from U.K., agreement on, **1952–53:** 6n.
  Prices, **1950:** 202
  Purchase and smelting, RFC operations, **1951:**
    82
  RFC policy on, **1952–53:** 2 [12]
  Shortage, **1945:** 128, 209
  Stockpiling, **1948:** 8 (p. 78)
  Texas City smelter, **1950:** 114
Tinian island, U.S. capture of, **1945:** 161
Tioga, N. Dak., campaign remarks, **1952–53:** 266
  [10]
Tipton, Ind., campaign remarks, **1948:** 240 [5]
Tiptonville, Tenn., **1945:** 164
Titian, *Portrait of Himself,* **1948:** 71 [1]
Tito, Josip Broz, **1948:** 86, 150 [8]; **1949:** 269 [13];
  1952–53: 107 [14]
Tobacco
  Exports, **1947:** 7 (p. 78); **1948:** 8 (p. 93), 31, 246;
    1950: 159
  Marketing quota, **1947:** 35
  Price supports, **1948:** 5 (p. 43); **1950:** 9 (p. 86)
Tobey, Sen. Charles W., **1946:** 143 [7]; **1948:** 15 [1],
  88 [7]; **1949:** 7 [34]; **1950:** 86 [13]; **1951:**
  54n.
Tobias, Channing H., **1951:** 266n.
Tobin, Maurice J., **1952–53:** 292n.
  See also Labor, Secretary of.
  News conference remarks on, **1948:** 88 [15], 174
    [7, 10]
Tojo, Hideki, **1948:** 256; **1951:** 138
Tokyo, **1945:** 45, 161; **1946:** 141 [11]; **1947:** 36 [20]
  War crimes trials, **1946:** 18 (pp. 46, 47)
Toledo, Ohio
  Campaign remarks in, **1948:** 183 [7], 257 [3];
    1952–53: 319 [1]
  Mayor Michael V. DiSalle, **1948:** 257 [3]
  Plan for labor-management peace, **1946:** 257 [17]
Tolono, Ill., campaign remarks, **1948:** 233 [5]

Tombstone, Ariz
  Epitaph in, **1948:** 136 [1]; **1952–53:** 98 [2], 123
    [12]
  Mayor Wally C. Foster, **1952–53:** 123 [12]
Tongass National Forest, Alaska, **1948:** 105
  Japanese logging operations in, **1952–53:** 247 [11]
Topeka, Kans.
  Flood control, **1952–53:** 18 (p. 88)
  35th Division reunion, **1951:** 108 [7], 113 [16]
Toronto Reservoir, Kansas, **1952–53:** 367 (p. 1146)
Torp, Oscar, visit of, **1952–53:** 258 [10]
Torquato, John R., **1948:** 251n.
Torresola, Griselio, **1950:** 278ftn. (p. 695)
Toscanini, Arturo, **1950:** 146 [21]
Totalitarianism, **1947:** 56, 76, 90 [1], 140, 210 [1],
  222; **1948:** 5 (p. 21), 49 [21], 266
  "Big lie" technique, **1952–53:** 251
  Comments on, **1950:** 21, 37, 80 [4], 92, 94, 155,
    162, 174, 185, 207, 254; **1951:** 135
Tour of Nation, the President's, comments on,
  1950: 135, 136, 137 [13, 15], 139, 157
Tours, battle of, **1951:** 8
Towers, Adm. John H., **1946:** 226 [14]
Town meetings, New England, **1947:** 90 [1]
  Anecdote on, **1948:** 259 [2]
Townsend, John G., Jr., nomination as Alternate
  U.S. representative to U.N. General As-
  sembly, **1945:** 219n.
Townsend plan, **1948:** 89
Tractors, shortage, **1947:** 18
Trade, international, **1945:** 2, 66, 128, 178, 228;
  1946: 2, 18 (pp. 43, 45, 46, 57, 85), 25, 67,
  76, 110 [4], 172, 174, 236, 248; **1947:** 2 (p.
  10), 4 (pp. 37, 38), 21, 51, 52, 55, 58, 122,
  138, 143, 155 [7], 172, 224, 242; **1948:** 2, 5
  (p. 29), 8 (pp. 69, 89, 93, 96, 97), 12, 23, 32,
  168, 177, 179, 202 [6], 234; **1949:** 6, 8 (p.
  53), 19, 68, 120, 151, 195, 263; **1950:** 42,
  81, 111, 130; **1952–53:** 366
  See also Balance of payments; Exports; Imports;
    Tariffs; Trade Agreements Act; *specific*
    commodities.
  Agricultural commodities, **1948:** 276; **1950:** 83
  Armaments, **1947:** 72
  Balance of payments.
    See main heading, Balance of payments.
  Barriers, reduction of, **1947:** 238; **1948:** 143, 160,
    213; **1949:** 88, 210, 263
  Campaign remarks, **1952–53:** 285
  China, **1945:** 216
  Committee for Financing Foreign Trade, **1946:**
    142
  Communist bloc, **1952–53:** 105, 180, 203
    Restrictions on trade with, **1951:** 117, 118 [14],
      224 [4]
    War materials, embargo on shipment to, **1950:**
      252

Trade, international — *continued*
  Customs procedures, simplification, **1951:** 13 (p. 105), 219
  Danish-Soviet, **1952–53:** 217
  Effect on domestic economy, **1948:** 213
  European dependence on, **1947:** 238
  Expansion, **1950:** 2, 6, 42, 119, 122, 126, 132, 159
  Geneva conferences on.
    See Geneva conferences.
  Japan, restoration of trade relations, **1951:** 216
  Latin American, **1951:** 59
  Liberalization, **1951:** 11, 126; **1952–53:** 190, 215
  News conference remarks, **1945:** 4 [5], 64 [2]; **1949:** 113 [5], 122 [7], 144 [16, 22, 24], 171 [3, 16]; **1950:** 86 [16], 253 [8]
  Policy study by Public Advisory Board for Mutual Security Program, **1952–53:** 203
  Raw materials, **1952–53:** 179
  Reciprocal agreements, **1950:** 42, 86 [16], 130; **1952–53:** 307, 322
    Escape clauses, **1952–53:** 10
  Relationship to farm economy, **1948:** 117
  Strategic and critical materials, **1951:** 13 (pp. 75, 76)
  Tariffs and Trade, General Agreement on, **1947:** 216; **1948:** 8 (p. 97), 42, 84 [23], 88 [6, 18, 21], 143; **1949:** 6, 120, 217; **1951:** 126
  Trade Agreements Act.
    See main heading, Trade Agreements Act.
  Trade Agreements Extension Act of 1948, approval, **1948:** 143
  Trade fair, proposed, **1949:** 171 [3, 16]
  Trade Organization, International, **1948:** 54
  U.N. conference on (1948), **1949:** 88
  U.S.-Argentina, **1949:** 113 [5], 144 [22]
  U.S. balance of trade, **1949:** 5
  U.S.-Canada, **1947:** 111
  U.S.-Cuba, **1948:** 81
  U.S.-Czechoslovakia, **1948:** 55 [6]
  U.S.-Italy, **1948:** 73
  U.S.-Latin America, **1948:** 69
  U.S.-Philippines, **1945:** 24; **1946:** 90; **1947:** 236 [7]
  U.S.-U.K., **1946:** 51
  U.S.-Venezuela, **1952–53:** 239
  Wartime controls, removal, **1945:** 209
  Wool, **1950:** 253 [8]
Trade Agreements Act, **1945:** 64 [2]; **1946:** 18 (p. 45), 25; **1947:** 39, 52, 111; **1948:** 2, 5 (p. 23), 99, 117, 165, 213, 231 [7], 233 [1], 236, 246; **1949:** 2, 5, 6, 40 [7], 88, 112 [15], 151, 161 [11], 202, 203, 217; **1950:** 34 [11], 42, 119, 130, 134; **1951:** 11, 33 [10], 165 [3]
  Expiration, **1952–53:** 203
  Extension, proposed, **1948:** 228 [1], 266
  Message to Congress, **1948:** 42
  Relationship to Marshall plan, **1948:** 88 [18, 21]

Trade Agreements Committee, **1950:** 34 [5]; **1952–53:** 10
Trade Agreements Extension Act of 1948, approval, **1948:** 143
Trade Agreements Extension Act of 1951, **1951:** 13 (p. 76), 126; **1952–53:** 10, 239
Trade Commission, Federal.
  See Federal Trade Commission.
Trade and Employment, International Conference on, **1946:** 18 (pp. 45, 46), 248
Trade Organization, International, **1946:** 236, 248; **1947:** 4 (p. 38), 7 (p. 67), 21, 51, 52, 111, 128, 138, 155 [7], 182 [7]; **1948:** 2, 8 (p. 97), 42, 54, 202 [6], 213; **1949:** 5, 8 (p. 55), 88, 217, 263; **1950:** 2, 6, 9 (p. 56), 42, 130, 159
Trade paper editors, news conference with, **1947:** 196
Trade Unions, Free, International Confederation of, **1951:** 153 [16]
Trademarks, legislation, **1947:** 7 (p. 88)
Trading with the Enemy Act, **1947:** 80; **1951:** 149
  Approval of amendment, **1948:** 154
Trades and Labor Assembly, New York, **1952–53:** 237
Traffic accidents, **1945:** 62, 208 [10], 224; **1946:** 96, 106; **1947:** 8, 27, 82, 86, 118; **1949:** 26, 114
  Reduction, **1950:** 229; **1951:** 9, 13 (p. 81), 42, 121
Traffic Club, Reading, Pa., **1948:** 227 [2]
Traffic laws, **1950:** 37
Traffic safety, **1948:** 279
Traffic safety, White House conference on, **1945:** 224
Training
  Driver, **1947:** 118
  Government employees, **1947:** 117
  Military.
    See Military training and education.
  Nurses, **1945:** 130
  President's Advisory Commission on Universal Training, **1946:** 268
  Scientific, **1947:** 183, 206, 211
  Seamen, **1947:** 123
Training Commission, National Security, **1952–53:** 18 (p. 73)
Transit strike, Washington, D.C., **1945:** 208ftn. (p. 528)
  Statement, **1945:** 195
Transjordan, U.S. diplomatic recognition of government, **1949:** 22 [15], 23
Transport pilot's license, honorary, the President's, **1949:** 253 [1]
Transportation, **1945:** 62, 68, 165; **1946:** 18 (pp. 46, 81, 82), 55, 56, 94; **1947:** 4 (pp. 20, 34), 7 (pp. 58, 61, 84, 86, 92), 51, 155 [6], 181 (pp. 399, 406), 224, 242; **1948:** 5, (pp. 20, 25, 47, 48, 50), 8 (pp. 62, 67, 81, 98), 9 [12],

Transportation — *continued*
 175; **1949:** 2, 8 (pp. 47, 84–88); **1950:** 9
 (pp. 91–96); **1951:** 13 (pp. 64, 80–83), 163,
 255
 See also Aviation, civil; Highways; Railroads;
 Ships.
 Air, **1947:** 19 [18], 115, 148, 161; **1948:** 5 (pp. 47,
  48, 50), 8 (pp. 81, 82), 168; **1950:** 9 (p. 94),
  171; **1952–53:** 18 (p. 83)
 Air Transport Agreement, U.S.-U.K., **1946:** 43
  [2], 44
 Alaska, **1948:** 105; **1950:** 9 (p. 91)
 Armed forces, repatriation, **1947:** 18
 Canada, **1948:** 105
 Carriers' Conference Committees, **1951:** 74
 Chinese system, **1946:** 265
 Common carrier rates, **1948:** 127
 Displaced persons migrating to U.S., **1945:** 225
 ECA cargoes, shipment on U.S. flag vessels,
  1948: 283 [9]
 Emergency exports, **1947:** 47
 European system, restoration of, **1947:** 238
 Facilities, allocation and use of, **1947:** 6 [33], 35,
  99; **1948:** 1, 8 (p. 74)
 Federal aid, **1948:** 5 (pp. 47, 48)
 Federal programs for, report, **1949:** 266; **1950:**
  53, 209 [16]; **1952–53:** 5, 18 (p. 81), 209,
  231, 367 (pp. 1142–1144)
 Five-year censuses of, **1952–53:** 367 (p. 1156)
 Freight charges, **1950:** 166; **1951:** 188 [17];
  1952–53: 266 [2], 270 [5]
 German system, **1946:** 6 [8]
 Highway, **1950:** 229
 Immigrants to U.S., **1952–53:** 182
 India, relief grain shipments to, **1951:** 34
 Interstate, **1948:** 20
 Korea, **1950:** 268
 Labor disputes, **1951:** 74
 Land, **1952–53:** 18 (p. 84)
 Latin American, **1948:** 69
 Less developed areas, **1950:** 177
 Mail, **1947:** 181 (p. 399); **1948:** 8 (p. 81)
  Proposed increase in rates by carriers, **1951:** 45
 Marine, **1948:** 179; **1952–53:** 367 (pp. 1142–1143)
 Mexico, air service to, **1952–53:** 246
 Railroad, **1947:** 143, 160; **1948:** 8 (pp. 80, 82), 95;
  1949: 148 [23]; **1950:** 221
 Railroad strike.
  See main heading, Railroad strike.
 Redeployment of armed forces, **1945:** 52 [3, 12]
  Letter to J. Monroe Johnson, **1945:** 53
  Statement, **1945:** 54
 Refugees to U.S., **1946:** 267
 Restrictions on civilian travel, **1945:** 54
 Taxes, **1949:** 151; **1950:** 18
 Urban, **1948:** 37
 Virgin Islands, **1949:** 141

Transportation — *continued*
 Water, **1949:** 8 (p. 86); **1950:** 9 (pp. 92–94), 76;
  1952–53: 18 (pp. 81–83)
 Coast Guard safety functions, **1948:** 62
Transportation, Office of Defense.
 See Defense Transportation, Office of.
Transportation Act of 1940, **1948:** 228 [12]
Traubel, Helen, **1950:** 146 [22]
Travel
 Foreigners in U.S., **1948:** 38; **1950:** 92, 185
 Freedom of, **1947:** 138
 International, **1948:** 168
 President's plans, **1947:** 141 [10], 145 [7], 174 [7];
  1948: 21 [2, 8], 84 [5], 88 [8], 110 [5], 150
  [10], 163 [18, 20], 170 [2], 174 [6, 8, 12], 178
  [2, 16]; **1949:** 39, 40 [14, 16], 45 [11], 52 [2],
  58 [19, 20, 23], 66 [5, 9], 93 [15], 112 [19],
  113 [14], 118 [3], 144 [8], 148 [8], 179 [12],
  192 [18, 20], 200 [4], 205 [18], 226 [20], 231
  [11], 234 [12], 236 [13, 19]; **1950:** 38 [5], 46
  [15, 16], 52 [3], 86 [20, 26, 28], 105 [16, 17,
  19], 137 [8], 146 [9], 169 [5–8, 10], 203 [16],
  309 [11]; **1952–53:** 31 [11], 49 [14, 18], 64
  [7], 88 [20, 21], 123 [15], 127 [3], 378
 U.S. abroad, **1950:** 159, 185; **1951:** 145 [5], 160
  Restrictions on travel to Communist countries,
   1950: 207
  State Department procedures governing,
   1952–53: 197 [10]
Travelers Aid Association, National, **1951:** 186
Travers, Howard K., **1951:** 193ftn. (p. 466)
Travis Air Force Base, Calif., **1952–53:** 135
Treason
 Constitutional definition, **1949:** 45 [20]
 Laws against, **1950:** 207
Treasury, Department of the, **1945:** 70, 213; **1946:**
  18 (pp. 72, 73, 85, 87), 35, 94, 116, 118,
  119 [3], 192 [6, 9, 11, 12, 19], 193, 194, 196,
  226 [2], 262 [4]; **1947:** 6 [14, 28, 35], 7 (pp.
  59, 60, 61, 64, 65, 75, 78, 80, 81, 82, 85, 88,
  90, 91, 93, 94, 95), 18, 23, 39, 60, 76, 80,
  135, 141 [5], 157, 158, 165, 180 [19, 20],
  181 (pp. 401, 402, 403, 405), 236 [9]; **1948:**
  4 [5, 10, 15, 16], 5 (pp. 23–25, 40, 44, 48,
  53, 57), 8 (p. 95), 21 [5], 25, 42, 46, 60, 89,
  101, 175; **1949:** 5, 8 (p. 51); **1950:** 114,
  196; **1952–53:** 11, 86, 211, 225, 226, 255
 Appropriations for, **1947:** 11
 Bell, Daniel W., **1945:** 202 [11]
 Cash surplus, **1947:** 36 [14]
 Cooperation with Senate crime investigation,
  1951: 63 [1]
 Daily statement, **1947:** 75
 Debt management operations, **1952–53:** 15
 Defense financing program, **1951:** 29
 Enemy war assets, receipt of proceeds from
  disposition of, **1948:** 154

Treasury, Department of the — *continued*
  Financing of election campaigns, proposed,
    1949: 148 [21]
  Fiscal policy, differences with Federal Reserve
    Board, **1951:** 56 [21], 113 [6]
  Joint accounting program for executive agencies,
    1951: 221
  News conference remarks, **1945:** 157 [14], 208
    [15]; **1949:** 7 [15, 50], 148 [21], 267 [3, 12];
    1950: 8 [29, 36, 38, 46], 34 [2]
  Reorganization, **1950:** 53–55, 149; **1952–53:** 11,
    84
  RFC, question of transfer to, **1951:** 33 [2]
  Savings bonds drive, **1948:** 26 [3, 10]; **1951:** 11,
    12 [13], 13 (p. 105), 60, 91, 133, 153 [1, 13],
    167, 210, 213, 290
  Silver purchase program, **1950:** 8 [29]
  Tax enforcement, **1950:** 8 [36, 38], 18
Treasury, Secretary of the (Henry Morgenthau, Jr).
  See also Morgenthau, Henry, Jr.
  Letters, **1945:** 76 [3], 82
  Morgenthau plan for Germany, **1945:** 22 [11]
  News conference remarks on, **1945:** 22 [11, 15],
    40 [1], 44 [1], 67 [3], 76 [9]
  Resignation, **1945:** 76 [2, 3, 9]
  Tax enforcement program, **1945:** 44 [1]
Treasury, Secretary of the (John W. Snyder), **1946:**
    144, 192 [3, 8], 229 [24, 26]; **1947:** 6, 35, 67
    [7], 94, 127 [3], 135, 180 [7, 13, 14, 17, 19,
    20], 181 (p. 404), 221 [1]; **1948:** 4, 9 [2, 4],
    15 [1], 166 [8]; **1949:** 7n., 8 (p. 93), 37, 54,
    58 [12], 64, 82, 98n., 149n., 210; **1950:** 8n.,
    9 (p. 51), 280, 281, 284; **1951:** 12, 28, 98,
    133, 202, 210; **1952–53:** 6, 27, 48, 193, 226,
    255, 292n., 331, 156ftn. (p. 403)
  Budget news conference, **1952–53:** 17
  Campaign remarks on, **1952–53:** 292 [11]
  Currency control, views on, **1950:** 97 [7]
  Defense contract financing, review of legislation,
    1951: 106
  Federal programs review, letter, **1950:** 196
  Fiscal policy, joint announcement with Chair-
    man of Federal Reserve Board, **1951:** 52
  Letter, **1952–53:** 225
  Memorandum, debt management and credit
    controls, **1951:** 44
  News conference remarks on, **1950:** 97 [7], 191
    [14], 217 [10], 309 [1]; **1951:** 7 [15], 153 [1],
    300 [6]; **1952–53:** 31 [17]
  Resignation, **1952–53:** 381
  Review of excess profits taxes, **1951:** 1
  RFC Loan Policy Board, ex-officio membership,
    1951: 39
  Statement on proposed tax increase, **1951:** 70
    [14]
Treasury, Secretary of the (Fred M. Vinson), **1945:**
    88; **1946:** 21 [9], 37 [14], 43 [12], 47, 72 [3],
    78 [3], 126 [13], 129 [1, 4]

Treasury, Secretary of the (Vinson) — *continued*
  See also Vinson, Fred M.
  Letter, **1945:** 176
  Memorandum, **1945:** 176
Treasury Committee, **1949:** 267 [3, 12]
Treaties.
  See International agreements.
Treaties and executive agreements, proposed leg-
    islation, **1952–53:** 140
Trees, value to nation, **1947:** 68
Trentini, Emma, **1951:** 99
Trenton, Mo., campaign remarks, **1948:** 194 [12]
Trenton, N.J., campaign remarks, **1952–53:** 303 [6]
Trials, military, in Munich, **1949:** 32 [12]
Tribble, Harold, **1951:** 256
Trieste, **1946:** 143 [15]
  Communism in, **1952–53:** 107 [2]
  Displaced persons in, immigration to U.S., **1950:**
    167
  Economic assistance, **1951:** 114
  Population growth, **1952–53:** 65
  Return to Italy, **1948:** 74
  Territorial settlement with Italy, **1951:** 232, 239
    [4]
Trimble, Repr. James W., **1952–53:** 32, 193n., 194
Trinity College, **1949:** 30 [12], 66 [5]
Tripoli, U.S. air base, **1948:** 9 [15]
Trotta, Fred, **1948:** 261 [7]
Trout, Robert, **1947:** 90n.
Trowel, silver, presentation to New York Avenue
    Presbyterian Church, **1951:** 68
Troy, Smith, **1952–53:** 274 [5]
Troy, Mont., campaign remarks, **1952–53:** 270 [8]
Troy, Ohio, campaign remarks, **1952–53:** 319 [4]
Truckee, Calif., campaign remarks, **1948:** 202 [3]
Truitt, Mrs. Max, **1949:** 15
Trujillo Molina, Rafael L., **1950:** 181 [2]
Truman, Maj. Gen. Benjamin C., **1950:** 29 [9]
Truman, Harry S., personal reminiscences
  Aberdeen Proving Ground, visits to, **1951:** 38
  Accession to Presidency, **1952–53:** 366, 378
  American Legion activities, **1951:** 191
  Attendance at Kansas City Law School while
    serving as County Judge, **1945:** 68
  Bankhead family, friendship with, **1948:** 247
  Bevin, Ernest, recollections of, **1951:** 88
  Boyhood chores, **1948:** 104
  British sovereigns, visits with, **1951:** 282
  Business losses in 1921 depression, **1948:** 117
  Campaigning for local offices and Senate, **1948:**
    138 [3], 216 [15, 16], 249, 268
  Congress. service in, **1947:** 6 [7], 46 [18], 127 [11],
    232 [12]
  Congressional Medal of Honor presentations,
    1951: 115; **1952–53:** 125
  Congressional Medal of Honor winners, con-
    versations with, **1950:** 165
  County fairs, attendance at, **1949:** 202

Truman, Harry S. — *continued*
  Democratic National Convention (1912), **1951:** 6
  Editorship of high school paper, **1952–53:** 63
  Election campaign (1892), **1948:** 233 [4]
  Election campaigns, **1950:** 110 [1], 160 [2];
      1952–53: 125, 126, 129, 143, 193, 321 [3]
  Employment in bank, **1951:** 21
  Employment with grain firm, **1947:** 196
  Family dentist in Independence, Mo., **1951:** 258
  Family letters, **1950:** 247
  Farming experiences, **1948:** 117, 194 [6, 8], 204
      [2], 246; **1950:** 110 [9], 127 [6], 145; **1951:**
      122; **1952–53:** 194, 315 [1]
  Father's interest in cattle market, **1948:** 212 [7]
  First "billion dollar Congress" (1892), **1947:** 6 [6]
  First elective office, **1947:** 9
  First honorary degree, **1948:** 194 [5]
  First sight of automobile, **1948:** 261 [8]
  First sight of a President (Theodore Roosevelt),
      1948: 246; **1951:** 290
  Ford, Henry, wartime interview with, **1951:** 38
  Forebears in Kentucky and Tennessee, **1948:** 222
      [1]
    Defense against Indians, **1951:** 289
  Grandfather's freighting business in Southwest,
      1948: 200 [1], 201
  Independence, Mo.
    Family and neighborhood ties in, **1948:** 287
    First homecoming as President, **1948:** 138 [1]
  Indian reservation, **1950:** 129 [2]
  Jackson County, Mo.
    4-H Club, **1949:** 123
    Public office in, **1948:** 231 [1]; **1949:** 54
    Road engineering, **1949:** 249
  Maine airbase, wartime inspection, **1950:** 121 [2]
  Military service, **1947:** 36 [7, 9]; **1948:** 89, 197,
      237 [5]
    National Guard, **1949:** 211 [7]; **1951:** 218, 270
    Reserve Officers Association, role in founding,
        1948: 243 [1]; **1949:** 234 [1]; **1951:** 218
    World War I, **1948:** 116 [1], 117, 126 [3], 200
        [2], 214 [4], 217, 249, 264 [5]; **1949:** 36,
        119, 223; **1950:** 21, 110 [9], 165, 272, 281;
        1951: 38, 298 [1]; **1952–53:** 125, 377 [2]
    World War II, offer to serve, **1948:** 200 [2], 214
        [4]; **1949:** 36; **1950:** 110 [9]; **1952–53:** 135
  Missouri, life in, **1950:** 14, 21, 121 [6], 127 [7],
      176, 281, 312, 314, 315
  Montgomery, Gen. Bernard L., visit to White
      House, **1952–53:** 250
  Musical interests, **1951:** 21, 99
  National Old Trails Association, leadership,
      1948: 137 [1], 233 [1]
  Nephew and family, visit to Washington, **1952–
      53:** 183
  Nieces, visit to Washington, **1950:** 247
  Pemiscot County fairs, **1945:** 163
  Philadelphia, first luncheon in, **1949:** 194

Truman, Harry S. — *continued*
  Picnics at Lonejack, Mo., opening Democratic
      campaigns, **1945:** 68
  Political career, **1952–53:** 89 [12], 117, 142, 292
      [11], 317 [5, 8]
  Political conventions, **1952–53:** 63, 218
  Presidency, succession to (1945), **1949:** 15
  Reelection to Senate (1940), **1948:** 183 [7]
  Rocky Mountains, visits to, **1950:** 124 [8]
  Rogers, Will, friendship with, **1948:** 216 [9]
  Roosevelt, Franklin D.
    Death of, **1949:** 76
    Meetings with, **1952–53:** 130
    Memories of, **1947:** 71
  Schooldays, anecdote from, **1952–53:** 268 [5]
  Senate, service in, **1948:** 122 [2], 214 [4], 228 [4],
      231 [1], 262, 267 [2]; **1949:** 38, 45 [21], 70,
      148 [15], 160, 192 [10]; **1950:** 12, 15, 38
      [12], 97 [10], 110 [9], 124 [4], 139; **1951:** 18,
      27, 32, 33 [2], 51, 56 [24], 98; **1952–53:**
      318, 377 [12]
  Truman committee, chairmanship of.
      See main heading, Truman Committee.
  Service as county judge, **1948:** 214 [8]
  Stephen Foster songs, **1950:** 139
  Tax distribution, essay on, **1949:** 54
  Teacher's anecdote, **1947:** 177 [9, 19]
  Thirty-fifth Division reunions, **1950:** 161 [2]
  Vandenberg, Senator, friendship with, **1952–53:**
      317 [2]
  Vaudeville in Kansas City, **1949:** 205 [6]
  Veterans hospitals, visits to, **1952–53:** 135
  Vice Presidency (1944), **1947:** 182 [8]
  Visits to
    Fort Bliss, Tex., **1949:** 223
    Fort Bragg, N.C., **1949:** 223
    Glasgow, Mont., **1950:** 129 [2]
    Oklahoma, **1948:** 214 [4]
    Reading, Pa. (1944), **1948:** 227 [2]
    South Carolina, **1949:** 186
    Texas, **1948:** 208 [7], 212 [4, 9, 10]
  Wooton, Paul, recollections of, **1951:** 18
  World War I, **1945:** 5
  Youth in Kansas City, **1948:** 194 [12]
Truman, Mrs. Harry S., **1945:** 26n., 168n., 196n.,
    202n.; **1946:** 78n., 173 [9], 229 [17]; **1947:**
    67 [15, 18], 74; **1948:** 85, 118 [1, 3, 6, 7],
    124 [1], 136 [2], 178 [16], 194 [3], 198 [7],
    204 [5], 212 [1], 216 [12, 13], 225 [1], 231
    [1], 250, 264 [3], 269; **1949:** 15n., 17, 20;
    1950: 87, 102, 104, 124 [8], 129 [7], 139;
    1951: 70 [11], 113 [3, 5], 136, 180, 223, 257,
    297; **1952–53:** 2 [2], 7 [10], 29, 73, 74n.,
    125, 197 [14], 258 [11, 14], 262, 377 [15],
    378
  News conference remarks on, **1945:** 4 [17], 52
      [19]

Truman, Mrs. John A. (the President's mother), **1945:** 211 [13]; **1947:** 52, 164
Truman, Lee, **1948:** 222 [6]
Truman, Margaret, **1945:** 26n., 202n.; **1947:** 243 [14]; **1948:** 118 [1, 3, 6, 7], 126 [4], 128 [4], 136 [2], 178 [16], 194 [5], 204 [5], 212 [1], 216 [12, 13], 225 [1], 227 [5], 231 [1], 250, 261 [3], 269; **1949:** 17, 20, 28 [21], 56, 123, 160, 176; **1950:** 21, 129 [7], 139, 145, 146 [22]; **1951:** 18, 21, 76, 99, 136, 223, 257, 282; **1952–53:** 73, 78n., 115 [4], 125, 149 [13], 156 [14], 197 [14], 233 [1, 6, 9], 258 [10], 266 [1], 269n., 270 [2, 4], 308 [6], 314, 319 [1], 377 [15, 19]
    News conference remarks on, **1951:** 63 [4], 70 [11]
Truman, Mary Jane, **1950:** 266, 314
Truman, Maj. Gen. Ralph E., **1949:** 119 [2]; **1950:** 161 [2]
Truman administration, distinctive name for, **1948:** 274 [4]
Truman-Barkley Club, Denver, **1948:** 198 [3]
Truman-Barkley Dinner, **1949:** 15
Truman buttons, 1948 campaign, **1947:** 205 [11]
Truman Committee, **1947:** 174 [8], 177 [21], 209 [8]; **1948:** 200 [5], 212 [7], 214 [4], 225 [3], 228 [2, 3], 231 [2–4], 235 [5], 236, 237 [1], 257 [1], 261 [1, 2, 7], 278 [23, 28]; **1949:** 4 [6], 28 [1], 144 [6], 161 [5], 260 [4]; **1950:** 29 [9], 152 [9], 247; **1951:** 7 [13], 33 [2], 46; **1952–53:** 158, 289 [8], 377 [2]
    Investigation of World War II defense program, **1948:** 118 [5], 128 [1], 206 [1]; **1950:** 121 [13]
Truman Day, **1949:** 250
Truman Doctrine, **1947:** 62 [10, 21], 67 [12], 74, 90 [1], 95 [11, 16, 26], 107 [2], 195; **1948:** 49 [3], 215, 260; **1949:** 22 [3], 86, 162, 184; **1950:** 94, 142
    Bill to implement, approval statement, **1947:** 100
    Message to Congress, **1947:** 56
    Statement, **1947:** 57
Truman Library, Independence, Mo., **1950:** 43n., 79n.; **1951:** 251 [27]; **1952–53:** 334ftn. (p. 1059)
Trust funds, **1946:** 18 (pp. 69, 83), 192 [2, 3, 6, 21], 193; **1947:** 6 [35], 7 (pp. 58, 62, 72, 73, 91), 116, 181 (p. 400); **1948:** 4 [8], 5 (pp. 22–25, 33–37, 56, 59), 175; **1949:** 7 [10, 22, 41], 8 (pp. 45, 48, 49, 66, 70, 71, 91); **1950:** 9 (pp. 54, 73, 103, 106); **1951:** 13 (pp. 98, 99); **1952–53:** 231
    Civil service retirement, **1952–53:** 18 (pp. 106, 113)
    Government employees retirement, **1950:** 9 (p. 76)
    Health insurance, **1949:** 7 [48]
    Interest accruals, **1952–53:** 18 (p. 114)

Trust funds — *continued*
    Life insurance, veterans, **1952–53:** 367 (p. 1160)
    Old age and survivors insurance, **1950:** 9 (pp. 54, 76); **1951:** 13 (p. 99); **1952–53:** 18 (pp. 104, 106), 367 (p. 1159)
    Railroad retirement, **1950:** 8 [10], 9 (pp. 50, 73, 74, 76); **1951:** 13 (p. 98); **1952–53:** 18 (pp. 104, 106), 231, 367 (pp. 1156, 1159)
    Unemployment insurance, **1945:** 42; **1949:** 151; **1950:** 9 (pp. 99, 100); **1951:** 13 (pp. 80, 81); **1952–53:** 18 (p. 95), 367 (pp. 1151, 1159)
    Veterans life insurance, **1950:** 9 (pp. 70, 71); **1951:** 13 (p. 103); **1952–53:** 18 (p. 110)
Trust territories, **1945:** 91; **1946:** 15 [4, 9], 21 [4, 15], 247; **1947:** 21, 119; **1950:** 9 (p. 102), 143
    Pacific Islands, **1947:** 119, 137, 151; **1949:** 101
Truth, Campaign of, **1950:** 227
Truth Squad, Republican, **1952–53:** 291
Tsaldaris, Constantine, **1949:** 261
Tubby, Roger, **1952–53:** 253 [2, 4], 345 [4], 359 [4]
Tuberculosis, **1951:** 135; **1952–53:** 249
    Control program, **1950:** 9 (p. 75), 286
Tuck, Gov. William M., **1947:** 138; **1948:** 41 [3]
Tucker, Ralph, **1948:** 138 [5]
Tucker, Richard, **1949:** 38
Tucson, Ariz., **1947:** 35
Tugwell, Gov. Rexford G., **1945:** 208 [6], 221 [15, 17]; **1946:** 141 [12], 143 [4], 163 [8], 240
Tulare, Calif., campaign remarks, **1948:** 204 [3]
Tullahoma, Tenn., **1951:** 138
Tulsa, Okla., **1949:** 22 [5]
    Campaign address, **1948:** 217
    Mayor Roy Lundy, **1948:** 217
Tunnell, Sen. James M., **1946:** 21 [3]
Turkey, **1945:** 132 [10]; **1946:** 53 [10]; **1947:** 62 [12], 107 [1]; **1949:** 78 [7]
    Assistance, **1947:** 56, 67 [2, 11, 12], 74, 90 [1], 95 [11, 16, 26], 100n., 107 [2], 138, 180 [10], 181 (pp. 398, 405), 188, 195, 220, 238; **1948:** 2, 28, 144, 160, 175, 202 [6], 228 [1], 231 [2], 244, 260, 263; **1949:** 8 (p. 54), 86, 162; **1950:** 9 (p. 59), 81, 86 [27], 142, 151, 201, 204, 232; **1952–53:** 18 (p. 75), 27, 55, 57, 75, 81, 242 [2], 288, 317 [2], 354, 366
        Economic, **1951:** 114, 138
        Military, **1951:** 114
    Communism in, **1951:** 138; **1952–53:** 69, 107 [2], 303 [2], 354, 378
    Defense, **1949:** 162, 184
    Filberts, shelled, exportation of, **1952–53:** 302
    Immigration to U.S., **1952–53:** 182
    Inonu, Ismet, **1948:** 263
    Korean war, participation, **1950:** 232, 296; **1951:** 170
    Lend-lease settlement, **1947:** 7 (p. 65)
    National holiday, statement, **1948:** 263

Turkey — *continued*
  NATO membership, **1951:** 227ftn. (p. 527);
    1952–53: 5, 8, 18 (p. 76), 77
  U.S. Ambassador Henry F. Grady, **1950:** 142
  U.S. Ambassador Edwin C. Wilson, **1947:** 100
  U.S. relations with, **1948:** 263
  U.S. relief for, **1947:** 220
Turner, Gov. Roy J., **1948:** 213, 214 [3–8], 216 [1–6,
    10–12], 217; **1951:** 118 [2], 145 [8]
Turner, Mrs. Roy J., **1948:** 214 [4], 216 [2, 5, 6, 12]
Tuttle Creek Dam, Kansas, **1952–53:** 18 (p. 88)
Tuskegee Institute, **1948:** 162n.
Tuten, Morrison, **1945:** 147n.
TVA.
  See Tennessee Valley Authority.
Twain, Mark, **1950:** 129 [1]; **1952–53:** 129
Two Harbors, Minn., improvement, veto, **1945:** 90
Two-party system, **1948:** 200 [7]
Tydings, Sen. Millard E., **1945:** 24; **1949:** 122 [13],
    148 [4], 161 [2]; **1950:** 82, 135, 171, 246;
    1952–53: 69n., 322
  Letters, **1950:** 79, 225
  Loyalty investigating subcommittee, **1951:** 22
    [14], 35
  News conference remarks on, **1950:** 52 [6], 105
    [7], 206 [17]
  1950 election campaign, **1951:** 49 [19]
Tydings-McDuffie Act, **1946:** 31, 116
Tyler, John, **1952–53:** 107 [10]
Tyrrhenian Sea, **1945:** 178
Typhus, Prevention, **1951:** 135

UAW.
  See United Automobile Workers.
Uintah Indian Reservation, **1951:** 198
Ukraine
  Political refugees from, **1947:** 140
  Relief for, **1948:** 186
Ulate, Otilio, **1950:** 181 [1]
Ulithi atoll, U.S. capture, **1945:** 161
Umatilla, Oreg., **1950:** 121 [11]
Umberto, King, **1946:** 126 [7]
UMT.
  See Universal Military Training.
UMW.
  See United Mine Workers.
Un-American Activities Committee, **1947:** 218
    [19]; **1948:** 86, 285 [20], 288 [2]; **1950:**
    152ftn. (p. 450); **1952–53:** 49 [7]
  Textbook investigation, **1949:** 122 [8]
Unconditional surrender of Axis powers, **1945:** 2,
    3, 37
  See also Cessation of hostilities *under* World War
    II.
  Germany, **1945:** 26 [1, 5], 28, 45, 91, 97
    Broadcast, **1945:** 27

Unconditional surrender — *continued*
  Germany — *continued*
    Messages, **1945:** 29
    Proclamation, **1945:** 26 [4], 27
    Rumor of, **1945:** 16
    Timing of announcement, statement, **1945:** 25
  Japan, **1945:** 100, 106 [3, 5, 9], 128, 143, 145,
    196n.
    Address to U.S. armed forces, **1945:** 123
    Broadcast, **1945:** 122
    Demanded, **1945:** 26 [2, 3], 28, 45, 93, 97
    Potsdam Declaration, **1945:** 100, 145, 216
    Proclamation, **1945:** 105
Underwood, Thomas R., **1948:** 222 [2–4]
Unemployment, **1945:** 128, 180, 202 [3], 226; **1946:**
    2, 17 [18], 18 (pp. 48, 49, 54, 71), 39, 73,
    124, 221, 226 [1], 252; **1947:** 4 (pp. 13, 34,
    37), 7 (pp. 57, 68), 68, 76, 98, 107 [2], 116,
    152; **1948:** 2, 8 (pp. 73, 87, 88, 98), 9 [18],
    32, 67, 80, 101, 115, 175, 176, 183 [5], 184,
    195, 227 [4], 228 [13]; **1949:** 5; **1950:** 84,
    106, 202, 279; **1951:** 11, 174; **1952–53:** 242
    [6]
  See also Depressed areas; Employment.
  Coal industry, **1952–53:** 305
  Decrease, **1948:** 228 [2, 4–6, 12], 268; **1951:** 167;
    1952–53: 15, 215, 349
  Depression years, **1948:** 255, 259 [1]
  Depressions and recessions.
    See Economy, national.
  Distilling industry, **1947:** 205 [14], 236 [1]
  Garment industry, **1951:** 239 [8]
  Increase, **1949:** 151, 154
  Insurance.
    See Unemployment compensation and insur-
      ance.
  Lawrence, Mass., **1949:** 78 [4]
  Lumber industry, **1950:** 121 [9]
  New England, **1950:** 137 [21]; **1952–53:** 294
  News conference remarks, **1949:** 32 [2, 7], 78 [4],
    118 [15], 122 [10, 14], 148 [2]
  Post-World War I, **1949:** 195
  Reduction, **1948:** 212 [10], 227 [5]; **1949:** 122 [10,
    14], 148 [2]
Unemployment compensation and insurance,
    1945: 99, 128; **1946:** 2, 18 (pp. 52, 53, 64,
    66, 69, 78, 79, 83); **1947:** 2 (p. 8), 4 (pp. 36,
    37), 7 (pp. 57, 58, 69, 73), 81, 177 [16], 232
    [1, 4]; **1948:** 2, 5 (pp. 34, 35, 37, 39), 8 (pp.
    68, 87), 10, 131, 175, 223, 255; **1949:** 8 (p.
    91), 127, 129, 154, 250 [3]; **1950:** 2, 6, 8 [2,
    3], 9 (pp. 46, 97), 127 [5], 157, 224, 281;
    1951: 13 (pp. 79–81); **1952–53:** 18 (p. 93),
    215, 237, 241, 292 [5], 293, 298 [3], 306 [6]
  Defense workers, **1951:** 11
  Expansion, proposed, **1950:** 9 (pp. 99, 102), 84,
    128, 135

Unemployment compensation — *continued*
  Extension of benefits, **1949:** 151, 161 [4]; **1951:** 4, 12 [33]
  Federal aid, **1949:** 32 [2], 54, 151
    For children of unemployed workers, **1948:** 107
  Government employees, **1948:** 107; **1952–53:** 18 (p. 113), 108, 137
  Legislation, **1945:** 128, 132 [3], 147 [8, 16], 157 [16], 180
  Message to Congress, **1945:** 42; **1950:** 84
  News conference remarks, **1945:** 44 [10], 132 [3], 147 [8, 16], 157 [16]; **1949:** 40 [3], 260 [12]
  State programs, Federal aid, **1952–53:** 15, 231, 367 (pp. 1150–1151)
  Trust fund, **1945:** 42; **1949:** 151; **1950:** 84; **1951:** 13 (p. 80); **1952–53:** 18 (p. 95), 367 (p. 1151)
  Veterans, **1948:** 5 (pp. 21, 32); **1949:** 8 (pp. 64, 91, 151); **1951:** 13 (pp. 99–102); **1952–53:** 231, 367 (p. 1160)
Unemployment Compensation Tax Act, **1947:** 4 (p. 37)
Unfair labor practices, **1947:** 120
Unification, armed forces.
  See under Armed forces, U.S.
Unification Act of 1947, **1949:** 241n.
Uniform Code of Military Justice, **1950:** 108
Union City, N.J., Mayor Harry J. Thourot, **1948:** 189n.
Union League Club, **1950:** 39
  Philadelphia, Pa., **1949:** 194
Union Pacific Railroad, construction of, **1948:** 198 [6]
Union of South Africa.
  See South Africa, Union of.
Union Station, Washington, dedication of Presidential Lounge as servicemen's center, **1951:** 186
Unions.
  See Labor organizations.
Unit rule, national party conventions, **1952–53:** 98 [41]
United Airlines, labor dispute, **1951:** 132 [1], 140 [10]
United Automobile, Aircraft and Agricultural Implement Workers of America, **1951:** 252
United Automobile Workers of America, **1946:** 2; **1948:** 110 [17]; **1949:** 122 [10], 269 [14]; **1950:** 146 [19], 202
  Labor dispute, **1945:** 204, 206
United Defense Fund, **1951:** 3, 180, 242; **1952–53:** 264
United Jewish Appeal, **1946:** 42
United Kingdom, **1945:** 45, 91, 97, 136, 150n., 178, 216; **1946:** 18 (pp. 41, 44, 45, 84), 25, 29, 57, 181, 247, 265; **1947:** 18, 23, 46 [3, 5], 74, 111, 132, 177 [4, 11], 181 (p. 400), 195;

United Kingdom — *continued*
  1948: 8 (pp. 96, 97), 126 [6], 198 [6]; **1949:** 84ftn. (p. 223); **1950:** 218, 275; **1951:** 18; **1952–53:** 38
Air Transport Agreement, **1946:** 43 [2], 44
Ambassador to, **1947:** 31 [5, 13, 15, 17, 19], 36 [6, 27], 210 [4]
Ambassador Sir Oliver Franks, **1949:** 11 [2, 8]; **1950:** 275n.
Anglo-American armies, junction with Soviet forces, **1945:** 12
Anglo-American Committee of Inquiry, **1945:** 193 [6], 208 [4], 210
Anglo-American financial and trade conference, **1945:** 202 [10]
Arabs, arms shipments to, **1950:** 38 [17]
Argentina, trade agreement with, **1949:** 122 [7], 144 [24]
Assistance, **1945:** 67 [4], 132 [4], 107 [22], 208 [11], 221 [4]; **1951:** 29, 238; **1949:** 40 [5, 11], 148 [5], 234 [11]; **1952–53:** 27, 358
Atomic bomb, cooperation in development, **1948:** 239
Atomic energy, **1945:** 156, 178
  Cooperation with U.S., **1949:** 161 [14], 166 [1], 179 [18]
  Development, **1945:** 93, 97, 181 [3]
  Possession of information, **1945:** 164 [1]
  Secrets, disclosure to Soviet Union, **1950:** 46 [20]
  U.S.-U.K.-Canada agreement, **1945:** 193 [8, 10]
Attlee, Clement R.
  See main heading Attlee, Clement R.
B-29 bombers, sale to, **1949:** 22 [8], 45 [15]
Balance of payments, **1952–53:** 15, 18 (p. 75)
Bevin, Ernest, **1945:** 91, 208 [2]; **1946:** 129 [11], 136 [14], 265; **1947:** 41, 46 [19]; **1949:** 68, 72 [14]; **1950:** 146 [13], 250ftn. (p. 640), 311; **1951:** 88
Big Three conference.
  See Heads of state and government, meetings.
Church of England, **1949:** 207
Churchill, Winston.
  See main heading, Churchill, Winston.
Coal production, **1947:** 238
Combined Chiefs of Staff, U.S.-U.K., **1945:** 197, 198; **1946:** 53 [5]
Combined committees and boards, U.S.-U.K., **1945:** 107ftn. (p. 234), 198, 199
Combined Food Board, **1946:** 108, 119 [16], 149
Commercial Policy, Joint Statement on, **1946:** 25
Constitution, British, comment on, **1951:** 88
Council of Foreign Ministers, membership, **1945:** 91, 97
Davies (Joseph E.) mission to, **1945:** 44 [8], 52 [15], 60 [6]
Death penalty, abolition, **1948:** 77 [17]

United Kingdom — *continued*
  Diplomatic recognition of Communist China,
      1949: 234 [5]
  Disarmament discussions, **1951:** 293
  Duke of Edinburgh, **1951:** 282, 288
  Economic discussion with foreign countries,
      1949: 192 [7, 24], 195, 205 [8], 211 [8], 214
      [5], 217
  Economic mission to U.S., question of, **1952–53:**
      247 [6]
  Economy, **1947:** 31 [16], 56; **1948:** 5 (p. 29), 21
      [13]; **1949:** 40 [5], 148 [5], 200 [22], 214 [5],
      234 [11]
  Eden, Anthony, **1945:** 22ftn. (p. 36), 31 [4], 91;
      1952–53: 6
  Egypt, withdrawal from, **1947:** 19 [17], 174 [10]
  Elections in, **1950:** 44 [13], 46 [17], 52 [14]
  Ethiopia, technical assistance to, **1951:** 259
  Europe, policy towards, **1951:** 149
  European coal and steel community, member-
      ship proposed, **1950:** 137 [19]
  Exchange teachers, **1949:** 187; **1951:** 194
      Remarks, **1952–53:** 234
  Financial Agreement.
      See Financial Agreement, U.S.-U.K.
  Food ration in, **1947:** 210 [6]
  Foreign ministers meeting.
      See main heading, Foreign ministers meetings.
  Germany
      Conventions on relations with, **1952–53:** 151
      Occupation zone in, **1947:** 7 (p. 67), 209 [13];
          1948: 5 (pp. 29, 30), 244
  Greece and Turkey, aid to, **1947:** 56
  Immigration of displaced persons and refugees,
      1945: 225
  Investments in U.S., **1952–53:** 218
  Iran
      Oil dispute with, **1952–53:** 5, 6
      Oil industry, negotiations on nationalization
          of, **1951:** 113 [8], 118 [11], 132 [11], 140 [4,
          6, 19], 150, 153 [19], 165 [11], 200 [2], 251
          [19], 275 [11]
  Italian colonies, accord with U.S. on disposition
      of, **1948:** 278 [14]
  Japan, peace treaty with, discussions, **1951:** 84n.
  Jay Treaty, **1952–53:** 45
  Jefferson papers, search for, **1950:** 12
  Jewish immigrants to Palestine, entry permits,
      1952–53: 297
  Joint declaration on Israeli arms policy, **1950:**
      147
  Joint report on Potsdam conference, **1945:** 91
  King George VI, **1945:** 91n.
      Death of, **1952–53:** 30, 31 [19]
  King James I, **1952–53:** 260
  Korean war, participation, **1950:** 193, 194, 232,
      296; **1951:** 170
  Lend-lease settlement, **1947:** 7 (p. 65)

United Kingdom — *continued*
  Loan to, proposed, **1947:** 78 [6]
  London.
      See main heading, London.
  Malaya, forces in, **1951:** 96, 114
  Meat, availability of, **1952–53:** 57
  Military strength, **1950:** 22, 206 [16], 301
  NATO participation, **1952–53:** 358
  News conference remarks, **1945:** 4 [22], 52 [9], 60
      [6, 8, 16], 67 [4], 76 [9], 100, 106 [18], 107
      [3, 18, 22], 118 [8, 13], 132 [4], 147 [19], 157
      [9, 11], 164 [1], 172 [10], 181 [3], 193 [6, 8,
      10], 202 [10], 208 [4, 11], 221 [4, 10]; **1946:**
      6 [8], 15 [22], 17 [4, 14, 22], 21 [18], 27 [12],
      30 [1], 41 [4, 19, 24], 43 [2], 53 [5, 20], 75
      [1], 84 [15, 21], 86 [22, 23, 29], 110 [4, 18],
      129 [11, 16], 136 [14], 163 [5], 192 [9, 19],
      199 [6], 215 [5, 11], 223 [3], 226 [5, 16], 229
      [11, 28], 257 [1], 266 [22]; **1949:** 11 [10], 22
      [8], 40 [5, 11], 45 [15], 122 [7], 144 [24], 148
      [5], 161 [14], 166 [1], 179 [18], 192 [7, 24],
      200 [22], 205 [8], 211 [8], 214 [5]; **1950:** 38
      [17], 44 [13], 46 [17, 20], 52 [14], 137 [19],
      206 [16,] 209 [1], 217 [13, 23]
  Overmantel for White House, presentation,
      1951: 288
  Palestine
      Policy toward, **1948:** 110 [9, 22]
      Withdrawal from, **1947:** 19 [17], 174 [10];
          1948: 55 [1], 71 [23], 93 [4]
  Palestine commission.
      See Anglo-American Committee of Inquiry.
  Palestine question.
      See Palestine.
  Petroleum agreement, **1945:** 76 [9], 107 [3], 214
  Polish army veterans in, immigration to U.S.,
      1950: 167
  Polish government in exile, **1945:** 60 [6, 8, 14, 16]
  Political crisis, **1947:** 174 [6]
  Princess Elizabeth, **1951:** 145 [3], 153 [11], 193
      [7], 282, 288
  Publishers and editors, remarks to, **1951:** 88
  Queen Elizabeth II, **1952–53:** 30, 74
      Coronation, **1952–53:** 342 [13]
  Ships, reactivation, **1950:** 217 [23]
  Steel purchases from U.S., question of, **1952–53:**
      6
  Strategic materials, exports to Communist bloc,
      1950: 230ftn. (p. 607); **1952–53:** 358
  Suez Canal dispute with Egypt, **1951:** 188 [12],
      275 [14]
  Syria and Lebanon, armed forces withdrawal
      from, **1948:** 202 [6]
  U.N. Security Council delegation, **1950:** 209 [1]
  U.S. Ambassador C. Douglas Dillon, **1950:** 23
      [10]
  U.S. Ambassador Lewis W. Douglas, **1948:** 110
      [9]; **1949:** 118 [7]

United Kingdom — *continued*
  U.S. Ambassador O. Max Gardner, **1948:** 246
  U.S. Ambassador John G. Winant, **1946:** 53 [17]
  U.S. bases in, **1952–53:** 6
  U.S. and Canada, trade agreement with, **1949:** 217
  U.S. relations with, **1950:** 275; **1951:** 288; **1952–53:** 4
  U.S. trade with, **1946:** 51
  Visit by the President, question of, **1951:** 70 [11]
  War casualties, **1947:** 210 [6]
  World Wars, financial drain on, **1952–53:** 218
United Labor Policy Committee, **1951:** 49 [2], 70 [9]
United Medical Administration, proposed, **1949:** 181
United Mine Workers, **1946:** 252; **1947:** 127 [15], 141 [9]; **1948:** 55 [9], 66n., 171, 248; **1950:** 16ftn. (p. 117), 27, 34 [2], 35, 49; **1951:** 153 [16]; **1952–53:** 341
United National Clothing Collection
  Letter to Henry J. Kaiser, **1945:** 144
  Statement, **1945:** 74
United Nations, **1945:** 2, 3, 9, 10, 27, 47, 66, 91, 97, 109, 110, 122, 123, 143, 156, 174, 177, 186, 214, 216, 218; **1946:** 18 (pp. 38, 39, 40–44, 87), 25, 52, 65, 67, 68, 76, 81, 83, 107, 113, 127, 140, 162, 169, 202, 218, 222, 241, 248, 251, 265, 271, 273; **1947:** 2 (p. 11), 7 (pp. 57, 66), 33, 34, 35, 39, 51, 52, 56, 108, 110, 111, 113, 117, 126, 129, 133, 136, 138, 178, 188, 189, 203, 234; **1948:** 8 (p. 97), 26 [9], 52, 53, 55 [7], 86, 92, 93 [18], 101, 114 [2]; **1950:** 17n., 42, 204, 206ftn. (p. 571), 267; **1951:** 30, 99n., 125, 170, 173, 197, 271, 272, 293, 295 [1]; **1952–53:** 69, 78, 101, 188, 284 [4], 299, 310, 320, 322
  See also United Nations General Assembly; United Nations Security Council.
  Address, **1946:** 236; **1950:** 271
  Admissions to membership, proposed
    Communist China, **1950:** 146 [13], 270 [2], 273 [7], 301; **1951:** 261 [1]
    Indonesia, **1949:** 272
    Israel, **1948:** 253
    Italy, **1951:** 235
    Japan, **1951:** 216
    Transjordan, **1949:** 23
  Aid for less developed countries, **1949:** 139; **1950:** 143
  Anglo-American cooperation in, **1951:** 88
  Anglo-Iranian oil dispute, question of role in, **1951:** 251 [19]
  Anniversaries, **1947:** 61, 129
  Anti-genocide convention, **1949:** 121
  Appropriations, **1951:** 184, 187
  Arms control, proposed, **1949:** 226 [22]

United Nations — *continued*
  Atomic energy control, **1950:** 42, 187; **1951:** 256, 293; **1952–53:** 170
    Proposed, **1949:** 226 [21], 234 [4]
  Balkan Commission, **1948:** 28
  Campaign remarks, **1952–53:** 281
  Children's programs, **1950:** 154; **1952–53:** 51
  Communist China, policy respecting, **1951:** 2 [7, 10], 16 [8], 261 [1]
  Communist nations, exclusion proposed, **1950:** 105 [15]
  Czech delegate, request for political asylum in U.S., **1950:** 137 [14]
  Disarmament efforts, **1951:** 54, 56 [16], 293; **1952–53:** 5, 170, 196
  East German and Czech refugees, relief for, **1950:** 146 [20]
  Economic agreements, **1945:** 66
  Economic and technical assistance program, **1951:** 13 (p. 75), 114, 170, 219, 259, 262; **1952–53:** 18 (p. 77), 55, 196
  Flag, **1950:** 189, 239n.
  Forced labor in Soviet Union, investigation, **1952–53:** 253 [1]
  Formosa, study of, **1950:** 223
  Founding, role of Adlai Stevenson, **1952–53:** 289 [5], 292 [1], 317 [4]
  General Assembly.
    See United Nations General Assembly.
  Gifts to, tax exemption, **1947:** 26
  Greece
    Military aid to, **1951:** 78
    Operations in, **1948:** 202 [6]
  Greek children detained in eastern Europe, efforts for repatriation, **1950:** 7, 90, 261
  Hull, Cordell, contribution to founding of, **1947:** 73
  Human rights, efforts for, **1947:** 21
  Indonesian operations, **1950:** 2, 143
  Information programs, **1950:** 92
  International Emergency Food Council, **1948:** 23
  International trade conference (1948), **1949:** 88
  Italian colonies, agreement on, **1948:** 278 [14]
  Jessup, Philip C., hearings on appointment as delegate, **1951:** 227 [15]
  Kashmir operations, **1950:** 143
  Korea
    Elections, sponsorship of, **1950:** 194
    Police action (1950–53).
      See Korean war.
    Reconstruction efforts in, **1950:** 264, 268, 269, 285
  Location, **1945:** 106 [20], 147 [17], 157 [13]; **1946:** 18 (p. 44), 86 [21], 123, 236, 257 [7]
    New York headquarters, **1947:** 26, 136; **1948:** 5 (p. 31), 68, 165, 168, 173, 174 [1]; **1949:** 8 (p. 55), 58 [1, 3, 22], 231 [11], 234 [12]
      Cornerstone, laying of, **1949:** 237, 238

United Nations — *continued*
Middle East, Economic Survey Mission, **1949:** 274
Military strength, **1950:** 162, 271
Natural resources, conference on, **1947:** 186
News conference remarks, **1945:** 22 [5], 26 [1], 67 [1], 106 [20], 147 [17], 157 [13], 193 [7, 8], 202 [6, 9, 13]; **1946:** 6 [6], 15 [4, 16], 17 [21], 21 [4], 41 [3], 53 [11], 61 [15], 66 [13, 14], 70 [9], 75 [1, 4], 86 [5, 14, 15, 21], 119 [9, 21], 126 [1], 143 [12], 237 [17], 257 [7]; **1947:** 46 [4], 90 [1], 174 [10], 191 [17], 243 [1, 14]; **1949:** 11 [8], 28 [13, 17], 40 [2], 58 [1, 3, 22], 66 [14], 89 [6, 11], 148 [1], 171 [2], 200 [16], 226 [21, 22], 231 [11]; **1950:** 23 [12, 17], 29 [10, 13], 34 [16, 18], 38 [20], 80 [1, 4, 12], 105 [15], 137 [14], 146 [13, 20], 152 [5], 186 [13], 209 [19], 238 [12], 258 [10], 270 [2, 4], 273 [7], 278 [14], 295 [1, 11, 14], 309 [12], 318 [6]
Palestine
Operations, **1948:** 55 [1], 71 [23], 84 [20], 93 [4], 97 [4, 5], 110 [7, 21], 178 [5], 281; **1950:** 2, 9 (p. 58), 25, 78, 143
Refugee relief, **1949:** 21, 57, 274; **1951:** 13 (p. 74), 172
U.N. Mediator (Count Folke Bernadotte), **1948:** 193 [2], 274 [7]
U.N. Mediator (Ralph Bunche), **1949:** 40 [2]
Palestine Conciliation Commission, **1949:** 11 [8], 40 [2], 57, 193, 274
Partisan attacks on, **1952–53:** 197 [3]
Police force, question of, **1948:** 9 [17, 19], 84 [20, 22]
Refugee agency, U.S. contribution, **1952–53:** 367 (p. 1140)
Refugee relief, **1947:** 43
Relief agencies, distribution of U.S. food surpluses to, **1950:** 249
Resolutions
China, **1950:** 3 [1]
Essentials of Peace, **1950:** 143
Greek children abducted by Communist guerrillas, **1950:** 90
Korea, **1950:** 172, 173, 179 [11], 186 [13], 189, 193, 194, 271, 287 [1], 295 [11, 16]
Spain, **1949:** 95ftn. (p. 248); **1950:** 278 [14]
War crimes (1946), **1950:** 174
Rules governing membership, **1945:** 91
San Francisco conferences, **1945:** 1n., 2, 22ftn. (p. 36), 33, 75, 97, 163, 177; **1946:** 236; **1947:** 74, 88 [1]; **1948:** 130 [3], 137 [4], 139 [3], 193 [2], 227 [5], 268; **1949:** 160, 210; **1950:** 80 [4], 127 [4], 174, 232, 269; **1952–53:** 196, 378
Addresses, **1945:** 10, 66

United Nations — *continued*
San Francisco conferences — *continued*
Foundation of U.N. (1945), **1951:** 56 [26], 150, 213, 215, 216
News conference remarks, **1945:** 4 [10, 11, 13], 26 [3], 44 [11, 17], 52 [15], 60 [1, 10], 64 [1], 67 [1]
Peace conference with Japan (1951), **1951:** 179 [9], 193 [3, 8, 10, 11], 200 [6], 209 [16], 216, 217
Veto powers, question of, **1945:** 52 [15], 60 [10]
Security Council.
See United Nations Security Council.
Soviet policy in, **1950:** 162, 269; **1951:** 140 [3, 5, 13, 18], 197; **1952–53:** 5, 196, 318, 366
Use of veto power, **1946:** 143 [12]; **1950:** 34 [18], 119, 193
Spain
Diplomatic relations by member states, question of, **1949:** 66 [14]
Membership, question of, **1950:** 278 [14]
Resolutions on, **1949:** 95ftn. (p. 248); **1950:** 278 [14]
Technical assistance programs, **1950:** 9 (p. 59), 177, 240
Trade conference, Geneva, **1947:** 128
Trusteeship territories, **1946:** 15 [4]; **1947:** 21, 137, 151; **1950:** 9 (p. 102), 143
Tunisia, debate on, **1952–53:** 98 [35]
U.S. appointments to, **1950:** 217 [1], 219, 258 [10]
U.S. participation and support, **1945:** 178; **1946:** 17 [21], 236; **1947:** 7 (p. 68), 21, 68, 72, 100, 210 [1], 238; **1948:** 2, 5 (p. 31), 34, 116 [1], 117, 120 [5], 124 [1], 126 [6], 129, 130 [1], 132, 136 [5], 137 [4], 139 [3], 158, 165, 168, 173, 193 [1], 202 [6], 212 [1], 227 [5], 231 [2, 3], 244, 256, 261 [13], 266; **1949:** 2, 8 (pp. 46, 53, 55), 19, 21, 27, 68, 75, 86, 120, 159, 163, 184, 210, 234 [8], 252, 254, 256, 273; **1950:** 2, 9 (p. 56), 21, 42, 78, 80 [1, 12], 87, 94, 105 [15], 110 [1], 119, 126, 132, 134, 139, 159, 160 [1], 162, 193, 197, 201, 202, 222, 232, 237, 239, 268, 269, 281, 285, 291, 299, 301, 303; **1951:** 2 [15, 17], 4, 6, 7 [5], 13 (pp. 68, 74), 25, 56 [26], 78, 80, 84, 96, 109, 116, 117, 138, 144, 170, 184, 223, 256, 293, 297; **1952–53:** 18 (p. 77), 61, 75 [1], 77, 98 [16], 144, 196, 197 [3], 218, 259, 279, 316, 317 [2], 354, 366, 378
Reports, **1949:** 97; **1950:** 143
U.S. representatives, nominations, message to Senate, **1945:** 219
United Nations, American Association for the, **1950:** 318ftn. (p. 762)
United Nations, Preparatory Commission of the, U.S. Representative (Edward R. Stettinius, Jr.), **1945:** 67 [1, 2], 96

United Nations, U.S. Representative (Warren R. Austin), **1947:** 1, 38, 62 [12], 133, 136n.; **1948:** 39, 55 [1], 68, 84 [20], 110 [21], 283 [4]; **1950:** 173, 219, 222, 296; **1951:** 22 [1], 184, 266
  Letter, **1950:** 223
  News conference remarks on, **1950:** 230 [7], 295 [1]
United Nations, U.S. Representative (Edward R. Stettiniius, Jr.), **1946:** 123, 126 [1, 14], 127
United Nations Atomic Energy Commission, **1945:** 191; **1946:** 18 (p. 42), 41 [3], 61 [15], 119 [21], 242 [2, 7]; **1947:** 1, 21; **1948:** 239; **1949:** 237; **1950:** 34ftn. (p. 152); **1951:** 54
United Nations Charter, **1945:** 66, 67 [1, 2], 91, 97, 143, 174; **1946:** 2, 18 (p. 42), 52, 65, 102, 236; **1947:** 2 (p. 10), 21, 51, 56, 61, 74, 88 [1], 90 [1], 101, 126, 129, 137, 138, 188, 189, 220, 238 243 [14]; **1948:** 28, 34, 52, 53, 55 [1], 86, 93 [18], 129, 130 [3], 137 [4], 193 [2], 202 [6], 227 [5], 256, 263; **1949:** 19, 68, 75, 97, 120, 139, 162, 184, 188, 210, 225, 237, 256; **1950:** 2, 42, 80 [1, 4], 143, 151, 162, 173, 174, 177, 193, 194, 223, 232, 269, 271, 301; **1951:** 2 [6, 17], 4, 25, 54, 59, 84, 88, 134, 144, 170, 174, 208, 215, 216, 232, 256, 270, 271; **1952–53:** 6, 55, 61, 111, 131, 144, 151, 196, 354, 366
  Joint statement with Foreign Minister Sofian-opoulos, **1945:** 75
  Preparatory Commission, **1945:** 67 [2]
  Ratification by Senate, **1945:** 69, 163
  Signing of, **1945:** 68
  Statute of International Court of Justice, **1945:** 68, 69
United Nations Children's Emergency Fund (UNI-CEF), **1951:** 187
  U.S. Committee for, report, **1949:** 257
  U.S. contribution, **1952–53:** 51
United Nations Commission on Genocide, **1950:** 2
United Nations Commission on Human Rights, **1947:** 130, 138; **1948:** 20, 30; **1949:** 256
United Nations Commission on Korea, **1950:** 194
United Nations Commission on the Status of Women, **1948:** 30; **1950:** 10
United Nations Conference on International Organization.
  See San Francisco Conferences *under* United Nations.
United Nations Day, **1949:** 237, 238; **1951:** 271, 272n.
United Nations Day, National Citizens Committee for, **1949:** 212; **1950:** 239; **1951:** 223; **1952–53:** 259
United Nations Declaration on Human Rights, **1950:** 2, 138, 174
United Nations Disarmament Commission, **1952–53:** 196

United Nations Economic and Social Council, **1946:** 236, 248; **1947:** 21, 38, 138, 186; **1949:** 139, 237; **1950:** 10, 143
United Nations Economic Survey Mission for the Near East, **1950:** 154
United Nations Educational, Scientific, and Cultural Organization (UNESCO), **1946:** 112, 236; **1947:** 21, 117, 138; **1948:** 30; **1950:** 87
  U.S. membership, **1946:** 184
  U.S. National Commission, remarks, **1946:** 222
United Nations Food and Agriculture Organization, **1946:** 2, 18 (p. 87), 25, 71, 149, 236; **1947:** 21; **1948:** 276; **1949:** 8 (p. 55), 263; **1950:** 287 [24]
United Nations Food and Drug Organization, **1951:** 296n.
United Nations General Assembly, **1945:** 91, 219; **1946:** 18 (p. 42), 123, 173 [1], 229 [19]; **1947:** 1, 136, 140, 196, 243 [14]; **1948:** 34, 55 [1], 202 [6]; **1949:** 212, 237; **1950:** 25, 143, 219, 264; **1951:** 173, 184, 293; **1952–53:** 196
  Address, **1946:** 236; **1950:** 271; **1951:** 170
  Atomic energy resolution, **1947:** 21
  Berlin blockade, communique on, **1948:** 274ftn. (p. 945)
  China, resolution on, **1950:** 3 [1]
  Disarmament plan, **1951:** 54
  Essentials of Peace, resolution on, **1950:** 143
  Greece, resolution on, **1948:** 129; **1949:** 162
  Greek children abducted by Communist guerrillas, resolution on, **1950:** 90
  Human Rights, Declaration of, **1950:** 174
  Korea, resolutions on, **1949:** 1, 117
  Korea, resolution on elections in (1947), **1952–53:** 323
  "Little Assembly," **1948:** 53, 129
  London meeting, **1945:** 221 [22]; **1946:** 15 [16]; **1947:** 21, 38
  Moscow meeting, proposed, **1950:** 46ftn. (p. 184)
  New York meeting, **1947:** 21, 38
  News conference remarks, **1945:** 67 [1], 193 [8], 221 [22]; **1950:** 3 [1], 186 [13], 209 [19], 217 [19], 278 [14]
  Palestine, resolution on, **1947:** 108
  Palestine refugees, resolution on aid for, **1948:** 281; **1949:** 21, 57, 274
  Paris meeting, **1948:** 178 [14], 202 [6], 230, 239, 243 [8, 10], 248, 274 [3]; **1949:** 11 [8]
  Spain, resolution on, **1950:** 278 [14]
  United Action for Peace, resolution, **1950:** 271
  U.S. delegate (Mrs. Franklin D. Roosevelt), **1949:** 171 [2, 17]
  U.S. delegation, **1950:** 217 [1], 219
    Instructions on Palestine question, **1948:** 274 [7]

United Nations General Assembly — *continued*
  U.S. delegation — *continued*
    Jessup, Philip C., recess appointment, **1951:**
      266
    Members of Congress, service on, **1951:** 266n.
    Report, **1946:** 65
    Stevenson, Adlai, service on, **1952–53:** 289 [5]
  War crimes resolution (1946), **1950:** 174
United Nations General Assembly, President (Herbert V. Evatt), **1948:** 274 [3, 6]
United Nations General Assembly, President
    (Paul-Henri Spaak), **1946:** 236n.
United Nations Korean Reconstruction Agency,
    1951: 114
United Nations Palestine Refugee Aid Act of 1950,
    1951: 172n.
United Nations Participation Act of 1945, **1951:**
    170; **1952–53:** 196
United Nations Relief and Rehabilitation Administration, **1945:** 50, 135, 144, 225; **1946:** 2,
    18 (pp. 45, 46, 80), 25, 68, 105, 124, 193,
    236; **1947:** 6 [27], 7 (pp. 66, 67, 78), 11, 15,
    37, 47, 181 (p. 400), 195; **1948:** 4 [3], 5 (pp.
    20, 30), 31
  Council meeting (London), **1945:** 128, 186
  Grain shipments to Poland, **1946:** 64
  Greece, assistance for, **1945:** 75
  News conference remarks, **1945:** 129 [6], 172 [14],
    202 [6]; **1946:** 30 [2], 70 [19], 119 [16], 143
    [3], 192 [25]
  U.S. contribution, **1946:** 18 (pp. 44, 74, 76, 77,
    84), 64
  U.S. participation, **1945:** 128
    Message to Congress, **1945:** 186
United Nations Relief and Rehabilitation Administration, Director General (Fiorello H.
    La Guardia), **1946:** 87n., 119 [16]
United Nations Relief and Rehabilitation Administration, Director General (Herbert H.
    Lehman), **1946:** 66 [9], 68, 70 [9]
  Memorandum, **1945:** 225
United Nations Relief and Works Agency for
    Palestine Refugees in the Near East,
    1950: 25n.
United Nations Secretariat, **1947:** 21
United Nations Secretary General (Trygve Lie),
    1946: 66 [14], 123; **1947:** 133, 136n.; **1948:**
    274 [3, 6]; **1949:** 139, 193, 237; **1950:** 105
    [8], 146 [2], 152 [11], 209 [13], 223, 226,
    271; **1951:** 173
  Election of, **1947:** 21
  Message, **1947:** 61
United Nations Security Council, **1945:** 91, 128,
    219; **1946:** 18 (p. 39), 76, 127, 247; **1947:**
    1, 21, 56, 119, 137, 151; **1948:** 34, 39, 55
    [1], 110 [7, 21], 202 [6], 230; **1949:** 68, 75,
    234 [4]; **1950:** 147, 296; **1951:** 54, 170, 184,
    266

United Nations Security Council — *continued*
  Korea, deliberations on, **1950:** 172, 173, 179 [11],
    181, 184, 189, 193, 194, 209 [1], 223, 271,
    287 [1], 295 [11]
  Military forces, proposed, **1946:** 236
  News conference remarks, **1945:** 67 [1], 193 [8];
    1946: 15 [4], 53 [15], 61 [14], 66 [5], 70 [2,
    11], 72 [17]; **1950:** 105 [8], 179 [11], 209 [1,
    19, 20], 287 [1], 295 [11]
  Soviet use of veto in, **1948:** 129
  Soviet and Western delegations, conduct of,
    1950: 209 [1, 20]
United Nations Special Committee on Palestine,
    1948: 55 [1]
United Nations Temporary Commission on Korea,
    1948: 129
  Report, **1949:** 1, 117
United Nations Trusteeship Council, **1947:** 21
United Nations War Crimes Commission, **1945:** 22
    [5]
United Press poll, **1951:** 56 [14]
United Rubber Workers Union, **1945:** 175 [18]
United Service Organizations (USO), **1945:** 122,
    154; **1946:** 225; **1948:** 221; **1949:** 34, 104,
    221; **1950:** 95n.; **1951:** 186, 242; **1952–53:**
    264, 297
United States, SS, sale of, **1952–53:** 177, 197ftn. (p.
    470)
United States Advisory Commission on Information, **1950:** 92
United States Attorney, Nevada, commission for,
    1952–53: 377 [22]
United States Attorneys, Conference of, **1951:** 115
United States Attorneys Association, remarks to,
    1952–53: 165
United States Bank, **1948:** 101
United States Cadet Nurse Corps, **1945:** 130n.
United States-Canadian Permanent Joint Board on
    Defense, **1947:** 111; **1952–53:** 23
United States Chamber of Commerce, **1947:** 88
    [14]; **1948:** 114 [3]; **1951:** 101 [5]
United States Circuit Court of Appeals, Third,
    1945: 132 [1]
United States Civil Defense Corps, **1951:** 96
United States Civil Service Commission, **1946:** 199
    [7], 216 [1, 10]
United States Civil Service Commission, President
    (Harry B. Mitchell), **1946:** 146
United States Coast Guard Academy, **1948:** 261 [6]
    Address, **1952–53:** 255
United States Code, **1948:** 20
United States Commercial Company, **1945:** 176;
    1947: 7 (pp. 67, 94), 181 (p. 400)
United States Committee for the United Nations
    International Children's Emergency
    Fund, report, **1949:** 257
United States Conciliation Service, **1945:** 104, 202
    [3], 204; **1946:** 18 (p. 50), 131; **1947:** 20,
    120, 221 [6]; **1948:** 134, 135, 232

United States Conference of Lawyers, **1950:** 37n.

United States Conference of Mayors, **1949:** 54

United States Court of Appeals for the District of Columbia, **1945:** 129 [4]

Appointments, **1945:** 132 [1]

United States Court of Claims, **1945:** 39, 40 [1]; **1946:** 151

United States Customs Court, **1945:** 157 [15]

United States Employees Compensation Commission, **1946:** 117

United States Employment Service, **1945:** 128, 180; **1946:** 18 (p. 52), 61 [2], 62, 118, 217; **1947:** 4 (p. 31), 81, 145 [23], 177 [16], 236 [1]; **1948:** 10, 101, 134, 135, 138 [4], 259 [1, 2]; **1949:** 129, 201; **1951:** 11

Bill providing for return to States, **1945:** 211 [11], 221 [6]

News conference remarks, **1945:** 137 [1], 211 [11], 221 [6]

United States Government Manual, **1945:** 120

United States High Commissioner in Austria, question of appointment, **1950:** 203 [19]

United States High Commissioner in Austria (Walter J. Donnelly), **1950:** 217 [2, 4], 218

United States High Commissioner in Austria (Lt. Gen. Geoffrey Keyes), **1950:** 274

United States High Commissioner in Germany (John J. McCloy), **1949:** 122 [3], 234 [6], 260 [15]; **1950:** 23 [18], 238 [9]

United States High Commissioner to the Philippines, termination of office, **1946:** 116, 119 [3]

United States High Commissioner to the Philippines (Paul V. McNutt), **1946:** 31, 63, 74, 122, 136 [11], 141 [15]

Letter, **1945:** 176

News conference remarks on, **1945:** 157 [2], 175 [2]

United States Housing Act of 1937, **1949:** 54

United States Housing Authority, **1946:** 116; **1947:** 102

United States Housing Corporation, **1946:** 116

United States Information Agency, **1950:** 92

United States Information and Educational Exchange Act of 1948, **1949:** 187n.; **1951:** 194n.

United States International Claims Commission, **1950:** 146ftn. (p. 439)

United States Lines, **1948:** 177; **1952–53:** 177

United States Maritime Commission, **1945:** 128; **1946:** 18 (pp. 53, 74, 77, 78, 82), 21 [16], 84 [11], 95 [6], 119 [19], 187, 192 [10], 193, 257 [12], 267; **1947:** 7 (pp. 85, 86), 18, 29, 35, 55, 181 (pp. 404, 406, 407), 228; **1948:** 4 [1, 13], 5 (pp. 25, 48, 50), 77 [11], 79n., 88 [19], 97 [5], 105, 175, 177; **1949:** 8 (p. 87), 84 [20], 127, 133; **1950:** 8 [12], 9 (pp. 92, 93), 76, 146 [8]

United States Maritime Commission, Chairman (Maj. Gen. Philip B. Fleming), **1949:** 156

United States Maritime Commission, Chairman (Vice Adm. Emory S. Land), **1946:** 3

United States Maritime Commission, Chairman (Vice Adm. William W. Smith), **1946:** 194n.; **1947:** 123, 124; **1948:** 79; **1949:** 78 [2]

United States Marshals, transfer to civil service, **1952–53:** 87

United States Military Academy, **1946:** 224; **1947:** 226 [2]; **1950:** 29 [9]; **1951:** 188 [14, 16], 200 [9]; **1952–53:** 142

Admission of Canadians, **1948:** 112

Luncheon remarks, **1952–53:** 130

Sesquicentennial convocation address, **1952–53:** 131

United States Naval Academy, **1945:** 132 [9]; **1947:** 35, 226 [2]; **1951:** 200 [9]

Admission of Canadians, **1948:** 112

Remarks at, **1952–53:** 130, 142

United States News, **1949:** 253 [3]

United States Park Police, **1947:** 165

United States representative for European Recovery Program, proposed, **1947:** 238

United States Rubber Co., **1947:** 19 [1], 174 [3]

United States Steel Corp., **1946:** 12, 16, 17 [19], 27 [9], 30 [4], 37 [16]; **1947:** 19 [1]; **1948:** 84 [1]; **1949:** 22 [10], 155 [12], 211 [6]; **1951:** 305; **1952–53:** 110

Labor dispute, **1945:** 204, 206

United States Supreme Court.

See Supreme Court of the United States.

United States Tariff Commission, **1947:** 7 (p. 87), 39; **1948:** 42; **1950:** 34 [11]; **1952–53:** 239

Ben D. Dorfman, **1945:** 24

United States Technical Conference on Air Pollution, **1950:** 101

United Steel Workers of America, **1946:** 12, 16; **1949:** 152, 209, 213; **1951:** 169, 277, 304, 305; **1952–53:** 22, 116n., 118n., 216

Labor dispute, **1945:** 204, 206

"Uniting for Peace" plan, **1950:** 269; **1951:** 170

Universal military training, **1945:** 218; **1946:** 18 (p. 52), 27 [6], 41 [20], 53 [4], 75 [3, 13], 76; **1947:** 2 (p. 12), 7 (p. 63), 36 [4, 7, 9], 46 [12], 88 [6], 106, 117, 127 [14]; **1948:** 2, 5 (pp. 20, 26–29), 52, 53, 71 [19], 80, 86, 88 [16], 89, 93 [16], 114 [2], 165, 175, 243 [1]; **1949:** 2, 7 [17], 8 (pp. 55, 56); **1950:** 8 [45], 138, 214 [2, 4, 15], 225n., 272, 318 [11]; **1951:** 4, 63 [22], 107, 191; **1952–53:** 18 (p. 72)

Address to Congress, **1945:** 174

News conference remarks, **1945:** 44 [3], 106 [14, 16]

Universal Military Training and Service Act, **1945:** 174n.

Universal Training, President's Advisory Commission on, **1946:** 268; **1947:** 2 (p. 12), 7 (p. 63), 106; **1948:** 5 (p. 26), 86, 190
Universities.
 See Colleges and universities.
Unknown Soldier, **1949:** 254
UNO.
 See United Nations.
UNRRA.
 See United Nations Relief and Rehabilitation Administration.
Upchurch, John D., **1948:** 218 [7]
Uranium, production increase, **1952–53:** 280 [4]
Uranium-235, separation at Oak Ridge, Tenn., **1949:** 166 [1]
Urban areas, **1949:** 2, 54, 249; **1950:** 110 [2], 111
 Airports, study of location and use, **1952–53:** 40
 Civil defense, **1950:** 303
 Housing, **1948:** 5 (p. 38), 160, 165, 219, 220, 227 [2], 229, 231 [2], 237 [4], 238, 258, 261 [2], 264 [1]; **1949:** 2, 5, 202; **1950:** 128
 Redevelopment, **1949:** 5, 8 (p. 72), 249; **1951:** 13 (pp. 90, 94), 116
 Streets and roads, **1950:** 69
 Water systems, **1950:** 69, 306
Urban renewal, **1945:** 128; **1946:** 18 (p. 63); **1947:** 7 (p. 74), 102, 131; **1948:** 5 (p. 38), 8 (pp. 67, 82, 83, 98), 172; **1949:** 2, 5, 8 (pp. 45, 72, 76), 54, 126, 151, 202; **1950:** 9 (pp. 77, 81), 37, 69, 134, 157; **1952–53:** 18 (pp. 95, 99), 293, 367 (p. 1154)
 See also Slum clearance.
Urey, Harold C., **1948:** 191n.
Urgent Deficiency Appropriation Bill, **1947:** 60
Uruguay
 Berreta, Tomás, **1947:** 30
 President-elect, visit by, **1947:** 31 [7]
 Rodriguez Larreta, Eduardo, **1950:** 137 [26]
USES.
 See United States Employment Service.
USIA.
 See United States Information Agency.
U.S. News and World Report magazine, **1952–53:** 277 [1], 295 [7], 315 [3]
USO.
 See United Service Organizations.
U.S.S.R.
 See Soviet Union.
Utah, **1948:** 56
 Campaign remarks, **1948:** 200 [3–7, 9], 201; **1952–53:** 280 [1–3], 281
 Candidates for public office, **1948:** 200 [5, 6]; **1952–53:** 280 [1, 3]
 Coal mining, in **1948:** 200 [3]
 Floods, control and relief, **1952–53:** 127 [5]
 Maw, Gov. Herbert B., **1948:** 200 [2,5, 7], 201, 259 [4]
 Power project, **1952–53:** 367 (p. 1146)

Utah — *continued*
 Primary elections, **1952–53:** 21 [10]
 Salt Lake City.
  See main heading, Salt Lake City, Utah.
 Shale deposits, **1949:** 226 [6]
 Thomas, Sen. Elbert L., **1945:** 114
 Weber Basin reclamation project, **1949:** 196
Ute Indian Tribe, use of tribal funds, approval, **1951:** 198
Utica, N.Y.
 Campaign remarks, **1948:** 228 [5]; **1952–53:** 289 [6]
 Mayor Boyd E. Golder, **1948:** 228 [5]

Vacation plans, the President's, **1946:** 141 [20], 173 [9]; **1949:** 113 [13], 236 [8], 267 [1]
Vaccaro, Ernest B., **1945:** 60ftn. (p. 123), 157ftn. (p. 367), 175ftn. (p. 418); **1946:** 43 [4]; **1947:** 95 [2], 141 [13], 218 [12], 243 [2]; **1948:** 71 [8], 166 [8], 178 [1], 243 [11]; **1949:** 22 [2], 32 [16], 58 [30], 84 [2], 161 [1], 166 [1], 182 [1], 236 [18], 265; **1950:** 179 [14, 24]; **1951:** 7 [5], 16 [15, 19], 22 [2], 33 [11, 15], 37 [11], 49 [23], 56 [18], 63 [1, 19], 70 [13], 101 [2], 118 [7, 13], 140 [19], 188 [1, 5], 193 [20], 200 [1], 224 [11], 251 [1]; **1952–53:** 7 [10], 44 [12], 64 [10], 98 [36], 107 [9], 123 [1], 197 [1], 233 [7, 11, 12, 13], 247 [1], 345 [1, 4], 377 [1, 5, 20]
Valentine, Alan, **1951:** 7 [13]; **1952–53:** 118
Valentine, Tex., campaign remarks, **1948:** 208 [5]
Valley Forge, Pa., **1947:** 240; **1950:** 121 [5], 185
Van Antwerp, Eugene I., **1948:** 184
Van Buren, Martin, **1951:** 251 [22]; **1952–53:** 78
Vandegrift, Gen. Alexander A., **1946:** 70 [1], 229 [2]
Vandenberg, Sen. Arthur H., **1945:** 10; **1946:** 61 [15], 80, 173 [1, 7], 266 [15]; **1949:** 103n., 144 [29], 148 [1], 179 [17]; **1950:** 29 [11], 80 [1, 5, 12], 89; **1951:** 53, 188 [4], 251 [25]; **1952–53:** 23, 242 [2], 259, 268 [5], 283, 291n., 292n., 295 [8], 298 [8], 307, 317 [2], 318, 322
 See also President Pro Tempore of the Senate.
 Death of, statement, **1951:** 86
 Nomination as U.S. representative to U.N. General Assembly, **1945:** 219n.
Vandenberg, Gen. Hoyt S., **1951:** 93n., 275 [15]; **1952–53:** 44 [3], 128, 320
Vanderbilt, W. H., **1950:** 157
Vanderbilt University, **1949:** 107
Van der Veer, McClellan, **1952–53:** 98 [15]
Van Fleet, Lt. Gen. James A., **1950:** 142; **1951:** 77n., 113 [13]; **1952–53:** 295 [8], 320
Van Hecke, Maurice T., **1950:** 153
Van Horn, Ezra, **1948:** 171

Van Nuys, Calif., Birmingham Veterans Hospital,
     1950: 137 [10], 146 [14]
Vanport, Oreg., **1948:** 111n.
Vargas, Getulio, **1950:** 273 [1], 287 [13]
Variety Clubs of America, **1945:** 88
Variety Clubs international, Humanitarian Award
     Dinner, **1948:** 196
Vassar College, **1948:** 30
Vatican
     Clark, Gen. Mark W., appointment as U.S.
          Ambassador, **1951:** 275 [7, 18, 20], 300
          [16]
     Minister to, question of appointment, **1950:** 206
          [8]
     Pope Pius XII, **1949:** 270
     Presidential emissary to, **1946:** 100, 136 [13], 173
          [16], 253; **1947:** 67 [13], 88 [12], 178, 185;
          1948: 286; **1949:** 269 [7], 270n.; **1950:**
          16ftn. (p. 116), 44 [3], 86 [11], 206 [8];
          1951: 188 [9]
     U.S. representation at, question of, **1952–53:** 21
          [7], 49 [2], 75 [12], 228 [4]
Vaudeville, **1949:** 205 [6]
Vaughan, Brig. Gen. Harry H., **1945:** 175 [5]; **1948:**
          285 [12]; **1949:** 36, 40ftn. (p. 152); **1950:**
          16 [22], 266; **1951:** 186; **1952–53:** 64 [15],
          75 [5]
     News conference remarks on, **1949:** 32 [3], 161
          [5, 13], 179 [9, 11, 13, 15, 19, 21], 182 [1,
          12, 14], 192 [1], 200 [6, 14, 19], 214 [4], 265
V-E Day, **1945:** 18; **1950:** 110 [1, 10]
     Broadcast, **1945:** 27
     First anniversary, **1946:** 107
     Messages, **1945:** 29
     News conference remarks, **1945:** 4 [21], 22 [9, 15],
          26
     Proclamation, **1945:** 26 [4], 27
Vegetables, exemption from price control, **1952–53:**
          190
Venereal disease, **1952–53:** 249
Venezuela
     Gallegos, Rómulo, **1948:** 150 [9], 158
     Iron ore deposits, **1951:** 11; **1952–53:** 175ftn. (p.
          433)
     New government, U.S. relations with, **1948:** 283
          [21]
     Petroleum products, importation, **1952–53:** 239
     Trade agreement with, **1952–53:** 239
     U.S. Ambassador Walter J. Donnelly, **1950:** 217
          [2, 4], 218
Venizelos, Sophocles, **1949:** 261
Vereide, Abraham, **1949:** 28 [15]
Vermejo reclamation project, N. Mex., **1949:** 185
Vermont, **1945:** 60 [2]; **1949:** 220
     Gov. Ernest W. Gibson, **1948:** 170 [7]; **1949:** 211
          [2]
Verne, Jules, **1947:** 74
Versailles peace conference, **1946:** 181

Vessels.
     See Ships.
Veterans, **1945:** 114, 154, 174, 180; **1946:** 1, 18 (pp.
          40, 49, 57, 69, 71), 50, 118, 166, 182; **1948:**
          2, 4 [1], 8 (p. 71); **1949:** 8 (pp. 47, 50, 62),
          78n., 154; **1950:** 9 (pp. 46, 48, 66–71), 170
     American Veterans of World War II, **1949:** 203,
          268n.
     Benefits.
          See Veterans benefits.
     Civic responsibilities, **1949:** 33, 49
     Dependents, **1948:** 175
     Disabled, **1950:** 8 [7], 9 (pp. 67, 70), 156, 298;
          1951: 13 (p. 101), 260; **1952–53:** 5, 135,
          138, 243
          Veto of bill to provide automobiles for, **1949:**
               247; **1951:** 260
     Education, **1947:** 181 (pp. 401, 405); **1948:** 2, 5
          (pp. 21, 32, 42), 175, 259 [4]; **1949:** 8 (p.
          63); **1951:** 13 (pp. 100, 101); **1952–53:** 18
          (p. 108), 231, 366
     Employment, **1945:** 128, 226; **1946:** 18 (p. 65), 61
          [2], 62, 119 [2], 164, 217, 226 [1], 232;
          1948: 2, 169; **1949:** 8 (p. 63), 129, 181;
          1952–53: 137
          Preference in Federal employment, **1945:** 108
          Reemployment rights, **1945:** 107 [4]
     Farm purchases by, **1947:** 97; **1950:** 121 [3]
     Groups, addresses or remarks to, **1951:** 36, 38,
          236, 272, 291
     Growth in number of, **1952–53:** 18 (p. 107), 367
          (p. 1159)
     Hospitals and medical care, **1945:** 112, 128;
          1947: 131, 181 (p. 404); **1948:** 2, 5 (pp. 21,
          33, 34), 175, 218 [5]; **1949:** 8 (pp. 47, 62,
          64, 65), 11 [11], 49n., 192 [17]; **1950:** 9 (p.
          70), 137 [10], 146 [14], 156, 203 [3], 233;
          1951: 13 (pp. 99–103), 101 [1], 102, 260;
          1952–53: 18 (pp. 107, 110), 135, 212, 333,
          367 (p. 1160)
     USO programs for, **1949:** 104, 221
     Housing, **1945:** 211 [1], 212; **1946:** 18 (p. 62), 32,
          46, 48, 67, 75 [30], 94, 116, 152, 153, 178,
          182, 193, 195, 226 [1], 249, 257 [6], 258,
          263; **1947:** 2 (p. 6), 4 (pp. 25, 30), 7 (pp.
          58, 69, 74, 75, 94), 18, 44, 60, 76, 131, 181
          (pp. 398, 405); **1948:** 2, 5 (pp. 25, 37, 40,
          41), 37, 150 [1], 165, 175, 183 [1, 2], 203,
          205, 220, 227 [7], 228 [10], 231 [3], 259 [3,
          4]; **1949:** 179 [9]; **1950:** 9 (pp. 69, 70, 78,
          79, 81); **1951:** 13 (pp. 93, 94), 111, 171 [6],
          174; **1952–53:** 18 (p. 98), 231, 366, 367
          (pp. 1152, 1153)
     Negro, discrimination against, **1952–53:** 290
     News conference remarks, **1945:** 44 [1], 107 [4],
          211 [1]; **1946:** 27 [11], 61 [2], 75 [30], 119
          [2], 192 [14, 25], 257 [6]; **1947:** 70 [4], 180
          [1]; **1949:** 7 [26, 30], 11 [11], 40 [13], 58
          [14], 72 [9], 192 [17]

Veterans — *continued*
  Occupational training, **1950:** 9 (pp. 68, 69), 36, 298; **1951:** 13 (pp. 99–103), 260; **1952–53:** 18 (p. 108), 243
  Peace conference, representation proposed, **1946:** 181
  Philippine Army, **1947:** 134
  Proportion of whole population, increase, **1951:** 12 [46]
  Recruitment for tax enforcement positions, **1945:** 44 [1]
  Red Cross services, **1947:** 5
  Selective Service records of, **1947:** 54
  Spanish-American War, **1946:** 188
    Veto of bill to broaden medical benefits, **1950:** 233
  Surplus property purchases, **1946:** 98
  Thirty-fifth Division, World War I, **1948:** 1, 117, 118 [3], 217
  Widows, veto of bill to revise eligibility standards, **1951:** 181
  World War II, promotion in postal service, veto, **1950:** 170
Veterans, Polish Legion of American, **1951:** 291
Veterans Administration, **1945:** 70, 128; **1946:** 1, 18 (p. 79), 91, 118, 122, 139, 192 [8]; **1947:** 7 (pp. 70, 74, 75, 93), 60, 181 (p. 403), 191 [19], 226 [1], 241; **1948:** 4 [1], 5 (pp. 31, 33, 37, 42), 37, 175; **1949:** 8 (p. 65); **1950:** 9 (pp. 67, 78, 79), 137 [10], 196, 233; **1951:** 101 [1], 181, 260; **1952–53:** 18 (p. 98), 31 [3, 16], 117, 138, 243, 249, 333
  Appropriations, **1952–53:** 135
  Employee pay rates, veto of bill, **1948:** 153
  Facility at Fort Logan, Colo., disapproval, **1952–53:** 212
  Hospital construction, **1945:** 112
  Ijams, George E., **1945:** 24
  Modernization, **1945:** 31 [6], 52 [8]
  News conference remarks, **1945:** 31 [6], 52 [8]; **1949:** 7 [30], 11 [11], 78 [18]
  Pay raise for certain employees, **1949:** 228
  Reorganization, **1952–53:** 18 (p. 116)
  Voluntary Services ceremonies, address, **1952–53:** 135
Veterans Affairs, Administrator of (Gen. Omar N. Bradley), **1945:** 112; **1946:** 1, 27 [11], 74, 182, 193, 224, 225; **1947:** 134, 184
  See also Bradley, Gen. Omar N.
  Letter, **1945:** 176
Veterans Affairs, Administrator of (Carl R. Gray), **1948:** 153; **1949:** 8 (p. 65), 156, 179 [9], 228, 247; **1950:** 36, 192, 196, 203 [3]; **1951:** 251 [26], 260; **1952–53:** 31 [3, 16], 135
Veterans Affairs, Administrator of (Brig. Gen. Frank T. Hines), resignation, **1945:** 52 [8], 112

Veterans and Armed Forces, Committee on Service to, **1950:** 95
Veterans benefits, **1945:** 42, 128, 176, 192; **1946:** 18 (pp. 53, 64, 78, 79, 84), 27 [11], 70, 91, 112, 139, 188, 192 [14, 25], 193, 195, 226 [1]; **1947:** 2 (p. 8), 4 (pp. 15, 19), 7 (pp. 56, 57, 68, 69, 70, 76, 92), 54, 60, 181 (pp. 398, 401, 405, 407); **1948:** 4 [8], 5 (pp. 20–22, 25, 31–33, 38), 9 [10], 175, 228 [10]; **1952–53:** 18 (pp. 107, 110), 138, 231, 376
  Bonds, terminal leave, **1947:** 181 (pp. 404, 406, 407)
  Bonus, question of, **1949:** 7 [26], 40 [13]
  Budget allocations for, **1951:** 221
  Disability compensation, **1952–53:** 18 (pp. 109, 110)
  Expenditures for, **1952–53:** 367 (pp. 1159–1161)
  Insurance, **1947:** 6 [2]; **1951:** 7 [30], 8 (pp. 48, 64, 65); **1950:** 9 (pp. 70, 71), 202, 236; **1951:** 12 [52], 13 (pp. 102, 103); **1952–53:** 5, 18 (p. 109), 367 (p. 1160)
  Klamath Indians, capital reserve fund, **1948:** 57
  Liberalization, **1952–53:** 367 (p. 1159)
  Loan guarantees, **1951:** 13 (p. 101); **1952–53:** 231, 366
  Pensions, **1947:** 6 [2]; **1949:** 8 (p. 64), 40 [13], 58 [14], 72 [9]; **1951:** 13 (pp. 102–103), 181, 182; **1952–53:** 18 (p. 109), 138, 367 (p. 1160)
  Philippine veterans, **1946:** 38, 74, 122
  Readjustment allowances, **1947:** 6 [4]; **1948:** 5 (p. 32), 63, 175, 228 [10]; **1949:** 8 (pp. 62–64), 151; **1952–53:** 18 (p. 108), 231, 367 (p. 1160)
  Red Cross services, **1948:** 40
  Unemployment allowances, **1949:** 8 (pp. 64, 91); **1951:** 13 (p. 102); **1952–53:** 231, 367 (pp. 1150, 1160)
Veterans Bureau (1920's), corruption in, **1948:** 228 [10]
Veterans Committee, American, **1946:** 214
Veterans Emergency Housing Act, **1947:** 18, 131; **1950:** 113
Veterans Employment Service, **1948:** 135; **1949:** 129
Veterans of Foreign Wars, **1946:** 181; **1949:** 33, 184; **1950:** 226; **1951:** 108 [4], 203n.
  Award dinner, **1952–53:** 29
Veterans Placement Service Board, **1949:** 129, 181
Veterans Readjustment Assistance Act of 1952, **1952–53:** 231 367 (pp. 1150, 1160)
Veterans of World War II, Amercan, **1949:** 203, 268n.
Veto Messages and Memorandums of Disapproval. *For citations to private bills see* Appendix A, **1945:** p. 591; **1946:** p. 515; **1947:** p. 543; **1948:** p. 973; **1949:** p. 595; **1950:** p. 765; **1951:** p. 657; **1952–53:** p. 1217.

Veto Messages — *continued*
  Agricultural workers, deferment, **1945:** 23
  Army Optometry Corps, **1946:** 109
  Atomic Energy Commission nominees, character investigations, **1948:** 102
  Bank of America National Trust and Savings Association, relief of, **1951:** 284
  Bureau of Reclamation, certain activities, disapproval, **1946:** 209
  Census records searching fee, proposed elimination, **1949:** 175
  Chiefs and Assistant Chiefs of naval bureaus, raise in rank, **1945:** 217
  Claims against Government, referees in, **1947:** 168
  Commemorative coins, **1947:** 162
  Contract Settlement Act of 1944, amendment, **1949:** 150
  Council Bluffs, Iowa, relief of, **1945:** 149
  Court of Claims, special jurisdiction, **1950:** 256
  District of Columbia, reimbursement of expenditures for U.S. Park Police, **1947:** 165
  Federal savings and loan insurance premiums, reduction, disapproval, **1946:** 208
  Federal Security Agency, supplemental appropriation, **1948:** 135
  Federal Trade Commission Act and Clayton Act, application to pricing practices, **1950:** 166
  Fish restoration and management projects, Federal aid, **1949:** 229
  Fish and wildlife development of Colorado-Big Thompson project, **1949:** 232
  Garbage, disposal in territorial waters, regulation, **1947:** 171
  Glacier National Park, acquisition of property, **1946:** 150
  Government real estate transactions, restrictions, **1951:** 105, 108 [1]
  Greenfields Division, Sun River irrigation project, Montana, **1952–53:** 80
  Hatch Act, amendment, **1950:** 182
  Immigration and Nationality Act, revision, **1952–53:** 182
  Improvement of certain harbors, **1945:** 90
  Income taxes, reduction, **1947:** 116, 145 [10], 147; **1948:** 63
  Indian claims against U.S., jurisdiction over, **1946:** 151
  Indian reservations, land disposal, **1948:** 25
  Indians, tax refund, **1947:** 163
  Internal security bill, **1950:** 254
  Interstate Commerce Act, amendment, **1947:** 160; **1948:** 127
  Law enforcement in District of Columbia, **1945:** 80
  Labor Management Relations Act of 1947, **1947:** 120

Veto Messages — *continued*
  Labor mediation facilities, **1946:** 131
  Merchant Ship Sales Act of 1946, amendment, **1950:** 257
  Miles City, Mont., conveyance of lands to, **1949:** 206
  Military personnel, promotion of former prisoners of war, **1946:** 135
  Mining subsidies, continuation, **1947:** 175
  Minnesota territory, commemorative coin, **1948:** 90
  National defense program, limitation of right to investigate, **1947:** 77
  National Science Foundation Bill, **1947:** 169
  Nationality Act of 1940, amendment, **1950:** 241
  Natural Gas Act of 1938, amendment, **1950:** 88
  Navajo and Hopi Indians, aid for, **1949:** 233
  News conference remarks, **1947:** 78 [14, 19, 24]
  News vendors, exclusion from social security, **1947:** 170
  Norwich University, conveyance of certain Weather Bureau property to, **1945:** 92
  Offshore lands
    Cession to States, **1952–53:** 146
    Renunciation of U.S. claims, **1946:** 189
  Panama Canal employees, compensation claims, **1952–53:** 208
  Parker River National Wildlife Refuge, abolishment, disapproval, **1946:** 211
  Post office quarters, leasing by Postmaster General, **1952–53:** 214
  Postal service, promotion of World War II veterans, **1950:** 170
  Price control bill, **1946:** 152
  Public land exchanges, **1946:** 190
  Railroads, financial readjustments of debtor corporations, disapproval, **1946:** 205
  Reduction of certain appropriations and contract authorizations, disapproval, **1945:** 226
  Reno, Nev., relief for, **1949:** 146
  Retirement credit for military enlistees performing foreign service between 1898–1912, **1945:** 205
  Retirement of reserve personnel, amendment, **1949:** 174
  Revenue cutter crews, veteran status, **1946:** 188
  St. Lawrence Bridge Commission, **1947:** 172
  San Luis Valley project, Colorado, **1949:** 245
  Schools on Federal property, segregation requirement, **1951:** 286
  Ship Warrants Act, repeal, **1947:** 167
  Social security
    News vendors, exclusion of, **1948:** 67
    Resolution respecting coverage, **1948:** 131
  Social Security Act, amendment, **1948:** 152
  South Parkersburg, W. Va., amendment of census records, **1950:** 210

[References are to items except as otherwise indicated]

Veto Messages — *continued*
  Spanish-American War veterans, broadening of medical benefits, **1950:** 233
  Swedish pioneers, commemorative stamps, **1948:** 59
  Taft-Hartley labor bill, broadcast following message, **1947:** 121
  Theodore Roosevelt National Park, disapproval, **1946:** 200
  Weather Bureau construction, disapproval, **1946:** 197
  Vermejo reclamation project, New Mexico, Federal aid, **1949:** 185
  Veterans, disabled, automobiles for, **1949:** 247; **1951:** 260
  Veterans Administration employees, pay rates, **1948:** 153
  Veterans Administration facility, Fort Logan, Colo., **1952–53:** 212
  Veterans pensions, bills respecting, **1951:** 181, 182
  War Contractors Relief Act, amendment, **1950:** 183, 216
  Wool bill, **1947:** 128
Veto record, the President's, comments on, **1948:** 212 [5, 6], 214 [5], 218 [13], 223, 228 [3, 5], 231 [3], 233 [5], 249, 256, 261 [9], 267 [3, 7]
Vetoes.
  See also Veto Messages and Memorandums of Disapproval.
  Frequency of use, **1948:** 249, 256, 261 [9], 267 [3]
  Pocket, use by the President, **1950:** 250 [14]
  Single item, question of, **1950:** 8 [9]
Viana, Melo, **1947:** 189n.
Vice Presidency
  Comments on, **1950:** 21, 29 [18]
  Expense allowances for, **1952–53:** 361
  Salary increase, question of, **1948:** 285 [10]; **1949:** 137
Vice President (Alben W. Barkley), **1949:** 19, 38, 70, 76, 93ftn. (p. 241), 103, 115n., 173, 190, 220, 222; **1950:** 4, 12, 15, 21, 29ftn. (p. 141), 134, 279; **1951:** 8, 24, 27, 67, 80, 130n., 136; **1952–53:** 2 [1], 32, 51n., 68, 69, 127 [1], 131, 143n., 144, 159n., 161, 218, 221 [9], 266n., 281, 324
  See also Barkley, Sen. Alben W.
  Conference with, **1948:** 288 [12]
  Gavel, presentation to, **1951:** 51
  Letters to President of Senate.
    See Congress, letters to Members of.
  News conference remarks on, **1949:** 226 [11], 234 [14]
  St. Lawrence Seaway project, resolution concerning (1945–46), **1952–53:** 23
  Visit to Europe, **1948:** 288 [4]
Vice Presidential candidacy (1944), **1947:** 182 [8]

Vice Presidential candidacy (1948), question of, **1947:** 218 [12]
  Victory Bond drive, proposed, **1945:** 171
Victory Clothing Collection for Overseas Relief, **1946:** 4
Victory gardens, **1945:** 49; **1946:** 40
Victory loan, **1946:** 17 [2], 18 (p. 72)
Videla, Gabriel González, **1952–53:** 123 [13]
Vienna, Allied Commission, **1945:** 91
Vienna, defeat of Mongols at, **1951:** 8
Vigilante Day, Helena, Mont., **1950:** 127 [4]
Vincennes, Ind
  Campaign remarks, **1952–53:** 321 [1]
  Post-election remarks, **1948:** 271 [2]
Vincent, John Carter, **1952–53:** 353 [12, 14], 359 [3], 362n.
Vinck, Senator (Belgium), **1949:** 54
Vinita, Okla., campaign remarks, **1948:** 216 [11]
Vinson, Repr. Carl, **1946:** 137; **1949:** 40 [12], 66 [12]; **1950:** 97 [12], 225, 246; **1952–53:** 27n., 66, 105, 180, 217, 358
  Letter, **1951:** 81
Vinson, Fred M., **1947:** 200
  See also Chief Justice of the United States; Treasury, Secretary of the; War Mobilization and Reconversion, Office of, Director.
  Appointment as Chief Justice of the United States, **1946:** 129 [1, 4], 136ftn. (p. 301)
  Appointment as Secretary of the Treasury, **1945:** 82
  News conference remarks on, **1945:** 52 [5, 7, 10], 132 [1]
  Service as Federal Loan Administrator, **1951:** 33 [2]
Virgin Islands, **1946:** 18 (p. 66); **1947:** 35, 119; **1948:** 20; **1950:** 53, 69, 70; **1951:** 243
  Assistance, **1949:** 40 [15]
  Economic and social development, **1948:** 146; **1949:** 141
  Gov. William H. Hastie, **1948:** 36, 38; **1949:** 40 [15]
  Visit to, **1948:** 36, 38
Virgin Islands Company, **1947:** 7 (p. 96); **1948:** 5 (p. 57), 38, 146; **1949:** 8 (p. 94)
Virgin Islands Corporation, **1950:** 69
  Incorporation, **1949:** 141
Virginia, **1947:** 138; **1950:** 9 (p. 102)
  Election laws, **1948:** 41 [3]
  Federal offices, question of dispersal to, **1950:** 214 [10]
  Gov. William M. Tuck, **1947:** 138; **1948:** 41 [3]
  Newport News, **1945:** 79n., 91n., 97n.
  News conference remarks, **1950:** 34 [1], 105 [19], 214 [10]
  Primary election, **1949:** 166 [2]
  Segregation, bill to abolish, **1950:** 34 [1]

Virginia Military Institute, **1952–53:** 242 [3], 387

Visas, issuance to European displaced persons and refugees migrating to U.S., **1945:** 225

Vishinsky, Andrei Y., **1947:** 191 [17]; **1951:** 261 [13], 295 [5]; **1952–53:** 5, 268 [5, 9], 269n., 270 [7], 318

Visitors, foreign leaders
Abdul Ilah, **1945:** 47
Alemán, Miguel, **1947:** 79, 83, 91n.
Ali Khan, Liaquat, **1950:** 102
Auriol, Vincent, **1951:** 58, 62, 63 [9], 65
Ben-Gurion, David, **1951:** 95 [1]
Berreta, Tomás, **1947:** 30, 31 [7]
Chiang Kai-shek, Madame, **1945:** 118 [6, 18]; **1948:** 283 [15], 285 [16], 288 [13]
Churchill, Winston, **1951:** 70 [10]; **1952–53:** 2 [7, 10, 17], 4, 7 [8], 359 [20]
De Gasperi, Alcide, **1947:** 15; **1951:** 231, 232
De Gaulle, Gen. Charles, **1945:** 113, 118 [4]
De Valera, Eamon, **1948:** 49 [20]
Drees, Willem, **1952–53:** 21 [21]
Dutra, Eurico Gaspar, **1949:** 102, 103, 105, 107, 108
Elizabeth, Princess, and Prince Philip, **1951:** 153 [11], 193 [7], 282, 288
Erlander, Tage, **1952–53:** 98 [37]
Figl, Leopold, **1952–53:** 127 [14]
González Videla, Gabriel, **1950:** 85
Juliana, Queen, **1952–53:** 73, 74
McBride, Sean, **1951:** 63 [5]
Nehru, Jawaharlal, **1949:** 227
Osmena, Sergio, **1945:** 172 [2]
Pahlavi, Shah Mohammad Reza, **1949:** 258, 259, 262, 273
Plaza, Galo, **1951:** 118 [3], 129, 130, 132 [4, 6, 8], 134, 136
Pleven, René, **1951:** 25
President's role as host, **1951:** 27
Prío Socarrás, Carlos, **1948:** 170 [5], 282, 283, [16]
Quirino, Elpidio, **1949:** 172, 173, 176, 178; **1951:** 207, 208, 224 [3]
Rios, Juan Antonio, **1945:** 56, 170
Romulo, Gen. Carlos P., **1951:** 49 [5]
Sofianopoulos, John, **1945:** 75
Somoza, Anastasio, **1952–53:** 115 [4]
Torp, Oscar, **1952–53:** 258 [10]
Tsaldaris, Constantin, **1949:** 261
Venizelos, Sophocles, **1949:** 261

Visits to foreign countries
Brazil, **1947:** 141 [3], 145 [20, 22], 155 [1], 174 [4, 7], 177 [15], 188, 189; **1949:** 102, 105, 107
Canada, **1947:** 19 [11], 46 [26], 67 [16], 111, 112
Chile, question of, **1950:** 46 [15], 137 [8], 270 [1]
Colombia, question of, **1947:** 221 [4]
Comments on, **1952–53:** 378
Coronation of Queen Elizabeth II, question of attendance, **1952–53:** 342 [13]
England (1945), **1951:** 282

Visits to foreign countries — *continued*
France (1951), plans for, **1950:** 152 [10]; **1951:** 56 [20]
Germany, **1947:** 74
Korea, proposed, **1952–53:** 345 [2, 4]
Latin America, **1947:** 95 [14]
Mexico, **1947:** 19 [16], 46 [25], 51, 79, 112; **1949:** 200 [1]

Vital statistics program, **1946:** 117

V-J Day, **1945:** 46, 128, 178; **1947:** 177 [8], 192, 214; **1948:** 8 (p. 92), 181 [1]
Address to armed forces, **1945:** 123
Broadcast, **1945:** 122
News conference remarks, **1945:** 100, 106 [3], 107 [4, 20]

Vocational education.
See Occupational training.

Vocational Education, Federal Board of, **1946:** 117

Vocational rehabilitation, **1946:** 18 (p. 79), 117; **1950:** 9 (p. 74), 74, 127 [7], 208
Merchant seamen, **1950:** 76
Veterans, **1950:** 9 (pp. 68, 69), 36, 298

Vocational Rehabilitation, Office of, **1946:** 117

Vocational Rehabilitation Act, **1950:** 74

Vogeler, Robert A., espionage charges by Hungary, **1951:** 153ftn. (p. 385)

Voice of America, **1950:** 44 [14], 92, 227; **1951:** 70 [1], 72, 188 [6], 197; **1952–53:** 5, 54, 166 [11], 242 [2], 367 (p. 1141)
Broadcast, controversy over, **1948:** 110 [10]

Voice of Democracy contest, remarks to winners, **1951:** 40; **1952–53:** 43

Volland, Georges, **1950:** 280, 281

Voluntary Credit Restraint Program, **1952–53:** 15

Voluntary Foreign Aid, Advisory Committee on, **1950:** 285

Von Steuben, Baron, **1950:** 185

Vorys, Repr. John M., **1951:** 266n.

Voting rights, **1947:** 130; **1948:** 2, 20 41 [3], 115; **1949:** 52 [6]; **1950:** 37, 255, 281; **1952–53:** 169
Alaska and Hawaii, **1950:** 291
Armed forces, **1952–53:** 38
District of Columbia, **1946:** 18 (p. 66), 237 [23, 25]; **1949:** 164
Washington Post poll, **1945:** 193 [4]
Duty to exercise, **1947:** 204; **1948:** 122 [1], 138 [3, 5–8], 139 [2, 3], 182, 183 [1, 2, 5–7], 184, 194 [1, 3–5, 10, 11, 13], 195, 198 [3–7], 199, 200 [1–6, 9], 201, 202 [1, 2, 4–6], 203, 204 [1, 3, 7], 205, 206 [2–4], 208 [8], 214 [5, 9], 216 [5–7, 13, 14, 16], 218, [1, 3], 220, 222 [9], 226, 227 [2–4, 6, 7, 9], 228 [1–5, 7–12], 229, 233 [3], 237 [1, 2, 4], 240 [3–5], 242 [2], 245, 250, 254, 257 [1, 3, 5], 259 [3–6], 260, 261 [1–3, 7, 9], 262, 264 [1, 5], 266, 267 [1, 4], 268, 269; **1952–53:** 221 [2], 277 [2], 280 [5], 282 [2, 6], 295 [2], 298 [5]

Voting rights — *continued*
  Military personnel, **1952–53:** 68, 96, 124
  Negroes, **1952–53:** 290
  Poll taxes, elimination of, **1952–53:** 290
  Proposed amendment, **1950:** 23ftn. (p. 134)
  Women, **1948:** 30, 118 [6], 211, 228 [10]; **1950:** 117 [1]
Vukelich, Thomas D., **1948:** 235 [5]

Waco, Tex., **1945:** 175 [6]; **1947:** 52n.
  Campaign remarks, **1948:** 212 [5]
Waesche, Adm. Russell R., **1946:** 70 [1]
Wage controls, **1945:** 104, 128, 202 [3], 204; **1946:** 2, 232, 237 [7, 10], 262 [3]; **1947:** 224, 232 [6]; **1948:** 5 (pp. 22, 51, 52), 11ftn. (p. 104), 71 [19], 163 [14], 176, 182, 183 [5], 184; **1949:** 5, 8 (p. 88); **1950:** 203 [6, 9, 22, 24] and ftn. (p. 560), 205, 206 [4], 209 [14], 215, 238 [13], 258 [5], 270 [13], 287 [19, 25], 318 [10]; **1951:** 2 [16, 19, 21, 27], 4, 7 [10], 11, 13 (p. 76), 16 [3], 23, 28, 44, 91, 98, 107, 118 [1], 123, 137n., 140 [2], 143, 167, 176, 179 [3], 199; **1952–53:** 5, 15, 18 (pp. 77, 80), 190, 218, 231, 305, 342 [7], 376
  See also Price controls; Rent control.
  Campaign remarks, **1952–53:** 287
  News conference remarks, **1947:** 19 [1]
  Republican opposition to, **1952–53:** 292 [9]
  Termination, **1946:** 249, 252; **1947:** 4 (pp. 16, 19), 18
Wage and Hour Act, **1948:** 252
Wage-hour bill, **1949:** 179 [8]
Wage Policy Committee, National, **1952–53:** 216
Wage Stabilization Board, National, **1946:** 35, 110 [8], 152, 153, 156, 179, 220, 229 [8, 23], 237 [14], 262 [4, 21]; **1950:** 243; **1951:** 11, 23, 49 [2], 85 [4, 6], 91, 161, 167, 169, 204, 209 [1], 252, 277, 304, 305; **1952–53:** 15, 18 (p. 80), 22, 37, 58, 64 [14], 70, 88 [5, 7], 110, 148, 161, 215, 341, 345 [5], 346
  Establishment, **1945:** 230
  Labor dispute mediation functions, **1952–53:** 82, 190
Wage Stabilization Board, Chairman (Archibald Cox), resignation, **1952–53:** 342 [4]
Wage Stabilization Board, Chairman (Nathan P. Feinsinger), **1951:** 252, 277, 305; **1952–53:** 22, 58
Wage Stabilization Board, Chairman (George Taylor), **1951:** 169, 204
Wages, **1946:** 2, 18 (pp. 40, 49–51, 62), 73, 125, 153, 226 [1], 249; **1947:** 4 (pp. 15, 21, 28, 29, 31), 35, 70 [15], 81, 87, 90 [5], 107 [2], 121, 127 [1], 147, 152, 214, 224; **1948:** 2, 8 (pp. 68, 70, 74, 87), 32, 80, 107, 115, 131 [1], 166 [6], 183 [5, 7], 218 [10], 222 [7, 9], 223,

Wages — *continued*
  227 [7], 228 [8], 235 [4]; **1949:** 5, 13, 66 [20], 120, 199, 218, 239; **1950:** 6, 157, 202, 253 [7]; **1951:** 154, 199, 279; **1952–53:** 5, 15, 69, 241, 272, 282 [8], 294, 298 [3], 312, 314, 321 [5]
  See also Pay.
  Automobile workers, increase, **1948:** 110 [17]
  Coal miners, **1947:** 142, 152; **1948:** 66, 171, 223; **1952–53:** 341, 342 [7]
  Cost-of-living adjustments, **1951:** 167
  Decrease, **1945:** 180
  Employees on public works or Federally assisted projects, **1950:** 53, 68, 74
  Guaranteed, report on, **1947:** 53
  Increase, **1945:** 104, 147 [16, 17], 180, 181 [11]; **1946:** 9, 16, 17 [19], 18 (p. 51), 35, 124, 179; **1947:** 4 (pp. 16, 28), 70 [15], 187, 224; **1948:** 2, 8 (pp. 64, 65, 73, 82, 90), 110 [17], 131 [1], 160, 165, 167, 182, 184, 216 [5], 227 [9], 228 [6, 12], 267 [3], 268; **1949:** 151, 239; **1950:** 2, 84, 122, 127 [4]; **1951:** 11, 159, 167
    Distribution, **1952–53:** 15, 82, 194, 215, 277 [5], 314, 315 [1]
    Wage increase bill, **1945:** 147 [15, 18]
  Industrial, **1952–53:** 215
  Labor disputes, **1945:** 221 [1, 3]
  Meat industry, **1946:** 21 [6]
  Minimum.
    See main heading, Minimum wage.
  News conference remarks, **1945:** 137 [11], 147 [15, 16, 17, 18], 157 [5], 172 [3], 181 [1, 11], 221 [1, 3]; **1946:** 17 [19], 21 [5, 6], 27 [9], 30 [4], 53 [2], 61 [9], 72 [2], 177 [9, 21], 216 [4], 226 [3], 257 [10], 262 [12]
  Overtime, **1947:** 93
  Portal-to-portal pay bill, **1947:** 62 [16], 88 [7], 93, 95 [3]
  Productivity allowances, **1951:** 167
  Protection against loss from sickness or disability, **1945:** 192
  Railroad industry, **1946:** 24, 124; **1948:** 5 (p. 37), 159n.; **1951:** 74; **1952–53:** 277 [5]
  Reconversion period, broadcast, **1945:** 180
    Hooper rating re, **1945:** 181 [1]
  Seamen, **1947:** 123
  Stabilization, **1945:** 128; **1946:** 124, 152, 179, 220; **1947:** 2 (pp. 3, 12), 20, 62 [17, 18]; **1951:** 11, 74, 91, 167; **1952–53:** 15, 33, 70, 82, 118, 129, 148, 161, 346, 367 (p. 1141)
  Standards, **1952–53:** 218
  Statistical survey, **1952–53:** 18 (p. 92)
  Steel industry, **1946:** 16, 21 [5], 27 [9], 53 [2], 61 [9]; **1947:** 19 [1]; **1948:** 84 [1]; **1952–53:** 70, 82, 88 [5, 13], 110, 129
  Textile workers, **1948:** 261 [4]

Wages — *continued*

Wage and hour statistics, international convention on, **1951:** 97

Wage-price policy, **1946:** 18 (p. 51), 30 [4], 35, 36, 67, 72 [2], 73; **1947:** 2 (p. 3), 62 [17], 76, 107 [2], 116, 224; **1948:** 8 (pp. 88–90), 101, 165, 167, 183 [6], 195, 212 [5], 216 [15], 217, 218 [3, 10], 226, 231 [6], 233 [3], 234, 240 [4, 6], 242 [3], 246, 251, 268; **1949:** 2, 5, 90, 151, 250 [3]; **1950:** 6, 84, 243, 303; **1951:** 23, 118 [1], 304; **1952–53:** 15, 82, 118, 161, 376

War workers, paid on holidays, **1945:** 115

Wagner, Lt. Col. Boyd D. (Buzz), **1948:** 251

Wagner, Earl T., **1952–53:** 320

Wagner, Sen. Robert F., **1946:** 61 [21], 116, 119 [3], 215 [6], 258, 263; **1947:** 95 [19], 131; **1948:** 184, 228 [2, 4], 261 [15], 262; **1949:** 78 [10], 148 [3], 251

Full employment bill, letter, **1945:** 222

Housing bill.

See Taft-Ellender-Wagner housing bill.

News conference remarks on, **1945:** 44 [16], 202 [4], 221 [2]

Resolution on Jewish national state in Palestine, **1945:** 202 [4]

Social security bill, **1945:** 44 [16]

Wagner, Robert F., Sr., **1952–53:** 290, 300

Wagner Act.

See National Labor Relations Act.

Wagner-Peyser Act, **1945:** 226; **1947:** 81; **1948:** 10

Wahlen, George E., Congressional Medal of Honor award, **1945:** 160n.

Wainwright, Gen. Jonathan M., **1948:** 110 [15]; **1951:** 115; **1952–53:** 250

Congressional Medal of Honor award, **1945:** 131; **1952–53:** 157

Wait, Sgt. Irving D., **1951:** 186

Waitt, Maj. Gen. Alden H., **1949:** 179 [11]

Wake Forest College, **1951:** 256, 275 [21]

Wake Island, **1950:** 264n., 268, 269, 273 [16]

Meeting with General MacArthur at, **1951:** 90 [6, 11, 16], 95 [6, 9, 11], 108 [2]; **1952–53:** 345 [1]

Wakefield, Ray C., **1947:** 127 [7]

Walcott, Charles D., **1946:** 201

Walker, Frank, **1947:** 182 [8]; **1948:** 248

Nomination as Alternate Representative to U.N. General Assembly, **1945:** 219n.

See also Postmaster General (Frank C. Walker).

Walker, Paul, **1952–53:** 49 [1]

Walker, Walter, **1948:** 200 [1]

Walker, Lt. Gen. Walton H., **1950:** 260, 320

Walker, William O., **1947:** 48n.

Walking stick, gift to the President, **1949:** 18

Walks, the President's, **1947:** 36 [1, 22]

Wall Street Journal, **1948:** 204 [4], 206 [3], 214 [7], 216 [5, 7], 259 [3], 261 [2], 264 [1]; **1949:**

Wall Street Journal — *continued*

171 [11], 260 [1]; **1950:** 279; **1952–53:** 266 [3], 277 [5], 289 [10], 306 [2], 308 [1]

Wallace, Mrs. David W. (the President's mother-in-law), **1945:** 211 [13]

Wallace, Henry A., **1946:** 226 [4], 229 [17]; **1947:** 70 [23], 78 [3], 209 [6], 243 [8, 17]; **1948:** 9 [20], 11 [6], 21 [14], 53, 181 [4, 18]; **1949:** 70, 155 [2]; **1950:** 209ftn. (p. 581); **1952–53:** 64 [3], 129

See also Commerce, Secretary of.

Attacks on supporters, **1948:** 71 [2]

Correspondence on 1944 Far Eastern trip, transmission to Congress, **1951:** 230

News conference remarks on, **1951:** 261 [9]

Wallace, Lew (Chairman, Oregon Democratic Committee), **1945:** 64 [1]; **1948:** 233 [3]

Wallace, Lewis, *Ben Hur*, **1945:** 64 [1]

Wallgren, Gov. Mon C., **1945:** 64 [1, 11, 14], 175 [12]; **1946:** 41 [13, 15]; **1947:** 95 [8]; **1948:** 122 [1, 2, 4–6], 124 [1, 2, 4, 5], 125, 278 [7]; **1950:** 121 [13], 266; **1952–53:** 274 [1, 3, 5]

Letter, **1949:** 100; **1951:** 55

News conference remarks on, **1949:** 22 [16], 28 [1], 45 [5, 10], 52 [3], 58 [8, 17], 66 [16], 78 [5], 179 [24], 205 [19], 231 [2, 5]; **1951:** 101 [6], 108 [10, 14], 165 [2]

Nomination as chairman of National Security Resources Board, **1949:** 28 [1], 45ftn. (p. 157), 58 [8, 17], 66 [16], 78 [5], 100

Wallgren, Mrs. Mon C., **1948:** 122 [5]

Wallingford, Conn., campaign remarks, **1952–53:** 292 [2]

Wallula, Wash., **1950:** 121 [11]

Walsh, Sen. David I., **1946:** 37 [4], 137

Walsh, Rev. Edmund A., **1946:** 268n.; **1948:** 116 [2]; **1949:** 73n., 110n.; **1950:** 32n.

Walsh, Maj. Gen. Ellard A., **1950:** 272n.

Walsh, Rev. Emmet M., **1951:** 22 [2], 278n.

Walsh, John R., **1948:** 240 [4, 5]

Walsh, Thomas W., **1949:** 250 [1]

Walsh-Healey Act, **1948:** 261 [4]; **1950:** 74; **1952–53:** 136 [12], 148

Walter, Repr. Francis E., **1948:** 227 [4, 5]; **1949:** 58 [5, 31]

Walter Reed Army Medical Center, **1952–53:** 135

Waltham Watch Co., **1949:** 32 [1]; **1950:** 34 [7]

"Wanted: A New Federal Power Policy," Repr. George A. Dondero, **1948:** 209

War

Nuclear, **1946:** 112, 242 [2]

Poll on possibility of, **1950:** 152 [5]

War, Secretary of (Robert P. Patterson), **1945:** 118ftn. (p. 250), 221 [7]; **1946:** 74, 82, 193, 194n., 242 [2]; **1947:** 12, 42, 50, 88 [10], 119, 127 [17], 134, 148, 151, 192

See also Patterson, Robert P.

Directives, **1946:** 19, 23

War, Secretary of (Patterson) — *continued*
  Letters, **1945:** 176, 201; **1946:** 138, 195; **1947:** 10
  Memorandums, **1945:** 176, 225
  News conference remarks on, **1946:** 119 [2], 126 [16], 136 [14], 141 [5], 192 [4, 10]
  Reports, **1946:** 63, 137, 138
  Resignation, **1947:** 150
War, Secretary of (Henry L. Stimson), **1945:** 93, 97, 118ftn. (p. 250)
  See also Stimson, Henry L.
  Distinguished Service Medal, citation, **1945:** 142
  News conference remarks on, **1945:** 107 [6, 17], 116, 118 [2, 12], 132 [11], 137 [5]
  Resignation, **1945:** 137 [5]
    Letter, **1945:** 139
War agencies, **1946:** 18 (p. 67), 101, 130, 145, 146; **1947:** 6 [5], 7 (p. 56), 80, 87, 180 [1]; **1948:** 4 [1], 46, 62
  Appropriations, **1945:** 51, 124
  Key personnel, retention proposed, **1945:** 18
  Letter to agency heads, **1945:** 35
  Liquidation, **1945:** 128
    Letter to George E. Allen, **1945:** 117
  Reduction in funds, **1945:** 22ftn. (p. 37), 124
War Assets Administration, **1946:** 98, 192 [8, 25], 263; **1947:** 7 (pp. 56, 91, 93), 80, 181 (p. 402), 226 [3]; **1948:** 45, 46, 71 [8, 14]; **1949:** 7 [19], 8 (p. 93)
War Assets Administrator (Lt. Gen. E. B. Gregory), **1946:** 141 [13], 192 [22]
War Assets Administrator (Jess Larson), **1947:** 229; **1949:** 89 [1]
War Assets Administrator (Maj. Gen. Robert M. Littlejohn), **1946:** 262 [11]
War Between the States, **1945:** 45, 164 [3]
War bonds, **1945:** 76 [3], 213
War Claims Act of 1948, **1950:** 100; **1951:** 149
War Claims Commission, **1949:** 144 [30]; **1950:** 16 [3], 100
  Establishment, **1948:** 154
War College, National, **1947:** 226 [2]
  Address, **1952–53:** 354
War contractors, reimbursement for wages paid on holidays, **1945:** 115
War Contractors Relief Act, amendment, vetoes, **1950:** 183, 216
War contracts, **1946:** 18 (pp. 71, 75, 77, 78), 116, 130n., 177ftn. (p. 357); **1947:** 7 (pp. 59, 65), 11, 18, 35, 80
  Termination, **1945:** 128
War Council, proposed, **1947:** 10n.
War crimes, **1946:** 236, 251, 265; **1947:** 21; **1948:** 283 [6], 288 [7]; **1952–53:** 292 [8], 312, 317 [7]
  Jackson (Justice Robert H.) report, **1945:** 52 [2, 9], 60 [9]
  Joint report, **1945:** 91
  U.N. resolution (1946), **1950:** 174

War crimes trials
  German, **1946:** 18 (pp. 46, 47), 42, 215 [1], 226 [13], 229 [13], 230, 233, 251; **1950:** 174
  Japanese, **1946:** 18 (pp. 46, 47)
    Soviet demand for trial of Emperor Hirohito, **1950:** 29 [14]
  Joint report, **1945:** 91
  News conference remarks, **1945:** 22 [5], 52 [9], 129 [8], 132 [1]
War criminals, **1945:** 2, 143
  Extradition, **1951:** 227 [12]
  German, **1951:** 33 [8], 227 [12]
  Joint report, **1945:** 91
  News conference remarks, **1945:** 22 [5, 14]
War Damage Commission, **1949:** 122 [20]
  Philippine, termination, **1951:** 64
War damage compensation, **1948:** 4 [10], 5 (pp. 25, 30, 52)
War Damage Corporation, **1947:** (p. 88); **1948:** 5 (p. 53)
War dead, return from overseas, **1947:** 7 (p. 91); **1948:** 5 (p. 56), 175
War Department, **1945:** 30, 70, 101, 114, 128, 140, 141, 143n., 198, 218; **1946:** 18 (pp. 47, 74–77), 29, 118, 84 [15], 119 [2, 4], 122, 130n., 176, 187, 192 [8], 193, 194, 223 [6], 229 [15], 238, 242 [2]; **1947:** 2 (p. 11), 6 [11, 14, 27, 32, 34, 39], 7 (pp. 56, 64, 85, 86, 91, 93), 11, 18, 35, 36 [24], 39, 47, 50, 75, 80, 92, 144, 150, 157, 181 (pp. 401, 403, 404), 195, 226 [1, 3]; **1948:** 4 [1]; **1949:** 50
  Appropriations, **1945:** 146
  Bruce, Howard, **1945:** 125n., 126
  Furlough of railroadmen to aid in manpower shortage, **1945:** 83
  Knudsen, Lt. Gen. William S., **1945:** 55
  Lovett, Robert A., **1945:** 137 [5]
  McCloy, John J., **1945:** 137 [5]
  News conference remarks, **1945:** 52 [8], 64 [7], 118 [16], 129 [1, 14], 137 [12], 181 [2]
  Patterson, Robert P., **1945:** 116n., 129 [4], 137 [5]
  Presidential flag, design of, **1945:** 175ftn. (p. 416)
  World War II defense contract, **1951:** 284
War Department Act, **1947:** 182 [1]
War of 1812, **1945:** 164 [3]; **1947:** 111
War emergency, **1946:** 27 [4], 53 [19], 86 [20], 95 [28], 262 [14, 18], 272; **1947:** 2 (p. 2), 6 [16], 14 [13], 35, 80
War expenditures, **1945:** 128; **1946:** 18 (pp. 74–76), 193; **1947:** 181 [1], 210 [1]; **1948:** 5 (pp. 19, 20)
War Food Administration, **1945:** 128; **1946:** 118
War Food Administrator (Marvin Jones), **1945:** 35n.
  Resignation, **1945:** 40 [1]
    Letter, **1945:** 39
War Fund, Community, campaign
  Address, **1945:** 154
  National Capital area, memorandum, **1945:** 171

War housing, **1948:** 5 (pp. 40, 41)
War industries, **1947:** 18
War Information, Office of, **1945:** 60 [4]
　Liquidation, **1945:** 120, 132 [1]
War Information, Office of, Director (Elmer
　Davis), **1945:** 120
　News conference remarks on, **1945:** 31 [1], 132
　[1]
　Resignation, **1945:** 132 [1]
War information, utilization, **1947:** 18
War Labor Board, National, **1945:** 104, 128; **1946:**
　143 [10]; **1951:** 74
　News conference remarks, **1945:** 106 [12], 137 [1],
　157 [5]
　Termination, **1945:** 230
War Labor Board, National, Chairman (Lloyd K.
　Garrison)
　Letter, **1945:** 230
　News conference remarks on, **1945:** 172 [3], 211
　[2]
War Labor Disputes Act, **1945:** 172 [6]; **1946:** 131,
　249, 272; **1947:** 87, 120
War Manpower Commission, **1945:** 48, 137 [1, 7];
　1946: 18 (p. 86); **1947:** 81; **1948:** 10
War materials.
　See Armaments.
War Memorial, Indianapolis, Ind., address, **1948:**
　241
War Memorial Park, Little Rock, Ark., dedication,
　1949: 120
War Mobilization and Reconversion, Office of,
　1945: 42, 128, 212; **1946:** 116, 160, 195,
　238; **1947:** 18, 24, 35, 53, 80, 96, 200
　Advisory Board, **1945:** 202 [3, 5]; **1946:** 51n., 95
　[8], 136 [1, 2], 177 [2], 220
　Housing Expediter, **1945:** 211 [1]
　News conference remarks, **1945:** 137 [2], 157 [5],
　202 [3, 5], 211 [1]; **1946:** 37 [10, 14], 72 [2,
　4, 7, 8], 95 [8], 119 [3], 129 [3, 21], 136 [1,
　2], 143 [2], 163 [2], 177 [2], 262 [8]
　Reports, **1946:** 18 (pp. 37, 52, 71), 72 [2, 4, 7, 8],
　73, 143 [2], 163 [2], 164, 226 [1, 6, 15]
　Termination, **1946:** 262 [3, 4, 8]
War Mobilization and Reconversion, Office of,
　Director (John W. Snyder), **1945:** 95,
　212n., 220, 223; **1946:** 12, 15n., 17, 23, 30
　[4], 37 [12, 14, 16], 51n., 72, 73, 123, 129 [1,
　3], 136 [1], 143 [2]
　See also Snyder, John W.
　News conference remarks on, **1945:** 106 [4], 129
　[6], 137 [2, 8], 211 [1]
　Report, **1945:** 128 and ftn. (p. 205)
War Mobilization and Reconversion, Office of,
　Director (John R. Steelman), **1946:** 163
　[2], 164, 166n., 177 [3], 192n., 193, 216 [7,
　11, 19, 23], 226 [1, 6, 15, 18], 234, 238
　See also Steelman, John R.

War Mobilization and Reconversion, Office of,
　Director (Fred M. Vinson), letter, **1945:**
　18
　See also Vinson, Fred M.
War Mobilization and Reconversion Act, **1945:** 41;
　1947: 96
War-Navy-State Coordinating Committee, **1945:**
　218
War orphans, immigration to U.S., **1950:** 167
War plants, curb on sale of, **1948:** 71 [8, 14]
War Plants Corporation, Smaller, **1947:** 181 (pp.
　400, 406)
War powers, **1945:** 128; **1946:** 2
　Termination, **1947:** 35, 156
　The President's, **1950:** 46 [9]
War Powers Acts, **1945:** 41, 128, 218; **1948:** 10, 14;
　1949: 133, 240 [15]
　First, **1947:** 18, 80, 81, 102; **1950:** 183, 216, 307;
　1951: 284
　News conference remarks, **1945:** 211 [1], 221 [21,
　23]
　Second, **1946:** 2, 18 (p. 55), 35, 262 [13]; **1947:** 18,
　24, 36 [18], 47, 58, 99
　Approval of extension, **1945:** 229
War Production Board, **1945:** 95, 128, 135; **1946:**
　43 [4], 86 [31], 93; **1947:** 179, 243 [2]
　Matthiessen, C. H., **1945:** 24
War Production Board, Chairman (J. A. Krug),
　1945: 35n., 45, 64 [4]
　Letters, **1945:** 95, 162
　Resignation, **1945:** 162
War profiteering, **1946:** 163 [10]
War Refugee Board, **1945:** 225
　Report on foreign relief activities, **1945:** 85
War relief, foreign, reports, letters, **1945:** 85
War Relocation Camp, **1945:** 225
War-risk insurance, maritime, **1950:** 236
War Shipping Administration, **1945:** 176; **1946:** 18
　(pp. 74, 77, 82), 29, 126 [15], 264; **1947:**
　167, 181 (p. 404); **1950:** 76
War Shipping Administrator (Capt. Granville Con-
　way), **1946:** 23
War Shipping Administrator (Vice Adm. Emory S.
　Land), **1946:** 3
　Letter, **1945:** 176
　Memorandum, **1945:** 225
War souvenirs, danger of, **1947:** 157
War structures, use as temporary housing, **1947:** 44
War time, end of, **1945:** 107 [23]
War workers, **1946:** 18 (pp. 40, 69, 71), 62
　Displacement, **1945:** 128, 180, 202 [3]
　Employment, **1945:** 226
　Housing shortage, **1945:** 212
　Wages paid on holidays, **1945:** 115
Ward, Angus, imprisonment by Communist Chi-
　nese, **1949:** 260 [3]
Ward, Artemus, **1952–53:** 249
Warfare, atomic, moral question of, **1949:** 231 [19]

Waring, Frank A., **1946:** 119 [1]; **1951:** 64n., 251 [16]

Waring, J. Waties, **1948:** 283 [2]; **1952–53:** 26 [11], 35 [7]

Warm Springs, Ga., **1945:** 172 [13]; **1947:** 78 [1]

Warm Springs Foundation, gift from White House Correspondents' Association, acceptance, **1945:** 208 [1]

Warner, Albert, **1947:** 90n.

Warner, J. C., **1948:** 191n.

Warren, Earl, **1947:** 31 [10]; **1948:** 150 [6], 170 [13], 231 [1], 242 [2], 261 [7], 267 [2]; **1951:** 216, 295 [6]; **1952–53:** 242 [4], 277 [3, 6], 278, 279

Warren, Gov. Fuller, **1949:** 51

Warren, Gertrude L., **1951:** 122

Warren, Lindsay C., **1949:** 174; **1950:** 9 (p. 51); **1951:** 221; **1952–53:** 177

Warrensburg, Mo., campaign remarks, **1948:** 138 [1]

Warrior River, barge transportation on, **1952–53:** 18 (p. 83)

Warrior River Lock and Dam, Ala., **1952–53:** 367 (p. 1143)

Warrior River Terminal Company, **1947:** 7 (p. 95)

Warsaw, Poland, **1945:** 77, 78

Waseca, Minn., campaign remarks, **1948:** 237 [2]

Washington, Booker T., **1946:** 196
Commemorative coin, **1947:** 162

Washington, George, **1945:** 227; **1947:** 30, 68, 110, 240; **1948:** 32, 86; **1950:** 41, 42, 82, 94, 138, 176, 185, 272, 312; **1951:** 191, 218, 255; **1952–53:** 5, 45, 136 [17], 174, 242 [6], 282 [7], 289, 296, 330
Coin throwing legend, **1951:** 290
News conference remarks on, **1951:** 90 [16], 165 [7]
Press criticism of, **1951:** 8, 56 [25]

Washington, Lt. John P., **1951:** 30n.

Washington
Addresses and remarks in, **1950:** 124 [1–6], 125, 126
Campaign remarks, **1948:** 122 [1–6], 124 [1, 2, 4, 5], 125; **1952–53:** 272, 274–276
Candidates for public office, **1951:** 108 [10, 14]; **1952–53:** 272, 274–276
Economic progress, **1952–53:** 274 [2], 276
Langlie, Gov. Arthur B., **1950:** 124 [1] 125, 126
Magnuson, Sen. Warren G., **1945:** 64 [3], 175 [12]
Mitchell, Sen. Hugh B., **1945:** 64 [5], 208 [21]
Olympia, **1945:** 64
Power projects, **1952–53:** 62, 367 (p. 1146)
Richland, **1945:** 93, 156
Seattle, **1945:** 64 [11, 12]
Wallgren, Gov. Mon C., **1945:** 64 [1, 11, 14], 175 [12]; **1947:** 95 [8]; **1948:** 122 [1–2, 4–6], 124 [1, 2, 4, 5], 125, 278 [7]

Washington, D.C.
See District of Columbia.

Washington Daily News, **1951:** 247 [1]

Washington Evening Star, **1947:** 107 [8], 221 [16]; **1948:** 11 [16], 15 [11], 55 [12], 181 [9], 212 [4]; **1949:** 40 [17], 72 [4], 122 [4], 144 [11]; **1951:** 33ftn. (p. 148), 275ftn. (p. 603)

Washington Hebrew Congregation temple, remarks at cornerstone laying, **1952–53:** 330

Washington Institute, Methodist Ministers, **1951:** 31

Washington and Lee University, **1949:** 144 [10]

Washington Monument, **1947:** 240

Washington Pilgrimage of American Churchmen, **1951:** 241

Washington Post, **1949:** 122 [8]; **1950:** 137 [11], 146 [4]; **1952–53:** 75 [4]
News conference remarks, **1945:** 132 [7], 193 [4]
Public opinion poll on voting rights in Washington, D.C., **1945:** 193 [4]

Washington State Press Club, **1948:** 125

Washington Student Citizenship Seminar, **1950:** 178

Washita River, **1952–53:** 194

Wassell, Sam, **1949:** 119 [3, 4], 120n.

Watches, importation of, **1949:** 32 [1]

Water carriers, **1947:** 18

Water conservation, **1948:** 99

Water pollution, **1945:** 192; **1947:** 78 [11], 171; **1948:** 5 (p. 35), 8 (p. 78)
Control, **1946:** 18 (p. 83); **1950:** 33, 53, 69, 71; **1952–53:** 292, [7]

Water Pollution Control Act of 1948, **1949:** 8 (p. 70); **1950:** 69

Water Power Act of 1920, Federal, **1952–53:** 388

Water resources development, **1945:** 7, 164 [8], 165; **1946:** 18 (pp. 60, 61), 97, 176; **1947:** 7 (pp. 58, 59), 31 [10], 68, 110, 144; **1948:** 2, 5 (pp. 44, 45), 6, 8 (pp. 66, 77, 78), 56, 149, 219; **1949:** 2, 5, 8 (pp. 81, 82), 39, 43, 77, 106, 154, 183, 196, 245; **1950:** 1, 9 (pp. 87, 89, 90), 99, 110 [4], 111, 116, 121 [3, 4], 125, 127 [1], 129 [5], 130, 135, 140, 265; **1951:** 13 (pp. 85, 86, 90), 55, 185; **1952–53:** 18 (pp. 87–89), 194, 231, 367 (pp. 1146–1147)
See also Flood control; Power projects; River and harbor development.
Agricultural, **1952–53:** 367 (pp. 1149–1151)
Campaign remarks, **1948:** 119, 120 [2, 3], 122 [6], 125, 126 [1], 128 [1], 134, 198 [4], 201, 202 [4], 203, 206 [1–4], 207, 214 [3, 4], 233 [6], 235 [4, 5], 237 [4]
Desalinization, **1950:** 9 (p. 90)
Research program, approval of legislation, **1952–53:** 199

Water resources development — *continued*
  Indian lands, **1952–53:** 18 (p. 90)
  Legislative and budgetary policy, **1952–53:** 367 (p. 1147)
  Message to Congress, **1952–53:** 388
  Missouri, **1952–53:** 3
  New England and New York, **1950:** 33
  News conference remarks, **1950:** 34 [17], 46 [2]
  Water Resources Policy Commission, **1949:** 236ftn. (p. 525); **1950:** 1, 9 (p. 90), 34 [17], 116; **1951:** 13 (pp. 85, 86), 55; **1952–53:** 18 (p. 89), 32, 194, 367 (p. 1147), 388
    Report, **1950:** 306
Water systems, urban, **1950:** 69
Water transportation, **1945:** 165
Water Utilization Treaty, U.S.-Mexico, statement, **1945:** 7
Waterloo, Iowa, campaign remarks, **1952–53:** 315 [1]
Waterman, Alan, **1951:** 89
Waters, Enoch P., **1947:** 48n.
Watershed Review Board, proposed, **1951:** 183n.
Waterways, navigation rights, **1945:** 178; **1946:** 18 (p. 43)
Waterways Corporation, Inland, **1949:** 8 (p. 87)
Watkins, Sen. Arthur V., **1952–53:** 345 [1], 377 [11]
Watkins, Gordon S., **1946:** 53 [1]
Watkins, John A., **1952–53:** 286 [1–3], 312, 321 [2], 349n.
Watson, Maj. Gen. Edwin M., Distinguished Service Medal, posthumous citation, **1945:** 57
Watson, Mrs. Edwin M., **1945:** 57n.
Watson, Wilson D., Congressional Medal of Honor award, **1945:** 160n.
Waukesha, Wis., campaign remarks, **1948:** 237 [7]
Waymack, William W., **1946:** 242 [2]; **1948:** 88 [1]
Wayne, Gen. Anthony, **1948:** 114 [2]
Waynick, Capus, **1950:** 23 [11], 146 [10], 278 [8]
Wayward Press, The, John Hersey, **1951:** 70ftn. (p. 216)
WBBM, radio station, **1947:** 48n.
Weapons, **1945:** 174; **1946:** 7, 17 [23], 18 (p. 75), 236; **1947:** 21, 101, 194
  See also Armaments; Atomic bomb; Missiles.
  Embargo on weapons to Communist bloc, **1950:** 252
  Hydrogen.
    See Hydrogen bomb.
  Korea, arms shipment to, **1950:** 179 [4]
  New, **1945:** 128
  Palestine
    British shipments to Arabs, **1950:** 38 [17]
    Purchase by Israel, question of, **1948:** 110 [7, 21, 22]
    Shipments to Israel, tripartite declaration on, **1950:** 147
  Poison gas, **1947:** 36 [3]
  Production, **1950:** 204, 301, 303

Weapons — *continued*
  Research and development, **1949:** 8 (p. 60); **1950:** 9 (p. 64), 138
  Soviet, use by North Korean forces, **1950:** 296
  Trade in, **1947:** 72
Weapons Evaluation Board, **1949:** 8 (p. 56)
Weather Bureau, **1946:** 197; **1947:** 7 (p. 59); **1949:** 8 (p. 91); **1950:** 9 (p. 102), 53, 76
  Conveyance or certain property to Norwich University, veto, **1945:** 92
Weather stations, ocean, **1948:** 5 (pp. 49, 50)
Weatherford, Robert P., Jr., **1950:** 280, 281
Webb, James E., **1946:** 177 [7]; **1949:** 4 [1], 7n., 122 [7], 167n., 260ftn. (p. 571); **1951:** 16 [2]; **1952–53:** 21 [24]
  See also Budget, Bureau of the, Director (James E. Webb).
Weber Basin, Utah, reclamation project, **1949:** 196
Webster, Daniel, **1948:** 119, 122 [2], 126 [1], 128 [2], 134, 198 [6]; **1949:** 80; **1952–53:** 268 [4]
Webster, William, **1950:** 29 [22]; **1951:** 89
Webster-Ashburton Treaty, **1950:** 121 [6]
Wedemeyer, Lt. Gen. Albert C., **1947:** 209 [4]; **1948:** 49 [21]; **1949:** 171 [1]; **1952–53:** 270 [8], 277 [2], 303 [10], 308 [3], 310, 316, 362n.
Weehawken, N. J., Mayor John G. Meister, **1948:** 189n.
Wehman, Edwin, **1945:** 147n.
Weight, the President's, **1948:** 274 [15]; **1949:** 52 [14]; **1951:** 56 [10]
Weigle, Luther, A., **1952–53:** 260n.
Weil, Frank L., **1949:** 73n., 110n.; **1950:** 32n., 95; **1951:** 17; **1952–53:** 259, 297
Weizmann, Chaim, **1948:** 110 [7, 21], 224, 274 [7]; **1949:** 58 [1], 84 [1, 15]; **1952–53:** 144, 297
Welch, Repr., Phil J., **1952–53:** 156 [1]
Welfare, Department of, proposed, **1947:** 2 (p. 8); **1949:** 94, 127, 128, 181, 182 [8]
Welfare Board, National Jewish, **1952–53:** 297
Welfare funds, labor unions, **1947:** 120, 142; **1948:** 171
  Electrical workers, **1946:** 110 [8]
Welfare programs, **1946:** 117; **1947:** 4 (pp. 35, 36), 7 (pp. 58, 71, 92), 152, 181 (p. 405); **1948:** 4 [8], 5 (pp. 20, 25, 37), 175, 181 [2]; **1949:** 5, 8 (pp. 47, 66–71), 181; **1950:** 9 (pp. 50, 71–77), 39, 42, 51, 110 [10], 134, 262; **1951:** 13 (pp. 64, 65, 96–99), 221, 238; **1952–53:** 18 (pp. 103–107), 292 [3], 293, 319 [3, 4]
  Alaska, **1950:** 9 (p. 91)
  Children and youth, **1949:** 151, 159, 198; **1950:** 5; **1951:** 187; **1952–53:** 218
  Expenditures for, **1952–53:** 231, 367 (pp. 1156–1159)
  Handicapped persons, **1948:** 152; **1949:** 151, 197; **1952–53:** 18 (p. 106), 367 (p. 1158)

Welfare programs — *continued*
  Home relief under social security, proposed,
    1949: 32 [2]
  Indians, **1952–53:** 18 (p. 106), 367 (p. 1158)
  Military personnel, **1949:** 73, 110; **1950:** 32;
    1951: 3, 17, 100
  Older persons, **1949:** 151; **1952–53:** 218
  Public assistance, **1952–53:** 367 (p. 1156)
  Republican opposition, **1952–53:** 292 [13]
  Selective Service inductees, **1948:** 190
  Special interest opposition, **1952–53:** 194
  Territories and possessions, U.S., **1948:** 146
  United Defense Fund, **1951:** 3
  Veterans, **1951:** 13 (pp. 99–103)
Welker, Sen. Herman, **1952–53:** 129
Wellington, New Zealand, **1951:** 84
Welsh, George, **1948:** 183 [1]; **1949:** 26, 54n.
Wenatchee, Wash., campaign remarks, **1948:** 122
    [4]; **1952–53:** 274 [2]
Wendover, Wyo., **1950:** 117 [1]
Wene, Elmer, **1948:** 227 [8]
Werner, Mrs. Stella B., **1952–53:** 308 [7]
West, Mrs. Elsie, **1949:** 219n.
West Executive Avenue, removal of pillars, **1947:**
    95 [1]
West Frankfort, Ill.,
  Coal mine explosion, **1952–53:** 18 (p. 94), 19
  Mayor Luther Burpo, **1948:** 218 [2]
  Wreath laying at war memorial, **1948:** 218 [2]
West Liberty, Iowa, campaign remarks, **1952–53:**
    315 [3]
West New York, N.J., Mayor Wilbur J. McGowan,
    1948: 189n.
West Point, **1946:** 224; **1950:** 29 [9]; **1951:** 188 [14,
    16], 200 [9]; **1952–53:** 130, 131, 142
  Admission of Canadians, **1948:** 112
West Virginia, **1947:** 104; **1952–53:** 26 [19]
  Campaign remarks in, **1948:** 222 [9, 10], 242;
    1952–53: 242 [2–6], 308 [1, 8]
  Candidates for public office, **1948:** 222 [9, 10],
    223, 242 [2, 3]; **1952–53:** 242 [3–6], 308 [1,
    8]
  Floods, control and relief, **1952–53:** 50
  Municipalities, veto of bill to amend census
    records, **1950:** 210
Westerly, R.I., campaign remarks, **1952–53:** 298 [5]
Western Air Lines, **1952–53:** 246
Western civilization, moral and spiritual values,
    1951: 8
Western Electric Co., **1950:** 43n.
Western Hemisphere, **1946:** 18 (p. 43), 76, 83, 102;
    1947: 30, 51, 73, 112; **1948:** 2, 8 (p. 96), 86,
    198 [1]; **1949:** 19, 35
  Communism in, **1948:** 77 [8]
  Copper imports from, **1950:** 209 [10]
  Defense, **1947:** 101; **1950:** 151, 318ftn. (p. 761);
    1951: 59, 76, 114, 125
  Economic assistance, **1951:** 4, 59

Western Hemisphere — *continued*
  Economic development, **1947:** 79; **1948:** 5 (p. 29)
  European exports to, **1947:** 238
  Foreign ministers, economic discussions, **1950:**
    309 [13]
  Foreign ministers meeting, **1951:** 16 [12], 59, 65,
    67, 76, 85 [12], 125
  Livestock disease control, **1947:** 45
  Marshall Plan participation, question of, **1947:**
    177 [22]
  Military cooperation, **1947:** 127 [17]
  Mutual security, **1947:** 188
  Technical cooperation with U.S., **1951:** 59
Western military alliance, question of formation,
    1948: 49 [16]
Western nations, federation, proposed, **1947:** 205
    [16]
Western States Conference, Democratic Party,
    1951: 110, 113 [2, 3]
Westinghouse Corp., **1949:** 44n.; **1950:** 48n.; **1951:**
    50n.; **1952–53:** 52n.
Westminster Presbyterian Church, Alexandria, Va.,
    cornerstone laying, **1952–53:** 337
Weston, Adelbert, **1950:** 266
Wetherby, Gov. Lawrence W., **1952–53:** 221 [1]
Wetmore, Alexander, **1946:** 201; **1948:** 27n.
Wewoka, Okla., campaign remarks, **1948:** 216 [3]
Whalen, Grover A., **1948:** 168n.
What Truman Would Do to Congress, Jonathan
    Daniels, **1951:** 70ftn. (p. 216)
Wheat **1946:** 29, 78 [14], 95 [17, 21]; **1947:** 217;
    1948: 175; **1952–53:** 321 [4]
  Conservation, **1948:** 14, 19
  Crops, **1947:** 210 [3], 236 [10]; **1948:** 167, 194 [5]
  Exports, **1947:** 7 (p. 78), 155 [6], 210 [3]; **1948:** 8
    (p. 93), 14, 195, 213; **1950:** 9 (p. 87), 130,
    159; **1951:** 13 (pp. 88, 89); **1952–53:** 367
    (p. 1148)
  Marketing quota, **1947:** 35
  Overseas relief, **1946:** 23, 30 [2], 86 [4, 27], 87, 95
    [1], 119 [16]; **1947:** 15, 29, 47, 107 [3], 191
    [7], 209 [11]
  Pakistan, U.S. loan for, **1952–53:** 252
  Prices, **1948:** 80, 213, 218 [11, 14], 276; **1949:** 5, 8
    (p. 79); **1952–53:** 18 (p. 91), 210, 282 [8],
    367 (p. 1148)
    Control, **1947:** 218 [6]
    Supports, **1947:** 76; **1948:** 195
  Production, **1952–53:** 367 (p. 1148)
    Need to increase, **1951:** 11
  Shipments, curtailment by railroad strike, **1950:**
    186 [4], 188n.
  Speculation in, **1947:** 196
  Storage, **1948:** 195
  Surplus, **1950:** 111, 191 [11]
Wheat Agreement, International, **1948:** 99, 165,
    213, 231 [7], 233 [1], 240 [5], 246, 276;
    1949: 5, 8 (p. 80), 202, 203, 263; **1950:**

Wheat Agreement, International — *continued*
  9 (p. 87), 130, 134; **1951:** 13 (pp. 88, 89);
  1952–53: 18 (p. 91), 367 (pp. 1148–1149)
Wheeler, Charles L., **1950:** 294n.
Wheeler, Sen. Burton K., **1946:** 163 [7], 199 [9], 237
  [3, 18]; **1947:** 78 [14, 19]; **1948:** 228 [12];
  1952–53: 143
Wheeler, Lt. Gen. Raymond A., **1947:** 141 [2];
  1948: 126 [1]
Wheeling, W. Va., campaign remarks, **1952–53:** 308
  [1]
Wheeling-Benwood, Ohio, **1952–53:** 367 (p. 1146)
Wheeling Steel Corp., **1951:** 305
Wherry, Sen. Kenneth S., **1946:** 6 [8], 152, 153, 179,
  232; **1948:** 213, 220, 226, 233 [3]; **1949:**
  74n., 76, 89 [5], 155 [4], 161 [7], 211 [5];
  1950: 80 [5], 214 [14, 17], 252; **1951:** 7 [5],
  298 [7]; **1952–53:** 290
  Letter, **1947:** 96
  Proposed amendment to Price Control Act,
    1945: 60 [13]
Whig Party, **1952–53:** 238 [14], 282 [7], 287, 289
Whisky distillers, foreign, use of U.S. corn, **1948:**
  15 [5]
Whitaker, Repr. John A., **1948:** 218 [11, 12]
Whitby Island, **1950:** 121 [13]
White, Cecil F., **1948:** 204 [1, 2]
White, Charles M., **1949:** 152n., 153; **1952–53:** 116
White, Gilbert, **1950:** 1n., 306n.
White, Robert M., **1952–53:** 26 [9, 10, 18]
White, Samuel, **1949:** 250 [3]
White, Sen. Wallace H., Jr., **1947:** 14 [4]
  Letter, **1948:** 12n.
White, Walter, **1947:** 130n.; **1952–53:** 253 [5]
White, William Allen, Jr., **1948:** 137 [4]
White, William Allen, Sr., **1948:** 137 [4]
White House, **1946:** 17 [27], 216 [2], 257 [21]; **1948:**
  26 [8, 19]
  Addition to building, **1946:** 15 [8], 21 [2]
  Antique furnishings, restoration, **1952–53:** 228
    [1], 229
  Architecture of, **1948:** 41 [5]
  Balcony, construction of, **1948:** 9 [9, 21], 26 [18,
    20], 71 [21], 77 [6, 13, 15]
  Destruction (1814), **1949:** 115
  Food conservation at, **1947:** 202
  Funds for, **1947:** 6 [16]
  Furniture, book on, **1950:** 29 [9]
  Gavels, memento, presentation, **1951:** 24, 27, 51
  Gifts for, acceptance, **1952–53:** 99, 171n., 260
  Invitation to General MacArthur, question of,
    1951: 85 [14]
  Lincoln mementos in, **1947:** 31 [1], 205 [1, 12]
  News conference remarks, **1949:** 11 [1], 89 [1],
    166 [7]
  News photographers, dinner, **1947:** 209 [1]
  Overmantel for, presentation, **1951:** 288
  Picketing of, **1949:** 166 [7]

White House — *continued*
  Police, **1952–53:** 134n.
  Public visiting hours, **1952–53:** 2 [2]
  Reconstruction, **1951:** 24, 27, 51
  Renovation and repair, **1949:** 31, 64, 86; **1950:**
    144; **1952–53:** 31 [4], 42, 98 [2], 168, 183,
    236, 378
    Commission to Superintend Construction,
      1949: 59n., 89 [1]
  Social functions, invitations to, **1950:** 206 [13]
  State dinners, cancellation, **1947:** 209 [1]
  Statement, rescission of appropriations, **1947:** 11
White House Architect, Office of, **1948:** 11 [16]
White House Conference on Children and Youth,
  1949: 198, 204
  Midcentury, **1950:** 5, 299
White House conference on traffic safety, **1945:**
  224
White House Correspondents' Association, **1949:**
  82
  Gift to Warm Springs Foundation, acceptance,
    1945: 208 [1]
White House News Photographers Association,
  1949: 52 [12, 17]
  Award presentations, **1951:** 43
White House Office
  Connelly, Matthew J., **1945:** 4 [2]
  Daniels, Jonathan, **1945:** 4 [2], 8 [3], 26 [2, 5]
  Early, Stephen T., **1945:** 4 [2], 8 [1], 31 [7], 43
  Hassett, William D., **1945:** 4 [2]
  Hopkins, Harry, **1945:** 44 [8, 18], 52 [15], 60 [6,
    10, 12, 15], 67 [2], 71
  McKim, Edward D., **1945:** 60 [3]
  Niles, David K., **1945:** 87, 100n.
  Rosenman, Samuel I., **1945:** 4 [2], 35, 44 [19], 46
  Ross, Charles G., **1945:** 60 [6], 64, 67n., 106, 116,
    132 [1], 164 [1, 2], 202 [4]
  Schoeneman, George J., **1945:** 100n., 107ftn. (p.
    229)
  Steelman, John R., **1945:** 175 [1]
  Vaughan, Brig. Gen. Harry H., **1945:** 175 [5]
White House press releases, list, Appendix A.,
  1945: p. 591; **1946:** p. 515; **1947:** p. 539;
  1948: p. 973; **1949:** p. 595; **1950:** p. 765;
  1951: p. 657; **1952–53:** p. 1217
White House statements
  Arkansas-White-Red River Basins Inter-Agency
    Committee, **1950:** 164
  Balance of payments, **1950:** 81n.
  Budget estimates, Veterans Administration,
    1946: 78n.
  Commission on Migratory Labor, establishment,
    1950: 153
  Congress
    Summary of action on the President's pro-
      gram, **1949:** 231 [16]
    Summary of action at special session, **1948:**
      165n.

White House statements — *continued*
    Greek Deputy Premiers, visit of, **1949:** 261
    Highway safety, **1951:** 42n.
    Israel, diplomatic recognition of government, **1949:** 24
    Korea
        Diplomatic recognition of government, **1949:** 1
        Military assistance and defense support, **1950:** 184
    MacArthur, Gen. Douglas, dismissal from commands, summary of background statements, **1951:** 77n.
    National emergency, meeting with Congressional leaders, **1950:** 302
    News conference remarks, clarifications, **1951:** 16ftn. (p. 113), 248
    Palestine refugees, aid to, **1948:** 281
    Shah of Iran, visit of, **1949:** 273
    Transjordan, diplomatic recognition of government, **1949:** 23
White River Basin, **1950:** 33, 140, 164; **1951:** 13 (p. 87)
White Russia, relief for, **1945:** 186
White Sands, N. Mex., **1947:** 141 [11]
White Sulphur Springs, W. Va., **1950:** 169ftn. (p. 485)
Whitefish, Mont., campaign remarks, **1952–53:** 270 [5]
Whitesboro, Tex., campaign remarks, **1948:** 214 [2]
Whiteside, Arthur D., **1947:** 148n.; **1948:** 7n.
Whitney, Alexander F., **1946:** 121, 124, 125, 126 [4]; **1948:** 11 [6]
Whitney, Cornelius Vanderbilt, **1947:** 191 [1]; **1949:** 40 [1]
Whitney, Maj. Gen. Courtney, **1951:** 90 [14]
Wholesale Price Index, **1952–53:** 33
Wholesalers, National Association of, **1947:** 85
Wichita, Kans., **1951:** 185
Wickard, Claude R., **1952–53:** 266 [7]
    Appointment as Rural Electrification Administrator, **1945:** 38, 40 [1], 44 [6]
    News conference remarks on, **1945:** 40 [1], 44 [6]
    Resignation as Secretary of Agriculture, **1945:** 40 [1], 44 [6]
        Letter, **1945:** 38
Wiener, Myron, **1950:** 16ftn. (p. 116)
Wier, Repr. Roy W., **1952–53:** 313 [5]
Wiggins, J. Russell, **1951:** 302
Wilberforce University, **1948:** 162n.
Wilbur, Wash., **1950:** 124 [4]
Wildlife resources, **1946:** 18 (p. 82), 118, 211; **1947:** 7 (p. 83); **1948:** 5 (p. 47), 8 (p. 78), 201
Wilentz, David T., **1952–53:** 303 [5]
Wiley, Sen. Alexander, **1950:** 44 [4], 214ftn. (p. 588); **1951:** 53, 113 [12]; **1952–53:** 129, 334 [1, 3]
Wilhelmina, Queen, **1948:** 87

Wilkes, John, **1948:** 249
Wilkes-Barre, Pa.
    Campaign address, **1948:** 249; **1952–53:** 306 [2]
    Mayor Luther M. Kniffen, **1948:** 249; **1952–53:** 306 [2]
Wilkie, Horace W., **1948:** 237 [8], 238
Wilkins, Roy, **1950:** 15n.
Wilkinson, Ernest L., **1952–53:** 281
Willamette River, **1952–53:** 97
Willard, Daniel, **1948:** 231 [9]; **1952–53:** 311 [1]
Willard, Ohio, campaign remarks, **1948:** 231 [9]; **1952–53:** 311 [1]
William, Doctor, **1949:** 95 [7]
William Chrisman High School, Independence, Mo., **1952–53:** 173
Williams, Clair A., **1952–53:** 315 [3, 4]
Williams, Gov. G. Mennen, **1951:** 174; **1952–53:** 317, 318
Williams, Hershel W., Congressional Medal of Honor award, **1945:** 160n.
Williams, Jack, epitaph at Tombstone, Ariz., **1952–53:** 98 [2], 123 [12]
Williams, Sen. John J., **1951:** 33 [7]; **1952–53:** 31 [17], 115 [21], 127 [7], 238 [2], 285
Williams, Kenneth P., *Lincoln Finds a General*, **1951:** 90 [16]
Williams, Llewellyn, **1951:** 224 [5]
Williams, Ralph L., **1952–53:** 282 [6–8]
Williams, Gov. Ransome J., **1945:** 147n.
Williams, Mrs. Robert C., **1950:** 263n.
Williams, Roger, **1951:** 241
Williams, Walter, **1952–53:** 98 [13]
Williamsburg, U.S.S., **1951:** 295 [8]; **1952–53:** 255
Williamsburg, Va., **1949:** 207n.
Williamsport, Pa., campaign remarks, **1952–53:** 306 [5]
Willis, Paul S., **1947:** 191 [3]
Williston, N. Dak., **1950:** 129 [3]
    Campaign remarks, **1952–53:** 266 [11]
Willkie, Philip, **1950:** 137ftn. (p. 421)
Willkie, Wendell L., **1945:** 68; **1952–53:** 233 [15], 289 [8], 295 [6], 306 [1], 313 [4]
    Journalism awards, **1947:** 48
Wills, William H., appointment to Federal Communications Commission, **1945:** 60 [2]
Wilmington, Del., campaign remarks, **1948:** 225 [1]; **1952–53:** 303 [1]
Wilmington, N.C., **1948:** 274 [10]
Wilmot Proviso, **1948:** 245
Wilson, Charles E., **1945:** 175 [11]; **1946:** 268n.; **1947:** 9, 236 [3], 237, 243 [2]; **1949:** 246; **1950:** 303, 307; **1952–53:** 34, 58, 70, 88 [8], 115 [5]
    See also Defense Mobilization, Office of, Director.
    Message, **1945:** 206
    President, General Electric Co, **1948:** 11 [2]
Wilson, Charles R., **1952–53:** 289n.

Wilson, Edmund, **1952–53:** 362n.
Wilson, Edwin C., **1947:** 100
Wilson, T. Sgt. Harold E., Congressional Medal of Honor, **1952–53:** 90
Wilson, Field Marshal Henry M., Distinguished Service Medal, citation, **1945:** 197
Wilson, Maj. Louis H., Congressional Medal of Honor award, **1945:** 160n.
Wilson, Ray, **1952–53:** 289 [4–6]
Wilson, William B., **1948:** 259 [2]
Wilson, Woodrow, **1945:** 66, 68, 175 [5]; **1946:** 199 [19]; **1947:** 68; **1948:** 32, 101, 126 [2], 211, 231 [10], 236, 242 [1], 245, 256, 259 [1, 2], 261 [4], 264 [5], 266; **1949:** 38, 252; **1950:** 4, 12, 82, 157, 162, 271, 312; **1952–53:** 21 [14], 63, 127 [18], 136 [17], 196, 285, 309, 366
    Press attacks on, **1951:** 8
    Recollections of, the President's, **1951:** 6
Wilson, Mrs. Woodrow, **1949:** 252n.
Wilson, Woodrow, School of Public and International Affairs, **1947:** 117
Wimberly, Harrington, **1945:** 132 [1]
Winant, John G., **1946:** 53 [17]
Winch, Robert F., **1951:** 251 [1]
Winchell, Walter, **1948:** 89
Windsor Locks, Conn., campaign remarks, **1952–53:** 292 [7]
Winchester, Ky., campaign remarks, **1948:** 222 [4]
Wine, Capt. Russell B., **1952–53:** 134n.
Winger, Albert E., **1952–53:** 351
Winona, Minn., campaign remarks, **1948:** 237 [4]; **1952–53:** 313 [1]
Winslow, Lorenzo S., **1946:** 21 [2]
Winslow, Ariz., campaign remarks, **1948:** 136 [1]
Winston-Salem, N.C., **1951:** 251, 255
Wiretapping, **1949:** 211 [12]
    Comments on, **1950:** 217 [12], 230 [8]
Wirtz, W. Willard, **1946:** 156, 229 [8]; **1947:** 87n.; **1950:** 27n., 36n.
Wisconsin, **1946:** 43 [4]; **1947:** 35, 162; **1948:** 90, 170 [2]; **1952–53:** 241
    Addresses and remarks in, **1950:** 131 [1, 2, 4], 132
    Campaign remarks in, **1948:** 235 [1–4], 237 [5–7], 238, 239
    Candidates for public office, **1948:** 237 [5, 7], 238, 239; **1950:** 44 [4]; **1952–53:** 253 [10]
    Gov. Walter J. Kohler, Jr., **1952–53:** 97
    Gov. Oscar Rennebohm, **1950:** 132n.
    Primary election, **1948:** 71 [11]; **1952–53:** 247 [2]
Wisconsin, University of, **1951:** 296n.
Wisconsin Power and Light Co., **1952–53:** 143
Wise, Rabbi Stephen S., **1946:** 155
Witherspoon, John, **1952–53:** 337
Withholding tax, **1950:** 46 [7], 200, 202
Witnesses in crime investigation, murder of, **1950:** 86 [2, 4, 12]
Witte, Edwin E., **1947:** 87n.; **1948:** 140n.; **1949:** 81

Wolcott, Jesse P., **1948:** 15 [5], 166 [8], 233 [4]
Wolf Point, Mont., campaign remarks, **1952–53:** 266 [13], 268 [1]
Woll, J. Albert, **1947:** 70 [8]
Woll, Matthew, **1950:** 4
Wolverton, Repr. Charles A., **1949:** 200 [11]
Women
    Ambassadorial appointments for, **1949:** 113 [11], 148 [18]
    Armed Forces, role in, **1952–53:** 248
    Business and Professional, International Federation of, **1952–53:** 188
    Democratic Party, political role in, **1951:** 238
    Democratic Women's Day, **1948:** 211
    Employment, **1947:** 4 (p. 31); **1950:** 243
    Equal rights, **1948:** 30
    Government positions for, **1949:** 11 [4]
    "Housewives for Truman," **1948:** 264 [3]
    In Congress, **1946:** 75 [21]
    Inter-American Convention on Granting Political Rights to, **1949:** 10
    Legal status, **1950:** 10
    Maternal health services, **1948:** 181 [2], 237 [3]; **1949:** 85; **1950:** 9 (p. 75); **1951:** 13 (p. 99)
    Message to, **1947:** 204
    National security, role in support of, **1951:** 11, 15, 193 [5], 294
    Political responsibilities of, **1950:** 255
    Politics and voting participation, **1949:** 219, 252
    Registration for defense service, proposed, **1950:** 105 [21]
    Role in politics, **1948:** 211
    Service on draft boards, **1948:** 174 [3]
    Social security benefits, **1948:** 107, 215
    Suffrage amendment to Constitution, statement, **1945:** 111
    U.S. vs. Soviet, **1945:** 60 [12]
    Voting rights, **1948:** 118 [6], 228 [10]; **1950:** 117 [1]
    Warwork, **1946:** 52
Women, United Nations Commission on the Status of, **1948:** 30; **1950:** 10
"Women in the Armed Services" commemorative stamp, remarks upon issuance, **1952–53:** 248
Women in the Services, Advisory Committee on, **1951:** 289
Women Voters, League of, **1947:** 121
Women's Army Corps, **1945:** 192; **1947:** 35
Women's Bureau Conference, address, **1948:** 30
Women's National Democratic Club, **1949:** 252; **1951:** 297
Women's Patriotic Conference on National Defense, **1950:** 21
Wood, Junius B., **1952–53:** 228 [1], 229
Wood, Maj. Gen. Leonard, **1948:** 81
Woodhouse, Mrs. Chase Going, **1948:** 261 [6]
Woodring, Harry, **1948:** 15 [7]

Woodrow Wilson School of Public and International Affairs, **1947:** 117

Woods, Tighe E. (Housing Expediter), **1948:** 71 [13, 15]; **1949:** 22 [5], 65, 182 [4]; **1950:** 93, 278 [5]; **1951:** 12 [55]

Woods, Rufus, **1952–53:** 274 [2]

Woods, Willis, **1949:** 205 [6]

Woodward, Stanley, **1949:** 32 [3]; **1950:** 97 [2], 138

Wool
    Exchanges, investigation and regulation of, **1947:** 209 [12], 226 [15]
    Imports, **1947:** 128
    Price supports, **1946:** 57; **1947:** 70 [18], 78 [25], 128; **1948:** 5 (p. 43); **1950:** 117 [4]
    Shortage of, **1950:** 230 [10], 253 [8]; **1951:** 11
    Veto of bill, **1947:** 128

Wooldridge, Rear Adm. E. T., **1952–53:** 310

Wooton, Paul, **1946:** 218; **1947:** 196; **1948:** 86; **1949:** 80; **1951:** 18, 21; **1952–53:** 339

Worcester, Mass.
    Campaign remarks, **1948:** 259 [5]; **1952–53:** 292 [10]
    Mayor Charles F. Sullivan, **1948:** 259 [5]

Work stoppages, **1952–53:** 15

Workweek, **1950:** 2, 243, 303; **1952–53:** 15, 376
    Coal miners, **1947:** 142; **1949:** 155 [16], 269 [10, 12]; **1950:** 29 [19]
    Employees of Government contractors, **1950:** 53
    Employees on public works or Federally assisted projects, **1950:** 68, 74
    Extension, **1948:** 11 [2]
    40-hour, **1950:** 18
        Enactment of, **1948:** 268
    Government employees, **1951:** 118 [9]
    Increase in defense industries, **1951:** 11, 167
    Public works projects, **1947:** 81
    Reduction, **1945:** 175 [11], 180; **1946:** 18 (pp. 65, 71); **1947:** 4 (p. 16), 152, 187
        Government employees, **1945:** 48, 70, 107 [1]
    Statistics, **1949:** 13
    Steel workers, **1947:** 142
    Wage and hour statistics, international convention on, **1951:** 97
    War Department employees, **1947:** 35

Workmen's compensation.
    See Disability compensation.

World Bank.
    See Bretton Woods agreements.

World Court.
    See International Court of Justice.

World citizenship courses, proposed, **1946:** 75 [26]

World Day of Prayer, broadcast, **1950:** 316

World Food Programs, Cabinet Committee on, **1947:** 47, 139, 191 [3, 5, 8]; **1948:** 1

World government conference, proposed, **1948:** 71 [3]

World Health Organization, **1946:** 236; **1947:** 7 (p. 67), 21, 59; **1950:** 177; **1951:** 135, 184; **1952–53:** 51, 55

World Health Organization — *continued*
    U.S. membership, **1948:** 132

World Land Tenure Conference, **1951:** 296

World Series, **1947:** 191 [23]
    President's hopes to attend, **1949:** 192 [18]

World Stabilization Fund, **1947:** 138

World War I, **1945:** 5, 45, 179; **1946:** 18 (p. 45), 236, 241; **1947:** 52, 97; **1948:** 2, 86, 89; **1949:** 252; **1950:** 18, 87; **1951:** 174, 181, 182, 294; **1952–53:** 307
    Battery D, 129th Field Artillery, reunion breakfast, **1949:** 18
    Brazil, participation in, **1949:** 102, 103n.
    Capital Issues Committee, **1951:** 44
    Casualties, **1950:** 138; **1951:** 56 [26], 65, 135
    Emergency powers, Presidential, **1951:** 13 (p. 65)
    Europe, financial drain on, **1952–53:** 218
    Farm price collapse following, **1947:** 76
    Intolerance in postwar era, **1952–53:** 288, 290
    Inflation and deflation of postwar period, **1945:** 128
    Lost Battalion, **1948:** 264 [5]
    Loyalty investigations following, **1949:** 122 [16]
    National debt at close of, **1949:** 95 [19]
    News conference remarks, **1945:** 31 [3, 6], 52 [8], 164 [3]
    Postwar era, **1948:** 94, 243 [1], 245, 266
        Crime wave, **1950:** 37
        Farm depression, **1950:** 121 [7]
        Isolationism, **1950:** 78, 110 [1], 162
        Tariffs, **1949:** 195; **1950:** 130
    President's service in, **1948:** 116 [1], 126 [3], 200 [2], 217, 249; **1949:** 36, 223; **1950:** 21, 110 [9], 165, 281; **1951:** 38, 298 [1]
    Thirty-fifth Division, **1948:** 117, 118 [3], 217; **1949:** 18, 36, 119
        Reunion, **1947:** 110; **1950:** 161; **1951:** 108 [7], 113 [16]
    Veterans, **1949:** 40 [13], 72 [9], 247

World War II, **1945:** 1, 2, 3, 6, 10, 12, 17, 18, 19, 28, 34, 41, 45, 49, 50, 53, 54, 55, 57, 58, 66, 91, 93, 97, 98, 111, 121, 125, 126, 128, 154, 160, 186, 190, 198, 200, 218; **1946:** 2, 7, 8, 18 (pp. 38, 42, 45, 69, 74, 87), 26, 50, 52, 68, 69, 76, 83, 93, 112, 113, 159, 162, 167, 171, 181, 193, 214, 236, 247, 265, 271; **1947:** 2 (p. 2), 7 (pp. 70, 91), 56, 74, 110, 129, 132, 135, 178, 179, 185, 188, 192, 200; **1948:** 8 (pp. 75, 96), 86, 101, 122 [6], 128 [4], 129, 137 [3], 182, 184, 218 [3], 235 [4]; **1949:** 160, 184, 252; **1950:** 87, 111, 121 [2, 13], 159, 183, 232, 271; **1952–53:** 101, 158, 196, 307, 366, 378
    Armed forces in, **1951:** 54, 57, 114, 275 [18]
    Armistice control commissions, termination, **1947:** 114
    Awards for service in, policy governing, **1947:** 103
    Bipartisan foreign policy, **1948:** 245

World War II — *continued*
  Brazilian participation, **1947:** 189; **1949:** 102
  Canadian participation, **1947:** 111
  Casualties, **1950:** 138; **1951:** 56 [26], 65, 135
    Civilian, **1946:** 268; **1947:** 140
    European, **1947:** 210 [6]
  Cemeteries, U.S., overseas, **1947:** 92
  Cessation of hostilities, **1947:** 2 (p. 2), 7 (p. 55),
    88 [1], 103, 156, 175, 180 [17], 210 [1];
    1948: 268; **1949:** 86; **1950:** 110 [1]
    See also Unconditional surrender of Axis
      powers.
    Japanese surrender, **1950:** 194, 216, 223
    Proclamation, **1946:** 273
    Statement, **1946:** 272
  Congressional Medal of Honor winners, **1950:**
    267
    See listing under Medals, presentations.
  Damage claims, **1949:** 8 (pp. 54, 70); **1950:** 9 (pp.
    56, 60), 100; **1951:** 64, 149
  Defense
    Contract, veto of bill relating to, **1951:** 284
    Housing units, disposition, **1952–53:** 367 (p.
      1154)
    Plants, use in Korean emergency, **1951:** 11
    Production, **1950:** 13, 202
    Program, **1951:** 38, 93, 98, 174
    Truman Committee investigation, **1948:** 118
      [5], 128 [1], 206 [1]; **1952–53:** 158, 289 [8],
      377 [2]
  Demobilization, postwar, **1948:** 236
  Dill, Field Marshal Sir John, contribution to
    Allied victory, **1950:** 275
  Draft rejectees, **1951:** 9, 258
  Economic effects, **1947:** 68; **1949:** 195; **1951:** 11,
    167
  Emergency powers, the President's, **1950:** 307;
    1951: 13 (p. 65)
    Termination, **1947:** 156
  Enemy assets, disposition, **1948:** 154
    Germany, disposition of confiscated property
      in U.S., **1952–53:** 258 [5]
    Italy, return of ships to, **1948:** 51
  Europe, financial drain on, **1952–53:** 128, 368
  Evacuation claims, Japanese-American, **1948:** 20
  Fiscal policy during, **1951:** 28
  Four Chaplains, heroism of, **1948:** 130 [1]
    Chapel of the Four Chaplains, dedication,
      1951: 30
  French resistance, **1945:** 109, 110
  Galapagos Islands, offer by Ecuador for use as
    base, **1951:** 136n.
  German spies in U.S. trial of, **1949:** 32 [15, 17]
  Housing, suspension of disposal, **1951:** 211
  Industrial cartels, contribution to German war
    effort, **1948:** 278 [23, 28]
  Industry, U.S., productivity, **1948:** 183 [6], 240 [1]
  Iranian participation, **1947:** 203

World War II — *continued*
  Italy, Stevenson rehabilitation mission, **1952–53:**
    292 [1]
  Jewish sufferings in, **1952–53:** 297
  Medical care facilities for military personnel,
    1952–53: 333
  Midway, Battle of, **1952–53:** 142
  Netherlands. resistance efforts, **1952–53:** 78
  News conference remarks, **1945:** 4 [21], 26, 31 [5],
    40 [1, 2, 3], 44 [2, 20], 52 [8], 60 [4], 94, 100,
    106 [3], 107 [4, 20]; **1946:** 6 [18], 27 [17], 53
    [5], 75 [7], 86 [20], 272; **1947:** 177 [8, 20]
  Norwegian participation, **1945:** 196
  Official termination, question of, **1945:** 114
  Outbreak of, 10th anniversary, **1949:** 200 [8]
  Peace treaties, **1951:** 49 [18], 149, 153 [22], 173,
    216, 217, 224 [8], 227ftn. (p. 527), 235;
    1952–53: 5, 38, 79, 95, 111, 342 [16]
    See also International agreements (1947).
    Proposed, **1950:** 179 [19], 250 [1, 6, 9, 17, 20],
      270 [14, 16]
  Postwar era
    Intolerance, **1952–53:** 298
    U.S. economy, **1952–53:** 289 [2], 292 [10], 293,
      294, 319 [1]
  President's offer to serve, **1948:** 200 [2], 214 [4];
    1949: 36
  Press censorship, **1946:** 13
  Price controls, **1951:** 7 [13]
  Prisoners of war.
    See main heading, Prisoners of war.
  Reconversion, postwar, **1950:** 14, 122
  Red Cross activities, **1949:** 215
  Refugee relief, **1947:** 43
  Rubber shortage, **1947:** 24, 31 [2]
  Saudi Arabian participation, **1947:** 33, 34
  Savings bond purchases, **1951:** 91
  Selective Service System in, **1947:** 63
  Souvenirs, danger of, **1947:** 157
  Soviet declaration of war on Japan, **1945:** 94, 97
  State of war with Germany, proposed termina-
    tion, **1951:** 149
  Stevenson, Gov. Adlai, services to Government,
    1952–53: 289 [5], 292 [1, 2], 317 [4]
  Surplus merchant ships, preservation, **1951:** 13
    (pp. 81–83)
  Temporary agencies, histories of, **1951:** 26
  Trained manpower, effectiveness of, **1945:** 174
  Transportation labor disputes, **1951:** 74
  USO services.
    See United Service Organizations.
  V-E Day.
    See main heading, V-E Day.
  Veterans.
    See main heading, Veterans.
  Victory in the East, proclamation, **1945:** 105
  Western Hemisphere defense, **1951:** 59

World Wars, Military Order of the, **1950:** 138n.; **1951:** 109n.
World's Christian Endeavor Union, **1950:** 197
Worthington, Hood, **1946:** 262 [1]
WPB.
   See War Production Board.
Wright, Gov. Fielding L., **1950:** 169 [2]
Wright, J. E., **1948:** 208 [7]
Wright, James L., **1947:** 191 [11, 14], 243 [4]; **1948:** 93 [11]
Wright, John I., **1948:** 219
Wright, Louis T., **1952–53:** 290n.
Wright, Theodore P., **1947:** 115n.; **1948:** 9 [8]
Wright Aeronautical Corp., **1951:** 252n.
Wright brothers, **1952–53:** 125, 328, 351
Wright Memorial Dinner, Aero Club of Washington, **1952–53:** 351
Wright Memorial Trophy, **1952–53:** 351n.
Wrong, H. H., **1952–53:** 23n.
Wyatt, Wilson W., **1947:** 60; **1948:** 32; **1949:** 38, 39, 74n.
   See also Housing Expediters.
   Appointment as Housing Expediter, **1945:** 211 [1]
      Letter, **1945:** 212
Wyoming, **1950:** 52 [3]
   Campaign remarks in, **1948:** 118 [5–7]; **1950:** 116, 117 [1, 4], 118, 119
   Gov. Arthur G. Crane, **1950:** 116, 117 [1, 4], 118
   Gov. Lester C. Hunt, **1948:** 118 [5, 7]
   Grand Teton National Park, reestablishment, **1950:** 248
   Woman suffrage in, **1950:** 117 [1]

Xerxes, attack on Greek city-states, **1951:** 8

Yacht, the President's, **1948:** 41 [13]
Yakima power project, **1952–53:** 367 (p. 1146)
Yale University, **1948:** 261 [7]
   Survey of classified information, **1951:** [1, 3, 14]
Yalta (Crimea) conference, **1945:** 13, 57n., 67 [1]; **1946:** 18 (p. 41); **1947:** 114; **1948:** 86; **1950:** 80 [4]; **1951:** 253
   Agreements, **1945:** 91, 97, 177, 211 [12]; **1946:** 6 [2], 27 [7, 12, 17]; **1947:** 56
   Decision on Poland, **1945:** 77, 78
   News conference remarks, **1947:** 236 [6]
Yalu River, Korea, **1951:** 63 [14, 16, 23], 95 [9]
Yangtze River defense line, breaching by Chinese Communists, **1949:** 84ftn. (p. 224)
Yankee Doodle, **1948:** 261 [9]
Yelle, Cliffe, **1952–53:** 274 [1]
Yellow fever epidemic, Philadelphia, **1948:** 104

Yonkers, N.Y., campaign remarks, **1948:** 264 [1, 2]; **1952–53:** 289 [11]
York, Pa., campaign remarks, **1948:** 139 [3]
Yorktown
   Anniversary of battle, **1951:** 165 [7]
   Battlefield, **1947:** 231
Yorktown, U.S.S., **1946:** 171n.
Young, Bill, **1948:** 137 [4]
Young, Brigham, **1952–53:** 280 [1]
Young, Clarence M., **1946:** 237 [1]; **1947:** 243 [4]
Young, E. Merl, **1951:** 227 [18]
Young, Mrs. E. Merl, **1951:** 49 [11], 56 [7]
Young, Brig. Gen. Gordon R., **1947:** 70 [7]
Young, James W., **1946:** 45n., 58n., 255n.
Young, John R., **1946:** 66 [1]; **1949:** 26n., 40 [8], 93 [2, 11], 113 [1]; **1952–53:** 31 [2], 88 [8]
Young, John S., **1946:** 119 [1]
Young, Sen. Milton R., **1949:** 226ftn. (p. 503); **1952–53:** 32
Young, Owen D., **1946:** 60; **1947:** 122
Young, P. Bernard, Jr., **1947:** 48n.
Young, Stephen M., **1948:** 258
Young American Medals, presentation, **1952–53:** 181
Young Democrats, **1948:** 101
Young Men's Christian Association, **1950:** 95n.; **1951:** 139n.; **1952–53:** 184
Young Women's Christian Association, **1951:** 139n.
Youngdahl, Gov. Luther W., **1949:** 250 [2, 3]; **1951:** 153 [8]
Youngstown Sheet & Tube Co., **1951:** 305
Youth, **1950:** 21, 262
   Apprentice training programs, **1952–53:** 367 (p. 1150)
   Boys Forum of National Government, American Legion, **1949:** 170
   Civic and political responsibilities, **1949:** 125, 191; **1952–53:** 220, 286 [6], 289 [1, 10]
   Crusade for Christian Citizenship, **1952–53:** 39
   Delinquency, **1946:** 52, 229 [21]; **1951:** 63 [1]
   Drug addiction, **1951:** 201, 287
   Employment, **1948:** 70; **1950:** 84, 154, 159, 185, 303
   Girl Scouts, 39th anniversary, statement, **1951:** 48
   Guidance, **1946:** 52
   Health and welfare, **1949:** 198, 204
   Home environment, **1950:** 37
   Indoctrination by totalitarian regimes, **1950:** 185, 299
   Keen Teen Club, **1946:** 75, 86 [33]
   Labor standards, **1952–53:** 18 (p. 95)
   Physical Fitness, **1945:** 192; **1946:** 268; **1948:** 89
   Political appeal of General Eisenhower, **1952–53:** 289 [10]
   Scholastic press, address to representatives of, **1952–53:** 63

Youth — *continued*
   Welfare programs, **1952–53:** 218
   White House conference on, **1949:** 198, 204;
      1950: 5, 299
Youth Administration, National, **1949:** 256
Youth Conference on Famine Relief, **1946:** 168
Yugoslav Emergency Relief Assistance Act, **1951:**
   81
Yugoslavia, **1946:** 6 [2, 4], 186 [12]; **1947:** 196;
   1948: 53, 129, 150 [8]
   Aggression against, U.S. attitude in event of,
      1949: 269 [13, 15]
   Armed forces, **1951:** 81
   Assistance, **1952–53:** 18 (p. 75), 27, 55
   Blooming mill, export to, **1949:** 182 [11]
   Communist aggression in, **1951:** 292; **1952–53:**
      107 [2]
   Defense, **1951:** 81, 292
   Economic assistance, **1951:** 81, 114, 292
   Nazi war criminal, demand for extradition of,
      1951: 227 [12]
   News conference remarks, **1949:** 182 [11], 200
      [10], 269 [13, 15]
   Partition of Trieste with Italy, proposed, **1951:**
      239 [4]
   Political refugees from, **1947:** 140
   Relief for, **1945:** 186
   Soviet Union, rift with, **1951:** 96
   Tito, Josip Broz, **1948:** 86, 150 [8]; **1949:** 269
      [13]; **1952–53:** 107 [14]

Yugoslavia — *continued*
   U.S. aid, **1950:** 290, 293, 295 [13]
   U.S. Ambassador George V. Allen, **1949:** 240 [4],
      269 [13]
   U.S. Ambassador Richard C. Patterson, **1947:** 62
      [5, 8]
   Violation of Greek border, **1947:** 56
Yuma, Ariz., **1947:** 35
   Campaign remarks, **1948:** 206 [4]

Zarubin, Gen. Georgi N., **1952–53:** 166 [18]
Zellerbach, James D., **1948:** 130 [1]
Zenkl, Dr. Petr, **1952–53:** 309
Ziemer, Gregor, **1947:** 90n.
Zimmerman, John W., **1952–53:** 303 [5]
Zimmerman, R. R., letter, **1945:** 203
Zinc
   Expansion of production, **1948:** 8 (p. 78)
   Subsidies, **1945:** 107 [10]; **1947:** 175
Zinsmaster, Harry W., **1947:** 191 [3]
Zionist movement, **1945:** 202 [4]
   Campaign to suppress in Soviet Union, **1952–53:**
      377 [28]
Zolkiewicz, Thaddeus S., **1952–53:** 43n.
Zook, George F., **1946:** 166n.; **1947:** 235n.
Zuckert, Eugene M., **1947:** 191 [1]; **1951:** 93n.